Encyclopedia of
African~American
Culture and History

Editorial Board

second edition

THE BLACK EXPERIENCE
IN THE AMERICAS

ENCYCLOPEDIA *of*

AFRICAN~AMERICAN

CULTURE *and* HISTORY

published in association with
THE SCHOMBURG CENTER FOR RESEARCH IN BLACK CULTURE

COLIN A. PALMER
Editor in Chief

3 *G-L*
VOLUME

MACMILLAN REFERENCE USA
An imprint of Thomson Gale, a part of The Thomson Corporation

THOMSON

GALE

Detroit • New York • San Francisco • San Diego • New Haven, Conn. • Waterville, Maine • London • Munich

Encyclopedia of African-American Culture and History, Second Edition

Colin A. Palmer, Editor in Chief

LIBRARY OF CONGRESS CATALOGING-IN-PUBLICATION DATA

Encyclopedia of African-American culture and history : the Black experience in the Americas / Colin A. Palmer, editor in chief.— 2nd ed.
    p. cm.
    Includes bibliographical references and index.
    ISBN 0-02-865816-7 (set hardcover : alk. paper) —
    ISBN 0-02-865817-5 (v. 1) — ISBN 0-02-865818-3 (v. 2) —
    ISBN 0-02-865819-1 (v. 3) — ISBN 0-02-865820-5 (v. 4) —
    ISBN 0-02-865821-3 (v. 5) — ISBN 0-02-865822-1 (v. 6)
    1. African Americans—Encyclopedias. 2. African Americans—History—Encyclopedias. 3. Blacks—America—Encyclopedias. 4. Blacks—America—History—Encyclopedias. I. Palmer, Colin A., 1942-

E185.E54 2005
973'.0496073'003—dc22   2005013029

This title is also available as an e-book.
ISBN 0-02-866071-4

Contact your Thomson Gale representative for ordering information.

Printed in the United States of America
10 9 8 7 6 5 4 3 2 1

Editorial and Production Staff

Contents

GABRIEL PROSSER CONSPIRACY

Gabriel Prosser worked in secret during 1800 to recruit and organize thousands of enslaved Virginians. He sketched out an elaborate plan to overthrow the slavery regime, and it came within hours of execution. But on the chosen day—Saturday, August 30—a hurricane destroyed bridges and flooded roads. The violent downpour washed out the proposed attack on the state capitol at Richmond, allowed time for word of the plan to leak to white authorities, and foiled what could have become a brilliant move in the dangerous chess game to force an end to slavery.

Gabriel was born into bondage about 1775, around the time that white Virginians declared their political independence. The authorities who executed him said he showed "courage and intellect above his rank in life." As the property of tavern-keeper Thomas Prosser, he worked regularly as a blacksmith in the Richmond area, where, inspired by stories of the recent Haitian Revolution, he framed his desperate plan. Aided by his wife and his brothers Martin and Solomon, he worked to procure weapons and rally recruits (Martin, a preacher, found recruits at funerals and secret religious gatherings, where he employed

biblical accounts of the Israelites' escape from Egypt to inspire potential conspirators). According to testimony in subsequent trials, from two to ten thousand African Americans knew of the design and looked to Gabriel as their leader to, in Solomon's words, "conquer the white people and possess ourselves of their property." The insurrectionists intended to spare Methodists, Quakers, and local Frenchmen because of their emancipationist leanings, and they expected poor whites and nearby Catawba Indians to join their cause when it gathered strength.

The plan called for several hundred participants (advised by a veteran from the successful siege at Yorktown) to gather at a spot outside Richmond. Behind a banner invoking the American, French, and Haitian Revolutions with the words Death or Liberty, they would march on the city in three contingents. One group would light fires in the dockside warehouses to divert whites from the heart of the city, while the other two groups would seize the capitol armory and take Governor James Monroe hostage. When the "white people agreed to their freedom," Gabriel "would dine and drink with the merchants of the city," and a white flag would be hoisted above the capitol, calling other blacks in the countryside to join them.

Betrayal by informers presented a huge danger, with so many persons approached about such an overwhelming plan. When torrential rains forced a last-minute postponement of the march on Richmond, several slaves had already alerted whites to the impending action, and Governor Monroe moved swiftly. The state militia arrested scores of suspects, and several dozen persons were executed. Prosser took refuge on the schooner *Mary,* captained by a sympathetic white Methodist. But in late September he was betrayed by two slave crewmen and captured in Norfolk. After a brief show trial in which the leader remained silent, he was hanged on October 7.

In the aftermath of the foiled insurrection, the Virginia Assembly acted to restrict the movement of all blacks—enslaved and free—and to set up a white public guard in Richmond. Such precautions proved ineffective, however. In 1802, authorities discovered further black plans to fight for freedom in Virginia and North Carolina.

In 1936 the publication of Arna Bontemps's novel *Black Thunder* offered an interesting literary treatment of Prosser's revolt.

See also Christiana Revolt of 1851; Haitian Revolution; Slavery

■ ■ *Bibliography*

Egerton, D. R. "Gabriel's Conspiracy and the Election of 1800." *Journal of Southern History* 56 (1990): 191–214.

Egerton, Douglas R. *Gabriel's Rebellion: The Virginia Slave Conspiracies of 1800 and 1802.* Chapel Hill: University of North Carolina Press, 1993.

Marszalek, John F. "Battle for Freedom: Gabriel's Insurrection." *Negro History Bulletin* 39 (1976): 540–543.

Mullin, Gerald W. *Flight and Rebellion: Slave Resistance in Eighteenth-Century Virginia.* New York: Oxford University Press, 1972.

Sidbury, James. *Ploughshares into Swords: Race, Rebellion, and Identity in Gabriel's Virginia, 1730–1810.* New York: Cambridge University Press, 1997.

PETER H. WOOD (1996)
Updated bibliography

GAINES, ERNEST J.

JANUARY 15, 1933

┣╋┫

The oldest son of a large family, Ernest Gaines, a writer, was born on the River Lake Plantation in Point Coupée Parish, Louisiana. His parents separated when he was young, and his father's absence led to a permanent estrangement. More important than his parents in his childhood was a maternal great-aunt who provided love and served as an example of strength and survival under extreme adversity. The older people in the close-knit community of the plantation "quarters" exemplified similar qualities, passing on to the child the rich oral tradition that figures prominently in his fiction.

At the age of fifteen Gaines moved from this familiar environment to Vallejo, California, where he could receive a better education. Lonely in these new surroundings, he spent much of his time in the town's public library and began to write. After high school he spent time in a junior college and the military before matriculating at San Francisco State College. An English major, he continued to write stories and graduated in 1957. Encouraged by his agent, Dorothea Oppenheimer, and (while in the creative writing program at Stanford) by Malcolm Cowley, Gaines committed himself to a literary career. In 1964 he published his first novel, *Catherine Carmier.* His subsequent books are *Of Love and Dust* (1967), *Bloodline* (1968), *The Autobiography of Miss Jane Pittman* (1971), *In My Father's House* (1978), and *A Gathering of Old Men* (1983). In a collection of interviews published as *Porch Talk with Ernest Gaines* (1990), he discussed his work in progress, a novel about an uneducated black man on death row and a black teacher in a Louisiana plantation school titled *A Lesson Before Dying* (1993).

In the 1960s and 1970s, except for a year at Denison University, Gaines lived and wrote in San Francisco. Since the early 1980s he has been associated with the University of Southwestern Louisiana, although he has continued to summer in San Francisco.

South Louisiana, the region of Gaines's youth and literary imagination, is beautiful and distinctive with unique cultural, linguistic, and social patterns. Like George Washington Cable and Kate Chopin before him, Gaines has been fascinated by the interplay of caste and class among the ethnic groups of the area: blacks, mixed-race Creoles, Cajuns, white Creoles, and Anglo whites. Once fairly stable as subsistence farmers, blacks and mixed-race Creoles have been dispossessed of the best land or displaced altogether by Cajuns, who are favored by the plantation lords because they are white and use mechanized agricultural methods. Under such socioeconomic conditions, young blacks leave, as Gaines himself did, though they often find themselves drawn back to Louisiana.

Such is the case in *Catherine Carmier.* In this novel the protagonist is the educated and alienated Jackson Bradley, who returns to his native parish to claim the love of the title character, the daughter of a mixed-race Creole whose racial exclusivism, attachment to the land, and semi-incestuous feelings toward her cannot condone such an alliance. Nor do Jackson's fellow blacks approve. Jackson cannot recapture his love or his homeland because, for all its pastoral charm, the world of his childhood is anachronistic. In *Of Love and Dust* Gaines moves from Arcadian nostalgia to a tragic mode. Marcus Payne, the rebellious protagonist, defies social and racial taboos by making love to the wife of a Cajun plantation overseer, Sidney Bonbon, after being rejected by Bonbon's black mistress. As Marcus and Louise Bonbon prepare to run away together, the Cajun, a grim embodiment of fate, kills him with a scythe.

If *Catherine Carmier* is a failed pastoral and *Of Love and Dust* a tragedy, *The Autobiography of Miss Jane Pittman* is a near-epic account of a centenarian whose life has spanned slavery, Reconstruction, Jim Crow, and the civil rights movement. Her individual story reflects the experience of oppression, resistance, survival, and dignity of an entire people. Although the protagonist of *In My Father's House* is a minister and civil rights leader in Louisiana and his unacknowledged son is an urban militant, this work's central theme is more private than public—the search for a father who has abdicated parental responsibility. In this grim tale, the son commits suicide and the father survives but without dignity. The mood of *A Gathering of Old Men,* on the other hand, is more comic than grim, but the old men who gather with shotguns to protect one of their own from unjust arrest achieve in this act of resistance the dignity that has been missing from their lives. White characters, too, achieve moral growth as social and racial change finally catches up with the bayou country. It is Gaines's most hopeful novel and in some ways his best.

In 1972 Gaines received the Black Academy of Arts and Letters Award. He was given the annual literary award of the American Academy and Institute of Arts and Letters in 1987. In 2000 he won the National Humanities Medal, the National Governors Association Award for Lifetime Contribution to the Arts, and Writer of the Year honors from the Louisiana Center for the Book.

See also Black Academy of Arts and Letters; Literature of the United States

■ ■ *Bibliography*

Babb, Valerie Melissa. *Ernest Gaines.* Boston: Twayne, 1991.

Doyle, Mary Ellen. *Voices from the Quarters: The Fiction of Ernest J. Gaines.* Baton Rouge: Louisiana State University Press, 2002.

KENNETH KINNAMON (1996)
Updatd by publisher 2005

GAIRY, ERIC

FEBRUARY 18, 1922
AUGUST 23, 1997

The trade unionist and politician Eric Matthew Gairy was born in Saint Andrew's Parish, Grenada, in 1922. He served as an acolyte in the local Roman Catholic Church and was educated in the island's public schools. He became chief minister in 1961, premier in 1967, and prime minister of independent Grenada in 1973. Initially a champion of workers' rights, Gairy later became a ruthless dictator whose actions led to a bloodless coup in 1979.

After leaving school, Gairy taught briefly before migrating, sometime between 1941 and 1942, to Trinidad, where he worked for the Americans who were constructing a military base. In 1943 he went to Aruba, where he worked for Lago Oil Company. He also taught at the evening school for workers operated by the Aruba branch of the Universal Negro Improvement Association. Gairy first became involved in trade union activities in Aruba, and it was there that he forged a close friendship with another Grenadian, Gascoigne Blaize, who later became one of his chief lieutenants in Grenada.

TRADE UNION ACTIVIST

When Gairy returned to Grenada in 1948, his blend of charisma and messianic vision allowed him to position himself as the champion of the working class. His successful 1950 defense of peasants evicted by the new proprietor of an estate in the northern portion of the island boosted his popularity among workers and peasants. After registering as a trade union in July, his newly formed Grenada Manual and Mental Workers' Union (GMMWU) demanded wage increases ranging from twenty percent to fifty percent for laborers on various estates. By January 1951, discontent among other union workers provided him with the opportunity to visit additional estates and recruit more members for his GMMWU. These visits resulted in strikes on some estates, followed by a successful month-long, island-wide strike beginning on February 19, which was a complete victory for the GMMWU.

The strike was not entirely peaceful. Looting and arson were commonplace, and some destruction of livestock and property also occurred. Using the codeword "sky-red" when he wished certain places to be set on fire, Gairy undoubtedly encouraged the violence. On February 21, he organized a massive demonstration that included busloads of people from all parts of the island, and his rhetorical skills inspired the crowd, who nicknamed him

Uncle Gairy. In addition to his following in Grenada, Gairy also received support from political leaders in Trinidad, Jamaica, Antigua, and Saint Kitts. With some six thousand Grenada workers supporting the strike, the island's economy quickly came to a halt. The acting governor eventually ordered the arrest and detention of both Gairy and Gascoigne Blaize. In desperation, the acting governor released Gairy and Blaize from detention after receiving a commitment that he would end the violence.

POLITICAL ACTIVITIES

At the age of barely twenty-nine, Gairy had become the indisputable leader of Grenada's working class, and he soon transformed this popularity into success at the polls. In 1950 he had formed the Grenada People's Party, which eventually became the Grenada United Labour Party (GULP). His personal popularity was evident in 1954, when his party captured all but two of the seats in the general elections. This electoral success continued in subsequent years, with Gairy's party winning six of the eight elections held between 1951 and 1976.

Gairy's charisma and popularity emboldened him to attempt a transformation of Grenada's society, but he soon ran afoul of British-appointed government officials. In 1957 he was accused of campaign irregularities, suspended from the Legislative Council, and prohibited from participating in elections for five years. Citing violations of financial regulations after 1961 (uncovered in the so-called *Squandermania Report*), as well as alleged browbeating of public servants, erosion of morale in the civil service, and illegal use of public money, the British government suspended the island's constitution and removed Gairy from office in 1962.

POWER AND OPPOSITION

On returning to office as premier in August 1967, Gairy sought to perpetuate his power by victimizing his political opponents through the lawless actions of a special police force that he personally recruited; by giving selective concessions to business people he favored; and by creating a highly centralized bureaucracy in which he was the primary decision maker. By acquiring the property of his political opponents, he promoted his land for the landless program. Various statutory boards were disbanded and replaced with pliant civil servants or party supporters. Charges of misrule by opponents began mounting.

From 1972 onwards, Gairy faced increasing opposition from progressives in the recently formed New Jewel Movement. Through protests and marches, they gained support for their fledgling organization. Government-sponsored beatings, imprisonment, and murders in 1973 resulted in the appointment of a commission of enquiry into the nature of law enforcement on the island. Protestors unsuccessfully sought to delay Gairy's plans for political independence without referendum. Island-wide strikes and protests in late 1973 and early 1974 led to the police killing of a popular businessman and the father of the New Jewel Movement's leader. Independence for Grenada came in 1974 amidst heightened violence and political polarization, and Gairy became prime minister under the new constitution. Knighted by Queen Elizabeth in 1977, he used the island's new status to forge alliances to enhance the country's visibility.

Between 1974 and 1979, Gairy used his government majority to make a mockery of parliament by using his majority merely to rubberstamp his agenda without seriously considering the opinions of others. On the rare occasions when the opposition received advance copies of papers that were up for parliamentary discussion, they received them on the very day the items were being introduced. Because the speaker invariably ruled on Gairy's behalf, they were effectively able to silence and frustrate the opposition. It was widely believed that his party's 1978 election victory stemmed from deliberately faulty voting lists and practices. Convinced that he could not be removed by constitutional means, the opposition New Jewel Movement overthrew his government in a bloodless coup on March 13, 1979, while Gairy was in the United States. Although he returned to Grenada in 1983, the GULP won only one seat in the 1984 elections and two in 1990. Gairy died peacefully in Grenada on August 23, 1997.

The architect of the long-overdue social revolution, Gairy had raised the level of political consciousness among Grenada's masses. By positioning himself as their champion against the excesses of the white- and brown-skinned oligarchy, he gave to the black masses considerable self-respect and gained from them a fanatical hero worship. He failed to win over large numbers of the urban middle class, however, and they found a home in Herbert Blaize's Grenada National Party.

See also Blaize, Herbert; International Relations in the Anglophone Caribbean; New Jewel Movement; Universal Negro Improvement Association

■ ■ *Bibliography*

Brizan, George. *Grenada, Island of Conflict: From Amerindians to People's Revolution, 1498–1979*. London: Zed, 1984.

DaBreo, D. Sinclair. *The Prostitution of a Democracy*. Barbados: Edgar Chris, 1977.

Emmanuel, Patrick. *Crown Colony Politics in Grenada. 1917–1951.* Barbados: Institute of Social and Economic Research, University of the West Indies, 1978.

Singham, Archie W. *The Hero and the Crowd in a Colonial Polity.* New Haven, Conn.: Yale University Press, 1968.

EDWARD L. COX (2005)

GAMA, LUIZ

JUNE 21, 1830
AUGUST 24, 1882

Brazilian abolitionist, republican, freethinker, and poet Luiz Gama was born in the city of Salvador da Bahia. His early life is the subject of some mystery and is likely to remain one, as all accounts of it are based on a single letter containing his own reminiscences. Gama's mother, Luiza Mahin, was an African-born freedwoman who made her living selling foodstuffs in the city market. Gama's father, whose name he declined to reveal, was the dissolute son of a prominent Bahian family. In 1837, when Gama was still a young boy, his mother was forced to flee Bahia, perhaps after being implicated in antislavery plotting. A few years later, in 1840, his father sold him into slavery after squandering his own inheritance.

Following this illegal sale, young Luiz was shipped south to the port of Rio de Janeiro, then to the neighboring province of São Paulo. He was a house slave in the city of São Paulo for nearly eight years, during the last years of which he befriended a boarder in his master's home, a law student who taught him to read.

Gama proved a quick study, using his newly acquired literacy to obtain documentation proving that he had been enslaved illegally and, in 1848, regaining his freedom. In the years that followed, he served in the military, worked as a clerk, and acquired a thorough, if informal, training in the law, eventually establishing his own practice.

Not content with having achieved his own freedom, Gama dedicated himself to the cause of human freedom more broadly, using his legal skills to liberate other enslaved men, women, and children through the courts and otherwise advancing the abolitionist cause as a lecturer, journalist, and fund-raiser. In all, Gama claimed to have assisted in the freeing of more than five hundred slaves.

Gama was not only an abolitionist, he was a republican during a period in which Brazil was ruled by a constitutional monarch, seeing the two struggles as joined and writing of his desire to see his country "without king and without slaves." He is said to have been the first Brazilian to use the phrase "United States of Brazil," and although he was deeply disappointed by the refusal of the rump leadership of the São Paulo Republican Party to take up the cause of immediate abolition, he never broke with the republican movement, as is often claimed.

Gama's abolitionism and republicanism are well known, but a further aspect of his intellectual formation has been overlooked. In matters religious, Gama was a freethinker, taking pride in the fact that his African-born mother had refused to allow him to be baptized as a Catholic. Although his father eventually had him baptized in the Church and he later expressed his belief in certain Christian tenets, Gama eschewed organized religion and expressed an admiration for Ernest Renan's iconoclastic *Life of Jesus.* Not coincidentally, this religious and political nonconformist was among the most prominent freemasons in São Paulo, a position he used to attract further support for the abolitionist cause.

Gama was also a poet, most famous for the doggerel with which he lampooned Brazilian racism, privilege, and hypocrisy. In "Quem sou eu?" ("Who am I?"), the most celebrated of his poems, he mocked the racial pretensions of his countrymen, playing on the nineteenth-century slang term for a male mulatto, *bóde* ("billy-goat"):

Se Negro sou, ou sou bóde
Pouco importa. O que isto póde?
Bódes ha de toda a casta,
Pois que a especie é muito vasta . . .
Ha cinzentos, ha rajados,
Bayos, pampas e malhados
Bódes negros, *bódes brancos,*
E, sejamos todos francos,
Uns plebeus, e outros nobres

[If I am black, or am billy-goat
It matters little. How can it?
There are goats of every caste,
For the species is very vast . . .
There are gray ones, there are spotted,
Chestnut-colored, streaked and mottled
Black goats, *white goats,*
And, let us all be frank,
Some plebian, and others noble]

In a further passage, the "billy-goat" proclaimed of his bleating, bucking countrymen:

Gentes pobres, nobres gentes
Em todos ha *meus parentes.*

[Persons poor, noble persons
Among one and all are *my relations.*]

But as a poet Gama also had a serious side, one clear in his ode to his mother, "Minha mãe" ("My Mother"), and in love poems like "A captiva" ("The Captive") and "Meus amores" ("My Loves"). These works, with their evocations of African and Afro-Brazilian beauty, were part of a larger effort on Gama's part to valorize blackness at a time in which African contributions to Brazilian society and culture were broadly ignored or denigrated. In his celebration of blackness, Gama was truly ahead of his time, anticipating the black-consciousness movements of the twentieth century.

Gama died in 1882, six years before the emancipation of all of Brazil's remaining slaves. His funeral cortège was among the most impressive that São Paulo had seen, with thousands of mourners accompanying the casket across the city to its final resting place.

Gama was married to Claudina Fortunata Sampaio, who survived him, as did his son—his only child—Benedicto. A collection of Gama's poems, titled *Primeiras trovas burlescas*, was published in two editions in his lifetime (1859, 1861) and in various posthumous editions (1904, 1944, 1954, 1981, 2000).

See also Emancipation in Latin America and the Caribbean; Literature; Rebouças, André

■ ■ *Bibliography*

Azevedo, Elciene. *Orfeu de carapinha: a trajetória de Luiz Gama na imperial cidade de São Paulo.* Campinas, Brazil: Editora da Universidade Estadual de Campinas, 1999.

Kennedy, James H. "Luiz Gama: Pioneer of Abolition in Brazil." *Journal of Negro History* 59, no. 3 (July 1974): 255–267.

Mennucci, Sud. *O precursor do abolicionismo no Brasil: Luiz Gama.* São Paulo: Companhia Editora Nacional, 1938.

JAMES P. WOODARD (2005)

GARDENS AND YARD ART

For African Americans, gardens and yards have been bound up with opportunities for stable living conditions, control over personal space, and home ownership amid threats to person and property extending from the seventeenth into the twenty-first centuries. Broadly, yards represent the American dream of independence and self-respect, the biblical notion of freedom to live under one's own vine and fig tree, and the ancestral bequest of roots for the living and their descendants in a home place. Plants, statuary, and artistic creations help to communi-

cate these themes and the unique visions of gardeners and yard makers. Even such ordinary activities as cutting grass and planting flowers can double as community building by showing passersby a home that is secure, successful, and welcoming.

GARDENS AND YARDS

Most Americans use the term *garden* to describe a relatively large area where vegetables or flowers are grown, *bed* for a smaller area of flowers, and *yard* to refer to domestic landscapes that surround residences. African diaspora history and experience also give meanings to these terms. In West and Central Africa, family gardens on lands surrounding a village are major sources of staple foods. People also own rights in individual fruit trees, palms, and herbs scattered through the community and the forest. Prior to European colonization, flowers generally were not grown solely for decoration but rather appreciated in relation to the total potential of the plant to feed, medicate, protect, or harm. Family compounds, often enclosed by a wall or fence, foreshadowed use of the yard in the Americas as an extension of the house, the site of practical activities as well as relaxation. Forest preserves that contained ritual sites, initiation compounds, sacred pools, memorials to ancestors, and important plants also influenced African-American landscape design.

On many North American and Caribbean plantations, the yard was a fenced or walled workspace adjacent to the planter's house. Access to the yard was strictly controlled, but some enslaved Africans and their descendants also had gardens that they tended in their meager spare time, enriching their diets and their pockets with the sale of crops. The forests and swamps beyond the plantation contained dangers but also routes for escape from forced labor.

WILDNESS AND CULTIVATION, EXUBERANCE AND MATURITY

On both sides of the Atlantic the complementary relationship between forest and settlement, wildness and cultivation, remains philosophically important, shaping both land and analogies between land use and the human body. Wild places like forests and swamps are associated with unpredictability, exuberance, and a hot emotional climate but are also exceptionally fertile and full of potential for healing and new growth. Cultivated places, like mature people, are orderly, discreet, and cool—in the sense of being emotionally balanced—as well as perfectly groomed. Wildness can burst forth spontaneously in any direction; cultivation channels this energy into mastery of all directions. Both orientations must be balanced for overall health; thus, both find places in yards, as do towers, posts, whirligigs, wheels, tires, balls, hubcaps, lighthouses, and other adornments that imply heights, depths, and movement through all points of the compass.

Thus, some carefully tended yards also include areas that seem wilder than the other parts, often located in back of the yard or on the far side of the driveway from the house. Traditionally, these are the areas in which memorials to loved ones and past generations are placed. Diverse African peoples, as well as African Americans, associate certain bodies of water, trees, inverted or pierced vessels, and otherworldly colors such as white and silver with ancestors and/or spirits. Items that some might call *yard art* not only decorate but display connections with the past and the staying power of forebears: old wheels, plows, sewing machines, bed heads, iron washing and cooking pots, stones, and even special roots, trees, and flowers like jonquils that return year after year, long after a home has been abandoned.

Trees contribute character to the landscape. The centerpiece of the yard for many southerners is a chinaberry tree that shades a cluster of chairs for work and sociability. Some yards also contain places of meditation beside a tree, carrying on the tradition of religious seekers selecting special trees and thickets for places of prayer. Widespread practices in the African diaspora link trees with individuals. For example, a "name tree" planted just as the morning sun crossed the horizon established the relationship near the time of a person's birth. The growth of the tree paralleled that of the child into maturity, eventually serving as a memorial after the individual's death. Sturdy "family trees" in rural yards symbolize "back home" for relatives spread throughout the country.

SIGNS OF CULTIVATION: BORDERS, SURFACES, AND THRESHOLDS

A widespread idea in the African diaspora holds that land is not empty space waiting to be claimed but rather must be *made* by eliminating wildness and negativity (thieves, gossip, jealousy, or disease) and must be kept up by treating every surface, plant, and ornament with care.

Surfaces, boundaries, and thresholds are key to these processes. In yards, fields, and burial grounds, earth is a passage, not a plane. Trees, plants, and posts that transect the surface of the yard connect the visible with the unseen. Borders (often of bottles before the mid-twentieth century), fences, and gates segment the land, functioning simultaneously as containers, barriers, decoration, and signs of ownership that mediate movement between inside and outside various areas.

In African-American yards, smooth, regular surfaces like swept sand, packed earth, raked gravel, and clipped grass are not so much blank as neutral (or cool): in a state of readiness and composure achieved against the vicissitudes of traffic and hurry. The surface of the ground is as much a "face" of the yard as is its façade from the street. Whether or not the preference for bare earth originated in Africa, it is widespread there and remained customary in American yards into the 1940s, when grass lawns became more common. A deterrent to insects and other pests, packed earth and raked sand also show that members of the household have paid attention to every square inch of the yard. It is combed and groomed like human hair, an analogy that Maya Angelou and others have drawn. Regular sweeping also obliterates the foot tracks of residents, for as anthropologist Zora Neale Hurston has discussed at length, in conjure, tracks can be picked up and used in rites to harm someone. Together, well-tended surfaces and boundaries contribute to a home that is sealed: impervious to assault, aesthetically pleasing, and functioning smoothly. The concept of sealing the house is virtually Pan-African. In the eighteenth century, the yards of enslaved Virginians in the Carter's Grove Plantation slave quarter used shells to seal the ground. Rather than sweeping the surface of the quarter bare, residents drew on an abundant supply of oyster shells that combined attractive whiteness with good drainage and announced the approach of visitors with loud crunching noises.

Boundaries and borders often have extra physical and visual anchors at the four corners. The corners of the yard as a whole and the beds inside it resonate with the corners of rooms inside the house, as well as with ritual space. The arrangements that mark the entrances to yards vary considerably, also implying the wide range of ways that the people who make them view their neighborhoods and potential visitors. Wrought gates, doors, and window coverings add "prestige and protection," according to an advertisement on WNOO radio in Chattanooga, Tennessee. A spiritual doctor from the 1930s recommended placing a fork by the door or gate to keep thieves away and stop people from gossiping. Traditional protections against conjure include a fork or broomstick over the kitchen door, sprinkling doors and gates with chamber lye and salt, and keeping a yard bird or frizzled chicken. Part of making a yard truly welcoming involves helping others avoid temptation so that visitors come only with good intentions.

EMBELLISHMENTS

Adding something extra, going a step beyond what's expected of an ordinary yard, fits well with an African-American aesthetic that Zora Neale Hurston called "deco-

African-American women sweeping their yards in Belton, South Carolina. *The preference for bare earth and smooth, regular surfaces, carefully tended, was common in Africa and remained customary in the yards of black Americans until the 1940s.* STILL PICTURE BRANCH (NWDNS), NATIONAL ARCHIVES AT COLLEGE PARK. REPRODUCED BY PERMISSION.

rating the decorations." This can mean expressing oneself by adding colorful trim, crafting small dramatic scenes with statuary, nurturing flowers that burgeon out of their beds, and a host of other ways of filling the yard with life. As more Americans moved into the cities, rural animals such as geese, deer, squirrels, and rabbits became popular ornaments. Cool, composed religious statues serve as role models and show awareness of blessings bestowed on the household. A secure yard is well looked after, and historically African Americans have had good reasons to be vigilant; thus, eagles can allude not only to patriotism but also to exceptional powers of sight. Indeed, in African-American yards, the eyes of statues almost always gaze at passersby, where they can remind potential transgressors that they have been seen and should behave accordingly.

In sum, African-American yard work is an extraordinarily rich and varied form of expressive culture combining beautification with communication and tradition with innovation.

See also Africanisms; Expressive Culture; Folk Arts and Crafts; Folk Religion

■ ■ *Bibliography*

Barton, Craig Evan, ed. *Sites of Memory: Perspectives on Architecture and Race.* Princeton, N.J.: Princeton Architectural Press, 2001.

Groth, Paul. "Lot, Yard, and Garden: American Distinctions." *Landscape* 30, no. 3 (1990): 29–35.

Gundaker, Grey, ed. *Keep Your Head to the Sky: Interpreting African American Home Ground.* Charlottesville: University Press of Virginia, 1998.

Thompson, Robert Farris. "The Circle and the Branch: Renascent Kongo-America Art." In *Another Face of the Diamond: Pathways Through the Black Atlantic South* (exhibition catalog). New York: INTAR Latin American Gallery, 1988.

Thompson, Robert Farris. "The Song that Named the Land: The Visionary Presence of African-American Art." In *Black Art: Ancestral Legacy.* Dallas: Dallas Museum of Art, 1989.

Thompson, Robert Farris. *Face of the Gods: Art and Altars of the Atlantic World*. New York: Museum for African Art; Munich: Prestel, 1993.

Westmacott, Richard. "Pattern and Practice in Traditional African-American Gardens in Rural Georgia." *Landscape Journal* 10, no. 2 (1991): 87–104.

Westmacott, Richard. *African-American Gardens and Yards in the Rural South*. Knoxville: University of Tennessee Press, 1992.

GREY GUNDAKER (2005)

GARNET, HENRY HIGHLAND

DECEMBER 23, 1815
FEBRUARY 12, 1882

Clergyman and abolitionist Henry Highland Garnet was one of the most formidable African-American leaders of the mid-nineteenth century. He was born on a slave plantation in New Market, Maryland, where his grandfather, likely a former Mandingo chief, was a leader of the slave community. At the age of nine he escaped from slavery with his family to New York City, where he was reared in an African-American community committed to evangelical Protestantism, "mental and moral improvement," and the antislavery cause. Young Garnet, whose father was a shoemaker and a leader of the African Methodist Episcopal Church, received an excellent education for a black youth in Jacksonian America in schools established by abolitionists, black and white. Beginning in 1825 he attended the famous African Free School on Mulberry Street. After several years as a seaman, followed by an apprenticeship to a Quaker farmer on Long Island (whose son became his tutor), Garnet in 1832 entered the Canal Street High School, which was directed by Theodore S. Wright and Peter Williams, Jr., two of the leading black clergymen and abolitionists of the era. Wright, who had been educated at Princeton, became his mentor, and in 1833 Garnet joined Wright's First Colored Presbyterian Church, a church that Garnet himself was later to pastor.

In 1835 Garnet, along with Alexander Crummell and another black youth, matriculated at the newly opened Noyes Academy in Canaan, New Hampshire. Not long after their arrival, following a harrowing journey on segregated transportation, a mob of neighboring farmers, angered by the boys' presence and their participation in local abolition meetings, dragged the makeshift school building into a nearby swamp and forced them to leave. The next

Henry Highland Garnet (1815–1882). One of the foremost African-American leaders of the nineteenth century, Garnett was a fugitive slave who became a prominent abolitionist and clergyman. PHOTOGRAPHS AND PRINTS DIVISION, SCHOMBURG CENTER FOR RESEARCH IN BLACK CULTURE, THE NEW YORK PUBLIC LIBRARY, ASTOR, LENOX AND TILDEN FOUNDATIONS.

year Garnet enrolled in Oneida Institute at Whitesboro, New York, from which he graduated in 1839.

In 1843 Garnet became an ordained minister in the Presbyterian church, although he had already pastored the Liberty Street Presbyterian Church in Troy, New York, since 1840, turning the church into a center of abolitionism and black self-help in the Troy area. He made his church an important station on the Underground Railroad; he set up a grammar school at the church, for education was the key to black progress; he preached temperance because drink undermined black advancement; and he edited two short-lived antislavery newspapers, the *Clarion* (1842) and the *National Watchman* (1847), so that African Americans could have their own voice. He also urged African Americans to leave the cities and pursue the greater independence of farm ownership.

During his Troy years, Garnet became heavily involved in radical antislavery politics. Shortly after joining in 1841, he became a leader in the newly formed Liberty Party, which pledged to end slavery through participation in the political process, an approach that contrasted with the moral suasionist, antigovernment approach of William Lloyd Garrison and his followers. At the same time, Garnet played a leading role in the struggle—unsuccessful until 1870—to eliminate property restrictions on the black franchise in New York State. In addition to state conventions, Garnet was active in the national Negro conventions movement, designed to establish policies on problems of slavery and race. It was at the Buffalo, New York, meeting in 1843 that he delivered his provocative "Address to the Slaves of the United States of America." In it he urged them to meet their moral obligation to the just God who had created all people in his image by using whatever means the situation dictated to throw off the oppressor's yoke. Garrisonians, led by Frederick Douglass, who interpreted Garnet's remarks as a call for slave rebellion, opposed a resolution authorizing the convention to distribute the speech. After heated debates the resolution was defeated. Garnet reintroduced the speech in the Troy convention in 1847 and shortly afterward published it, together with David Walker's *Appeal to the Coloured Citizens of the World* (1829), from which he had drawn some of the ideas contained in the "Address." By 1849 Douglass himself, no longer a Garrisonian, was stating publicly that he welcomed news of a rising of the slaves.

In 1850, following two years of successful mission work in Geneva, New York, Garnet left for England to lecture in the free-produce movement, whose major object was to strike at slavery through the boycott of goods produced by slave labor. Garnet remained in the British Isles until 1853 and then served as a missionary in Jamaica until illness forced his return to the United States in 1856. He then was named pastor at the Shiloh (formerly First Colored) Presbyterian Church in New York City and remained there until 1864, when he was called to the Fifteenth Street Presbyterian Church in Washington, D.C.

Garnet's restless search for ways to liberate African Americans from the bonds of slavery and color prejudice took another turn in 1858, when he became president of the newly formed and black-led African Civilization Society (ACS). Its grand design was the development of an "African nationality" through the "selective" emigration of African Americans to the Niger Valley, there to embark upon the civilizing mission of introducing evangelical Protestantism, expanding trade and commerce, and cultivating cotton and other crops that would compete with slave-grown produce to undermine slavery. His incipient Pan-Africanism was enhanced by his early contacts with Africans in New York City and his years in Jamaica, and

Henry Highland Garnet

"You cannot be more oppressed than you have been—you cannot suffer greater cruelties than you have already. Rather die freemen, than live to be slaves. Remember that you are three millions."

ADDRESS TO THE SLAVES OF THE UNITED STATES OF AMERICA, DELIVERED BEFORE THE NATIONAL CONVENTION OF COLORED CITIZENS. BUFFALO, NEW YORK, AUGUST 16, 1843. IN *THE BLACK ABOLITIONIST PAPERS*. VOL.3., *THE UNITED STATES, 1830-1846*, EDITED BY C. PETER RIPLEY. CHAPEL HILL: UNIVERSITY OF NORTH CAROLINA PRESS, 1991, 403-412.

it is likely that only illness prevented him from shifting his ministry to Africa in 1856, following the example of his longtime friend Alexander Crummell, who had earlier undertaken a mission to Liberia. Although opposed by anti-colonizationists such as Frederick Douglass, Garnet eventually won the support of many African nationalists, including Martin Delany, who joined the African Civilization Society in 1861. Even as the ACS gradually turned its missionary impulse toward meeting the relief and educational needs of the freed people during and after the Civil War, Garnet never relinquished his vision of African redemption.

Garnet also viewed the Civil War as a grand opportunity for African Americans, who were destined for freedom, to lead in the redemption of the United States. This faith was sorely tested, however, by the New York City Draft Riots in July 1863, which took a heavy toll on black lives and property, endangering Garnet's life and resulting in the sacking of his church. He was a leader in the organized effort to aid victims of the violence. Undeterred, he continued at great personal risk to recruit black volunteers for the Union armies. Soon after he became minister to Washington, D.C.'s Fifteenth Street Presbyterian Church in 1864, he took up missionary work among the recently freed slaves flocking into the national capital. In February 1865 he was invited to deliver a sermon in the U.S. House of Representatives commemorating passage of the Thirteenth Amendment, the first African American so asked. His message was a call for national atonement: *"Emancipate, enfranchise, educate, and give the blessings of the gospel to every American citizen"* (Garnet's italics).

After the Civil War, those who had long been in the forefront of the liberation struggle were gradually replaced by another generation. Garnet left Washington in 1868 to assume the presidency of Avery College in Pittsburgh; he remained there for a year before returning to Shiloh Presbyterian. His beloved wife, Julia, died in 1871, and in 1878 he married Sarah Thompson, a feminist and educator. During the 1870s he continued to champion civil rights and other reform causes, notably the emancipation of blacks in Cuba. He also grew increasingly disillusioned by the failures of Reconstruction and was especially upset by the government's refusal to distribute land to the freedpeople. And he came to believe that his lifelong efforts in the cause of liberation had gone largely unappreciated by his own people. In 1881, tired, in ill health, and against the advice of friends, he accepted the appointment as American minister to Liberia. He died in Liberia, and as was his wish, he was buried in the soil of Africa.

See also Abolition; African Civilization Society (AfCS); Delany, Martin R.; Douglass, Frederick; Pan-Africanism; Thirteenth Amendment

■ *Bibliography*

Litwack, Leon F., and August Meier, eds. *Black Leaders in the Nineteenth Century*. Urbana: University of Illinois Press, 1988.

Miller, Floyd J. *The Search for a Black Nationality: Black Colonization and Emigration, 1787–1863*. Urbana: University of Illinois Press, 1975.

Ofari, Earl. *"Let Your Motto Be Resistance": The Life and Thought of Henry Highland Garnet*. Boston: Beacon Press, 1972.

Pasternak, Martin B. *Rise Now and Fly to Arms: The Life of Henry Highland Garnet*. New York: Garland, 1995.

Pease, Jane H., and William H. Pease. *Bound with Them in Chains*. Westport, Conn.: Greenwood Press, 1972.

Schor, Joel. *Henry Highland Garnet: A Voice of Radicalism in the Nineteenth Century*. Westport, Conn.: Greenwood Press, 1977.

Stuckey, Sterling. *Slave Culture: Nationalist Theory and the Foundations of Black America*. New York: Oxford University Press, 1987.

Swift, David E. *Black Prophets of Justice: Activist Clergy Before the Civil War*. Baton Rouge: Louisiana State University Press, 1989.

OTEY M. SCRUGGS (1996)
Updated bibliography 2005

GARRIDO, JUAN
C. 1480
C. 1547

From the onset of the Spanish exploration and invasion of the Americas in the 1490s, Africans were brought across the Atlantic as slaves and servants. Many fought as black conquistadors against native warriors, thereby earning their freedom and a subordinate place in Spanish colonial society. Juan Garrido was one such African.

The details of Garrido's birth, including his original name, are not known, but most likely he was born in West Africa in the early 1480s and sold as a boy to Portuguese slave traders. He was baptized in Lisbon in the 1490s and then moved to Seville, perhaps when he was purchased by a Spaniard named Pedro Garrido. Around 1503 Pedro Garrido brought Juan across the Atlantic to Santo Domingo, on the island of Hispaniola. Juan Garrido later claimed to have arrived in the Americas a free man, but it is probable that he earned his freedom fighting in the conquest of Puerto Rico, where he then settled. Garrido's biography becomes clearer from this point on, for he later summarized it himself in a letter to the King of Spain, in his *probanza de mérito*, or "proof of merit," requesting a royal pension (the letter is preserved in the Archive of the Indies in Seville or AGI). Between 1508 and 1519, Garrido "went to discover and pacify" the Caribbean islands of Puerto Rico, Cuba, Guadalupe, and Dominica, and he participated in the Spanish discovery of Florida (Restall, 2000, p. 171).

In 1519 Garrido joined the expedition led by Hernando Cortés into Mexico, serving "in the conquest and pacification of this New Spain from the time when the Marqués del Valle (Cortés) entered it; and in his company I was present at all the invasions and conquests and pacifications which were carried out, always with the said Marqués, all of which I did at my own expense without being given either salary or *repartimiento de indios* (allotment of tribute-paying natives)" (Restall, 2000, p. 171). Garrido's lack of salary had nothing to do with his origins; the conquistadors, whether African or Spanish, were armed investors, not salaried soldiers, and they fought for the spoils of war. Only the higher-ranking Spaniards were allotted native communities, but Garrido might have hoped for some of the lesser rewards and benefits that he did indeed receive. In the wake of the fall of the Mexica (Aztec) imperial capital of Tenochtitlán in 1521, Garrido settled temporarily on the outskirts of the ruined city, by the Tacuba causeway. Here he built a small chapel commemorating the Spaniards and their allied native warriors who had died in "La Noche Triste"—the bloody escape from Tenochtitlán in 1520.

It was also at this time that he had "the inspiration to sow maize [i.e., wheat] here in New Spain and to see if it took; I did this and experimented at my own expense" (Restall, 2000, p. 171). Although Cortés and several other Spaniards also took credit for the first planting of wheat on the American mainland, Garrido successfully made it his claim to fame, and he is usually associated with it to this day.

Meanwhile, Garrido continued to participate in the Spanish Conquest, joining the expedition under Antonio de Carvajal to Michoacán and Zacatula from 1523 to 1524. Upon his return to Mexico City, now rising from the ruins of Tenochtitlán, he was made a *portero* (doorkeeper) and a *pregonero* (town crier), both positions typically given to free blacks and mulattoes in colonial Spanish America. For a time he was also guardian of the important Chapultepec aqueduct. Perhaps most significantly, on February 10, 1525, Garrido was granted a house plot within the rebuilt capital, where he settled for his remaining two decades. He remained active, heading a gold-mining expedition to Zacatula in 1528, complete with an African slave gang, and also leading a mine-labor gang of black and native slaves, of whom he was part owner, on the Cortés expedition to Baja California from about 1533 to 1536. But he also enjoyed domestic life, marrying and having three children, before dying in Mexico City around 1547.

▪▪ *Bibliography*

Alegría, Ricardo E. *Juan Garrido, el conquistador negro en las Antillas, Florida, México, y California, c.1503–1540.* San Juan, Puerto Rico: Centro de Estudios Avanzados de Puerto Rico y el Caribe, 1990.

Gerhard, Peter. "A Black Conquistador in Mexico." *Hispanic American Historical Review* 58, no. 3 (1978): 451–459. Reprinted in *Slavery and Beyond: The African Impact on Latin America and the Caribbean,* edited by Darien J. Davis. Wilmington, Del.: Scholarly Resources, 1995.

Restall, Matthew. "Black Conquistadors: Armed Africans in Early Spanish America." *The Americas* 57, no. 2 (2000): 171–205.

Restall, Matthew. *Seven Myths of the Spanish Conquest.* New York: Oxford University Press, 2003.

MATTHEW RESTALL (2005)

GARVEY, AMY ASHWOOD

JANUARY 18, 1897
MAY 3, 1969

Pan-Africanist Amy Ashwood was born in Port Antonio, Jamaica. Educated in Panama and Jamaica, she first met Marcus Garvey in 1914 while attending high school in Jamaica. Garvey launched the United Negro Improvement Association (UNIA) a few days after the two met; Ashwood, considered by some a cofounder of the organization, was at least its second member. An excellent public speaker, she worked actively to establish and promote the incipient movement in Jamaica and served as its executive secretary.

Ashwood left for Panama in 1916 and did not meet Garvey again until 1918, when she came to New York. In the United States, she busied herself with UNIA work: traveling across the country making speeches and recruiting new members, working on its journal, *Negro World,* and helping manage the new Black Star Line Steamship Corporation. In 1919 she is reported to have saved Garvey's life by placing her body between him and a disgruntled former employee who wanted to shoot him and then wrestling the would-be assassin to the ground.

Ashwood married Garvey in New York City at Liberty Hall on December 25, 1919. However, by the middle of the following year, the marriage ended acrimoniously, with accusations of infidelity on both sides. Garvey, in addition, charged Ashwood with misappropriating funds; she countered that the UNIA leader was politically inept. Garvey received a divorce in 1922, which Ashwood later contested, and promptly married his secretary and Ashwood's childhood friend, Amy Jacques.

Following the breakup with Garvey, Ashwood left the UNIA but remained a committed Pan-Africanist all her life, taking Garvey's message to many parts of the world. In 1924 she helped found the Nigerian Progress Union in London. In New York, in 1926, she collaborated with Caribbean musician Sam Manning on the musicals *Brown Sugar, Hey! Hey!,* and *Black Magic,* intended to introduce calypso to Harlem audiences. In 1929 she left with Manning for London, where she lived until 1944.

In London Ashwood's Pan-African activities resulted in friendships with such people as C. L. R. James, George Padmore, Kwame Nkrumah, and Jomo Kenyatta; all of them frequented the West Indian restaurant she ran from 1935 to 1938, which became a famous Pan-Africanist meeting place. In 1935 she was active in organizing protests against the Italian invasion of Ethiopia. In 1945 she chaired the sessions of the fifth Pan-African Congress in Manchester along with W. E. B. Du Bois.

Ashwood returned to New York briefly in 1944 and campaigned hard on behalf of Adam Clayton Powell, Jr., who was seeking his first term in the House of Representatives. Ashwood spent the next few years in West Africa. In 1947 she went to Liberia on the invitation of President William Tubman. The two became close friends, and with Tubman's help Ashwood wrote an official history of Liberia, which has never been published. In 1949 she spent some time in Ghana and researched her Ashanti roots.

Ashwood divided the rest of her life between the United States, England, the Caribbean, and West Africa. A lifelong feminist, she paid greater attention to women's issues in the later years of her life. She also continued antiracist agitation in England, forming a chapter of the Association for the Advancement of Colored People in London in 1958.

Ashwood was in England in 1964 when Garvey's body was returned to Jamaica; she participated in the official ceremonies marking the occasion. During these years she also tried, unsuccessfully, to find a publisher for her biography of Garvey and the movement, which is yet to be published. Ashwood died destitute in London.

See also Garvey, Marcus; *Negro World*; Pan-Africanism; Universal Negro Improvement Association

▪▪ *Bibliography*

Martin, Tony. *Amy Ashwood Garvey: Pan-Africanist, Feminist and Wife No. 1.* Dover, Mass.: Majority Press, 1988.

Yard, Lionel M. *Biography of Amy Ashwood Garvey, 1897–1969.* New York: Association for the Study of Afro-American Life and History, 1989.

KEVIN PARKER (1996)

GARVEY, AMY JACQUES

DECEMBER 31, 1896
JULY 25, 1973

╺┣┫╸

Journalist Amy Jacques Garvey was the second wife of Marcus Mosiah Garvey, founder of the Universal Negro Improvement Association (UNIA). She was born in Kingston, Jamaica, to Charlotte and George Samuel Jacques, who were from the Jamaican middle class. Plagued by ill health, Amy Jacques, in need of a cooler cli-

mate, migrated in 1917 to the United States. She became affiliated with the UNIA in 1918 and served as Marcus Garvey's private secretary and office manager at the UNIA headquarters in New York. After Marcus Garvey divorced his first wife, Amy Ashwood Garvey, he married Amy Jacques on July 27, 1922, in Baltimore, Maryland.

During Marcus Garvey's several periods of incarceration for alleged mail fraud (1923–1927), Amy Jacques Garvey assumed an unofficial leadership position, although she was never elected to a UNIA office. She nevertheless functioned as the major spokesperson for the UNIA and was the chief organizer in raising money for Marcus Garvey's defense. In addition, she served as the editor of the woman's page, "Our Women and What They Think," in the *Negro World*, the UNIA's weekly newspaper, published in New York. Her editorials demonstrated her political commitment to the doctrine of Pan-Africanism and also her belief that women should be active within their communities.

After Marcus Garvey's deportation from the United States in 1927, Amy Jacques Garvey packed their belongings and joined him in Jamaica. After Marcus Garvey died on June 19, 1940, in London, Amy Jacques Garvey continued to live in Jamaica and to serve the UNIA, headquartered in Cleveland, Ohio. Her edited books include *The Philosophy and Opinions of Marcus Garvey* in two volumes (1923, 1925). Her biographical memoir *Garvey and Garveyism*, published in 1963, helped to stimulate a rebirth of interest in Garveyism. Amy Jacques Garvey was awarded a prestigious Musgrave Medal in 1971 by the Board of Governors at the Institute of Jamaica for her distinguished contributions on the philosophy of Garveyism.

See also Garvey, Marcus; *Negro World*; Pan-Africanism; Universal Negro Improvement Association

▪▪ *Bibliography*

Hill, Robert, ed. *The Marcus Garvey and Universal Negro Improvement Association Papers.* 7 vols. Berkeley: University of California Press, 1984.

Taylor, Ula Yvette. *The Veiled Garvey: The Life and Times of Amy Jacques Garvey.* Chapel Hill: University of North Carolina Press, 2002.

ULA Y. TAYLOR (1996)
Updated bibliography

GARVEY, MARCUS

AUGUST 7, 1887
JUNE 10, 1940

Marcus Mosiah Garvey was the founder and leader of the Universal Negro Improvement Association (UNIA), the largest organized mass movement in black history. Hailed in his own time as a redeemer, a "black Moses," Garvey is now best remembered as champion of the back-to-Africa movement that swept the United States in the aftermath of World War I.

FROM JAMAICA TO THE UNITED STATES

Garvey was born in Saint Ann's Bay, on the north coast of the island of Jamaica. He left school at fourteen, worked as a printer's apprentice, and subsequently joined the protonationalist National Club, which advocated Jamaican self-rule. He participated in the printers' union strike of 1912, and following its collapse went to Central America, working in various capacities in Costa Rica, Honduras, and Panama. He spent over a year in England during 1913 and 1914, where he teamed up for a time with the pan-Negro journalist and businessman Duse Mohamed Ali, publisher of the influential *African Times and Orient Review*. After a short tour of Europe, he returned to England and lobbied the Colonial Office for assistance to return to Jamaica.

Garvey arrived back in Jamaica on the eve of the outbreak of World War I. He lost little time in organizing the UNIA, which he launched at a public meeting in Kingston on July 20, 1914. Content at first to offer a program of racial accommodation while professing strong patriotic support for British war aims, Garvey was a model colonial. He soon aspired to establish a Tuskegee-type industrial training school in Jamaica. In spring 1916, however, after meeting with little success and feeling shut out from political influence, he moved to the United States—ostensibly at Booker T. Washington's invitation, although he arrived after Washington died.

Garvey's arrival in America coincided with the dawn of the militant New Negro era, the ideological precursor of the Harlem Renaissance of the 1920s. Propelled by America's entry into World War I in April 1917, the New Negro movement quickly gathered momentum from the outrage African Americans felt in the aftermath of the infamous East Saint Louis race riot of July 2, 1917. African-American disillusionment with the country's failure to make good on the professed democratic character of American war aims became widespread.

Marcus Garvey (1887–1940). Born in Jamaica, Garvey was the founder and leader of the Universal Negro Improvement Association (UNIA), which quickly grew to become the largest mass movement in African American history, and the largest Pan-African movement of all time. © CORBIS. REPRODUCED BY PERMISSION.

Shortly after his arrival in America, Garvey embarked on a period of extensive travel and lecturing, which provided him with a firsthand sense of conditions in African-American communities. After traveling for a year he settled in Harlem, where he organized the first American branch of the UNIA in May 1917.

RADICALIZATION

With the end of the war, Garvey's politics underwent a radical change. His principal political goal now became the redemption of Africa and its unification into a United States of Africa. To enrich and strengthen his movement, Garvey envisioned a black-owned and -run shipping line to foster economic independence, transport passengers between America, the Caribbean, and Africa, and serve as a symbol of black grandeur and enterprise.

Accordingly, the Black Star Line was launched and incorporated in 1919. The line's flagship, the SS *Yarmouth*, renamed the SS *Frederick Douglass*, made its maiden voyage to the West Indies in November 1919; two other ships were acquired in 1920. The Black Star Line would prove to be the UNIA's most powerful recruiting and propaganda tool, but it ultimately sank under the accumulated weight of financial inexperience, mismanagement, expensive repairs, Garvey's own ill-advised business decisions, and, ultimately, insufficient capital.

Meanwhile, by 1920 the UNIA had hundreds of divisions and chapters operating worldwide. It hosted elaborate annual conventions at its Liberty Hall headquarters in Harlem and published *Negro World*, its internationally disseminated weekly organ, which was soon banned in many parts of Africa and the Caribbean.

At the first UNIA convention in August 1920, Garvey was elected to the position of provisional president of Africa. To lay the groundwork for launching his program of African redemption, Garvey sought to establish links with Liberia. In 1920 he sent a UNIA official to scout out prospects for a colony in that country. Following the official's report, in the winter of 1921 a group of UNIA technicians was sent to Liberia.

LEGAL AND POLITICAL DIFFICULTIES

Starting in 1921, however, the movement began to unravel under the economic strain of the Black Star Line's collapse, the failure of Garvey's Liberian program, opposition from black critics, defections caused by internal dissension, and official harassment. The most visible expression of the latter was the federal government's indictment of Garvey in early 1922 on charges of mail fraud stemming from Garvey's stock promotion of the Black Star Line, although by the time the indictment was presented the Black Star Line had already suspended all operations.

The pressure of his legal difficulties soon forced Garvey into an ill-advised effort to neutralize white opposition. In June 1922 he met secretly with the acting imperial wizard of the Ku Klux Klan in Atlanta, Edward Young Clarke. The revelation of Garvey's meeting with the KKK produced a major split within the UNIA, resulting in the ouster of the "American leader," Rev. J. W. H. Eason, at the August 1922 convention. In January 1923 Eason was assassinated in New Orleans, but his accused assailants, who were members of the local UNIA African Legion, were subsequently acquitted. After their acquittal and as part of the defense campaign in preparation for the mail fraud trial, Garvey's second wife, Amy Jacques Garvey (1896–1973), edited and published a small volume of Garvey's sayings and speeches under the title *Philosophy and Opinions of Marcus Garvey* (1923).

Shortly after his trial began, Garvey unwisely undertook his own legal defense. He was found guilty on a single count of fraud and sentenced to a five-year prison term,

> ### Marcus Garvey
>
> "We believe in the freedom of Africa for the Negro people of the world, and by the principle of Europe for the Europeans and Asia for the Asiatics; we also demand Africa for the Africans at home and abroad."
>
> DECLARATION OF RIGHTS OF THE NEGRO PEOPLES OF THE WORLD, DRAFTED AND ADOPTED IN NEW YORK, 1920. PUBLISHED IN GARVEY, AMY JACQUES, ED. *PHILOSOPHY AND OPINIONS OF MARCUS GARVEY*, NEW YORK, 1974.

although his three Black Star Line codefendants were acquitted. (The year following his conviction, Garvey launched a second shipping line, the Black Cross Navigation and Trading Company, but it too failed.)

JAMAICA AND LONDON

Thanks to an extensive petition campaign, Garvey's sentence was commuted after he had served thirty-three months in the Atlanta federal penitentiary. Upon his release in November 1927, he was immediately deported to Jamaica and was never allowed to return to the United States. A second and expanded volume of *Philosophy and Opinions of Marcus Garvey* was edited and published by Amy Jacques Garvey in 1925 as part of Garvey's attempt to obtain a pardon.

Back in Jamaica, Garvey soon moved to reconstitute the UNIA under his direct control. This move precipitated a major split between the official New York parent body and the newly created Jamaican body. Although two conventions of the UNIA were held in Jamaica, Garvey was never able to reassert control over the various segments of his movement from his base in Jamaica.

Although he had high hopes of reforming Jamaican politics, Garvey was defeated in his 1930 bid to win a seat on the colonial legislative council. He had to content himself with a seat on the municipal council of Kingston. Disheartened and bankrupt, he abandoned Jamaica and relocated to London in 1935. A short time after he arrived in England, however, fascist Italy invaded Ethiopia, producing a crisis that occasioned a massive upsurge of pro-Ethiopian solidarity throughout the black world, in which movement UNIA divisions and members were at the forefront. Garvey's loud defense of the Ethiopian emperor,

BIG MASS MEETING

A CALL TO THE

COLORED CITIZENS

OF

ATLANTA, GEORGIA

To Hear the Great West Indian Negro Leader

HON. MARCUS GARVEY

President of the Universal Negro Improvement Association
of Jamaica, West Indies.

Big Bethel A. M. E. Church

Corner Auburn Avenue and Butler Street

SUNDAY AFTERNOON, AT 3 O'CLOCK

MARCH 25, 1917

He brings a message of inspiration to the
12,000,000 of our people in this country.

SUBJECT:

"The Negroes of the West Indies, after
78 years of Emancipation." With a
general talk on the world position of
the race.

An orator of exceptional force, Professor Garvey has spoken
to packed audiences in England, New York, Boston, Washington,
Philadelphia, Chicago, Milwaukee, St. Louis, Detroit, Cleveland,
Cincinatti, Indianapolis, Louisville, Nashville and other cities. He
has travelled to the principal countries of Europe, and was the
first Negro to speak to the Veterans' Club of London, England.
   This is the only chance to hear a great man who has taken
his message before the world. **COME OUT EARLY TO
SECURE SEATS.** It is worth travelling 1,000 miles to hear.

All Invited. Rev. R. H. Singleton, D.D., Pastor.

Handbill inviting "colored citizens of Atlanta, Georgia" to hear Marcus Garvey speak, March 25, 1917. Garvey was known for his fiery oratory as an advocate of black nationalism and the back-to-Africa movement. © DAVID J. & JANICE L. FRENT COLLECTION/ CORBIS. REPRODUCED BY PERMISSION.

Haile Selassie, soon changed, which met with scathing public criticism, alienating many of Garvey's followers.

Throughout the thirties Garvey tried to rally his greatly diminished band of supporters through his monthly magazine, *Black Man*. Between 1936 and 1938 he convened a succession of annual meetings and conventions in Toronto, Canada, where he also launched a school of African philosophy as a UNIA training school. He undertook annual speaking tours of the Canadian maritime provinces and the eastern Caribbean.

LEGACY

In 1939 Garvey suffered a stroke that left him partly paralyzed. The indignity of reading his own obituary notice precipitated a further stroke that led to his death on June 10, 1940. Although his last years were spent in obscurity, in the decades between the two world wars Garvey's ideology inspired millions of blacks worldwide with the vision of a redeemed and emancipated Africa. The importance of Garvey's political legacy was acknowledged by such African nationalists as Nnamdi Azikiwe of Nigeria and Kwame Nkrumah of Ghana. In 1964 Garvey was declared Jamaica's first national hero.

Although he failed to realize his immediate objectives, Garvey's message represented a call for liberation from the psychological bondage of racial subordination. Drawing on a gift for spellbinding oratory and spectacle, Garvey melded black aspirations for economic and cultural independence with the traditional American creed of success to create a new and distinctive black gospel of racial pride.

See also Garvey, Amy Ashwood; Garvey, Amy Jacques; *Negro World*; Pan-Africanism; Universal Negro Improvement Association

■ ■ *Bibliography*

Cronon, Edmund David. *Black Moses: The Story of Marcus Garvey and the Universal Negro Improvement Association.* Madison: University of Wisconsin Press, 1955.

Garvey, Amy Jacques, ed. *Philosophy and Opinions of Marcus Garvey* (1923–1925). With an introduction by Robert A. Hill. New York: Atheneum, 1992.

Garvey, Marcus. *Selected Writings and Speeches of Marcus Garvey,* edited by Bob Blaisdell. Mineola, N.Y.: Dover, 2004.

Hill, Robert A., ed. *The Marcus Garvey and Universal Negro Improvement Association Papers.* Los Angeles and Berkeley: University of California Press, 1983–1991.

Lewis, Rupert. *Marcus Garvey: Anti-Colonial Champion.* Trenton, N.J.: Africa World Press, 1988.

Martin, Tony. *Race First: The Ideological and Organizational Struggles of Marcus Garvey and the Universal Negro Improvement Association.* Westport, Conn.: Greenwood, 1976.

Stein, Judith. *The World of Marcus Garvey: Race and Class in Modern Society.* Baton Rouge: Louisiana State University Press, 1986.

Vincent, Theodore G. *Black Power and the Garvey Movement,* 2nd ed. Trenton, N.J., 1992.

ROBERT A. HILL (1996)
Updated bibliography

GARVEY MOVEMENT

See Garvey, Marcus; Universal Negro Improvement Association

GARY CONVENTION

From March 10 to 12, 1972, eight thousand African Americans from every region of the United States attended the first National Black Political Convention in Gary, Indiana. Organized largely by Michigan congressman Charles C. Diggs, Mayor Richard Hatcher of Gary, and the writer and activist Amiri Baraka, who chaired the event, the convention sought to unite blacks politically—"unity without uniformity" was the theme—and looked toward the creation of a third political party. Hatcher, who had been elected mayor in 1968, was the keynote speaker. Many delegates had been elected in conventions in their home states. The convention approved a platform that demanded reparations for slavery, proportional congressional representation for blacks, the elimination of capital punishment (which resulted in the execution of a disproportionate number of African Americans), increased federal spending to combat crime and drug trafficking, a reduced military budget, and a guaranteed income of $6,500 (a figure above the then-current poverty level) for a family of four.

After much debate and some walkouts by delegates, the convention also rejected integration as an idea, supporting local control of schools instead, and passed a resolution favoring the establishment of an independent Palestinian state. However, the convention took no position on any of that year's presidential candidates, including black congresswoman Shirley Chisholm, who was then running for the Democratic nomination. Chisholm had been left out of the convention planning, and believing that many black male leaders did not support her, she did not attend the Gary convention. Roy Wilkins and the National Association for the Advancement of Colored People (NAACP) denounced the convention as "openly separatist and nationalist." The mainstream media, which had been barred from the event, were also critical.

The National Black Assembly, not a third political party, emerged from the convention. It met in October 1972 and again in March 1973. A second National Black Political Convention was held in 1974 in Little Rock, Arkansas, with follow-up meetings the next year. Thereafter, interest in further conventions petered out.

See also Baraka, Amiri (Jones, LeRoi); Diggs, Charles, Jr.; Hatcher, Richard Gordon; National Association for the Advancement of Colored People (NAACP); Wilkins, Roy

"A Black political convention, indeed all truly Black politics, must begin from this truth: The American system does not work for the masses of our people, and it cannot be made to work without radical, fundamental changes."

FROM THE AGENDA OF THE FIRST NATIONAL BLACK POLITICAL CONVENTION, GARY, INDIANA 1972.

■ ■ Bibliography

Hampton, Henry, and Steve Fayer. *Voices of Freedom.* New York: Bantam, 1990.

Low, W. Augustus, and Virgil A. Clift, eds. *Encyclopedia of Black America.* New York: McGraw-Hill, 1981.

JEANNE THEOHARIS (1996)

GASKIN, WINIFRED

MAY 10, 1916
MARCH 5, 1977

Winifred Maria Ivy Gaskin was a public servant, journalist, politician, diplomat, and founding member of Guyana's first women's political organization, the Women's Political and Economic Organisation (WPEO). She was born in Buxton, East Coast Demerara, to Stanley and Irene Thierens. Gaskin's education began at St. Anthony's Roman Catholic School, where her father was the headmaster. She won the Buxton Scholarship in 1927, attended St. Joseph's Convent High School in Georgetown, Guyana, obtained a middle school scholarship, and proceeded to Bishop's High School, the premier girls' secondary school. Gaskin was a runner-up for the prestigious British Guiana Scholarship but never attended university. Instead, she pursued a life's work of public service.

Initially, Gaskin, a dark-complexioned working-class woman of African descent, was denied an appointment at Georgetown's General Post Office, then part of the British Colonial Public Service, because of protests by the mostly white colonial workforce. It was only after the intervention of the white headmistress of Bishop's High School, who pointed out Gaskin's academic excellence, that she was hired. In 1939 she married E. Berkeley Gaskin, and the union produced her only child, Gregory. The union also ended her work at the post office because married women were not eligible for appointment to or to hold postal service positions.

Unarguably, Gaskin's discriminatory treatment helped to influence her in striving to improve women's conditions. In a June 30, 1946, article in the newspaper the *Chronicle,* she encouraged women to improve their conditions by initiating identifiable changes. Less than a month later the WPEO was established, aiming to encourage the political education of women and their participation in national life. It addressed issues relating to day-care facilities for working-class women, housing, price control of food items, better wages, transportation, health care, and education. Gaskin actively participated in public meetings and demonstrations held by the WPEO. She was active in submitting petitions to the local legislature and the British government as part of the WPEO's advocacy for reforms.

Gaskin became a journalist for *The Argosy,* and later subeditor, and editor of *Bookers News,* the organ of Bookers-McConnell Ltd., the largest British plantation, commercial proprietors, and slave owners in British Guiana during colonial times. Gaskin also served as president of the British Guiana Press Association. She was an original member of the Political Affairs Committee, the precursor of the People's Progressive Party (PPP). After a split occurred in the PPP in 1955, Gaskin became a founding member of the People's National Congress (PNC) and rose to the rank of chairman. She was instrumental in forming the Women's Revolutionary Socialist Movement (WRSM) of the PNC. Gaskin was a party delegate to the British Guiana Independence Conferences held in London in October 1962 and October 1963.

The PNC and another political party, the United Force, formed a coalition government after the general elections of December 1964. Gaskin was elected to the House of Assembly and became the minister of education and race relations. She introduced policies that provided free education for students from kindergarten to university. In 1968 she became Guyana's first high commissioner to the Commonwealth Caribbean. She was awarded the Order of Distinction of Jamaica for distinguished diplomatic service. For her outstanding public service, Gaskin also received one of the highest Guyanese national honors, the Cacique Crown of Honour of Guyana. In 1976 she returned to Guyana and headed the Foreign Affairs and Economic Section, Ministry of National Development, before she died in 1977. The former president of Guyana, the late Linden Forbes S. Burnham, lauded Gaskin as a pioneer in the women's movement. He emphasized that, at a time when few women dared, she was a politician and socialist

whose determination and work made her one of the nation's most distinguished daughters.

See also Journalism; People's National Congress; Politics

■ ■ *Bibliography*

Chronicle (Georgetown, Guyana), June 30, 1946.

Foreign Service Despatch, American Consulate, Georgetown, Guyana, The Department of State, Washington, Decimal File (1910–1963), Numeric File (1963–1973), 741D, 841D, 844B, Record Group 59, National Archives at College Park (Archives II), Md.

Joseph, Valerie. "Winifred Gaskin, Public Servant." In *The African-Guyanese Achievement: 155th Anniversary of African Slave Emancipation,* vol. 1, p. 18. Georgetown, Guyana: Free Press, 1993.

New Nation (official organ of the People's National Congress), 1957–1980s.

Sunday Graphic, June 12, 1960.

"Winifred Gaskin." In *Guynews #2,* vol. 1. Georgetown, Guyana: Government Information Services, 1977.

Woolford, Hazel M. "Women in Guyanese Politics, 1812–1964." In *Themes in African-Guyanese History,* edited by Winston F. McGowan, James G. Rose, and David A. Granger, pp. 327–350. Georgetown, Guyana: Free Press, 1998.

BARBARA P. JOSIAH (2005)

GATES, HENRY LOUIS, JR.
SEPTEMBER 16, 1950

■ ■ ■

Teacher, scholar, and writer Henry Louis Gates, Jr., was born in Keyser, West Virginia. He attended Yale and Clare College, Cambridge, where he received a doctorate in literature in 1979. He taught at Yale, Cornell, and Duke before going to Harvard in 1991. Gates came to public attention in 1981 when he received one of the first MacArthur Foundation "genius" grants, and again in 1983, when he published a rediscovered 1859 novel by an African-American woman, *Our Nig,* the first such work of its kind to be found. His major scholarly work, *The Signifying Monkey: A Theory of African American Literary Criticism* (1998), links literary analysis with black vernacular expression. Critic Ismael Reed called it "the Rosetta Stone of the American multicultural Renaissance."

Gates emerged in the 1990s as a popularizer of black scholarship and a spokesperson on racial issues. His work in establishing and chairing Harvard University's Department of African-American Studies helped give the field legitimacy. He has also successfully championed the inclusion of black writers in the American literary cannon, serving as co-editor of *The Norton Anthology of African American Literature* (1996). He is also co-editor of *Africana 2000,* a massive CD-ROM encyclopedia of the African diaspora, as well as its print version, *Africana: The Encyclopedia of the African and African American Experience* (1999).

Gates has distinguished himself as an effective fundraiser, a prolific writer and editor of books and articles, a spokesperson for cultural diversity, reparations, and affirmative action, and as the host of a six-part BBC/PBS television series, *Wonders of the African World.*

Gates was the 2002 Jefferson Lecturer in the Humanities for the National Endowment for the Humanities. In 2004 he co-edited *African American Lives.*

See also Black Studies; English, African-American; Intellectual Life; Literary Criticism, U.S.

■ ■ *Bibliography*

Bigelow, Barbara Carlisle, ed., *Contemporary Black Biography*, vol. 3. Detroit, Mich.: Gale, 1993.

Clarke, Breena, and Susan Tifft. "A 'Race Man' Argues for a Broader Curriculum: Henry Louis Gates Jr. Wants W. E. B. DuBois, Wole Soyinka and Phyllis Wheatley on the Nation's Reading Lists." *Time* 137, no. 16 (April 1991): 16–17.

Smothers, Bonnie. "The Booklist Interview: Henry Louis Gates Jr." *Booklist* 93, no. 12 (February 15, 1997): 972–973.

RICHARD NEWMAN (2001)
Updated by publisher 2005

GAYE, MARVIN (GAY, MARVIN PENTZ)

APRIL 2, 1939
APRIL 1, 1984

Singer and songwriter Marvin Gaye grew up in Washington, D.C., and began his musical career singing in the choir and playing organ in the church where his father, Marvin Gay, Sr., was a Pentecostal minister. In a radical rejection of his father's expectations, the younger Gaye became a secular musician.

Gaye's career as a professional musician began in 1958 when he became friendly with Harvey Fuqua, a record promoter for Chess Records who was impressed with his performance at a local high-school talent contest. After hearing Gaye's 1957 recordings with a group called the Marquees ("Wyatt Earp" and "Hey Little Schoolgirl") on the Columbia rhythm-and-blues label Okeh, Fuqua invited Gaye to Chicago and signed him to the Chess label in 1959. From the beginning of his career Gaye altered his last name, adding an *e* to the end for reasons he never explained.

In 1960 Gaye and Fuqua relocated to Detroit, where Fuqua established contacts with Berry Gordy, founder of the fledgling Motown Records. The next year Gaye and Fuqua married two of Gordy's sisters (Anna and Gwen, respectively), Fuqua joined Motown, and Gaye was signed to the label. Even though Gaye was part of the Gordy family, it was several years before he began recording as a Motown solo artist. From 1960 to 1962 he was a backup singer and session drummer for various Motown performers. In 1962 Motown released his debut solo album, *The Soulful Mood of Marvin Gaye,* a collection of jazz-influenced, middle-of-the-road ballads. It was two years until Gaye had a hit single with "Hitch Hike" (1964). That same year he released "Pride and Joy," which climbed to the top ten on both the pop and the rhythm-and-blues charts.

During his time with Motown, Gaye recorded such hit records as "Ain't That Peculiar" (1965), "It Takes Two" (1967), "Your Precious Love" (1967), "Ain't Nothing Like the Real Thing" (1968), "You're All I Need to Get By" (1968), and, most successful of all, "Heard It Through the Grapevine" (1968) and "What's Going On" (1971). As one of Motown's soul-music emissaries, Gaye perfected the style, its ballad idiom, emotional lyrics, and use of gospel techniques in a secular context.

Gaye's most successful album was *What's Going On* (1971), which included three top ten hits ("Inner City Blues," "Mercy Mercy Me," and the title song). As Motown's first "concept album," *What's Going On* was musically diverse and a forum for Gaye to articulate his views on contemporary political issues, with particular attention to pollution in the nuclear age and the challenges facing inner-city blacks.

The year *What's Going On* was released, Gaye received honors from *Billboard* and *Cashbox* magazines as trendsetter and male vocalist of the year, respectively. He also won an Image Award from the NAACP. Motown released his next album, *Let's Get It On,* in 1973, and the title song immediately reached number one on the charts as Gaye's most successful single.

The last ten years of Gaye's life were marked by his divorce from Anna Gordy, marriage to Janis Hunter, relocation to Europe because of tax debts, dismissal from Motown in 1981, and increased dependence on drugs. His long-term feuds with his father and ongoing depression erupted on April 1, 1984, when an argument between the men resulted in Gay shooting and killing his son in Los Angeles. Gaye's father was acquitted because a brain tumor contributed to his irrational and violent behavior.

Gaye's soulful aesthetic, with his light, crooning tenor voice full of emotion, earnestness, and often guttural sensuality, was ideally suited to both his contemplative and ecstatic performance modes. In 1983, the year before his death, Gaye continued to reveal his gifts as a performer, winning two Grammy Awards, for best male vocalist and best instrumental performance, with his gold record "Sexual Healing."

See also Music in the United States; Rhythm and Blues

■■ *Bibliography*

Dyson, Michael Eric. *Mercy, Mercy Me: The Art, Loves, and Demons of Marvin Gaye.* New York: Basic Civitas Books, 2004.

Edmonds, Ben. *What's Going On and the Last Days of the Motown Sound.* Edinburgh: Mojo Books, 2001.

Gaye, Frankie, and Fred E. Basten. *Marvin Gaye, My Brother.* San Francisco: Backbeat Books, 2003.

George, Nelson. *Where Did Our Love Go: The Rise and Fall of the Motown Sound.* New York: St. Martin's Press, 1985.

Hardy, Phil, and Dave Laing. *Encyclopedia of Rock.* New York: Schirmer Books, 1988.

Pareles, Jon, and Patricia Romanowski. *The Rolling Stone Encyclopedia of Rock & Roll.* New York: Summit Books, 1986.

Ritz, David. *Divided Soul: The Life of Marvin Gaye.* New York: Da Capo Press, 1985.

MICHAEL D. SCOTT (1996)
Updated bibliography

GAY MEN

The history of African-American gay men is far from a linear progression in status from social pariahs to more or less accepted and acceptable members of both the black and gay communities. Rather, it is a troubling and often painful story of the attempt to find an identity and build a visible community within the white and heterosexual power structures. On the one hand, the post–World War II economic boom and the gains of the civil rights movement have contributed to increased financial stability and social mobility for many black Americans. At the same time, relatively relaxed attitudes toward sex have prevailed in contemporary society. These circumstances have led to a broader range of black gay identity becoming visible and have reduced in some respects the stigma on such activity. However, black gays and lesbians experienced the large increase in poverty, drug addiction, homelessness, and other ills that afflicted other blacks during the 1980s and early 1990s; moreover, they have been plagued by antigay violence and by the epidemic of AIDS.

Although black civil rights leaders and elected officials have sometimes pushed for legal protections for gays and lesbians, homosexuality was not and is not generally accepted in the black community, which shares white society's negative attitudes toward sexual minorities. Various explanations have been propounded for the black community's response to homosexuality. First, the black church, as an important and historically independent institution, has had great prominence in African-American life, and its ministers and clergy have traditionally evinced a patriarchal, homophobic stance. For instance, in 1993 black minister Eugene Lumpkin, a member of San Francisco's Human Rights Commission, referred to homosexuality as an "abomination." (He was forced to resign soon after.) The same year, conservative black ministers in Cincinnati played a crucial role in overturning a local antidiscrimination ordinance covering sexual orientation. At the same time, the black church's music, ritual, and message of love and community have served an important nurturing role for the many gay men who retain a strong bond with their church and community.

Another example of homophobia is the traditional disdain of homosexuals as effeminate. Ironically, large numbers of black men, particularly those in prison, have same-sex contact but remain strongly antihomosexual and refuse to consider themselves gay. Black militant politics has often had a homophobic side, a famous example being Eldridge Cleaver's attack on James Baldwin, and numerous militant cultural figures, such as rap musicians, have included antigay slurs in their work. Many African Americans who tolerate private same-sex conduct oppose public affirmation of homosexuality. They fear it is an embarrassment to the larger black community, which is trying to overcome white stereotyping of black crime, immorality, and sexual excess. A notable example is civil rights activist Bayard Rustin's dismissal from the Southern Christian Leadership Conference (SCLC) in the early 1960s, due in part to concern over his homosexuality.

Perhaps the most crucial element in the black community's homophobia is the widespread assumption that gayness and gay men are white ("the white man's weakness" as Amiri Baraka termed it in 1970). Since many blacks do not realize that their own friends and relatives may be gay, they have no reason to change their negative outlook, and they resent the gay movement's appropriation of the civil rights movement's tactics and rhetoric as an attempt to divert attention from the cause of African-American liberation. All too often, white gay activists reinforce this belief by projecting a white image for the gay community and by refusing to incorporate black leadership and culture. In 1993, when the subject of admitting gays and lesbians into the military was being nationally debated, the contributions and the important legal precedent of Sargeant Perry Watkins, an African American who had successfully litigated his discharge on grounds of sexual orientation, were largely ignored by activists and the media. Similarly, the media and public all but ignored the life and tragic death in 1995 of Glenn Burke, an openly gay major league baseball player for the Los Angeles Dodgers and Oakland Athletics.

Some black scholars claim that same-sex desire is the result of the alienating forces of modern life or merely a more or less recent white intrusion into and against "African" values. Nevertheless, while we know little about its early history, same-sex contact by African Americans has existed since at least as far back as 1646, when Jan Creoli, "a Negro" in New Netherland (now New York State) was sentenced to be "choked to death, and then burned to ashes" for a second sodomy offense. Similarly, in 1712, Massachusetts authorities executed "Mingo, alias Coke," the slave of a magistrate, for "forcible buggery" (presumably sodomy). Through the nineteenth century the subject remained almost completely hidden except for what can be gathered from criminal records or the shrill exhortations of elite editors and writers in antebellum black newspapers warning blacks to curb both their sexual appetites and their tendency toward revelry and erotic abandon. In 1892 a report on "perversion" by Dr. Irving Rosse discussed such topics as African Americans arrested for performing oral sex in Washington D.C.'s Lafayette Square (still a popular cruising area in the 1990s) and the rituals of a "band of Negro men of androgynous character." In 1916 Dr. James Kiernan reported on blacks who solicited men in Chicago cafés and performed fellatio and sometimes "pederasty" on them in a "resort" under a popular dime museum.

The Great Migration of the 1910s and 1920s and the consequent urbanization of African Americans led to the creation and expansion of gay spaces—bars, dance clubs (including "drag balls," dances where men dressed as women), bathhouses, and theaters—in the black communities of larger cities. These served as meeting places for black gay men and sometimes for white gay men trying to escape the rigid sexual mores of white society or seeking black male prostitutes. Popular songs such as "Foolish Man Blues" and "Sissy Man Blues" (sung by such singers as Ma Rainey and Bessie Smith, both bisexual women), though disdainful in tone, testified to the existence and attractiveness of homosexuals.

At the same time, black gay men assumed important positions in American cultural and intellectual life, a primacy they have maintained ever since. Cultural movements—notably that brief concatenation of artists and intellectuals known as the Harlem Renaissance—were heavily gay flavored. Socialite hostess A'Lelia Walker surrounded herself with gay men whose work she promoted, and Carl Van Vechten, a gay white man, helped sponsor the movement's artistic products. Countee Cullen, Alain Locke, Wallace Thurman, Lawrence Brown, Claude McKay, and Richard Bruce Nugent were gay or bisexual men who were some of the brightest lights of the Harlem Renaissance. Significantly, Nugent published the first explicit piece of black gay literature, "Smoke Lilies and Jade" (1926), a short story published in the short-lived Harlem Renaissance journal *Fire.* Claude McKay's novel *Home to Harlem* (1928) features a scene in a recognizably gay bar.

Despite the high visibility of gay men in black culture, many aspects of gay life itself remained secret, forbidden, and indeed alienating to many black gay men themselves. The idea that black gays actually composed a community that intersected, but was not subsumed in, either the black or gay communities would have seemed altogether odd to earlier generations of black gay intellectuals. James Baldwin, a literary giant of the latter part of the twentieth century whose works included homosexual characters and complex meditations on sexuality and race, commented as late as 1984 in a *Village Voice* interview that he felt uncomfortable with the label "gay" and presumably with the idea of belonging to a (black) gay community. "The word 'gay' has always rubbed me the wrong way. . . . I simply feel it's a world that has very little to do with me, with where I did my growing up. I was never at home in it."

Despite the presence of such openly gay individuals as Baldwin and science fiction writer Samuel Delany during the 1950s and 1960s, the emergence of gay African Americans as a political group did not occur until the late 1960s and 1970s, when the success of the civil rights movement in empowering and enfranchising blacks led other groups to struggle publicly for their liberation. Fittingly, African Americans had a large hand in the Stonewall rebellion, traditionally considered the founding event of the gay liberation movement. In June 1969, the Stonewall Inn, a New York gay bar, was raided by police. Many of the patrons were black, largely drag queens and effeminate gay men. Tired of police harassment, they fought back, throwing bottles and bricks. News of the incident quickly spread and led to the formation of political groups, notably the short-lived Gay Liberation Front (GLF). Sensitive to the revolutionary nature of the gay struggle, the GLF formed alliances with radical black groups, such as the Black Panther Party. However, as most gay political groups abandoned their radical beginnings and reverted to a predominantly white, middle-class outlook and membership, gay black activists became alienated from and less involved in their activities. Many blacks continue to feel unwelcome in the white gay community. Bars, dance clubs, and other spaces in gay areas sometimes discourage black patronage through discriminatory "carding" and harassment policies.

Split between the black and gay communities, many African-American homosexuals continue to feel obliged to choose. Writers such as Max C. Smith and Julius Johnson have noted the rough division of African-American homosexuals into two groups, "black gays" and "gay blacks." Black gays remain primarily active in the black community and have mostly black male friends and lovers. Many of them remain private about their gayness, and some lead bisexual "front lives." Gay blacks, on the other hand, identify with the gay community. They more frequently date and socialize with whites, and they tend to be more open about their sexuality.

Black gays and lesbians have worked to create a community and to mold a distinctively black gay culture. An important ingredient of the drive has been to construct independent black gay institutions. Black gay men, often in cooperation with black lesbians, have, since the late 1970s, created a number of political, social, and cultural institutions. The founding of the National Coalition of Black Gays (later the National Coalition of Black Lesbians and Gays) in 1979 demonstrated a profound belief in the viability of the black lesbian and gay community. Indeed, the creation of such a national coalition by a handful of Washington, D.C.-based activists showed just how secure some black gays had become in their assumption of black gay cultural and political unity. This initial effort was followed by the founding of black gay organizations throughout the country, including several black gay churches (the Pentecostal Faith Temple of Washington, D.C., among them); a writers collective called Other Countries; music groups, such as the Lavender Light Gospel Choir; and a number of social institutions, including Gay Men of African Descent (New York), Black Gay Men United (Oakland), Adodi, and Unity (both of Philadelphia).

A notable example of organizing within the larger black community was the founding of a gay student group at Howard University, the first of several gay organizations at historically black colleges. Black gay men have also branched out into fighting racism in the gay community through work in such groups as Men of All Colors Together (formerly Black and White Men Together). They have also been active in AIDS education, Philadelphia's Blacks Educating Blacks About Sexual Health Issues (BEBASHI) being a noted example. Bars, bathhouses, and restaurants catering mainly to a black gay clientele have been set up, and black gay men have organized plays, musical performances, and dances (including the drag balls immortalized in white filmmaker Jennie Livingston's 1991 documentary *Paris Is Burning*).

In addition, there has been an explosion since the early 1980s of black gay (and lesbian) literature. Black gay and lesbian literature was regularly collected in special issues of gay and lesbian magazines. Moreover, a number of independent black gay and lesbian publications— namely, *Habari Daftari, Other Countries Journal, Pyramid Review, Blacklight, Blackheart, BLK, Yemonja, Black/Out, Moja: Black and Gay, B*, and *Real Read*—were started with the express purpose of providing an outlet for the broadest possible group of black gay and lesbian writers. Many of the most prominent and successful pieces of black gay literature have been anthologies, beginning with the foundation collections *In the Life* (1986) and *Brother to Brother* (1991), and continuing through the 1990s with *Shade* (1996) and *Fighting Words* (1999). In the early twenty-first century, collections such as *Black Like Us* (2002) and *Freedom in this Village* (2005) continue to survey and catalogue an ever-growing canon of black gay men's writing.

Several black writers have become prominent outside the community. Randall Kenan's *Visitation of Spirits* (1989) and *Let the Dead Bury Their Dead* (1992) and Melvin Dixon's *Vanishing Rooms* (1991) were published by major presses. Essex Hemphill has not only had his 1992 collection *Ceremonies* published by a major press, but he has also achieved renown through his appearance in Marlon Riggs's popular nonfiction films, such as *Tongues Untied* (1991). E. Lynn Harris's stirring novelistic explorations of bisexuality, which he at first sold himself door to door, became a major publishing phenomenon. At the same time, black gay publishing concerns produced more and more literature just as black gay men began to organize new mediums of expression on the Internet. After working in President Bill Clinton's administration during the early 1990s, Keith Boykin started exploring the invisibility of black bisexual and gay life in novels and then nonfiction: he now keeps a regular "blog" detailing his experiences as an urban black gay man. The Internet has provided black gay men a virtual space for promoting events such as film festivals and parades. The Internet also has served as a forum for community and support networks and has established an arena for creative and private expressions separate from publishing firms.

Black gay artists and intellectuals have established inroads into areas of expression outside of literature. Alvin Ailey helped revolutionize modern dance with his integration of black folk music and motifs and strong sensual elements, while Bill T. Jones was a pioneer in New Wave—including openly gay—choreography. Films such as Isaac Julien's *Looking for Langston* (1988) and Marlon Riggs's *Anthem* (1994) and *"Non, Je Ne Regrette Rien"* (*No Regret*, 1992) have been enthusiastically received by gay and straight audiences throughout the world. Thomas Allen Harris's two short videos, *Splash* (1991) and *Black Body* (1992), have established a strong black gay presence in video, while his brother Lyle Harris has enriched the field of photography through such works as *Confessions of a Snow Queen.* The San Francisco performance troupe Pomo Afro Homos has offered a powerful testimony on the black gay experience. Performer RuPaul has become a major singer and cultural icon. Jazzman Billy Strayhorn collaborated with Duke Ellington to produce immortal songs. Harvard theologian Peter Gomes has elucidated biblical teachings on sexuality. Actor Howard Rollins, star of such films as *A Soldier's Story* (1984) and the television series *In the Heat of the Night* (1988–1994), was a major sex symbol before disease cut short his career. Producer/director/playwright George C. Wolfe has made major contributions to American theater, including direction of the landmark drama *Angels in America* (1993). In an attempt to focus and unify critical study of these diverse artists and genres, black literary and cultural critics have been brought together at the Los Angeles–based African-American Gay and Lesbian Studies Center, founded by Gil Gerard in 1992.

As the twenty-first century begins, the dilemma facing black gays, particularly black gay artists and intellectuals, is whether they will be able to maintain and develop their autonomous institutions while continuing to push into the mainstream of American political and cultural life. Already very serious questions have been raised about who can and should control the image of the black gay man. For example, black critics bell hooks and Robert Reid-Pharr have questioned the political and cultural imperatives underpinning the representation of black gay men in the film *Paris Is Burning.* Furthermore, black gay men still face explicit harassment and isolation from more visible African-American men, particularly from conservative political and religious leaders and in hip-hop and reggae lyrics. The cultural atmosphere for black gay men remains ambiguous and uncertain, marked on the one hand by huge amounts of gay political and cultural activity along with abundant representations of black gay men in books and online but on the other hand by disproportionate invisibility in other arenas, which makes the persistence of violence, disease, poverty, and despair problematic.

See also Identity and Race in the United States; Lesbians; Masculinity

■■ *Bibliography*

Beam, Joseph, ed. *In the Life: A Black Gay Anthology.* Boston: Alyson, 1986.

Boykin, Keith. *Beyond the Down Low: Sex, Lies, and Denial in Black America.* New York: Carroll & Graf, 2005.

Carbado, Devon W., Dwight A. McBride, and Donald Weise, eds. *Black Like Us: A Century of Lesbian, Gay, and Bisexual African American Fiction.* San Francisco: Cleis Press, 2002.

Cleaver, Eldridge. *Soul on Ice.* New York: McGraw-Hill, 1968.

D'Emilio, John. *Sexual Politics, Sexual Communities: The Making of the Homosexual Minority in the United States, 1940–1970.* 2d ed. Chicago: University of Chicago Press, 1998.

Duberman, Martin, Martha Vicinus, and George Chauncey Jr., eds. *Hidden from History: Reclaiming the Gay and Lesbian Past.* New York: New American Library, 1990.

Harris, E. Lynn, ed. *Freedom in this Village: Twenty-Five Years of Black Gay Men's Writing, 1969 to the Present.* New York: Carroll & Graf, 2005.

Hemphill, Essex, ed. *Brother to Brother: New Writings by Black Gay Men.* Boston: Alyson, 1991.

hooks, bell. "Is Paris Burning?" *Black Looks: Race and Representation.* Boston: South End Press, 1992.

Katz, Jonathan Ned. *Gay/Lesbian Almanac: A New Documentary.* New York: Carroll & Graf, 1994.

Morrow, Bruce, and Charles H. Rowell, eds. *Shade: An Anthology of Fiction by Gay Men of African Descent.* New York: Avon, 1996.

Peterson, John L. "Black Men and Their Same-Sex Desires and Behaviors." In Gilbert Heratt, ed. *Gay Culture in America: Essays from the Field.* Boston: Beacon Press, 1992.

Reid-Pharr, Robert. "The Spectacle of Blackness." *Radical America* 24, no. 4 (Winter 1992).

Smith, Charles Michael, ed. *Fighting Words: Personal Essays by Black Gay Men.* New York: Avon, 1999.

ROBERT REID-PHARR (1996)
JUSTIN ROGERS-COOPER (2005)

George, David

c. 1743
1810

David George was born a slave in Sussex County, Virginia, around 1743. He died a world away, a free man, in Sierra

Leone, West Africa, not quite seventy years later. Along with David Liele, Andrew Bryan, Jessie Peter, Hannah Williams, and others, George is best known as one of the progenitors of an Afro-Baptist faith developed and articulated across the British Atlantic world by a cadre of black Christians in the aftermath of the American Revolution. For his part, George established and nurtured pioneering Baptist congregations in South Carolina, Georgia, Nova Scotia, and Sierra Leone. His missionizing and institution building during the Revolutionary period—when Christianity was of little real consequence to most blacks in British America—foreshadowed the later development of the black church and of black evangelicalism as formidable social and cultural forces in African-American life.

George was born to African parents and spent the first nineteen years of his life as a slave on the Chappell plantation in southeastern Virginia. He ran away from the property before his twentieth birthday, and in an odyssey illustrating many of the complexities of colonial American life and society, he spent the next two or three years trekking farther into the Deep South, straining desperately to stay ahead of a thirty-guinea reward that his former master had offered for his capture and return. During this long flight George worked for a succession of white traders on the Pee Dee and Savannah Rivers, was for a time enslaved by a Creek headman in the Georgia interior, subsequently sojourned among the Natchez Indians, and just as the son of his former master finally tracked him down, arranged to have himself purchased by a frontier merchant, Indian trader, and planter named George Gaulphin.

George eventually settled at Gaulphin's Silver Bluff property in the South Carolina upcountry. There he married, began a family, and moved, as he put it, from having "no serious thoughts" about his soul to distressing constantly over where he might spend eternity. Ultimately, George became one of eight blacks on the Gaulphin property to be baptized, a rite performed by a white preacher who occasionally visited the plantation. Sometime between 1773 and 1775 this band was formed into a congregation and the Silver Bluff Baptist Church became, quite likely, the first black church in North America.

During the American Revolution George and other members of the church sought refuge, and their liberty, behind British lines in and around Savannah, Georgia. As the tide of the war turned against the British, George and others joined successive British evacuations and settled eventually with thousands of other Loyalists, black and white, in Nova Scotia in late 1782. During the next seven years George planted and watered Baptist chapels throughout the British Maritime colonies of Nova Scotia and New Brunswick. As did other black immigrants to Nova Scotia, however, George suffered mightily from white violence and discrimination, which joined with a harsh physical environment made life in the Maritimes nearly unbearable. When British philanthropists and the British government—responding to agitation from blacks in Nova Scotia—offered to resettle dissatisfied black Nova Scotians to Sierra Leone, George threw his considerable influence behind the scheme. David George joined a Maritime exodus of more than a thousand blacks and arrived in Sierra Leone in 1792. Except for a subsequent trip to London, George lived the rest of his life in West Africa, continuing the pioneering missionary efforts that had defined his life. During the last years of his life, though, George's close associations with British officialdom in Sierra Leone worked to lessen his influence among the larger black emigrant community who over time came to see the kinds of broken promises and equivocations that had defined their Nova Scotia experience make themselves manifest at Sierra Leone as well.

See also Baptists; Free Blacks, 1619–1860

■■ *Bibliography*

Brooks, Walter H. "The Priority of the Silver Bluff Church and Its Promoters." *Journal of Negro History* 7, no. 2 (1922): 127–96.

George, David. "An Account of the Life of Mr. David George, from Sierra Leone in Africa; Given by Himself in a Conversation with Brother Rippon of London and Brother Pearce of Birmingham." In *Unchained Voices: An Anthology of Black Authors in the English-Speaking World of the 18th Century*, edited by Vincent Carretta, pp. 333–350. Lexington: The University Press of Kentucky, 1996.

Gordan, Grant. *From Slavery to Freedom: The Life of David George: Pioneer Black Baptist Minister*. Hantsport, Nova Scotia: Lancelot Press Limited, 1992.

Sobel, Mechal. *Trabelin' On: The Slave Journey to an Afro-Baptist Faith*. Westport, Conn.: Greenwood Press, 1979.

Walker, James St. G. *The Black Loyalists*. New York: Africana Publishing Company, 1976.

Walker, James St. G. "David George." In *Dictionary of Canadian Biography Online*. Available from <http://www.biographi.ca/EN/>.

ALEXANDER X. BYRD (2005)

GIBSON, ALTHEA

AUGUST 25, 1927
SEPTEMBER 28, 2003

Althea Gibson was the first black tennis player to win the sport's major titles. Born in Silver, South Carolina, to a garage hand and a housewife, she came to New York City at age three to live with an aunt. The oldest of five children, she was a standout athlete at Public School 136 and began playing paddleball under Police Athletic League auspices on West 143rd Street in Harlem. In 1940 she was introduced to tennis by Fred Johnson, a one-armed instructor, at the courts (now named after him) on 152nd Street. She was an immediate sensation.

Gibson became an honorary member of Harlem's socially prominent Cosmopolitan Tennis Club (now defunct) and won her first tournament—the American Tennis Association (ATA) junior girls title—in 1945. (The ATA is the oldest continuously operated black noncollegiate sports organization in America). Although Gibson lost in the finals of the ATA women's singles in 1946, she attracted the attention of two black physicians: Dr. Hubert Eaton of Wilmington, North Carolina, and Dr. R. Walter Johnson of Lynchburg, Virginia, who tried to advance her career.

In September 1946 Gibson entered high school in Wilmington while living with the Eatons, and she graduated in 1949. She won the ATA women's single title ten years in a row, from 1947 to 1956. As the best black female tennis player ever, she was encouraged to enter U.S. Lawn Tennis Association (the white governing body of tennis) events. Jackie Robinson had just completed his third year in major league baseball, and pressure was being applied on other sports to integrate. Although she was a reluctant crusader, Gibson was finally admitted to play in the USLTA Nationals at Forest Hills, New York, on August 28, 1950.

Alice Marble, the former USLTA singles champion, wrote a letter, published in the July 1950 issue of *American Lawn Tennis* magazine, admonishing the USLTA for its reluctance to admit Gibson when she was clearly more than qualified. Gibson's entry was then accepted at two major events in the summer of 1950 before her Forest Hills debut. She was warmly received at the Nationals, where she lost a two-day, rain-delayed match to the number-two-seeded Louise Brough in the second round.

Gibson's breakthrough heralded more to come. The ATA began a serious junior development program to provide opportunities for promising black children. (Out of that program came Arthur Ashe, who became the first black male winner of the sport's major titles.) Sydney Llewelyn became Gibson's coach, and her rise was meteoric. Her first grand slam title was the French singles in Paris in 1956. Before she turned professional, she added the Wimbledon and the U.S. singles in both 1957 and 1958, and the French women's doubles and the U.S. mixed doubles. She was a Wightman Cup team member in 1957 and

1958. After her Wimbledon victory, she was presented her trophy by Queen Elizabeth II, she danced with the queen's husband, Prince Philip, at the Wimbledon Ball, and New York City accorded her a ticker-tape parade.

The poise she showed at Wimbledon and at other private clubs where USLTA-sanctioned events were played was instilled by Dr. Eaton's wife and by her time spent as an undergraduate at Florida A&M University in Tallahassee, Florida. Jake Gaither, FAMU's famed athletic director, helped secure a teaching position for her in physical education at Lincoln University in Jefferson City, Missouri. In the winter of 1955–56, the State Department asked her to tour Southeast Asia with Ham Richardson, Bob Perry, and Karol Fageros.

In 1957 Gibson won the Babe Didrickson Zaharias Trophy as Female Athlete of the Year, the first black female athlete to win the award. She also began an attempt at a career as a singer, taking voice lessons three times a week. While singing at New York City's Waldorf-Astoria Hotel for a tribute to famed songwriter W. C. Handy, she landed an appearance on the *Ed Sullivan Show* in May 1958. Moderately successful as a singer, she considered a professional tour with tennis player Jack Kramer, the American champion of the 1940s. She also became an avid golfer, encouraged by Joe Louis, the former world heavyweight champion, who was a golf enthusiast. Louis had also paid her way to her first Wimbledon championships.

The Ladies Professional Golfers Association (LPGA) was in its infancy and purses were small. But Gibson was a quick learner and was soon nearly a "scratch" player. She received tips from Ann Gregory, who had been the best black female golfer ever. Gibson, a naturally gifted athlete, could handle the pressure of professional sports. But the purses offered on the LPGA tour were too small to maintain her interest.

In 1986 New Jersey governor Tom Kean appointed Gibson to the state's Athletic Commission. She became a sought-after teaching professional at several private clubs in central and northern New Jersey and devoted much of her time to counseling young black players. The first black female athlete to enjoy true international fame, Gibson was elected to the International Tennis Hall of Fame in 1971.

In 1997 Gibson was honored with a ceremony at the U.S. Open. At about this time her health was failing and she was living in near poverty because of her medical bills when a group of athletes and coaches staged a benefit that raised $100,000 to help defray her expenses. While her health initially improved somewhat, it gradually deteriorated until her death in 2003. On September 7, 2004 she was honored posthumously at a ceremony at the U.S. Open tennis tournament in New York.

See also Tennis; Williams, Venus and Serena

■ ■ Bibliography

Gibson, Althea. *I Always Wanted to Be Somebody.* New York: Harper & Row, 1958.

Gibson, Althea, with Richard Curtis. *So Much to Live For.* New York: G. P. Putnam's Sons, 1968.

Schoenfeld, Bruce. *The Match: Althea Gibson and Angela Buxton: How Two Outsiders—One Black, the Other Jewish—Forged a Friendship and Made Sports History.* New York: Amistad Press, 2004.

ARTHUR R. ASHE JR. (1996)
Updated by publisher 2005

GIBSON, JOSH

DECEMBER 21, 1911
JANUARY 20, 1947

If any one man personified both the joy of Negro League baseball and the pathos of major league baseball's color line, it was catcher Josh Gibson, black baseball's greatest hitter. Born Joshua Gibson to sharecroppers Mark and Nancy (Woodlock) Gibson in Buena Vista, Georgia, Josh moved to Pittsburgh in 1924 when his father found employment at the Homestead Works of the Carnegie-Illinois Steel Company. On the diamond, the solidly built Gibson astounded fans and players with his feats for two decades, but he never got the chance to play in the major leagues.

As a youth on the north side of Pittsburgh, Gibson attended a vocational school where he prepared for the electrician's trade. But it was on the city's sandlots, playing for the Gimbel Brothers and Westinghouse Airbrake company teams, that he prepped for his life's work. Joining the Pittsburgh Crawfords in 1927 when this team of local youths was still a sandlot club, Gibson soon attracted the attention of Homestead Grays owner Cumberland Posey.

Gibson starred for the Grays in the early 1930s, returning to the Pittsburgh Crawfords for the 1934–1936 campaigns. By then, the Crawfords were owned by numbers baron Gus Greenlee, who remade them into the 1935 Negro National League champions. With future Hall of Famers Gibson, Satchel Paige, Judy Johnson, Oscar Charleston, and "Cool Papa" Bell on the team, the Crawfords were quite possibly the best team ever assembled.

In 1937, after breaking his contract and joining many of his Crawford teammates in the Dominican Republic,

Gibson was traded back to the Grays. There, he and Buck Leonard were considered black baseball's equivalent to Babe Ruth and Lou Gehrig. The Grays won nine pennants in a row after Gibson returned, a mark equaled only by the Tokyo Giants.

Although a fine defensive catcher, the muscular six-foot one-inch, 215-pound Gibson is remembered best for his legendary swings at the plate. Perhaps the greatest slugger ever, he hit balls out of parks across the United States and the Caribbean basin, where he played each winter between 1933 and 1945. His home runs at Forbes Field and Yankee Stadium are thought to have been the longest hit at each. During his career, Gibson never played for a losing team.

His lifetime .379 batting average in the Negro and Caribbean leagues is the highest of any Negro Leaguer. He won batting championships, most-valuable-player awards, and/or home run titles in the Negro Leagues, Cuba, Mexico, the Dominican Republic, and Puerto Rico. His home run blasts are still recalled throughout these lands.

The second-highest-paid Negro Leaguer, Gibson also was the league's second-best attraction, behind Satchel Paige in both categories. Promoters often advertised for Negro League games by guaranteeing that Gibson would hit a home run. He rarely let them down.

Although fellow Negro Leaguers remember Gibson with fondness and a respect that borders on awe, his personal life was touched by tragedy. His young bride, Helen, died delivering their twin children, Josh Jr. and Helen, in 1930. Gibson himself died in 1947, soon after the Brooklyn Dodgers signed Jackie Robinson. He was only thirty-five at the time. In 1972 he joined batterymate Satchel Paige in the Baseball Hall of Fame.

See also Baseball; Paige, Satchel

■ ■ Bibliography

Holway, John B. *Josh and Satch: The Life and Times of Josh Gibson and Satchel Paige.* Westport, Conn.: Meckler, 1991.

Ribowsky, Mark. *The Power and the Darkness: The Life of Josh Gibson in the Shadows of the Game.* Replica Books, 2001.

Ruck, Rob. *Sandlot Seasons: Sport in Black Pittsburgh.* Urbana: University of Illinois Press, 1987.

ROB RUCK (1996)
Updated bibliography

GILLESPIE, DIZZY

OCTOBER 21, 1917
JANUARY 6, 1993

John Birks Gillespie, or "Dizzy," as he was later known, was born in Cheraw, South Carolina. He took up the trombone in his early teens and began playing the trumpet shortly thereafter. When he began to play the trumpet, he puffed out his cheeks, a technical mistake that later became his visual trademark. Starting in 1932, Gillespie studied harmony and theory at Laurinburg Institute, in Laurinburg, North Carolina, but in 1935 he broke off studies to move with his family to Philadelphia. The bandleader Frank Fairfax gave Gillespie his first important work, and it was in Fairfax's band that Gillespie earned his nickname, Dizzy, for his clowning onstage and off.

In 1937 Gillespie moved to New York and played for two years with Teddy Hill's band. Through the early 1940s his experience was mostly with big bands, including those of Cab Calloway, Ella Fitzgerald, Benny Carter, Charlie Barnet, Les Hite, Lucky Millinder, Earl Hines, Duke Ellington, and Billy Eckstine. Among his important early recordings were "Pickin' the Cabbage" (1940) with Calloway and "Little John Special" (1942) with Millinder. Gillespie married Lorraine Willis in 1940, and he began leading small ensembles in Philadelphia and New York shortly thereafter. In 1945 he joined with saxophonist Charlie Parker (1920–1955) to lead a bebop ensemble that helped inaugurate the modern jazz era.

Although younger jazz musicians had played in a bebop style in the early 1940s in big bands and in after-hours jam sessions at clubs in Harlem, it was not until Parker and Gillespie's 1945 recordings, including "Dizzy Atmosphere," "Shaw 'Nuff," and "Groovin' High," that the new style's break from swing became clear. Bebop reacted to the sometimes stodgy tempos of the big bands and was instead characterized by adventurous harmonies and knotty, fast lines played in stunning unison by Gillespie and Parker, with solos that emphasized speed, subtlety, and wit.

Gillespie's trumpet style during this time was enormously influential. By the mid-1940s he had broken away from his earlier emulation of Roy Eldridge (1911–1989) and arrived at a style of his own, one which he maintained for the next five decades. He had a crackling tone, and his endless flow of nimble ideas included astonishing runs and leaps into the instrument's highest registers. Although many of Gillespie's tunes were little more than phrases arrived at spontaneously with Parker, Gillespie composed many songs during this time that later became jazz stan-

Dizzy Gillespie (1917–1993). © WILLIAM COUPON/CORBIS

dards, including "A Night in Tunisia" (1942), "Salt Peanuts" (1942), and "Woody 'n' You" (1943). In addition to his virtuosity on trumpet, Gillespie continued to display his masterful sense of humor and instinct for gleeful mischief. Starting in the mid-1940s he affected the role of the jazz intellectual, wearing a beret, horn-rimmed glasses, and a goatee. He popularized bebop slang and served as the hipster patriarch to the white beatniks.

After his initial successes with Parker in the mid-1940s, Gillespie went on to enormous success as the leader of his own big band, for which he hired Tadd Dameron, George Russell, Gil Fuller, and John Lewis as composers and arrangers. Some of the band's recordings include "Things to Come" (1946), "One Bass Hit" (1946), and "Our Delight" (1946). The band's celebrated appearance at the Salle Pleyel in Paris, France, in 1948, yielded recordings of "'Round about Midnight," "I Can't Get Started," and "Good Bait." This appearance included the Cuban percussionist Chano Pozo, and during this time Gillespie began to explore Afro-Cuban rhythms and melodies. Gillespie's composition "Manteca" (1947) and his performance of George Russell's "Cubana Be, Cubana Bop" (1947) were among the first successful integrations of jazz and Latin music, followed later by his composition "Con Alma" (1957). In the late 1940s and early 1950s Gillespie also continued to work on small-group dates, including reunions with Charlie Parker in 1950, 1951, and 1953 and a return to the Salle Pleyel as a leader in 1953.

Although Gillespie never lost his idiosyncratic charm and sense of humor—after 1953 he played a trumpet with an upturned bell, supposedly the result of someone having bent the instrument by sitting on it—he outgrew the role of practical joker and instead became a figure of respect and genial authority. He released "Love Me" and "Tin Tin Deo" in 1951 on his own short-lived Dee Gee record label, and he became a featured soloist on many performances by the popular traveling sessions known as Jazz at the Philharmonic (JATP). In 1956 Gillespie's integrated band became the first to tour overseas under the sponsorship of the U.S. State Department, and in the following years he took the band on tours to the Middle East, South America, and Europe. In 1959 Gillespie, always an outspoken opponent of segregation, performed at the first integrated concert in a public school in his hometown of Cheraw, South Carolina. The next year he refused to back down when Tulane University in New Orleans threatened to cancel a concert unless he replaced his white pianist with an African American. Gillespie's political activities took another twist in 1964 when he went along with a tongue-in-cheek presidential campaign. During this time Gillespie continued to record, both with small groups (*Swing Low, Sweet Cadillac,* 1967) and with big bands (*Reunion Big Band,* 1968). He also worked extensively in film and television.

In the 1970s and 1980s, Gillespie maintained his busy schedule of touring and recording both in the United States and abroad as a leader of small and large bands and as a guest soloist. He appeared with the Giants of Jazz tour (1971-1972) and recorded with Mary Lou Williams (1971), Machito (1975), Count Basie (1977), Mongo Santamaria (1980), Max Roach (1989), and often with his trumpet protégé, John Faddis (b. 1953). During this time he also appeared on television shows such as *Sesame Street* and *The Cosby Show.* In 1979 he published his autobiography, *To BE or Not to BOP,* in which he explained his longstanding interest in Africa, which influenced his politics, music, and style of dress, and also recounted his involvement in the Bahá'í faith, to which he had converted in the late 1960s.

By the late 1980s Gillespie had long been recognized as one of the founding figures of modern jazz. In 1989 he won the U.S. National Medal of the Arts and was made a French Commandeur d'Ordre des Arts et Lettres. Although his instrumental style was largely fixed by the mid-1940s, he won four Grammy Awards in the 1970s and 1980s, and his career as a trumpeter ranked in influence and popularity with Louis Armstrong (1901–1971) and Miles Davis (1926–1991); along with Armstrong he became jazz's unofficial ambassador and personification around the world. Gillespie, who lived in Queens, New York, and then in Camden, New Jersey, continued giving hundreds of concerts each year in dozens of countries until his death at the age of seventy-four.

See also Davis, Miles; Jazz; Parker, Charlie

■ ■ *Bibliography*

Gillespie, Dizzy, and Al Fraser. *To BE or Not to BOP.* New York: Doubleday, 1979.

Gitler, Ira. *Jazz Masters of the Forties.* New York: Macmillan, 1966.

Horricks, Raymond. *Dizzy Gillespie.* Tunbridge Wells, UK: Spellmount, 1984.

Shipton, Alyn. *Groovin' High: The Life of Dizzy Gillespie.* New York: Oxford University Press, 1999.

Vail, Ken. *Dizzy Gillespie: The Bebop Years, 1937–1952.* Lanham, Md.: Scarecrow Press, 2003.

JONATHAN GILL (1996)
Updated bibliography

GIOVANNI, NIKKI

JUNE 7, 1943

Poet Nikki Giovanni was born Yolanda Cornelia Giovannia in Knoxville, Tennessee. Her father, Jones Giovanni, was a probation officer; her mother, Yolanda Cornelia Watson Giovanni, was a social worker. The Giovannis were a close-knit family, and Nikki felt a special bond with her younger sister, Gary, and her maternal grandmother, Louvenia Terrell Watson. Watson instilled in Giovanni a fierce pride in her African-American heritage.

After graduating from Fisk University in 1967, Giovanni was swept up by the Black Power and black arts movements. Between 1968 and 1970 she published three books of poetry reflecting her preoccupation with revolutionary politics: *Black Judgment* (1968), *Black Feeling, Black Talk* (1970), and *Re: Creation* (1970).

But *Re: Creation* also introduced more personal concerns. In the spring of 1969 Giovanni gave birth to a son, Tom. The experience, she said, caused her to reconsider her priorities. Her work through the middle 1970s concentrated less overtly on politics and confrontation and more on personal issues such as love and loneliness. Yet Giovanni would always deny any real separation between her "personal" and her "political" concerns. During this time she began writing poetry for children. *Spin a Soft Black Song: Poems for Children* appeared in 1971, *Ego-Tripping and Other Poems for Young People* in 1973, and *Vacation Time: Poems for Children* in 1980.

In the 1970s Giovanni expanded her horizons in other ways. Between 1971 and 1978 she made a series of six records, speaking her poetry to an accompaniment of gospel music (the first in the series, *Truth Is on Its Way,* was the best-selling spoken-word album of 1971). She published essays and two books of conversations with major literary forebears: *A Dialogue: James Baldwin and Nikki Giovanni* (1973) and *A Poetic Equation: Conversations Between Nikki Giovanni and Margaret Walker* (1974). She was also a sought-after reader and lecturer.

Critical reaction to Giovanni's work has often been mixed. While some have praised her work for its vitality and immediacy, some have felt that her early popularity and high degree of visibility worked against her development as a poet. Others have criticized her work as politically naive, uneven, and erratic. Some of these reactions were due in part to Giovanni's very public growing up as a poet and the diversity of her interests. These criticisms have never bothered Giovanni, who believes that life is "inherently incoherent."

Other works of Giovanni's include *My House* (1972), *The Women and the Men* (1972), *Cotton Candy on a Rainy Day* (1978), *Those Who Ride the Night Winds* (1983), a collection of essays titled *Sacred Cows and Other Edibles* (1988), *The Genie in the Jar* (1996), *The Sun Is So Quiet* (1996), *Love Poems* (1997), *Blues: For All the Changes: New Poems* (1999), *Quilting the Black-Eyed Pea: Poems and Not Quite Poems* (2002), and *Girls in the Circle* (2004). In 2002 she won the first Rosa Parks Woman of Courage award.

See also Black Arts Movement; Literature of the United States; Poetry, U.S.

■ ■ *Bibliography*

Bailey, Peter. "I Am Black, Female, Polite, . . .". *Ebony* (February 1972): 48–56.

Josephson, Judith P. *Nikki Giovanni: Poet of the People.* Berkeley Heights, N.J.: Enslow, 2003.

Tate, Claudia. *Black Women Writers at Work.* New York: Continuum, 1983.

MICHAEL PALLER (1996)
Updated by publisher 2005

GLASSPOLE, FLORIZEL

SEPTEMBER 25, 1909
NOVEMBER 25, 2000

▐▐▐ ▬▬▬▬▬▬

Sir Florizel Glasspole enjoyed the distinction of being the second native Governor General of an independent Jamai-

ca. He was born in Kingston, Jamaica's capital city, on September 25, 1909, the elder son of the late Methodist Minister the Rev. Theophilus Glasspole and his wife, Florence. He received his early education at the Buff Bay infant school in the parish of St. Mary and the Central Branch Primary School in Kingston. He received his secondary education at Kingston's prestigious Wolmers High School for Boys. At that time Jamaica was still a British colony and secondary education in the Island was then geared to prepare students for overseas examinations administered by the Universities of Cambridge and London. After completing secondary education, he acquired his tertiary education in Accounts by means of correspondence courses from the Scottish School of Accountancy in Scotland.

In his younger days, Glasspole was at one time Secretary of the Coke Young Men's Club and represented it in many debating contests. He was one of the leading personalities in the National Reform Association (1937) and in the Kingston and St. Andrew Literary and Debating Society. He served on several public boards and committees, including the Wage Board, the Apprenticeship Committee, the Industrial Relations Committee, and the Minimum Wage Boards for the baking, printing, and dry goods trades.

Glasspole was also a member of the Coke Methodist Church, and, in spite of a full public programme, he maintained an interest in sports and gardening and was a keen dog lover. In 1944 he married Ina Josephine Kinlocke. The marriage produced one daughter, Sara Lou.

Before entering the political arena, young Glasspole had a long and distinguished career in the trade union movement where he worked for more than eighteen years beginning with a three year stint as general secretary of the Jamaica United Clerks Association in 1937. He served eight years as general secretary for the Trade Union Advisory Council beginning in 1939. The Water Commission Manual Workers Union named him general secretary in 1941, a position he held concurrent with the presidency of the Jamaica's Printers and Allied Workers Union until 1948. From 1945 until 1955 he held a handful of other presidencies or was general secretary for the following organizations: the Machado Employees Union, Jamaica Trade Union Congress (1947–1952), Mental Hospital Workers Union (1944–1947), Municipal and Parochial General Workers Union (1945–1947), General Hospital and Allied Workers Union (1944–1947), and National Workers Union (1952–1955). Glasspole was also an ex-officio member of the Kingston and St Andrew Corporation from 1944 until 1955, a director of the Institute of Jamaica from 1944 through 1950, and a director of City Printery Ltd from 1944 until 1950.

Taking a job as an accounting clerk at the Serge Island Sugar Estate in St. Thomas in 1930 played a pivotal role in his life. "My heart shuddered with sympathy for the canefield workers," he recalled later. They worked long hours for very low wages. Conditions in the country were poor. The rumblings of social dissent, at first quiet, erupted and became the 1938 riots. The 1930s and 1940s were a turbulent period in Jamaica's history with strikes occurring regularly in the depressed economy, organized by labor and political organizations which were taking root in the Island.

Glasspole was one of the founding members of the People's National Party (PNP) in 1938. And in 1939, he became general secretary of the Trade Union Advisory Council. This was the peak of labor and political unrest in Jamaica with riots occurring in several parishes. In 1946, because of the impressive role Sir Glasspole played in the movement, the British Trade Union Congress assisted him in being awarded a scholarship to study trade unionism at Ruskin College in Oxford, England.

As an important leader in the trade union movement in Kingston, Glasspole was the ideal candidate for the PNP in their bid to win the East Kingston and Port Royal seat in the general elections of 1944. He was one of the only four PNP candidates to win a seat in those elections, which were the first to be held under Universal Adult Suffrage in Jamaica. Thereafter, he was appointed leader of Opposition Business in the House of Representatives and became secretary of the PNP's Parliamentary Group.

His role took a dramatic turn in 1955 when the PNP won the general elections. At the time he was a vice president of the party. He was also appointed leader of Government Business in the House of Representatives and became secretary of the local executive committee of the Commonwealth Parliamentary Association.

During a two-year tenure as Minister of Labour, he achieved far-reaching success in reviving the Jamaica Farm Work Programme in the United States.

As a member of the Standing Federation Committee on the West Indian Federation from 1953 through 1958, Glasspole made a valuable contribution to the regional integration movement. He was also a member of the Jamaica House of Representatives Committee, which prepared the Independence Constitution and the delegation which finalized the constitution with the British government in London.

Glasspole served as Minister of Education from 1957 to 1962 and from 1972 to 1973 until he was appointed governor general. Jamaicans looked to education to point the way forward, and Sir Glasspole was called upon to provide the leadership. His tenure as Minister of Education

was a time of political and social renaissance, ideas contended, visions of nationhood expanded, and dreams of social equity, upward mobility, and prosperity fulfilled.

The Ministry of Education constructed its headquarters at National Heroes Circle. Children of the "no-moneyed class" were enabled to obtain quality secondary education with the introduction of Common Entrance free places to high school—equivalent to a ticket to social equity and upward mobility. This democratization and expansion of secondary education helped meet the country's growing demand for qualified personnel in every field of activity. Furthermore, the ministry instituted an In-service Teachers Education Thrust (ISTET), which allowed educators to upgrade their qualification while on the job. The College of Arts, Science and Technology (CAST)—now the University of Technology (UTECH)—opened as a multifaceted tertiary institution. Spanish was declared a second official language in Jamaica to help to break down barriers between Jamaica and its Spanish-speaking neighbors.

Meanwhile, Glasspole's social conscience continued to play out as patron of a range of civic organizations, including the Jamaica Red Cross Society, the Scouts Association, the YMCA and the YWCA, the Jamaica Cancer Society, and the United Nations Association of Jamaica. His life work earned him a long and impressive list of national and international awards and honors, culminating in the Order of the Nation, Jamaica's second highest honor (after National Hero). Other awards include the Order of Andres Bello, one of Venezuela's highest, which he received in 1970; the Order of Liberator in 1978, also from Venezuela; and the first honor award from Jamaica's national newspaper, *The Daily Gleaner*, in 1979. In 1981 Glasspole was knighted by Queen Elizabeth II of England, receiving the Grand Cross of the Most Distinguished Order of St. Michael and St. George in a private function at Buckingham Palace. The University of the West Indies bestowed upon him an Honorary Doctor of Laws degree in 1982. The following year he was made the Grand Commander of the Royal Victorian Order by the Queen of England.

Sir Glasspole retired from the office of governor general in 1990 and spent his last days working on his memoirs. He died on November 25, 2000, at the age of 91. As governor general he was a pivotal participant in the country's journey from colonialism, through self-government, and finally to independence.

See also Education in the Caribbean; Farm Worker Program; People's National Party

■ ■ *Bibliography*

The Jamaica Information Service (JIS). March, 1982.

E. LEO GUNTER (2005)

GLISSANT, EDOUARD

SEPTEMBER 21, 1928

Born in Sainte-Marie, Martinique, Edouard Glissant and his contemporary Frantz Fanon are the best known of the generation of writers who came after the founding father of *Négritude*, Aimé Césaire. Like Fanon, Glissant was educated at the Lycée Schoelcher and later left for Paris after participating in Césaire's electoral campaign. Unlike that of many of his contemporaries in the 1950s, Glissant's early poetry was not overtly political but a dense exploration of Caribbean landscape. His first book of essays, *Soleil de la conscience* (*Sun of Consciousness*), in 1956 is essentially a travel book dealing with his relation to France as an insider and an outsider. This "ethnography of the self," as he called it, was written as a series of prose poems and contained the major themes of his later work: the importance of place, the idea of an open insularity, and the fundamentally interconnected nature of all cultures. The theme of individual self-discovery is continued in Glissant's early novels *La Lezarde* (*The Ripening*), which won the Prix Renaudot in 1958, and *Le quatrième siècle* (*The Fourth Century*) in 1965. Both brought him to prominence because of their original evocations of Martinican space and history and their experimental treatment of generic conventions.

Glassant spent nineteen years in Paris, during which he produced a number of essays on the most influential writers of the Americas, Saint-John Perse, Aimé Césaire, William Faulkner, and Alejo Carpentier, which later became the basis for the 1969 book of essays *L'intention poétique* (*The Poetic Intention*). He also became involved in anticolonial politics through the Front Antillo-Guyanais formed with Paul Niger, and he returned to Martinique in 1965 and founded the Institut Martiniquais d'Études. By inviting artists such as Roberto Matta from Chile and Agustín Cárdenas from Cuba and with the publication of the magazine *Acoma*, Glissant tried to counter the rapid Europeanization of Martinique, which had become a French Department in 1946. His bleak view of Martinique's future as a department is recorded in the 1975 novel, significantly titled *Malemort* (*Undead*).

In 1980 Glissant left Martinique to become the editor of the *UNESCO Courier* in Paris. In the following year he published his well-known *Le discours Antillais* (*Caribbean Discourse*) and the novel *La case du commandeur* (*The Driver's Cabin*). In his essays he established himself as the major Caribbean theorist of the post-*Négritude* period, proposing a view of the Caribbean as an exemplary site of creolization that transcended racial and linguistic divisions. He left Paris in 1988 for a teaching position in the United States, and his interrelated novels evolved into narratives of nomadic wanderings and an exploded sense of place in *Mahagony* (1987) and *Tout monde* (1993). Similarly, his later essays, *Poétique de la Relation* (*Poetics of Relating*) in 1990 and *Faulkner, Mississippi* (1996), develop his theories of rhizomatic identity and the Americas as a site of pervasive *métissage,* or intermixing of peoples. Glissant's ideas have spawned a movement of cultural affirmation in Martinique called the *créolité* movement of which Patrick Chamoiseau is the most prominent literary figure.

See also Césaire, Aimé; Chamoiseau, Patrick; Diasporic Cultures in the Americas; Négritude

■ ■ *Bibliography*

Baudot, Alain. *Bibliographie annotee d'Edouard Glissant.* Toronto: Éditions du Gref, 1993.

Dash, J. Michael. *Edouard Glissant.* Cambridge, UK: Cambridge University Press, 1995.

Glissant, Edouard. *Caribbean Discourse.* Translated by J. Michael Dash. Charlottesville: University Press of Virginia, 1989.

J. MICHAEL DASH (2005)

GLOBETROTTERS, HARLEM

See Harlem Globetrotters

GLOVER, DANNY

JULY 22, 1947

Born in San Francisco, the son of two postal workers who were both union organizers and members of the NAACP, actor Danny Glover attended San Francisco State University, where he majored in economics. During the 1960s he became a student activist, and he worked as an economic planner for the city after graduation. He began taking acting classes in the 1960s at the Black Actor's Workshop sponsored by the American Conservatory Theatre in Oakland. In the 1970s he acted with Sam Shepard's Magic Theater, the San Francisco Eureka Theater, and the Los Angeles Theater and made guest appearances on such television series as *Lou Grant, Chiefs,* and *Gimme a Break.*

In 1979 Glover made his New York theater debut in Athol Fugard's *The Blood Knot,* for which he won a Theater World Award. He also played in the 1982 Broadway production of Fugard's *Master Harold . . .and the Boys,* where he was seen by writer and director Robert Benton, who cast him as a sharecropper in the motion picture *Places in the Heart* (1984). Glover also appeared in Fugard's *A Lesson from Aloes* (1986) at the Steppenwolf Theater Company in Chicago.

In 1985 Glover appeared in three films: *Witness, Silverado,* and *The Color Purple,* Steven Spielberg's adaptation of Alice Walker's novel, in which he appeared as the sadistic "Mister," opposite Whoopi Goldberg. In 1987 Glover starred as a Los Angeles detective who is partners with Mel Gibson in *Lethal Weapon.* The action-adventure movie was a major commercial success and led to three sequels.

In 1990 Glover produced and starred in Charles Burnett's *To Sleep with Anger,* a film about middle-class black life in South-Central Los Angeles. The same year he was inducted into the Black Filmmakers Hall of Fame and received the Phoenix Award from the Black American Cinema Society. Glover appeared in *Predator 2* (1991) and *The Saint of Fort Washington* (1992), and in 1993, he starred as a police officer in *Bopha!,* a film set in South Africa and filmed in Zimbabwe, about the 1976 Soweto uprisings. In 1994 Glover starred in the popular film *Angels in the Outfield,* and in 1998, he won critical praise for his featured role in *Beloved,* Jonathan Demme's adaptation of Toni Morrison's novel. Later credits include *The Prince of Egypt* (1998), *The Royal Tenenbaums* (2001), and *Saw* (2004). Glover has been the recipient of two NAACP Image Awards, both in 1987, for his performance in *Lethal Weapon* (1987) and in HBO's *Mandela* (1987), for which he also received an ACE Award. In recent years he has attracted controversy for his political activism, speaking out against the death penalty and the U.S.-led war in Iraq.

See also Burnett, Charles; Film in the United States, Contemporary

■■ *Bibliography*

"Danny Glover." In *Contemporary Black Biography*, Vol. 24. Edited by Shirelle Phelps. Detroit: Gale, 2000.

"Danny Glover." *Current Biography* 53 (April 1992): 29–32.

SABRINA FUCHS (1996)
SUSAN MCINTOSH (1996)
Updated by publisher 2005

GLOVER, SAVION
NOVEMBER 19, 1973

Tap veteran Gregory Hines called Savion Glover "the best tap dancer that ever lived." Born in Newark, New Jersey, Glover grew up in a housing project with his mother. From age two he showed an affinity for rhythm, beating out sounds on pots and pans at will. Yvette Glover enrolled Savion in tap dance at age seven at New York City's Broadway Dance Center. Savion recalls tapping in cowboy boots—the only hard-soled shoes his mother could afford—for seven months before receiving his first pair of tap shoes.

At age twelve Glover secured the lead role in Broadway's *The Tap Dance Kid.* In 1989 he was nominated for his first Tony Award for his performance in *Black and Blue.* In the same year he starred with Gregory Hines and Sammy Davis Jr. in the movie *Tap.* In 1992 he became the youngest recipient of a National Endowment for the Arts (NEA) grant for choreography. From 1991 to1994, he starred in the Broadway production of *Jelly's Last Jam* and taught children's tap classes wherever he traveled. From 1991 to 1995 he was a regular guest on *Sesame Street.*

Glover's greatest accomplishment has been his involvement in the original *Bring in 'da Noise, Bring in 'da Funk,* which began late in 1995. The show, a dramatic display of black musical styles including hip-hop and new styles of tap dance, garnered nine Tony nominations in 1996. Serving as the Broadway show's choreographer and star, Glover won one of the show's four awards for Best Choreographer.

In 2004, after three years away from the spotlight, and mourning the death of his friend Gregory Hines, Glover reemerged with a renewed enthusiasm as a dancer, actor, and dance instructor.

See also Davis, Sammy, Jr.; Hines, Gregory; Musical Theater; Tap Dance; Theatrical Dance

■■ *Bibliography*

Acocella, Joan. "Taking Steps. (Glover, Savion)" *The New Yorker* 79, no. 42 (January 12, 2004): 77–78.

Hildebrand, Karen. "A Conversation. (Savion Glover)" *Dance Magazine* 78, no. 5 (May 2004): 35.

Winship, Frederick M. "Savion Glover's Career Explodes." *United Press International* (January 17, 2004).

RACHEL ZELLARS (2001)
Updated by publisher 2005

GOLDBERG, WHOOPI

NOVEMBER 13, 1950

▌▌▌

Actress Whoopi Goldberg was born Caryn Johnson in New York City and raised in a housing project by her mother. She received her earliest education at a parish school, the Congregation of Notre Dame. She gained her first stage experience at the Helena Rubinstein Children's Theatre at the Hudson Guild, where she acted in plays from the age of eight to ten.

In the mid-1960s Goldberg dropped out of high school and worked on Broadway as a chorus member in the musicals *Hair, Jesus Christ Superstar,* and *Pippin.* She was married briefly in the early 1970s and had a daughter from the marriage, Alexandrea Martin.

In 1974 Goldberg moved to Los Angeles and has since maintained California residence. She became a founding member of the San Diego Repertory Theatre and later joined Spontaneous Combustion, an improvisation group. It was about this time that she adopted the name Whoopi Goldberg.

In 1981 Goldberg, with David Schein, wrote the extended comedy sketch *The Last Word.* The eclectic ensemble of characters in her sketches includes a self-aborting surfer girl, a panhandling ex-vaudevillian, a junkie, and a Jamaican maid. Goldberg's style, a blend of social commentary, humor, and improvisation, earned her both critical acclaim and a large audience. In 1983 she developed an hour-long piece entitled *The Spook Show,* which played in London and New York to great acclaim. After appearing in Berkeley, California, in a one-woman show called *Moms,* based on the life of comedian Moms Mabley, Goldberg opened on Broadway in 1984 in a new version of her comedy sketches, *Whoopi Goldberg,* produced by Mike Nichols.

The following year Goldberg starred as Celie in Steven Spielberg's film of Alice Walker's *The Color Purple.* She received an Academy Award nomination for her performance, which propelled her into the Hollywood mainstream. She subsequently starred in such films as *Jumping Jack Flash* (1986), *Burglar* (1987), *Fatal Beauty* (1987),

Whoopi Goldberg. *Born Caryn Johnson in 1950 and raised in a New York City housing project, Goldberg has risen to fame as an Oscar and Grammy Award-winning actor and entertainer.* PHOTOGRAPH BY CHRIS BRANDIS. AP/WIDE WORLD PHOTOS.

Clara's Heart (1988), and *The Long Walk Home* (1990). She appeared in a continuing role on the television series *Star Trek: The Next Generation* from 1988 through 1993. In 1990 she received an Academy Award for best supporting actress for her role as a psychic in *Ghost.* Goldberg became only the second black woman—the first since Hattie McDaniel in 1939—to win an Oscar in a major category. Subsequently she appeared in *Soapdish* (1991), *Sister Act* (1992), and *Sarafina!* (1992), becoming the first African-American to star in a film shot on location in South Africa.

In 1992 Goldberg cofounded the annual comedy benefit "Comic Relief" on the cable television network Home Box Office to raise money for the homeless. That same year she launched her own syndicated television talk show. In 1993 Goldberg appeared in the films *Sister Act 2* and *Made In America,* a comedy about an interracial relationship. In 1994, Goldberg hosted the Oscar Awards. Her subsequent film appearances include *The Player* (1995), *Boys on the Side* (1996), *How Stella Got Her Groove Back*

(1998), *The Ghosts of Mississippi* (1998), *Girl, Interrupted* (1999), and *Kingdom Come* (2001). In 1997, following a short-lived late-night talk show, *The Whoopi Goldberg Show,* she returned to Broadway in *A Funny Thing Happened on the Way to the Forum.* In 1998 she revived the television quiz show "Hollywood Squares" as a starring vehicle. Her career in television continued in 2003, when she launched a sitcom titled *Whoopi,* and she returned to the stage once again in 2004, reviving her original one-woman Broadway show with *Whoopi: The 20th Year.*

See also Comedians; Mabley, Jackie "Moms"; McDaniel, Hattie; Film in the United States, Contemporary

■ ■ *Bibliography*

Hine, Darlene Clark. *Black Women in America.* Brooklyn, N.Y.: Carlson, 1993, pp. 491–493.

Moritz, Charles. *1985 Current Biography Yearbook.* New York: H.W. Wilson, 1993.

Parish, James Robert, *Whoopi Goldberg: Her Journey from Poverty to Mega-Stardom,* Secaucus, N.J.: Birch Lane Press, 1997.

SUSAN MCINTOSH (1996)
Updated by publisher 2005

GOMES, PETER JOHN

MAY 22, 1942

❚❚❚

Theologian Peter Gomes, whom *Time* magazine called "one of America's great preachers," was born in Boston and grew up in Plymouth, Massachusetts. His father was a Cape Verdean immigrant who labored in the local cranberry bogs, while his mother was a fourth-generation African-American Bostonian, from an affluent family, who had studied music at the New England Conservatory before becoming the first African American to work in Cambridge's city hall. Gomes attended Bates College in Lewiston, Maine, where he received his B.A. in 1965, then attended Harvard University Divinity School. After Gomes earned an S.T.B. degree from Harvard in 1968, he was ordained a minister in the American Baptist Church. He subsequently took a position as professor of history and director of Freshman Studies at the Tuskegee Institute.

In 1970 Gomes accepted the post of assistant minister at Harvard's prestigious Memorial Church and was named professor of Christian morals. Over the following two decades he was a notable figure at Harvard for his dynamic

preaching and thoughtful biblical exegesis and for his conservative Republican politics. In 1984 and 1988 Gomes was selected to deliver sermons at the inaugurations of Presidents Ronald Reagan and George H. W. Bush.

In 1991, at a rally held in protest of an antigay piece in the conservative Harvard magazine *Peninsula,* Gomes came out as "a Christian who happens as well to be gay." He thereafter became an important figure in the gay rights movement. In 1998, two years after he published a bestselling Bible analysis, *The Good Book,* Gomes announced that Memorial Church would solemnize same-sex unions.

Gomes was named Clergy of the Year in 1998 by *Religion in American Life.* Gomes has spoken and delivered sermons all over the world, has been a guest on numerous television programs, and has been the subject of many magazine articles.

See also Baptists; Gay Men; Lesbians; Theology

■ ■ *Bibliography*

Gomes, Peter J. *The Good Book: Reading the Bible with Mind and Heart.* New York: Morrow, 1996.

Higgins, Richard. "Polishing the Truth. (Interview)" *The Christian Century* 119, no. 11 (May 22, 2002): 19–20.

Ostling, Richard N. "Christians Spar in Harvard Yard." *Time* 139, no. 11 (March 16, 1992): 49.

GREG ROBINSON (2001)
Updated by publisher 2005

GÓMEZ, JUAN GUALBERTO

JULY 12, 1854
MARCH 5, 1933

❚❚❚

Juan Gualberto Gómez y Ferrer was born on a Cuban sugar plantation to the slaves Fermín Gómez and Serafina Ferrer. Known throughout his life as a man of letters and a nationalist intellectual par excellence, he argued, perhaps more fervently than any other Cuban nationalist, that the problem of Cuban freedom was as much about the socioeconomic progress and political participation of African-descended Cubans as it was a struggle for sovereignty. Indeed, for many of his peers his pronouncements on race progress undermined the ideal of national racelessness and marked him as a troubling player in the national political arena.

In 1869, at age fifteen, Gómez traveled to Paris in the company of a wealthy Cuban landowner to learn carriage making, but his obvious scholarly aptitude quickly led to his enrollment at Paris's Munge School of Engineering and the Central School of Arts and Manufacture. For several years Gómez studied assiduously while also witnessing French revolutionary fervor and the devastation of the Franco-Prussian War (1870–1871). In the evenings he mixed with tradesmen at workers' clubs and attended parliamentary and public debates about citizens' rights.

The Pact of Zanjón (1878), which ended Cuba's Ten Years War and brought a partial and unsatisfactory peace to the island, coincided with the return home of a young man of considerable ideological maturity. Gómez's return, in fact, coincided with significant shifts in Cuba's social and political terrain: The Moret law (1870) of gradual abolition had granted slaves only partial emancipation; Cuban political parties had finally emerged (1878), albeit without Cubans' representation at the Spanish *cortes;* and repression by the crown rose even as liberal reforms established freedoms in the press, public assembly, and education. Gómez proved a formidable adversary for the state, founding and editing several publications that opposed colonial rule and supported socioeconomic advancement for the "colored race," until he was deported to Spain from 1880 to 1890 for sedition. Though Gómez organized all classes and colors, he proselytized in particular among black and mulatto artisans, insisting that African-descended Cubans, especially former slaves, would gain full political participation through education and enlightened thinking and behavior. In 1886, despite his exile in Spain, Gómez galvanized hundreds of black and mulatto social club members on the island to form a political bloc known as the Central Directorate of Societies of the Colored Race.

In the decades following the end of colonialism in Cuba in 1898, Gómez received prestigious appointments to Havana's Board of Education and the Cuban Academy of History, and he spearheaded a hearty but unsuccessful protest among fellow constitutional assemblymen to prevent the adoption of the U.S.-authored Platt Amendment in the new Cuban constitution. He also served in national leadership in the house (1914–1916) and senate (1916–1924). Gómez continued to advocate race progress and denounce political corruption in his newspaper, *Patria* (1925–1927), even attacking the despotism of President Gerardo Machado (1925–1933). Until 1932, when Gómez retired in relative poverty near Havana, Cubans from all sectors continued to request his counsel and intervention in employment, social, and political matters. Juan Gualberto Gómez died from pulmonary edema in 1933.

See also Afrocubanismo

■ ■ *Bibliography*

Estuch, Leopoldo Horrego. *Juan Gualberto Gómez: un gran inconforme.* Havana: Editorial Mecenas, 1954.

Gómez, Juan Gualberto. *Por Cuba libre.* Havana: Editorial de Ciencias Sociales, 1974.

Scott, Rebecca. *Slave Emancipation in Cuba: The Transition to Free Labor, 1860–1899.* Princeton, N.J.: Princeton University Press, 1985.

MELINA ANN PAPPADEMOS (2005)

GORDON, GEORGE WILLIAM

C. 1820
OCTOBER 23, 1865

George William Gordon, the son of Scottish planter Joseph Gordon and a slave woman whose name is unknown, was born into slavery around 1820. Gordon's father kept him nominally in servitude until the general Emancipation Act freed slaves in 1834, encouraging his interest in books and figures and sending him as a teenager to live with James Daly, a businessman in Black River, Jamaica. Gordon mastered commerce, and by 1842 he was a successful merchant and produce dealer in Kingston.

In 1844, Gordon entered public life, winning a seat in the Jamaican Assembly for the parish of St. Thomas in the Vale. Ironically (given his later career) he contested the seat as a defender of the Established Church, against the sustained campaign of the Baptists and other dissenters who advocated its disestablishment. At the same time, Gordon benefited from the support of the planters in the parish where his father, who was also a member of the Assembly, had connections to coffee and sugar properties. Although the younger Gordon strongly supported the planters' immigration proposals in the Assembly, he, given his own slave background and his very close attachment to his mother, strenuously opposed proposals of the 1840s to reintroduce whipping. Further, in 1848 and the following year, Gordon joined other coloureds of the Assembly in their "nationalist" opposition to the planters' reckless retrenchment strategies to effect the restoration of protection for colonial produce. This stance cost Gordon the planters' support, and he declined to seek re-election to the Assembly in 1849.

Gordon returned to the Assembly in 1863 for the parish of St. Thomas in the East, with the solid support of Paul Bogle and other small freeholders. They looked to Gordon as a genuine spokesperson for their interests, and he launched a broadside against the administration of Governor Edward Eyre and the local Magistrates in the parish who, with Governor Eyre's unqualified support, victimized Gordon in an attempt to silence his strident criticisms of their administration and of the established church.

Nonetheless, Gordon continued to speak out vehemently against injustice and the political elites' disregard and contempt for the peoples' hardships, which were worsened by the dramatic decline in the sugar industry (a primary source of employment) and the ravages of drought and floods that destroyed provision crops. It was clear for all but the blinkered that people were starving and ground down by high taxation on imported food, the supply and cost of which was further affected by the American Civil War.

In 1865, Gordon's speeches in the Assembly and at public meetings focused on the deteriorating social state of the island and the failure of the Assembly and the Governor to address the matter. Against Gordon's passionate protests, legislators instead approved the reintroduction of whipping for predial larceny, at a time when many were starving. Furthermore, when the Crown neglected the peoples' plea for access to tracts of unused crown lands and the local administration cruelly dismissed poverty as the result of laziness, Gordon's speeches at public meetings in various parts of the island pointed to the absence of work, low wages, injustice in the courts, the denial of political rights and the general insensitivity of the political administration. Gordon organized one such meeting in Morant Bay in August 1865, where his political allies, including Paul Bogle, echoed his sentiments and applied them to the corrupt local administration of that parish. Planters in the vestry at Morant Bay had frustrated Gordon's efforts to expose the inadequacy of their poverty relief, and later prevented him from taking up an elected post as churchwarden because he was not a practicing member of the Church of England, even though the small freeholders had elected him. These tensions boiled over into the Paul Bogle-led rebellion in Morant Bay on October 11, 1865, and despite the absence of dispassionate evidence linking Gordon with its planning or execution, Eyre blamed his most determined political detractor's speeches and political associations for inspiring the rebels. Accordingly, Eyre had Gordon arrested in Kingston and transported to Morant Bay, where he was tried under martial law, found guilty of high treason, and was hanged on October 23, 1865.

One hundred years later, in 1965, the Jamaican Government elevated George William Gordon to the status of National Hero for his passionate advocacy for the poor in the immediate post-slavery period of Jamaican history.

See also Bogle, Paul; Morant Bay Rebellion

■ ■ *Bibliography*

Bakan, Abigail. *Ideology and Class Conflict in Jamaica: The Politics of Rebellion.* Montreal and Kingston: McGill-Queen's University Press, 1990.

Curtin, Philip D. *Two Jamaicas: The Role of Ideas in a Tropical Colony, 1830–1865.* Cambridge, Mass: Harvard University Press, 1955.

Heuman, Gad. "Post-Emancipation Protest in Jamaica: The Morant Bay Rebellion, 1865." In *From Chattel Slaves to Wage Slaves: The Dynamics of Labour Bargaining in the Americas,* edited by Mary Turner. Kingston: Ian Randle, 1995.

SWITHIN WILMOT (2005)

GORDON, ODETTA HOLMES FELIOUS

See Odetta (Gordon, Odetta Holmes Felious)

GORDY, BERRY
NOVEMBER 28, 1929

The music executive Berry Gordy Jr., the third in his family to carry that name, was born in Detroit. He was attracted to music as a child, winning a talent contest with his song "Berry's Boogie." He also took up boxing, often training with his friend Jackie Wilson, who would later become a popular rhythm-and-blues singer. Gordy quit high school to turn professional, but he soon gave up boxing at the urging of his mother. After spending 1951 to 1953 in the army, Gordy married Thelma Louise Coleman and began to work in the Gordy family printing and construction business.

In 1953 Gordy opened a jazz record store in Detroit. However, since rhythm-and-blues records were more in demand, the business closed after only two years. Gordy then began working at a Ford Motor Company assembly line, writing and publishing pop songs on the side, including "Money, That's What I Want" (1959). During this time, Gordy, who had separated from his wife, wrote some of Jackie Wilson's biggest hits, including "Lonely Teardrops" (1958), "That Is Why I Love You So" (1959), and "I'll Be Satisfied" (1959). He also sang with his new wife, Raynoma Liles, whom he married in 1959, on a number

Berry Gordy, founder of Motown Records. AP/WIDE WORLD PHOTOS. REPRODUCED BY PERMISSION.

of records by the Detroit singer Marv Johnson. In the late 1950s Gordy met and worked with Smokey Robinson and the Matadors, who at Gordy's suggestion changed their name to the Miracles. Gordy recorded them on their first record, "Got a Job" (1958).

During this period Gordy became increasingly dissatisfied with leasing his recordings to larger record companies, who often would take over distribution. At the urging of Robinson, Gordy borrowed eight-hundred dollars and founded Tamla Records and Gordy Records, the first companies in what would become the Motown empire. He released "Way Over There" (1959) and "Shop Around" (1961) by the Miracles. Gordy began hiring friends and family members to work for him, and he began to attract young unknown singers, including Diana Ross, Marvin Gaye, Mary Wells, and Stevie Wonder. The songwriting team of Eddie Holland, his brother Brian, and Lamont Dozier began to write songs for Gordy, who had formed a base of operations at 2648 Grand Boulevard in Detroit. From that address Gordy also formed the publishing and management companies that would constitute the larger enterprise known more generally as Motown. Over the next ten years, Motown, with Gordy as chief executive and chief shareholder (and often producer and songwriter as

well), produced dozens of pop and rhythm-and-blues hits that dominated the new style known as soul music.

In the mid-1960s Gordy began to distance himself from the company's day-to-day music operations, spending more and more time in Los Angeles, where he was growing interested in the film and television industries. He divorced Raynoma in 1964 and married Margaret Norton, whom he also later divorced. (Gordy again married in 1990, but that marriage, to Grace Eton, ended in divorce three years later.)

In the late 1960s, many Motown performers, writers, and producers complained about Gordy's paternalistic and heavy-handed management of their finances. Some of them—including the Jackson Five, Holland-Dozier-Holland, and the Temptations—left the company, claiming that Gordy had misled and mistreated them. By this time he was quite wealthy, living in a Los Angeles mansion that contained a portrait of himself dressed as Napoleon Bonaparte. He resigned as president of the Motown Records subsidiary in 1973 in order to assume the chair of Motown Industries, a new parent corporation. The following year he completed what had been a gradual move of Motown to Los Angeles and produced several successful television specials. His film ventures—including the Diana Ross vehicles *Lady Sings the Blues* (1973), *Mahogany* (1975), and *The Wiz* (1978)—were not as successful.

Despite the departure of its core personnel over the years, the company Gordy presided over in the 1980s remained successful, with more than one-hundred-million dollars in annual sales in 1983, making it the largest black-owned company in the United States. In 1984 Gordy allowed MCA to begin distributing Motown's records, and the company bought Motown in 1988 for sixty-one million dollars. Gordy kept control of Gordy Industries, which ran Motown's music publishing, film, and television subsidiaries. His net worth in 1986, as estimated by *Forbes,* was more than $180 million, making him one of the wealthiest people in the United States at that time. In the late 1980s and the 1990s, Gordy branched out into other fields, including sports management and the ownership and training of racehorses.

Although Gordy, who was inducted into the Rock and Roll Hall of Fame in 1988, began his career as a successful songwriter and producer, his greatest achievement was selling soul music to white pop audiences, thus helping to shape America's youth into a single, huge, multiracial audience. In 2004, Gordy sold the last piece of his Motown legacy: EMI Music Publishing bought the rights to fifteen hundred compositions for eighty million dollars.

See also Jackson Family; Music in the United States; Recording Industry

■ ■ *Bibliography*

George, Nelson. *Where Did Our Love Go? The Rise and Fall of the Motown Sound.* New York: St. Martin's, 1985.

Posner, Gerald. *Motown: Money, Music, Sex, and Power.* New York: Random House, 2002.

Waller, Don. *The Motown Story.* New York: Scribner, 1985.

JONATHAN GILL (1996)
Updated by publisher 2005

GOSPEL MUSIC

The African-American religious music known as gospel, originating in the field hollers, slave songs, spirituals, and Protestant hymns sung on southern plantations, and later at camp meetings and churches, has come to dominate not only music in black churches but singing and instrumental styles across the spectrum of American popular music, including jazz, blues, rhythm and blues, soul, and country. Exemplified in songs such as "Take My Hand, Precious Lord" and "Move On Up a Little Higher," gospel music encourages emotional and jubilant improvisation on songs of thanksgiving and praise as well as sorrow and suffering.

Musically, gospel is distinguished by its vocal style, which in both male and female singers is characterized by a strained, full-throated sound, often pushed to guttural shrieks and rasps suited to the extremes of the emotion-laden lyrics. Melodies and harmonies are generally simple, allowing for spontaneity in devising repetitive, expressive fills and riffs. The syncopated rhythms of gospel are typically spare, with heavy, often hand-clapped accents.

THE FOUNDING YEARS

Although the roots of gospel can be traced to Africa and the earliest arrival of Africans in the New World, the main antecedent was the "Dr. Watts" style of singing hymns, named for British poet and hymnist Isaac Watts (1674–1748), who emphasized a call-and-response approach to religious songs, with mournful but powerful rhythms. Thus, in the nineteenth century, African-American hymnody in mainstream denominations did not differ considerably from music performed in white churches. The earliest African-American religious denominations date back to the late eighteenth century, when black congregations split off from white church organizations in Philadelphia. In 1801 the minister Richard Allen, who later founded the African Methodist Episcopal (AME) denomination, published two collections of hymns designed for use in black

churches. These collections were the forerunners of similar collections that formed the basis for the music performed in most nineteenth-century black churches, yet they were quite similar to the slow-tempo, restrained white Protestant hymnody. Around the middle of the nineteenth century a new type of music known as "gospel hymns" or "gospel songs" was being composed in a new style, lighter and more songlike than traditional hymnody, written by white composers such as Dwight Moody (1837–1899), Ira Sankey (1840–1908), Philip Paul Bliss (1838–1876), Robert Lowry (1826–1899), and William Batchelder Bradbury (1816–1868).

Another important nineteenth-century influence on gospel music was the idea, increasingly popular at a minority of nineteenth-century black churches, that spiritual progress required a deeper and more directly emotional relationship with God, often through the singing of white "gospel hymns," although gospel as an African-American form would not take that name for decades. These congregations, often led by charismatic ministers, began searching for a religion based on "Holiness or Hell" and were early participants in the Latter Rain movement, which sought to "irrigate the dry bones" of the church. The first congregation known to accept this doctrine, based on the activities of the Day of Pentecost (though, confusingly, this is *not* what is now called Pentecostalism) was the United Holy Church of Concord, South Carolina, which held its first meeting in 1886 and had its first convention in 1894 under the leadership of Brother L. M. Mason (1861–1930). Another early congregation to accept that doctrine and encourage early forms of gospel music was the Church of the Living God, in Wrightsville, Arkansas, under the leadership of William Christian (1856–1928) in 1889.

The Holiness doctrine proved controversial within black churches, as did the music associated with Holiness. In 1895 Charles Harrison Mason and Charles Price Jones were forced from the Baptist church, and together they proceeded to organize the Church of God in Christ in Lexington, Mississippi, where the music was heavily influenced by the performance style at Los Angeles's Azusa Street Revival, a black congregation that marked the beginning of Pentecostalism, under the leadership of William Joseph Seymour. The Azusa Street Revival featured highly charged services involving "speaking in tongues" as a manifestation of the Holy Ghost. Such activities were eventually integrated into the mainstream of black church activity, but around the turn of the century, Holiness-style services, and even the singing of spirituals, were strenuously opposed by conservative black church elders who had fought to "elevate" the musical standards of their con-

"homemade" harmonies came hand-clapping, foot-stomping, and holy dancing, also known as "shouting."

Holiness, Sanctified, and Pentecostal congregations sprang up rapidly all over the South, particularly in rural, poor communities, starting around the turn of the century, and in less than a decade gospel music, then known as church music, was being sung in Baptist and Methodist congregations as well. During this time the most popular gospel hymns were by a new generation of black composers, including William Henry Sherwood; Jones, who composed "Where Shall I Be?" and "I'm Happy with Jesus Alone"; Mason, who in addition to "I'm a Soldier" wrote "My Soul Loves Jesus" and the chant "Yes, Lord"; and Charles Albert Tindley, who composed "What Are They Doing in Heaven," "Stand by Me," and "I'll Overcome Someday," which was the forerunner of the civil rights anthem "We Shall Overcome." Since at this time there were no publishing houses for black gospel, these composers began to establish their own. They also depended on recordings and traveling preachers to spread their music. Preachers who popularized their own songs included J. C. Burnett ("Drive and Go Forward," 1926), Ford Washington McGhee ("Lion of the Tribe of Judah," 1927), J. M. Gates ("Death's Black Train Is Coming," 1926), and A. W. Nix ("The Black Diamond Express to Hell," 1927).

THE BIRTH OF GOSPEL MUSIC

The 1920s were a crucial time in the development of gospel music. In 1921 the National Baptist Convention, USA, the largest organization of black Christians in the world, not only formally recognized gospel as a legitimate sacred musical form but published a collection of hymns, spirituals, and gospel songs under the title *Gospel Pearls*, edited by Willa A. Townsend (1885–1963). That hymnal contained six songs by Tindley, the first gospel composer successfully to combine the conventions of white evangelical music with the simple, often sentimental melodies of black spirituals. The 1921 convention also marked the emergence of the composer Thomas A. Dorsey (1899–1993), who would go on to become known as the Father of Gospel because of his indefatigable songwriting, publishing, organizing, and teaching. Three years later the National Baptist Convention published the *Baptist Standard Hymnal,* another important step toward bringing gospel into the mainstream of African-American church worship. Other important gospel composers who came to prominence during this time were Lucie Campbell (1885–1963) and William Herbert Brewster (1897–1987).

Despite the publication of these hymnals and the dissemination of individual songs in both print and by record, it was by word of mouth that gospel spread, particu-

American pianist, clergyman, and composer Thomas Andrew Dorsey with his female gospel quartet, Chicago, Illinois, 1934. Chicago became an important center for gospel music by the 1930s, in part due to the efforts of Dorsey. HULTON ARCHIVE/GETTY IMAGES

gregations. Jones, for example, was opposed to the Azusa Street style and eventually split from Mason to organize the Church of Christ, Holiness.

Early forms of gospel music such as sung or chanted testimonials and sermons were used to complement prayers in Holiness churches. Drawing on the call-and-response tradition that dated back to slavery times, members of a congregation would take inspiration from a phrase from the sermon or testimony and out of it spontaneously compose a simple melody and text. A chorus of congregants would repeat the original phrase, while the leader interpolated brief extemporized choruses. For example, in Charles Harrison Mason's 1908 "I'm a Soldier," the leader and congregation begin by alternating the following lines: "I'm a soldier/In the army of the Lord/I'm a soldier/In the army." Succeeding choruses differ only in the lead line, with the leader interpolating such phrases as "I'm fighting for my life," "I'm a sanctified soldier," or "I'll live and I'll die," and the congregation repeating "In the army" as a refrain. The length of such songs often stretched to fifteen minutes or more. Along with simple larly in working-class communities in the rural South. In Jefferson County, Alabama, workers in coal mines and factories used their lunch hours to organize quartets to sing this new type of religious song. In some respects these groups were inspired by the tradition of the secular Fisk Jubilee and Tuskegee vocal quartets, but the new groups emphasized the powerful emotional experiences of conversion and salvation. One of the first such groups, the Foster Singers, organized in 1916, stressed equality between the vocal parts. However, it was a Foster Singers spinoff group, the Birmingham Jubilee Singers, led by one of the members of the Foster Singers, that inspired gospel quartets that soon started all over the South. The Birmingham Jubilee Singers allowed the bass and tenor more prominence and freedom, raised tempos, and used more adventurous harmonies, including "blue" notes. The vocal quartets organized in this style in the 1920s include the Fairfield Four (1921), which as of 1992 still included one of its original members, the Rev. Samuel McCrary; the Blue Jay Singers (1926); the Harmonizing Four (1927); and the Dixie Hummingbirds (1928). In the 1930s new quartets included the Golden Gate Quartet (1934), which went on to become the most popular group of the 1930s and 1940s, and the Soul Stirrers (1936). The following year, Rebert H. Harris (b. 1916) joined the groups, and over the next fourteen years he became their most famous singer. In 1938 Claude Jeter Harris (b. 1914) organized the Four Harmony Kings, who later changed their name to the Swan Silvertones to acknowledge their sponsorship by a bakery.

By the 1930s gospel music had been firmly planted in northern cities. This was due not only to the Great Migration of rural blacks following World War I but also to the fact that, increasingly, record companies and publishing houses were located in northern cities, and particularly in Chicago, then the focal point for gospel music. Thomas Andrew Dorsey opened his publishing house in 1932, the same year he composed "Take My Hand, Precious Lord" (popularly known as "Precious Lord, Take My Hand"). Through composing, publishing, organizing, and teaching gospel choirs, Dorsey was given the sobriquet Father of Gospel.

Starting in the 1920s, gospel music was taken up by many different types of ensembles in addition to vocal quartets. In urban areas blind singers often came to prominence by performing on street corners and in churches. One of the most important of these was Connie Rosemond, for whom Lucie Campbell composed "Something Within Me." Others were Mamie Forehand and the guitarists and singers Blind Joe Taggard and Blind Willie Johnson. The blind Texan singer Arizona Dranes accom-

panied herself on piano and is credited with introducing that instrument to recorded gospel music. Among the gospel singers who sang with piano accompaniment as early as the 1920s were Willie Mae Ford Smith, Sallie Martin, Clara Hudmon (1900–1960), Madame Ernestine B. Washington (1914–1983), and guitarist and singer Sister Rosetta Tharpe, the first important performer to find a large audience outside the gospel circuit. Male-accompanied singers included Brother Joe May (1912–1973) and J. Robert Bradley (b. 1921). The greatest of the accompanied singers was Mahalia Jackson, who was born in New Orleans and found her calling in Chicago at age sixteen. Her 1947 recording of "Move On Up a Little Higher," by Herbert Brewster, featuring her soaring contralto, came to define the female gospel style.

In the late 1930s accompanied gospel ensembles consisting of four to six women, four or five men, or a mixed group of four to six singers, became popular. Clara Ward (1924–1973) organized the earliest notable accompanied ensemble, the Ward Singers, in 1934. The year before, Roberta Martin had joined with composer Theodore Frye (1899–1963) to form the Martin-Frye Quartet, later known as the Roberta Martin Singers. Sallie Martin organized the Sallie Martin Singers in 1940. Three years later the Original Gospel Harmonettes were formed, with pianist Evelyn Stark. They later came to prominence when singer Dorothy Love Coates joined the group and introduced "hard" gospel techniques, such as singing beyond her range and straining the voice for dramatic effects. Other accompanied ensembles included the Angelic Gospel Singers and the Davis Sisters, with pianist Curtis Dublin.

During this time vocal quartets and quintets continued to be popular. Archie Brownlee (1925–1960) organized the Five Blind Boys of Mississippi in 1939, the same year that Johnny L. Fields (b. 1927) formed the Five Blind Boys of Alabama, featuring Clarence Fountain (b. 1929). James Woodie Alexander (b. 1916) began leading the Pilgrim Travelers in 1946.

In the years between the wars, women, who from the start had been pillars of African-American religious institutions, became increasingly involved as publishers and organizers. In 1932, Dorsey, Sallie Martin, and Willie Mae Ford Smith formed the National Convention of Gospel Choirs and Choruses. Roberta Martin, the composer of "God Is Still on the Throne," opened her own publishing house in 1939. Sallie Martin opened hers along with Kenneth Martin (1917–1989), the composer of "Yes, God Is Real," in 1940.

Gullah Gospel Singers, Beaufort, South Carolina, May 1997. © CATHRINE WESSEL/CORBIS

THE GOLDEN AGE

By 1945 gospel was becoming recognized not only as a spiritual experience but also as a form of entertainment, and this became known as gospel's golden era. Singers, appearing on stage in attractive uniforms, had established and refined a popular and recognizable vocal sound. Gospel pianists such as Mildred Falls (1915–1975), Herbert Pickard, Mildred Gay, Edgar O'Neal, James Herndon, and James Washington and organists such as Little Lucy Smith, Gerald Spraggins, Louise Overall Weaver, and Herbert "Blind" Francis were working in exciting styles derived from ragtime, barrelhouse, and the blues, with chordal voicing, riffs, and complicated rhythms. Finally a group of composers including Doris Akers (b. 1923), Sammy Lewis, and Lucy Smith could be depended on to come up with fresh material. Just as early gospel composers relied on traveling from church to church to popularize their songs, so too did the first early popular gospel

singers find it necessary to go on the road. Sister Rosetta Tharpe performed at nightclubs and dance halls, but far more typical was the experience of Mahalia Jackson, who by 1945 had quit her regular job and joined a growing number of traveling professional gospel singers performing in churches and schools, moving on to auditoriums and stadiums. These singers were able to support themselves, and some, like Jackson, were quite successful, especially in the context of touring companies.

After the war the recording industry and radio played a large part in popularizing gospel. At first, small companies such as King, Atlantic, Vee-Jay, Dot, Nashboro, and Peacock were the most active in seeking out gospel singers. Apollo Records recorded Jackson and Roberta Martin before they moved to larger labels. The Ward Sisters, the Angelic Gospel Singers, and the Davis Sisters first recorded for Gotham Records. The Original Gospel Harmonettes recorded first for RCA Victor. With the proliferation of re-

The Beamon Singers Gospel Choir performs at the presentation of the U.S. Postal Service's newest stamps honoring four of gospel's most innovative female vocalists, August 30, 1998. The "Gospel Singer" stamps, pictured at the House of Blues musical venue in Cambridge, Massachusetts, feature Mahalia Jackson, Roberta Martin, Clara Ward, and Sister Rosetta Tharpe. AP/WIDE WORLD PHOTOS. REPRODUCED BY PERMISSION.

cordings, gospel radio programs became popular. In New York, the gospel disk jockey Joe Bostic was extraordinarily successful, as were Mary Manson in Philadelphia, Irene Joseph Ware in Chicago, Mary Dee in Baltimore, Goldie Thompson in Tampa, and John "Honeyboy" Hardy in New Orleans. Other cities with gospel shows in the postwar years included Atlanta, Los Angeles, Louisville, and Miami.

Among the more prominent performers and leaders who emerged during gospel's postwar golden era were Madame Edna Gallmon Cooke (1918–1967), Julius "June" Cheeks (1928–1981), who joined the Sensationales in 1946, "Professor" Alex Bradford (1927–1978), Robert Anderson (b. 1919), and Albertina Walker (b. 1930), who in 1952 formed the Caravans. Among the members of the Caravans were Shirley Caesar and Inez Andrews (b. 1928), who had a hit record with "Mary, Don't You Weep." Marion Williams left the Ward Singers in 1958 to form the Stars of Faith. Willie Joe Ligon (b. 1942) organized the Mighty Clouds of Joy in 1959. Perhaps the best-known singer to emerge from the golden era was Sam Cooke, who joined the Soul Stirrers in 1950 and revitalized the male gospel quartet movement with his hits "Nearer to Thee"

and "Touch the Hem of His Garment" before going on to fame as a popular singer starting in 1956.

The most significant figure from this time was the Rev. James Cleveland, who began singing in Dorsey's children's choir at the age of eight. By the age of sixteen, Cleveland had composed his first hit for the Roberta Martin Singers. He accompanied the Caravans, formed his own group, and in 1963 began recording with the Angelic Choir of Nutley, New Jersey. Cleveland's recordings were so successful that they sparked a new phase in gospel music dominated by gospel choirs. Prominent choirs following Cleveland's lead included those led by Thurston Frazier, Mattie Moss Clark (b. 1928), and Jessy Dixon (b. 1938).

By the end of the 1950s gospel was becoming ubiquitous, not only in black communities but as a part of mainstream American culture. Mahalia Jackson recorded "Come Sunday" as part of Duke Ellington's *Black, Brown and Beige* in 1958 and the next year appeared in the film *Imitation of Life*. Langston Hughes, who in 1956 wrote *Tambourines to Glory: A Play with Spirituals, Jubilees, and Gospel Songs*, wrote the gospel-song play *Black Nativity* in 1961, for a cast that included Marion Williams and Alex Bradford. In 1961 a gospel category was added to the Grammy awards, with Mahalia Jackson the first winner. During the 1960s costumed groups and choirs began to appear on Broadway, at Carnegie Hall, and in Las Vegas, as well as on television shows. In addition to Sam Cooke, many singers trained in the gospel tradition helped popularize gospel-style delivery in popular music. Rhythm-and-blues doo-wop groups from the late 1940s and 1950s, such as the Ravens, the Orioles, and the Drifters, used close harmonies and a high-crooning-male-lead style borrowed from gospel. Singers such as Dinah Washington, Ray Charles, Al Green, Aretha Franklin, James Brown, Little Richard, and Stevie Wonder used gospel techniques to cross over to enormous international popularity on the rock, soul, and rhythm-and-blues charts.

Gospel music was a crucial part of the civil rights movement. There had been a political thrust in sacred black music since the abolitionist hymnody of the nineteenth-century, and in the 1960s musicians such as Mahalia Jackson, Fannie Lou Hamer, Guy Carawan, the Montgomery Trio, the Nashville Quartet, the CORE Freedom Singers, the SNCC Freedom Singers, and Carlton Reese's Gospel Freedom Choir appeared at marches, rallies, and meetings. Gospel musicians had always reworked traditional material at will, and in the 1960s gospel songs and spirituals originally intended for religious purposes were changed to apply to secular struggles. For example, "If You Miss Me from Praying Down Here" became "If

You Miss Me from the Back of the Bus." Other popular songs were "We Shall Overcome," "This Little Light of Mine," "We'll Never Turn Back," "Eyes on the Prize," "Ninety-Nine and a Half Won't Do," "O Freedom," and "Ain't Nobody Gonna Turn Me Around." For many leaders of the civil rights movement, such as Hamer, the Rev. Dr. Martin Luther King Jr., and the Rev. Wyatt Tee Walker, gospel music was an essential part of their organizing work. "Precious Lord" was a favorite of Martin Luther King Jr., so Mahalia Jackson sang it at his funeral.

THE CONTEMPORARY SOUND AND BEYOND

The next phase in the history of gospel music came in 1969, when Edwin Hawkins released his rendition of "Oh Happy Day," a white nineteenth-century hymn, in which he eschewed the gritty timbres of Cleveland in favor of smooth pop vocals, soul harmonies, and jazz rhythms, including a conga drum. The song, which became the number one song on *Billboard*'s pop chart, represented a fusion of the traditional gospel style of Mahalia Jackson, Thomas Andrew Dorsey, and the Dixie Hummingbirds with elements of jazz, rhythm and blues, and soul. Record producers, inspired by the crossover potential of what became known as contemporary gospel, began encouraging gospel groups toward a more contemporary sound, igniting a long-running controversy within the gospel community.

After Hawkins, one of the principal figures of contemporary gospel throughout the 1970s was the composer and pianist Andraé Crouch, the cousin of critic Stanley Crouch. Also important were Myrna Summers, Danniebell Hall, Douglas Miller, Bebe and Cece Winans, the Clark Sisters, and the ensemble Commissioned. At the same time, gospel came to Broadway again in the widely acclaimed musical *Your Arms Too Short to Box with God* (1976).

In 1983 *The Gospel at Colonus* was a popular stage production in New York, and in the 1980s and 1990s gospel, particularly contemporary, has continued to attract large audiences. The unaccompanied vocal sextet Take 6 combined gospel-style harmonies with mainstream jazz rhythms to achieve huge popular success in the late 1980s. Other popular contemporary singers from this time included Richard Smallwood, who uses classical elements in his songs, Bobby Jones, Keith Pringle, and Daryl Coley. Walter Hawkins (b. 1949), the brother of Edwin Hawkins, combines elements of traditional and contemporary styles, especially on recordings with his wife, Tremaine (b. 1957). The Hawkins style was taken up by the Thompson Community Choir, the Charles Fold Singers, the Barrett Sisters, and the Rev. James Moore, as well as mass choirs in Florida, New Jersey, and Mississippi. The choral ensemble

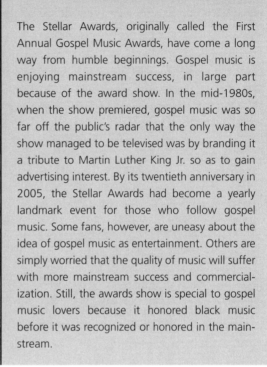

The Stellar Awards

The Stellar Awards, originally called the First Annual Gospel Music Awards, have come a long way from humble beginnings. Gospel music is enjoying mainstream success, in large part because of the award show. In the mid-1980s, when the show premiered, gospel music was so far off the public's radar that the only way the show managed to be televised was by branding it a tribute to Martin Luther King Jr. so as to gain advertising interest. By its twentieth anniversary in 2005, the Stellar Awards had become a yearly landmark event for those who follow gospel music. Some fans, however, are uneasy about the idea of gospel music as entertainment. Others are simply worried that the quality of music will suffer with more mainstream success and commercialization. Still, the awards show is special to gospel music lovers because it honored black music before it was recognized or honored in the mainstream.

Sounds of Blackness has been popular in recent years, as have contemporary vocal quartets such as the Williams Brothers, the Jackson Southernaires, and the Pilgrim Jubilees. These groups often use synthesizers and drum machines in addition to traditional gospel instruments. Prominent contemporary gospel composers include Elbernita Clark, Jeffrey LeValle, Andrae Woods, and Rance Allen.

Gospel-style singing, at least until the advent of rap music, dominated African-American popular music. One indication of the importance of gospel to the music industry is the fact that as of 1993 six Grammy categories were devoted to gospel music. Gospel, which started out as a marginal, almost blasphemous form of musical worship, now has a central place in African-American church activity. Not only Holiness and Pentecostal churches but Baptist and Methodist denominations have fully accepted gospel music. Its striking emotional power has enabled gospel music to remain a vital part of African-American culture.

In the early 2000s gospel music became a half-billion-dollar-per-year industry and held a 6.7 percent share in the music market. In a 2002 *Ebony* music poll, 21.2 percent of the respondents cited gospel music as their favorite, whereas 9.2 percent chose easy listening and 6.5 percent noted hip-hop. Because of gospel music's increasing popularity, retail chain restaurants in the southeast United States began instituting "Gospel Nights" in 2002. The program, which brings live gospel music to food establishments, has been met with increasing enthusiasm from patrons.

See also African Methodist Episcopal Church; Allen, Richard; Caesar, Shirley; Cleveland, James; Fisk Jubilee Singers; Holiness Movement; Music in the United States; Religion; Spirituals

■■ *Bibliography*

Boyer, Horace Clarence. "A Comparative Analysis of Traditional and Contemporary Gospel Music." In *More Than Dancing: Essays on Afro-American Music and Musicians*, edited by Irene W. Jackson, pp. 127–146. Westport, Conn.: Greenwood Press, 1985.

Burnim, Mellonee V. "The Black Gospel Music Tradition: A Complex of Ideology, Aesthetic and Behavior." In *More Than Dancing: Essays on Afro-American Music and Musicians*, edited by Irene W. Jackson, pp. 147–167. Westport, Conn.: Greenwood Press, 1985.

Carpener, Delores, and Nolan Williams, eds. *African American Heritage Hymnal*. Chicago: Gia Publications, 2001.

Harris, Michael W. *The Rise of Gospel Blues: The Music of Thomas Andrew Dorsey in the Urban Church.* New York: Oxford University Press, 1992.

Heilbut, Anthony. *The Gospel Sound: Good News and Bad Times.* New York, Simon & Schuster, 1971. Revised, New York: Harper & Row, 1985.

Lovell, John, Jr. *Black Song: The Forge and the Flame: The Story of How the Afro-American Spiritual Was Hammered Out.* New York: Macmillan, 1972.

Maultsby, Portia K. *Afro-American Religious Music: A Study in Musical Diversity.* Springfield, Ohio: Hymn Society of America, 1986.

Reagon, Bernice Johnson, ed. *We'll Understand It Better By and By.* Washington, D.C.: Smithsonian Institution Press, 1992.

Ricks, George R. *Some Aspects of the Religious Music of the U.S. Negro: An Ethnomusicological Study with Special Emphasis on the Gospel Tradition.* New York: Arno Press, 1977.

Walker, Wyatt Tee. *"Somebody's Calling My Name": Black Sacred Music and Social Change.* Valley Forge, Pa.: Judson Press, 1979.

HORACE CLARENCE BOYER (1996)
Updated by publisher 2005

GOSSETT, LOUIS, JR.

MAY 27, 1936

Actor Louis Gossett Jr. was born in Brooklyn, New York, the son of Louis Sr., a porter, and Hattie Gossett, a maid. He was raised in Bath Beach, an ethnically mixed neighborhood of Jewish, Italian, and African-American residents.

In high school Gossett was encouraged by his English teacher to pursue acting. In 1953 he captured a role in the Broadway play *Take a Giant Step* and won the Donaldson Award as best newcomer of the year for his performance. He helped support the family with his earnings from acting, allowing his mother to give up her work as a maid.

From 1956 to 1958 Gossett attended New York University on an athletic and drama scholarship. Though invited to try out for the New York Knicks basketball team, he instead chose to accept the part of George Murchison in the 1959 Broadway premiere of *A Raisin in the Sun*, a role he assumed in the film version in 1961.

Gossett's most important roles include "Fiddler" in the television miniseries *Roots* (1977) and Sergeant Foley in the film *An Officer and a Gentleman* (1982), a part that was not written expressly for a black actor. When he received an Academy Award for best supporting actor for his portrayal of Sergeant Foley, he became only the third black actor ever to be so honored, after Sidney Poitier and Hattie McDaniel.

Gossett has starred in two short-lived television series, *The Powers of Matthew Star* (1982) and *Gidion Oliver* (1989). In the 1980s and early 1990s Gossett played a hard-nosed military officer, modeled on the Sergeant Foley character, in the films *Iron Eagles* (1986), *Iron Eagles II* (1988), and *Aces: Iron Eagles III* (1992). In 1992 Gossett starred as an out-of-shape boxer who revives his career in the film *Diggstown*. He subsequently appeared in the television movies *Captive Heart: The James Mink Story* (1996), *In His Father's Shoes* (1997), *Inside* (1997), and *The Inspectors* (1998). In the new century Gossett continued to be in demand for television movies, with roles in at least ten through 2005, including *The Inspectors II: A Shred of Evidence* (2000), *For Love of Olivia* (2001), *Jasper, Texas* (2003), and *Lackawanna Blues* (2005). He also starred in the television series *Resurrection Blvd*.

See also Film in the United States, Contemporary; McDaniel, Hattie; Poitier, Sidney; Television

Bibliography

Bogle, Donald. *Blacks in American Film and Television: An Illustrated Encyclopedia.* New York: Garland, 1988.

"Louis Gossett, Jr." *Contemporary Black Biography*, Volume 7. Detroit, Mich: Gale, 1994.

ELIZABETH V. FOLEY (1996)
Updated by publisher 2005

GOVEIA, ELSA V.

APRIL 12, 1925
MARCH 18, 1980

Elsa Vesta Goveia, a pioneering historian of Caribbean slave societies, was born in the colony of British Guiana (now Guyana) in 1925, and she died in Jamaica in 1980. Winning the prestigious British Guiana Island Scholarship (the first woman to do so) in 1944 enabled her to study for a degree in history at University College, London. After earning a First Class degree in 1948, she immediately began research for her Ph.D. at the University of London.

In 1950 Goveia was recruited as the first West Indian member of the Department of History at the newly established University College of the West Indies (UCWI; renamed the University of the West Indies [UWI] in 1962) at Mona, Jamaica. Rising steadily up the academic ranks, she was appointed Professor of West Indian History in 1961, becoming the first West Indian professor in the History Department and the first female professor at UCWI/UWI.

Goveia's major achievements involve her contribution to the emerging historiography of the Caribbean and her leading role in introducing and encouraging the teaching of the region's history at the secondary and tertiary levels.

Her most important work, *Slave Society in the British Leeward Islands at the End of the Eighteenth Century* (1965), is a pioneering study of the social history of a group of small sugar islands at the height of the institution of slavery in the Caribbean. She was perhaps the most influential historian of this period to conceptualise "slave society" as consisting of "the whole community based on slavery"—meaning free blacks, free coloreds, and whites as well as the enslaved. Indeed, she was one of the originators of the concept of a "slave society," which has subsequently become a commonplace term of Caribbean (and New World) historiography. Goveia also contributed significantly to the emerging concept of "Creole society" through her careful analysis of the social and cultural interaction of white, black, and mixed-race persons (enslaved and free) in islands dominated by African slavery.

Of importance, too, is her pioneering 1956 study of the major writings on the history of the English-speaking territories from the sixteenth century to the end of the nineteenth century. This work can be said to mark the beginning of serious analysis of the region's historiographical tradition.

At UWI, Goveia designed, and taught for many years, the first full-fledged university courses on Caribbean history. A superb teacher, she influenced several generations of students by her erudition, her passionate interest in her subject, and her meticulous scholarship. Nor did she confine her work to academia. With her colleagues, she encouraged and assisted secondary school teachers all over the region to introduce Caribbean history into the curricula. She also played a major role in the establishment or upgrading of archives in the different territories in the 1950s and the 1960s.

Elsa Goveia was clearly the most influential historian of the Caribbean in the period between 1950 and 1980, and she made a major contribution to the emerging historiography and scholarship on New World slave societies. She played a pioneering role in the teaching of the region's history at the multicampus University of the West Indies, which she served for thirty years.

See also Education in the Caribbean; University of the West Indies

Bibliography

Higman, Barry H. *Writing West Indian Histories.* Warwick University Caribbean Studies. London and Basingstoke, UK: Macmillan, 1999.

Goveia, Elsa V. *A Study on the Historiography of the British West Indies to the End of the Nineteenth Century.* Mexico City: Instituto Panamericano de Geografía y Historia, 1956. Reprint, Washington D.C.: Howard University Press, 1980.

Goveia, Elsa V. *Slave Society in the British Leeward Islands at the end of the Eighteenth Century.* New Haven, Ct.: Yale University Press, 1965. Reprint, Westport, Ct.: Greenwood Press, 1980.

Marshall, W.K. "History Teaching in the University of the West Indies." In *Before and After 1865: Education, Politics, and Regionalism in the Caribbean*, edited by Brian L. Moore and Swithin R. Wilmot. Kingston, Jamaica: Ian Randle Publications, 1998.

BRIDGET BRERETON (2005)

GRACE, SWEET DADDY

JANUARY 25, 1881
JANUARY 12, 1960

▮▮▮

Religious leader Bishop Charles Emmanuel Grace, better known as Sweet Daddy, was born Marceline Manoël de Graça in the Cape Verde Islands of mixed African and Portuguese descent. Around 1908 he immigrated to New Bedford, Massachusetts, where he engaged in several occupations, including cranberry picking, before a journey to the Holy Land inspired him to found a church in West Waltham, Massachusetts, around 1919. In religious revivals in Charlotte, North Carolina, in the mid-1920s, Daddy Grace gathered several thousand followers and in 1926 incorporated in the District of Columbia the United House of Prayer for All People of the Church on the Rock of the Apostolic Faith.

A flamboyant and charismatic leader, Grace wore his hair and fingernails long, the latter painted red, white, and blue. He baptized converts with fire hoses and sold his followers specially blessed products, such as soap, coffee, eggs, and ice cream. He specialized in acquiring expensive real estate, particularly mansions and hotels, but he also supported church members with housing, pension funds, and burial plans. At his death in Los Angeles in 1960, there was an estate of some $25 million, but it was unclear what was owned by the church and what was his personal estate. An Internal Revenue Service lien of $6 million in back taxes was settled for $2 million in 1961.

Sweet Daddy never overtly claimed the divinity his followers attributed to him. "I never said I was God," he once noted, "but you cannot prove to me I'm not." At Daddy's death in 1960, Bishop Walter T. McCullogh took over the House of Prayer following a successful lawsuit against rival James Walton.

See also Christian Denominations, Independent; Protestantism in the Americas

▪▪ *Bibliography*

Fauset, Arthur Huff. *Black Gods of the Metropolis: Negro Religious Cults of the Urban North.* Philadelphia: University of Pennsylvania Press, 1944.

Halter, Marilyn. *Between Race and Ethnicity: Cape Verdean American Immigrants, 1860–1965.* Urbana: University of Illinois Press, 1993.

RICHARD NEWMAN (1996)

GRACIA REAL DE SANTA TERESA DE MOSE

▮▮▮

In 1687 eight men, two women, and a nursing child escaped from Carolina to Spanish St. Augustine and requested baptism into the "True Faith." Florida's governor sheltered the runaways out of Christian obligation and refused to return them when an agent from Carolina came to reclaim them.

The slaves' "telegraph" quickly reported this outcome, and soon other runaways began arriving in St. Augustine. Florida officials repeatedly solicited Spain for guidance, and finally, on November 7, 1693, Charles II issued a royal proclamation "giving liberty to all . . . the men as well as the women . . . so that by their example and by my liberality others will do the same."

Although some later freedom seekers were re-enslaved by a governor who tried to appease the Carolinians and avoid war, those not freed persisted in claiming the freedom promised by Spain's king. Led by the Mandinga commander of the black militia, a man baptized as Francisco Menéndez, they repeatedly petitioned the governors and church officials, but to no avail. As war with England threatened, however, Florida's new governor reviewed their petitions and granted all the enslaved runaways unconditional freedom.

In 1738 the newly freed men and women established the town of Gracia Real de Santa Teresa de Mose about two miles north of St. Augustine. Mose was considered a town of "new Christians," and its residents were the "subjects" of Captain Francisco Menéndez. The founding population of thirty-eight men, "most of them married," suggests a total population of about 100 people. Because so few men came with wives, the remainder had formed unions with local African and Indian women, making Mose a multiethnic and multicultural settlement.

Florida's governor clearly considered the benefits of a northern outpost of ex-slaves carrying Spanish arms. The freedmen also understood their expected role and vowed to be "the most cruel enemies of the English," and to risk their lives and spill their "last drop of blood in defense of the Great crown of Spain and the Holy Faith." Mose was a valuable military resource for the Spaniards but also a continuing provocation to English planters.

In 1739 "Angolan" slaves revolted near Stono, South Carolina, killing more than twenty whites before heading for St. Augustine. The following year General James Oglethorpe of Georgia led a massive invasion of Florida, supported by Carolina troops and volunteers, allied Indians, black "pioneers," and seven warships of the Royal Navy.

The Mose militia joined Spanish troops and Indian militias in guerrilla operations against the invaders and also in retaking Mose, which had been occupied. Just before daybreak on June 14, 1740, Spanish forces, Indians, and free blacks led by Menéndez launched a surprise attack on Mose. The combined Florida forces killed about seventy-five of the unprepared invaders in bloody hand-to-hand combat. British accounts refer to the event as "Bloody" or "Fatal" Mose, and the Spanish victory there led to Oglethorpe's subsequent withdrawal from Florida.

Mose was badly damaged in the fighting and was not resettled until 1752. It was finally abandoned at the end of the Seven Years' War in 1763, when Spain ceded Florida to the British. Menéndez and his "subjects" joined the Spanish exodus to Cuba, where they became homesteaders on the Matanzas frontier.

Mose was the earliest free black town in what became the United States, and it provides an important example of initiative, agency, and empowerment in the colonial history of African Americans. The enslaved Africans who risked their lives to become free and establish Mose also shaped the geopolitics of the southeast and the Caribbean. The Spanish Crown subsequently extended the religious sanctuary policy to other areas around the Caribbean and applied it to the disadvantage of Dutch and French slaveholders, as well as the British. The lives and sacrifices of the people of Mose thus took on a long-term international political significance that they could not have foreseen. The sanctuary policy they helped implement was only abrogated in 1790, under pressure from the new government of the United States.

Kathleen Deagan and a research team from the Florida Museum of Natural History excavated Mose and found artifacts including pottery, pipes, musket balls, and a handmade St. Christopher medal in or around the fort. This material evidence augments English and Spanish documentary sources for Mose's history, including a village census and petitions written and signed by Menéndez. In 1994 the state of Florida purchased the Mose site, and in 1996 it was designated a National Historic Landmark.

See also Black Towns; Free Blacks, 1619–1860; Maroon Arts; Runaway Slaves in the United States

■ ■ *Bibliography*

Deagan, Kathleen, and Darcie MacMahon. *Fort Mose: Colonial America's Black Fortress of Freedom.* Gainesville: University Press of Florida, 1995.

Landers, Jane. "Gracia Real de Santa Teresa de Mose: A Free Black Town in Colonial Florida." *American Historical Review* 95 (1990): 9–30.

Landers, Jane. *Black Society in Spanish Florida.* Urbana: University of Illinois Press, 1999.

JANE LANDERS (2005)

GRAJALES CUELLO, MARIANA

JUNE 12, 1815
NOVEMBER 27, 1893

Mariana Grajales Cuello is a legendary figure in Cuba. She was born a free woman of color in 1815 in the eastern city of Santiago de Cuba, the daughter of émigrés from Santo Domingo, and she died in 1893 in exile in Kingston, Jamaica. She is best known as the "glorious mother of the Maceos," the most famous of whom was her son, General Antonio Maceo (1845–1896), and much of what is known about her is filtered through him. She herself left no written documents, and, in contrast to the voluminous accounts of her son, comparatively little has been written about her. She was, however, an extraordinary woman in her own right.

While free women of color were often stereotypically portrayed in slave times as a buffer group, as moral matriarchal stalwarts of upwardly mobile families, or as sensual and licentious, Grajales refused to compromise herself or her family. She gave up an established position with three small farms and a Santiago de Cuba townhouse not for economic reasons but to fight against slavery and Spanish colonialism and to pursue a vision of a politically and racially free Cuba.

Free people of color were numerically strong in nineteenth-century eastern Cuba, and they were the only racial grouping in which women outnumbered men, as the Hispanic white settler and African slave populations were more predominantly male. In the more racially fluid society of Santiago de Cuba, Grajales's formative years were spent among free people of color of some property. They saw a relative erosion of their position, however, with the rapid expansion of sugar and slavery and a growing "fear of the black" on the part of the white planter class.

In these turbulent times, Grajales brought up thirteen children, four by her first husband Fructuoso Regueiferos, who died in 1840, and nine by Marcos Maceo (1808–1869), with whom she lived beginning in 1843 and whom she married after the death of his first wife. She and her family were catapulted to the heart of Cuba's late nineteenth-century struggles. It took thirty years of intermittent war (1868–1878, 1879–1880, and 1895–1898) to break the slave regime (emancipation became inevitable in 1886) and achieve independence from Spain (in 1898, though this ushered in the first U.S. military occupation of 1898 to 1902). War broke out in the less wealthy, more creole and free-colored eastern part of the country and culminated in an invasion of the western section, led by Maceo. While dogged by racial fears, the struggle brought together the races, and for many the old regime was as much a social (i.e., racial) as political anathema.

Memoirs and campaign diaries of the first war of Cuban independence (1868–1878) testify to how Grajales (with her daughters Baldomera and Dominga) and Maceo's wife María Cabrales, with whom Grajales maintained a close relationship, ran base camps, tending the wounded and seeing to the provision of food and clothing. When Marcos Maceo died in battle in 1869 and Antonio Maceo was wounded, Grajales sent a younger son off to fight. In 1878, after heading the Baraguá Protest against capitulation to Spain under the Zanjón Truce, Antonio Maceo agreed to leave Cuba with his family only when he had been entrusted by the revolutionary government to muster support for the cause among Cuban communities abroad. The family was given a Spanish amnesty and escort to sail from Santiago to Kingston, Jamaica. From 1878 until his return to Cuba to fight (and die) in the 1895–1898 war, Antonio Maceo was in and out of Jamaica, but Grajales was to remain there, part of a Cuban émigré community organizing for the renewed independence effort. When she died there in 1893, she was buried in St. Andrews Roman Catholic Cemetery. Thirty years later, in 1923, her remains were ceremonially exhumed and returned to Cuba, where they were laid to rest, alongside others of her family, in Santiago's Santa Efigenia Cemetery.

One of several statues to her memory in Cuba was erected in 1937 in the capital city of Havana. It depicts her with her small son, her arm pointing into the distance, and bears the inscription: "To Mariana Grajales, Mother of the Maceos. The people of Cuba." In 1957 she was declared the "official mother of Cuba," though she was portrayed as a Catholic, Marianist mother, and thus was whitened in the process. After the 1959 revolution, she was revered as the defiant and heroic, revolutionary mother-leader, whose loyalty was to causes beyond her own image and those of husband, father, or son. Due recognition was also accorded to her color. For many Afro-Cubans, Grajales symbolizes the spirit power of women of color to lead and commune with the *orishas* (spirits) to redress imbalance through ritual and action. To exhort others to kill and to die for a cause is seen as being within the power and right of a strong nurturer-warrior woman, and such a figure can resonate through history to take on mythical proportions.

See also Emancipation in Latin America and the Caribbean; Maceo, Antonio

▪▪ *Bibliography*

La Mujer Cubana en los Cien Años de Lucha, 1868–1968. Havana, Cuba: Instituto del Libro, 1969.

Portuondo, Olga. "El padre de Antonio Maceo: ¿Venezolano?" *Del Caribe* 19 (1992).

Sarabia, Nydia. *Historia de una Familia Mambisa: Mariana Grajales.* Havana, Cuba: Editorial Orbe, 1975.

Stubbs, Jean. "Social and Political Motherhood of Cuba: Mariana Grajales Cuello." In *Engendering History: Caribbean Women in Historical Perspective*, edited by Verene Shepherd, Bridget Brereton, and Barbara Bailey. New York: St. Martin's Press, 1995.

Stubbs, Jean. "Race, Gender, and National Identity in Nineteenth-Century Cuba: Mariana Grajales Cuello and the Revolutionary Free Browns of Cuba." In *Blacks, Coloureds, and the Formation of National Identity in Nineteenth-Century Latin America*, edited by Nancy Naro. London: ILAS/Palgrave, 2003.

JEAN STUBBS (2005)

GRANDFATHER CLAUSE
▪▪▪

The grandfather clause was among the legal devices designed by southern legislatures to limit African-American suffrage following Reconstruction. Literacy and property tests were imposed on potential voters, except for those who had been entitled to vote before black enfranchisement as well as their sons and grandsons. The grandfather clause was thus technically an exemption written into laws restricting suffrage but an exemption that allowed virtually all whites to retain the vote and that effectively disfranchised almost all African Americans.

The Mississippi constitution of 1890 represented the first attempt to eliminate black voting, and by World War I almost all the ex–Confederate states had adopted some form of black disfranchisement legislation. These included poll taxes, literacy requirements, property-holding requirements, the white primary, and an array of similar provisions designed to circumvent the Fifteenth Amendment to the U.S. Constitution, which prohibits states from limiting suffrage on the basis of race.

In 1898 Louisiana introduced the first grandfather clause, which stated that "no male person who was on January 1st 1867 or at any date prior thereto entitled to vote . . . and no son or grandson of any such person . . . shall be denied the right to register and vote in this state by reason of his failure to possess the educational or property qualifications." Variants of this approach were the fighting grandfather clause, which exempted descendants of veterans, or Mississippi's "understanding" clause, which exempted those who could verbally interpret the state constitution to the satisfaction of white registration officials.

The grandfather clauses' effects were temporary. Only current white voters were exempted, and all new voters had to meet the literacy test. In practice, literacy tests resulted in a substantial reduction in white as well as black voting, since few whites would publicly proclaim their illiteracy to take the exemption. In 1914 the U.S. Supreme Court found grandfather clauses unconstitutional, and the southern states shifted to other forms of disfranchisement legislation.

See also Black Codes; Jim Crow

■ ■ *Bibliography*

Key, V. O., Jr. *Southern Politics in State and Nation.* New York: Knopf, 1949.

Keyssar, Alexander. *The Right to Vote: The Contested History of Democracy in the United States.* New York: Basic Books, 2000.

Kousser, Morgan. *The Shaping of Southern Politics: Suffrage Restriction and the Establishment of the One-Party South, 1880–1910.* New Haven, Conn., and London: Yale University Press, 1974.

MICHAEL W. FITZGERALD (1996)
Updated bibliography

GRANDMASTER FLASH (SADDLER, JOSEPH)

JANUARY 1, 1957

━┃┃┃━━━━━━━━━━━━━━━

Born in Barbados as Joseph Saddler, Grandmaster Flash got his start in the vibrant street-party scene of the Bronx in 1970s New York. A prominent DJ, Flash pioneered a number of record-mixing innovations, including "scratching," "break mixing," "punch phasing," and the "beat box." Flash's mastery of these techniques placed him at the forefront of the rap music scene, which exploded into national popularity in the early 1980s.

Flash's innovations centered around the use of multiple turntables to combine the best parts of songs to create an exciting new combination of beats and melodies. In addition to creating new sounds, Flash added an element of showmanship to his performances, mixing records behind his back and including friends who "shouted out" to excite the audience. These shout outs evolved into complex rhyming lyrics and became a permanent part of Flash's act when he formed Grandmaster Flash and the Furious Five. The group's 1981 single, "The Adventures of Grandmaster Flash on the Wheels of Steel," introduced a national audience to the exciting rhythmic montage of sound made possible by Flash's technological innovations. Their 1982 hit, "The Message," won critical acclaim and demonstrated that rap music could tackle the pressing issues of urban poverty and violence. Although the group broke up in 1982, their work remained influential to rap and hip-hop music. Flash remained active in the hip-hop scene and is known for his role as music director on the *Chris Rock Show.* Grandmaster Flash received the Founder's Award at the 2003 Billboard-AURN R&B/Hip-Hop Awards Show.

See also Hip Hop; Rap

■ ■ *Bibliography*

George, Nelson. *Hip Hop America.* New York: Viking, 1998.

Rose, Tricia. *Black Noise: Rap Music and Black Culture in Contemporary America.* Hanover, N.H.: University Press of New England, 1994.

Toop, David. *Rap Attack 3.* London: Serpent's Tail,1999.

MICHAEL WADE FUQUAY (1996)
Updated by publisher 2005

GRAVENBERCH, ADOLF FREDERIK

FEBRUARY 1, 1811
NOVEMBER 16, 1906

━┃┃┃━━━━━━━━━━━━━━━

Adolf Frederik Gravenberch was born in Suriname and was originally named simply Adolf Frederik. His parents were slaves, and his master lent him to a plantation physician, A. Steglich, from whom he learned a number of medical skills. He acquired even more medical knowledge when after Steglich's death his master allowed him to work in the hospital directed by Dr. George Cornelis Berch Gravenhorst, a leading surgeon and authority on the treatment of leprosy and elephantiasis. Then, in 1847, Gravenhorst helped him buy his freedom and made him an assistant surgeon in the hospital on Gravenstraat. It was in honor of his benefactor that he came to take the name Gravenberch. After Gravenhorst's permanent departure for the Netherlands soon afterwards, Gravenberch set out to pursue a medical career on his own. Toward that end he petitioned King William III for a license to practice medicine, through the colony's governor, O. G. Stuart von Schmidt auf Altenstadt, whom he had met. Despite Gravenberch's lacking the usual formal education and certification by examination, the king responded in 1855 with a royal appointment as a municipal physician in the colony of Suriname. This action was applauded by some, but resented by others, who cited professional standards and his color and slave origins in opposing the appointment.

Gravenberch thereupon set up a hospital in Paramaribo and developed a large practice, including all classes of the urban population, as well as patients drawn from the plantations. He was especially recognized by the black community for providing vital medical advice and treatment, at times free of charge, that they would never otherwise have received because of the prevailing racial attitudes. He also had a successful marriage, with several children, and for a time he prospered financially. He lived in the district of Boven-Commewijne, acquired other buildings in town, and in the late 1850s and early 1860s bought a sugar plantation called La Jaloussie along the Boven-Commewijne River. He also acquired two tracts of forestland, Osembo on the Para River and Libanon on the Saramacca. However, he lost most of his fortune with the fall in sugar prices in the wake of the emancipation of slaves that had occurred in 1863. His financial plight was compounded in 1875, when colonial officials, after having allowed him to extend his practice into the districts, now brought charges against him for crossing the restrictive racial boundaries. With the help of a legal adviser, Colaço Belmonte, he was exonerated, and his request to legally practice in the districts was granted. In 1879 he moved his residence to Paramaribo for the rest of his life. In 1880, thousands of well-wishers joined in the silver jubilee celebration of his career as a physician, and he continued on to celebrate the golden jubilee in 1905.

Gravenberch died in Paramaribo on November 16, 1906, at the age of ninety-five, and he was buried in the Willem Jacobus Rust Cemetery there. Gravenberch's son, Rudolf Johan, also achieved a notable reputation. On March 23, 1908, a petition submitted to Queen Wilhelmina on his behalf requested that he also be licensed to practice medicine. At the time he was an assistant inspector at the slaughterhouse, and for sixteen years he had served as a medic in the military hospital in Paramaribo. He had attended, but not completed, medical school. His petition, initiated by a Surinamer Baptist minister, Carl P. Rier, was launched at a memorial service aimed at keeping alive the humanitarian legacy of his father. While its nearly 3,000 signers eventually included physicians, politicians, clergymen, civil servants, and plantation directors, the petition was not approved. It nevertheless demonstrates that Adolf Frederik Gravenberch's career inspired others to continue the struggle for social justice in Suriname.

See also Free Blacks, 1619-1890

■ ■ *Bibliography*

Neck-Yoder, Hilda van. "Surinam's Cultural Memory: of Crown and Knife." *CLA Journal* 24 (1980): 173–183.

Oudschans Dentz, Fred. "Eenige bladzijden uit het leven van Dr. George Cornelis Bergh Gravenhorst." *Nederlandsch Tijdschrift voor Geneeskunde* 86 (1942): 1430–1436.

Rier, C. P. *The Biography of Dr. Adolf Frederik Gravenberch, Municipal Physician*. Paramaribo, Suriname: C. P. Rier, 1908.

Unpublished translation of *De levensgeschiedenis van dr. A. F. Gravenberch* by Hilda van Neck-Yoder, found in the Moorland-Spingarn Research Center, Howard University, Washington, D.C.

ALLISON BLAKELY (2005)

GRAVEYARDS

See African Burial Ground Project; Cemeteries and Burials

GRAY, WILLIAM H., III

AUGUST 20, 1941

━┃┃┃━━━━━━━━━━━━━━━━

Congressman and administrator William Herbert Gray III was born in Baton Rouge, Louisiana, the son of William H. Gray Jr., a minister and president of Florida A&M University, and Hazel Yates, a high school teacher. In 1963 he received a B.A. from Franklin and Marshall College in Lancaster, Pennsylvania, in 1966 a master of divinity from Drew Theological Seminary in Madison, New Jersey, and a master of theology from Princeton Theological Seminary in 1970. In 1964 he became pastor of Union Baptist Church, in Montclair, New Jersey, where he was active in helping to initiate low-income housing projects. In 1972, as both his father and grandfather before him, he became pastor of Bright Hope Baptist Church in Philadelphia, where he developed a politically active ministry and continued his interest in housing and mortgage issues.

Gray was first elected to Congress from Pennsylvania's Second District as a Democrat in 1978. During his time in Congress, he served on the House Appropriations, Foreign Affairs, and District of Columbia committees. His most important post was chair of the House Budget Committee in 1985, from which he steered the passage of the country's first trillion-dollar budget through controversies and differences between Congress and President Ronald Reagan.

A centrist within the Democratic Party, Gray's primary focus in domestic policy was federal support of black private-sector development. On foreign issues he served as a leading spokesman on U.S. policy toward Africa and was a congressional sponsor of the anti-apartheid movement. Gray sponsored an emergency aid bill for Ethiopia in 1984 and helped secure passage of the Anti-Apartheid acts of 1985 and 1986, overriding presidential vetoes.

Gray's mainstream domestic politics and energetic party politicking helped pave the way for his ascendance to the Democratic leadership. In 1985 he was elected chairman of the Democratic caucus in the House, and in 1989 he became majority whip, the number three leadership position in the House and the highest rank held by an African-American congressman at that time.

In 1991 Gray resigned from Congress to become president of United Negro College Fund (UNCF) in New York City. That year he oversaw the inauguration of the UNCF's Campaign 2000, a drive to raise $250 million by the year 2000. With the support of President George H. W. Bush and a $50 million gift from media magnate Walter Annenberg, the campaign raised $86 million in its first year. In May 1994 Gray was named temporary envoy to Haiti by President Bill Clinton but retained his position at the UNCF.

In 2003, after transforming the UNCF into a powerful philanthropic organization, Gray stepped down as president to spend more time with his family.

See also Politics in the United States; United Negro College Fund

■ ■ *Bibliography*

Clay, William L. *Just Permanent Interests: Black Americans in Congress, 1870–1991.* New York: Amistad, 1992.

RICHARD NEWMAN (1996)
Updated by publisher 2005

GREAT DEPRESSION AND THE NEW DEAL

The Great Depression was a period of enormous economic upheaval that affected the lives of all Americans. Rich and poor alike experienced the hardships of a contracting economy. The political and economic status of African Americans made them particularly vulnerable, and they felt the effects of the Depression earlier than other groups. During the booming 1920s, blacks had made modest gains because there was a need for their labor. These gains were achieved even though the jobs available were, for the most part, unskilled, low-paying positions, jobs that white workers no longer wanted.

EMPLOYMENT AMONG AFRICAN AMERICANS

According to the 1930 census, 37 percent of working African Americans were employed as agricultural laborers and 29 percent as personal-service and domestic workers. Only 2 percent were classified as professionals (lawyers, doctors, teachers, and clergy). Because such a large proportion of black workers were involved in agriculture, the collapse of the cotton industry brought devastating results. As early as 1926, the National Urban League was advising unemployed southern black workers not to come north unless they were certain they had a job. White workers were already displacing black workers in jobs that had traditionally belonged to African Americans.

Unemployment increased rapidly in the early 1930s. It was thought that approximately 15 percent of the workforce was unemployed in 1930, and this percentage increased as the depression lengthened. African-American organizations estimated that the percentage of unemployed black workers was at least twice the rate of the country as a whole. Private social-service agencies, as well as state and local relief organizations, became overwhelmed with requests for help from people seeking work and public assistance. President Herbert Hoover's administration paid little attention to the plight of those in need, however, assuring the country that "prosperity is just around the corner."

ROOSEVELT AND THE NEW DEAL

Most of the country regarded Franklin D. Roosevelt's election as president in 1932 with hope and anticipation. He had run on a platform that promised to turn the economy around and put America back to work, and, in fact, Roosevelt moved swiftly to enact legislation that would provide

A young girl looks out from a newspaper-lined window in her log cabin home in Gee's Bend, Alabama, 1937. The widespread impoverishment caused throughout the United States by the Great Depression of the 1930s brought about a further decline in living standards for many southern blacks. THE LIBRARY OF CONGRESS

quick temporary measures to alleviate the economic distress experienced by the unemployed and to stimulate the private sector of the economy. This legislation seemed, at first, to be promising to the African-American population. Programs in Roosevelt's plan—known as the New Deal—that were of special interest to blacks included the National Recovery Administration (NRA), the Agriculture Adjustment Administration (AAA), the Civilian Conservation Corps (CCC), the Public Works Administration (PWA), and the Civil Works Administration (CWA)—all federal programs created in 1933. In addition, the Federal Emergency Relief Administration (FERA) provided federal funds to the states to enable them to provide relief and work relief to the poor. This was the first federal program to give direct grants to the states; it included incentives that encouraged states to improve public-assistance policies.

The Works Progress Administration (WPA) and the National Youth Administration (NYA) were created in 1935. The WPA provided work relief to those out of work but employable; meanwhile, FERA was phased out, giving the responsibility for providing public assistance back to the states. The NYA provided work relief for young people living at home or attending college.

In addition, significant New Deal reform legislation was enacted during the Great Depression that was of great concern to African Americans. This included the Social Security Act of 1935, a watershed in social-welfare policy, which established old-age and unemployment insurance administered by the federal government and categorical relief programs administered by the states; the National Labor Relations Act of 1935, which gave considerable power to organized labor by guaranteeing the right of workers to organize on their own behalf without interference from employers; and the Fair Labor Standards Act of 1938, which established a minimum wage and maximum hours of work.

NATIONAL INDUSTRIAL RECOVERY ACT

The National Industrial Recovery Act (NIRA) of 1933 was an omnibus act designed to stimulate the private-sector economy, relieve economic distress, and resolve conflicts between labor and management. African Americans believed that the NIRA had the potential to be very helpful. Several black organizations, including the National Urban League and the National Association for the Advancement of Colored People (NAACP), tried unsuccessfully to have an antidiscrimination amendment attached to it. The NIRA created the National Recovery Administration (NRA), and one of its immediate tasks was to establish industrial codes with minimum-wage rates and maximum hours of work in all industries, an anti-inflationary measure meant to control a wage-price spiral. The first problem that African Americans encountered in this program was the exclusion of domestic and agricultural workers from coverage. This meant that for two-thirds of the black workforce, there was very little hope of receiving any increase in wages or improvement in working conditions.

Furthermore, during the process of establishing codes, it became apparent that industries were submitting codes that amounted, in effect, to differential wages in occupations with a majority of black workers. The proposed wages for these occupations were 20 percent to 40 percent lower than the wages in occupations whose workers were predominantly white. When Roosevelt issued a blanket "blue eagle" agreement to promote support of the codes, it caused widespread displacement of black workers, especially in the South, where employers refused to pay a minimum wage to them. In order to counteract these policies, the Joint Committee on National Recovery was founded, composed of twenty-two national African-American fraternal, civic, and church groups. The Joint Committee, cochaired by John P. Davis and Robert Weaver (1907–1997), closely monitored the establishment of codes in all industries where there were a substantial number of black workers, and they submitted briefs against a different wage based on geographic areas.

Section 7A of the NIRA gave workers the right to organize and bargain collectively without interference from employers. Organized labor was able to use section 7A to expand its membership and help workers take advantage of collective bargaining, particularly in the coal industry and needle trades. Some African Americans had reservations about this policy, not because they were against the principle of collective bargaining, which they saw as very positive, but because of the policies of local unions that prevented blacks from becoming part of the organized labor movement.

WORKPLACE DISCRIMINATION

African-American organizations, especially the National Urban League and the NAACP, pressured the American Federation of Labor (AFL) to abolish segregation and discrimination, but these practices continued. As labor gained more control over jobs in New Deal work programs, more black workers were denied jobs because they were not union members. The Joint Committee, along with National Urban League officials Eugene Kinkle Jones and T. Arnold Hill and NAACP executive secretary Walter White, argued that this was a violation of the NRA codes, but discrimination continued. In 1935, when the Supreme Court ruled that the NRA's regulation of the private sector was unconstitutional, African Americans did not regard this as a significant loss.

THE AGRICULTURAL ADJUSTMENT ADMINISTRATION

The Agricultural Adjustment Administration (AAA) was established to alleviate the problems associated with depressed prices for farm products and mounting crop surpluses. The AAA had a decentralized administration that gave a great deal of power to local areas. In spite of clear federal guidelines as to how benefits were to be allocated between owner and tenant, there were great variations in the treatment of black sharecroppers—people who lived and farmed on land that was owned by another person and shared their earnings, based on acreage and production, with the landowner.

Too frequently, large landowners controlled the AAA benefits (incentives to reduce cotton acreage), and tenant farmers and sharecroppers were not given their fair share. The Southern Tenant Farmers' Union, an interracial organization, was formed to fight for fair treatment under the AAA and received considerable support from the NAACP. But it was difficult for these organizations to compete with the southern bloc of the Democratic Party in Congress, and little was accomplished. The AAA was replaced by the Soil Conservation Act and the Domestic Allotment Act when, in 1936, the Supreme Court ruled that the AAA's processing tax was unconstitutional.

THE CIVILIAN CONSERVATION CORPS

The Civilian Conservation Corps (CCC) was one of the most enduring and popular New Deal work-relief programs, lasting until the 1940s. It served three purposes: (1) it provided relief to young men and their families; (2) it removed young people from the private labor market; and (3) it provided basic education and job training. The young men lived in CCC camps run by the War Depart-

Children of sharecropper, Arkansas, 1935. *The Great Depression of the 1930s brought about a further decline in living standards for many southern blacks in the United States. While the average yearly household income in the United States was $1,500 at that time, a study of sharecroppers in four Southern states found their average income to be $294 annually.* PHOTOGRAPHS AND PRINTS DIVISION, SCHOMBURG CENTER FOR RESEARCH IN BLACK CULTURE, THE NEW YORK PUBLIC LIBRARY, ASTOR, LENOX AND TILDEN FOUNDATIONS.

ment, and they worked on conservation projects such as reforestation.

African Americans did not have equal access to this program. Although it was federally financed and administered, local social-service staffs selected participants. In some areas, this resulted in the exclusion of African-American youths. Since the camps were administered by the War Department, the segregated policies of the armed forces were often followed. In addition, there was a racial quota that limited the number of black youth according to the proportion of blacks in the population.

Furthermore, the camps did not hire black personnel. Through pressure brought to bear by such African-American organizations as the National Urban League and the NAACP, some of these policies were changed. All-black camps were set up in areas where segregation was the law of the land; in other areas, the camps were integrated. Some black reserve officers were placed at all-black camps. In spite of these changes, local autonomy and quo-

tas continued to limit the participation of African Americans.

THE PUBLIC WORKS ADMINISTRATION

The intent of the Public Works Administration in the Department of the Interior was to stimulate industry through the purchase of materials and wage payments. The program was designed to construct large projects such as dams, government buildings, and low-rent housing. It was a federal employment program that paid set wages based on levels of skill and prevailing wages in local areas. Federal administration was more likely to ensure that African-American workers would be treated fairly, but projects were awarded to local contractors, who then negotiated with organized labor for the selection of workers. This resulted in the exclusion of many black workers because local AFL craft unions did not admit blacks, and there was no enforcement against discrimination.

Robert Weaver, special adviser for Negro affairs in the Department of the Interior, proposed a plan to correct this situation based on the percentage of skilled and unskilled African-American workers in each of the cities involved in low-rent-housing construction. Eighteen months after the plan had been implemented, Weaver expressed the belief that it had helped to overcome discrimination against black workers. Unfortunately, the plan was never extended to other PWA projects or other New Deal programs.

THE FEDERAL EMERGENCY RELIEF ADMINISTRATION

The Federal Emergency Relief Administration (FERA) was a relief and work-relief program administered by the states through federal grants. Designed as a temporary program to meet emergency needs, it had many attributes that promised to be helpful to African-American workers. It provided jobs with a specific wage rate based on skill; there was no racial quota; it had a white-collar component that provided work for black professionals; it funded self-help projects; and federal regulations attached to the program raised relief standards and discouraged discrimination. FERA also established eligibility with means testing (i.e., one's income had to be below a set amount so that one could quality for benefits), which ensured that those most in need would be given priority.

But there was no rule to enforce nondiscrimination. Since eligibility was established locally, local prejudices prevailed, making it difficult for African Americans to participate. It was therefore easier for them to get relief than to obtain work on FERA projects. FERA's wage rates were established according to geographic zones and were disliked by many employers, who thought the rates increased labor costs. A great deal of pressure to rescind or lower the wage rates came from the southern states, where the rates were above the average wage paid to most black workers in the private sector. African Americans were appalled when this pressure proved effective, arguing that one of the goals of the New Deal was to attain a decent standard of living for all Americans.

THE CIVIL WORKS ADMINISTRATION

The Civil Works Administration (CWA) was a temporary program that was created because the PWA was slow in getting work projects started. Winter was approaching, and many people faced extreme hardship because the CCC, FERA, and the PWA were not meeting the needs of all the unemployed. The CWA had the capacity to provide four million jobs on projects that could be started quickly, were labor-intensive, and required a minimal use of

equipment and material. The program had a white-collar component but did not have racial quotas, and although it was not means-tested, it gave preference to those most in need. This initiative appears to have been more helpful to African Americans than other New Deal programs, but it was of short duration. It was created as a temporary measure to help the unemployed survive the winter of 1933, and it was slowly dismantled as the cold weather passed.

THE NATIONAL YOUTH ADMINISTRATION

The National Youth Administration (NYA) was established in 1935 to help young men and women who were living at home. It helped those young people who were not attending school to receive job training and those in school to continue their education. African-American youth fared fairly well under the NYA, in spite of a great deal of local autonomy in the administration of the programs. This relative success may have been the result of the influence of Mary McLeod Bethune (1875–1955), the head of the Negro Affairs section of the NYA, who was able to funnel thousands of dollars to black youths.

THE WORKS PROGRESS ADMINISTRATION

New Deal administrators began to fear that FERA was creating a permanent dependent class. There was a general consensus that relief for the able-bodied unemployed should be in the form of work relief. Thus, FERA was dismantled in 1935 and the Works Progress Administration (WPA; later called the Work Projects Administration) was established to serve as a coordinating agency for work-relief programs in the states. Instead, however, it became a giant work-relief program itself, assuming responsibility for providing work to over three and a half million people and emphasizing the desirability of work over relief. Responsibility for providing relief was returned to the states, many of which reverted to "poor-law standards" that had been in place prior to FERA.

After the experiences that African Americans had had with earlier New Deal programs, they regarded the WPA very cautiously. It had attributes that appeared to be helpful, such as federal administration, an emphasis on work, a white-collar component, and set wage rates, and it gave preference to those most in need by establishing eligibility with means testing.

But the WPA also had policies that were disturbing to the black population, including wage rates that were lower than those in the private sector and with geographic differentiations. The states in the Southeast, where the majority of African Americans lived, had the lowest wage rate

African-American sharecropper working with one-horse plow, Georgia, 1937. Most African Americans became sharecroppers out of necessity, providing their own labor and depending on credit for everything from animals and equipment to food and other necessities. Photograph by Dorothea Lange. PHOTOGRAPHS AND PRINTS DIVISION, SCHOMBURG CENTER FOR RESEARCH IN BLACK CULTURE, THE NEW YORK PUBLIC LIBRARY, ASTOR, LENOX AND TILDEN FOUNDATIONS.

(sixty-five cents per day for unskilled workers). Although discrimination was forbidden, there was no enforcement mechanism to prevent it. The WPA was a federal program, but most of the projects were developed at the local level and gave a great deal of control to local officials. Organized labor again controlled hiring on many of the projects.

Since the WPA was not allowed to compete with private industry, and because the cost of materials was to be kept to a minimum, many of its jobs were regarded as make-work assignments, and thus of very little value. Harry Hopkins, the administrator of the WPA, was creative in his development of projects and actually accomplished a great deal—the program built or improved hospitals, schools, farm-to-market roads, playgrounds, and landing strips. The white-collar component proved especially beneficial to African-American professionals. Hopkins created the WPA Federal Theatre Project, which presented plays and dances for children and adults, many of whom had never seen a live theatrical production. The WPA Federal Writers' Project resulted in the development of numerous brochures, guides, and other publications, such as the Life in America series, which included ethnic studies such as *The Negro in Virginia*. The Federal Arts Project gave jobs to unemployed artists, who taught at community centers, produced artistic works, and painted murals in government buildings. Many African-American actors, writers, and artists were employed in these WPA projects. Charles White (1918–1979) and Hale Woodruff (1900–1980), for example, were accomplished artists who taught in WPA programs in the South.

As the private sector expanded, WPA policies became more restrictive. Workers could not remain on projects longer than eighteen months. This was especially hard on black workers because the private labor market was not absorbing them as quickly as it was absorbing whites. The WPA was curtailed sharply in 1940, although over eight million people remained unemployed. These individuals were forced to return to relief for help.

The National Urban League and the NAACP thought it imperative for African Americans to be gainfully employed, and they advocated some kind of permanent public-works program to provide jobs for those workers who could not find employment in the private sector. They predicted that a large proportion of African Americans would become permanently dependent on relief without a work program to help them remain employed. They also recognized that the WPA was costly and had its faults, but they thought that it was worth the price in the human dignity and self-respect that regular employment provided.

SOCIAL WELFARE LEGISLATION

In addition to creating temporary programs to alleviate the economic distress and stimulate the private-sector economy, the New Deal produced some permanent, significant social-welfare legislation. Legislation of the greatest concern to African Americans included the National Labor Relations Act and the Social Security Act, both in 1935, and the Fair Labor Standards Act in 1938.

THE NATIONAL LABOR RELATIONS ACT. The National Labor Relations Act had its beginning with section 7A of the NIRA. When the NRA was ruled unconstitutional, many of the policies in section 7A were transferred to a labor bill that was introduced by Senator Robert Wagner of New York in 1935. African Americans were especially concerned about a clause stating that "the employer and a labor organization may agree that an applicant for employment shall be required to join a labor organization as a condition of employment." They feared that this clause would have very negative consequences for black workers because it seemed to legalize closed shops. If this was to be the law, the African-American population believed it was mandatory to have a mechanism to prevent unions from discriminating against black workers.

T. Arnold Hill, the industrial secretary of the National Urban League, testified against Wagner's labor bill, prefacing his testimony with a statement supporting the labor movement and the concept of collective bargaining. The crux of his testimony was that the league could not support the bill as written because it permitted closed shops, denied black workers the right to engage in strikebreaking in occupations where they were also prohibited from joining the striking union; and failed to protect them from racial discrimination by labor unions.

Wagner was very much aware of the discriminatory practices of organized labor, but he was reluctant to include any kind of antidiscrimination clause in the labor bill because he thought this would jeopardize its passage. In the end, the bill was passed without such a clause. This issue continued to be a major concern among blacks, however, and enforcement against employment discrimination was finally accomplished with Title 7 of the 1964 Civil Rights Act.

THE SOCIAL SECURITY ACT. The Social Security Act established federal responsibility for a broad range of social-welfare programs to help individuals meet the loss of earnings or absence of income caused by unemployment, old age, death of a family's wage earner, and other hazards of life. The initial act provided old-age insurance, unemployment compensation, aid to destitute blind and elderly persons, and aid to destitute children in one-parent families. In 1939 the act was amended to include survivors' insurance.

This act was of special importance to President Roosevelt, whose primary concerns were old-age security and unemployment insurance. He insisted on worker contributions, because he thought this would make old-age insurance different from relief and ensure the permanence of these programs. Benefits would be regarded as a right by those who had contributed through the social security payroll tax, and the programs would be viewed as self-supporting. This would make it less likely for Congress, in later years, to dismantle them.

The Social Security Act has had a lasting and profound effect on African Americans because it created a two-tier social-welfare system. The first, and preferred, tier is a system to which workers and/or their employers contribute (old-age and survivors' insurance and unemployment compensation). The second tier is a stigmatized system that consists of public-assistance programs (aid to the poor elderly, the blind, and dependent children).

African-American organizations closely monitored the debates leading to the passage of the Social Security Act. The three issues that were of most concern to them were administrative responsibility, coverage, and methods of financing. They preferred federal administration of all programs, universal coverage, and financing by a means other than worker contributions. The original bill covered all workers, but the Treasury Department objected because of the difficulties involved in collecting a payroll tax from agricultural and domestic workers; they were thus

A thirteen-year-old sharecropper plows a field near Americus, Georgia, 1937. *The Great Depression intensified the severe poverty of many rural farmers.* THE LIBRARY OF CONGRESS

excluded from coverage under the first tier. This exclusion may have been for political reasons also, since it was anticipated that farmers, especially in the South, would have strong objections to contributing to social insurance benefits for black farm laborers and would fight against passage of the bill.

African Americans testified while the bill was being debated in Congress, advocating the inclusion of domestic and agricultural workers, federal administration of all programs, and financing through general revenues. The exclusion of agricultural and domestic workers under the first tier meant that about two-thirds of the black workforce would not be eligible for old-age insurance or unemployment compensation. Such people would have to rely on public assistance when they were unable to support themselves by working. The act gave the states the administrative responsibility for public-assistance programs under the second tier, something that was especially difficult for the African-American population in the Southeast.

Local autonomy meant that many black individuals and families who were eligible for old-age assistance, blind assistance, or aid to dependent children would be denied it by local agencies with discriminatory policies. Many would be forced to work in the cotton fields without the protection of any labor statutes.

African Americans paid very little attention to the public-assistance components of the act. Their main concerns were the programs tied to employment. The NAACP and the National Urban League pointed out that relief rolls were no substitute; relief was a dole that stigmatized and robbed an individual of self-respect and initiative. These organizations continued to try to amend the act to provide coverage for agricultural and domestic workers under the first tier.

THE FAIR LABOR STANDARDS ACT. The Fair Labor Standards Act established a minimum wage and maximum hours of work. As with the NLRA, many aspects of this act had been part of the code policies under the National Recovery Administration. The African-American population was generally in favor of the bill, although geographic wage differentials were seriously considered and it was quite likely that agricultural and domestic workers would once again be excluded. The National Urban League favored the bill but decided not to support it openly because of the likelihood of a racist backlash. The NAACP attempted to ally with the AFL, hoping that such an alliance would result in the inclusion of agricultural and domestic workers, but the AFL did not join it on this issue.

The bill barely passed because it had no strong backing from any group; indeed, it might never have been reported out of committee if Senator Claude Pepper, who supported it, had not won a senatorial primary in Florida over a congressman who campaigned against the bill. It was then brought to the floor and quickly passed.

The Fair Labor Standards Act was very weak because too many concessions had been given to diverse groups to ensure its passage. This meant that several occupations had been excluded from coverage, including domestic and agricultural workers. It left the differential wage question to the administrator of the law. This eventually resulted in a federal set wage of 25 cents per hour and a maximum workweek of 44 hours; after two years, industry would reach a minimum wage of 40 cents and a 40-hour maximum workweek.

AFRICAN AMERICANS IN THE GOVERNMENT

The New Deal administration was the first to include a substantial number of African Americans. Several black leaders served as advisers for Negro affairs in the various cabinet departments—a group frequently referred to as the "black cabinet" or the "black brain trust." Some of the prominent appointees were Robert Weaver, Mary McLeod Bethune, William Hastie, Forrester Washington, Eugene Kinkle Jones, and Robert Vann. Historians are not in agreement regarding the amount of influence this group exercised. Black advisers were able to expand employment opportunities for black professionals in civil-service positions and perhaps, from time to time, focus some attention on civil rights. But for the most part, the black cabinet was not a cohesive group and never made any strong policy statements.

Advisers for Negro affairs were seldom involved in the formulation of policy. However, it is clear that the presence of such advisers was a positive force. Robert Weaver was able to devise policies that helped more black workers gain jobs under the PWA. Mary McLeod Bethune, head of the Negro Affairs section of the NYA, was a highly re-spected woman who was able to help thousands of black youths take advantage of NYA benefits. In addition, Bethune had a close relationship with Eleanor Roosevelt and explained the needs, concerns, and aspirations of the African-American population to her. Mrs. Roosevelt, as the president's wife, was perceived by the black community as a friend who was willing to intervene and be an advocate for them. She was sympathetic to the plight of African Americans but, like the president, did not believe that the government could eliminate racial obstacles.

AFRICAN-AMERICAN ORGANIZATIONS

The leadership that was most helpful to African Americans came from outside the administration, in the form of black organizations such as the National Urban League and the NAACP. These groups attempted to monitor the development of New Deal legislation and programs, to testify in favor of certain policies, to keep the African-American population abreast of New Deal initiatives, and to help them take advantage of the programs. These organizations frequently made attempts to mobilize the African-American population to support or fight against certain legislation. However, they were not very successful in persuading Congress to support policies that would have been more helpful to African Americans. This was largely due to a lack of political power.

THE SWITCH TO THE DEMOCRATIC PARTY

Most African Americans who voted in 1932 were loyal to the Republican Party, the party believed to be responsible for the emancipation of the slaves. By 1936, however, most of the voting black population had switched their loyalties to the Democrats. This switch occurred in spite of the fact that the Democratic Party paid very little attention to the needs of blacks. The party tended to be beholden to its southern bloc, which was adamantly racist and against the federal government's exercising authority in matters traditionally left to the states. This meant, of course, that the southern states would be able to continue their segregation laws and patterns.

Yet New Deal legislation had the potential to provide more for blacks than had any recent Republican administration legislation. It did provide at least a segment of the black population with public-works jobs and with relief. There was an effort in at least some of the New Deal programs to prevent discrimination on the basis of race. More than any previous administration, it appointed African Americans to meaningful positions. These events appear to be a plausible explanation for the switch from the "party of Lincoln" to the Democratic Party.

Even though most African Americans made this switch in 1936, they continued to lack the political clout needed to influence New Deal legislation, mostly because the largest proportion of the black population was in the South and disfranchised. Blacks in the South lived under a repressive political system; fear of lynching made it difficult to mobilize any southern protest movement. Throughout the 1930s, the NAACP strongly advocated legislation that would make lynching a federal crime, but its attempts were never supported by New Deal administrators. Nor did the New Deal support the NAACP's efforts to eliminate the poll tax in southern states, a tax designed to disfranchise the black population.

Throughout the Depression, New Deal legislation had to meet a litmus test that would ensure the support of the southern bloc of the party. This was to the detriment of African-American workers because, too often, legislation was enacted with policies that limited their access to programs and entitlements. In 1940, as the WPA was dismantled, a substantial portion of the black population remained unemployed and on relief, and no significant change had occurred in discriminatory employment practices. Thus, the New Deal did not become the panacea the African-American population had hoped it would.

See also Bethune, Mary McLeod; Federal Writers' Project; Labor and Labor Unions; National Association for the Advancement of Colored People (NAACP); National Urban League; Weaver, Robert Clifton; White, Walter Francis; Woodruff, Hale

■ ■ *Bibliography*

Cayton, Horace, and George Mitchell. *Black Workers and the New Unions.* Chapel Hill: University of North Carolina Press, 1939. Reprint, Westport, Conn.: Negro Universities Press, 1970.

Kirby, John B. *Black Americans in the Roosevelt Era: Liberalism and Race.* Knoxville: University of Tennessee Press, 1980.

Powell, Jim. "Why Did FDR's New Deal Harm Blacks?" Cato Institute. Available from http://www.cato.org.

Sitkoff, Harvard. *A New Deal for Blacks: The Emergence of Civil Rights as a National Issue.* New York: Oxford University Press, 1978.

Weiss, Nancy J. *Farewell to the Party of Lincoln: Politics in the Age of FDR.* Princeton, N.J.: Princeton University Press, 1983.

Wolters, Raymond. *Negroes and the Great Depression.* Westport, Conn.: Greenwood, 1970.

DONA COOPER HAMILTON (1996)
Updated bibliography

GREAT MIGRATION, THE

See Migration/Population, U.S.

GREEN, AL
APRIL 13, 1946

━ ▮ ▮ ▮ ━━━━━━━━━━━

Singer and songwriter Albert Leomes Green was born in Forrest City, Arkansas, where at age nine he began singing in a family gospel quartet called the Green Brothers. For six years the group toured gospel circuits, first in the South and then in the Midwest when the family relocated to Grand Rapids, Michigan, first recording in 1960. Green formed his own pop group, Al Green and the Creations, in 1964 after his father expelled him from the gospel quartet for listening to what he called the "profane music" of singer Jackie Wilson. The group toured for three years before changing their name in 1967 to Al Greene and the Soulmates (the *e* was briefly added to Green's name for commercial reasons). That year Green made his record debut with the single "Back Up Train," which went to number five on the national soul charts in 1968. However, there were no follow-up successes, and Green was plunged back into obscurity, playing small clubs again.

While touring in Midland, Texas, in 1969, Green met Willie Mitchell, vice president of Hi Records in Memphis, Tennessee. Mitchell produced Green's version of "I Can't Get Next to You," which went to number one on the national soul charts in 1971. Continuing to collaborate with Mitchell and drummer Al Jackson, Jr. (of Booker T. and the MGs), Green went on to record a string of million-selling singles and LPs throughout the early 1970s. Combining sensuous, emotive vocals with strings, horns, and hard-driving backbeats, Green helped define the sound of soul music in the 1970s. His hits included "Let's Stay Together" (1971), "Look What You've Done for Me" (1972), "I'm Still in Love with You" (1972), and "You Ought to Be with Me" (1972).

At the height of his career, Green began to reconsider his pop music orientation and shifted back toward gospel music. A turning point was an incident in 1974 in which his girlfriend scalded him with a pot of boiling grits before killing herself with his gun. When Green recovered from his burns, he became a minister, and in 1976 he purchased a church in Memphis and was ordained pastor of the Full Gospel Tabernacle, where he would perform services nearly every Sunday. He did not immediately give up pop music, but his attempts to mix gospel themes with secular soul music fared poorly.

In 1979 Green decided to sing only gospel music, and the next year he released his first gospel album, *The Lord Will Make a Way.* In 1982 he costarred in a successful Broadway musical with Patti LaBelle, *Your Arms Too Short to Box with God.* The lines between gospel music and love songs remained somewhat blurred for Green, who in his shows would lose himself in religious ecstasy one moment and toss roses into the audience the next.

Throughout the 1980s and early 1990s, Green continued to record gospel records and pastor the Full Gospel Tabernacle. In 1994 he rerecorded a duet, "(Ain't It Funny) How Time Slips Away," on the compilation disc *Rhythm, Country, and Blues* with country-pop singer Lyle Lovett. In the 1990s fan interest in Green was renewed when one of his songs was featured in the 1994 movie *Pulp Fiction* and he made guest appearances on the popular television show *Ally McBeal.* In 2003 he released the album *I Can't Stop,* and in 2004 he was inducted into both the Gospel Hall of Fame and the Songwriters Hall of Fame.

See also Gospel Music

■ ■ *Bibliography*

"Al Green." In *Contemporary Black Biography.* Vol. 47. Detroit: Thomson Gale, 2005.

Heilbut, Anthony. *The Gospel Sound: Good News and Bad Times.* New York: Simon and Schuster, 1985.

Hoerburger, Rob. "The Gospel According to Al." *Rolling Stone* 27 (March 1986): 27–28.

JOSEPH E. LOWNDES (1996)
Updated by publisher 2005

GREGORY, DICK

OCTOBER 12, 1932

╺┨┠┨╾────────────

Comedian, activist, and rights advocate Richard Claxton Gregory was born and raised in a St. Louis slum. Abandoned by his father when he was a child, Gregory worked at odd jobs to help support his family. In high school he distinguished himself as a talented runner and demonstrated the quick wit and gift for satire that would ultimately catapult him toward stardom. With the aid of an athletic scholarship, he attended Southern Illinois University at Carbondale (1951–1954 and 1956), where he became a leading track star and began to dream of becoming a comedian.

Drafted into the army in 1954, Gregory returned briefly to Carbondale after completing his term of service in 1956 and then traveled to Chicago to pursue his goal of becoming a comedian. He admired and was influenced by Timmie Rogers, Slappy White, and Nipsey Russell. In the late 1950s Gregory worked in small black clubs like the Esquire Show Lounge, where he met his future wife, Lillian Smith, and struggled to gain popular recognition. His efforts won him a cameo appearance in *Cast the First Stone,* a 1959 ABC television documentary.

Gregory's breakthrough occurred in January 1961, when the Playboy Club in Chicago hired him to replace the unexpectedly ill white comedian "Professor" Irwin Corey. Gregory's bold, ironic, cool, and detached humor completely disarmed and converted his audience, which included many white southern conventioneers. After this success, his contract with the Playboy Club was quickly extended from several weeks to three years. Against the backdrop of the intensifying pace of the civil rights movement Gregory's candid, topical humor signaled a new relationship between African-American comedians and white mainstream audiences. By 1962 he had become a national celebrity and the first black comic superstar in the modern era, opening the doors for countless black comedians. He also became an author, publishing *From the Back of the Bus* (1962) and, with Robert Lipsyte, *Nigger: An Autobiography* (1964).

His celebrity status secured, Gregory emerged as an outspoken political activist during the 1960s. As an avid supporter of the civil rights movement, he participated in voter registration drives throughout the South, marched in countless parades and demonstrations, and was arrested numerous times. He also began to entertain at prisons and for civil rights organizations, using his biting humor as a powerful tool to highlight racism and inequality in the United States. The assassinations of John. F. Kennedy, the Rev. Dr. Martin Luther King, Jr., and others led Gregory to believe in the existence of a large framework of conspiracies to thwart civil rights and liberties in the United States. He took to the lecture circuit, espousing the ideas of Mark Lane, a leading conspiracy theorist.

Gregory found numerous ways to dramatize his chosen causes. He fasted for lengthy periods to demonstrate his commitment to civil rights and to protest the Vietnam War, the abuse of narcotics, and world hunger. In 1967 he campaigned unsuccessfully in a write-in effort to be mayor of Chicago, and in 1968 he was the presidential candidate for the U.S. Freedom and Peace Party, a split-off faction within the Peace and Freedom party, whose candidate for president in 1968 was Eldridge Cleaver. By the late 1960s Gregory was increasingly devoting his attention to the youth of America, lecturing at hundreds of college campuses each year and making fewer and fewer night club appearances; he released his last comedy album, *Caught in the Act,* in 1973.

During the 1970s Gregory wrote several books, including *No More Lies: The Myth and Reality of American History* (published as by Richard Claxton Gregory with James R. McGraw, 1971); *Code Name Zorro: The Murder of Martin Luther King, Jr.* (with Mark Lane, 1971); and *Dick Gregory's Political Primer* (1972). After moving with his wife and ten children to a farm in Massachusetts in 1973, he became a well-known advocate of vegetarianism. Often limiting himself to a regimen of fruit and juices, he became a nutritional consultant, often appearing on talk shows in his new role, and wrote (with Alvenia Fulton) *Dick Gregory's Natural Diet for Folks Who Eat, Cookin' with Mother Nature* (1974). He also wrote *Up from Nigger* with James R. McGraw, the second installment of his autobiography (1976).

In 1984 Gregory founded Health Enterprises, Inc., successfully marketing various weight-loss products. Three years later he introduced the Slim-Safe Bahamian Diet, a powdered diet mix that proved extremely popular, and expanded his financial holdings to hotels and other properties. These economic successes were abruptly reversed after the failure of a financing deal and conflicts with his business partners. Gregory was evicted from his Massachusetts home in 1992. In the same year, he returned to his hometown of St. Louis to organize the Campaign for Human Dignity, whose stated purpose was to reclaim predominantly African-American neighborhoods from drug dealers and prostitutes. In October 1993 Gregory was arrested for illegally camping—along with members of his "Dignity Patrol"—in a crime-ridden park in Washington, D.C. In 1993 he also coauthored, with Mark Lane, *Murder in Memphis,* another book about the assassination of Rev. Dr. Martin Luther King, Jr.

In 1995 Gregory staged a hunger strike to protest the Republican welfare reform bills, and in 1998 he joined conservative Republicans to demand an investigation of the "murder" of Commerce Secretary Ron Brown. During the mid-1990s, he also returned to performing, notably in a limited run off-Broadway show, *Dick Gregory Live,* in October 1995.

After Gregory achieved the pinnacle of success in the world of stand-up comedy, he made a decision to place his celebrity status in the service of his fierce and uncompromising commitment to human rights. Throughout the various shifts and turns of his career for more than three decades, he has kept faith with those commitments.

As part of his commitment to human rights, Gregory was arrested in July 2004 as he protested outside the Sudanese Embassy in New York. Gregory, along with other well-known activists, was protesting the Sudanese government's support of its militia, who were killing hundreds of black Africans daily.

See also Civil Rights Movement, U.S.; Comedians

■ ■ *Bibliography*

Gregory, Dick, with Martin Lipsyte. *Nigger: An Autobiography.* New York: Dutton, 1964.

Gregory, Dick, with James R. McGraw. *Up from Nigger.* New York: Stein and Day, 1976.

Gregory, Dick, with Sheila P. Moses. *Callus on my Soul.* Atlanta, Ga.: Longstreet Press, 2000.

Hendra, Tony. *Going Too Far.* New York: Doubleday, 1987.

Watkins, Mel. *On the Real Side: Laughing, Lying and Signifying—The Underground Tradition of African-American Humor That Transformed American Culture from Slavery to Richard Pryor.* New York: Simon and Schuster, 1994.

JAMES A. MILLER (1996)
Updated by publisher 2005

GRIGGS, SUTTON ELBERT

1872
JANUARY 2, 1933

Novelist and preacher Sutton Elbert Griggs was born in Chatfield, Texas, raised in Dallas, and attended Bishop College in Marshall, Texas. Following the path of his father, the Rev. Allen R. Griggs, he studied for the Baptist ministry at the Richmond Theological Seminary (later part of Virginia Union University) and was ordained in 1893. Griggs's first pastorate was in Berkley, Virginia, and he went on to serve for more than thirty years as a Baptist minister in Nashville and Memphis, Tennessee. In addition to his career as a pastor, he soon established himself as an author of novels, political tracts, and religious pamphlets. In the period following Reconstruction, marked by a fierce resurgence of segregation, disfranchisement, and antiblack violence in the South, Griggs—along with such African-American writers as Charles W. Chesnutt, Paul Laurence Dunbar, W. E. B. Du Bois, and Frances Ellen Watkins Harper—responded with positive portrayals of black Americans and demands for civil rights.

Griggs wrote more than thirty books, most of which he published himself and vigorously promoted during preaching tours of the South, as he describes in *The Story of My Struggles* (1914). His five novels are technically unimpressive, weakened by stilted dialogue, flat characterizations, and sentimental and melodramatic plot lines. Even as flawed polemics, however, they are distinguished by their unprecedented investigation of politically charged themes of African-American life in the South, such as black nationalism, miscegenation, racial violence, and suffrage. Above all else a religious moralist, Griggs was critical of assimilationist projects, calling instead for social equality and black self-sufficiency, but he was equally impatient with radical militancy in the quest for civil rights.

His fiction often centers on such ethical concerns. In *Imperium in Imperio* (1899), Griggs's best-known work and one of the first African-American political novels, the integrationist Belton Piedmont chooses to die rather than support a militaristic plot to seize Texas and Louisiana from the United States as a haven for African Americans. In *Overshadowed* (1901), Astral Herndon, discouraged by the "shadow" of racial prejudice both in the United States and in Africa, chooses exile as a "citizen of the ocean." Dorlan Worthell in *Unfettered* (1902) wins the hand of the beautiful Morlene only by offering a plan for African-American political organization. *The Hindered Hand* (1905) is pessimistic about the possibilities of reforming southern race relations: The Seabright family encounters violent tragedy in striving to "pass" in white society in order to transform white racist opinions, and their one dark-skinned daughter, Tiara, flees to Liberia with her husband, Ensal, who has refused to participate in a "Slavic" conspiracy to destroy the Anglo-Saxons of the United States through germ warfare. While Baug Peppers attempts inconclusively to fight for voting rights for southern blacks before the Supreme Court in *Pointing the Way* (1908), Letitia Gilbreth, who believes that "whitening" the race through assimilation is the only way to effect racial equality, is driven mad when her niece refuses the mulatto Peppers and marries a dark-skinned man.

Similar themes also appear in Griggs's political treatises, most notably *Wisdom's Call* (1909), an eloquent argument for civil rights in the South that comments on lynching, suffrage, and the rights of black women, and *Guide to Racial Greatness; or, The Science of Collective Efficiency* (1923), with a companion volume of biblical verses entitled *Kingdom Builders' Manual* (1924); these together offer a project for the political organization of the African-American southern population, stressing education, religious discipline, employment, and land ownership. At the end of his life, Griggs returned to Texas to assume the position his father had held, the pastorate of the Hopewell Baptist Church in Denison. He soon departed for Houston and, at the time of his death, was attempting to found a national religious and civic institute there.

See also Chesnutt, Charles W.; Dunbar, Paul Laurence; Du Bois, W. E. B.; Harper, Frances Ellen Watkins; Literature of the United States

■ ■ *Bibliography*

Fleming, Robert E. "Sutton E. Griggs: Militant Black Novelist." *Phylon* 34 (March 1973): 73–77.

Gloster, Hugh M. "Sutton E. Griggs: Novelist of the New Negro." *Phylon* 4 (fourth quarter 1943): 333–345.

BRENT EDWARDS (1996)

GRIMKÉ, ANGELINA WELD

FEBRUARY 27, 1880
JUNE 10, 1958

The poet and playwright Angelina Weld Grimké was born in Boston, the daughter of Archibald Grimké and Sarah Stanley Grimké. She attended integrated schools in Hyde Park, Massachusetts, and graduated in 1902 from Boston Normal School of Gymnastics, later part of Wellesley College. Grimké worked as a teacher in Washington, D.C., from that time until her retirement in 1926. In 1930, she moved to Brooklyn, where she lived for the rest of her life.

Grimké's best-known work is a short play entitled *Rachel*, first presented in 1916 and published in book form in 1920. The play portrays a young African-American woman who is filled with despair and, despite her love of children, despondently resolves not to bring any of her own into the world. With its tragic view of race relations, *Rachel* was staged several times by the National Association for the Advancement of Colored People (NAACP) as a response to D. W. Griffith's racist 1915 film *The Birth of a Nation*.

But Grimké's most influential work was her poetry. Publishing first as a teenager, she initially wrote in the sentimental style of late-nineteenth-century popular poetry. In the early years of the twentieth century, however, she began to display an interest in experimentation, both formal and thematic. She openly took up sexual themes, with a frankness that was not common among African-American poets of her time. Only occasionally addressing racial issues, she nevertheless did so with a militance and subjectivity that looked toward the Harlem Renaissance. Although she was not to be a major figure in that movement, such work did much to contribute its foundations.

(Angelina Weld Grimké should not be confused with the nineteenth-century abolitionist Angelina Grimké Weld, though they were related. The former's father was the nephew of the latter.)

See also Grimké, Archibald Henry; Harlem Renaissance; Poetry, U.S.

■ ■ *Bibliography*

Hull, Gloria T. *Color, Sex and Poetry: Three Women Writers of the Harlem Renaissance.* Bloomington: Indiana University Press, 1987.

DICKSON D. BRUCE JR. (1996)

GRIMKÉ, ARCHIBALD HENRY

AUGUST 17, 1849
FEBRUARY 25, 1930

❚❚❚ ─────────────

The writer and activist Archibald Henry Grimké was born a slave in Charleston, South Carolina. He was the nephew of the noted abolitionists Sarah Grimké and Angelina Grimké Weld. Receiving some education during his childhood, after Emancipation he attended Lincoln University and, supported by his aunts, Harvard Law School, from which he graduated in 1874. In 1884 he became editor of the *Boston Hub,* a Republican newspaper. In 1886, disillusioned by the growing indifference of Republican Party to the problems of African Americans and by the party's conservative economic program, Grimké switched allegiances. He soon became the most prominent African-American democrat in Massachusetts.

After 1890, Grimké removed himself from politics and, focusing on scholarship, wrote major biographies of William Lloyd Garrison and Charles Sumner. Then, in 1894, he was appointed consul to the Dominican Republic, where he served until 1898.

Upon his return to the United States, Grimké also returned to writing, and he published widely on racial questions. In 1903, he became president of the leading African-American intellectual organization, American Negro Academy, a post he held until 1919. As an activist he was deeply involved in the debate over the leadership of Booker T. Washington, although, despite a general opposite to Washington's views, he was unwilling to commit himself fully to either side.

But his activism became particularly notable when, in 1913, he became president of the District of Columbia branch of the National Association for the Advancement of Colored People (NAACP). The branch was the organization's largest, representing the NAACP on all issues involving federal legislation and policy. As president, Grimké led its efforts into the 1920s, lobbying Congress and federal agencies to inhibit the segregationist policies of Woodrow Wilson's administration, while fighting against discrimination in the Washington community itself. In 1919, in recognition of these efforts and of his lifetime of service defending the rights of African Americans, he received the Spingarn Medal, the NAACP's highest honor.

See also American Negro Academy (ANA); National Association for the Advancement of Colored People (NAACP); Spingarn Medal; Washington, Booker T.

■ ■ *Bibliography*

Archibald Henry Grimké Papers. Manuscript Division, Moorland-Spingarn Research Center, Howard University, Washington, D.C.

Bruce, Dickson D., Jr. *Archibald Grimké.* Baton Rouge: Louisiana State University Press, 1993.

DICKSON D. BRUCE JR. (1996)

GRIMKÉ, CHARLOTTE L. FORTEN

AUGUST 17, 1837
JULY 22, 1914

❚❚❚ ─────────────

Charlotte L. Forten Grimké, an abolitionist, teacher, and writer, was born into one of Philadelphia's leading African-American families. Her grandfather, James Forten, was a well-to-do sail-maker and abolitionist. Her father, Robert Bridges Forten, maintained both the business and the abolitionism.

Charlotte Forten continued her family's traditions. As a teenager, having been sent to Salem, Massachusetts, for her education, she actively joined that community of radical abolitionists identified with William Lloyd Garrison. She also entered enthusiastically into the literary and intel-

Charlotte L. Forten Grimke (1837–1914). PHOTOGRAPHS AND PRINTS DIVISION, SCHOMBURG CENTER FOR RESEARCH IN BLACK CULTURE, THE NEW YORK PUBLIC LIBRARY, ASTOR, LENOX AND TILDEN FOUNDATIONS.

lectual life of nearby Boston, and even embarked on a literary career of her own. Some of her earliest poetry was published in antislavery journals during her student years. And she began to keep a diary, published almost a century later, which remains one of the most valuable accounts of that era.

Completing her education, Forten became a teacher, initially in Salem and later in Philadelphia. Unfortunately, she soon began to suffer from ill health, which would plague her for the rest of her life. Nevertheless, while unable to sustain her efforts in the classroom for any length of time, she did continue to write and to engage in antislavery activity. With the outbreak of the Civil War, she put both her convictions and her training to use, joining other abolitionists on the liberated islands off the South Carolina coast to teach and work with the newly emancipated slaves.

On the Sea Islands, she also kept a diary, which was also later published. This second diary, and two essays she wrote at the time for the *Atlantic Monthly,* are among the most vivid accounts of the abolitionist experiment. Like many teachers, Forten felt a cultural distance from the freedpeople but worked with dedication to teach and prove the value of emancipation. After the war, she continued her work for the freedpeople, accepting a position in Massachusetts with the Freedmen's Union Commission.

She also continued her literary efforts, which included a translation of the French novel *Madame Thérèse,* published by Scribner in 1869. In 1872, after a year spent teaching in South Carolina, Forten moved to Washington, D.C., where she worked first as a teacher and then in the Treasury Department. There she met the Reverend Francis Grimké, thirteen years her junior and pastor of the elite Fifteenth Street Presbyterian Church. They were married at the end of 1878.

The marriage was long and happy, despite the death in infancy of their only child. Apart from a brief residence in Jacksonville, Florida, from 1885 to 1889, the Grimkés lived in Washington, D.C. and made their Washington home a center for the capital's social and intellectual life. Although Charlotte Grimké continued to suffer from poor health, she maintained something of her former activism, serving briefly as a member of the Washington school board and participating in such organizations as the National Association of Colored Women. She did a small amount of writing, although little was published. Finally, after about 1909, her failing health led to her virtual retirement from active life.

See also Abolition; Forten, James; Grimké, Francis James; Gullah; National Association of Colored Women

■ ■ *Bibliography*

"Charlotte Forten Grimké Papers." In *Francis James Grimké Papers,* Manuscript Division, Moorland-Spingarn Research Center, Howard University, Washington, D.C.

Cooper, Anna J. *Life and Writings of the Grimké Family.* 2 vols. 1951.

Stevenson, Brenda, ed. *The Journals of Charlotte Forten Grimké.* New York: Oxford University Press, 1988.

DICKSON D. BRUCE JR. (1996)

GRIMKÉ, FRANCIS JAMES

OCTOBER 4, 1850
NOVEMBER 11, 1937

The minister and author Francis James Grimké was born on Caneacres, a rice plantation near Charleston, South Carolina. He was the son of Henry Grimké, a wealthy white lawyer, and his African-American slave Nancy Weston, who also bore the elder Grimké two other sons, Archibald (1849–1930) and John (b. 1853). Henry Grimké died in September 1852, and the mother and children lived for several years in a de facto free status. This ended in 1860 when E. Montague Grimké, the boys' half-brother, to whom ownership had passed, sought to exercise his "property rights." Francis Grimké ran away from home and joined the Confederate Army as an officer's valet. Montague Grimké eventually sold him to another officer, whom Francis Grimké served until Emancipation. In 1866, he began his educational journey at Lincoln University (Pennsylvania), where he came to the notice of his white abolitionist aunts, Angelina Grimké Weld (1805–1879) and Sarah Moore Grimké (1792–1873), who acknowledged his kinship and encouraged his further study, providing moral and material support.

Francis Grimké began the study of law at Lincoln after graduating at the head of his undergraduate class in 1870. He continued to prepare for a legal career, attending Howard University in 1874, but felt called to the ministry and entered Princeton Theological Seminary in 1875. Upon graduation from the seminary in 1878, Grimké began his ministry at the 15th Street Presbyterian Church in Washington, D.C., and married Charlotte L. Forten of Philadelphia. In 1880, Theodora Cornelia, their only child, died in infancy. From 1885 to 1889, Grimké served the Laura Street Presbyterian Church in Jacksonville, Florida. He then returned to Washington and remained as pastor at the 15th Street Church until 1928, when he became pastor emeritus.

Grimké's pulpit afforded him access to one of the most accomplished African-American congregations in America; the members expected and received sermons that addressed issues of faith and morals with ethical insight, literary grace, and prophetic zeal. He practiced what he preached, earning himself the sobriquet "Black Puritan." Through printed sermons and articles, Grimké encouraged a national audience to agitate for civil rights "until justice is done." He campaigned against racism in American churches and helped form the Afro-

Francis James Grimke (1850–1937). *The son of a white lawyer and an African-American slave, Grimke became an influential minister and civil rights advocate.* GENERAL RESEARCH AND REFERENCE DIVISION, SCHOMBURG CENTER FOR RESEARCH IN BLACK CULTURE, THE NEW YORK PUBLIC LIBRARY, ASTOR, LENOX AND TILDEN FOUNDATIONS.

Presbyterian Council to encourage black moral uplift and self-help. He also participated in the creation of organizations such as the American Negro Academy, which nurtured African-American development.

While not normally an activist outside the church, Grimké was an active supporter of Booker T. Washington's self-help efforts. However, in the early years of the twentieth century, he joined the group of African-American "radicals" led by W. E. B. Du Bois. He sided with Du Bois against Washington at the Carnegie Hall Conference (1906), which led to the schism between Washington and the radicals, and he later became a strong and longtime supporter of the NAACP.

In 1923 Grimké aroused a storm of controversy with his Howard University School of Religion convocation address, "What Is the Trouble with Christianity Today?" In the address he denounced groups such as the YMCA and the "federation of white churches" for their racist practices, and he also challenged the sincerity of the faith of former president Woodrow Wilson. Legislators, led by Representative James Byrnes of South Carolina, protested the address and tried to remove Grimké from Howard's board of trustees by threatening Howard's federal budget appropriation. Grimké retired in 1925 and lived in Washington, D.C., until his death in 1937.

See also American Negro Academy (ANA); Du Bois, W. E. B.; Grimké, Angelina Weld; Grimké, Archibald Henry; Grimké, Charlotte L. Forten; Washington, Booker T.

■ ■ *Bibliography*

Woodson, Carter G., ed. *The Works of Francis James Grimké.* 4 vols. Washington, D.C.: Associated Publishers, 1942.

HENRY J. FERRY (1996)

GUARDIAN, THE

The *Guardian* (1901–1960), an African-American weekly newspaper, served primarily as a forum for its founder and editor, William Monroe Trotter. Self-billed as "America's greatest race journal," it carried the motto "For Every Right with All Thy Might," setting the militant tone for its notorious page 4 editorials on racial issues. While the Guardian attracted a national audience by including social gossip from other major cities, its agenda was explicitly political, emphasizing integration, legal rights, and the importance of strong and persistent agitation. Trotter found it fitting that the *Guardian* came to occupy the very building where William Lloyd Garrison's abolitionist paper, the *Liberator,* had been produced.

Born into a wealthy Boston family, the Harvard-educated Trotter abandoned a successful business career, convinced that the pursuit of prosperity by African Americans was "like building a house upon the sands" so long as racial discrimination and persecution persisted. Trotter, with fellow Massachusetts Racial Protective Association member George W. Forbes, launched the *Guardian* on November 9, 1901, in order to aggressively challenge Booker T. Washington's accommodationist model of post-Reconstruction race relations.

Under Trotter's stewardship, the *Guardian*'s reportage featured his bellicose forays into the political arena, most prominently a public confrontation with Washington in 1903, which was dubbed the "Boston Riot." After the fracas, Forbes quit the paper, significantly weakening its literary quality. Soon thereafter, Washington himself launched a secret campaign to undermine Trotter's political legitimacy and the *Guardian* itself. But neither smear tactics nor infiltration of Trotter's circle of activists nor the subsidizing of rival publications succeeded in silencing Washington's nemesis. Even those who disagreed with Trotter's methods, such as W. E. B. Du Bois, nonetheless expressed sympathy with his point of view.

The *Guardian* continued to reflect Trotter's commitment to independent politics, militant integration, and direct action. Presidential endorsements were based on candidates' records on race issues, not on party loyalties. The newspaper gave ample coverage to campaigns Trotter led or supported, including the Niagara Movement, the fight against racial discrimination in the armed forces during World War I, and the public protests against D. W. Griffith's controversial film *The Birth of a Nation* (1915). In later years, the *Guardian* defended the Scottsboro Boys and supported New Deal economic policies.

The *Guardian*, said Trotter, was "not a mere money-making business, but a public work for equal rights and freedom." Intent on preserving the *Guardian*'s independence, he refused to sell shares in or incorporate the paper; because he relied on the black community for support, he did not raise the annual subscription rate until 1920. But the *Guardian* was Trotter's sole source of income, and he and his wife, Geraldine, made enormous personal sacrifices to keep the paper afloat, mortgaging and selling off property piece by piece until not even their house remained.

While the *Guardian* bore its founder's personal imprint for many years —both politically and financially—it did survive him. After Trotter's death in 1934, his sister, Maude Trotter Steward, edited the *Guardian* until she died in 1957.

See also *Liberator, The*; Niagara Movement; Scottsboro Case; Trotter, William Monroe; Washington, Booker T.

■ ■ *Bibliography*

Bennett, Lerone, Jr. *Pioneers in Protest.* Chicago: Johnson Publishing, 1968.

Campbell, Georgetta Merritt. *Extant Collections of Early Black Newspapers: A Research Guide to the Black Press, 1880–1915, with an Index to the Boston "Guardian," 1902-1904.* Troy, N.Y.: Whitestone Publishing, 1981.

Fox, Stephen R. *The Guardian of Boston: William Monroe Trotter*. New York: Atheneum, 1970.

TAMI J. FRIEDMAN (1996)
RENEE TURSI (1996)

GUILLÉN, NICOLÁS

JULY 10, 1902
JULY 16, 1989

▪ ▪ ▪

Nicolás Guillén was Cuba's most important and most popular twentieth century poet and one of Spanish America's most capacious and signally original poetic voices. Born in the eastern provincial city of Camagüey, his poetry's conscientiously Afro-Hispanic character, thematic foci, patterns of stress and inflection—with its distinctively Afro-Hispanic modulations and syncretic quality—became the personification and, as he early on intended, "perhaps the most apt" emblematic sign of his lyric articulation and unwavering defense of a national identity and cultural sensibility at once ethnically creole, distinctively Cuban, and broadly Antillean.

Guillén was a compelling chronicler of his island's historic odyssey under two colonial regimes (Spanish and American). His poetry served as a lyric barometer of his country's general condition, persisting inequities, and determined aspirations to a more racially egalitarian society and an authentically national sovereignty. It also reflected the political, social, and racial dramas unfolding on the wider global stage, apparent in such poems as "Soldiers in Abyssinia" (1935), *Spain: A Poem in Four Agonies and One Hope* (1937), "My Last Name" (1953), "Maus Maus" (1953), the poet's affecting "Elegy to Emmett Till" (1956), "Little Rock" (1957), "The Flowers Grow High" (1963), and "Small Ode to Vietnam" (1966). Guillén's verse deftly combines its author's characteristically elegiac, prophetically epic vision and radical Marxist temper with an appealingly subversive ironic wit and a wily, incisive humor.

Guillén's first published book of poems, *Motivos de son* (1930), revealed an unprecedented realism in the perception of black life in Havana's slums. The collection's socially complex and critically compassionate monologues brought unwonted, strikingly new dimensions to the shades of exoticism more typical of the *negrista* movement then coming into vogue. In the introduction to *Sóngoro cosongo* (1931), he wrote that in Cuba "we all have a touch of the ebony" and that, in consequence, "a Creole poetry . . . would not be truly such were it to ignore the Negro." The major collections which followed—*West Indies, Ltd.*

(1934), *Cantos para soldados y sones para turistas* (1937), *El son entero* (1943), his several *Elegías* (1948-58), and *La paloma de vuelo popular* (1958)—gave a sharper quality and pitch to the poet's pioneering of his *son* poem, a "mulatto verse," as Guillén defined it, and the increasingly distressed "voice of rage" which the title poem of *West Indies, Ltd.* announces. Guillén's piercing ironies and "singing plain" censure of the "blood and weeping / [lie] behind easy laughter" take regular aim at all manner of racial and colonial or colonizing presumption. They reveal the ignominy and daily humiliations of a social system wherein "to get enough to eat / you work 'til you're almost dead," and "it's not just bending you're back, / but also bowing your head." There is also an intimation of the coming of the society's revolutionary transformation, wherein all citizens would be treated more humanely.

Guillén greeted the 1959 Cuban Revolution enthusiastically. Its impact, unfolding, achievements, and difficulties immediately became one of his work's central themes. The poems in *El gran Zoo* (1967), *La rueda dentada* (1972), *El diario que a diario* (1972), and *Por el mar de las Antillas anda un barco de papel* (1977) were infused with a new celebratory tone, and the poet's characteristically elegiac mood became both more provocative and playful. The intimate passion and longing poignancies of *En algún sitio de la primavera: elegía* (1986) with its chronicling of love's loss and one's own mortality, likewise gave unaccustomed inflections and resonance to an already varied corpus of poetry of love and romantic yearning.

The communicative efficacy, artistic rigor, innovative virtuosity, and lyric range that, over the course of his long career, epitomized Guillén's Afro-Hispanic poetic synthesis and critical gaze, effectively produced, in one critic's words, "a general poetic revision at the core of modern poetry written in the Spanish language" (González Echevarría, p. 302). Universally regarded as the greatest of the *negrista*, or black theme, poets, he also stands with César Vallejo and Pablo Neruda as one of the three most representatively original Latin American poets of his era. A national icon, he was officially proclaimed Cuba's *Poeta Nacional* in 1961. Elected first president of the Union of Cuban Artists and Writers just two years later, he served in that office until his death in 1989. Selections of his prose and journalistic writings can be found in the three volumes of *Prosa de prisa 1929-1972* (1975–1976) and in *Páginas vueltas* (1982).

See also Literature

■ ■ *Bibliography*

Branche, Jerome, ed. *Lo que teníamos que tener: Raza y revolución en Nicolás Guillén.* Pittsburgh, Pa.: University of Pittsburgh: Instituto Internacional de Literatura Iberoamericana (Serie Antonio Cornejo Polar), 2003.

González Echevarría, Roberto. "Guillén as Baroque: Meaning in *Motivos de son,*" *Callaloo* 10, no. 2 (spring 1987): 302.

Márquez, Roberto, and David Arthur McMurray, trans. and eds. *Man-Making Words: Selected Poems of Nicolás Guillén,* 2d ed. Amherst: University of Massachusetts Press, 2003.

ROBERTO MÁRQUEZ (2005)

GULF WAR

See Military Experience, African-American

GULLAH

The Gullah are a community of African Americans who have lived along the Atlantic coastal plain and on the Sea Islands off the coast of South Carolina and Georgia since the late seventeenth century. Comprised of the descendants of slaves who lived and worked on the Sea Islands, Gullah communities continued to exist into the early twenty-first century, occupying small farming and fishing communities in South Carolina and Georgia. The Gullah are noted for their preservation of African cultural traditions, which was made possible by the community's geographic isolation and its inhabitants' strong community life. They speak an English-based creole language also called Gullah, or among Georgia Sea Islanders called Geechee.

ORIGINS

The etymology of the term *Gullah* is uncertain. Among the most widely accepted theories is that it is a shortened form of *Angola,* a region of coastal central Africa with different boundaries from the contemporary nation-state and former Portuguese colony of the same name. Many of South Carolina's slaves were imported from the older Angola. Equally plausible is the suggestion that the term is a derivation of the West African name *Golas* or *Goulah,* who were a large group of Africans occupying the hinterland of what is present-day Liberia. Large numbers of slaves were brought to South Carolina from both western and central Africa, lending both explanations credibility. The word *Geechee* is believed to have originated from *Gidzi,*

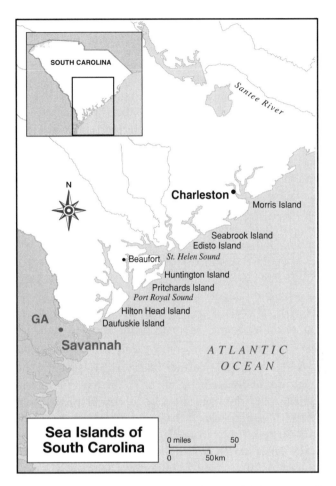

Map of the Sea Islands of South Carolina. Gullah language and culture, with its roots in the coastal, rice-producing regions of West Africa, flourished in the Sea Islands of South Carolina long after slavery was abolished, partly because access to much of the territory in this swampy, semi-tropical region was by water only until the middle of the twentieth century. THE GALE GROUP

the name of the language spoken in the Kissy country of present-day Liberia. Whatever the origins of these terms, it is clear that the Gullah community that developed in the Sea Islands embodied a mixture of influences from the coastal regions of West Africa.

The slave communities of the Sea Islands developed under unique geographic and demographic conditions that permitted them to maintain a degree of cohesion and autonomy denied to slave communities in other regions of the South. A geographical shift in the production of rice within the South Carolina low country during the mid-1700s brought a major shift in population. South Carolina's slave population had been concentrated in the parishes surrounding Charleston, but in the 1750s South Carolina rice planters abandoned the inland swamps for the tidal and river swamps of the coastal mainland. At the same time, new methods in the production of indigo stimulated settlement of the Sea Islands, where long-staple cotton also began to be produced in the late eighteenth century.

As a result, the coastal regions of South Carolina and the adjacent Sea Islands became the center of the plantation economy, and the demand for slave labor soared. Concurrent with this shift in agricultural production was a change in the African origins of the slaves imported into South Carolina. During the last half of the eighteenth century, imports from the Kongo–Angola region declined, and the majority of slaves introduced into the Sea Islands came from the Windward Coast (present-day Sierra Leone, Senegal, and Gambia) and the Rice Coast (part of present-day Liberia). South Carolina planters apparently preferred slaves from these regions because of the Africans' familiarity with rice and indigo production. These African bondsmen and -women brought with them the labor patterns and technical skills they had used in Africa. Their knowledge of rice planting had a major impact in transforming South Carolina's methods of rice production.

The geographic isolation of the Sea Islands and the frequency of disease in the region's swampy, semitropical climate kept white settlement in the area to a minimum. Meanwhile, a growing demand for slaves and their concentration on tremendous plantations created a black majority in the South Carolina coastal region. In 1770 the population in the South Carolina low country was 78 percent black, and the proportion of blacks along the coast and the Sea Islands probably was even higher.

The relative isolation and numerical strength of the slaves and their freedom from contact with white settlers permitted them to preserve many native African linguistic patterns and cultural traditions. The constant influx of African slaves into the region throughout the remainder of the eighteenth century likewise permitted the Gullah to maintain a vital link to the customs and traditions of West Africa.

THE POST-CIVIL WAR ERA

The end of slavery brought significant changes to the Gullahs' traditional way of life, but the unique geographic and demographic conditions on the Sea Islands ensured that the Gullah community would retain its distinctiveness well beyond the Civil War. Blacks remained a majority in the South Carolina low country. In 1870, the population was 67 percent black; by 1900 it had decreased only marginally.

The Gullahs' experiences during and after the Civil War differed from those of blacks across the South. Although the Port Royal Experiment, established on the Sea

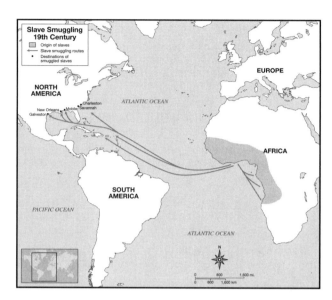

Routes and key destinations for slaves smuggled into the United States, 1808–1865. *Although the Atlantic slave trade legally came to an end in 1808, slaves were still brought into major southern port cities directly from West Africa or by way of the Caribbean. In places like the Gullah Sea Islands of South Carolina, newly arriving Africans helped to sustain the influence of African culture on the religions, music, and speech patterns of American blacks.* MAP BY XNR PRODUCTIONS. THE GALE GROUP.

Islands during the Union's wartime occupation to provide the Gullah with experience in independent farming, was ultimately a failure, many Gullah in the decades following the Civil War nevertheless were able to become independent farmers.

Due to the declining market for the Sea Islands' long-staple cotton, many white landowners began to desert the area shortly after the war's end. Agricultural production in the low country first suffered from war-related devastation of the land; then, in the early 1900s, competition from rice plantations in the western United States further crippled South Carolina's market position. As whites abandoned their former plantations and blacks took over the land, some cotton production for the market continued, but subsistence farming and fishing dominated the Sea Island economy.

Whites' abandonment of the coastal region and the Sea Islands left the Gullah even more isolated than before. During the first half of the twentieth century, black residents of the Sea Islands, like other African Americans across the South, were denied basic civil rights, but they benefited from their geographic isolation and numerical dominance. Unlike blacks in most other regions of the South, the Gullah were able to maintain cohesive, largely independent communities well into the twentieth century.

GULLAH CULTURE

Most of what we know of the Gullah comes from studies conducted by anthropologists and linguists in the 1930s and 1940s. The Gullah culture described by these observers reflects a blending of various African and American traditions. Gullah handicrafts such as basket weaving and wood carving demonstrate African roots, both in their design and their functionality. Wooden mortars and pestles, rice "fanners," and palm-leaf brooms were introduced into the Sea Islands by the Gullah and were used in ways that reflected African customs. The Gullah, for example, used their palm-leaf brooms to maintain grass-free dirt yards—a tradition they still maintained early in the twenty-first century. The Gullah diet is based on rice and similarly reflects the African origins of the original community. The Gullah make gumbos and stews similar to West African dishes such as jollof and plasas.

The distinctiveness of the Gullah community is perhaps best reflected in its language. Gullah, or Geechee, a predominantly oral language, is the offspring of the West African pidgin English that developed along the African coast during the peak of the slave trade. The pidgin was a merger of English and the native languages spoken on the African coast and served as a means of communication among Africans and British slave traders. Many of the slaves from the coastal regions of West Africa who were brought to South Carolina in the eighteenth century were familiar with pidgin English and used it to communicate with one another in the New World. Over time, the pidgin mixed with the language spoken by the South Carolina planter class and took on new form. Gullah, the creole language that developed, became the dominant and native language of the slave community of the Sea Islands. Like most unwritten creole languages, Gullah rapidly evolved, and by the time it was first seriously studied in the 1930s it undoubtedly had more in common with standard English than with antebellum or eighteenth-century Gullah.

The Gullah language derives most of its vocabulary from English, but it also incorporates a substantial number of African words, especially from the Krio language of present-day Sierra Leone. The Gullah used names, for example, that reflected personal and historical experiences and that carried specific African meanings. Naming practices of the Gullah served, as they do for West Africans, as symbols of power and control over the outside world. The pronunciation of Gullah and its sentence and grammatical structures, moreover, deviate from the rules of standard English, reflecting instead West African patterns. Gullah is spoken with a Caribbean cadence, reflecting the common African background of the Gullah and West Indian slaves.

Gullah, though less widely spoken by the end of the twentieth century, remains prevalent throughout the Sea Islands. Lorenzo Dow Turner, the first linguist to study Gullah speech in the 1940s, found a number of African words and phrases being used among the inhabitants of the Sea Islands in the 1940s. In 1993, William A. Stewart, a linguist at the City University of New York, estimated that 250,000 Sea Islanders still spoke Gullah and at least a tenth of this number spoke no other language. Gullah also has had a significant impact upon the language spoken across the southeastern region of the United States. Such Gullah words as *buckra* (a white person), *goober* (peanut), and *juke* (disorderly) can be found in the vocabulary of black and white southerners.

Other aspects of Gullah language observed by Turner and such scholars as Ambrose E. Gonzales and Guy B. Johnson also exhibit African roots. Gullah proverbs demonstrate an adaptation of the African tradition of speaking in parables, and the oral tradition of storytelling among the Gullah also has been identified with African patterns. Trickster tales such as those about Brer Rabbit, which were popularized in the late nineteenth and early twentieth centuries by the white folklorist Joel Chandler Harris, are still part of Gullah and Geechee folklore. These tales, often moral in tone and content, are an important form of entertainment.

RELIGION AND COMMUNITY

Religion played a dominant role within the Gullah slave community and continued to regulate community life into the twentieth century. Church membership predicated membership in the community at large, and one was not considered a member of the plantation community until one had joined the "Praise House." Praise Houses, originally erected by planters in the 1840s as meeting-houses and places of worship for slaves, functioned as town halls among the Gullah well into the late twentieth century, possibly as late as the 1970s. The Praise House essentially took the place of the white-controlled Baptist churches as the slave community's cultural center. Even after blacks assumed control of their churches during and after the Civil war, the Praise House remained the locus of community power.

Everyone in the community was expected to abide by the Praise House customs and regulations, enforced by a Praise House committee, which held them to certain standards of behavior and trust. This method of defining the borders of the community reinforced the Gullahs' close-knit community structure; some argue that it mirrored West African traditions of establishing secret societies.

This utilization of the Praise House to fit the needs of the Gullah community illustrates the adaptive nature of the Gullah's religious practices. Gullah slaves applied a mixture of African customs and beliefs to the Christian principles introduced by their masters, creating a religion that served a vital function within their community. Even as they accepted Christianity, for example, they maintained their belief in witchcraft, called *wudu, wanga, joso,* or *juju,* and continued to consult "root doctors" for protection and for their healing powers.

The Gullahs' physical forms of worship also continued to follow West African patterns. Gullah spirituals, both religious and secular in nature, for example, incorporated a West African pattern of call and response. In addition to being sung in church and at work, these highly emotional spirituals were often used as accompaniments to the Gullah "ring shout," a syncretic religious custom that combined Africanisms with Christian principles. During the ring shout, onlookers sang, clapped, and gesticulated, while others shuffled their heels in a circle. The performance started slowly but gained speed and intensity as it progressed. The ring shout, which had largely disappeared by the late twentieth century, served as a religious expression linked to natural and supernatural forces. While the trancelike atmosphere of the ring shout is believed to be of West African origin, the practice itself and the way it functioned within the community are Gullah creations.

The strength and endurance of the Gullah community and culture is evident in the cultural traditions of the Seminole Blacks, a group strongly tied to the original Sea Island Gullah community. From the late 1700s to the early nineteenth century, Gullah slaves escaped from the rice plantations and built settlements along the remote, wooded Florida frontier. Over time, these maroon communities joined with other escaped slaves and surrounding Native Americans to form a loosely organized tribe with shared customs, food, and clothing. Along with the Native Americans, the escaped slaves were removed from Florida in the nineteenth century and were resettled on reservations in the West. During the late twentieth century, groups of these Seminole Blacks were found throughout the West, especially in Oklahoma, Texas, and Mexico. Some of them, who have retained numerous African customs, continue to speak Afro-Seminole, a creole language descended from Gullah.

LOSS OF ISOLATION; LOSS OF COHESION

While Gullah communities still exist in the Sea Islands of Georgia and South Carolina, they have begun to disintegrate in recent decades. The social cohesion of the com-

Drummers at the Gullah Festival in Beaufort, South Carolina. *The festival, conceived as a way to celebrate and recognize Gullah culture, has been held annually since 1987.* © BOB KRIST/CORBIS

munity was first threatened in the 1920s, when bridges were built between the mainland and the islands. Outmigration from the Sea Islands accelerated during World War II as defense spending created new economic opportunities. During the 1950s and 1960s, outside influence increased as wealthy developers began buying up land at cheap rates and building resorts on Hilton Head and other islands. This development opened some job opportunities for black Sea Islanders, but the openings tended to be in low-paying service jobs with little opportunity for advancement.

One benefit of this development has been to break down the Gullahs' isolation and to increase their awareness of trends within the larger African-American community. In the 1940s, Esau Jenkins, a native of Johns Island, led a movement to register voters, set up community centers, and provide legal aid to members of the island's African-American community. In an effort to register black voters, Jenkins, with the help of Septima Clark, of Charleston, established the South's first citizenship school on Johns Island in 1957. Jenkins' efforts helped break down the isolation of black Sea Islanders and involved them more directly in the struggle for civil rights among African Americans across the country.

The modernization of the Sea Islands and the Gullahs' subsequent loss of isolation, however, has caused the community to lose some of its cultural distinctiveness and cohesion. From a predominantly black population on Hilton Head in 1950, whites came to outnumber blacks five to one by 1980. Many Gullah traditions, such as the ring shout, have largely disappeared, and many community members criticize the now predominantly white public schools for deemphasizing the history and culture of the Gullah people. In response to the negative impact of these modernizing changes, efforts have been made to increase public awareness of Gullah traditions and to preserve them.

In 1948, the Penn Center on Saint Helena Island, South Carolina, formerly a school for freed slaves, was converted into a community resource center. It offers programs in academic and cultural enrichment and teaches Gullah to schoolchildren. In 1979, the Summer Institute of Linguistics, a professional society of linguists, and the nondenominational Wycliffe Bible Translators undertook projects on Saint Helena Island to translate the Bible into Gullah, to develop a written system for recording Gullah, and to produce teaching aids for use in schools. In 1985 Beaufort, South Carolina, began an annual Gullah Festival to celebrate and bring recognition to the rich Gullah culture.

Increasingly, national attention has been focused on the Sea Islands. In 1989, *In Living Color*, a dance-theater piece about Gullah culture on Johns Island, South Carolina, premiered in New York City at the Triplex Theater. Set in a rural prayer meeting, the piece offers a memoir of life among the Gullah during the late 1980s. *Daughters in the Dust*, a 1992 film about a Gullah family at the turn of the century, perhaps provided the greatest national recognition for the Gullah. Written and directed by Julie Dash, whose father was raised in the Sea Islands, the film's dialogue is primarily in Gullah, with occasional English subtitles.

Such projects have helped increase public awareness of the importance of understanding and preserving Gullah traditions, and in 1994 the children's network Nickelodeon began work on a new animated series called *Gullah Gullah Island*, which focused on a black couple who explored the culture of the Sea Islands. The show ran for three years. Black Sea Islanders hope that these efforts will bring the necessary national recognition to help protect the Gullah community from further cultural erosion.

See also Africanisms; Clark, Septima; Maroon Wars; Slave Trade

■ ■ *Bibliography*

Burch, Audra D. S. "Threatened by Change, Gullah Fighting to Preserve their Culture." *The Miami Herald* (November 30, 2003).

Burden, Bernadette. "A Bible to Call Their Own: Gullah Speakers Put Verses in Native Tongue." *Atlanta Journal and Constitution*, June 11, 1993.

Creel, Margaret Washington. *A Peculiar People: Slave Religion and Community-Culture among the Gullahs.* New York: New York University Press, 1988.

Crum, Mason. *Gullah: Negro Life in the Carolina Sea Islands* (1940). New York: Negro Universities Press, 1968.

Curry, Andrew. "The Gullah's Last Stand?" *U.S. News & World Report* (June 18, 2001): 40.

Glanton, Dahleen. "Gullah Culture in Danger of Fading Away." *Chicago Tribune* (June 3, 2001).

Jacobs, Sally. "The Sea Islands' Vanishing Past." *Boston Globe*, March 24, 1992.

Joyner, Charles. *Down by the Riverside: A South Carolina Slave Community.* Urbana: University of Illinois Press, 1984.

Pollitzer, William S. *The Gullah People and Their African Heritage.* Athens: University of Georgia Press, 1999.

Rose, Willie Lee. *Rehearsal for Reconstruction: The Port Royal Experiment.* Indianapolis, Ind.: Bobbs-Merrill, 1964.

Turner, Lorenzo D. *Africanisms in the Gullah Dialect.* Chicago: University of Chicago Press, 1949.

Wood, Peter H. *Black Majority: Negroes in Colonial South Carolina from 1670 through the Stono Rebellion.* New York: Knopf, 1974.

LOUISE P. MAXWELL (1996)
Updated bibliography

Hair and Beauty Culture

This entry has two unique essays about the same topic, differing mainly in their geographical focus.

> Hair and Beauty Culture in Brazil
> *Ângela Figueiredo*
>
> Hair and Beauty Culture in the United States
> *Robyn Spencer*

Hair and Beauty Culture in Brazil

Travelers to Brazil were the first to recognize how headgear, hairstyles, makeup, and body tribal marks are used as signifiers of ethnic identity in that nation. However, except for tribal scarifications, which are permanent, such signifiers can easily be modified in different parts of the world where interactions between blacks and whites take place.

Hair and Skin Color as Racial Identifiers

In Brazil, as in any other country of the African diaspora, hair is both an ethnic-identity marker and an indicator of beauty or ugliness. Historically, blacks have been discriminated against both in show business and the world of beauty, two spheres that have been particularly active in the construction of negative stereotypes associated with black phenotypes.

In Brazil, unlike the United States, it is skin colors and hair textures that are mainly used in defining the place individuals occupy in what might be called a racial classification table. For example, the term *morena* refers to a half-caste whose hair is smooth and curled, while *mulato* refers to a half-caste with kinky hair. *Cabo verde* refers to dark-complexioned persons with curled hair, which makes them resemble Indians. Such people are generally considered very beautiful by Brazilian standards. There are, of course, regional variants of this classification scheme.

Comparing the situation in Brazil with that in the United States, where racial classification is defined by lineage, Oracy Nogueira (1985) observed that racial discrimination in Brazil is based more on physical marks—meaning outward marks and appearance—and not on the racial origins of the individuals concerned. In Brazil, markers of racial identification are constantly used in daily interactions to indicate a person's closeness to or distance from other individuals, as well as similarities or dissimilarities with others.

Seen from this perspective, straightening one's hair in Brazilian society may not only be a beauty exercise, it can also be seen as an attempt to move up the racial classification scale—that is, to become less "black." Given the importance of hair in determining one's place in this racial classification, the black activist movements that rose to prominence in Brazil from the 1970s onward elected to use natural hairstyles as a symbol of racial affirmation.

The posture of the black Brazilian activists during that period was basically antagonistic by its very nature, for it was aimed at destroying the dual image constructed by Western society in which black was always associated with ugliness, stupidity, dirtiness, or other negative qualities. The objective of black activism was therefore to establish a standard that would go contrary to the existing one. So if the rule was to wear smooth, permed, and jerry-curled hair in order to disguise one's ethnic and racial identity, the counter-rule would be to show that one is proud of one's phenotype by not straightening one's hair (Olívia Cunha, 1991).

By proposing racial affirmation through the use of natural hair, black activists did not isolate the hair phenomenon from other elements, such as dress and makeup, that were part of the new aesthetic. However, the perming of hair had been in practice as a symbol of beauty and modernity at least since the late 1920s. Petrônio Domingues (2002) demonstrated this by uncovering newspaper advertisements published by blacks in São Paulo at that time. He also found that this same hair-straightening practice had at one time been condemned among women involved in Candomblé. This means that certain symbols consciously used in a given period to affirm racial identity may once have had other significations within the same society, or other connotations within different societies.

Blacks in the United States have used hair straightening or permanent curls for some time, even though these practices were criticized by important black leaders, including Malcolm X. Black activists in Brazil, however, have never considered such practices as taking away from their blackness.

In Brazil, hair dressing has always been extremely popular in the day-to-day life of black women. Many black women spend a considerable part of their earnings on making their hair "beautiful," and from a very young age, black women are socialized to wear their hair curled and permed. Among adults, some black women treat their hair because they are convinced that it makes them look more beautiful, while others justify the practice with the claim that treated hair is easier to manage in their day-to-day activities.

From the point of view of black activism, as pointed out elsewhere, hair is of utmost importance in Brazil in staking out one's ethnic identity. Many Brazilians claim that, of all the black phenotypes, hair stands out as the one that should be given attention as often as one wishes. They also believe that the method used in treating hair is dependent upon different factors, such as the occasion being prepared for, the cost of treatment, and one's financial situation.

Until the 1970s, options for hair treatment were very limited, with the most common being hair straightening with the aid of a hot comb, the use of henna leaves to color and straighten the hair, and the use of headgear or a turban. It is noteworthy that the head scarves used by women in the early twenty-first century no longer have the elegance of the elaborate headgear documented earlier by various travelers, with such scarves now serving more for concealment of the hair than for aesthetic purposes. The very few chemical products available in the past basically consisted of high soda concentrates, which demanded expertise in their application. They were therefore restricted to use by professional hairdressers, and they had to be purchased at specialized stores. By the 1980s, however, changes in the political situation in Brazil led to the further internationalization of its economy, which opened the way for the exposure of Brazilians to more modern hair products. This led to a wider variety of hair products and hair-treatment options.

TYPES OF HAIR TREATMENTS

In trying to identify the diverse types of hair treatment from the 1990s onward, three distinct categories of hairdressing professionals can be recognized: hot-comb specialists, hair-braid specialists, and hairdressers.

The hot-comb specialists employ a hair-straightening comb, a kind of flat iron that, when heated, serves to stretch the hair, thereby making the strands straighten out. The hair then looks as if it had gone through some type of chemical treatment. This kind of hair treatment is usually done in the kitchen of houses, and the customers that undergo such treatment usually come from the immediate vicinity. This hair treatment is the least expensive of the three techniques.

In the 1970s, partly due to the influence of the Black Power movement and the emphasis it placed on hair aesthetics, and partly due to the first black cultural movement in the city of Salvador (capital of the state of Bahia)—

Guided by their instructor, two students braid a young woman's hair in Rio de Janeiro, Brazil, 2000. *The 1970s marked a revival in the use of braids by black women, partly due to the influence of Ilê Aiyê, the black cultural movement that began in the city of Salvadore in 1974* © RICARDO AZOURY/CORBIS

namely, the Ilê Aiyê—there was a revival of the use of braids by black women. Initially, the use of such braids was restricted to the period of Carnival, but as the years rolled by, the vogue among black women of wearing braids became more constant. In the state of Bahia, the Carnival association Ilê Aiyê plays an important role in the construction of a positive image concerning both the beauty of black women and the general affirmation of black identity. Even though the field has witnessed a boom in recent times, hair-braiding activities have always been a craft practiced mostly by women. Unlike their colleagues who work with the hot-comb, braiding professionals usually have a more expansive clientele, with some coming from outside the immediate vicinity, including white tourists.

The art of hair braiding has always required the use of human or artificial hair attachments, which are meant to add to the volume and length of the hairdo. The laws of supply and demand and the taste of clients has led to widely varying prices, and the process can be expensive. The hair attachments used for such operations originate from diverse sources. Natural human hair generally comes from India, while hair treated with chemicals generally comes from the United States. Synthetic braids are mostly obtained from Taiwan or China. However, the rise in demand for braid attachments has placed Brazil within the network of international braids markets, which is also a reflection of the dynamics of globalization.

One other important issue concerning hairdressing has to do with its naturalness. The quest for naturalness in hair treatments does not in any way signify letting go, in real terms, of products and technologies that modify the hair. Rather, the issue concerns the naturalness of the end result—that is, the appearance. In essence, hair that is considered natural is that which does not betray the treatment it has undergone. Apart from appearance, what distinguishes naturalness from artificiality is whether or not chemical products have been employed. A good example is the fact that the use of kanekalon hair (a type of synthetic hair used to augment hair volume) makes one's hair less natural than if human hair attachments had been used.

When Soft Sheen, a multinational cosmetic industry, set up shop in Rio de Janeiro in the late 1980s, a range of hair relaxers and permanent afro-wave products were introduced to Brazil. To maintain such hair treatments, however, other products must be used to keep the hair looking wet. Besides being expensive, these products became scarce. This forced manufacturers, cosmetologists, and hairdressers to look for alternative Brazil-made products that are both less expensive and equally effective.

With regards to beauty products in general, the launching of the magazine *Raça Brasil* in September 1996 literally led to the discovery of a new black consumership. According to Roberto Melo, producer of the magazine, "the sales record attained by *Raça Brasil* gave the lie to three existing dogmas in the Brazilian editorial market: (1) that blacks did not have enough purchasing power to indulge in secondary consumer products; (2) that magazines that carry the pictures of blacks on their front covers would not sell; and (3) that black Brazilians are not proud of their racial origins" (*Jornal da Tarde*, October 13, 1996).

The astounding success of *Raça Brasil* (its premier issue sold 300,000 copies) served as a catalyst for the debate on the existence of specific products exclusively for the black consumer. More than anything else, the magazine *Raça Brasil* greatly contributed to the increased visibility of the black middle class by showing how much purchasing power the class controlled (see Fry, 2002).

Following the lead of *Raça Brasil,* other diverse print media have brought to the forefront the emergence of specific products for the black segment of the society. Curiously, even in the early twenty-first century, the discovery of the black consumer has been highly restricted to products meant for the body, such as creams, makeup, and cosmetics, and products for hair conditioning. In 2000 the Brazilian Association of the Personal Hygiene, Perfume, and Cosmetics Industry reported a growth of 60 percent in the market of products for black consumption, while the overall market for beauty and general cosmetic products only increased 11 percent. In early 2002 the daily newspaper *Jornal da Tarde* announced that in the previous year the Brazilian market for shampoo and hair-conditioning products generated R$680 [*reais*] million, while hair relaxers brought in another R$280 million. The production of the pioneering manufacturer Cravo & Canela ("clove and cinnamon"—a popular way to refer to black and brown skin) grew dramatically, from a modest 20,000 units to 200,000 units in eight years.

In previous years, despite the fact that the products were consumed mostly by blacks, the manufacturers were still reluctant to put pictures of black people on their labels. By the late twentieth century, however, virtually all hair-care products available on the market, be they hair conditioners, relaxers, or even shampoos, either had images of black women on the label or the label explicitly stated that the product was made especially for use by black people.

According to the Brazilian press, there is a consensus concerning the greater preference of blacks in general (compared to white people) for the consumption of clothes and other objects connected to body care and physical appearance. The veracity of this alleged preference of black consumers for the acquisition of body-care products notwithstanding, after the launching of *Raça Brasil,* the beauty-products market for black people in Brazil grew as it never had before. Initially, it was the same traditional manufacturers that introduced cosmetic products specifically for black consumers, as was the case with the Davene and O Boticário companies. Later, manufacturers had to adapt their products to the standards of those that had come to be identified with black consumers, as was the case with Shen hair pomades, which are manufactured by Avon. Curiously, only recently did Avon start to openly appeal to black consumers in Brazil.

The emergence of an ethnically segmented market was propelled by the Umidfica manufacturing company, the pioneer in the domain of hair-care products in Bahia. Founded in 1994, Umidfica produces up to fifteen different hair-treatment products, fourteen of which are exclusively for black hair, while only one product is meant for all types of hair. Umidfica's mission has thus been different from that of manufacturers that offer specific products for consumption by blacks, especially as Umidfica originally set out to service the black sector of the economy. Only recently did its management think of diversifying by extending their products to the white sector as well.

The transformation undergone by the cosmetic market for blacks in Brazil has so far yielded two important trade fairs: Cosmoétnica and Étnic. The latter made its debut during the International Fair for Cosmetics and Afro-Ethnic Products in São Paulo in December 1997, while Cosmoétnica came on the scene in December 2000 with its first fair dubbed the International Trade Fair for Black Beauty, also held in São Paulo.

Black hair manipulation in Brazil shows the universal character of the black condition in different parts of the Americas, as well as the specificity of the Brazilian system of race relations, which is based on a color continuum that offers many opportunities for the individual manipulation of physical appearance.

See also Representations of Blackness in Latin America and the Caribbean

■ ■ *Bibliography*

Bacelar, Jéferson. *Etnicidade: ser negro em Salvador.* Salvador, Brazil: Pemba/Ianamá, 1989.

Black, Paula, and Ursula Sharma. "Men Are Real, Women Are 'Made Up': Beauty Therapy and the Construction of Femininity." *Sociological Review* 49, no. 1 (2001): 100–116.

Cunha, Manuela Carneiro da. *Antropologia do Brasil: Mito, história, e etnicidade.* São Paulo, Brazil: Editora Brasiliense, 1986.

Cunha, Olívia M. dos Santos. "Corações Rastafari: Lazer, política, e religião em Salvador." Master's Thesis, Museu Nacional, Universidade Federal do Rio de Janeiro, 1991.

Domingues, Petrônio José. "Negros de Almas Brancas? A ideologia do Branqueamento no Interior da Comunidade Negra em São Paulo, 1915–1930." *Estudos Afro-Asiáticos* 24, no. 3 (2002): 563–600.

Figueiredo, Ângela. "Beleza pura: Símbolos e economia ao redor do cabelo do negro." Master's Thesis, Dept. of Social Sciences, Universidade Federal da Bahia, Brazil, 1994.

Figueiredo, Ângela. *Cabelo, cabeleira, cabeluda, descabelada: Identidade, consumo, e manipulação da aparência.* A paper presented at the XXVI Annual Congress of Anpocs, Caxambu (MG), mimeo, 2002.

Fry, Peter. "Estética e política: Relações entre 'Raça,' publicidade, e a produção da beleza no Brasil." In *Nú & Vestido: Dez antropólogos revelam a cultura do corpo carioca,* edited by Miriam Goldenberg. Rio de Janeiro: Record, 2002.

Landes, Ruth. *The City of Women.* Edited with introduction by Sally Cole. New York: Macmillan, 1947. Reprint, Albuquerque: University of New Mexico Press, 1994.

Maués, Maria Angélica Motta. "Da 'Branca senhora' ao 'negro herói': A trajetória de um discurso racial." *Estudos Afro-Asiáticos* 21 (1991): 119–130.

Nogueira, Oracy. *Tanto preto quanto branco: Estudo de relações raciais.* São Paulo, Brazil: T.A. Queiroz, 1985.

Sansone, Livio. *Blackness Without Ethnicity: Constructing Race in Brazil.* New York: Palgrave Macmillan, 2003.

Santos, Jocélio Teles. "O negro no espelho: Imagens e discursos nos salões de beleza étnicos." *Estudos Afro-Asiáticos* 38 (2000): 49–66.

Viana, Hildegards. *A Bahia já foi assim.* São Paulo, Brazil: Edições GRD, 1978.

Vieira, Hamilton. "Tranças: a nova estética negra." In *Identidade negra e educação,* edited by Marco Aurelio Luz. Salvador, Brazil: Ianamá, 1989.

ÂNGELA FIGUEIREDO (2005)

HAIR AND BEAUTY CULTURE IN THE UNITED STATES

African-American men and women have often used their hair and faces as sites of artistry and as a means of self-expression. Enslaved Africans brought diverse notions of beauty to North America. In America, African hair and beauty traditions underwent a complex process of cultural continuity, acculturation, and transformation. Although there was much diversity in black skin color and hair texture and curl structure, to whites, black hair type—generally thick, tightly curled hair—rivaled skin color as one of the most distinctive features of Africans. These physical characteristics were perceived as the very antithesis of beauty by many whites who conformed to a European standard of beauty that placed primacy upon white skin and straight hair. For many whites, blacks' social, economic, and political subordination as slaves was justified by physical appearance. The images, drawings, and depictions of slave men's and women's hair that remain in the historical record are often colored by these racist assumptions. Stereotypical caricatures about African Americans that relied on exaggerated depictions of thick black lips, unkempt black hair, and dark black skin—most notably in minstrel shows—pervaded white popular culture in the eighteenth and nineteenth centuries. Advertisements for runaway slaves, for example, often contained descriptions of black hair characterizing it as "bushy" or "woolly."

Slaves in close contact with whites—northern slaves, urban slaves, and house slaves—were constantly confronted with white beauty aesthetics and at times adopted white beauty practices. Evidence exists, for example, that urban male slaves in New York in the seventeenth century styled their hair to resemble the popular wigs worn at the time by white men. However, the vast majority of African Americans maintained their own conception of hairstyle and adornment. Forced into an unfamiliar environment, slave men and women became innovators, using natural substances such as berries and herbs for hairdressing and skin care. The hair of slave women was often covered and wrapped with rags and other pieces of cloth. Hair braiding, a strong tradition in West Africa, remained common for slave women.

Some slave men and women served as stylists and barbers for other blacks, as well as some whites, during slavery. Northern free black men and women, such as Pierre Dominique Toussaint and the sisters Cecilia, Caroline, and Maritcha Remond Putnam, pioneered in white hair care in the nineteenth century and continued in that role after Emancipation. Barbering, in particular, was an occupation that provided crucial economic support for many black men. In 1885 there were five hundred black barbers—three hundred of whom ran their own shops—in Philadelphia. About 150 or so were able to attract white customers. Barbering was also a preferred occupation for free blacks in the South. Many barbers, including William Johnson of Natchez, Mississippi, made barbering a stepping-stone to later entrepreneurial success. Others, such as Robert Delarge and Joseph Rainey, both Reconstruction congressmen from South Carolina, used barbering to further their political ambitions. The successful early twentieth-century insurance company founders John Merrick and Alonzo Herndon both received their start in business through the ownership of barbershops. These politicians made use of the political contacts they were able to make as barbers for whites to familiarize themselves with white elites.

The solidification of Jim Crow segregation by the turn of the twentieth century resulted in black beauty salons and barbershops losing their white client base. For example, Philadelphia's black population had doubled by the early twentieth century, but the number of barbershops had been reduced to 116. This factor, coupled with rising spending power among a growing black middle class, led to the genesis of a formalized black hair and beauty culture industry offering commercial beauty products and services to the growing market.

After slavery, many black men and women—who equated grooming with respectability and freedom—experimented with a vast array of hairstyles and beauty techniques. Both black-owned and white-owned companies responded to the diverse hair and beauty needs of black consumers. Black entrepreneurs vigorously competed for dominance in the black hair and beauty culture industry. In the early twentieth century, the Overton Hygienic Manufacturing Company, founded in 1898 by entrepreneur Anthony Overton, became successful when it expanded into the cosmetics industry selling "High Brown" facial powder. Annie Turnbo Malone's Poro Company was one of the leading manufacturers of hair-care products for black women. In 1905 Madam C. J. Walker revolutionized the hair and beauty culture industry by creating a treatment for hair loss—a common ailment that plagued black women as a result of poor diet, dandruff, scalp disease, and harsh hair-care treatments. She also pioneered a hair-straightening system for black women's hair called the Walker system, which used a heated metal comb to straighten black women's hair.

European aesthetics pervaded the black community in many ways—from social hierarchies based on skin color to cultural expressions categorizing hair as "good" or "bad" based on its texture—and shaped the context in which African Americans made their hair and beauty choices. There was much debate about hair and beauty within the black community. Black men also had a crucial stake in these debates. Although skin lighteners and hair straighteners found their greatest market among black women, some black men chemically processed their hair to relax the curl structure. Skin care was relatively simple for black men. However, razor-shaving facial hair was often a painful process for black men. The tight curl pattern of their hair resulted in ingrown hairs, informally known as "razor bumps," on the face and neck. This condition was irritated each time the shaving process was repeated. To avoid this, many black men turned to harsh chemical depilatories or chose to wear a beard.

Many in the beauty culture industry argued that the standards of beauty they promoted—lighter skin and straighter hair—were linked to personal success and racial progress and could therefore counter negative stereotypes about black people. Some blacks agreed, arguing that altering the natural state of their hair and skin was a way to challenge the correlation between black hair and unkemptness, poor grooming, or a lack of professionalism in an employment situation. Others saw a direct link between hair straightening and skin-lightening creams and cosmetics—often with names such as "Black-No-More" and "No Kink"—and the acceptance of white standards of beauty and a lack of black self-esteem. Pointing out the often painful and damaging effects of chemicals on black hair, scalp, and skin, these blacks argued that leaving hair in its unprocessed state was a way to embrace their African heritage and challenge white domination by reversing notions of beauty. In the 1920s Marcus Garvey, black activist and advocate of Pan-Africanism, refused to accept advertisements for hair straighteners and skin lighteners in his publication *Negro World*.

Hair straightening, however, cannot simply be equated with the adoption of a European aesthetic and the rejection of African cultural heritage. Many Africans conceptualized their hair as a headdress to be adorned and manipulated as a site of artistic and cultural construction. Through the styling of their straightened hair, African Americans struggled to define a space for themselves within the framework of the dominant aesthetic that could challenge, oppose, and undermine it while reaffirming black cultural values. Although some middle-class blacks wore their straightened hair in styles similar to those popular among middle-class whites, others combined their straightened heads of hair with pomades and hairdressing creams to explore bold, innovative, and creative styling options.

Often, the straightening of hair was a statement of rebellion. Finger waves and pin curls (waves and circular curls sculpted on hair slicked close to the scalp), popular among black women and some men, were emblematic of the Harlem Renaissance period. The process—a style called the "conk," achieved by using a lye-based chemical to straighten black men's hair—was integral to the subculture that formed among many young, black urban males during the 1940s. Although conks were popular among the black middle class, working-class blacks styled their conks with heavy pomade, a center part, and a ducktail, often pairing them with flamboyant zoot suits to articulate an oppositional political and cultural identity that challenged both white and black middle-class sensibilities.

Beauty parlors and barbershops were important within the internal African-American service economy of the middle decades of the twentieth century. In the 1940s black women owned 96.7 percent of black-held beauty shops and 88 percent of related business schools. Black beauticians criticized the racist assumption in the beauty-culture industry that black beauticians could style and care for only black hair and agitated against segregated beauty schools. They fought for equality in training and licensing for black and white beauticians and argued that black beauticians should be held to the same standards as white ones. Beauty trade associations often took public positions on civil rights matters. The National Beauty Culturalists League, founded in 1919, for example, adopted the slogan "Every Beautician a Registered Voter" in the 1950s.

Beauty parlors and barbershops were sites of debates and information sharing, where black people created networks of mutual support that could be used in social fraternization or political organizing. Black politicians, for example, often targeted beauty parlors and barbershops as key community institutions on the campaign trail. Poorer black men and women often opened unlicensed beauty parlors and barbershops in their homes as a vehicle toward economic self-sufficiency. Unable to afford professional beauty schools, these men and women passed on skills of hairstyling and haircutting through apprenticeships. These unlicensed shops were criticized as unprofessional and unqualified by many middle-class shop owners who resented the competition they believed was unfair. Despite these challenges, however, unlicensed shops continued to survive alongside licensed shops as community institutions.

In the 1960s hairstyle took on additional meaning for both blacks and whites who defined hair not only as a badge of self-identity but as an indicator of political consciousness. During the period of militant pride and cultural awareness that characterized the Black Power move-ment of the mid-1960s, many African Americans began to style their hair in an unprocessed state to symbolize the connection to their African past and challenge white beauty standards. In 1966 Black Power leader Stokely Carmichael militantly asserted, "We have to stop being ashamed of being black. A broad nose, a thick lip and nappy hair is us, and we are going to call that beautiful . . . we are not going to fry our hair anymore." Guided by the slogan "Black is Beautiful," many black men and women abandoned hairstyles that required chemical processing.

The Afro—unprocessed black hair arranged in a circular symmetry around the head—was one of the most popular hairstyles of the mid to late 1960s for both men and women. Afros—also called "naturals"—varied with black hair texture and ranged in height from low, scalp-hugging cuts to styles elaborately shaped and coiffed several inches away from the scalp. Political activist Angela Davis's large Afro was a political statement that symbolized her militancy and her rejection of the conventional cultural practices of mainstream America.

The beauty industry created new products aimed at the maintenance of natural hairstyles and marketed them alongside its more traditional products. In the late 1960s, for example, Johnson Products, the leading black-owned company in the beauty culture industry, introduced a no-lye relaxer (thought to be less damaging to the scalp) to straighten hair, as well as the popular Afro-Sheen line of products aimed at the maintenance of Afros. Advertisements in black magazines such as *Ebony* and *Jet* began to feature darker-skinned models with unprocessed hair and slogans such as "Rows. Fros. Anything Goes." Cornrows—a hairstyle traditionally worn by black girls in which hair is braided in rows along the scalp and often weaved into elaborate designs and decorated with ornaments ranging from beads to cowrie shells to tinfoil—became popular among many black women and some black men. In the early 1970s, for example, Stevie Wonder was one of many musicians who donned intricately styled and adorned braided hairstyles. White actress Bo Derek's cornrows in the 1979 movie *10* caused outrage among many in the black community, who believed that she had appropriated the style devoid of its cultural meaning.

Facial hair was integral to black men's self-presentation in the early 1970s. For some black men, moustaches were more than an aesthetic choice but instead a symbol of virility. Black actor Richard Roundtree's character Shaft—popularized in the blaxploitation film genre of the 1970s—sported a thick moustache that was as integral to his depiction of black male power as his leather jacket and streetwise attitude. Isaac Hayes, who achieved considerable renown as the composer and performer of the Academy Award–winning title song from *Shaft* (1971), helped pioneer another popular black male style of the 1970s, the shaved head. Jheri Curls, a chemical process that loosened and lengthened the curl pattern in the hair and required that the hair be constantly saturated by a curl-activating lotion, was popular for both men and women in the late 1970s and early 1980s. During this period, the Afro—especially in its lower-cut form—achieved a more mainstream acceptance.

In the 1980s and early 1990s, a rising cultural-consciousness movement created space for a diversity of natural hairstyles for blacks. Although this movement continued in the tradition of the "Black is Beautiful" movements of the mid-1960s, the popularity and limited mainstream acceptance of unprocessed hairstyles made the former link between hairstyle and political consciousness a hotly debated issue in the black community. There was a rise in popularity and cultural acceptance of dreadlocks—a style common among Jamaican Rastafarians, in which unprocessed hair is sectioned off and long braids of it are allowed to grow together unhampered. These sections "lock" because of black hair's tight curl pattern. Folksinger Tracy Chapman and author Alice Walker are two prominent black women who have embraced this hairstyle.

Hair braiding was increasingly accepted as a skilled art form as braids grew in popularity, diversity of style, and form in the 1980s and 1990s. The use of human or synthetic hair extensions for braiding to augment the length or the width of the individual braids increased in the 1980s. Hair weaves (extensions of synthetic or human hair either sewn or glued on the scalp) were used by some black women to achieve straight-textured, long hair. Others used extensions to add flexibility in the creation of elaborately braided Afrocentric hairstyles and boldly sported styles called "Senegalese twists" or "African goddess braids." Other women chose to wear their hair closely cropped and low to the scalp, unprocessed or slightly relaxed in a process called "texturization."

Hair braiding for African-American men had increased visibility as well. Hip-hop culture of the 1980s and 1990s popularized daring haircuts for young African-American men that ranged from shaved heads—a style long embraced by many older black men as an alternative to thinning hair—to a texturized version of the Afro called the "blow out." Also popular was the fade haircut, in which the sides and back of the hair are cut lower than the top, and the back of the head is used as a palette for everything from intricate designs to commercial symbols or even the wearer's initials. A new generation of stylists specializing in the maintenance of unprocessed black hair and the creation of bold new cuts for men developed alongside traditional salons as the hair and beauty culture industry created new products to meet the needs of these consumers.

These products were increasingly supplied by white-owned companies such as Revlon and Alberto Culver. These white companies—often better financed than their black counterparts and therefore able to offer lower prices—adopted aggressive Afrocentric marketing strategies to attract black consumers. By 1993 fourteen of the nineteen cosmetics companies in the lucrative black hair-care market were white-owned.

Hair and beauty culture remained a creative area for black men and women in the 1990s. Acutely aware that physical appearance has an impact on almost every arena, from social life to employment opportunities, black people have always had to grapple with the broader implications of their hair and beauty culture. In the 1980s and 1990s, an increasing number of black men and women took to the courts to register complaints about discrimination in employment due to hairstyle. Issues of politics, economics, and aesthetics—along with age, regional location, and class—continue to guide the choices black men and women make for their hair and beauty needs. By 2000, a wide range of natural hairstyles—locs, two-strand twists, and Afros—gained increased acceptance by the black mainstream. Pop culture icons, such as singers Lauryn Hill, India Arie, Jill Scott, Alicia Keys, and others, showcased the versatility of black hair's natural textures. Black companies forayed into the natural hair-care market to offer products and services to meet this rising need.

See also Representations of Blackness in the United States

■ ■ ■ *Bibliography*

Jones, Lisa. *Bulletproof Diva: Tales of Race, Sex and Hair*. New York: Doubleday, 1994.

Morrow, Willie. *400 Years Without a Comb*. San Diego, Calif.: Black Publishers of San Diego, 1973.

Peiss, Kathy. "Making Faces: The Cosmetics Industry and the Cultural Construction of Gender, 1890–1930." *Genders* (Spring 1990): 372–394.

Rooks, Noliwe M. *Hair Raising: Beauty, Culture, and African American Women*. New Brunswick, N.J.: Rutgers University Press, 1996.

Weathers, Natalie R. "Braided Sculptures and Smokin' Combs: African-American Women's Hair Culture." *SAGE* 8, no. 1 (Summer 1991): 58–61.

White, Shane. *Somewhat More Independent: The End of Slavery in New York City, 1770–1810*. Athens: University of Georgia Press, 1991.

Wolf, Naomi. *The Beauty Myth: How Images of Beauty Are Used Against Women*. New York: Anchor, 1991.

ROBYN SPENCER (1996)
Updated by author 2005

HAITIAN CREOLE LANGUAGE

Haitian Creole, also known as *Kreyòl*, is a member of the French-based creole language groups with a considerable part of its lexicon coming directly from seventeenth-century French. Its grammar differs from French, however, and reflects closely the West African languages, such as Ewe, Fon, Yoruba, and Ibo. *Kreyòl* is similar to the creoles spoken in the French overseas departments of Martinique and Guadeloupe, as well as in Dominica, Saint Lucia, and parts of Trinidad. *Kreyòl* also has much in common with the creole spoken in Louisiana and with the popular languages of Mauritius and the Seychelles islands in the Indian Ocean. *Kreyòl* is the native language of about 7.5 million Haitians and is spoken and understood by over one million people outside of Haiti.

Various theories have been advanced to explain the origin of French-based creole language groups. Early theorists claimed that they developed as the result of attempts by African slaves to imitate the language of their French masters. These early theorists also held that the white overseers and the crews of slave ships deliberately used simplified forms of European languages when speaking to a people they believed to be mentally inferior and incapable of learning the "civilized" variety. A second theory suggested that French-based creoles developed in three stages: The African slave attempted to copy the language of the master or foreman; the colonizer simplified his or her language in imitation of the slave; and finally the slave imitated the French speaker's own modification of French. A third theory rejects the idea that French-based creoles developed on the plantations, ascribing their origin to Afro-Portuguese pidgin, the lingua franca spoken by seamen and traders of the seventeenth century. The French sailors later replaced Portuguese words with French words, which were then acquired by the slaves, who further developed the language. Debate continues over the contention that all creole languages developed from an identical pidgin stage called the Afro-Portuguese pidgin, which originated along the western and southern coasts of Africa and became extremely useful from the early fifteenth century to traders from a multitude of nations in the Mediterranean basin.

Most modern linguists agree that Haitian Creole developed as a result of attempts by African slaves to communicate with their masters and with each other. Haitian Creole, or *Kreyòl*, is a language created in the French colony of Saint Domingue as a result of the unequal relations between the mass of slaves drawn from over forty different African ethnic groups and their French masters. Some of the early literary works in Haitian Creole include the well-known poem "*Lisette quitté la plaine*" (Lisette leaves the plain), by Duvivier de La Mahotière, and the Félicite Sonthonax Declaration of 1794, the communiqué of the French envoy sent to reestablish peace in revolutionary Saint Domingue and ordering "*liberté*" for the slaves. On January 1, 1804, Haiti became the only independent nation founded by African ex-slaves; it had a turbulent political history and experienced a long period of isolation from Western colonial powers. Thus the need to forge a national language was tantamount.

The Haitian Constitution of 1987 (Chapter I, Article 5) gave *Kreyòl* an official status, along with French, which had been the sole official language for more than 180 years, since Haiti's independence, although only about fifteen percent of the population can read and write French fluently. The true national language of all Haitians is *Kreyòl*, which is written and read by well over sixty percent of the population, including the minority of bilingual *Kreyòl* and French speakers.

Haitian Creole today exhibits three main dialectical variations: northern, southern, and central. In spite of the presence of these regional variations, however, Haitian Creole presents a high degree of standardization and normalization given that dialectical boundaries are not rigid and Haitians tend to be bidialectal. There is, however, a significant distinction between the *Kreyòl rèk* of the countryside and the somewhat more French sounding *Kreyòl swa* of Port-au-Prince. This variation has had an impact on arguments regarding how Haitian Creole should be spelled. Prior to 1980, two positions dominated the debate over orthography and the use of *Kreyòl* for adult literacy or as a means of instruction in primary schools. One position advocated a phonetic spelling system, which uses the International Phonetic Alphabet and diacritic signs. The other advocated a spelling system as near to French as possible. The proponents of the latter position view *Kreyòl* as a stepping stone to French (a "*passage au Français*"). Following the educational reform of the 1980s, a new spelling system was adopted and used widely. This spelling system corresponds to the speech patterns of Port-au-Prince and its surroundings. It is generally agreed that French and *Kreyòl* are mutually unintelligible. Haitian Creole is a distinct language with a unique morpho-phonological structure; it is not a French dialect.

"Sèl lang ki simante tout Ayisyen ansanm, se lang kreyòl.... Kreyòl ak fransè se lang ofisyèl Repiblik Dayiti."

"Only one language unites all Haitians—it is the Kreyol language.... Kreyol and French are the official languages of Haiti."

KONSTITISYON REPIBLIK DAYITI (HAITIAN CONSTITUTION), 1987, CH.I, ART.5.

See also Creole Languages of the Americas

■ ■ *Bibliography*

DeGraff, Michel, ed. *Language Creation and Language Change: Creolization Diachrony, and Development.* Cambridge, Mass.: MIT Press, 1999.

Dejean, Yves. *Comment é écrire le Créole d'Haiti.* Montreal, Canada: Collectifs Paroles, 1980.

Dejean, Yves. "Diglossia Revisited: French and Creole in Haiti." *Word* 34 (1983): 189–213.

Hall, Robert. *Pidgin and Creole Languages.* Ithaca, NY: Cornell University Press, 1966.

Holm, John. *Pidgins and Creoles,* vols. 1 and 2. Cambridge, U.K.: Cambridge University Press, 1988-1989.

Lefebvre, Claire. *Creole Genesis and the Acquisition of Grammar: The Case of Haitian Creole.* Cambridge, U.K.: Cambridge University Press, 1998.

Muhlhausler, Peter. *Pidgin and Creole Linguistics.* New York: B. Blackwell, 1986.

Valdman, Albert. *Le créole: structure, statut et origine.* Paris: Éditions Klinscksieck, 1978.

Valdman, Albert, et al. *A Learner's Dictionary of Haitian Creole.* Bloomington, Ind.: Creole Institute, 1996.

MARC E. PROU (2005)

■ ■ ■ HAITIAN REVOLUTION

This entry consists of two distinct articles. The first provides an overview of the Haitian Revolution and the second focuses on the reaction to the revolution in the United States.

OVERVIEW
Laennec Hurbon

AMERICAN REACTION TO THE HAITIAN REVOLUTION
James Alexander Dun

OVERVIEW

Haiti is the ancient Taino name for the Caribbean island that was first named St. Domingue by the French after the 1697 Treaty of Ryswick granting Spain the western portion of the island. It was Jean-Jacques Dessalines, commander in chief of the victorious army against the French expeditionary forces (1802–1804), who chose the name of Haiti for St. Domingue. He wanted to consign to oblivion the French colonial domination of the island. The series of events that unfolded in St. Domingue were new and unprecedented, and they constituted, after the French Revolution of 1789 and the American Revolution of 1776, a third revolution that had immense implications for the countries still under the yoke of slavery and colonialism. However, it seems that history books have done everything possible to underestimate and obscure the fact that this transition from St. Domingue to Haiti was indeed an authentic revolution. What did it consist of exactly? What was at stake in the struggle undertaken to reach the creation of an independent nation? What are the explanations for the causes of this independence of 1804? Why can historians and why should historians state that it was about a revolution that had its own specificity, originality, and orientations?

To address these questions, one must first attempt to review the situation in St. Domingue from 1789 to 1804 and the different strategies put in place by the actors.

THE GENERAL SLAVE INSURRECTION OF AUGUST 1791: ITS FACTORS AND ITS STAKES

On the eve of 1789, St. Domingue was the most prosperous French colony, furnishing 70 percent of the revenue that France obtained from the totality of its possessions in the New World. One in eight French people lived off St. Domingue, from which fifteen hundred boats departed each year, loaded with 200,000 tons of sugar, coffee, and indigo. From just 1785 to 1789, 150,000 slaves were imported from Africa, with 55,000 slaves imported in one year alone, 1789. This clearly demonstrates that the system of slavery already begun two centuries before on the island was implacable and in full force near the end of the eighteenth century. The slaves numbered approximately 400,000 in contrast to 35,000 whites and 50,000 freed people (mulattos and blacks). One must be careful, however, not to see things in black and white, since among the slaves, there were mulattos, even if they were small in number, and among the freed slaves there were slave owners. Thirteen thousand men served in militias to prevent sabotage on sugar plantations, slave rebellions, and the running away of slaves. The Black Codes, instituted in 1685 to prevent the crossing of these racial lines, strictly enforced relations among the three large social groups.

News of the storming of the Bastille and the declaration that "all men are born free and equal in rights" created immediate panic among St. Domingue's colonists, especially its merchants and administrators. For them, the best way of safeguarding the institution of slavery was to regain autonomy for St. Domingue, thus ending the practice of trading exclusively with metropolitan France. Above all, they sought to prevent the freed mulattos from exercising their civil rights. In the midst of this maneuvering by the whites (planters, managers, artisans, traders, and civil servants), came the news that on March 8, 1790, a decree issued in France proclaimed the right of all individuals age twenty-five and older to French citizenship. This victory for the free people of color suddenly created a giant rift in the institution of slavery. The white colonists did their best to avoid the implementation of this decree, which could pave the way for demands for freedom by the slaves. Faced with the refusal of the colonial administration to directly implement the decree, one of the mulatto leaders, Vincent Ogé, who had recently spent a year in France and who would thus have been in contact with the Society of the Friends of Blacks, disembarked in the colony with weapons and ammunition to free the enslaved mulattos. But he was captured, tortured, and executed. Some of his companions succeeded in fleeing to the western part of the island.

Would the slaves stand by passively watching as conflict developed between the white colonists and the freed mulattos? Since their arrival in the colony, slaves had been in search of freedom, running away to escape their masters, and they were waiting for a propitious moment to organize a general uprising and put an end to the system of slavery. Vodou was practiced among the slaves: It was an inherited system of belief from Africa integrating the traditions of diverse ethnic groups represented on the colony. In one of their vodou ceremonies, the slaves swore to put an end to slavery. It was during the night of August 22–23, 1791, that a general slave insurrection in the north of the country exploded, with disastrous repercussions: numerous fatalities among the colonists and the torching of 161 sugarcane refineries and 1,200 coffee plantations, with damage estimated at 600 million pounds.

The first accounts of the insurrection emphasized the element of surprise and the influence of exterior forces on the society of St. Domingue; the slaves were never presented as having made the deliberate choice of freedom by and for themselves. The colonists sought to ensure the failure of the insurrection by requesting widespread assistance from abroad. Those who fled after the insurrection and who sought refuge in Philadelphia spread the idea that barbarism was rampant in St. Domingue and that it was essential to avoid the radicalism of emancipation by planning for a gradual abolition. All of the slave powers (Holland, Spain, Portugal, England, and the United States) wanted to ensure that a similar insurrection did not happen in their colonies.

The factors that led to the insurrection have been the object of endless questioning. Certain reports mention the influence of the Society of the Friends of Blacks; others declare that the word "revolution" was already on everyone's lips. The first factor was most certainly the condition of life for the slaves. The text of the royal edicts of 1685, known as the Code Noir, or the slave code, regulated daily life and demanded the absolute obedience of slaves to their masters. Laws were futile in limiting the power of the masters; they did not permit slaves to lodge any complaints against their masters. A number of slaves died of starvation or of the harsh conditions where they worked, on the plantation or in some cases in the household. As for the female slaves, they were routinely raped or in any case lived in constant fear of rape, since by definition to be a slave meant to be the property of one's master. It was under these conditions, and the permanent threat of the whip brandished by the overseer, that the slaves worked. Those who escaped and became fugitives were severely punished and submitted to various tortures (feet chained, mutilations, arms hacked off), and these tortures could lead to the death of the slave with no consequences for the masters. In short, daily life for the slaves was akin to the experience of a concentration camp. One can understand why the occasion for an insurrection was therefore particularly waited for and sought out. Vodou was a religion practiced far from the masters' eyes as a veritable system of mutual recognition that favored the collective conscience and a sense of solidarity. In fact, it was a religious leader, Boukman, who led the insurrection and who had recourse to the blood oath made to the gods to keep the plans completely secret. This pact was a tradition among the Ewe, the Adja, the Mahi, and the Fon of Dahomey (contemporary Benin).

Although Catholic missionaries were used to control the slaves by justifying the institution of slavery itself—all slaves had to be baptized upon the arrival of the Church—there were several priests who sided with the insurgent slaves and who acted on their behalf in negotiations with the colonists. All things considered, vodou and the Catholic Church, as well as the rumors about the rights of man, played a role in serving as a catalyst for the slave insurrection.

But what allowed the insurrection to achieve its full significance was the fighting led by Toussaint-Louverture, former slave and coachman on the Breda plantation in the north. He knew how to ally himself very early on with the leaders of the insurrection and worked to make the suppression of slavery decided by the slaves irreversible by putting into practice the principles of equality and freedom affirmed in the declaration of the rights of man: "Brothers and friends," he said. "I am Toussaint-Louverture, my name is perhaps known among you. I have undertaken to avenge myself. I want freedom and equality to reign in St. Domingue. I will work to realize this. Let us unite, brothers, and join us in fighting for the same cause." (Letter of Toussaint-Louverture, National Library of Paris, cited by James, 1938, p. 109).

TOUSSAINT-LOUVERTURE AND THE FOUNDATIONS OF AN INDEPENDENT HAITIAN NATION

A review of the essential stages of the politics conducted by Toussaint-Louverture reveals the following: He patiently constructed his own army, allied himself when necessary with Spain, then with England, and imposed himself as the incontestable leader of the various groups and factions struggling in the colony. When the colonists joyously greeted the British from Jamaica who would support the system of slavery shaken by the insurrection, Toussaint chose to fight with the French, and he rejoined their side. He was backed by the new assembly in France, the National Convention, which ratified the abolition of slavery on February 4, 1794, already proclaimed by decree in 1793 by its high commissioner, Sonthonax. Appointed commander in chief of the army in St. Domingue, Toussaint instilled discipline among his troops of fugitive slaves. In 1801 he succeeded in placing the entire colony under his command and triumphantly entered Santo Domingo, capital of the western region of the island no longer under Spain's control, and proclaimed the emancipation of the slaves. Toussaint effectively functioned as if the island were already independent. He reorganized the government administration and the judiciary, abolished useless taxes, created regulations against smuggling, and strove to convince former slaves to return to work. Finally, he took the risk of establishing the Constituent Assembly, therefore laying the foundation for an independent nation. This is the meaning of the 1801 constitution, cornerstone of the nation, even if the texts declare that St. Domingue remained associated with France. One of the founding principles of this constitution was thus articulated: "In this land, slaves cannot exist, slavery is forever abolished."

Toussaint-Louverture, leader of the Haitian Revolution. PHOTOGRAPHS AND PRINTS DIVISION, SCHOMBURG CENTER FOR RESEARCH IN BLACK CULTURE, THE NEW YORK PUBLIC LIBRARY, ASTOR, LENOX AND TILDEN FOUNDATIONS.

It was the expedition of Napoleon Bonaparte in 1802 to reinstate slavery on the island that hastened the brutal rupture with France, for Toussaint-Louverture's plan had been to establish a nation associated with France in a sort of commonwealth before the fact. However, Napoleon would resort to all the schemas and codes of a racist ideology and assemble one of the largest armadas of that epoch (eighty-six battleships and 35,000 soldiers) to regain control of St. Domingue and deport Toussaint-Louverture to France with his generals. The determination of the former slaves and the subordinate officers made the task impossible for the head of the expedition, General Leclerc. With Toussaint arrested and deported to the Fort de Joux in France, the war ran its course. News of the reinstatement of slavery in Guadeloupe, known in St. Domingue thanks to the slaves who accompanied the French troops and who escaped from the warships, had the effect of fomenting insurrection among all of the soldiers and the masses of farmers. Finally, in the course of a victorious battle, the new Haitian flag was raised on May 18, 1803. Jean-Jacques

Dessalines, new chief of the army following the arrest of Toussaint, announced to Thomas Jefferson in the United States that Haiti would be proclaimed independent on January 1, 1804.

THE REPERCUSSIONS OF THE HAITIAN REVOLUTION

The events in St. Domingue had an influence that one must learn to decipher, even two hundred years later. In the quest to comprehend the repercussions of the successful slave insurrection of St. Domingue on the slave colonies of the Caribbean, one realizes that this was a revolution that concerned the destiny of all the black communities of the Americas, the African diaspora, and Africa itself.

News of the insurrection of 1791 and Haitian independence reached the slave colonies, unleashing various revolts and insurrections. Even if it had been difficult to assist Guadeloupe and Martinique, one must note that the constitution of 1805 stipulated that all slaves who arrived in Haiti became free and Haitian and that "Haitians will from now on only be known under one designation, Black." On the one hand, Haiti was considered a welcoming nation for all of the fugitive slaves of the Caribbean; on the other, the appellation of black was rehabilitated, an appellation that slavery had transformed into a stigma and a mark of barbarism. One must suppose that a fear of contagion provoked by the Haitian Revolution dominated the minds of colonial administrators in Guadeloupe and Martinique. Dessalines himself believed he had to organize an expedition in February 1805 to Santo Domingo to pursue the occupation that Toussaint had undertaken because the French forces stationed in the east of the island represented a danger to the independence of Haiti. The suppression of slavery in the east had therefore to be consolidated by a Haitian occupation; this was the motive offered by the new Haitian government.

Yet it was Spanish America, above all, that was most directly influenced by the Haitian Revolution in its quest for independence. In 1806 Francisco de Miranda departed from the southern Haitian town of Jacmel with significant aid for Venezuela, where he hoped to foment an insurrection and proclaim independence. At the time, however, he claimed to be mobilizing a nonviolent political movement that would not follow the model of the Haitian Revolution. Later, with Simón Bolívar, he made an appeal to five hundred Haitians and about a thousand slaves to join the Venezuelan army, but the problem of the abolition of black slavery, which was rife in South America, did not appear to be a preoccupation. In 1815 Bolívar again obtained assistance and asylum in Haiti on the southern coast, in the town of Les Cayes. President Alexandre Pétion received him on January 2, 1816, and assured him he would receive support in weapons, soldiers, and money. It was from the port of Les Cayes that Bolívar departed with six hundred refugees to undertake a new stage in the liberation of Spanish America. Pétion, in return, solicited from Bolívar the proclamation of the abolition of slavery in the countries of the continent that were liberated. On June 3, 1816, Bolívar honored the promise made to Pétion and proclaimed the abolition of slavery under the principle of equality among all men.

Research on the repercussions of the Haitian Revolution still needs to be undertaken with greater precision. In fact, Great Britain did not delay in proclaiming the abolition of slavery in its colonies (Barbados, Jamaica, and others) and all participation in the slave trade under punishment of death, by parliamentary decree in 1827. In 1814 Holland prohibited the slave trade. At any rate, the colonists from other countries in the Caribbean were henceforth on the defensive.

In the United States, news of the Haitian antislavery revolution was met with a guarded reception. The American government did not recognize Haiti's independence before 1862, that is, before the end of the Civil War, so that the black slaves of the South would not be tempted into a violent revolution for an immediate abolition of slavery. However, the trade that had flourished under the government of Toussaint-Louverture between 1794 and 1802 was pursued without interruption. The United States understood that the failure of General Leclerc's expedition to St. Domingue would benefit them both in political and economic terms. Bonaparte's ambitions for Louisiana to help realize his dream of a colonial project that would dominate the Caribbean and the Gulf of Mexico represented an obstacle to American expansionism. This obstacle was soon discarded; with the loss of the colony of St. Domingue, Bonaparte had to renounce Louisiana. On the other hand, among black Americans freed and enslaved, Toussaint-Louverture became a historical figure, and the news of Haitian independence sustained the vision of black self-determination and the possibility of vanquishing racist ideology.

THE HAITIAN REVOLUTION: A TURNING POINT IN THE HISTORY OF HUMANITY

While it is closely linked to the French Revolution, the Haitian Revolution retains its own specificity. The problem of the application of the principles articulated in the Declaration of the Rights of Man and of the Citizen arises principally from the notion of "man." The dominant mentality in France and among the majority of the revolutionaries of the eighteenth century led to an understanding of human rights based on parameters from the culture of the West (language, religion, and race). Thus, there was considerable delay in the recognition of blacks as whole human beings to whom one can apply the principles of freedom and equality. There was the problem of anthropology, which seems to be the principal obstacle for the abolition of black slavery, as if blacks were not yet ready to enjoy the rights of humanity. Even so, the insurrection of St. Domingue on August 23 and the success of the Haitian Revolution in 1804 was a magnificent demonstration of just how much the slaves were attached to those very principles of freedom and equality. Abolition was not something that was to be granted by others; the process of emancipation was deliberated and organized by the slaves themselves. This was the first such emancipation to succeed in history, and it attests to the fact that there are no human beings who can be classified as less than human on the basis of a racial hierarchy of cultures. For this reason, the Haitian Revolution had far-reaching consequences for its resolutely antiracist, antislavery, and anticolonialist orientation. It was a watershed in the history of human rights and freedom, and it ushered in a new era. Wherever racial ideology is still rampant, wherever the independence of nations in the region is menaced by superpowers bent on political domination just as in the days of slavery, wherever dictatorship reigns, there the memory of the Haitian Revolution must be revived.

See also Black Codes; Dessalines, Jean-Jacques; Toussaint-Louverture

■ ■ *Bibliography*

Benot, Yves. *La révolution française et la fin des colonies.* Paris: Édition La Découverte, 1987.

Benot, Yves. *La démence coloniale sous Napoléon.* Paris: Édition La Découverte, 1992.

Benot, Yves, and Marcel Dorigny, eds. *Le rétablissement de l'esclavage dans les colonies françaises (1802). Aux origines d'Haiti.* Paris: Édition Maisonneuve et Larose, 2003.

Cauna, Jacques de. "La révolution à St Domingue (1789–1793)." In *La révolution aux Caraïbes,* edited by Lucien Abenon, Jacques de Cauna, and Liliane Chauleau. Publications des annales historiques de la révolution française. Paris: Société des études robespierristes, 1989.

David, Davis Brion. *The Problem of Slavery in the Age of Revolution (1770–1823).* Ithaca, N.Y.: Cornell University Press, 1975.

Dorigny, Marcel, ed. *Haiti première république noire.* Paris: Publications de la société française d'histoire d'outre-mer, 2003.

Fick, Carolyn. *The Making of Haiti: The Revolution from Below.* Knoxville: University of Tennessee Press, 1991.

Fouchard, Jean. *Les marrons de la liberté.* Paris: Édition de l'Ecole, 1972.

Geggus, David. "The Haitian Revolution." In *The Modern Caribbean,* edited by Franklin Knight and Colin A. Palmer. Chapel Hill: University of North Carolina Press, 1989.

Genovese, Eugene, D. *From Rebellion to Revolution: Afro-American Slave Revolts in the Modern World.* Baton Rouge: Louisiana State University Press, 1979.

Hurbon, Laennec, ed. *L'insurrection des esclaves à St Domingue.* Paris: Édition Karthala, 2000.

James, C. L. R. *Les Jacobins noirs. Toussaint Louverture et la Révolution de St Domingue.* Translated from English by Pierre Naville. Paris: Édition Caribéennes, 1938.

Moise, Claude. *Toussaint Louverture et la Constitution de 1801.* Montréal: Edition du CIDHICA, 2001.

Trouillot, Michel-Rolph. *Silencing the Past: Power and the Production of History.* Boston: Beacon Press, 1995.

LAENNEC HURBON (2005)
Translated from French by Nadine Pinède

AMERICAN REACTION TO THE HAITIAN REVOLUTION

Americans avidly followed the events that transpired on the French Caribbean island of Saint Domingue between 1789 and 1804—events historians later would collectively demarcate as a "Haitian Revolution." In an age when the movement of information was tied directly to patterns of trade, Saint Domingue's status as a juggernaut among Caribbean sugar-producing islands ensured that numerous American shippers would constantly be doing business on its wharves. Beginning in the years after the American Revolution, news from Saint Domingue moved regularly to ports along the North American littoral as producers, merchants, and consumers evaluated goings-on there for their impact on American markets. The advent of violence did not dampen economic opportunities; contact would continue throughout the 1790s and into the early nineteenth century.

In addition to economic motives, Americans were fixated on events in Saint Domingue because of their implications for political and sociocultural issues at home. Beginning in 1789, the French colony experienced a series of disruptions as various white factions battled over conflicting agendas related to changes brought about by the French Revolution. As events in France unfolded, the island's free colored population (which Americans usually termed "mulatto") attempted to secure the rights and benefits of the newly enlarged French citizenry. Violence erupted in 1790 and 1791 as various groups struggled over the degree of the colony's autonomy, over racial equality, and even over the propriety of the revolution in France itself. In August 1791 the island's slaves rose in unprecedented numbers in an attempt to vanquish the slave system. As anarchy increased, the British and Spanish invaded the island in 1793, and violence and warfare continued over the rest of the decade. In 1804, after turning away the Spanish, the British, and finally the French national armies, the black and free colored inhabitants of the island declared themselves independent, replacing the region's preeminent slave colony with an independent republic in which citizenship was defined around blackness.

These developments made Saint Domingue, today called Haiti, integral to American discussions about France and its revolution, about the implications of Americans' own recent revolutionary past, about slavery, and about race and citizenship. With important exceptions the general trend of American reactions is one of bifurcation along racial lines. African Americans, free and enslaved, were intimately aware of events on the island and incorporated them into their own struggles for equality and liberty. Free black communities, such as those in Philadelphia and New York City, cautiously made reference to Saint Domingue as a warning to American slaveholders and to the nation at large if the nation continued to flout its egalitarian ideals. In Philadelphia in 1793, for example, African-American leaders Absalom Jones and Richard Allen mentioned Saint Domingue obliquely as a referent in their larger plea for justice. By 1804, however, frustrated black youths marched through Philadelphia's streets chanting, "give them St. Domingo!"

The reactions of American slaves are more difficult to gauge because of the increasingly hysterical tenor of white observations of their behavior in relation to events on Saint Domingue. Especially after the onset in August 1791 of the slave revolts in Saint Domingue, white Americans were prone to see the risk of "the horrors of St. Domingo" in any sort of slave resistance. Rumors of "French negroes" terrified Thomas Jefferson in 1793 and spurred the white citizens of Charleston, South Carolina, to restrict the entry of black mariners into the port. Moreover, fragmentary evidence suggests that there were links between increased American slave rebelliousness and Saint Domingue. A large group of slaves rose in Pointe Coupée, Louisiana, in 1795, shortly after the arrival of white and black refugees from the island, followed by a larger revolt in 1811 in the same area. Rumors of connections between Saint Domingue and slave conspiracies abounded in Virginia toward the end of the 1790s and were a large part of the ways whites understood Gabriel's revolt in Richmond in 1800. Denmark Vesey's rumored plot in Charleston in 1822 centered around the notion that he had been in contact with Haitian leaders.

During the violence and afterwards, events on Saint Domingue served as a counter to white portraits of black subservience and subhumanity. Equally important, Haiti provided useful tactical advantages for African Americans. A number of black sailors and escaped slaves made the island a sanctuary in the nineteenth century. For the greater community of color, the island developed as an emblem of possibility and helped bolster morale and engender action. White fear when exposed to this more abstract sense of black collectivity, however, tended to mask a tentativeness and ambivalence that American people of color may also have had toward Haitian realities. Religious, cultural, and language differences, for example, served to retard the incorporation of slaves and people of color from the island into African-American communities. Ironically, white hysteria may have helped to forge a pan-black consciousness around Haiti where one did not immediately exist.

White hysteria itself, however, merits closer attention. While many white communities, slave holding and otherwise, understood Saint Domingue/Haiti only as an expression of black violence, at various points during the 1790s white reactions contained some ambiguity. Emergent Republicans in the mid-Atlantic and New England states voiced a degree of support for the notion of free colored equality in interpreting the early struggles on the island. More hesitant but still discernable was white support for the French policy of emancipation after 1794. Federalist president John Adams, engaged in the Quasi War with the French Republic later in the decade, supported the separatist inclinations of Haitian leader Toussaint-Louverture. Such reactions, however, had strong political motives; they had as much to do with American ideas about France and the French Revolution as they did with sensibilities about the universality of the rights of man or the injustice of slavery. White antislavery activists experienced a similar two-mindedness. Many seized on the slave violence on the island as proof of slavery's dangers. In a few instances these concerns fueled calls for immediate emancipation, but most often they translated into self-congratulatory sentiments regarding either gradual emancipation in the states north of Maryland or the perceived mildness of slavery in the American South.

In the end, white reactions to the Haitian Revolution demonstrate the fact that unfettered black freedom and citizenship were inconceivable to most white minds in the nineteenth century. As commercial contact between the island nation and the United States dwindled in the antebellum period, Haiti was reduced to a symbol in American minds. Among white commentators, this was made evident in the repeated invocation of "Hayti" as a place of violence and despair. Both Nat Turner's revolt in 1831 and

John Brown's raid of 1859, neither of which had any demonstrable connection to Haiti, were discussed in relation to the island. A similar symbolic use of the Caribbean nation by African Americans is evident in writings such as David Walker's *Appeal* (1829) and in efforts such as those mounted by Prince Saunders to facilitate emigration of free African Americans to Haiti in the 1810s and 1820s. "Hayti," therefore, as a place of anarchy or as a beacon of hope, was imagined by Americans more than it was experienced. As such, exploring its meaning in American minds tells as much about the observers as the observed.

See also Allen, Richard; Haitian Revolution; Jones, Absalom; Nat Turner's Rebellion; Toussaint-Louverture

■ ■ *Bibliography*

Bolster, W. Jeffrey. *Black Jacks: African American Seamen in the Age of Sail.* Cambridge, Mass.: Harvard University Press, 1997.

Dixon, Chris. *African America and Haiti: Emigration and Black Nationalism in the Nineteenth Century.* Contributions in American History, no. 186. Westport, Conn., and London: Greenwood Press, 2000.

Geggus, David P., ed. *The Impact of the Haitian Revolution in the Atlantic World: The Carolina Lowcountry and the Atlantic World.* Columbia: University of South Carolina Press, 2001.

Trouillot, Michel-Rolph. *Silencing the Past: Power and the Production of History.* Boston: Beacon Press, 1995.

JAMES ALEXANDER DUN (2005)

HALEY, ALEX

AUGUST 11, 1921
FEBRUARY 10, 1992

▮ ▮ ▮

Journalist and novelist Alexander Palmer Haley was born in Ithaca, New York, and raised in Henning, Tennessee. He attended Elizabeth City State Teachers College in North Carolina from 1937 to 1939. At age seventeen he left college and enlisted in the Coast Guard, where he eventually served as editor of the official Coast Guard publication, *The Outpost.* In 1959 he retired as chief journalist, a position that had been expressly created for him.

After leaving the Coast Guard, Haley became a freelance writer, contributing to *Reader's Digest, The New York Times Magazine, Harper's, Atlantic,* and *Playboy* (for which he inaugurated the "Playboy Interview" series). He first received widespread attention for *The Autobiography of Malcolm X* (1965). His collaboration with the black na-

tionalist Malcolm X consisted of a series of extended interviews transcribed by Haley; the result was an autobiography related to Haley that was generally praised for vibrancy and fidelity to its subject. The book quickly achieved international success and was translated into many different languages, selling millions of copies in the United States and abroad. As a result, Haley received honorary doctorates in the early 1970s from Simpson College, Howard University, Williams College, and Capitol University.

Haley is best known, however, for his epic novel *Roots: The Saga of an American Family* (1976). Based on Haley's family history as told to him by his maternal grandmother, *Roots* traces Haley's lineage to Kunta Kinte, an African youth who was abducted from his homeland and forced into slavery. Combining factual events with fiction, Roots depicts the African-American saga from its beginnings in Africa, through slavery, emancipation, and the continuing struggle for equality. The novel was an immediate best-seller, and two years after its publication had won 271 awards, including a citation from the judges of the 1977 National Book Awards, the NAACP's Spingarn Medal, and a special Pulitzer Prize. Presented as a television miniseries in 1977, Roots brought the African-American story into the homes of millions. The book and the series generated an unprecedented level of awareness of African-American heritage and served as a spur to black pride.

The reception of Haley's book, however, was not devoid of controversy. Two separate suits were brought against Haley for copyright infringement: One was dismissed, but the other, brought by Harold Courlander, was settled after Haley admitted that several passages from Courlander's book *The African* (1968) appeared verbatim in *Roots.* In addition, some reviewers expressed doubts about the reliability of the research that had gone into the book and voiced frustration at the blend of fact and fiction. After Haley's death, more evidence came to light to suggest that he had inflated the factual claims and plagiarized material for *Roots.*

The unparalleled success of *Roots* gave rise to a widespread interest in genealogy as well as to a proliferation of works dealing specifically with the African-American heritage. *Roots: The Next Generation* was produced as a miniseries in 1979. Haley formed the Kinte Corporation in California and became involved in the production of films and records, the first of which was *Alex Haley Speaks,* which included advice on how to research family histories. In 1980 Haley helped produce *Palmerstown U.S.A.,* a television series loosely based on his childhood experiences in the rural South in the 1930s. In the 1980s Haley lectured widely, made numerous radio and television appearances, and wrote prolifically for popular magazines.

In his last years Haley concentrated on writing a narrative of his paternal ancestry, *Queen: The Story of an American Family.* The book, which Haley intended to be a companion volume to *Roots,* was published and adapted for television the year following his 1992 death in Seattle. Since his death, Haley's reputation, which had suffered in the late 1970s because of the charges of plagiarism, was again attacked, as information came to light that he may have invented parts of his story as presented in *Roots* and presented them as fact.

A subsequent posthumous work, *Mama Flora's Family,* was published and adapted into a television movie in 1998.

See also Literature of the United States; Television

■ ■ *Bibliography*

Baye, Betty Winston. "Alex Haley's Roots Revisited." *Essence* 22, no. 10 (February 1992): 88–92.

Fiedler, Leslie A. *The Inadvertent Epic: From Uncle Tom's Cabin to Roots.* New York: Simon and Schuster, 1982.

Nobile, Philip. "Uncovering Roots." *Village Voice* 38, no. 8 (February 23, 1993): 31–38.

ALEXIS WALKER (1996)
Updated by publisher 2005

HALL, PRINCE

1735?
DECEMBER 4, 1807

┼┼┼─────────────────────

The place and date of civic leader Prince Hall's birth are not known. Recent research has cast doubt on the traditional versions of his early years, which placed his birth in the West Indies. Current evidence indicates that Hall became a member of the School Street Congregational Church of Boston in 1762. In 1770 he was manumitted by William Hall, a Boston craftsman, who probably had owned him since the 1740s. In 1775 Hall petitioned to join Boston's St. John's Lodge of Freemasons and was turned down. Hall and fourteen other free African-American men then sought and received admission to a Masonic lodge affiliated with an Irish regiment in the British army stationed in Boston. Obtaining a permit from the military lodge to participate in some Masonic activities as an independent body, Hall and the others continued as Masons in a limited capacity throughout the Revolutionary War.

Throughout his adult life Hall worked in the Boston area, both as a leather crafter in his shop, the Golden Fleece, and as a caterer. During the Revolutionary War he supplied leather drumheads to the Continental army, and it is also possible that he joined it as a combatant. Discussions of him in the letters of his white and black contemporaries show that they looked upon him as the social and political leader of African Americans in Boston. Thus, in the early years of the war Hall signed petitions to the Continental Congress requesting permission for African Americans to fight in the war. Employing arguments analogous to those used by the revolutionaries to justify their revolt against the British, on January 13, 1777, Hall and others also petitioned the Massachusetts legislature to outlaw slavery.

In 1784 Hall, as master of the provisional African Lodge, applied for a charter from the London Grand Lodge. Although the charter establishing African Lodge 459 was granted in September of that year, Hall did not receive it until April 1787. He then served as its Grand Master until his death at the age of seventy-two. (Several of his annual addresses to the lodge, placing the history of the lodge in the context of Masonic and African history, were published during his lifetime.) In the year after his death, Hall's followers adopted his name for what remains the largest and most highly regarded African-American fraternal order, the Prince Hall Masons.

During Shays's Rebellion in 1786, Hall, acting as a spokesperson for Boston's black community, wrote to assure the Massachusetts state government of his and his fellow Masons' political loyalty and willingness to serve against Shays's followers. However, only months later, Hall formally submitted a suggestion to the legislature that it consider financially assisting blacks who wished to return to Africa and establish an independent state. In both instances the state government declined to act on Hall's petitions.

In his capacity as Grand Master and leader of Boston's African-American community, Hall protested the seizure of three free blacks (one a Mason) in Boston by slave traders, and in February 1788 successfully petitioned the Massachusetts government for their return. In the same document he denounced the slave trade, which contributed significantly to the March 26, 1788, decision banning such trade in Massachusetts. In other letters and petitions to the state government, the politically active Hall demanded full citizenship and the establishment of public schools for blacks. (In 1800 Hall opened in his own home one of the first schools in Boston for free black children.) Hall died in Boston in 1807.

See also Fraternal Orders; Slave Trade

■ ■ *Bibliography*

Grimshaw, William H. *Official History of Freemasonry Among the Colored People in North America.* New York: Macoy, 1903.

Logan, Rayford W., and Michael R. Winston. *Dictionary of American Negro Biography.* New York: Norton, 1982.

Wesley, Charles H. *Prince Hall: Life and Legacy,* 2nd ed. Washington, D.C.: United Supreme Council, 1983.

PETER SCHILLING (1996)

HAMER, FANNIE LOU (TOWNSEND, FANNIE LOU)

OCTOBER 6, 1917
MARCH 14, 1977

▪▪▪

Civil rights activist Fannie Lou Townsend was born to Ella Bramlett and James Lee Townsend in Montgomery County, Mississippi. Her parents were sharecroppers, and the family moved to Sunflower County, Mississippi, when she was two. Forced to spend most of her childhood and teenage years toiling in cotton fields for white landowners, Townsend was able to complete only six years of schooling. Despite wrenching rural poverty and the harsh economic conditions of the Mississippi Delta, she maintained an enduring optimism. She learned the value of self-respect and outspokenness through her close relationship with her mother. In 1944 she married Perry Hamer, moved with him to Ruleville, and worked as a sharecropper on a plantation owned by W. D. Marlowe.

During her years on the Marlowe plantation, Hamer rose to the position of time- and recordkeeper. In this position she acquired a reputation for a sense of fairness and a willingness to speak to the landowner on behalf of aggrieved sharecroppers. She began to take steps to directly challenge the racial and economic inequality that had so circumscribed her life after meeting civil rights workers from the Student Nonviolent Coordinating Committee (SNCC) in 1962. In Mississippi SNCC was mounting a massive voter registration and desegregation campaign aimed at empowering African Americans to change their own lives.

Inspired by the organization's commitment to challenging the racial status quo, Hamer and seventeen other black volunteers attempted to register to vote in Indianola, Mississippi, on August 31, 1962, but were unable to pass the necessary literacy test, which was designed to prevent blacks from voting. As a result of this action, she and her family were dismissed from the plantation, she was threatened with physical harm by Ruleville whites, and she was constantly harassed by local police. Eventually, she was forced to flee Ruleville and spent three months in Tallahatchie County, Mississippi, before returning in December.

In January 1963 Hamer passed the literacy test and became a registered voter. Despite the persistent hostility of local whites, she continued her commitment to civil rights activities and became an SNCC field secretary. By 1964 Hamer had fully immersed herself in a wide range of local civil rights activities, including SNCC-sponsored voter registration campaigns and clothing- and food-distribution drives. At that time she was a central organizer and vice-chairperson of the Mississippi Freedom Democratic Party (MFDP), a parallel political party formed under the auspices of SNCC in response to black exclusion from the state Democratic Party. Hamer was one of the sixty-eight MFDP delegates elected at a state convention of the party to attend the Democratic National Convention in Atlantic City in the summer of 1964. At the convention the MFDP delegates demanded to be seated and argued that they were the only legitimate political representatives of the Mississippi Democratic Party because unlike the regular party, which formed and operated at the exclusion of blacks, their party was open to all Mississippians of voting age.

Hamer's televised testimony to the convention on behalf of the MFDP propelled her into the national spotlight. A national audience watched as she described the economic reprisals that faced African Americans who attempted to register to vote and recounted the beating that she and five other activists had received in June 1963 in a Winona County, Mississippi, jail. Hamer's proud and unwavering commitment to American democracy and equality inspired hundreds of Americans to send telegrams supporting the MFDP's challenge to the southern political status quo. Although the MFDP delegates were not seated by the convention, Hamer and the party succeeded in mobilizing a massive black voter turnout and publicizing the racist exclusionary tactics of the state Democratic Party.

By the mid-1960s SNCC had become ideologically divided and Hamer's ties to the organization became more tenuous. However, she continued to focus her political work on black political empowerment and community development. Under her leadership the MFDP continued to challenge the all-white state Democratic Party. In 1964 Hamer unsuccessfully ran for Congress on the MFDP ticket, and one year later she spearheaded an intense lobbying effort to challenge the seating of Mississippi's five congressmen in the House of Representatives. She played an integral role in bringing the Head Start Program for children to Ruleville and organized the Freedom Farm Cooperative for displaced agricultural workers. In 1969 she founded the Freedom Farm Corporation in Sunflower, a cooperative farming and landowning venture to help poor blacks become more self-sufficient. It fed well over five thousand families before collapsing in 1974. Three years later, after over a decade of activism, she died from breast cancer and heart disease.

Fannie Lou Hamer was a symbol of defiance and indomitable black womanhood that inspired many in the civil rights movement. Morehouse College and Howard University, among others, have honored her devotion to African-American civil rights with honorary doctoral degrees. Her words "I'm sick and tired of being sick and tired" bear testament to her lifelong struggle to challenge racial injustice and economic exploitation.

See also Civil Rights Movement, U.S.; Mississippi Freedom Democratic Party; Student Nonviolent Coordinating Committee (SNCC)

■ ■ *Bibliography*

Collier-Thomas, Bettye, and Franklin, V. P., eds. *Sisters in the Struggle: African American Women in the Civil Rights–Black Power Movement.* New York: New York University Press, 2001.

Crawford, Vicki L., Jacqueline Anne Rouse, and Barbara Woods. *Women in the Civil Rights Movement.* Brooklyn: Carlson, 1990.

Jordan, June. *Fannie Lou Hamer.* New York: Crowell, 1972.

Kling, Susan. *Fannie Lou Hamer.* Chicago: Women for Racial and Economic Quality, 1979.

Lee, Chana Kai. *For Freedom's Sake: The Life of Fannie Lou Hamer.* Urbana: University of Illinois Press, 1999.

CHANA KAI LEE (1996)
Updated bibliography

HAMILTON, WILLIAM

1773
DECEMBER 9, 1836

The abolitionist William Hamilton was born in New York sometime in 1773. He was reputed to be the illegitimate son of the American statesman Alexander Hamilton, the nation's first secretary of the treasury, though evidence for the accuracy of this rumor is lacking. He made a living as a carpenter, but he made his name as a powerful orator working to improve the conditions of African Americans. In 1808 he cofounded and became president of the New York African Society for Mutual Relief, which provided funds for the widows and children of its members.

One of the country's earliest black abolitionists, Hamilton delivered an antislavery speech, *An Address to the New York African Society for Mutual Relief,* on January 2, 1809. The address was published a week later at his listeners' request. In the speech, Hamilton celebrated the recent ending of the American slave trade and promoted the education of African Americans. He expressed confidence that "soon shall that contumelious assertion of the proud be proved false, to wit, that Africans do not possess minds as ingenious as other men."

In 1820 Hamilton was one of the founding members of the African Methodist Episcopal Zion (AMEZ) Church in New York City. On July 4, 1827, he gave a major oration at the church to commemorate the New York State emancipation statute. While in his earlier speech he insisted on the equality of the races, in this oration he proclaimed the superiority of blacks, noting that "if there is any difference in the species, that difference is in favour of the people of colour." Arguing that no white American could claim superiority to African Americans as long as he continued to hold slaves, Hamilton asked, "Does he act in conformity to true philosophy?"

Having made clear his contempt for the true motives of white men—"authority and gold"—and having accomplished his expressed goal "to unravel this mystery of superiority," Hamilton proceeded to exhort the young men of his audience to further study and education, and to rouse themselves from "frivolity and lethargy." Giving the lie to the supposed lethargy of African Americans, Hamilton was tireless in his endeavors on their behalf. He helped to organize the first annual Convention for the Improvement of Free People of Color held in Philadelphia on September 20, 1830. As president of the fourth annual convention, held in New York in June, 1834, he gave a well-received speech published as Minutes of the Fourth Annual Convention, for the Improvement of the Free People of Color. As a member of the Phoenix and Philomathean societies he worked towards improving the education of African Americans.

Strongly opposed to the American Colonization Society, Hamilton was a staunch supporter of the abolitionist William Lloyd Garrison, whom he knew personally. He publicized Garrison's *Liberator,* and helped in the publication of Garrison's *Thoughts on Colonization.* Hamilton died in or near New York City in 1836. His sons, Robert and Thomas, established two newspapers *The People's Press* and *The Anglo-African.*

See also Abolition; African Methodist Episcopal Zion Church; *Liberator, The*; Slave Narratives; Varick, James

■ ■ *Bibliography*

Boardman, Helen M. "First Families of Manhattan." *Phylon* (Second Quarter 1944): 138–142.

Ottley, Roi, and William J. Weatherby. *The Negro in New York.* New York: New York Public Library, 1967.

Porter, Dorothy, ed. *Early Negro Writing: 1760–1837.* Boston: Beacon Press, 1971. Reprint: Baltimore, MD: Black Classic Press, 1994.

Ripley, C. Peter, ed. *The Black Abolitionist Papers.* Volume III, *The United States, 1830–1846.* Chapel Hill: University of North Carolina Press, 1991.

Walls, William. *The African Methodist Episcopal Zion Church: Reality of the Black Church.* Charlotte: A.M.E. Zion Publishing House, 1974.

LYDIA MCNEILL (1996)

HAMMON, BRITON

C. 18TH CENTURY

❙❙❙

All that is known about the writer Briton Hammon is gleaned from his publication, *A Narrative of the Uncommon Sufferings, and Surprising Deliverance of Briton Hammon, A Negro Man,—Servant to General Winslow, of Marshfield, in New England; Who Returned to Boston, after Having Been Absent Almost Thirteen Years* (Boston, 1760).

Hammon was either a servant or a slave of General Winslow of Marshfield, Massachusetts. In 1747 he sailed, with Winslow's consent, from Plymouth, Massachusetts, to the West Indies. He stayed several weeks in Jamaica, was shipwrecked on the coast of Florida, and was captured by Native Americans. He escaped with a Spanish schooner and was imprisoned in a Spanish dungeon in Havana for almost five years because he refused to serve on board a Spanish ship. Hammon then escaped again and went to England; he signed on a ship bound for Boston and found his former master, General Winslow, also on board. Both returned to Marshfield, where Hammon wrote his account of thirteen years of traveling.

Hammon's narrative has long been considered the first prose work by an African-American writer. Some literary historians credit him with writing the first slave narrative. His status is vague. In the title he used the word *servant,* and from his description it is not clear whether he was a privileged slave or a servant in a more modern sense. According to Hammon, he was paid to be a cook and to do other jobs. There is no information about the purposes of his travels. In the preface to his *Narrative,* Hammon explains "To the Reader" that his "capacities and conditions of life are very low" and asks for the reader's understanding.

See also Autobiography, U.S.

■ ■ *Bibliography*

Logan, Rayford W., and Michael R. Winston, eds. *Dictionary of American Negro Biography.* New York: Norton, 1982.

DORIS DZIWAS (1996)

HAMMON, JUPITER

1711
C. 1806

❙❙❙

Poet and preacher Jupiter Hammon was born on Long Island, New York, and raised in slavery to the Lloyd family. Little is known about his personal circumstances; scholars speculate that he attended school and was permitted access to his master's library. He is known to have purchased a Bible from his master in 1773. A favored slave in the Lloyd household, he worked as a servant, farmhand, and artisan. In early 1761 Hammon published the first poem by a black person to appear in British North America, titled "An Evening Thought. Salvation by Christ with Penitential Cries: Composed by Jupiter Hammon, a Negro belonging to Mr. Lloyd of Queen's Village, on Long Island, the 25th of December, 1760." When British troops invaded Long Island, Hammon fled with the Lloyd family to Hartford, where he remained for the duration of the Revolutionary War. His second extant poem, "An Address to Miss Phillis Wheatly [sic], Ethiopian Poetess, in Boston, who came from Africa at eight years of age, and soon became acquainted with the gospel of Jesus Christ," was published there in 1778. In 1779 a work called "An Essay on Ten Virgins" was advertised, but no copy of it remains. Hammon's sermon, "A Winter Piece: Being a Serious Exhortation, with a Call to the Unconverted; and a Short Contemplation on the Death of Jesus Christ," to which is appended the seventeen-quatrain verse, "A Poem for Children, with Thoughts on Death," appeared in Hartford in 1782. Hammon returned to Oyster Bay, Long Island, later that year, and a second prose work, "An Evening's Improvement, Shewing the Necessity of Beholding the Lamb of God," which concludes with "A Dialogue, Entitled, the

ENCYCLOPEDIA of AFRICAN-AMERICAN CULTURE and HISTORY
second edition

Kind Master and the Dutiful Servant," was published in 1786. Hammon spoke to members of the African Society in New York on September 24, 1786. The text of that speech, "An Address to the Negroes of the State of New York," was printed in New York early in 1787.

Hammon's poems follow a strict, mechanical rhyme scheme and meter, and, like his sermons, exhort the reader to seek salvation by obeying the will of God. He appears to have extended this notion of Christian piety to his domestic situation and refused to speak out in public against slavery. However, even as he urged African Americans to "obey our masters," he questioned whether slavery was "right, and lawful, in the sight of God." "I do not wish to be free," he said at age seventy-five, "yet I should be glad, if others, especially the young negroes were to be free." The exact date of his death, and the place of his burial, are not known.

See also Poetry, U.S.; Wheatley, Phillis

■ ■ *Bibliography*

Kaplan, Sidney, and Emma Nogrady Kaplan. *The Black Presence in the Era of the American Revolution 1770–1800.* Revised edition. Amherst: University of Massachusetts Press, 1989.

Ransom, Samuel A., Jr. *America's First Negro Poet: The Complete Works of Jupiter Hammon of Long Island.* Port Washington, NY: Kennikat Press, 1970. Includes Oscar Wegelin, "Biographical Sketch of Jupiter Hammon" (1915) and Vernon Loggins, "Critical Analysis of the Works of Jupiter Hammon" (1900).

QUANDRA PRETTYMAN (1996)

HAMMONS, DAVID

1943

Born in Springfield, Illinois, artist David Hammons moved to Los Angeles to study graphic design and fine arts in 1964. He met his most influential teacher, Charles White, at Otis Art Institute, where he studied from 1968 to 1972. In the late 1960s and early 1970s Hammons produced body prints that investigated African-American identity. Recurring motifs included self-portraiture, the American flag, and the spade shape. In the early and mid-1970s Hammons moved into assemblage sculpture, continuing the use of culturally charged symbols for African Americans including spades (shovels), chains, barbecue bones, and African-American hair.

Hammons moved to New York City in 1975. He showed in galleries but also on the streets of Harlem and the East Village. Well-known to the avant-garde art world and in the African-American art community, he took on something of legendary status, amplified by his inaccessibility (he never had a telephone) and his flair for the dramatic. Benchwork works included *Higher Goals* (1983), a series of six-story-tall basketball hoop sculptures with a typically punning title, and *How Do You Like Me Now?*, a controversial portrait of the Rev. Jesse Jackson as a white man with blond hair.

In the early 1990s Hammons reluctantly accepted international recognition with shows at venues such as the Museum of Modern Art (New York) and Documenta (Kassel, Germany) and grants including the MacArthur Award.

See also Art in the United States, Contemporary

■ ■ *Bibliography*

Cannon, Steve, Tom Finkelpearl, and Kellie Jones. *David Hammons: Rousing the Rubble.* Cambridge, Mass.: MIT Press, 1991.

TOM FINKELPEARL (1996)

HAMPTON, LIONEL LEO

APRIL 12, 1908
AUGUST 31, 2002

Jazz vibraphonist and bandleader Lionel Hampton was born in Louisville, Kentucky, and raised in Birmingham, Alabama, then in Chicago. Most sources list his birth year as 1909; his autobiography, however, states that he was born in 1908. Hampton introduced the vibraphone to jazz and was widely regarded as a virtuoso performer. Like many jazz musicians, he received his first musical experiences in the black church, learning to play drums in his grandmother's Birmingham Holiness congregation. He received his first formal lessons on percussion while in elementary school. Hampton later joined the Chicago Defender Youth Band, directed by Major N. Clark Smith, an influential educator who nurtured many famous jazz musicians, among them Milt Hinton and Nat "King" Cole. By his second year of high school, Hampton was playing drums regularly with local musicians, including Les Hite and Detroit Shannon.

In the mid-1920s Hampton moved to Culver City, California., where he joined Reb's Legion Club Forty-Fives and made some of his first recordings. On the West Coast he met Gladys Riddle, who later became his wife and business partner until her death in 1971. In 1930 he began a series of recordings with Louis Armstrong and His Sebastian's Cotton Club Orchestra, his first recordings on vibraphone. During this time, he also made appearances in movies with Les Hite (the Columbia film *Depths Below*) and Louis Armstrong (*Pennies from Heaven*).

In the mid-1930s Hampton formed his own group and worked regularly along the West Coast. In 1936 he joined Benny Goodman's Quartet, which included Teddy Wilson, Gene Krupa, and later guitarist Charlie Christian. The series of Goodman engagements (such as the famous 1938 Carnegie Hall concert) and recordings catapulted him to stardom as jazz's most influential vibraphonist. Through Hampton's performances the vibraphone became a jazz instrument of recognition. During this same period he also continued to record as the leader of his own sessions until leaving Goodman in 1940. Hampton performed and recorded continuously with great commercial success for the next forty-five years in the United States and abroad with various groups, one of the jazz world's most popular and highly regarded musicians.

Throughout his long career Hampton recognized and nurtured young talent. A partial list of musicians who have played in his groups over the years reads like a who's who of jazz history: Howard McGhee, Dexter Gordon, Fletcher Henderson, Oscar Peterson, Ben Webster, Coleman Hawkins, Johnny Griffin, Quincy Jones, Benny Carter, Dinah Washington, Betty Carter, Nat "King" Cole, and Joe Williams, among others. Hampton is perhaps best known for his showy, energetic stage presence and his hard-driving swing style, which can be heard in such compositions as "Flying Home," "Stompology," and "Down Home Stomp." Over the years he joined Goodman and Wilson for reunion concerts and remained actively engaged in philanthropic and civic activities.

Hampton suffered personal tragedy when his New York apartment was destroyed by fire in January 1997. However, he continued to perform, and in 1998 he was the star of a gala concert on his ninetieth birthday. After suffering a series of strokes and being in ill health for a number of years, Hampton died at the age of ninety-four in 2002.

See also Armstrong, Louis; Jazz

■ ■ *Bibliography*

Hampton, Lionel, with James Haskins. *Hamp: An Autobiography*. New York: Amistad, 1993.

GUTHRIE P. RAMSEY JR. (1996)
Updated by publisher 2005

HAMPTON INSTITUTE

In 1868 in Hampton, Virginia, Samuel Chapman Armstrong founded Hampton Normal and Agricultural Institute as a nondenominational and coeducational school where young African Americans were to be trained as teachers. Armstrong, a white man, was convinced that most freedmen's schools were failures because they did not address blacks' most pressing needs. He believed that the experience of slavery had caused African Americans to degenerate into a morally deficient caste, and he accepted the stereotypical image of the freedman as poor, lazy, insolent, and lawless. To succeed, he argued, educators had to respond to these harsh realities by developing an entirely new approach to education for blacks. In addition to offering academic instruction, schools had to contribute to their pupils' moral development and help them attain material prosperity. Armstrong intended Hampton to be a model school, where generations of black teachers would be indoctrinated with his ideas.

Because Armstrong believed that blacks would continue to serve as the South's laboring class in the foreseeable future, Hampton Institute became the first school for African Americans to adopt a comprehensive system of industrial education. All students were required to labor in the school's farms and trade shops for two full days each week. The stated goal of this manual-education program was not to train skilled craftsmen but to develop "character" and to foster a spirit of self-reliance among the students. Hampton's white teachers reported that the work system helped their pupils to appreciate the dignity of labor and to understand that prosperity could be gained only through hard work.

Students' academic pursuits were closely coordinated with their work in the shops and fields. Hampton's supporters argued that "book learning" was useful to most African Americans only to the extent to which it could make them more productive and prosperous workers. Therefore, the institute's teachers emphasized only the development of "practical" skills such as writing, botany, and simple arithmetic. As a result, by the time students completed the three-year normal program, they had received educations equivalent only to grammar-school programs in the North.

To supplement the institute's academic and industrial work, Armstrong developed a system of social instruction designed to "civilize" the students. Since Hampton was primarily a boarding school, its teachers could control their students' behavior every hour of the day. In their dormitories, students received instruction in Christian morality, personal hygiene, housekeeping, and etiquette.

Students in carpentry shop class at Hampton Institute, c. 1900. THE LIBRARY OF CONGRESS

Above all, they learned to emulate the behavior and seek the respect of their white neighbors.

The influence of Armstrong's educational philosophy, known as the Hampton Idea, soon spread throughout the South as Booker T. Washington and hundreds of other graduates applied the lessons they had learned at the institute to their own schools. Substantial financial support from whites in the North enabled Hampton and its imitators to grow rapidly. Many whites found Hampton's pragmatic approach, with its emphasis on manual labor and self-help rather than social and political activism, enormously appealing. The institute offered the hope that the nation's "race problem" could be solved without disrupting the socioeconomic status quo. The General Education Board and other philanthropic foundations used their financial influence to guide Hampton's growth along even more conservative directions, and to encourage other schools to adopt similar curriculums. Their support helped the institute to develop into one of America's larg-

est and wealthiest black schools, and guaranteed that the Hampton Idea would become ascendant in the field of African-American education by the start of the twentieth century.

Hampton Institute has always been criticized by African Americans who believe that it served only to perpetuate their socioeconomic subordination. The school appeared to be training its students to fill precisely the same roles that blacks held under slavery. As the Hampton Idea gained widespread support among whites, it seemed increasingly likely that industrial education would soon be the only form of schooling available to blacks. As a result, criticism of the institute grew sharper, especially among black intellectuals.

In 1903 W. E. B. Du Bois published his first major attack on industrial education, and was soon recognized as the leading critic of the Hampton Idea. While Du Bois and other critics conceded that many African Americans could benefit from "practical" education, they felt that blacks

A mathematics class paces off distances at Hampton Institute, Virginia, c. 1900. Founded by General Samuel Chapman Armstrong in 1868, Hampton Institute became the model for industrial education for African Americans throughout the South. THE LIBRARY OF CONGRESS.

also needed access to higher education in order to progress. They urged the institute to place greater emphasis on academics and to encourage its students to aspire to something more than life as manual laborers. They complained that in its pursuit of material prosperity and white approval, Hampton too often sacrificed black dignity.

These criticisms had little direct impact on the institute's curriculum until the 1920s. After World War I, many states embarked on crusades of educational reform and began to demand that teachers be better educated. Increasing numbers of Hampton's graduates failed to meet these higher standards. Institute officials first attempted to solve the problem by making only slight modifications to the academic program; eventually, however, they were forced to raise their admissions standards and to offer college-level courses. By 1927 over 40 percent of Hampton students were enrolled in the collegiate program. These students, who were more sympathetic to Du Bois's argu-

ments than their predecessors had been, became increasingly critical of their school.

In 1927 a protest over a relatively minor social issue quickly grew into a general strike. Student leaders demanded that the institute raise the quality of its teaching, abolish key elements of the industrial system, hire more African Americans, and grant students an expanded role in administration. The strike was quickly crushed, but Hampton officials had no alternative but to respond to the students' demands. In 1929 the institute declared that it would no longer accept students who had not already completed high school. The following year, to emphasize its shift from Armstrong's industrial model to a more traditional program of higher education, the school formally changed its name from Hampton Normal and Agricultural Institute to Hampton Institute. In 1984 the school—having developed into a prominent liberal-arts and teachers' college with over four thousand students—changed its name to Hampton University.

See also Du Bois, W. E. B.; Education in the United States; Washington, Booker T.

■■ *Bibliography*

Anderson, James D. *The Education of Blacks in the South, 1860–1935.* Chapel Hill: University of North Carolina Press, 1988.

Lovelace, Carey. "Carrie Mae Weems at the International Center of Photography, Uptown." *Art in America* 89, no. 6 (June 2001): 123.

Peabody, Francis G. *Education for Life: The Story of Hampton Institute.* Garden City, N.Y.: Doubleday, Page & Co., 1918.

GREGORY J. MURPHY (1996)
Updated bibliography

HANCOCK, GORDON BLAINE

JUNE 23, 1884
JULY 24, 1970

▐▐▐

The sociologist and minister Gordon Hancock was born in rural Ninety-Six, a township in Greenwood County, South Carolina. He was educated in Newberry, a neighboring town, by a private instructor and acquired a teacher's certificate in 1902. In 1904 he matriculated at Benedict College in Columbia, South Carolina, receiving a bachelor of arts degree in 1911 and a bachelor of divinity in 1912. Ordained in 1911, he became pastor of Bethlehem Baptist Church in Newberry. He was named principal of Seneca Institute, a coed Baptist boarding school for blacks in Seneca, South Carolina, in 1912. Hancock left South Carolina in 1918 to attend Colgate University in Hamilton, New York. One of only two blacks enrolled in the school, Hancock earned his second B.A. in 1919 and his second B.D. in 1920.

That same year, Hancock entered Harvard as a graduate fellow in sociology and earned a master's degree in 1921. Shortly thereafter, he accepted a professorship at Virginia Union University in Richmond, Virginia, where he organized one of the first courses on race relations at any black college. In 1925 he accepted the pastorship at Richmond's Moore Street Baptist Church. He also wrote a weekly column for the Associated Negro Press that appeared in 114 black newspapers and preached the merits of interracial cooperation and black self-help.

In 1931 Hancock founded the Torrance School of Race Relations at Virginia Union. During the Depression, he originated the Double Duty Dollar idea, encouraging blacks to patronize black-owned businesses. Disdainful of what he viewed as overambition among blacks, he also promoted a Hold Your Job campaign, emphasizing the importance of maintaining a solid black working class.

Characterized by some as an accommodationist, Hancock looked for support from southern white moderates in trying to end segregation without sacrificing black identity, self-help, and racial solidarity. Hancock believed that blacks should be accorded full equality, and he advocated black economic, cultural, social, and political self-development.

Alarmed by the growing racial tension and aggression in the South during World War II, Hancock convened fifty-two black southern leaders at the Southern Conference on Race Relations in Durham, North Carolina, in October 1942 to propose a "New Charter of Race Relations" for the South. Serving as director of the conference, Hancock helped produce the Durham Manifesto, a statement issued by the conference in December of that year, outlining the leaders' carefully nuanced demands for improvements in the position of African Americans in the South. Following this, the black leaders met with white moderates at a conference in Richmond and, with Hancock again serving as director, agreed to form the Southern Regional Council.

Hancock took a slightly more aggressive approach to racial issues in the years following the Durham conference, questioning the merits of interracial cooperation with southern whites and more openly attacking racial segregation. Hancock's position as a spokesperson for the black community began to fade just as the civil rights movement started to receive national attention. He was named professor emeritus at Virginia Union and retired from there in 1952, removing himself almost entirely from the public spotlight. In 1963, Hancock left his pastorship at Moore Street Baptist Church. He spent his later years collecting black spirituals as well as composing and publishing his own songs (*Two Homeward Songs,* 1965). Hancock died at his home in Richmond, Virginia, in 1970.

See also Durham Manifesto; Sociology

■■ *Bibliography*

Gavins, Raymond. *The Perils and Prospects of Southern Black Leadership: Gordon Blaine Hancock, 1884–1970.* Durham, N.C.: Duke University Press, 1977.

LOUISE P. MAXWELL (1996)
LYDIA MCNEILL (1996)

HANCOCK, HERBIE

APRIL 12, 1940

Born and raised in Chicago, jazz pianist and composer Herbert Jeffrey Hancock started formal piano lessons at the age of seven and became a prodigy, performing the first movement of Mozart's D major "Coronation" piano concerto (K. 537) with the Chicago Symphony Orchestra at the age of eleven. He formed his own jazz ensemble at Hyde Park High School, and went on to study engineering while he wrote for the big band at Grinnell College (1956–1960) and attended Roosevelt University (1960).

After graduation, Hancock played as a sideman in Chicago for saxophonist Coleman Hawkins, and in 1961 he was hired by trumpeter Donald Byrd. Hancock also played with saxophonist Phil Woods and bandleader and saxophonist Oliver Nelson, and in 1962 he made his recording debut as a leader on *Takin' Off*, which featured his gospel-tinged "Watermelon Man," a tune later popularized by percussionist Mongo Santamaria.

In 1962 Hancock moved to New York and worked with Eric Dolphy and Clark Terry before joining Miles Davis's quintet in 1963, contributing artfully atonal improvisations and modal compositions to the trumpeter's *My Funny Valentine* (1964), *E.S.P.* (1965), *Miles Smiles* (1966), *Nefertiti* (1967), *In a Silent Way* (1969), and *Big Fun* (1969). During this time Hancock continued recording as a leader on *Empyrean Isles* (containing his "Cantaloupe Island," 1964), *Maiden Voyage* (including "Dolphin Dance," 1965), and *Speak like a Child* (1968).

Introduced to electric instruments during his eight years with Davis's landmark quintet, Hancock formed his own sextet, and from 1971 to 1973 he further explored the assimilation of the rhythms and electric textures of rock and funk with jazz, a style that came to be known as "fusion." In 1973 Hancock released *Headhunters*, an album that gained him a wider audience, and gave him his first hit single, "Chameleon." His subsequent albums, *Thrust* (1974) and *Manchild* (1975), experimented with popular rhythm-and-blues dance idioms and were deplored by many jazz critics. During this time, however, Hancock led a double career as he continued to work in the same hard-bop vein he had pursued with Davis in the 1960s. In 1976 and 1977 he reunited with his former colleagues from Davis's quintet, touring and recording under the name V.S.O.P. In 1983 Hancock released his second hit single, "Rockit," on the rap-influenced *Future Shock* (1983). Hancock has also gained renown as a composer for films, including *Blow Up* (1966), *Death Wish* (1975), *A Soldier's Story* (1984), and *Round Midnight*, for which he won an Academy Award for best score in 1986. In the 1990s he continued to pursue parallel careers with his own electric groups, as well as in mainstream jazz contexts that include solo performances, duos with Chick Corea, a trio with bassist Buster Williams and Al Foster, and with V.S.O.P. In 2004 Hancock won the National Endowment of the Arts Award and received the National Endowment for the Arts Jazz Masters Fellowship, the highest honor bestowed upon jazz musicians.

See also Davis, Miles; Jazz

■ ■ *Bibliography*

Mandel, Howard. "Herbie Hancock: Of Films, Fairlights, Funk . . . and All That Other Jazz." *Down Beat* 53, no. 7 (July 1986): 16–19.

Mehegan, John. "Discussion: Herbie Hancock Talks to John Mehegan." *Jazz* 3, no. 5 (1964).

Townley, R. "Hancock Plugs In." *Down Beat* 41, no. 17 (1974).

SCOTT DEVEAUX (1996)
Updated by publisher 2005

HANSBERRY, LORRAINE

MAY 19, 1930
JANUARY 12, 1965

Playwright Lorraine Hansberry was the youngest child of a nationally prominent African-American family. Houseguests during her childhood included Paul Robeson and Duke Ellington. Hansberry became interested in theater while in high school, and in 1948 she went on to study drama and stage design at the University of Wisconsin. Instead of completing her degree, however, she moved to New York, worked at odd jobs, and wrote. In 1959 her first play, *A Raisin in the Sun*, was produced and was both a critical and commercial success. It broke the record for longest-running play by a black author and won the New York Drama Critics Circle Award. Hansberry was the first African American and the youngest person ever to win that award. The play, based on an incident in the author's own life, tells the story of a black family that attempts to move into a white neighborhood in Chicago. Critics praised Hansberry's ability to deal with a racial issue and at the same time explore the American dream of freedom and the search for a better life. The play was turned into a film in 1961, and then was adapted as a musical, *Raisin*, which won a Tony Award in 1974.

Hansberry's second play, *The Sign in Sidney Brustein's Window*, focuses on white intellectual political involvement. Less successful than *A Raisin in the Sun,* it closed after a brief run at the time of Hansberry's death from cancer in 1965. After her death, Hansberry's former husband, Robert B. Nemiroff, whom she had married in 1953, edited her writings and plays, and produced two volumes: *To Be Young, Gifted and Black* (1969) and *Les Blancs: The Collected Last Plays of Lorraine Hansberry* (1972). Her unproduced screenplay for *A Raisin in the Sun* was published in 1992. *To Be Young, Gifted and Black* was presented as a play and became the longest-running Off-Broadway play of the 1968–1969 season.

See also Drama

■ ■ *Bibliography*

Johnson, Brett. "Recasting a Classic: Lorraine Hansberry's *A Raisin in the Sun*—45 Years Later." *Essence* 35, no. 12 (June 2004): 126.

Keppel, Ben. *The Work of Democracy: Ralph Bunche, Kenneth B. Clarke, Lorraine Hansberry, and the Cultural Politics of Race.* Cambridge, Mass: Harvard University Press, 1995.

"Lorraine Hansberry." *Concise Dictionary of American Literary Biography: The New Consciousness, 1941–1968.* Detroit, Mich: Gale, 1987.

LILY PHILLIPS (1996)
Updated bibliography

HARLEM, NEW YORK

Harlem, New York, is bounded roughly by 110th Street on the south, 155th Street on the north, Morningside Drive on the west, and Saint Nicholas Avenue and the East River on the east. During the twentieth century Harlem became the most famous African-American community in the United States. Prior to 1900, Harlem had been primarily a white neighborhood. In the 1870s, with the growth of commuter rail service, it evolved from an isolated, impoverished village in the northern reaches of Manhattan into a wealthy residential suburb.

THE CREATION OF A BLACK ENCLAVE

With the opening of a subway line extending along Lenox Avenue in the early years of the twentieth century, a flurry of real estate speculation contributed to a substantial increase in building. At the time, the population of Harlem was largely English and German, with increasing numbers of Jewish immigrants. By 1904, however, Harlem's economic prosperity and expansion ceased as a result of high rental costs and excessive construction. In that same year, Phillip A. Payton Jr., a black realtor, founded the Afro-American Realty Company with the intention of leasing vacant white-owned buildings and renting them to African Americans. Although the company survived for only four years, due to Payton's unwise investments, it played a pivotal role in opening up Harlem to African Americans.

Coupled with this development, black migration from the South during the early years of the new century dramatically altered Harlem's composition until by 1930 it had become a largely all-black enclave. In 1890 there were approximately 25,000 African Americans in Manhattan. By 1910 that number had more than tripled to 90,000. In the following decade the black population increased to approximately 150,000 and more than doubled by 1930 to over 325,000. In Harlem itself the black population rose from approximately 50,000 in 1914 to about 80,000 in 1920 to about 200,000 by 1930.

Harlem was called a city within a city, because it contained the normal gamut of classes, businesses, and cultural and recreational institutions traditionally identified with urban living. By the 1920s, moreover, Harlem's place in American intellectual and political history had progressed significantly. This transition was fueled on the cultural scene by the literary and artistic activity collectively called the Harlem Renaissance. Emerging after renewed racism and a series of race riots during the Red Summer of 1919 squelched the promise that African Americans would gain racial equality in return for military service in World War I, the Harlem Renaissance reflected the evolution of what was called a New Negro spirit and determination. As Alain Locke, one of its acknowledged leaders, explained, self-respect and self-dependence became characteristics of the New Negro movement, which were exemplified in every facet of cultural, intellectual, and political life.

THE AFRICAN-AMERICAN CULTURAL CAPITAL

Represented by poets such as Claude McKay, Langston Hughes, and Countee Cullen; novelists like Zora Neale Hurston, Jean Toomer, and Jessie Fauset; artists like Aaron Douglas; photographers like James VanDerZee; and social scientists and philosophers like E. Franklin Frazier, Alain Locke, and W. E. B. Du Bois, the Harlem Renaissance was national in scope but came to be identified with the emerging African-American cultural capital, Harlem. The outpouring of literary and artistic production that comprised the Harlem Renaissance also led to a number of social gatherings at which the black intelligentsia mingled and exchanged ideas. Many of the most celebrated of

Lenox Avenue, Harlem, June 14, 1938. *Photographer Berenice Abbott included this image of Lenox Avenue in her collection* Changing New York: Photographs by Berenice Abbott, 1935–1938. PHOTOGRAPHY COLLECTION, MIRIAM AND IRA D. WALLACH DIVISION OF ART, PRINTS AND PHOTOGRAPHS, THE NEW YORK PUBLIC LIBRARY, ASTOR, LENOX AND TILDEN FOUNDATIONS.

these events were held at the home of A'Lelia Walker, daughter of Madame C. J. Walker, who had moved the base of her multimillion-dollar beauty care industry to Harlem in 1913.

Also fostering Harlem's growth in the 1920s were a series of political developments. Both the National Association for the Advancement of Colored People (NAACP) and the National Urban League established offices in the area. Moreover, by 1920 two major New York black newspapers, the *New York Age* and the *Amsterdam News,* moved their printing operations and editorial offices to Harlem. Socialists A. Philip Randolph and Chandler Owen established their offices in Harlem as well and from there they edited and published their newspaper, the *Messenger,* beginning in 1917. Nothing, however, caught the attention of Harlemites as quickly as the 1916 arrival of Marcus Garvey, who established the headquarters of the Universal

Negro Improvement Association (UNIA) in the district. Garvey's emphasis on race pride and the creation of black businesses and factories, and his appeal to the masses, awakened and galvanized the Harlem community.

By 1915 Harlem had become the entertainment capital of black America. Performers gravitated to Harlem and to New York City's entertainment industry. Musicians such as Willie "The Lion" Smith, Fats Waller, and James P. Johnson created a version of early jazz piano known as the Harlem Stride around the time of World War I. After 1920, bandleaders such as Fletcher Henderson, Duke Ellington, and Chick Webb laid the foundation for big-band jazz. (Early in the 1940s, at clubs such as Minton's Playhouse and Monroe's, a revolution would occur in jazz. Individuals such as Thelonious Monk, Charlie Parker, and Dizzy Gillespie moved away from swing, using advanced harmonies and substitute chords, creating bebop jazz.)

Lafayette Theatre in Harlem. CORBIS

Harlem also became a major center of popular dance. On the stage, Florence Mills was perhaps Harlem's most popular theatrical dancer in the 1920s; 150,000 people turned out for her funeral in 1927. Tap dance flourished in Harlem as well. The roster of well-known performers included the Whitman Sisters, Buck and Bubbles, the Nicholas Brothers, Earl "Snake Hips" Tucker, and Bill "Bojangles" Robinson, who carried the honorary title the Mayor of Harlem.

Harlem's theatrical life was also vibrant. From the early years of the century through the Great Depression, the center of popular entertainment in Harlem was the Lincoln Theater, on 135th Street off Lenox Avenue. After 1934 the Lincoln was superseded by the Apollo Theater. Harlem attracted vaudevillians such as Bert Williams, George W. Walker, Flournoy Miller, and Aubrey Lyles, and a later generation of comedians including Dewey "Pigmeat" Markham and Dusty Fletcher, who popularized the "Open the door, Richard" routine.

After 1917 the Lafayette Theater grew in prominence as a home of serious drama, due to the success of such ac-

tors as Paul Robeson, Richard B. Harrison (famous for his role as "De Lawd" in *Green Pastures*), and Abbie Mitchell. Harlem was also a center of nightclubs. The best known included the black-owned Smalls' Paradise, the Cotton Club, and the mobster-connected and racially exclusive Connie's Inn. The best-known dance hall was the Savoy Ballroom, which billed itself as the "Home of Happy Feet" and presented the best in big-band jazz after 1926. Harlem's cultural vitality was celebrated in plays including Wallace Thurman's *Harlem* (1929), Langston Hughes's *Mulatto* (1935), *Little Ham* (1935), and *Don't You Want to be Free?* (1936–1937), and Abram Hill's *On Strivers' Row* (1939). Musical performers celebrated Harlem's social scene through such compositions as "The Joint is Jumping," "Stompin' at the Savoy," "Harlem Airshaft," "Drop Me Off in Harlem," and "Take the *A* Train."

CHURCHES AND POLITICS

As Harlem became a political and cultural center of black America, the community's black churches became more

A "Back to Africa" announcement, Harlem. Harlem at the time of the great migration was home to many people of the African Diaspora, who had come to the city from the Caribbean, South America, Africa, and the American South. Movements to reclaim their African heritage and bring unity to the disparate groups had great appeal. GENERAL RESEARCH AND REFERENCE DIVISION, SCHOMBURG CENTER FOR RESEARCH IN BLACK CULTURE, THE NEW YORK PUBLIC LIBRARY, ASTOR, LENOX AND TILDEN FOUNDATIONS.

influential as well. Most were Protestant, particularly Baptist and Methodist, and the Abyssinian Baptist Church became the most famous during the interwar period. The Rev. Adam Clayton Powell Sr. moved the church from West 40th Street in midtown Manhattan to West 138th Street in Harlem in 1923. He combated prostitution, organized classes in home economics, built a home for the elderly, and organized soup kitchens and employment networks during the Great Depression. He was succeeded as senior pastor in 1937 by his son, Adam Clayton Powell Jr., who expanded the scope of the church's community activism. Harlem's scores of storefront churches, many of which proliferated during the interwar period, imitated Abyssinian's community aid efforts on a smaller scale. Harlem's most famous heterodox religious leader of the 1930s, Father Divine, established a series of soup kitchens and stores in the community through his Peace Mission and his Righteous Government political organization.

The 1930s were a period of stagnation and decline in Harlem, as they were throughout the nation. Civil rights

protest increased during the decade, and much of it originated in Harlem. In response to white businessmen's unwillingness to hire black workers for white-collar jobs in their Harlem stores, a series of "Don't Buy Where You Can't Work" boycott campaigns commenced in 1933 and became an effective method of protesting against racial bigotry throughout the decade. Harlem community leaders such as Adam Clayton Powell Jr. often joined with the NAACP, the National Urban League, the Communist Party, and the Citizens' League for Fair Play (CLFP) in leading these protests. Under the aegis of the Communist Party, major demonstrations were also held on Harlem streets in the early 1930s in support of the Scottsboro Boys and Angelo Herndon.

Major-party politics thrived in Harlem as much as radical politics did during the first half of the century. In the 1920s the Republican Party (led in black communities by Charles Anderson) and the Democratic Party (led by Ferdinand Q. Morton under Tammany Hall's United Colored Democracy) competed fiercely for black votes. Within the black community itself, African Americans and Caribbean Americans competed for dominance over the few available instruments of political control. Caribbean Americans were particularly prominent in the struggle to integrate Harlem blacks into the main organization of the Democratic Party; J. Raymond Jones (an immigrant from the Virgin Islands who would ultimately become head of Tammany Hall) led an insurgent group called the New Democrats in this effort during the early 1930s.

Civil disturbances played an important role in Harlem's growing political consciousness. In 1935 a riot, fueled by animosity toward white businesses and the police, left three dead and caused over $200 million in damage. New York City Mayor Fiorello LaGuardia later assigned his Mayor's Commission on Conditions in Harlem (led by E. Franklin Frazier) to study the uprising; the commission revealed a great number of underlying socioeconomic problems that were giving rise to racial animosities. In 1943 Harlem experienced another major race riot, which left five dead. This second riot was fueled by racial discrimination in war-related industries and continuing animosities between white police officers and Harlem's black citizens.

These events helped shape the emerging political career of Adam Clayton Powell Jr., who was elected to the New York City Council in 1941 and to the United States Congress in 1944, representing Harlem's newly created Eighteenth District. Powell's intolerance of race discrimination, along with his vocal and flamboyant style, brought national attention to the community, and he remained a symbol of Harlem's strength and reputation until his expulsion from Congress in 1967. He was reelected by his loyal Harlem constituency in 1968.

Post–World War II Era

By the end of World War II, Harlem experienced another transition. The migration of middle-class blacks to more affluent neighborhoods destabilized the class balance of earlier decades. Many of the remaining businesses were owned not by black residents but by whites who lived far removed from the ghetto. At the same time, most of the literati associated with the Harlem Renaissance had left the district. However, Harlem's literary life was preserved by a number of dedicated authors, including Ralph Ellison (whose 1952 novel, *Invisible Man,* was centered in Harlem) and Harlem native James Baldwin. The Harlem Writers Guild was founded in 1950 by John Oliver Killens, Maya Angelou, John Henrik Clarke, and others, and has for over four decades offered writers in the community a forum for the reading and discussion of their works. Photographers such as Austin Hansen and Gordon Parks Sr. continued to capture and celebrate Harlem's community on film.

For most of those who remained in Harlem after the war, however, a sense of powerlessness set in, exacerbated by poverty and a lack of control over their community. The quality of Harlem housing continued to be an acute problem. Paradoxically, as the quality of Harlem's inadequately heated, rat-infested buildings deteriorated, and as health ordinances related to housing were increasingly ignored, the rents on those units rose. People were evicted for being unable to keep up with their rent, and having no other place to go many either entered community shelters or joined the swelling ranks of the homeless.

Heroin addiction and street crime were increasingly serious problems. The 1950s saw Harlem deteriorate, both spiritually and physically. Dependent on welfare and other social services, many Harlemites longed for a chance to reassert some degree of hegemony over their community.

The 1964 Harlem Youth Opportunities Unlimited Act (HARYOU) represented an attempt to provide solutions. After an intensive study of the community from political, economic, and social perspectives, HARYOU proposed a combination of social action to reacquire political power and an influx of federal funds to redress the increasing economic privation of the area. From the beginning, however, the project suffered from personnel conflicts among the leadership. Social psychologist Dr. Kenneth B. Clark, who originally conceived and directed the project, resigned after a struggle with Adam Clayton Powell Jr. Following Clark's tenure, a Powell ally, Livingston Wingate,

led the project through a period of intensifying government scrutiny of its finances.

HARYOU was an attempt to increase local control through community action while remaining dependent upon government largess for organizational funding, and it failed. It was also unable to ameliorate the alienation and decline into delinquency that plagued Harlem's youth. Illustrative of its failure was the 1964 riot, ignited like its predecessors by an incident of alleged police brutality, which underscored the troubles that continued to plague the community.

By the late 1960s, Harlem precisely fit the conclusion reached by the 1968 National Commission of Civil Disorders report. It was a ghetto, created, maintained, and condoned by white society. Literary works of the postwar era, from Ann L. Petry's *The Street* (1946) to Claude Brown's *Manchild in the Promised Land* (1965), reflected this progressively deteriorating state of affairs as well.

It was in this period of decay that another charismatic organization emerged in the community, the Nation of Islam. Malcolm X, the head of Harlem's mosque, blended the intellectual acumen of the 1920s literati with the political sophistication and charisma of Marcus Garvey. He galvanized the masses and rekindled in them a sense of black pride and self-determination, appealing to their sense of disgruntlement with a message that was far angrier and less conciliatory than that offered by other major civil rights leaders. He was assassinated on February 21, 1965, in the Audubon Ballroom in Upper Manhattan.

Harlem since the 1960s

Harlem since the 1960s has been severely affected by the same external forces that have plagued many other American urban centers. As the U.S. economy underwent a critical transition from a focus heavy manufacturing to a focus on service and information technologies, large-scale industry left urban areas. Large numbers of Harlem residents followed this exodus, settling in suburban areas in Queens, the Bronx, and other boroughs. The resultant unemployment among those who remained further eviscerated Harlem. The community had long since lost its position as the population center of black New York to the Bedford-Stuyvesant area of Brooklyn. Community vital statistics have been no more encouraging. It was estimated in 1992 that the average African-American male born in Harlem would have a life expectancy of sixty-four years, dying before becoming eligible for most Social Security or retirement benefits.

The Harlem Commonwealth Council, a nonprofit corporation begun in 1967 and founded through the Of-

One of Harlem's main intersections, 125th Street and 7th Avenue, in 1943. *On the left is Blumstein's Department Store, the site of a major "Don't Buy Where You Can't Work" protest in 1934. On the right, farther up the block, is the Apollo Theater.* PHOTOGRAPHS AND PRINTS DIVISION, SCHOMBURG CENTER FOR RESEARCH IN BLACK CULTURE, THE NEW YORK PUBLIC LIBRARY, ASTOR, LENOX AND TILDEN FOUNDATIONS.

fice of Economic Opportunity and the private sector, sought to develop Harlem economically and empower its community leaders politically. Yet in its first twenty-five years, bad investments and an uncertain economy have reduced its real estate holdings, and virtually all its large-scale enterprises have gone bankrupt.

In 1989 David N. Dinkins, a product of Harlem's Democratic Clubs, became the first African-American mayor of New York. One of his biggest supporters was Charles Rangel, who in 1970 had succeeded Adam Clayton Powell Jr. as Harlem's congressman. In his four years as mayor, Dinkins sought to reestablish an atmosphere of racial harmony and cooperation to realize his vision of New York City as a "gorgeous mosaic" of diverse ethnicities.

Harlem residents continued their efforts to reassert control over their community in the 1990s, as the Harlem Chamber of Commerce led efforts to revitalize Harlem's businesses and reclaim the community's physical infra-

structure (a process sometimes referred to as "ghettocentrism"). A plan to spend over $170 million to build permanent housing for the poor and homeless began early in the decade, and such landmark structures as the Astor Row houses, on 130th Street, were rehabilitated as well. The Schomburg Center for Research in Black Culture, on 135th Street, established in 1926 as a branch of the New York Public Library, remained the nation's leading resource of African-American scholarship, as well as the location of academic conferences and meetings of the Harlem Writers Guild. The Studio Museum of Harlem, on 125th Street, was a focus for African-American and Caribbean-American folk art. The Apollo Theater, on 125th Street, was reopened in 1989, and it continued to showcase the current and future leaders of black entertainment. The nearby Hotel Theresa no longer served as a hotel but continued as the Theresa Towers, a modern office center and community landmark.

Throughout Harlem's history there has been a wide gap between the social, intellectual, and artistic accomplishments of the community's elite and the poverty and neglect experienced by its masses. This gap was dramatically demonstrated by debates during the mid-1990s over the use of community development funds to bring large supermarkets to the 125th Street area, a plan that community activists favored as a way to bring lower-cost goods to Harlem but that small shop owners opposed as unfair competition.

Harlem was marked by a series of crises revolving around race and economics in the mid-1990s. In 1994, following complaints by local merchants, police forcibly removed street peddlers selling African artifacts and other wares from 125th Street. In 1995, after the Jewish landlord of a space in a building owned by an African-American church announced plans to terminate the sublease of a popular African-American clothing store, violent protests broke out, and an arsonist shot himself and four others before setting fire to the store. In 1998 national attention was again fixed on Harlem when former Nation of Islam activist Khalid Abdul Muhammad announced plans for a Million Youth March. New York Mayor Rudolph Giuliani refused a permit on the pretext that the city could not afford police protection. Organizers ultimately won a court order authorizing the march, which drew an estimated 40,000 people. At the same time, however, Harlem continues to maintain, as it has in every decade of its existence, an inner energy and spirit.

See also Abyssinian Baptist Church; Apollo Theater; Black Middle Class; Dinkins, David; Garvey, Marcus; Great Depression and the New Deal; Harlem Renaissance; Harlem Writers Guild; Jazz; Lincoln Theater; Malcolm X; Migration; Nation of Islam; New Negro; Riots and Popular Protests; Savoy Ballroom; Universal Negro Improvement Association

■ ■ *Bibliography*

Anderson, Jervis. *This Was Harlem: A Cultural Portrait, 1900–1950*. New York: Farrar, Straus & Giroux, 1981.

Boyd, Herb, ed. *The Harlem Reader: A Celebration of New York's Most Famous Neighborhood: From the Renaissance Years to the Twenty-first Century*. New York: Three Rivers, 2003.

Capeci, Dominic. *The Harlem Riot of 1943*. Philadelphia: Temple University Press, 1977.

Clarke, John Henrik, ed. *Harlem: A Community in Transition*. New York: Citadel, 1969.

Cruse, Harold. *The Crisis of the Negro Intellectual: From Its Origins to the Present*. New York: Morrow, 1967.

Greenberg, Cheryl. *"Or Does It Explode?" Black Harlem in the Great Depression*. New York: Oxford University Press, 1991.

Hamilton, Charles V. *Adam Clayton Powell, Jr.: The Political Biography of an American Dilemma*. New York: Atheneum, 1991.

Huggins, Nathan. *Harlem Renaissance*. New York: Oxford University Press, 1971.

Johnson, James Weldon. *Black Manhattan* (1930). New York: Da Capo, 1991.

Lewis, David Levering. *When Harlem Was in Vogue*. New York: Knopf, 1981.

Locke, Alain, ed. *The New Negro* (1925). Reprint. New York: Atheneum, 1970.

McKay, Claude. *Harlem: Negro Metropolis* (1940). New York: Harcourt Brace Jovanovich, 1968.

Naison, Mark. *Communists in Harlem during the Depression*. Urbana: University of Illinois Press, 1986.

Osofsky, Gilbert. *Harlem: The Making of a Ghetto*. New York: Harper & Row, 1963.

MARSHALL HYATT (1996)
Updated by publisher 2005

HARLEM GLOBETROTTERS

The Harlem Globetrotters were founded in 1926. At that time Abe Saperstein (1902–1966), an English-born Jewish Chicagoan who had coached semipro basketball in the Chicago area, took over the coaching duties of an African-American team, the Savoy Big Five (formerly Giles Post American Legion). Saperstein decided the team would be more popular with better marketing. To emphasize its racial composition and its barnstorming, he renamed the team the Harlem Globetrotters, although they had no connection to the New York City neighborhood. The newly renamed team debuted on January 7, 1927, in Hinckley, Illinois, wearing read, white, and blue uniforms that Saperstein had sewn in his father's tailor shop. The first starting team consisted of Walter "Toots" Wright, Byron "Fat" Long, Willis "Kid" Oliver, Andy Washington, and Al "Runt" Pullins.

The Globetrotters played the itinerant schedule of barnstorming basketball teams, taking on black and white squads of greatly varying levels of ability, with many memorable games against their archrivals, the New York Rens. Players boosted the team's popularity by clowning—drop-kicking balls, spinning them on fingertips, and bouncing them off teammates' heads. In 1939 the Globetrotters finished third in the *Chicago Herald American*'s World Professional Tournament; in 1940, they became World Champions. In 1943 the team traveled to Mexico City (the first indication that the team would soon justify its "Globetrotter" name) and won the International Cup Tournament. During the mid-1940s, a white player, Bob Karstens, joined the Globetrotters (the team has briefly had two other white players).

After World War II, as professional all-white basketball leagues began slowly integrating, the Globetrotters, led by Marques Haynes, were so popular that rumors spread that Saperstein opposed integration in order to keep control of the market for black players. Meanwhile, they continued to hold their own against white teams in exhibition games. In February 1948 the Globetrotters, following a fifty-two-game winning streak, played George Mikan and the Minneapolis Lakers evenly in two exhibition games in Chicago. The team's skill and popularity belied black exclusion policies.

By 1950 NBA teams had three black players, including ex-Globetrotter Nat "Sweetwater" Clifton. After the integration of professional basketball, the Globetrotters' playing style changed dramatically. Clowning now became predominant. Players such as Reece "Goose" Tatum, Meadowlark Lemon, and Fred "Curly" Neal were hired not only for playing ability but for trick shooting, dribbling, and comedic talent. The Globetrotters, now billed as "The Clown Princes of Basketball," became best known for already familiar routines, such as the pregame "Magic Circle." In this act, players stand in a loose circle and display their skill and deftness with the ball, accompanied by the team's theme song, "Sweet Georgia Brown."

In 1950 the Globetrotters began annual coast-to-coast trips with squads of college All-Americans, which lasted until 1962. The same year, the team began annual European summer tours, playing to enormous crowds. In 1951 they played before seventy-five thousand spectators in Berlin's Olympic Stadium, still one of the largest crowds ever to see a basketball game. During this period, they appeared in two movies, *Go Man Go* (1948) and *The Harlem Globetrotters* (1951). In the early 1950s, after the Globetrotters lost consecutive games to Red Klotz's Philadelphia Spas, Abe Saperstein decided to dispense with playing local teams and to barnstorm with the Spas (later renamed the Washington Generals), who play some 250 games with the Globetrotters each year and serve as straight men for their stunts. The Generals, following an agreement with the Globetrotters, allow several trick-shot baskets per game. The last time the Generals beat their rivals was in 1971. In the 1950s the Globetrotters split into two squads, one of which played on the East Coast while the other focused on the West. In 1958–1959, the same year that Wilt Chamberlain, after the end of his college career, spent playing with the team (often as a seven-foot one-inch guard!), the Globetrotters toured the Soviet Union as

goodwill ambassadors. Other famous athletes who played with the team included Bob Gibson and Connie Hawkins. The team has retained its interracial popularity, although during the 1960s some blacks criticized team members for their clownish image, which reinforced racial stereotypes, and the team's silence on civil rights issues.

After Saperstein's death in 1966, the team was sold to three Chicago businessmen for $3.7 million. In 1975 Metromedia purchased the team for $11 million. The Globetrotters remained popular into the 1970s, when they starred in cartoon and live-action TV series, but their popularity declined some years later, especially after stars such as Meadowlark Lemon left the team after contract disputes. In 1985 the first female Globetrotter, Lynette Woodward, was hired. In December 1986 Metromedia sold the team (as part of a package that included the Ice Capades) to International Broadcasting Corp. (IBC) for $30 million. In 1993 IBC entered bankruptcy and Mannie Johnson, a former Globetrotter, bought the team. It was another Globetrotter, Curly Neal, who best captured the team's appeal: "How do I know when we played a good 'game'?" he said. "When I look up at the crowd and I see all those people laughing their heads off. It's a hard world and if we can lighten it up a little, we've done our job."

In 1998 the Globetrotters played their 20,000th game. Globetrotters great Meadowlark Lemon was inducted into the basketball Hall of Fame in 2003.

See also Basketball; Renaissance Big Five (Harlem Rens)

■ ■ *Bibliography*

Gutman, Bill. *The Harlem Globetrotters*. Champaign, Ill.: Garrard, 1977.

Lemon, Meadowlark. *Meadowlark*. Nashville, Tenn.: Nelson, 1987.

Weiner, Jay. "Meadowlark Lemon Comes Home to Roost with Globetrotters." *Chicago Star Tribune*, March 1, 1993.

GREG ROBINSON (1996)
Updated by publisher 2005

Harlem Renaissance

∎∎∎

If the Harlem Renaissance was neither exclusive to Harlem nor a rebirth of anything that had gone before, its efflorescence above New York City's Central Park was characterized by such sustained vitality and variety as to influence by paramountcy and diminish by comparison the similar cultural energies in Boston, Philadelphia, and Washington, D.C. During its earliest years, beginning about 1917, contemporaries tended to describe the Harlem phenomenon as a manifestation of the New Negro Arts Movement. However, by the time it ended in the winter of 1934–1935—with both a whimper and a bang—the movement was almost universally regarded as indistinguishable from its Harlem incarnation.

As the population of African Americans rapidly urbanized and its literacy rate climbed, Harlem, New York, the "Negro capital of America," rose out of the vast relocation under way from South to North. A combination of causes propelled the Great Black Migration: southern white mob violence, the economics of discrimination, crop failure, the interruption of European immigration after 1914 and a consequent labor vacuum in the North, and the aggressive recruitment of black labor for work at wartime wages by northern industrialists. With the vast welling of black people from Georgia, the Carolinas, Virginia, and elsewhere, their numbers rose from 60,534 in all of New York City in 1910 to a conservative 1923 estimate of the National Urban League (NUL) that placed the number at 183,428, with probably two-thirds in Harlem. Although this section of the city was by no means wholly occupied by people of color—never more than 60 percent during the 1930s—it soon became distinctively black in culture and in the mainstream perception. If the coming of black Harlem was swift, its triumph had been long anticipated by the increasing numbers of African Americans living in midtown Manhattan's teeming Tenderloin and San Juan Hill districts. The Tenderloin (so called from a police captain's gustatory graft), stretching roughly from West Fourteenth to Forty-second streets, had become home to the city's nonwhites during the early nineteenth century, after they forced their way out of the old Five Points area east of today's Foley Square, where City Hall stands.

By the 1890s blacks were battling the Irish for scarce turf north of Fiftieth Street in what came to be called San Juan Hill, in honor of African-American troops in the Spanish-American War. Influx and congestion had, as the African-American newspaper the *New York Age* predicted, great advantages: "Influx of Afro-Americans into New York City from all parts of the South made . . . possible a great number and variety of business enterprises." The example of Lower East Side Jews accumulating money and moving on, in the 1890s, to solid brownstones on wide, shaded streets in Harlem was enviously watched by African Americans. The area had undergone a building boom in anticipation of the extension of the subway, but by the turn of the century many apartment buildings were sparsely occupied. A few white landlords broke ranks

around 1905 to rent or sell to African Americans through Philip A. Payton's pioneering Afro-American Realty Company.

Two institutional activities were outstandingly successful in promoting the occupation of Harlem—churches and cabarets. Saint Philip's Episcopal Church sold its West Twenty-fifth Street holdings for $140,000 in 1909 and disposed of its Tenderloin cemetery for $450,000 two years later. The Abyssinian Baptist Church, presided over by the charismatic Adam Clayton Powell, Sr., negotiated a comparable disposal of its property in order to build one of Protestant America's grandest temples on 138th Street. Nightclubs such as Banks's, Barron's, and Edmond's transported music and a nightlife style from the Tenderloin that gave Harlem its signature. Barron's Little Savoy featured "Jelly Roll" Morton, Willie "the Lion" Smith, James P. Johnson, Scott Joplin, and other legends of the era. Barron Wilkins took his club uptown before the country entered the European war.

Precisely why and how the Harlem Renaissance materialized, who molded it and who found it most meaningful, as well as what it symbolized and what it achieved, raise perennial American questions about race relations, class hegemony, cultural assimilation, generational-gender-lifestyle conflicts, and art versus propaganda. Notwithstanding its synoptic significance, the Harlem Renaissance was not, as some students have maintained, all inclusive of the early twentieth-century African-American urban experience. There were important movements, influences, and people who were marginal or irrelevant to it, as well as those alien or opposed. Not everything that happened in Harlem from 1917 to 1934 was a Renaissance happening. The potent mass movement founded and led by the charismatic Marcus Garvey was to the Renaissance what nineteenth-century populism was to progressive reform: a parallel but socially different force, related primarily through dialectical confrontation. Equally different from the institutional ethos and purpose of the Renaissance was the black church. An occasional minister (such as the father of poet Countee Cullen) or exceptional Garveyites (such as Yale-Harvard man William H. Ferris) might move in both worlds, but black evangelism and its cultist manifestations, such as Black Zionism, represented emotional and cultural retrogression in the eyes of the principal actors in the Renaissance. If the leading intellectual of the race, W. E. B. Du Bois, publicly denigrated the personnel and preachings of the black church, his animadversions were merely more forthright than those of other New Negro notables like James Weldon Johnson, Charles S. Johnson, Jessie Redmon Fauset, Alain Locke, and Walter Francis White.

The relationship of music to the Harlem Renaissance was problematic, for reasons exactly analogous to its elitist aversions to Garveyism and evangelism. When Du Bois wrote, a few years after the beginning of the New Negro movement in arts and letters, that "until the art of the black folk compels recognition they will not be rated as human," he, like most of his Renaissance peers, fully intended to exclude the blues of Bessie Smith and the jazz of "King" Oliver. Spirituals sung like lieder by the disciplined Hall Johnson Choir—and, better yet, lieder sung by conservatory-trained Roland Hayes, recipient of the NAACP's prestigious Spingarn Medal—were deemed appropriate musical forms to present to mainstream America. The deans of the Renaissance were entirely content to leave discovery and celebration of Bessie, Clara, Trixie, and various other blues-singing Smiths to white music critic Carl Van Vechten's effusions in *Vanity Fair*. When the visiting film director Sergei Eisenstein enthused about new black musicals, Charles S. Johnson and Alain Locke expressed mild consternation in the Urban League's *Opportunity* magazine. They would have been no less displeased by Maurice Ravel's fascination with musicians in Chicago dives. As board members of the Pace Phonograph Company, Du Bois, James Weldon Johnson, and others banned "funky" artists from the Black Swan list of recordings, thereby contributing to the demise of the African-American-owned firm. But the wild Broadway success of Miller and Lyles's musical *Shuffle Along* (it helped to popularize the Charleston) or Florence Mills's *Blackbirds* revue flaunted such artistic fastidiousness.

The very centrality of music in black life, as well as of black musical stereotypes in white minds, caused popular musical forms to impinge inescapably on Renaissance high culture. Eventually, the Renaissance deans made a virtue out of necessity; they applauded the concert-hall ragtime of "Big Jim" Europe and the "educated" jazz of Atlanta University graduate and big-band leader Fletcher Henderson, and they hired a Duke Ellington or a Cab Calloway as drawing cards for fund-raising socials. Still, their relationship to music remained beset by paradox. New York ragtime, with its "Jelly Roll" Morton strides and Joplinesque elegance, had as much in common with Chicago jazz as Mozart with "Fats" Waller. The source of musical authenticity and the reservoir of musical abundance lay in those recently urbanized and economically beleaguered men and women whose chosen recreational environments were raucous, boozy, and lubricious. Yet these were the men and women whose culture and condition made Renaissance drillmasters (themselves only a generation and a modest wage removed) uncomfortable and ashamed, men and women whose musical pedigrees went back from

Prominent figures of the Harlem Renaissance, 1924. From left to right: Langston Hughes, Charles S. Johnson, E. Franklin Frazier, Rudolph Fisher, and Hubert T. Delany. PHOTOGRAPHS AND PRINTS DIVISION, SCHOMBURG CENTER FOR RESEARCH IN BLACK CULTURE, THE NEW YORK PUBLIC LIBRARY, ASTOR, LENOX AND TILDEN FOUNDATIONS.

Louis Armstrong and Sidney Bechet through Chicago to New Orleans's Storyville and its colonial-era Place Congo.

The Renaissance relished virtuoso performances by baritone Jules Bledsoe or contralto Marian Anderson, and pined to see the classical works of William Grant Still performed in Aeolian Hall. It took exceeding pride in the classical repertory of the renowned Clef Club Orchestra. On the other hand, even if and when it saw some value in the music nurtured in Prohibition joints and bleary rent parties, the movement found itself pushed aside by white ethnic commercial co-optation and exploitation—by Al Capone and the mob. Thus, what was musically vital was shunned or deplored in the Harlem Renaissance from racial sensitivity; what succeeded with mainstream audiences derived from those same shunned and deplored sources and was invariably hijacked; and what was esteemed as emblematic of racial sophistication was (even when well done) of no interest to whites and of not much more to the majority of blacks. Last, with the notable exception of Paul Robeson, most of the impresarios as well as the featured personalities of the Renaissance were more expert in literary and visual-arts matters than musical.

The purpose of emphasizing such negatives—of stressing whom and what the Harlem Renaissance excluded or undervalued—serves the better to characterize the essence of a movement that was an elitist response to a rapidly evolving set of social and economic conditions demographically driven by the Great Black Migration beginning in the second decade of the twentieth century. The Harlem Renaissance began "as a somewhat forced phenomenon, a cultural nationalism of the parlor, institutionally encouraged and constrained by the leaders of the civil rights establishment for the paramount purpose of improving 'race relations' in a time of extreme national reaction to an annulment of economic gains won by Afro-Americans during the Great War" (Lewis, 1981). This mobilizing elite emerged from the increasing national cohesion of the African-American bourgeoisie at the turn of the century, and of the migration of many of its most educated and enterprising to the North about a decade in advance of the epic working-class migration out of the South. Du Bois indelibly labeled this racially advantaged minority the "Talented Tenth" in a seminal 1903 essay. He fleshed out the concept biographically that same year in "The Advance Guard of the Race," a piece in *Booklover's Magazine:* "Widely different are these men in origin and method. [Paul Laurence] Dunbar sprang from slave parents and poverty; [Charles Waddell] Chesnutt from free parents and thrift; while [Henry O.] Tanner was a bishop's son."

Students of the African-American bourgeoisie—from Joseph Willson in the mid-nineteenth century through Du Bois, Caroline Bond Day, and E. Franklin Frazier during the first half of the twentieth to Constance Green, August Meier, Carl Degler, Stephen Birmingham, and, most recently, Adele Alexander, Lois Benjamin, and Willard Gatewood—have differed about its defining elements, especially that of pigment. The generalization seems to hold that color was a greater determinant of upper-class status in the post–Civil War South than in the North. The phenotype preferences exercised by slaveholders for house slaves, in combination with the relative advantages enjoyed by illegitimate offspring of slavemasters, gave a decided spin to mulatto professional careers during Reconstruction and well beyond. Success in the North followed more various criteria, of which color was sometimes a factor. By the time of Booker T. Washington's death in 1915, however, a considerable amount of ideological cohesion existed among the African-American leadership classes in such key cities as Atlanta, Washington, Baltimore, Philadelphia, Boston, Chicago, and New York. A commitment to college preparation in liberal arts and the classics, in contrast to Washington's emphasis on vocational training, prevailed. Demands for civil and social equality were espoused again after a quietus of some fifteen years.

The once considerable power of the so-called Tuskegee Machine now receded before the force of Du Bois's propaganda, a coordinated civil rights militancy, and rapidly altering industrial and demographic conditions in the nation. The vocational training in crafts such as brickmaking, blacksmithing, carpentry, and sewing prescribed by Tuskegee and Hampton institutes was irrelevant in those parts of the South undergoing industrialization, yet industry in the South was largely proscribed to African Americans who for several decades had been deserting the dead end of sharecropping for the South's towns and cities. The Bookerites' sacrifice of civil rights for economic gain, therefore, lost its appeal not only to educated and enterprising African Americans but to many of those white philanthropists and public figures who had once solemnly commended it. The Talented Tenth formulated and propagated the new ideology being rapidly embraced by the physicians, dentists, educators, preachers, businesspeople, lawyers, and morticians comprising the bulk of the African-American affluent and influential—some ten thousand men and women, out of a total population in 1920 of more than ten million. (In 1917, traditionally cited as the natal year of the Harlem Renaissance, there were 2,132 African Americans in colleges and universities, probably no more than 30 of them attending "white" institutions.)

It was, then, the minuscule vanguard of a minority—0.02 percent of the racial total—that constituted the Talented Tenth that jump-started the New Negro Arts Movement. But what was extraordinary about the Harlem Renaissance was that its promotion and orchestration by the Talented Tenth were the consequence of masterful improvisation rather than of deliberate plan, of artifice imitating likelihood, of aesthetic deadpan disguising a racial blind alley. Between the 1905 "Declaration of Principles" of the Niagara Movement and the appearance in 1919 of Claude McKay's electrifying poem "If We Must Die," the principal agenda of the Talented Tenth called for investigation of and protest against discrimination in virtually every aspect of national life. It lobbied for racially enlightened employment policies in business and industry; the abolition through the courts of peonage, residential segregation ordinances, Jim Crow public transportation, and franchise restrictions; and enactment of federal sanctions against lynching. The vehicles for this agenda, the NAACP and the NUL, exposed, cajoled, and propagandized through their excellent journals, the *Crisis* and *Opportunity,* respectively. The rhetoric of protest was addressed to ballots, courts, legislatures, and the workplace: "We urge upon Congress the enactment of appropriate legislation for securing the proper enforcement of . . . the thirteenth, fourteenth and fifteenth amendments," the Niagara Movement had demanded and the NAACP continued to reiterate. Talented Tenth rhetoric was also strongly social-scientific: "We shall try to set down interestingly but without sugarcoating or generalizations the findings of careful scientific surveys and facts gathered from research," the first *Opportunity* editorial would proclaim in January 1923, echoing the objectives of Du Bois's famous Atlanta University studies.

It is hardly surprising that many African Americans, the great majority of whom lived under the deadening cultural and economic weight of southern apartheid, had modest interest in literature and the arts during the first two decades of the twentieth century. Even outside the underdeveloped South, and irrespective of race, demotic America had scant aptitude for and much suspicion of arts and letters. Culture in early twentieth-century America was paid for by a white minority probably not a great deal larger, by percentage, than the Talented Tenth. For those privileged few African Americans whose education or leisure inspired such tastes, therefore, appealing fiction, poetry, drama, paintings, and sculpture by or about African Americans had become so exiguous as to be practically nonexistent. With the rising hostility and indifference of the mainstream market, African-American discretionary resources were wholly inadequate by themselves to sustain even a handful of novelists, poets, and painters. A tubercular death had silenced poet-novelist Dunbar in 1906, and poor royalties had done the same for novelist Chesnutt after publication the previous year of *The Colonel's Dream.* Between that point and 1922, no more than five African Americans published significant works of fiction and verse. There was *Pointing the Way* in 1908, a flawed, fascinating civil rights novel by the Baptist preacher Sutton Griggs. Three years later, Du Bois's *The Quest of the Silver Fleece,* a sweeping sociological allegory, appeared. The following year came James Weldon Johnson's well-crafted *The Autobiography of an Ex-Colored Man,* but the author felt compelled to disguise his racial identity. A ten-year silence fell afterward, finally to be broken in 1922 by McKay's *Harlem Shadows,* the first book of poetry since Dunbar. In "Art for Nothing," a short, trenchant think piece in the May 1922 *Crisis,* Du Bois lamented the fall into oblivion of sculptors Meta Warwick Fuller and May Howard Jackson, and that of painters William E. Scott and Richard Brown.

Although the emergence of the Harlem Renaissance seems much more sudden and dramatic in retrospect than the historic reality, its institutional elaboration was, in fact, relatively quick. Altogether, it evolved through three stages. The first phase, ending in 1923 with the publication of Jean Toomer's unique prose poem *Cane,* was dominated by white artists and writers—bohemians and revolutionaries—fascinated for a variety of reasons with the life of black people. The second phase, from early 1924 to mid-1926, was presided over by the civil rights establishment of the NUL and the NAACP, a period of interracial collaboration between "Negrotarian" whites and the African-American Talented Tenth. The last phase, from mid-1926 to 1934, was increasingly dominated by African-American artists themselves—the "Niggerati."

When Charles S. Johnson, new editor of *Opportunity,* sent invitations to some dozen African-American poets and writers to attend an event at Manhattan's Civic Club on March 21, 1924, the movement had already shifted into high gear. At Johnson's request, William H. Baldwin III, a white Tuskegee trustee, NUL board member, and heir to a railroad fortune, had persuaded Harper's editor Frederick Lewis Allen to corral a "small but representative group from his field," most of them unknown, to attend the Civic Club affair in celebration of the sudden outpouring of "Negro" writing. "A group of the younger writers, which includes Eric Walrond, Jessie Fauset, Gwendolyn Bennett, Countee Cullen, Langston Hughes, Alain Locke, and some others," would be present, Johnson promised each invitee. All told, in addition to the "younger writers," some fifty persons were expected: "Eugene O'Neill, H. L. Mencken, Oswald Garrison Villard, Mary Johnston, Zona Gale, Robert Morss Lovett, Carl Van Doren, Ridgely Torrence, and about twenty more of this type. I think you might find this group interesting enough to draw you away for a few hours from your work on your next book," Johnson wrote the recently published Jean Toomer almost coyly.

Although both Toomer and Langston Hughes were absent in Europe, approximately 110 celebrants and honorees assembled that evening, included among them Du Bois, James Weldon Johnson, and the young NAACP officer Walter Francis White, whose energies as a literary entrepreneur would soon excel even Charles Johnson's. Locke, professor of philosophy at Howard University and the first African-American Rhodes scholar, served as master of ceremonies. Fauset, literary editor of the *Crisis* and Phi Beta Kappa graduate of Cornell University, enjoyed the distinction of having written the second fiction (and first novel) of the Renaissance, *There Is Confusion,* just released by Horace Liveright. Liveright, who was present, rose to praise Fauset as well as Toomer, whom he had also published. Speeches followed in rapid succession—Du Bois, James Weldon Johnson, Fauset. White called attention to the next Renaissance novel: his own, *The Fire in the Flint,* shortly forthcoming from Knopf. Albert Barnes, the crusty Philadelphia pharmaceutical millionaire and art collector, described the decisive impact of African art on modern art. Poets and poems were commended—Hughes, Cullen, Georgia Douglas Johnson of Washington,

D.C., and, finally, Gwendolyn Bennett's stilted yet appropriate "To Usward," punctuating the evening: "We claim no part with racial dearth,/We want to sing the songs of birth!" Charles Johnson wrote the vastly competent Ethel Ray Nance, his future secretary, of his enormous gratification that Paul Kellogg, editor of the influential *Survey Graphic,* had proposed that evening to place a special number of his magazine at the service of "representatives of the group."

Two compelling messages emerged from the Civic Club gathering. Du Bois asserted that the literature of apology and the denial to his generation of its authentic voice were now ending; Van Doren said that African-American artists were developing at a uniquely propitious moment. They were "in a remarkable strategic position with reference to the new literary age which seems to be impending," Van Doren predicted. "What American literature decidedly needs at this moment is color, music, gusto, the free expression of gay or desperate moods. If the Negroes are not in a position to contribute these items," Van Doren could not imagine who else could. It was precisely this "new literary age" that a few Talented Tenth leaders had kept under sharp surveillance and about which they had soon reached a conclusion affecting civil rights strategy. Despite the baleful influence of D. W. Griffith's *The Birth of a Nation* and the robust persistence of Uncle Tom, "coon," and Noble Savage stereotypes, literary and dramatic presentations of African Americans by whites had begun, arguably, to change somewhat for the better.

The African American had indisputably moved to the center of mainstream imagination with the end of the Great War, a development crucially assisted by chrysalis of the Lost Generation–Greenwich Village bohemia. The first issue of Randolph Bourne's *Seven Arts* (November 1916), featuring, among others of the Lyrical Left, Waldo Frank, James Oppenheim, Paul Rosenfeld, Van Wyck Brooks, and the French intellectual Romain Rolland, incarnated the spirit that informed a generation without ever quite cohering into a doctrine. The inorganic state, the husk of a decaying capitalist order, was breaking down, these young white intellectuals believed. They professed contempt for "the people who actually run things" in America. Waldo Frank, Toomer's bosom friend and literary mentor, foresaw not a bloody social revolution in America but that "out of our terrifying welter or steel and scarlet, a design must come." There was another Village group decidedly more oriented toward politics: the Marxist radicals (John Reed, Floyd Dell, Helen Keller, Max Eastman) associated with *Masses* and its successor magazine, *Liberator,* edited by Max and Crystal Eastman. The inaugural March 1918 issue of *Liberator* announced that

it would "fight for the ownership and control of industry by the workers."

Among the Lyrical Left writers gathered around *Broom, S4N,* and *Seven Arts,* and the political radicals associated with *Liberator,* there was a shared reaction against the ruling Anglo-Saxon cultural paradigm. Bourne's concept of a "trans-national" America, democratically respectful of its ethnic, racial, and religious constituents, complemented Du Bois's earlier concept of divided racial identity in *The Souls of Black Folk.* Ready conversance with the essentials of Freud and Marx became the measure of serious conversation in MacDougal Street coffeehouses, Albert Boni's Washington Square Book Shop, or the Hotel Brevoort's restaurant. There Floyd Dell, Robert Minor, Matthew Josephson, Max Eastman, and other *enragés* denounced the social system, the Great War to which it had ineluctably led, and the soul-dead world created in its aftermath, with McKay and Toomer, two of the Renaissance's first stars, participating.

From such conceptions, the Village's discovery of Harlem followed logically and, even more, psychologically. For if the factory, campus, office, and corporation were dehumanizing, stultifying, or predatory, the African American—largely excluded from all of the above—was a perfect symbol of cultural innocence and regeneration. He was perceived as an integral, indispensable part of the hoped-for design, somehow destined to aid in the reclamation of a diseased, desiccated civilization. The writer Malcolm Cowley would recall in *Exile's Return* that "one heard it said that the Negroes had retained a direct virility that the whites had lost through being overeducated." Public annunciation of the rediscovered Negro came in the fall of 1917, with Emily Hapgood's production at the old Garden Street Theatre of three one-act plays by her husband, Ridgely Torrence. *The Rider of Dreams, Simon the Cyrenian,* and *Granny Maumee* were considered daring because the casts were black and the parts were dignified. The drama critic from *Theatre Magazine* enthused of one lead player that "nobody who saw Opal Cooper—and heard him as the dreamer, Madison Sparrow—will ever forget the lift his performance gave." Du Bois commended the playwright by letter, and James Weldon Johnson excitedly wrote his friend, the African-American literary critic Benjamin Brawley, that *The Smart Set*'s George Jean Nathan "spoke most highly about the work of these colored performers."

From this watershed flowed a number of dramatic productions, musicals, and several successful novels by whites, and also, with great significance, *Shuffle Along,* a cathartic musical by the African Americans Aubrey Lyles and Flournoy Miller. Theodore Dreiser grappled with the

W. E. B. Du Bois (top right) and others working in the offices of the NAACP magazine **The Crisis.** The Crisis, *together with another leading black journal, the National Urban League's* Opportunity, *published the work of Harlem Renaissance writers and artists, and also sponsored literary contests that brought much-needed recognition and rewards to many talented African Americans.* © UNDERWOOD & UNDERWOOD/ CORBIS. REPRODUCED BY PERMISSION.

explosive subject of lynching in his 1918 short story "Nigger Jeff." Two years later, the magnetic African-American actor Charles Gilpin energized O'Neill's *The Emperor Jones* in the 150-seat theater in a MacDougal Street brownstone taken over by the Provincetown Players. *The Emperor Jones* (revived four years later with Paul Robeson in the lead part) showed civilization's pretensions being moved by forces from the dark subconscious. In 1921 *Shuffle Along* opened at the 63rd Street Theatre, with music, lyrics, choreography, cast, and production uniquely in African-American hands, and composer Eubie Blake's "I'm Just Wild About Harry" and "Love Will Find a Way" entering the list of all-time favorites. Mary Hoyt Wiborg's *Taboo* was also produced in 1921, with Robeson in his theatrical debut. Clement Wood's 1922 sociological novel *Nigger* sympathetically tracked a beleaguered African-American family from slavery through the Great War into urban adversity. T. S. Stribling's *Birthright,* that same year, was remarkable for its effort to portray an African-American male protagonist of superior education (a Harvard-educated physician) martyred for his ideals after returning to the South. "Jean Le Negre," the black character in e. e. cummings' *The Enormous Room,* was another

Noble Savage paradigm observed through a Freudian prism.

But Village artists and intellectuals were aware and unhappy that they were theorizing about Afro-America and spinning out African-American fictional characters in a vacuum—that they knew almost nothing firsthand about these subjects. Sherwood Anderson's June 1922 letter to H. L. Mencken spoke for much of the Lost Generation: "Damn it, man, if I could really get inside the niggers and write about them with some intelligence, I'd be willing to be hanged later and perhaps would be." At least the first of Anderson's prayers was answered almost immediately when he chanced to read a Jean Toomer short story in *Double-Dealer* magazine. With the novelist's assistance, Toomer's stories began to appear in the magazines of the Lyrical Left and the Marxists, *Diak, S4N, Broom,* and *Liberator.* Anderson's 1925 novel *Dark Laughter* bore unmistakable signs of indebtedness to Toomer, whose work, Anderson stated, had given him a true insight into the cultural energies that could be harnessed to pull America back from the abyss of fatal materialism. Celebrity in the Village brought Toomer into Waldo Frank's circle, and with it criticism from Toomer about the omission of African Americans from Frank's sprawling work *Our America.* After a trip with Toomer to South Carolina in the fall of 1922, Frank published *Holiday* the following year, a somewhat overwrought treatment of the struggle between the races in the South, "each of which . . . needs what the other possesses."

Claude McKay, whose volume of poetry *Harlem Shadows* made him a Village celebrity also (he lived on Gay Street, then entirely inhabited by nonwhites), found his niche among the *Liberator* group, where he soon became coeditor of the magazine with Michael Gold. The Eastmans saw the Jamaican poet as the kind of writer who would deepen the magazine's proletarian voice. McKay increased the circulation of *Liberator* to sixty thousand, published the first poetry of e. e. cummings (over Gold's violent objections), introduced Garvey's Universal Negro Improvement Association (UNIA), and generally treated the readership to experimentation that had little to do with proletarian literature. "It was much easier to talk about real proletarians writing masterpieces than to find such masterpieces," McKay told the Eastmans and the exasperated hard-line Marxist Gold. McKay attempted to bring Harlem to the Village, as the actor Charlie Chaplin discovered when he dropped into the *Liberator* offices one day and found the editor deep in conversation with Hubert Harrison, Harlem's peerless soapbox orator and author of *When Africa Awakes.* Soon all manner of Harlem radicals began meeting at the West Thirteenth Street offices, while the Eastmans fretted about Justice Department surveillance. Richard B. Moore, Cyril Briggs, Otto Huiswood, Grace Campbell, W. A. Domingo, *inter alios,* represented Harlem movements ranging from Garvey's UNIA and Brigg's African Blood Brotherhood to the Communist Party, with Huiswood and Campbell. McKay also attempted to bring the Village to Harlem, in one memorable sortie taking Eastman and another Villager to Ned's, his favorite Harlem cabaret. Ned's, notoriously antiwhite, expelled them.

This was part of the background to the Talented Tenth's abrupt, enthusiastic, and programmatic embrace of the arts after World War I. In 1924, as Charles Johnson was planning his Civic Club evening, extraordinary security precautions were in place around the Broadway theater where *All God's Chillun Got Wings,* O'Neill's drama about miscegenation, starring Paul Robeson, was playing. With white Broadway audiences flocking to O'Neill plays and shrieking with delight at *Liza, Runnin' Wild,* and other imitations of *Shuffle Along,* the two Johnsons, Du Bois, Fauset, White, Locke, and others saw a unique opportunity to tap into the attention span of white America. If they were adroit, African-American civil rights officials and intellectuals believed, they stood a fair chance of reshaping the images and repackaging the messages out of which mainstream racial behavior emerged.

Bohemia and the Lost Generation suggested to the Talented Tenth the new approach to the old problem of race relations, but their shared premise about art and society obscured the diametrically opposite conclusions white and black intellectuals and artists drew from it. Stearns's Lost Generation *révoltés* were lost in the sense that they professed to have no wish to find themselves in a materialistic, Mammon-mad, homogenizing America. Locke's New Negroes very much wanted full acceptance by mainstream America, even if some—Du Bois, McKay, and the future enfant terrible of the Renaissance, Wallace Thurman—might have immediately exercised the privilege of rejecting it. For the whites, art was the means to change society before they would accept it. For the blacks, art was the means to change society in order to be accepted into it.

For this reason, many of the Harlem intellectuals found the white vogue in Afro-Americana troubling, although they usually feigned enthusiasm about the new dramatic and literary themes. Most of them clearly understood that this popularity was due to persistent stereotypes, new Freudian notions about sexual dominion over reason, and the postwar release of collective emotional and moral tensions sweeping Europe and America. Cummings, Dreiser, O'Neill, and Frank may have been well intentioned, but the African-American elite was quietly rather infuriated that Talented Tenth lives were frequently reduced to music, libido, rustic manners, and an incapacity for logic. The consummate satirist of the Renaissance, George Schuyler, denounced the insistent white portrayal of the African American in which "it is only necessary to beat a tom tom or wave a rabbit's foot and he is ready to strip off his Hart, Schaffner & Marx suit, grab a spear and ride off wild-eyed on the back of a crocodile." Despite the insensitivity, burlesquing, and calumny, however, the Talented Tenth convinced itself that the civil rights dividends of such recognition were potentially greater than the liabilities were.

Benjamin Brawley put this potential straightforwardly to James Weldon Johnson: "We have a tremendous opportunity to boost the NAACP, letters, and art, and anything else that calls attention to our development along the higher lines." Brawley knew that he was preaching to the converted. Johnson's preface to his best-selling anthology *The Book of American Negro Poetry* (1922) proclaimed that nothing could "do more to change the mental attitude and raise his status than a demonstration of intellectual parity by the Negro through his production of literature and art."

Reading Stribling's *Birthright,* an impressed Fauset nevertheless felt that she and her peers could do better. "We reasoned," she recalled later, "'Here is an audience waiting to hear the truth about us. Let us who are better qualified to present that truth than any white writer, try to do so.'" The result was *There Is Confusion,* her novel about genteel life among Philadelphia's aristocrats of color. Walter Francis White, similarly troubled by *Birthright* and other two-dimensional or symbolically gross representations of African-American life, complained loudly to H. L. Mencken, who finally silenced him with the challenge, "Why don't you do the right kind of novel. You could do it, and it would create a sensation." White did. The sensation turned out to be *The Fire in the Flint* (1924), the second novel of the Renaissance, which he wrote in less than a month in a borrowed country house in the Berkshires.

Meanwhile, Langston Hughes, whose genius (like Toomer's) had been immediately recognized by Fauset, published several poems in the *Crisis* that would later appear in his collection The Weary Blues. The euphonious "The Negro Speaks of Rivers" (dedicated to Du Bois) ran in the *Crisis* in 1921. With the appearance of McKay's *Harlem Shadows* in 1922 and Toomer's *Cane* in 1923, the officers of the NAACP and the NUL saw how real the possibility of a theory being put into action could be. The young New York University prodigy Countee Cullen, already published in the *Crisis* and *Opportunity,* had his mainstream breakthrough in 1923 in *Harper's* and *Century* magazines. Two years later, Cullen won the prestigious Witter Bynner poetry prize, with Carl Sandburg as one of the three judges. Meanwhile, the *Survey Graphic* project moved apace under the editorship of Locke.

Two conditions made this unprecedented mobilization of talent and group support in the service of a racial arts and letters movement more than a conceit in the minds of its leaders: demography and repression. The Great Black Migration produced the metropolitan dynamism undergirding the Renaissance. The Red Summer of 1919 produced the trauma that led to the cultural sublimation of civil rights. In pressure-cooker fashion, the increase in Harlem's African-American population caused it to pulsate as it pushed its racial boundaries south below 135th Street to Central Park and north beyond 139th ("Strivers' Row"). Despite the real estate success of the firms of Nail and Parker and the competition given by Smalls' Paradise to the Cotton Club and Connie's (both off-limits to African-American patrons), however, this dynamic community was never able to own much of its own real estate, sustain more than a handful of small, marginal merchants, or even control the profits from the illegal policy business perfected by one of its own, the literary Caspar

1925 broadside advertising Cotton Club on Parade, *featuring Cab Calloway and his orchestra.* PHOTOGRAPHS AND PRINTS DIVISION, SCHOMBURG CENTER FOR RESEARCH IN BLACK CULTURE, THE NEW YORK PUBLIC LIBRARY, ASTOR, LENOX AND TILDEN FOUNDATIONS.

Holstein. Still, both the appearance of and prospects for solid, broad-based prosperity belied the inevitable consequences of Harlem's comprador economy. The Negro Capital of the World filled up with successful bootleggers and racketeers, political and religious charlatans, cults of exotic character ("Black Jews"), street-corner pundits and health practitioners (Hubert Harrison, "Black Herman"), beauty culturists and distinguished professionals (Madame C. J. Walker, Louis T. Wright), religious and civil rights notables (Reverends Cullen and Powell, Du Bois, Johnson, White), and hard-pressed, hardworking families determined to make decent lives for their children. Memories of the nightspots in "The Jungle" (133rd Street), of Bill "Bojangles" Robinson demonstrating his footwork on Lenox Avenue, of raucous shows at the Lafayette that gave Florenz Ziegfeld some of his ideas, of the Tree of Hope outside Connie's Inn where musicians gathered as at a labor exchange, have been vividly set down by Arthur P. Davis, Regina Andrews, Arna Bontemps, and Hughes.

In the first flush of Harlem's realization and of general African-American exuberance, the Red Summer of 1919 had a cruelly decompressing impact on Harlem and Afro-America in general. The adage of peasants in Europe—"City air makes free"—was also true for sharecropping blacks, but not even the cities of the North made them equal or rich, or even physically secure. Charleston, South Carolina, erupted in riot in May, followed by Longview, Texas, and Washington, D.C., in July. Chicago exploded on July 27. Lynchings of returning African-American soldiers and expulsion of African-American workers from unions abounded. In the North, the white working classes struck out against perceived and manipulated threats to job security and unionism from blacks streaming north. In Helena, Arkansas, a pogrom was unleashed against black farmers organizing a cotton cooperative; outside Atlanta the Ku Klux Klan was reconstituted. The message of the white South to African Americans was that the racial status quo ante bellum was on again with a vengeance. Twenty-six race riots in towns, cities, and counties swept across the nation all the way to Nebraska. The "race problem" definitively became an American dilemma and no longer a remote complexity in the exotic South.

The term "New Negro" entered the vocabulary in reaction to the Red Summer, along with McKay's poetic catechism: "Like men we'll face the murderous, cowardly pack/Pressed to the wall, dying, but fighting back!" There was a groundswell of support for Marcus Garvey's UNIA. Until his 1924 imprisonment for mail fraud, the Jamaican immigrant's message of African Zionism, anti-integrationism, working-class assertiveness, and Bookerite business enterprise increasingly threatened the hegemony of the Talented Tenth and its major organizations, the NAACP and NUL, among people of color in America (much of Garvey's support came from West Indians). The UNIA's phenomenal fund-raising success, as well as its portrayal of the civil rights leadership as alienated by class and color from the mass of black people, delivered a jolt to the integrationist elite. "Garvey," wrote Mary White Ovington, one of the NAACP's white founders, "was the first Negro in the United States to capture the imagination of the masses." *The Negro World,* Garvey's multilingual newspaper, circulated throughout Latin America and the African empires of Britain and France. To the established leadership, then, the UNIA was a double threat because of its mass appeal among African Americans and because "respectable" civil rights organizations feared the spillover from the alarm Garveyism caused the white power structure. While Locke wrote in his introductory remarks to the

special issue of *Survey Graphic* that "the thinking Negro has shifted a little to the left with the world trend," he clearly had Garveyism in mind when he said of black separatism, "this cannot be—even if it were desirable." Although the movement was its own worst enemy, the Talented Tenth was pleased to help the Justice Department speed its demise.

No less an apostle of high culture than Du Bois, initially a Renaissance enthusiast, vividly expressed the far-fetched nature of the arts movement as early as 1923: "How is it that an organization of this kind [the NAACP] can turn aside to talk about art? After all, what have we who are slaves and black to do with art?" Slavery's legacy of cultural parochialism, the agrarian orientation of most African Americans, systematic underfunding of primary education, the emphasis on vocationalism at the expense of liberal arts in colleges, economic marginality, the extreme insecurity of middle-class status—all strongly militated against the flourishing of African-American artists, poets, and writers. It was the brilliant insight of the men and women of the NAACP and NUL that although the road to the ballot box, the union hall, the decent neighborhood, and the office was blocked, there were two paths that had not been barred, in part because of their very implausibility, as well as their irrelevancy to most Americans: arts and letters. These people saw the small cracks in the wall of racism that could, they anticipated, be widened through the production of exemplary racial images in collaboration with liberal white philanthropy, the robust culture industry located primarily in New York, and artists from white bohemia (like themselves, marginal and in tension with the status quo).

If in retrospect, then, the New Negro Arts Movement has been interpreted as a natural phase in the cultural evolution of another American group—a band in the literary continuum running from New England, Knickerbocker New York, and Hoosier Indiana to the Village's bohemia, East Side Yiddish drama and fiction, and the southern Agrarians—such an interpretation sacrifices causation to appearance. The other group traditions emerged out of the hieratic concerns, genteel leisure, privileged alienation, or transplanted learning of critical masses of independent men and women. The Renaissance represented much less an evolutionary part of a common experience than it did a generation-skipping phenomenon in which a vanguard of the Talented Tenth elite recruited, organized, subsidized, and guided an unevenly endowed cohort of artists and writers to make statements that advanced a certain conception of the race—a cohort of whom most would never have imagined the possibility of artistic and literary careers.

Toomer, McKay, Hughes, and Cullen possessed the rare ability combined with personal eccentricity that defined them as artists; the Renaissance needed not only more like them but a large cast of supporters and extras. American dropouts heading for seminars in garrets and cafés in Paris were invariably white and descended from an older gentry displaced by new moneyed elites. Charles Johnson and his allies were able to make the critical Renaissance mass possible. Johnson assembled files on prospective recruits throughout the country, going so far as to cajole Aaron Douglas and others into coming to Harlem, where a network staffed by his secretary, Ethel Ray Nance, and her friends Regina Anderson and Louella Tucker (assisted by the gifted Trinidadian short story writer Eric Walrond) looked after them until a salary or fellowship was secured. White, the self-important assistant secretary of the NAACP, urged Robeson to abandon law for an acting career, encouraged Nella Larsen to follow his own example as a novelist, and passed the hat for artist Hale Woodruff. Fauset continued to discover and publish short stories and verse, such as those of Wallace Thurman and Arna Bontemps.

Shortly after the Civic Club evening, both the NAACP and the NUL announced the creation of annual awards ceremonies bearing the titles of their respective publications, *Crisis* and *Opportunity*. The award of the first *Opportunity* prizes came in May 1925 in an elaborate ceremony at the Fifth Avenue Restaurant with some three hundred participants. Twenty-four judges in five categories had ruled on the worthiness of entries. Carl Van Doren, Zona Gale, Fannie Hurst, Dorothy Canfield Fisher, and Alain Locke, among others, judged short stories. Witter Bynner, John Farrar, Clement Wood, and James Weldon Johnson read the poetry entries. Eugene O'Neill, Alexander Woollcott, Thomas M. Gregory, and Robert Benchley appraised drama. The judges for essays were Van Wyck Brooks, John Macy, Henry Goodard Leach, and L. Hollingsworth Wood. The awards ceremony was interracial, but white capital and influence were crucial to success, and the white presence in the beginning was pervasive, setting the outer boundaries for what was creatively normative. Money to start the *Crisis* prizes had come from Amy Spingarn, an accomplished artist and poet and the wife of Joel Spingarn, chairman of the NAACP's board of directors. The wife of the influential attorney, Fisk University trustee, and Urban League board chairman L. Hollingsworth Wood had made a similar contribution to initiate the *Opportunity* prizes.

These were the whites Zora Neale Hurston, one of the first *Opportunity* prize winners, memorably dubbed "Negrotarians." These comprised several categories: political

Negrotarians such as progressive journalist Ray Stannard Baker and maverick socialist types associated with *Modern Quarterly* (V. F. Calverton, Max Eastman, Lewis Mumford, Scott Nearing); salon Negrotarians such as Robert Chanler, Charles Studin, Carl and Fania (Marinoff) Van Vechten, and Elinor Wylie, for whom the Harlem artists were more exotics than talents; Lost Generation Negrotarians drawn to Harlem on their way to Paris by a need for personal nourishment and confirmation of cultural health, in which their romantic or revolutionary perceptions of African Americans played a key role—Anderson, O'Neill, Georgia O'Keeffe, Zona Gale, Waldo Frank, Louise Bryant, Sinclair Lewis, Hart Crane; commercial Negrotarians such as the Knopfs, the Gershwins, Rowena Jelliffe, Liveright, V. F. Calverton, and music impresario Sol Hurok, who scouted and mined Afro-America like prospectors.

The philanthropic Negrotarians, Protestant and Jewish, encouraged the Renaissance from similar motives of principled religious and social obligation and of class hegemony. Oswald Garrison Villard (grandson of William Lloyd Garrison, heir to a vast railroad fortune, owner of the *New York Evening Post* and the *Nation,* and cofounder of the NAACP), along with foundation controllers William E. Harmon and J. G. Phelps-Stokes, and Mary White Ovington of affluent abolitionist pedigree, looked on the Harlem Renaissance as a movement it was their Christian duty to sanction, as well as an efficacious mode of encouraging social change without risking dangerous tensions. Jewish philanthropy, notably represented by the Altmans, Rosenwalds, Spingarns, Lehmans, and Otto Kahn, had an additional motivation, as did the interest of such scholars as Franz Boas and Melville Herskovits, jurists Louis Brandeis, Louis Marshall, and Arthur Spingarn, and progressive reformers Martha Gruening and Jacob Billikopf. The tremendous increase after 1900 of Jewish immigrants from Slavic Europe had provoked nativist reactions and, with the 1915 lynching of Atlanta businessman Leo Frank, both an increasingly volatile anti-Semitism and an upsurge of Zionism. Redoubled victimization of African Americans, exacerbated by the tremendous outmigration from the South, portended a climate of national intolerance that wealthy, assimilated German-American Jews foresaw as inevitably menacing to all American Jews.

The May 1925 *Opportunity* gala showcased the steadily augmenting talent in the Renaissance—what Hurston pungently characterized as the "Niggerati." Two laureates, Cullen and Hughes, had already won notice beyond Harlem. The latter had engineered his "discovery" as a Washington, D.C., bellhop by placing dinner and three poems on Vachel Lindsay's hotel table. Some prize winners were

Zora Neale Hurston. AP/WIDE WORLD PHOTOS. REPRODUCED BY PERMISSION.

barely to be heard from again: Joseph Cotter, G. D. Lipscomb, Warren MacDonald, Fidelia Ripley. Others, such as John Matheus (first prize in the short story category) and Frank Horne (honorable mention), failed to achieve first-rank standing in the Renaissance. But most of those whose talent had staying power were also introduced that night: E. Franklin Frazier, winning the first prize for an essay on social equality; Sterling Brown, taking second prize for an essay on the singer Roland Hayes; Hurston, awarded second prize for a short story, "Spunk"; and Eric Walrond, third short-story prize for "Voodoo's Revenge." James Weldon Johnson read the poem taking first prize, "The Weary Blues," Hughes's turning-point poem combining the gift of a superior artist and the enduring, music-encased spirit of the black migrant. Comments from Negrotarian judges ranged from O'Neill's advice to "be yourselves" to novelist Edna Worthley Underwood's exultant anticipation of a "new epoch in American letters," and Clement Wood's judgment that the general standard "was higher than such contests usually bring out."

Whatever their criticisms and however dubious their enthusiasms, what mattered as far as Charles Johnson and his collaborators were concerned was success in mobilizing and institutionalizing a racially empowering crusade and cementing an alliance between the wielders of influence and resources in the white and black communities, to which the caliber of literary output was a subordinate, though by no means irrelevant, concern. In the September 1924 issue of *Opportunity* inaugurating the magazine's departure from exclusive social-scientific concerns, Johnson had spelled out clearly the object of the prizes: they were to bring African-American writers "into contact with the general world of letters to which they have been for the most part timid and inarticulate strangers; to stimulate and foster a type of writing by Negroes which shakes itself free of deliberate propaganda and protest." The measures of Johnson's success were the announcement of a second *Opportunity* contest, to be underwritten by Harlem "businessman" (and numbers king) Caspar Holstein; former *Times* music critic Carl Van Vechten's enthusiasm over Hughes, and the subsequent arranging of a contract with Knopf for Hughes's first volume of poetry; and, one week after the awards ceremony, a prediction by the *New York Herald Tribune* that the country was "on the edge, if not already in the midst of, what might not improperly be called a Negro renaissance"—thereby giving the movement its name.

Priming the public for the Fifth Avenue Restaurant occasion, the special edition of *Survey Graphic* edited by Locke, "Harlem: Mecca of the New Negro," had reached an unprecedented forty-two thousand readers in March 1925. The ideology of cultural nationalism at the heart of the Renaissance was crisply delineated in Locke's opening essay, "Harlem": "Without pretense to their political significance, Harlem has the same role to play for the New Negro as Dublin has had for the New Ireland or Prague for the New Czechoslovakia." A vast racial formation was under way in the relocation of the peasant masses ("they stir, they move, they are more than physically restless"), the editor announced. "The challenge of the new intellectuals among them is clear enough." The migrating peasants from the South were the soil out of which all success would come, but soil must be tilled, and the Howard University philosopher reserved that task exclusively for the Talented Tenth in liaison with its mainstream analogues—in the "carefully maintained contacts of the enlightened minorities of both race groups." There was little amiss about America that interracial elitism could not set right, Locke and the others believed. Despite historical discrimination and the Red Summer, the Rhodes scholar assured readers that the increasing radicalism among African Americans was superficial. The African American was only a "forced radical," a radical "on race matters, conservative on others." In a surfeit of mainstream reassurance, Locke concluded, "The Negro mind reaches out as yet to nothing but American events, American ideas." At year's end, Albert and Charles Boni published Locke's *The New Negro*, an expanded and polished edition of the poetry and prose from the *Opportunity* contest and the special *Survey Graphic*.

The course of American letters was unchanged by the offerings in *The New Negro*. Still, the book carried several memorable works, such as the short story "The South Lingers On," by Brown University and Howard Medical School graduate Rudolph Fisher; the acid "White House-(s)" and the euphonic "The Tropics in New York," poems by McKay, now in European self-exile, and several poetic vignettes from Toomer's *Cane*. Hughes's "Jazzonia," previously published in the *Crisis*, was so poignant as to be almost tactile as it described "six long-headed jazzers" playing while a dancing woman "lifts high a dress of silken gold." In "Heritage," a poem previously unpublished, Cullen outdid himself in his grandest (if not his best) effort with its famous refrain, "What is Africa to me." The book carried distinctive silhouette drawings and Egyptian-influenced motifs by Aaron Douglas, whose work was to become the artistic signature of the Renaissance. With thirty-four African-American contributors—four were white—Locke's work included most of the Renaissance regulars. (The notable omissions were Asa Randolph, George Schuyler, and Wallace Thurman.) These were the gifted men and women who were to show by example what the potential of some African Americans could be and who proposed to lead their people into an era of opportunity and justice.

Deeply influenced, as were Du Bois and Fauset, by readings in German political philosophy and European nationalism (especially Herder and Fichte, Palacky and Synge, Herzl and Mazzini), Locke's notion of civil rights advancement was a "cell group" of intellectuals, artists, and writers "acting as the advance guard of the African peoples in their contact with Twentieth century civilization." By virtue of their symbolic achievements and their adroit collaboration with the philanthropic and reform-minded mainstream, their augmenting influence would ameliorate the socioeconomic conditions of their race over time and from the top downward. It was a Talented Tenth conceit, Schuyler snorted in Asa Randolph's *Messenger* magazine, worthy of a "high priest of the intellectual snobbocracy," and he awarded Locke the magazine's "elegantly embossed and beautifully lacquered dill pickle." Yet Locke's approach seemed to work, for although the objective conditions confronting most African Americans in Harlem and elsewhere were deteriorating, optimism remained high. Harlem recoiled from Garveyism and social-

ism to applaud Phi Beta Kappa poets, university-trained painters, concertizing musicians, and novel-writing officers of civil rights organizations. "Everywhere we heard the sighs of wonder, amazement and sometimes admiration when it was whispered or announced that here was one of the 'New Negroes,'" Bontemps recalled.

By the summer of 1926, Renaissance titles included the novels *Cane, There is Confusion, The Fire in the Flint,* and Walter White's *Flight* (1926), and the volumes of poetry *Harlem Shadows,* Cullen's *Color* (1924), and Hughes's *The Weary Blues* (1926). The second *Opportunity* awards banquet, in April 1926, was another artistic and interracial success. Playwright Joseph Cotter was honored again, as was Hurston for a short story. Bontemps, a California-educated poet struggling in Harlem, won first prize for "Golgotha Is a Mountain," and Dorothy West, a Bostonian aspiring to make a name in fiction, made her debut, as did essayist Arthur Fauset, Jessie's able half-brother. The William E. Harmon Foundation transferred its attention at the beginning of 1926 from student loans and blind children to the Renaissance, announcing seven annual prizes for literature, music, fine arts, industry, science, education, and race relations, with George Edmund Haynes, African-American official in the Federal Council of Churches, and Locke as chief advisers. That same year, the publishers Boni & Liveright offered a $1,000 prize for the "best novel on Negro life" by an African America. Caspar Holstein contributed $1,000 that year to endow *Opportunity* prizes; Van Vechten made a smaller contribution to the same cause. Amy Spingarn provided $600 toward the *Crisis* awards. Otto Kahn underwrote two years in France for the young artist Hale Woodruff. There were the Louis Rodman Wanamaker prizes in music composition.

Both the Garland Fund (American Fund for Public Service) and the NAACP's coveted Spingarn Medal were intended to promote political and social change rather than creativity, but three of eight Spingarn Medals were awarded to artists and writers between 1924 and 1931, and the Garland Fund was similarly responsive. The first of the Guggenheim Fellowships awarded to Renaissance applicants went to Walter White in 1927, to be followed by Eric Walrond, Nella Larsen (Imes), and Zora Neale Hurston. The Talented Tenth's more academically oriented members benefited from the generosity of the new Rosenwald Fund fellowships.

The third *Opportunity* awards dinner was a vintage one for poetry, with entries by Bontemps, Sterling Brown, Hughes, Helene Johnson, and Jonathan H. Brooks. In praising their general high quality, the white literary critic Robert T. Kerlin added the revealing comment that their effect would be "hostile to lynching and to jim-crowing."

Walrond's lush, impressionistic collection of short stories, *Tropic Death,* appeared from Boni & Liveright at the end of 1926, the most probing exploration of the psychology of cultural underdevelopment since Toomer's *Cane.* If *Cane* recaptured in a string of glowing vignettes (most of them about women) the sunset beauty and agony of a pre-industrial culture, *Tropic Death* did much the same for the Antilles. Hughes's second volume of poetry, *Fine Clothes to the Jew* (1927), spiritedly portrayed the city life of ordinary men and women who had traded the hardscrabble of farming for the hardscrabble of domestic work and odd jobs. Hughes scanned the low-down pursuits of "Bad Man," "Ruby Brown," and "Beale Street," and shocked Brawley and other Talented Tenth elders with the bawdy "Red Silk Stockings." "Put on yo' red silk stockings,/Black gal," it began, urging her to show herself to white boys. It ended wickedly with "An' tomorrow's chile'll/Be a high yaller."

A melodrama of Harlem life that had opened in February 1926, *Lulu Belle,* produced by David Belasco, won the distinction for popularizing Harlem with masses of Jazz Age whites. But the part of Lulu Belle was played by Lenore Ulric in blackface. Drama quickened again in the fall of 1927 with Harlemite Frank Wilson (and, for one month, Robeson) in the lead role in Du Bose and Dorothy Heyward's hugely successful play *Porgy. Porgy* brought recognition and employment to Rose McClendon, Georgette Harvey, Evelyn Ellis, Jack Carter, Percy Verwayne, and Leigh Whipper. Richard Bruce Nugent, Harlem's most outrageous decadent, and Wallace Thurman, a Utah-born close second, newly arrived from Los Angeles, played members of the population of "Catfish Row." Frank Wilson of *Porgy* fame wrote a play himself, *Meek Mose,* which opened on Broadway in February 1928. Its distinction lay mainly in the employment it gave to Harlem actors and secondarily in an opening-night audience containing Mayor James Walker, Tuskegee principal Robert Russa Moton, Alexander Woollcott, Harry T. Burleigh, Otto Kahn, and the Joel Spingarns. There was a spectacular Carnegie Hall concert in March 1928 by the ninety-voice Hampton Institute Choir, followed shortly by W. C. Handy's Carnegie Hall lecture on the origins and development of African-American music, accompanied by choir and orchestra.

Confidence among African-American leaders in the power of the muses to heal social wrongs was the rule, rather than the exception, by 1927. Every issue of *Opportunity,* the gossipy *Inter-State Tattler* newspaper, and, frequently, even the mass-circulation *Chicago Defender* or the soi-disant socialist *Messenger* trumpeted racial salvation through artistic excellence until the early 1930s. *Harper's*

for November 1928 carried James Weldon Johnson's article reviewing the strategies employed in the past for African-American advancement: "religion, education, politics, industrial, ethical, economic, sociological." The executive secretary of the NAACP serenely concluded that "through his artistic efforts the Negro is smashing" racial barriers to his progress "faster than he has ever done through any other method." Charles Johnson, Jessie Fauset, Alain Locke, and Walter White fully agreed. Such was their influence with foundations, publishing houses, the Algonquin Round Table, and various godfathers and godmothers of the Renaissance (such as the mysterious, tyrannical, fabulously wealthy Mrs. Osgood Mason) that McKay, viewing the scene from abroad, spoke derisively of the artistic and literary autocracy of "that NAACP crowd."

A veritable ministry of culture now presided over African America. The ministry mounted a movable feast to which the anointed were invited, sometimes to Walter and Gladys White's apartment at 409 Edgecombe Avenue, where they might share cocktails with Sinclair Lewis or Mencken; often (after 1928) to the famous 136th Street "Dark Tower" salon maintained by beauty-culture heiress A'Lelia Walker, where guests might be Sir Osbert Sitwell, the crown prince of Sweden, or Lady Mountbatten; and very frequently to the West Side apartment of Carl and Fania Van Vechten, to imbibe the host's sidecars and listen to Robeson sing or Jim Johnson recite from "God's Trombones" or George Gershwin play the piano. Meanwhile, Harlem's appeal to white revelers inspired the young physician Rudolph Fisher to write a satiric piece in the August 1927 *American Mercury* called "The Caucasian Storms Harlem."

The third phase of the Harlem Renaissance began even as the second had just gotten under way. The second phase (1924 to mid-1926) was dominated by the officialdom of the two major civil rights organizations, with their ideology of the advancement of African Americans through the creation and mobilization of an artistic-literary movement. Its essence was summed up in blunt declarations by Du Bois that he didn't care "a damn for any art that is not used for propaganda," or in exalted formulations by Locke that the New Negro was "an augury of a new democracy in American culture." The third phase of the Renaissance, from mid-1926 to 1934, was marked by rebellion against the civil rights establishment on the part of many of the artists and writers whom that establishment had promoted. Three publications during 1926 formed a watershed between the genteel and the demotic Renaissance. Hughes's "The Negro Artist and the Racial Mountain," appearing in the June 1926 issue of the *Nation,* served as a manifesto of the breakaway from the arts and letters party line. Van Vechten's *Nigger Heaven,* released by Knopf that August, drove much of literate Afro-America into a dichotomy of approval and apoplexy over "authentic" versus "proper" cultural expression. Wallace Thurman's *Fire!!,* available in November, assembled the rebels for a major assault against the civil rights ministry of culture.

Hughes's turning-point essay had been provoked by Schuyler's *Nation* article "The Negro Art-Hokum," which ridiculed "eager apostles from Greenwich Village, Harlem, and environs" who made claims for a special African-American artistic vision distinctly different from that of white Americans. "The Aframerican is merely a lamp-blacked Anglo-Saxon," Schuyler had sneered. In a famous peroration, Hughes answered that he and his fellow artists intended to express their "individual dark-skinned selves without fear or shame. If white people are pleased we are glad. . . . If colored people are pleased we are glad. If they are not, their displeasure doesn't matter either." And there was considerable African-American displeasure. Much of the condemnation of the license for expression Hughes, Thurman, Hurston, and other artists arrogated to themselves was generational or puritanical, and usually both. "Vulgarity has been mistaken for art," Brawley spluttered after leafing the pages of *Fire!!* "I have just tossed the first issue of *Fire!!* into the fire," the book review critic for the *Baltimore Afro-American* snapped after reading Richard Bruce Nugent's extravagantly homoerotic short story "Smoke, Lillies and Jade." Du Bois was said to be deeply aggrieved.

But much of the condemnation stemmed from racial sensitivity, from sheer mortification at seeing uneducated, crude, and scrappy black men and women depicted without tinsel or soap. Thurman and associated editors John Davis, Aaron Douglas, Gwendolyn Bennett, Arthur Huff Fauset, Hughes, Hurston, and Nugent took the Renaissance out of the parlor, the editorial office, and the banquet room. *Fire!!* featured African motifs drawn by Douglas and Nordic-featured African Americans with exaggeratedly kinky hair by Nugent, poems to an elevator boy by Hughes, jungle themes by Edward Silvera, short stories about prostitution ("Cordelia the Crude") by Thurman, gender conflict between black men and women at the bottom of the economy ("Sweat") by Hurston, and a burly boxer's hatred of white people ("Wedding Day") by Bennett; and a short play about pigment complexes within the race (*Color Struck*) by Hurston, shifting the focus to Locke's "peasant matrix," to the sorrows and joys of those outside the Talented Tenth. "Let the blare of Negro jazz bands and the bellowing voice of Bessie Smith . . . penetrate the closed ears of the colored near-intellectuals," Hughes exhorted in "The Negro Artist and the Racial Mountain."

Van Vechten's influence decidedly complicated the reactions of otherwise worldly critics such as Du Bois, Jessie Fauset, Locke, and Cullen. While his novel's title alone enraged many Harlemites who felt their trust and hospitality betrayed, the deeper objections of the sophisticated to *Nigger Heaven* lay in its message that the Talented Tenth's preoccupation with cultural improvement was a misguided affectation that would cost the race its vitality. It was the "archaic Negroes" who were at ease in their skins and capable of action, Van Vechten's characters demonstrated. Significantly, although Du Bois and Fauset found themselves in the majority among the Renaissance leadership (ordinary Harlemites burned Van Vechten in effigy at 135th Street and Lenox Avenue), Charles Johnson, James Weldon Johnson, Schuyler, White, and Hughes praised the novel's sociological verve and veracity and the service they believed it rendered to race relations.

The younger artists embraced Van Vechten's fiction as a worthy model because of its ribald iconoclasm and its iteration that the future of African-American arts lay in the culture of the working poor, and even of the underclass—in bottom-up drama, fiction, music, poetry, and painting. Regularly convening at the notorious "267 House," Thurman's rent-free apartment on 136th Street (alternately known as "Niggerati Manor"), the group that came to produce *Fire!!* saw art not as politics by other means—civil rights between book covers or from a stage or an easel—but as an expression of the intrinsic conditions most people of African descent were experiencing. They spoke of the need "for a truly Negroid note," for empathy with "those elements within the race which are still too potent for easy assimilation," and they openly mocked the premise of the civil rights establishment that (as a Hughes character says in *The Ways of White Folks*) "art would break down color lines, art would save the race and prevent lynchings! Bunk!" Finally, like creative agents in society from time immemorial, they were impelled to insult their patrons and to defy conventions.

To put the Renaissance back on track, Du Bois sponsored a symposium in late 1926, inviting a wide spectrum of views about the appropriate course the arts should take. His unhappiness was readily apparent, both with the overly literary tendencies of Locke and with the bottom-up school of Hughes and Thurman. The great danger was that politics was dropping out of the Renaissance, that the movement was turning into an evasion, sedulously encouraged by certain whites. "They are whispering, 'Here is a way out. Here is the real solution to the color problem. The recognition accorded Cullen, Hughes, Fauset, White, and others shows there is no real color line,'" Du Bois charged. He then announced that all *Crisis* literary prizes would henceforth be reserved for works encouraging "general knowledge of banking and insurance in modern life and specific knowledge of what American Negroes are doing in these fields." Neither James Weldon Johnson nor White (soon to be a Guggenheim fellow on leave from the NAACP to write another novel in France) approved of the withdrawal of the *Crisis* from the Renaissance, but they failed to change Du Bois's mind.

White's own effort to sustain the civil-rights-by-copyright strategy was the ambitious novel *Flight,* edited by his friend Sinclair Lewis and released by Knopf in 1926. A tale of near-white African Americans of unusual culture and professional accomplishment who prove their moral superiority to their oppressors, White's novel was considered somewhat flat even by kind critics. Unkind critics, such as Thurman and the young Frank Horne at *Opportunity,* savaged it. The reissue the following year of *The Autobiography of an Ex-Colored Man* (with Johnson's authorship finally acknowledged) and publication of a volume of Cullen's poetry, *Copper Sun,* continued the tradition of genteel, exemplary letters. In a further effort to restore direction, Du Bois's *Dark Princess* appeared in 1928 from Harcourt, Brace; it was a large, serious novel in which the "problem of the twentieth century" is taken in charge by a Talented Tenth International whose prime mover is a princess from India. But the momentum stayed firmly with the rebels.

Although Thurman's magazine died after one issue, respectable Afro-America was unable to ignore the novel that embodied the values of the Niggerati—the first Renaissance best-seller by a black author: McKay's *Home to Harlem,* released by Harper & Brothers in the spring of 1928. No graduates of Howard or Harvard discourse on literature at the Dark Tower or at Jessie Fauset's in this novel. It has no imitations of Du Bois, James Weldon Johnson, or Locke—and no whites at all. Its milieu is wholly plebeian. The protagonist, Jake, is a Lenox Avenue Noble Savage who demonstrates (in marked contrast to the book-reading Ray) the superiority of the Negro mind uncorrupted by European learning. *Home to Harlem* finally shattered the enforced literary code of the civil rights establishment. The *Defender* disliked McKay's novel, and Du Bois, who confessed feeling "distinctly like needing a bath" after reading it, declared that *Home to Harlem* was about the "debauched tenth." Rudolph Fisher's *The Walls of Jericho,* appearing that year from Knopf, was a brilliant, deftly executed satire that upset Du Bois as much as it heartened Thurman. Fisher, a successful Harlem physician with solid Talented Tenth family credentials, satirized the NAACP,

the Negrotarians, Harlem high society, and easily recognized Renaissance notables, while entering convincingly into the world of the working classes, organized crime, and romance across social strata.

Charles Johnson, preparing to leave the editorship of *Opportunity* for a professorship in sociology at Fisk University, now encouraged the young rebels. Before departing, he edited an anthology of Renaissance prose and poetry, *Ebony and Topaz,* in late 1927. The movement was over its birth pangs, his preface declared. Sounding the note of Hughes's manifesto, he declared that the period of extreme touchiness was behind. Renaissance artists were "now less self-conscious, less interested in proving that they are just like white people. . . . Relief from the stifling consciousness of being a problem has brought a certain superiority" to the Harlem Renaissance, Johnson asserted. Johnson left for Nashville in March 1928, four years to the month after his first Civic Club invitations.

Meanwhile, McKay's and Fisher's fiction inspired the Niggerati to publish an improved version of *Fire!!* The magazine, *Harlem,* appeared in November 1928. Editor Thurman announced portentously, "The time has now come when the Negro artist can be his true self and pander to the stupidities of no one, either white or black." While Brawley, Du Bois, and Fauset continued to grimace, Harlem benefited from significant defections. It won the collaboration of Locke and White; Roy de Coverly, George W. Little, and Schuyler signed on; and Hughes contributed one of his finest short stories, based on his travels down the west coast of Africa—"Luani of the Jungles," a polished genre piece on the seductions of the civilized and the primitive. Once again, Nugent was wicked, but this time more conventionally. The magazine lasted two issues.

The other Renaissance novel that year from Knopf, Nella Larsen's *Quicksand,* achieved the distinction of being praised by Du Bois, Locke, and Hughes. Larsen was born in the Danish Virgin Islands of mixed parentage. Trained in the sciences at Fisk and the University of Copenhagen, she would remain something of a mystery woman, helped in her career by Van Vechten and White but somehow always receding, and finally disappearing altogether from the Harlem scene. *Quicksand* was a triumph of vivid yet economical writing and rich allegory. Its very modern heroine experiences misfortunes and ultimate destruction from causes that are both racial and individual; she is not a tragic mulatto, but a mulatto who is tragic for both sociological and existential reasons. Roark Bradford, in the *Herald Tribune,* thought *Quicksand*'s first half very good, and Du Bois said it was the best fiction since Chesnutt.

There were reviews (*Crisis, New Republic, New York Times*) that were as laudatory about Jessie Fauset's *Plum*

Countee Cullen. THE BETTMANN ARCHIVE/CORBIS-BETTMANN. REPRODUCED BY PERMISSION.

Bun, also a 1928 release, but they were primarily due to the novel's engrossing reconstruction of rarefied, upper-class African-American life in Philadelphia rather than to special literary merit. If Helga Crane, the protagonist of *Quicksand,* was the Virginia Slim of Renaissance fiction, then Angela Murray (Angele, in her white persona), Fauset's heroine in her second novel, was its Gibson Girl. *Plum Bun* continued the second phase of the Renaissance, as did Cullen's second volume of poetry, *The Black Christ,* published in 1929. Ostensibly about a lynching, the lengthy title poem lost its way in mysticism, paganism, and religious remorse. The volume also lost the sympathies of most reviewers.

Thurman's *The Blacker the Berry,* published by Macaulay in early 1929, although talky and awkward in spots (Thurman had hoped to write the Great African-American Novel), was a breakthrough. The reviewer for the *Chicago Defender* enthused, "Here at last is the book for which I have been waiting, and for which you have been waiting." Hughes praised it as a "gorgeous book," mischievously writing Thurman that it would embarrass those who bestowed the "seal-of-high-and-holy approval of Harmon awards." The ministry of culture found the novel distinctly distasteful: *Opportunity* judged *The Blacker the Berry* to be fatally flawed by "immaturity and gaucherie." For the first time, color prejudice within the race was the central theme of an African-American novel. Emma Lou, its heroine

(like the author, very dark and conventionally unattractive), is obsessed with respectability as well as tortured by her pigment. Thurman makes the point on every page that Afro-America's aesthetic and spiritual center resides in the unaffected, unblended, noisome common folk and the liberated, unconventional artists.

With the unprecedented Broadway success of *Harlem,* Thurman's sensationalized romp through the underside of that area, the triumph of Niggerati aesthetics over civil rights arts and letters was impressively confirmed. The able theater critic for the *Messenger,* Theophilus Lewis, rejoiced at the "wholesome swing toward dramatic normalcy." George Jean Nathan lauded Harlem for its "sharp smell of reality." Another equally sharp smell of reality irritated establishment nostrils that same year with the publication of McKay's second novel, *Banjo,* appearing only weeks after *The Blacker the Berry.* "The Negroes are writing against themselves," lamented the reviewer for the *Amsterdam News.* Set among the human flotsam and jetsam of Marseilles and West Africa, McKay's novel again propounded the message that European civilization was inimical to Africans everywhere.

The stock market collapsed, but reverberations from the Harlem Renaissance seemed stronger than ever. Larsen's second novel, *Passing,* appeared. Its theme, like Fauset's, was the burden of mixed racial ancestry. But, although *Passing* was less successful than *Quicksand,* Larsen again evaded the trap of writing another tragic-mulatto novel by opposing the richness of African-American life to the material advantages afforded by the option of "passing." In February 1930, white playwright Marc Connelly's dramatization of Roark Bradford's book of short stories opened on Broadway as *The Green Pastures.* The Hall Johnson Choir sang in it, Richard Harrison played "De Lawd," and scores of Harlemites found parts during 557 performances at the Mansfield Theatre, and then on tour across the country. The demanding young critic and Howard University professor of English Sterling Brown pronounced the play a "miracle." The ministry of culture (increasingly run by White, after James Weldon Johnson followed Charles Johnson to a Fisk professorship) deemed *The Green Pastures* far more significant for civil rights than Thurman's *Harlem* and even than King Vidor's talking film *Hallelujah!* The NAACP's Spingarn Medal for 1930 was presented to Harrison by New York's lieutenant governor, Herbert Lehman.

After *The Green Pastures* came *Not Without Laughter,* Hughes's glowing novel from Knopf. Financed by Charlotte Osgood Mason ("Godmother") and Amy Spingarn, Hughes had resumed his college education at Lincoln University and completed *Not Without Laughter* his senior year. The beleaguered family at the center of the novel represents Afro-Americans in transition within white America. Hughes's young male protagonist learns that proving his equality means affirming his distinctive racial characteristics. Not only did Locke admire *Not Without Laughter*, the *New Masses* reviewer embraced it as "our novel." The ministry of culture decreed Hughes worthy of the Harmon gold medal for 1930. The year ended with Schuyler's ribald, sprawling satire *Black No More,* an unsparing demolition of every personality and institution in Afro-America. Little wonder that Locke titled his retrospective piece in the February 1931 *Opportunity* "The Year of Grace." Depression notwithstanding, the Renaissance appeared to be more robust than ever.

The first Rosenwald fellowships for African Americans had been secured, largely due to James Weldon Johnson's influence, the previous year. Beginning with Johnson himself in 1930, most of the African Americans who pursued cutting-edge postgraduate studies in the United States over the next fifteen years would be recipients of annual Rosenwald fellowships. Since 1928 the Harmon Foundation, advised by Locke, had mounted an annual traveling exhibition of drawings, paintings, and sculpture by African Americans. The 1930 installment introduced the generally unsuspected talent and genius of Palmer Hayden, William H. Johnson, Archibald Motley, Jr., James A. Porter, and Laura Wheeler Waring in painting. Sargent Johnson, Elizabeth Prophet, and Augusta Savage were the outstanding sculptors of the show. Both Aaron Douglas and Romare Bearden came to feel that the standards of the foundation were somewhat indulgent and therefore injurious to many young artists, which was undoubtedly true. Nevertheless, the Harmon made it possible for African-American artists to find markets previously wholly closed to them. In 1931 more than two hundred works of art formed the Harmon Travelling Exhibition of the Work of Negro Artists, to be seen by more than 150,000 people.

Superficially, Harlem itself appeared to be in fair health well into 1931. James Weldon Johnson's celebration of the community's strengths, *Black Manhattan,* was published near the end of 1930. "Harlem is still in the process of making," the book proclaimed, and the author's confidence in the power of the "recent literary and artistic emergence" to ameliorate race relations was unshaken. In Johnson's Harlem, redcaps and cooks cheered when Renaissance talents won Guggenheim and Rosenwald fellowships; they rushed to newsstands whenever the *American Mercury* or *New Republic* mentioned activities above Central Park. In this Harlem, dramatic productions unfolded weekly at the YMCA; poetry readings were held regularly at Ernestine Rose's 135th Street Public Library (today's

Schomburg Center); and people came after work to try out for Du Bois's Krigwa Players in the library's basement. It was the Harlem of amateur historians such as J. A. Rogers, who made extraordinary claims about the achievements of persons of color, and of dogged bibliophiles such as Arthur Schomburg, who documented extraordinary claims. It was much too easy for Talented Tenth notables Johnson, White, and Locke not to notice in the second year of the Great Depression that for the vast majority of the population, Harlem was in the process of unmaking. Still, there was a definite prefiguration of its mortality when A'Lelia Walker suddenly died in August 1931, a doleful occurrence shortly followed by the sale of Villa Lewaro, her Hudson mansion, at public auction.

Meanwhile, the much-decorated Fifteenth Infantry Regiment (the 369th during World War I) took possession of a new headquarters, the largest National Guard armory in the state. The monopoly of white doctors and nurses at Harlem General Hospital had been effectively challenged by the NAACP and the brilliant young surgeon Louis T. Wright. There were two well-equipped private sanitariums in Harlem by the end of the 1920s: the Vincent, financed by numbers king Caspar Holstein, and the Wiley Wilson, equipped with divorce settlement funds by one of A'Lelia Walker's husbands. Rudolph Fisher's X-ray laboratory was one of the most photographed facilities in Harlem.

Decent housing was becoming increasingly scarce for most families; the affluent, however, had access to excellent accommodations. Talented Tenth visitors availed themselves of the Dumas or the Olga, two well-appointed hotels. By the end of 1929 African Americans lived in the 500 block of Edgecombe Avenue, known as "Sugar Hill." The famous "409" overlooking the Polo Grounds was home at one time or another to the Du Boises, the Fishers, and the Whites. Below Sugar Hill was the five-acre, Rockefeller-financed Dunbar Apartments complex, its 511 units fully occupied in mid-1928. The Dunbar eventually became home for the Du Boises, E. Simms Campbell (illustrator and cartoonist), Fletcher Henderson, the A. Philip Randolphs, Leigh Whipper (actor), and, briefly, Paul and Essie Robeson. The complex published its own weekly bulletin, the *Dunbar News,* an even more valuable record of Talented Tenth activities during the Renaissance than the *Inter-State Tattler.*

The 1931 Report on Negro Housing, presented to President Hoover, was a document starkly in contrast to the optimism found in *Black Manhattan.* Nearly 50 percent of Harlem's families would be unemployed by the end of 1932. The syphilis rate was nine times higher than white Manhattan's; the tuberculosis rate was five times greater; those for pneumonia and typhoid were twice those of whites. Two African-American mothers and two babies died for every white mother and child. Harlem General Hospital, the area's single public facility, served 200,000 people with 273 beds. Twice as much of the income of a Harlem family went for rent as a white family's. Meanwhile, median family income in Harlem dropped 43.6 percent in two years by 1932. The ending of Prohibition would devastate scores of marginal speakeasies, as well as prove fatal to theaters such as the Lafayette. Connie's Inn would eventually migrate downtown. Until then, however, the clubs in "The Jungle," as 133rd Street was called (Bamville, Connor's, the Clam House, the Nest Club), and elsewhere (Pod's and Jerry's, Smalls' Paradise) continued to do a land-office business.

Because economic power was the Achilles' heel of the community, real political power also eluded Harlem. Harlem's Republican congressional candidates made unsuccessful runs in 1924 and 1928. Until the Twenty-first Congressional District was redrawn after the Second World War, African Americans were unable to overcome Irish, Italian, and Jewish voting patterns in order to elect one of their own. In state and city elections, black Harlem fared better. African-American aldermen had served on the city council since 1919; black state assemblymen were first elected in 1917. Republican Party patronage was funneled through the capable but aged Charles W. ("Charlie") Anderson, collector of Internal Revenue for the Third District. Although African Americans voted overwhelmingly for the Republican ticket at the national level, Harlemites readily voted for Democrats in city matters. Democratic patronage for Harlem was handled by Harvard-educated Ferdinand Q. Morton, chairman of the Municipal Civil Service Commission and head of the United Colored Democracy—"Black Tammany." In 1933 Morton would bolt the Democrats to help elect Fusion candidate Fiorello La Guardia mayor. Despite a growing sense of political consciousness, greatly intensified by the exigencies of the depression, Harlem continued to be treated by City Hall and the municipal bureaucracies as though it were a colony.

The thin base of its economy and politics eventually began to undermine the Renaissance. Mainstream sponsorship, direct and indirect, was indispensable to the movement's momentum, and as white foundations, publishers, producers, readers, and audiences found their economic resources drastically curtailed (the reduced value of Sears, Roebuck stock chilled Rosenwald Fund philanthropy), interest in African Americans evaporated. With the repeal of the Eighteenth Amendment, ending Prohibition, honorary Harlemites such as Van Vechten sobered up and turned to other pursuits. Locke's letters to Charlotte Os-

good Mason turned increasingly pessimistic in the winter of 1931. In June 1932 he perked up a bit to praise the choral ballet presented at the Eastman School of Music, *Sahdji,* with music by William Grant Still and scenario by Richard Bruce Nugent, but most of Locke's news was distinctly downbeat. The writing partnership of two of his protégés, Hughes and Hurston, their material needs underwritten in a New Jersey township by "Godmother," collapsed in acrimonious dispute. Each claimed principal authorship of the only dramatic comedy written during the Renaissance, *Mule Bone,* a three-act folk play that went unperformed (as a result of the dispute) until 1991. Locke took the side of Hurston, undermining the affective tie between Godmother and Hughes and essentially ending his relationship with the latter. The part played in this controversy by their brilliant secretary, Louise Thompson, the strong-willed, estranged wife of Wallace Thurman, remains murky, but it seems clear that Thompson's Marxism had a deep influence on Hughes in the aftermath of his painful breakup with Godmother, Locke, and Hurston.

In any case, beginning with "Advertisement for the Waldorf-Astoria," published in the December 1931 *New Masses,* Hughes's poetry became markedly political. "Elderly Race Leaders" and "Goodbye Christ," as well as the play *Scottsboro, Limited,* were irreverent, staccato offerings to the coming triumph of the proletariat. The poet's departure in June 1932 for Moscow, along with Louise Thompson, Mollie Lewis, Henry Moon, Loren Miller, Theodore Poston, and thirteen others, ostensibly to act in a Soviet film about American race relations, *Black and White,* symbolized the shift in patronage and the accompanying politicization of Renaissance artists. If F. Scott Fitzgerald, golden boy of the Lost Generation, could predict that "it may be necessary to work inside the Communist party" to put things right again in America, no one should have been surprised that Cullen and Hughes united in 1932 to endorse the Communist Party candidacy of William Z. Foster and the African American James W. Ford for president and vice-president of the United States, respectively. One Way to Heaven, Cullen's first novel—badly flawed and clearly influenced by *Nigger Heaven*—appeared in 1932, but it seemed already a baroque anachronism with its knife-wielding Lotharios and elaborately educated types. An impatient Du Bois, deeply alienated from the Renaissance, called for a second Amenia Conference to radicalize the ideology and renew the personnel of the organization.

Jessie Fauset remained oblivious to the profound artistic and political changes under way. Her final novel, *Comedy: American Style* (1933), was technically much the same as *Plum Bun.* Once again, her subject was skin pigment and the neuroses of those who had just enough of it to spend their lives obsessed by it. James Weldon Johnson's autobiography, *Along This Way,* was the publishing event of the year, an elegantly written review of his sui generis public career as archetypal Renaissance man in both meanings of the word. McKay's final novel also appeared that year. He worried familiar themes, but *Banana Bottom* represented a philosophical advance over *Home to Harlem* and *Banjo* in its reconciliation through the protagonist, Bita Plant, of the previously destructive tension in McKay's work between the natural and the artificial, soul and civilization.

The publication at the beginning of 1932 of Thurman's last novel, *Infants of the Spring,* had already announced the end of the Harlem Renaissance. The action of the book is in the characters' ideas, in their incessant talk about themselves, Booker T. Washington, W. E. B. Du Bois, racism, and the destiny of the race. Its prose is generally disappointing, but the ending is conceptually poignant. Paul Arbian (a stand-in for Richard Bruce Nugent) commits suicide in a full tub of water, which splashes over and obliterates the pages of Arbian's unfinished novel on the bathroom floor. A still legible page, however, contains this paragraph that was in effect an epitaph:

> He had drawn a distorted, inky black skyscraper, modeled after Niggerati Manor, and on which were focused an array of blindingly white beams of light. The foundation of this building was composed of crumbling stone. At first glance it could be ascertained that the skyscraper would soon crumple and fall, leaving the dominating white lights in full possession of the sky.

The literary energies of the Renaissance finally slumped. McKay returned to Harlem in February 1934 after a twelve-year sojourn abroad, but his creative powers were spent. The last novel of the movement, Hurston's beautifully written *Jonah's Gourd Vine,* went on sale in May 1934. Charles Johnson, James Weldon Johnson, and Locke applauded Hurston's allegorical story of her immediate family (especially her father) and the mores of an African-American town in Florida called Eatonville. Fisher and Thurman could have been expected to continue to write, but their fates were sealed by the former's professional carelessness and the latter's neurotic alcoholism. A few days before Christmas 1934, Thurman died, soon after his return from an abortive Hollywood film project. Ignoring his physician's strictures, he hemorrhaged after drinking to excess while hosting a party in the infamous house at 267 West 136th Street. Four days later, Fisher expired from intestinal cancer caused by repeated exposure to his own X-ray equipment. A grieving Locke wrote

Charlotte Mason from Howard University, "It is hard to see the collapse of things you have labored to raise on a sound base."

Locke's anthology had been crucial to the formation of the Renaissance. As the movement ran down, another anthology, English heiress Nancy Cunard's *Negro,* far more massive in scope, recharged the Renaissance for a brief period. Enlisting the contributions of most of the principals (though McKay and Walrond refused, and Toomer no longer acknowledged his African-American roots), Cunard captured its essence, in the manner of expert taxidermy.

Arthur Fauset attempted to explain the collapse to Locke and the readers of *Opportunity* at the beginning of 1934. He foresaw "a socio-political-economic setback from which it may take decades to recover." The Renaissance had left the race unprepared, Fauset charged, because of its unrealistic belief "that social and economic recognition will be inevitable when once the race has produced a sufficiently large number of persons who have properly qualified themselves in the arts." James Weldon Johnson's philosophical tour d'horizon appearing that year, *Negro Americans, What Now?,* asked precisely the question of the decade. Most Harlemites were certain that the riot exploding on the evening of March 19, 1935, taking three lives and causing $2 million in property damage, was not an answer. By then, the Works Progress Administration had become the major patron of African-American artists and writers. Writers like William Attaway, Ralph Ellison, Margaret Walker, Richard Wright, and Frank Yerby would emerge under its aegis, as would painters Romare Bearden, Jacob Lawrence, Charles Sebree, Lois Maillou Jones, and Charles White. The Communist Party was another patron, notably for Richard Wright, whose 1937 essay "Blueprint for Negro Writing" would materially contribute to the premise of Hughes's "The Negro Artist and the Racial Mountain." And for thousands of ordinary Harlemites who had looked to Garvey's UNIA for inspiration, then to the Renaissance, there was now Father Divine and his "heavens."

In the ensuing years much was renounced, more was lost or forgotten; yet the Renaissance, however artificial and overreaching, left a positive mark. Locke's *New Negro* anthology featured thirty of the movement's thirty-five stars. They and a small number of less gifted collaborators generated twenty-six novels, tne volumes of poetry, five Broadway plays, countless essays and short stories, three performed ballets and concerti, and a considerable output of canvas and sculpture. If the achievement was less than the titanic expectations of the ministry of culture, it was an artistic legacy, nevertheless, of and by which a beleaguered Afro-America could be both proud and sustained. Though more by osmosis than by conscious attention, mainstream America was also richer for the color, emotion, humanity, and cautionary vision produced by Harlem during its Golden Age. "If I had supposed that all Negroes were illiterate brutes, I might be astonished to discover that they can write good third-rate poetry, readable and unreadable magazine fiction," was the flinty judgment of a contemporary white Marxist. That judgment was soon beyond controversy largely because the Harlem Renaissance finally, irrefutably, proved the once-controversial point during slightly more than a single decade.

See also Abyssinian Baptist Church; Cullen, Countee; Du Bois, W. E. B.; Garvey, Marcus; Harlem, New York; Hughes, Langston; Jim Crow; Johnson, James Weldon; Joplin, Scott; National Urban League; Niagara Movement; Spingarn Medal; Universal Negro Improvement Association; White, Walter Francis

■ ■ Bibliography

Beckman, Wendy Hart. Artists and Writers of the Harlem Renaissance. Berkeley Heights, N.J.: Enslow, 2002.

Bloom, Harold, ed. The Harlem Renaissance. Philadelphia: Chelsea House, 2004.

Bontemps, Arna, ed. The Harlem Renaissance Remembered: Essays Edited with a Memoir. New York: Dodd, Mead, 1972.

Egar, Emmanuel E. Black Women Poets of the Harlem Renaissance. Lanham, Md.: University Press of America, 2003.

Huggins, Nathan I. Harlem Renaissance. New York: Oxford University Press, 1971.

Huggins, Nathan I, ed. Voices from the Harlem Renaissance. New York: Oxford University Press, 1976.

Lewis, David L. When Harlem Was in Vogue. New York: Vintage, 1981.

Schwarz, A. B. Christa. Gay Voices of the Harlem Renaissance. Bloomington: University of Indiana Press, 2003.

Wagner, Jean. Black Poets of the United States: From Paul Laurence Dunbar to Langston Hughes. Urbana: University of Illinois Press, 1973.

DAVID LEVERING LEWIS (1996)
Updated bibliography

HARLEM RENS

See Renaissance Big Five (Harlem Rens)

HARLEM WRITERS GUILD

In the late 1940s, a number of talented and ambitious young African Americans were seeking a way to simultaneously express their creativity and promote social change. Two such figures were Rosa Guy (b. 1925/28) and John Oliver Killens (1916–1987), who had studied literature and writing at prominent institutions like New York University, but realized that the mainstream literary world was largely inaccessible to blacks. Consequently, they began meeting with the writers Walter Christmas and John Henrik Clarke (1915–1998) in a Harlem storefront to critique each other's ideas and stories. By the early 1950s this workshop became known as the Harlem Writers Guild. During the guild's early years, meetings were frequently held in Killens's home, as well as at the home of the artist Aaron Douglas. As membership grew, the Guild influenced several generations of African-American writers.

Killens's Youngblood (1954) was the first novel published by a guild member. Appearing to critical acclaim at the beginning of the civil rights movement, it told the story of a southern black family struggling for dignity in the early twentieth century. Although Killens was a native of Georgia and a tireless voice protesting racial injustice in the United States, he was also involved in left-wing politics as a young man, and guild participants, many of whom were union organizers or Progressive Party members, were encouraged to think globally. Christmas and Clarke were both contributors to Communist periodicals, while other writers, such as novelists Julian Mayfield (1928–1984) and Paule Marshall (b. 1929), called attention to the lives and struggles of slave descendants in Cuba and the West Indies.

Although its main goals were literary, the guild believed in political action. In 1961, for example, Guy, Marshall, and the poet Maya Angelou staged a sit-in at the United Nations to protest the assassination of the first Congolese premier, Patrice Lumumba. That same year, when the Cuban leader Fidel Castro and the Soviet premier Nikita Khrushchev met in Harlem, guild members joined another organization, Fair Play for Cuba, in welcoming them to the African-American capital of the world.

During the 1960s a number of guild members found work as professional writers, journalists, and editors in the publishing industry. As a consequence, the guild, in addition to offering workshops, began sponsoring writers' conferences and book parties. The celebration at the United Nations for Chester Himes's biography The Quality of

Hurt drew 700 people, while more than a thousand people attended a 1965 conference, "The Negro Writer's Vision of America," which was cosponsored by the New School for Social Research. This event featured a widely reported debate between Killens and Clarke and two white intellectuals, Herbert Aptheker and Walter Lowenfels, on the proper role of the artist in the fight against racism. The actor and playwright Ossie Davis (1917–2005), a participant at the conference, summed up his viewpoint when he wrote in *Negro Digest* that the black writer "must make of himself a hammer, and against the racially restricted walls of society he must strike, and strike, and strike again, until something is destroyed—either himself—or the prison walls that stifle him!"

In 1970, guild member Louise Meriwether published *Daddy Was a Numbers Runner,* and the next two decades saw the publication of acclaimed books by Grace Edwards-Yearwood, Doris Jean Austin, Arthur Flowers, and Terry McMillan, famed for her popular third novel, *Waiting to Exhale* (1992). Other guild members, such as Guy, Joyce Hansen, Brenda Wilkinson, and Walter Dean Myers, focused on writing literature for children and young adults.

In the early 1990s the guild sponsored several literary celebrations including a centennial salute to Zora Neale Hurston; "The Literary Legacy of Malcolm X," and two tributes to Rosa Guy for her leadership in the organization. Some former guild members also received national attention after the election of Bill Clinton as U.S. president. Maya Angelou was chosen to read her poem "On the Pulse of the Morning" at the 1993 presidential inauguration. In addition, Clinton made it known that his favorite mystery character was Walter Mosley's Easy Rawlings.

In 1991, guild director William H. Banks Jr. began hosting "In Our Own Words" for the MetroMagazine section on WNYE, a television station owned by the New York City Department of Education. This weekly program brought many guild members exposure in six viewing areas in the United States and Canada. Since 1988, writing workshops have met most frequently at the Schomburg Center for Research in Black Culture of the New York Public Library.

See also Angelou, Maya; Caribbean/North American Writers (Contemporary); Children's Literature; Davis, Ossie; Harlem Renaissance; Himes, Chester; Killens, John Oliver; Literature in the United States

■ ■ *Bibliography*

Cruse, Harold. *The Crisis of the Negro Intellectual.* New York: Morrow, 1967. Reprint, New York: New York Review Books, 2005.

Johnson, Abby Arthur, and Ronald Maberry. *Propaganda and Aesthetics: The Literary Politics of Afro-American Magazines in the Twentieth Century.* Amherst: University of Massachusetts Press, 1979.

SHARON M. HOWARD (1996)
Updated bibliography

HARPER, FRANCES ELLEN WATKINS

SEPTEMBER 24, 1825
FEBRUARY 20, 1911

One of the most prominent activist women of her time in the areas of abolition, temperance, and women's rights, Frances Ellen Watkins Harper also left an indelible mark on African-American literature. Frances Watkins was born in Baltimore and raised among the city's free black community. She was orphaned at an early age, so her uncle, the Rev. William Watkins, took responsibility for her care and education, enrolling her in his prestigious school for free blacks, the Academy for Negro Youth. Here Watkins received a strict, classical education, studying the Bible, Greek, and Latin. Although she left school while in her early teens to take employment as a domestic, she never ceased her quest for additional education. She remained a voracious reader; her love of books contributed to her beginnings as a writer.

Frances Watkins published her first of several volumes of poetry in 1845. This early work, *Forest Leaves,* has been lost, however. From 1850 until 1852 she taught embroidery and sewing at Union Seminary, an African Methodist Episcopal Church school near Columbus, Ohio. She then moved on to teach in Pennsylvania. Both teaching situations were difficult because the schools were poor and the facilities overtaxed. During this period she was moved by the increasing number of strictures placed on free people of color, especially in her home state of Maryland, a slave state. From this point, she became active in the anti-slavery movement.

In 1854 Watkins moved to Philadelphia and became associated with an influential circle of black and white abolitionists. Among her friends there were William Still and his daughter Mary, who operated the key Underground Railroad station in the city. The same year another collection of Watkins's verse, *Poems on Miscellaneous Subjects,* was published. Many of the pieces in this volume dealt with the horrors of slavery. The work received popular acclaim and was republished in numerous revised, enlarged editions. Watkins also published poems in prominent abolitionist papers such as *Frederick Douglass' Paper* and the *Liberator*. Later would come other collections—*Sketches of Southern Life* (1872), the narrative poem *Moses: A Story of the Nile* (1889), *Atlanta Offering: Poems* (1895), and *Martyr of Alabama and Other Poems* (1895).

With her literary career already on course, Watkins moved to Boston and joined the antislavery lecture circuit, securing a position with the Maine Anti-Slavery Society. She later toured with the Pennsylvania Anti-Slavery Society. Watkins immediately distinguished herself, making a reputation as a forceful and effective speaker, a difficult task for any woman at this time, especially an African American. Public speaking remained an important part of her career for the rest of her life, as she moved from antislavery work to other aspects of reform in the late nineteenth century.

In 1860 Frances Watkins married Fenton Harper and the two settled on a farm near Columbus, Ohio. Their daughter, Mary, was born there. Fenton Harper died four years later, and Frances Harper resumed her public career. With the close of the Civil War, she became increasingly involved in the struggle for suffrage, working with the American Equal Rights Association, the American Woman Suffrage Association, and the National Council of Women. Harper also became an active member of the Women's Christian Temperance Union. Despite her disagreements with many of the white women in these organizations and the racism she encountered, Harper remained steadfast in her commitment to the battle for women's rights. She refused to sacrifice any aspect of her commitment to African-American rights in seeking the rights of women, however. She was also a key member of the National Federation of Afro-American Women and the National Association of Colored Women.

In addition to the many poems, speeches, and essays she wrote, Harper is probably best known for her novel, *Iola Leroy; or, Shadows Uplifted,* published in 1892. The work tells the story of a young octoroon woman who is sold into slavery when her African-American heritage is revealed. It is a story about the quest for family and for one's people. Through Iola Leroy and the characters around her, Harper addresses the issues of slavery, relations between African Americans and whites, feminist concerns, labor in freedom, and the development of black intellectual communities. In this book, she combined many of her lifelong interests and passions.

Harper's public career ended around the turn of the century. She died in Philadelphia in 1911, leaving an enduring legacy of literary and activist achievement.

See also Abolition; *Frederick Douglass' Paper*; *Liberator, The*; National Association of Colored Women; National Federation of Afro-American Women; Underground Railroad

■ ■ *Bibliography*

Boyd, Melba Joyce. *Discarded Legacy: Politics and Poetics in the Life of Frances E. W. Harper, 1825–1911.* Detroit: Wayne State University Press, 1994.

Carby, Hazel V. *Reconstructing Womanhood: The Emergence of the Afro-American Woman Novelist.* New York: Oxford University Press, 1987.

Smith, Frances Foster, ed. *A Brighter Coming Day: A Frances Ellen Watkins Harper Reader.* New York: Feminist Press, 1990.

JUDITH WEISENFELD (1996)
Updated bibliography

HARRIS, ABRAM LINCOLN, JR.

JANUARY 17, 1899
NOVEMBER 16, 1963

The economist Abram Harris was born in Richmond, Virginia. He left his mark on developments in the areas of economic anthropology, black studies, institutional economics, and the history of economic thought.

A 1922 graduate of Virginia Union University in Richmond, Harris completed his M.A. in economics at the University of Pittsburgh in 1924, and he received his Ph.D. in economics in 1930 from Columbia University. After teaching briefly at West Virginia State University (1924–1925) and working at the Minneapolis Urban League (1925–1926), where he served as research director coordinating a report on the status of black working people in Minnesota's Twin Cities, Harris taught at Howard University from 1927 through 1945. He then went to the University of Chicago, where he taught for the rest of his life. Although his appointment was in the undergraduate college and he never taught graduate courses, any appointment at Chicago was a rarity for a black scholar in the 1940s.

In his early years at Howard, Harris and his colleagues Ralph Bunche (1904–1971) and E. Franklin Frazier (1894–1962) were the leading figures among the young intellectuals who attacked the traditional tactics and outlooks of the older generation of "race men." In 1931 Harris published, in collaboration with the Jewish political scientist Sterling

Spero, his most famous work, *The Black Worker*, which examined race relations in the American labor movement. In 1935, following preliminary discussions at the the the National Association for the Advancement of Colored People's Amenia Conference of 1933, he was the main author of the so-called Harris Report, which urged the NAACP to adopt a more activist protest strategy and a class-based rather than a race-based approach to social change. While the report was not enacted, Harris continued to advocate a multiracial working-class movement as the only real solution to race problems in the United States.

In 1935, Harris and Bunche sponsored a conference at Howard University on the condition of blacks during the Great Depression, out of which came a special issue of the *Journal of Negro Education* (1935). The issue contained an article inspired by Harris, developed further the next year in his publication *The Negro as Capitalist* (1936) in which he argued that black businessmen and black-owned financial institutions were as harmful to the black masses as white capitalists. He claimed that black-owned banks, in particular, subjected the black working class to usurious interest rates, high rates of mortgage loan foreclosures, and an extremely high risk of outright bank failure. He urged the black working class to rely instead upon financial cooperatives of their own making. Futhermore, in light of negligible black ownership of the nation's industrial sector, he viewed notions of the development of "black capitalism" as sheer fantasy. Finally, Harris declared that civil rights efforts by existing black organizations were doomed to inadequacy in light of the fundamental economic disparities between the races.

Into the 1940s, Harris was the intellectual leader of the left-leaning Social Science Division at Howard, which he helped found in 1937. His influence on Bunche was especially pronounced, reflected in numerous papers in which Bunche virtually echoed positions that Harris had taken earlier. Harris's vision of the history of capitalist development and the role of slavery and the slave trade also had a profound effect on Eric Williams's analysis of the origins of the British Industrial Revolution in his classic study *Capitalism and Slavery* (1944).

In 1945 Harris left Howard to accept an appointment at the University of Chicago, where he appeared to undergo an intellectual conversion to anti-Marxism. He had never been naive about his earlier endorsement of radical change, and he had expressed deep concerns about the totalitarian direction of the Soviet Revolution as early as 1925, when he wrote "Black Communists in Dixie" for the Urban League's magazine *Opportunity*.

During Harris's years at Chicago, he became largely silent on the race question. His published research efforts concentrated on the history of economic theory, notably in essays such as "The Social Philosophy of Karl Marx" (1948) and in the volume *Economics and Social Reform* (1958), an exploration of John Stuart Mill's moderate liberalism. Harris also wrote on Mill's views of mid-nineteenth-century British colonial policy, chiefly with regard to India. He had begun to write a reinterpretation of *The Black Worker*, to be called *The Economics and Politics of the American Race Problem*, when he died. In keeping with his later views, his thesis in this work was that blacks had to improve their own skills and "human capital" in order for integration efforts to succeed. He had moved wholly away from a focus on working-class political movements.

Harris had a marked influence on both black radical and neoconservative thought, and his works display one of the most discerning critical voices of the twentieth century.

See also Black Studies; Bunche, Ralph; Howard University; Intellectual Life; National Association for the Advancement of Colored People (NAACP)

■ ■ *Bibliography*

Darity, William, Jr. "Soundings and Silences on Race and Social Change: Abram Harris Jr. in the Great Depression." In *A Different Vision*, vol. 1, *African American Economic Thought*, edited by Thomas D. Boston. New York: Routledge, 1997.

Darity, William, Jr. "Harris, Abram Lincoln, Jr." In *Encyclopedia of African American Business History*, edited by Juliet E. K. Walker. Westport, Ct.: Greenwood Press, 1999.

Darity, William, Jr., and Julian Ellison "Abram Harris Jr.: The Economics of Race and Social Reform." *History of Political Economy* 22, no.4 (1990): 611–627.

Harris, Abram L., Jr. *The Negro As Capitalist: A Study of Banking and Business among American Negroes*. Philadelphia, Pa.: American Academy of Political and Social Science, 1936.

Harris, Abram L., Jr. *Race, Radicalism, and Reform: Selected Papers*, edited by William Darity Jr. New Brunswick, N.J.: Transaction Publishers, 1989.

Spero, Sterling, and Abram L. Harris Jr. *The Black Worker: The Negro and the Labor Movement*. New York: Columbia University Press, 1931.

WILLIAM A. DARITY JR. (1996)
Updated by author 2005

HARRIS, BARBARA CLEMENTINE

JUNE 12, 1930

❙❙❙

Barbara Harris was the first female bishop of the Protestant Episcopal Church. She was born in Philadelphia, where her father, Walter Harris, was a steelworker and her mother, Beatrice, was a church organist. A third generation Episcopalian, Harris was very active in the St. Barnabas Episcopal Church. While in high school she played piano for the church school and later started a young adults group.

After graduating from high school, Harris went to work for Joseph V. Baker Associates, a black-owned public relations firm. She also attended and graduated from the Charles Morris Price School of Advertising and Journalism in Philadelphia. In 1968 she went to work for Sun Oil Company and became community relations manager in 1973.

During the 1960s Harris participated in several civil rights events. She was part of the 1965 Freedom March from Selma, Alabama, to Montgomery, Alabama, with the Rev. Dr. Martin Luther King, Jr., and was also a member of a church-sponsored team of people who went to Mississippi to register black voters. Harris began attending North Philadelphia Church of the Advocate in 1968. That same year, the Union of Black Clergy was established by a group of black Episcopalian ministers. Harris and several other women lobbied for membership. Eventually, they were admitted and the word *laity* was added to the organization's name. Later it became the Union of Black Episcopalians.

Once the Episcopal Church began to ordain women in 1976, Harris began to study for the ministry. From 1977 to 1979 she took several courses at Villanova University in Philadelphia, and spent three months in informal residency at the Episcopal Divinity School in Cambridge, Massachusetts. She was named deacon in 1979, served as a deacon-in-training in 1979–1980, and was ordained to the priesthood in 1980. She left Sun Oil Co. to pursue her new career full-time.

The first four years of Harris's ministry were spent at St. Augustine-of-Hippo in Norristown, Pennsylvania. She also worked as a chaplain in the Philadelphia County Prison System, an area in which she had already spent many years as a volunteer. In 1984 she became the executive director of the Episcopal Church Publishing Co. Her writings were critical of church policies, which she believed to be in contrast to social, political, and economic fairness.

In 1988 the Episcopal Church approved the consecration of women as bishops. Harris was elected to become bishop of the Massachusetts diocese in the fall of 1988. Her election was ratified in January 1989 and she was ordained in a ceremony in Boston on February 11, 1989, with over seven thousand in attendance.

As the first female Episcopal bishop, Harris was surrounded by controversy centered on three issues: her gender, her lack of traditional seminary education and training, and her liberal viewpoints. Policies toward women, black Americans, the poor, and other minorities were always at the forefront of Harris's challenges to the church and its doctrines. Harris overcame the objections and focused her attention on her duties as a bishop. She served the diocese of Massachusetts, where she was extremely active in local communities and prison work. Greatly concerned with the prison ministry, she represented the Episcopal Church on the board of the Prisoners Visitation and Support Committee. She continued to speak out about gender discrimination in the church; in 1999 at the Church of the Advocate in Philadelphia, she spoke on the twenty-fifth anniversary of the ordination of the church's first eleven women priests, lambasting male bishops for the lack of support for women priests. In 2003 Harris retired at the age of seventy-two, the mandatory retirement age for bishops in the church.

See also Episcopalians; King, Martin Luther, Jr.; Protestantism in the Americas

■ ■ *Bibliography*

"Harris, Barbara (Clementine)." *Current Biography* 5 (June 1989): 24–28.

Harris, Barbara Clementine. *Parting Words: A Farewell Discourse.* Cambridge, Mass.: Cowley Publications, 2003.

Jessie Carney Smith, ed. *Notable Black American Women.* Detroit: Gale, 1992.

DEBI BROOME (1996)
Updated by publisher 2005

HARRIS, PATRICIA ROBERTS

MAY 31, 1924
MARCH 23, 1985

❙❙❙

Educator, lawyer, and politician Patricia Roberts was born in the blue-collar town of Mattoon, Illinois, where her father was a Pullman porter. She attended high school in Chicago and then enrolled at Howard University in Washington, D.C. She became active in civil rights causes at Howard, participating in one of the nation's first student sit-ins at a segregated Washington cafeteria and by serving as the vice chairman of a student chapter of the National Association for the Advancement of Colored People (NAACP).

After graduating in 1945, Roberts returned to Chicago, where she briefly attended graduate school at the University of Chicago and worked as program director at the Chicago Young Women's Christian Association. In 1949 she returned to Washington and accepted a position as the assistant director of the American Council on Human Rights. In 1953 she became executive director of Delta Sigma Theta, a black sorority, and two years later, she married Washington lawyer William Beasley Harris.

Patricia Roberts Harris entered George Washington Law School in 1957. Upon graduation in 1960 she accepted a position as an attorney at the U.S. Department of Justice. The following year she joined the Howard University Law School faculty, where she also served as the associate dean of students. In 1963, with the support of the Kennedy administration, Harris was chosen to cochair the National Women's Committee for Civil Rights, a clearinghouse and coordinating committee for a wide range of national women's organizations. She also served on the District of Columbia advisory committee to the United States Commission on Civil Rights.

In 1965 Harris became the first African-American woman to hold an ambassadorship when she was appointed envoy to Luxembourg. She held the post until September 1967, when she rejoined the faculty at Howard University. In 1969 she was appointed dean of Howard Law School, becoming the first black woman to head a law school, but her tenure lasted only thirty days. Caught between disputes with the faculty and the president of the university over student protests, Harris resigned.

Harris then accepted a position with a private law firm—Fried, Frank, Harris, Shriver & Kampelman—and also held a number of positions in the Democratic Party during the 1970s, such as the temporary chairmanship of the credentials committee. Harris became the first black woman cabinet member when she was nominated by President Jimmy Carter to head the Department of Housing and Urban Development in 1976. She held the job for two years, and in 1979 she became secretary of health, education, and welfare (renamed the Department of Health and Human Services in 1980), serving until 1981.

In 1982 Harris ran for mayor of Washington, D.C. Running against Marion S. Barry in the Democratic primary, she lost a bitter contest in which she was depicted as an elitist who could not identify with the city's poorer blacks. She spent her remaining years as a professor at George Washington National Law Center before her death in 1985.

See also Barry, Marion; National Association for the Advancement of Colored People (NAACP); Politics in the United States; United States Commission on Civil Rights

■ ■ *Bibliography*

Boyd, Gerald M. "Patricia R. Harris, Carter Aide, Dies." *New York Times* (March 1985): 366–367.

Greenfield, Meg. "The Brief Saga of Dean Harris." *Washington Post* (March 23, 1969): C1, C5.

Harris, Patricia Roberts. *Papers.* Library of Congress, Washington, D.C.

JAMES BRADLEY (1996)

HARRIS, WILSON
MARCH 24, 1921

The first recipient of the Guyana Prize for Fiction (1985–1987), Wilson Harris was born in New Amsterdam, a coastal city in the Berbice region of British Guiana (Guyana after 1966). Since 1945 he has published twenty-three novels, two collections of novellas, two volumes of poetry, and several books of essays and interviews.

Harris's writings engage the intellectual and spiritual resources that reside in the depths of what he calls, in his novel *Carnival,* the "universal plague of violence" that exists in the twentieth century (p. 14). His novels dramatize how this legacy of violence can be transformed into powerfully creative energy. For instance, death is not an end for Harris's characters but a necessary "cancellation" of one's "fear of strangeness and catastrophe in a destitute world" (p. 116). Instead of Conradian "horror," Harris's protagonists typically experience spiritual fulfillment and self-knowledge only when they embrace otherness.

Unlike V. S. Naipaul and other Caribbean writers, Harris does not believe in "historylessness" and irreversible cultural destitution. For him the Caribbean's landscape itself *is* history. Harris's fictional landscapes abound with traces and echoes of eclipsed histories—of African slaves, East Indian indentured laborers, and Amerindians—sometimes to the point of sensory overload for some readers. Harris's early career as a surveyor familiarized him with his native South American landscape. After graduating from Queen's College of the University of Guyana in 1939, he led countless survey expeditions along Guyana's coast and into its interior. These experiences resonate in most of his novels, even in those not specifically set in Guyana. The first and most acclaimed of these novels is *Palace of the Peacock* (1960). Harris wrote *Palace* in 1959, the year he emigrated to the United Kingdom, where he still resides.

Harris's characters, many of whom are fictional personae, are best described as activated archetypes, or "character-masks," as he prefers. Their sense of selfhood is complicated by the fact that, according to Harris, memory is never just individual recollection. Rather, it always includes traces of other, "strange" presences, both dead and alive. When characters embark on their "voyage[s] in the straits of memory" (*Palace*, p. 62), they come to acknowledge their "inner problematic ties" to the rest of the world. Although they inhabit different times and universes, they can encounter each other intuitively and imaginatively through the "world's unconscious," something of a Jungian network. In his *Carnival Trilogy,* for example, Harris's Dantesque characters, led by Virgilian guides from the realm of the dead, move in and out of Inferno, Purgatorio, and Paradiso, all three of which he conceives as overlapping modes of existence that represent relative states of consciousness and unconsciousness. As their inner spaces of consciousness overlap more and more with the outer realms of the phenomenal world, characters are freed from ingrained patterns of thought and behavior. A character's individual identity eventually gives way to a state of spiritual freedom, or true personhood, through an awareness of "parallel" universes. The joint, multiple conception of authorship that follows from such an awareness is at the heart of Harris's re-visionary strategies.

Harris believes that writers of literature have the moral responsibility to interrogate areas of intellectual and emotional self-deception without resorting to political dogma. Applying this premise has led him to imagine and experiment with alternatives to traditional narrative. His "new density" of language eschews clear political messages and easy access to categories such as otherness and cultural authenticity. Harris's work is a poetics of imaginative cross-cultural reassembly that is also a sustained critique of realist modes of representation, in literature and elsewhere. As early as 1952, in "Form and Realism in the West Indian Artist," Harris insists that realism is central to imperial ideologies and that its literary manifestations constitute a troubling residue of imperialism's cultural politics. This residue significantly includes "protest realism," which Harris deems an ineffective form of intellectual resistance to conceptual and physical violence. Harris's writings on realism and imperialism anticipate major arguments in the work of postcolonial theorists such as of Edward Said and Homi Bhabha.

See also Literature of the English-Speaking Caribbean

▪ ▪ *Bibliography*

Durrant, Sam. *Postcolonial Narrative and the Work of Mourning: J.M. Coetzee, Wilson Harris, and Toni Morrison / Sam Durrant*. Albany: State University of New York Press, 2004.

Maes-Jelinek, Hena. "The Wilson Harris Bibliography." Available online at <www.ulg.ac.be/facphl/uer/d-german/L3/whone.html> (March 2005).

Webb, Barbara J. *Myth and History in Caribbean Fiction: Alejo Carpentier, Wilson Harris, and Edouard Glissant*. Amherst: University of Massachusetts Press, 1992.

FICTION AND POETRY BY HARRIS

Fetish (1951); *Eternity to Season* (1954, rev. 1978); *Palace of the Peacock* (1960); *The Far Journey of Oudin* (1961); *The Whole Armour* (1962); *The Secret Ladder* (1963); *Heartland* (1964); *The Eye of the Scarecrow* (1965); *The Waiting Room* (1967); *Tumatumari* (1967); *Ascent ot Omai* (1970); *The Sleepers of Roraima: A Carib Trilogy* (1970); *The Age of the Rainmakers* (1971); *Black Marsden* (1972); *Companions of the Day and Night* (1975); *Da Silva da Silva's Cultivated Wilderness: and Genesis of the Clowns* (1977); *The Tree of the Sun* (1978); *The Angel at the Gate* (1982); *Carnival* (1985); *The Guyana Quartet* (1985); *The Infinite Rehearsal* (1987); *The Four Banks of the River of Space* (1990); *Resurrection at Sorrow Hill* (1993); *The Carnival Trilogy* (1993); *Jonestown* (1996); *The Dark Jester* (2001); *The Mask of the Beggar* (2003).

ESSAYS BY HARRIS

Tradition, the Writer and Society (1967); *Explorations: A Selection of Talks and Articles, 1966–1981*, edited by Hena Maes-Jelinek (1981); *The Womb of Space: The Cross-Cultural Imagination* (1984); *The Radical Imagination: Lectures and Talks*, edited by Alan Riach and Mark Williams (1992); *Selected Essays of Wilson Harris*, edited by Andrew Bundy (1999).

VERA M. KUTZINSKI (2005)

HARRISON, HUBERT HENRY

APRIL 27, 1883
DECEMBER 17, 1927

Hubert Harrison, a self-educated working-class intellectual, writer, orator, editor, and political activist, played signal roles in what became the largest class-radical movement (socialism) and the largest race-radical movement (the "New Negro"/Garvey movement) in U.S. history. He profoundly influenced a generation of class and race activists including A. Philip Randolph, Chandler Owen, Cyril Briggs, Richard B. Moore, and Marcus Garvey and was described by Randolph as the father of Harlem radicalism. Considered by historian J. A. Rogers to be "perhaps the foremost Afro American intellect of his time" (Rogers, 1972, p. 432), Harrison also edited and reshaped Garvey's *Negro World* into a powerful international political and cultural force that fostered a mass interest in literature and the arts. In addition, he was the nation's first regular black book reviewer (1920–1922) and an important cofounder and developer (with Arthur Schomburg and others) of the Department of Negro Literature and History of the 135th Street Public Library (1925–1927), which subsequently grew into the internationally famous Schomburg Center for Research in Black Culture.

Harrison was born in Concordia, St. Croix, Danish West Indies (now the U.S. Virgin Islands) and immigrated to New York in 1900 as a seventeen-year-old orphan. He worked low-paying jobs, attended high school, and participated in black intellectual circles before becoming a postal worker in 1907. During his first decade in New York, the critical thinking Harrison became an agnostic and humanist, studied history, science, freethought, languages, and social and literary criticism, was attracted to the protest philosophy of W. E. B. Du Bois and socialism, and had letters on numerous historical, cultural, and literary subjects published in the *New York Times*. In 1909 he married Irene Louise Horton, and in 1911, after he wrote several letters critical of Booker T. Washington in the New York *Sun,* he was fired by the post office and hired by the Socialist Party.

From 1911 to 1914 Harrison served as the leading black orator, organizer, writer, campaigner, and theoretician in the Socialist Party. His oratory was famous from Wall St. to Madison Square to Harlem, where he developed the soapbox tradition later continued by Owen, Randolph, Garvey, Moore, and Malcolm X. In 1911 he served as an editor of *The Masses,* which subsequently grew into America's foremost left-literary publication. In his theoretical series on "The Negro and Socialism" (*New York Call,* 1911) and on "Socialism and the Negro" (*International Socialist Review,* 1912) he advocated that Socialists champion the cause of the Negro as a revolutionary doctrine, develop a special appeal to Negroes, and affirm the duty of Socialists to oppose race prejudice. He initiated the Colored Socialist Club, a pioneering effort at organizing African Americans, but soon concluded that Socialist Party leaders, like the leaders of organized labor, put the

white "race first and class after." Harrison increasingly supported the more egalitarian, direct action-oriented Industrial Workers of the World and spoke at the 1913 Paterson Silk Strike. After Socialist leaders moved to restrict his speaking, he left the Socialist Party, became active in the free speech movement, and developed his own Radical Lecture Forum with talks on subjects as diverse as evolution, birth control, comparative religion, and the racial implications of the Great War. Then, prompted in part by his analysis of how the developing black theater revealed "the social mind of the Negro," he began to concentrate his work in Harlem.

In 1917 Harrison founded the *The Voice* and the Liberty League, the first newspaper and first organization of the militant "New Negro" movement. *The Voice* called for a "race first" approach, full equality and enforcement of the Fourteenth and Fifteenth Amendments, federal antilynching legislation, labor organizing, support of socialist and anti-imperialist causes, and armed self-defense in the face of racist attacks. *The Voice* was soon followed by other New Negro publications including Randolph and Owens's *Messenger* (1917), Garvey's *Negro World* (1918), and Briggs's *Crusader.* The Liberty League's program was aimed at the "common people" and emphasized internationalism, political independence, and class and race consciousness. The league developed the core features (race radicalism, self-reliance, tricolor flag, outdoor and indoor lectures, a newspaper, and protests in terms of democracy) and the core leadership individuals Marcus Garvey used in his Universal Negro Improvement Association (UNIA). Harrison later claimed that from the Liberty League, "Garvey appropriated every feature that was worthwhile in his movement."

After *The Voice* failed in November 1917, Harrison organized for the American Federation of Labor, rejoined and then left the Socialist Party, and then cochaired the 1918 Colored National Liberty Congress with William Monroe Trotter. The Liberty Congress was the major black protest effort during World War I, and it petitioned both houses of the U.S. Congress for federal antilynching legislation at a time when the National Association for the Advancement of Colored People (NAACP) did not advocate such legislation and when Du Bois advocated forgetting "special grievances" and closing ranks behind the government's war effort. Following the failure of a resurrected *Voice* in 1919, Harrison became editor of the *New Negro,* "an organ of the international consciousness of the darker races."

In January 1920 Harrison became principal editor of the *Negro World,* the organ of Garvey's UNIA. He reshaped that paper with the "Poetry for the People," book review, and "West Indian News Notes" sections that he initiated and with the numerous reviews, editorials, and articles he wrote pertaining to Africa, peoples of African descent, and international affairs. Selections from his writings through the summer of 1920 appear in his two books, *The Negro and the Nation* (1917) and *When Africa Awakes* (1920). By the UNIA's August 1920 convention Harrison was highly critical of Garvey and, though he continued to write for the *Negro World* into 1922, he worked against Garvey while attempting to build a Liberty Party to run black candidates for political office.

Harrison became a U.S. citizen in 1922, and from 1922 to 1926 he was a featured lecturer for the New York City Board of Education's "Trends of the Times" and "Literary Lights of Yesterday and Today" series. He was also active in anticensorship and anti–Ku Klux Klan efforts, worked with the American Negro Labor Congress and the Urban League, wrote widely for the black press and many of the nation's leading periodicals, and promoted the efforts of a number of poets and artists including Claude McKay, Charles Gilpin, Eubie Blake, and Augusta Savage. In 1924 he founded the International Colored Unity League, which stressed the need for black people to develop "race-consciousness," called for broader-based unity of action and cooperative efforts, and advocated a separate state for African Americans. His 1927 effort to develop a new publication, *The Voice of the Negro,* lasted several months. Harrison died in New York City after an appendicitis attack, leaving his wife and five young children virtually penniless.

During the 1910s and 1920s when Harlem became an international center of radical black thought and literary influence, Hubert Harrison was the most class conscious of the race radicals and the most race conscious of the class radicals and an intellectual of seminal influence. The militant "New Negro" movement he founded marked a major shift from the white-patron-based leadership approach of Booker T. Washington and the "Talented Tenth" orientation of W. E. B. Du Bois, it prepared the ground for the Garvey movement, and it was qualitatively different from the more middle-class, more arts-based literary movement associated with the 1925 publication of Alain Locke's *New Negro.* Harrison's emphasis on education of "the common people" was much appreciated in his day, and thousands attended his Harlem funeral.

See also Garvey, Marcus; Intellectual Life; Literary Magazines; New Negro; *Negro World*; Pan-Africanism

■ ■ *Bibliography*

Harrison, Hubert Henry. *When Africa Awakes: The "Inside Story" of the Stirrings and Strivings of the New Negro in the Western World.* Baltimore: Black Classics Press, 1997.

James, Portia. "Hubert H. Harrison and the New Negro Movement," *The Western Journal of Black Studies* 13 (1989): 82–91.

James, Winston. *Holding Aloft the Banner of Ethiopia: Caribbean Radicalism in Early Twentieth-Century America.* New York: Verso, 1998.

Perry, Jeffrey B., ed. *A Hubert Harrison Reader.* Middletown, Conn.: Wesleyan University Press, 2001.

Rogers, J. A. "Hubert Harrison: Intellectual Giant and Free-Lance Educator (1883–1927)." In J. A. Rogers. *World's Great Men of Color,* vol. 2, edited by John Henrik Clarke, pp. 432–443. New York: Collier, 1972.

JEFFREY B. PERRY (1996)
Updated by author 2005

HART SISTERS OF ANTIGUA
■■■

Sisters Elizabeth Hart Thwaites (1772–1833) and Anne Hart Gilbert (1773–1833) were born on Antigua to free colored parents. As educators, abolitionists, and Methodists, both sisters were very engaged with the various representations of blacks and slaves circulating in the West Indies and used their writing to effectively challenge the patriarchal order, which construed blacks, women, and slaves as lowly.

The sisters are commonly understood to be the first female African-Caribbean writers to publish. Anne Hart Gilbert wrote a solicited short history of Antiguan Methodism and completed the biography of her husband, John Gilbert. Elizabeth Hart Thwaites also wrote a solicited history of Antiguan Methodism. In addition she wrote poetry, hymns, and letters, including one that was republished and circulated as an antislavery tract. Elizabeth was more strident about emancipation in her writing than her sister because she had associations with mainstream British pro-emancipation circles.

Both sisters were baptized into the Methodist faith in 1786 as young women. After this point both would become outspoken members of the Methodist community in Antigua. They advocated a kind of Christianity that sought to challenge rather than enforce the status quo. More specifically, both insisted that God's work was not just a male preserve but that women had the right to pursue holy work as well. In advocating the political equality inherent in Christianity, the sisters proposed that through

Methodism and Christianity blacks and slaves were equal to whites. In a certain sense their work can be linked to the upsurge of evangelical women's activism in England, where most women's work was associated with the heart and feeling, or the womanly arts. In emulating their British counterparts, they offered a black Methodist female paradigm.

The sisters were committed to education. They traveled to Montserrat to observe the Lancastrian system of education based on the factory model and drew upon it as they defiantly educated slaves, proposing that slaves were educable and smart. Elizabeth founded a private school in St. John's in 1801. Then in 1809 they opened the first Caribbean Sunday school for boys and girls, without regard for race. Anne Hart held her Sunday school meetings in the dark so people would not feel ashamed of their clothes.

Anne and Elizabeth constructed a new kind of public identity for black women in the Caribbean. In doing so they refuted stereotypes of the depraved or licentious enslaved black woman. Both sisters were committed to helping women and children. They founded a society for orphans and women called the Female Refuge Society in 1816. In particular, Anne condemned prostitution and blamed it on the institution of slavery. Elizabeth argued that by eliminating sexual predation, black women could become socially mobile.

As the first black women to write and agitate against slavery, the sisters transform a reader's sense of the nineteenth century in that they show black women participating in discourses that sought to exclude them. In addition, they also provide evidence of the creolization of religions in the West Indies as they reshaped Methodism to reflect their lives.

See also Education in the Caribbean; Emancipation in Latin America and the Caribbean; Protestantism in the Americas; Representations of Blackness in Latin America and the Caribbean

■ ■ *Bibliography*

Ferguson, Moira, ed. *The Hart Sisters: Early African Caribbean Writers, Evangelicals, and Radicals.* Lincoln: Nebraska University Press, 1993.

Ferguson, Moira, ed. *Nine Black Women: An Anthology of Nineteenth-Century Writers from the United States, Canada, Bermuda, and the Caribbean.* New York: Routledge, 1997.

Gilbert, Anne Hart. *The History of Methodism in Antigua.* 1804.

Twaites, Elizabeth Hart. *The History of Methodism in Antigua.* 1804.

NICOLE N. ALJOE (2005)

Hastie, William Henry

November 17, 1904
April 14, 1976

The lawyer and educator William Henry Hastie was considered one of the best legal minds of the twentieth century. He was once suggested for the presidency of Harvard University and twice considered as a nominee for the U.S. Supreme Court, reflections of the high regard in which he was held.

Hastie was born in Knoxville, Tennessee, where he spent his early years. His father, a clerk in the United States Pension Office, and his mother, a teacher until his birth, offered him early examples of resistance to discrimination. Rather than ride on segregated streetcars, they provided alternative means for young Hastie to go to school, which sometimes meant walking.

In 1916 the family moved to Washington, D.C., which gave Hastie the opportunity to attend Dunbar High School, the best secondary school in the nation for African Americans. There he excelled athletically and academically, graduating as valedictorian of his class in 1921. He went on to Amherst College, where he again established an excellent athletic and academic record. In addition to winning prizes in mathematics and physics, he was elected to Phi Beta Kappa as a junior, serving as its president during his senior year. In 1925 he graduated magna cum laude as class valedictorian.

After teaching mathematics and general science for two years at the Bordentown Manual Training School in New Jersey, Hastie pursued legal studies at Harvard Law School, where he distinguished himself as a student. He was named to the editorial board of the *Harvard Law Review,* the second African American to earn that distinction, and was one of its most active editors. Hastie received his LL.B. degree from Harvard in 1930, and he returned there to earn an S.J.D. in 1933.

His academic career closely followed that of his second cousin Charles Hamilton Houston, who had also excelled at Dunbar High, Amherst College, and Harvard Law School. Upon completion of his legal studies, Hastie became a lawyer and went into practice with his father, William, in the Washington, D.C., firm of Houston and Houston. He also became an instructor at Howard University Law School, where Houston was vice dean. Working together, the two men transformed the law school from a night school into a first-class institution. As Robert C. Weaver recalled, "It was during this time that the Houston-Hastie team became the principal mentors of Thurgood Marshall, as well as symbols for, and teachers of, scores of black lawyers, many of whom played a significant role in Civil Rights litigation" (Weaver, 1976, p. 267).

In 1930, the year that Hastie completed his first law degree, the National Association for the Advancement of Colored People (NAACP) decided on its legal strategy for fighting against racism: to attack the "soft underbelly" of segregation, the graduate schools. Hastie, Houston, and Marshall became the principal architects of that strategy. In 1933 Hastie was one of the lawyers who argued the first of these cases, *Hocutt v. University of North Carolina*. Although the case was lost, his performance won him immediate recognition. More important, it laid the groundwork for future cases that would lead to the end of legal segregation in the United States.

As assistant solicitor for the Department of the Interior (1933–1937), Hastie challenged the practice of segregated dining facilities in the department. He also played a role in drafting the Organic Act of 1936, which restructured the governance of the Virgin Islands. In 1937, as a result of his work on the Organic Act, he was appointed federal judge of the U.S. District Court for the Virgin Islands, the first African American to be appointed a federal judge. He left this post in 1939 and returned to Howard Law School as a professor and dean. In 1946 he went back to the Virgin Islands as its first black governor.

In 1940 Hastie was appointed civilian aide to the secretary of war and given the charge of fighting discrimination in the armed services. While he was able to make some progress after a little more than two years, conditions remained intolerable. Hastie decided that he could fight segregation more effectively if he were outside the constraints of an official position, and he resigned in January 1943.

In 1949 Hastie left the position of governor of the Virgin Islands to take a seat as judge on the Third Circuit Court of Appeals, where he established a positive reputation. His cases were never overturned, and they often established precedents that were upheld by the Supreme Court. He served the Third Circuit as chief justice for three years before retiring in 1971 and taking a position as senior judge.

Hastie received over twenty honorary degrees, including two from Amherst College (1940, 1960) and one from Harvard (1975). He was the recipient of the NAACP's Spingarn Medal (1943), the Philadelphia Award (1975), and the Washington Bureau Association's Charles Hamilton Houston Medallion of Merit (1976). He was elected a fellow of the American Academy of Arts and Sciences (1952) and was made a lifetime trustee of Amherst College

(1962). His alma maters have also honored him with portraits: One, dedicated in 1973, hangs in the Elihu Root Room of the Harvard Law Library; the other, a gift of the Amherst College class of 1992, hangs in Johnson's Chapel at Amherst.

See also Marshall, Thurgood; National Association for the Advancement of Colored People (NAACP)

■ ■ *Bibliography*

Wade, Harold, Jr. *Black Men of Amherst.* Amherst, Mass., 1976.

Ware, Gilbert. *William Hastie: Grace under Pressure.* New York, 1984.

Weaver, Robert C. "William Henry Hastie, 1904-1976." *The Crisis* (October 1976): 267–270.

ROBERT A. BELLINGER (1996)

HATCHER, RICHARD GORDON

JULY 10, 1933

Politician Richard Gordon Hatcher was born and raised in Michigan City, Indiana, the son of Carleton and Catherine Hatcher. He received his bachelor of science degree from Indiana University in 1956 and a law degree from Valparaiso University in Indiana in 1959. From 1961 to 1963 he served as a deputy prosecuting attorney in Lake County, which includes the city of Gary, Indiana. In 1963 he became a member of Gary's city council. In 1967, as an independent Democrat, Hatcher defeated both his Republican opponent and the regular Democratic Party machine when he was elected mayor of Gary. With Carl Stokes, who was elected mayor of Cleveland, Ohio, on the same day, Hatcher became one of the first two African Americans elected mayor of a major city. In all, Hatcher served a five-term, twenty-year tenure in office.

When Hatcher came into office, Gary was suffering from the decline of the local steel industry, which was the core of the town's economy. This decline led to a loss in factory jobs and the exodus of the middle class from the city. These trends caused Gary's total population to decrease from 180,000 in the late 1960s to 116,000 in the late 1980s. During the same period, however, the city's African-American population rose from about 50 percent of the total to more than 80 percent. Hatcher sought to deal with the resulting racial tensions by integrating the police force and encouraging black businesses, but these efforts often brought him into conflict with white neighborhoods in surrounding suburbs.

Hatcher's leadership role in Gary's black community led him to address racial issues in a national context. In 1969 Hatcher joined a citizens' investigation of violence against the Black Panther Party. In 1972 he presided over the plenary session of the first National Black Political Convention, held in Gary. Although he supported the convention's moves to establish a new black political agenda, distinct from the agendas of the two major parties, he rejected the convention's resolution against busing to achieve integrated schools as well as its attacks on the state of Israel.

Hatcher was a close associate of the Rev. Jesse Jackson. From 1982 to 1984 he was chairman of the National Board of Directors for Operation PUSH (People United to Save Humanity), resigning his chairmanship (but retaining his board membership) to assist Jackson's presidential campaigns. In 1984 he was national chairman of the Jackson for President Committee, and in 1988 he served as national vice chair of the Jackson for President Campaign.

Hatcher lost the Democratic primary for reelection in 1987 to Thomas V. Barnes, an African American who promised new economic initiatives and whose supporters believed that Hatcher was racially divisive. Hatcher saw Barnes elected mayor in November 1987 and failed in his attempt to take the nomination back from Barnes in 1991.

Following his electoral defeat in 1987, Hatcher became president of his own law firm in Gary, known as Hatcher and Associates. Nelson Mandela invited Hatcher to South Africa in 1991 and praised him for helping convince the United States to impose sanctions on the apartheid regime. Hatcher also began work in 1991 on a "black common market" program for the purpose of strengthening and coordinating black businesses nationwide.

Since 1989 Hatcher has worked as an adjunct professor at Indiana University, and continues to work with various political, urban, and civil rights organizations.

See also Black Panther Party for Self-Defense; Gary Convention; Jackson, Jesse; Operation PUSH (People United to Serve Humanity); Politics in the United States; Stokes, Carl Burton

■ ■ *Bibliography*

Clay, William L. *Just Permanent Interests: Black Americans in Congress, 1870–1991.* New York: Amistad Press, 1992.

Terry, Don. "Hatcher Begins Battle to Regain Spotlight in Gary." *New York Times,* May 6, 1991, p. A12.

DURAHN TAYLOR (1996)
Updated by publisher 2005

HAYES, ISAAC

AUGUST 20, 1942

Singer, musician, composer, and record producer Isaac Hayes was born in Covington, Tennessee, and attended Memphis public schools. He played saxophone in his high school band, sang in church choirs, and began playing saxophone and piano in local clubs as early as the 1950s, completing his first solo recording in 1962. From 1962 to 1965 he played in the Memphis-area rhythm-and-blues club circuit, including Sir Isaac and the Doo-Dads. He soon formed a songwriting and producing partnership with his friend David Porter. The team worked together for several years at Stax Records in Memphis, establishing the Memphis Sound.

Hayes and Porter together wrote and produced numerous recordings, and Hayes personally worked as arranger, pianist, organist, and producer, with major Stax artists such as Otis Redding and Carla Thomas. Their hit songs of the period 1965–1968 included "Son Man" and "Hold On, I'm Coming," followed by the *Hot Buttered Soul* album, which went platinum in 1969. Perhaps the crowning achievement of this period was Hayes's 1971 score for the film *Shaft,* an instant hit for both the film and the subsequent record releases. *Shaft* earned Hayes an Academy Award, two Grammys, and a Golden Globe award. Next came *Black Moses,* another Grammy winner, in 1972.

Hayes's style blends rhythm and blues with jazz elements, including sampling and a liberal use of synthesizers and overdubbing. He fits his music to his artists (including himself), and the result often crosses over various performing styles, including blues, jazz, and gospel. The movie *Shaft 2000* follows in this vein, and Hayes's artistic efforts continue. In 2004 he won the Trumpet Award and was signed to act in the television series *Stargate SG-1* and in the movie *Hustle and Flow.*

See also Blaxploitation Films; Music in the United States; Recording Industry

■ ■ *Bibliography*

Floyd, Samuel, ed. *International Dictionary of Black Composers.* Chicago: Fitzroy Dearborn, 2000.

Hardy, Phil, and Dave Laing. *Encyclopedia of Rock.* New York: Schirmer, 1987.

Hitchcock, H. Wiley, and Stanley Sadie, eds. *The New Grove Dictionary of American Music.* New York: Grove, 1986.

DARIUS L. THIEME (1996)
Updated by publisher 2005

HAYWOOD, HARRY

FEBRUARY 4, 1898
JANUARY, 1985

Communist activist and theoretician Harry Haywood was born in South Omaha, Nebraska, the youngest child of former slaves. In 1913 his family moved to Minneapolis, Minnesota, and in the same year, at the age of fifteen, Haywood dropped out of school and worked at a string of menial jobs, including bootblack, barbershop porter, bellhop, and busboy. In 1914 he moved to Chicago, where he worked as a waiter on the Michigan Central Railroad. During World War I he fought in France with the 370th Infantry. After the war Haywood settled in Chicago, and in 1923 he was recruited into the African Blood Brotherhood, a secret black nationalist organization, and then into the Young Workers League, both associated with the Communist Party (CPUSA). Two years later he became a full-time party organizer and soon came to be a leading proponent of black nationalism and self-determination within the party, seeking to reconcile Marxism-Leninism with what the party called the national-colonial question.

Haywood traveled with a delegation of young black cadres to the Soviet Union in 1926 and studied there until 1930, when he returned to the U.S. While in the Soviet Union, Haywood was strongly influenced by the first generation of anticolonial revolutionaries who were his fellow students, including M. N. Roy of India, Tan Malaka of Indonesia, and the future Vietnamese revolutionary Ho Chi Minh. In 1928 Haywood authored a resolution on what the party called the Negro question, which was presented to the Comintern's Sixth World Congress. Haywood argued for the "national minority status" of the African-American people. He advocated a "national revolutionary" movement for self-determination and an autonomous republic to be established in the "black belt" of the American South. By 1930 Haywood's formulation had become the official position of the party in its attempt to organize African Americans.

Harry Haywood, c. 1950. *Haywood joined the Communist Party during the 1920s, and quickly came to be a leading proponent of black nationalism within the party, contending that blacks in the deep South constituted an oppressed nation, with full rights to self-determination.* PHOTOGRAPHS AND PRINTS DIVISION, SCHOMBURG CENTER FOR RESEARCH IN BLACK CULTURE, THE NEW YORK PUBLIC LIBRARY, ASTOR, LENOX AND TILDEN FOUNDATIONS.

In 1931 Haywood was chosen to head the Communist Party's Negro Department. He helped lead the party's campaign to defend the Scottsboro Boys, eight black teenagers convicted and sentenced to death for allegedly raping two white women in Alabama. In 1934 Haywood was appointed to the politburo of the CPUSA and became national secretary of the party's civil rights organization, the League of Struggle for Negro Rights. In 1937 he fought in the Spanish Civil War with the Abraham Lincoln Brigade, a volunteer force organized by the CPUSA to aid the Spanish Republic against the insurrection by Francisco Franco's fascist armies. In 1938 he was removed from the politburo for alleged mistakes in Spain, but Haywood suspected that this removal was due to his uncompromising support of black nationalism, which was losing favor in the party leadership. During World War II, Haywood served as a seaman in the Merchant Marine and worked as an organizer for the communist-led National Maritime Union from 1943 until the war ended.

Harry Haywood

"The Black Freedom struggle is a revolutionary movement in its own right, directed against the very foundations of U. S. imperialism, with its own dynamic pace and momentum, resulting from the unfinished democratic and land revolutions of the South. It places the Black liberation movement and the class struggle of U. S. workers in their proper relationship as two aspects of the fight against the common enemy—U. S. capitalism. It elevates the Black movement to a position of equality in the battle."

BLACK BOLSHEVIK: AUTOBIOGRAPHY OF AN AFRO-AMERICAN COMMUNIST (CHICAGO: LIBERATOR PRESS, 1978), P. 234.

The Communist Party's support of national self-determination in the black belt was officially dropped in 1944 but had been muted since the adoption of the popular front strategy in 1935. Despite this shift in party policy, Haywood continued to vigorously promote his theory that the black population in the United States represented a colonized people who should organize as a nation before being integrated into American society. He argued that self-determination and territorial autonomy were the only mechanisms that would guarantee the security of African Americans. His position finally caused him to be expelled from the party in 1959.

Haywood lived in Mexico City from 1959 to 1963 and thereafter returned to Chicago. In the 1960s Haywood supported various black nationalist movements, such as the Nation of Islam under the leadership of Malcolm X, the Revolutionary Action Movement, and the League of Revolutionary Black Workers. Throughout his later years, Haywood remained critical of the integrationist politics of "petit-bourgeois" civil rights leaders such as the Rev. Dr. Martin Luther King Jr. and the Rev. Jesse Jackson. In the 1970s Haywood was a leading figure in a small Maoist organization, the Communist party (Marxist-Leninist), which called for self-determination for African Americans in the Deep South. Haywood attempted to apply Mao Zedong's theories of peasant revolution to African Americans, influencing a number of younger black nationalists, including Amiri Baraka (LeRoi Jones) and Stokely Car-

michael (Kwame Toure). His public activities declined in his final years, and he died in Chicago in 1985.

See also African Blood Brotherhood; Baraka, Amiri (Jones, LeRoi); Carmichael, Stokely; Communist Party of the United States; League of Revolutionary Black Workers; Malcolm X; Revolutionary Action Movement

■ ■ *Bibliography*

Buhle, Mari Jo, Paul Buhle, and Dan Georgakas. *Encyclopedia of the American Left.* New York: Garland, 1990.

Haywood, Harry. *Black Bolshevik: Autobiography of an Afro-American Communist.* Chicago: Liberator, 1978.

THADDEUS RUSSELL (1996)

HEADLEY, GEORGE

MAY 30, 1909
NOVEMBER 30, 1983

The son of migrant workers from Barbados and Jamaica, George Alphonso Headley was born in Colón, Panama. When he was ten, he was taken to Jamaica, where he grew up in the care of his aunt, as his parents migrated to Cuba and then to the United States. Exposed to cricket in Jamaica, he quickly developed a passion for the sport. By age seventeen he was already making his mark in local competitive cricket and was first selected to represent Jamaica in 1928 against a visiting English team led by Lord Tennyson. His innings of 252 runs in the first match announced his arrival to the entire region, and it was utterly surprising that he was not selected for the first West Indies test tour to England that summer. However, he made his test debut on the England tour of the West Indies in 1930. In his very first match he became the first West Indian to score a test century with his innings of 176 runs in Barbados, and then "immortalized" himself by scoring centuries in each innings of the British Guiana test match. His mammoth innings of 223 in the final test in Jamaica was the highest score by any cricketer in the fourth innings of a test match.

His prodigious talent, however, was severely tested when the West Indies toured Australia in 1930–1931. But after initially struggling against the best bowlers in the world, he rose to the challenge to score two centuries in the third and fifth tests. He again distinguished himself on a gruelling tour of England in 1934 with a magnificent 169 not out in the second test, and when England visited in 1935 he crowned his very successful series with 270 not

West Indies cricket player George Headley batting against England in Manchester, 1939. GETTY IMAGES.

■ ■ *Bibliography*

Burrowes, S. I., and J. A. Carnegie. *George Headley*. London: Nelson, 1971.

Goodwin, Clayton. *Caribbean Cricketers: From the Pioneers to Packer*. London: Harrap, 1980.

James, C. L. R. *Beyond the Boundary*. London: Hutchinson, 1963.

Lawrence, Bridgette. *100 Great West Indian Test Cricketers: From Challenor to Richards*. London: Hansib, 1988.

Manley, Michael. *A History of West Indies Cricket*. London: Andre Deutsch, 1988.

Richards, Jimmy, and Mervyn Wong. *Red Stripe Statistics of West Indies Cricket, 1865-1989*. Kingston, Jamaica: Heinemann Publishers Caribbean, 1990.

Ross, Gordon. *A History of West Indies Cricket*. London: A. Baker, 1976.

White, Noel, and George Headley. *George 'Atlas' Headley*. Kingston: Institute of Jamaica, 1974.

BRIAN L. MOORE (2005)

out in the final match in Jamaica. His outstanding batting performances were instrumental in helping the West Indies win their first ever test series. If the 1939 tour of England was less successful for the West Indies, Headley once again wrote himself into record books by becoming the first player to score centuries in each innings at Lords, then considered the mecca of world cricket.

The Second World War, however, more or less put an end to Headley's test career. Although he played in three test matches after the war and became the first black man to captain a West Indian test team in the Barbados match against England in 1948, injury and disagreement with the selectors combined to limit his performances. He played his last test match in Jamaica in 1953. But his career statistics speak for themselves. In just twenty-two test matches, he amassed 2,190 runs, including ten centuries, for an average of 60.83.

George Headley was not simply the best West Indian batsman of his generation, earning him the pseudonym "Atlas" for literally carrying the rest of the team on his shoulders, he was revered by the mass of black West Indians who, fondly calling him "Mas George," identified their own struggles for social equality and political self-determination with his performances on the cricket field. The dedication of the largest pavilion at Sabina Park in Jamaica, and the national award of the Order of Jamaica, were therefore fitting tributes to a great West Indian.

See also Sports

HEALING AND THE ARTS IN AFRO-CARIBBEAN CULTURES

The Creole religions of the Caribbean—Haitian Vodou, Cuban Santería, Jamaican Rastafarianism, among others—are wide-ranging spiritual practices whose impact can be felt in virtually every aspect of the cultures of the region, from language and music to healing and the arts. The healing cultures associated with Creole religiosity in the Caribbean evolved out of the fusion of the native healing systems of the indigenous Arawak and Carib peoples of the Antilles and the herbal medicine and folk curative practices brought to the region by African slaves and European colonizers. Together they developed into hybrid and pluralistic magico-religious practices that have maintained a most tenacious hold on the Caribbean cultural imagination. They represent complex systems of physical, spiritual, and cultural healing that allowed conquered Amerindian and enslaved African communities that had already suffered devastating cultural losses to preserve a sense of group and personal identity.

From the early years of European colonization in the Caribbean, Creole healing traditions have relied on a multiplicity of objects—fragments of material culture produced by the clash and fusion of folk art traditions. These objects are credited with the ability to heal diseases of the body and the spirit, as well as with empowering a population suffering from the ills of colonialism and slavery.

These objects, because they function as links between humans and their gods, exemplify the principle of reciprocity that is the foundation of the crucial relationship between humans and the spirit world in Caribbean religiosities. Many of these objects, such as the various representations of spirits (orishas in Santería and lwas in Vodou) through the imagery of Catholic saints and the sequined flags whose entrance marks the beginning of a Vodou ceremony, have become highly valued items in the international art market, losing in the process their connection to religion and ritual.

The earliest manifestation of the creolized healing arts of the Caribbean is that of santos, carved-wood religious figures that have been produced in Puerto Rico and other Caribbean islands since the early sixteenth century. These polychrome figurines, roughly eight to twenty inches in height, were introduced by Spanish friars as aids to the conversion of the Arawak (and later the African) population, and soon replaced the traditional Taíno cemís as objects of veneration in homes and of magical fertilization in the fields. Like the santos, Taíno cemís (small triangle-shaped carved figurines fashioned out of stone or wood) had served as conduits for the forces of the spirit world to enter into communion with humans in rituals of fertility, healing, or divination.

Initially carved by Spaniards in a style highly influenced by Romanesque and Gothic art, the santos were appropriated and simplified as they were incorporated within Creole religious and healing practices. The santos are believed to be imbued with the spirit of the saint, lwa, or the orisha they represent, which can be invoked to bring about physical healing or spiritual comfort. In isolated rural communities with little or no access to medical care, most people relied on their devotion to these images for protection against disease. For example, a common figure, that of St. Raymond Nonnatus (San Ramón Nonato), a thirteenth-century saint considered the protector of pregnant women and newborn babies, would be placed on the abdomens of women in labor to assure their safety and that of the child. Santeros, as the carvers of these images are still known, developed an island-specific iconography that allowed the peasantry to quickly recognize and contextualize the carved images through symbolic forms and attributes. Saint Blaise (San Blás), the fourth-century saint that protects against diseases of the throat, for example, is immediately recognizable for his pastoral staff, red and yellow miter, black cassock with a white alb, and black shoes.

The carved wooden santos and other representations of Catholic saints made their way into the altars, rituals, and healing practices of Santería and Vodou through the associations made by slaves between the mythology of the African-derived orishas and lwa (spirits) and attributes or qualities identified with Catholic saints. On Santería and Vodou altars they joined a variety of objects—sequined flags, bottles, dolls, among others—linked to curative practices. Although African-derived ethnomedical therapeutics in the Caribbean are essentially plant-based and consist of decoctions, infusions, aromatics, and/or baths prescribed to cleanse an evil spell or attract beneficent healing spirits, they are often aided by a variety of forms of folk art.

One of the best known forms of religious art in the Caribbean are the sequined and beaded Vodou flags (drapo Vodou) whose ritual entrance into the ounfò or temple marks the beginning of the Vodou ceremony. The flags depict specific lwa, recreating their dynamic iconography through specific elements and color combinations attributed to the various spirits, sometimes using a printed chromolithograph of the corresponding Catholic saint as the basis of the piece. Their connection to healing practices is both ritualistic and tangible. Their ritual use as devices for saluting the spirits and summoning the spiritual force of the devotees or serviteurs opens the path to ceremonies of initiation, possession, and personal and communal healing. They are important elements in a complex summoning of the spirits to join their devotees through the phenomenon of possession, when the voice of the lwa can articulate for the devotees present the steps necessary for spiritual and physical healing. Equally important is the close connection between the making of these sacred flags and service to the lwa, as many flagmakers attribute the originality of their designs to the inspiration of the gods and propose the labor of creating the intricate patterns as healing work in and of itself in which various members of the community can engage. When done well and in the proper spirit of devotion, flagmaking is work that can be pleasing to the lwa and can embody the ideal relationship between the spirit world and human devotees. Flags are also of importance in the Anglophone Caribbean practice of Obeah, although their production is not elaborate and their healing powers limited. An Obeah flag, a diagonal red cross on a black background, may be displayed in some Caribbean gardens as a guarantor of protection from thieves and Obeah spells. The Vodou flags, together with the other objects that crowd the space of the Vodou altar—calabashes for food offerings painted with the vévé or secret signs of the lwa, sequined bottles offered in honor of the spirits, undecorated libation bottles, among them—represent the creative material culture of Santería and Vodou. Yoruban-inspired beadwork, examples of which we find in beaded bottles or necklaces on Vodou and Santería altars, is never simply decorative but part of a sacred language where the patterns, colors, and other design elements correspond to specific iconographies and ritual functions.

These objects often share their space with a variety of dolls that range from carefully handcrafted cloth dolls to mass-produced reproductions of "action figures" such as Darth Vader. Whereas the commercially made figures usually represent *lwa* such as Bawon Samdi (Baron Samedi)—the head of the Gede (or Guédé) family of raucous spirits whose activities are confined to the world of the dead, whom they are said to personify—cloth dolls are used chiefly as mediums, as conduits of messages to the spirit world or as repositories of the spirits of ancestors. As in the making of Vodou flags, the making of dolls for healing and ritual purposes is a spiritual process through which the dolls are imbued with the *aché* or *pwén* (power) of the spirits. As such, only those trained in healing practices or working selflessly for the good of others can produce dolls with the proper attributes for helping in the healing process. The process is as intrinsic a sign of devotion as the ritual work in which the objects themselves will be used.

In Santería, as in Vodou, the ancestors play an essential role in healing practices. The spirits of the dead do not comprise a single category, however, but include, in addition to the ritual family ancestors, deceased spirits that form one's "spiritual picture" or spirit field and that appear in dreams or through divination and mediumship. These spirit guides, as represented through dolls, paintings, photographs, lithographs, and statues of saints, can range from deceased members of one's biological family to Gypsies, Indians, and old Congo slaves. Their preparation, as that of the carving of *santos* or the embroidery of a *drapo Vodou,* follows a detailed iconographic pattern in order to imbue the figure with the power of the spirit it represents. The dolls can be consulted for advice and prescriptions for dealing with a variety of physical, spiritual, or psychological maladies. In the Mayombe (Congo-derived) practices of Santería, for example, the *mayombero* will work to transfer the evil that attacks his patient to a doll. The doll is given the sick person's name and is buried in an effort to trick death into believing that the doll is the patient's corpse. In another variation of the use of healing dolls, a doll, properly prepared or baptized, is placed on the bed next to the patient. The doll is later placed in a box and buried, while the patient is cleansed three times with a rooster that is passed over the entire body. The rooster is expected to die after absorbing the patient's illness.

Aspects of African-derived healing practices surface through many other art forms throughout the Caribbean.

The work of Cuban artist Wilfredo Lam, for example, has always been understood as incorporating elements of Palo Monte, a Congo-derived Cuban religious tradition that observes a different interaction with the spirits than Yoruba-based religions; focused less on a pantheon of deities, the Reglas Congas emphasize control of the spirits of the dead and healing with the use of charms (*prendas*), formulas, and spells. Healing ceremonies are a frequent topic in Haitian painting, where they appear as colorful, community-based rituals that remind the viewer of the vitality of the Haitian healing arts. Denis Vergin's *Interior Ceremony* (1946), Ernst Prophète's *Chez un Docteur Feuille* (At the Herb Doctor's House, 1973), and Jean Léandre's *Healing Ceremony with Music* (c. 1976) show the range of depictions of healing cultures in Haitian art. Vergin focuses on the moment when the *lwa* has become manifest through the *oungan* or priest and offers a *pakét* (a bundle containing materials that can transmit the power of the spirits) to a pregnant woman. Prophète's work shows the interior of a Dokté Fé or leaf doctor's healing room, which displays the variety of materials and techniques used for healing. Léandre's painting depicts a healing ceremony conducted by a secret society in which animals are being readied for sacrifice as offering to the *lwa* in exchange for a man's health. Haitian paintings of *lwa* believed to have curative powers appear often in home altars and *ounfò*.

Many artists throughout the region have inserted healing themes and imagery in paintings, sculpture, and photography that record the devastating impact of AIDS on the peoples of the Caribbean islands. Although technically not involved with physical healing—this art, particularly notable in Puerto Rico—has focused on chronicling the impact of the illness on the human body and seeks to either channel the rage and impotence of many of its victims or to depict the coming to terms with premature mortality. Puerto Rican photographer Victor Vázquez's work is perhaps the most eloquent example of the haunting quality of AIDS-related art in the Caribbean. His book of photographs, *El reino de la espera* (1991), offers a pictorial narrative of the last months and death of a friend stricken with AIDS. His subsequent work draws on imagery and themes borrowed from the healing practices of Santería, especially through the depiction of *ebbó*, the offerings or sacrifices that are a vehicle for the cleansing and purification that are basic to the healing traditions of the region. Fellow Puerto Rican artist Anaida Hernández's traveling show, *Hasta que la muerte nos separe* (Till Death Do Us Part, 1994), is intended as a healing work to help women face the trauma of domestic violence. Consisting of one hundred square niches filled with photographs, votive candles, flowers, and other objects in altarlike arrangements, each dedicated to a different woman who died as a result of domestic violence in Puerto Rico between 1990 and 1993, the work means to focus attention on an important social issue while offering a healing tribute to the dead women and their families. The work is one of the most important examples of a vital new subject in the Caribbean healing arts in the twenty-first century.

See also Santería; Voodoo

■ ■ *Bibliography*

Cosentino, Donald. *Sacred Arts of Haitian Vodou.* Los Angeles, Calif.: UCLA Fowler Museum of Cultural History, 1995.

Dayan, Joan. *Haiti, History, and the Gods.* Berkeley: University of California Press, 1997.

Fernández Olmos, Margarite, and Lizabeth Paravisini-Gebert, eds. *Sacred Possessions: Vodou, Santería, Obeah, and the Caribbean.* New Brunswick, N.J.: Rutgers University Press, 1997.

Fernández Olmos, Margarite, and Lizabeth Paravisini-Gebert, eds. *Healing Cultures: Art and Religion as Curative Practices in the Caribbean and Its Diaspora.* New York: Palgrave, 2001.

Fernández Olmos, Margarite, and Lizabeth Paravisini-Gebert. *Creole Religions of the Caribbean: An Introduction from Vodou and Santería to Obeah and Espiritismo.* New York: New York University Press, 2003.

Gossai, Hemchand, and Nathaniel Samuel Murrell. *Religion, Culture, and Tradition in the Caribbean.* Basingstoke, UK: Macmillan, 2000.

Lindsay, Arturo. *Santería Aesthetics in Contemporary Latin American Art.* Washington, D.C.: Smithsonian Institution Press, 2001.

Matibag, Eugenio. *Afro-Cuban Religious Experience: Cultural Reflections in Narrative.* Gainesville: University Press of Florida, 1996.

Murphy, Joseph M. *Working the Spirit: Ceremonies of the African Diaspora.* Boston: Beacon Press, 1994.

Taylor, Patrick. *Nation Dance: Religion, Identity, and Cultural Difference in the Caribbean.* Bloomington: Indiana University Press, 2001.

LIZABETH PARAVISINI-GEBERT (2005)

HEARNE, JOHN (CAULWELL, EDGAR)
FEBRUARY 4, 1926
DECEMBER 12, 1994

John Hearne was born in Montreal, Canada, the son of Maurice Vincent Hearne and Doris Delisser-Hearne. He attended Jamaica College in Kingston, Jamaica, and at the

age of seventeen he joined the Royal Air Force as an air gunner, seeing duty between 1943 and 1946. After the war, Hearne studied at Edinburgh University (M.A. in history, 1949), and the University of London (Diploma of Education, 1950). He then joined the growing community of West Indian students in postwar London who would later distinguish themselves in several fields of endeavor. His passion for and skill at writing was soon recognized, and he became one of the young contributors of short stories to Edna Manley's pioneering literary magazine *FOCUS*, which began publication in Kingston during the 1940s. To support his early writing, Hearne taught in various schools in England and Jamaica (where he taught for several years at Calabar High School). In 1956 Hearne married Leeta Hopkinson.

In 1955 Hearne's first full-length novel, the slightly autobiographical *Voices under the Window,* was published in London, eliciting favorable reviews from a wide cross-section of the British press. *Voices* brilliantly illustrates the enduring strengths of Hearne's creative writing—a vivid, elaborate verbal artistry; a tight, economically written plot; strongly drawn characters; highly sophisticated, class-cadenced dialogue; and endless observations on the essentially Caribbean themes of love, violence, politics, social class, color, and race. He won the John Llewellyn Rhys Memorial Prize in 1956, awarded for the best novel by a British Commonwealth author under thirty, and the Musgrave Silver Medal, awarded by the Institute of Jamaica, in 1964. His achievements placed him in the forefront of the Caribbean literary boom of the 1950s and 1960s. *Voices,* set in Jamaica, was quickly succeeded by four additional novels, all closely following the same recipe of *Voices*: *Stranger at the Gate* appeared in 1956; *The Faces of Love* (published in the United States as *The Eye of the Storm*) in 1957; *The Autumn Equinox* in 1959; and *Land of the Living* in 1961. These second four novels are all set on the fictitious Caribbean island of Cayuga, a thinly disguised, imaginative re-creation of Jamaica.

After 1961, Hearne busied himself teaching, working for the government, writing plays and commentaries for radio and television, and producing a regular newspaper column in one of the leading daily papers of Jamaica. His articles appeared in *Public Opinion, News Week, New Statesman, Nation, Pagoda,* and *Spotlight.* Several of his radio plays were aired by the British Broadcasting Corporation (BBC). Between 1962 and 1992 Hearne served as director of the Creative Arts Center at the University of the West Indies, and as chair of the Institute of Jamaica. He also taught for short periods at several universities in Canada and the United States.

In 1969 Hearne collaborated with fellow journalist Morris Cargill to write a novel of international intrigue under the pseudonym John Morris. Set in Jamaica, *Fever Grass* was the first of three such collaborations. Hearne's final novel, *The Sure Salvation*, appeared in 1981. This was a historical novel dealing with slavery and the slave trade, and it revealed much of the creative power that exemplified his earlier novels. Hearne retired from the University of the West Indies in 1992, and he died on December 12, 1994.

See also Literature of the English-Speaking Caribbean

■ ■ *Bibliography*

Jones, Joseph, and Johanna Jones. *Authors and Areas of the West Indies.* Austin, Tex.: Steck-Vaughn, 1970.

Ramchand, Kenneth. *The West Indian Novel and Its Background.* London: Faber and Faber, 1970.

Ramchand, Kenneth. *West Indian Narrative: An Introductory Anthology,* rev. ed. London: Nelson Caribbean, 1980.

FRANKLIN W. KNIGHT (2005)

HECTOR, TIM

NOVEMBER 24, 1942
NOVEMBER 12, 2002

▬ ▬ ▬

Leonard Timoshenko "Tim" Hector was an Antiguan activist and social critic well known throughout the Caribbean for his radical politics and his contributions to Caribbean cricket. He credited his mother, Mabel Hector, and a local educator, Mildred Richards, as being the primary contributors to his personal and intellectual growth. He also identified several important male role models and influences, a list that included many local personalities, his grandfather, and regional contemporaries Walter Rodney, George Lamming, and Cheddi Jagan. Reflecting on his radicalism and socialism, Hector once stated, "I did not become a socialist, but was bred one from age 6, or thereabout" (Hector, 2000–2001, p. 113). Hector's politics were a regional variation on socialism, communism, and Marxism. As a student of C. L. R. James, he advocated greater popular participation and organization for the masses and was increasingly concerned that Caribbean politicians seek political and social alternatives more appropriate for their societies and not continue to mimic the systems of Europe and the United States. While his home environment was crucial in forming his social and intellectual base, it was the social and political ideologies of Trinidadian scholar and political activist C. L. R. James (1901–1989) that influenced Hector's politics.

Born in St. Johns Antigua to a single mother, Hector distinguished himself early as a "bright boy." While his formal colonial education taught him the basics it was the informal education at his home—a place where many local thinkers and educators came to discuss both local and world affairs, where he insisted he was truly educated. As a child he was allowed to listen and even to participate in debates with adults. Hector, a commonwealth scholar, distinguished himself as an extraordinary teacher until 1973, when he was fired from his job as a teacher at a public school, largely because of his political activism against the labour party. He continued to teach after 1973 at a private high school and expanded his political activism and his journalism. Hector had joined other leftists in 1972 to form a radical pan-African group, which they transformed by 1973 into a political party—the Antigua-Caribbean Liberation Movement (ACLM). The ACLM was committed to African liberation and to forming and maintaining linkages across the African diaspora. In 1972 the first *African Liberation Day* was organized and by 1973 the group was networking with similar organizations throughout the Americas and Africa to orchestrate simultaneous marches throughout the world. The ACLM also established relations with socialist Cuba and Libya, creating a great deal of concern in the Richard Nixon administration in the United States.

The ACLM's biweekly publication, *The Outlet,* played a crucial role in Antiguan politics for some thirty years. Hector's column, *Fan the Flames,* became a regular feature in which he wrote on a range of political and social topics. Several of Hector's articles triggered investigations by the British government, and in the mid-1970s Hector disclosed a scandal involving the Canadian company Space Research Corporation (SRC), which was engaged in the shipment of arms to the apartheid government of South Africa via Antigua.

As a political party from 1972 to 1993 the ACLM never sought to win elections on the island, instead existing for over thirty years as an ideological opposition to the governing party. This was Hector's response to the two-party syndrome and other problems of party politics in the West Indies. This political system had emerged in the Caribbean region, where two political parties dominated the political landscape, fighting each other for control of the government using whatever means necessary, including character assassination and unjust arrest. Until its demise in 1993, the ACLM achieved its aim of constituting a permanent and viable opposition to Antiguan politics. Despite numerous arrests and law suits brought against *The Outlet,* it survived until 2002, almost ten years after the ACLM. Hector's articles, with titles that included "Independence: Yes! The Old Mess: No!" and "Cricket Is More than Meets the Eye" reflected the range of his interest in Caribbean societies. In addition to his educational and political contributions, Hector made a contribution to the development of Caribbean culture, in particular to Caribbean cricket and to the survival of steel band, a musical form he described as "the solitary new musical instrument created in the entire 20th century" (Hector, 2000).

See also James, C. L. R.; Journalism; Politics

■ ■ *Bibliography*

Hector, Leonard Tim. "The Steelband as Nationalism and Art." *The CLR James Journal* vol. 8, issue 1 (winter 2000–2001): 108–115.

CHRISTOLYN A. WILLIAMS (2005)

HEIGHT, DOROTHY
MARCH 24, 1912

Dorothy Height's career as an activist and reformer has been dedicated to working for African Americans through women's organizations, ranging from girls' clubs and sororities to the YWCA and the National Council of Negro Women (NCNW). Height was born in Richmond, Virginia; her family moved to Rankin, Pennsylvania, when she was four. In this mining town she and her family were active in the life of their church and community groups. As a young woman Height participated in local girls' clubs and the YWCA, moving into leadership at a young age. This was the beginning of her successful combination of religious and community work, part of a long African-American tradition.

Height graduated from New York University in 1932. She was able to complete the degree in three years through hard work and the support of an Elks scholarship. During this period she also took on a number of part-time jobs in restaurants, in a factory, in laundries, writing newspaper obituaries, and doing proofreading for Marcus Garvey's newspaper, *Negro World*. She then spent an additional year at the university to earn a master's degree in educational psychology. From there she took a position as assistant director of the Brownsville Community Center in Brooklyn and became involved with the United Christian Youth Movement. She traveled to England and Holland to represent her group at Christian youth conferences in 1937; she was also introduced to Eleanor Roosevelt and

helped Roosevelt plan the 1938 World Youth Congress held at Vassar College.

From 1935 until 1937 Height was a caseworker for the New York City Department of Welfare. In the wake of the 1935 Harlem riots, she became the first black personnel supervisor in her department. Seeking a position that would give her a broader range of work experience, she left the Department of Welfare in 1937 to work for the Harlem YWCA as the assistant director of its residence, the Emma Ransom House. In this position Height gained expertise in issues facing many African-American women in domestic labor and learned to administer a community-based organization. She also became involved with the NCNW through her friendship with Mary McLeod Bethune.

In 1939 Height accepted the position of executive secretary of the Phillis Wheatley YWCA in Washington, D.C. She also began to work with the Delta Sigma Theta sorority, encouraging both organizations to improve the lives of working African-American women. Her outstanding efforts led Height to a position with the national board of the YWCA in 1944. She was involved in organizing the YWCA's watershed conference in 1946 at which the organization took a stand for the racial integration of its programs. From 1947 until 1956 she served as president of Delta Sigma Theta, making it an international organization in addition to expanding its work at home.

Height became president of the National Council of Negro Women in 1957. Under her leadership the NCNW, an umbrella group for a wide variety of black women's organizations, became an active participant in the civil rights struggles in the United States. She also involved the YWCA in civil rights issues through her position as secretary of the organization's Department of Racial Justice, a job she assumed in 1963.

Although she was moderate in her approach to the question of civil rights, Height has never ceased her activities in search of equality. Her commitment has been to a struggle carried on through the widest possible range of organizations, and so she has served as a consultant to many private foundations and government agencies. She was a major force in moving the YWCA to be true to its 1946 declaration on interracial work. At the group's 1970 convention, she helped to write a new statement of purpose for the YWCA, declaring its one imperative to be the elimination of racism.

Through Dorothy Height's involvement, the YWCA has taken many steps forward in its attitudes and actions concerning African-American women. The organization's full commitment to integration and parity in its operation owes much to her work. She continues to guide the NCNW, and has made it an important voice in articulating the needs and aspirations of women of African descent around the world. In 1993 she was awarded the Spingarn Medal by the National Association for the Advancement of Colored People. In 1996, in a break with moderate colleagues, she addressed the Million Man March. In December 1997 Height resigned from the National Council of Negro Women.

In 2003 Height published her memoirs, *Open Wide the Freedom Gate*. In 2004 she received the Congressional Gold Medal and was honored by Barnard College, seventy-five years after being turned away from the college.

See also Bethune, Mary McLeod; Garvey, Marcus; National Council of Negro Women

■ ■ *Bibliography*

Giddings, Paula. *In Search of Sisterhood*. New York: Morrow, 1988.

Height, Dorothy. *Open Wide the Freedom Gates: A Memoir*. New York: Public Affairs, 2003.

Hill, Ruth Edmonds, and Patricia Miller King, eds. *The Black Women Oral History Project*. Westport, Conn.: Meckler, 1991.

JUDITH WEISENFELD (1996)
Updated by publisher 2005

HEMPHILL, ESSEX

APRIL 16, 1957
NOVEMBER 4, 1995

Essex Hemphill was an author, poet, performance artist, and black gay activist who challenged silence, exclusion, and homophobia within black communities and institutions. The eldest of five children, he was born in Chicago and grew up in Washington, D.C. Hemphill fought to create an accessible African-American gay history. In 1978, he founded the *Nethula Journal of Contemporary Literature,* and he ran the journal for several years before becoming increasingly involved in performance poetry. He performed at the Kennedy Center for Performing Arts, the Folger Shakespeare Library, the 1994 National Black Arts Festival, and at the Whitney Museum. Hemphill self-published three books—*Diamonds in the Kitty* (1982), *Plums* (1983), and *Earth Life* (1985)—and a larger collection, *Conditions* (1986).

His work may be seen in the film *Looking for Langston* and in two docudramas by Marlon Riggs, *Tongues Untied*

and *Black Is, Black Ain't*. Hemphill won the National Library Association's New Authors in Poetry Award for *Ceremonies,* published by Penguin in 1992. His radical poems, prose, and expository writing in *Ceremonies* explored African-American urban and gay realities. He also won a Lambda Award for editing the 1991 anthology *Brother to Brother: New Writings by Black Gay Men*—his best-known work. In 1986 he received a fellowship for poetry from the National Endowment for the Arts. Hemphill died from AIDS complications on November 5, 1995.

See also Gay Men; Poetry, U.S.

■ ■ *Bibliography*

Walsh, Sheila. "Essex Hemphill Dies." *Washington Blade*, November 10, 1995.

RACHEL ZELLARS (1996)

HENDRIX, JIMI

NOVEMBER 27, 1942
SEPTEMBER 18, 1970

In a professional career that lasted less than a decade, rock guitarist, singer, and songwriter James Marshall "Jimi" Hendrix created music that would establish him as the most innovative and influential guitarist rock music produced.

Born in Seattle, Washington, Hendrix started to play the guitar at age eleven and was playing with local rock groups as a teenager. He left school at sixteen, and with his father's permission joined the army as a paratrooper a year later. While in the service he met bass player Billy Cox, with whom he would later join forces as a civilian. Hendrix's army career ended when he was injured on a practice jump.

Once out of the army, he hit what was known as the chitlin circuit as a backup guitarist for a host of popular rock and rhythm-and-blues artists including Little Richard, the Isley Brothers, Curtis Knight, Wilson Pickett, Ike and Tina Turner, King Curtis, and James Brown. During this period, which lasted from 1962 to 1964, he began incorporating his trademark crowd-pleasers: playing his guitar with his teeth, behind his back, and between his legs. Early in his career, Hendrix played ambidextrously but he eventually settled on using a right-handed Fender Stratocaster, restrung upside down and played left handed. He manipulated the tone and volume controls (which were

Jimi Hendrix (1942–1970). © HENRY DILTZ/CORBIS

now on top) to make unique effects and sounds. Hendrix's huge hands allowed him a phenomenal reach and range; his ability to play clean leads and distorted rhythm simultaneously remains a musical mystery.

In 1964 Hendrix moved to New York and using the name Jimmy James fronted his own band, called the Blue Flames. In the mid-sixties, at the height of the folk music era, he became known in New York. Holding forth as a solo act at the Cafe Wha?, a basement cafe on MacDougal Street in Greenwich Village, he also found time to play local venues as a sideman with a group called Curtis Knight and the Squires, and in Wilson Pickett's band, where he met the young drummer Buddy Miles. In 1967 Chas Chandler (formerly the bassist of the Animals) convinced Hendrix to return with him to London. On the promise that he would meet Eric Clapton, Hendrix agreed. In England, in just three weeks, the Jimi Hendrix Experience was formed, with Mitch Mitchell on drums and Noel Redding on bass. "Hey Joe," their first single, went all the way to number six on the British charts in 1967, and an appearance on the British television show *Ready, Steady, Go* attracted wide attention when Hendrix played their new single, "Purple Haze."

The same year, Paul McCartney persuaded the Monterey Pop Festival officials to book Hendrix even though his first album had yet to be released. He ended a riveting musical performance by his setting his guitar on fire, transforming himself, at twenty-four, into a rock superstar. Later in 1967 his debut album *Are You Experienced?* was called by *Guitar Players'* Jas Obrecht "the most revolutionary debut album in rock guitar history."

In 1968 he released his second album, *Axis: Bold as Love,* which contained more of his distinctive sounds in such songs as "Little Wing," "If 6 was 9," and "Castles Made of Sand." His third album, a double set titled *Electric Ladyland,* was released just nine months later. Hendrix created a recording studio of the same name in Greenwich Village, a reflection of his belief that he was connected to a female spirit/muse of fire and electricity.

In 1969 Hendrix performed at the Woodstock Festival, the only black performer of his time to penetrate the largely white world of hard and psychedelic rock. He was pressured by black groups to take a more political stance but took no part in formal politics; his political statement was in his music, and his electric version of the "Star-Spangled Banner," which he played at Woodstock, was in itself a political statement.

Later that year Hendrix formed the all-black Band of Gypsys with former army friend Bill Cox on bass and Buddy Miles on drums. Although the group lasted only a few months, a live performance was captured on the album *Band of Gypsys.* Hendrix's management believed it was a mistake for him to forsake his white rock side, and he was pressured to make an adjustment. Hendrix finally settled on Mitch Mitchell on drums with Billy Cox on bass. They performed at the club Isle of Fehmarn in West Germany on September 6, 1970. Twelve days later Hendrix died in London after complications resulting from barbiturate use.

Although Hendrix's period as a headline performer lasted only three years, his influence on popular music has been considerable. In helping to establish the prime role of the electric guitar soloist, he was an inspiration for several generations of heavy metal musicians. His improvisatory style has inspired both jazz musicians and practitioners of avant-garde "new music."

See also Brown, James; Little Richard (Penniman, Richard); Music in the United States

■ ■ *Bibliography*

Henderson, David. *Jimi Hendrix: Voodoo Chile'.* New York: Doubleday, 1978.

Henderson, David. *'Scuse Me While I Kiss the Sky: The Life of Jimi Hendrix.* New York: Bantam, 1981.

Lawrence, Sharon. *Jimi Hendrix: The Man, the Magic, the Truth.* New York: Harper, 2005.

DAVID HENDERSON (1996)
Updated bibliography

HENSON, JOSIAH

JUNE 15, 1789
MAY 5, 1883

Josiah Henson, an abolitionist clergyman, was born a slave in Charles County, Maryland. He gained a reputation as a diligent worker with a capacity for leadership, and his role as a slave preacher was eventually recognized by the Methodist Episcopal Church. Henson's last owner, Isaac Riley, made him a plantation manager and entrusted him on one occasion with the transportation of eighteen slaves to Kentucky. He remained a loyal slave until he was duped by his master in negotiations to purchase his freedom. In October 1830, he escaped to Canada with his wife, Charlotte, and their four children.

Once in Canada, Henson found work as a farm laborer and slowly established an itinerant ministry. He served as a captain in a company of the Essex Coloured Volunteers during the Canadian Rebellion of 1837. Henson devoted much of his efforts to assisting fugitive slaves. Working as a conductor on the Underground Railroad, he brought fugitives from Kentucky to the Canadian haven. He envisioned racial progress under the protection of British law, and he therefore encouraged black settlement in Canada. With the financial backing of several New England philanthropists, he helped found a manual labor school, the British-American Institute, at the Dawn settlement, near Chatham, Canada West (present-day Ontario). The Dawn school and the settlement's sawmill provided educational and employment opportunities, respectively, for African Americans fleeing southern slavery and northern racial oppression.

Henson toured England in 1849 and 1851, lecturing on slavery, meeting with prominent reformers, and raising funds for the British-American Institute. He presented some of the Dawn settlement's products, including walnut lumber, at the Great Exhibition of 1851. His management of the school and his fund-raising tours in England sparked criticism from some Canadian blacks, and upon his return he became embroiled in a decade-long struggle for control of the British-American Institute property. The school eventually closed in 1868.

Henson's international notoriety increased dramatically with the publication of *Uncle Tom's Cabin* in 1852.

In her research for the novel, Harriet Beecher Stowe (1811–1896) interviewed Henson and read his biography, a seventy-six-page pamphlet published in 1849, titled *The Life of Josiah Henson, Formerly a Slave, Now an Inhabitant of Canada, as Narrated by Himself.* Despite some initial equivocations on the part of Henson and Stowe, he became identified in the public mind as the model for the fictional Uncle Tom, and he is best remembered for this connection with Stowe's widely read antislavery novel. Stowe wrote the introduction to his second narrative, *Truth Stranger than Fiction: Father Henson's Story of His Own Life,* in 1858. On his final tour of England, in 1876, he received an audience with Queen Victoria and was celebrated as "Mrs. Stowe's Uncle Tom."

See also Abolition; Canada, Blacks in; Christian Methodist Episcopal Church; Free Blacks, 1619–1860; Literature of the United States; Underground Railroad

■■ *Bibliography*

Beattie, Jessie Louise. *Black Moses: The Real Uncle Tom.* Toronto: Ryerson Press, 1957.

Hartgrove, W. B. "The Story of Josiah Henson." *Journal of Negro History* 3 (1918): 1–21.

MICHAEL F. HEMBREE (1996)

HENSON, MATTHEW A.

AUGUST 8, 1866
MARCH 9, 1955

Explorer Matthew Alexander Henson was born in rural Charles County, Maryland, the son of freeborn sharecroppers. At the age of four Henson and his family moved to Washington, D.C. When he was still a young child both of his parents died, and Henson and his siblings were put under the care of an uncle in Washington. At the age of twelve he left school, traveled to Baltimore, and started his career as a seaman when he was hired as a cabin boy on a ship sailing out of the port city. Henson spent the remainder of his adolescence traveling around the world as a merchant sailor and working menial jobs when back on the East Coast.

At the age of twenty, while working as a clerk in a Baltimore hat store, Henson was hired by U.S. Navy Lt. Robert E. Peary to be Peary's personal servant on a survey expedition for the building of a Central American canal. When the expedition returned to the United States in

1888, Henson followed Peary to the League Island Navy Yard, where he worked as a courier.

In 1891 Peary received a commission to explore northern Greenland and again hired Henson as a personal assistant, despite Peary's concern that a "son of the tropics" would not be able to withstand Arctic weather. While surveying Greenland Henson grew close to the native Inuits, learned the Inuit language, became the expedition's most able dogsled driver, and acted as liaison with the Inuits, who were used as guides and porters by the survey team. Henson and Peary returned to the United States in the summer of 1892 and spent a year touring the country presenting lectures and reenactments of their Greenland expedition. On a second exploration of Greenland, from 1893 to 1895, Peary and Henson led an aborted attempt at reaching the North Pole. For the next eleven years, Peary, with Henson as his chief assistant, led five more unsuccessful attempts at the North Pole, each time succumbing to frostbite or Arctic storms.

In July 1908 Peary, Henson, and a crew of twenty-seven aboard a specially made icebreaking ship left New York for a final attempt at the pole. In February 1909, having arrived at Cape Sheridan, between the northern tip of Greenland and the frozen edge of the Arctic Ocean, Peary led a team of twenty-two, with Henson as one of his chief lieutenants, across the polar ice cap. On April 6, 1909, Peary, Henson, and four Eskimos became the first people to reach the North Pole.

Upon returning to the mainland, Peary was confronted with the news that Frederick Cook had claimed to have reached the North Pole one year earlier. Thus began a protracted and bitter public controversy over the veracity of each man's claim. By the end of 1910, however, most scientific societies had rejected Cook's account and accepted Peary's.

Although celebrated by African-American leaders for many years, Henson was largely unrecognized by the white public as the codiscoverer of the North Pole. After the historic expedition of 1909 Henson spent the rest of his working life as a messenger in the U.S. Customs House and in a New York City post office. In his later years he finally won some of the honors he deserved. The Explorers Club made Henson its first African-American member in 1937. In 1944 Congress awarded him a medal for his codiscovery of the North Pole. In 1948 he was given the Gold Medal of the Geographical Society of Chicago. In 1950 he was honored at the Pentagon, and in 1954, a year before his death, he was received at the White House by President Eisenhower. A U.S. postage stamp commemorating his achievement was issued in 1986.

When Henson died in 1955, his wife was unable to afford a burial site and he was buried in a shared grave in Woodlawn Cemetery in New York. In 1988 his remains were moved to Arlington National Cemetery and buried next to those of Peary. In 2001 Henson was posthumously awarded the Hubbard Medal.

■ ■ *Bibliography*

Counter, S. Allen. *North Pole Legacy: Black, White and Eskimo.* Amherst: University of Massachusetts Press, 1991.

Henson, Matthew A. *A Negro Explorer at the North Pole.* New York: Stokes, 1912.

Miller, Floyd. *Ahdoolo! The Biography of Matthew A. Henson.* New York: Dutton, 1963.

Robinson, Bradley. *Dark Companion.* New York: Fawcett, 1947.

THADDEUS RUSSELL (1996)
Updated by publisher 2005

HIGGINBOTHAM, A. LEON, JR.

FEBRUARY 25, 1928
DECEMBER 14, 1998

A. Leon Higginbotham Jr., one of the nation's most prominent African-American judges, was born in Trenton, New Jersey. In 1944, he enrolled at Purdue University but left after the college president informed him that the college would not provide heated dormitories to black students. Higginbotham graduated from Antioch College in 1949. He then attended Yale Law School, graduating with honors in 1952. In 1954, after serving briefly as assistant district attorney in Philadelphia, he helped to found Norris, Green, Harris, and Higginbotham, a Philadelphia law firm. Higginbotham also became active in the local chapter of the National Association for the Advancement of Colored People (NAACP) and served as chapter president starting in 1960.

In 1962 Higginbotham was named commissioner of the Federal Trade Commission. Two years later he was appointed to the U.S. District Court by President Lyndon Johnson. He soon became an outstanding member of the court and he distinguished himself by his liberal opinions on abortion and prisoner's rights. In 1977 Higginbotham was elevated to the U.S. Court of Appeals for the Third Circuit by President Jimmy Carter. In 1989, the year after he published *In the Matter of Color,* a study of race and the legal process, he became chief judge of the U.S. Court of Appeals, the third African American to hold such a position. After retiring from the bench in 1993, he was named law professor at Harvard University. He also served as counsel to the elite New York law firm of Paul, Weiss, Rifkind, Wharton, and Garrison. In 1995 he was awarded the Presidential Medal of Freedom and the NAACP's Spingarn Medal. In 1996 he published a second study of race and law, *Shades of Freedom.*

See also National Association for the Advancement of Colored People (NAACP); Politics in the United States

GREG ROBINSON (1996)

HIGHLANDER CITIZENSHIP SCHOOL

Myles Horton, the cofounder of the Highlander Folk School, described it as a place where "people can share their experience and learn from each other." This precursor of the Highlander Citizenship School, founded in Grundy County, Tennessee, in 1932 to serve industrial and rural workers in southern Appalachia, quickly became a regional center for worker education and labor organization. The racial dissension in the labor movement soon persuaded Highlander officials that racism was the primary obstacle to securing economic justice in the South. Uniquely situated to respond to racial developments in the 1950s, and anticipating the U.S. Supreme Court decision in *Brown v. Board of Education,* Highlander began to focus on desegregating public schools. A series of workshops initiated in 1953 trained an interracial group of civic, labor, and church groups to lead the transition. Out of these workshops was born the Highlander Citizenship School.

Bernice Robinson and Septima Poinsette Clark, the coordinators of the Citizenship Schools, developed their curricula around the lived experiences and specific needs of the students in the communities from which they came. The Citizenship Schools provided instruction in areas ranging from adult literacy to voter registration, local voting requirements, political parties, social security, taxes, the functions of local school boards, and a host of other immediately relevant issues.

Citizenship Schools sprang up throughout the South. Among the hundreds who attended them were Rosa Parks, Ella Baker, Dorothy Cotton, Ruby Doris Smith, and Diane Bevel Nash, all of whom became active in the civil rights movement of the 1950s and 1960s. In May 1961 Tennessee state officials, who for years had harassed Highlander, succeeded in revoking the school's charter and confiscating its property following a ruling by the Tennessee Supreme Court. Highlander transferred its programs to the Southern Christian Leadership Conference and, under the direction of Clark and Robinson, continued to thrive. It was later reincorporated as the Highlander Research and Education Center, now located in New Market, Tennessee.

See also *Brown v. Board of Education of Topeka, Kansas*; Baker, Ella J.; Clark, Septima; Education in the United States; Labor and Labor Unions; Nash, Diane; Parks, Rosa; Southern Christian Leadership Conference (SCLC)

■ ■ *Bibliography*

Glen, John M. *Highlander: No Ordinary School, 1932–1962.* Lexington: University Press of Kentucky, 1988.

Langston, Donna. "The Women of Highlander." In *Women in the Civil Rights Movement: Trailblazers and Torchbearers, 1941–1965,* edited by Vicki L. Crawford et al., pp. 145–168. Brooklyn, N.Y.: Carlson, 1990.

CHRISTINE A. LUNARDINI (1996)

HILL, ERROL
AUGUST 5, 1921
SEPTEMBER 15, 2003

Errol Hill was the foremost scholar, historian, and advocate of theater in the Caribbean and African America. These roles were founded on his practical involvement in the theater as actor, director, playwright, and teacher in a career that spanned some six decades and contributed significantly to the growth and appreciation of this art in his native Caribbean.

Born in Trinidad, West Indies, Hill, along with actor Errol John and others, founded the island's first indigenous theater company, the Whitehall Players, in 1947. Graduating from the Royal Academy of Dramatic Art in 1951, Hill was appointed Extra-Mural Tutor in Drama at the University of the West Indies, where he stimulated and facilitated much of the development of Caribbean theater across the region. Following this assignment, Hill taught at the University of Ibadan, Nigeria, for two years before taking up appointments in the United States, where he would settle for the rest of his life. He retired after thirty-five years at Dartmouth College as John D. Willard Professor of Drama and Oratory, Emeritus.

Hill's work and contribution to theater internationally represent the very emergence of the West Indies as a region from colonialism to nationalism and political independence to cultural affirmation on the world stage.

The son of a Methodist minister, Hill benefited from a sound colonial education, which involved an early exposure to the performing arts, one of his schoolmasters being the Trinidad playwright DeWilton Rogers. Theater for Hill, as for the majority of practitioners of the day, meant British theater. In Hill's case, this influence was reinforced by his links with the British Council, where he worked as secretary and whose premises at Whitehall lent its name to the company he formed. But the West Indian masses had emerged in the literature of the region at least a decade before, and as Hill pointed out, "critics called for native plays" (1972, p. 29). Hill responded to this mandate with *Ping Pong* (1950), the first play on the steelband, Trinidad's indigenous musical orchestra, which had emerged in the late 1930s.

Through his appointment in 1953 to the University of the West Indies, itself a symbol and instrument of a nascent nationhood, Hill championed and propagated the idea of an indigenous theater that would crown a federated West Indies. He undertook the herculean task himself, teaching enthusiastically among the countries between British Honduras and British Guiana the skills such an enterprise demanded. The year the political Federation fell apart, Hill wrote *Man Better Man* (1960), a play reflecting the composition and traditions of Trinidadian folk. The play represented the newly independent state at the 1965 Commonwealth Festival in Britain. Other dramas in this period, *Dance Bongo* (1964) and *Whistling Charlie and the Monster* (1964), a political satire, continued to demonstrate the possibilities of an indigenous West Indian theater.

Hill's two-year appointment at the University of Ibadan in 1965 and thereafter in the United States allowed him to consolidate his theories and pursue further research into the history of the largely unrecorded theater of the African diaspora. He wrote extensively on the constituent arts of Trinidad Carnival, authenticating them theatrically and placing them on the agenda for further academic study. This he accomplished most authoritatively in his seminal thesis, *The Trinidad Carnival: Mandate for a National Theatre* (1972).

In this and in his other papers on Caribbean theater, Hill's stand is clear and consistent. He argues that there is a role in the Caribbean for a purposeful and professional theater as an expression of national identity and social cohesion and that Caribbean society is the poorer for not yet possessing it. This theater, he contests, belongs to all people, not just a social elite, and the people regionally should have access to it. Moreover, Caribbean theater must be based on indigenous sources that the people of the region recognize as their own. In fact, the definition of theater in the African experience incorporates a multiplicity of forms quite unlike modern Western theater, and this multiplicity must be reflected on the national stage.

Professor Hill's scholarly, academic, and artistic achievements are recognized in the many prestigious awards he received in America, Europe, and the Caribbean.

See also Carnival in Brazil and the Caribbean; University of the West Indies

■ ■ *Bibliography*

Hill, Errol. "Emergence of a National Drama in the West Indies." *CQ* 18, no. 4 (1972): 9–40.

Hill, Errol. *The Jamaica Stage, 1665–1990: Profile of a Colonial Theatre.* Amherst: University of Massachusetts Press, 1992.

Hill, Errol. *Shakespeare in Sable: A History of Black Shakespearean Actors.* Amherst: University of Massachusetts Press, 1992.

Hill, Errol. *The Trinidad Carnival: Mandate for a National Theatre.* London: New Beacon, 1997.

Hill, Errol G., and James V. Hatch. *A History of African American Theatre.* Cambridge, UK: Cambridge University Press, 2003.

RAWLE GIBBONS (2005)

HILL, KEN

1909
1979

■ ■ ■

Kenneth George Hill started public life in the 1930s as a journalist for Jamaica's largest newspaper, the *Daily Gleaner.* This was a time of ferment in Jamaica's nationalist movement, when important trade unions, political parties, and newspapers emerged. Hill played an important role in all of these.

In 1937 Hill founded a mildly nationalist organization, the National Reform Association (NRA). The NRA was a precursor to the early trade unions and most notably to Jamaica's first modern political party, the Peoples National Party (PNP), founded in 1938. Hill was also a vice president of the Bustamante Industrial Trade Union (led by Alexander Bustamante) but resigned in 1939 to become secretary of the Tramway, Transport, and General Workers Union, affiliated with the Trade Union Council, which was sympathetic to the PNP.

In 1939 Hill joined a Marxist group in the PNP, which became known simply as the left. One member, Richard

Hart, wrote, "Ken Hill, by far the most influential, was more pragmatic and less concerned with political theory than most members of the left. He probably began to consider himself a communist both as a result of the influence of his brother Frank and also his observation of the course of world events" (Hart, 1999, p. 56).

In November 1942 the Governor of Jamaica, Sir Arthur Richards, ordered the detention of Kenneth Hill, his younger brother Frank, Richard Hart, and Arthur Henry (popularly remembered as the Four Hs), whom he regarded as subversives. Richards used his wartime emergency powers to single out Ken Hill as "probably the most dangerous subversive agent in Jamaica" (Hart, 1999, p. 202). Hill became second vice president of the PNP (1947–1952) and the colonial government's fears that the party was being taken over by communists increased. It also feared the influence of the left in the trade union movement and claimed that Ken Hill (among others) was a revolutionary communist, as well as anti-British, anti-American, and racist.

Upon his release from detention in 1943, Hill returned to trade union and political work, becoming president of the Garage, Foundry, and Allied Workers Union and general secretary of the Caterers and Hotel Employees Union. He was a PNP candidate in Jamaica's 1944 general elections, the first in which Jamaicans aged twenty-one and over exercised the right to vote (adult suffrage) after the removal of property, gender, and literacy qualifications. Hill lost to Alexander Bustamante, leader of the opposing Jamaica Labour Party (JLP). Hill was a candidate again in the first local government elections under adult suffrage in 1947, again for the PNP, and defeated Rose Agatha Leon. He again won a seat in the 1949 general elections for the PNP and also became mayor of Kingston in 1951.

The PNP, however, had lost both general elections and sought to moderate its image in time for the next general election. The Four Hs were asked to resign in 1952. The PNP also disassociated itself from Hill's radical Trade Union Congress (TUC, formerly the Trade Union Council) to form a more moderate working-class union, the National Workers Union.

The PNP won the general elections in 1955 but Kenneth and Frank Hill ran as members of the National Labour Party (NLP), a party they formed in 1955. It ran four candidates but all lost and the party was dissolved.

Hill became a member of the Bustamante-led JLP after 1955 and was a candidate of the party's federal alliance, the West Indies Democratic Labour Party, for which he won a seat in the federal parliament in 1958 and of which he remained a member until the dissolution of the federation in 1962.

The JLP won Jamaica's elections in 1962 but Hill did not run. However, he remained a trade union activist in the TUC. By the mid-1960s, bridges with the PNP were rebuilt. In 1967 he was appointed by the PNP to the Jamaican Senate, signifying that he had once again become a member of that party. Hill served as senator until 1972, when he retired from public life. His picture is displayed at the headquarters of the PNP as one of the founders of the party.

See also Bustamante, Alexander; Jamaica Labour Party; Peoples National Party; West Indies Democratic Labour Party

■ ■ *Bibliography*

Hart, Richard. *Towards Decolonisation: Political, Labour, and Economic Developments in Jamaica, 1938–1945.* Mona, Jamaica: Canoe Press, University of the West Indies, 1999.

ROBERT MAXWELL BUDDAN (2005)

HILLIARD, EARL FREDERICK
APRIL 9, 1942

Congressman and lawyer Earl Hilliard, an activist in the modern civil rights movement in Alabama, was the first African American elected as representative to the U.S. Congress since the Reconstruction. Born in Birmingham to William and Iola Frazier Hilliard, he was educated at Morehouse College (B.A., 1964), Howard University School of Law (J.D., 1967), and Atlanta University School of Business (M.B.A., 1970). Hilliard began his career as a teacher at Miles College (1967–1968) and then was assistant to the president of Alabama State University (1968–1970).

Hilliard's work with voter-registration drives and participation in protest marches during the civil rights era of the 1960s gave him access to many blacks in the area. Elected to the Alabama House of Representatives in 1974, he chaired the first Alabama Black Legislative Caucus. He ran for office again in 1980, winning election to the state senate. Redistricting in Alabama after the 1990 census made possible the new Seventh Congressional District, which encompassed black neighborhoods around Birmingham and Montgomery. In a runoff election in 1992, Hilliard narrowly won a seat in the U.S. Congress.

In Congress Hilliard served on the House Agriculture Committee and the Committee on International Relations. He was first vice chair of the Congressional Black Caucus and later vice chair of the Progressive Caucus. He aggressively represented the interests of his home state, as demonstrated by the federal transportation grant that he obtained to restore ferry service in the predominantly black town of Gees Bend. He also enabled Alabama to receive three of the federal government's "enterprise zones," which provided tax incentives to promote business in depressed areas.

In 1999 Hilliard was investigated by the House Ethics Committee for possible personal and campaign finance violations. In 2002 he was defeated in the Alabama Democratic runoff race by Arthur Davis.

See also Civil Rights Movement, U.S.; Congressional Black Caucus; Politics in the United States

■ ■ *Bibliography*

Phelps, Shirelle, ed. *Contemporary Black Biography*, vol. 24. Detroit, Mich.: Gale, 2000.

Who's Who Among African Americans, 12th ed. Detroit, Mich.: Gale, 1999.

RAYMOND WINBUSH (1996)
Updated by publisher 2005

Hill-Thomas Hearings

▪▪▪

In September 1991, U.S. District Judge Clarence Thomas, nominated to the U.S. Supreme Court by President George H. W. Bush, began his confirmation hearing by the Senate Judiciary Committee. On September 27, the committee, tied in its vote on the nomination, sent the nomination to the Senate floor without a recommendation. Despite the committee's failure to issue a recommendation, most commentators believed the Senate would confirm Thomas. On October 6, 1991, National Public Radio and *New York Newsday* ran a story about Anita Faye Hill (b. 1956), a law professor at the University of Oklahoma, who had been a staff attorney under Thomas at the Department of Education and the Equal Employment Opportunity Commission in the early 1980s and who had told FBI investigators that Thomas had sexually harassed her during her tenure. The story was based on the leak of a confidential affidavit Hill had provided the committee on September 23. Her story made public, Hill openly repeated her accusations. In a comment later echoed by many women,

Hill claimed the all-male Judiciary Committee had been insensitive to the importance of sexual harassment and had not questioned Thomas about it. Meanwhile, Thomas categorically denied any such conduct. On October 8, following a long debate in the Senate, the vote on Thomas's confirmation was delayed. Committee Chair Joseph R. Biden scheduled further hearings in order to provide Hill and Thomas an opportunity to testify publicly on the issue.

On October 11, 1991, before a nationwide television audience, the hearings on Thomas's conduct began. Hill described Thomas's repeated sexual overtures to her, charging that he had boasted of his sexual prowess, frequently used prurient sexual innuendos, and had insisted on describing to her the plots of pornographic movies he had seen. When asked why, if Thomas had harassed her in such a fashion, Hill had accepted a position under him at the Equal Employment Opportunity Commission, she explained that the harassment had stopped for a period, and she feared she would be unable to find another job without his recommendation.

Thomas's testimony flatly contradicted Hill's. Although Thomas asserted he had not listened to Hill's testimony, which he angrily referred to as lies, he denied any wrongdoing and repeatedly refused to discuss his private life. He denounced the committee's confirmation process as "un-American" and assailed it for staging what he called a "high-tech lynching" of him as an independent conservative black intellectual.

During the following days, as the Senate debated the hearings, Senate Republicans launched a furious assault on Hill's character and truthfulness in order to discredit her. Senators charged her with "fantasizing" about Thomas's interest in her. At the same time, many observers felt the Judiciary Committee had not investigated Thomas's veracity with equal zeal. Nationwide argument, which crossed ideological and gender lines, raged over whether Thomas or Hill was telling the truth, and whether Thomas's alleged sexual harassment was relevant to his confirmation.

Within the black community, debate was particularly pointed, although few, if any, blacks altered their position on Thomas's confirmation as a result of the revelations. Many, perhaps most, blacks saw the affair as an embarrassment, reviving stereotypes of blacks as sexually rapacious, vulgar, and mendacious, and the stigma of black males as rapists. Harvard sociologist Orlando Patterson assumed the essential truth of Hill's version, but thought Thomas's conduct was an example of "Rabelaisian humor," a harmless example of "down-home courting." Some suspected conspiracies, as did black conservative Arthur Fletcher, chair of the U.S. Civil Rights Commission, who claimed the hearings were a racist plot to pit blacks against each other. Yale law professor Stephen Carter called both parties victims of the confirmation process. Many black men and women considered Hill a traitor to the race for accusing Thomas publicly, and for trying to block a black man's ascension to the Supreme Court. Others defended Hill's courage. Jesse Jackson called her the Rosa Parks of sexual harassment. Toni Morrison asserted that black men such as Thomas wished to rise on the backs of black women, whose needs and feelings were ignored. Countless women, black and white, were inspired by the public discussion of sexual harassment to share their own feelings and stories of harassment.

On October 15, the Senate confirmed Thomas by a vote of fifty-two to forty-eight, the second narrowest winning margin in history. Public opinion polls published at the time showed that the majority of Americans believed Thomas and suspected Hill's allegations. Still, many women were politically energized by the hearings, and many women were elected to public office in 1992 with the support of their campaign contributions and activism. Within a year after the hearings, however, new opinion polls suggested that a majority of Americans now believed Anita Hill had told the truth. By that time, continuing public interest in the affair had been reflected in the publication of several books on the trials, including two notable anthologies of essays written by African Americans.

See also Jackson, Jesse Louis; Morrison, Toni; Politics in the United States; Thomas, Clarence

■■ *Bibliography*

Brock, David. *The Real Anita Hill.* New York: Free Press, 1993.

Chrisman, Robert, and Robert L. Allen, eds. *Court of Appeal: The Black Community Speaks Out on the Racial and Sexual Politics of Thomas v. Hill.* New York: Ballantine, 1992.

Morrison, Toni, ed. *Race-ing Justice, Engendering Power.* New York: Pantheon, 1992.

GREG ROBINSON (1996)

HIMES, CHESTER

JULY 29, 1909
NOVEMBER 12, 1984

■■■

The novelist and short-story writer Chester Himes was born in Jefferson City, Missouri. The youngest of three sons, he spent his first fourteen years in the South. His mother, the former Estelle Bomar, was the daughter of former slaves who had achieved considerable success in the construction business. She was educated at a black Presbyterian finishing school in North Carolina and taught music from time to time at African-American colleges and academies. Her husband, Joseph Himes, also born of former slaves, grew up in poverty in North Carolina but acquired a diploma at Claflin College in Orangeburg, South Carolina. A skilled blacksmith and wheelwright, he taught mechanical arts at black institutions in Georgia, Missouri, Mississippi, and Arkansas. Both parents appear as thinly disguised characters whose conflicting social and racial views bewilder the protagonist in Himes's autobiographical novel *The Third Generation* (1954).

In 1923 a freak accident blinded Himes's older brother, causing the family to move from Pine Bluff, Arkansas, to St. Louis to seek specialized medical treatment. Two years later they moved to Cleveland, where Chester graduated from East High School in January 1926. Following graduation he worked as a busboy at a Cleveland hotel, where he suffered a traumatic fall that left him with permanent back and shoulder injuries. In September 1926 he enrolled as a liberal arts student at Ohio State University, but he was expelled the following February for failing grades and unseemly behavior. Thereafter he drifted into a life of crime in the black ghettos of Cleveland and Columbus. In December 1927, he was sentenced to serve twenty years in the Ohio State Penitentiary for armed robbery.

While in prison, Himes began a lifelong career writing fiction; his first stories were printed in African-American publications in early 1932. In 1934 he reached a national audience in *Esquire* for "To What Red Hell," describing the 1930 fire that swept through the Ohio penitentiary, killing more than 330 convicts. He was paroled in 1936, and in August 1937 he married Jean Lucinda Johnson, a longtime friend. From 1936 to 1940 he worked mainly at manual jobs and for the Federal Writers' Project, departing for California in the fall of 1940 in hopes of writing for Hollywood. Repeated rejections at the studios, however, led him to seek work at the racially tense California shipyards. These experiences are reflected in several articles he wrote in the 1940s, as well as in two bitter novels, *If He Hollers Let Him Go* (1946) and *Lonely Crusade* (1947). The interethnic, economic, social, and sexual consequences of racism are treated at some length in these books.

From 1945 to 1953 Himes lived mainly in New York and New England; he sailed for France several months after the publication of his prison novel *Cast the First Stone*

(1952). For the rest of his life he lived mainly in France and Spain, making only occasional visits to the United States, and much of his subsequent fiction was published first in France before appearing elsewhere. Among his books written abroad were seven Harlem police thrillers involving the characters Cotton Ed Johnson and Grave Digger Jones; one of these books won a French literary award in 1958. Two incomplete novels, *Plan B,* dealing with a future race war, and *The Lunatic Fringe* have not yet been printed in the United States. Himes's own favorite among his works was *The Primitive* (1955), which depicts an intense, troubled relationship between a black man and a white woman in post–World War II New York. Himes's only published novel with a non-American setting, *A Case of Rape* (1985), focuses on four black men being tried in Paris for the violation and death of a white woman. Because the fictional characters were modeled on well-known African Americans living in Europe, the book caused something of a stir in the expatriate community. Himes's other works written in Europe were *Pinktoes* (1961), an interracial sex comedy about the activities of a celebrated Harlem hostess, and *Run Man Run* (1966), a thriller telling of a black man's flight from a murderous New York policeman. In 1978 Himes obtained a divorce in absentia and married Lesley Packard, an English journalist.

While living in Spain, Himes wrote two volumes of an autobiography, *The Quality of Hurt* (1973) and *My Life of Absurdity* (1976). Toward the end of his life he came to view his writings as being in the absurdist tradition. Racism, he said, made blacks and whites behave absurdly. He envisioned organized violence as the only means of ending racial oppression in America. Because his literary reputation was never as high in the United States as it was in Europe, Himes lived precariously for most of his authorial years, but a resurgence of interest in his writings in the 1970s brought him a measure of financial security. Upon his death in Alicante, Spain, he left a number of unfinished projects.

See also Federal Writers' Project; Literature of the United States

■ ■ *Bibliography*

Lundquist, James. *Chester Himes.* New York: Ungar, 1976.

Milliken, Stephen F. *Chester Himes: A Critical Appraisal.* Columbia: University of Missouri Press, 1976.

Muller, Gilbert H. *Chester Himes.* Boston: Twayne, 1989.

Sallis, James. *Chester Himes: A Life.* New York: Walker & Co., 2001.

Skinner, Robert. *Two Guns from Harlem: The Detective Fiction of Chester Himes.* Bowling Green, Ohio: Bowling Green State University Popular Press, 1989.

EDWARD MARGOLIES (1996)
Updated bibliography

HINES, GREGORY

FEBRUARY 14, 1946
AUGUST 9, 2003

Jazz tap dancer, singer, actor, musician, and creator of improvised tap choreography, Gregory Oliver Hines was born in New York City, the son of Maurice Hines Sr. and Alma Hines. He began dancing at the age of three, turned professional at age five, and for fifteen years performed with his older brother Maurice as The Hines Kids, making nightclub appearances across the country. While the Broadway teacher and choreographer Henry LeTang created the team's first tap dance routines, the brothers learned to dance by watching such great tap masters as Charles "Honi" Coles, Howard "Sandman" Sims, the Nicholas Brothers, and Teddy Hale, wherever and whenever they performed in the same theaters. In 1964 Maurice Sr. joined his sons' act as a drummer, changing the group's name to Hines, Hines, and Dad, and they toured internationally, frequently appearing on *The Tonight Show.* After years of on-the-road travel, the younger Hines became restless and left the group in his early twenties, "retiring" to Venice, California, where he formed the jazz-rock band Severence. He released an album of original songs in 1973.

When he moved back to New York City in the late 1970s, Hines immediately landed a role in *The Last Minstrel Show.* The show closed in Philadelphia but launched him back into performing; just a month later came *Eubie* (1978), a certified Broadway hit that earned him the first of four Tony nominations. *Comin' Uptown* (1980) led to another nomination, and *Sophisticated Ladies* (1981) a third. In 1992 Hines received the Tony Award for Best Actor in a Musical for his riveting portrayal of the jazz man Jelly Roll Morton in George C. Wolfe's production of *Jelly's Last Jam,* sharing a Tony nomination for choreography for that show with Hope Clark and Ted Levy.

Hines made his initial transition from dancer-singer to film actor in Mel Brooks' hilarious *The History of the World, Part I* (1981), playing the role of a Roman slave who in one scene sand-dances in the desert. He followed that in quick succession playing the role of a coroner in *Wolfen,* an allegorical mystery directed by Michael

Wadleigh. In 1984 he starred in Francis Ford Coppola's film *The Cotton Club* (1984), which reunited him with his brother, Maurice. The fierce virtuosity of Hines's tap dancing is seen in the *White Nights* (1985), in which he played an American defector to the Soviet Union opposite Mikhail Baryshnikov. In 1988 Hines starred in a film that combined his penchant for both dance and drama, *Tap*, the first dance musical to merge tap dancing with contemporary rock and funk musical styles; it featured a host of tap legends, including Sandman Sims, Bunny Briggs, Harold Nicholas, and Hines's costar and show business mentor, Sammy Davis Jr.

Hines's extensive and varied film resume includes teaming with Billy Crystal in director Peter Hyam's hit comedy *Running Scared,* and with Willem Dafoe in the Southeast Asia military thriller *Off Limits*. He starred in William Friedkin's dark comedy *Deal of the Century* with Sigourney Weaver and Chevy Chase; Penny Marshall's military comedy *Renaissance Man*, costarring with Danny DeVito; *The Preacher's Wife* with Denzel Washington and Whitney Houston, once again directed by Marshall; *Waiting to Exhale*, with Angela Bassett and Whitney Houston for director Forest Whittaker; and *Good Luck*, with costar Vincent D'Onofrio. In 1994 Hines made his directorial debut in the independent feature *Bleeding Hearts*, a contemporary romantic drama exploring the precarious relationship between a thirty-year-old white male radical and a black female high school student.

Hines's work in television was equally diverse. In 1989 he created and hosted *Tap Dance in America,* a Public Broadcasting Service television special that featured veteran tap dancers, established tap dance companies, and the next generation of tap dancers. The film was nominated for an Emmy Award, as was his performance on *Motown Returns to the Apollo*. Hines made his television series debut in 1998, playing Ben Stevenson, a loving single father hesitantly reentering the dating world on the series *The Gregory Hines Show*. Throughout an amazingly varied career, Hines continued to be a tireless advocate for tap dance in America and in 1988 lobbied successfully for the creation of National Tap Dance Day, now celebrated in forty cities in the United States and in eight other nations.

Like a jazz musician who ornaments a melody with improvisational riffs, Hines improvised within the frame of the dance. His tap "improvography" demanded the percussive phrasing of a composer, the rhythms of a drummer, and the lines of a dancer. While being the inheritor of the tradition of black rhythm tap, he was also a proponent of the new. "He purposely obliterated the tempos," wrote Sally Sommer, "throwing down a cascade of taps like pebbles tossed across the floor. In that moment, he

aligned tap with the latest free-form experiments in jazz and new music and postmodern dance."

Hines died in Los Angeles at the age of fifty-seven.

See also Davis, Sammy, Jr.; Glover, Savion; Musical Theater; Tap Dance

■ ■ *Bibliography*

Bandler, Michael J. "Tapping into Stardom." *American Way* (December 10, 1985): 21–26.

Dunning, Jennifer. "Gregory Hines, Versatile Dancer and Actor, Dies at 57." *New York Times* (August 11, 2003).

Graustark, Barbara. "Tapped For Stardom." *American Film* (December 1984): 28–34.

Sommer, Sally. "Tap Happy: Hines On Tap." *Dance Magazine* (December, 1988): 46–50.

Sommer, Sally. "Gregory Hines: From Time Step to Timeless." *New York Times* (August 14, 2003).

CONSTANCE VALIS HILL (1996)
Updated by author 2005

HIP-HOP

Hip-hop, in its most contemporary and uniform manifestation, emerged in 1973. Though various elements of hip-hop culture—both culturally and aesthetically—are found in African culture, the Harlem Renaissance, and the black arts movement of the 1960s, it was not until 1973 with the legendary DJ Kool Herc's first block party that hip-hop truly began to emerge. Many factors are responsible for the creation and development of hip-hop culture in the South Bronx:

1. American urban planning and later, Reaganomics;

2. the postindustrial urban landscape;

3. the crack epidemic of the 1980s;

4. technological advances, namely sampling and synthesizers; and

5. major cuts in funding for the arts in and around New York City (Rose, 1994).

Today, hip-hop culture and its constituents have crystallized into what Bakari Kitwana (2002) has appropriately labeled the "Hip-Hop Generation."

Hip-hop culture consists of at least seven elements, four primary and three secondary. The original, primary elements of hip-hop culture are DJ-ing (by nontraditional disc jockeys who were the first technicians to isolate and

Hip-hop graffiti mural. *One of the primary elements of hip-hop culture, graffiti (graf) was practiced by visual artists who reclaimed public space by "vandalizing" trains, bridges, and other visible, open canvases.* © HENRY DILTZ/CORBIS. REPRODUCED BY CORBIS CORPORATION.

sample the break-beats from popular songs of the 1970s); break dancing (by early dance athletes who borrowed moves from *capoeira,* ballet, and the martial arts, among other dance forms and kinesthetic techniques); graffiti, or graf (practiced by visual artists with no outlets who reclaimed public space by "vandalizing" trains and other visible, public canvases with spray paint); and MC-ing (referring to masters of ceremonies; the earliest rappers were mere background lyricists usually allowed only to give shoutouts to DJs, area crews, and announcements of upcoming hip-hop parties, originally referred to as jams). The second tier of elements developed as the culture grew into a worldwide phenomenon. These elements include fashion and modes of dress, entrepreneurship, and complex systems of knowledge (particularly elaborate language and other semiotic codes).

Each of the four primary elements centers around legendary historical figures within the culture. The figure credited with establishing the culture through a unique utilization of two turntables is DJ Kool Herc (Clive Campbell). Born in Kingston Jamaica, Kool Herc migrated to the west Bronx in 1967. By the early 1970s Kool Herc (who claims American soul and reggae as his seminal musical influences) had integrated elements of Jamaican yard culture into spontaneous parties (indoor and outdoor) that are now considered the first hip-hop jams. These parties were distinct for a number of reasons:

1. They were cheaper than most disco parties of the time period;

2. Kool Herc isolated and looped break-beats from 1970s soul classics and popular disco tunes in order to make the jam eminently danceable;

Grandmaster Flash, one of the founding fathers of hip-hop. *Born Joseph Saddler in Barbados, West Indies, and raised in the Bronx, Grandmaster Flash was one of rap's earliest technical pioneers. The deejay (DJ) innovative turntable techniques he experimented with in the 1970s have become synonymous with rap and hip-hop artistry.* PHOTOGRAPH BY PETER NOBLE. © S.I.N./CORBIS. REPRODUCED BY PERMISSION.

3. The looped break-beats provided extended opportunities for breakdancers to showcase their amazing acrobatic skills; and

4. MCs became the voice of hip-hop culture through shoutouts and party announcements.

Eventually the role of the MC developed into that of the central entertainer of hip-hop culture: the rapper. The first rap record that achieved mainstream radio attention was titled "Rappers Delight," performed by the Sugar Hill Gang and released by Sylvia Robinson's Sugar Hill Records in 1979. However, some of the lyrics of this historical record were actually written by Grand Master Caz, one of the original rappers from the South Bronx, who performed his raps in and around the same jams initiated by DJ Kool Herc.

There were several crews of young folk who participated in the development of break dancing and graffiti. One of the earliest and now most legendary breaking crews is the Rock Steady Crew. Bronx b-boys (b-boys and b-girls are imbibers of hip-hop culture who creatively participate in two or more primary elements of the culture) Jimmy D. and Jojo established the legendary Rock Steady Crew, joined by Crazy Legs and Lenny Len in 1979.

The earliest documented graf label belongs to Greece-born Demetrius from 183th Street in the Bronx. He made himself famous by tagging Taki 183 throughout the five boroughs of New York City via subway trains. There are several other dates and historical figures of note. In 1974 Afrika Bambaataa transformed one of New York City's largest and most violent gangs into hip-hop culture's first organization, the ZULU Nation. Even today the ZULU Nation is one of the most publicly active, communally oriented organizations in hip-hop. Bambaataa, along with DJ Busy Bee Starski, is credited with coining the term hip-hop (in reference to those original parties/jams) in the same year. In 1975 Grand Wizard Theodore discovered the scratch, a monumental DJ-ing technique by which DJs deliberately rupture a vinyl sound recording to produce the

Rappers engaged in battle, Harlem, New York, 2003. Featured from left are Hip Hop artists Peanut, Gotti, Trigg, and Little Foo. © BRENDA ANN KENNEALLY/CORBIS

now legendary scratching sound so often associated with hip-hop DJs and music producers.

From these origins, hip-hop's development can appropriately be broken down into three eras: The Old School Era, Golden Age Era, and the Platinum Present.

The Old School Era, from 1979 to 1987, is when hip-hop culture cultivated itself in and through all of its elements, usually remaining authentic to its countercultural roots in the postindustrial challenges manifested in the urban landscape of the late twentieth century. Artists associated with this era include Grandmaster Flash and the Furious Five, The Sugarhill Gang, Lady B, Big Daddy Kane, Run DMC, Kurtis Blow, and others.

The Golden Age Era, from 1987 to 1993, marked a time when rap and rappers began to take center stage as the culture splashed onto the mainstream platform of American popular culture. The extraordinary musical production and lyrical content of rap songs artistically eclipsed most of the other primary elements of the culture (break dancing, graf art, and DJ-ing). Eventually the recording industry began contemplating rap music as a potential billion-dollar opportunity. Mass-mediated rap

music and hip-hop videos displaced the intimate, insulated urban development of the culture. Artists associated with this era include Run DMC, Boogie Down Productions, Eric B and Rakim, Salt N Pepa, Queen Latifah, De La Soul, A Tribe Called Quest, Public Enemy, NWA, and many others.

The last era is the Platinum Present. From 1994 on, hip-hop culture has enjoyed the best and worst of what mass-mediated popularity and cultural commodification have to offer. The meteoric rise to popular fame of gangsta rap in the early 1990s set the stage for a marked content shift in the lyrical discourse of rap music toward more and more violent depictions of inner-city realities. Millions of magazines and records were sold, but two of hip-hop's most promising artists, Biggie Smalls and Tupac Shakur, were literally gunned down in the crossfire of a media-fueled battle between the so-called East and West Coast constituents of hip-hop culture. With the blueprint of popular success for rappers laid bare, several exceptional artists stepped into the gaping space left in the wake of Biggie and Tupac. This influx of new talent included Nas,

Jay-Z, Master P, DMX, Big Pun, Snoop Doggy Dogg, Eminem, and Outkast.

By the mid-1990s hip-hop culture also emerged as an area of serious study on the university level. Courses on hip-hop culture, history, and aesthetics were offered on college campuses across America. Due largely to student demand and interest, these courses analyzed the origins and significance of hip-hop culture. Currently housed at Harvard University's W. E. B. Du Bois Institute, the Hiphop Archive, founded in 2002 by Marcyliena Morgan, is an example of this important pedagogical development.

See also Music in the United States; Rap

∎∎ *Bibliography*

Forman, Murray. *The 'Hood Comes First: Race, Space, and Place in Rap and Hip Hop.* Middletown, Conn.: Wesleyan University Press, 2002.

Kitwana, Bakari. *The Hip-Hop Generation: Young Blacks and the Crisis in African-American Culture.* New York: Basic Civitas Books, 2002.

The Original Hip-Hop (Rap) Lyrics Archive. Available from <http://www.ohhla.com>.

Rose, Tricia. *Black Noise: Rap Music and Black Culture in Contemporary America.* Hanover, N.H.: University Press of New England, 1994.

Toop, David. *Rap Attack #3.* London: Serpent's Tail Press, 2000.

WILLIAM BOONE (2005)
JAMES PETERSON (2005)

HISTORIANS AND HISTORIOGRAPHY, AFRICAN AMERICAN

▪▪▪

The writing of African-American history began as a quest to understand the status and condition of black people in the United States. The first works on the subject, James W. C. Pennington's *A Textbook of the Origin and History of the Colored People* (1841) and Robert Benjamin Lewis's *Light and Truth: Collected from the Bible and Ancient and Modern History, Containing the Universal History of the Colored Man and Indian Race, from the Creation of the World to the Present Time* (1836), sought to explain the enslavement of Africans in the western hemisphere. They recounted black achievement in ancient Africa, particularly Egypt and Ethiopia, to justify racial equality. These early black writers, similar to many of the first chroniclers of the

United States, searched for the "hidden hand" of God in human affairs. History for them was the revelation of divine providence in the activities of people and nations.

Although African Americans suffered from enslavement, prejudice, and discrimination, Pennington and Lewis considered their status and condition as temporary because of the biblical prophecy that "Ethiopia shall soon stretch forth her hands unto God" (*Ps.* 68:31). For many African Americans, including black historians prior to the twentieth century, this prophecy was a promise of divine deliverance from the chains of slavery and the shackles of racial discrimination.

Histories written after Pennington and Lewis, such as William C. Nell's *The Colored Patriots of the American Revolution* (1855), and William Wells Brown's *The Black Man: His Antecedents, His Genius, and His Achievements* (1863), were intended to convince black and white Americans that African Americans deserved freedom, justice, and equality. If given the opportunity, an idea argued and illustrated in their books, African Americans could excel in all areas of life and contribute to the country's development and progress. They wrote to inspire African Americans to lead exemplary lives and not to provide any excuse for racial prejudice and discrimination.

George Washington Williams, at different times a soldier, pastor, editor, columnist, lawyer, and legislator, was the first black historian to write a systematic study of the African-American past. He bridged the gap between early chroniclers of African-American history and the more scientific writers of the twentieth century. Although Williams employed methods of research similar to professional historians of his day in conducting interviews, examining newspapers, using statistics, and culling archives, he still wrote to discern the plans of God in studying the past. His impressive two-volume work, *History of the Negro Race in America from 1619 to 1880* (1883), was flawed by its often literal reproduction of documentation and lack of analysis and interpretation. The publication, however, was a remarkable achievement for its time and earned Williams recognition as a pioneer in modern African-American historiography.

Almost a decade after Williams's pathbreaking work, W. E. B. Du Bois became the first African American to earn a doctorate in history, receiving the degree in 1895 from Harvard University. A year later, his dissertation, "The Suppression of the African Slave Trade to the United States of America, 1638–1870," was the first volume published in the Harvard Historical Studies series. In his now classic *The Souls of Black Folk: Essays and Sketches* (1903), Du Bois was one of the first historians to explore the interior lives of African Americans and their distinctive culture. As was the case with much of his scholarship, Du Bois was ahead of his time. Because of the effort to achieve freedom, justice, and equality, black historians, in the main, paid greater attention to revising the errors, omissions, and distortions of white historians and to glorifying the contributions of African Americans to American life than to identifying and defining a distinctive African-American culture.

Carter G. Woodson was the foremost proponent of the revisionist and contributionist school of African-American historiography. He earned the title "Father of Black History" for institutionalizing the revisionist and contributionist interpretation of the African-American past and for popularizing the study of black history. Woodson was the second African American to earn a doctorate in history, also from Harvard University, in 1912. He organized the Association for the Study of Negro Life and History (ASNLH) in 1915 to preserve the African-American heritage, promote interracial harmony, and inspire black youth to greater achievement. In 1916 Woodson launched the *Journal of Negro History* to publish scholarship about the African-American past. He established the Associated Publishers in 1921 to publish books of black history and initiated Negro History Week in 1926 (expanded to Black History Month in 1976). To reach a more popular audience, Woodson started the *Negro History Bulletin* in 1937. Until his death in 1950, Woodson and his colleagues in the ASNLH (William M. Brewer, Lorenzo J. Greene, Luther Porter Jackson, James Hugo Johnston, Rayford W. Logan, W. Sherman Savage, Alrutheus A. Taylor, and Charles H. Wesley) virtually dominated the field of African-American history.

Few historians wrote about the black experience before World War II. Gunnar Myrdal's two-volume study *An American Dilemma: The Negro Problem and Modern Democracy* (1944) and John Hope Franklin's *From Slavery to Freedom: A History of American Negroes* (1947) sparked interest in the subject. Myrdal's report for the Carnegie Corporation on black life in the United States was completed with the assistance of several leading black and white scholars. The work was more sociological than historical, as it looked to resolve the problem of race and to avoid racial conflict similar to the riots that broke out in some twenty-five cities and towns after World War I. Franklin's book was an example of meticulous research that demonstrated the central role African Americans played in the development of the United States. These two trailblazing works influenced scholars to take greater note of African-American history for understanding the American past. World War II, in large measure, destroyed the traditional ideology of white supremacy and with it the

justification for excluding African Americans from full citizenship as well as from the story of the nation's past.

Although white scholars now paid greater attention to the African-American experience, they used more of a sociological or race relations approach to black history. Many historians, black and white, wrote in the abolitionist tradition of revealing injustices heaped on African Americans. Black people became victims more than shapers of history. The legacy of slavery, for example, supposedly explained all the problems that beset the black population, from underachievement to illegitimacy, family instability, crime, illiteracy, and self-hatred. African Americans allegedly internalized the oppression of slavery and were mired in a culture of poverty.

With the growth of the civil rights and black consciousness movements of the 1950s and 1960s, black historians in particular began to explore African-American resistance and the creation of a viable culture that sustained black people from the brutality of slavery, segregation, and subordination. If ordinary African Americans braved often violent assaults to desegregate buses, lunch counters, drinking fountains, swimming pools, restrooms, and voting booths, then how strong was the legacy of slavery? What were the real historical patterns of black behavior? Earl E. Thorpe, who wrote prolifically about African-American historiography, suggested that "It is because the past is a guide with roads pointing in many directions that each generation and epoch must make its own studies of history" (1957, p. 183). It therefore becomes necessary to go back in time, to understand what some writers referred to as the "Second Reconstruction," and to appreciate the origins of the struggle for civil rights and black power.

By the late 1960s, historians of the African-American experience largely abandoned the sociological or race relations interpretation. They adopted a more anthropological and psychological approach to the African-American past, a concern about black people as agents of history and not as helpless victims. They explored the interior lives of African Americans, their culture, and its antecedents in Africa. Ironically, it was the white anthropologist Melville J. Herskovits who insisted that African Americans had retained elements of African culture, while the black sociologist E. Franklin Frazier argued that black people had been stripped of their past and started anew in the United States. The place of Africa loomed larger in the scholarship of the 1960s and 1970s, as historians studied emigration, black nationalism, religion, music, dance, folklore, and the family in the context of African persuasion.

In many respects, Benjamin Quarles, a venerable black historian at Morgan State University, originated the new writing of African-American history with the publication of *Black Abolitionists* (1969). Quarles wrote that the African American was abolition's "different drummer," a participant in, as well as a symbol of, the movement, and one of its pioneers. John W. Blassingame's *The Slave Community: Plantation Life in the Antebellum South* (1972) soon followed with an original interpretation of slavery in which the slaves helped define the peculiar institution and possessed some discretion over the shape of their daily lives. The work of Barbara J. Fields, Eugene D. Genovese, Herbert G. Gutman, Vincent Harding, Nathan I. Huggins, Norrece T. Jones, Charles W. Joyner, Wilma King, Lawrence W. Levine, Daniel C. Littlefield, Leslie H. Owens, Albert J. Raboteau, Brenda Stevenson, Sterling Stuckey, Margaret Washington, Thomas L. Webber, and Peter H. Wood has broadened and deepened an understanding of slave life and culture. Genovese's *Roll, Jordan, Roll: The World the Slaves Made* (1974), in particular, influenced the study of the dialectical relationship between slave and master (and by extension blacks and whites) as one governed not by race relations but by reciprocal duties and obligations. This give-and-take in determining the status and condition of African Americans in slavery and freedom has been advanced in the work of Ira Berlin, David W. Blight, Eric Foner, Thomas C. Holt, James O. Horton, Gerald D. Jaynes, Leon F. Litwack, Waldo E. Martin, Nell I. Painter, James L. Roark, Willie Lee Rose, Julie Saville, and Joel Williamson.

The new African-American historiography has been applied to themes of migration, urbanization, the working class, and protest. Historians have examined the causes and consequences of black migration from the rural South to urban areas of the North and South, finding them to be primarily the result of family decisions and kinship networks more than outside forces. They have studied both the physical and the institutional ghetto. Segregation produced the former, while African Americans created the latter to meet their own religious, economic, cultural, political, and social needs. The ghetto of the early twentieth century was not necessarily a slum. It was often a vibrant community in which African Americans carried out their daily lives. Studies of black business development by Raymond Gavins, Alexa B. Henderson, Michael E. Lomax, Juliet E. K. Walker, Walter Weare, and Robert E. Weems Jr. have depicted that vibrancy.

A growing body of research on African Americans and European immigrants suggests that black workers enjoyed some advantages in education, skills, and language facility that eroded over time as immigrants organized labor along ethnic and racial lines. Although the Congress of Industrial Organizations' embrace of black workers during the late 1930s brought some absolute change for African Americans, there was little relative change in comparison with white workers. African Americans, moreover, experienced the Great Depression earlier and suffered longer than any other segment of the population. Historians such as John E. Bodnar, Dennis C. Dickerson, William H. Harris, Earl Lewis, August Meier and Elliott M. Rudwick, Richard B. Pierce, Christopher Reed, Nikki Taylor, Joe William Trotter Jr., and Lillian Williams have illuminated the fate of the black working class.

Although they have faced great odds in racism, segregation, lynching, disfranchisement, and discrimination, African Americans have been resilient in not succumbing to oppression. As James D. Anderson, Herbert Aptheker, Lerone Bennett Jr., Mary F. Berry, Richard J. M. Blackett, John H. Bracey Jr., John Henrik Clarke, John E. Fleming, V. P. Franklin, Vincent Harding, Robert A. Hill, Jonathan Scott Holloway, August Meier and Elliott M. Rudwick, Daryl Scott, Donald Spivey, Arvarh Strickland, and Quintard Taylor have shown, the protest tradition among African Americans has endured. One of the strong tenets of recent African-American historiography is that black people retained their integrity as a people despite the potential of slavery and racism to break them. They resisted brutalization, although they could not always avoid brutality. They fashioned a distinctive and viable culture in opposition to oppression. Their culture was rooted in Africa but given form and substance in the United States. Their tradition of resistance and protest burst forth in an unprecedented manner during the modern civil rights movement of the 1950s and 1960s. Taylor Branch, Clayborne Carson, William H. Chafe, John Dittmer, David J. Garrow, Vincent Harding, Darlene Clark Hine, Steven F. Lawson, David L. Lewis, Manning Marable, August Meier and Elliott M. Rudwick, Charles Payne, Linda Reed, Harvard Sitkoff, Patricia Sullivan, Julius Thompson, and Robert Weisbrot have recorded the critical events, organizations, and personalities that constituted the "Second Reconstruction."

A younger generation of historians, such as Scot Brown, Rod Bush, Sundiata Cha-Jua, William Jelani Cobb, Eddie S. Glaude Jr., Winston Grady-Willis, Jeffrey Ogbar, and Komozi Woodward, has emerged during the early twenty-first century to explain the "post–civil rights era," and especially the rise of Black Power and black nationalism. African-American cultural history in the work of Kevin Gaines, Adam Green, Mitch Kachun, Robin D. G. Kelley, Nick Salvatore, William L. Van Deburg, and Craig Werner has taken on greater import to understand the global reach and influence of African-American art, dance, literature, and music.

Although African-American historiography has broken away from explaining the past as divine providence, revising the errors, omissions, and distortions of racist white writers, celebrating the contributions of famous black men to the growth and development of the United States, depicting the endless horrors of racism and segregation, and analyzing race relations, it has until recently had a blind spot. The new African-American historiography has studied black people as agents rather than as victims of the past but has, for some time, ignored the issue of gender. The work of Elsa Barkley Brown, Bettye Collier-Thomas, Gloria Dickinson, Sheila Flemming, Paula Giddings, Sharon Harley, Evelyn Brooks Higginbotham, Darlene Clark Hine, Tera W. Hunter, Jacqueline Jones, Chana Kai Lee, Cynthia Neverdon-Morton, Barbara Ransby, Jacqueline Rouse, Stephanie Shaw, Ula Y. Taylor, Rosalyn Terborg-Penn, Deborah Gray White, and Rhonda Y. Williams has brought gender to the forefront of African-American historiography. As a result, fresh insight into the African-American past, the forebearers of black culture, and the builders of black progress has been gained. Gender has begun to take on greater compass than the study of black women as scholars have started to explore masculinity and black sexuality. The writing of African-American history has become more multidimensional as historians probe class, sexuality, color, gender, religion, region, and profession.

Growing immigration to the United States by black people from Africa, the Caribbean, Europe, and Central and South America has raised new questions about African Americans and the African diaspora. This new immigration has reinvigorated African-American culture and enriched the conversation about what it means to be an African American. Ralph Crowder, Thomas J. Davis, George Fredrickson, Michael Gomez, Robin D. G. Kelley, Manning Marable, Tony Martin, Brenda Gayle Plummer, and William R. Scott have expanded the scope of African-American history to embrace what Earl Lewis has referred to as "overlapping diasporas." This broader scope has included studying how the international position of the United States has affected the domestic civil rights movement in the work of Carol Anderson, Thomas Borstelmann, Mary L. Dudziak, and Penny Von Eschen.

Maghan Keita, Wilson J. Moses, and Clarence Walker have explored popular interpretations of African-American history and the concept of Afrocentrism as a challenge to universalism and as a quest for a distinctive black identity emanating from Africa. Given that there is no scientific certainty for the category of race, historians such as Evelyn Brooks Higginbotham, Thomas C. Holt, Earl Lewis, and David Roediger have confronted the meaning of race as a broad framework that often obscures African-American multidimensionality.

From a field innovated by less than two dozen black historians prior to 1940, African-American historiography has grown to embrace a large corps of black and white scholars who have produced a new and exciting body of scholarship. The writing of African-American history has given voice and agency to a people for too long almost invisible, who were assumed to have no past worthy of study. African-American historiography has not only rescued the thought and action of black people over time and space in the United States, but it has also made the writing of U.S. history impossible without the voice and agency of African Americans.

See also Anthropology and Anthropologists; Du Bois, W. E. B.; Education; Franklin, John Hope; Frazier, Edward Franklin; Pennington, James W. C.; Quarles, Benjamin; Sociology; Woodson, Carter G.

■ ■ *Bibliography*

Blassingame, John W. "The Afro-Americans: From Mythology to Reality." In *The Reinterpretation of American History and Culture,* edited by William H. Cartwright and Richard L. Watson Jr. Washington, D.C.: National Council for the Social Studies, 1973.

Harris, Robert L., Jr. "Coming of Age: The Transformation of Afro-American Historiography." *Journal of Negro History* 67, no. 2 (Summer 1982): 107–121.

Higginbotham, Evelyn Brooks. "African American Women's History and the Metalanguage of Race." *Signs* 17 (1992): 251–274.

Hine, Darlene Clark, ed. *The State of Afro-American History: Past, Present, and Future.* Baton Rouge: Louisiana State University Press, 1986.

Holt, Thomas C. "African-American History." In *The New American History,* edited by Eric Foner. Philadelphia: Temple University Press, 1990; rev. and expanded ed., 1997.

Lewis, Earl. "To Turn As on a Pivot: Writing African Americans into a History of Overlapping Diasporas." *American Historical Review* 100 (1995): 765–787.

Meier, August, and Elliott M. Rudwick. *Black History and the Historical Profession, 1915–1980.* Urbana: University of Illinois Press, 1986.

Quarles, Benjamin. "Black History's Antebellum Origins." *Proceedings of the American Antiquarian Society* 89 (1979): 89–122.

Redding, Jay Saunders. "The Negro in American History: As Scholar, as Subject." In *The Past Before Us: Contemporary Historical Writing in the United States,* edited by Michael Kammen. Ithaca, N.Y.: Cornell University Press, 1980.

Thorpe, Earl E. "Philosophy of History: Sources, Truths, and Limitations." *Quarterly Review of Higher Education Among Negroes* 25, no. 3 (1957): 172–185.

Thorpe, Earl E. *Black Historians: A Critique.* New York: Morrow, 1969.

Wood, Peter H. "I Did the Best I Could for My Day: The Study of Early Black History During the Second Reconstruction,

1960 to 1976." *William and Mary Quarterly* (3rd series) 35, no. 2 (1978): 185–225.

ROBERT L. HARRIS JR. (1996)
Updated by author 2005

HOLDER, GEOFFREY

AUGUST 20, 1930

▌▌▌————————————

Born in Port-of-Spain, Trinidad, dancer, choreographer, and painter Geoffrey Holder was one of four children in a middle-class family. He attended Queens Royal College, a secondary school in Port-of-Spain, and received lessons in painting and dancing from his older brother Boscoe.

When Holder was seven, he debuted with his brother's dance troupe, the Holder Dance Company. When Boscoe moved to London a decade later, Geoffrey Holder took over direction of the company. In 1952 Agnes de Mille saw the group perform on the island of St. Thomas, U.S. Virgin Islands, and invited Holder to audition for impresario Sol Hurok in New York City. Already an accomplished painter, Holder sold twenty of his paintings to pay for passage for the company to New York City in 1954. When Hurok decided not to sponsor a tour for the company, Holder taught classes at the Katherine Dunham School to support himself. His impressive height (six feet six inches) and formal attire at a dance recital attracted the attention of producer Arnold Saint Subber, who arranged for him to play Samedi, a Haitian conjurer, in Harold Arlen's 1954 Broadway musical *House of Flowers.* During the run Holder met fellow dancer Carmen DeLavallade, and the two married in 1955. During 1955 and 1956 Holder was a principal dancer with the Metropolitan Opera Ballet in New York. He also appeared with his troupe, Geoffrey Holder and Company, through 1960. The multitalented Holder continued to paint throughout this time, and in 1957 he was awarded a Guggenheim Fellowship in painting.

In 1957 Holder acted in an all-black production of *Waiting for Godot.* Although the show was short-lived, Holder continued to act, and in 1961 he had his first film role in the movie *All Night Long,* a modern retelling of *Othello.* His career as a character actor flourished with appearances in *Everything You Always Wanted to Know About Sex* (1972), *Live and Let Die* (1973), and as Punjab in *Annie* (1982).

Holder has also been an active director. His direction of the Broadway musical *The Wiz,* (1975), an all-black retelling of *The Wizard of Oz,* earned him Tony Awards for best director and best costume design. In 1978 he directed and choreographed the lavish Broadway musical *Timbuktu!* He has choreographed pieces for many companies, including the Alvin Ailey American Dance Theater, for which he choreographed *Prodigal Prince* (1967), a dance based on the life of a Haitian primitive painter. Dance Theater of Harlem has in its repertory Holder's 1957 piece *Bele,* which like most of his work combines African and European elements.

Holder cowrote (with Tom Harshman) and illustrated the book *Black Gods, Green Islands* (1959), a collection of Caribbean folklore; and *Geoffrey Holder's Caribbean Cookbook* was published in 1973. He also gained widespread recognition in the late 1970s and 1980s for his lively commercials. In 1992 Holder appeared in the film *Boomerang* with Eddie Murphy, and in 1999 he appeared in *Goosed* with Jennifer Tilly. His deep, rich voice—he is perhaps best known to the public for his rolling laugh in a series of 7UP soda commercials—has placed him in demand for voice-overs, including episodes of the television series *Cyberchase* in 2002 and 2003. He resides in New York, where he continues to paint, choreograph, and act.

See also Ailey, Alvin; Ballet; Dunham, Katherine

■ ■ *Bibliography*

Dunning, Jennifer. *Geoffrey Holder: A Life in Theater, Dance and Art.* New York: Abrams, 2001.

Emery, Lynne Fauley. *Black Dance from 1619 to Today.* Princeton, N.J.: Princeton Book Co., 1988.

Moss, Allyn. "Who Is Geoffrey Holder?" *Dance* (August 1958): 36–41.

ZITA ALLEN (1996)
Updated by publisher 2005

HOLIDAY, BILLIE

APRIL 7, 1915
JULY 17, 1959

▌▌▌————————————

The singer Billie Holiday was born Eleanora Fagan, the daughter of Sadie Fagan and jazz guitarist Clarence Holiday. She was born in Philadelphia and grew up in Baltimore, where she endured a traumatic childhood of poverty and abuse. As a teenager, she changed her name (after screen star Billie Dove) and came to New York, where she began singing in speakeasies, influenced, she said, by Louis Armstrong (1901–1971) and Bessie Smith (1894?–1937).

In 1933 she was spotted performing in Harlem by the critic and producer John Hammond, who brought her to Columbia Records, where she recorded classic sessions with such jazz greats as pianist Teddy Wilson (1912–1986) and tenor saxophonist Lester Young (1909–1959), who gave Holiday her nickname, "Lady Day".

Following grueling tours with the big bands of Count Basie and Artie Shaw, Holiday became a solo act in 1938, achieving success with appearances at Cafe Society in Greenwich Village, and with her 1939 recording of the dramatic antilynching song "Strange Fruit." Performing regularly at intimate clubs along New York's Fifty-second Street, she gained a sizable income and a reputation as a peerless singer of torch songs.

A heroin addict, Holiday was arrested for narcotics possession in 1947 and spent ten months in prison. This made it illegal for her to work in New York clubs. Yet despite such hardships and her deteriorating health and voice, she continued to perform and make memorable, and sometimes challenging, recordings on the Decca, Verve, and Columbia labels until her death in 1959.

Although riddled with inaccuracies, Holiday's 1956 autobiography, *Lady Sings the Blues,* remains a fascinating account of her mercurial personality. A 1972 film of the same title, starring pop singer Diana Ross, further distorted Holiday's life, though it also introduced her to a new generation of listeners. Holiday was one of America's finest and most influential jazz singers. Though her voice was light and had a limited range, her phrasing, in the manner of a jazz instrumentalist, places her among the most consummate of jazz musicians. She was distinguished by her impeccable timing, her ability to transform song melodies through improvisation, and her ability to render lyrics with absolute conviction. While she was not a blues singer, her performances were infused with the same stark depth of feeling that characterizes the blues.

See also Jazz; Jazz Singers; Smith, Bessie

■ ■ *Bibliography*

Blackburn, Julia. *With Billie.* New York: Pantheon, 2005.

Chilton, John. *Billie's Blues: The Billie Holiday Story, 1933–1959.* Foreword by Buck Clayton. New York: Da Capo, 1975.

Kliment, Bud. *Billie Holiday.* New York: Chelsea House, 1990.

O'Meally, Robert. *Lady Day: The Many Faces of Billie Holiday.* New York: Arcade, 1991.

BUD KLIMENT (1996)
Updated bibliography

The Church of God, Holiness, in Mexico, Missouri, 1950. *A significant event in African American religious history, the Holiness movement advocated a simple, antiworldly approach to life, as well as adherence to a strict, moralistic code of behavior. Breaking away from the Methodist Church, Holiness movement followers founded their own congregations, primarily "Church of God" denominations, throughout the south.* GEORGE SKADDING/GETTY IMAGES

HOLINESS MOVEMENT

The Holiness movement is a significant religious movement in African-American religious history. The term *Holiness* can be confusing due to the multiplicity of its uses. Many publications use the term somewhat broadly to include Pentecostalism and the Apostolic movement; however, properly used, it specifically describes that distinct Holiness movement that resulted in the founding of the Holiness church denomination.

The Holiness movement in the post–Civil War era was the result of an internal conflict within the Methodist Church. Eschewing the new, less austere standards of the postwar church, followers of the Holiness movement advocated a simple, antiworldly approach to life, as well as adherence to a strict, moralistic code of behavior. The followers of the Holiness movement believed in the theological framework of John Wesley (1703–1791), but they then went a step further in their interpretation of his writings. In addition to the first blessing of conversion—

justification by faith—accepted by most Protestants, adherents of the movement declared that a second experience, or blessing, of complete sanctification was necessary in order to achieve complete emotional peace. The second blessing purified the believer of his inward sin (the result of Adam's original sin), and gave the believer a perfect love toward God and man. A state of earthly holiness (or perfection) was seen as possible to achieve. This experience was attained through devout prayer, meditation, the taking of Holy Communion, and fellowship with other believers. Those who had received the second blessing were characterized by a deep inner feeling of joy and ecstasy, as well as by lives that reflected a moral and spiritual purity.

At first, the Methodist Church leaders welcomed the new movement as one which would instill more pious behavior in its members. By 1894, however, those who had experienced the "second blessing" began to press for changes to church doctrine, literature, and even songs used in worship services. As a result, the followers of the new movement split from Methodism and founded their own churches throughout the South, North, and Midwest. In the early Holiness churches, racial lines were obscured. Many blacks and whites served together as officials, preachers, and church members. However, under pressure to conform to social norms of segregation, divisions along racial lines were well in place by the 1890s.

Black Holiness congregations, often calling themselves the Church of God, sprang up throughout the South after 1890. One of the largest and most influential was the Church of God in Christ, founded by C. H. Mason (1866–1961) and C. P. Jones (1865–1945), which was incorporated in Memphis in 1897. It was the first Holiness church of either race to be legally chartered. Mason and Jones had come out of a Baptist Church background, as had many other black converts to the Holiness movement. Like their counterparts from the Methodist Church, they longed for a purer expression of their faith and a religion that was unfettered by the push toward worldly materialism. Because it was legally chartered, the Church of God in Christ could perform marriage ceremonies and ordinations, and many independent white Holiness ministers were ordained by Jones and Mason. It was also the denomination most receptive to musical experimentation, encouraging the use of instruments, ragtime, jazz, and the blues as a part of worship.

Both the black and white Holiness congregations were split after a black Holiness convert named William J. Seymour (1870–1922) organized a church in Los Angeles in 1906, where he espoused a third blessing—the Baptism of the Holy Ghost—which would be evidenced by the Pentecostal gift of speaking in tongues. Seymour taught that it was only after having received this third blessing that a believer was truly sanctified and perfected. Thousands of Holiness believers were converted to the new Pentecostal church. Pentecostalism has gone on to attract millions of converts, eventually overshadowing its founding Holiness faith.

In 1907 Mason was converted, which resulted in a schism between him and Jones over doctrinal differences. While Mason adhered to the tenet of a required third blessing in order to receive the Holy Spirit, Jones maintained that the gift of the Holy Spirit was given by God at the time of conversion. They split into two churches and Mason's new Church of God in Christ became the largest Pentecostal church in the United States. Jones founded the Church of Christ (Holiness) USA in 1907. By 1984 there were 170 congregations with approximately 10,000 members. One of the offshoot congregations that sprang from the Church of Christ (Holiness) USA is the Churches of God, Holiness. Founded in Atlanta in 1920, by 1967 there were forty-two churches with a reported membership total of about 25,000. There are several other, smaller Holiness churches, as well.

Besides serving as the birthplace of the Pentecostal Church, the Holiness movement was very important and influential in the lives of those who believed in it. The movement was brought north during the Great Migration of the first two decades of the twentieth century and continued to thrive throughout the era of the Great Depression. Simplicity and continuity were stressed over consumption and liberalization of religious standards. The Holiness movement also stressed that anyone, regardless of race or gender, could participate in church hierarchy, including preaching, on an equal basis. The believers of the Holiness movement sought to undo the materialistic and divisive nature of American society by beginning with their own lives and their own hearts.

See also Baptists; Christian Denominations, Independent; Pentecostalism in North America

■ ■ *Bibliography*

Ayers, Edward L. *The Promise of the New South: Life after Reconstruction.* New York: Oxford University Press, 1992.

Clemmons, Ithiel C. *Bishop C. H. Mason and the Roots of the Church of God in Christ.* Bakersfield, Calif.: Pneuma Life, 1996.

DuPree, Sherry Sherrod, ed. *Biographical Dictionary of African-American Holiness-Pentecostals: 1880–1990.* Washington, D.C.: Middle Atlantic Regional Press, 1989.

Murphy, Larry G., J. Gordon Melton, and Gary L. Ward, eds. *Encyclopedia of African American Religions.* New York: Garland, 1993.

Paris, Arthur. *Black Pentecostalism: Southern Religion in an Urban World.* Amherst: University of Massachusetts Press, 1982.

Payne, Wardell J., ed. *Directory of African-American Religious Bodies,* 2d ed. Washington, D.C.: Howard University Press, 1995.

Sanders, Cheryl J. *Saints in Exile: The Holiness-Pentecostal Experience in African American Religion and Culture.* New York: Oxford University Press, 1996.

Synan, Vinson. *The Holiness-Pentecostal Tradition: Charismatic Movements in the Twentieth Century,* 2d ed. (originally published in 1971 as *The Holiness-Pentecostal Movement in the United States*). Grand Rapids, Mich.: W. B. Eerdmans, 1997.

DEBI BROOME (1996)
Updated bibliography

HOLLAND, JEROME HEARTWELL

JANUARY 6, 1916
JANUARY 13, 1985

▐ ▬ ▬

The educator and diplomat Jerome Holland was born and raised in Auburn, New York, and in 1935 became the first African American to play football at Cornell University, where he was twice selected as an All American. Holland graduated with honors in 1939 and received a master's degree in sociology two years later. After teaching sociology and physical education at Lincoln University in Pennsylvania, he received his Ph.D. from the University of Pennsylvania in 1950. He served as president of Delaware State College in Dover, Delaware (1953–1959), and of Hampton Institute in Hampton, Virginia (1960–1970). Holland also authored a number of economic and sociological studies on African Americans, including "Black Opportunity" (1969), a treatise supporting the full integration of African Americans into the mainstream of the American economy.

In 1970 President Richard M. Nixon appointed Holland U.S. ambassador to Sweden, and he served until 1972. He was a board member of nine major United States companies, including the Chrysler Corporation, American Telephone and Telegraph, and General Foods, as well as a member of the board of directors of the National Urban League and the United Negro College Fund. In 1972 Holland became the first African American to sit on the board of directors of the New York Stock Exchange, a position he held until 1980. Holland was inducted into the National Football Foundation's College Hall of Fame in 1965, and in 1985 he posthumously received the Presidential

Medal of Freedom for his contributions in education and public service.

See also National Urban League; United Negro College Fund

■ ■ *Bibliography*

Ashe, Arthur R., Jr. *A Hard Road to Glory: A History of the African-American Athlete.* New York: Warner, 1988.

Young, A. S. "Doc." *Negro Firsts in Sports.* Chicago: Johnson Publishing, 1963.

SASHA THOMAS (1996)

HOLLY, JAMES T.

1829
MARCH 13, 1911

▐ ▬ ▬

Emigrationist and missionary James Theodore Holly was born to free parents in a free black settlement in Washington, D.C. At fourteen, the family moved to Brooklyn, New York, where Holly learned shoemaking under the direction of his father. In 1848 he began working as a clerk for Lewis Tappan, the renowned abolitionist, who furthered his interest in the antislavery movement.

In 1851, in reaction to the Fugitive Slave Act of 1850, Holly and his wife, Charlotte, moved to Windsor, Canada. He became coeditor of Henry Bibb's newspaper, *The Voice of the Fugitive,* and began to encourage black emigration through his writing. Holly endorsed Bibb's controversial Refugee Home Society, a program designed by Bibb to train and rehabilitate fugitive slaves.

Holly became increasingly involved in the emigration movement. In 1854 the first National Emigration Convention was held in Cleveland, Ohio, where Holly was named a delegate and represented the National Emigration Board as its commissioner; the following year he made his first trip to Haiti. During the 1850s Holly also championed the American Colonization Society in its efforts to remove African Americans from the United States.

Holly was raised a Catholic, but in 1855 he converted from Roman Catholicism, becoming a deacon in the Protestant Episcopal Church. The following year he became a priest and moved to New Haven, Connecticut, where he served at St. Luke's Church and continued to promote the idea of emigration to Haiti. During this period he wrote his major work, *Vindication of the Capacity of the Negro Race for Self-Government and Civilized Progress,* which was published in 1857. Writing against the grain of American nationalism, Holly called the United States a "bastard democracy," and asserted that emigration to Haiti would provide far more personal liberty and general well-being for black men and women. Emigration would be a grand experiment in progress even in "monarchical" Haiti, Holly contended, and would demonstrate African-American capacities for political and social progress. Ironically, Holly also believed in English cultural supremacy. He was an anglophile who asserted that providence was directing black men and women in the New World in a vanguard struggle for independence and black pride that would promote European cultural ideals. His Christian expansionism and emigration plans were linked to a great respect for the developed arts and sciences of the "Anglo-American race."

In May 1861 Holly left the United States with 110 followers, made up of family and church members, and established a colony in Haiti. Yellow fever and malaria took their toll on the colony, however, and during the first year, the diseases killed his mother, his wife, their two children, and thirty-nine other members of the group. Others returned to the United States, leaving Holly with only a handful of followers. In 1862 Holly returned to the United States seeking financial assistance from the Episcopal Church to establish a mission. His request was granted.

In 1874, at Grace Church in New York City, Holly became the first African American to be consecrated bishop by the Episcopal Church. He served as head of the Orthodox Apostolic Church of Haiti, a church in communion with other Episcopal churches. He published a number of articles in the *AME Church Review* and continued to believe, until his death in 1911, that black Americans should emigrate to Haiti.

See also African Methodist Episcopal Church

■ ■ *Bibliography*

Dean, David M. *Defender of the Race.* Boston: Lambeth Press, 1978.

"James T. Holly." *Notable Black American Men.* Detroit, Mich.: Gale, 1998.

Logan, Rayford W., and Michael R. Winston, eds. *Dictionary of American Negro Biography.* New York: Norton, 1982.

SUSAN MCINTOSH (1996)
Updated bibliography

HOLT, PATRICIA LOUISE

See LaBelle, Patti (Holt, Patricia Louise)

HOMOSEXUALITY

See Gay Men; Lesbians

HOOD, JAMES WALKER

MAY 30, 1831
OCTOBER 30, 1918

■ ■ ■

The minister James Walker Hood was born in Kennett Township, Chester County, Pennsylvania, and moved with his family to Wilmington, Delaware, in 1841. His father was a tenant farmer who helped found the local Methodist church. In 1852 Hood moved to New York City and was licensed to preach there in 1856 by the African Methodist Episcopal Zion (AMEZ) Church. In 1857 he moved to New Haven, Connecticut, where he joined the local AMEZ church. Three years later he was ordained a deacon in that denomination and sent as a missionary to Nova Scotia. He returned to the United States in 1863, and served a congregation at Bridgeport, Connecticut. The following year he was sent to North Carolina to minister to freedmen within Union lines. He remained in North Carolina for the rest of his life, working in New Bern, Charlotte, and Fayetteville, where he finally settled.

Hood was a delegate to North Carolina's Constitutional Convention in 1868, and that same year was appointed assistant superintendent of public instruction in North Carolina, a position he held for three years. In 1872 he was ordained a bishop of the AMEZ church. In 1879 he was instrumental in the founding of Zion Wesley Institute (later Livingston College) in Salisbury, North Carolina. He served as chairman of the institute's board of trustees until his retirement in 1916.

Hood traveled to London as a delegate to the interdenominational 1881 Ecumenical Conference, and to Washington as the first black president of the 1891 conference. In 1884 a collection of his sermons appeared under the title *The Negro in the Christian Pulpit*. It was the first publication of its kind by an African-American clergyman. Hood's other published work includes *One Hundred Years* of the *African Methodist Episcopal Zion Church* (1895) and *The Plan of the Apocalypse* (1900). From 1901 to 1909 Hood was an informal advisor to Theodore Roosevelt. Hood Theological Seminary, established in 1912 at Livingston College, was named in his honor.

See also African Methodist Episcopal Zion Church

■ ■ *Bibliography*

"James Walker Hood." *Religious Leaders of America*, 2nd ed. Detroit: Gale Group, 1999.

Murphy, Larry G., J. Gordon Malton, and Gary L. Ward. *Encyclopedia of African-American Religions*. New York: Garland, 1993.

Simmons, William J. *Men of Mark*. Cleveland: O. G. M. Rewell, 1887. Reprint, New York: Arno Press, 1968

LYDIA MCNEILL (1996)
Updated bibliography

HOODOO

See Voodoo

Blues legend John Lee Hooker (1917–2001). © NEAL PRESTON/CORBIS

HOOKER, JOHN LEE

AUGUST 22, 1917
JUNE 21, 2001

Blues singer and guitarist John Lee Hooker learned the guitar from his stepfather and began playing blues in Memphis nightclubs. He moved to Detroit in the 1940s; there he worked in a factory, continued playing in clubs, and began recording for Modern Records in 1948, achieving great success there with "Boogie Chillun." Hooker recorded for different companies under a variety of pseudonyms on some seventy recordings between 1949 and 1953. He began to temper his sound in the 1950s by using a full band to back up his rhythmically driving guitar and deep voice, which yielded the commercially successful "Boom Boom" in 1961. A remake of the song by the Animals in 1964 introduced Hooker to a much broader audience. An active performer through the 1970s and 1980s, he recorded for several labels, and his music was featured in the 1985 film *The Color Purple*. In 1991 Hooker was inducted into the Rock and Roll Hall of Fame.

In 1995 Hooker retired from performing on a regular basis. His last release was *Don't Look Back* in 1997, the same year he opened John Lee Hooker's Boom Boom Room, a blues club in San Francisco. In 2000 he received a Grammy Lifetime Achievement Award. He died just five days after his last performance.

See also Blues, The

■ ■ *Bibliography*

Hochman, Steve, ed. *Popular Musicians*. Pasadena, Calif.: Salem Press, 1999.

Neely, Kim. "Rock and Roll Hall of Famers Tapped." *Rolling Stone* (November 29, 1990): 36.

Obrecht, Jas. "John Lee Hooker." *Guitar Player* (November 1989): 50ff.

DANIEL THOM (1996)
Updated by publisher 2005

HOOKS, BENJAMIN L.

JANUARY 31, 1925

The lawyer, minister, and civic leader Benjamin Lawson Hooks (also known as Benjamin Lawrence Hooks) was born in Memphis, Tennessee, where he attended public schools. Upon graduation from Booker T. Washington High School, Hooks pursued prelaw studies at Howard University, graduating in 1944. In 1948 he earned a juris doctor degree from De Paul University in Chicago and returned to Memphis to practice law, hoping to help end legal segregation.

In 1961 Hooks was appointed assistant public defender of Shelby County, Tennessee. Four years later, he was appointed to fill a vacancy in the Shelby County Criminal Court (a position to which he was subsequently elected on the Republican ticket), becoming the first black criminal court judge in the state. In addition to practicing law, Hooks was active in the civil rights movement in the 1950s and 1960s, serving as one of thirty-three members of the board of directors of the Southern Christian Leadership Conference from its inception in 1957 until 1977. Hooks also cofounded and sat on the board of the Mutual Federal Savings and Loan Association from 1955 to 1969. He was ordained a Baptist minister in 1956 and became pastor of the Middle Baptist Church in Memphis, serving the church in that capacity for 45 years. 1972, President Richard M. Nixon nominated Hooks to the Federal Communications Commission, where became the first African American member and actively sought to improve employment and ownership opportunities of African Americans and worked for more positive depictions of blacks in the electronic media.

Hooks became executive director of the National Association for the Advancement of Colored People (NAACP) in 1977 at a difficult moment in the organization's history. Since the 1960s, militant organizations had begun to eclipse the prominence of the NAACP, which had come under increasing attack for being too conservative. Viewed by its critics as a stodgy bastion of the middle class, the NAACP suffered a decline in membership and financial contributions. When Hooks replaced Roy Wilkins, who had served as executive director for twenty-two years, the organization was $1 million in debt and controlled by a faction-ridden board of directors.

As executive director, Hooks sought to revitalize the organization's finances and image, becoming more involved in such national issues as the environment, national health insurance, welfare, urban blight, and the criminal justice system. He announced his intention to forge new alliances with corporations, foundations, and businesses, in addition to strengthening the NAACP's traditional alliances with liberals, the government, and labor groups. Hooks led the fight for home rule in Washington, D.C., and was instrumental in securing the passage of important legislation such as the Humphrey-Hawkins bill of 1978,

which mandated a dramatic lowering of the unemployment rate through the use of federal fiscal and monetary policy. Under his direction the NAACP also encouraged the withdrawal of U.S. businesses from South Africa.

In 1980 Hooks became the first African American to address both the Republican and Democratic national conventions. As executive director, Hooks upheld the NAACP's tradition of focusing on political activity, but he also tried to steer the organization toward helping African Americans on an everyday level through programs such as the Urban Assistance Relief Fund, which he founded in the wake of the 1980 Miami riot. In conjunction with his position at the NAACP, Hooks also served as chairman of the Leadership Conference on Civil Rights (LCCR), a coalition of organizations devoted to civil rights issues.

In 1992 Hooks stepped down as executive director of the NAACP amid disputes between his supporters and those of board chairman William F. Gibson over the organization's leadership and direction. Many members expressed the view that the NAACP had continued to lose its effectiveness, although Hooks and his supporters maintained that it had upheld its heritage of civil rights activism. After leaving the NAACP, Hooks continued to serve as chairman of the LCCR until 1994, when he resumed his position as pastor of Middle Street Baptist Church on a full-time basis. In June 1992 Hooks was chosen to serve as the president of the board of directors of the National Civil Rights Museum in Memphis.

In 2000 the University of Memphis created the Benjamin Hooks Institute for the study of civil rights. The university also made Hooks' papers available online.

See also Civil Rights Movement, U.S.; National Association for the Advancement of Colored People (NAACP); Southern Christian Leadership Conference (SCLC); Wilkins, Roy

■ ■ *Bibliography*

Delaney, P. "Struggle to Rally Black America." *New York Times Magazine,* July 15, 1979.

Hooks, Benjamin. *The March for Civil Rights: The Benjamin Hooks Story.* Chicago: American Bar Association, 2003.

"New Voice of the NAACP." Interview. *Newsweek,* November 22, 1976.

LOUISE P. MAXWELL (1996)
Updated by publisher 2005

HOPE, JOHN

JUNE 2, 1868
FEBRUARY 20, 1936

The educator and civil rights activist John Hope was born in Augusta, Georgia, to Mary Frances (Fanny) and James Hope. His mother was the daughter of an emancipated slave and his father was a native of Scotland. James Hope bequeathed a substantial estate to his family, but Fanny and her children were deprived of their inheritance.

John Hope completed the eighth grade in 1881; five years later he entered Worcester Academy in Massachusetts, where he graduated with honors in June 1890. That fall, he enrolled at Brown University in Rhode Island on a scholarship. It was at Brown that Hope began to hone his writing and speaking skills and to develop race consciousness. (Although he could pass for white, he always identified himself as black.) He was the orator for his graduating class in 1894. Shortly afterward, he married Lugenia Burns, a Chicago social worker; they later had two sons.

Hope entered the field of education at a time when Booker T. Washington was advocating vocational training for African Americans. Hope rejected that philosophy, insisting that black people must acquire higher learning if they were to make a convincing case for social equality. He turned down an offer to teach at Washington's Tuskegee Institute. Instead, from 1894 to 1898 he taught Greek, Latin, and the natural sciences at Roger Williams College in Nashville, Tennessee. He went on to teach classics at Atlanta Baptist College (which became Morehouse College in 1913). In 1906, Hope became the college's first black president.

Hope's views were shared by W. E. B. Du Bois, with whom Hope nurtured a lifelong friendship. Like Du Bois, Hope was willing to join with others to achieve common objectives. He was the only college president to participate in the Niagara Movement in 1906, and the only one to attend the initial meeting that resulted in the formation of the National Association for the Advancement of Colored People (NAACP) three years later.

As president of Atlanta Baptist College, Hope faced obstacles to his goals. Just before school was set to begin in September 1906, an antiblack riot swept through Atlanta; Hope demonstrated his leadership by ensuring that classes went on as scheduled. He was also unable to obtain financial support from some white philanthropists until a colleague approached Booker T. Washington for help. Over the years, however, he proved extraordinarily suc-cessful in increasing enrollment, raising money, and attracting leading black scholars. His educational achievements culminated in his 1929 appointment as president of the new Atlanta University, a consortium including Atlanta University, Morehouse College, and Spelman College. In 1934, Hope convinced W. E. B. Du Bois to head the department of sociology.

Hope did not, however, restrict his activities to the university setting. He traveled to France during World War I, where he insisted that the Young Men's Christian Association (YMCA) adopt new policies to ensure equitable treatment for black soldiers; this effort initiated a lasting commitment to the YMCA's work. Hope served as president of the National Association of Teachers in Colored Schools, and he acted as honorary president of the Association for the Study of Negro Life and History. In addition, he was a member of both the NAACP's advisory board and the Urban League of New York's executive committee. In 1920, he joined the Commission on Interracial Cooperation (CIC), a moderate, liberal integrated group of Atlanta civic leaders; he was elected CIC president in 1932.

In the late 1920s and early 1930s, through his considerable organizational connections, Hope traveled widely in Europe, the Soviet Union, the Middle East, Latin America, and the Caribbean. His commitment to cooperation across national and racial boundaries reinforced his vision of education as a tool for gaining equality. Hope was a pioneer in developing outstanding graduate and professional programs for black people. At the same time, it was under his tutelage that Atlanta University's faculty offered training to public school teachers and established citizenship schools to encourage voter registration. Hope died in Atlanta in 1936.

See also Bethune, Mary McLeod; Civil Rights Movement, U.S.; Du Bois, W. E. B.; Education in the United States; Franklin, John Hope; Hope, Lugenia Burns; National Association for the Advancement of Colored People (NAACP); Niagara Movement; Washington, Booker T.

■ ■ *Bibliography*

Davis, Leroy. *A Clashing of the Soul: John Hope and the Dilemma of African American Leadership and Black Higher Education in the Early Twentieth Century.* Athens: University of Georgia Press, 1998.

Torrence, Ridgely. *The Story of John Hope.* New York: Macmillan, 1948.

SASHA THOMAS (1996)
TAMI J. FRIEDMAN (1996)
Updated bibliography

HOPE, LUGENIA BURNS

FEBRUARY 19, 1871
AUGUST 14, 1947

▮▮▮

Reformer Lugenia Burns Hope was one of the key members of a group of southern African-American activists in the late nineteenth and early twentieth centuries. Born in St. Louis, Missouri, Burns came from a line of free black Mississippians on both sides. She grew up in Chicago and was educated in the public schools. She also studied art at the Chicago School of Design and the Chicago Art Institute. As a young woman Burns bore the responsibility of supporting her family when her siblings were out of work. It was during this period that she became involved in reform work as a paid worker. She also became acquainted with the pioneering settlement work of Chicago's Hull House.

In 1897 Lugenia Burns married John Hope, a college professor. Within a year John Hope accepted a teaching position at his alma mater, Atlanta Baptist College (later Morehouse College). In Atlanta Hope blossomed as an activist, focusing on the needs of black children in the city. Her concern with children's issues became sharpened through the birth of the Hopes' two children, Edward and John.

In 1908 Hope was a driving force in the founding of the Neighborhood Union, with which she remained active until 1935. She was active in the work of the YWCA in the South and was a vocal opponent of the segregationist policies of the organization in this period. She was also a prominent member of the National Association of Colored Women, the National Council of Negro Women, and the International Council of Women of the Darker Races.

After her husband's death in 1936, Hope moved to New York City, where she continued to be involved in reform organizations. During this period she worked as an assistant to Mary McLeod Bethune, then with the National Youth Administration. Hope was not able to continue with her demanding schedule through the 1940s as her health began to fail. Lugenia Burns Hope, dedicated activist for equality, died in 1947 after a long and influential career.

See also Bethune, Mary McLeod; Hope, John; Morehouse College; National Association of Colored Women; National Council of Negro Women

▪▪ *Bibliography*

Hine, Darlene Clark, and Thompson, Kathleen. *A Shining Thread of Hope.* New York: Broadway Books, 1999.

Rouse, Jacqueline A. *Lugenia Burns Hope: A Black Southern Reformer.* Athens: University of Georgia Press, 1989.

JUDITH WEISENFELD (1996)
Updated bibliography

HOPKINS, PAULINE ELIZABETH

1859
AUGUST 13, 1930

▮▮▮

Born in Portland, Maine in 1859, writer Pauline Hopkins and her family settled in Boston, Massachusetts. At the age of fifteen, she won a contest with her essay "Evils of Intemperance and Their Remedies." In 1879 she completed her first play, *Slaves' Escape, or The Underground Railroad.* This musical drama was produced the following year by the Hopkins' Colored Troubadours. Hopkins was an actress and singer in the production and became known as "Boston's favorite soprano."

During the early 1890s Hopkins pursued a profession in stenography. She passed the civil service exam and was employed for four years at the Bureau of Statistics, where she worked on the Massachusetts Decennial Census of 1895. In May 1900 Hopkins's literary career was launched with the founding of *The Colored American* magazine by the Colored Cooperative Publishing Company (CCPC). The premiere issue published Hopkins's short story "The Mystery Within Us."

Throughout the life of *The Colored American* (1900–1909), Hopkins had six other short stories featured and three novels serialized. It was during *The Colored American*'s first year of publication that the CCPC also released her first and best remembered novel, *Contending Forces: A Romance Illustrative of Negro Life North and South.* Her writing, reflective of the historical conditions and cultural images of her day, advocated racial justice and the advancement of African-American women.

A frequent contributor to *The Colored American*, Hopkins was employed as an editor. She also helped increase circulation by creating the Colored American League in Boston. Twenty prominent African-American citizens were organized to generate subscriptions and business. During 1904 she raised additional support by lecturing throughout the country. By September she left the magazine, apparently because she was afflicted with neuritis. She continued writing, and her sociocultural survey series, "The Dark Races of the Twentieth Century," was featured in *Voice of the Negro* in 1905.

Hopkins's last published literary work, "Topsy Templeton," appeared in *New Era* magazine in 1916. Returning to stenography, she was employed at the Massachusetts Institute of Technology until August 1930. She died on August 13, 1930, when her bandages, worn to relieve her painful illness, accidentally caught fire.

See also Literature in the United States

■ ■ *Bibliography*

Campbell, Jane. *Mythic Black Fiction: The Transformation of History*. Knoxville: University of Tennessee Press, 1986.

Carby, Hazel. *Reconstructing Womanhood: The Emergence of the Afro-American Woman Novelist*. New York: Oxford University Press, 1987.

Shockley, Ann Allen. "Pauline Elizabeth Hopkins: A Biographical Excursion into Obscurity." *Phylon* 33 (1972): 22–26.

Shockley, Ann Allen. *Afro-American Women Writers, 1746–1933: An Anthology and Critical Guide*. Boston: G. K. Hall, 1988.

Tate, Claudia. "Pauline Hopkins: Our Literary Foremother." In *Conjuring: Black Women, Fiction, and Literary Tradition*, edited by Marjorie Pryse and Hortense J. Spillers. Bloomington: Indiana University Press, 1985.

JANE SUNG-EE BAI (1996)

HORNE, LENA

JUNE 30, 1917

Born in New York, singer and actress Lena Horne accompanied her mother on a tour of the Lafayette Stock Players as a child and appeared in a production of *Madame X* when she was six years old. She received her musical education in the preparatory school of Fort Valley College, Georgia, and in the public schools of Brooklyn. Horne began her career at the age of sixteen as a dancer in the chorus line at the Cotton Club in Harlem. She also became a favorite at Harlem's Apollo Theatre and was among the first African-American entertainers to perform in "high-class" nightclubs. Appearing on stages and ballrooms from the Fairmont in San Francisco to the Empire Room at the Waldorf-Astoria in New York, Horne was among the group of black stars—including Sammy Davis, Jr., Eartha Kitt, and Diahann Carroll—who had musicals especially fashioned for them on Broadway.

Horne made her first recording in 1936 with Noble Sissle and recorded extensively as a soloist and with others. She toured widely in the United States and Europe. In 1941 she became the first black performer to sign a contract with a major studio (MGM). Her first film role was in *Panama Hattie* (1942), which led to roles in *Cabin in the Sky* (1942), *Stormy Weather* (1943), *I Dood It* (1943), *Thousands Cheer* (1943), *Broadway Rhythm* (1944), *Two Girls and a Sailor* (1944), *Ziegfeld Follies* of 1945 and 1946, *The Duchess of Idaho* (1950), and *The Wiz* (1978). Horne was blacklisted during the McCarthy era of the early 1950s, when her friendship with Paul Robeson, her interracial marriage, and her interest in African freedom movements made her politically suspect. Her Broadway musicals include *Blackbirds* of 1939, *Jamaica* (1957), and the successful one-woman Broadway show *Lena Horne: The Lady and Her Music* (1981). The record album of the latter musical won her a Grammy Award as best female pop vocalist in 1981.

Horne's spectacular beauty and sultry voice helped to make her the first nationally celebrated black female vocalist. Her powerful and expressive voice is perhaps captured best in the title song of *Stormy Weather*. In 1984 she was a recipient of the Kennedy Center honors for lifetime achievement in the arts. She published two autobiographies: *In Person: Lena Horne* (1950) and *Lena* (1965).

Horne remained active through the 1990s, and at the age of eighty declared she had expanded her style to sing jazz. She recorded a best-selling tribute to Billy Strayhorn, *We'll Be Together Again* (1994), a live performance at Carnegie Hall, *An Evening with Lena Horne* (1997), and a jazz album, *Being Myself* (1998).

Horne continued to perform on occasion into the twenty-first century. The first volume of a collection of her music was released in 2004.

See also Apollo Theater; Carroll, Diahann; Cotton Club; Davis, Sammy, Jr.; Kitt, Eartha Mae; Music in the United States; Robeson, Paul

■ ■ *Bibliography*

Buckley, Gail Lumet. *The Hornes: An American Family*. New York: Knopf, 1986.

JAMES E. MUMFORD (1996)
Updated by publisher 2005

HORTON, GEORGE MOSES

C. 1797
C. 1883

▸▸▸

The poet George Moses Horton was born a slave on a farm in Northampton County, North Carolina. When he was six years old, his master moved to Chatham County, near the University of North Carolina. At an early age, Horton began to compose poems based on biblical themes. Although Horton taught himself to read, he did not learn to write until he was in his thirties. He probably made his initial contact with university students while peddling produce from his master's farm. Soon he was peddling poems he had dictated—acrostics and love poems, written to order. By paying a regular fee to his master for the privilege, he was, eventually, permitted to work as a janitor at the university.

Horton's reading was augmented by university students, who provided him with books, and he received formal writing instruction from Caroline Lee Hentz, the Massachusetts-born wife of a literature professor and novelist, who was instrumental in his initial publication. Horton sought to purchase his freedom; his two antebellum collections were made specifically, though unsuccessfully, toward that end. With the help of southern friends, *Hope of Liberty* (1829) was published to raise "by subscription, a sum sufficient for his emancipation, upon the condition of his going in the vessel which shall first afterwards sail for Liberia." *Poetical Works of George Moses Horton, the Colored Bard of North Carolina* (1845) was underwritten by the president, faculty, and students of the University of North Carolina. His last and largest collection, *Naked Genius* (1865), was published with the assistance of Captain Will Banks, whom Horton met when he fled to the Union army in Raleigh (April 1865).

Horton is regarded as the first professional black poet in America, and it is certainly the case that he wrote for money. His poetry clearly reveals a conscious craftsmanship. The heavy influence of his early exposure to Wesleyan hymnal stanzas and his fondness for Byron are evident, but Horton's work shows variety in stanzaic structure, tone, and theme. Although his contemporary local reputation rested largely on his love poems, he addressed a wide variety of topics, including religion, nature, death, and poetry. Historical events and figures associated with the Civil War appear in the last volume, as do some rather misogynistic poems, which are generally seen as evidence of an unhappy marriage. Horton's dominant tone is senti-

mental, plaintive, or pious, but his work exhibits irony, satire, humor, bitterness, and anger as well.

In spite of the circumstances of his publication, which discouraged direct abolitionist poems, some of Horton's most effective poems treat the devastating experience of slavery, especially "On Liberty and Slavery," "Slavery," and "The Slave's Complaint."

Little is known about Horton's later years except that after Emancipation he moved to Philadelphia, where some sources report that he wrote short stories for church magazines and where he is thought to have died.

See also Civil War, U.S.; Poetry, U.S.

■ ■ *Bibliography*

Sherman, Joan. "George Moses Horton." In *Invisible Poets: Afro-Americans of the Nineteenth Century,* 2nd ed. Urbana: University of Illinois Press, 1989, pp. 5–20.

QUANDRA PRETTYMAN (1996)

HOSPITALS IN THE UNITED STATES, BLACK

▸▸▸

Black hospitals have been of three broad types: segregated, black controlled, and demographically determined. Segregated black hospitals included facilities established by whites to serve blacks exclusively, and they operated predominantly in the South. Black-controlled facilities were founded by black physicians, fraternal organizations, and churches. Changes in population led to the development of demographically determined hospitals. As was the case with Harlem Hospital, they gradually evolved into black institutions because of a rise in black populations surrounding them. Historically black hospitals—the previously segregated and the black-controlled hospitals—are the focus of this article.

Until the advent of the civil rights movement, racial customs and mores severely restricted black access to most hospitals. Hospitals—both in the South and in the North—either denied African Americans admission or accommodated them, almost universally, in segregated wards, often placed in undesirable locations such as unheated attics and damp basements. The desire to provide at least some hospital care for black people prompted the establishment of the earliest segregated black hospitals. Georgia Infirmary, established in Savannah in 1832, was the first such facility. By the end of the nineteenth century, several others had been founded, including Raleigh, North Carolina's St. Agnes Hospital in 1896 and Atlanta's MacVicar Infirmary in 1900. The motives behind their creation varied. Some white founders expressed a genuine, if paternalistic, interest in supplying health care to black people and offering training opportunities to black health professionals. However, white self-interest was also at work. The germ theory of disease, widely accepted by the end of the nineteenth century, acknowledged that "germs have no color line." Thus the theory mandated attention to the medical problems of African Americans, especially those whose proximity to whites threatened to spread disease.

Following the precedent set by other ethnic groups, African Americans themselves founded hospitals to meet the particular needs of their communities. Provident Hospital, the first black-controlled hospital, opened its doors in 1891. The racially discriminatory policies of Chicago nursing schools provided the primary impetus for the establishment of the institution. In addition, the hospital proved beneficial to black physicians, who were likewise barred from Chicago hospitals. Several other black-controlled hospitals opened during the last decade of the nineteenth century. These included Tuskegee Institute and Nurse Training School at Tuskegee Institute, Alabama, in 1892; Provident Hospital at Baltimore, in 1894; and Frederick Douglass Memorial Hospital and Training School at Philadelphia, in 1895. The establishment of these institutions also represented, in part, the institutionalization of Booker T. Washington's political ideology. These hospitals would advance racial uplift by improving the health status of African Americans and by contributing to the development of a black professional class.

By 1919 approximately 118 segregated and black-controlled hospitals existed, 75 percent of them in the South. Most were small, ill-equipped facilities that lacked clinical training programs. Consequently, they were inadequately prepared to survive sweeping changes in scientific medicine, hospital technology, and hospital standardization that had begun to take place at the turn of the century.

The most crucial issue faced by the historically black hospitals between 1920 and 1945 was whether they could withstand the new developments in medicine. In the early 1920s a group of physicians associated primarily with the National Medical Association (NMA), a black medical society, and the National Hospital Association (NHA), a black hospital organization, launched a reform movement to ensure the survival of at least a few quality black hospitals. The leaders of these organizations feared that the growing importance of accreditation and standardization would lead to the elimination of black hospitals and with

it the demise of the black medical profession. For most African-American physicians, black hospitals offered the only places in which they could train and practice.

The NMA and NHA engaged in various activities to improve the quality of black hospitals, including the provision of technical assistance and the publication of educational materials. They also worked to raise funds for black hospitals. But funds were not readily forthcoming. Indeed, the depression forced all hospitals to grapple with the problem of financing. However, three philanthropies, the Julius Rosenwald Fund, the General Education Board, and the Duke Endowment, responded to the plight of black hospitals and provided crucial financial support.

The activities of the black hospital reformers and the dollars of white philanthropists produced some improvements in black hospitals by World War II. One prominent black physician hailed these changes as the "Negro Hospital Renaissance." This, however, was an overly optimistic assessment. The renaissance was limited to only a few hospitals. In 1923 approximately 200 historically black hospitals operated. Only six provided internships, and not one had a residency program. By 1944 the number of hospitals had decreased to 124. The AMA now approved nine of the facilities for internships and seven for residencies; the American College of Surgeons fully approved twenty-three, an undistinguished record at best. Moreover, the quality of some approved hospitals was suspect. Representatives of the American Medical Association freely admitted that a number of these hospitals would not have been approved except for the need to supply at least some internship opportunities for black physicians. This attitude reflected the then accepted practice of educating and treating black people in separate, and not necessarily equal, facilities.

The growth of the civil rights movement also played a key role in limiting the scope of black hospital reform. In the years after World War II, the energies of black medical organizations, even those that had previously supported separate black hospitals, shifted toward the dismantlement of the "Negro medical ghetto" of which black hospitals were a major component. Their protests between 1945 and 1965 posed new challenges for the historically black hospitals and called into question their very existence.

The NMA and the NAACP led the campaign for medical civil rights. They maintained that a segregated health care system resulted in the delivery of inferior medical care to black Americans. The organizations charged that the poorly financed facilities of the black medical ghetto could not adequately meet the health and professional needs of black people and rejected the establishment of additional

Facility	Beds 1990	Beds 2005	Total* revenues (millions)	Net* income (millions)	Patient* discharges	Founded
Howard University Hospital, Washington, DC	491	282	173.7	−149.3	8,155	1862
Richmond (VA) Community Hospital	88	104	84.6	−1.9	3,105	1902
Nashville General Hospital at Meharry, Nashville, TN (formerly George W. Hubbard Hospital)	240	120	118.8	−8.2	6,546	1910
Newport News (VA) General Hospital	40	0	—	—	—	1915
Norfolk (VA) Community Hospital	117	135	7.8	−2.3	454	1915
L. Richardson Memorial Hospital, Greensboro, NC	59	0	—	—	—	1923
Riverside General Hospital, Houston, TX	86	83	15.3	+1.9	1,031	1925
Southwest Detroit Hospital, Detroit MI	156	0	—	—	—	1974

* CMS-HCRIS, *Hospital Cost Report* (CMS-2552-96)

ones to remedy the problem. Instead, the NMA and the NAACP called for the integration of existing hospitals and the building of interracial hospitals.

Legal action was a key weapon in the battle to desegregate hospitals. Armed with the precedent set by the Supreme Court ruling in *Brown v. Board of Education of Topeka, Kansas,* the medical civil rights activists began a judicial assault on hospital segregation. *Simkins v. Moses H. Cone Memorial Hospital* proved to be the pivotal case. The 1963 decision found the separate-but-equal clause of the 1946 Hill-Burton Act, which provided federal monies for hospital construction, unconstitutional. The *Simkins* decision represented a significant victory in the battle for hospital integration. It extended the principles of the *Brown* decision to hospitals, including those not publicly owned and operated. Its authority, however, was limited to those hospitals that received Hill-Burton funds. The 1964 federal court decision in *Eaton v. Grubbs* broadened the prohibitions against racial discrimination to include voluntary hospitals that did not receive such funds.

The 1964 Civil Rights Act supplemented these judicial mandates and prohibited racial discrimination in any programs that received federal assistance. The 1965 passage of the Medicare and Medicaid legislation made most hospitals potential recipients of federal funds. Thus, they would be obligated to comply with federal civil rights legislation.

The predominant social role of the historically black hospitals before 1965 had been to provide medical care and professional training for black people within a segregated society. The adoption of integration as a societal goal has had an adverse effect on the institutions. Civil rights legislation increased the access of African Americans to previously white institutions. Consequently, black hospitals faced an ironic dilemma. They now competed with hospitals that had once discriminated against black patients and staff. In the years since the end of legally sanctioned racial segregation, the number of historically black hospitals has sharply declined. In 1944, 124 black hospitals operated. By 1990 the number had decreased to eight, and for several of them the future looks grim.

Desegregation resulted in an exodus of physicians and patients from black hospitals. Where white physicians had once used these facilities to admit and treat their black patients, they abruptly cut their ties. Furthermore, since 1965, black physicians have gained access to the mainstream medical profession and black hospitals have become less crucial to their careers. This loss of physician support contributed to declines in both patient admissions and revenues at many black hospitals. As a result of changing physician referral practices and housing patterns, black hospitals have also lost many of their middle-class patients. They have become facilities that treat, for the most part, poor people who are uninsured or on Medicaid. This pattern of decreased physician support, reduced patient occupancy, and diminished patient revenues forced many black hospitals to close after 1965. It also makes the few surviving institutions highly vulnerable.

The historically black hospitals have had a significant impact on the lives of African Americans. Originally created to provide health care and education within a segregated society, they evolved to become symbols of black pride and achievement. They supplied medical care, provided training opportunities, and contributed to the development of a black professional class. The hospitals were once crucial for the survival of African Americans. They have now become peripheral to the lives of most Americans and are on the brink of extinction.

The push for cost containment and vertical integration in the 1990s saw many firms in the entire health care environment either consolidate or close. The survival of these institutions was even more in question as they faced the same challenges as their counterparts in more traditional institutions. Government reimbursement regulations, improved health care access for more affluent African Americans, and increasing competition from HMOs (health maintenance organizations) had more adverse affects on the black hospitals. Of the remaining facilities, in 1990, none had positive profit margins and half had deficits in excess of $1.75 million, while the median profit margin for all hospitals in the United States was a positive 2.73 percent, or about $300,000.

The individuals that black hospitals serviced were most in need of care and least likely to be able to pay. These facilities served as the safety net and the primary-care providers for a large population of persons of color, a business condition that created mounting financial instabilities. Many black hospitals, and equally many major general hospitals in urban areas, had to seek bankruptcy protection and were eventually subsumed into the indigent-care mechanisms of the communities they served or purchased by larger health care systems.

As of 2005, five of the eight facilities that remained in 1990 were still operating (this was the number that submitted a required report on their prior year's financial activity to the CMS). There has been significant expansion in some, and three of the five have maintained or acquired affiliation with a medical school. While only one of the five remaining black hospitals turned a profit in fiscal year 2004, the firms did manage to survive the very turbulent health care environment of the 1990s. These institutions are poised to remain viable and effective institutions in the health care continuum well into the twenty-first century.

See also Brown v. Board of Education of Topeka, Kansas; Civil Rights Movement, U.S.; Freedmen's Hospital; National Association for the Advancement of Colored People (NAACP); Nursing

■ ■ *Bibliography*

Centers for Medicare and Medicaid Services, Healthcare Cost Report Information System, Hospital Cost Report (CMS-2552-96), 12/31/04.

Cobb, W. Montague. "Medical Care and the Plight of the Negro." *Crisis* 54 (1947): 201–211.

Downing, L. C. "Early Negro Hospitals." *Journal of the National Medical Association* 33 (1941): 13–18.

Gamble, Vanessa Northington. *The Black Community Hospital: Contemporary Dilemmas in Historical Perspective.* New York: Garland, 1989.

Gamble, Vanessa Northington. "The Negro Hospital Renaissance: The Black Hospital Movement." In *The American General Hospital,* edited by Diana E. Long and Janet Golden, pp. 182–205. Ithaca, N.Y.: Cornell University Press, 1989.

Julius Rosenwald Fund. *Negro Hospitals: A Compilation of Available Statistics.* Chicago: Author, 1931.

Kenney, John A. "The Negro Hospital Renaissance." *Journal of the National Medical Association* 22 (1930): 109–112.

Payne, Larah D. "Survival of Black Hospitals in the U.S. Health Care System: A Case Study." In *Black Organizations: Issues on Survival Techniques,* edited by Lennox S. Yearwood, pp. 205–211. Lanham, Md.: University Press of America, 1980.

Taravella, Steve. "Black Hospitals Struggle to Survive." *Modern Healthcare* 20 (July 2, 1990): 20–26.

VANESSA NORTHINGTON GAMBLE (1996)
NORRIS WHITE GUNBY, JR. (2005)

HOUSTON, CHARLES HAMILTON

SEPTEMBER 3, 1895
APRIL 22, 1950

Charles Hamilton Houston, a lawyer, was born in the District of Columbia, the son of William L. Houston, a government worker who attended Howard University Law School and became a lawyer, and Mary Hamilton Houston, a teacher who later worked as a hairdresser. He attended Washington's M Street High School and then went to Amherst College in Amherst, Massachusetts. He graduated Phi Beta Kappa in 1915, then taught English for two years at Howard University. In 1917 Houston joined the army and served as a second lieutenant in a segregated unit of the American Expeditionary Forces during World War I. Following his discharge, he decided on a career in law and entered Harvard Law School. Houston was the first African-American editor of the *Harvard Law Review.* He received an L.L.B. degree cum laude (1922) and an S.J.D. degree (1923). He received the Sheldon Fellowship for further study in civil law at the University of Madrid (1923–1924).

In 1924 Houston was admitted to the Washington, D.C., bar, and he entered law practice with his father at Houston & Houston in Washington, D.C. (later Houston & Hastie, then Houston, Bryant, and Gardner), where he handled domestic relations, negligence, and personal injury cases, as well as criminal law cases involving civil rights matters. He remained with the firm until his death. Throughout his career Houston served on numerous committees and organizations, including the Washington Board of Education, the National Bar Association, the National Lawyers Guild, and the American Council on Race Relations. He also wrote columns on racial and international issues for *The Crisis* and the *Baltimore Afro-American.* In 1932 he was a delegate to the NAACP's second Amenia Conference.

In 1927 and 1928, after receiving a grant from the Rockefeller Foundation, Houston wrote an important report, "The Negro and His Contact with the Administration of Law." The next year, he was appointed vice dean at Howard University, where he served as professor of law and as head of the law school. He transformed the law program into a full-day curriculum that was approved by both the American Bar Association and the Association of American Law Schools. Houston mentored such students as Thurgood Marshall, William Bryant, and Oliver Hill. Under his direction, Howard Law School became a unique training ground for African-American lawyers to challenge segregation through the legal system.

In 1935 Houston took a leave of absence from Howard to become the first full-time, salaried special counsel of the NAACP. As special counsel Houston argued civil rights cases and traveled to many different areas of the United States, sometimes under trying conditions, in order to defend blacks who stood accused of crimes. He won two important Supreme Court cases, *Hollins v. Oklahoma* (1935) and *Hale v. Kentucky* (1938), which overturned death sentences given by juries from which blacks had been excluded because of their race.

Houston persuaded the joint committee of the NAACP and the philanthropic American Fund for Public Service to support an unrelenting but incremental legal struggle against segregation, with public education as the main area of challenge. In 1896 the U.S. Supreme Court had ruled in *Plessy v. Ferguson* that "separate but equal" segregated facilities were constitutional. Houston realized that a direct assault on the decision would fail, so he designed a strategy of litigation of test cases and a slow build-up of successful precedents based on inequality within segregation. He focused on combating discrimination in graduate education, a less controversial area than discrimination in primary schools, as the first step in his battle in the courts. *University of Maryland v. Murray* was his first victory and an important psychological triumph. The Maryland Supreme Court ordered that Donald Murray, an African American, be admitted to the University of Maryland Law School because there were no law schools for blacks in the state. Two years later, Houston successfully argued *Missouri ex rel. Gaines v. Canada* in the U.S. Supreme Court. The Court ordered that Lloyd Gaines be admitted to the University of Missouri, which had no black graduate school, ruling that granting scholarships for black students to out-of-state schools did not constitute equal admission.

In 1938, suffering from tuberculosis and heart problems, Houston resigned as chief counsel, and two years later he left the NAACP. However, he remained a prime adviser over the next decade through his membership on the NAACP Legal Committee. His position as special counsel was taken over by his former student and deputy Thurgood Marshall, who formed the NAACP Legal Defense and Education Fund, Inc. (LDF), to continue the struggle Houston had begun. Their endeavor culminated with the famous 1954 Supreme Court decision in *Brown v. Board of Education of Topeka, Kansas,* which overturned school segregation. Houston remained active in the effort. Shortly before his death, he initiated *Bolling v. Sharpe* (1954), a school desegregation suit in Washington, D.C., which later became one of the school cases the Supreme Court consolidated with and decided in *Brown.*

In 1940 Houston became general counsel of the International Association of Railway Employees and of the Association of Colored Railway Trainmen and Locomotive Firemen. He and his co-counsel investigated complaints of unfair labor practices and litigated grievances. Houston successfully argued two cases, *Steele v. Louisville & Nashville Railroad* and *Tunstall v. Brotherhood of Locomotive Firemen and Enginemen,* involving racial discrimination in the selection of bargaining agents under the Railway Labor Act of 1934. Houston also worked as an attorney for hearings of the President's Fair Employment Practices Committee (FEPC). Appointed to the FEPC in 1944, he dramatically resigned in December 1945 in protest over President Truman's refusal to issue an order banning discrimination by Washington's Capital Transit Authority, and of the committee's imminent demise.

In the late 1940s Houston led a group of civil rights lawyers in bringing suit against housing discrimination. He helped draft the brief for the LDF's Supreme Court case *Shelley v. Kramer* and argued a companion case, *Hurd v. Hodge,* in which the Supreme Court barred enforcement of racially restrictive covenants in leases.

In 1948 Houston suffered a heart attack, and died of a coronary occlusion two years later. He received the NAACP's Spingarn Medal posthumously in 1950. In 1958 Howard University named its new main law school building in his honor.

See also *Brown v. Board of Education of Topeka, Kansas;* Civil Rights Movement, U.S.; Marshall, Thurgood; NAACP Legal Defense and Educational Fund; National Association for the Advancement of Colored People (NAACP); *Plessy v. Ferguson*

■ ■ *Bibliography*

Kluger, Richard. *Simple Justice.* New York: Vintage, 1975.

McNeil, Genna Rae. "'To Meet the Group Needs': The Transformation of Howard University School of Law, 1920–1935." In *New Perspectives on Black Educational History,* edited by

V. P. Franklin and James D. Anderson, pp. 149–172. Boston: G. K. Hall, 1978.

McNeil, Genna Rae. *Groundwork: Charles Hamilton Houston and the Struggle for Civil Rights.* Philadelphia: University of Pennsylvania Press, 1983.

Ogletree, Charles J. *All Deliberate Speed: Reflections on the First Half Century of Brown v. Board of Education.* New York: W. W. Norton, 2004.

Rowan, Carl. *Dream Makers, Dream Breakers: The World of Justice Thurgood Marshall.* Boston: Little, Brown, 1993.

Segal, Geraldine. *In Any Fight Some Fall.* Rockville, Md.: Mercury, 1975.

Tushnet, Mark V. *The NAACP's Legal Strategy Against Segregated Education, 1925-1950.* Chapel Hill: University of North Carolina Press, 1987.

GENNA RAE MCNEIL (1996)
Updated bibliography

HOUSTON, WHITNEY

AUGUST 9, 1963

▮▮▮ ━━━━━━━━━━━━

Singer, actress, and model Whitney Houston was born in Newark and grew up in East Orange, New Jersey. She comes from a family of performers: Her mother, Cissy Houston, is a long-time gospel performer, and her husband, Bobby Brown, is also a singer. As a child Houston sang in the choir of her church, New Hope Baptist Church, and sang her first solo at the age of twelve. After working briefly as a teen model, she returned to music following her graduation from high school. She performed in minor capacities such as backup singing and advertising, but she did not sign a record contract until 1985. Her first album, *Whitney Houston* (1985), became the best-selling debut album for any solo artist, selling thirteen million copies and winning a Grammy Award and two National Music Awards. Her follow-up albums, *Whitney* (1987) and *I'm Your Baby Tonight* (1990), succeeded in similar fashion.

Houston's fourth album accompanied her acting debut in *The Bodyguard* (1992), in which she performed the Dolly Parton song "I Will Always Love You," the longest running number-one single in history. The film grossed $390 million, the soundtrack sold twenty-four million copies, and Houston's fame was at its peak.

Houston's career slowed down somewhat after that. She continued to appear in occasional acting roles and released only one album, *My Love is Your Love* (1998), in addition to several singles. In late 1999 she became the subject of rampant drug abuse rumors because of her erratic public behavior. Houston adamantly denied the rumors.

The rumors proved correct, however, and Houston was eventually admitted to a Georgia rehabilitation center. During this time her husband, Bobby Brown, was often in trouble with the law (including an assault against Houston). In 2004 Houston announced that her addiction days were in the past. She and Brown were still together and had signed to do a ten-part reality television program.

See also Music in the United States; Rhythm and Blues

■ ■ *Bibliography*

Bigelow, Barbara Carlisle, ed. *Contemporary Black Biography*, vol. 7. Detroit, Mich.: Gale, 1994.

Current Biography Yearbook. New York: H. W. Wilson, 1986.

Smith, Jessie Carney, ed. *Notable Black American Women*, Book II. Detroit, Mich.: Gale, 1996.

JESSIE CARNEY SMITH (2001)
Updated by publisher 2005

HOWARD, ETHEL

See Waters, Ethel

HOWARD UNIVERSITY

▮▮▮ ━━━━━━━━━━━━

In December 1866 a group of Congregationalists in Washington, D.C., proposed establishing the Howard Normal and Theological Institute for the Education of Teachers and Preachers to train ministers and educators for work among newly freed slaves. After receiving some support and funding, Howard University was chartered on March 2, 1867, and given the mission of establishing a university "for the education of youth in the liberal arts and sciences."

Howard received its name from Gen. Oliver Otis Howard, head of the Freedmen's Bureau. General Howard, along with several other Civil War generals and U.S. congressmen, was largely responsible for the organization of the university and its campaign to secure an annual appropriation for its maintenance from Congress. Despite substantial federal funding, Howard was governed by a privately selected board of trustees and has always maintained its independent status. In keeping with its religious mission, the board of the university decreed that anyone chosen for any position in the university "be a member of some Evangelical church."

In the first years of Howard University's operation, very few African Americans were involved in its administration or on the board of trustees. The first students enrolled at Howard, four or five young women, were also white; they graduated from the three-year Normal Department in 1870. George B. Vashon, the first black faculty member at Howard, taught in a short-lived evening school in 1867–1868. One of the first black female leaders at Howard was Martha B. Briggs (1873–1879, 1883–1889). At first an instructor in the Normal Department, Briggs would become principal of the department in 1883.

In 1868 the trustees created a Preparatory Department, which served as preparation for entrance into undergraduate course work by ensuring a minimum level of achievement in basic subjects like reading and writing. They also added a collegiate department, which included a four-year curriculum; it would eventually become the mainstay of the university. In its inaugural year, the collegiate department only had one student and two professors. The first three graduates of the department received their degrees in 1872. One of the two blacks in this class, James Monroe Gregory, became a tutor in Latin and math; in 1876 he became a professor of Latin.

Several other departments rounded out the university in its early years. A medical department was established in 1868. Its first graduating class of five, in 1871, included two blacks. The nearby Freedmen's Hospital was invaluable for medical students and doctors who were often unable to secure medical privileges at other institutions. Charles Burleigh Purvis, who worked virtually without compensation for many years as a professor in the medical department, was largely responsible for guiding both the medical school and its students during his long career.

Under the tutelage of Dean John Mercer Langston, a future congressman, the Law Department first enrolled students in the spring of 1869. It graduated its first class of ten in February 1871, including African-American John Cook, a future dean of the law school. An integral part of Howard from its founding, the theology department, opened officially in 1870, never used federal funds; instead, it relied upon contributions from the American Missionary Association, which was associated with the Congregational Church.

The university struggled financially for the first several years. Much of its original funding came from the Freedmen's Bureau, which provided capital for operation as well as money for the purchase of land and the construction of a campus. Before the bureau closed it channeled more than $500,000 to Howard, from 1867 until 1872. After the bureau's demise, the university received no additional federal funds until 1879, when Congress began granting Howard a small appropriation.

Howard University in the 1880s. *Founded in Washington, D.C., in 1867, Howard soon became a center of African-American intellectual life. In the early decades of the twentieth century, the university boasted a faculty that included many of the nation's leading black scholars.* PHOTOGRAPHS AND PRINTS DIVISION, SCHOMBURG CENTER FOR RESEARCH IN BLACK CULTURE, THE NEW YORK PUBLIC LIBRARY, ASTOR, LENOX AND TILDEN FOUNDATIONS.

After several years Howard's operations increased in scope. From 1875 to 1889 more than five hundred students received professional degrees in medicine, law, and theology, and almost three hundred students received certificates from the normal, preparatory, and collegiate departments. The board of trustees also made efforts to expand and increase the African-American representation among its membership. In 1871 they appointed Frederick Douglass to become a trustee; he served until his death in 1895. Several other blacks were named trustees in this period. Booker T. Washington became a trustee in 1907.

By 1900 Howard University had more than seven hundred students. Along with Fisk and Atlanta universities, Howard was one of the most prominent black academic colleges in the country. Under the administration of President Wilbur P. Thirkield (1906–1912), the university began to stress more industrial courses of study and the sciences. Howard established one of the first engineering programs at a predominantly black college; Howard's other science programs were also generally superior. The eminent biologist Ernest E. Just (1907–1941), who taught at Howard for several decades, helped further develop Howard's reputation in the sciences.

Another leader at Howard—and one of the most important black educators in the early twentieth century—was Kelly Miller. Miller, who served Howard in various capacities from 1890 to 1934, was dean of the College of Arts and Sciences from 1908 to 1919 and fought for the introduction of courses on African-American life as early as the turn of the century.

The 1920s was a decade of great growth and change. The high school that prepared students for entrance into Howard closed in 1920. Under the administration of President J. Stanley Durkee, the university budget grew from $121,937 in 1920 to $365,000 only five years later. Lucy Slowe Diggs (1922–1937) was the first dean of women at Howard; she helped to transform the role of female university officials to that of active administrators participating in shaping university policy. In 1925 students took part in a weeklong strike for greater student participation in university policy-making and an end to mandatory chapel services. Another focus of student and intellectual agitation was the growing demand for the appointment of a black president to lead Howard. Mordecai W. Johnson, a Baptist minister, became Howard's first African-American president on September 1, 1926; he served until 1960.

In the 1920s and 1930s Howard became a center of African-American intellectual life and attracted a brilliant faculty committed to finding new directions for black America. Many black scholars trained at Ivy League schools and other predominantly white institutions were unable to find employment other than in historically black colleges and universities (HBCUs). Howard attracted the cream of the crop.

One of the leading figures at Howard in the 1920s was philosopher Alain Locke (1912–1925, 1927–1954), popularizer of the New Negro movement. Several administration officials and faculty members urged the implementation of a curriculum that explicitly acknowledged the cultural accomplishments of African Americans. Kelly Miller had been doing so for years; William Leo Hansberry (1922–1959) became the first African-American scholar to offer comprehensive courses in the civilization and history of Africa in the 1920s.

The 1930s were a period of intellectual accomplishment at Howard, with a faculty that included the leading black scholars in the country. Led by political scientist Ralph J. Bunche (1928–1933), English professors Sterling Brown (1929–1969) and Alphaeus Hunton (1926–1943), sociologist E. Franklin Frazier (1934–1959), and economist Abram Harris, Jr. (1927–1945), the Howard faculty

looked for ways to transcend the division between accommodationism and black nationalism. While proud exponents of the distinctiveness of black culture, they often espoused industrial unionism and multiracial working-class harmony, and were sensitive to the internal divisions and class differences within the black community. Historian Rayford Logan (1938–1982), largely responsible for strengthening the history department, wrote the most comprehensive history of Howard from its founding until its centennial. Logan also served the larger cause of African-American studies by producing the ground-breaking *Dictionary of American Negro Biography* (1982). The distinguished African-American pianist Hazel Harrison (1936–1955) was one of the leading women faculty members of the period.

Charles H. Houston (1929–1935), who helped to strengthen the curriculum at the law school and became one of the most important civil rights lawyers of the 1930s and 1940s, added to Howard's position as the best black law school in the country at the time. Under Houston's capable guidance, the law school strengthened its curriculum and received accreditation from the American Association of American Law Schools in late 1931. Graduates included Thurgood Marshall (1933), future justice of the U.S. Supreme Court.

The 1930s were also marked by administrative controversy. President Johnson came under harsh criticism from many who felt that his managerial style was heavy-handed and autocratic. Johnson had removed several administration officials and had fired several university employees. The alumni association criticized Johnson and the board of trustees as well, arguing that the alumni should have more of a voice in choosing trustees and constructing university policy.

Given their reliance on federal funds for operation, Howard officials were often held accountable by members of Congress for perceived ideological aberrations like socialism or communism. In the early 1940s, investigations into the activities of some faculty members, among them Alphaeus Hunton, by the House Committee on Un-American Activities (HUAC) brought unwanted attention to Howard. When another HUAC inquiry occurred in the early 1950s, President Mordecai Johnson did not attempt to derail the various investigations but declared his confidence that the faculty members being investigated would be vindicated; all were. The administration at Howard often urged moderation and discouraged university employees from making overtly political statements.

Several prominent black scholars taught at Howard during the 1940s and 1950s. Margaret Just Butcher, daughter of biologist Ernest Just, taught English at How-

President Lyndon Johnson talks with Patricia R. Harris, Associate Professor of Constitutional Law at Howard University, after attending commencement exercises at the school, June 4, 1965.
© BETTMANN/CORBIS

ard from 1945 until 1955; she collaborated with Alaine Locke on *The Negro in American Culture* (1956). Prominent civil rights leader Anna Arnold Hedgeman was dean of women from 1946 until 1948; she would later be instrumental in helping to plan the 1963 March on Washington. Mercer Cook (1927–1936, 1944–1960, 1966–1970), an influential translator of the *Négritude* poets, and the Afrocentrist Cheikh A. Diop, taught in the Department of Romance Languages for several generations.

While the 1950s was a time of relative quiet at Howard, the university experienced intellectual and political turmoil during the 1960s. In 1962 Vice President Lyndon B. Johnson spoke at the commencement; returning to Howard three years later, this time as president, Johnson renewed his pledge to struggle for equal rights for all and outlined the tenets of what would become his plans for the Great Society. Students vocally disrupted a 1967 speech by Gen. Lewis Hershey, director of the Selective Service System. They further disrupted campus operations in 1968 when students all over the country took part in demanding an end to the war in Vietnam. Howard students were also urging the implementation of a more radical curricu-

lum. In 1969 Howard inaugurated its African-American Studies program.

President James M. Nabrit, Jr., one of the attorneys who crafted one of the briefs used to justify the decision by the U.S. Supreme Court to end segregation in the landmark 1954 *Brown v. Board of Education of Topeka, Kansas,* led Howard from 1960 until 1969, some of its most turbulent years. Notable faculty members included Patricia Roberts Harris (1961–1963, 1967–1969), who was an attorney, the first African-American woman to become an ambassador, and a professor in the Howard Law School for several years. Her tenure as the first black female dean of the law school, however, lasted only thirty days; outcry over student protests and conflicts with other university administrators compelled her to resign (1969).

In the mid-1980s Howard was one of the first universities in the United States to initiate divestment from South Africa. Republican Party chairman Lee Atwater resigned from the board of trustees in 1989 after protests by hundreds of students. Howard received more unfavorable publicity in early 1994 after the appearance on campus by former Nation of Islam official Khalid Muhammad.

Howard has many notable facilities. The Moorland-Spingarn Center, one of the premier archival resources for studying African-American history and culture, had accumulated over 150,000 books and more than four hundred manuscript collections. The center was a result of the donation of collections from trustee Jesse Moorland in 1914 and NAACP official Arthur Spingarn in 1946; they included "books, pictures, and statuary on the Negro and on slavery." An art gallery includes an extensive African-American collection of painting, sculpture, and art. A university radio and television station sought to bring in revenue and offer a valuable educational service to the larger community of the District of Columbia. The Howard University Press has published more than a hundred works since its inception in 1972. Howard University Hospital, a five-hundred-bed teaching hospital, is responsible for, among other things, pioneering research by the Howard University Cancer Center and the Center for Sickle Cell Disease.

For fiscal year 2001 the operation budget of Howard University was $419 million, and the university employed more than 6,000 people. (In 1975 the budget was about $100 million.) Howard still receives more than 50 percent of its budget from the federal government—about $232 million for 2001. Its enrollment in 1993 stood at almost 12,000 students distributed among various colleges, programs, and institutes. A decade later enrollment stood at about 11,000 students, including 7,000 undergraduates.

The future, however, holds uncertainty for Howard and other HBCUs. Howard has consistently dedicated itself to providing an intellectual haven for African Americans denied opportunities elsewhere. In 1963, the board of trustees promised that

> As a matter of history and tradition, Howard University accepts a special responsibility for the education of capable Negro students disadvantaged by the system of racial segregation and discrimination, and it will continue to do so as long as Negroes suffer these disabilities.

As bars against entry of blacks into primarily white universities have disappeared, a crisis has arisen for those schools which historically relied upon having the brightest African-American students and faculty. Partly to address this problem, Howard launched its Howard 2000 reorganization program in the early 1990s. Its goal was to help Howard remain fiscally and academically competitive into the next century.

See also Brown v. Board of Education of Topeka, Kansas; Bunche, Ralph; Douglass, Frederick; Education in the United States; Fisk University; Freedmen's Hospital; Johnson, Mordecai Wyatt; Just, Ernest; Langston, John Mercer; Locke, Alain Leroy; Logan, Rayford W.; Marshall, Thurgood

■ ■ *Bibliography*

Ashley, Dwayne, and Juan Williams. *I'll Find a Way or Make One: A Tribute to Historically Black Colleges and Universities.* Martinsburg, W.V.: Amistad Press, 2004.

Dyson, Walter. *Howard University, the Capstone of Negro Education: A History, 1867–1940.* Washington, D.C.: Howard University Graduate School, 1941.

Janken, Kenneth Robert. *Rayford W. Logan and the Dilemma of the African-American Intellectual.* Amherst: University of Massachusetts Press, 1993.

Leavy, Walter. "Howard University: A Unique Center of Excellence." *Ebony* 40 (September 1985): 140–142.

Logan, Rayford. *Howard University: The First Hundred Years, 1867–1967.* New York: New York University Press, 1969.

Wolters, Raymond. *The New Negro on Campus: Black College Rebellions in the 1920s.* Princeton, N.J.: Princeton University Press, 1975.

ESME BHAN (1996)
Updated by publisher 2005

HOYTE, DESMOND

MARCH 9, 1929
DECEMBER 22, 2002

Hugh Desmond Hoyte was born into a family of modest circumstances in Georgetown, British Guiana, and became president of the Cooperative Republic of Guyana in 1985. His life reflected the process of social transformation that accompanied the transition of the colony—British Guiana—to an independent state—Guyana—over the course of the twentieth century. Hoyte was both a product of the colonial order and an agent of the new nationalist political order that sought to grapple with the challenges of independence in the late twentieth century.

EDUCATION AND EARLY CAREER

Hoyte attended Saint Barnabas Anglican School and the Progressive High School at a time when the education of children represented a major investment for parents, since public education was not widely available in the colony. He later obtained an external B.A. degree from the University of London and after a stint of teaching in Grenada studied law in London beginning in 1957. He received an LL. B. in London in 1959 and was called to the bar. He returned to Guyana in 1960 to begin practice as a lawyer. In his education and career path, Hoyte was representative of the commitment to education and professional development that marked the generation of Guyanese who emerged as the standard bearers of the nationalist struggle. His erudition and commitment to education were never compromised by his pursuit of a political career.

In 1961 Hoyte joined the legal firm of Clarke and Martin, among whose members were Forbes Burnham, Fred Wills, and Fenton Ramsahoye, who would all go on to prominent political careers in the nationalist era. Forbes Burnham became his professional and political mentor—a relationship that led to Hoyte's eventual ascension to the presidency of Guyana upon the death of Burnham in 1985. Hoyte's legal career lasted until 1968, when he was elected to parliament on the People's National Congress (PNC) slate in the first of a series of fraudulent elections that allowed Burnham to consolidate his power in an independent Guyana.

Hoyte's formal entry into parliament as a result of the 1968 election was preceded by his 1966 appointment to the National Elections Commission, the agency that supervised the disputed elections of 1968. He had also served as a legal advisor to the pro-PNC Guyana Trades Union Congress and as a member of the General Council of the

PNC since 1962. His entry into national politics reflected his close collaboration with Burnham and the grooming process he had undergone as a prelude to his entry into the cabinet as minister of home affairs in 1969, with responsibility for the police and a section of the state security apparatus. Hoyte's portfolio was critical to another major post-independence political transition in 1970, when Guyana became a republic, with an appointed president serving as ceremonial head of state.

A Major Influence

Hoyte served as finance minister from 1970 to 1972; as minister of works and communications from 1972 to 1974; and as minister of economic development from 1974 to 1980. He was also elevated to membership of the central committee of the PNC in 1973. He had emerged as a major figure within the government and ruling party. The 1970s saw another fraudulent election in 1973, and the introduction of a new constitution creating, by way of a rigged 1978 referendum, an executive presidency.

The 1970s also saw a rapprochement between the PNC and the opposition Marxist-Leninist People's Progressive Party (PPP) as the country's political trajectory allowed it to foster closer relations with the Soviet Union, China, and Cuba. Hoyte, as minister of economic development, oversaw the nationalization of the bauxite and sugar industries and the expansion of the public sector. The increasing state control of the economy was driven by a desire to use profits from the export sectors to promote the diversification of the economy as a whole. Unfortunately, this strategy was adopted as the oil shocks of the 1970s wreaked havoc with the global financial and trading systems and undermined the economies of all exporters of primary commodities. This expansion of state control led to the imposition of limits upon freedom of the press and the ruling party's resort to militarization of the state through the creation of the Guyana National Service and the Guyana People's Militia. It also led to capital flight and the migration of skilled Guyanese.

Presidency

Hoyte's increasing influence was evident when he was appointed vice president to Burnham, who became executive president in 1980. Hoyte was named prime minister and first vice president in 1984. A year later Hoyte became president upon Burnham's death. His accession to the presidency in 1985 was the capstone of his political career. In a surprising turnaround and disavowal of his mentor, and despite a flawed election in 1985, Hoyte initiated an era of political reform. Intimately aware of the possibility

of state financial collapse due to its debt burden and the crisis of management at all levels of the vastly expanded public sector, Hoyte abandoned Burnham's flirtation with the socialist bloc. He adopted International Monetary Fund advice and a structural adjustment program. He also re-established freedom of the press, encouraged the establishment of the Iwokrama project to support sound environmental management of Guyana's rain forest, and created the Guyana Prize for Literature. The changes he introduced extended to the electoral reforms that led to his ouster in 1992 in an election at which former U.S. President Jimmy Carter was the lead international observer. Hoyte's decision to embark upon the process of reform reversed the course of economic decline that had preceded his assumption of the presidency.

After 1992 Hoyte remained leader of the opposition until his death in 2002, although he lost the general elections of 1992, 1997, and 2001 to the PPP. His death marked the passage of the generation nationalists who led Guyana to independence but whose legacy for the future of the country remains ambiguous.

See also Burnham, Forbes; People's National Congress; Politics and Politicians in Latin America

▪▪ *Bibliography*

Ferguson, Tyrone. *Structural Adjustment and Good Governance: The Case of Guyana.* Georgetown, Guyana: Public Affairs Consulting, 1995.

Ferguson, Tyrone. *To Survive Sensibly or to Court Heroic Death: Management of Guyana's Political Economy, 1965–1985.* Georgetown, Guyana: Guyana National Printers, 1999.

Fraser, Cary. *Ambivalent Anti-Colonialism.* Westport, Conn.: Greenwood, 1994.

Glasgow, R.A. *Guyana: Race and Politics among Africans and East Indians.* The Hague: Nijhoff, 1970.

Hintzen, Percy C. *The Costs of Regime Survival: Racial Mobilization, Elite Domination, and Control of the State in Guyana and Trinidad.* Cambridge, U.K.: Cambridge University Press, 1989.

Singh, Chaitram. *Guyana: Politics in a Plantation Society.* New York: Praeger, 1988.

Spinner, Thomas J., Jr. *A Political and Social History of Guyana, 1945–1983.* Boulder, Colo.: Westview, 1984.

CARY FRASER (2005)

HUDSON, HOSEA

1898
1988

∎∎∎

Union leader and communist activist Hosea Hudson was born into an impoverished sharecropping family in Wilkes County in the eastern Georgia black belt. He became a plow hand at ten, which sharply curtailed his schooling. The combination of a boll-weevil infestation and a violent altercation with his brother-in-law prompted Hudson in 1923 to move to Atlanta, where he worked as a common laborer in a railroad roundhouse. A year later he moved to Birmingham, Alabama, and commenced his career as an iron molder.

Although he remained a faithful churchgoer, Hudson harbored persistent doubts about God's goodness and power, given the oppression of African Americans as workers and as Negroes. As a working-class black, however, he lacked a focus for his discontent until the Communist Party, U.S.A. (CPUSA) began organizing in Birmingham in 1930. In the wake of the conviction of the Scottsboro Boys and the Camp Hill massacre, both in Alabama in 1931, Hudson joined the CPUSA. Within a year he had lost his job at the Stockham foundry. Although he was able to earn irregular wages through odd jobs and iron molding under assumed names, much of the burden of family support in the 1930s fell on his wife, who never forgave him for putting the welfare of the Communist Party before that of his wife and child.

During the Great Depression, Hudson was active with a series of organizations in and around the CPUSA. He helped the Unemployed Councils secure relief payments and fight evictions on behalf of the poor. In his first trip outside the South, he spent ten weeks in New York State at the CPUSA National Training School in 1934, during which he learned to read and write. As a party cadre in Atlanta from 1934 to 1936, he worked with neighborhood organizations and helped investigate the lynching of Lint Shaw. Returning to Birmingham in 1937, he worked on a Works Project Administration project (WPA), served as vice president of the Birmingham and Jefferson County locals of the Workers Alliance, and founded the Right to Vote Club (which earned him a key to the city of Birmingham in 1980 as a pioneer in the struggle for black civil rights).

After the creation of the Congress of Industrial Organizations, Hudson joined the campaign to organize unorganized workers. As the demand for labor during World War II eased his way back into the foundries, he became recording secretary of Steel Local 1489, then organized United Steel Workers Local 2815. He remained president of that local from 1942 to 1947, when he was stripped of leadership and blacklisted for being a communist. He was underground in Atlanta and New York City from 1950 to 1956, during the height of the cold war and McCarthyism. Imbued with a justified sense of the historical importance of his life, Hudson wrote two books on his experiences: *Black Worker in the Deep South* (1972) and *The Narrative of Hosea Hudson* (1979). Active in the Coalition of Black Trades Unionists until his health failed in the mid-1980s, Hudson died in Gainesville, Florida.

See also Communist Party of the United States; Great Depression and the New Deal

■■ *Bibliography*

Painter, Nell Irvin. *The Narrative of Hosea Hudson: His Life as a Negro Communist in the South,* 2nd ed. New York: W. W. Norton, 1994.

NELL IRVIN PAINTER (1996)

HUGHES, LANGSTON

FEBRUARY 1, 1902
MAY 22, 1967

∎∎∎

Writer James Langston Hughes was born in Joplin, Missouri, and grew up in Lawrence, Kansas, mainly with his grandmother, Mary Langston, whose first husband had died in John Brown's raid at Harpers Ferry and whose second, Hughes's grandfather, had also been a radical abolitionist. Hughes's mother, Carrie Langston Hughes, occasionally wrote poetry and acted; his father, James Nathaniel Hughes, studied law, and then emigrated to Mexico around 1903. After a year (1915–1916) in Lincoln, Illinois, Hughes moved to Cleveland, where he attended high school (1916–1920). He then spent a year with his father in Mexico. In June 1921 he published a poem that was to become celebrated, "The Negro Speaks of Rivers," in *The Crisis* magazine. Enrolling at Columbia University in New York in 1921, he withdrew after a year. He traveled down the west coast of Africa as a mess man on a ship (1923), washed dishes in a Paris nightclub (1924), and traveled in Italy and the Mediterranean before returning to spend a year (1925) in Washington, D.C.

Poems in journals such as *The Crisis* and *Opportunity* led to Hughes's recognition as perhaps the most striking new voice in African-American verse. Steeped in black

American culture, his poems revealed his unswerving admiration for blacks, especially the poor. He was particularly inventive in fusing the rhythms of jazz and blues, as well as black speech, with traditional forms of poetry. In 1926 he published his first book of verse, *The Weary Blues,* followed by *Fine Clothes to the Jew* (1927), which was attacked in the black press for its emphasis on the blues culture. A major essay, "The Negro Artist and the Racial Mountain," expressed his determination to make black culture the foundation of his art. In 1926 he enrolled at historically black Lincoln University, and graduated in 1929. With the support of a wealthy but volatile patron, Mrs. Charlotte Osgood Mason (also known as "Godmother"), he wrote his first novel, *Not Without Laughter* (1930). The collapse of this relationship deeply disturbed Hughes, who evidently loved Mrs. Mason but resented her imperious demands on him. After several weeks in Haiti in 1931, he undertook a reading tour to mainly black audiences, starting in the South and ending in the West. He then spent a year (1932–1933) in the Soviet Union, where he wrote several poems influenced by radical socialism, including "Goodbye Christ," about religious hypocrisy. In Carmel, California (1933–1934) he wrote most of the short stories in *The Ways of White Folks* (1934). After a few months in Mexico following the death of his father there, Hughes moved to Oberlin, Ohio.

In New York Hughes's play *Mulatto,* about miscegenation in the South, opened on Broadway in 1935 to hostile reviews but enjoyed a long run. Several other plays by Hughes were produced in the 1930s at the Karamu Playhouse in Cleveland. He spent several months as a war correspondent in Spain during 1937. Returning to New York in 1938, he founded the Harlem Suitcase Theater, which staged his radical drama *Don't You Want to Be Free?* In 1939, desperately needing money, he worked on a Hollywood film, *Way Down South,* which was criticized for its benign depiction of slavery. However, he was able to settle various debts and write an autobiography, *The Big Sea* (1940).

In 1940, when a religious group picketed one of his appearances, Hughes repudiated "Goodbye Christ" and his main ties to the left. In *Shakespeare in Harlem* (1942) he returned to writing poems about blacks and the blues. After two years in California he returned to New York. Late in 1942, in the *Chicago Defender,* he began a weekly newspaper column that ran for more than twenty years. In 1943 he introduced its most popular feature, a character called Jesse B. Semple, or Simple, an urban black Everyman of intense racial consciousness but also with a delightfully offbeat sense of humor. In 1947 his work as lyricist with Kurt Weill and Elmer Rice on the Broadway

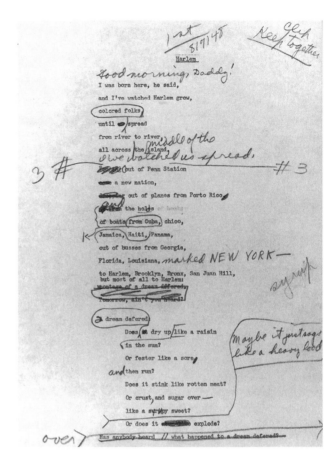

Typewritten manuscript of the poem "Good Morning" by Langston Hughes, with his editorial remarks, notations, and corrections. *"Good Morning" was featured in Hughes's collection* Montage of a Dream Deferred *(1951), which captures the mood of an increasingly troubled Harlem.* REPRODUCED BY PERMISSION OF THE YALE COLLECTION OF AMERICAN LITERATURE, BEINECKE RARE BOOK AND MANUSCRIPT LIBRARY. AND HAROLD OBER ASSOCIATES INCORPORATED FOR THE ESTATE OF LANGSTON HUGHES.

musical play *Street Scene* enabled him finally to buy a home and settle down in Harlem. Hughes, who never married, lived there with an old family friend, Toy Harper, and her husband, Emerson Harper, a musician.

As a writer, Hughes worked in virtually all genres, though he saw himself mainly as a poet. In *Fields of Wonder* (1947), *One-Way Ticket* (1949), and *Montage of a Dream Deferred* (1951), he used the new bebop jazz rhythms in his poetry to capture the mood of an increasingly troubled Harlem. With Mercer Cook, he translated the novel *Gouverneurs de la rosée* (*Masters of the Dew,* 1947) by Jacques Roumain of Haiti; he also translated poems by Nicolás Guillén of Cuba (*Cuba Libre,* 1948), Federico García Lorca of Spain (1951), and Gabriela Mistral of Chile (*Selected Poems,* 1957). The first of five collections of Simple sketches, *Simple Speaks His Mind,* appeared in 1950, and another collection of short stories, *Laughing to Keep from Crying,* came in 1952. Working first with composer William Grant Still and then with Jan Meyerowitz, Hughes composed opera libretti and other texts to be set to music.

Right-wing groups, which were anticommunist and probably also motivated by racism, steadily attacked Hughes—despite his denials—for his alleged membership in the Communist Party. In 1953, forced to appear before Sen. Joseph McCarthy's investigating committee, he conceded that some of his radical writing had been misguided. Criticized by some socialists, he pressed on with his career and later toured Africa and elsewhere for the State Department. He published about a dozen books for children on a variety of topics, including jazz, Africa, and the Caribbean. With photographer Roy DeCarava he published an acclaimed book of pictures accompanied by a narrative, *The Sweet Flypaper of Life* (1955). His second volume of autobiography, *I Wonder as I Wander,* was published in 1956.

Perhaps the most innovative of Hughes's later work came in drama, especially his gospel plays such as *Black Nativity* (1961) and *Jericho-Jim Crow* (1964). He was also an important editor. He published (with Arna Bontemps) *Poetry of the Negro, 1746–1949* (1949), as well as *An African Treasury* (1960), *New Negro Poets: U.S.A.* (1964), and *The Book of Negro Humor* (1966). Hughes was widely recognized as the most representative African-American writer and perhaps the most original of black poets. In 1961 he was admitted to the National Institute of Arts and Letters. He died in New York City.

See also *Chicago Defender*; Harlem Renaissance; *Opportunity: Journal of Negro Life*; Decarava, Roy; Lincoln University; Poetry, U.S.; Still, William

■ ■ *Bibliography*

Bloom, Harold. *Langston Hughes.* New York: Chelsea House, 1989.

Mikolyzk, Thomas A. *Langston Hughes: A Bio-Bibliography.* Westport, Conn.: Greenwood Press, 1990.

Rampersad, Arnold. *The Life of Langston Hughes,* 2nd ed. New York: Oxford University Press, 2002.

ARNOLD RAMPERSAD (1996)
Updated bibliography

HUIE, ALBERT

DECEMBER 31, 1920

Albert Huie was born in Falmouth, Trelawny, on the north coast of Jamaica. In 1936, he moved to Kingston, Jamaica's capital, where he decided to pursue a career as an artist. It was an occupational path very few black Jamaicans followed at that time. Young Huie's talents were cultivated by a group of contemporaries who were interested in creating and supporting Jamaica's national art and culture. The Jamaica Arts Society awarded him a scholarship to study watercolor painting at Armenian artist Koren der Harootian's school in Kingston in 1938. Huie subsequently received informal training, including an introduction to linocutting, from a group of artists who gathered at sculptor Edna Manley's residence. In 1944 he left Jamaica to attend art school at the Ontario College of Art and University College of Toronto in Canada. The recipient of a British Council Scholarship three years later, he trained in painting and graphic techniques at Camberwell School of Arts, London. Exhibitions he encountered in London, especially the Van Gogh exhibition at the Tate in 1948, would also inform his work. Huie returned to Jamaica in 1948, where he worked as an artist and art educator at Clarendon College, Wolmers' Boys' School, and Excelsior High School.

The British colony of Jamaica underwent fundamental sociopolitical changes in the late 1930s and 1940s that informed Huie's art, including worker riots, anticolonial protests, union formation, and universal suffrage. Starting in the 1930s, the African diasporic movements of Ethiopianism, Rastafarianism, and Garveyism challenged colonial and imperial power, politically, socially, and culturally, on the island. Although each of these movements was very different, they were united in their critique of colonialism and promotion of the long denigrated African aspects of Jamaican society. Marcus Garvey, in particular, inspired Huie to see black people and their communities as beautiful and representable as the subjects of art. At a time when popular cultural forms caricatured blacks, he used portraiture and oil painting to present a respectable image of black subjects. Moreover, by creating portraits in a post-impressionist style, which frequently concentrated squarely on the face of his sitters, he forced viewers to confront the subjectivity and humanity of his models. Huie also sensitively rendered his sitters' skin color, paying close attention to the reflection and radiation of light on black skin. He made black skin, something long devalued in colonial Jamaica, the very focus of his art. Frequently the subject of praise, his representations of blacks also sparked controversy. Huie scandalized many viewers who attended the annual All-Island exhibition with his frank portrayal of a black female nude in 1960.

Starting in the 1940s Huie also began to represent black Jamaican religious and secular expressions in the form of linocuts, using a silhouetted style that recalls the work of French artist Henri Matisse. Inspired by the new interest in black Jamaican culture, he published images on a range of subjects, from the African-Jamaican religion *Pocomania* to the jitterbug dance, in the cultural nationalist magazine *Public Opinion*. The periodical issued prints of his work, making them accessible and affordable to a wide audience.

Huie also made a name for himself as a landscape painter. Like his interest in seeing artistic value in black subjects and cultural expressions, Huie was equally devoted to representing the specific color and light of different parts of Jamaica's landscape with accuracy and sensitivity, recording how landscapes changed in appearance at different parts of the day and during different local seasons. Trained in Canada by J. E. H. McDonald and Frank Carmichael, two founding members of the Group of Seven, a "national school" devoted to art inspired by and reflective of Canada, Huie sought to reapply their lessons to his island home. He used the qualities derived from keen observation of Jamaica's unique geography to create his landscape paintings.

Since the late 1930s, Huie has worked prolifically as an artist, exhibiting locally and internationally, winning acclaim at home and abroad. As early as 1939, he won the Bronze Prize for the painting *Counting Lesson* at the New York World's Fair. He was also nationally recognized with a Musgrave Silver Medal in 1958, Gold Musgrave Medal of the Institute of Jamaica in 1974, the Order of Distinction in 1975, and with a retrospective exhibition at the National Gallery of Jamaica in 1979.

See also Art in the Anglophone Caribbean; Painting and Sculpture

■ ■ *Bibliography*

Burke, Shirley Maynier. "Strength and Subtle Shades." *Jamaica Journal* 21, no. 3 (August–October 1988): 30–38.

Lucie-Smith, Edward. *Albert Huie.* Kingston: Ian Randle Publishers, 2001.

Thompson, Krista. "Visualizing Blackness in Modern Jamaican Art 1922–1938." *Small Axe: A Caribbean Journal of Criticism* 16 (September 2004): 1–31.

KRISTA A. THOMPSON (2005)

HUISWOUD, OTTO

OCTOBER 28, 1893
FEBRUARY 20, 1961

Otto Huiswoud (sometimes spelled Huiswood) was born in 1893 in Suriname, the grandson of a slave. In 1912 he moved to the United States, where he worked as a trader in tropical products and, later, as a printer in Harlem. He then became involved with American socialist and Negro organizations. His earliest known affiliation was with a group surrounding the *Messenger,* a monthly magazine established by A. Philip Randolph (1889–1979) and Chandler Owen (1889–1967) and published from 1917 to 1928. While urging American negroes to support the Russian Revolution, this group's leaders rejected the Communists' greater emphasis on class struggle, rather than on racism, in addressing the plight of blacks. Also associated with the *Messenger* were Cyril Briggs and Richard B. Moore, who in 1919 founded a nationalist organization called the African Blood Brotherhood, which Huiswoud also joined briefly. He accompanied its more radical members when they left the *Messenger* group and joined the American Communist Party, which was just taking shape.

Huiswoud is most often mentioned as the first black member of the Communist Party USA. In 1922 he was a member of the American delegation to the Fourth Congress of the Communist International (Comintern). While there, he was elected an honorary member of the Moscow City Council and had a rare audience with Lenin, who was already mortally ill. Huiswoud was elected to the Central Committee of the Communist Party USA, and later to the Executive Committee of Comintern. In 1927 he studied at the Lenin School in Moscow, one of the political institutions founded to train elite communist leaders. Comintern then assigned him as its primary organizer for the Caribbean region. At the meeting of the Sixth Comintern Congress in 1928 he was one of the several black delegates who helped formulate the official policy on nationalism, urging creation of independent black soviet republics in the southern United States and in southern Africa. This policy, called "Self-Determination in the Black Belt," stressed that the "Negro question" had to be viewed as primarily a class question related to colonialism and not as a race question. It was adopted despite having scant support from black delegates. Two years later Huiswoud openly challenged this position in an article titled "World Aspects of the Negro Question," published in the February 1930 issue of *The Communist.*

Another important post with Comintern followed in 1934 when he became the editor of the *Negro Worker,* the organ of the International Trade Union Committee of Negro Workers. In this he succeeded the Trinidadian George Padmore (1902–1957) the founder of the *Negro Worker,* who was expelled from the Communist Party for failing to follow the party line. This monthly had been based in Hamburg, but flight from the Nazis prompted moves to Copenhagen and then Paris from 1936 to 1938. During these years Huiswoud and his British-Guianese wife, H. A. Dumont, traveled through the European cities with uncertainty concerning the welcome they would receive from nervous local authorities. In 1935 they were in the Netherlands, only to move back to New York in 1938, then back to Suriname in 1941, when Huiswoud's health required a warmer climate. Upon his arrival in Paramaribo in January, however, the authorities arrested him without charges and detained him for twenty-two months in an internment camp whose mixed population of Nazis, Jewish refugees, and antifascists reflected the political uncertainty common to a number of European colonies during World War II. After the war, he and his wife moved finally to the Netherlands. There he took a job with PTT, the national communications company, and he was a leader in the Surinamer community, serving for years as president of the nationalistic association *Ons Suriname* (Our Suriname), and collaborating with the two other main like-minded groups, *Wie Eegie Sanie* (Our Own Things) and the *Surinaamse Studenten Vereniging* (The Surinamer Student Union). He died in the Netherlands in 1961.

See also African Blood Brotherhood; Communist Party of the United States; *Messenger, The*

■ ■ *Bibliography*

Huiswoud, Otto E. "World Aspects of the Negro Question." *The Communist* (February 1930): 132–147.

Oostindie, Gert. "Kondreman in Bakrakondre." In *In het land van de overheerser,* edited by Gert Oostindie and E. Maduro. Dordrecht, Germany: Floris, 1986.

Solomon, Mark. *The Cry Was Unity: Communists and African Americans, 1917-1936.* Jackson: University Press of Mississippi, 1998.

Van Enckevort, Maria Gertrudis. "The Life and Work of Otto Huiswoud: Professional Revolutionary and Internationalist (1893-1961)." Ph.D. diss., University of the West Indies, Mona Campus, 2000.

ALLISON BLAKELY (2005)

HUNTER-GAULT, CHARLAYNE

FEBRUARY 27, 1942

As the creator and chief of the Harlem bureau of the *New York Times* in the late 1960s, journalist Charlayne Hunter-Gault sought to move media coverage of African Americans away from stereotypes to in-depth, realistic, and accurate stories. Born in Due West, South Carolina, Hunter-Gault became the first black woman admitted to the University of Georgia, graduating in 1963 with a degree in journalism. Her career has included work with *The New Yorker* magazine, NBC News in Washington, D.C., and PBS's *MacNeil/Lehrer Newshour.* Hunter-Gault has also taught at the Columbia University School of Journalism. Her distinguished career has brought her a number of important honors: She has won two Emmy Awards, for national news and documentary film; was named the Journalist of the Year in 1986 by the National Association of Black Journalists; and was the 1986 recipient of the George Foster Peabody award. In 1992 she published her autobiography, *In My Place.* In 1999, Hunter-Gault became the Johannesburg Bureau Chief for CNN South Africa, where she continues to create award-winning reports about African people, society, culture, and politics.

See also Journalism

■ ■ *Bibliography*

Fraser, C. Gerald. "Charlayne Hunter-Gault: From Frontline to Firing Line." *Essence* 17 (March 1987): 40–42, 110.

Hunter-Gault, Charlayne. *In My Place.* New York: Farrar, Straus and Giroux, 1992.

Lanker, Brian. *I Dream a World: Portraits of Black Women Who Changed the World.* New York: Stewart, Tabori & Chang, 1989.

Trillin, Calvin. *An Education in Georgia: Charlayne Hunter, Hamilton Holmes, and the Intergration of the University of Georgia.* Athens: University of Georgia Press, 1991.

JUDITH WEISENFELD (1996)
Updated by publisher 2005

HUNTON, WILLIAM ALPHAEUS, JR.

SEPTEMBER 18, 1903
JANUARY 13, 1970

Political activist and educator William Alphaeus Hunton Jr., was born in Atlanta, Georgia. After the Atlanta race riot of 1906 Hunton's parents, William Hunton Sr., and Addie Waites Hunton, moved the family to Brooklyn, New York. He received his B.A. from Howard University in 1924. Two years later, Hunton graduated from Harvard University with an M.A. in English and accepted a position as an assistant professor in Howard's English department.

Hunton taught at Howard for over fifteen years, earning a Ph.D. from New York University in 1938 in the process. As a member of Howard's faculty, Hunton participated in the general intellectual activism prevalent at Howard during this period. He was a member of the national executive board of the National Negro Congress (NNC) and remained involved even after the moderates left the NNC and the organization was increasingly dominated by the Communist Party. Thereafter, Hunton was closely associated with the public positions of the party. In 1941 the House Committee on Un-American Activities (HUAC), a congressional committee investigating supposed subversive behavior, accused Hunton of Communist Party membership. After leaving Howard in 1943, Hunton moved to New York City, got married, and became the director of education for the Council on African Affairs (CAA).

While with the council, Hunton prepared and wrote pamphlets, produced news releases, and lobbied international organizations on African issues. In the late 1940s he was active in lobbying the United Nations to prohibit South Africa from annexing South West Africa (now Namibia); he also protested the visit of South African prime minister Jan Smuts to the United States in 1946. Other South African campaigns included an attempt to improve conditions for black South African mineworkers.

In 1951 Hunton and other leftists formed the Civil Rights Bail Fund, which provided bail for those unwilling to give names to HUAC. After refusing himself to provide the names of contributors to the fund, Hunton was sentenced to six months in jail for contempt of court in July 1951. In 1953 the federal government, citing the CAA's aid to the African National Congress and its ongoing ties to the Communist Party, ordered the council to register as a subversive organization. Continued harassment led Hunton to disband the CAA two years later.

Despite the closing of CAA, Hunton remained interested in African affairs, and in 1957 he published *Decision in Africa: Sources of Current Conflict.* Late the following year he attended the All African People's Conference in Ghana and did not return to the United States until August 1959, after extensive tours of Africa, Europe, and his first of many trips to the Soviet Union. In May 1960 Hunton and his wife moved to Conakry, Guinea, where he taught English in a lycée. After less than two years, the Huntons moved to Accra, Ghana, at the behest of W. E. B. Du Bois, who required Hunton's aid with his *Encyclopedia Africana* project. Du Bois died in 1963 before the project was complete. Hunton and his wife were deported after Kwamé Nkrumah's government fell during a military coup in 1966. After briefly returning to the United States, the Huntons settled in Lusaka, Zambia, in 1967. He lived there until his death from cancer in early 1970.

See also Atlanta Riot of 1906; Intellectual Life

■■ *Bibliography*

Hunton, Dorothy. *Alphaeus Hunton: The Unsung Valiant.* New York: Eppress Speed Print, Inc., 1986.

Hunton, William Alphaeus, Jr. *Decision in Africa: Sources of Current Conflict.* New York: International Publishers, 1957.

Von Eschen, Penny. *Race Against Empire: Black Americans and Anticolonialism, 1937–1957.* Ithaca, N.Y.: Cornell University Press, 1997.

JOHN C. STONER (1996)
Updated bibliography

HURSTON, ZORA NEALE

JANUARY 7, 1891
JANUARY 28, 1960

The folklorist Zora Neale Hurston was born in Notasulga, Alabama, and grew up in Eatonville, Florida, the first black incorporated town in America. For reasons that remain unknown, she claimed 1901 as the date of her birth, increasing the mystery and complexity of the woman who in the 1930s produced the single most significant novel on the nature of black female identity in the group's journey from slavery to freedom. Her father, a carpenter and Baptist preacher and a signer of Eatonville's charter, was elected mayor for three terms in succession. Her mother, formerly a country schoolteacher, taught Sunday school but spent most of her time raising her eight children. In Ea-

Zora Neale Hurston. *The novelist and anthropologist is seen here during her period of greatest productivity, the late 1930s and early 1940s, when she wrote* Mules and Men, Their Eyes Were Watching God, *and* Dust Tracks on a Road. THE LIBRARY OF CONGRESS

tonville, unlike in most of the South at the turn of the century, African Americans were not demoralized by the constant bombardment of poverty and racial hatred, and Hurston grew up surrounded by a vibrant and creative secular and religious black culture. There she first learned the dialect, songs, folktales, and superstitions that are at the center of her works. Her stories focus on the lives and relationships among black people within their communities.

HARLEM RENAISSANCE

The death of Hurston's mother in 1904 disrupted her economically and emotionally stable home life, and a year later, at fourteen, she left home to take a job as a maid and wardrobe assistant in a traveling Gilbert and Sullivan company. She separated from the company in Baltimore, found other work, and attended high school there. In 1918 she graduated from Morgan Academy, the high school division of Morgan State University, and entered Howard

University in Washington, D.C., where she took courses intermittently until 1924. The poet Georgia Douglas Johnson and the philosopher Alain Locke were two of her teachers. Her first story, "John Redding Goes to Sea" (1921), appeared in *Stylus,* Howard's literary magazine.

Hurston arrived in New York in 1925, at the height of the Harlem Renaissance. She soon became an active part of the group of painters, musicians, sculptors, entertainers, and writers who came from across the country to participate in Harlem's unprecedented flowering of black arts. She also studied at Barnard College under anthropologist Franz Boas and graduated with a B.A. in 1928. Between 1929 and 1931, with support from a wealthy white patron, Mrs. Osgood Mason, Hurston returned to the South and began collecting folklore in Florida and Alabama. In 1934 she received a Rosenwald Fellowship and in 1936 and 1937 received Guggenheim Fellowships that enabled her to study folk religions in Haiti and Jamaica. She was a member of the American Folklore Society, the Anthropological Society, the Ethnological Society, the New York Academy of Sciences, and the American Association for the Advancement of Science. Based on her extensive research, Hurston published *Mules and Men* (1935), the first collection (seventy folktales) of black folklore published by an African American. A second volume, *Tell My Horse* (1938), came out of a two-month stay in Haiti and contains a poetic account of Haitian history, political analyses of contemporary events in the region, and a vivid and exciting section on Vodou as a sophisticated religion of creation and life. Her most academic study, *The Florida Negro* (1938), written for the Florida Federal Workers Project, was never published.

Franz Boas and Mrs. Mason stimulated Hurston's anthropological interests—interests that gave her an analytical perspective on black culture that was unique among black writers of her time—but she was also fully vested in the creative life of the cultural movement around her. Her close friends included Carl Van Vechten, Locke, Langston Hughes, and Wallace Thurman, with whom she coedited and published the only issue of the journal *Fire!!* Appearing in November 1926, its supporters saw it as a forum for young writers who wanted to break with traditional black ideas. Coincidentally, *Fire!!* was destroyed by a fire in Thurman's apartment.

BODY OF WORK

Hurston's first novel, *Jonah's Gourd Vine* (1934), the story of a Baptist preacher with a personal weakness that leads to his unfortunate end, reveals the lyrical quality of her writing and her mastery of dialect. Her protagonist, modeled on her father, is a gifted poet/philosopher with an en-

> ## Zora Neale Hurston
>
> "What all my work shall be, I don't know either, every hour being a stranger to get as you live it. I want a busy life, a just mind and a timely death."
>
> DUST TRACKS ON A ROAD: AN AUTOBIOGRAPHY. PHILADELPHIA: J.B. LIPPINCOTT, 1942, P. 294.

viable imagination and speech filled with the imagery of black folk culture. He is also a vulnerable person who lacks the self-awareness to comprehend his dilemma.

For its beauty and richness of language, *Their Eyes Were Watching God* (1937) is Hurston's art at its best. Her most popular work, it traces the development of its heroine from innocence to the realization that she has the power to control her own life. An acknowledged classic since its recovery in the 1970s, it has been applauded by both black and white women scholars as the first black feminist novel. *Moses, Man of the Mountain* (1939), Hurston's third and most ambitious novel, makes of the biblical Israelite deliverance from Egypt an exploration of the black transition from slavery to freedom. Taking advantage of the pervasiveness of Moses mythology in African and diaspora folklore, Hurston removes Moses from scripture, demystifies him, and relocates him in African-American culture, where he is a conjure man possessed with magical powers and folk wisdom. The novel tells the story of a people struggling to liberate themselves from the heritage of bondage. In *Seraph on the Suwanee* (1948), Hurston's last and least successful work, she turns away from black folk culture to explore the lives of poor white southerners. The story revolves around a husband and wife trapped in conventional sexual roles in a marriage that dooms the wife's search for herself.

Dust Tracks on a Road (1942), Hurston's autobiography, is the most controversial of her books; even some of her staunchest admirers consider it a failure. Critics who complain about this work identify its shortcomings as its lack of self-revelation, the misleading personal information Hurston gives about herself, and the significant roles that whites play in the text. Other critics praise it as Hurston's attempt to invent a narrative self as an alternative to the black identity inherited from the slave narrative tradition. Poised between the black and white worlds, not as victim of either but as participant-observer in both, her narrative self in *Dust Tracks* presents positive and negative qualities from each. From this perspective, *Dust Tracks* is a revisionary text, a revolutionary alternative women's narrative inscribed into the discourse of black autobiography.

Reviews of Hurston's books in her time were mixed. White reviewers, often ignorant of black culture, praised the richness of her language but misunderstood the works and characterized them as simple and unpretentious. Black critics in the 1930s and 1940s, in journals like the *Crisis,* objected most to her focus on positive aspects of black folk life. Their most frequent criticism was the absence of racial terror, exploitation, and misery from her works. Richard Wright expressed anger at the "minstrel image" he claimed Hurston promoted in *Their Eyes Were Watching God.* None of her books sold well while she was alive, and throughout her lifetime she experienced extreme financial stress.

Hurston and her writings disappeared from public view from the late 1940s until the early 1970s. Interest in her revived after writer Alice Walker went to Florida "in search of Zora" in 1973 and reassembled the puzzle of Hurston's later life. Walker discovered that Hurston's final return to the South occurred in the 1950s when, still trying to write, she supported herself with menial jobs. Without resources and suffering from the effects of a stroke, in 1959 she entered a welfare home in Fort Pierce, Florida, where she died in 1960 and was buried in an unmarked grave. On Walker's pilgrimage, she marked a site where Hurston might be buried with a headstone that pays tribute to "a genius of the South." Following her rediscovery, the once-neglected Hurston rose into literary prominence and enjoys wide acclaim as the essential forerunner of black women writers who came after her.

See also Caribbean/North American Writers (Contemporary); Harlem Renaissance; Literary Magazines; Literature of the United States

■ ■ *Bibliography*

Gates, Henry Louis, Jr. and K. A. Appiah, eds. *Zora Neale Hurston: Critical Perspectives Past and Present.* New York: Amistad, 1993.

Hemenway, Robert E. *Zora Neale Hurston: A Literary Biography.* Urbana: University of Illinois Press, 1977.

Kaplan, Carla, ed. *Zora Neale Hurston: A Life in Letters.* New York: Doubleday, 2002.

Lowe, John. *Jump at the Sun: Zora Neale Hurston's Cosmic Comedy.* Urbana: University of Illinois Press, 1994.

Wall, Cheryl A. "Zora Neale Hurston: Changing Her Own Words." In *American Novelists Revisited: Essays in Feminist*

Criticism, edited by Fritz Fleischmann. Boston: G. K. Hall, 1982.

Wall, Cheryl A., ed. *Zora Neale Hurston's* Their Eyes Were Watching God: *A Casebook.* New York: Oxford University Press, 2000.

NELLIE Y. MCKAY (1996)
Updated bibliography

HUTSON, JEAN BLACKWELL

SEPTEMBER 7, 1914
FEBRUARY 4, 1998

Curator and later chief of the Schomburg Center for Research in Black Culture of the New York Public Library for thirty-two years, Hutson was responsible from 1948 to 1980 for developing the world's largest collection of materials by and about people of African descent. She also publicized the poor physical condition of the building in which Schomburg's rare materials were stored. The result was a new climate-controlled building, quadruple the size of the old, which opened in September 1980.

Jean Blackwell was born in Summerfield, Florida, to Paul and Sarah Blackwell. Her father was a farmer and produce merchant and her mother a teacher. From the age of four she lived in Baltimore, where she graduated from Douglass High School as valedictorian in 1931. After three years at the University of Michigan, she transferred to Barnard College, graduating in 1935. She received a master's degree in library service from Columbia University the following year, and in 1941 a teacher's certificate, also from Columbia. After twelve years of working at various branches of the New York Public Library, Blackwell came to the Schomburg Collection on a six-month assignment in 1948. She was married to Andy Razaf, the song lyricist, from 1939 to 1947, and to John Hutson, a library colleague, from 1952 until his death in 1957. She stayed until 1980, when she was named assistant director of collection management and development for black culture for the research libraries. She retired in February 1984.

Hutson lectured on black history at New York's City College from 1962 to 1971. Invited by Kwame Nkrumah, Ghana's president, she was at the University of Ghana from 1964 to 1965 to help build their African collection. She held memberships in the American Library Association, the NAACP, the Urban League, and Delta Sigma Theta sorority. She was a founder and first president of the Harlem Cultural Council. Among many awards, Hutson received an honorary doctorate from King Memorial College in Columbia, South Carolina, in 1977, and was one of the seventy-five women portrayed in the photographic exhibition "I Dream a World" in 1989. She was honored by Barnard College in 1990 and by Columbia University's School of Library Service in 1992. The State University of New York (SUNY) at Buffalo offers a library residency program named for her. On January 28, 1995, at Hutson's eightieth birthday celebration, the Schomburg Center named the main reading room for her to recognize her contribution.

See also Archival Collections; Schomburg, Arthur

■ ■ *Bibliography*

Jean Blackwell Hutson: An Appreciation. New York: Schomburg Center for Research in Black Culture, 1984.

Smith, Dinitia. "Jean Hutson, Schomburg Chief, Dies at 83." *New York Times* (February 7, 1998): B18.

BETTY KAPLAN GUBERT (1996)
Updated by author 2005

IDENTITY AND RACE IN THE UNITED STATES

Personal identities are created through individuals' interactions with their social and material worlds. This view of identity suggests that individuals neither rely solely on their own resources nor simply succumb to definitions imposed on them by others to make sense of whom they are. Identity, or the processes of defining one's self in a world where others are doing the same, is a complex, interactive dynamic that involves the interplay of psychological (internal) and social (external) forces. In addition, in a world that is characterized by unequal power relationships, the question of identity is an inherently political one. This is especially true in the United States, where questions of identity are thoroughly implicated in America's culture wars and in what it means to be a respectable member of society.

In addition, matters of race have always been central to what it means to be American. That this process is subject to negotiation is perhaps best illustrated in James Baldwin's 1985 essay "The Price of the Ticket." The "ticket," according to Baldwin, is the granting of rights and privileges by which we define what it means to be a citizen of the United States; the "price" is to become "white," a decision that entails sacrificing any cultural markers that designate one as different from the mainstream of society. From this perspective, the question of race and identity in America, on the one hand, is a matter of assimilation. On the other hand, the question of race and identity concerns the possibility of challenging the cost of admission to mainstream society, or altering the terms of what Baldwin calls the "dimwitted ambition [that] has choked many a human being to death here" (1985, p. xx). Whatever the case, the psychological, social, material, and political dimensions that shape race and identity in America are brought into particular relief when viewed through the lens of black history and life in the United States.

AFRICANS IN ANTEBELLUM AMERICA

There is general agreement among historians that approximately ten million African captives were brought to the Americas between the sixteenth and the mid-nineteenth century. The first Africans brought to North America were members of agrarian polities of West and West Central Africa. Africans from the more organized states with central governments and armies were also among the initial wave of captives, but, being more elusive, they were captured in fewer numbers. After the legislative end of America's participation in the slave trade in 1808, Africans were still illegally brought to the United States until the 1850s. Later captives were largely "unseasoned" Africans who were imported mainly from Central Africa directly to the southern regions of the United States.

Societal perceptions of Africans in America changed during the 1700s from a multiform population of "different" people to a uniform population of "inferior" people. This change was spurred by shifting demographics in the New World and by the desire of the elites to maintain social order in ways that served their interests. Order was established through the creation of a racial social hierarchy that was enacted through interrelated political, economic, and cultural processes. Politically, legislators passed laws that denied black people en masse basic rights and privileges accorded to most white Americans. Economically, black people were denied the right to own property, even to the extent that it meant control over their own bodies. Culturally, governmental, religious, and literary institutions converged to produce widespread imagery that shaped popular views of black people as essentially inferior to white people and as deserving of their political disenfranchisement and economic subordination. These societal views of black people were reinforced during the late nineteenth century as academic disciplines became professionalized and university-trained experts disseminated "scientific" knowledge that only reinforced extant imagery that depicted people of African descent as inferior.

Of course, black people themselves always have had a say about whom they were and forged identities to combat social prescriptions from a myriad of resources they had at their disposal. Some of these resources originated in the autochthonous African cultures from which they were removed and which they offered as the distinctive lore of black culture that was transmitted to each generation of New World Africans. Black people also tapped into the cultures of the Americas, those of European ethnic populations as well as those of indigenous populations, to make sense of who they were. In short, captive Africans forged a range of colonial and antebellum black identities. For example, in a 1792 letter to Thomas Jefferson, then secretary of state, the celebrated mathematician Benjamin Banneker wrote, "Sir, I freely and cheerfully acknowledge, that I am of the African race, and in that color which is natural to them of the deepest dye" (Aptheker, 1990, p. 24). The grandson of a former indentured white female servant and a manumitted slave of African nobility, Banneker chided Jefferson for his failure to extend liberty to the masses of the enslaved Africans in his midst. Or, consider George Bentley. In 1859 a Tennessee newspaper writes that Bentley, a slave, was "black as the ace of spades"

and a "preacher in charge" of a large congregation comprised almost exclusively of slaveholders. In contrast to the ideology espoused by Banneker some seven decades earlier, Bentley was an enslaved southern proslavery parson who refused to allow the church he led to purchase him from his master's family.

The elegies of eighteenth-century poet Phillis Wheatley and the slave narratives of captive women such as Harriet Jacobs and Elizabeth Keckley further extend and complicate questions of race and identity among Americans of African descent in colonial and antebellum America. In addition, clandestine antislavery activities among captive and free Africans during the same periods, black religious and social organizations of the late eighteenth century, and the network of African Free Schools of the late-1800s also provided resources for black people to establish a wider range of identities than those imposed on them by the broader society. The means and capacity for black people to speak for themselves notwithstanding, their almost absolute political and economic subordination prior to Emancipation, prevented them from altering their dominant social identities as a uniform class of inferior human beings.

BLACK IDENTITY AND DOUBLE CONSCIOUSNESS

The Souls of Black Folk by W. E. B. Du Bois, written at the turn of the twentieth century, remains the most influential work to engage both the dominant scholarship on and popular notions about black identity. Du Bois's notion of black identity is captured in the widely quoted passage from the 1903 classic:

> After the Egyptian and Indian, the Greek and Roman, the Teuton and Mongolian, the Negro is a sort of seventh son, born with a veil, and gifted with second-sight in this American world—a world which yields him no true consciousness, but only lets him see himself through the revelation of the world. It is a peculiar sensation, this double-consciousness, this sense of always looking at the self through the eyes of others, of measuring one's soul by the tape of a world that looks on in amused contempt and pity. One ever feels his twoness—an American, a Negro; two souls, two thoughts, two unreconciled strivings; two warring ideals in one dark body, whose dogged strength alone keeps it from being torn asunder.
>
> The history of the American Negro is the history of this strife—this longing to attain self-conscious humanhood, to merge this double self into a better and truer self. (Du Bois, 1903, p. 3)

In Du Bois's conception of identity, American culture and Negro, or black, culture represent two distinct and irreconcilable spheres of life. This notion is not a novel idea, however. Scholars point to the strong influence of the philosophical ideas of romanticism and of the concepts of early American psychology on Du Bois's formulation of double-consciousness. Scholars such as Hazel Carby also argue that Du Bois's intellectual formulations were restricted by his uncritical commitment to social norms that privileged both the perspectives of white men and the culture of the white upper-middle class. Though such commitments manifested at times in Du Bois's disparaging view of women and black folk culture, the influence of his work on black-identity scholarship in all fields representing the humanities and social sciences is nonetheless remarkable. The Du Boisian conundrum that characterizes what it means to be black in America is evident in diverse contributions, such as Ralph Ellison's novel *Invisible Man* (1952), E. Franklin Frazier's sociology, and Kenneth and Mamie Clark's psychology. Du Bois's notion of double-consciousness also shaped public life, as was evident in the U.S. Supreme Court's consideration of the Clarks' social scientific research in its 1954 landmark ruling in *Brown v. Board of Education*.

Of course, Du Bois's conception of identity did not go uncontested by contemporaneous scholars and social movements. For example, social and cultural black nationalist movements from 1900 to 1950, such as the Harlem Renaissance, the Universal Negro Improvement Association, and the Nation of Islam, complicated popular notions of identity shaped by the influence of Du Bois. In addition, such individuals as anthropologist Zora Neale Hurston and linguist Lorenzo Dow Turner produced scholarship that demonstrated the essential role of distinct black cultures, even those that originated in Africa, in the formation of African-American identity. These and other cultural influences allowed black women, for instance, to carve out the psychic space for what Darlene Clark Hine called the development of a new, but unheralded, collective black women's oppositional consciousness that was appropriate in the era of Jim Crow.

IDENTITY AND BLACK POWER

The black social movements of the first half of the twentieth century paved the way for those movements of the 1960s and 1970s that provided an even greater challenge to dominant characterizations of black identity in the United States. Of course, the 1954 Supreme Court ruling was significant along these lines, contributing to the increase in the number of black students at white universities and colleges by the late 1960s. However, black students did not simply gain access to these institutions. Once there, they also challenged normative assumptions about society, including those about race and identity in America. Such a challenge necessarily entailed an examination of what it meant to be white. In his famous 1963 essay "A Talk to Teachers," James Baldwin brought into bold relief the relational character of identity and how the assertion of black identities necessarily called into question the nature of white identities. According to Baldwin, "So where we are now is that a whole country of people believe that I'm a 'nigger' and I *don't*, and the battle's on! Because if I am not what I've been told I am, then it means that *you're* not what *you* thought you were *either!* And that is the crisis" (Baldwin, 1985, p. 329). In ideological terms, students attended more to matters of self-definition and self-determination than to those of integration. The pressures that these students exerted on their institutions eventually resulted in the eruption of black studies programs at predominately white colleges and universities across the country, beginning with San Francisco State University in 1968 and many others, including Harvard, Yale, and Ohio State, in 1969.

Significantly, in the 1970s William E. Cross began to develop his theory of *nigrescence*, or of "becoming black," to explain the development of identity among black college students. This theory, which enjoys great currency among contemporary researchers, educators, and counselors, charts the movement of individuals through five to six stages of ideological metamorphosis. These stages of identity development generally occur across three major levels of awareness or cognitive organization: *pre-encounter, encounter,* and *post-encounter*. During the pre-encounter stage, societal values and conceptions of what it means to be black dominate an individual's sense of self. Movement onto a subsequent level occurs when individuals encounter an event or events that compel them to confront questions of race in society. This stage describes a transitional period in which individuals may reassert their identification with the dominant white culture or resort to uncritically accepting things associated with black culture and repudiating institutions and values associated with the white culture. Some individuals remain in the stages of the encounter level, while others move on to a post-encounter level. Here, individuals come to terms with black culture in ways that do not necessarily entail the rejection of white culture. In addition, persons on the post-encounter level are less reactionary and generally refocus their energy from wanton aggression toward groups and individuals that they perceive to be different to directed anger against racist and oppressive groups and institutions.

Scholars such as Darlene Clark Hine, Paula Giddings, Elizabeth Higginbotham, and others demonstrate in their respective works that most models of identity produced in the wake of the Black Power movement, such as Cross's, typically equated the experiences of black males with the experiences of black people. They argue that, consequently, these models imposed yet another restrictive social identity on African Americans, especially black women. In contrast to its typical treatment in history, psychology, black cultural studies, and popular culture, identity, according to some writers, is shaped by the "intersecting" or "interlocking" experiences of race, gender, class, and sexuality in the everyday lives of individuals. For instance, the social and material processes that shape the identities of black women are likely to be qualitatively different from those that shape the identities of black men. In addition, the various aspects of one's social location, or "positionality," may contribute to one's identification with ideas, beliefs, goals, attitudes, or opinions shaped by different and, in some instances, even conflicting, ideological systems. For example, it is conceivable that during the high-profile O. J. Simpson trials of the mid-1990s, a black woman could simultaneously identify with the defendant, a black male, based on shared experiences around racial injustice, and empathize with the victim, a white woman, based on shared experiences around domestic violence.

Some writers, such as Higginbotham, point to similar restrictions placed on the identities of black women in women's studies programs that are rooted in the discipline's almost exclusive focus on gender relations as a source of oppression. Other writers, such as Audre Lorde and E. Frances White, point to the heterosexism of dominant notions of black identities and the concomitant erasure of gay and lesbian experiences in the scholarship. Similarly, filmmaker Marlon Riggs confronted the identification of blackness with a hypermasculinity born of the 1960s Black Power movement in *Black Is. . .Black Ain't* (1994). Finally, White critiqued identity models born of these movements and points to respectability—that is, the conventions that regulate sexual norms in Western Europe and the United States—as undermining the capacity of these movements and the scholarly traditions they inform to embrace the full range of identities that constitute black humanity.

MULTIRACIAL IDENTITIES IN THE TWENTY-FIRST CENTURY

The idea of race and identity in America is further complicated by the fact that nature knows no color lines, which has resulted in the creation of an African-American population whom the award-winning journalist and writer Itabari Njeri calls the "New World Black." Njeri believes that all African Americans with nonblack ancestry, especially

white, should own up to and embrace their diverse heritage. In her view, since this implicates the vast majority of black people in the western hemisphere, such a move would normalize what African Americans often construe as exotic within their communities (e.g., offspring of interracial unions) and would put an end to what she calls "the official silence on America's historically miscegenated identity" (1993, p. 38). Certainly, most Americans of African descent recognize their diverse racial lineage, or at least have some sense of the possibility of it. However, at the same time they may be loathe to identify themselves as other than black or African American. That many black people do not socially identify with the multiple aspects of their racial or ethnic heritage may be attributable to any number of reasons. For instance, some argue that to do so is meaningless in a world of fixed categories in which the one-drop rule is in full effect.

As evidence of this, they might point to golfing sensation Eldrick "Tiger" Woods and his run at the 1997 Masters Tournament at Augusta National Golf Club in Augusta, Georgia. During the media fanfare surrounding the event, Woods consistently pointed out to journalists that he was both black and Asian, owing to the respective backgrounds of his father and mother. However, as Woods approached the final rounds en route to a record victory at this major professional golf tournament, the media typically pointed to his significance as the first African American to win such an event and rarely, if ever, acknowledged his Asian ancestry or multiracial heritage. Perhaps the most memorable incident that reified the media's treatment of Woods's race occurred when fellow golfer Fuzzy Zoeller commented on the phenom's impending victory. Addressing the media throng at the end of his own thirty-fourth-place run at the title, Zoeller made the following remarks about the eventual Masters champion: "That little boy is driving well and he's putting well. He's doing everything it takes to win. So, you know what you guys do when he gets in here? You pat him on the back and say congratulations and enjoy it and tell him not to serve fried chicken next year. Got it? Or collard greens or whatever the hell they serve" (Cable Network News, 1997). In addition to pointing to the intransigent nature of race and identity in America, as evident in the accounts of the media's and Zoeller's behavior toward Woods, black individuals might point out that their nonblack ancestors are too remote in their lineage to identify them with any precision. Or, in the event that such ancestors could be identified, with rare exception, the relationships are such as to render them socially and culturally meaningless in contemporary society.

A related matter concerns other black individuals who challenge normative assumptions about race. These are black persons who are presumptively white; that is, black people who, because of their physical characteristics, are assumed to be white on first meeting them. In such instances, the black self-identities of such individuals may be dramatically inconsistent with the white identities that others, black and nonblack alike, reflexively and inflexibly impose on them. Challenging normative assumptions about race has profound psychological, social, and political implications, as brought into bold relief in James Weldon Johnson's classic *The Autobiography of an Ex-Coloured Man* (1912), the equally memorable Douglas Sirk film *Imitation of Life* (1959), and the landmark 1896 *Plessy v. Ferguson* Supreme Court ruling that established as federal policy "separate but equal." Kathe Sandler's film documentary *A Question of Color* (1992) and the autobiographies *Black Notebooks* (1997) by Toi Derricotte and *Life on the Color Line* (1995) by Gregory Williams provide examples of this phenomenon in contemporary American society. That some of the individuals in the aforementioned examples, as well as in society in general, deny their black heritage and "pass" for white highlights the fact that race and identity in America also involve some element of choice. In a related vein, Creoles of Louisiana comprise a mixed-heritage "black" population that challenges normative assumptions about race. Although the use of Creole among African Americans fell from common usage after the Louisiana Purchase (1803), it was revived after the Civil War, when former free blacks sought to distinguish themselves from emancipated slaves, and the term is still used as a marker of racial hybrid identity in contemporary society.

It is clear that the masses of black people have always acknowledged the fluid sexual boundaries that have resulted in a sizable mixed-race population within the race. Since the late 1980s, however, a growing multiracial social movement has become more vocal along these lines and has given voice to the non-Creole black population of mixed racial heritage. Proponents of contemporary multiracial social movements, such as the Association of Multiethnic Americans and the Multiracial Category Movement, advocate on behalf of persons born of interracial unions and those who self-identify as either biracial or multiracial. In addition, they advocate federal recognition of multiracial categories, arguing that the racial and ethnic makeup of the country has changed considerably since 1977 when the United States Office of Management and Budget (OMB) authorized Statistical Policy Directive Number 15. Directive 15 established the standards for the four racial categories that have since become commonplace in the United States: American Indian or Alaskan Native, Asian or Pacific Islander, Black, and White. In addition, the directive established two categories of ethnicity: Hispanic origin and Not of Hispanic origin.

The multiracial social movement was given a boost in 1997 when, following his victory at the Masters Tournament and in the wake of the Fuzzy Zoeller fiasco, Tiger Woods and his father appeared on *The Oprah Winfrey Show*. During the taped session, Winfrey asked Woods and his father about their views on the racial significance that the media had attached to the tournament. Woods replied by expressing dismay with the media's insistence on labeling him simply as African American, noting that he was black, Thai, Chinese, white, and American Indian. He also recalled that, as a child, in an effort to capture his rich heritage when identifying himself, he created a new label. Elaborating on this point, Woods stated: "Growing up, I came up with this name. I'm a 'Cablinasian.'" Members and sympathizers of multiracial social movements, including lawmakers, seized on Woods's comments in support of their advocacy to change the 2000 U.S. census to reflect the changing demographics of America. However, some civil rights organizations, such as the NAACP, argued that the myriad combinations resulting from the new categories could dilute estimates of historically protected racial populations. Not only would underestimation of these populations result in the loss of their political clout, opponents of changes to the census argued that new formulas could also curtail the enforcement of civil rights laws and the allocation of funding for such governmental programs as health care, education, and public transportation in ways that would disproportionately burden black people, other people of color, and the poor.

In response to growing criticism of its 1977 standards, in 1997 the OMB initiated a review of Directive 15 and in October of that year announced revised measures for collecting federal data on race and ethnicity. The minimum categories for race as of 2005 were: American Indian or Alaska Native; Asian; Black or African American; Native Hawaiian or Other Pacific Islander; and White. The 2000 census also included a sixth racial category: Some Other Race. The two minimum categories for ethnicity remained intact: Hispanic or Latino and Not Hispanic or Latino. Also, instead of allowing a multiracial category, as was originally suggested in public and congressional hearings, the OMB began to allow respondents to select one or more races when they self-identify.

Despite the public rhetoric and legislative activity that contributed to the revision of OMB Directive 15, the multiracial population counted in the 2000 census was relatively small—only 6.8 million people or slightly more than 2 percent of the total population. This group included a considerable number of Latinos; in fact, 2.2 million Latinos selected more than one box—nearly one-third of the 6.8 million who selected two or more races. This is not unusual, as "Hispanic" or "Latino" represents an ethnic category on the census and historically those who have identified with this group also have chosen additional categories to qualify their ethnic identities in accordance with their diverse racial identities as Mexican-American, Cuban-American, Dominican, or Puerto Rican, to name several.

CONCLUSION

As indicated in the introduction, matters of race and identity have always been central to what it means to be American. Further, these matters are thoroughly imbricated with psychological, social, and material significance. Given the power dimensions that inhere in the ways identities are created and re-created, these matters have always been contested, with the battle occurring largely on cultural fronts. It is notable, then, that nearly 97 percent of those who checked more than one box in the 2000 census identified themselves at least partially as white, such as white and American Indian, white and Asian, white and black, and white and other. The significance of these choices remains to be seen. However, they do raise important questions about the character that race and identity will assume in twenty-first-century America: Do such decisions augur badly for a nation of Americans still willing to pay the price of the ticket? Or, do they point to democratic possibilities in which difference is embraced as a norm in the new millennium?

See also Afrocentrism; Black Power Movement; Civil Rights Movement, U.S.; Folklore; Masculinity; Migration; Race, Scientific Theories of; Social Psychology, Psychologists, and Race

■ ■ *Bibliography*

Aptheker, Herbert, ed. *A Documentary History of the Negro People in the United States, vol. 1: From Colonial Times through the Civil War.* New York: Citadel, 1951–1994.

Baker, Lee D. *From Savage to Negro: Anthropology and the Construction of Race, 1896–1954.* Berkeley and London: University of California Press, 1998.

Baldwin, James. *The Price of the Ticket: Collected Nonfiction 1948–1985.* New York: St. Martin's/Marek, 1985.

Blassingame, John W. *The Slave Community: Plantation Life in the Antebellum South.* New York and Oxford: Oxford University Press, 1979.

Cable Network News. "Golfer Says Comments about Woods 'Misconstrued'." (April 21, 1997): video interview is available at <http://www.cnn.com/us/9704/21/fuzzy>.

Carby, Hazel. *Race Men: The W. E. B. Du Bois Lectures.* Cambridge: Harvard University Press, 1998.

Cross, William E. *Shades of Black: Diversity In African-American Identity.* Philadelphia: Temple University Press, 1991.

Derricotte, Toi. *The Black Notebooks: An Interior Journey.* New York: Norton, 1997.

Du Bois, W. E. B. *The Souls of Black Folk.* New York, 1903. Reprint. New York: Bantam Books, 1989.

Early, Gerald, ed., *Lure and Loathing: Essays on Race, Identity, and the Ambivalence of Assimilation.* New York: Allen Lane, Penguin Press, 1993.

Ellison, Ralph. *Invisible Man.* New York: Random House, 1952.

Higginbotham, Elizabeth. *Too Much to Ask: Black Women in the Era of Integration.* Chapel Hill: University of North Carolina Press, 2001.

Hine, Darlene Clark. "'In the Kingdom of Culture': Black Women and the Intersection of Race, Gender, and Class. In *Lure and Loathing: Essays on Race, Identity, and the Ambivalence of Assimilation,* edited by Gerald Early. New York: Allen Lane, Penguin Press, 1993.

Johnson, James Weldon. *The Autobiography of an Ex-Coloured Man* (1912). New York: Vintage, 1989.

Njeri, Itabari. "Sushi and Grits: Ethnic Identity and Conflict in a Newly Multicultural America." In *Lure and Loathing: Essays on Race, Identity, and the Ambivalence of Assimilation,* edited by Gerald Early. New York: Allen Lane, Penguin Press, 1993.

Njeri, Itabari. *The Last Plantation: Color, Conflict, and Identity: Reflections of a New World Black.* Boston and New York: Houghton Mifflin Company, 1997.

Williams, Gregory Howard. *Life on the Color Line: The True Story of a White Boy Who Discovered He Was Black.* New York: Dutton, 1995.

GARRETT ALBERT DUNCAN (2005)

IMMIGRATION

See Migration

INDIAN, AMERICAN

See Black-Indian Relations

INNIS, ROY
JUNE 6, 1934

Civil rights activist Roy Emile Alfredo Innis was born in St. Croix, U.S. Virgin Islands, and moved to New York City with his mother in 1946. He served in the army for two years during the Korean War and attended the City College of New York from 1952 to 1956, majoring in

chemistry. He worked as a chemist at Montefiore Hospital in New York City. In 1963, Innis joined the Harlem chapter of the Congress of Racial Equality (CORE), an interracial civil rights organization committed to nonviolent direct action. In 1964 he became chairman of the chapter's education committee. He advocated community control of public schools as an essential first step toward black self-determination. He was elected chapter chairman the following year and proposed an amendment to the New York State constitution that would provide an independent school board for Harlem. In 1967 he was one of the founders of the Harlem Commonwealth Council, an organization committed to supporting black-owned businesses in Harlem. He served as the organization's first executive director.

Innis became one of the leading advocates of black nationalism and Black Power within CORE, and in 1968 he was elected CORE's national director. He took control of the organization during a period in which its influence and vitality were declining. Under his leadership, which was characterized by tight centralization of organizational activities and vocal advocacy of black capitalism and separatism, CORE's mass base further declined. Despite this fact, Innis remained in the public eye.

Innis popularized his ideas as coeditor of the *Manhattan Tribune*—a weekly newspaper focusing on Harlem and the Upper West Side—which he founded with white journalist William Haddad in 1968. Later that year he promoted a Community Self-Determination bill, which was presented before Congress. He received national attention in 1973 when he debated Nobel Prize–winning physicist William Shockley on the issue of black genetic inferiority on NBC's late-night *Tomorrow Show*.

In 1980, after former CORE members led by James Farmer mounted an unsuccessful effort to wrest control of the organization from Innis, he consolidated his hold over the organization by becoming national chairman. By this time Innis's polemical oratory, his argument that societal racism had largely abated, and his support of Republican candidates placed him in the vanguard of black conservatism. In 1987 he received much notoriety for his support for Bernhard Goetz, a white man who shot black alleged muggers on a New York subway, and his championing of Robert Bork, a controversial U.S. Supreme Court nominee who had opposed the Civil Rights Act of 1965.

Innis entered the political arena in 1986 when he unsuccessfully ran for Congress from Brooklyn as a Democrat. In the 1993 Democratic primary, he unsuccessfully challenged David Dinkins, the first African-American mayor of New York City, and he then became a vocal supporter of Dinkins's Republican challenger, Rudolph Giuli-

ani, who won the election. In 1994 Innis celebrated his twenty-fifth year of leadership of CORE. Innis has remained active, traveling to Nigeria from 1996 to 1998 to monitor elections.

See also Black Power Movement; Civil Rights Movement, U.S.; Congress of Racial Equality (CORE); Dinkins, David; Farmer, James

■ ■ *Bibliography*

Jones, Charles. "From Protest to Black Conservatism: The Demise of the Congress of Racial Equality." In *Black Political Organizations in the Post-Civil Rights Era*, edited by Ollie A. Johnson III and Karin L. Stanford. New Brunswick, N.J.: Rutgers University Press, 2002.

Meier, August, and Elliott Rudwick. *CORE: A Study in the Civil Rights Movement, 1948–1968*. New York: Oxford University Press, 1973.

Van Deburg, William. *New Day in Babylon: The Black Power Movement and American Culture, 1965–1975*. Chicago: University of Chicago Press, 1992.

ROBYN SPENCER (1996)
Updated by author 2005

INSTITUTE OF THE BLACK WORLD

❚ ❚ ❚

A research institute in black studies, located in Atlanta, the Institute of the Black World was originally a project of the Martin Luther King Jr. Center for Nonviolent Social Change. In 1969 the institute became an independent organization. Committed to scholarly engagement in social and political analysis and advocacy, the institute sought to foster racial equality as well as African-American self-determination and self-understanding. It placed particular emphasis on exploring the role of education in the African-American movement for social change. In the 1990s, under the leadership of historian Vincent Harding, the institute conducted research, trained scholars, organized conferences and lectures, and issued publications, as well as produced radio programs, a taped lecture series, and other audiovisual materials. It also encouraged black artists and developed teaching materials for black children. One of its projects was the Black Policy Studies Center. The institute was located in a house where W. E. B. Du Bois once lived.

See also Black Studies

DANIEL SOYER (1996)

INSURANCE COMPANIES

Historically, African-American-owned insurance companies have their roots in the numerous fraternal orders and mutual aid societies that existed in the early history of the United States. These societies were formed among free blacks to provide security during times of hardship. African Americans banded together to care for the sick, widowed, and orphaned, and to administer burial rites. In 1780 free blacks formed the African Free Society in Newport, Rhode Island, to care for indigent members of their community. Seven years later Richard Allen and Absalom Jones formed the Free African Society of Philadelphia, which operated under a formal constitution. Members paid one shilling monthly. Mutual aid societies also existed in the South. In 1790 free mulattoes in Charleston, South Carolina, organized the Brown Fellowship Society, which, aside from caring for widows and orphans, maintained a cemetery and credit union.

Often church related, these mutual aid societies were the only place to which blacks could turn for financial protection. Evidence of the need for such security was given by the fact that over a hundred such societies existed in Philadelphia alone in 1849. Premiums ranged from about $.25 to $.35 and benefits from $1.50 to $3 per week for sickness, $10 to $20 for death.

The late nineteenth and early twentieth centuries witnessed the transformation of mutual and fraternal aid societies into modern insurance companies—though fraternal societies such as the Masons, the Knights of Pythias, and the Oddfellows would remain an important source of insurance among the African-American community until the 1930s. One of the most important African-American reformers was William Washington Browne, who in 1881 founded the Grand United Order of the True Reformers in Richmond, Virginia. Browne, a former slave and preacher, formed the True Reformers to promote "happiness, peace, plenty, thrift, and protection." The society became quite popular, reaching a membership in the 1890s of 100,000 people in eighteen states. Browne's reforms included using mortality tables—though based on crude statistics—to set premium rates. Like other successful black entrepreneurs, he used the income from his organization to found other businesses, including a bank, a hotel, a department store, and a newspaper.

A great number of insurance associations founded in the upper South during the late nineteenth century can be traced to former associates and employees of Browne. These include Samuel Wilson Rutherford, who founded the National Benefit Insurance Company of Washington, D.C., in 1898; Booker Lawrence Jordan, who helped to create the Southern Aid Society of Richmond in 1893; and John Merrick, who founded what became the North Carolina Mutual Life Insurance Company in 1898. Newer insurance companies lost the fraternal and ritualistic side of the earlier societies; they were, for the most part, state-chartered insurance corporations.

Another entrepreneur, Thomas Walker, brought similar innovations to mutual aid associations in the lower South. Walker, also a former slave and preacher, organized the Union Central Relief Association of Birmingham in 1894 (it had previously been known as the Afro-American Benevolent Association). Walker tied benefits to premiums and selected policyholders with care; he sent a stream of African-American agents traveling throughout the South to secure insurees.

These enterprises were formed at least in part out of expediency. Many white-owned insurance companies refused to insure blacks, whom they regarded as too high a risk. The reluctance of white companies to insure black lives was based in part on the widespread poverty and the higher mortality rate among blacks. Those that did sell insurance to African Americans usually offered them inferior policies. In 1881 the white-owned Prudential Insurance Company calculated a mortality rate among blacks that was 50 percent higher than that of whites. In turn, it offered policies to blacks that paid only one-third of the benefits whites received for the same premiums. Despite these policies, most black-owned firms had trouble competing with their larger white-owned counterparts, even among black insurees. Calls for support of black-owned businesses had only limited appeal. National white-owned firms appeared to offer a stability and security that black firms could not match. In 1928 the white-owned Metropolitan of New York had twenty times more insurance on African-American lives than the largest black-owned insurance company.

The difficulties of black insurers were magnified by the fact that, due to the relative poverty of their policyholders, they were forced to compete almost exclusively in the field of industrial insurance—a type of insurance in which insurees paid a small weekly premium of only a few cents and received a small return. Industrial insurance had been introduced in the United States by the white-owned firms The Provident and John Hancock in the 1870s. It was popular among working-class people who could not afford large annual premiums for term and whole life insurance; for blacks, industrial insurance was most often purchased to provide money for proper burial ceremonies. Industrial insurance incurred high operating costs, largely because agents had to make weekly trips to the homes of policyholders. This cost was made worse for black agents,

CHICAGO CONTAINS A FRACTION MORE THAN 1% OF THE NEGRO POPULATION OF AMERICA, AND ABOUT 4½% OF AMERICAN NEGRO WEALTH, ESTIMATING THE WEALTH OF THE NEGRO IN THE UNITED STATES AT TWO BILLION DOLLARS.

HOME OF "LIBERTY LIFE"

Home of Liberty Life Insurance Company, first Old Line Legal Reserve Insurance Company to be operated by Negroes in the North. Organized by Frank L. Gillespie; incorporated June 30th, 1919, under the laws of the State of Illinois; capital, $200,000.00; resources, $360,000.00. Branch offices are maintained in Illinois, Michigan, Kentucky, Missouri and Washington, D. C. "Liberty Life" owns its present home at 35th Street and Grand Blvd, and is contemplating a skyscraper improvement on the same site at a cost of $5,000,000.00.

Liberty Life Insurance Building, Chicago, c. 1925. Founded in 1919 by Frank L. Gillespie, Liberty Life was the first black-owned insurance company in the northern United States. GENERAL RESEARCH AND REFERENCE DIVISION, SCHOMBURG CENTER FOR RESEARCH IN BLACK CULTURE, THE NEW YORK PUBLIC LIBRARY, ASTOR, LENOX AND TILDEN FOUNDATIONS.

who, at the turn of the century, were forced to travel on Jim Crow cars and stay in out-of-the-way, unsanitary hotels.

Industrial insurance also lent itself to fraud and abuse, including especially forfeiture, whereby customers who missed two or more consecutive payments would lose their entire policies. Complaints about the improprieties of insurance companies—both industrial and ordinary—led to a series of investigations throughout the industry. The best known were the 1905 Armstrong investigations, which revealed malpractice, fraud, and mismanagement in the workings of New York State's (and the nation's) largest life insurance companies. The trials led to stricter regulation in many states, such as larger cash reserve requirements, which many black-owned companies found difficult to meet.

Given these new requirements, the higher costs of selling industrial insurance, and the lack of reliable data on black mortality, many black-owned firms were unsuccessful. A small number of black-owned insurance companies founded in the early twentieth century proved more enduring. These included North Carolina Mutual (1898) and Atlanta Life (1905). The North Carolina Mutual Life Insurance Company was founded in Durham, North Carolina, by John Merrick. Its agents worked strictly on commission and sold industrial insurance almost exclusively. It formed offices in surrounding cities—Chapel Hill, Hillsborough, Raleigh, Greensboro—and after five years of business had over 40,000 policyholders. North Carolina Mutual also began the practice of reinsuring financially distressed black-owned societies. This became particularly true when stricter state regulation of mutual-assessment organizations came about in the early twentieth century.

By 1907 it claimed, with some justification, to be the "Greatest Negro Insurance Company in the World."

One reason North Carolina Mutual was able to secure such business was the strength of its agency force. Charles Clinton Spaulding, who would later serve as president of North Carolina Mutual, was made general manager in charge of agents in 1900. He advised the company to publish a monthly newspaper to advertise and motivate agents. He also oversaw devotional meetings at which agents and other employees sang such songs as "Give Me That Good Ol' Mutual Spirit" to the tune of "Give Me That Old-Time Religion." These sales meetings, along with other trappings of modern business culture, straddled the line between the church-bound mutual aid societies of the past and the secularized business practices of the present. Because of its prominence, North Carolina Mutual was important in the black community—even outside of business circles. It established a savings bank and employment bureau, and erected a highly visible headquarters. By 1920 North Carolina Mutual had grown to the extent that it employed 1,100 people.

Another successful black-owned insurance company founded in the early twentieth century was the Atlanta Life Insurance Company, organized by Alonzo Herndon in 1905. Herndon, born in 1858 in Georgia, had spent seven and a half years of his life as a slave. Like North Carolina Mutual's founder, John Merrick, Herndon had made a fortune through the ownership of barbershops. Active in black intellectual movements, Herndon became friends with Booker T. Washington and attended the first Niagara Conference in 1905 under the leadership of W. E. B. Du Bois. In the company's first year, Atlanta Life secured 6,324 policyholders. Between 1922 and 1924 Atlanta Life entered a half dozen new states, most in the lower South. Although the majority of its business was in industrial insurance, Atlanta Life opened an ordinary department in 1922. That same year, it became the first black company to create an educational department to teach agents salesmanship and the technical aspects of insurance and accounting.

Less successful in the long term than either of these was the Standard Life Insurance Company, founded in 1913 by Herman Perry. Standard Life was the first black company organized for the purpose of selling exclusively ordinary life insurance. It had an explosive beginning, with phenomenal sales that by 1922 had brought the company more than $22 million of insurance in force. Perry, however, expanded the operation to include a number of different businesses, including real estate, printing, pharmaceutical, and construction firms. This expansion proved ruinous to cash reserves, and Perry was forced to

sell to the white-owned Southeastern Trust Company in 1924, despite the efforts of several black businessmen to retain ownership within the African-American community.

The migration of blacks to northern cities after World War I brought new opportunities for black-owned insurance companies. Several northern companies were founded: The Supreme Life Insurance Company (1921) and the Chicago Metropolitan Mutual Association (1927) were founded in Chicago; the United Mutual Life Insurance Company (1933) was founded in New York. Some southern-based companies, such as Atlanta Life, began selling policies in the North (in this case, in Ohio, and later, Michigan). In 1938 North Carolina Mutual, for the first time, sent agents north of Baltimore.

Black insurance enterprises suffered greater losses during the depression than did white enterprises, in part because they dealt almost exclusively in industrial insurance. A total of 63 percent of all insurance carried by Negro companies in 1930 was industrial, in contrast to only 17 percent for white companies. Black industrial policyholders generally had very little wealth and were forced to give up policies at the onset of hard times. The major black firms of the 1930s experienced a lapse rate for industrial insurance nearly 350 percent higher than for ordinary insurance. Victory Life and National Benefit Life, which had been founded in 1898 by Samuel Rutherford, both failed, while Supreme Liberty Life switched from ordinary insurance to enter the industrial market. Throughout its relatively brief history as a business, insurance had largely been dominated by men, but women had held high positions in companies, and black-owned insurance companies seemed to offer more opportunities to women than did their white counterparts. In 1912 nearly one-fourth of North Carolina Mutual's agents were women; at the white-owned Metropolitan Life Insurance Company, only one woman was employed as an agent before the mid-1940s. At the start of World War II, as more and more men entered war-related industries or were drafted, opportunities for women agents increased. In Philadelphia, a woman, Essie Thomas, led all other agents in sales for North Carolina Mutual.

With improved prosperity at the end of World War II, black families became better prospects for insurance sales. More and more white-owned firms courted blacks and eliminated or reduced premium differentials. White firms began to hire agents away from black-owned firms to solicit the new black middle class. In 1940 the vast majority of white underwriters still refused to insure blacks at all, and of the fifty-five that did, only five did so at standard rates. By contrast, in 1957, over 100 white companies competed for black policyholders, often at standard rates. While the overall growth rate of black-owned insurance companies slowed after 1960, there was a corresponding rise in the number of black-owned companies from fifteen in 1930 to forty-six in 1960.

Some black-owned firms, such as North Carolina Mutual, began to lessen their appeals to black solidarity—to the annoyance of black separatists. In the 1960s North Carolina Mutual was allowed to join the American Life Convention and Life Insurance Association. Black-owned companies also began selling other forms of insurance, such as group insurance offered to large employers. Although group insurance was first introduced early in the twentieth century, it did not become popular until the 1930s. The group insurance market proved a difficult one for minority-owned companies to enter. Few, if any, black enterprises employed a hundred or more workers, and white-owned companies were reluctant to sign on with a black-owned company. For this reason, many black-owned insurers had to remain outside the group market until the 1970s, when they were aided by affirmative action laws.

Golden State Mutual of Los Angeles became the second largest black insurance company in the United States, largely due to its success in group sales. Founded in 1925 by William Nickerson, Jr., Norman O. Houston, and George A. Beavers, Jr., Golden State Mutual had remained fairly small for several decades, with operations in only six states. Between 1968 and 1970, its group business grew tremendously, expanding from $59 million to $202 million. North Carolina Mutual also recorded great increases in business due to group insurance; in 1971 it became the first black company with over $1 billion insurance in force.

The 1980s saw difficulties continue for black-owned insurance firms. Reduced federal aid to low-income families (the main policyholders of black insurers) made even industrial policies difficult to afford. Premium receipts dropped 0.92 percent from 1987 to 1988 for the insurance industry as a whole; for black-owned insurance companies, the drop in premium receipts was 7.83 percent. Two strategies for survival emerged among black-owned insurance firms. The first, practiced by North Carolina Mutual and Atlanta Life, was to acquire new insurees through acquisition of smaller black-owned insurance companies. In 1985 Atlanta acquired Mammoth Life and Accident Insurance Company (founded in 1915 in Louisville, Kentucky), and in 1989 it acquired Pilgrim Health and Life Insurance Company (founded in 1898 in Augusta, Georgia). In all, from 1977 to 1989, eleven black-owned insurance companies were merged or acquired. Golden State Mutual—

operating in California, Hawaii, Florida, and Minnesota—followed another strategy. It attempted to sell term, whole life, and universal life to the middle-income market rather than the low-income market, which was the mainstay of Atlanta Life and North Carolina Mutual. Golden State greatly reduced the number of its personnel (from 760 employees in 1984 to 410 in 1988, not including commissioned sales staff), and hired college-educated agents. It also began television advertising campaigns starring football star Herschel Walker.

With the onset of a recession, the early 1990s proved particularly hard for many black-owned insurance companies. At that time twenty-nine black-owned insurance companies were operating in the United States; together, they held $23 billion of insurance in force. The largest were North Carolina Mutual, Atlanta Life Insurance, and Golden State Mutual Insurance. United Mutual Life, the eleventh largest black-owned insurance company in the country, was acquired by the white-owned Metropolitan Life Insurance Company of New York in 1992. It was the last black-owned insurance company in the Northeast.

See also Allen, Richard; Du Bois, W. E. B.; Economic Condition, U.S.; Entrepreneurs and Entrepreneurship; Fraternal Orders; Jim Crow; Jones, Absalom; Mutual Aid Societies; North Carolina Mutual Life Insurance Company; Spaulding, Charles Clinton

■ ■ *Bibliography*

Henderson, Alexa B. *Atlanta Life Insurance Company, Guardian of Black Economic Dignity.* Tuscaloosa: University of Alabama Press, 1990.

Weare, Walter B. *Black Business in the New South: A Social History of the North Carolina Mutual Life Insurance Company.* Urbana: University of Illinois Press, 1973.

WALTER FRIEDMAN (1996)

INTELLECTUAL LIFE

Whether cast as attempts to document African-American mind, worldview, racial philosophies, or cultural mythos, nearly all scholarly studies of black intellectual life have acknowledged—as this article will—the functional importance of formal and informal educational institutions and the central ideological role of the quest for freedom and equality. The diffusion of this latter complex of ideas through African-American communities, its crystallization in folk thought, in religion, in popular culture, and in social movements, plays as important a role in understanding African-American intellectual life as studying the history of black intellectuals as a social entity; and this article attempts to balance these approaches. It also recognizes that in African-American life and throughout the modern world, intellectuals themselves, as a professional category, employ, with relatively greater frequency and dexterity than most of their peers, symbol systems of broad scope and abstract reference concerning humanity, society, nature, and the cosmos. But because the social history of black Americans has severely restricted their formal practice of intellectual occupations, the performance of these roles has frequently been assumed by individuals practicing nonintellectual occupations. Accordingly, the deeply rooted human need to perceive, experience, and express value and meaning in particular events—through words, colors, shapes, or sounds—has manifested itself in black intellectual life only partially in professional works of science, scholarship, philosophy, theology, law, literature, and the arts. Without implying any absolute separation of literature, music, and the arts from African-American intellectual life, the task of delineating the fuller role of these expressive modes and their individual intellectual expositors will be left to the various specialized articles devoted to them particularly.

Despite contrary misconceptions, African Americans originated in Old World African societies with a wide spectrum of intellectual traditions, literate as well as oral, and in which even the most rudimentary and relatively undifferentiated communities created recognized institutional niches for the intellectual functions that are expressed in art and interpretive speculation. In the large, highly differentiated kingdoms of the Western Sudan and Central Africa, specialized intellectual leaders—ofttimes institutionalized in guilds or professional castes—defined the cosmologies in which the individual and group were conceptually located; they helped to identify and regulate the occurrence of evil; to legitimate the powers and responsibilities of authority; to preserve and explain society's past; to transmit analytical and expressive skills to the young; to guide and critique aesthetic and religious experiences; and to foster the control of nature.

The era of European New World colonization and the accompanying Atlantic slave trade dramatically disrupted the intellectual lives of Africans caught up in it; but throughout the history of the United States, African Americans have created syncretic intellectual lives often at the cutting edge of literary, artistic, and scientific creativity. Slavery notwithstanding, every era has produced individual representatives of what Benjamin Brawley termed "the Negro genius," whose intellectual and moral capaci-

ties provided crucial armaments in the ongoing "literature of vindication" that reformers and abolitionists initially mounted to defend African Americans against persisting theories of their innate inferiority. Inevitably, developments in African-American intellectual life have continuously been shaped by the problems and possibilities affecting American intellectual life generally. These have included the modernizing, secularizing forces that have moved the life of the mind in America from a colonial intellectual setting dominated by Christian divines and isolated scientific prodigies to a twentieth-century context variously identified with communities of bohemians, exiles, government-service intellectuals, and university professors. African-American intellectual life has evidenced also the tendency before the mid-twentieth century for intellectuals to believe themselves to be agents of progress, whether in the form of millennialism, republicanism, high culture, or social science methodology. This Enlightenment legacy has persisted in contradistinction to the modern tendency for the earlier progressivist faith to be replaced by doubt, and the formerly unifying vision and influence of American thinkers to be diminished by fragmentation and narrow expertise. Not surprisingly, the phases of African-American intellectual life have been delimited by the shifting conditions and recurring crises in black social history as well as by such larger contrapuntal developments; though manifest social exigencies have lent the progessivist faith and the struggle for a unifying vision more than conventional staying power in the intellectual world of African-American communities.

COLONIAL AND REVOLUTIONARY AMERICA

During the colonial and Revolutionary era, the circumstances of slavery shaped African-American intellectual life in specific ways. First, slavery rigorously suppressed African culture, its languages and institutions of intellectual discourse, and drove surviving oppositional intellectual forms underground. Second, the repudiation in the American colonies of the Greco-Roman tradition of the erudite slave and the corollary prohibitions against literacy, stultified the development of Western intellectual skills and opportunities for the vast majority of African Americans. Third, strict social control of even quasi-free black intellectuals was attempted through both de jure laws and de facto discrimination. Fourth, as a consequence, an African-American tradition of sacred and secular folk thought in sermons, tales, aphorisms, proverbs, narrative poems, sacred and secular songs, verbal games, and other linguistic forms became the primary matrix for historicizing, interpreting, and speculating about the nature and meaning of society and the cosmos. Toward the end of the colonial period, however, the emergence of the earliest professional black intellectual voices was fostered by two broad cultural developments in the British colonies—the Great Awakening (approximately 1735–1750) with its unifying religious fervor, millennial progressivism, and missionary appeal to African Americans and Native Americans; and then the revolutionary political ferment that accompanied the spreading Enlightenment doctrine of the Rights of Man: life, liberty, and equality. African Americans quickly grasped the relevance to their own circumstances of the democratic dogma and revolutionist rhetoric that transfixed colonial legislatures and the Continental Congress; and during the War of Independence, while weighing the loyalist appeals and promises of emancipation from British colonial governors, black men and women sponsored petitions to legislatures, court cases for individual freedom, and platform oratory calculated to convert the professed revolutionary faith of rebel American slaveholders into direct challenges to American slavery itself.

During the decades following the War of Independence, the growth of autonomous black churches, schools, and fraternal and burial societies in the free North (Philadelphia, New York, and Boston, especially) and in selected southern cities (New Orleans; Charleston S.C.; and Savannah) created the initial context for formal development of group intellectual life. In early African-American churches a vital intellectual tradition of intense striving for contact with the sacred focused on the mastery, interpretation, and exposition of biblical writings, with a distinctive strain of exegetical "Ethiopianism" apparent as early as the 1780s. Identifying Africans in American bondage with Israel in biblical Exodus became a controlling metaphor in secular as well as sacred African-American literature; and the Ethiopian prophecy of Psalms 68:31—"Princes shall come out of Egypt; Ethiopia shall yet stretch out her hands unto God"—became the dominant sermonic text offered to answer the omnipresent question of theodicy. This problem of explaining the divine purpose of black suffering—while simultaneously separating the slaveholders' religion from "true Christianity"—became the pivotal heuristic of antebellum black religious thought and the foundation of a distinctive African-American theology. Some of the initial virtuoso intellectual action by African Americans arose out of such religious preoccupations or out of conversion experiences fused with the political ferment of revolution: the neoclassicist verse of Phillis Wheatley; the sermons and letters of the Congregationalist minister Lemuel Haynes; the antislavery autobiography of Olaudah Equiano, for example. Prior to the establishment of black secular education, the quest for literacy was fueled by religious impulses and facilitated by free black churches or by the "invisible church" in slave communities. And in

New York City between 1787 and 1820, the African Free School, with white missionary support, provided formal education for hundreds of students such as Ira Aldridge, who went on to international fame as a Shakespearean actor.

But Free African societies and fraternal orders like the Prince Hall Masons also provided a counterconventional intellectual matrix—for mastering the secular and sacred freethought traditions of the Radical Enlightenment, in which the proselytizing mythographers of freemasonry and Renaissance hermeticism offered African-American free thinkers secret access to a "perennial philosophy" that hypothesized an unbroken continuity with, and a reverential attitude toward, the esoteric symbol systems and pagan wisdom literatures of ancient North Africa and the Orient. No less significant, the influence of Enlightenment science and technological innovation created a milieu in which perhaps the most variegated black intellectual career of the eighteenth century could evolve—that of Benjamin Banneker, mathematician, naturalist, astronomer, inventor, almanac compiler, surveyor, and essayist.

THE AGE OF ABOLITION

In the nineteenth century the movement toward autonomous institutions in free black communities, North and South, continued. But the most significant developments for African-American intellectual life were the successive appearances of, first, widespread protest between 1817 and 1830 against the mass black deportation schemes of the American Colonization Society; second, the opening phase of the National Negro Convention Movement, from 1830 to 1840; and third, the emergence of militant black abolitionism, from 1843 to the onset of the Civil War. Alongside the growth of stable, northern free black communities, these developments provided the broadest context to date for the fruition of African-American intellectual skills and activities. Besides spurring the general acquisition of forensic and oratorical prowess, the anticolonization movement helped forge a vital journalistic tradition with the development of the nation's first black newspaper, *Freedom's Journal*—cofounded in 1827 by the college-trained, Jamaica-born John Russwurm, and Samuel cornish, a Presbyterian minister. Anticolonization activities also provided the impetus for the strain of radical political exhortation that erupted in David Walker's insurrectionist Appeal in Four Articles (1829), the nineteenth-century prototype for militant repudiation of white racism and black acquiescence.

The National Negro Convention Movement, which began with six annual aggregations between 1830 and 1835 (all save the fifth in Philadelphia), gave African-

American intellectual life its first major coordinated organizational thrust—by providing linkages between the roughly fifty black antislavery societies then in existence; by creating a rationale for boycotts organized by newly established "Free Produce Societies" against the products of slave labor; and by founding temperance and moral reform societies and African missionary groups. With the revitalization of American abolitionism after the emancipation of slaves in the British West Indies in 1833, the ground was laid for a militant black abolition struggle that, beginning with the Negro national convention of 1843, developed increasing intellectual autonomy from the antislavery program of William Lloyd Garrison. Over the next two decades, black abolitionism moved ideologically toward programmatic insurrectionism and nationalist emigrationism, as the Fugitive Slave Act of 1850 and the Dred Scott Decision of 1857 made central in African-American philosophical debate the political issues surrounding the juridical denial of American citizenship rights and nationality to even native-born free black people.

The final three antebellum decades also witnessed an array of organized intellectual activities by newly formed African-American literary societies and lyceums in northern free black communities. The New York Philomathean Society, founded in 1830, the Philadelphia Library Company of Colored Persons, in 1833, as well as groups in midwestern and border cities, like the Ohio Ladies Education Society, started private libraries and organized debating and elocution contests, poetry readings, and study classes variously devoted to promoting "a proper cultivation for literary pursuits and improvement of the faculties and powers" of the mind. As early as 1832 the African-American Female Intelligence Society of Boston provided a platform for pioneering moral reformer and black feminist lecturer Maria Stewart; and the Benjamin Banneker Society in Philadelphia sponsored regular lecture series on political, scientific, religious, and artistic issues.

These expanding institutional supports for black intellectual life facilitated the careers of the two most extensively educated figures of the antebellum era—Alexander Crummell, Episcopal clergyman and Liberia mission leader; and James McCune Smith, university-trained physician, abolitionist, editor, essayist, and ethnologist—both products of the African Free School and of advanced training outside restrictive American borders. The early pan-African scholarship of St. Thomas-born Edward Wilmot Blyden; the pioneering political essays and fiction of Martin Delany; the voluminous racial uplift, moral reform, and women's rights lectures and belletristic works of Frances Ellen Watkins Harper—all reflect the expanding audiences and material support for African-American intellectual actions and performances that accompanied the broader ferment in American culture during the era of romanticist and transcendentalist ascendancy. No less than their Euro-American counterparts, Jacksonian-era black intellectual leaders espoused a providential view of history that afforded them a special worldwide mission and destiny. Beginning with Robert Benjamin Lewis's *Light and Truth; Collected from the Bible and Ancient and Modern History* (1836, 1844) and James Pennington's *Text Book of the Origin and History of the Colored People* (1841), a tradition evolved of popular messianic historiography by self-trained "scholars without portfolio," many of them Christian ministers, who drew eclectically on sacred and profane sources in ecclesiastical accounts, in the new romantic national histories, and in the archaeological and iconographic data vouchsafed by the rise of modern Egyptology during the early nineteenth century, following the discovery and decipherment of the Rosetta stone.

Although racial codes through the South greatly restricted black intellectual life, in Louisiana the language and intellectual traditions of French culture persisted during the antebellum era, with members of the African-American elite ofttimes acquiring an education in France itself and choosing expatriate status there over caste constraints in America. The career of New Orleans scientist-inventor Norbert Rillieux, whose innovations in chemical engineering revolutionized the international sugar-refining industry, developed in this context, as did the dramaturgy of Victor Séjour, a leading figure in the black Creole literary enclave, *Les Cenelles* (The Hollyberries), which emerged in New Orleans during the 1840s. Although no specifically belletristic literary movement appeared in northern free black communities, literary traditions in poetry, autobiography, and the essay extended back into the eighteenth century; and the final antebellum decade witnessed the publication of the earliest extant African-American novels and stage plays. The northern free black community of New York City served as the site of Thomas Hamilton's pioneering *Anglo-African Magazine* (1859), an outgrowth of the publisher's lifelong ambition to provide an independent voice representing African Americans in "the fourth estate," and a vehicle for skilled historical essays, biographical sketches, fiction, critical reviews, scientific studies, and humor by such eminent antebellum black luminaries as Edward Wilmot Blyden, Martin Delany, Frances Harper, James Theodore Holly, George Vashon, Mary Ann Shadd Cary, and John Mercer Langston.

The most influential product of African-American intellectual life during the era, however, was the twin stream of slave narratives and spiritual autobiographies that apotheosized the complementary ideologies of abolition and moral reform through biblical motifs of captivity and providential redemption related compellingly by such figures as William Wells Brown, Frederick Douglass, Harriet Jacobs, Jarena Lee, and Solomon Northrup. In their assault on the legal and historical pretexts for slavery, self-authored slave narratives in particular (as opposed to those transcribed by white amanuenses) cultivated an assertive facticity about the horrors of bondage and a subjective ethos of faith, adaptability, and self-reliance that gave expressive mythic structure to an evolving African-American corporate identity. In the narratives by black abolitionist leaders like Douglass, Samuel Ringgold Ward, and Sojourner Truth, slave autobiographies revealed their close alliance also with oratory as a political instrument and a molder of group consciousness. Evidencing often distinctive uses of the "plain style" or the flamboyant rhetoric of the golden age in American platform oratory, formal public utterances by African Americans during the final antebellum decades lend greater credence to the claims of intellectual historians that the national consciousness was created and stabilized, policies for westward expansion formulated, the rights of women conceived, the slave power consolidated and then broken, all through the egalitarian processes of public address—ceremonial, hortatory, deliberative. Black Americans during the years leading to the Civil War heard, pondered, read aloud, and committed to memory their favorite orators. And passages learned from Wendell Phillips's thousandfold lectures on Toussaint Louverture, from annual West Indian Emancipation Day observances, from Frederick Douglass's Fourth of July oration, and from African School texts of classical rhetoric prepared African Americans intellectually to respond, with arms and labor, when Lincoln finally appealed for their support to help save the Union.

RECONSTRUCTION THROUGH THE 1890S

The Civil War and Emancipation dramatically recast the contours of African-American intellectual life. The decade of Reconstruction optimism focused the thought of black communities largely on the equalitarian possibilities of the franchise, on education, on the acquisition of property and wealth, and on the cultivation of those qualities of character and conduct conducive to "elevating the race" within the body politic. Freedmen's Bureau professional occupations and the emerging constellation of black colleges and universities created new matrices for black intellectual life within corporate intellectual or practical institutions. During the following decade, one index to the shifting intellectual balance appeared with the publication

of the *AME Church Review* (1884), which for the next quarter century, under the successive editorships of Benjamin Tucker Tanner, Levi Coppin, and Hightower Kealing, would become the premier magazine published by and for African Americans and would be transformed from a church newspaper to a national scholarly journal of public affairs. It featured biblical criticism and theology, wide-ranging editorial opinions, articles on pan-African history and American civic issues, as well as black poetry and fiction and popular essays, all attuned to "the intellectual growth of our people" and carefully uniting sectarian and increasingly nonsectarian interests in the purpose of giving to the world "the best thoughts of the race, irrespective of religious persuasion or political opinion." Coterminously, a stream of articles and books on biblical interpretation by authors such as the Reverend James Theodore Holly, John Bryan Small, and Sterling Nelson Brown (father to the poet) confronted the hermeneutical practices and canonical assumptions of late nineteenth-century biblical higher criticism with allegorical, christological, typological, and historical challenges to traditionally anti-black exegeses of Jahwist traditions such as the so-called curse of Ham.

While black institutions like churches, fraternal societies, and conventions continued to foster intellectual activities, perhaps a better index of post-Reconstruction developments—and of the secularizing intellectual tendencies in particular—appeared with the formation in 1897 of the first major African-American learned society, the American Negro Academy, in Washington, D.C. It was constituted as "an organization of authors, scholars, artists, and those distinguished in other walks of life, men of African descent, for the promotion of Letters, Science, and Art." The Academy published twenty-two occasional papers over the next quarter century on subjects related to African-American culture, history, religion, civil and social rights. Its all-male membership spanned the fields of intellectual endeavor; and besides its first president, Alexander Crummel, it ultimately included such important intellectual leaders as Francis J. Grimké, a Princeton-trained Presbyterian clergyman; W. E. B. Du Bois, professor of economics and history at Atlanta University; William H. Crogman, professor of classics at Clark University; William S. Scarborough, philologist and classicist at Wilberforce University; John W. Cromwell, lawyer, politician, and newspaper editor; John Hope, president of Morehouse College; Alain Locke, Harvard-trained philosopher, aesthetician, and Rhodes Scholar; Carter Woodson, historian and Howard University dean; and James Weldon Johnson, poet, novelist, songwriter, and civil rights leader. Interrelated developments in institutionalized black intellectual life included the founding of the Atlanta University

Studies of the Negro Problems in 1896, the American Negro Historical Society of Philadelphia in 1897, the Negro Society for Historical Research in 1912, and the Association for the Study of Negro Life and History in 1915. Moreover, these institutions were frequently closely linked to the nationwide orbit of educational and reform activities sponsored by the more than one hundred local black women's clubs that had been founded by leaders such as Mary McLeod Bethune, Lucy Laney, Charlotte Hawkins Brown, Ida Wells-Barnett, and Nannie Burroughs and then federated in 1896 as the National Association of Colored Women. Nannie Burroughs, for instance, demonstrated the various intellectual intersections in her subsequent coterminous service as a life member of Woodson's Association for the Study of Negro Life and History.

No less important, the expanding literacy of the black audience during the educational fervor that followed Emancipation generated new opportunities for black intellectual entrepreneurs like the minister-pamphleteer-novelist Sutton Griggs and artist-intellectuals like dramatist-journalist-fictionist Pauline Hopkins. They created intellectual products and performances devoted to racial solidarity and to a widening interracial marketplace of progressivist art and ideas. Following a decade of post-Reconstruction struggle against reaction, in the 1890s a cluster of significant events coalesced that expressed in a variety of intellectual and artistic media the new dynamic of black independence and self-assertion: In 1895, Booker T. Washington galvanized national attention with his Atlanta Exposition speech. In 1895 also, "Harry" Burleigh was assisting Antonín Dvořák with the black folk themes of the *New World Symphony* and at the same time making his entry into the New York concert world. In 1896 Paul Laurence Dunbar emerged as a leading poetic voice; and painter Henry Ossawa Tanner marked the beginning of his first substantial Paris recognition. In the same year a pioneering black musical comedy premiered on Broadway. In 1898 Will Marion Cook introduced "serious syncopated music" with *Clorindy*; and the Anglo-African composer, Samuel Coleridge Taylor, achieved maturity and fame with the first part of his *Hiawatha Trilogy*. And in 1898 and 1899 Charles Chesnutt, the novelist, inaugurated the first fully professional career of a black fiction writer. The appearance in 1903 of W. E. B. Du Bois's *The Souls of Black Folk* became a synthesizing artistic event of this period and one that spurred, perhaps for the first time, an ascendancy to black national leadership on the basis of intellectual performance alone.

The era's famous Washington–Du Bois controversy highlighted not just the partisan intraracial ideological differences over political, educational, and economic strategies but the changing role and increasing prominence of secular intellectuals in black America generally—Washington's rise paralleling the emergence of an anti-intellectual, industrial-minded, managerial Euro-American elite and Du Bois's ascendancy paralleling that of a coterie of Arnoldian "elegant sages" who assumed the roles of national culture critics and prophets. Between African-American and Euro-American intellectuals of either orientation, however, the continuing predominance of conflict rather than the consensus over issues of racial justice also continued to parallel the still entrenched segregation of American intellectual and institutional life; and such conflict expressed itself through the continuing ideological and iconographical war over racial imagery in all the artistic and scholarly media of the period, a pattern that remained essentially unaltered until the intercession of World War I.

RENAISSANCE AND WAR

The emergence after World War I of the first major African-American cultural movement gave evidence of a self-identified intellectual stratum of "New Negroes." It was structured, first, by new sources of financial support and patronage for the performers of intellectual actions. Second, a cadre of secular leaders had developed—university-trained philosophers and social scientists such as W. E. B. Du Bois, Alain Locke, and Charles S. Johnson and activist organizers like Marcus Garvey—who superintended the intellectual performances from bases in corporate intellectual institutions (primarily black colleges and universities) or in practical institutions like the NAACP, the Urban League, and the Universal Negro Improvement Association (UNIA). These developments were reinforced by the less formal creation of salons like A'Lelia Walker's "Dark Tower," of the "Negro Sanhedrin" at Howard University, and of coteries of artists in Philadelphia, Washington, D.C., and cities distant from the "Negro Mecca" in Harlem. Third, the movement responded to patterns of rising consumer demand from white and black audiences alike for black intellectual objects and intellectual-practical performances. Fourth, new relationships had emerged between tradition and creativity in the various fields of intellectual action—modernism in the arts, and the rise in academia of the social sciences, the "new history," and new paradigms in physical science.

The increasing urbanization and industrialization of the nation generally, and the country-to-city Great Migration of African Americans in particular, combined with the emergence of popular culture and the new media technologies (radio, cinema, phonograph, graphic arts, etc.) to provide the culturally nationalistic "Black Renaissance," as

Langston Hughes termed it, an unprecedentedly "creativogenic" milieu with specific intellectual characteristics. The growth of mass audiences, and of new technical means for communicating with them, expanded the field of action for black intellectuals. The general reaction against standardization and conformity in American life, and the postwar openness to diverse cultural stimuli, which accompanied the further decline of prewar Victorianism, lowered the barriers to cross-cultural exchange. A modernist "cult of the new," which stressed *becoming* and not just being as a creative value, fostered experimental attitudes and improvisational styles for which jazz became an acknowledged exemplar. The growing shift of moral authority in vernacular culture from religious spirituals and parlor songs to secular blues and cabaret lyrics undergirded a pronounced generational rebellion against conventional sexual attitudes and gender roles in black communities and beyond. The freer access to cultural media for American citizens generally facilitated the emergence of independent African-American motion picture and recording companies. Among the cadre of Black Renaissance intellectuals, the conscious sense of greater freedom, following a legacy of severe oppression and near-absolute exclusion, had created a collective compensatory incentive to creativity. A movement ethos that apotheosized youth, a self-conscious exposure to different and even contrasting cultural stimuli from black immigrants and ideas elsewhere in the African diaspora, and a now-fashionable tolerance for diverging views and intense debate helped make the Black Renaissance manifestly creativogenic, despite its manifold constraints.

A destabilizing facet of African-American intellectual life during the period, however, was the widening gulf between intellectuals and traditional patterns of authority and religious orthodoxy inside and outside black communities. As intellectual historians generally concur, at the end of Reconstruction the lives of most Americans were still dominated by the values of the village, by conventional nineteenth-century beliefs in individualism, laissez-faire, progress, and a divinely ordained social system. But in the closing decades of the century the spread of science and technology, industrialism, urbanization, immigration, and economic depression eroded this worldview. Black intellectuals experienced increasingly the same tension with ecclesiastical and temporal authority that modern intellectuals in general have felt—the intellectual urge to locate and acknowledge an *alternative* authority which is the bearer of the highest good, whether it be science, order, progress, or some other measure, and to resist or condemn *actual* authority as a betrayer of the highest values. Traditions for defining or seeking new "sacred" values that won stronger allegiance among African-American intellectuals

included: (1) the tradition of scientism, that of the new social sciences in particular, because of their attention to the race problem and their role in public policy; (2) the romantic tradition, specifically the cults of "Negro genius," of an Herderian apotheosis of "the folk," of countercultural bohemianism and the "hip"; (3) the apocalyptic tradition of revolutionism, millenarianism, and radical Pan-Africanism adapted to the contours of American life; (4) the populist tradition with its themes of the moral and creative superiority of the uneducated and unintellectual and its critique of bourgeois/elite society by its disaffected offspring; (5) the feminist tradition, variously reformist or radical, with its revisionary assault on conventional gender roles and on the hegemony of an ostensibly patriarchal social matrix rooted in female subordination; and (6) the anti-intellectual tradition of order (dissensual political and religious sects built on charismatic models and revitalizationist discipline—Garveyism, Father Divine, and the Nation of Islam), which ofttimes deems pronounced intellectualism to be disruptive.

Among these traditions of alternative authority, scientism, despite the increasing popularization of scientific ideas in the mass media, had acquired the broadest social prestige but the least democratized mechanisms of evaluation and reward. To the extent that its accomplishments were achieved through formal research in laboratory settings by research-degree holders, it retained the most uncertain footing in African-American intellectual life at the same time that it more and more supplanted achievement in the high arts as the greatest potential symbol of group capacities and progress. At the turn of the twentieth century, the most highly honored of all black scientists, the agricultural chemist George Washington Carver (1864–1943), symbolized the ambiguities that the issue of race introduced into scientific culture in America. The tensions between theoretical and applied science contributed to Carver's being derided by partisans of the former as more a concoctionist than a contributor to genuine scientific knowledge. The tensions between science and the Christian faith he espoused as a spur of his Tuskegee research placed him in conflict with the cult of scientific objectivity. And despite the revolutionary impact of that research on peanut and soybean derivatives for the economy of both the nation and the South, to many black proponents of nationalistic racial uplift, his characteristic humility and racial deference made problematic the role of such black scientists in group progress.

At the time, however, Carver's uncertain place in African-American intellectual life mirrored the uncertain place of scientists generally in American culture and progress, as revealed in the apparent "inferiority complex" of

American scientific culture in the international intellectual community at the turn of the century. That sense of national deficiency crystallized in a widely discussed article from the *North American Review* in 1902; this article lamented the inferiority of American scholarship and science relative to the European and noted that none of the great scientific achievements of the preceding century—the theory of evolution, the atomic structure of matter, the principles of electromagnetic induction and electrolytic action, the discovery of microorganisms, and the concept of the conservation of energy—had been the work of Americans, whose successes instead were largely derivative in the major sciences or were located in minor fields such as astronomy, geology, and meteorology.

Perceived deficiencies in the life of the scientific mind—and the manifest need for greater achievement—functioned analogously at the levels of nation and race, then, in the early decades of the twentieth century. Among African Americans, despite the pioneering doctorate degree in physics awarded Edward Bouchet at Yale University in 1876, a total of only thirteen physical or biological science doctorates had been earned prior to 1930. But in the next decade and a half a more than tenfold increase in earned science doctorates occurred, fueled primarily by doctors of medicine, among whom were pioneering research scientists such as Charles Drew (1904–1950; hematology) and Hildrus Poindexter (1901–1987; microbiology). An estimated 850 African Americans earned natural science doctorates by 1972; and at a fairly constant rate approximately one out of every one hundred American science doctorate holders would be African American into the 1990s. But because the social history of African-American scientists confined about 75 percent of them, as late as 1981, to employment at predominantly black institutions of higher learning—with limited laboratory facilities and research support and heavy instructional responsibilities—their primary role in African-American intellectual life has been to teach the sciences at those institutions, where the majority of black science doctorate holders have continued to receive their undergraduate training. Nevertheless, as recipients of scientific awards, as office holders or journal editors in scientific societies, as members of scientific advisory or research grant review committees, and as authors of textbooks, African-American scientists have achieved distinction in fields as diverse as aerospace science (NASA astronauts Drs. Ronald McNair and Mae Jemison, for example), organic chemistry, marine and cell biology. In the mathematical theory of games and statistical decisions, for instance, David H. Blackwell, the first black mathematician elected to the National Academy of Sciences, coauthored a pioneering textbook for the field in 1954, won the Von Neu-

mann theory prize in 1979, and, for work as a Rand Corporation consultant, has been cited as one of the pioneers in the theory of "duels"—a two-person, zero-sum game involving the choice of the moment of time for firing in military conflict.

Besides the prestige and inherent intellectual attractions of the sciences and scientism, these fields, despite the persistence of racial discrimination within the world of professional researchers, offered African-American intellectuals careers in which the links between merit and acclaim were presumably established by "objective" standards of authority with "universal" provenience. The scientific tradition of rejecting tradition if it does not correspond with the "facts of verifiable experience" provided some black intellectuals the kind of "higher" authority that freed them to an increasing extent from the "priest-governed" black communities described by W. E. B. Du Bois. Such an outlook focused necessarily on the *methods* of science; but for natural scientists in particular, it failed to define concrete social objectives and social roles.

African-American intellectuals drawn to the social sciences, by contrast, found the then unquestioned social utility of the new sciences of society a source of continuity with the pre-twentieth-century "gospel" of progress and with associated meliorist, progressivist, or millenialist philosophies of racial uplift. Unlike the natural sciences, the place of the social sciences in African-American intellectual life was firmly established early during the development of black post-Reconstruction practical and educational institutions; and a tradition of prominent African-American achievement in the fields of economics, political science, anthropology, sociology, and psychology developed almost coterminously with the emergence and professionalization of these fields within the modern academy.

During the 1890s the earliest formal departments of sociology appeared in America, as did the first contributions of African Americans to the new discipline—both emerging amid a climate of extreme racism in popular and academic thought. The half century between the appearance in 1899 of W. E. B. Du Bois's *The Philadelphia Negro* and of St. Clair Drake and Horace Cayton's *Black Metropolis* in 1945 has been described as the golden age in the sociology of black America, with a series of path-breaking works by social scientists based at black colleges and universities. Du Bois's classic study of black Philadelphia was both the first scientific study of an African-American community—a precursor of the Atlanta University Publications series he later founded—and the pioneer work of American urban sociology. It spurred similar projects such as *The Negro at Work in New York City: A Study in Economic Progress* (1912), conducted by George Edmund

Haynes, one of the earliest black Ph.D. holders in sociology and an early proponent of black migration research. The period from World War I to the mid–1930s was dominated by the famous University of Chicago school of American sociology; and out of it a group of distinguished black sociologists and anthropologists—Charles S. Johnson, E. Franklin Frazier, Bertram Doyle, St. Clair Drake, and Horace Cayton—emerged with major research works on black family sociology, race relations, social stratification, community development, southern plantation systems, migration patterns, and related topics. At Atlanta University, Ira De A. Reid, a specialist on West Indian immigration and rural plantation studies, succeeded Du Bois in conducting studies on urban African-American life and in training new researchers. E. Franklin Frazier, at Howard University (where a sociology department had earlier been established by Kelly Miller) and Charles Johnson at Fisk University commanded, like Reid, the resources necessary to develop strong sociology departments with graduate research programs. But at black institutions without resources for graduate study, strong undergraduate programs were built nonetheless by sociologists such as St. Clair Drake at Roosevelt College, Oliver Cox at Lincoln University, W. S. M. Banks and Earl Pierro at Fort Valley State College, and Mozell Hill at Langston University.

Though sociologists have outnumbered black social scientists in other fields, the middle decades of the twentieth century witnessed an expanding representation of African-American scholars in economics, political science, psychology, and anthropology. During the period from the 1930s to the 1960s economists such as Booker T. McGraw, Frederick Jackson, Rodney G. Higgins, Frank G. Davis, and Winfred Bryson Jr. developed careers as scholars and advisers to service organizations, businesses, and government, while Abram Harris, perhaps the most widely known black economist of the era, combined early service as an Urban League official with an academic career of research scholarship on the labor movement and black business development that culminated in his series of studies on social reform strategies in the economic philosophies of Thorstein Veblen, Werner Sombart, John Commons, Karl Marx, and John Stuart Mill. From the 1960s to the 1990s, as the sphere of black entrepreneurial activities and service opportunities expanded in the wake of the civil rights movement, African-American economists such as Bernard Anderson, Andrew Brimmer, Samuel Myers, Thomas Sowell, Clifton Wharton, and Walter Williams have played increasingly diverse roles in the academy, in private and public foundations, in conservative or liberal "think tanks," in political organizations such as the Congressional Black Caucus, and in a publishing industry eager for certified expertise in "the dismal science."

In economics, as in other social sciences like psychology and anthropology, however, black practitioners faced—with a difference—the dilemma that perplexed all fields of knowledge after the 1920s and 1930s, when scientism's leading edge—physics and mathematics—no longer epitomized the discovery of immutable natural laws but instead struggled with new uncertainties that undermined belief in fixed laws and principles. Albert Einstein's theory of relativity, Werner Heisenberg's "uncertainty principle," Kurt Gödel's demonstration that mathematical theories could not be verified without referring back to their own premises, all marked science, despite its spectacular technical achievements, as in some ways as metaphorical as the arts and incapable of vouchsafing ultimate principles for human action and judgment. Economic models that postulated rational patterns of buying and selling ignored irrational personal motivations such as race prejudice and circumvented central issues such as the effects of racist institutions on individual behavior.

In psychology, psychometric measures, regarded at the turn of the century as empirical propositions of enormous accuracy, had become so interwoven with ideological nativism, elitism, social class bias, and racism that as early as 1927 Horace Mann Bond found it necessary to denounce as "invidious propaganda" the then widespread psychometric "game" of testing black children for standardized notions of intelligence, for "racial temperament," and for dubious "mulatto hypotheses." Between 1920 and 1950 the roughly thirty black doctorate holders in psychology, beginning with Francis Cecil Sumner and his work on the psychoanalytical theories of Sigmund Freud and Alfred Adler, were drawn to a variety of research modes, from G. Henry Alston's experimental neurological examination of the "psychophysics of the spatial conditions for the fusion of warmth and cold into heat" to May Pullins Claytor's construction of questionnaires for detecting symptoms of juvenile delinquency. The training of African-American psychologists during the era was strongly influenced by the urgent social need for black teachers and social service workers. Corresponding tendencies led black colleges and universities to deemphasize the ascendant German-derived laboratory science curriculum in psychology that, at white institutions, subordinated the practical and applied sphere. Throughout this period Howard University's program in psychology, under the leadership of Francis Sumner, was the only black school providing graduate and undergraduate training in laboratory-experimental psychology. In the course of preparing such outstanding scholars as Mamie Clark and Kenneth Clark, it developed a strong curriculum based on the behaviorism of John Watson and the dynamic psychology of Freud and William McDougall. However, in psychology as in the other social science disciplines, the diminishing likelihood that any one theory could ultimately disprove any other made relatively arbitrary such procedural choices; and the growing uncertainty of the concept of race itself as an operative term made the incursions of relativism even more pronounced.

In stressing the "cultural significance" of psychology—its importance for understanding "literature, religion, philosophy, art, crime, genius, mental derangement, history, biography, and all creations of the human mind"—the Howard program implicitly aligned itself with developing traditions of anthropological and folkloric study in African-American life that embraced the new notions of "cultural relativism" promoted by social scientists such as Franz Boas. Boas believed that "the idea of a 'cultured' individual is merely relative" to the system of meanings in which that individual grows up and lives and that such a belief liberates us from the normative prejudice that Western civilization is absolutely superior to others. After World War I, Boas and his students (who included the writer-folklorist Zora Neale Hurston) rejected genteel Victorian notions of culture that focused exclusively on the highest stratum of artistic expression by educated elites. They adopted instead a presumably detached viewpoint of culture as endemic to all human communities and perhaps better observed in everyday life and common emotions than in superordinate ideals or formalities.

The corresponding emphasis on folklore and folklife reinforced practices of cultural preservation that had become established in African-American intellectual life decades earlier. Groups of black scholars and students had been working actively to document and preserve African-American folk traditions since the 1880s and 1890s, when a black folklore group formed at Hampton Institute in Hampton, Va., to collect African-American sacred and secular songs, proverbs, tales, and wisdom lore. In the 1920s and '30s, in conjunction with a burst of interest in American folklore scholarship generally, a group of professionally trained black folklorists emerged who gave new regional and genre focuses to the enterprise. In 1922 Fisk professor Thomas Talley published a large collection of play songs, proverbs, and verbal art in his *Negro Folk Rhymes*; in 1925 an African musicologist and composer from Sierra Leone, Nicholas Ballanta-Taylor, who had come to the Gullah communities of coastal Georgia and the Carolinas to study links between African and African-American music, published his transcriptions of religious songs in *St. Helena Island Spirituals*. Arthur Huff Fauset, who earned a Ph.D. from the University of Pennsylvania, specialized in the folk narratives and riddles of the South and the West Indies and in the urban religious cults of

Philadelphia. James Mason Brewer, a Texas-based folklorist who studied at Indiana University with folktale specialist Stith Thompson, published a ground-breaking slave tale collection, *Juneteenth*, and subsequent volumes of South Carolina humor, as well as preacher and ghost tales from the Texas Brazos region. And Zora Neale Hurston, trained in Boas's anthropology program at Columbia University, fused her ongoing folklore collecting and research with a developing career as a creative writer that led to a series of works on American hoodoo, Jamaican obeah, Haitian vodoun and to the southern songs, jokes, games, tales, and conjure lore of her classic *Mules and Men* in 1935. In the works of all these scholars the underlying premises of the new cultural relativism provided a scientistic source of authority for the pragmatic labors of documenting and preserving the communal traditions of African-American life.

In analogous ways the practice and study of law and politics in African-American intellectual life responded also to the influence of the new sciences of society. Early black lawyers like George B. Vashon (1824–1878) in pre–Civil War New York and his pupil, Oberlin graduate John Mercer Langston, later the founder of the law school at Howard University, struggled for the rights of African Americans and for recognition as professionals in a nineteenth-century American culture in which the dignity, prosperity, formal cultivation, and pervasive influence of the legal profession were some of its most striking phenomena. Vashon had studied law in an age when jurisprudence, the liberal arts, and the sciences remained parts of a unified higher education, as testified to in his own multifaceted career as lawyer, mathematician, linguist (with fluency in Greek, Latin, Hebrew, German, French), and author of the masterful epic poem *Vincent Oge*, on the Haitian revolutionary hero. Powerful contrasts were emerging, however, between the scientific worldview affirmed in his *Anglo-African Magazine* essay on "The Successive Advances of Astronomy"—an encomium to the triumph of Laplacean mathematics and Newtonian physics—and the religious folk cosmology of unlettered preacher John Jasper's legendary 1880 sermon "The Sun Do Move," with its fervent experiential rejection of the counterintuitive postulates of Newtonian science. Modern legal science had embraced those postulates in the course of its rise to intellectual dominance; and more than their British or continental European counterparts, American lawyers dominated political life, and to a large extent, business. And as Alexis De Tocqueville had early noted, in America the language and ideas of judicial debate and the spirit of the law penetrated "into the bosom of society."

The pervasive influence of legal ideas and attitudes in American thought, however, was inherently a force for conservatism, a conservatism rooted in the "natural law" philosophy that laws, as in Newtonian science, are to be discovered, not made, that they are patterned in "the nature of things," not on changing human needs. Sanctified in the U.S. Constitution, perhaps no theory of law was better fitted, as Henry Steele Commager noted and as black litigants quickly discovered, to restrict government to negative functions, to put property rights on a par with human rights, to invest the prevailing practices of industrial capitalism with legal sanction, and to provide protection for slavery in the natural law limitations of the due process clause. The U.S. Supreme Court's *Dred Scott Decision* of 1857, nullifying black citizenship rights, and the *Plessy v. Ferguson* decision of 1896, sanctioning "separate but equal" facilities as amenable to the Fourteenth Amendment, reverberated throughout African-American intellectual life; but through their manifest justice, such decisions helped inculcate a pragmatic tradition of protestant legalism in black thought, which eschewed the cult of veneration for the law that, for many other Americans, "made constitutionalism a religion and the judiciary a religious order surrounded with an aura of piety."

At the turn of the twentieth century, as a conflict developed between fixed, Newtonian concepts of law and dynamic, progressive ideas in politics and science, African Americans, guided by their painful experience of law as a fixed system of predation and social control, aligned themselves understandably with the new "sociological jurisprudence" that Roscoe Pound inaugurated as "a process, an activity, not merely a body of knowledge or a fixed order of construction." In accord with the new jurisprudence, as they established practices in local areas and aided in the development of national organizations of racial uplift such as the NAACP, black lawyers like Frederick McGhee (1861–1912), who was admitted to the bar in Illinois and Minnesota and who helped initiate the Niagara Movement (1905), conceived law more and more as an evolving social science, even as a method of social engineering—one that was required to conform to the whole spectrum of social needs and was dependent on society and capable of improvement. W. Ashbie Hawkins (b. 1862) and Scipio Africanus Jones (1863–1943), counsels in World War I–era NAACP civil rights cases, helped establish patterns of case research grounded no less in social facts than in legal rules. Such patterns were intensified by a subsequent generation of constitutionally trained attorneys led by Charles Hamilton Houston, William Hastie, James Nabrit, Raymond Pace Alexander, and Thurgood Marshall—whose collective work on classic civil rights cases spanned the 1930s, 1940s, and 1950s, culminating in *Brown v. Board of Education, Topeka, Kansas* (1954), which ended legal segregation.

Houston, who had specialized in the study of constitutional law, absorbed the philosophy of "sociological jurisprudence" at Harvard Law School under Roscoe Pound's deanship; and on later becoming Dean of Law at Howard University, he promoted the philosophy of legal advocacy as a pragmatic tool available to groups unable to achieve their rightful place in society through direct action. Trained at Howard under Houston's mentoring dictum that "a lawyer's either a social engineer or . . . a parasite on society," Thurgood Marshall, whose nomination to the U.S. Supreme Court by President Lyndon Johnson in 1967 marked the high point of African-American achievement in the judiciary, reaffirmed his own integral place in the new jurisprudential tradition by pointedly reminding celebrants of the 1987 bicentennial of the U.S. Constitution that the nation's founding fathers had held "a woefully incomplete conception of the people" and that their vision of the law, as reflected in the Constitution, had only been expanded through unceasing social struggle that had entailed a bloody civil war.

Because the law had retained its Newtonian character longer than any of the social sciences, the intellectual shift among African-American legal minds toward a pragmatic and evolutionary philosophy of the Constitution and the judiciary was part of a late phase in the broad scientistic conversion of American social thought. Since the tradition of moral reform in black political thought had even deeper roots in the Newtonian worldview—faith that the very perfection of liberty and a just social order was possible if human beings were but reasonable enough to affirm those concepts and virtuous enough to conform to them—the rise of a new anti-Newtonian science of politics posed significant problems for African-American intellectuals. The history of abolitionism and moral reform movements had given black communities a rich tradition of extraofficial political practice anchored in ethical appeals to the "Newtonian" political theory—and the accompanying rhetoric of natural law, social compacts, inalienable rights, immutable laws, eternal principles of justice, and so forth—to which the founding fathers had subscribed. But the new science of politics had been jarred into being by the stark disharmony between those eighteenth-century abstractions and the undeniable late nineteenth-century reality of widespread governmental corruption and incompetence amidst profound changes in society, economy, and technology—changes beyond the ken of the founding fathers. Besides the failed logical legerdemain of the Constitution's three-fifths clause on slavery, the dissonance between eighteenth-century political theory and twentieth-century political reality was nowhere more apparent than in the original failure of the Constitution, and the corollary refusal of the law, to recognize the existence of the country's most important political institution—the political party.

The living realities of party politics—the spoils system, political pluralism, organizational inertia, mass and individual emotionalism or irrationality—therefore dominated the attentions of a statistically minded new political science that its practitioners addressed less to theory of any sort than to "the intimate study of the political process, dealing with interest groups and power relations, with skills and understandings, forms of communications, and personalities." Eschewing progressivist moral reformism as analytically bankrupt, the new science of politics aligned itself with Walter Lippmann's assertion in 1914 that "before you can begin to think about politics at all, you have to abandon the notion that there is a war between good men and bad men . . . [and that] politics is merely a guerilla war between the bribed and the unbribed." No less pertinent to a potential shift in black political strategies, Lippman's concept of the "stereotype" as an adaptive mechanism in mass psychology and public opinion underscored the new scientific orientation away from the Newtonian model of the "rational man" and toward the driven, irrational creature of Freud and the behaviorists.

Between the 1930s and the '60s, as a group of university-trained African-American political scientists emerged, which included Ralph Bunche, G. James Fleming, Robert E. Martin, Erroll Miller, Robert Gill, and Alexander J. Walker, this new orientation to political life became a complicating facet of the ongoing tactical debates in black communities—particularly as it implicated patterns of personal and organizational leadership. The problem of leadership had preoccupied African-American intellectual life from the era of nineteenth-century abolitionism and the National Negro Convention Movement to the Reconstruction era to the turn-of-the-century Washington-Du Bois controversy and the New Negro-Garveyite clashes of the 1920s. Beginning with the Washington-Du Bois controversy, so-called conservative and radical political traditions in African-American life became intensely polarized, though in the later view of scholars such as John Brown Childs, these categories reveal less about the various competing black strategies for social change than does a focus on their underlying materialist or idealist worldviews and related cooperative versus elitist conceptions of political leadership. As became evident in the wave of crusading black political journalism between World Wars I and II, African-American social and intellectual life had been transformed by northern migration and urbanization and

by a rapidly diversifying array of organizations and ideologies advocating a wide spectrum of political strategies. Leading the journalistic upsurge was the NAACP magazine *The Crisis*, begun in 1910 under the editorship of W. E. B. Du Bois, through whom black social thinkers "talked to white America as America had never been addressed before." Other new journals and newspapers had expanded the ideological spectrum: the anarchist *Challenge*, edited by William Bridges, a former Black Nationalist Liberty Party member, in 1916; the socialist *Messenger*—the "Only Radical Magazine in America," edited by labor leaders A. Philip Randolph and Chandler Owen, in 1917; Marcus Garvey's *Negro World*, the organ of the Universal Negro Improvement Association, in 1918; and *Opportunity*, from the Urban League, edited by the sociologist Charles S. Johnson, in 1923.

In this new communicative arena of proliferating print media, a cluster of competing but not mutually exclusive social philosophies in African-American life—several of them with antebellum antecedents—had now acquired formulaic structures and programmatic agendas: (1) liberal integrationism and "cultural pluralism"; (2) conservative bourgeois economic nationalism and black capitalism; (3) Pan-African cultural nationalism; (4) political separatism and emigrationist territorial nationalism; and (5) revolutionary nationalism. Alongside the official leadership of the rising black middle class's civil rights and racial uplift organizations, a popular tradition of millenarian cult heroes, religious revivalists, charismatic revolutionaries, and skilled confidence men had evolved. And parallel to and interpenetrating both of these from below, black folk beliefs, shifting and diversifying with migration, urbanization, and industrialization, articulated a vernacular pantheon of proto-political leadership in tales, toasts, blues, and ballads. Political manifestoes, essays, and fiction by literary intellectuals conversant with social science concepts, such as Richard Wright ("Blueprint for Negro Writers," 1937, and *Native Son*, 1941), Langston Hughes ("The Need for Heroes," 1941), Zora Neale Hurston (*Moses, Man of the Mountain*, 1939), and Ralph Ellison (*Invisible Man*, 1952), meditated metaphorically on the problems of leadership and helped reshape the political imaginations of a growing black audience.

But political scientists like Ralph Bunche, by his own admission, "cultivated a coolness of temper, and an attitude of objectivity" grounded in Darwinian concepts of social evolution, comparative analysis, pragmatism, and emphasis on economic and psychic factors. The first black holder of a political science doctorate, and the founder of Howard University's program in the field, Bunche symbolized a new political role for African-American intellectuals; and starting in 1935 he initiated a probing critique of black organizational leadership and programmatic policies that anatomized their limitations relative to (1) a society that was only "theoretically democratic," to (2) group antagonisms that capitalist economic competition made a "natural phenomenon in a modern industrial society," and to (3) "the stereotyped racial attitudes and beliefs of the masses of the dominant population." Characterizing the entire spectrum of racial advancement organizations—from the NAACP to Garvey's UNIA—as bound to anachronistic assumptions about the nature of the modern world, Bunche's assessment marked a new divide between academic analysts and political practitioners that would become an enduring feature of African-American intellectual life, a divide made clear, for instance, in the contrast between Bunche's *A World View of Race* (1936), a model of economics-based evolutionary pragmatism, and *The Philosophy and Opinions of Marcus Garvey* (1925), with its Newtonian apotheosis of idealist nationalism and racial purity by the architect of urban black America's first mass movement. Ultimately, Bunche's worldview, elaborated through subsequent fieldwork on colonial policy in Africa, led him to play a pivotal role in the formation of the United Nations (drafting the trusteeship sections of the UN Charter in 1945) and to a Nobel Peace Prize for being the architect of the 1949 Near East accord between Jews and Arabs in Palestine.

The urban black world into which Ralph Bunche had been born, and to which Marcus Garvey had immigrated, experienced, during the years their political views were moving toward collision, a flowering of African-American architects on the most literal level. Mass migration had spurred a rising nexus of formal black city-based institutions—businesses, political and educational organizations, churches, fraternal and sororal orders—and with them the New Negro "dream of a Black Metropolis." A paying clientele had evolved for the generation of professionally trained African-American architects who had matriculated at the turn of the twentieth century in the self-help artisan curricula at Tuskegee and Hampton Institute, and later at Howard University. Before these schooled professionals a long history of antebellum slave artisans and free black "master builders" had produced a tradition of vernacular architecture in African-American intellectual life that had left traces of African spatial sense, ornamental motifs, and compositional utility on American buildings as disparate as the 1712 Dutch Jansen House on the Hudson River; various plantation mansions in Old South cities like Savannah, Charleston, and New Orleans; or the early nineteenth-century "African House" built in Louisiana for Isle Brevelle, a settlement of free people of color, by Louis Metoyer, a wealthy ex-slave who had studied architecture in Paris.

During the period from 1880 to 1900, as formal schools of architecture were being founded in America and as black institutions emerged in new southern and northern environments, the most significant American architectural achievements were not so much in monumental buildings as in railroads, grain elevators, bridges, powerhouses, dams, factories, and schools, where the focus on function helped American architects minimize the devitalizing influence of aesthetic imitation fostered by successive Eurocentric academic revivals of Greek, Romanesque, and Gothic styles. In 1892 Booker T. Washington recruited Robert R. Taylor, one of the earliest black graduates in architecture from the Massachusetts Institute of Technology, to develop (without formal accreditation at the time) mechanical industries at the school; and the group of architectural students he trained, including John Lankford, Wallace Rayfield, William Pittman, and Vertner Tandy, became leading designers of the new black religious, educational, and commercial architecture. Modernist style was not yet in the ascendancy in the academy or the public sphere; and African-American architects were caught like their professional peers in the prevailing cultural schism that permitted boldly expressive engineering in bridges or commercial buildings while limiting time-honored cultural institutions at the top of the social hierarchy—the church and the college—to conventional colonial, Romanesque, or Gothic molds. Working within these constraints, Lankford became national supervising architect for the AME Church, designing such landmarks as Atlanta's Big Bethel; Rayfield became supervising architect for the AME Zion Church; and Pittman designed the Negro Building for the 1907 Jamestown Tricentennial.

Some African-American architects who had been trained outside the black college orbit, like William Moses and Julian Abele, mastered the design ethos of public sphere architecture and achieved noteworthy successes outside the black institutional milieu. Moses, awarded a degree in architecture from Pennsylvania State in 1924, won, while on the faculty at Hampton Institute, the open competition to design the Virginia Pavillion at the 1939 New York World's Fair, though this winning design was not used once his racial identity was discovered. Abele, a graduate of the Pennsylvania School of Fine Arts and Architecture, turned his flair for the Gothic revival style into a prominent career as chief designer for the large white architectural firm Horace Trumbauer & Associates in Philadelphia, superintending such projects as Philadelphia's Free Library and Museum of Fine Arts, Harvard University's Widener Library, and the designs for Duke University and the Duke family mansions. Albert Cassell, a 1919 graduate of Cornell University, planned five trade buildings at Tuskegee Institute before assuming leadership of Howard University's Department of Architecture and, deploying a Georgian style, literally transformed the physical appearance of its entire campus.

Perhaps because of the institutional constraints within which most black architects have functioned, and because of the decline of the vernacular tradition, a distinctively African-American philosophy of architecture was slow to evolve, although by 1939 John Louis Wilson, the first black graduate (1928) of Columbia University's school of architecture, hinted at the possibility in his assertion that architecture is a "lithic history of social conditions; [and] the monuments of a race—never the result of chance—survive as indices of the fundamental standards of a people, a locality, and an epoch." During the Harlem Renaissance, as a small black elite gained access to the expressive possibilities of "power architecture," the design choices made in domestic and recreational buildings by figures such as Madame C. J. Walker took on broad symbolic significance. The "cosmopolitan ideal" current among fashionable New Negroes asserted itself in Vertner Tandy's Italianate design for Walker's Irvington-on-the-Hudson palazzo, Villa Lewaro; and a counterpointing "race ideal" manifested itself in the Egyptianizing art deco ornamental motifs created for the flatiron-shaped Walker theater and business center in Indianapolis by the white firm of Rubush & Hunter. In the decades during and after World War II, as black architectural, engineering, and construction firms such as McKissack & McKissack began to win government awards for design contracts, and as educational opportunities in architecture diversified, clusters of black architects and black-owned firms developed in the large urban centers of California, New York, and the District of Columbia, with periodic calls for an African-American style and "soul" in architecture echoing the cycles of cultural consciousness in the nation's increasingly black urban centers.

As secular sources of alternative intellectual authority, all the aforementioned fields of African-American scientistic activity have experienced these cycles of black cultural consciousness in tandem with the shifts in historicism and popular and professional historiography that have figured prominently in black intellectual life during the twentieth century. The nature and intellectual contexts of American history writing in general underwent dramatic changes at the end of the nineteenth century. African-American historians grappled, as did all their peers, both with the growing secularization of ideas that undermined the providential design of older, theologically based ro-

mantic historiography and with the rise of scientific methods and standards of research that accompanied the professionalization of history writing in modern universities. Self-trained George Washington Williams, whose *A History of the Negro Race in America from 1619 to 1880* (1882) constituted the first work of modern historical scholarship by an African American, bridged the old and the new worlds of historiography. His commitment to rigorous citation, to archival research, to cross-checked source materials, and to new primary sources such as newspapers and statistical and oral data placed him in the advance guard of historians. But his political partisanship, his missionary Christianity, and his optimistic faith in the discernability of God's providential design in history set him against the intellectual tendencies that were teaching sociologists, economists, political scientists, and historians alike that they could no longer reveal God's and Newton's laws or construct grand systems. Unlike Harvard-trained W. E. B. Du Bois, whose pioneering monograph, *Suppression of the African Slave Trade* (1896), placed its dispassionate faith in "the empirical knowledge which, dispelling ignorance and misapprehension, would guide intelligent social policy," Williams attuned his work less to reasoned pragmatism than to the rhetoric of popular inspiration— "not as a blind panegyrist" to his race, he wrote, but to satisfy with "the truth, the whole truth, and nothing but the truth," his black readers' "keen sense of intellectual hunger."

Predicated on the need to combat the pejorative Anglo-Western practice that, from David Hume to Arnold Toynbee, denied historical significance to African peoples entirely, both the academic and popular strains of African-American historiography expanded their roles in black intellectual life at the onset of the twentieth century. Such expansion built on the growing black audiences fostered by the rise of public education and mass literacy, by the awakening interest in "race history" encouraged through spreading concepts of nation and nationality, and by the emergence of a group of historical writers based in black colleges and universities or at newspapers and the journals of racial uplift organizations. In Western society generally, the period following World War I saw an explicit ideal of popular history promoted on a mass scale, with an exploding market for sweeping, unflinchingly speculative accounts written in highly dramatic, nontechnical language made evident in the vast sales of H. G. Wells's *Outline of History* (1920), Hendrik Van Loon's *The Story of Mankind* (1921), and Oswald Spengler's *The Decline of the West* (1918–1922). Correspondingly, among nonacademic New Negro historians such as Hubert Harrison, Drusilla Dunjee Houston, J. A. Rogers, and Arthur Schomburg, an inspirational philosophy of race history asserted itself in historical essays and books that were broad in scope and speculative appeal rather than narrowly monographic, that were assertively value-laden and judgmental, and that professed the social utility and moral edification appropriate to black renaissance. Appeals to racial solidarity helped modulate in African-American communities the schism that elsewhere led academic historians to confront the 1920s' and 1930s' vogue of nonprofessional historiography with perjorative contrasts between "popular writing" and "profound systematic treatment." But at mid-century, the contrasts between the works of black academic historians like John Hope Franklin, Benjamin Quarles, and Rayford Logan and those of the "scholars without portfolio" clearly reflected the impact on the former group of the dispassionate ethos and limiting assumptions of authoritative social science methodologies, and the persisting influence on the latter of alternative intellectual authorities mentioned earlier in this article, whose "sacred values" often resided in the romantic, populist, and apocalyptic traditions of "Negro genius," "the folk," and Ethiopianist or Egyptianist revivalism.

In an attempt to characterize the evolution of historical scholarship in postbellum African-American life, John Hope Franklin has proposed the following four-generation typology: (1) a generation of largely nonprofessional historiography beginning with the publication in 1882 of Williams's *History of the Negro Race*, ending around 1909 with Booker T. Washington's *Story of the Negro*, and concerned primarily with explaining the process of adjustment African Americans made to American social conditions; (2) a second generation marked by the publication of Du Bois's *The Negro* in 1915 but dominated from that year forward by the books, organizational entities, periodical enterprises, and scholarly protégés of Carter G. Woodson, who produced a stream of monographs on labor, education, Reconstruction, art, music, and other topics before his death in 1950; (3) a third generation inaugurated by the appearance of Du Bois's *Black Reconstruction* in 1935, and impelled by the intellectual impact of the Great Depression and the World War II global crisis, to focus less on black achievements than on race relations and international contexts, authoring an impressive body of work on slavery and urban and intellectual history and closing the 1960s with a significant number of white historians in the field; and finally (4) the largest and best-trained generation, beginning around 1970, approaching comprehensiveness in their range of specializations, passionately revisionist regarding both conventional *and* black historiographical traditions, and buttressed conceptually and institutionally by the black studies movement and the nationwide integration of American colleges and universities.

Focused less on the developing cadre of professional historians and more on the various uses and diversifying clientele of black history, Benjamin Quarles suggests an alternative typology to describe the different publics that, by the 1970s, dictated the content and style of black history writing: (1) the black rank and file; (2) the black revolutionary nationalists; (3) the black academicians; and (4) the white world, lay and scholarly. First in this scheme, black history for the rank and file, was designed to create a sense of pride and personal worth; and it stressed victories and achievements in a "great man/woman" theory of history highlighted by heroic individuals from African antiquity to the present. Conveyed increasingly by such mass media vehicles as television and radio, magazines, newspapers, coloring books, postcards, games, and comic books, it has emphasized optimistic biographical sketches of black leaders in politics, business, athletics, and the lively arts, with special appeals to youth. By contrast, the black history espoused by revolutionary nationalists has constructed a core narrative of contrapuntal white oppression and black rebellion, has been apocalyptic and polemical in temper, and has compounded elements of Marxist, Pan-Africanist, and anticolonialist ideologies in a studiously historicized but partisan call to black liberation and nation building. Characterized more by radical interpretation than by original research, revolutionary nationalist historiography has eschewed the academic cult of objectivity as inherently conservative and typically selected topics of exploration consonant with its political objectives.

One issue in African-American intellectual life that the historiographical presence of black revolutionary nationalism crystallizes is the role of apocalyptic, millenarian, radical communitarian, socialist, Marxist, and neo-Marxist ideas and ideologies generally in the thought of black communities. Although still understudied as a facet of black intellectual life, the utopian antebellum communitarian movements in which American socialism originated—the Shaker villages, the Owenite communes such as New Harmony and Francis Wright's Nashoba, the Fourieristic phalanxes, and the like—ofttimes had black members (like Shaker elder Rebecca Cox Jackson [1795–1871], for example), even if at the margins; and they characteristically proposed a combination of socialist and colonizationist schemes to end slavery and reconstruct society. The Communist Clubs of "scientific" or Marxian socialists took more radical abolitionist stances and as early as the 1850s were inviting African Americans to join as equal members in the "realization and unification of a world republic" that would recognize "no distinction as to nationality or race, caste or status, color or sex."

Equally important, indigenous African-American dreams of independent black communities or of a "black nation"—to be achieved through internal migration, insurrection, or emigration elsewhere—date back at least to the efforts of Paul Cuffe (1759–1817) to colonize Sierra Leone. In the postbellum era given imaginative expression in narratives such as Sutton Griggs's *Imperium in Imperio* (1899) and organizational form in pre-Garveyite "Back to Africa" schemes such as the Oklahoma exodus of Chief Alfred Sam, they became fused with various strains of programmatic socialism popularized by Edward Bellamy's utopian *Looking Backward* (1888) and *Equality* (1897). Reformist socialism and revolutionary Marxism gained broader appeal in early twentieth-century black communities through the sermons of black socialist preachers such as George Washington Woodbey (b. 1854); through the radical journalism of Cyril Briggs's *The Crusader*, Philip Randolph and Chandler Owen's the *Messenger*; through Hubert Harrison's public oratory, newspaper columns, and Colored Unity League; and through an expanding body of Marxist polemics and historiography written by black members of socialist or communist organizations or by Marxian academics like W. E. B. Du Bois. During the interregnum between the two world wars, the pre-Stalinist "romance of communism," which influenced American liberal intellectuals generally after the 1917 Bolshevik Revolution, won the allegiance of performing artists such as Paul Robeson and black literary intellectuals such as Claude McKay, Langston Hughes, and Richard Wright. And between 1928 and 1943, grounded in party member Harry Haywood's subcommittee advocacy of a "national revolutionary" movement for black self-determination, the Communist Party of the U.S.A. based its mass appeal to African Americans on the proposal to establish an independent "Black Belt" nation in the South. Though the Stalinist era disillusioned many black radicals, as it did many of their nonblack colleagues, the apocalyptic ideological appeal of revolutionary Marxism has persisted in the post–World War II decades, revitalized in African-American intellectual life by the emergence of anticolonialist African socialism (an eclectic mixture primarily of African traditionalism, classical European Marxism, and Chinese socialism) and the Tanzanian socialism of Julius Nyerere in particular, whose *ujamaa* principles of family-centered communal enterprise and nationalized industries were assimilated into the Kwanza celebrations of contemporary African Americans during the apogee of Black Power–era cultural nationalism. After the founding of the Black Panther Party for Self Defense in 1966 by Huey Newton (1942–1989) and Bobby Seale (b. 1936), its paramilitary orchestration of ideas drawn from the Marxist-Leninist corpus, from black nationalist writings, and from anticolonial revolutionary movements in Asia and Africa became the most visible manifestation of black political militancy. Along with the evolving revolutionary nationalism of Malcolm X after his separation from Elijah Muhammad's Nation of Islam, and with the cause célèbre of inmate George Jackson and academically trained Angela Davis, the Black Panther phenomenon helped create a mystique of romantic revolutionism in African-American intellectual life that, among college and university students in particular, remained intense into the 1990s.

The intensity of that mystique is one of the forces that has frequently inclined African-American academic historians to differentiate their work conceptually from that of revolutionary nationalists. Black academicians, inclined by professional training to see history less as inspiration or ideological weapon than as a discipline, have been consistently impelled, by the demand for original and controlled research, away from the obvious and well known toward the study of processes more than persons and to the identification and solution of methodological and conceptual problems apparent in the African-American past. Considering emotionally charged, highly provocative discourse to be, by convention, more the province of the poet, the orator, and the charismatic leader than the professional historian, they have characteristically tried to subordinate their private wishes and values to social science imperatives presumed to be often counterintuitive and counterideological; and they have continued to seek, in the terms of their own understandings, "balanced" treatments of the past rather than the selectively self-gratifying or politically efficacious. Among academic historians, as the uses and clientele of African-American history have increasingly involved white and non-African-American communities, lay and academic, the dual objectives of demythologizing the American past and demonstrating the centrality of black Americans in the national experience have been complicated by the broadening conceptual challenges inherent in the newer historiography of social movements, feminism, and American cultural pluralism. One sign of the intellectual maturation of African-American historical studies in the 1980s and '90s has been their growing awareness of, first, the heuristic value of diversified uses and clienteles for history, and, second, the need for cross-fertilizing perspectives, multimedia modes of presentation, and multidisciplinary methods that recognize the changing character of historical evidence and the array of new techniques and technologies available to record the human journey through time and space.

FACING THE TWENTY-FIRST CENTURY

As suggested earlier, the emergence by the mid-twentieth century of a more stable black middle class fostered the development of an African-American intellectual stratum with functions analogous to those evident in varying degrees in modern societies around the world. Historian John Hope Franklin, himself a leading figure in the generation of professional black scholars who gained prominence during the first postwar decade, by 1979 could write that the years since 1925 had seen an increase, not only in the number of black artist-intellectuals that was unimaginable a half-century earlier, but also in the styles and forms by which they could communicate. The increasing security, solidarity, and self-esteem of their work as intellectuals during "the most productive period in the history of Afro-American literature and culture" derived in large measure from their status as members of a professional intellectual class based increasingly at large, newly integrated white colleges and universities. And the foci of their intellectual activities, at least five of which seem manifest, increasingly paralleled those of intellectuals elsewhere—at the same time that conscious affirmations of difference figured more centrally in their worldview.

First, growing numbers of black intellectuals devoted themselves to creating and diffusing high culture—or a new synthesis of vernacular and high-culture traditions intended to supplant older artistic forms and mythologies. Creativity and originality in the arts and letters was increasingly perceived to be a primary intellectual obligation; and during the 1960s and '70s a "second Black Renaissance" or "Black Arts Movement"—the "aesthetic sister of the Black Power Movement"—became the focus of a concerted effort to link African-American art and politics to the currents of Pan-African intellectual activism in the Third World. Following the opening of Leroi Jones/ Imamu Amiri Baraka's Black Arts Theatre in Newark, N.J., in 1965, shortly after the assassination of Malcolm X, self-proclaimed "New Breed" poets, dramatists, and fiction writers assertively manifested a self-conscious cultural nationalism, influenced partly by the poetics and varying anticolonial philosophies of Francophone black African and Caribbean artist-intellectuals such as Leopold Sedar Senghor of Senegal and Frantz Fanon of Martinique.

Larry Neal, a coleader of the movement along with Amiri Baraka, described the new attitudes toward tradition as stemming from (1) "the historic struggle to obliterate racism in America"; (2) "the general dilemma of identity which haunts American cultural history"; and (3) "an overall crisis in modern intellectual thought in Western society, where values are being assaulted by a new generation of youth around the world as it searches for new standards and ideals." Blending the aesthetic postulates of Francophone *négritude,* the rhythmic lyricism of contemporary blues-derived "soul" music, and the warrior ethos and scatological invective of urban street gangs, Black Arts

intellectuals also developed cross-cultural analogies between their imperatives and those of turn-of-the-century radical Irish Renaissance poets and playwrights who had felt compelled to modulate the influence of English literature on their own works by plunging into Celtic mythology and folklore. Leading figures in the black arts movement, dispersed nationwide in urban artists' collectives that communicated the black arts in new "little magazines" like the *Journal of Black Poetry* and *Black Dialogue,* and through independent publishing houses like Dudley Randall's Broadside Press in Detroit and Don L. Lee/Haki Madhubuti's Third World Press in Chicago, helped sponsor a proliferation of black theaters and bookstores along with a self-consciously performative intellectual style that garnered unprecedentedly large audiences for spoken word recordings like those of The Last Poets and for a new wave of highly stylized urban-based black cinema presented by filmmakers such as Gordon Parks, Melvin Van Peebles, and Gordon Parks Jr.

A second forward-looking focus of African-American intellectual activity developed as global communications and rapid transport intensified the process by which black intellectuals provided national and cross-national models of development for aesthetically sensitive intellectuals all over the world. That process acquired new significance with the expanding power of the international mass media and the emotional appeal of the civil rights and Black Power movements as paradigms for social change among marginalized groups worldwide. A diversifying spectrum of ideologies and cultural modes, associated with groups ranging from the NAACP and CORE (the Congress of Racial Equality) to the Nation of Islam and the Republic of New Africa, influenced youth and social protest movements in Britain and Eastern Europe; and as far away as India, a politico-artistic resistance movement among dark-skinned "untouchables"—the "Dahlit Panthers"—modeled itself on the feline iconography, Marxist-Leninist rhetoric, and community activism of the Black Panthers.

Third, black intellectuals assumed a programmatic commitment to developing common culture and a tradition of cultural criticism. As early as 1925 Alain Locke had described the New Negro movement as an effort to turn the common problem African Americans faced into a common consciousness and culture. William Stanley Braithwaite, W. E. B. Du Bois, Benjamin Brawley, Sterling Brown, Jessie Fauset, Gwendolyn Bennett, and Eric Walrond, among others, helped establish a magazine tradition of critical reviews of literature and the arts during the era; and Theophilus Lewis's columns in the *Messenger* offered pioneering critiques of African-American theater. Maude Cuney-Hare, trained at the New England Conservatory of

Music, founded and directed the Allied Arts Centre in Boston in 1927, dedicating it to "discover and encourage musical, literary, and dramatic talent, and to arouse interest in the artistic capabilities of the Negro child." Superseding James Monroe Trotter's *Music and Some Highly Musical People* (1878), her *Negro Musicians and Their Music* (1936) presented the first comprehensive critical history of the diasporic black creative tradition in a single artistic medium, delineating African music from its earliest phases and explicating the New World influence of African instruments, rhythms, and dances on such forms as the Argentinian tango, the Cuban habañera, and the bamboula of Louisiana (*see* Dance).

Alain Locke's own annual *Opportunity* magazine, defined as "retrospective reviews of the literature of the Negro," from 1928 to midcentury, composed the first sustained attempt at cross-disciplinary, cross-media black cultural criticism—and provided as well an intellectual-history-in-miniature of the era. During these and subsequent decades, the growth of the black population and its dispersion through mass migration and urbanization had created a subsociety too large to be united through kinship connection or firsthand experience. The development of common culture depended increasingly on "reproductive" intellectual institutions such as schools, churches, and newspapers—through which a sense of identity and symbolic group traditions were promoted by African-American teachers, clergy, and journalists. In contrast to the youth-conscious efforts of the New Negro era, during the Great Depression and World War II years a representative group of black intellectuals, including Alain Locke, W. E. B. Du Bois, Ira Reid, Sterling Brown, Ralph Bunche, and Eric Williams, founded an elaborate project of adult education and intergroup relations called the Associates in Negro Folk Education, which, in the course of combatting adult illiteracy, was intended "to bring within the reach of the average reader basic facts and progressive views about Negro life" by publishing a series of "Bronze Booklets" on black fiction, poetry and drama, the visual arts, music, social history, and so forth.

At midcentury, Locke's call for an introspective cultural criticism that would supply the missing "third dimension" of black intellectual life was first met by Margaret Just Butcher's posthumous synthesis, in *The Negro in American Culture* (1956), of Locke's own cumulative explorations of African-American contributions to American music, dance, folklore, poetry, polemics, fiction, drama, painting, sculpture, education, and regional nationalism. However, with the urban rebellions and cultural nationalism of the 1960s and '70s, the ensuing clash of ideas over the concept of racial integration magnified what

Harold Cruse called the "crisis of the Negro intellectual"—the problem of forging a cultural philosophy and a sense of tradition upon which a politics of liberation and a systematic criticism of the arts could be erected. The search for an irreducibly "black aesthetic" began in this context as a fragmentary critical movement grounded in separatist polemics and coalesced outside the academy under the black arts leadership of Amiri Baraka, Larry Neal, Hoyt Fuller, Addison Gayle, Don L. Lee, and Ron Karenga. The "black aestheticians" came closest to discovering a viable indigenous sense of cultural tradition in Baraka's theoretical, ethnomusicologically focused social history, *Blues People* (1963), and his cultural essays. But the more comprehensive and systematic achievements in cultural criticism came after the eclipse of the black arts movement, during the late 1970s and '80s, *within* the academy, as a generation of African-American scholars trained in the theoretical postulates and practices of structuralism, poststructuralism, deconstruction, hermeneutics, dialogics, feminism, and neo-Marxist criticism adapted these modes of analysis to African-American cultural texts and contexts. Academy-based critical theorists such as Houston Baker, Barbara Christian, and Henry Louis Gates became leading figures, as did hip-hop theorists and popular culture critics like Greg Tate, Michele Wallace, and Nelson George in avant-garde mass media newspapers and journals.

Besides the aforementioned emphases on creating art, on building cross-cultural alliances, and on developing a common African-American sense of tradition, a fourth intellectual impulse—to effect broad social change—has persisted in African-American intellectual life as a "sacred value." Continuing racial conflict has kept the degree of intellectual consensus in American society within strict limits; and the different social situations of the recipients of high culture, and the extreme discrepancies in educational preparation and receptive capacity, have fostered diverse paths of creativity and impelled a partial rejection of Western civilization's cultural values among African-American intellectuals. In the post–World War II decades, this rejection of prevailing intellectual traditions has included both nihilistic repudiation of popular or high-culture traditions tainted with ideological racism and the observance or development of an alternative stream of tradition, sometimes of suppressed or forgotten traditions of syncretized or authentic African origin. Guided by the philosophical anthropology of works such as Janheinz Jahn's *Muntu: The New African Culture* and Cheikh Anta Diop's *The African Origin of Civilization*, the theory of social change espoused in the mid-1980s by the proponents of Afrocentricity is rooted in ideological advocacy of the original unity of African culture, and in the need for a revitalizing new ethnocultural consciousness among the peoples of the modern African diaspora, as a prerequisite for a unifying politics of liberation. Although the validity of Jahn's and Diop's views have been challenged by other specialists in African studies, and though debate about the "essentialist" postulates and racialist implications of Afrocentricity has intensified among intellectuals inside and outside African-American communities, the growing pervasiveness of the concept and its texts and iconography cannot be dismissed.

Three other recent developments in African-American intellectual life merit attention with respect to concepts of social change—the growth of black liberation theology, the emergence of African-American critical legal theory, and the consolidation of black neoconservative ideology. Regarding the first of these, under the leadership of James Cone, and in dialogue with other theologians such as James De Otis Roberts, Cain Felder, and philosopher Cornel West, black religious thinkers who matured in the Black Power era have moved beyond the black church tradition of Christian ecumenism, espoused by such earlier leaders as Benjamin Mays (1894–1984) and Howard Thurman (1900–1981), and beyond the synthesis with Gandhian nonviolence effected by Martin Luther King Jr. (1929–1968). As a forerunner to contemporary African-American theologians, Benjamin Mays, a Southern sharecropper's son who rose to become a Baptist minister and president of Morehouse College, devoted part of his early career to scholarship for the Institute of Social and Religious Research and authored books such as *The Negro's Church* (1933) and *The Negro's God as Reflected in His Literature* (1938), which provided pioneering descriptions of African-American religious life "as scientifically exact as the nature of the material permits." In addition, as a religious teacher advocating Christian practice in race relations, he became one of the spiritual progenitors of the civil rights movement, urging students such as Andrew Young and Julian Bond into public service and considering "his greatest honor [to be] having taught and inspired Martin Luther King Jr." Howard Thurman, also an ordained Baptist minister, became dean of Rankin Chapel, professor of theology at Howard University, and one of the twelve "Great Preachers" of this century. But his unorthodox "inward journey" in quest of a spiritual liberation beyond race and ethnicity led him to develop a unique mystical ecumenism that drew on spiritual experiences in India (with Mohandas Gandhi), Sri Lanka, and Myanmar as well as on the cosmology of African-American spirituals and on Native American belief systems in his own ancestry. The most prolific of African-American religious writers, Thurman authored a long succession of richly metaphorical meditations on love, temptation, spiritual discipline, creative encounter, and the search for religious

common ground, which influenced generations of black seminarians, among them Martin Luther King Jr.

Because King has influenced African-American intellectual life perhaps more than any other religious thinker, it is important to understand his theology of the "beloved community" as a complex fusion of African-American church traditions and advanced formal training in the philosophies of such diverse thinkers as Henry David Thoreau, Mohandas Gandhi, G. W. F. Hegel, Walter Rauschenbusch, and Reinhold Niebuhr. In James Cone's view, King's ministry of social transformation through creative, nonviolent confrontation embodied publicly the central ideas of black religious thought—love, justice, liberation, hope, and redemptive suffering—terms used in common with other Christian communities but given a distinctively black meaning by particular social and political realities. In Cone's own work, however, the preeminence King gave to love in this cluster of mutually dependent values was shifted to the concept of liberation; and in the wake of the Black Power era and under the influence of Malcolm X's nationalist, Islamicist critique of white Christian supremacism, Cone and other black liberation theologians have increasingly turned away from the texts of European Christian theology and toward African-American vernacular religion as a thematic locus. By drawing partly on the work of Latin American theologians of liberation, and by reformulating aspects of the African-American Ethiopianist tradition, they have posited a new Christocentric black theology, centered on a biblical witness of God's commitment to the poor and oppressed, which "places our *past* and *present* actions toward Black liberation in a theological context, seeking to create value-structures according to the God of black freedom." Cultivating a global worldview and sensitivities to other oppressed social groups, black liberation theologians have acknowledged the strengths and the weaknesses of traditional black theology: "For example, Africans showed the lack of knowledge black theologians had about African culture; Latin theologians revealed the lack of class analysis; Asia showed the importance of a knowledge of religions other than Christianity; feminist theology revealed the sexist orientation of black theology; and other minorities in the United States showed the necessity of a coalition in the struggle for justice in the nation and around the globe."

The import acknowledged herein of religions other than Christianity points to a related facet of African-American intellectual life—the long-lived and currently increasing role of non-Christian concepts of liberation, from Islamic, Judaic, Buddhist, Bahai, Rastafarian, traditional African beliefs, and occult traditions, among others. In developing a spectrum of relating thought that, as Cone recognizes, "is neither exclusively Christian . . . nor primarily African," African Americans have frequently chosen to profess other world religions or various nonconformist and free-thought beliefs ostensibly better suited to liberate them from white Christian nationalism and the maladies of modern living. As early as Edward Wilmot Blyden's *Christianity, Islam, and the Negro Race* in 1887, selected black religious thinkers have lauded the elevating and unifying potential of Islam, the benefits of its world civilization, and its vaunted capacity for incorporating Africans without creating in them a sense of inferiority. The perceived historic continuity with West African Islam has been a contributing factor to its appeal, just as the antecedent historical tradition of Ethiopian "Falashas" has lent Judaism greater appeal to orthodox as well as heterodox African-American converts and believers.

By contrast, the reception of Bahaism, which treats religious truth as relative, not absolute, and as evolving through successive revelations provided by prophets from many different traditions, suggests the intellectual appeal of newer religious worldviews to African-American adherents. A much-persecuted, heretical nineteenth-century Persian offshoot of Islam, the Bahai faith developed a distinctly modern theology rooted in the professedly indivisible oneness of humankind, the necessary accord of religion with science and reason, the absolute equality of men and women, and the abolition of prejudice of all kinds. As it spread to America early in the twentieth century, Bahaism distinguished itself to African Americans by identifying the race problem as a major *spiritual* problem and by openly sponsoring "racial amity" conferences and unification through intermarriage at a time when American Christianity remained thoroughly segregated. The Bahai faith attracted African-American artist-intellectuals as different as the philosopher Alain Locke, the *Chicago Defender* publisher Robert Abbott, the jazz musician "Dizzy" Gillespie, and the poet Robert Hayden, offering a vision of progressive social change through priestless, "democratic theocracy" that by 1983 saw African Americans accounting for more than 30 percent of its U.S. membership.

At some remove from the religious worldview, in the decidedly secular thought of contemporary legal theorists such as Derrick Bell, Patricia Williams, and Stephen Carter, the importance of law as a locus for social change theories has been reemphasized; and the transformative powers *and* limits of the law have been reconceptualized in highly original mixtures of allegory, case law, social history, and autobiographical meditation that defy the positivist conventions of the older sociologist jurisprudence. A recurrent feature of this new legal discourse is a powerful intellectual skepticism that confronts the older African-American tradition of millenarian hope with the specter of racism as "an integral, permanent, and indestructible component of this society." Among black legal theorists on both the political left and right, the law itself is seen less as an edifice of immutable truths or a blueprint for social engineering than as a chaotic mythological text; and the manifest contradictions of such legal remedies as affirmative action serve to underscore the narrowed possibilities for progressive social change through legal construction. The challenge such a perspective mounts to the activist traditions of African-American intellectual life are multiple, not the least of which is the very definition of the intellectual's proper function. Accordingly, as construed by constitutional lawyer Stephen Carter, "the defining characteristic of the intellectual is not (as some seem to think) a particular level of educational or cultural attainment, and certainly not a political stance," but rather "the drive to learn, to question, to understand, to criticize, not as a means to an end but as an end in itself."

In the wake of the civil rights and Black Power eras, the rise of a cohesive black neoconservative movement has given skeptical, iconoclastic criticism of African-American life high visibility, particularly through the scholarly writings of authors such as economist Thomas Sowell and cultural commentators Stanley Crouch and Shelby Steele. The movement has some historical precedent in early forms of black economic nationalism, capitalist and socialist, that have sought various degrees of economic and social autonomy from the larger society through (1) controlling the black segment of the marketplace through black businesses and "buy black campaigns"; (2) establishing a full-scale black capitalist economy parallel to that of the dominant society; or (3) forming black producer and consumer cooperatives or reviving preindustrial communalism. Such ideas have figured significantly in the outlooks of Booker T. Washington, W. E. B. Du Bois, Marcus Garvey, the Nation of Islam, and others; and they defy conventional "conservative" and "radical" categorization. But as early as 1903 sociologist Kelly Miller had highlighted the ideological warfare between black "radicals and conservatives" in order to interpret the Washington–Du Bois controversy over political, economic, and educational strategies for racial uplift. Acknowledging the ambiguities therein, Alain Locke in 1925 described the psychology of the "New Negro" in part by asserting that "for the present the Negro is radical on race matters, conservative on others, a 'forced radical,' a social protestant rather than a genuine radical." And giving these psychopolitical tensions the most emphatic personal configuration, *Pittsburgh Courier* journalist and satirist George Schuyler, having renounced his 1920s allegiances to leftist politics, ultimately embraced autobiographically a reformulated new public identity as *Black and Conservative* (1966), establishing further precedent for the phenomenon of the 1970s and 1980s that saw growing numbers of African-American intellectuals joining the "neoconservative" flight from liberal-radical social philosophies and public policy.

Because conservatism has typically been identified—often wrongly—with Republican party politics, and because critics have often failed to distinguish properly conservatives from neoconservatives (the distinction is ideological more than chronological), African Americans have often chafed at the latter label. But whatever differentiates them from nominal neoconservatives, the writings of intellectuals like Sowell and Steele do share some pivotal neoconservative stances about social policy: (1) though less likely than conservatives to condemn governmental manipulation of the citizenry as fundamentally immoral regardless of the intended social improvements, they are more likely than liberals to be disillusioned by the failures of public policy and to insist that there is little public policy leverage for changing the relevant human behaviors and conditions of modern life; (2) they tend to agree with neoconservatives that the limitations of our knowledge about the consequence of any given policy, and the basic inefficiency of bureaucratic government in implementing policy, make the liberal agenda indefensible and unachievable.

Largely in accord with these stances, Thomas Sowell has elaborated the black neoconservative position in more than a dozen books that compare the economic performance of ethnic groups around the world and advocate laissez-faire economics, with minimal government regulation, as more amenable to black progress than the bureaucratic manipulations of the liberal welfare state. And in *A Conflict of Visions: Ideological Origins of Political Struggle* (1987), he has attempted to identify two perennial diametrically opposed visions of human nature and society, one "constrained" and the other "unconstrained," as the root of political turmoil in the modern era. The "constrained" vision with which Sowell has allied himself eschews "unconstrained" notions of human rationality and perfectibility for an emphasis on the limitations of human altruism and reason and on the pragmatic necessity for disciplined cultural traditions and a society ordered and stabilized by the free marketplace. Shelby Steele's corollary "new vision of race in America," articulated in *The Content of Our Character* (1990), lacks Sowell's theoretical sweep and supporting data but offers provocative speculations about the tangle of psychopathological guilt, fear, damaged self-esteem, and false ethnic pride that, in his view, has prevented African Americans from taking advantage of real opportunities for success and misdirected their energies away from meaningful social competition and into black

nationalist fantasies, chauvinistic educational enterprises, and ineffective affirmative action programs. However controversial, the arguments of Sowell, Steele, and other black neoconservatives have enhanced the sophistication of policy debates in African-American communities; and, capitalizing on the strategic and philosophical quandaries traditional liberal-radical civil rights organizations faced during the Reagan-Bush era, they have forced black thinkers across the political spectrum to consider anew the basic concepts and practical methods of social conservatism and social change.

Perhaps the most far-reaching recent developments in black intellectual life with respect to concepts of social change, however, have come through the flowering and dispersion of black feminist thought in the 1970s and '80s, building on a long tradition of African-American female leadership, creative activity, and political activism. The emergence of a cohesive and consummately skilled group of black female literary artists, in the wake of the black arts and women's liberation movements of the 1960s and '70s, helped galvanize the formation of black women's studies as an autonomous academic discipline in the middle 1970s, epitomized by the appearance in 1982 of Gloria Hull, Patricia Scott, and Barbara Smith's ground-breaking critical anthology *All the Women Are White, All the Blacks Are Men, But Some of Us Are Brave*. Organized as an interdisciplinary field of theoretical and practical study that is unified by black female perspectives on the conceptual triumvirate of "race, class, and gender," advocates of black women's studies have reconstructed an historical continuity of black feminist expression—from Maria Stewart's 1830s African-American Female Society addresses to Sojourner Truth's famous "Ain't I a Woman?" speech in 1851 to the 1890s manifestoes of Anna Julia Cooper and Victoria Earle Matthews; and from Amy Jacques Garvey's mid-1920s nationalist/feminist editorials and the Depression-era fiction and folklore of Zora Neale Hurston to the contemporary "womanist" prose, poetry, and drama of Alice Walker and her peers.

Walker's concept of the "womanist" as one who "acknowledges the particularistic experiences and cultural heritage of black women, resists systems of domination, and insists on the liberty and self-determination of all people" comes close to providing a consensual definition of the range of ideologies and praxis of black women's feminism. But the proliferation of black feminist ideas across the spectrum of lay and professional intellectual activities defies any narrow construction of its purposes and practices; and its versatility and growing popular appeal have become evident in the diverse audiences for such black feminist cultural critics as Hazel Carby, the writer bell hooks, and Michele Wallace, for popular and academic historians of black female experience such as Paula Giddings and Darlene Clark Hine, for social scientists such as Joyce Ladner, Patricia Hill Collins, and MacArthur prize-winner Sara Lawrence Lightfoot, whose *Balm in Gilead: Journey of a Healer* (1988), an intergenerational biography of her mother, the pioneering child psychiatrist Margaret Lawrence, consummates the formal valorization of black female family traditions.

As a final focus of contemporary practical and theoretical activity, black intellectuals, spurred by an expanding African-American electorate and corollary concentrations of local and national political power, have increasingly found themselves playing explicitly political roles in grassroots and electoral mobilization for city, state, and federal offices, for black third-party conventions, and for presidential campaigns such as those of the Rev. Jesse Jackson in 1984 and 1988 and Gov. Bill Clinton in 1992. However, inasmuch as the political elite needs the approbation and services of intellectuals but remains loath to share the highest authority with them, the separation of black intellectuals from the higher executive and legislative branches of government parallels more starkly the marginal situation of American intellectuals generally as it has evolved from the time of the Jacksonian revolution until the "New Liberalism" of Woodrow Wilson and afterward. Nonetheless, liberal and constitutional politics in modern states have to a large extent been "intellectuals' politics"—that is, politics vaguely impelled by ideals precipitated into programs. Racial exclusion has made even more pronounced for African Americans the intellectuals' major political vocation of enunciating and pursuing the ideal. And as part of the "crisis of the Negro intellectual" articulated by Harold Cruse at the height of the Black Power movement during the late 1960s, the vitiation of this political vocation among black intellectuals has been exacerbated by their problematic sense of continuity with their cultural, creative, and ideological antecedents.

Such a crisis notwithstanding, however, by no means have black intellectuals been uniformly attracted by ideological politics, even those of civil rights and Black Power. Moderation and devotion to the rules of civil polity, quiet and apolitical concentration on specialized intellectual tasks, cynical or antipolitical passivity, and faithful acceptance of, and service to, the existing order are all to be found in substantial proportions among modern black intellectuals, just as among their nonblack peers. Although their work in scientific and scholarly spheres remains subject to much stricter regulation than in the fields of expressive intellectual action, some black intellectuals have influenced realignments of the social structure, within the intellectual subsociety in particular, supplanting the incumbents of leadership roles in professional intellectual associations and garnering previously unattainable allocations of intellectual awards and prizes—one of the most noteworthy being the award of the 1993 Nobel Prize for Literature to novelist Toni Morrison. And new fields of inquiry have been pioneered by black intellectuals such as Harry Edwards in the sociology of sport and the prolific critic Nathan Scott Jr. in religious literary criticism. Nonetheless, in the closing decade of the twentieth century, the long-lived function of black intellectuals in supplying the doctrines and some of the leaders of protest and social change movements remained one of their most widely accepted and effective roles. And from the evidence of the imaginative and theoretical roles played by contemporary writers such as Octavia Butler and Samuel R. Delany in the immensely popular realm of fantasy and science-based "speculative fiction," black intellectuals in the closing years of the second millennium were poised also to help formulate and guide a global society's creative vision of its possible futures.

See also Abolition; Afrocentrism; Anthropology and Anthropologists; Architecture; Art; Black Arts Movement; Black Middle Class; Black Power Movement; Black Studies; Civil War, U.S.; Communist Party of the United States; Dance; Education in the United States; Feminist Theory and Criticism; Film; Folklore; Free Blacks, 1619–1860; Great Depression and the New Deal; Harlem Renaissance; Historians and Historiography; Identity and Race in the United States; Journalism; Kwanza; Literature; Masculinity; Mathematicians; Music; Nationalism in the United States in the Nineteenth Century; New Negro; Pan-Africanism; Political Ideologies; Politics; Race and Science; Religion; Representations of Blackness in the United States; Science; Slavery; Social Psychology, Psychologists, and Race; Sociology; Spirituality; Woodson, Carter Godwin

■ ■ *Bibliography*

Banks, William M. *Black Intellectuals: Race and Responsibility in American Life*. New York: W. W. Norton, 1996.

Barksdale, Richard, and Kenneth Kinnamon, eds. *Black Writers of America*. New York: Macmillan, 1972.

Bell, Bernard W. *The Afro-American Novel and Its Traditions*. Amherst: University of Massachusetts Press, 1987.

Buhle, Mari Jo, et al., eds. *Encyclopedia of the American Left*. 2d ed. New York: Oxford University Press, 1998.

Bullock, Penelope. *The Afro-American Periodical Press, 1838–1909*. Baton Rouge: Louisiana State University, 1981.

Buterfield, Stephen. *Black Autobiography in America*. Amherst: University of Massachusetts Press, 1974.

Childs, John Brown. *Leadership, Conflict, and Cooperation in Afro-American Social Thought.* Philadelphia: Temple University Press, 1989.

Coles, Robert. *Black Writers Abroad: A Study of Black American Writers in Europe and Africa.* New York: Garland, 1999.

Commager, Henry Steele. *The American Mind: An Interpretation of American Thought and Character since the 1880s.* New Haven, Conn.: Yale University Press, 1950.

Cone, James. "Black Religious Thought." In Charles Lippy and Peter Williams, eds., *Encyclopedia of the American Religious Experience.* Vol. 2. New York: Scribner, 1988.

Cruse, Harold. *The Crisis of the Negro Intellectual: A Historical Analysis of the Failure of Black Leadership.* New York: New York Review Books, 2005.

Diedrich, Maria, Henry Louis Gates, and Carl Pedersen, eds. *Black Imagination and the Middle Passage.* New York: Oxford University Press, 1999.

Dozier, Richard. "Black Architecture." In Charles Wilson and William Ferris, eds., *Encyclopedia of Southern Culture.* Chapel Hill: University of North Carolina Press, 1989.

Elder, Arlene. *The "Hindered Hand": Cultural Implication of Early African American Fiction.* Westport, Conn.: Greenwood Press, 1978.

Ellison, Ralph. *Shadow and Act.* New York: Random House, 1964.

Foner, Philip S. *American Socialism and Black Americans, from the Age of Jackson to World War II.* Westport, Conn.: Greenwood Press, 1977.

Franklin, John Hope. *Race and History: Selected Essays 1938–1988.* Baton Rouge: Louisiana State University Press, 1989.

Fullinwider, S. P. *The Mind and Mood of Black America.* Homewood, Ill.: Dorsey Press, 1969.

Guthrie, Robert V. *Even the Rat Was White: A Historical View of Psychology.* 2d ed. Boston: Allyn and Bacon, 2004.

Jackson, Blyden. *A History of Afro-American Literature. Vol. 1, The Long Beginning, 1746–1895.* Baton Rouge: Louisiana State University Press, 1989.

James, Joy. *Transcending the Talented Tenth: Black American Intellectuals.* New York: Routledge, 1997.

Loewenberg, Bert James, and Ruth Bogin, eds. *Black Women in Nineteenth-Century American Life.* University Park: Pennsylvania State University Press, 1976.

Logan, Rayford, and Michael R. Winston, eds. *Dictionary of American Negro Biography.* New York: Norton, 1982.

Loggins, Vernon. *The Negro Author: His Development in America.* New York: Columbia University Press, 1931.

Meier, August. *Negro Thought in America, 1880–1915.* Ann Arbor: University of Michigan Press, 1963.

Miller, Perry. *The Life of the Mind in America, from the Revolution to the Civil War.* New York: Harcourt, Brace, 1965.

Moses, Wilson. *Afrotopia: The Roots of African American Popular History.* New York: Cambridge University Press, 1998.

Moses, Wilson. *The Wings of Ethiopia: Studies in African-American Life and Letters.* Ames: Iowa State University Press, 1990.

Moss, Alfred A. *The American Negro Academy: Voice of the Talented Tenth.* Baton Rouge: Louisiana State University Press, 1981.

Perry, Lewis. *Intellectual Life in America: A History.* New York: F. Watts, 1984.

Napier, Winston. *African American Literary Theory: A Reader.* New York: New York University Press, 2000.

Porter, Dorothy B. "The Organized Educational Activities of Negro Literary Societies, 1828–1846." *Journal of Negro Education* 5 (1936): 555–76.

Posnock, Ross. *Color & Culture: Black Writers and the Modern Intellectual.* Boston: Harvard University Press, 1998.

Quarles, Benjamin. *Black Mosaic: Essays in Afro-American History and Historiography.* Amherst: University of Massachusetts Press, 1988.

Robinson, Cedric. *Black Marxism: The Making of the Black Radical Tradition.* Chapel Hill: University of North Carolina Press, 2000.

Sammons, Vivian Ovelton. *Blacks in Science and Medicine.* New York: Hemisphere, 1990.

Shils, Edward. "Intellectuals." In *International Encyclopedia of the Social Sciences,* 7: 399–415. New York: Macmillan, 1968–1991.

Smith, Jesse Carnie, ed. *Notable Black American Women.* 3 vols. Detroit: Gale, 1992–2003.

Smith, Jesse Carnie, ed. *Notable Black American Men.* Detroit: Gale, 1998.

Smythe, Mabel, ed. *The Black American Reference Book.* Englewood Cliffs, N.J.: Prentice-Hall, 1976.

Thorpe, Earl, *The Mind of the Negro.* Westport, Conn.: Negro Universities Press, 1961.

Vincent, Theodore, ed. *Voices of a Black Nation: Political Journalism in the Harlem Renaissance.* San Francisco: Ramparts Press, 1973.

Wilmore, Gayraud. *Black Religion and Black Radicalism.* 3d ed. Maryknoll, N.Y.: Orbis Books, 1998.

JOHN S. WRIGHT (1996)
Updated bibliography

INTERNATIONAL RELATIONS OF THE ANGLOPHONE CARIBBEAN

❙❙❙

The history of the Caribbean is a mosaic of conquests by European powers, starting with the arrival of Christopher Columbus in 1492. However, from the promulgation of the Monroe Doctrine in 1823, the United States gradually assumed a greater influence in the region that fit within the wider context of the growth of colonialism and the increasing struggle among powerful states to secure a dominant position in the global political economy. Given its proximity and regional hegemony, it is the United States that has been able to influence the agenda of issues that Caribbean nations face, as well as shape the context and contours of decisions made by the various governments. So, in order to understand the nature of Caribbean international relations, one needs to take into consideration the historical, geostrategic, economic, and political power realities of the region.

The geography of the Caribbean combines with a shared history to provide an appearance of a homogenized region, but the reality is that Caribbean states have struggled on similar but separate tracks to find a foreign policy approach. Size, type of government, and at times the role of political and government leaders all figure in the complex dynamics of interactions among various actors, including states, organizations, and individuals at the domestic, regional, and international levels. National differences of wealth, developmental level, and politics have also had a direct bearing on Caribbean foreign policies. Haiti, for example, was the first Caribbean country to become independent (in 1804), but it has been plagued with a legacy of dictatorship. On the other hand, the nations of the English-speaking Caribbean gained independence during the 1960s and have relatively stable variants of the British parliamentary system. Overall, there is a dependence on foreign trade and a reliance on a narrow economic base comprised of agricultural production of cash crops such as sugar and bananas; mining and the manufacturing of oil, bauxite, gold, and apparel; and service industries. This dependency is reflected in a number of ways as the region struggles to break old patterns and seek greater influence in the global arena. The Caribbean has therefore operated under a variety of political and economic constraints that limit what Caribbean governments can accomplish and that reduce their control over events.

INDEPENDENCE AND THE COLD WAR ERA

In the immediate years after independence, some Caribbean governments sought to develop relations with other developing states outside of the region. Reflecting the ethnic heritage of the people, Trinidad and Tobago and Guyana developed ties with India and, along with Jamaica, created diplomatic links with some African countries. Despite the fact that these efforts were well intended, they have been mostly symbolic. The majority of Caribbean states gained independence during the 1960s, a period filled with the tensions and conflicts of East-West rivalry. The Cold War thus set the tone for foreign relations as the countries gained in importance, not because of anything intrinsic to them but because of their links with the wider struggle between the United States and the Soviet Union. The character of Caribbean relations during the Cold War was de-

fined by security concerns within the framework of the containment of communism, especially after the 1959 Cuban Revolution. The ensuing threat of Cuba as an exporter of revolution—and its growing alliance with the Soviet Union—led to the 1961 Bay of Pigs invasion, the Cuban Missile Crisis, and the resulting policy of political and economic isolation of Cuba. In 1965 the United States engaged in direct military intervention in the Dominican Republic, and by 1983 the anticommunist strategy had intensified under President Ronald Reagan with a military intervention in Grenada. The Reagan administration also launched the Caribbean Basin Initiative as a means of increasing trade and investment, but the initiative rewarded only those countries that implemented free-market economic reforms and served as a manifestation of a growing dependence on the United States.

By the 1970s, the Cold War atmosphere also witnessed the rise of a new set of leaders (such as Michael Manley of Jamaica, Forbes Burnham of Guyana, and Maurice Bishop of Grenada) who sought new solutions for the old problems of colonialism and neocolonialism. Their foreign policies, couched in anti-imperialist rhetoric, coincided with the U.S. strategy of constant opposition to radical regimes in the region. With issues of development a common theme, these leaders turned increasingly to Third World and North-South forums to address issues of development. The Non-Aligned Movement, which first sought to avoid the trappings of the Cold War, embarked on a strategy of maximizing the gains from the bipolar competition between the United States and the Soviet Union. Armed with the solidarity gained from the Non-Aligned Movement, the Caribbean and developing nations in other regions used the Group of 77 in the United Nations to demand a New International Economic Order in a special session of the United Nations in May 1974. This helped to set the economic agenda for over a decade, but it eventually gave way to neoliberal strategies. Their influence was reduced in the multilateral arena, however, with the shift in the North-South dialogue from the political arenas of the United Nations to the financial and trade institutions of the International Monetary Fund (IMF) and the World Trade Organization (WTO).

NEGOTIATING CAPACITY, INSTITUTIONAL RELATIONS, AND ECONOMIC SURVIVAL

The international and global agenda for the Caribbean changed rapidly with the beginning of the 1980s. The end of the Cold War and the decline of communism helped to dramatically accelerate powerful trends that required changes in the policies and behaviors of states. Toward the end of the twentieth century, severe financial crises caused by rising debt, falling exports, and shrinking economies in an increasingly global economy influenced the tone and style of Caribbean foreign policy and relations. These ideological and policy changes have led to a shift toward developing appropriate domestic policies. The bargaining leverage enjoyed in the Cold War era, and the confrontational tactics geared toward international regulation, have given way to market-oriented economic policies and political pluralism as the basis for economic development. Private and commercial entities and multilateral financial institutions such as the IMF have become major actors in the planning and implementation of policy for all the Caribbean states. In addition, globalization, structural adjustment, and reforms have posed a challenge for the small, open economies that are very vulnerable to external shocks.

The preferential arrangements that guaranteed duty-free access to European markets under the ACP (African, Caribbean, and Pacific) Lomé Convention, the Caribbean Basin Initiative, and the Caribbean-Canada Trade Agreement (CARIBCAN) are now challenged by new rules enforced by the WTO and created to promote a liberalized global trading regime and facilitate negotiations on trade-related issues. The "banana dispute," in which the United States joined with Mexico and Central American countries to pressure the European Union to liberalize its banana trade with the Caribbean, exemplifies the new realities. This has resulted in increasing competition and marginalization of the Caribbean, especially for the eight small island economies of the Organization of Eastern Caribbean States. In addition, the United States is the Caribbean's largest trading partner, accounting for most of the imports into the region. Yet the countries all compete to get access to a U.S. market that has become increasingly protectionist. The economies of the Caribbean (except Trinidad and Tobago) have also become dependent on services for export. Tourism constitutes the greater portion of service exports and is very vulnerable to natural disasters, travel patterns of tourists, and competition within and outside of the region.

Given the increasing vulnerability and the failure of reform advocated by the New International Economic Order, Caribbean states have turned to regional and subregional groupings with the hopes of finding their own identity and a basis for common action to take advantage of growing economic interdependence and to address the realities of global competition. The first attempt toward regionalism dates back to 1966 with the formation of the Caribbean Free Trade Association (CARIFTA). Then, in 1973, the Treaty of Chaguaramas created the Caribbean Community and Common Market (CARICOM). The treaty was revised in 1992 to facilitate the creation of the Caribbean Single Market and Economy (CSME), which includes a common external tariff; functional cooperation in agriculture, energy, transportation, tourism, meteorology, natural disaster, education and law; regional cooperation in infrastructure; and a Caribbean Court of Justice. In an effort toward wider relations in the region, the Association of Caribbean States (ACS) was formed in 1996. Its membership of thirty-six nations includes Cuba, the Dominican Republic, Haiti, Mexico, Colombia, Venezuela, and the Isthmus states. The CSME is expected to remove barriers to the movement of labor, capital, goods, and services between the signatories of the fifteen member states—the agreement came into effect in January 2005 between Jamaica, Trinidad and Tobago, and Barbados, with the expectation that the other members would join by the end of the year. However, the region still has to deal with problems of sovereignty and commitments to the integration process.

The Free Trade Area of the Americas (FTAA) is another regional/hemispheric vehicle touted as one way in which Caribbean economies would be able to make positive adjustments in an era of globalization. A basic framework is in place, but a number of difficult issues are unresolved. There are different interpretations of whether the FTAA should be a primarily market-access agreement or a broader rules-based pact. Caribbean governments have emphasized the need for fair trade to address the issue of special and differential treatment. Furthermore, since September 11, 2001, security has displaced trade on the U.S. agenda, and the merging of the war on terrorism with the war on drugs has resulted in an emphasis on creating "smart" borders and denying safe havens for terrorists. There are now fears that commitments to hemispheric security will override the importance of economic development of the region.

AN UNCERTAIN FUTURE

The parameters of Caribbean international relations have now shifted to the promotion of interests in an environment that is dominated by (and challenged with) concerns of globalization, economic competition, and terrorism. The Caribbean also exists in a world dominated by the most powerful state, which has historically influenced the image and fate of its relations. The pervasive nature of economic crises and increasing constraints on the state have reduced any semblance of autonomy derived from the rights of sovereignty and the ability to formulate independent positions in foreign policy. The future of the Caribbean nations in international politics will greatly depend on the dynamic mix between the demands that external chal-

Fidel Castro, president of Cuba (left), with Keith Mitchell, prime minister of Grenada. *Grenada was the last stop for Castro during a six-day tour of the Caribbean in 1998, fifteen years after U.S. troops invaded the island nation to put down a Marxist coup.* PHOTOGRAPH BY KIMBERLY WHITE. HULTON/ARCHIVE, GETTY IMAGES. REPRODUCED BY PERMISSION.

lenges and internal politics simultaneously place on the governments of the region. As a people, the Caribbean extends beyond its geographical boundaries to the various metropolitan centers of Europe and North America. These overseas aggregations—in the form of a diaspora—are larger than many of the member states in the region. The survival and development of the Caribbean in international affairs may have to rely, in the final analysis, on the creativity of its people both within and beyond the confines of the Caribbean Sea.

See also Bishop, Maurice; Burnham, Forbes; Caribbean Community and Common Market (CARICOM); Manley, Michael; Media and Identity in the Caribbean; Natural Resources of the Caribbean

■ ■ *Bibliography*

Atkins, G. Pope. *Latin America and the Caribbean in the International System,* 4th ed. Boulder, Colo.: Westview, 1999.

Grant-Wisdom, Dorith. "US-Caribbean Relations." In *Caribbean Security in the Age of Terror: Challenge and Change,* edited by Ivelaw Griffith. Kingston, Jamaica: Ian Randle, 2004.

Griffith, Ivelaw, ed. *Caribbean Security in the Age of Terror: Challenge and Change.* Kingston, Jamaica: Ian Randle, 2004.

Haar, Jerry, and Anthony Bryan, eds. *Canadian-Caribbean Relations in Transition: Trade, Sustainable Development, and Security.* New York: St. Martin's Press, 1999.

Hall, Kenneth, and Dennis Benn, eds. *Contending with Destiny: The Caribbean in the 21st Century.* Kingston, Jamaica: Ian Randle, 2000.

Thomas, Clive Y. *The Poor and the Powerless: Economic Policy and Change in the Caribbean.* New York: Monthly Review Press, 1988.

Watson, Hilbourne, ed. *The Caribbean in the Global Political Economy.* Boulder, Colo.: Lynne Reiner, 1994.

DORITH GRANT-WISDOM (2005)

INVENTIONS

See Inventors and Inventions; Patents and Inventions

INVENTORS AND INVENTIONS

Historians are just beginning to uncover some of the ways in which African Americans have contributed to the development of American technology. Seventeenth-century African-American inventors left no written records of their own. But many of them were skilled in crafts and created new devices and techniques in the course of their work. Africans brought a store of technological knowledge with them to the Americas. In the West elements of African technology merged with European and Native American technology to create new American traditions in technology. This is particularly evident in the areas of boat building, rice culture, pharmacology, and musical instrument making.

More is known about black inventors in the eighteenth and nineteenth centuries, particularly those who enjoyed some celebrity in their time, such as Norbert Rillieux, a Louisianan who invented the multiple-effect vacuum evaporation system for producing sugar from sugarcane. The Rillieux method revolutionized the sugar industry and came to be the accepted method of sugarcane juice evaporation. Though blacks contributed to the technological development that resulted, there was little public recognition of their achievements.

In the North many African-American men turned to the maritime trades for employment, and from these ranks came several outstanding inventors such as James Forten, the wealthy Philadelphia black abolitionist whose fortune was built upon his invention around the turn of the nineteenth century of a sail-handling device, and Lewis Temple, who introduced the toggle harpoon to commercial whaling in Massachusetts in the 1840s.

Craftsmen who invented new devices discovered innovative techniques that improved the quality of their products or reduced the cost of producing them often went into business for themselves instead of hiring them-

Elijah McCoy (1843–1929). *McCoy automated the maintenance of locomotive and stationary engines by inventing a self-lubricating device—a small cup that supplied drops of oil to moving parts while they operated.* THE GRANGER COLLECTION, NEW YORK. REPRODUCED BY PERMISSION.

selves out for wages. But these craftsmen-inventors still faced the problems of patenting the invention or protecting it somehow from competitors, financing its production, and marketing it.

The enactment of the U.S. Patent Act in 1790 provided for some documentation of black inventors and their inventions, but this documentation is incomplete. Because the race of the inventor was not generally recorded by the U.S. Patent Office, it is not known for certain how many blacks received patents. Thomas L. Jennings, a New York abolitionist, is the earliest African-American patent holder to have been identified so far. He received a patent for a dry-cleaning process on March 3, 1821. Further research may uncover earlier black patent holders. Slaves were legally prohibited from receiving patents for their inventions, and there are few surviving accounts in which slave inventors are fully identified.

The slave inventor found himself in an unlikely position that must have strained the assumptions of slavery to the utmost. Nothing illustrates the slave inventor's dilemma more clearly than the situation of two such inventors:

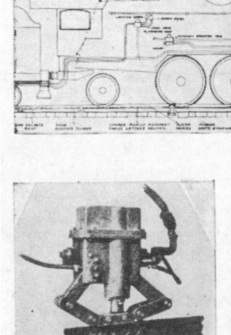

Parts of The Brookins Automatic Train Control System to prevent wrecks. 1446 South Wabash Avenue. " . . . Our Bureau of Safety is familiar with the Brookins Device and has found that it contains elements of strength and merit sufficient to warrant test installations." John J. Esch, Interstate Commerce Commission, May 19, 1923.

Photo by Woodard
A. J. BROOKINS
Inventor

A. J. Brookins, inventor of the Brookins Automatic Train Control System, designed to help prevent train wrecks. The image is from John Taitt's Souvenir of Negro Progress, 1779–1925 (1925). GENERAL RESEARCH AND REFERENCE DIVISION, SCHOMBURG CENTER FOR RESEARCH IN BLACK CULTURE, THE NEW YORK PUBLIC LIBRARY, ASTOR, LENOX AND TILDEN FOUNDATIONS.

"Ned" and Benjamin Montgomery. They were responsible for the federal government and the Confederate government formally taking up the "problem" of slave inventors.

Ned's owner, O. J. E. Stuart, wrote to the secretary of the interior requesting that he receive a patent for the invention of a cotton scraper that his slave mechanic, Ned, had invented. Although Stuart admitted that the concept for the invention came entirely from Ned, he reminded the secretary that "the master is the owner of the fruits of the labor of the slave both intillectual [sic], and manual." The U.S. attorney general rendered a final opinion on June 10, 1858, "that a machine invented by a slave, though it be new and useful, cannot, in the present state of the law, be patented." The attorney general also prohibited the masters of slaves from receiving patents for their slaves' inventions. The decision not to allow either slaves or their owners to receive patents for slave inventions meant that such inventions could not enjoy any legal protection or any formal recognition. The attorney general's opinion stood until the end of the Civil War and the passage of the Thirteenth and Fourteenth Amendment. Further mention of Ned is absent from the historical record, and nothing is known of what became of him.

Benjamin Montgomery was also a slave inventor. He was the slave of Joseph Davis (brother of Jefferson Davis, later president of the Confederacy). Montgomery served as general manager and mechanic on Davis's plantation in Mississippi. In the late 1850s Montgomery invented a propeller for a river steamboat, specifically designed for the shallow waters around the plantation. Montgomery's biographers write that both Joseph and Jefferson Davis tried to have the propeller patented, but they were prevented from doing so by the attorney general's 1858 decision barring slave inventions from being patented. After he became president of the Confederate States, Jefferson Davis oversaw Confederate legislation that allowed a master to receive patents for his slaves' inventions. Many other slaves, lost to history, invented labor-saving devices and innovative techniques.

After the Civil War significant numbers of black inventors began to patent their inventions. The list of inventions patented by blacks reveals what kinds of occupations African Americans held and in which sectors of the labor force they were concentrated. Agricultural implements, devices for easing domestic chores, musical instruments,

Selected Inventions by African Americans

Inventor	Invention	Year
Ashbourne, A.P.	Biscuit cutter	1875
Bailey, L.C.	Folding bed	1899
Bath, P.E.	cataract Laserphaco	1988
Beard, A.J.	Rotary Engine	1892
Beard, A.J.	Car-coupler	1897
Becket, G.E.	Letter box	1892
Bell, L.	Locomotive smokestack	1871
Benjamin, M.E.	Gong and signal chairs for hotels	1888
Binga, M.W.	Street sprinkling apparatus	1879
Blackburn, A.B.	Railway signal	1888
Blair, Henry	Corn planter	1834
Blair, Henry	Cotton planter	1836
Boone, Sarah	Ironing board	1892
Boykin, Otis	Burglar-proof cash register	1961
Brooks, C.R.	Street-sweeper	1896
Brooks, Phil	Disposable syringe	1974
Brown, Marie	Video home security system	1969
Brown, O.E.	Horseshoe	1892
Burr, J.A.	Lawn mower	1899
Butts, J.W.	Luggage carrier	1899
Carter, W.C.	Umbrella stand	1885
Church, T.S.	Carpet beating machine	1884
Cook, G.	Automatic fishing device	1899
Cooper, J.	Elevator device	1895
Cornwall, P.W.	Draft regulator	1893
Cralle, A.L.	Ice-cream mold	1897
Crum, George	Potato chip	1853
Davis, W.R., Jr.	Library table	1878
Demon, Ronald	©Smart Shoe	1998
Dorticus, C.J.	Machine for embossing photos	1895
Downing, P.B.	Street letter drop mailbox with hinged door	1891
Drew, C.R.	Blood bank	c.1938
Elkins, T.	Refrigerating apparatus	1879
Flemming, F., Jr.	Guitar (variation)	1886

Selected Inventions by African Americans *(continued)*

Inventor	Invention	Year
Goode, S.S.	Folding cabinet bed	1885
Grant, G.F.	Golf tee	1899
Gregory, J.	Motor	1887
Headen, M.	Foot power hammer	1886
Jackson, B.F.	Gas burner	1899
Johnson, L.G.	©Supersoaker	1988
Joyner, Majorie	Permanent wave machine	1928
Latimer and Nichols	Electric lamp	1881
Marshall, T.J.	fire extinguisher (variation)	1872
McCoy, E.	Lubricator for steam engines	1872
Morgan, Garrett	Gas mask	1914
Morgan, Garrett	Traffic signal	1923
Spears, H.	Portable shield for infantry	1870
Sutton, E.H.	Cotton cultivator	1878
Woods, G.T.	Electromechanical brake	1887
Woods, G.T.	Railway telegraphy	1887
Woods, G.T.	Induction telegraph system	1887
Woods, G.T.	Overhead conducting system for railway	1888
Woods, G.T.	Electromotive railway system	1888
Woods, G.T.	Railway telegraphy	1888

and devices related to the railroad industry were common. These inventions served as a source of financial security, personal pride, achievement, and spiritual "uplift" for African Americans. Much of the struggle for black inventors of that era revolved around the battle to assert themselves upon the national consciousness. On August 10, 1894, on the floor of the House of Representatives, Representative George Washington Murray from South Carolina rose to read the names and inventions of ninety-two black inventors into the *Congressional Record*. Representative Murray hoped that it would serve as a testament to the technological achievement of a people so recently emancipated.

Many African Americans made contributions to the new technologies and industries developed in the nineteenth century. Jan Matzeliger invented a shoe-lasting machine that made the skill of shoe lasting (i.e., shaping) by hand obsolete. Elijah McCoy designed hydrostatic oil lubricators that were adopted by railroad and shipping companies. His standard of quality was so rigorous that the term "the real McCoy" came to be applied to his lubricators and to stand for the highest quality product available. Garrett A. Morgan patented a safety hood (a precursor to the modern gas mask) and an automatic traffic signal. He once donned his safety hood himself to save the lives of men trapped in an underground explosion. Granville T. Woods and Lewis H. Latimer were pioneers in the newly emerging fields of electrical engineering. Woods patented many electrical and railway telegraphy systems; Latimer, with several patents to his credit, was one of the "Edison pioneers," the group of researchers who worked most closely with Thomas A. Edison.

The twentieth century brought many changes to industrial engineering and design. The rise of corporate enterprise led to more centralized research. Many of the most important inventions began to come from teams of researchers employed by large companies. As technology became more complicated, inventors in emerging fields began to have more formal education.

Today, advanced degrees in engineering and the sciences have become prerequisites for doing innovative work in some fields. Despite these changes, important inventions are still being patented by inventors who work alone—individuals who are suddenly struck by a solution to a daily encountered problem, or who laboriously work out a cheaper, quicker, or better means of producing something.

See also Carver, George Washington; Forten, James; Latimer, Lewis Howard; Patents and Inventions; Science

■ ■ *Bibliography*

Baker, Henry E. *The Colored Inventor: A Record of Fifty Years.* 1915. Reprint, New York: Arno Press and *New York Times*, 1968.

Carter-Ives, Patricia. *Creativity and Invention: The Genius of Afro-Americans and Women in the United States and Their Patents.* Arlington, Va.: Research Unlimited, 1988.

Gibbs, C. R. *The Afro-American Inventor.* Washington, D.C.: Gibbs, 1975.

Haber, Louis. *Black Pioneers of Science and Invention.* New York: Harcourt, 1970.

Hayden, Robert. *Eight Black American Inventors.* Reading, Mass.: Addison-Wesley, 1972.

Hermann, Janet Sharp. *Pursuit of a Dream.* New York: Oxford University Press, 1981.

James, Portia P. *The Real McCoy: African American Invention and Innovation, 1619–1930.* Washington, D.C.: Smithsonian Institution, 1989.

Klein, Aaron. *Hidden Contributors: Black Scientists and Inventors in America.* Garden City, N.Y.: Doubleday, 1971.

PORTIA P. JAMES (1996)

ISLAM

■ ■ ■

This entry has two unique essays about the same topic, differing mainly in their geographical focus.

ISLAM IN NORTH AMERICA
Lawrence H. Mamiya

ISLAM IN THE CARIBBEAN
Nasser Mustapha

ISLAM IN NORTH AMERICA

Originating in the seventh century CE through the revelations, visions, and messages received by the prophet Muhammad in Arabia, Islam spread rapidly throughout North Africa. Black African converts to Islam were called Moors and not only helped conquer southern Spain but also gained a reputation as skilled navigators and sailors. The Moors who accompanied the Spanish explorers in the fifteenth and sixteenth centuries were among the first to introduce the Islamic religion to the Americas. However, the greater impact of Islam in British North America occurred with the arrival of African Muslims (adherents of Islam) from the Islamized parts of West Africa who had been captured in warfare and sold to the European traders of the Atlantic slave trade.

MUSLIM SLAVES IN NORTH AMERICA

The presence of Muslim slaves has been ignored by most historians, who have tended to focus on the conversion of Africans to Christianity or on the attempts to preserve aspects of traditional African religions. Yet their presence has been attested to by narrative and documentary accounts, some of which were written in Arabic. Yarrow Mamout, Job Ben Solomon, and Lamine Jay arrived in colonial Maryland in the 1730s. Abdul Rahaman, Mohammed Kaba, Bilali, Salih Bilali, and "Benjamin Cochrane" were enslaved in the late eighteenth century. Omar Ibn Said, Kebe, and Abu Bakr were brought to southern plantations in the early 1800s; two others, Mahommah Baquaqua and Mohammed Ali ben Said, came to the United States as freemen about 1850. Abdul Rahaman, a Muslim prince of the Fula people in Timbo, Fouta Djallon, became a slave for close to twenty years in Natchez, Mississippi, before he was freed; he eventually returned to Africa through the aid of abolitionist groups.

Court records in South Carolina described African slaves who prayed to Allah and refused to eat pork. Missionaries in Georgia and South Carolina observed that some Muslim slaves attempted to blend Islam and Christianity by identifying God with Allah and Muhammad with Jesus. A conservative estimate is that close to 30,000 Muslim slaves came from Islamic-dominated ethnic groups such as the Mandingo, Fula, Gambians, Senegambians, Senegalese, Cape Verdians, and Sierra Leoneans in West Africa. Although the African Muslim presence in North America was much larger than previously believed, Islamic influence did not survive the impact of the slave period. Except for the documents left by the Muslims named above, only scattered traces and family memories of Islam remained among African Americans. In his novel *Roots,* Alex Haley's ancestral Muslim character, Kunta Kinte of the Senegambia, exemplifies these survivals.

LOSS AND REDISCOVERY

By the late nineteenth century, black Christian churches had become so dominant in the religious and social life of black communities that only a few African-American leaders who had traveled to Africa knew anything about Islam. Contacts between immigrant Arab groups and African Americans were almost nonexistent at this time. After touring Liberia and South Africa, Bishop Henry McNeal Turner of the African Methodist Episcopal church recognized the "dignity, majesty, and consciousness of worth of Muslims" (Austin, p. 24; Hill and Kilson, p. 63). But it was Edward Wilmot Blyden, the West Indian educator, Christian missionary, and minister for the government of Liberia, who became the most enthusiastic supporter of Islam for African Americans. Blyden, who began teaching Arabic in Liberia in 1867, wrote a book, *Christianity, Islam, and the Negro Race* (1888), in which he concluded that Islam had a much better record of racial equality than Christianity did—a conclusion that struck him especially strongly after he compared the racial attitudes of Christian and Muslim missionaries whom he had encountered in Africa. Islam, he felt, could also be a positive force in improving conditions for African Americans in the United States. Although he lectured extensively, Blyden did not become a leader of a social movement that could establish Islam effectively in America. That task awaited the prophets and forceful personalities of the next century.

The massive rural-to-urban migrations by more than four million African Americans during the first decades of the twentieth century provided the conditions for the rise of a number of black militant and separatist movements, including a few that had a tangential relationship to Islam. These proto-Islamic movements combined the religious trappings of Islam—a few rituals, symbols, or items of dress—with a core message of black nationalism.

In 1913 Timothy Drew, a black deliveryman and street-corner preacher from North Carolina, founded the first Moorish Holy Temple of Science in Newark, New Jersey. Rejecting Christianity as the white man's religion, Drew took advantage of widespread discontent among the newly arrived black migrants and rapidly established temples in Detroit, Harlem, Chicago, Pittsburgh, and cities across the South. Calling himself Prophet Noble Drew Ali, he constructed a message aimed at the confusion about names, national origins, and self-identity among black people. He declared that they were not "Negroes" but "Asiatics," or "Moors," or "Moorish Americans" whose true home was Morocco, and that their true religion was Moorish Science, whose doctrines were elaborated in a sixty-page book, written by Ali, called the *Holy Koran* (which should not be confused with the Qur'an of orthodox Islam).

Prophet Ali issued "Nationality and Identification Cards" stamped with the Islamic symbol of the star and crescent. There was a belief that these identity cards would prevent harm from the white man, or European, who was in any case soon to be destroyed, with "Asiatics" then in control. As the movement spread from the East Coast to the Midwest, Ali's followers in Chicago practiced "bumping days," on which aggressive male members would accost whites on the sidewalks and surreptitiously bump them out of the way—a practice that reversed the Jim Crow custom of southern whites forcing blacks off the sidewalks. After numerous complaints to the police, Noble Drew Ali ordered a halt to the disorders and urged his followers to exercise restraint. "Stop flashing your cards before Europeans," he said, "as this only causes confusion. We did not come to cause confusion; our work is to uplift the nation" (Lincoln, p. 54). The headquarters of the movement was moved to Chicago in 1925.

The growth of the Moorish Science movement was accelerated during the post–World War I years by the recruitment of better educated but less dedicated members who quickly assumed leadership positions. These new leaders began to grow rich by exploiting the less educated membership of the movement and selling them herbs, magical charms, potions, and literature. When Ali intervened to prevent further exploitation, he was pushed aside, and this interference eventually led to his mysterious death in 1929. Noble Drew Ali died of a beating; whether it was done by the police when he was in their custody or by dissident members of the movement is not known. After his death, the movement split into numerous smaller factions, with rival leaders claiming to be reincarnations of Noble Drew Ali.

The Moorish Science Temple movement has survived, with active temples in Chicago, Detroit, New York, and a few other cities. In present-day Moorish temples, membership is restricted to "Asiatics," or non-Caucasians, who have rejected their former identities as "colored" or "Negro." The term *el* or *bey* is attached to the name of each member as a sign of his or her Asiatic status and inward transformation. Friday is the Sabbath for the Moors, and they have adopted a mixture of Islamic and Christian rituals in worship. They face Mecca when they pray, three times a day, but they have also incorporated Jesus and the singing of transposed hymns into their services. The Moorish Science Temple movement was the first proto-

Islamic group of African Americans and helped to pave the way for more orthodox Islamic practices and beliefs. Many Moors were among the earliest converts to the Nation of Islam, or Black Muslim movement.

ISLAMIC MISSIONARIES

While the Moors were introducing aspects of Islam to black communities, sometime around 1920 the Ahmadiyyah movement sent missionaries to the United States, who began to proselytize among African Americans. Founded in India in 1889 by Mizra Ghulam Ahmad, a self-proclaimed Madhi, or Muslim messiah, the Ahmadiyyahs were a heterodox sect of Islam that was concerned with interpretations of the Christian gospel, including the Second Coming. The Ahmadiyyahs also emphasized some of the subtle criticisms of Christianity that were found in the Qur'an, such as the view that Jesus did not really die on the cross (Surah 4:157–159).

As an energetic missionary movement, the Ahmadiyyah first sent missionaries to West Africa, then later to the diaspora in the United States. Sheik Deen of the Ahmadiyyah mission was influential in converting Walter Gregg, who became one of the first African-American converts to Islam and changed his name to Wali Akram. After a period of studying the Qur'an and Arabic with the sheik, Akram founded the First Cleveland Mosque in 1933. He taught Islam to several generations of Midwesterners, including many African Americans. He also worked as a missionary in India. Although it was relatively unknown and unnoticed, the Ahmadiyyah mission movement is significant in that it provided one of the first contacts for African Americans with a worldwide sectarian Islamic group, whose traditions were more orthodox than the proto-Islamic black-nationalist movements.

About the same time that the Ahmadiyyah movement began its missionary work in the United States, another small group of orthodox Muslims, led by a West Indian named Sheik Dawud Hamed Faisal, established the Islamic Mission to America in 1923 on State Street in Brooklyn. At the State Street Mosque, Sheik Dawud taught a more authentic version of Islam than the Ahmadiyyahs because he followed the Sunna (practices) of the prophet Muhammad; whereas the Ahmadiyyahs believed in the tradition of the Mahdi, or Islamic messianism, Dawud belonged to the tradition of Sunni orthodoxy. The sheik welcomed black Americans to mingle with immigrant Muslims. He taught Arabic, the Qur'an, the Sunna-Hadith tradition, and *sharia*, or Islamic law, emphasizing the five pillars of Islam: the credo (*shahadah*) of Islam that emphasizes belief in one God and Muhammad as the messenger of Allah; prayer (*salat*) five times a day facing Mecca; charity tax

(*zakat*); fasting (*saum*) during the month of Ramadan; and pilgrimage to Mecca (*hajj*) if it is possible. Sheik Dawud's work was concentrated mainly in New York and New England. He became responsible for converting a number of African-American Muslims.

A smaller group and third source of African-American Sunni Muslims was the community in Buffalo, New York, that was taught orthodox Islam and Arabic by an immigrant Muslim, Professor Muhammad EzalDeen, in 1933. EzalDeen formed several organizations, including a national one, Uniting Islamic Societies of America, in the early 1940s.

ORTHODOX ISLAM

The work of the Ahmadiyyah movement, Sheik Dawud's Islamic Mission to America and the State Street Mosque, Imam Wali Akram's First Cleveland Mosque, and Professor EzalDeen's Islamic Societies of America was important in establishing a beachhead for a more orthodox and universal Sunni Islam in African-American communities.

During the turmoil of the 1960s, young African Americans traveled abroad and made contact with international Muslim movements such as the Tablighi Jamaat. The Darul Islam movement began in 1968 among dissatisfied African-American members of Sheik Dawud's State Street Mosque in Brooklyn and was led by a charismatic black leader, Imam Yahya Abdul Karim. Sensing the disenchantment with the lack of leadership, organization, and community programs in Sheik Dawud's movement, Imam Karim instituted the Darul Islam, the call to establish the kingdom of Allah. The movement spread to Cleveland, Baltimore, Philadelphia, and Washington, D.C. A network of over forty mosques was developed between 1968 and 1982. After a schism in 1982, the Darul Islam movement declined in influence, but it has since been revived under the charismatic leadership of Imam Jamin al-Amin of Atlanta (the former H. Rap Brown of the Student Nonviolent Coordinating Committee). Other smaller Sunni organizations also came into existence during the 1960s, such as the Islamic Party and the Mosque of the Islamic Brotherhood. It is ironic, however, that the greatest impact and influence of Islam among black people were exerted by another proto-Islamic movement called the Nation of Islam.

NATION OF ISLAM

In 1930 a mysterious peddler of sundry goods who called himself Wali Fard Muhammad began to spread the word of a new religion, designed for the "Asiatic black man." He soon developed a following of several hundred people and

Joseph X, a member of the Nation of Islam, selling The Final Call *on a street in Chicago in 1995.* © RALF-FINN HESTOFT/CORBIS

established Temple No. 1 of the Nation of Islam. Focusing on knowledge of self as the path to individual and collective salvation, Master Fard explained that black people were members of the lost-found tribe of Shabazz and owed no allegiance to a white-dominated country, which had enslaved and continuously persecuted them. When Fard mysteriously disappeared in 1934, his chief lieutenant—the former Robert Poole, now called Elijah Muhammad—led a segment of followers to Chicago, where he established Muhammad's Temple No. 2 as the headquarters for the fledgling movement.

Elijah Muhammad deified Master Fard as Allah, or God incarnated in a black man, and called himself the Prophet or Apostle of Allah, frequently using the title *the honorable* as a designation of his special status. Although the basic credo of the Nation of Islam stood in direct contradiction to the tenets of orthodox Islam, the movement's main interests were to spread the message of black nationalism and to develop a separate black nation. The Honorable Elijah Muhammad emphasized two basic principles: to know oneself (a development of true self-knowledge based on the teachings of the Nation of Islam); and to do for self (an encouragement to become economically independent). He also advocated a strict ascetic lifestyle, which

included one meal per day and a ban on tobacco, alcohol, drugs, and pork. From 1934 until his death in 1975, Muhammad and his followers established more than one hundred temples and Clara Muhammad schools, and innumerable grocery stores, restaurants, bakeries, and other small businesses. During this period, the Nation of Islam owned farms in several states, a bank, a fleet of trailer trucks for its fish and grocery businesses, and an ultramodern printing plant. Muhammad's empire was estimated to be worth more than eighty million dollars.

Elijah Muhammad's message of a radical black nationalism, which included the belief that whites were devils, was brought to the American public by a charismatic young minister who had converted to the Nation of Islam after his incarceration in a Boston prison in 1946 for armed robbery. Upon his release from prison in 1952 and until his assassination in 1965, Minister Malcolm X, the former Malcolm Little, had an enormous impact on the growth of the movement.

Extremely intelligent and articulate, Malcolm X was an indefatigable proselytizer for the Nation of Islam, founding temples throughout the country and establishing the newspaper *Muhammad Speaks*. For his efforts, he was awarded the prestigious post of minister of Temple No. 7 in Harlem and appointed the national representative by Elijah Muhammad. Malcolm X led the Nation of Islam's attack on the word *negro* as a reflection of a slave mentality and successfully laid the ideological basis for the emergence of the black consciousness and Black Power movements of the late 1960s. However, a dispute with Elijah Muhammad about future directions and personal moral conduct led Malcolm X to leave the Nation of Islam in 1964. Louis Farrakhan, another charismatic speaker, took Malcolm's place as the national representative and head minister of Temple No. 7. On a *hajj* to Mecca, Malcolm X became convinced that orthodox Sunni Islam was a solution to the racism and discrimination that plagued American society. On February 21, 1965, the renamed el Hajj Malik el Shabazz was assassinated in the Audubon Ballroom in Harlem while delivering a lecture for his newly formed Organization for Afro-American Unity.

SCHISM AND UNITY

When Elijah Muhammad died a decade later, in February 1975, the fifth of his six sons, Wallace Deen Muhammad, was chosen as his father's successor as supreme minister of the Nation of Islam. In April 1975, Wallace Muhammad shocked the movement by announcing an end to its racial doctrines and black nationalist teachings. He disbanded the Fruit of Islam and the Muslim Girls Training, the elite internal organizations, and gradually moved his followers toward orthodox Sunni Islam. His moves led to a number of schisms, which produced several competing black nationalist groups: Louis Farrakhan's resurrected Nation of Islam in Chicago, the largest and best known of the groups; Silas Muhammad's Nation of Islam in Atlanta; and a Nation of Islam led by John Muhammad, brother of Elijah Muhammad, in Detroit.

In the evolution of his movement, Wallace Muhammad took the Muslim title and name Imam Warith Deen Muhammad (in 1991 the spelling of his surname was changed to the British Mohammed). The movement's name and the name of its newspaper also changed several times: from the World Community of Al-Islam in the West (*Bilalian News*) in 1976 to the American Muslim Mission (*American Muslim Mission Journal*) in 1980; then in 1985 Warith Deen Muhammad decentralized the movement into independent *masjids*, which means "place of prayer"(*Muslim Journal*). Farrakhan's Nation of Islam also published its own newspaper, the *Final Call*. With several hundred thousand followers—predominantly African Americans—who identify with his teachings, Mohammed has continued to deepen their knowledge of the Arabic language, the Qur'an, and the Sunna, or practices of the Prophet. Immigrant Muslims from Africa, Pakistan, and Middle Eastern countries also participate in the Friday Jum'ah prayer services.

Although it adheres to the basic tenets of orthodox Sunni Islam, the movement has not yet settled on a particular school of theological thought to follow. Since every significant culture in Islamic history has produced its own school of thought, it is Mohammed's conviction that eventually an American school of Islamic thought will emerge in the United States, comprising the views of African-American and immigrant Muslims. Imam Warith Deen Mohammed has been accepted by the World Muslim Council as a representative of Muslims in the United States and has been given the responsibility of certifying Americans who want to make the pilgrimage to Mecca. In 2000, Imam Mohammed again dissolved his movement, the Muslim American Society, because he wanted to shake up his followers who were becoming too complacent. However, the major African-American Muslim leaders and their *masjids* have chosen to support Imam Mohammed's Mosque Cares Ministry, so his movement continues to exist but under a different name.

At the beginning of the twenty-first century, the leaders of the two largest African-American Muslim movements, Imam Warith Deen Mohammed and the Honorable Louis Farrakhan, have made a rapprochement by holding joint prayer services in Chicago during the last weekend of February, the traditional time of the Nation of Islam's Savior's Day celebration. Imam Mohammed has accepted Farrakhan as a true Muslim because he led his movement to hold the formal Friday Jum'ah prayer service and to adhere to other practices of orthodox Islam, such as following the lunar calendar for the Ramadan celebration and reciting the formal prayers in Arabic. Although both leaders are friendly, they have agreed to keep their movements separate rather than merge them.

In its varying forms, Islam has had a much longer history in the United States, particularly among African Americans, than is commonly known. In the last decade of the twentieth century, about one million African Americans belonged to proto-Islamic and orthodox Islamic groups. Islam has become the fourth major religious tradition in American society, alongside Protestantism, Catholicism, and Judaism. In black communities, Islam has re-emerged as the dominant religious alternative to Christianity.

See also Al-Amin, Jamil Abdullah (Brown, H. "Rap"); Fard, Wallace D.; Farrakhan, Louis; Islam in the Caribbean; Malcolm X; Muhammad, Elijah; Muslims in the Americas; Nation of Islam; Noble Drew Ali

■ ■ *Bibliography*

Austin, Allen. *African Muslim Slaves in Ante-Bellum America: A Sourcebook.* New York: Garland, 1984.

Blyden, Edward Wilmot. *Christianity, Islam and the Negro Race* (1888). Edinburgh, Scotland: Edinburgh University Press, 1967.

Essien-Udom, E. U. *Black Nationalism: A Search for Identity in America.* Chicago: University of Chicago Press, 1962.

Farrakhan, Louis. *Seven Speeches.* Chicago: Muhammad's Mosque of Islam No. 2 (in-house publication), 1974.

Fauset, Arthur Huff. *Black Gods of the Metropolis: Negro Religious Cults of the Urban North* (1944). Philadelphia: University of Pennsylvania Press, 1971.

Haddad, Yvonne, ed. *The Muslims of America.* New York: Oxford University Press, 1991.

Hill, Adelaide C. and Martin Kilson. *Apropos of Africa: Sentiments of Negro American Leaders on Africa from the 1800's to the 1950's.* Garden City, N.Y.: Frank Cass Publishers, 1969.

Hill, Robert A., ed. *The Marcus Garvey and the Universal Improvement Association Papers.* 3 vols. Berkeley: University of California Press, 1983–1984.

Lincoln, C. Eric. *The Black Muslims in America.* Boston: Beacon, 1961.

Malcolm X and Alex Haley. *The Autobiography of Malcolm X.* New York: Grove, 1965.

Mamiya, Lawrence H. "From Black Muslim to Bilalian: The Evolution of a Movement." *Journal for the Scientific Study of Religion* 21, no. 2 (June 1982): 138–152.

Muhammad, Elijah. *Message to the Black Man in America*. Chicago: Muhammad Mosque of Islam No. 2 (in-house publication), 1965.

Muhammad, Warith Deen. *As the Light Shineth from the East*. Chicago: WDM Publishing Co. (in-house publication), 1980.

Perry, Bruce. *Malcolm: The Life of a Man Who Changed Black America*. Barrytown, N.Y.: Station Hill, 1991.

Turner, Richard B. *Islam in the United States in the 1920s: The Quest for a New Vision in Afro-American Religion*. Ph.D. diss., Princeton University, 1986.

Waugh, Earle H., Baha Abu-Laban, and Regula B. Qureshi, eds. *The Muslim Community in North America*. Edmonton, Canada: University of Alberta Press, 1983.

LAWRENCE H. MAMIYA (1996)
Updated by author 2005

ISLAM IN THE CARIBBEAN

The experiences of plantation slavery were not conducive to the continuity of most cultural traits brought from Africa. Thus within a few generations, all traces of Islam virtually disappeared in the Caribbean. Historical evidence shows that there were many Muslims among these slaves, mainly from the Mandingo, Hausa, and Fulani peoples. Evidence also shows that there was a latent, suppressed attachment to ancestral religions, including Islam.

In one of the ironies of Caribbean history, many Afro-Caribbean people converted to Islam centuries after all traces of this religion were destroyed by the European cultural dominance faced by their ancestors. This acculturative process took place systematically throughout slavery and may have varied in intensity from one Caribbean country to another as Melville Herskovits observed.

Islam was once more introduced to the Caribbean through the indentured laborers from India from 1845 to 1917. This community was largely concerned with its own survival, had limited contact with the wider society, and thus was not engaged in missionary activity. Nevertheless, a few individuals of African descent converted to Islam as early as 1940. Among these were Pir Robinson and Yusuf Mitchell, who both became leaders in what was perceived at that time as an Indian religion. Robinson was a wealthy businessman from the southern part of the island of Trinidad. He accepted Islam through his own search, eventually became a leader at his mosque, and was known to be engaged in many social welfare activities. Mitchell, a nationally known architect from north Trinidad, became a Muslim in 1950. Being influenced by religious missionaries, Mitchell initially practiced many local traditions. He was a founding member of the Islamic Missionaries Guild (c. 1969) and the Islamic Trust (c. 1975).

A significant influx of African converts began in the early 1970s, spurred by an increased black consciousness among the Afro-Caribbean community. This phenomenon was inspired by events in North America and particularly by the teachings of Malcolm X. While the Nation of Islam did have a small following in Port of Spain, Trinidad, and in other Caribbean territories, the majority of Africans in the Caribbean who accepted Islam joined the orthodox Muslim community. These new Afro-Caribbean Muslims came mainly from grassroots urban communities, and they did not find ready acceptance by the middle-class leadership of the traditional Muslim community. However, among the younger members of the Muslim community, who were generally more fundamentalist in their religious orientation, there was no significant race or class barrier.

Though Afro-Caribbean Muslims were warmly accommodated by the Islamic Missionaries Guild of the Caribbean and South America (with branches in Guyana, Barbados, and Trinidad) and the Islamic Trust of Trinidad and Guyana, as a group they were still uncomfortable with the Indian Muslim community. They were especially concerned with the Indian cultural traditions, which they felt were influenced by Hinduism. In February 1977, Afro-Trinidadian Muslims in Trinidad established their own group under the influence of the Islamic Party of North America. The Jamaat-al-Muslimeen, an Islamic organization with a predominantly Afro-Trinidadian membership, evolved out of this group. In July 1990, led by Yasin Abu Bakr, the group attempted to remove the democratically elected government. They took Prime Minister A. N. R. Robinson and other government ministers hostage, but the coup attempt failed after seven days. Many of the Jamaat's members then left to form the Islamic Resource Society. This group has very cordial relations with the Indian Muslim community and belongs to the United Islamic Organizations, a coordinating body of Muslim groups in Trinidad. Afro-Trinidadian Muslims frequently worship at most of the Indian-dominated mosques in Trinidad and Tobago and in Guyana, but there are a few urban mosques that are predominantly Afro-Trinidadian in their congregation. The other Muslim communities in the Caribbean, with the exception of Barbados, are predominantly Afro-Caribbean in their membership.

MIDDLE EASTERN INFLUENCE

There were Muslims, Jews, and Christians among the early Syrian and Lebanese immigrants to the Caribbean. These groups came as traders to the Caribbean in the 1930s. Those who remained Muslims often intermingled, and sometimes intermarried, with Indian Muslims. One of the

Yasin Abu Bakr, August 1, 1990. *Abu Bakr rides with fellow prisoners after Trinidadian and Tobagoan forces arrest him in Port-of-Spain following an attempted coup d'etat by his militant Muslim group Jamaat-al-Muslimeen* © LES STONE/CORBIS.

first Muslim missionaries from the Middle East was Abdel Salaam, who came from Egypt around 1966. He taught Arabic at several centers in Trinidad. In the 1970s, nationals from Trinidad, Guyana, and Barbados were awarded scholarships to pursue studies in Egypt and Saudi Arabia. Their return provided a new turn of events for the Muslim community in the Caribbean. As might have been expected, their interpretations of Islam did not find favor with the traditional Muslims. They nevertheless found tremendous support from among the youth of the region, who were largely disenchanted with the leadership of traditional Muslims. These new and radical fundamentalist-type approaches, which emphasized a return to the original sources in the practice of Islam, provided an exciting escape from the traditionalism of the mainstream Muslim community.

The Iranian Revolution of 1979 further kindled the flames of fundamentalism among Caribbean Muslims. Young Muslims took pride in openly identifying with Islam. It was only around the mid-1970s that Muslim women began wearing the *hijab,* or veil. Prior to this, the *ohrni,* an Indian head covering, was worn by older women only (Niehoff and Niehoff, 1961).

In some Caribbean countries, organizations bringing together different Muslim traditions have been established. These "ecumenical" attempts have achieved some degree of success at the formal level, where groups of different orientations sit together to address the needs of the Muslim community. However, the more traditional Muslims show little inclination to change traditional religious practices.

In countries such as Guyana, Trinidad and Tobago, and Suriname, the major strength of the community lies in its numerous institutions. There are Muslim cooperatives, a credit union, a housing cooperative, several primary and secondary schools, and three religious institutes. The mosques of the region have also served as important institutions over the years. As of 1998, Guyana had 154 mosques; Trinidad and Tobago, 112; Suriname, 100; Jamaica, 6; and Barbados, 4. In addition to serving as places of worship, many mosques serve as both places of worship and educational institutions, known as *maktabs* (literally, a place of writing) or *madrasahs* (literally, a place for studying). Both terms are used to refer to educational institutions. In Guyana, *madrasah* is preferred, while in

Trinidad, *maktab* is preferred. In most of the smaller Muslim communities of the Caribbean, members (largely of Afro-Caribbean descent) formed a regional body, the Association of Islamic Communities of the Caribbean and Latin America (AICCLA), in 1982 to coordinate their activities. They have received some financial and other forms of assistance from outside the Caribbean.

The Muslim community in the Caribbean has successfully struggled to maintain a visible presence in the face of numerous forces that have threatened its very existence. And yet a marked diversity exists within the community, even among those who claim to have the same orientation. There are many variations in the approach to Islam. These are usually based on matters of religious practice and jurisprudence (*fiqh*) and not basic beliefs. There is, however, much need for further research on the historical background and unique characteristics of Caribbean Muslims.

See also Islam in North America; Muslims in the Americas; Slave Religions

■ ■ *Bibliography*

Afroz, Sultana. "Unsung Slaves: Islam in the Plantation Society." *Caribbean Quarterly* 41, nos. 2, 3 (1995): pp. 30–44.

Caribbean Islamic Secretariat. *Muslims in the Caribbean.* Port of Spain: CIS Caribbean Islamic Secretariat, 1998.

De Waal Malefijt, A. "Animism and Islam among the Javanese in Surinam." In *Peoples and Cultures of the Caribbean*, edited by Michael M. Horowitz. New York: Natural History Press, 1971.

Diouf, Sylviane A. *Servants of Allah: African Muslims Enslaved in the Americas.* New York: New York University Press, 1998.

Hadith: Sahih al Bukhari. Chicago: Kazi Publications, 1980.

Hamid, A.W. "Muslims in the West Indies." Paper presented to the Muslim Minorities Seminar, Islamic Council of Europe, 1978.

Kasule, Omar Hassan. "Muslims in Trinidad and Tobago." *Journal of the Institute of Muslim Minority Affairs*, 7, no. 1 (1986): 195–224.

Khan, F. "Islam as a Social Force in the Caribbean." Paper presented at the Conference of the History Teachers' Association of Trinidad and Tobago, June 1987.

Khan, N. Personal communication, September 1998.

Mansingh, A. and Mansingh, L. "Hosay and its Creolization." *Caribbean Quarterly* 41, no. 1 (1995): 25–39.

The Muslim Standard, no. 3 (December 1975).

Niehoff, A., and J. Niehoff. "East Indians in Trinidad and Tobago." *Milwaukee Public Museum Publications in Anthropology*, no. 6 (1961).

Quick, A. H. Abdullah Hakim. *Deeper Roots: Muslims of the Caribbean from before Columbus to the Present.* Nassau, Bahamas: AICCLA, 1990. Reprint, London: Ta-Ha Publishers Ltd., 1996.

Samaroo, Brinsley. "The Indian Connection: The Influence of Indian Thought and Ideas on East Indians in the Caribbean." In *India in the Caribbean*, edited by David Dabydeen and Brinsley Samaroo. London: Hansib Publishing House, 1987.

Samaroo, Brinsley. "Early African and East Indian Muslims in Trinidad and Tobago." In *Across the Dark Waters*, edited by David Dabydeen and Brinsley Samaroo. London: Macmillan Caribbean, 1996.

Sanyal, U. *Devotional Islam and Politics in British India.* Delhi: Oxford University Press, 1996.

Sharif, Ja'far. *Islam in India*, translated by G. A. Herklots. London: Humphrey Milford, 1921.

NASSER MUSTAPHA (2005)

ISLAM, NATION OF

See Nation of Islam

JACK AND JILL OF AMERICA

❚❚❚

Jack and Jill of America, a nonprofit philanthropic organization, was founded in 1938 in Philadelphia by Marion T. Stubbs Thomas with the primary aim of serving African-American children from the ages of two to nineteen. The group grew out of volunteer community work by African-American women during the Great Depression. Along with several other women of the Philadelphia black elite, Thomas agreed that most of the women who associated socially and professionally had children who did not know one another, so the women sponsored cultural events and created a network for parents and children. In 1939 Jack and Jill of America expanded to New York, and by 1988, its fiftieth anniversary, it had expanded to 187 chapters across the nation.

Through the 1940s and 1950s, Jack and Jill of America raised funds for a variety of charities, including those concerned with children's health. The leaders of Jack and Jill, without representation on the boards of charities that they supported, decided to form their own Jack and Jill of America Foundation. It began in 1968 and is involved in a variety of efforts in areas such as health, education, science, and culture. It works with local chapters of Jack and Jill and other groups in most of the United States and in the District of Columbia.

See also Philanthropy and Foundations

■■ *Bibliography*

Baker, Adelle W. *Jack and Jill of America, Incorporated: Into the New Millennium*. Orlando, Fla.: LBS Publications, 2000.

Hine, Darlene Clark. *Black Women in America: An Historical Encyclopedia*. Brooklyn, N.Y.: Carlson, 1993.

Roulhe, Nellie C. *Work, Play, and Commitment: A History of the First Fifty Years, Jack and Jill of America, Incorporated*. 1989.

THOMAS PITONIAK (1996)
Updated bibliography

Jackson, George Lester

September 23, 1941
August 21, 1971

▌▌▌

Activist George Jackson was born in Chicago and moved to Los Angeles with his family when he was fourteen. One year later he was convicted of attempted robbery and sent to California's Youth Authority Corrections facility in Paso Robles. After his release Jackson was again arrested and convicted for attempted robbery, and at age sixteen he was incarcerated in a California county jail. In 1960 Jackson was accused of stealing $71 from a gas station and received an indeterminate sentence of one year to life. After he served the statutory minimum of one year, his case was reconsidered yearly. Jackson was never granted parole, and he spent the rest of his life in prison.

Jackson was incarcerated in Soledad State Prison in Salinas, California. He was politicized by his experiences in prison and began to study the theories of third-world communists Mao Zedong, Frantz Fanon, and Fidel Castro. He became a strong supporter of communist ideas, viewing capitalism as the source of the oppression of people of color. Jackson soon became a leader in the politicization of black and Chicano prisoners in Soledad Prison. In part as the result of his prison activities, he was placed in solitary confinement for extended periods of time.

On January 16, 1970, in response to the death of three black inmates in Soledad Prison, a white guard—John Mills—was killed. George Jackson, John Clutchette, and Fleeta Drumgo were accused of the murder. All three were regarded as black militants by prison authorities. The extent of their involvement in the murder has never been clarified.

The fate of the "Soledad Brothers" became an international cause célèbre that focused investigative attention and publicity on the treatment of black inmates. Jackson's eloquence and dignity made him a symbol of militant pride and defiance. Massive grassroots rallies and protests popularized the plight of the Soledad Brothers.

The publication in 1970 of *Soledad Brother: The Prison Letters of George Jackson* greatly contributed to Jackson's visibility. The book traced his personal and political evolution and articulated the fundamental relation he saw between the condition of black people inside prison walls and those outside. Jackson believed that the building of a revolutionary consciousness among imprisoned people was the first step in the overall development of an anti-capitalist revolutionary cadre in the United States.

For many of Jackson's supporters in the Black Power movement and the New Left, the guilt or innocence of the Soledad Brothers was not the issue. They perceived the Soledad Brothers as political prisoners who were victims of a conspiracy by prison authorities. Angela Davis, spokesperson for the Soledad Brothers Defense Committee, argued that the Soledad Brothers were being persecuted solely because they had helped create an anti-establishment consciousness among black and Chicano inmates.

On August 7, 1970, Jackson's teenage brother, Jonathan, entered the Marin County Courthouse in San Rafael, held the courtroom at gunpoint, distributed weapons to three prisoners present, and attempted to take the judge, assistant district attorney, and three jurors as hostages to bargain for his brother's freedom. In the ensuing struggle, Jonathan Jackson was killed, along with two of the prisoners and the judge. Angela Davis was accused of providing him with the four weapons and was arrested on October 13, 1971. Davis's trial gained international attention, and after spending sixteen months in jail, she was acquitted in 1972.

During 1970 the Soledad Brothers had been transferred to San Quentin Prison. Jackson was killed by prison guards on August 21, 1971, three days before his case was due to go to trial, The official report said that Jackson was armed; that he had participated in a prison revolt earlier in the day, which had left two white prisoners and three guards dead; and that he was killed in an apparent escape attempt. However, accounts of this incident are conflicting, and many argue that Jackson was set up for assassination and had nothing to do with the earlier melee.

Jackson was eulogized by many in the Black Power movement and the New Left as a martyr and a hero. After his death, *Soledad Brother* was published in England, France, Germany, and Sweden. In March 1972 the remaining two Soledad Brothers were acquitted of the original charges.

See also Black Power Movement; Davis, Angela

■ ■ *Bibliography*

Durden-Smith, Jo. *Who Killed George Jackson? Fantasies, Paranoia, and the Revolution.* New York: Knopf, 1976.

Szulc, Tad. "George Jackson Radicalizes the Brothers in Soledad and San Quentin." *New York Times Magazine,* August 1, 1971.

ROBYN SPENCER (1996)

JACKSON, JANET

MAY 16, 1966

The last of nine children, Janet Damita Jo Jackson was born in Gary, Indiana; her brothers had already begun performing as The Jackson 5. In 1977 she was cast in the Norman Lear televised sitcom *Good Times*. She moved to *Diff'rent Strokes* in 1981 and *Fame* in 1983. Directed by a father she later called distant and controlling, she recorded two albums, *Janet Jackson* and *Dream Street*, before her graduation from high school in 1984. Although both yielded minor hit singles, neither sold particularly well.

When she turned eighteen, Jackson took more control over her musical direction. Her 1986 album *Control*, made with the writing and producing team of Jimmy Jam and Terry Lewis, projected a persona of steely independence against spare, mechanical rhythms. The album sold more than five million copies, and spawned six hit singles. "What Have You Done for Me Lately" reached number one on the *Billboard* Hot 100. In 1989 she released *Rhythm Nation 1814*. The title track's plea for racial unity sits somewhat uneasily over the record's pulsating rhythms and sexual themes, but the album sold over six million copies, won a Grammy Award, and led to a world tour in which Janet showed off her precisely choreographed ensemble dancing. In 1993 she starred in director John Singleton's film *Poetic Justice* and released *janet.*, an album that traded in the independent stance and urban funk of her previous two records for a more relaxed groove and even more explicit sexuality. Another huge hit, with seven million sold, *janet.* also spawned a run of hit singles, including "That's the Way Love Goes," her best-seller.

In 1995 Janet joined her brother Michael on the hit single "Scream," and her hit single "Runaway" in 1996 became her sixteenth gold-certified single, placing her among an exclusive club of female artists. After battling with depression, she released *The Velvet Rope* in 1997. A curious mix of social commentary and raunchy sexuality, *The Velvet Rope* sold only half as many copies as *janet.* A duet with rapper Busta Rhymes landed Jackson back near the top of the charts in 1999. The next year she starred with Eddie Murphy in *Nutty Professor II: The Klumps*; her single from the soundtrack, "Doesn't Really Matter," reached number one. After a bitter divorce, her *All for You*, another frankly sexual album, entered the charts at number one in 2001, yielding two huge singles, "All for You" and "Someone to Call My Lover." After two years of nearly constant touring, Jackson returned to the studio in 2003 to record *Damita Jo*.

A misguided publicity stunt at the halftime show of the 2004 Super Bowl, however, clouded her future. At the end of a duet with singer Justine Timberlake, Jackson's right breast, adorned with a star-shaped nipple medallion, was exposed. A firestorm of controversy erupted, including 200,000 angry complaints to the Federal Communications Commission. Timberlake apologized, denying any foreknowledge of the "wardrobe malfunction." Jackson coyly proclaimed her innocence for several days before acknowledging that she had planned to bare her breast. The stunt did little to help the sales of *Damita Jo,* which sold only half as many copies as Jackson's previous record in its first week and quickly stalled on its way up the charts. Its impact on her career remains uncertain.

See also Jackson Family; Jackson, Michael; Music in the United States

▪ ▪ *Bibliography*

Andrews, Bart. *Out of the Madness: The Strictly Unauthorized Biography of Janet Jackson.* New York: HarperCollins, 1994.

Brown, Geoff. *The Complete Guide to the Music of Michael Jackson and the Jackson Family.* New York: Omnibus Press, 1996.

Ritz, David. "Sex, Sadness & the Triumph of Janet Jackson." *Rolling Stone* (October 1, 1998).

HARRIS FRIEDBERG (2005)

JACKSON, JESSE

OCTOBER 8, 1941

Minister, politician, and civil rights activist Jesse Louis Jackson was born Jesse Burns in Greenville, South Carolina, to Helen Burns and Noah Robinson, a married man who lived next door. In 1943 his mother married Charles Henry Jackson, who adopted Jesse in 1957. Jesse Jackson has recognized both men as his fathers. In 1959 Jackson graduated from Greenville's Sterling High School. A gifted athlete, he was offered a professional baseball contract; instead, he accepted a scholarship to play football at the University of Illinois, at Champaign-Urbana. When he discovered, however, that African Americans were not allowed to play quarterback, he enrolled at North Carolina Agricultural and Technical College in Greensboro. There, besides being a star athlete, Jackson began his activist career as a participant in the student sit-in movement to integrate Greensboro's public facilities.

Jackson's leadership abilities and charisma earned him a considerable reputation by the time he graduated with a B.S. in sociology in 1964. After graduation he married Jacqueline Brown, whom he had met at the sit-in protests. During his senior year he worked briefly with the Congress of Racial Equality (CORE), quickly being elevated to the position of director of southeastern operations. Jackson then moved north, eschewing law school at Duke University in order to attend the Chicago Theological Seminary in 1964. He was later ordained to the ministry by two renowned figures: gospel music star and pastor Clay Evans and legendary revivalist and pulpit orator C. L. Franklin. Jackson left the seminary in 1965 and returned to the South to become a member of the Rev. Dr. Martin Luther King Jr.'s staff of the Southern Christian Leadership Conference (SCLC).

Jackson initially became acquainted with SCLC during the famous march on Selma, Alabama in 1965. In 1966 King appointed him to head the Chicago branch of SCLC's Operation Breadbasket, which was formed in 1962 to force various businesses to employ more African Americans. In 1967, only a year after his first appointment, King made Jackson the national director of Operation Breadbasket. Jackson concentrated on businesses heavily patronized by blacks, including bakeries, milk companies, soft-drink bottlers, and soup companies. He arranged a number of boycotts of businesses refusing to comply with SCLC demands of fair employment practices and successfully negotiated compromises that soon gained national attention.

Jackson was in King's entourage when King was assassinated in Memphis in 1968. After King's death, however, Jackson's relationship with SCLC became increasingly strained over disagreements about his independence and his penchant for taking what was considered to be undue initiative in both public relations and organizational planning. He was also criticized for the direction in which he was leading Operation Breadbasket. Finally, in 1971, Jackson left SCLC and founded Operation PUSH, which he would lead for thirteen years. As head of PUSH, he continued an aggressive program of negotiating black employment agreements with white businesses, as well as promoting black educational excellence and self-esteem.

In 1980 Jackson demanded that an African American step forward as a presidential candidate in the 1984 election. On October 30, 1983, after carefully weighing the chances and need for a candidate, he dramatically announced, on the television program *60 Minutes,* his own candidacy to capture the White House. Many African-American politicians and community leaders, such as Andrew Young, felt that Jackson's candidacy would only divide the Democrats and chose instead to support Walter Mondale, the favorite for the nomination. Jackson, waging a campaign stressing voter registration, carried a hopeful message of empowerment to African Americans, poor

people, and other minorities. This constituency of the "voiceless and downtrodden" became the foundation for what Jackson termed a "Rainbow Coalition" of Americans—the poor, struggling farmers, feminists, gays, lesbians, and others who historically, according to Jackson, had lacked representation. Jackson, offering himself as an alternative to the mainstream Democratic Party, called for, among other things, a defense budget freeze, programs to stimulate full employment, self-determination for the Palestinians, and political empowerment of African Americans through voter registration.

Jackson's campaign in 1984 was characterized by dramatic successes and equally serious political gaffes. In late 1983 U.S. military flyer Robert Goodman was shot down over Syrian-held territory in Lebanon while conducting an assault. In a daring political gamble, Jackson made Goodman's release a personal mission, arguing that if the flyer had been white, the U.S. government would have worked more diligently toward his release. Traveling to Syria, Jackson managed to meet with President Hafez al-Assad and Goodman was released shortly afterwards; Jackson gained great political capital by appearing at the flyer's side as he made his way back to the United States.

The 1984 campaign, however, was plagued by political missteps. Jackson's offhand dubbing of New York as "Hymietown" while eating lunch with two reporters cost him much of his potential Jewish support and raised serious questions about his commitment to justice for all Americans. Although Jackson eventually apologized, the characterization continued to haunt him and remains a symbol of strained relations between African Americans and Jews. Another issue galling to many Jews and others was Jackson's relationship with Louis Farrakhan, head of the Nation of Islam. Farrakhan had appeared with Jackson and stumped for him early in the campaign. Jackson, despite advice to the contrary, refused to repudiate Farrakhan; it was only after one speech, in which Farrakhan labeled Judaism a "dirty" religion, that the Jackson campaign issued a statement condemning both the speech and the minister. Another controversy, and a source of special concern to Jews, was Jackson's previous meetings with Yasir Arafat, head of the Palestine Liberation Organization (PLO), and his advocacy of self-determination for the Palestinians.

Jackson ended his historic first run with an eloquent speech before the Democratic National Convention in San Francisco, reminding black America that "our time has come." In a strong showing in a relatively weak primary field, Jackson had garnered almost 3.3 million votes out of the approximately 18 million cast.

Even more impressive than Jackson's first bid for the presidency was his second run in 1988. Jackson espoused a political vision built upon the themes he first advocated in 1984. His campaign once again touted voter registration drives and the Rainbow Coalition, which by this time had become a structured organization closely overseen by Jackson. His new platform, which included many of the planks from 1984, included the validity of "comparable worth" as a viable means of eradicating pay inequities based on gender, the restoration of a higher maximum tax rate, and the implementation of national health care. Jackson also urged policies to combat "factory flight" in the Sun Belt and to provide aid to farmworkers in their fight to erode the negative effect of corporate agribusiness on family farms. Further, he railed against the exploitative practices of U.S. and transnational corporations, urging the redirection of their profits from various foreign ventures to the development of local economies.

While he failed to secure the Democratic nomination, Jackson finished with a surprisingly large number of convention delegates and a strong finish in the primaries. In thirty-one of thirty-six primaries, Jackson won either first or second place, earning almost seven million votes out of the approximately 23 million cast. In 1988 Jackson won over many of the black leaders who had refused to support him during his first campaign. His performance also indicated a growing national respect for his oratorical skills and his willingness to remain faithful to politically progressive ideals.

In the 1992 presidential campaign, Jackson, who was not a candidate, was critical of Democratic front-runners Bill Clinton and Al Gore and did not endorse them until the final weeks of the campaign. Since his last full-time political campaign in 1988, Jackson has remained highly visible in American public life. He has crusaded for various causes, including the institution of a democratic polity in South Africa, statehood for the District of Columbia, and the banishment of illegal drugs from American society.

Jackson has also been an outspoken critic of professional athletics, arguing that more African Americans need to be involved in the management and ownership of professional sports teams and that discrimination remains a large problem for many black athletes. Further, on the college level, the institution of the NCAA's Proposition 42 and Proposition 48 have earned criticism from Jackson as being discriminatory against young black athletes. Through the medium of a short-lived 1991 television talk show, Jackson sought to widen his audience, addressing pressing concerns faced by African Americans.

Jackson's various crusades against illegal drugs and racism, while often specifically targeted toward black teenagers, have exposed millions of Americans to his message. His powerful oratorical style—pulpit oratory that empha-

> ### Reverend Jesse Jackson
>
> "My constituency is the damned, disinherited, disrespected and the despised."
>
> SPEECH DELIVERED TO THE DEMOCRATIC NATIONAL CONVENTION IN SAN FRANCISCO, JULY 17, 1984.

sizes repetition of key phrases like "I am somebody"—often impresses and challenges audiences regardless of their political beliefs. In late 1988 Jackson became president of the National Rainbow Coalition, Inc.; he remains involved in the activities of numerous other organizations.

During the early 1990s Jackson remained largely outside the national spotlight. He was disappointed by the failure of his bid to assume leadership of the National Association for the Advancement of Colored People following the resignation of Rev. Benjamin Chavis. Jackson returned to widespread public prominence in the mid-1990s. In 1996 he supported the successful congressional campaign of his son, Jesse Jackson Jr. In 1998 he became a close adviser to President Bill Clinton following reports of Clinton's extramarital affair. Later that year he announced that he was considering another presidential run in 2000.

Jackson has been the most prominent civil rights leader and African-American national figure since the death of Martin Luther King Jr. The history of national black politics in the 1970s and 1980s was largely his story. He has shown a great ability for making alliances, as well as a talent for defining issues and generating controversy. The essential dilemma of Jackson's career, as with many of his peers, has been the search for a way to advance and further the agenda of the civil rights movement as a national movement at a time when the political temper of the country has been increasingly conservative.

As the new century began, Jesse Jackson continued to be a strong figure in American politics, with his influence spreading across the globe. In 2004 he visited Libya and the Sudan, urging Sudanese leaders to put an end to the civil war that had killed so many people.

See also Chavis, Benjamin Franklin, Jr.; Civil Rights Movement, U.S.; Congress of Racial Equality (CORE); King, Martin Luther, Jr.; National Association for the Advancement of Colored People (NAACP); Operation PUSH (People United to Serve Humanity); Politics in the United States; Rainbow Coalition; Southern Christian Leadership Conference (SCLC)

▪ ▪ *Bibliography*

Faw, Bob, and Nancy Skelton. *Thunder in America*. Austin: Texas Monthly Press, 1986.

Frady, Marshall. *Jesse: The Life and Pilgrimage of Jesse Jackson*. New York: Random House, 1996.

Gibbons, Arnold. *Race, Politics, and the White Media: The Jesse Jackson Campaigns*. Lanham, Md.: University Press of America, 1993.

Hatch, Roger D., and Frank E. Watkins, eds. *Reverend Jesse L. Jackson: Straight from the Heart*. Philadelphia: Fortress Press, 1987.

Reynolds, Barbara. *Jesse Jackson: The Man, the Movement, the Myth*. Chicago: Nelson-Hall, 1975.

MICHAEL ERIC DYSON (1996)
Updated by publisher 2005

JACKSON, JIMMY LEE

1939
FEBRUARY 26, 1965
▪▪▪

The activist Jimmy Lee Jackson was the first black person to die during the violence surrounding the Southern Christian Leadership Conference's (SCLC) 1965 Alabama Project for voting rights. Little is known about his background. He was a twenty-six-year-old woodcutter when, on February 18, 1965, he traveled with his mother and grandfather to Marion, Ala., a small town outside Selma, to participate in a rally and march in support of James Orange, an SCLC leader jailed during a voting rights drive. Shortly after the march began, the marchers were attacked by Alabama state troopers, and Jackson's grandfather was injured during the confrontation. Attempting to help his grandfather and protect his mother, Jackson was shot in the stomach at close range by a state trooper. The wounded Jackson was forced to run a gauntlet of troopers swinging their nightsticks before he was taken to the Negro Good Samaritan Hospital in Selma.

Jackson died of his wounds on February 26. The Reverend Dr. Martin Luther King Jr. preached at his funeral on March 3 and led a procession of one thousand marchers to Jackson's grave. At the funeral, an activist (accounts differ as to whom) suggested a march from Selma to Montgomery, the state capital, to demand an explanation for Jackson's death from Governor George Wallace.

While not widely publicized at the time, Jackson's death galvanized activists to undertake the march from Selma to Montgomery on March 7, 1965. Known as "Bloody Sunday" for the way it was violently broken up by Selma police, the march was a turning point in alerting the national consciousness to the black struggle for equal rights.

See also Civil Rights Movement, U.S.; King, Martin Luther, Jr.; Southern Christian Leadership Conference (SCLC)

▪ ▪ *Bibliography*

Garrow, David J. *Bearing the Cross: Martin Luther King, Jr. and the Southern Christian Leadership Conference*. New York: William Morrow, 1986.

MICHAEL PALLER (1996)

JACKSON, JOSEPH HARRISON

SEPTEMBER 11, 1900
AUGUST 18, 1990
▪▪▪

The minister Joseph H. Jackson was born in Jamestown, Mississippi, and received a B.A. from Jackson College in Jackson, Mississippi and a bachelor of divinity degree from Colgate-Rochester Divinity School. He later received an honorary doctor of divinity degree from Jackson College. From 1922 to 1941, he served as a minister in churches in Mississippi, Nebraska, and Pennsylvania. In 1934 he became corresponding secretary of the Foreign Mission Board of the National Baptist Convention (NBC) and vice president of the World Baptist Alliance. In 1941 he became pastor of the Olivet Baptist Church in Chicago, perhaps the largest Baptist church in the country.

In 1953 Jackson was elected president of the National Baptist Convention, the country's largest black religious group, with five million members. He campaigned as a reformer, pledging to eliminate presidential self-succession. Ironically, he remained president for twenty-nine years, a tenure marked by controversy over his opposition to civil rights activism and his autocratic leadership.

Although Jackson supported legal efforts in support of civil rights, he strongly believed that blacks should concentrate on "self-development" through advancing economic opportunity, and that civil disobedience would inflame racial differences. In January 1961 he denounced the sit-in movement and referred to the Rev. Dr. Martin Luther King Jr. as a "hoodlum." In 1963 he denounced the planned March on Washington as "dangerous and unwarranted." Attempting to speak at a National Association for the Advancement of Colored People (NAACP) rally that year, he was booed off the stage. Jackson actively pursued an African uplift program. In 1961 he developed a land investment program through which Baptists used 100,000 acres in Liberia to encourage settlement and raise money for missionaries. For his efforts, Jackson was made a Royal Knight of the Republic of Liberia, and received an honorary degree from Bishop College in Monrovia. He also led the Baptists to create Freedom Farm, a model farming community in Somerville, Tennessee.

Jackson faced several challenges to his leadership of the NBC. In 1957, despite his repeated promises to resign, he had his supporters suspend the convention's rules and was reelected by a voice vote. Angered opponents brought suit against the NBC board, but to no avail.

In 1960, at the NBC convention in Philadelphia, civil rights advocates led by Dr. King supported the Rev. Gardner Taylor for president. When Jackson's supporters attempted to reelect him by a voice vote, pandemonium broke out and Jackson left the hall. Taylor won a roll call vote, and the two factions brought injunctions against each other. Jackson retained the support of the NBC board and retained his presidency. At the 1961 NBC convention in Kansas City, Missouri, Jackson was reelected in a disputed vote that resulted in a riot. Banished from the NBC, King and Taylor formed the Progressive National Baptist Convention, a group committed to social action.

As president of the NBC, Jackson toured widely, visiting Africa, the Middle East, Asia, and Russia. In 1962 he attended the Second Vatican Council in Rome and had a private meeting with Pope John XXIII. He wrote several books, including *Stars in the Night* (1950), *The Eternal Flame* (1956), *Many but One: The Ecumenics of Charity* (1964), and *Unholy Shadows and Freedom's Holy Light* (1967), as well as *A Story of Christian Activism: The History of the National Baptist Convention, U.S.A., Inc.* (1980). In 1973 the NBC's library in Chicago was named for him. In 1982 Jackson retired, and in 1989, he established a $100,000 scholarship fund at Howard University.

See also Howard University; King, Martin Luther, Jr.; Missionary Movements; National Association for the Advancement of Colored People (NAACP); National Baptist Convention, U.S.A., Inc.

■ ■ *Bibliography*

Branch, Taylor. *Parting the Waters: America in the King Years, 1954–1963.* New York: Simon & Schuster, 1988.

Paris, Peter J. *Black Religious Leaders: Conflict in Unity,* 2nd ed. Louisville, Ky.: Westminster/John Knox Press, 1991.

GREG ROBINSON (1996)

JACKSON, LILLIE MAE CARROLL

MAY 25, 1889
JULY 6, 1975

Born in Baltimore, Maryland, civil rights leader Lillie Mae Carroll was the daughter of former slave Charles Carroll, who was an eponymous descendant of one of the signers of the Declaration of Independence. In 1903 the Carrolls bought a house in the prosperous Druid Hill section of Baltimore, where much of that city's black middle class resided. Lillie Mae Carroll graduated from the Colored High and Training School in 1908 and began teaching. She married Kieffer Jackson, a traveling salesman, in 1910, and the two spent the next eight years on the road throughout the South. They returned to Baltimore in 1918 to raise their four children.

Jackson's involvement in civil rights activism began in 1931, when her daughter Juanita returned from college in Pennsylvania and organized the Baltimore Young People's Forum. Lillie Jackson formed an adults' advisory board for the group. They sponsored a successful "Buy Where You Can Work" campaign against businesses that refused to employ African Americans. Shortly thereafter, following a series of lynchings in the area, the National Association for the Advancement of Colored People (NAACP) named Jackson to revive the floundering Baltimore branch. She then began a thirty-five-year career with the NAACP that resulted in many landmark civil rights victories. One of the Baltimore branch's first actions was a lawsuit to desegregate the University of Maryland law school, which was argued by Thurgood Marshall in his first case. Under Jackson, the NAACP also brought lawsuits throughout the 1940s and 1950s that resulted in the desegregation of public schools, parks, beaches, and swimming pools.

Under "Fearless Lil," Baltimore NAACP membership saw enormous growth in the 1940s, rising to eighteen thousand in 1946. Jackson organized and was elected president of the Maryland NAACP state conference in 1942. She helped organize demonstrations against police brutality in Annapolis that year. In response, the governor appointed her to the newly formed Interracial Commission, but she resigned shortly afterward, explaining that the commission was an ineffectual body that censored her opinions. She organized and participated in the Maryland Congress Against Discrimination in Baltimore in 1946. An extensive voter registration drive throughout the 1940s doubled the number of black voters and made registration more accessible. In 1956 Jackson received an honorary doctorate from Morgan State College (now Morgan State University) in Baltimore. During the 1950s she also worked to make Baltimore the first city to comply with the 1954 *Brown v. Board of Education* Supreme Court decision. When the civil rights movement accelerated in the late 1950s, Jackson often contributed her own money to bail out arrested activists when the NAACP's funds were depleted.

Jackson was a devout Christian and a lifelong member of Baltimore's Stark Street United Methodist Church, as well as the first woman to serve on its board of trustees. She believed that the NAACP was "God's workshop" and was instrumental in uniting different congregations and denominations for civil rights activism. After she retired from the NAACP in 1970 at age eighty, she formed Freedom House, a network of inner-city community activists. She died in Baltimore in 1975.

See also National Association for the Advancement of Colored People (NAACP)

■ ■ *Bibliography*

"Dr. Lillie M. Jackson: Lifelong Freedom Fighter." *Crisis* 82 (1975): 279–300.

Greene, Susan Ellery. *Baltimore: An Illustrated History.* Woodland Hills, Calif.: Windsor Publications, 1980.

ALLISON X. MILLER (1996)

JACKSON, LUTHER PORTER

1892
APRIL 20, 1950

Luther Porter Jackson, an educator, civic leader, and historian, was born to the former slaves Edward and Delilah Jackson in Lexington, Kentucky, sometime in 1892. He graduated from Chandler Normal School in 1910 and attended Fisk University, where he received his B.A. in 1914 and his M.A. in 1916. Years later, in 1937, he received a Ph.D. in history from the University of Chicago.

Jackson's teaching career began in South Carolina, where he taught at the Voorhees Industrial School from 1915 to 1918. He then taught at the Topeka Industrial Institute until 1920. In 1922 he joined the staff of the Virginia Normal and Industrial Institute in Petersburg (renamed Virginia State College in 1930), and was named associate professor of history in 1925. In 1929 he was promoted to full professor and chair of the History and Social Science Department, a position he held for the rest of his life.

Jackson became an expert on blacks in Virginia, scrupulously studying courthouse documents. In 1942 he published *Free Negro Labor and Property Holding in Virginia, 1830–1860.* He went on to publish numerous scholarly works, including *Virginia Negro Soldiers and Seamen in the Revolutionary War* (1944) and *Negro Office Holders in Virginia, 1860–1895* (1945).

Jackson was a vocal advocate for black suffrage, and beginning in 1942 he published *The Voting Status of Negroes in Virginia,* a pamphlet intended to encourage African Americans to vote. He also founded the Petersburg League of Negro Voters, which later became the Virginia Voters League. In 1947 the Southern Regional Council commissioned Jackson to study black voting in the South, the results of which were published in a pamphlet, *Race and Suffrage in the South Since 1940* (1948).

Jackson was very involved with the Petersburg Negro Business Association, which eventually became the Virginia Trade Association. He also was an accomplished musician—he played the cornet—and founded the Petersburg Community Chorus, which he directed in yearly concerts from 1933 to 1941.

Jackson was an active participant in Carter G. Woodson's Association for the Study of Negro Life and History. He was also very active in fund-raising for the NAACP. In 1948 his efforts resulted in an award from the Virginia NAACP "for unselfish and devoted services in enhancing the voting status of Negroes." Jackson was a driven man who, in addition to his other activities, served on numerous boards and councils and often worked late into the night. He died of a heart attack in 1950. Luther Jackson High School was dedicated in his memory on April 17, 1955, in Merrifield, Virginia.

See also Association for the Study of African American Life and History; National Association for the Advancement of Colored People (NAACP)

■ ■ *Bibliography*

Logan, Rayford W., and Michael R. Winston, eds. *Dictionary of American Negro Biography.* New York: Norton, 1982.

DEBI BROOME (1996)

JACKSON, MAHALIA

OCTOBER 26, 1911
JANUARY 27, 1972

◂▸◂▸

When sixteen-year-old Mahala Jackson (as she was named at birth) arrived in Chicago in 1927, she had already developed the vocal style that was to win her the title of "world's greatest gospel singer." Though born into an extremely religious New Orleans family, she spent hours listening to the recordings of blues singers Bessie Smith and Ma Rainey and could be found at every parade that passed her neighborhood of Pinching Town in New Orleans.

In later life she would admit that although she was a thoroughgoing Baptist, the Sanctified church next door to her house had had a powerful influence on her singing, for although the members had neither choir nor organ, they sang accompanied by a drum, tambourine, and steel triangle. They clapped and stomped their feet and sang with their whole bodies. She recalled that they had a powerful beat she believed was retained from slavery, and once stated, "I believe blues and jazz and even rock 'n' roll stuff got their beat from the Sanctified church."

Jackson's style was set early on: From Bessie Smith and Ma Rainey she borrowed a deep and dark resonance that complemented her own timbre; from the Baptist church she inherited the moaning and bending of final notes in phrases; and from the Sanctified church she adopted a full-throated tone, delivered with a holy beat. Surprisingly, although gospel in its early stages was being sung in New Orleans, none of her vocal influences came from gospel singers.

Upon arriving in Chicago with her Aunt Hannah, Jackson joined the Johnson Singers, an a cappella quartet. The group quickly established a reputation as one of Chicago's better gospel groups, appearing regularly in concerts and gospel-song plays with Jackson in the lead. In time Mahalia, as she now chose to call herself, became exclusively a soloist. In 1935 Thomas A. Dorsey persuaded her to become his official song demonstrator, a position she held until 1945. Dorsey later stated that Jackson "had a lot of soul in her singing: she meant what she sang."

Although she made her first recordings in 1937 for Decca, it was not until 1946, when she switched to the small Apollo label, that Jackson established a national reputation in the African-American community. Her 1947 recording of "Move On Up a Little Higher" catapulted her to the rank of superstar and won her one of the first two gold records for record sales in gospel music. (Clara Ward won the other.) Accompanied on this recording by her longtime pianist, Mildred Falls, Jackson demonstrated her wide range and ability to improvise on melody and rhythm. As a result of this recording, she became the official soloist for the National Baptist Convention and began touring throughout the United States. She was the first gospel singer to be given a network radio show when, in 1954, CBS signed her for a weekly show on which she was the host and star. In the same year she moved to the Columbia label, becoming a crossover gospel singer through her first recording on that label, "Rusty Old Halo." Several triumphs followed in rapid succession. She appeared on the Ed Sullivan and Dinah Shore television shows, at Carnegie Hall, and in 1958 for the first time at the Newport Jazz Festival. Tours throughout the world began, with Jackson garnering accolades in France, Germany, and Italy.

A crowning achievement of Jackson's was the invitation to sing at one of the inaugural parties of President John F. Kennedy in 1961. In 1963 she was asked to sing just before Rev. Dr. Martin Luther King, Jr. was to deliver his famous "I Have a Dream" speech at the March on Washington. Her rendition of "I've Been Buked and I've Been Scorned" contributed to the success of King's speech. During her career, she appeared in such films as *St. Louis Blues* (1958), *Imitation of Life* (1959) and *Jazz on a Summer's Day* (1958), sang "Precious Lord, Take My Hand" at the funeral of Dr. King, and recorded with Duke Ellington. Toward the end of her life, she suffered from heart trouble but continued to sing until her death in Chicago. Jackson appeared on a United States postage stamp in 1998.

See also Blues, The; Gospel Music

■ ■ *Bibliography*

Goreau, Laurraine. *Just Mahalia, Baby: The Mahalia Jackson Story*. Gretna, La: Pelican, 1984.

Heilbut, Tony. *The Gospel Sound: Good News and Bad Times*. New York: Simon & Schuster, 1971. Revised, New York: Limelight Editions; Distributed by Harper & Row, 1985.

Jackson, Mahalia, and E. M. Wylie. *Movin' On Up*. New York: Hawthorn Books, 1966.

HORACE CLARENCE BOYER (1996)

JACKSON, MAYNARD HOLBROOK, JR.

MARCH 23, 1938
JUNE 23, 2003

▐▐▐ ▬▬▬▬▬▬▬▬▬▬▬▬▬▬▬▬▬▬▬▬▬

Maynard Jackson, a lawyer, businessman, former three-term mayor of Atlanta, and the first African-American mayor of a major southern city, was born in Dallas, Texas. At the age of seven he moved with his family to Atlanta, Georgia, where the elder Jackson served as pastor of Friendship Baptist Church until his death in 1953. As a Ford Foundation Early Admissions scholar, Jackson graduated from Morehouse College in Atlanta in 1956 at the age of eighteen with a B.A. in political science and history.

After graduation, Jackson worked for one year in Cleveland, Ohio, as a claims examiner for the Ohio State Bureau of Unemployment Compensation, then as an encyclopedia salesman, and later as assistant district sales manager for the P. F. Collier Company in Buffalo, Boston, and Cleveland. In 1964 he received an LL.B. from North Carolina College at Durham and returned to Atlanta to practice law with the U.S. National Labor Relations Board (NLRB), where he handled representation cases and unfair labor practice cases. In 1967 Jackson left the NLRB to work for the Community Legal Services Center of Emory University. Specializing in housing litigation and providing free legal services to the poor in Atlanta's Bedford-Pine neighborhood, he developed a reputation as a civil rights activist.

In 1968, following the deaths of Martin Luther King Jr. and Senator Robert Kennedy, Jackson decided to enter politics and made a bid for a seat in the U.S. Senate against Senator Herman Talmadge, Georgia's longtime senator, who was running unopposed. Appealing to those whom Talmadge had traditionally neglected, namely blacks and white liberals, Jackson lost the election but succeeded in outpolling Talmadge in Atlanta, carrying the city by more than 6,000 votes. Despite Jackson's defeat, this election provided him political exposure and helped him build a base of support among blacks and white liberals, a following that contributed to his later electoral victories. Jackson also developed as a gifted speaker and orator.

In 1969 Jackson ran for vice mayor of Atlanta against Milton Farris, a white alderman, on a coalition campaign that built upon his previous support from black and white liberal voters. In the 1969 campaign both Jackson and the mayoral winner, Sam Massell, received crucial support from the city's growing number of black voters. While Jackson recognized the importance of his support from blacks, he avoided any direct appeals to race consciousness for fear of alienating the city's white voters. Jackson won the election and was sworn in as Atlanta's first black vice mayor in 1970, and in conjunction with this position, as the first black president of the board of aldermen. In the same year, he cofounded the law firm of Jackson, Patterson, and Parks. As vice mayor, Jackson was a strong supporter of grassroots organizations, urging the formation of neighborhood coalitions.

In 1973 Jackson entered the mayoral race against eleven candidates, including incumbent mayor Sam Massell and the powerful black state senator and favorite of the old-guard black leadership, Leroy Johnson. Jackson defeated Massell in the runoff election, in which Massell, a liberal Democrat and traditionally a moderate on racial issues, ran a racially divisive campaign. Jackson, however, continued to build upon the support he had received from blacks and white liberals in earlier elections and campaigned on a people-oriented platform. The major issues he addressed were crime, law enforcement, housing, and a jobs training and placement program. Jackson pledged to end racism in the city's hiring policies but stated his opposition to any program that favored blacks as racially or legally superior.

Jackson was inaugurated as Atlanta's first black mayor in January 1974. At the age of thirty-four, he was also the city's youngest mayor. In his first inaugural address, Jackson proclaimed full citizen participation in his new administration. He served two consecutive terms, holding the office from 1974 to 1982 and serving the maximum number of consecutive terms allowed by the city's charter. During this period, Atlanta transformed itself into a growing international city.

Jackson entered office in 1974 under a new city charter, the first in one hundred years, which replaced the former weak mayor-council form of government with one that gave the mayor increased administrative powers. The charter required all agencies and departments to report to the mayor and abolished the position of vice mayor. The charter also augmented Jackson's power by providing him the opportunity to reorganize the city government.

As mayor, Jackson worked to break down discriminatory barriers in the city's hiring policies and in securing city contracts. He created the city's first minority business program, ensuring opportunities for minorities and women in major city contracts and in administrative posts in the city government while at the same time maintaining links to the city's traditional white business elite. In 1973, prior to Jackson taking office, blacks received less than one percent of city contracts. He insisted on minority participation on a major airport expansion, requiring joint ven-

> ## Maynard Jackson
>
> "We must learn and remember that Atlanta's strength lies not in the power of its government, but in the power of the governed, and they demand the removal of the social cataracts from our governmental eyes."
>
> INAUGURAL ADDRESS AS MAYOR OF ATLANTA, JANUARY 7, 1974.

ture participation with minority firms. By the time Jackson had finished his second term, minorities received over thirty-six percent of city business. Rebuffing white business leaders, Jackson insisted that white firms integrate their boards and management teams. Jackson also opened the lines of communication between his office and Atlanta's neighborhoods, creating a monthly "People's Day," in which he traveled to various neighborhoods to listen to residents' concerns and complaints. Jackson's affirmative action programs were later modeled by cities across the country.

After leaving office, Jackson became a managing partner of Chapman and Cutler, a Chicago-based municipal law firm, building a lucrative bond practice and founding Jackson Securities Inc., an investment banking firm, in 1987. In 1989 Jackson reentered Atlanta politics, winning a landslide election to serve his third term as mayor. During this period he guided the city through the initial steps of preparation for the summer centennial Olympic Games in 1996. At the close of his term at the end of 1993, Jackson decided not to seek reelection despite a seventy percent approval rating and returned to Jackson Securities Inc. as full-time chairman of the board and majority stockholder.

Always restless away from elective office, Jackson in 2001 ran unsuccessfully for the chairmanship of the Democratic National Committee on a platform to reenergize the grassroots supporters. The *New York Times* endorsed his candidacy. He became the National Development chair of the Democratic Party and chair of the Voting Rights Institute. In spring of 2003 Jackson contemplated but decided against another run for the U.S. Senate from Georgia.

On June 23, 2003, Maynard Jackson died in Washington D.C., of a heart attack after arriving on a plane from Atlanta. The Atlanta City Council later renamed its airport the Hartsfield-Jackson Airport, after Atlanta's two long-sitting mayors.

See also Mayors; Politics in the United States

■ ■ *Bibliography*

Atlanta Journal Constitution (June 24, 2003): A1.

Bass, Jack. *The Transformation of Southern Politics.* New York: Basic Books, 1976.

Benson, Christopher. "Hail and Farewell: Maynard Holbrook Jackson Jr., 1938–2003: Throngs Celebrate Life of Atlanta's Visionary Black Mayor." *Ebony* 58, no. 11 (September 2003): 142–45.

Dingle, Derek T. "The Ultimate Champion for Black Business." *Black Enterprise* 34, no. 2 (September 2003): 72–78.

Jamieson, Duncan R. "Maynard Jackson's 1973 Election as Mayor of Atlanta." *Midwest Quarterly* 18 (October 1976): 7–26.

"Maynard Jackson, Atlanta's First Black Mayor, Dies in D.C." *Jet* 104, no. 2 (July 7, 2003): 16–17.

Pomerantz, Gary. *Where Peachtree Meets Sweet Auburn: The Saga of Two Families and the Making of Atlanta.* New York: Scribner, 1996.

Washington Post (June 24, 2003): B7.

White, Gayle. "Maynard Jackson: A Champion for Atlanta." *Atlanta Journal Constitution* (June 29, 2003), section E (special 14 page memorial section).

DEREK M. ALPHRAN (1996)
Updated by author 2005

JACKSON, MICHAEL

AUGUST 29, 1958

■ ■ ■

The pop singer, dancer, and cultural icon Michael Jackson had a dominant influence on American popular music from the 1970s through the 1990s. For more than a decade, starting in the late 1970s, Michael Jackson created dance music with an electrifying synthesis of street rhythms and lush arrangements. His music was supported by exquisitely crafted music videos featuring Jackson's eye-popping choreography that virtually defined the emerging form of the music video genre. But Jackson's own demons eventually spurred him to engage in bizarre, and allegedly, criminal behavior that chipped away at his enormous popularity and began to overshadow his signal achievements as a performer.

Jackson began singing with his four brothers in 1963, and he quickly became the lead singer and dancer for the Jackson 5, the last of the great Motown acts (and perhaps its greatest crossover success). Jackson begin to release solo albums in 1971, but his solo career did not take off until he began to work with producer and arranger Quincy

Jones, whom he had met and collaborated with on *The Wiz* (1977), an all-black musical version of *The Wizard of Oz.* Coproducing with Jones, Jackson wrote three of the ten songs on his breakthrough 1979 album, *Off the Wall.* With Jackson resplendent in tuxedo and glowing white socks on the cover, *Off the Wall* proclaimed his emergence as an adult entertainer. Quincy Jones drew on Los Angeles's top pop-funk session players, and he and Jackson assembled an exquisitely crafted amalgam of disco, soul, and pop, putting to rest Jackson's bubblegum image. It yielded four Top Ten singles—including scorching dance cuts like "Don't Stop 'Til You Get Enough," as well as libidinous ballads—and sold eleven million copies. The next year Michael reunited with his brothers on *Triumph*, but by this time it was clear that his superstar status virtually relegated his brothers to a supporting role.

In 1982 Jackson again teamed up with Jones to make *Thriller*, a more rock-oriented album with funkier dance tracks but more soulful ballads. The record yielded seven Top Ten singles, including "Wanna Be Startin' Somethin'"; a duet with Paul McCartney, "The Girl is Mine"; "Beat It"; "Billie Jean"; and the title track, with a campy rap by the actor Vincent Price. Spending over two years on the charts and claiming a record eight Grammy awards, *Thriller* eventually sold more than forty million copies, making it the best-selling album of all time. The music videos for *Thriller* brought an end to MTV's refusal to feature African-American music, and the "Beat It" video brought special acclaim due to its choreographed gang fight, which evoked the production numbers of a Broadway musical scored for rock and roll and was dubbed "Michael's West Side Story."

As a result, Jackson, who had always been a witty and talented stage performer, began to attract attention as a dancer. In a 1983 television special celebrating Motown's twenty-fifth anniversary, Jackson electrified a huge broadcast audience with his rendition of the African-American vernacular dance step known as "the backslide." His version, renamed "the moonwalk," combined the traditional forward-stepping, back-sliding routine with James Brown's signature spins (which he had copied as a child) and the robotic "locking" motions long popular among hip-hop street performers. In 1984 Jackson joined his brothers to record and tour in support of the album *Victory.* In 1985 he coauthored the song "We Are the World" with Lionel Ritchie, and they recorded it with an all-star cast for the album *USA for Africa*, with the proceeds benefiting famine relief. The single and video of the song were a huge success.

Jackson's 1987 album, *Bad*, attempted, but failed, to reproduce the unprecedented success of *Thriller.* On the

Michael Jackson with Quincy Jones during the 1984 Grammy Awards. *Jackson won six Grammys that year, including Record of the Year ("Beat It") and Album of the Year (Thriller).* AP/WIDE WORLD PHOTOS. REPRODUCED BY PERMISSION.

title track, Jackson toughened the street persona he had often affected, but *Bad* was a slicker record with weaker songs and an increasingly split personality, veering from talking trash on "Bad," "Dirty Diana," and "Smooth Criminal" to soulful introspection on "Man in the Mirror" and "I Just Can't Stop Loving You," a lush duet with the singer Siedah Garrett. Although it yielded five number one singles, *Bad* sold only a fifth as many copies as *Thriller.*

Jackson did not produce a new album until *Dangerous* in 1991. Now widely known as the "King of Pop," he brought in Teddy Riley, a new producer associated with the updated New Jack Swingan amalgam of hip-hop rhythms, samplings, and vocals that emerged in the late-1980s, combining the melodies of soul with funkier street rhythms of rap. Its first single, "Black or White," went to number one, as did the album, but the video, premiering in prime time on network TV, was criticized for its violence and lasciviousness, which clashed with its message of racial harmony.

In the years since the triumph of *Thriller* and Jackson's ascension to the role of "King of Pop," Jackson's many personal quirks have drawn increasing critical attention. Shy and soft-spoken, he has seemed frail in public appearances. Numerous plastic surgeries and his lightening skin tone led some in the African-American community (and others) to question his racial solidarity; Jackson's claim to suffer from the pigmentation disorder vitiligo did not explain his many trips to plastic surgeons in search of a smaller, more sculpted nose. Labeled "wacko Jacko" by the aggressive British tabloids, Jackson sought refuge from his detractors in the company of celebrities like Elizabeth Taylor and, increasingly, children. In particular, he began to have many children, especially boys, as overnight guests at his fabulous Neverland Valley Ranch, a 2,600-acre pleasure dome northwest of Santa Barbara, California. Named for the magical kingdom in the children's book *Peter Pan,* the estate sports amusement park rides, a petting zoo, its own narrow-gauge railroad, and statues of children.

Rumors and then charges swirled around Jackson's conduct with his young friends.

On September 3, 2004, the television news magazine *Dateline NBC* reported that in 1990 he secretly paid a two million dollar settlement to the son of an employee to avoid an accusation of child molestation. In a press release issued the next day, Jackson acknowledged the payment but denied any wrongdoing. In September, 1993, a thirteen-year-old boy and his father filed a civil suit against Jackson alleging sexual battery, seduction, willful misconduct, emotional distress, fraud, and negligence. In a sworn declaration made in December, 1993, the boy accused Jackson of multiple counts of sexual contact, including open-mouth kissing, fondling, and oral sex. The suit was withdrawn when Jackson paid a total of twenty-five million dollars to the boy and his family. Two marriages, widely rumored to be marriages of convenience, followed the humiliating settlement. In May 1994, Jackson married Lisa Marie Presley, the daughter of Elvis Presley; the marriage ended in divorce in January, 1996. In November 1996, Jackson married Debbie Rowe, an employee of his dermatologist, who was expecting his child at the time. She bore him two children before they were divorced in October 1999.

In 1995 Jackson released a double album, *HIStory*; however, only the second disk, *HIStory Continues*, consisted of new material. Although it contained the scorching dance hit "Scream," recorded with his sister Janet, anti-Semitic slurs in "They Don't Care About Us" led MTV and VH1 to ban the video. The record did not match the success of Jackson's earlier efforts, though it had sold eighteen million copies by 2004. In 2001, Jackson released *Invincible*, an album of all-new material, his first since *Dangerous*. Rumored to be the most expensive album ever made, it sold only two million copies in the United States and spawned only one hit single, "You Rock My World,"

which cracked the top ten for only one week and received little video airplay. A compilation of hits, *Number Ones*, released in 2003, also included a new single, "One More Chance." Written by R. Kelly, one of the best-selling R&B singer/songwriter/producers of the 1990s, the song reached number one on billboard's R&B/Hip-Hop Singles chart and stayed there for three weeks.

But Jackson's many troubles were coming to a head. In early 2002 Jackson had another son by a surrogate mother. Staying in a hotel in Berlin, Jackson dangled the child over a fourth-floor balcony to show him off to fans, earning widespread condemnation for endangering the child. In 2002 and 2003, Jackson was sued by concert promoters and his own financial advisers. On November 18, 2003, law enforcement agents searched Jackson's Neverland Ranch, and the following day he was charged with multiple counts of felony child molestation involving a thirteen-year-old cancer survivor. Jackson allegedly gave the boy and his brother wine, showed them pornography, and had "substantial sexual contact" with the child. Jackson was arrested, forced to surrender his passport, and released on three million dollars bail. A new ten-count grand jury indictment, unsealed on April 30, 2004, expanded the charges to include allegations of child abduction, false imprisonment, and extortion. Jackson was acquitted of all charges by a California jury in June, 2005.

See also Jackson Family; Jackson, Janet; Jones, Quincy; Music in the United States

▪ ▪ *Bibliography*

Brown, Geoff. *The Complete Guide to the Music of Michael Jackson and the Jackson Family.* New York: Omnibus Press, 1996.

George, Nelson. *The Michael Jackson Story.* New York: Dell, 1984.

Jackson, Michael. *Moonwalk.* New York: Doubleday, 1988.

Mercer, Kobena. "Monster Metaphors: Notes on Michael Jackson's 'Thriller.'" In *Sound and Vision: the Music Video Reader,* edited by Simon Frith, Andrew Goodwin, and Lawrence Grossberg. London: Routledge, 1993.

Orth, Maureen. "Neverland's Lost Boys." *Vanity Fair* 523 (March 2004): 384–389, 415–421.

Swenson, J. "Michael Jackson." In *The Rolling Stone Illustrated History of Rock & Roll,* 3d ed., edited by A. DeCurtis and James Henke with Holly George-Warren. New York: Random House, 1976.

HARRIS FRIEDBERG (2005)

JACKSON FAMILY

A dominant influence on American popular music since the 1960s, the Jackson family consists of the nine children of Joseph and Katherine Jackson. The couple's first three sons, Sigmund "Jackie" (May 4, 1951–), Toriano "Tito" (October 15, 1953–), and Jermaine (December 11, 1954–), began singing in 1962; Marlon (March 12, 1957–) and Michael (August 29, 1958–) joined a year later. Their other children, Maureen "Rebbie" (May 29, 1950–), LaToya (May 29, 1956–), Steven "Randy" (October 29, 1962–), and Janet (May 16, 1966–) began entertaining publicly with their siblings in the 1970s. By the 1980s the Jackson family was generating a nonstop stream of recordings, music videos, movies, television shows, and concerts that were hugely popular among both African-American and white audiences. In the 1990s, however, public attention turned to squabbles within the family and the increasingly questionable public behavior of some of the family members.

All of the Jackson children were born and raised in the Midwestern industrial city of Gary, Indiana, where they led a sheltered existence in a working-class neighborhood. The five oldest sons were driven by their father, a steel mill crane operator and one-time rhythm-and-blues guitarist, to practice music three hours a day. They began to perform in local talent contests in 1963 and rapidly advanced to amateur contests in Chicago. In 1967 Michael's lead soprano and irresistible dance moves, borrowed from James Brown, helped the brothers win the famed amateur night contest at Harlem's Apollo Theater. The next year the Jacksons signed with Motown, the black-owned Detroit recording company. Motown's owner, Berry Gordy, took complete control of the group, choosing their songs, managing their performances, and gaining the rights to their name, then The Jackson 5. The group's first singles, including "I Want You Back" (1969) and "ABC" (1970), were popular, layering Michael's vocals over funky, stutter-step bass lines.

In 1970 the family moved to Los Angeles, and in the years that followed, the Jacksons made numerous television appearances. Although their recordings from this time suffered from a sense of forced cuteness, their popularity never flagged, and the brothers began to insist on performing much of the instrumental backing themselves. Their recordings from this time include *Lookin' Through the Windows* (1972) and *Get It Together* (1973). In 1974 the Jacksons broke with the formulaic routine of Motown recordings and produced "Dancing Machine," a frenetic dance hit that presaged the disco era. In 1975 the group broke with Motown and signed with Epic, which offered them five times more in royalties. Because Motown owned the name The Jackson 5, they called themselves The Jacksons. Jermaine, having married Hazel Gordy, the daughter of Motown's founder, remained with Motown to pursue a solo career.

Like Motown, Epic at first refused to let the Jacksons, who had replaced Jermaine with Randy, write or produce their own material. Instead, their densely layered pop hits, bridging the gap between soul and disco, were written by the Philadelphia-based team of Kenny Gamble and Leon Huff. Only in 1977 were they finally allowed to fully control their own recordings. The resulting album, *Destiny*, mixed Michael's gospel-style vocals with disco rhythms and yielded the hit single "Shake Your Body (Down to the Ground)," written by Michael and Randy.

Meanwhile, although Michael was concentrating on his spiraling solo character, he reunited with his brothers in 1980 on *Triumph*, but by this time it was clear that his superstar status virtually relegated his brothers to a backup role. After *Triumph*, the Jacksons brought Michael back in 1984 for the enormously successful *Victory* album and tour. Since then the Jacksons as a group have been less active, concentrating on solo careers, although Jackie, Marlon, Tito, and Randy did record the largely unsuccessful *2300 Jackson Street* (1989).

After Michael, Jermaine Jackson has been the most successful male singer in the family. He released *Jermaine* in 1972 and recorded almost a dozen more solo albums over the next decade. In 1991 he recorded "You Said, You Said" and "Word to the Badd," a scalding attack on Michael. Marlon Jackson's solo album, *Baby Tonight*, was released in 1987. Randy Jackson, badly injured in a 1980 auto accident, recovered in time for the Jacksons' reunion in 1984. He released his first solo album in 1989. In 1997 The Jackson 5 was admitted to the Rock & Roll Hall of Fame.

The Jackson daughters have also had solo careers. The oldest, Rebbie, continued performing after the 1970s but without the popularity of her two younger sisters. LaToya Jackson released four undistinguished solo albums. In 1991 she countered her mother's 1990 memoirs, *The Jacksons: My Family*, by publishing *LaToya: Growing Up in the Jackson Family*, which portrayed a childhood dominated by fear and abuse. Janet has gone on to parlay modest singing abilities with hot choreography and even hotter lyrics into a vastly popular career.

Despite internal family conflicts, the Jacksons remain, collectively and individually, the most prominent and productive family in African-American popular music.

See also Jackson, Janet; Jackson, Michael; Music in the United States; Rhythm and Blues

The Jackson 5. *Jackson family brothers (from left) Tito, Marlon, Michael, Jackie, and Jermaine perform on* The Sonny and Cher Comedy Hour. AP/WIDE WORLD PHOTOS. REPRODUCED BY PERMISSION.

■ ■ *Bibliography*

Brown, Geoff. *The Complete Guide to the Music of Michael Jackson and the Jackson Family.* New York: Omnibus Press, 1996.

Jackson, La Toya. *La Toya: Growing Up in the Jackson Family.* New York: Dutton, 1991.

McDougal, Weldon A. *The Michael Jackson Scrapbook: The Early Days of the Jackson 5.* New York: Avon Books, 1984.

HARRIS FRIEDBERG (1996)
Updated by author 2005

JACOBS, HARRIET ANN

1813
MARCH 7, 1897

┣┃┃

Harriet Jacobs—slave narrator, reformer, antislavery activist, and Civil War and Reconstruction relief worker— was born a slave in Edenton, North Carolina. Jacobs's major contribution is her narrative, *Incidents in the Life of a Slave Girl: Written by Herself* (1861). The most comprehensive antebellum autobiography by an African-American woman, *Incidents* is the first-person account of Jacobs's pseudonymous narrator, who writes of her struggle against sexual oppression and her fight for freedom. After publishing her book, Jacobs devoted her life to providing relief for the black Civil War refugees in Alexandria, Virginia, and Savannah, Georgia.

Writing as "Linda Brent," Jacobs tells the story of her life in the South as a slave and as a fugitive, and of her life as a fugitive slave in the North. Breaking taboos forbidding women to discuss their sexuality, she writes of the abuse she suffered from her licentious master, Dr. James Norcom, whom she calls "Dr. Flint." She confesses that to prevent him from making her his concubine, at sixteen she became sexually involved with a white neighbor. Their alliance produced two children, Joseph (c. 1829–?), whom she calls "Benny," and Louisa Matilda (1833–1917), called "Ellen." Jacobs describes running away from Norcom in 1835 and the almost seven years she spent in hiding in a tiny crawlspace above a porch in her grandmother's Edenton home.

Jacobs further recounts her 1842 escape to New York City, her reunion with her children, who had been sent north, and her subsequent move to Rochester, where she became part of the circle of abolitionists around Frederick Douglass' newspaper *The North Star*. Condemning the compliance of the North in the slave system, she describes her North Carolina masters' attempts to catch her in New York after passage of the 1850 Fugitive Slave Law. Jacobs explains that despite her principled decision not to bow to the slave system by being purchased, in 1853 her New York employer, Mrs. Nathaniel Parker Willis (called "Mrs. Bruce") bought her from Norcom's family. Like other slave narrators, she ends her book with her freedom and the freedom of her children.

Most of the extraordinary events that "Linda Brent" narrates have been documented as having occurred in Jacobs's life. In addition, letters that Jacobs wrote while composing her book present an unique glimpse of its inception, composition, and publication and recount her complex relationships with black abolitionists such as William C. Nell and white abolitionists such as Amy Post and Lydia Maria Child. They also form an interesting commentary on Jacobs's northern employer, the litterateur Nathaniel Parker Willis, and on Harriet Beecher Stowe, author of the runaway best-seller *Uncle Tom's Cabin*, whom Jacobs tried to interest in her narrative.

Although *Incidents* was published anonymously, Jacobs's name was connected with her book from the first; only in the twentieth century were its authorship and its autobiographical status disputed. *Incidents* made Jacobs known to northern abolitionists, and with the outbreak of the Civil War she used this newfound celebrity to establish a new career for herself. Jacobs collected money and supplies for the "contraband"—black refugees crowding behind the lines of the Union army in Washington, D.C., and in occupied Alexandria, Virginia—and returned south.

Supported by Quaker groups and the newly formed New England Freedmen's Aid Society, in 1863 Jacobs and her daughter moved to Alexandria, where they distributed emergency relief supplies, organized primary medical care, and established the Jacobs Free School—a black-led institution providing black teachers for the refugees. In 1865 mother and daughter moved to Savannah, where they continued their relief work. Throughout the war years Harriet and Louisa Jacobs reported on their southern re-

lief efforts in the northern press and in newspapers in England, where Jacobs's book had appeared as *The Deeper Wrong: Incidents in the Life of a Slave Girl: Written by Herself* (1862). In 1868 they sailed to England and successfully raised money for Savannah's black orphans and aged.

But in the face of the increasing violence in the South, Jacobs and her daughter then retreated to Massachusetts. In Boston they were connected with the newly formed New England Women's Club. Later, in Cambridge, Jacobs ran a boardinghouse for Harvard faculty and students for several years. Harriet and Louisa Jacobs later moved to Washington, D.C., where they established a series of boardinghouses and the daughter was employed at Howard University. In 1896, when the National Association of Colored Women held its organizing meetings in Washington, D.C., Harriet Jacobs was confined to a wheelchair, but it seems likely that Louisa was in attendance. The following spring Harriet Jacobs died at her Washington home. She is buried in Mount Auburn Cemetery, Cambridge.

See also Douglass, Frederick; Howard University; National Association of Colored Women; Nell, William Cooper; Slave Narratives

■ ■ *Bibliography*

Garfield, Deborah M., and Rafia Zafar, eds. *Harriet Jacobs and Incidents in the Life of a Slave Girl: New Critical Essays.* New York: Cambridge University Press, 1996.

Yellin, Jean Fagan. "Text and Contexts of Harriet Jacobs's *Incidents in the Life of a Slave Girl: Written by Herself.*" In *The Slave's Narrative*, edited by Charles T. Davis and Henry Louis Gates, Jr., pp. 262–282. New York: Oxford University Press, 1985.

Yellin, Jean Fagan. Introduction to *Incidents in the Life of a Slave Girl: Written by Herself.* Cambridge: Harvard University Press, 1987, pp. xiii–xxxiv.

Yellin, Jean Fagan, *Harriet Jacobs: A Life.* New York: Basic Books, 2004.

JEAN FAGAN YELLIN (1996)
Updated by author 2005

JAMAICA LABOUR PARTY

■ ■ ■

The Jamaica Labour Party (JLP) is one of the two remaining political parties in Jamaica. Its influence upon Jamaica is due primarily to the skillful leadership of William Alexander Clarke, otherwise known as Alexander Bustamante.

Bustamante was born in Blenheim in the parish of Hanover, Jamaica, on February 24, 1884, and migrated to Cuba in 1905 at the age of twenty-one.

After Bustamante returned from Cuba in 1934 he wrote frequent letters to the Jamaican newspapers, most of them focusing on topical issues and demonstrating his concern for the condition of poor black laborers. By 1937 he had developed such a large readership that he could turn most of his attention to traveling and holding small private meetings in response to the incidence of labor riots on the island. At one meeting in Kingston, Bustamante charged that he was attacked because of his support for improvement in the working conditions of the masses. By then his magnetic personality and charisma endeared him to his followers. On May 23, 1938, he addressed a large crowd of striking workers under Queen Victoria's statue in South Parade, Kingston. Security forces moved in to break up the crowd, and Bustamante challenged them to shoot him instead of the workers he led. He and other labor leaders were arrested. His pugnacity, however, cemented his place in their hearts and minds and many became his ardent supporters.

BIRTH AND DEVELOPMENT

Bustamante, to be sure, was not the founder of Jamaica's first political party. Dr. Robert Love's People's Convention of 1894 and Marcus Garvey's People's Political Party of 1929 were two of Jamaica's earlier political parties. Both parties had only limited success because their leaders preached a message of black nationalism, which was not appealing to the middle class. In addition, both individuals were staunchly opposed by British colonial officials. The Moyne Report, commissioned by the British government regarding the labor riots of the 1930s, however, advocated sweeping political reforms. As a result, the masses, along with trade unions, could openly participate in the political process. This led to several black intellectuals organizing the first "legitimate" political party, the People's National Party (PNP), on September 18, 1938, led by Norman Manley, one of Jamaica's most eminent barristers. The PNP sought a political union of the middle and lower classes. It relied on the charismatic and influential Bustamante to lead a trade union of workers as an auxiliary organization. By the end of June 1938, Bustamante launched his union, the Bustamante Industrial Trade Union (BITU), from a merger of five others. The growth of the BITU was so rapid that within two months its membership more than doubled.

The colonial authorities in Jamaica realized that Bustamante had become a dangerous political agitator because his trade union activities were unorthodox but very effective. They arrested him a second time and incarcerated him for seventeen months. His release on February 8, 1942, is shrouded in controversy, since some scholars argue that the government released him to form a political party in opposition to the PNP, which had become allegedly prosocialist. On July 8, 1943, Bustamante launched the Jamaica Labour Party.

In Jamaica's first general elections held under universal adult suffrage on December 14, 1944, the JLP defeated the PNP by capturing twenty-three of the thirty-two seats to the PNP's four—independent candidates captured the other five. Bustamante then became Jamaica's first chief minister. The JLP was reelected with a national majority in 1949 but was defeated by the PNP in the elections of 1955 and 1959. The JLP defeated the PNP on the referendum to determine Jamaica's future in the West Indies Federation on September 19, 1961, and in the 1962 general elections, which led Jamaica into political independence. Since postindependence the JLP has only formed the government from 1967 to 1972 and from 1980 to 1988.

ORGANIZATIONAL STRUCTURE

The highest decision-making body in the JLP is the annual national conference, which is made up of delegates from all over the country. At this conference the leader/president of the party and deputy leaders are chosen and major changes to the party's constitution, policy, and organizational structure are ratified. The next highest body is the Central Executive, which is chaired by the chairman of the JLP and administers the party's affairs during the year, normally meeting quarterly. Elections for other important posts, such as trustees, secretaries, treasurers, and the party's chairman, are done at the Central Executive level. This body has the power to appoint candidates and caretakers for constituencies and parish council divisions, as well as members of subcommittees. It comprises the chairman of the party and all the secretaries, along with the president, deputy leaders, elected parliamentarians, senators, and leaders of the affiliate organizations, such as the BITU, the G2K (the youth arm of the party), and the JLP's National Women's Organization.

The Standing Committee consists of officers of the party and chairmen of national committees. This committee acts for and reports to the Central Executive and meets as required. The Standing Committee, which is chaired by the JLP's chairman, supervises the work of over fifteen national committees. These include Finance, BITU, Disciplinary Organizational Policy, Legal and Constitutional, Public Relations, Property, Equipment, Campaign, Membership, Electoral, Selection, and International Relations. The Area Council leaders, who are the deputy leaders of

Jamaica Labour Party (JLP) supporters rally in support of candidate Edward Seaga, Kingston, Jamaica, 2002. *Seaga, leader of the JLP from 1974 until his retirement in 2005, served as prime minister of Jamaica from 1980 to 1989. The People's National Party, Jamaica's other primary political organization, has held the majority in the Jamaican parliament since that date.* AP/WIDE WORLD PHOTOS. REPRODUCED BY PERMISSION.

the party, also sit on the Standing Committee. On a micro level, the party is organized into four Area Councils, each of which has its own secretariat and is managed by one of the four deputy leaders of the party. Each Area Council is subdivided into around fifteen constituencies.

FUNDING

The party is funded predominantly by the business community and through fund-raising activities. Each constituency is expected to raise its own funds through membership fees and other means. Each constituency elects a management team consisting of persons in the following areas: finance, campaign, and public relations. These persons raise the necessary funds to carry out the programs of the constituency and by extension the party.

To ensure that the JLP remains solvent on the macro level it operates a trust company (Greenbelt Trust) through its trustees. The treasurers of the JLP also ensure that income from the trust company and from financial contributions are well spent, since proceeds from the business community and from membership fees are not always consistent.

FOREIGN POLICY

The JLP is primarily a conservative party and not fully a labor party in the traditional sense, as is the British Labour Party. The JLP is thus aligned with other conservative political parties around the world, such as the Republican Party in the United States. It also shares with other conservative governments a faith in a market economy and in small or minimal state ownership. Any government entity that is not most essential for the state to manage has to be privatized, since the JLP views the private sector as the main engine for national development.

As an example of the JLP's conservative links, a German conservative party, the National Democratic Union, funds their political think tank, the Jamaica Institute for Political Education. It is responsible for initiating research and utilizing the services of independent scholars to draft papers in relation to political education, public policy, and changes in social, economic, and political thought.

REGIONALISM

The conservative politics of the JLP led to its heading the campaign for Jamaica's withdrawal from the West Indies

Federation in 1961. The party advocated independence and an alliance with Western democracies, since it felt that the Federation's leaders were pro-socialism. Currently, the JLP supports a limited Caribbean integration but remains highly critical of an emerging Caribbean Court, which would replace the British Privy Council. It also opposes any attempt to recreate a federation of the islands.

See also Bustamante, Alexander; Manley, Norman; Moyne Commission; People's National Party; West Indies Federation

▪ ▪ *Bibliography*

Brown, Orville. *The History of the Jamaica Labour Party.* Unpublished document, JLP headquarters, Kingston, Jamaica, 1986.

Bustamante, Gladys. *The Memoirs of Lady Bustamante.* Kingston, Jamaica: Kingston Publishers, 1997.

Eaton, George E. *Alexander Bustamante and Modern Jamaica.* Kingston, Jamaica: Kingston Publishers, 1975.

Hamilton, B. St. J. *Bustamante: Anthology of a Hero.* Kingston: Jamaica: Publication and Productions, Ltd., 1977.

Ramocan, George. Interview by Dave Gosse, August 15, 2004.

Ranston, Jackie. *From We Were Boys: The Story of the Magnificent Cousins, Manley and Bustamante.* Kingston, Jamaica: Bustamante Institute of Public and International Affairs, 1989.

Seaga, Edward. *The Fiftieth Year Anniversary of the Jamaica Labour Party.* Kingston, Jamaica: Jamaica Institute of Political Education, 1983.

Shearer, Hugh. *Alexander Bustamante: Portrait of a Hero.* Unpublished document, JLP headquarters, Kingston, Jamaica, n.d.

DAVE ST. A. GOSSE (2005)

JAMAICA PROGRESSIVE LEAGUE
▪▪▪

The Jamaica Progressive League (JPL) of New York, formed in 1936 by a group of Jamaican men and women residing in New York City, set in motion the movement for self-government on the island of Jamaica, which gained its independence from Britain in 1962. The organization survives into the present and owes its longevity in part to its distinctive political relationship to the homeland and to the Jamaican diaspora. One of the first organizational strategies of the New York–based JPL was to establish a political party in Jamaica (the People's National Party, or PNP) devoted to universal suffrage and self-government. In its early history, the PNP served as the JPL's political voice on the island. The New York JPL also formed a branch in Kingston in 1937 and later in other U.S. cities, the Panama Canal Zone, and other key locations where Jamaicans had settled. The JPL functioned as a vehicle through which the Jamaican diaspora could participate in Jamaica's long-term self-determination as well in as its struggle for independence from Britain. Significantly, the league, as its name implies, relied upon the Jamaican associations, community networks, and fundraising skills already established in New York to promote its political agenda. Added to this core political dimension was the league's capacity to also address social welfare concerns, emergency relief, and other needs of Jamaicans at home and in its migrating communities.

FORMATION

The group of compatriots who met at the headquarters of the Jamaica Benevolent Association on September 1, 1936, to formally organize the Jamaica Progressive League had held several preliminary meetings. They wanted to create a consensus about the league's objective—self-government for Jamaica—and they wanted to identify key individuals to participate in and promote the project. Notably, they met with an organized group of Jamaican women who had just completed several successful fundraising campaigns, with a prominent Jamaican physician, and with an outspoken but moderate Jamaican journalist. The actual leaders of the league were long-time activists committed to socialist politics and well known in the Harlem community. They included Adolphe Roberts, a writer, who became president; W. A. Domingo, an intellectual and importer of Caribbean food products, who became vice president; and Rev. E. Ethelred Brown, a Unitarian pastor of the Harlem Community Church, who became secretary. Other founding members included T. E. Hanson, Dr. Lucien Brown, A. Wendell Malliett, Ivy Essien, James O'Meally, Thomas R. Bowen, (Mrs.) T. D'Aguilar, Agatha Fraser, and Ben and Theophilus Burrell.

The founding members thus comprised a broad coalition of Jamaicans, and this united front reflected the migrant community's response to a series of insurgencies that occurred all over the Caribbean between 1935 and 1938. Anticolonial labor riots erupted in Saint Kitts, Trinidad, British Guiana, Saint Vincent, and Saint Lucia in 1935, and in 1937 and 1938 in Trinidad, Barbados, British Guiana, Saint Lucia, and Jamaica. Demonstrators protested widespread unemployment, poor health and sanitary conditions, low wages, and many other social conditions. The colonial authorities' response was military and punitive, and many workers were killed, wounded, or arrested.

These events created a diaspora-wide response from Harlem to London, helped mobilize pan-Caribbean organizations, and inspired demands for self-government and immediate reform.

In this political climate, the Jamaica Progressive League launched its movement for universal suffrage and self-government. Designing a banner emblematic of the laboring masses and adopting the motto "From the Ground Up," the organization spread its message through mass meetings, pamphleteering, leafleting, and lectures. Among the widely distributed publications were O'Meally's "Why We Demand Self-Government for Jamaica," and the JPL's "Onward Jamaica," published in 1937. E. Ethelred Brown wrote an expose of civil services abuses and in 1938 represented the league before the West Indies Royal Commission, which convened in Jamaica in the wake of the region-wide disturbances. Domingo and Roberts spent six months in Jamaica in 1937 and 1938. Their arrival preceded the widespread labor rebellions that erupted in May 1938 and facilitated the JPL's fundraising in New York for the legal defense of workers arrested during the uprising. They also met with the Jamaican branch of the JPL and acted as advisers to the group that formed the People's National Party, headed by Norman W. Manley. The PNP, with financial backing from the league (E. Ethelred Brown served as its chief fundraiser in New York), began an aggressive campaign for self-government and reform. Amid labor strikes and mass protests, the colonial government made important concessions. The Legislative Council approved league's resolution to reinstate competitive civil service examinations. In 1944, universal adult suffrage, without property qualifications, went into effect, accompanied by a new constitution allowing Jamaicans to elect representatives to a legislative assembly. Jamaica was among the first colonies in the British Empire to win the right to choose its own representatives to a legislative assembly on the basis of universal suffrage.

In New York, the Jamaica Progressive League, guided by the socialist intellectuals Domingo and Brown, worked with other anticolonialists during the 1940s and 1950s. Their activities were deemed "subversive" and were subject to surveillance; many key activists were arrested while traveling in their home countries, were detained in the United States, or were deported. Colonial officials arrested Domingo on his arrival in Jamaica in June of 1941 after FBI agents intercepted letters identifying his work for the PNP. He was detained for twenty months and remained in Jamaica for an additional four years after U.S. officials refused to grant him a visa. The New York JPL rallied to support Domingo's family financially while he took advantage of this period by stepping up his work for the PNP

and writing articles for the local press, particularly *Public Opinion,* the main organ of the Jamaica self-government movement. Domingo returned to the United States in 1947 and continued to work for the JPL.

INDEPENDENCE

In the politically charged period just before and just after Jamaica won its independence, membership in the New York Jamaica Progressive League reached its peak. Even Jamaicans who had been skeptical about the movement for self-government rejoiced in their country's independence and joined in the league's celebratory activities. However, the league soon entered a transitional phase. Brown, who died in 1956, and Domingo, who died in 1968, no longer guided the League's politics. The organization's new leadership, drawn from the ranks of the professional and business classes, turned more and more to the "the needs of Jamaicans where they live now." An important example was the league's increased campaign to remove immigration barriers during the 1960s, which was led by its president, Beryl Henry. Before he died, Domingo also worked on this project. To advance the concerns of an expanding immigrant community, Henry cultivated political ties with powerful local, state, and national elected officials in the United States. The league played an active role in the introduction of the 1965 Hart-Celler Bill, which repealed the national origins quota system. Once race-based immigration restrictions were lifted, new waves of migrants arrived from Jamaica and other parts of the Caribbean and developing world. This new generation of Jamaican migrants both insured the League's survival and complicated its identity as a political organization.

By the 1960s and 1970s, Jamaicans were more difficult to unite around a single political agenda. Furthermore, the JPL's diverse membership, which now included a new generation of migrants who arrived after 1965, did not all agree with the league's position on the PNP. Although the JPL maintained its official affiliation, its leaders distanced the organization from any single political party.

Perhaps because of its adaptive strategies, the JPL remained a vital organization in the early 1970s. In 1973 the league purchased a twelve-story building in Manhattan, at a cost of $2 million, to serve as its new headquarters, Jamaica House. According to a history of the league, the Workers Bank of Jamaica extended the loan. The building housed numerous JPL services, including its adult education program, which provided opportunities for migrants to acquire high school equivalency certificates, as well as immigration advising services, student advising services, and a free legal clinic. The league sold Jamaica House in

1979 to pay its debts and to free the organization from cumbersome real estate management responsibilities.

Since the 1980s, the New York JPL has struggled to sustain a political and social relationship with recent migrant generations and the organization has experienced decline. The league reached its zenith when its leadership appealed to multiple constituencies and effectively combined its political goals with the immediate social needs of Jamaicans. Still, the Jamaica Progressive League's history provides an unusual opportunity to examine diaspora politics within one organization that links colonial and postcolonial communities among several generations of Jamaican migrants.

See also Anti-Colonial Movements; Manley, Norman; People's National Party

■ ■ *Bibliography*

Bolles, A. Lynn. *We Paid Our Dues: Women Trade Union Leaders of the Commonwealth Caribbean.* Washington, D.C.: Howard University Press, 1996.

Brown, E. Ethelred. "My Recent Visit to Jamaica." *Ambassador* 2, no. 2 (1952–1953): 39

Brown, E. Ethelred. "The Jamaica Progressive League of New York." *Ambassador* 2, no. 2 (1952–1953): 21

Brown, E. Ethelred. Papers. Box 4, folder 7, flyers. Schomburg Center for Research in Black Culture.

Domingo, W. A. "The Jamaica Progressive League. Jamaica's Outpost of Goodwill and Friendship in the United States." *Souvenir Journal.* In E. Ethelred Brown Papers, box 4, folder 7. Schomburg Center for Research in Black Culture.

Henry, Beryl. "Notes and Jottings on the League's Struggle with Immigration." *Souvenir Journal.* In E. Ethelred Brown Papers, box 4, folder 7. Schomburg Center for Research in Black Culture.

Henry, Keith. "Caribbean Political Dilemmas in North America and in the United Kingdom." *Journal of Black Studies* 7, no. 4 (June 1977): 373–786.

Henry, Keith. "The Political Tradition in New York: A Conjunction of Political Cultures." *Journal of Black Studies* 7, no. 4 (June 1977): 455–484.

Hill, Robert, ed. *Marcus Garvey and Universal Negro Improvement Association Papers,* vol. 1. Berkeley: University of California Press, 1983.

Kasinitz, Philip. *Caribbean New York. Black Immigrants and the Politics of Race.* Ithaca, N.Y.: Cornell University Press, 1992.

Moore, W. Burghardt, and Joyce Moore Turner. *Richard B. Moore, Caribbean Militant in Harlem: Collected Writings 1920–1974.* Bloomington: Indiana University Press, 1988.

Morrison-Reed, Mark D. *Black Pioneers in a White Denomination.* Boston: Skinner House, 1980

Reid, Ira De A. "The Negro in the British West Indies." *Journal of Negro Education* 10, no. 3 (July 1941): 524–535.

Watkins-Owens, Irma. *Blood Relations: Caribbean Immigrants and the Harlem Community, 1900–1930.* Bloomington: Indiana University Press, 1996.

Young, John S. *Lest We Forget: The Jamaica Progressive League.* New York: Isidor Books, 1981.

Zeidenflet, Alex. "Political and Constitutional Developments in Jamaica." *Journal of Politics* 14, no. 3 (August 1952): 512–540.

IRMA WATKINS-OWENS (2005)

JAMES, A. P. T.

1901
JANUARY 5, 1962

■ ■ ■

Alphonso Philbert Theophilus James was born in Patience Hill, Tobago. He later migrated to Trinidad, where he worked as a laborer with the Brighton Lake Asphalt Company and rose in the ranks to become a foreman, before eventually becoming an independent contractor. He was involved with the Uriah Butler labor movement in the 1930s and was an advocate for labor issues, though he is best known for being the most ardent advocate for political, social, and economic development in Tobago. James was a member of the Trinidad Labour Party, and he won the Tobago seat in the Legislative Council of Trinidad and Tobago in 1946. His tenure in office lasted until 1961.

James believed that Tobago, though disadvantaged by years of neglect, was an equal partner in the former united colony of Trinidad and Tobago, not a subordinate, dependent adjunct. He demanded that Tobago have separate representation and a separate voice on all issues and in all forums, even in the parliament of the British West Indies Federation. He contended that if Tobago's infrastructure, sea communication, and social services were improved, and if its agricultural, fishing, and tourism resources developed, the island would achieve economic viability and thus free itself from dependence on the Trinidad treasury. Probably the most significant of James's convictions was that Tobago should once again be granted administrative autonomy and become a separate entity, independent of Trinidad. At the end of his career he advocated secession from Trinidad.

His advocacy for Tobago resulted in several victories, including the purchase of two new steamships for the inter-island route in 1960, the construction of the North Coast Road, the appropriation of more money for the improvement of medical service and equipment at the Tobago hospital, and the construction of at least two elementary schools in Tobago. James strongly believed that Tobago could regain economic viability, mainly through the development of its agricultural and fishing industries and by encouraging tourism. Thus, in 1948, he visited the secretary of state for the colonies and presented a memorandum for the economic and political development of Tobago from the Tobago Citizens Political and Economic Party (TCPEP), which recommended, inter alia, that the Colonial Development Corporation provide fifteen million dollars towards the development of Tobago. James also lobbied for the extension of water distribution and the provision of electricity to Tobago. In 1952, Scarborough, Tobago's capital, was finally electrified.

By 1947 the uneven development in Tobago led James to threaten to work toward the separation of the island from Trinidad. In 1948 James also championed the cause for full responsible government—that all members of the Legislative Council should be elected, and that Tobago should have two seats in the council and representation on the Executive Council and the Estimates Committee, which created the colony's annual budget. James believed that because Tobago was separated from Trinidad by the ocean, Tobagonians knew best what the island needed. Thus, their increased representation in the corridors of power was essential for the progress of the island. Further, James and the TCPEP demanded that a special ministry to handle Tobago affairs be created, and the Ministry of Tobago Affairs was duly established in 1964.

In 1956 the People's National Movement (PNM), led by Eric Williams (1911–1981), came to power. James was optimistic about Williams' "Tobago Development Programme," with its 9.2 million dollars promised for economic development in Tobago. Williams also proposed a Ministry of Tobago Affairs, with a minister who would be a member of the Executive Council. James soon became impatient with the pace of progress in the development program, however, and that and other matters led to strained relations with the PNM. By 1960 James had formed a group called the Tobago Independence Movement (TIM) to explore the possibility of Tobago gaining internal self-government status within the West Indies Federation. The group proposed a referendum on separation from Trinidad. The proposal was condemned by the PNM government, which James charged with having a colonial mentality toward Tobago.

In 1961 James lost his seat in the general elections. One month later, on January 5, 1962, he died of a cerebral hemorrhage and hypertension. To James's credit, Tobago was a better place because of his unrelenting advocacy on its behalf. The political pressure he put on the central government forced Trinidadian officials to abandon the view that Tobago should only be considered a rural backwater with little economic potential, not worthy of much administrative attention and devoid of political consciousness.

See also Peoples National Movement; West Indies Federation; Williams, Eric

■ ■ *Bibliography*

Luke, Learie B. "Identity and Autonomy in Tobago: From Union to Self- Government, 1889–1980." Ph.D. diss., Howard University, Washington, D.C., 2001.

Phillips, Andre. *Governor Fargo: A Short Biography of Alphonso Philbert Theophilus James.* Scarborough, Tobago: Tobago Printery.

"Resolution Passed at the General Meeting of the Tobago Citizens Political and Economic Party." CO 295/654/70778/1/1: Public Records Office, Kew, England.

LEARIE B. LUKE (2005)

JAMES, C. L. R.

JANUARY 4, 1901
MAY 31, 1989

The political activist Cyril Lionel Richard James was born in Tunapuna, Trinidad. He attended Queen's Royal College in Trinidad, where he later taught English and history. He started to write fiction while he was teaching. In 1929 his controversial story about women in a slum, "Triumph," appeared in the short-lived magazine *Trinidad,* which James co-edited. In the early 1930s James moved to England, where he supported himself by writing articles on cricket, a sport in which he was skilled. In England he became politically active as an anti-Stalinist Marxist, and joined the Trotskyite faction of the International Labour Party. His first political book, *The Life of Captain Cipriani* (1932), treated questions of colonialism. In it, James called for West Indian independence.

In the mid-1930s James turned his attention to Pan-Africanism, joining forces with the theorist and orator George Padmore (c. 1902–1959). After the Italian invasion of Ethiopia in 1935, James became editor of *International African Opinion* and chaired the International Friends of Abyssinia. His Pan-African thought was further developed in his historical work *The Black Jacobins* (1938), in which he analyzed the 1791 Haitian slave revolt led by Toussaint-Louverture (1743–1803) as a model of revolutionary struggle.

James, an internationally known figure, came to the United States on a Trotskyist lecture tour in 1938. He decided to stay and work in America's small anti-Stalinist Marxist circle. While he admired Trotsky, James associated himself with the independent Socialist Worker's Party

(SWP). In 1940, however, he broke with the SWP to join the new Worker's Party. Using the party pseudonym "J. P. Johnson," James formed the Johnson-Forest Tendency with Raya Dunayevskaya. Within the group, he organized sharecroppers and workers and wrote theoretical articles.

During the 1940s James formed his mature ideas. Some he circulated in mimeographed form and in the *New Internationalist* (and published later as *Notes on Dialectics*). Others appear in State Capitalism and World Revolution (1950). James attacked the theory that state property equaled socialism. Refuting the principle of a vanguard party, he warned that bureaucracy, even if communist in name, was an obstacle to change in social relations of production. He argued that people of color were the lever for successful social change, because of their numerical superiority and the communitarian nature of African institutions. James, who considered socialism a vehicle for Pan-Africanism, felt American blacks would serve to unite workers in the West and the Third World.

In 1950 the Johnsonites left the Worker's Party and returned to the Socialist Worker's Party. In 1952 James was labeled an undesirable alien by the U.S. State Department and interned on Ellis Island. In 1953, the same year he published his study of Herman Melville, *Mariners, Renegades, and Castaways*, James was expelled from the United States. He returned to Trinidad to become secretary of the Federation Labour party and to work for West Indian independence. His later books include *Modern Politics* (1960) and *Party Politics in the West Indies* (1962). James left Trinidad in 1962 after falling out with the West Indies Federation. He spent his last years in England, where he lectured and wrote historical articles and essays on Caribbean politics and culture.

James died in 1989. In 1984, the C.L.R. James Institute was founded in New York City with his authorization. The institute was still active in the early 2000s, providing information about James and acting as a community library for gatherings and research.

See also Anti-Colonial Movements; Pan-Africanism; Toussaint-Louverture

■ ■ *Bibliography*

Buhle, Paul. *C. L. R. James: The Artist as Revolutionary.* New York: Verso, 1988.

Dhondy, Farrukh. *C. L. R. James: A Life.* London: Orion, 1996.

Farred, Grant. *Rethinking C. L. R. James.* Cambridge, Mass: Blackwell, 1996.

Grimshaw, Anna, ed. *The C. L. R. James Reader.* Cambridge, Mass: Blackwell, 1992.

Nielsen, Aldon Lynn. *C. L. R. James: A Critical Introduction.* Jackson: University Press of Mississippi, 1997.

Worcester, Kent. *C. L. R. James and the American Century, 1938–1953.* San Juan, P.R., 1980.

Worcester, Kent. *C. L. R. James: A Political Biography.* Albany: State University of New York Press, 1995.

NANCY GAGNIER (1996)
Updated by publisher 2005

JAMES, DANIEL "CHAPPIE"

FEBRUARY 11, 1920
FEBRUARY 25, 1978

The first black four-star general, Daniel "Chappie" James Jr. joined Tuskegee's pioneer black Army Air Corps unit in 1937. He served in World War II and led a fighter group in Korea, inventing air tactics to support ground forces and receiving the Distinguished Service Medal. In Vietnam he was vice commander of the Eighth Tactical Fighter Wing, earning the Legion of Merit award. National attention accompanied his speeches supporting the war and black soldiers' reasons to fight.

Afterward he commanded Wheelus Air Force Base in Libya, then became Defense Department public affairs officer and a popular speaker. He received his fourth star with command of the crucial North American Air Defense, monitoring possible air and missile attacks.

Skills and overwhelming personality smoothed James's unprecedented ascent. Generally opposed to mass movements to improve blacks' situation, he cited his mother's dictum that personal excellence could overcome all barriers. He applauded peaceful demonstrations, however; indeed, the violence at Selma, Alabama, made him consider resigning. He brushed off personal experiences with racism, although he seldom wore civilian clothes so his uniform might shield him. Blacks sometimes criticized him, but many Americans liked his support of the Vietnam War and his view of race relations that emphasized individualism.

See also Military Experience, African-American; Tuskegee University

■ ■ *Bibliography*

Bracey, Earnest M. *Daniel "Chappy" James: The First African American Four Star General.* Jefferson, N.C.: McFarland, 2003.

McGovern, James R. *Black Eagle: General Daniel "Chappie" James, Jr.* University: University of Alabama Press, 1985.

Phelps, J. Alfred. *Chappie: America's First Black Four-Star General: The Life and Times of Daniel James, Jr.* Novato, Calif.: Presidio, 1991.

ELIZABETH FORTSON ARROYO (1996)
Updated bibliography

JAMES, ETTA

JANUARY 5, 1938

■ ■ ■

Rhythm and blues singer Etta James, born Jamesetta Hawkins in Los Angeles, sang during her childhood in the choir of Saint Paul's Baptist Church. She began to sing professionally at the age of fourteen, when she worked with a rhythm and blues ensemble led by Johnny Otis. Her first recording, "Roll with Me Henry" (1954), was originally banned by radio stations because of its salacious content. However, the record became a hit, and it was rereleased in 1955 under the title "Wallflower."

In the mid- to late 1950s, James was one of the most popular singers in rhythm and blues, trailing only Dinah Washington and Ruth Brown in the number of hit rhythm and blues records she had. Nominally a blues shouter, her gospel-influenced voice was also by turns sweet, pouting, or gruff. Among her hit records, many of which were recorded for Chicago's Chess Records, were "Good Rockin' Daddy" (1955), "W-O-M-A-N" (1955), "How Big a Fool" (1958), "All I Could Do Was Cry" (1960), "Stop the Wedding" (1962), "Pushover" (1963), and "Something's Got a Hold on Me" (1964). James toured with Little Richard, James Brown, Little Willie John, and Johnny "Guitar" Watson.

Heroin addiction forced James to quit recording in the mid- to late 1960s. She eventually entered a rehabilitation program that enabled her to return to the music industry in 1973 with the album *Etta James,* which won a Grammy Award. James then recorded numerous albums, including *Come a Little Closer* (1974), *Etta Is Betta Than Evvah* (1976), *Deep in the Night* (1978), *Blues in the Night with Eddie "Cleanhead" Vinson* (1986), *Seven Year Itch* (1988), and *Stickin' to My Guns* (1990). Nonetheless, her pioneering role as a rhythm and blues singer was often overlooked until the 1990s. In 1990 she won an NAACP Image Award, and in 1993 she was inducted into the Rock and Roll Hall of Fame.

In 1998 James published her memoirs, *Rage to Survive: The Etta James Story.* James had suffered from a lifelong weight problem and in recent years was forced to perform in a wheelchair because of her weight. In 2003 she had gastric bypass surgery and lost two hundred pounds, bringing new energy and enthusiasm to her performances. In 2003 she received a star on Hollywood's Walk of Fame.

See also Rhythm and Blues

■ ■ *Bibliography*

Hess, Norbert. "Living Blues Interview: Etta James." *Living Blues* 54 (1982): 12.

James, Etta, and David Ritz. *Rage to Survive: The Etta James Story.* New York: Da Capo, 1998.

ROBERT W. STEPHENS (1996)
Updated by publisher 2005

JAMISON, JUDITH

MAY 10, 1943

■ ■ ■

Born the younger of two children in Philadelphia, Pennsylvania, dancer Judith Jamison studied piano and violin as a child. Tall by the age of six, Jamison was enrolled in dance classes by her parents in an effort to complement her exceptional height with grace. She received most of her early dance training in classical ballet with master teachers Marion Cuyjet, Delores Brown, and John Jones at the Judimar School of Dance. Jamison decided on a career in dance only after three semesters of coursework in psychology at Fisk University, and she completed her education at the Philadelphia Dance Academy. In 1964 she was spotted by choreographer Agnes de Mille and invited to appear in de Mille's *The Four Marys* at the New York–based American Ballet Theatre. Jamison moved to New York in 1965 and that same year joined the Alvin Ailey American Dance Theater (AAADT).

Jamison performed with AAADT on tours of Europe and Africa in 1966. When financial pressures forced Ailey briefly to disband his company later that year, Jamison joined the Harkness Ballet for several months and then returned to the re-formed AAADT in 1967. She quickly became a principal dancer with that company, dancing a variety of roles that showcased her pliant technique, stunning beauty, and exceptional stature of five feet, ten inches. Jamison excelled as the goddess Erzulie in Geoffrey Holder's *The Prodigal Prince* (1967), as the Mother in a revised version of Ailey's *Knoxville: Summer of 1915* (1968), and as the Sun in the 1968 AAADT revival of Lucas Hoving's *Icarus.* These larger-than-life roles fit neatly with Jamison's regal bearing and highly responsive emotional center, and critics praised her finely drawn dance interpretations that were imbued with power and grace. Jamison and Ailey's collaboration deepened, and she created a brilliant solo in his *Masekela Language* (1969). Set to music of South African trumpeter Hugh Masekela, Jamison portrayed a frustrated and solitary woman dancing in a seedy saloon. Her electrifying performances of Ailey's fifteen-minute solo *Cry* (1971) propelled her to an international stardom unprecedented among modern dance artists. Dedicated by Ailey "to all black women everywhere—especially our mothers," the three sections of *Cry* successfully captured a broad range of movements, emotions, and images associated with black womanhood as mother, sister, lover, goddess, supplicant, confessor, and dancer.

In 1976 Jamison danced with ballet star Mikhail Baryshnikov in Ailey's *Pas de Duke* set to music by Duke Ellington. This duet emphasized the classical line behind Jamison's compelling modern dance technique and garnered her scores of new fans. Jamison's celebrity advanced, and she appeared as a guest artist with the San Francisco Ballet, the Swedish Royal Ballet, the Cullberg Ballet, and the Vienna State Ballet. In 1977 she created the role of Potiphar's wife in John Neumeier's *Josephslegende* for the Vienna State Opera, and in 1978 she appeared in Maurice Béjart's updated version of *Le Spectre de la Rose* with the Ballet of the Twentieth Century. Several choreographers sought to work with Jamison as a solo artist, and important collaborations included John Parks's *Nubian Lady* (1972), John Butler's *Facets* (1976), and Ulysses Dove's *Inside* (1980).

In 1980 Jamison left the Ailey company to star in the Broadway musical *Sophisticated Ladies,* set to the music of Duke Ellington. She later turned her formidable talent to choreography, where her work has been marked by a detached sensuality and intensive responses to rhythm. Jamison founded her own dance company, the Jamison Project, to explore the opportunities of getting a group of dancers together, for both my choreography [and] to commission works from others. Alvin Ailey's failing health caused Jamison to rejoin the AAADT as artistic associate for the 1988–1989 season. In December 1989 Ailey died, and Jamison was named artistic director of the company. She has continued to choreograph, and her ballets include *Divining* (1984), *Forgotten Time* (1989), *Hymn* (1993), *Double Exposure* (2000), and *Here . . . and Now* (2002), all performed by the AAADT.

Jamison has received numerous awards and honors, including a Presidential Appointment to the National Council of the Arts, the 1972 *Dance Magazine* Award, and the Candace Award from the National Coalition of One Hundred Black Women. Her great skill as an administrator has led the AAADT to the forefront of American dance, operating consistently without a large deficit, and in residence at the largest single facility devoted to dance in the country. Her greatest achievement as a dancer was an inspiring ability to seem supremely human and emotive within an elastic and powerful dance technique.

See also Ailey, Alvin; Ballet; Dove, Ulysses; Ellington, Duke

■ ■ *Bibliography*

"Jamison, Judith." *Current Biography Yearbook.* New York: H.W. Wilson, 1973, pp. 202–205.

Jamison, Judith, with Howard Kaplan. *Dancing Spirit: An Autobiography.* New York: Doubleday, 1993.

Jowitt, Deborah. "'Call Me a Dancer': (Judith Jamison)." *New York Times,* December 5, 1976, sec. 6, pp. 40–41, 136–148.

Maynard, Olga. *Judith Jamison: Aspects of a Dancer.* New York: Doubleday, 1982.

THOMAS F. DEFRANTZ (1996)
Updated by author 2005

JAZZ

This entry consists of three distinct but interrelated articles.

OVERVIEW
Leonard Goines

JAZZ IN AFRICAN-AMERICAN CULTURE
John Gennari

JAZZ SINGERS
Linda Dahl

OVERVIEW

Despite complex origins, the status of jazz as a distinctively African-American music is beyond question. Nonetheless, in its development from folk and popular sources in turn-of-the-twentieth-century America, jazz has transcended boundaries of ethnicity and genre. Played in every country of the globe, it is perhaps twentieth-century America's most influential cultural creation, and its worldwide impact, on both popular and art music, has been enormous. Jazz has proved to be immensely protean and has existed in a number of diverse though related styles, from New Orleans– and Chicago-style Dixieland jazz, big band or swing, bebop, funky cool jazz, hard bop, modal jazz, free jazz, and jazz rock. One reason for the variety in jazz is that it is basically a way of performing music rather than a particular repertory. It originated in blends of the folk music, popular music, and light classical music being created just prior to 1900, and now embraces a variety of popular musical styles from Latin America, the Caribbean, Asia, and Africa, as well as diverse modern, classical, and avantgarde performance traditions.

Jazz also has an inescapable political thrust. It originated during a time of enormous oppression and violence in the South against African Americans. The early African-American practitioners of jazz found racial discrimination in virtually every aspect of their lives, from segregated dance halls, cafés, and saloons to exploitative record companies. Like blackface minstrelsy, early jazz was popular with whites, in part because it reinforced "darkie" stereotypes of African Americans as happy-go-lucky and irrepressibly rhythmic. Nonetheless, many black jazz musicians used jazz as a vehicle for cultural, artistic, and economic advancement, and were able to shape their own destinies in an often hostile environment. African-American jazz was, from its earliest days, often performed for or by whites, and it was assimilated into the overall fabric of popular music, to the uneasiness of some on both sides of the racial divide. It has continued to mirror and exemplify the complexities and ironies of the changing status of African Americans within the broader culture and polity of the United States.

EARLY JAZZ

Although its origins are obscure, early forms of jazz began to flourish around the turn of the century in cities such as New Orleans, Chicago, and Memphis. The long prehistory of jazz begins with the rhythmic music slaves brought to America in the sixteenth and seventeenth centuries and developed on southern plantations. Since the traditional drums, flutes, and horns of West Africa were largely forbidden, call-and-response singing and chanting, field hollers, foot stomping, and handclapping were common, especially in the context of fieldwork and church worship. Under those restrictions, among the earliest African-American instruments adopted were European string instruments such as the violin and guitar. The African-derived banjo was also a popular instrument. Eventually the publicly performed music that Reconstruction-era city-dwellers made an essential part of urban life demanded brass and woodwind instruments, not only for their volume but also to accompany the Spanish American War–era military marches, popular songs, and light classics that were so popular among all classes and races in the late nineteenth century.

While it is difficult to draw a precise line between jazz and its precursors, its immediate predecessors were two forms of African-American folk and popular music known as blues and ragtime. Ragtime is primarily piano music that integrates complex African-derived rhythmic practices with the harmonies of light classics, parlor music, show tunes, and popular songs. The virtuosic practice of "ragging"—altering rhythms to, in effect, "tease" variety and humor out of formal, strict patterns—was widespread by the 1880s, especially in towns along the Mississippi River like St. Louis and (eventually) New Orleans. Ragtime was also being played before the turn of the century in eastern cities such as New York and Baltimore. The greatest ragtime players, Scott Joplin, Eubie Blake, Tony Jackson, and Jelly Roll Morton, also composed, and sheet music became a central feature of home entertainments among families, black and white, who could afford pianos. Ragtime was also played by instrumental ensembles; the syncopated orchestras led in New York City by James Reese Europe and Will Marion Cook during the first two decades of the century owed much to the precise, contrapuntal style of piano rags. The ragtime-derived piano style proved influential on later jazz styles, especially since many of the best bandleaders of the swing era, including Duke Ellington, Earl "Fatha" Hines, and Count Basie, were heavily influenced by Harlem stride pianists such as James P. Johnson, Fats Waller, Willie "The Lion" Smith, and Luckey Roberts. Also deeply indebted to stride were later pianists such as Teddy Wilson, Art Tatum, and Thelonious Monk.

The blues similarly began along the Mississippi River in the 1880s and 1890s. Among the first published blues, "Memphis Blues" (1912), by W. C. Handy, was broadly derived from black rural folk music. The sexual frankness and suggestiveness, its recognition of suffering and hardship of all kinds, and the slow, insinuating melodies soon had an impact on popular music. The 1920s saw the rise of such blues singers as Ma Rainey, Bessie Smith, and Mamie Smith, but long before that the blues had a palpable influence on the music of early New Orleans jazz.

It was New Orleans that gave its name to the earliest and most enduring form of jazz and bred its first masters. That Buddy Bolden, Bunk Johnson, Kid Ory, Jelly Roll Morton, King Oliver, Sidney Bechet, and Freddy Keppard all came from New Orleans attests to the extraordinary fertility of musical life in what was then the largest southern city. In New Orleans, blacks, whites, and the culturally distinct light-skinned African Americans known as Creoles supported various kinds of musical ensembles by the mid-nineteenth century. Other influences included traveling cabaret and minstrel shows, funeral, carnival, and parade bands. A more or less direct African influence on New Orleans was also pervasive, no more so than in Congo Square, a onetime site of slave auctions that later became an important meeting place and open-air music hall for New Orleans blacks.

The various layers of French, Spanish, Haitian, Creole, Indian, and African-American culture in New Orleans created a mixed social environment, and not only in Storyville, the legendary red-light district whose role in the birth of jazz has probably been overemphasized. Nonetheless, it was in Storyville that legalized prostitution encouraged a proliferation of brothels, gambling houses, and saloons where many of the early New Orleans jazz musicians first performed. Though many of the early New Orleans jazz bands and performers, including Sidney Bechet and Jelly Roll Morton, were Creoles, very soon non-Creoles such as King Oliver and Louis Armstrong were integrated into Creole ensembles.

By the end of the first decade of the twentieth century, these diverse musical styles had evolved into the style of music that was almost exclusively associated with New Orleans. Although there are no recordings of jazz from this period, what the music sounded like can be inferred from photographs of the period, later reminiscences, and later recordings. A typical early New Orleans jazz ensemble might include one or more cornets, trombone, clarinet, and a rhythm section of string or brass bass, piano, and guitar or banjo. The cornets, which were eventually replaced by the trumpets, took the melodic lead, while an elaborate countermelody was contributed by the clarinet, and the trombone provided a melodic bass line. The rhythm section filled in the harmonies and provided the beat. The typical repertory of these ensembles consisted largely of blues-based songs.

The two main types of improvisation in early jazz were solo and collective improvisation. Solo improvisation takes place when one musician at a time performs solo. In collective improvisation, which was the key feature of the New Orleans early jazz sound and later Chicago-related Dixieland style, more than one musician improvises simultaneously. This style can be heard in the early recordings of Kid Ory, King Oliver, and Jelly Roll Morton, as well as music made by whites such as the Original Dixieland Jazz Band, the New Orleans Rhythm Kings, the Wolverines, and Chicago's Austin High School Gang.

Jazz no doubt existed in some recognizable form from about 1905—the heyday of the legendary and never-recorded New Orleans cornetist Buddy Bolden—but the first recording by a group calling itself a "jazz" band was made in 1917, in New York, by the white, New Orleans–based ensemble the Original Dixieland Jazz Band. Though

as early as 1913 James Reese Europe had recorded with his black syncopated orchestra, and by the early 1920s Johnny Dunn and Kid Ory had recorded, it was not until 1923 that the first representative and widely influential New Orleans–style jazz recordings by African Americans were made in the Midwest, by King Oliver and Jelly Roll Morton.

The movement of the best New Orleans musicians to Chicago is often linked to the closing of Storyville in 1917. Much more important was the Great Migration of southern blacks to northern cities during the World War I years. In Chicago, jazz found a receptive audience, and jazz musicians were able to develop profitable solo careers while enjoying a more hospitable racial climate than in the South.

Big Band Jazz

Jazz underwent significant changes on being transplanted to the North. By the early 1920s, when the New York–based band of Fletcher Henderson made its first recordings, jazz was being presented in a manner akin to the refined dance band orchestras of the time, with larger ensembles of ten pieces or more, working within carefully written arrangements. Whereas the early jazz repertory consisted largely of original blues, in the 1920s jazz musicians began performing waltzes and popular songs. The style of playing changed as well. In place of the thrilling but often unwieldy polyphony of New Orleans jazz came the antiphonal big-band style, in which whole sections traded off unison or close-harmony riffs, often in a call-and-response format with a single soloist. In contrast to the instrumentation of the typical New Orleans early jazz ensemble of three horns and a rhythm section, big bands generally had a brass section consisting of three trumpets and one trombone, and three or four reeds (a variety of saxophones and clarinets). In the 1930s the size of big bands often grew to fifteen or more musicians. Providing the pulse for the swing big bands was a rhythm section, usually containing a piano, string bass and drums, and often an acoustic guitar.

If the big bands regimented and reined in the sounds of New Orleans jazz, it also permitted the emergence of the soloist, particularly on the saxophone and trumpet, probably the most important development of the era. Though featured soloists were not unknown in the New Orleans jazz style, big band jazz arrangements often used themes as mere preludes to extended solo improvisations, with both the rhythm section and the orchestra as a whole often serving as accompanists to whoever was soloing. No figure exemplified this change better than Louis Armstrong. Although bred in New Orleans, his stay in Chicago taught him much about the theatrical possibilities of a

Duke Ellington and Louis Armstrong, 1946. AP/WIDE WORLD PHOTOS INC. REPRODUCED BY PERMISSION

well-constructed solo. During 1924 and 1925 he performed with the Henderson band in New York, where his majesty tone and unfailingly fresh phrasing almost single-handedly turned that ensemble from a straitlaced dance band toward a New Orleans–influenced style that would eventually become known as swing. Armstrong's recordings with his own ensembles in the 1920s feature not only his brilliant trumpet but also his voice. By singing the same way that he played the trumpet, Armstrong became the model for superb jazz phrasing and popularized scat singing—using nonsense syllables instead of words. In the 1930s his recordings of such emerging standards as "Body and Soul" and "Stardust" proved that jazz could redefine pop tunes.

In 1929 Armstrong fronted a big band in New York, a move that signaled the decline of both Chicago and Chicago-style jazz in favor of Harlem as the new capital and swing big bands as the dominant sound. By the mid-1930s Harlem was the undisputed center of the jazz world, and the swing era coincided with the rise of Harlem as the focal point for African-American culture. The largest black community in the world made its home along 125th Street in Manhattan, attending elegant and inexpensive dance palaces and buying recordings also made in New York. However, it would be a mistake to focus exclusively on New York or Chicago. Many of the greatest swing big bands, known as territory bands, came from elsewhere. The Southwest, in particular Kansas City, an important railroad switching station as well as host to an extensive collection of mob-owned after-hours nightclubs, was the most important center for territory bands. In the early 1920s Bennie Moten's group had already inaugurated a Kansas City style, in its mature phase marked by looser, four-to-the-bar rhythms and freer styles of soloing. The pianist in the band, a student of Harlem stride named Count Basie, brought the core of that band to New York in 1936, and brought to prominence a whole new generation of hard-swinging soloists such as Lester Young, Herschel Evans, and Buck Clayton, as well as vocalist Jimmy Rushing.

The big band era was the only time jazz was truly America's popular music. Starting in the late 1920s, the dance bands of Ellington, Henderson, Basie, Jimmie Lunceford, Andy Kirk, Teddy Hill, Earl "Fatha" Hines, as well as those of Chick Webb, Cab Calloway, and Lionel Hampton, competed with white bands led by Benny Goodman, Paul Whiteman, Tommy Dorsey, and Artie Shaw. The prominence of the soloist during the swing era marks the emergence of celebrity jazz musicians like Louis Armstrong, who became "stars" almost on a par with the most popular white entertainers of the day, such as Bing Crosby, in both white and black communities, in Europe as well as in America. The big band era also marks the emergence of tenor saxophonist stars such as Coleman Hawkins and Ben Webster, as well as vocalists such as Billie Holiday and Ella Fitzgerald.

Jazz in the swing era gave numerous African-American performers a largely unprecedented degree of acceptance, fame, and financial success. Still, these achievements occurred within a society that was uncomfortable at best with both public and private racial interaction in any but the most controlled settings. Although some dance halls and nightclubs were integrated, many others, including the most famous ones, such as the Cotton Club, were not. Musicians often appeared there in less than flattering contexts, and audiences clamored for Duke Ellington's "exotic" side, known as jungle music, and for the comic, minstrel side of performers such as Louis Armstrong and Fats Waller. Through the end of the 1930s almost all jazz bands were segregated, with white bands such as those led by the Dorsey brothers, Paul Whiteman, Benny Goodman, Glenn Miller, Woody Herman, and Artie Shaw making considerably more money than their African-American counterparts.

Goodman's ensemble was the first integrated jazz band. He hired Fletcher Henderson as an arranger and in 1936 hired Teddy Wilson as pianist and Lionel Hampton on vibes for his quartet. Goodman, the most popular bandleader of the late 1930s, played in a style quite similar to the best of the black bands, and was unfairly crowned the "King of Swing" by critics. This raised the ire of many black musicians. Although Armstrong, Ellington, Basie, and Waller became genuine celebrities, the white musicians who played in a "black" style often captured a market unavailable to blacks. This would be a persistent grievance among black jazz musicians.

BEBOP

In the early 1940s one of the last major bands from the Southwest to reach prominence in New York was led by Jay McShann, whose band contained the seeds of the next development in jazz (primarily through the innovations of its own saxophonist, Charlie Parker). Although the emergence of the frenetic and rarified style of jazz that became known as "bebop"—so named because of the final, two-note phrase that often ended bebop solos—is frequently seen as a revolt against big band swing, all of the early bebop giants drew upon their experiences playing with swing musicians, often in big bands. Earl Hines, Billy Eckstine, Coleman Hawkins, and Cootie Williams nurtured many beboppers, and one of the first great bebop groups was a big band led by Dizzy Gillespie in 1945 and 1946. After Parker left Jay McShann, he worked with Gillespie in bands led by Hines and Eckstine. Thelonious Monk worked with Cootie Williams, as did Bud Powell.

The very first stirrings of bebop had come in the late 1930s, when drummer Kenny Clarke, who had worked in big bands led by Teddy Hill and Roy Eldridge, began keeping time on the high-hat cymbal rather than on the bass drum, which was reserved for rhythmic accents, a style adopted by young drummers such as Max Roach and Art Blakey. Just as timekeepers were experimenting with the rhythmical palate of the drum kit, so too were soloists extending the limits of the harmonies of standard popular songs and blues, and aspiring to a new and recondite tonal vocabulary. Inspired by the virtuosic playing and harmonic sophistication of pianist Art Tatum and tenor saxophonist Lester Young, in the early 1940s Gillespie and Parker were creating a music for musicians, noted for its complexity, with a whole new, difficult repertory. Trumpeter Fats Navarro, bassist Charles Mingus, and pianists Thelonious Monk and Bud Powell were also prime architects of bebop, as were such white musicians as pianists Lennie Tristano and Al Haig, and alto saxophonist Lee Konitz.

Disgruntled swing musicians complained that bebop was an elitist style that robbed jazz of its place as America's popular music. Certainly, the refusal of bebop musicians to adhere to a four-to-the-bar bass drum rhythm meant that the music was no longer suitable for dancing. As bebop lost its function as dance music, tempos quickened even more, and solos became more rhythmically adventurous. Bebop's quirky, sophisticated compositions and fleet, witty improvisations demanded the serious and more or less undivided attention that concert music requires. Bebop came of age and reached its height of popularity not in "high-toned" Harlem dance halls but in the nightclubs and after-hours clubs of Harlem and 52nd

Street, and often the audience consisted of a small coterie of white and black jazz fans and sympathetic jazz musicians. In retrospect, however, it was not bebop that dealt the deathblow to jazz as a popular music. The big bands were struggling to survive long before the bebop era began, and by the 1950s, not even Count Basie and Duke Ellington's bands could keep up with the dance rhythms of rhythm and blues and early rock and roll.

Just as New Orleans–style jazz established the basic language for what is generally considered "classic jazz," so too did the beboppers define what is still considered modern jazz. Bebop was inherently music for small ensembles, which usually included a rhythm section of piano, bass, and drums, and two or three horns, playing a new repertory of jazz standards often derived from the chord changes of Ray Noble's "Cherokee" or George Gershwin's "I Got Rhythm." In the standard bebop ensemble, after the initial statement of the theme in unison, each soloist was given several choruses to improvise on that theme. The beboppers, ever restless innovators, also experimented with Latin music, string accompaniments, and the sonorities of twentieth-century European concert music.

The latter influenced pianist John Lewis and trumpeter Miles Davis, bebop pioneers who forged a new style known as "cool jazz." In the late 1940s Davis began listening to and playing with white musicians, especially arranger Gil Evans, associated with Claude Thornhill's band. Davis formed an unusual nine-piece band, including "non-jazz" instruments such as tuba and French horn for club and record sessions later known as Cool Jazz. The ensemble's elegant, relaxed rhythms, complex and progressive harmonies, and intimate solo styles proved enormously influential to white musicians such as Gerry Mulligan, Chet Baker, Lennie Tristano, Dave Brubeck, George Shearing, and Stan Getz, as well as to Lewis's Modern Jazz Quartet.

Davis, a prodigious creator of jazz styles, helped launch the other major trend of the 1950s, "hard bop." Inaugurated by "Walkin'" (1954), hard bop was marked by longer, more emotional solos reminiscent of 1930s cutting contests and reaffirmation of the gospel and blues. Charles Mingus, Sonny Rollins, Clifford Brown, Horace Silver, Art Blakey, and Thelonious Monk were all major exponents of hard bop, as were Cannonball Adderley, Eric Dolphy, Mal Waldron, Jackie McLean, and Wes Montgomery later. During the late 1950s Davis led an ensemble that included some of the finest and most influential of all hard bop players, including John Coltrane, Cannonball Adderley, and white pianist Bill Evans. Davis's landmark *Kind of Blue* (1959) introduced a popular and influential style of playing known as modal, in which modes or scales, rather than chord changes, generate improvisation. Davis also never gave up his interest in large-ensemble, arranged music, and he experimented in the late 1950s, collaborating with Gil Evans, with orchestrations derived from modern European concert music. This music, which white composer Gunther Schuller dubbed as "Third Stream," was never popular among jazz audiences, although black jazz composers such as John Lewis and George Russell embraced its concepts.

Bebop, cool jazz, hard bop, Third Stream music, and "soul" or "funk" jazz, pioneered by Horace Silver, dominated jazz in the late 1950s. However, the giants of the previous decades, playing what was to be called "mainstream" jazz, had some of their greatest popular, if not musical, successes. During that decade Louis Armstrong toured regularly in small and large ensembles and had several enormously popular records. Basie organized a new orchestra, and also had several hit records. Ellington, who had triumphantly introduced new extended works annually in the 1940s, continued to compose for his orchestra and also had several hits.

AVANT-GARDE JAZZ

By the early 1960s jazz had reached a crucial turning point. Many of the jazz masters of the swing era, such as Lester Young and Billie Holiday, were dead. Many of the most important musicians, including Charlie Parker, Bud Powell, and Clifford Brown, had died tragically young or had been devastated by heroin addiction, mental illness, or accidents. Musicians had pushed the rhythmic and harmonic conventions that had been established during the swing era to their breaking point. During the 1960s Coltrane, Ornette Coleman, and Cecil Taylor led the way in beginning to abandon the swinging rhythms and melodies of traditional jazz in favor of implied tempos and harmonies, drawing on the largely unexplored reaches of their instruments, often in epic-length solos. By the mid-1960s a whole new generation of avant-garde or free jazz musicians, including Albert Ayler, Archie Shepp, Marion Brown, Bill Dixon, Sun Ra, and Don Cherry, began to abandon even the bedrock jazz convention of theme and improvisation in favor of dissonant collective improvisations related to the energetic polyphony of New Orleans–style jazz. These musicians, inspired by the civil rights movement, also began to address politics, especially race problems and black nationalism, in their music. They were often joined by musicians from the previous generation, such as Max Roach and Charles Mingus. Also in the 1960s, many jazz musicians visited Africa, and some converted to Islam, although some musicians—for example, Sadik Hakim—had converted as early as the 1940s. Many figures

Lifetime Achievement Grammy Awards

Ever since the first jazz Grammy was given to Ella Fitzgerald in 1958, numerous other black jazz musicians have collected Grammy Awards as well. A special category called the Lifetime Achievement Award is reserved for the most influential musicians who have maintained a high standard of quality over a long period of time.

Duke Ellington was the first jazz musician to be recognized with a Lifetime Achievement Award in 1966. Considered by many to be the most prolific composer of the twentieth century, Ellington was an obvious choice. He wrote nearly 2,000 compositions before his death in 1975.

Ella Fitzgerald received hers in 1967. The quintessential female lounge singer, she had an extremely wide vocal range to offset her small voice. This vocal range gave her a gift for mimicry enabling her to imitate jazz instruments and other famous singers.

After his death, Louis Armstrong was honored with a lifetime achievement Grammy in 1972. Most famous for his ability on the cornet and gravelly voice, he is considered the most important improviser in jazz and, like Fitzgerald above, had a keen sense of swing. His sense of humor and positive disposition made him an extremely likable performer.

Billie Holiday was honored in 1987, also after her death, in 1959. Her influence on later female singers is matched only by Fitzgerald. Whereas Fitzgerald was more adept at handling light material, Holiday's signature was slow, melancholic songs of unrequited love. "Gloomy Sunday" (1941), a song about suicide, and "Lover Man" (1944) are her most highly regarded songs.

Charlie Parker received his lifetime achievement award in 1984, also posthumously. An influential improvising soloist on the saxophone, perhaps the most influential, and a central figure of bop in the 1940s, Parker was idolized by his peers. He and Dizzy Gillespie (another lifetime achievement winner in 1989) formed the nucleus of Billy Eckstine's band.

Among the other African-American jazz artists receiving the Lifetime Achievement Award were: Benny Carter (1987), Lena Horne (1989), Art Tatum (1989), Sarah Vaughan (1989), Miles Davis (1990), John Coltrane (1992), Thelonious Monk (1993), and Charles Mingus (1997).

---

in the black arts movement, such as Amiri Baraka, hailed the extended solos of musicians such as John Coltrane as an authentic African-American art form. Ironically, at the same time, almost any connection to a large black audience in America was sundered.

The "further out" jazz became, the more harshly it was attacked by traditional musicians and listeners alike. In response, by the late 1960s many free jazz musicians were searching for ways to recapture a mass black audience. Once again, it was Miles Davis who led the way. Starting in the late 1960s, Davis began using electric instruments in his bands and incorporating funk, rhythm and blues, and rock rhythms into his albums. Members of Davis's electric ensembles, such as Herbie Hancock, Wayne Shorter, and Chick Corea, later enjoyed tremendous popular success.

If the electric music Davis created, known as "fusion" or "jazz rock," inspired accusations that he was selling out,

in the 1970s, the purist mantle would be carried by a group of musicians who had been playing in Chicago since the early 1960s. Striving toward the implicit racial pride and artistic and economic independence preached by Sun Ra, Mingus, and Taylor, the Association for the Advancement of Creative Musicians (AACM) was founded in 1965. The AACM, and its offshoot, the St. Louis–based Black Artists Group, have been responsible for many of the most important developments in jazz since the mid-1970s. The Art Ensemble of Chicago, pianist Muhal Richard Abrams, and saxophonist Anthony Braxton and Henry Threadgill have all been important exponents of what they term "creative music," which idiosyncratically and unpredictably draws upon everything from ragtime to free jazz.

Jazz in the 1990s

In the 1980s, the institutionalization of jazz accompanied the more general interest of universities, symphonies, and museums in many areas of African-American culture. Since the 1970s, many jazz musicians, including Mary Lou Williams, Archie Shepp, Jackie McLean, Bill Dixon, and Anthony Braxton, have held university positions. Although there is a long history of formally trained jazz musicians, from Will Marion Cook to Miles Davis, a large proportion of the best young jazz musicians now come from conservatories. Such training has resulted not only in avant-gardists like Anthony Davis and David Murray, who have a healthy appreciation for the roots of jazz, but bebop-derived traditionalists like Wynton Marsalis, who have brought mainstream jazz to the public prominence it has lacked for forty years. Further, although independent scholars compiled discographies and wrote biographies as early as the 1930s, since the 1980s there has been a burst of institutional scholarly activity, accompanied by the integration of jazz into traditional symphony repertories, as well as the creation of jazz orchestras dedicated to preserving the repertory, and developing new compositions, at the Smithsonian Institution and Lincoln Center. Jazz, as perhaps the greatest of all African-American cultural contributions, always captured the imagination of great African-American writers like Langston Hughes and Ralph Ellison, and it continues to suffuse the work of contemporary writers like Ishmael Reed, Toni Morrison, Albert Murray, and Stanley Crouch.

The Second Century

Jazz has been a pluralistic music since its inception. From the "Spanish tinge" of the New Orleans period to the world music explorations of John Coltrane, Don Cherry, and Collin Walcott, jazz has absorbed anything it needed to extend its boundaries. Latin music, for example, decisively influenced jazz innovators from Jelly Roll Morton to Dizzy Gillespie. Further, by the mid-1960s, Cuban and Brazilian rhythms, scales from India and the near east, along with musical instruments from many areas of the world, were enjoying a significant place in jazz performance. Before the 1970s, jazz history followed a straightforward narrative—constantly gravitating toward the next new thing. Consequently, one was able to match each decade with a dominant style. Suddenly this all changed. Jazz became syncretistic, eclectic, and enormously diverse. In addition, groups like Shakti, the Codono trio, and Oregon emerged with the mission of building bridges between cultures and incorporating elements of ethnic music into their performances. By the end of the 1980s, a search was on for common roots and a universal musical energy.

Technological advances, the burgeoning recording reissue industry, and a plethora of new educational materials had prepared many artists to view the jazz tradition as a whole rather than through the lens of one particular style. Some looked backward to tradition while others looked forward to change. An ever-increasing diversity of styles and tendencies resulted—each marketing to its own specific audience. As jazz approached its second century, a new generation of musicians, including pianist Geri Allen and tenor saxophonist Joshua Redman, continued to improvise on the history of jazz to further address and define issues central to this particular African-American experience.

As the twenty-first century arrived, fusions of jazz with ethnic, popular, and other contemporary musical genres ranged from the jazz flavored offerings of smooth jazz to cutting edge free improvisations on funk and hip hop foundations. By the mid-1990s, for instance, established jazz players such as legendary drummer Max Roach and saxophonist Branford Marsalis, along with saxophonists Steve Coleman and Greg Osby of Brooklyn's M-BASE collective, had experimented with the sounds of funk and hip hop in ambitious but traditionally oriented ways. By the year 2000, trumpeter Dave Douglas, while continuing to be inspired by jazz's historical tradition, had also included Balkan and European folk elements in some of his work. Concurrently, versatile vocalist Cassandra Wilson established herself as an artist of great promise, singing everything from jazz standards and funk to unusual pop.

See also Jazz in African-American Culture; Jazz Singers; Music in the United States

■ ■ *Bibliography*

Berendt, Joachim E. *The Jazz Book: From Ragtime to Fusion and Beyond*. Westport, Conn.: Greenwood Press, 1982.

Blesh, Rudi. *Shining Trumpets: A History of Jazz*, 4th ed. New York: Knopf, 1958.

Charters, Samuel B., and Leonard Kunstadt. *Jazz: A History of the New York Scene*. Garden City, N.Y.: Doubleday, 1962.

Dahl, Linda. *Stormy Weather: The Music and Lives of a Century of Jazz Women*. New York: Proscenium, 1984.

Driggs, Frank, and Harris Lewine. *Black Beauty, White Heat: A Pictorial History of Classic Jazz*. New York: William Morrow, 1982.

Feather, Leonard. *Encyclopedia of Jazz*, rev. ed. New York: Da Capo, 1970.

Gioia, Ted. *The History of Jazz*. New York: Oxford University Press, 1997.

Gitler, Ira. *Jazz Masters of the Forties*. New York: Macmillan, 1966.

Goldberg, Joe. *Jazz Masters of the Fifties*. New York: Macmillan, 1966.

Hadlock, Richard. *Jazz Masters of the Twenties*. New York: Macmillan, 1965.

Hodeir, Andre. *Jazz: Its Evolution and Essence.* Translated by David Noakes. New York: Grove, 1956.

Jost, Ekkehard. *Free Jazz.* New York: Da Capo, 1981.

Leonard, Neil. *Jazz and White Americans: The Acceptance of a New Art Form.* Chicago: University of Chicago Press, 1962.

Russell, Ross. *Jazz Style in Kansas City and the Southwest.* Berkeley: University of California Press, 1971.

Schuller, Gunther. *Early Jazz: Its Roots and Musical Development.* New York: Oxford University Press, 1968.

Schuller, Gunther. *The Swing Era: The Development of Jazz, 1930–1945.* New York: Oxford University Press, 1989.

Shipton, Alyn. *A New History of Jazz.* New York: Continuum, 2001.

Stearns, Marshall. *The Story of Jazz.* New York: Oxford University Press, 1970.

Stewart, Rex. *Jazz Masters of the Thirties.* New York: Macmillan, 1972.

Weinstein, Norman C. *A Night in Tunisia: Imaginings of Jazz in Africa.* Metuchen, N.J.: Scarecrow Press, 1992.

Williams, Martin. *Jazz Masters of New Orleans.* New York: Da Capo, 1967.

Williams, Martin, ed. *Jazz Panorama.* New York: Collier, 1964.

Williams, Martin, ed. *The Art of Jazz: Ragtime to Bebop.* New York: Da Capo, 1981.

LEONARD GOINES (1996)
Updated by author 2005

JAZZ IN AFRICAN-AMERICAN CULTURE

Jazz was born in the street parades and sporting houses of early twentieth-century New Orleans; nurtured in the rent parties, speakeasies, and dance halls of 1920s and 1930s Chicago, New York, St. Louis, Washington, Baltimore, and Boston; seasoned in the corner saloons and barber shops of Philadelphia, Detroit, and Los Angeles in the 1940s and 1950s; and refined in the concert halls, conservatories, and universities of post–World War II cultural capitals the world over. Jazz was forged in the cauldron of Jim Crow segregation by the descendants of slaves, who transformed antebellum spirituals, work songs, hollers, and ring shouts into the witness-bearing, intensely expressive truthfulness of the blues, as well as the effervescent spirit of ragtime. Marrying these currents of sorrow and joy, oppression and resistance, jazz captured and heralded the struggle for African-American freedom. Jazz's rhythmic finesse, melodic inventiveness, and improvisational energy expressed the dreams and desires of a modernizing people, a people anxious to cast off the chains of slavery and segregation in order to catch the pulse of America's emergence as a twentieth-century beacon of technological and cultural innovation. Jazz was the soundtrack for the Great Migration of African Americans from the rural plantation culture of the Old South to the modern urban culture of the North, Midwest, and West.

As the sound of migration and modernity, jazz was the seed-bed for a new African-American urban vernacular culture of dance, style, and language that became the envy of musicians, artists, writers, intellectuals, and culturally aware ("hip") people everywhere. The African-American jazz musician, John Szwed has written, was "the first truly nonmechanical metaphor for the twentieth-century," successor to the English Gentleman as a globally-emulated model of humanness, grace, and elegance (Szwed, p. 2). African-American jazz pioneers such as Buddy Bolden, Jelly Roll Morton, King Oliver, Sidney Bechet, Louis Armstrong, Coleman Hawkins, Eubie Blake, Fletcher Henderson, Duke Ellington, Bessie Smith, Billie Holiday, Count Basie, Jimmie Lunceford, Mary Lou Williams, and The International Sweethearts of Rhythm struggled to transform an American entertainment business still rooted in traditions of blackface minstrelsy and vaudeville. African-American entertainers were expected to cater to white fantasies of happy-go-lucky black servility as embodied in such minstrel-stage stock characters as Sambo and Mammy. Through the 1920s and into the early 1930s, the so-called "Jazz Age," black jazz musicians worked in venues whose names—Cotton Club, Plantation Club, Kentucky Club, Club Alabama—drew expressly on mythic southern images, recreating for northern white elite audiences ("slummers") a plantation-derived aura of white supremacy. First in the big-band swing movement of the mid-1930s to the mid-1940s, and then in the bebop, cool, and free jazz movements from the late 1940s to the early 1960s, African-American jazz musicians like Ellington, Holiday, Hawkins, Williams, Lester Young, Charlie Parker, Dizzy Gillespie, Thelonious Monk, Sarah Vaughan, Ornette Coleman, John Coltrane, Cecil Taylor, Max Roach, Abbey Lincoln, and Archie Shepp actively criticized and resisted old-fashioned stereotypes associated with black entertainment, insisting on jazz's status as an art form and projecting themselves as cultural heroes and heroines. Much like W. E. B. Du Bois, Alain Locke, James Weldon Johnson, Mary McLeod Bethune, Richard Wright, Ralph Ellison, and other African-American political and cultural leaders—but perhaps with even greater influence among the black masses—African-American jazz musicians embodied and proselytized an image of the "New Negro," of urbane, cultured, and savvy black men and women fit to lead not just African America but America itself.

JAZZ AS CREATIVE TECHNIQUE AND CULTURAL EQUIPMENT

Jazz musicians have become known as the most creative of creative artists, and this has much to do with the boundary-crossing agility and improvisational inventiveness of African-American culture more generally. The best jazz—whether performed by black or non-black musicians—combines a deep immersion in local folk or vernacular idioms (community-based stories and states of feeling communicated through distinctive rhythms of speech, gesture, and performance) with a broad artistic awareness that absorbs ideas and techniques from an array of cultures and experiences. Just as jazz musicians have crossed ethnic social barriers while remaining true to their roots, so jazz music itself has always been engaged in a process of expanding cultural frontiers beyond the limitations of race. Through jazz, African-American culture has effected a New World synthesis of Africa, Europe, the Caribbean, and South and North America; it is this synthesis, indeed, that has made jazz the quintessential cultural expression of the modern world. Jazz began as a world music—early New Orleans jazz polyphony and rhythms had more in common with the music of Martinique, Brazil, and Argentina than anything that was heard in the rest of North America in the 1900s and 1910s—and it continued to grow as a world music throughout the twentieth-century. From Jelly Roll Morton's dictum that all jazz must have a "Latin tinge" to the Afro-Latin jazz innovations of Chano Pozo, Tito Puente, Celia Cruz, and Paquito D'Rivera; from Charlie Parker's love for Stravinsky and strings to the Modern Jazz Quarter's use of Baroque fugues and counterpoint; from John Coltrane's absorption of the Indian raga to Duke Ellington's "Far East Suite," jazz has been a primary vehicle by and through which African-American culture has functioned as a—perhaps *the*—world culture.

Anchoring jazz's global reach is a set of characteristics intrinsic to African-American culture and especially informed by jazz's African roots:

DANCE-BEAT ORIENTATION AND RHYTHMIC GROOVE. Most jazz, not just the music played expressly for dancers, is animated by the spirit of the body in motion, harkening back to African performance traditions in which music and dance are inseparable and mutually reinforcing. The swing music of Ellington, Basie, Lunceford, and Chick Webb extended the African ideal of dance as a celebration of life, a source of energy, joy, inspiration, and social community. Bebop and other forms of modern jazz moved the music off the dance floor but retained a strong connection to body language—as expressed, for instance, in Thelo-

nious Monk's idiosyncratic shuffling dances around his piano, or in Cecil Taylor's athletic sweeps and swoons over the keys and into the bowels of his piano. Central to this dance-beat orientation is the jazz musician's keen ability to establish and continually enrich the rhythmic groove—to know where the downbeat is even if it is not stated, to master and manipulate subtle shadings of phrasing and pulse. Whether the rhythmic figures of a jazz piece are complicated or simple, skilled players and listeners learn to lock into a shared sense of group time. Jazz *moves*.

CALL-AND-RESPONSE CONVERSATION. As in an African dance ritual or in an African-American preacher's sermon to the congregation, jazz performance functions as a dialogue among the musicians, as well as between the musicians and the dancing or listening audience. Jazz musicians learn to listen and communicate with each other, deeply attuned to the nuances of time, gesture, attitude, and sound that each player brings to the performance. This spirit of interactive collaboration often makes the instruments of the band sound like so many voices engaged in a conversation–horn sections spraying riffs (short melodic-rhythmic figures) across the bandstand; a pianist "comping" (jazz slang for accompanying) behind a soloist; a drummer "dropping a bomb" (breaking up his steady cymbal rhythm with between-the-beat figures on the snare and bass drum) to kick the band forward; horn players and the drummer "trading fours" or eights (alternating four-bar or eight-bar solos) like sentences building themselves into a paragraph. Jazz *speaks*.

IMPROVISATION WITHIN A COMMUNAL CONTEXT. Centrally important to jazz performance is the improvised solo, the space in the music where the individual musician steps forward into the spotlight to craft a personalized statement out of the basic materials (chord structure, melody, rhythmic pattern) of the song. Jazz improvisation grants freedom to the featured soloist, but requires that soloist to work within the established context of the performance. An improvised solo is a spontaneous composition, an on-the-spot creation. But to succeed—both musically and culturally—the improvised solo must honor and abide by rules and conventions analogous to those of public speech. It must fit itself into the social flow, shaping itself to the distinctive characteristics of each performance situation, answering the particular challenges imposed by fellow musicians and the audience. It must achieve a stamp of individuality, a personal signature, while also enhancing and enriching the social whole. Improvisation is itself a form of call-and-response within the communal rhythmic groove. "True jazz," said Ralph Ellison, "is an art of individual assertion within and against the group" (O'Meally, 2001, p. 36). Jazz *stylizes*.

CREOLIZATION AND HETEROGENEOUS SOUND. Jazz has inherited from African culture a profoundly pluralistic sensibility, an ability to choose eclectically from a variety of sources, to embrace multiplicity, tension, and even contradiction. This sensibility operates on the social level, with jazz culture's fluid openness and flexibility—the jazz world brings diverse bodies and minds together. It also operates as an aesthetic—the sound of jazz is the sound of high contrast, clashing colors, overlapping layers, timbral variety. Jazz *synthesizes*.

These characteristics inform not just jazz music, but a wide range of African-American expressive culture that in turn has profoundly shaped the broader American culture. When Ralph Ellison asserted that "all American culture is jazz-shaped" (O'Meally, 2001, p. ix), he was thinking about American speech, American humor, American politics (jazz as a model for participatory democracy), American popular culture—movies, cartoons, advertising, and sports (think of Michael Jordan as a master improviser, deepening the rhythmic groove and the high style of a basketball game). Many of the most interesting artists of the twentieth and twenty-first centuries—writers such as Langston Hughes, James Weldon Johnson, Frank Marshall Davis, Amiri Baraka, Jayne Cortez, Sonia Sanchez, Elizabeth Alexander, John Edgar Wideman, Yusef Komunyakaa, and Major Jackson; actors such as Marlon Brando, Robert DeNiro, Denzel Washington, and Don Cheadle; comedians such as Jackie "Moms" Mabley, Dewey "Pigmeat" Markham, Lenny Bruce, and Bill Cosby; painters such as Henri Matisse, Romare Bearden, Archibald Motley Jr., and Jean-Michel Basquiat; photographers such as Eugene Smith, Gordon Parks, Roy DeCarava, Gjon Mili, and William Gottlieb; filmmakers such as Oscar Micheaux, Orson Welles, Robert Altman, Martin Scorsese, Woody Allen, and Spike Lee; choreographers such as Alvin Ailey, Judith Jameson, and Arthur Mitchell—have embraced jazz as the cornerstone of the modern cultural imagination, an artistic model for new ways of writing, moving, seeing, and sounding.

Jazz is the story of, the sound of, and the cultural equipment for African-American creative freedom.

See also Jazz; Jazz Singers; Music in the United States

■ ■ *Bibliography*

Baraka, Amiri (Leroi Jones). *Blues People: Negro Music in White America.* New York: William Morrow, 1963.

Monson, Ingrid. *Saying Something: Jazz Improvisation and Group Interaction.* Chicago: University of Chicago Press, 1996.

Murray, Albert. *Stomping the Blues.* New York: Da Capo, 1976.

O'Meally, Robert, ed. *The Jazz Cadence of American Life.* New York: Columbia University Press, 1998.

O'Meally, Robert, ed. *Living with Music: Ralph Ellison's Jazz Writings.* New York: Modern Library, 2001.

Porter, Eric. *What Is This Thing Called Jazz? African American Musicians as Artists, Critics, and Activists.* Berkeley: University of California Press, 2002.

Ramsey, Guy. *Race Music: Black Cultures from Bebop to Hip Hop.* Berkeley: University of California Press, 2003.

Szwed, John, "Really the (Typed-Out) Blues: Jazz Fiction in Search of Dr. Faustus." *Village Voice* (July 2, 1979): 2.

Tucker, Sherrie. *Swing Shift: "All-Girl Bands" of the 1940s.* Durham, N.C.: Duke University Press, 2000.

JOHN GENNARI (2005)

JAZZ SINGERS

In 1928, when Louis Armstrong lifted his trumpet and then set it down to sing on the record "West End Blues," he set a gold standard for jazz vocalists to come. Armstrong had a horn that sang and a voice that sounded like a horn and improvised with both, sailing beyond the words and the melody. Armstrong and other singers in the early twentieth century such as Bessie Smith and Ethel Waters drew their inspiration from African-American musicians who performed field hollers, spirituals, blues, vaudeville and early musical show tunes, marches and pop numbers, as well as European-based classical music. And whatever the source, black singers infused the music with what Armstrong called "singing his soul, with feeling." That was to remain a prized component of good jazz. Black vaudeville shows and dance bands became popular across the land. Radio helped propel a number of black vocalists and orchestras to fame nationwide on the airwaves. Among them were Ivie Anderson with Duke Ellington, Jimmy Rushing with Count Basie, and Pha Terrell with the Clouds of Joy.

By the time World War II ended, America entered an era of shifting expectations and technological advances, including those in jazz. As the swing era withered, bebop, a modern, more complex style of jazz, was featured in many smaller clubs, where people came to listen rather than dance. Among the singers who had come of age during the swing era and became known as great soloists in the postwar years were Billie Holiday, Ella Fitzgerald, and Sarah Vaughan. During the 1940s, Holiday, called Lady Day, was the headliner at one of America's first integrated nightclubs, Café Society in New York. Though Lady Day

Jazz singing legend Billie Holiday (1915–1959).
© BETTMANN/CORBIS

had a limited vocal range and did not employ scat—wordless vocalizing—in her technique, she was arguably the greatest jazz singer ever, timeless in her exquisite expression of feelings and subtle use of dynamics, color, phrasing, and shading. The rhythmically intrepid Ella Fitzgerald, on the other hand, took scat singing to a pinnacle, as well as serving up shimmering, perfect ballads, as her many songbook recordings of popular composers attest. Another towering talent was Sarah Vaughan, with a gorgeous and unusually supple vocal instrument, dazzling musicians and audiences with her mastery of pitch, color, rhythm, and grasp of bebop harmonies in her scat singing. Immediately following these three greats was Carmen McRae, one of the greatest interpreters of lyrics, with a judicious use of behind-the-beat phrasing and a dramatic gift that spanned icy disdain, tenderness, and fiery passion.

Romantic "black baritones" were numerous among male singers in the 1940s. Billy Eckstine's modern jazz big band showcased his creamy voice and matinee idol looks as he smoothly maneuvered bebop changes. Earl Coleman had a hit with "Dark Shadows," and Johnny Hartman became widely known after an album of ballads with John Coltrane. Joe Williams's highly polished, lithe voice produced a number of hits with Count Basie's band, such as "Every Day I Have the Blues." Williams, who cited wide-ranging influences among black singers, including country

blues singers Bill Broonzy and Memphis Slim, big band shouters Joe Turner and Jimmy Rushing, and concert singers Paul Robeson and Roland Hayes, went on to international success as a soloist. However, *the* baritone to emerge in the 1940s was that of an excellent pianist with a limited vocal range and rather raspy quality. But when Nat "King" Cole sang, he communicated great depth, swing, perfect intonation and enunciation, and a natural butterscotch charm. His many hit records, among them "Unforgettable," "It's Only a Paper Moon," "Mona Lisa," and "Nature Boy," made him a household name in the 1950s. As hugely popular as he was, Cole became the first African-American entertainer to get his own television show, but the show folded during that period of growing demand for civil rights in America because he could not secure a national sponsor. His legacy lived on, however: Both his brother Freddie Cole and his daughter Natalie Cole achieved successful singing careers.

Also in the 1950s Dinah Washington, the "Queen of the Blues," sublimely blended bluesy gospel with "worldly" music, as in "What a Difference a Day Makes." Hypertalented, Washington, who could and did sing just about anything, made fine jazz-based recordings in an intimate style, paving the way for many other singers, including Esther Philips, Nancy Wilson, Gloria Lynne, Etta James, Ernestine Anderson, and Dee Dee Bridgewater. Washington's crown, though, went to Aretha Franklin, who, like Washington, made a brilliant crossover from gospel to "worldly" music in 1960, and recorded some jazz-based material. Arguably the greatest crossover talent, however, was Ray Charles, "the Genius." Trained as a pianist, a devotee at first of Nat Cole and soulful singer Charles Brown, Ray Charles made a series of memorable hits from the 1960s on, ranging from jazz standards such as "Georgia," country classics including "You Don't Know Me," gospel-blues rousers such as "What'd I Say," and possibly the best "God Bless America" ever.

Other singers experimented with the angular, jagged complexities of bebop in scat singing. Leo Watson improvised melodies and witty lyrics with the speed of a whirling dervish, while Babs Gonzales, of Three Bips and a Bop, was a vivid presence. It was Eddie Jefferson who first composed lyrics to already existing instrumental solos, but it was King Pleasure who had a jazz hit with Jefferson's lyric to "Moody's Mood for Love." A bit later came Jon Hendricks, who formed the popular vocal trio Lambert, Hendricks & Ross, going on as a soloist to write and perform many vocalized pieces set to jazz players' solos.

When it came to wordless vocalizing, arguably no one was more riveting than Betty Carter. After working with Ray Charles in 1961, Carter raised the bar for innovations in jazz singing by radically reassembling lyrics of standards through scatting, tonal distortions, wide-ranging tempos, and quick changes, producing unexpected emotional resonance in the process. Such singers as Jeanne Lee ran with the baton in the 1970s, pioneering free jazz techniques by using the syllables of lyrics for freeform scatting. Other black female singers were strikingly dramatic in different ways. Nina Simone included jazz in a wide repertoire that combined raw emotional power with political militancy, as in her composition "Mississippi Goddam." Abbey Lincoln developed into a socially and politically acute commentator in the 1960s, becoming a well-known international presence by the 1990s.

The 1960s and 1970s saw the emergence of several standout male vocalists, including Joe Lee Wilson, an ebullient blues and jazz singer, and Leon Thomas, whose huge voice scat yodeling on "The Creator Has a Master Plan" was memorable. Gil Scott-Heron emerged as a jazz-funk poet-visionary, while the superlative soulful pianist and baritone Andy Bey left a spiritual high-water mark on jazz singing, though laboring on in relative obscurity for many years before becoming an international presence by the 1990s.

There were talented singers who achieved a more limited or local recognition, among them the ebullient veteran Dakota Staton and Ethel Ennis on the East Coast and the warmly understated Lorez Alexandria on the West Coast. Alexandria remained in fine voice into the 1990s, while Ennis was content to work in her hometown of Baltimore. Teri Thornton, who had made a few well-received albums in the early 1960s, made a fine comeback album not long before her death in the late 1990s. And Shirley Horn, based in Washington, D.C., eventually achieved international acclaim for her nuanced, subtle, yet insistent swing and appealing romanticism, both as pianist and vocalist.

As the twentieth century segued into the twenty-first, a new crop of vocalists emerged. Paula West spanned jazz and cabaret with an imaginative program. Some singers included an ever-wider range of pop recordings with material drawn from what has become known as *The Great American Songbook,* the jazz canon that comprises compositions by Duke Ellington, Billy Strayhorn, George Gershwin, Cole Porter, Irving Berlin, and others. Along with selections from the canon, Dianne Reeves included Motown tunes in her performance, while Vanessa Rubin's tastes ranged from established jazz material to soul, Nnenna Freelon recorded an album of Stevie Wonder compositions, and Carla Cook sang bossa nova and bop, funk, gospel, and the 1960s folk-pop hit "Scarborough Fair." Many singers included their own originals, such as the excellent Carmen Lundy.

A Selective Discography

Andy Bey: *Shades of Bey*

Betty Carter: *Inside Betty Carter*

Ray Charles: *The Very Best of Ray Charles*

Nat King Cole: *Cool Cole*

Billy Eckstine: *Verve Jazz Masters 22: Billy Eckstine*

Ella Fitzgerald: *Pure Ella*

Giacamo Gates: *Remembering Eddie Jefferson*

Johnny Hartman: *John Coltrane and Johnny Hartman*

Billie Holiday: *The Billie Holiday Story* (6 volumes)

Lambert, Hendricks and Ross: *Sing a Song of Basie*

Abbey Lincoln: *Straight Ahead*

Kevin Mahogany: *Big Band*

Bobby McFerrin: *Spontaneous Inventions*

Carmen McRae: *Carmen Sings Monk*

Sarah Vaughan: *At Mister Kelly's*

Dinah Washington: *Dinah Jams*

Joe Williams: *Havin' A Good Time*

Cassandra Wilson: *Blue Skies*

Compilation: *Smithsonian Collection: The Jazz Singers 1919-1984*

Among male singers, Kevin Mahogany developed his big, Joe Williamsy baritone in exciting forays into blues, ballads, and standards, while Bobby McFerrin, who had a huge hit with "Don't Worry, Be Happy," took a page from the Leo Watson school of stream-of-consciousness scat singing. Noted for a huge range and an uncanny ability to closely imitate other sounds, including musical instruments and maintain two melodic lines at once, McFerrin went on to record with classical cellist Yo-Yo Ma, as well as jazz with pianist Chick Corea. Another singer, Gia-

Jazz singer Betty Carter performs at the Monterey Jazz Festival.
© CRAIG LOVELL/CORBIS

camo Gates, a disciple of the Eddie Jefferson style, was one of the hardest swinging vocalists on the scene.

As the twenty-first century progressed, definitions continued to shift and blur within the capacious category of music called jazz singing. Lizz Wright steered a course between R&B and jazz, Typhanie Monique recorded an evocative version of the 1960s rock group the Doors' "Light My Fire," while the acclaimed contralto Cassandra Wilson was lauded for recording material by legendary bluesman Robert Johnson. Styles of music from around the world continued to weave even more colorful strands into the tapestry of jazz singing. Though no one could predict where jazz singing would evolve, the roots of jazz, however, remained the same: Africa uprooted and transplanted on American soil. African-American jazz singing was, then and now, both a uniquely American art form and a gift given to the world.

See also Blueswomen of the 1920s and 1930s; Charles, Ray (Robinson, Ray Charles); Cole, Nat "King"; Coltrane, John; Eckstine, Billy; Fitzgerald, Ella; Holiday, Billie; Jazz in African-American Culture; Jazz: Overview; Lincoln, Abbey; McRae, Carmen; Music in the United States; Vaughan, Sarah; Waters, Ethel

■■ *Bibliography*

Balliett, Whitney. *American Singers.* New York: Oxford University Press, 1979.

Dahl, Linda. *Stormy Weather: A History of Women in Jazz.* New York: Limelight Editions, 1984.

Friedwald, Will. *Jazz Singing.* New York: Da Capo Press, 1990.

Cassandra Wilson. *Wilson won the 1997 Grammy Award for Best Jazz Vocal Performance for* New Moon Daughter. © MITCHELL GERBER/CORBIS

Gourse, Leslie. *Louis' Children: American Jazz Singers.* New York: Cooper Square Press, 2001.

Lees, Gene. *Singers and the Song II.* New York: Oxford University Press, 1998.

LINDA DAHL (2005)

JEFFERS, AUDREY

FEBRUARY 12, 1896
JUNE 24, 1968

■ ■ ■

Born to parents of Trinidad and Tobago's small, black property-owning class, Audrey Layne Jeffers completed her primary and secondary education at Tranquillity Girls' Practising School before proceeding to London in 1913 to complete a diploma in social science at Alexander College, North Finchley. During World War I she served among the West African troops and through the West India Committee organized a West African Soldiers Fund and Cigarette Fund. After the war she joined the Society of Peoples of African Origin, formed by fellow Trinidadian F. E. M. Hercules.

Upon her return to Trinidad and Tobago in 1920, Jeffers established a school serving black middle-class children, earning a reputation as a teacher of excellence. Deeply affected by the poverty in wider Port of Spain (the capital of Trinidad and Tobago) and influenced by religion and social work—upper- and middle-strata women's only legitimate spheres of public activity—in 1921 she founded Trinidad and Tobago's most important women's organization of the early twentieth century, the Coterie of Social Workers (COSW).

The COSW allowed Jeffers to combine her concern with women, her compassion for the less fortunate, and her ongoing concern with persons of African descent. Coterie membership comprised women of the respectable black and colored communities, who by the mid-1930s were being excluded from careers in teaching and the civil service. The Trinidad and Tobago Education Act of 1934, for example, prohibited married women from permanent employment except in certain circumstances.

Coterie activities included the establishment of the St. Mary's Home for Blind Girls and Women in 1928, the Maud Reeves Hostel for Working Girls in 1935, Anstey House for Respectable Young Ladies, and in the 1940s, Faith House, a rest house and training center for women.

A high point in Jeffers's career came in 1936. In March of that year, she was an honored guest of the Negro Progress Convention in British Guiana, marking the one hundredth anniversary of slave emancipation. She addressed the convention's women's session on the topic "Women and their Responsibility to the Race." In May the Coterie hosted the First Conference of British West Indies and British Guiana Women Social Workers in Port of Spain, the first major women's conference in the English-speaking Caribbean. The conference's recommendations included the introduction of a girl's open scholarship for higher education, the establishment of a women's police force, and increased employment for educated black women.

In October, after a challenge to her eligibility, Jeffers became the first woman elected to the Port of Spain Municipal Council. In 1946 she would become the first woman nominated to the Legislative Council. She also served as honorary counsel for the Republic of Liberia. The COSW submission to the 1938 West India Royal Commission called for the establishment of a girls' college to prepare girls for the Island Scholarship, government provision of clothing to needy children, and equal numbers of women and men on the Board of (Film) Censors. One blot on Jeffers's career was her failure to support universal adult suffrage in 1946.

In 1956, in response to the political federation of the British Caribbean colonies, a Caribbean Women's Association was formed at Jeffers's instigation "to provide the women of the Caribbean with a representative national organization dedicated to the principle that women must play a vital role in the development and life of the Caribbean community" (Henderson, 1973, p. 14). In 1953 Amy Ashwood Garvey hailed Jeffers as "a long-standing feminist and No. 1 social worker in the West Indies" (*Port of Spain Gazette,* May 30). Jeffers received the MBE (Member of the Order of the British Empire) in 1929, the OBE (Officer of the Order of the British Empire) in 1959, and Trinidad and Tobago's Chaconia Gold Medal for social service posthumously in 1969.

See also Social Work

■ ■ *Bibliography*

Comma-Maynard, Olga. *The Brierend Pattern: The Story of Audrey Jeffers O.B.E. and the Coterie of Social Workers.* Port of Spain, Trinidad and Tobago: Busby Printerie, 1971.

Henderson, Thelma. "The Role of Women in Politics in Trinidad and Tobago: 1925–1972." Caribbean Studies thesis. St. Augustine, Trinidad and Tobago: University of the West Indies, 1973.

Port of Spain Gazette (May 30, 1953).

Reddock, Rhoda. *Women, Labour, and Politics in Trinidad and Tobago: A History.* London: Zed Books, and Kingston, Jamaica: Ian Randle Publications, 1984.

RHODA E. REDDOCK (2005)

JEFFERSON, BLIND LEMON
JULY 1897
DECEMBER 1929

■ ■ ■

Although the circumstances of his birth are obscure, the blues guitarist and singer Blind Lemon Jefferson's birthplace is often given as Couchman, Texas. He is thought to have been born blind, but several of his songs indicate that he lost his sight in childhood. Jefferson learned to play guitar as a teenager, and he was soon performing on the streets of nearby Wortham, as well as at barber shops and parties. He also sang spirituals at the family's church, Shiloh Baptist Church in Kirvin.

Jefferson moved to Dallas in 1912. He weighed almost 250 pounds at the time, and for a brief time earned money as a novelty wrestler in theaters. He met Huddie "Leadbelly" Ledbetter (1885–1949) in Dallas's Deep Ellum neighborhood, and they played and traveled together throughout East Texas until Leadbelly was jailed for murder in 1918. Jefferson also performed for spare change on Dallas streets, at times assisted by T-Bone Walker (1910–1975) and Josh White (1915–1969). He was noted for his ability to hear pennies (and reject them) by the sound they made in his tin cup. In the early 1920s Jefferson married and had a son.

Jefferson's first recordings were spirituals, including "All I Want is That Pure Religion" and "I Want to be Like Jesus in my Heart," made under the name Deacon L. J. Bates. "Long Lonesome Blues" (1926), his first popular success, displayed his clear, high-pitched voice, accentuated by hums and moans. His guitar playing was marked by a subtle, almost contrapuntal use of hammered bass and treble lines. Like many East Texas and Delta bluesmen, Jefferson sang of day-to-day life ("Corinna Blues" [1926], "Jack of Diamonds" [1926], "Rising High Water Blues" [1927], "Piney Woods Money Mama" [1928], "See That My Grave Is Kept Clean" [1928], "Pneumonia Blues" [1929]) as well as travel ("Sunshine Special" [1927], "Rambler Blues" [1927], "Matchbox Blues" [1927]). He sang lyrics filled with sexual innuendo ("That Black Snake Moan" [1926], "Oil Well Blues" [1929], "Baker Shop Blues" [1929]), and many of his songs were about jail ("Blind Lemon's Penitentiary Blues" [1928], "Hangman's Blues" [1928]), although he was never incarcerated. In the late 1920s Jefferson's recordings made him a wealthy, nationally recognized figure. He traveled throughout the South and Midwest, and even kept an apartment in Chicago. However, his popularity lasted only briefly, and by 1929 he was no longer performing and recording as frequently. In December 1929, on a date that has never been verified, Jefferson froze to death in a Chicago blizzard. His body was transported back to Wortham, Texas, after his death, but his grave was poorly marked. In 1967 friends of Jefferson put a marker in the approximate location of his grave, and in 1997 money was raised for a real headstone to be placed in the spot.

See also Blues, The; Leadbelly (Ledbetter, Hudson William)

■ ■ *Bibliography*

Govenar, Alan. "That Black Snake Moan: The Music and Mystery of Blind Lemon Jefferson." In *Bluesland,* edited by Peter Welding and Toby Byron. New York: Dutton, 1991.

Groom, Bob. *Blind Lemon Jefferson.* Knutsford, UK: Blues World, 1970.

Uzzel, Robert L. *Blind Lemon Jefferson: His Life, His Death, and His Legacy.* Austin, Tex.: Eakin, 2002.

JONATHAN GILL (1996)
Updated by publisher 2005

JESÚS, ÚRSULA DE

1604
1666

■ ■ ■

Úrsula de Jesús, a mystic who spent most of her life in the Convent of Saint Clare in Lima, Peru, gained a reputation for sanctity that only a few achieved during the seventeenth century. Even more unusual is that in 1647 the Catholic confessor of this humble, black religious servant *(donada)* ordered her to record her religious experiences, which she did until several years before her death.

As a young slave, Úrsula and her mother resided with their owner, Gerónima de los Ríos, and in 1617 she entered the Convent of Saint Clare to serve her owner's niece. Founded in 1605, this convent attracted scores of elite women aspiring to become nuns of the black veil (the highest rank) or the more modest white veil. However, the only possibility for women of color to become "nuns" was by taking simple vows of obedience and enclosure as *donadas*, or religious servants, who would then continue to serve individual nuns and perform communal labor.

For twenty-eight years Úrsula was one of hundreds of slaves and servants whose exhausting daily work regime afforded no time to seriously contemplate religious matters. However, according to a religious biography *(vida)* of Úrsula written in 1686, a brush with death in 1642 transformed her life. Úrsula then gained a greater sense of purpose, she beseeched God to instruct her in spiritual matters, and the nuns began referring to her as a "servant of God." By 1645 a nun of the black veil purchased Úrsula's freedom, and she then took her vows as a *donada*.

From 1647 until her death in 1666, Úrsula's spiritual abilities, and particularly her ability to intercede on behalf of souls trapped in purgatory—a punitive domain where Catholics believed sins were purged before the soul entered heaven—continued to grow. Over two decades Úrsula became intimately familiar with the interior worlds of dead souls communicating with her in the belief that her prayers might alleviate their suffering in purgatory. In her diary she recorded the "visits" from priests revealing their sundry peccadilloes, nuns mourning their impudent conduct, or slaves and servants recounting the excessive work they had endured. For Úrsula, saving souls in purgatory presented an opportunity to perform charitable labor and to gain an authority that, under other circumstances, might evade her.

In fact, after Úrsula had prayed ardently to ensure their safe passage from purgatory, many transfigured souls appeared to thank her before ascending to heaven. Once, in a vision, the slave María Bran appeared to Úrsula dressed in an ecclesiastical garment and wearing a crown of flowers, and assured Úrsula that blacks and *donadas* went to heaven. The fact that a slave would occupy a space in the lofty heights of purgatory—and then enter heaven—reveals Úrsula's (and perhaps, others') conception of purgatory as a space where social justice prevailed.

Near the end of her life Úrsula was told that, because of her efforts to help others, she too would be granted direct and safe passage to heaven. When she died in 1666, the Saint Clare nuns deeply mourned her passing and a number of high secular and ecclesiastical authorities attended her funeral. The nuns commissioned an artist to paint her portrait, and an anonymous friar wrote her *vida,* based largely upon her diary.

Úrsula's text is the only extant seventeenth-century spiritual autobiography written by a woman of color in Latin America. In her fifty-seven-folio diary, she recorded her innermost thoughts, which she wrote or dictated to several scribes in both the first and third person. The text is filled with repetitious narrative, vivid imagery, and above all, incredibly rich dialogues with celestial figures ranging from her guardian angel disguised as a friar, to Christ, Mary, and God.

Although Úrsula never gained the recognition that Saint Rosa of Lima (1586–1617) achieved in seventeenth-century Peru, she served as a model for other humble women to emulate. To this day, the memory of Úrsula lives on among the Saint Clare nuns in Lima, who continue to recount tales of her miracles and the fervent desire of this remarkable mystic to placate others.

See also Catholicism in the Americas; Egipcíaca, Rosa

■ ■ *Bibliography*

Jesús, Úrsula de. *The Souls of Purgatory: The Spiritual Diary of a Seventeenth-Century Afro-Peruvian Mystic, Úrsula de Jesús.* Translated and edited by Nancy E. van Deusen. Albuquerque: University of New Mexico Press, 2004.

van Deusen, Nancy E. "Ursula de Jesús: A Seventeenth-Century Afro-Peruvian Mystic." In *The Human Tradition in Colonial Latin America,* edited by Kenneth J. Andrien. Wilmington, Del.: Scholarly Resources, 2002.

Wood, Alice L. "Religious Women of Color in Seventeenth-Century Lima: Estefanía de San Joseph and Ursula de Jesu Christo." In *Beyond Bondage: Free Women of Color in the Americas,* edited by David Barry Gaspar and Darlene Clark Hine. Urbana: University of Illinois Press, 2004.

NANCY E. VAN DEUSEN (2005)

JET

■ ■ ■

The magazine *Jet,* founded by John H. Johnson in November 1951, is the leading African-American newsweekly. In 2003 its paid subscriptions were over 912,000 and its weekly readership was estimated at 11 million. Among the publications of the Johnson Publishing Company, it ranks second in circulation to *Ebony,* the popular large-format monthly magazine it was designed to complement.

Jet, whose title carries the connotation both of dark skin color and of speedy airplanes, was meant as a quick, pocket-sized review of black news. Founded on the model of *Life* magazine's unsuccessful pocket-sized feature magazine *Quick, Jet* was originally only 5¾" x 4". Within six issues of its founding, it had a weekly circulation of 300,000. By the 1990s circulation was 900,000 per week, and the magazine had grown to a 7 3/8" x 5¼" format.

By the early 1990s, *Jet* was distributed throughout the United States and in forty foreign countries, including many African nations. Its appeal stems from its coverage of important issues in the African-American community and from its concise style. *Jet*'s articles are meant to cover important issues in readable form, for people who neither have the time nor wish to read deeply on current events but want to stay informed. Its reputation for news and commentary on social events was best expressed by a character in a play by writer Maya Angelou, who claimed, "If it didn't happen in *Jet,* it didn't happen anywhere."

See also Angelou, Maya; *Ebony*; Journalism

■ ■ *Bibliography*

Johnson, John H. and Lerone Bennett. *Succeeding Against the Odds.* New York: Warner, 1989.

KAREN BENNETT HARMON (1996)
Updated by publisher 2005

JIM CROW

As a way of portraying African Americans, *Jim Crow* first appeared in the context of minstrelsy in the early nineteenth century. Thomas "Daddy" Rice, a white minstrel, popularized the term. Using burnt cork to blacken his face, attired in the ill-fitting, tattered garments of a beggar, and grinning broadly, Rice imitated the dancing, singing, and demeanor generally ascribed to Negro character. Calling it "Jump Jim Crow," he based the number on a routine he had seen performed in 1828 by an elderly and crippled Louisville stableman belonging to a Mr. Crow. "Weel about, and turn about / And do jis so; / Eb'ry time I weel about, / I jump Jim Crow." The public responded with enthusiasm to Rice's caricature of black life. By the 1830s minstrelsy had become one of the most popular forms of mass entertainment, *Jim Crow* had entered the American vocabulary, and many whites, north and south, came away from minstrel shows with their distorted images of black life, character, and aspirations reinforced.

Less clear is how a dance created by a black stableman and imitated by a white man for the amusement of white audiences would become synonymous with a system designed by whites to segregate the races. The term *Jim Crow* as applied to separate accommodations for whites and blacks appears to have had its origins not in the South but in Massachusetts before the Civil War. Abolitionist newspapers employed the term in the 1840s to describe separate railroad cars for blacks and whites. Throughout the North, blacks, though legally free, found themselves largely the objects of scorn, ridicule, and discrimination. Most northern whites shared with southern whites the conviction that blacks, as an inferior race, were incapable of assimilation as equals into American society. Racial integrity demanded that blacks, regardless of class, be segregated in public transportation—that they be excluded from the regular cabins and dining rooms on steamboats, compelled to ride on the outside of stagecoaches, and forced to travel in special Jim Crow coaches on the railroads. Only in pre–Civil War New England did blacks manage to integrate transportation facilities, but only after prolonged agitation during which blacks and white abolitionists deliberately violated Jim Crow rules and often had to be dragged from the trains.

Before the Civil War, enslavement determined the status of most black men and women in the South, and there was little need for legal segregation. Several Radical Republican state governments outlawed segregation in their new constitutions during Reconstruction but did not try to force integration on unwilling whites. Custom, habit, and etiquette defined the social relations between the races and enforced separation. The determination of blacks to improve their position revolved largely around efforts to secure accommodations that equaled those provided to whites.

But in the 1890s, even as segregation became less rigid and pervasive in the North, the term *Jim Crow* took on additional force and meaning in the South. It came to represent an expanded apparatus of segregation sanctioned by law. Economic and social changes had multiplied the places and situations in which blacks and whites might come into contact, and whites had become alarmed over a new generation of blacks undisciplined by slavery, unschooled in racial etiquette, less fearful of whites, and more inclined to assert their rights as citizens.

Jim Crow, then, came to the South in an expanded and more rigid form in the 1890s and the early twentieth century in response to white perceptions of a new generation of blacks and to growing doubts that this generation could be trusted to stay in its place without legal force. Some whites, caught up in the age of Progressive reform, preferred to view legal segregation as reform rather than repression, as a way to resolve racial tensions and maintain the peace. For most whites, however, it was nothing less than racial self-preservation, deeply rooted in the white psyche. "If anything would make me kill my children," a white woman told a northern visitor, "it would be the possibility that niggers might sometime eat at the same table and associate with them as equals. That's the way we feel about it, and you might as well root up that big tree in front of the house and stand it the other way up and expect it to grow as to think we can feel any different" (Johnson, 1904, p. 352).

Between 1890 and 1915 the racial creed of the white South manifested itself in the systematic disfranchisement of black men, in rigid patterns of racial segregation, in unprecedented racial violence and brutality, and in the dissemination of racial caricatures that reinforced and comforted whites in their racial beliefs and practices. The white South moved to segregate the races by law in practically every conceivable situation in which they might come into social contact. The signs WHITE ONLY and COLORED would henceforth punctuate the southern scenery: from public transportation to public parks and cemeteries; from the workplace to hospitals, asylums, orphanages, and prisons; from the entrances and exits at theaters, movie houses, and boardinghouses to toilets and water fountains. Oftentimes, Jim Crow demanded exclusion rather than separation, as with municipal libraries and many sports and recreational facilities. Jim Crow legislation tended to be thorough, far-reaching, even imaginative: from separate public school textbooks for black and white children to

A sign points the way to a separate waiting room for blacks at the Illinois Central Railroad in Jackson, Missippi. The term Jim Crow *first appeared in the context of minstrelsy in early nineteenth century America, a popular form of entertainment that fostered a distorted view of blacks. Later, Jim Crow came to be associated with various laws segregating blacks in the South.* © BETTMANN/CORBIS

Jim Crow Bibles for black witnesses in court, from separate telephone booths to Jim Crow elevators. New Orleans adopted an ordinance segregating black and white prostitutes.

In *Plessy v. Ferguson* (1896) the U.S. Supreme Court employed the "separate-but-equal" principle to affirm the constitutionality of Jim Crow, confirming what most black southerners already knew from personal experience—that the quality of their life and freedom depended on the whims and will of a majority of whites in their locality or state. The court decision, along with the elaborate structure of Jim Crow, remained in force for more than half a century. In the 1950s and 1960s a new climate of political necessity and a new generation of black Americans helped to restructure race relations. With an emboldened and enlarged civil rights movement in the vanguard, the federal government and the courts struck down the legal barriers of racial segregation and ended Jim Crow. But a far more intractable and elusive kind of racism, reflected in dreary economic statistics and a pervasive poverty, lay beyond the reach of the law and the growing civil rights movement.

See also Abolition; Minstrels/Minstrelsy; *Plessy v. Ferguson*

■ ■ *Bibliography*

Cell, John W. *The Highest Stage of White Supremacy: The Origins of Segregation in South America and the American South.* Cambridge, UK: Cambridge University Press, 1982.

Johnson, Clifton. *Highways and Byways of the South.* New York: Macmillan, 1904.

McMillan, Neil R. *Dark Journey: Black Mississippians in the Age of Crow.* Urbana: University of Illinois Press, 1989.

Patler, Nicholas. *Jim Crow and the Wilson Administration: Protesting Federal Segregation in the Early Twentieth Century.* Boulder: University Press of Colorado, 2004.

Rabinowitz, Howard. *Race Relations in the Urban South, 1865–1890.* New York: Oxford University Press, 1978.

Toll, Robert C. *Blacking Up: The Minstrel Show in Nineteenth-Century America.* New York: Oxford University Press, 1974.

Williamson, Joel. *The Crucible of Race: Black-White Relations in the American South since Emancipation.* New York: Oxford University Press, 1984.

Woodward, C. Vann. "The Strange Career of a Historical Controversy." In *American Counterpoint: Slavery and Racism in the North-South Dialogue.* Boston: Little, Brown, 1971.

Woodward, C. Vann. *The Strange Career of Jim Crow.* 3rd ed. New York: Oxford University Press, 1974.

LEON F. LITWACK (1996)
Updated bibliography

JOHN HENRY

A towering, legendary American working-class folk heroes, John Henry represents not only the nineteenth-century struggle of the human spirit against the coming industrial era but also African-American resistance to white labor domination. It is not clear how the legend represents actual events surrounding the construction of the Big Bend tunnel of the Chesapeake & Ohio railroad in Summers County, West Virginia, in the 1870s. In the legend John Henry, an enormously strong black steel driver, pits himself in a contest against a steam drill intended to replace workers. Wielding only a hammer, John Henry wins by drilling holes along fourteen feet of granite, compared to the machine's nine feet, but the effort kills him.

The story exists in many different musical versions, often with different melodies. The text, which was first printed around the turn of the century, also exists in different versions, but all combine thematic aspects of the African-American work song with the narrative structure of British folk ballads. It is one of the most popular American folk songs and has been recorded hundreds of times, most often by blues singers. The first recording was by country music pioneer Fiddlin' John Carson in 1924. The first recording by black musicians was by the Francis and Sowell duo in 1927. Since then, versions have been released by Leadbelly, Paul Robeson, Brownie McGhee and Sonny Terry, Fred McDowell, Memphis Slim, Odetta, Mississippi John Hurt, Big Bill Broonzy, and Harry Belafonte.

See also Folklore; Folk Music

■■ *Bibliography*

Chappell, Louis W. *John Henry: A Folk-Lore Study.* Port Washington, N.Y.: Kennikat Press, 1968.

Cohen, Norm. *Long Steel Rail.* Urbana: University of Illinois Press, 1981.

ANDREW BIENEN (1996)
GREG ROBINSON (1996)
Updated bibliography

JOHNSON, CARYN

See Goldberg, Whoopi

JOHNSON, CHARLES RICHARD

APRIL 23, 1948

Novelist Charles Johnson was born in Evanston, Illinois, and studied at Southern Illinois University and SUNY at Stony Brook in New York, majoring in philosophy. As he writes in his essay "Where Philosophy and Fiction Meet" (1988), he was inspired by a campus appearance of LeRoi Jones (Amiri Baraka) to turn toward literary expression (after some work as a cartoonist). His flirtation with cultural nationalism was intense but brief: He came to recognize that its built-in danger "is the very tendency toward the provincialism, separatism, and essentialist modes of thought that characterize the Anglophilia it opposes." If the utopianism and the mix of social hope and colorful individual expression of the 1960s inspired him to become a writer, he was attracted to the tradition of the philosophical novel, which he began to write at the postmodern moment when parody, comedy, and tongue-in-cheek improvisation in the face of disaster came together. He worked under the supervision of novelist John Gardner and remained closely associated with him for many years. Johnson draws freely on Indian and Japanese Buddhist sources, Western philosophy, and literary precursors from Cervantes to slave narratives and from Saint Augustine to Hermann Hesse's *Siddhartha*. He has also been deeply influenced by the ways in which the African-American writers W. E. B. Du Bois, Jean Toomer, Richard Wright, and Ralph Ellison approached fundamental questions of culture and consciousness. Johnson traced their legacy in the essay "Being & Race: Black Writing Since 1970" (1988), a subtly yet firmly argued survey of the contemporary literary scene, for the title of which Martin Heidegger served as an inspiration.

After writing a number of increasingly accomplished short stories that were collected in *The Sorcerer's Appren-*

tice (1986) and publishing a first novel, *Faith and the Good Thing*, in 1974 (several others exist in manuscript but were never published), Johnson achieved an artistic breakthrough with his novel *Oxherding Tale* (1982). A meditation on the representation of the eighth of the "Oxherding Pictures" by Zen artist Kakuan-Shien (in which both the ox and herdsman are gone), the novel also continues the tradition of autobiographical fiction as embodied in James Weldon Johnson's *The Autobiography of an Ex-Colored Man*. *Oxherding Tale* represents the education of Andrew Hawkins, who is raised by a transcendentalist tutor on a southern plantation—a plantation that is visited by Karl Marx in the novel. As Andrew (like Saint Augustine before him) learns to free himself from dualism, another figure, that of the Soulcatcher, grows in importance. Johnson draws the philosophical issues out of love, education, or enslavement. It is a stylistically brilliant novel, both comic and profound, picaresque and self-reflexive. It parodies the eighteenth-century novel and the genre of the slave narrative yet manages to remain faithful to both these inspirations. Johnson received the Governor's Award for Literature from the state of Washington for *Oxherding Tale* in 1983.

Johnson's novel *Middle Passage* (1990) continued the exploration of a nineteenth-century setting for unusual purposes. It is the tale of Rutherford, who eludes collectors of gambling debts and the offer of redemption by marriage in New Orleans when he takes the place of a sailor, only to find himself aboard a slave ship headed for Africa. Johnson manages to revitalize what have become fixtures in imagining the nineteenth century by concerning himself with the human issues he locates in particular spaces. The enslaved Almuseri add some elements of magical realism to the text, which may be the most imaginative modern thematization of the experience that the title refers to, free from the clichéd ways in which this historical period has sometimes been fictionalized. *Middle Passage* was awarded the National Book Award in 1990. Johnson's novel *Dreamer* (1998), an exploration of the mind of Martin Luther King Jr., was not a critical success.

Johnson has continued to publish books, including *Soulcatcher and Other Stories* in 2001, and a book of interviews, *Passing Three Gates* (2004), edited by Jim McWilliams.

See also Caribbean/North American Writers (Contemporary); Du Bois, W. E. B.; Ellison, Ralph; Literature of the United States; Toomer, Jean; Wright, Richard

■ ■ *Bibliography*

Johnson, Charles. "Where Philosophy and Fiction Meet." *American Visions* 36 (June 1988): 47–48.

Johnson, Charles. *Passing Three Gates: Interviews with Charles Johnson.* Edited by Jim McWilliams. Seattle: University of Washington Press, 2004.

Kutzinski, Vera. "Johnson Revises Johnson: *Oxherding Tale* and *The Autobiography of an Ex-Colored Man.*" *Pacific Philology* (Spring 1989): 39–46.

WERNER SOLLORS (1996)
Updated by publisher 2005

JOHNSON, CHARLES SPURGEON

JULY 24, 1893
OCTOBER 27, 1956

■■■

Sociologist and editor Charles Spurgeon Johnson was born in Bristol, Virginia, and was given a classical education by his father, Rev. Charles Henry Johnson, a Baptist minister who had been taught to read English, Latin, Greek, and Hebrew by his former slave-master. In 1916 the younger Johnson earned a B.A. from Virginia Union University in Richmond.

In 1917 Johnson moved to Chicago to pursue graduate studies in sociology at the University of Chicago, where he became associated with a group of influential scholars who made up the Chicago School of Sociology, including Robert E. Park and W. I. Thomas. Johnson had a profound regard in particular for Park, his lifelong mentor who specialized in race relations and urban sociology. He received a Ph.B. in 1918, while serving as a director of research and records for the Chicago Urban League, of which Park was the president.

After the race riot of 1919, Johnson was appointed to the interracial Chicago Commission on Race Relations, coauthoring the committee report, "The Negro in Chicago: A Study in Race Relations and a Race Riot" (1922). Written under Park's supervision, this was Johnson's first major research project. It was also one of the first significant sociological studies indicating the persistence of racial segregation and discrimination within northern cities, and it warned that the pervasive barriers to black economic and social equality might provoke additional riots.

In 1921 Johnson moved to New York City to become director of research for the National Urban League. Two years later he founded the league's magazine, *Opportunity:*

A *Journal of Negro Life,* which he edited from 1923 to 1928. This journal proved to be an important cultural force in the Harlem Renaissance, publishing many of the black poets and writers of the time and organizing literary contests and awards ceremonies to gain recognition for these authors and encourage white publishers to support them. As an editor, Johnson was also concerned with bringing social science research to a black general readership.

The bulk of Johnson's sociological contribution was made from 1927 to 1947, the period during which he served as chairman of the department of social sciences at Fisk University. In various publications, Johnson made a major contribution to the understanding of the South as a region, the economic foundation of race relations, and contemporary debate on racial problems. One of his most important books is *Shadow of the Plantation* (1934), a study of the collapse of southern cotton tenancy, in which he demonstrated that racial discrimination was compounded by the economic exploitation that existed in the South during the Great Depression. Johnson argued that sharecropping created an ongoing economic basis for racial discrimination, and demonstrated how powerful agrarian and industrial interests shaped the "human relations" of race and racism. In *The Negro College Graduate* (1938) he described in great detail how difficult it was for blacks to gain entrance to college and to advance professionally after graduation, and the economic and psychological problems this caused. *Growing Up in the Black Belt* (1941) showed black adolescence to be at once a product of the omnipresent "color system" and of the socialization process as it works out in any complex society with differences among young people in age, sex, class, and urban or rural background.

In 1947 Johnson became the first black president of Fisk University. Over the years, he was a consultant on race relations to presidents Franklin D. Roosevelt, Herbert Hoover, and Dwight D. Eisenhower. In 1930 Johnson was a member of the League of Nations Commission whose mission was to investigate human rights violations in Liberia, and he served on the Tennessee Valley Authority in 1934. From 1936 to 1937 he was a consultant to the U.S. Department of Agriculture on the issue of farm tenancy and in 1946 a U.S. delegate to the United Nations Educational, Scientific and Cultural Organization (UNESCO). Johnson died suddenly in 1956.

See also Harlem Renaissance; National Urban League; *Opportunity: Journal of Negro Life*; Sociology

▪ ▪ *Bibliography*

Blackwell, James, and Morris Janowitz, eds. *Black Sociologists: Historical and Contemporary Perspectives.* Chicago: University of Chicago Press, 1974.

Gilpin, Patrick J. *Charles S. Johnson: Leadership beyond the Veil in the Age of Jim Crow.* Albany: State University of New York Press, 2003.

Kellner, Bruce. *The Harlem Renaissance: A Historical Dictionary for the Era.* Westport, Conn.: Greenwood, 1984.

Rauschenbush, Winfred. *Robert E. Park: Biography of a Sociologist.* Durham, N.C.: Duke University Press, 1979.

JO H. KIM (1996)
Updated bibliography

JOHNSON, EARVIN "MAGIC"

AUGUST 14, 1959

Earvin "Magic" Johnson Jr. was born and raised in Lansing, Michigan, where he soon demonstrated an unusual aptitude for basketball. Despite the flair suggested by his nickname (which was given to him in 1974 by Fred Stabley Jr., a reporter for the *Lansing State Journal*), Johnson's playing style was crafted out of devotion to basketball fundamentals and endless hours of practice. After leading his high school team to the state championship in his senior year, Johnson chose to attend college at nearby Michigan State University. He electrified crowds with his dazzling playmaking and the enthusiasm he displayed on the court while leading the Spartans to a national collegiate championship as a sophomore in 1979. At 6'9", he was perhaps the most agile ball handler for anyone of his size in the history of the game, and his combination of height, athletic skills, and passing ability brought a new dimension to the position of guard.

Johnson left Michigan State after his sophomore year, and at the age of twenty he joined the professional ranks, leading the Los Angeles Lakers to the National Basketball Association (NBA) Championship in 1980—a feat they achieved four more times during the decade (in 1982, 1985, 1987, and 1988). Johnson holds the NBA record for assists (9,921) and was named the league's Most Valuable Player three times (1987, 1989, 1990), playoff MVP three times (1980, 1982, 1987), and All-Star Game MVP twice (1990, 1992). His desire to win translated into an unselfish style of play that elevated passing to an art form (his 10,141 career assists ranks him second in NBA history) and stressed teamwork over individual accolades. His charisma and court savvy helped to revive interest in the NBA, while his versatility transformed the game to one dominated by multitalented guards and forwards. Johnson's contributions on the court have been matched by his efforts and leadership away from it: He has worked for numerous charitable organizations and has raised several million dollars for the United Negro College Fund over the course of his career. With an engaging personality and smile, Johnson became one of the most famous and recognizable Americans in the 1980s.

Johnson retired from professional basketball in November 1991 when he revealed that he had tested positive for HIV, the virus that causes AIDS (acquired immunodeficiency syndrome). Following his announcement Johnson assumed a leadership role once again in working to raise research funds for, and awareness of, the disease. In 1992 he was appointed to the President's National Commission on AIDS, but he resigned soon thereafter when he became disillusioned with the government's efforts on behalf of AIDS research. Johnson kept AIDS in the public eye when he resumed his career shortly after guiding the U.S. basketball team to a gold medal at the 1992 Olympics. He attempted a comeback with the Lakers in the fall of 1992, but after some players in the league expressed reservations about playing with him because of his virus, he retired again. In that same year Johnson authored *What You Can Do to Avoid AIDS,* the net profits from which went to the Magic Johnson Foundation, which Johnson established for prevention, education, research, and care in the battle against AIDS. In mid-season 1995–1996 Johnson rejoined the badly faltering Lakers as a player-coach. He once again retired at the end of the season.

During his retirement Johnson continued his AIDS education efforts, and he encouraged businesses to enter inner-city neighborhoods, notably through his successful Magic Johnson Cineplex movie theater in South Central Los Angeles, opened in 1995. In 1997 he hosted a short-lived late-night talk show.

By 2001 Johnson had expanded his foundation's mission to include business ventures with Starbucks and a series of initiatives to increase minority homeownership, educational opportunities, and computer literacy. Because of the sophisticated drugs available to treat HIV-AIDS in the United States, Johnson is currently living with what many now consider a chronic disease, instead of a terminal condition.

See also AIDS in the Americas; Basketball

■ ■ *Bibliography*

Aldridge, David. "Thankfully, Earvin's Obit Far from Written." Available from <http://espn.go.com/nba/columns/aldridge/1274716.html>.

Friend, Tom. "Still Stunning the World 10 Years Later." Available from <http://espn.go.com/gen/s/2001/1105/1273720.html>.

Johnson, Earvin "Magic," and Roy S. Johnson. *Magic's Touch.* Reading, Mass.: Addison-Wesley, 1989.

Pascarelli, Peter F. *The Courage of Magic Johnson: From Boyhood Dreams to Superstar to His Toughest Challenge.* New York: Starfire, 1991.

JILL DUPONT (1996)
Updated by author 2005

JOHNSON, JACK

MARCH 31, 1878
JUNE 10, 1946

The third of six surviving children, boxer Jack Johnson was born John Arthur Johnson in Galveston, Texas, to Henry Johnson, a laborer and ex-slave, and Tiny Johnson. He attended school for about five years, then worked as a stevedore, janitor, and cotton picker. He gained his initial fighting experience in battle royals, brutal competitions in which a group of African-American boys engaged in no-holds-barred brawls, with a few coins going to the last fighter standing. He turned professional in 1897. In his early years Johnson mainly fought other African-American men. His first big win was a sixth-round decision on January 17, 1902, over Frank Childs, one of the best black heavyweights of the day. The six-foot, 200-pound Johnson developed into a powerful defensive boxer who emphasized quickness, rhythm, style, and grace.

In 1903, Johnson defeated Denver Ed Martin in a twenty-round decision, thus capturing the championship of the unofficial Negro heavyweight division, which was created by West Coast sportswriters to compensate for the prohibition on blacks fighting for the real crown. Johnson, who was then the de facto leading heavyweight challenger, sought a contest with champion Jim Jeffries but was rebuffed because of the color line. Racial barriers largely limited Johnson's opponents to black fighters like Joe Jeanette, whom he fought ten times. Johnson's first big fight against a white contender was in 1905, against Marvin Hart, which he lost by the referee's decision, despite having demonstrated his superior talent and ring mastery. Hart became champion three months later, knocking out Jack Root to win Jeffries's vacated title. Johnson's bid to get a title fight improved in 1906, when he hired Sam Fitzpatrick as his manager. Fitzpatrick knew the major promoters and could arrange fights that Johnson could not when he managed himself. Johnson enhanced his reputation with victories in Australia, a second-round knockout of forty-four-year-old ex-champion Bob Fitzsimmons in Philadelphia, and two wins in England.

In 1908 Canadian Tommy Burns became champion, and Johnson stalked him to Australia, looking for a title bout. Promoter Hugh McIntosh signed Burns to a match in Sydney on December 26 for a $30,000 guarantee with $5,000 for Johnson. Burns was knocked down in the first round by Johnson, who thereafter verbally and physically punished Burns until the police stopped the fight in the fourteenth round. White reaction was extremely negative, with journalists describing Johnson as a "huge primordial ape." A search began for a "white hope" who would regain the title to restore to whites their sense of superiority and to punish Johnson's arrogant public behavior. To many whites Johnson was a "bad nigger" who refused to accept restrictions placed upon him by white society. A proud, willful man, Johnson recklessly violated the taboos against the "proper place" for blacks, most notoriously in his relationships with white women. Although much of the black middle class viewed his lifestyle with some disquiet, he became a great hero to lower-class African Americans through his flouting of conventional social standards and his seeming lack of fear of white disapproval.

Johnson defended his title five times in 1909, most memorably against middleweight champion Stanley Ketchell, a tenacious 160-pound fighter. Johnson toyed with Ketchell for several rounds, rarely attacking. Ketchell struck the champion behind the ear in the twelfth round with a roundhouse right, knocking him to the canvas. An irate Johnson arose, caught the attacking challenger with a right uppercut, and knocked him out. Johnson's only defense in 1910 was against Jim Jeffries, who was encouraged to come out of retirement by an offer of a $101,000 guarantee, split three to one for the winner, plus profits from film rights. When moral reformers refused to allow the match to be held in San Francisco, it was moved to Reno, Nevada. The former champion, well past his prime, was overmatched. Johnson taunted and humiliated him, ending the fight with a fifteenth-round knockout. Fears that a Johnson victory would unleash racial hostilities were quickly realized as gangs of whites randomly attacked blacks in cities across the country. Some states and most cities barred the fight film for fear of further exacerbating racial tensions. Overnight the national press raised an uproar over the "viciousness" of boxing and clamored for its prohibition. Even Theodore Roosevelt, himself an avid

boxer, publicly hoped "that this is the last prizefight to take place in the United States." The reaction to Johnson's victory over a white champion proved a significant event in the history of American racism, as white fears of black male sexuality and power were manifested in a wave of repression and violence.

In 1910 Johnson settled in Chicago, where he enjoyed a fast lifestyle; he toured with vaudeville shows, drove racing cars, and in 1912 opened a short-lived nightclub, the Cafe de Champion. Johnson defended his title once during the two years following the Jeffries fight, beating "Fireman" Jim Flynn in nine rounds in a filmed fight in Las Vegas, New Mexico. Subsequently, in response to anti-Johnson and antiboxing sentiment and concern about films showing a black man pummeling a white, the federal government banned the interstate transport of fight films.

In 1911 Johnson married white divorcee Etta Terry Duryea, but their life was turbulent and she committed suicide a year later. Johnson later married two other white women. His well-publicized love life caused much talk of expanding state antimiscegenation statutes. More important, the federal government pursued Johnson for violation of the Mann Act (1910), the so-called "white slavery act," which forbade the transportation of women across state lines for "immoral purposes." The law was seldom enforced, but the federal government chose to prosecute Johnson, even though he was not involved in procuring. Johnson was guilty only of flaunting his relationships with white women. He was convicted and sentenced to one year in the penitentiary but fled the country to Europe through Canada. He spent several troubled years abroad, defending his title twice in Paris and once in Buenos Aires, and struggled to earn a living.

In 1915 a match was arranged with Jess Willard (six feet six inches and 250 pounds) in Havana. By then Johnson was old for a boxer and had not trained adequately for the fight; he tired and was knocked out in the twenty-sixth round. The result was gleefully received in the United States, and thereafter no African American was given a chance to fight for the heavyweight title until Joe Louis. Johnson had hoped to make a deal with the government to reduce his penalty, and four years later he claimed that he threw the fight. Most boxing experts now discount Johnson's claim and believe it was an honest fight. Johnson returned to the United States in 1920 and served a year in Leavenworth Penitentiary in Kansas. He subsequently fought a few bouts, gave exhibitions, trained and managed fighters, appeared onstage, and lectured. His autobiography, *Jack Johnson: In the Ring and Out,* appeared in 1927; a new edition was published, with additional material, in 1969. Johnson died in 1946 when he drove his car off the road in North Carolina.

Johnson's life was memorialized by Howard Sackler's play *The Great White Hope* (1969), which was made into a motion picture in 1971. Johnson finished with a record of 78 wins (including 45 by knockout), 8 defeats, 12 draws, and 14 no-decisions in 112 bouts. He was elected to the Boxing Hall of Fame in 1954. In 1987 *Ring* magazine rated him the second greatest heavyweight of all time, behind Muhammad Ali.

See also Boxing

■ ■ *Bibliography*

Gilmore, Al-Tony. *Bad Nigger! The National Impact of Jack Johnson.* Port Washington, N.Y.: Kennikat Press, 1978.

Hietala, Thomas R. *The Fight of the Century: Jack Johnson, Joe Louis, and the Struggle for Racial Equality.* Armonk, N.Y.: M.E. Sharpe, 2002.

Johnson, Jack. *Jack Johnson: In the Ring and Out.* Chicago: National Sports Publishing Company, 1927. Revised, Chicago, 1969.

Johnson, Jack. *Jack Johnson Is a Dandy: An Autobiography*, edited by Dick Schaap. New York: Chelsea House, 1969.

Roberts, Randy. *Papa Jack: Jack Johnson and the Era of White Hopes.* New York: Free Press, 1983.

Wiggins, William H. "Jack Johnson as Bad Nigger: The Folklore of His Life." *Black Scholar* 2 (January 1971): 4–19.

STEVEN A. RIESS (1996)
Updated bibliography

JOHNSON, JAMES WELDON

JUNE 17, 1871
JUNE 26, 1938

Writer and political leader James William Johnson, who changed his middle name to Weldon in 1913, was born in Jacksonville, Florida. James, Sr., his father, the head-waiter at a local hotel, accumulated substantial real estate holdings and maintained a private library. Helen Dillet Johnson, his mother, a native of Nassau in the Bahamas, was the only African-American woman teaching in Jacksonville's public schools. Through his parents' example, the opportunity to travel, and his reading, Johnson developed the urbanity and the personal magnetism that characterized his later political and literary career.

Johnson graduated in 1894 from Atlanta University, an all-black institution that he credited with instilling in him the importance of striving to better the lives of his people. Returning to Jacksonville, he traveled many different roads to fulfill that sense of racial responsibility. Appointed principal of the largest school for African Americans in Florida, he developed a high-school curriculum. At the same time he founded a short-lived newspaper, the *Daily American* (1895–1896); studied law; passed the bar examination; and wrote lyrics for the music of his brother, J. Rosamond Johnson. In 1900 the brothers collaborated on "Lift Ev'ry Voice and Sing," a song that is regarded as the Negro National Anthem.

Johnson moved to New York in 1902 to work on the vaudeville circuit with his brother and his brother's partner, Robert Cole. Called by one critic the "ebony Offenbachs," the songwriting team of Cole, Johnson, and Johnson was one of the most successful in the country. (The 1902 song "Under the Bamboo Tree" was their greatest success.) The team tried to avoid stereotypical representations of blacks and invest their songs with some dignity and humanity, as well as humor.

While his brother toured with Cole, James Weldon Johnson studied literature at Columbia University and became active in New York City politics. In 1904, in a political association dominated by Booker T. Washington, Johnson became the treasurer of the city's Colored Republican Club. The Republican Party rewarded his service with an appointment to the U.S. Consular Service in 1906. Johnson served first as U.S. consul at Porto Cabello, Venezuela, and then, from 1908 to 1913, in Corinto, Nicaragua.

In Venezuela Johnson completed his first and only novel, *The Autobiography of an Ex-Colored Man* (1912). Published anonymously, it was taken by many readers for a true autobiography. That realism marks an important transition from the nineteenth- to the twentieth-century African-American novel. Johnson brought modern literary techniques to his retelling of the popular nineteenth-century "tragic mulatto" theme.

The election of Woodrow Wilson, a Democrat, to the presidency blocked Johnson's advancement in the consular service. He returned to New York, where in 1914 he joined the *New York Age* as an editorial writer. While he was associated with the politics of Booker T. Washington, Johnson's instincts were more radical and he gravitated toward the NAACP. In 1916 the NAACP hired him as a field secretary, charged with organizing or reviving local branches. In that post, he greatly expanded and solidified the still-fledgling organization's branch operations and helped to increase its membership, influence, and revenue. He also took an active role organizing protests against racial discrimination, including the racial violence of the "Red Summer" of 1919, a phrase he coined.

James Weldon Johnson (1871–1938). *Johnson, a venerated figure of the Harlem Renaissance, believed that artistic achievement was a key to racial uplift, and urged fellow African American artists to assimilate black folk culture into their work. A successful novelist, poet, educator, lawyer, administrator, and diplomat, Johnson was also a talented songwriter who penned the lyrics to "Lift Ev'ry Voice and Sing" (1900).* CORBIS

Shortly after he joined the staff of the NAACP, Johnson published his first collection of poetry, *Fifty Years and Other Poems* (1917). Like the work of Paul Laurence Dunbar, Johnson's poetry falls into two broad categories: poems in standard English and poems in a conventionalized African-American dialect. Although he used dialect, he also argued that dialect verse possessed a limited range for racial expression. His poems in standard English include some of his most important early contributions to African-American letters. Poems such as "Brothers" and "White Witch" are bitter protests against lynching that anticipate the poetry of Claude McKay in the 1920s and the fiction of Richard Wright in the 1930s and 1940s.

During the 1920s Johnson's political and artistic activities came together. He was appointed secretary of the NAACP's national office in 1920. His tenure brought coherence and consistency to the day-to-day operations of the association and to his general political philosophy. He led the organization in its lobbying for the passage of the Dyer Anti-Lynching Bill and in its role in several legal

cases; his report on the conditions of the American occupation of Haiti prompted a Senate investigation. Johnson's leadership helped to establish the association as a major national civil rights organization committed to accomplishing its goals through lobbying for legislation and seeking legal remedies through the courts. In 1927–1928 and again in 1929, he took a leave of absence from the NAACP. During the latter period he helped organize the consortium of Atlanta University and Spelman and Morehouse Colleges.

Also in the 1920s Johnson, with such colleagues at the NAACP as W. E. B. Du Bois, Walter White, and Jessie Fauset, maintained that the promotion of the artistic and literary creativity of African Americans went hand-in-hand with political activism, that the recognition of blacks in the arts broke down racial barriers. Their advocacy of black artists in the pages of *Crisis,* and with white writers, publishers, and critics, established an audience for the flourishing of African-American literature during the Harlem Renaissance. Johnson himself published an anthology of African-American poetry, *The Book of Negro Poetry* (1922, rev. 1931), and he and his brother edited two volumes of *The Book of American Negro Spirituals* (1925 and 1926). In his introductions to these anthologies and in critical essays, he argued for a distinct African-American creative voice that was expressed by both professional artists and the anonymous composers of the spirituals. *Black Manhattan* (1930) was a pioneering "cultural history" that promoted Harlem as the cultural capital of black America.

Johnson was not in the conventional sense either a pious or a religious man, but he consistently drew on African-American religious expressions for poetic inspiration. In such early poems as "Lift Ev'ry Voice and Sing," "O Black and Unknown Bards," and "100 Years," he formulated a secular version of the vision of hope embodied in spirituals and gospel songs. His second volume of poetry, *God's Trombones* (1927), drew on the African-American vernacular sermon. Using the rhythms, syntax, and figurative language of the African-American preacher, Johnson devised a poetic expression that reproduced the richness of African-American language without succumbing to the stereotypes that limited his dialect verse.

In 1930 Johnson resigned as secretary of the NAACP to take up a teaching post at Fisk University and pursue his literary career. His autobiography, *Along This Way,* was published in 1933; his vision of racial politics, *Negro Americans, What Now?*, was published in 1934; and his third major collection of poetry, *Saint Peter Relates an Incident,* was published in 1935. He was killed in an automobile accident.

See also Du Bois, W. E. B.; McKay, Claude; National Association for the Advancement of Colored People (NAACP); Negro National Anthem; Poetry, U.S.; Politics in the United States; Red Summer; Washington, Booker T.; Wright, Richard

■ ■ ■ *Bibliography*

Andrews, William L., ed. *James Weldon Johnson: Writings*. New York: Library of America, 2004.

Fleming, Robert E., ed. *James Weldon Johnson and Arna Wendell Bontemps: A Reference Guide*. Boston: G. K. Hall, 1978.

Fleming, Robert E. *James Weldon Johnson*. Boston: Twayne, 1987.

Levy, Eugene. *James Weldon Johnson: Black Leader, Black Voice*. Chicago: University of Chicago Press, 1973.

GEORGE P. CUNNINGHAM (1996)
Updated bibliography

JOHNSON, JOSHUA

c. 1761–1763
c. 1830s

▮▮▮

In the field of American art, one of the most important revelations of the early twenty-first century has been the discovery of documentation for the parentage and race of Joshua Johnson, one of the most important early African-American painters. In contrast to twentieth-century speculation about his life, his parents have now been positively identified, as have certain elements of his professional training.

Johnson was born between 1761 and 1763, son of George Johnson of Baltimore County, Maryland, and an unidentified enslaved woman. In 1764 he was purchased by his father from William Wheeler Sr., a farmer and the presumed owner of his mother. His father apprenticed him to learn the trade of blacksmithing from William Forepaugh of Baltimore. In July 1782, George Johnson recorded that "a certain Mulatto child named Joshua Johnson which I acknowledge to be my son" should be manumitted, given his freedom, "as soon as he shall be out of his said Apprenticeship or arrive at the age of 21 years which shall first happen." It is evident one of these two events had taken place—either Joshua was twenty-one years old, or he had completed his apprenticeship to Forepaugh—on July 15, when his father had his manumission recorded, providing Joshua Johnson his freedom. Although Johnson was trained as a blacksmith, none of his

work in this medium has been located. Further, the manner and extent of his training as a painter is not known, though hints of the difficulties he faced are evident in the first of his three known newspaper advertisements, published on December 19, 1798, in the *Baltimore Intelligencer*:

> The subscriber, grateful for the liberal encouragement which an indulgent public have conferred on him, in his first essays, in PORTRAIT PAINTING, returns his sincere acknowledgements. He takes liberty to observe, That by dint of industrious application, he has far improved and matured his talents, that he can insure the most precise and natural likenesses. As a *self-taught genius*, deriving from nature and industry his knowledge of the Art; and having experienced many insuperable obstacles in the pursuit of his studies, it is highly gratifying to him to make assurances of his ability to execute all commands, with an effort, and in a style, which must give satisfaction. He therefore respectfully solicits encouragement. Apply at His house, in the alley leading from Charles to Hanover Street, back of Sear's Tavern. JOSHUA JOHNSTON [Johnson's name is found spelled with and without the "t" in nineteenth-century records].

It is speculated that the earliest dated works by Joshua Johnson were not painted before the mid- to late 1780s, if not the early 1790s, a chronology supported by his advertisement and the life dates of the sitters depicted in many of his earliest paintings. Johnson was to continue his activity as a portrait painter through the early 1820s. Among his finest paintings of family groups are *Mrs. Thomas Everette and Her Children* (1818, oil on canvas, 38 7/8 by 55 3/16 inches, held by the Maryland Historical Society) and *Mrs. Hugh McCurdy and Her Daughters* (1806-1807, oil on canvas, 41 by 34 1/2 inches, held by the Corcoran Gallery of Art). Johnson's best-known portraits of children include *The Westwood Children* (1807); *Portrait of Edward Pennington Rutter and Sarah Ann Rutter* (1804); and *Charles John Stricker Wilmans* (1803-1805). Only two Johnson paintings of African-American sitters have been identified. One of these, *Portrait of Daniel Coker* (1805–1810, collection of the American Museum in Bath, England), is considered Johnson's most important work, a rendering of the prominent early black Methodist and advocate of African emigration.

Joshua Johnson and his portraits were rediscovered by the art world in the 1930s through the work of Dr. J. Hall Pleasants, a doctor and historian/genealogist. By 1939, Dr. Pleasants had located thirteen paintings related

Portrait of Daniel Coker (Joshua Johnson, 1805–1810). *A rendering of the prominent black Methodist and advocate of African emigration, Johnson's portrait of Coker is one of only two Johnson paintings of African-American sitters that have been identified, and is considered the artist's most important work.* © AMERICAN MUSEUM IN BRITAIN, BATH

by style and family traditions. His first article, "Joshua Johnson, the First Black American Painter?" in the *Walpole Society Note Book* ended with a question mark because the evidence did not conclusively identify the painter's race. For decades this question continued to be raised by artists and historians, including the artist Romare Bearden (1911–1988) in his *History of African-American Artists from 1792 to the Present* (1993). Johnson's paintings have been widely collected and exhibited. Noted examples are found in private collections and major museums including the National Gallery of Art, Metropolitan Museum of Art, Corcoran Gallery of Art, Maryland Historical Society, Baltimore Museum, Philadelphia Museum of Art, and the Fine Arts Museums of San Francisco.

Although some descendants of Johnson's portrait subjects have recollected family traditions of a black artist painting their ancestral portrait, there was only one Baltimore city directory entry that identified a race for Johnson, in spite of the same name being listed in nine additional directories. The 1817–1818 edition listed him under "Free Householders of Colour." It appears that different clerks recorded his race according to varying interpretations of his appearance.

During the late eighteenth and early nineteenth centuries, Baltimore was home to a community of free blacks as well as aristocratic abolitionists, a situation that appears to have helped Johnson's career as a portrait painter. Johnson's residencies at various locations around the center of Baltimore were often in the same neighborhoods as many of his sitters.

Johnson is presumed to have died sometime after 1824, the last year he is found in Baltimore municipal records. No date of death or burial records have been located for him, although records indicate that his second wife, Clara (or Clarissa), whom he had wed before 1803, probably survived him. Johnson's first marriage—to Sarah, sometime before 1798—resulted in two daughters, both of whom died in childhood, and two sons, who grew up in Baltimore. (The surnames of his wives are unknown.)

Johnson's training as an artist has never been documented, although visual comparisons relate his work to that of members of the Peale family, which was active in the Baltimore region. These include the inventor and museum founder Charles Willson Peale, his sons Rembrandt and Raphaelle, and their cousin Charles Peale Polk. All of these men were painters, and Johnson very likely knew portraits painted by Polk during the late 1780s into the mid 1790s. Johnson and Polk used similar compositional devices and props and were interested in both the physical and psychological relationships between sitters. Thus, although Polk was never Johnson's owner or master, he is related to Johnson stylistically. Polk occasionally depicted women wearing white dresses as well as others in a variety of outfits that included scarves, fichus (light triangular scarves), and other accessories. Research has shown that many of the items included in Polk's portraits related specifically to the sitter, and the same is likely to have been true for their clothing. Johnson's style, from his earliest to his latest works, visually incorporates elements that are likely to be the result of influence of the Peales, specifically Polk.

Johnson's "signature" elements include women and girls wearing white empire dresses; carrying accessories such as strawberries, red shoes, or umbrellas; and usually seated or arranged beside pieces of distinctive Baltimore upholstered furniture. A mother, her daughters, and occasionally her young sons, are captured in a thin silvery atmosphere, linked by their gestures as a family group, and further unified by the repetition of details such as the white dresses.

Interestingly, Johnson often painted portraits of children, many of which survive. These include his signature

Portrait of Mr. and Mrs. James McCormick and Their Children (Joshua Johnson, 1804–1805). *The painting of the McCormicks is considered to be one of Johnson's finest family portraits.* NATIONAL ARCHIVES

style, with such elements as books, fruit, and red shoes. His depictions of children probably indicate an area actively cultivated for his patrons. These works are dynamic and share elements and details of composition. Each places the child in a stage-like environment, often with draperies and patterned stone floors in ambiguous indoor-outdoor settings. Each child appears to have been dressed in his or her best outfit. The attractiveness of these endearing portrayals would have served as a good advertisement of Johnson's abilities and likely brought him additional work.

Part of Johnson's style, thought to be drawn from his training and work as a blacksmith, is a sharp curving linearity. Translations of the curves and turns of ornamental ironwork are suggested by the sinuous lines of the furniture and the rigid columnar quality of the human forms. Further, the light of Baltimore, a seaport undiminished by pollution, must be acknowledged as one possible source for the silvery palette often seen in Johnson's paintings. These elements of palette and form combine with a precision of details, a tautness of line, and a thin application of paint in the areas of the laces and diaphanous fabrics to produce in Johnson's mature works a style that did not merely mimic that of the painters of the Peale family and other Baltimore competitors, but that provided a fashionable and attractive alternative to them.

See also Painting and Sculpture

■ ■ *Bibliography*

Bearden, Romare, and Henry Henderson. "The Question of Joshua Johnston." In *A History of African-American Artists from 1792 to the Present.* New York: Pantheon Books, 1993.

Bryan, Jennifer, and Robert Torchia. "The Mysterious Portraitist Joshua Johnson." *Archives of American Art Journal* 36 (1996): 2–7.

Hartigan, Linda Roscoe. *Sharing Traditions: Five Black Artists in Nineteenth-Century America.* Washington, D.C.: Smithsonian Institution Press, 1985.

Hunter, Wilbur Harvey, Jr. "Joshua Johnston: 18th-Century Negro Artist." *American Collector* 17 (February 1948): 6–8.

Perry, Mary Lynn, "Joshua Johnston: His Historical Context and His Art." Master's thesis, George Washington University, 1983.

Pleasants, J. Hall. "An Early Baltimore Negro Portrait Painter, Joshua Johnston." *Walpole Society Note Book* (1939): 37–73 (reprinted as a pamphlet in 1940).

Pleasants, J. Hall. "Joshua Johnston, The First American Negro Portrait Painter." Baltimore, Md.: Maryland Historical Society, 1942.

Pleasants, J. Hall. *Catalogue of an Exhibition of Portraits by Joshua Johnston.* Baltimore, Md.: Peale Museum, 1948.

Simmons, Linda Crocker. "The McCurdy Family by Joshua Johnson." In *A Capital Collection, Masterworks from the Corcoran Gallery of Art,* edited by Eleanor Heartney. Washington, D.C.: Corcoran Gallery of Art, 2002.

Weekley, Carolyn J., Stiles Tuttle Colwill, Leroy Graham, and Mary Ellen Hayward. *Joshua Johnston, Freeman and American Portrait Painter.* Baltimore, Md.: Maryland Historical Society, 1987.

LINDA CROCKER SIMMONS (1996)
Updated by author 2005

JOHNSON, MORDECAI WYATT

JANUARY 12, 1890
SEPTEMBER 10, 1976

❙❙❙————————

Born in Paris, Tennessee, Mordecai Johnson, an educator, received his first bachelor of arts degree from Morehouse College in 1911. A second B.A. came from the University of Chicago in 1913, followed by a bachelor of divinity degree from Rochester Theological Seminary in 1916 and graduate degrees from Harvard University, Howard University, and Gammon Theological Seminary. Johnson began his career teaching English at Morehouse College in Atlanta.

After leaving Morehouse, Johnson served as a Baptist minister in New York and in West Virginia, where he or-

ganized Charleston's first branch of the National Association for the Advancement of Colored People (NAACP). Never one to back down from an injustice, he was merciless in his attacks on what he called the "Jim Crow churches" of America and worked to integrate all denominations. A gifted speaker, Johnson traveled throughout the Southwest with the YMCA, making detailed studies of many black schools and colleges.

In 1926 Johnson was unanimously recommended by Howard University's board of trustees to serve as the school's first African-American president. Three years later he was honored as the fifteenth recipient of the NAACP Spingarn Medal. A fighter for equal rights, Johnson promoted a policy of academic freedom at Howard for both students and faculty. While president, he could be heard quoting the principles of Mohandas K. Gandhi to his students in the 1930s and rallying for African independence in the 1940s. In 1952 Johnson called for a nonviolent solution to the cold war that culminated in a peace mission to Moscow in 1959. On June 30, 1960, he retired as president of Howard. Thirteen years later, the university honored him with a building in his name. Johnson died in 1976 at the age of eighty-six.

See also Education in the United States; Howard University; Spingarn Medal

■ ■ *Bibliography*

Low, W. Augustus, and Virgil A. Clift. *Encyclopedia of Black America.* New York: McGraw-Hill, 1981.

McKinney, Richard I. *Mordecai: The Man and His Message. The Story of Mordecai Wyatt Johnson.* Washington, D.C.: Howard University Press, 1997.

Thompson, Charles H. "Howard University Changes Leadership." *Journal of Negro Education* 29, no. 4 (fall 1960): 409–411.

MICHAEL A. LORD (1996)
Updated bibliography

JOHNSON, NOBLE AND GEORGE

❙❙❙————————

Little is known about the early lives or later years of Noble Mark Johnson (April 18, 1881–January 9, 1978) and George Perry Johnson (October 29, 1885–October 17, 1977), two brothers who in 1916 founded Lincoln Motion Pictures, the second black American film company. The brothers were raised in Colorado Springs, Colorado (Noble was born in Missouri, before the family moved to Colorado). Noble Johnson first worked as an actor in Philadelphia, while George attended Hampton Institute, in Hampton, Virginia, before moving to Oklahoma, where he worked at one of the region's early black newspapers in 1906. After moving to Tulsa, he produced the *Tulsa Guide,* another early black regional newspaper, and then became the first black clerk at the Tulsa post office.

At the time that they founded Lincoln Motion Pictures, George Johnson was working as a mailman in Omaha, Nebraska, and his brother was playing bit parts in Universal Studios films. They formed the studio, which was among the earliest Hollywood film companies, in order to avoid the financial domination of whites in the film industry and to protest the racist attitudes embodied in D. W. Griffith's *The Birth of a Nation* (1915). Noble ran Lincoln's studio in Los Angeles, while George Johnson continued to work as a postman in Lincoln, Nebraska, directing the company's booking office there.

The company was one of the first independent film companies to make black films with black financing for black audiences, offering black actors and actresses some of the era's few opportunities to play characters other than servile domestics or heartless villains. Lincoln made about one film per year between 1915 and 1922, including *The Realization of a Negro's Ambition* (1916), *The Trooper of Troop K* (1916), and *A Man's Duty* (1921), all of which starred Noble Johnson. Despite large turnouts and excited responses in some cities, the company never gained a big enough audience for its films and lacked a national distribution system. This, combined with a depression that followed World War I, led to the company's failure in 1921.

Even before Lincoln Motion Pictures closed, George Johnson had started an informal news service devoted to black films and filmmakers. Eventually, he moved to Hollywood, changed his name to George Perry, and turned what had been at first a simple collection of newspaper clippings into the Pacific Coast Bureau, which documented production and financial activities and spread gossip about dozens of black film companies. George Johnson gave his archive to the University of California and completed an oral history there before his death in 1977.

After the demise of Lincoln Motion Pictures, Noble Johnson continued to work in film. He acted in many prominent films of the 1920s and 1930s, including *Four Horsemen of the Apocalypse* (1921), *Ben Hur* (1925), and *King Kong* (1933), but almost always in the "exotic" roles, such as that of the Native American, African, Latino, or Asian "primitive." He also appeared in *Tropic Fury* (1939), *The Desert Song* (1943), and *North of the Great Divide* (1950) before retiring in 1950.

See also Film in the United States, Contemporary

■ ■ *Bibliography*

Cripps, Thomas. *Slow Fade to Black: The Negro in American Film.* New York: Oxford University Press, 1977.

Diawara, Manthia, ed. *Black American Cinema.* New York: Routledge, 1993.

Leab, Daniel J. *From Sambo to Superspade: The Black Experience in Motion Pictures.* Boston: Secker and Warburg, 1975.

MICHAEL PALLER (1996)

JONES, ABSALOM

1746
1818

The minister and community leader Absalom Jones was among the enslaved African Americans who gained their freedom in the era of the American Revolution. He made some of the most important contributions to black community-building at a time when the first urban free-black communities of the United States were taking form. Enslaved from his birth in Sussex County, Delaware, Jones served on the estate of the merchant-planter Benjamin Wynkoop. Taken from the fields into his master's house as a young boy, he gained an opportunity for learning. When his master moved to Philadelphia in 1762, Jones, at age sixteen, worked in his master's store but continued his education in a night school for blacks. In 1770 he married, and through unstinting labor he was able to buy his wife's freedom in about 1778 and his own in 1784.

After gaining his freedom, Jones rapidly became one of the main leaders of the growing free-black community in Philadelphia—the largest urban gathering of emancipated slaves in the post-Revolutionary period. Worshiping at Saint George's Methodist Episcopal Church, Jones soon began to discuss a separate black religious society with other black Methodists such as Richard Allen and William White. From these tentative steps toward community-based institutions came the Free African Society of Philadelphia, probably the first independent black organization in the United States. Although mutual aid was its purported goal, the Free African Society was quasi-religious in character; beyond that, it was an organization where people emerging from the house of bondage could gather strength, develop their own leaders, and explore independent strategies for hammering out a postslavery existence that went beyond formal legal release from thralldom.

Once established, the Free African Society became a vehicle for Jones to establish the African Church of Phila-

BLACK SAINTS

Sheet music for "Black Saints," a hymn honoring Absalom Jones. Written in the 1990s by Harold T. Lewis, the lyrics celebrate Jones's rise from slavery to become priest and principal founder of St. Thomas's African Episcopal Church in Philadelphia, the first black Episcopal church. THE CHURCH HYMNAL CORPORATION, 1993. WORDS BY HAROLD T. LEWIS. MUSIC BY JOHN GOSS. WORDS COPYRIGHT © 1992 BY HAROLD T. LEWIS. REPRODUCED BY PERMISSION.

delphia, the first independent black church in North America. Planned in conjunction with Richard Allen and launched with the assistance of Benjamin Rush and several Philadelphia Quakers, the African Church of Philadelphia was designed as a racially separate, nondenominational, and socially oriented church. But in order to gain state recognition of its corporate status, it affiliated with the Protestant Episcopal Church of North America and later took the name Saint Thomas's African Episcopal Church. Jones became its minister when it opened in 1794, and he served in that capacity until his death in 1818. For decades, Saint Thomas's was emblematic of the striving for dignity, self-improvement, and autonomy of a generation of African Americans released or self-released from bondage, mostly in the North. In his first sermon at the African Church of

Philadelphia, Jones put out the call to his fellow African Americans to "arise out of the dust and shake ourselves, and throw off that servile fear, that the habit of oppression and bondage trained us up in." Jones's church, like many others that emerged in the early nineteenth century, became a center of social and political as well as religious activities, and a fortress from which to struggle against white racial hostility.

From his position as the spiritual leader at Saint Thomas's, Jones became a leading educator and reformer in the black community. Although even-tempered and known for his ability to quiet controversy and reconcile differences, he did not shrink from the work of promoting the rights of African Americans. He coauthored, with Richard Allen, *A Narrative of the Proceedings of the Black People, During the Late Awful Calamity in Philadelphia, in the Year 1793*, a resounding defense of black contributions in the yellow fever epidemic of 1793 (Jones himself assisted Benjamin Rush in ministering to the sick and dying in the ghastly three-month epidemic) and a powerful attack on slavery and white racial hostility. In 1797 he helped organize the first petition of African Americans against slavery, the slave trade, and the federal Fugitive Slave Law of 1793. Three years later he organized another petition to President Jefferson and the Congress deploring slavery and the slave trade. From his pulpit he orated against slavery, and he was responsible in 1808 for informally establishing January 1 (the date on which the slave trade ended) as a day of thanksgiving and celebration, in effect an alternative holiday to the Fourth of July for black Americans.

Typical of black clergymen of the nineteenth century, Jones functioned far beyond his pulpit. Teaching in schools established by the Pennsylvania Abolition Society and by his church, he helped train a generation of black youth in Philadelphia. As Grand Master of Philadelphia's Black Masons, one of the founders of the Society for the Suppression of Vice and Immorality (1809), and a founder of the literary Augustine Society (1817), he struggled to advance the self-respect and enhance the skills of the North's largest free African-American community. By the end of Jones's career, Saint Thomas's was beginning to acquire a reputation as the church of the emerging black middle class in Philadelphia. But he would long be remembered for his ministry among the generation emerging from slavery.

See also Allen, Richard; Free Blacks, 1619–1860; Runaway Slaves in the United States; Slavery

■ ■ *Bibliography*

Nash, Gary B. " 'To Arise Out of the Dust': Absalom Jones and the African Church of Philadelphia, 1785-95." In *Race, Class, and Politics: Essays on American Colonial and Revolutionary Society,* edited by Gary B. Nash, pp. 323–355. Urbana: University of Illinois Press, 1986.

GARY B. NASH (1996)

■ ■ *Bibliography*

Johnson, Buzz. *"I Think of My Mother": Notes on the Life and Times of Claudia Jones.* London: Karia, 1985.

Thomas, Elean. "Remembering Claudia Jones." *World Marxist Review* (March 1987).

THADDEUS RUSSELL (1996)

JONES, CLAUDIA
FEBRUARY 21, 1915
DECEMBER 25, 1964

■┃■┃■

Communist Party leader Claudia Jones was born in Port of Spain, Trinidad, and moved with her family to Harlem, in New York, in 1924. While Jones was still a teenager, her mother died, which forced Jones to leave school and work in a factory. In the early 1930s she became involved in the campaign to free the nine Scottsboro Boys, a campaign led by the Communist-dominated International Labor Defense, and she was recruited into the Harlem branch of the Young Communist League (YCL). Shortly afterward, Jones became editor of the YCL's *Weekly Review* and the *Spotlight.* In 1940 she was elected chair of the YCL's national council.

During the 1930s and 1940s Jones was active in the party's civil rights campaigns and supported the National Negro Congress, a civil rights organization that increasingly came under the influence of the Communist Party. She was also a leading voice within the party for women's rights and, after World War II, was appointed to the party national executive committee's commission on women, briefly serving as its secretary.

In 1948 Jones and several other party leaders were arrested on charges of sedition and she was nearly deported before a protest campaign compelled the federal government to free her on bail. Two years later Jones was rearrested under the Smith Act, along with fifteen other party leaders, for "teaching and advocating Marxism." In 1951 she was convicted and imprisoned in a federal penitentiary for one year.

In 1955 Jones was deported. She settled in London, where she renewed her work with the Communist Party. During the late 1950s and early 1960s she also served as the editor of the left-wing *West Indian Gazette* and worked for the Caribbean Labour Congress. Jones died in London in 1964.

See also Communist Party of the United States; National Negro Congress; Scottsboro Case

JONES, GAYL
NOVEMBER 23, 1949

■┃■┃■

Born in Lexington, Kentucky, novelist, poet, and critic Gayl Jones grew up listening to the African-American oral tradition that is prominent in her narratives. Storytelling, both oral and written, was a part of her family experience. Her grandmother wrote religious dramas, and her mother composed stories to entertain the children. Jones herself began writing fiction when she was seven or eight. She received several prizes for poetry while an English major at Connecticut College. She then studied creative writing at Brown University under William Meredith and Michael Harper. She published her first novel while still a graduate student. She taught creative writing and African-American literature at the University of Michigan until 1983; since then she has lived primarily in Paris and Lexington.

Jones's early novels focus on women driven to or over the edge of madness by the abuses they endure. The originality of her work lies in allowing these women to speak for themselves. *Corregidora* (1975), *Eva's Man* (1976), and the stories in *White Rat* (1977) are narrated by characters whose racial and sexual experiences are rendered in voices that are simultaneously obsessive in their concerns and ordinary in their idiom. Her later narratives are poems that present the history of blacks in the New World, including Brazil. *Song for Anninho* (1981), *The Hermit-Woman* (1983), and *Xarque and Other Poems* (1985) continue the focus on the suffering of black women but without the obsessive voices. Her work of criticism, *Liberating Voices: Oral Tradition in African American Literature* (1991), explores folk traditions in the major writers of poetry and fiction. Two later novels, *The Healing* (1998) and *Mosquito* (1999), move in a more positive direction by depicting strong, articulate women capable of telling their own stories and creating meaningful relationships despite the difficulties of life. These works continue Jones's practice of being highly experimental in the ways these stories are told.

See also Literature of the United States; Poetry, U.S.

■ ■ *Bibliography*

Bramen, Carrie Tirado. "Speaking in Typeface: Characterizing Stereotypes in Gayl Jones's *Mosquito*." *Modern Fiction Studies* 49, no. 1 (2003): 124–154.

Byerman, Keith E. "Beyond Realism: The Fictions of Gayl Jones and Toni Morrison." In *Fingering the Jagged Grain: Tradition and Form in Recent Black Fiction*. Athens: University of Georgia Press, 1986, pp. 171–184.

Dubey, Madhu. "Gayl Jones and the Matrilineal Metaphor of Tradition." *Signs: Journal of Women in Culture and Society* 20, no. 2 (1995): 245–267.

Ward, Jerry W. "Escape from Trublem: The Fiction of Gayl Jones." *Callaloo* 5 (1982): 95–104.

KEITH E. BYERMAN (1996)
Updated by publisher 2005

JONES, JAMES EARL

JANUARY 17, 1931

■ ■ ■

James Earl Jones, an actor renowned for his broad, powerful voice and acting range, was born as Todd Jones in Arkabutla, Mississippi, the son of actor Robert Earl Jones. He was raised by his grandparents, who moved to Michigan when Jones was five. Soon afterwards, Jones developed a bad stutter, and remained largely speechless for the following eight years. When he was fourteen, a high school English teacher had him read aloud a poem he had written, and Jones gradually regained the use of his voice. He subsequently starred on the school's debating team. In 1949 Jones entered the University of Michigan as a premedical student, but he soon switched to acting and received his bachelor's degree in 1953. Two years later he moved to New York City and studied at the American Theater Wing. He made his professional debut in 1957.

Jones first became well known in the early 1960s. His first leading role was in Lionel Abel's *The Pretender* in 1960. That same year he became a member of Joseph Papp's New York Shakespeare Festival; he remained with the company until 1967, performing on and off Broadway in numerous theatrical productions. He also played several small parts on Broadway. Between 1961 and 1963 he appeared in eighteen different plays off Broadway. His most notable performances came in Shakespeare Festival productions, as well as in an all-black production of Jean Genet's *The Blacks*, in Josh Greenfield's *Clandestine on the Morning Line*, and in Jack Gelber's *The Apple*. In 1962 Jones won an Obie Award for best actor of the season based on his performances in the latter two productions and in Errol John's *Moon on a Rainbow Shawl*. He subse-

quently won both a Drama Desk Award (1964) and a second Obie (1965) for his performance in the title role of *Othello* at the New York Shakespeare Festival. Jones also made his screen debut at this time, in a small role in Stanley Kubrick's *Dr. Strangelove* (1964).

In 1967 Jones received his first widespread critical and public recognition when he was cast as the boxer Jack Jefferson (a fictionalized version of heavyweight champion Jack Johnson) in a Washington, D.C., production of Howard Sackler's play *The Great White Hope*. In 1968 the play moved to Broadway. The following year, it won a Pulitzer Prize and Jones received a Tony Award. He also starred in the 1970 film based on the play and was nominated that year for an Oscar.

During the 1970s Jones appeared in a variety of stage and screen roles, including such movies as *The Man* (1972), *Claudine* (1974)—for which he was nominated for a Golden Globe Award—*The River Niger* (1975), *The Bingo Long Travelling All-Stars and Motor Kings* (1976), and *A Piece of the Action* (1977); he also provided the voice of Darth Vader in *Star Wars* (1977) and its sequels. On stage, Jones starred in Lorraine Hansberry's *Les Blancs* (1970), in Athol Fugard's *Boesman and Lena* (1970), in an adaptation of John Steinbeck's *Of Mice and Men* (1974), and in various Shakespearean roles.

In 1977 Jones appeared on Broadway in a one-man show in which he portrayed singer/activist Paul Robeson. The show (which opened soon after Robeson's death) was denounced as a distortion of Robeson's life by Paul Robeson, Jr., and was picketed by a committee of black artists and intellectuals who complained that the play had soft-pedaled Robeson's political radicalism. Jones countered that the committee was engaged in censorship. The play's Broadway run and subsequent appearance on public television served to revive public interest in Robeson's life and career.

During the 1980s and 1990s Jones continued to act in various media. On stage, he starred on Broadway in 1981–82 in a highly acclaimed production of *Othello* with Christopher Plummer as Iago and Cecilia Hart (Jones's wife) as Desdemona, in Athol Fugard's *A Lesson from Aloes* (1980) and *Master Harold . . . and the Boys* (1982), and in August Wilson's *Fences*, for which he received a second Tony Award in 1987. He also appeared in more than thirty films during this period, including such movies as *Matewan* (1984), *Soul Man* (1985), *Gardens of Stone* (1985), *Coming to America* (1988), *Field of Dreams* (1989), *The Hunt for Red October* (1990), *Sommersby* (1993), and the animated feature *The Lion King* (1994) as well as *A Family Thing* (1998).

Jones also has had considerable experience in television. He appeared in several episodes of such dramatic series as *East Side, West Side* in the early 1960s. In 1965 his role on *As the World Turns* made him one of the first African Americans to regularly appear in a daytime drama. In 1973 he hosted the variety series *Black Omnibus*. In 1978 Jones played author Alex Haley in the television miniseries *Roots: The Next Generations*. In the late 1990s and into the 2000s he has made numerous appearances in such popular television shows as *Touched by an Angel, Frasier, Will and Grace,* and *Everwood.* He also has starred in two short-lived dramatic series, *Paris* (1979–80) and *Gabriel's Fire* (1990–1992) for which he won an Emmy in 1990, and has made many television movies, including *The Cay* (1974), *The Atlanta Child Murders* (1984), and *The Vernon Johns Story* (1994). In 1993 Jones published a memoir, *Voices and Silences.*

See also Film in the United States; Johnson, Jack; Robeson, Paul; Television

■■ ■ *Bibliography*

Bogle, Donald. *Blacks in American Film and Television: An Illustrated Encyclopedia.* New York: Garland, 1988.

Jones, James Earl, and Penelope Niven. *Voices and Silences.* New York: Scribner's, 1993.

SABRINA FUCHS (1996)
Updated by publisher 2005

JONES, LEROI

See Baraka, Amiri (Jones, LeRoi)

JONES, PHILIP MALLORY
1947

▐ ▐ ▐

Philip Mallory Jones is a media artist whose work explores the significance of the black diaspora experience. His videos make reference to African sensibilities such as the constant flow of life energy, the ageless wisdom of elders, and the permanence of meanings found in artistic forms of expression. These components are used to tell stories centered on space and time. The notion of ancestral memory and the salience of the spiritual world are other themes commonly found in his work. They are also paramount to his central figures, who struggle with the sexual and ra-

cial tensions that problematize everyday interactions with others and self.

Jones earned his B.A. from Beloit College and acquired an M.F.A. in creative writing from Cornell University. He has achieved such accolades as the 2002 Batza Chair in Art and Art History at Colgate University. From 1991 to 2000 he was artist-in-residence at the Institute for Studies in the Arts at Arizona State University. In addition, he has taught at several academies, including Howard University. As the former cofounder and director of *Ithaca Video Project* (1971–1984), his contributions to the field of media arts have been twofold: He is an artist and an advocate. Jones's artistic expression incorporates writing, photography, video, filmmaking, and digitized media. Some of his works include: *The Trouble I've Seen* (1976), *Black/White and Married* (1979), *Soldiers of a Recent and Forgotten War* (1981), *Ghosts and Demons* (1987), *Footprints* (1988), *Jembe* (1989), *Paradigm Shift* (1992), *Crossroads* (1993), and three collaborative performance pieces: *Drummin'* (1997), *Mirrors and Smoke* (2000), and the *Vo-Du Macbeth Opera* (2001).

Described as an impressionistic documentary that dismantles prescribed cultural boundaries, one of Jones's most prominent works, a 1994 video titled *First World Order,* shows, "the connections between group creativity and individual emotions and desires" (Powell, p. 181). In an excerpt from this film, an aged Belizean woman states, "I laugh to myself," as she ponders over her relationship with an estranged son. The fractured bond between this mother and child mirrors the disconnect that exists between non-Western cultures of the African diaspora and the rest of the world. Jones uses this metaphor to challenge the commonly held trope that Western society is the "first world order." His work inverts the structure of this global power dynamic by decoding various cultural expressions whose meanings originated outside of Western society. The dispersion of these cultural expressions is visually articulated through the use of freeze frames that slowly move images in and out of spaces to show how they changed over time. This sequencing achieves two things. It reveals how non-Western artistic expressions of the African diaspora were appropriated, and it presents these "third world" cultures as the original "first world order."

As the curator for the annual Ithaca Film Festival, which toured nationally from 1975 to 1984, Jones provided a venue for fellow artists to display their work and find the artistic, moral, and financial support needed to persevere in the independent filmmaking industry. To this end, his campaigning for venues extends beyond the plight for more black visibility and representation. It echoes the necessity for convergence between the display demands of digital arts and a revamping of traditional structures of exhibition space. His vision to improve spatial barriers, cross-culturally and (inter)nationally, also challenges the propensity for the media to perpetuate historical misrepresentations of black people.

Jones resides in Atlanta, Georgia, where he serves as a consultant to the Center for African American Archival Preservation. He is the artistic director of Alchemy Media and Marketing, Inc., and is working on a book, *Lissen Here!*

See also Art in the United States, Contemporary; Film in the United States, Contemporary

■ ■ *Bibliography*

Bambara, Toni Cade. "Reading the Signs, Empowering the Eye: Daughters of the Dust and the Black Independent Cinema Movement." In *Black American Cinema*, edited by Manthia Diawara, pp. 118–144. New York and London: Routledge, 1993.

Electronic Art Intermix. "Philip Mallory Jones." Available from <www.eai.org/eai/>.

Jones, Philip Mallory. *First World Order*. 28 min., color, sound. New York: Electronic Arts Intermix, 1994.

Muhammad, Erika Dayla. "Race in Digital Space: Conceptualizing the Media Project." *Art Journal* 60, no. 3 (fall 2001): 92–95.

Powell, Richard J. *Black Art and Culture in the 20th Century*. London: Thames and Hudson, 1997.

Zimmerman, Patricia R. "States of Emergency." In *Key Frames: Popular Cinema and Cultural Studies*, edited by Matthew Tinkcom and Amy Villarejo, pp. 377–394. London and New York: Routledge, 2001.

SAADIA NICOE LAWTON (2005)

JONES, QUINCY

MARCH 14, 1933

The music producer and composer Quincy Delight Jones Jr. was born in Chicago and learned to play the trumpet in the public schools in Seattle, Washington, where his family moved in 1945. Jones sang in church groups from an early age, and he wrote his first composition at the age of sixteen. While in high school he played trumpet in rhythm-and-blues groups with his friend Ray Charles (1930–2004). After graduating from high school, Jones attended Seattle University, after which he enrolled in the Berklee School of Music in Boston. He traveled with Jay McShann's band before being hired by Lionel Hampton

(1908–2002) in 1951. Jones toured Europe with Hampton and soloed on the band's recording of his own composition, "Kingfish" (1951).

After leaving Hampton in 1953, Jones, who had an undistinguished solo style on trumpet, turned to studio composing and arranging, working with Ray Anthony, Tommy Dorsey, and Hampton. During the 1950s, Jones also led his own big bands on albums such as *This Is How I Feel About Jazz* (1956). In 1956 Jones helped the trumpet player Dizzy Gillespie (1917–1993) organize his first State Department big band. From 1956 to 1960 he worked as the music director for Barclay Records in Paris, where he also studied arranging with the renowned teacher Nadia Boulanger (1887–1979). He also worked with Count Basie, Charles Aznavour, Billy Eckstine, Sarah Vaughan, Dinah Washington, and Horace Silver, and he led a big band for recording sessions such as *The Birth of a Band* (1959). Jones served as music director for Harold Arlen's blues opera *Free and Easy* on its European tour. Back in the United States in the early 1960s, Jones devoted his time to studio work, attaining an almost ubiquitous presence in the Los Angeles and New York music scenes.

Jones began working as a producer at Mercury Records in 1961. After producing Leslie Gore's hit record "It's My Party" (1963), he became Mercury's first African-American vice president in 1964. He increasingly made use of popular dance rhythms and electric instruments. In 1964 he also scored and conducted an album for Frank Sinatra and Count Basie, *It Might As Well Be Swing*. He recorded with his own ensembles, often in a rhythm-and-blues or pop-jazz idiom, on albums such as *The Quintessence* (1961), *Golden Boy* (1964), *Walking in Space* (1969), and *Smackwater Jack* (1971). Jones also branched out into concert music with his *Black Requiem*, a work for orchestra (1971). Jones was the first African-American film composer to be widely accepted in Hollywood, and he scored dozens of films, including *The Pawnbroker* (1963), *Walk, Don't Run* (1966), and *In Cold Blood* (1967).

In 1974, shortly after recording *Body Heat*, Jones suffered a cerebral stroke and underwent brain surgery. After recovering he formed his own record company, Qwest Productions. Throughout the 1970s Jones remained in demand as an arranger and composer. He also wrote or arranged music for television shows (*Ironside*, *The Bill Cosby Show*, the miniseries *Roots*, and *Sanford and Son*), and for films (*The Wiz*, 1978). During the 1980s Jones expanded his role in the film business. In 1985 he co-produced and wrote the music for the film *The Color Purple* and served as executive music producer for Sidney Poitier's film *Fast Forward* (1985).

Jones's eclectic approach to music, and his ability to combine gritty rhythms with elegant urban textures, is perhaps best exemplified by his long association with Michael Jackson. Their collaborations on *Off The Wall* (1979) and *Thriller* (1984) resulted in two of the most popular recordings of all time. Jones also produced Jackson's *Bad* (1987). During this time, Jones epitomized the crossover phenomenon by maintaining connections with many types of music. His eclectic 1982 album *The Dude* won a Grammy Award, and in 1983 he conducted a big band as part of a tribute to Miles Davis at Radio City Music Hall. The next year he produced and conducted on Frank Sinatra's recording, *L.A. Is My Lady*. He conceived of USA for Africa, a famine relief organization that produced the album and video *We Are The World* (1985). In 1991 Jones appeared with Davis at one of the trumpeter's last major concerts, in Montreux, Switzerland, a performance that was released on album and video in 1993 as *Miles and Quincy Live at Montreux*. During this time Jones also continued to work with classical music, and in 1992 he released *Handel's Messiah: A Soulful Celebration*.

By 1994, with twenty-two Grammy Awards to his credit, Jones had become the most honored popular musician in the history of the awards. He also wielded enormous artistic and financial power and influence in the entertainment industry and was a masterful discoverer of new talent. In 1990 his album *Back on the Block*, which included Miles Davis and Ella Fitzgerald in addition to younger African-American musicians such as Ice-T and Kool Moe Dee, won six Grammy awards. He continued to expand his activities into the print media, including the magazine *Vibe*, aimed primarily at a youthful African-American readership. He also produced the hit television series *Fresh Prince of Bel Air*, which began in 1990. That same year Jones was the subject of a video biography, *Listen Up: The Lives of Quincy Jones*.

Jones won the Jean Hersholt Humanitarian Award in 1995 and the Henry Mancini and Oscar Micheaux Awards in 1999. In 2001 Jones published *Q: The Autobiography of Quincy Jones*. Celebrities and musicians paid tribute to Jones in October 2004 at the United Negro College Fund's "Evening of Stars," honoring his lifetime achievements and commitment to helping others.

See also Jackson, Michael; Music in the United States; Recording Industry

■ ■ *Bibliography*

Horricks, Raymond. *Quincy Jones*. Tunbridge Wells, UK: Spellmount, 1985.

Jones, Quincy. *Q: The Autobiography of Quincy Jones*. New York: Doubleday, 2001.

Sanders, Charles Leonard. "Interview with Quincy Jones." *Ebony* (October 1985): 33–36.

Shah, Diane K. "On Q." *New York Times Magazine* (November 18, 1990): 6.

JONATHAN GILL (1996)
Updated by publisher 2005

JONGO

Jongo, also known as *caxambu* or *tambu*, is a dance and musical genre of black communities from southeast Brazil. It originated from the dances performed by slaves who worked at coffee plantations in the Paraíba Valley, between Rio de Janeiro and São Paulo, and also at farms in some areas of Minas Gerais and Espírito Santo. Jongo is a member of a larger group of Afro-Brazilian dances, such as *batuque, tambor de crioula,* and *zambê,* which feature many elements in common, including the use of fire-tuned drums, the call-and-response form of group singing, the poetical language used in the songs, and the *umbigada,* a distinctive step whereby two dancers hit their bellies. These elements suggest strong ties with the cultural practices of Bantu-speaking peoples of central and southern Africa, especially Congo, Angola, and Mozambique, from where came most of the slaves who worked at the farms in southeast Brazil.

Jongos usually take place during a nightlong party in which several people dance in pairs or in a circle, to the sound of two or more drums, while a soloist sings short phrases answered by the group. The drums, built from hollow tree trunks covered with animal hide in one of the extremities and tuned by the heat of a bonfire, are called *caxambu* or *tambu* (the bigger one) and *candongueiro* (the smaller one). Other instruments can also be used, such as a large and low-pitched friction drum, called *puíta* or *angoma-puíta,* and a rattle made of straw and small beads, called *guaiá, inguaiá,* or *angóia*. Jongo songs, also called *pontos,* are sung in Portuguese but may include words of African origin. Often improvised, they are of several types, each one with a particular function: the *pontos de louvação* are used to salute spiritual entities, the owners of the house and the ancestors; the *pontos de visaria* or *bizarria* are sung for fun purposes, to enliven the dancers or as a vehicle for satirical commentaries; the *pontos de demanda, porfia,* or *gurumenta* are used by singers who challenge each other with riddles that must be deciphered by the opponent.

On the coffee plantations during the nineteenth century, jongos occupied an intermediate position between religious ceremony and secular diversion. Performed on weekends or on the eve of holidays, they were often the only form of entertainment available to the slaves, and also the only opportunity to perform forbidden African religious rites, even if disguised as profane dances. The use of African terms, combined with a rich metaphorical language, made jongo songs obscure to the white masters, thus providing a means for the expression of social criticism and cryptic messages from one slave to the others.

Slavery was abolished in 1888, and in the following decades many former slaves and their descendants moved to the cities of southeast Brazil, bringing jongo with them. In Rio de Janeiro, at the beginning of the twentieth century, jongos were performed regularly in several *favelas* (shantytowns) such as Salgueiro, Mangueira, and Serrinha. Because many of the founders of the first samba schools from Rio were also *jongueiros*, it is likely that jongo influenced the birth of samba as a modern, urban musical genre. This influence can be noticed, for example, in *partido-alto*, a subgenre of samba in which two or more singers challenge each other by means of improvised verses, and in the *cuíca* friction drum widely used in samba, probably a higher-pitched version of the ancient *puíta*. Though in the twentieth century jongo became essentially a profane diversion, it never lost completely its religious aspects, and is closely related to *umbanda*, a syncretic religion mixing African, Catholic, and spiritist beliefs born in the first decades of the twentieth century. Jongo and umbanda share a common cosmology, and many *jongueiros* are devout *umbandistas*.

Today, jongos continue to be performed by descendants of slaves in a least a dozen communities, in rural settings as well as in the periphery of cities. Since the 1990s jongo has experienced a revival and become more widely known as a hallmark of Afro-Brazilian culture. This was due largely to Darcy Monteiro (1932–2001), also known as Mestre Darcy do Jongo. A professional musician and heir of a traditional family of *jongueiros* from Serrinha, Rio de Janeiro, Mestre Darcy introduced jongo to a larger audience through recordings and concerts.

See also Capoeira; Dance, Diasporic

■ ■ *Bibliography*

Dias, Paulo. "A outra festa negra." In *Festa: cultura e sociabilidade na América Portuguesa,* edited by I. Jancsó and I. Kantor. São Paulo, Brazil: Hucitec/Edusp/Fapesp/Imprensa Oficial, 2001.

Ribeiro, Maria de Lourdes Borges. *O Jongo.* Rio de Janeiro, Brazil: FUNARTE/Instituto Nacional do Folclore, 1984.

Stein, Stanley J. *Vassouras: A Brazilian Coffee County.* 2d ed. Princeton, N.J.: Princeton University Press, 1985.

GUSTAVO PACHECO (2005)

JOPLIN, SCOTT
C. 1867
APRIL 1, 1917

■┃┃■─────────────

Born in eastern Texas, some 35 miles (56 kilometers) south of present-day Texarkana, to an ex-slave father and a freeborn mother, ragtime composer Joplin rose from humble circumstances to be widely regarded as the "King of Ragtime Composers." The frequently cited birth date of November 24, 1868, is incorrect; census records and his death certificate show that he was born between June 1, 1867, and mid-January, 1868.

In the early years of his career he worked with minstrel companies and vocal quartets, in bands as a cornetist, and as a pianist. His earliest published compositions (1895–1896) were conventional songs and marches. In 1894 he settled in Sedalia, Missouri, where he attended the George R. Smith College. His "Maple Leaf Rag" (1899), which memorializes a black social club in Sedalia, became the most popular piano rag of the era. By 1901 he was famous and moved to St. Louis, where he worked primarily as a composer.

Despite his success in ragtime, he wanted to compose for the theater. In 1903 he formed a company to stage his first opera, *A Guest of Honor* (now lost). He started on a tour through midwestern states in August 1903, but the box office receipts were stolen after an early performance. Out of money, he was unable to pay the troupe's boardinghouse bill and was forced to abandon his property, including the opera score, and he terminated the tour. He returned to St. Louis and resumed composing piano rags. In 1907 he moved to New York, where major music publishers were eager to issue his rags, but he still aspired to be a "serious" composer. In 1911 he completed and self-published his second opera, *Treemonisha,* in which he expressed the view that his race's problems were exacerbated by ignorance and superstition and could be overcome by education. He never succeeded in mounting a full production of this work.

Despite his efforts with larger musical forms, Joplin is today revered for his piano rags, these being the most sophisticated examples of the genre. His published output includes fifty-two piano pieces, of which forty-two are rags (including seven collaborations with younger colleagues); twelve songs; one instructional piece; and one opera. Several songs, rags, a symphony, and several stage works—his first opera, a musical, and a vaudeville—were never published and are lost.

A Joplin revival began in late 1970 when Nonesuch Records, a classical music label, issued a recording of Joplin rags played by Joshua Rifkin. For the record industry, this recording gave Joplin the status of a classical composer. This status was enhanced a year later when the New York Public Library issued the two-volume *Collected Works of Scott Joplin*. Thereafter, a number of classical concert artists included Joplin's music in their recitals. In 1972 his opera *Treemonisha* received its first full performance, staged in Atlanta in conjunction with an Afro-American Music Workshop at Morehouse College, and in 1975 the opera reached Broadway. (Joplin's orchestration is lost; there have been three modern orchestrations of the work—by T. J. Anderson, William Bolcom, and Gunther Schuller.) In 1974 the award-winning movie *The Sting* used several Joplin rags in its musical score, bringing Joplin to the attention of an even wider public. "The Entertainer" (1902), the film's main theme, became one of the most popular pieces of the mid-1970s. Further recognition of Joplin as an artist came in 1976 with a special Pulitzer Prize and in 1983 with a U.S. postage stamp bearing his image.

See also Opera; Musical Theater; Ragtime

■ ■ *Bibliography*

Berlin, Edward A. *King of Ragtime: Scott Joplin and His Era.* New York: Oxford University Press, 1994.

Haskins, James, and Kathleen Benson. *Scott Joplin.* Garden City, NY: Doubleday, 1978.

Ping-Robbins, Nancy R. *Scott Joplin: A Guide to Research.* New York and London: Garland Publishing, 1998.

EDWARD A. BERLIN (1996)
Updated bibliography

JORDAN, BARBARA

FEBRUARY 21, 1936
JANUARY 17, 1996

Congresswoman and professor Barbara Charline Jordan was born in Houston, Texas, the daughter of Arlyne Jordan and Benjamin M. Jordan, a Baptist minister. She spent her childhood in Houston and graduated from Texas Southern University in Houston in 1956. After receiving a law degree from Boston University in 1959, she was engaged briefly in private practice in Houston before becoming the administrative assistant for the county judge of Harris County, Texas, a post she held until 1966.

In 1962 and again in 1964, Jordan ran unsuccessfully for the Texas State Senate. In 1966, helped by the marked increase in African-American registered voters, she became the first black since 1883 elected to the Texas State Senate. The following year she became the first woman president of the Texas Senate. That year, redistricting opened a new district in Houston with a black majority. Jordan ran a strong campaign, and in 1972 she was elected to the U.S. House of Representatives from the district, becoming the first African-American woman elected to Congress from the South.

Jordan's short career as a high-profile congresswoman took her to a leadership role on the national level. In her first term she received an appointment to the House Judiciary Committee, where she achieved national recognition during the Watergate scandal, when in 1974 she voted for articles of impeachment against President Richard M. Nixon. A powerful public speaker, Jordan eloquently conveyed to the country the serious constitutional nature of the charges and the gravity with which the Judiciary Committee was duty-bound to address the issues. "My faith in the Constitution is whole, it is complete, it is total," she declared. "I am not going to sit here and be an idle spectator to the diminution, the subversion, the destruction of the Constitution."

Jordan spent six years in Congress, where she spoke out against the Vietnam War and high military expenditures, particularly those earmarked for support of the war. She supported environmental reform as well as measures to aid blacks, the poor, the elderly, and other groups on the margins of society. Jordan was a passionate campaigner for the Equal Rights Amendment and for grassroots citizen political action. Central to all of her concerns was a commitment to realizing the ideals of the Constitution.

Public recognition of her integrity, her legislative ability, and her oratorical excellence came from several quarters. Beginning in 1974 and for ten consecutive years, the *World Almanac* named her one of the twenty-five most influential women in America. *Time* magazine named her one of the Women of the Year in 1976. Her electrifying keynote address at the Democratic National Convention that year helped to solidify her stature as a national figure.

In 1978, feeling she needed a wider forum for her views than her congressional district, Jordan chose not to seek reelection. Returning to her native Texas, she accepted a professorship in the School of Public Affairs at the University of Texas at Austin in 1979, and beginning in 1982 she held the Lyndon B. Johnson Centennial Chair in Public Policy. Reflecting her interest in minority rights, in 1985 Jordan was appointed by the secretary-general of the United Nations to serve on an eleven-member commission charged with investigating the role of transnational corporations in South Africa and Namibia. In 1991 Texas governor Ann Richards appointed her "ethics guru," charged with monitoring ethics in the state's government. In 1992, although confined to a wheelchair by a degenerative disease, Jordan gave a keynote speech at the Democratic National Convention, again displaying the passion, eloquence, and integrity that had first brought her to public attention nearly two decades earlier.

In January 1996, two years after she received the Presidential Medal of Freedom, Jordan died. Her obituaries explained much that she had kept private during her lifetime, confirming that she had suffered from multiple sclerosis. They named her longtime companion and discussed her lesbianism.

After her death, a terminal at the Austin-Bergstrom International Airport in Austin was dedicated to Jordan, and in 2002 a seven-foot statue of Jordan was placed in the terminal.

See also Politics in the United States

■ ■ *Bibliography*

Haskins, James. *Barbara Jordan*. New York: Dial, 1977.

Rogers, Mary Beth. *Barbara Jordan: American Hero*. New York: Bantam, 1998.

CHRISTINE A. LUNARDINI (1996)
Updated by publisher 2005

JORDAN, JUNE

JULY 9, 1936
JUNE 14, 2002

Born in Harlem to Jamaican immigrants Granville and Mildred Jordan, writer June Jordan grew up in Brooklyn's Bedford-Stuyvesant, where poverty and racism were rampant. She absorbed quite early, as she records in the introduction to her first collection of essays, *Civil Wars* (1981), her community's belief in the power of the word. In her family, literature was important, so that by age seven she was writing poetry. She attended an exclusive New En-

gland white high school and went to Barnard College in 1953, both of which she found alienating experiences.

In college Jordan met Michael Meyer, a student at Columbia, whom she married in 1955. They had a son, Christopher David, in 1958 and were divorced by 1965, experiences she explores in later essays. In the 1960s Jordan, by then a single working mother, actively participated in and wrote about African-American political movements in New York City. Her first book-length publication, *Who Look at Me* (1969); her poems collected in *Some Changes* (1971); and her essays in *Civil Wars* (1995) exemplify her illumination of the political as intimate, the personal as political change, poetry as action—concepts central to all Jordan's work.

Jordan's writing workshop for Brooklyn children in 1965 resulted in the anthology *Voice of the Children* (1970) and anticipated her many books for children: *His Own Where* (1971), written in black English; *Dry Victories* (1972); *Fannie Lou Hamer* (1972); *New Life: New Room* and *Kimako's Story* (1981), while her organizing of poets in the 1960s resulted in the anthology *SoulScript Poetry* (1970). Her collaboration with Buckminster Fuller in 1964 to create an architectural design for Harlem indicates her concern with black urban environments, a theme evident in *His Own Where* and *New Life: New Room*. Jordan's work as an architect won her a Prix de Rome scholarship in 1970, a year she spent in Rome and Greece, geographical points for many poems in *New Days: Poems of Exile & Return* (1974).

Jordan's teaching at City College, New York City, and the State University of New York at Stony Brook were her starting points for theoretical essays on black English, of which she is remembered as a major analyst. Her reflections on her mother's suicide in 1966 were the genesis for black feminist poems such as "Getting Down to Get Over," in *Things That I Do in the Dark: Selected Poems* (1977). In the 1970s Jordan contributed to black feminism with major essays and poems. Her "Poem about My Rights" in *Passion: New Poems, 1977–80,* written while she was a professor at Yale University, also indicated her growing internationalism, as she related the rape of women to the rape of Third World countries by developed nations.

In the 1980s, through poetry in *Living Room* (1985) and *On Call: Political Essays* (1985), as well as *Naming Our Destiny* (1989), Jordan wrote about oppression in South Africa, Lebanon, Palestine, and Nicaragua as she widened her personal vision as an African-American woman to include more of the struggling world. The growth of her international audience was indicated by the translation of her work into many languages (including Arabic and Japanese), by British publications of *Lyrical Campaigns: Poems*

(1985) and *Moving Towards Home: Political Essays* (1989), and by recordings of her poems as sung by Sweet Honey in the Rock.

In 1978 and 1980 Jordan recorded her own poems, and in the 1980s she began writing plays, a genre she called "a living forum." Her play *The Issue* was produced in 1981. Jordan also widened her audience by being a regular columnist for the *Progressive* magazine.

In her writing, Jordan dramatized how life seems to be an increasing revelation of the "intimate face of universal struggle." Jordan began teaching at the University of California at Berkeley in 1986, and she taught there until her death in 2002 from breast cancer, a disease she had been fighting since the 1970s.

See also Poetry, U.S.

■ ■ *Bibliography*

Jordan, June. *Kissing God Goodbye: Poems, 1991–1997.* New York: Doubleday, 1997.

Jordan, June. *Soldier: A Poet's Childhood.* New York: Basic Books, 2001.

Freccero, Carla. "June Jordan." In *African American Writers*, edited by Lea Baechler and A. Walton Litz, pp. 245–261. New York: Scribner's, 1991.

BARBARA T. CHRISTIAN (1996)
Updated by publisher 2005

JORDAN, MICHAEL
FEBRUARY 17, 1963

Widely acknowledged as one of the greatest players in the history of the NBA, Michael Jeffrey Jordan was born in Brooklyn, New York, the fourth of James and Deloris Jordan's five children and the last of their three boys. He grew up in North Carolina, first in rural Wallace and later in Wilmington.

Jordan was released from the Laney High School varsity basketball team in his sophomore year. Even after an impressive junior season, he received only modest attention from major college basketball programs and chose to attend the University of North Carolina.

On March 29, 1982, the nineteen-year-old freshman sank the shot that gave his school a 63–62 victory over Georgetown and its first NCAA men's basketball championship in twenty-five years. Jordan followed that by winning the college Player of the Year award from the *Sporting*

News in each of the next two seasons. After announcing that he would enter the NBA draft after his junior season, he capped his amateur career by captaining the U.S. men's basketball team to a gold medal at the 1984 Olympic Games in Los Angeles.

Jordan was the third pick in the 1984 NBA draft, chosen by the woeful Chicago Bulls. The six-foot-six-inch guard immediately set about reversing their fortunes and was named the NBA Rookie of the Year after leading the team in scoring, rebounding, and assists.

After sitting out most of his second season with a broken foot, Jordan put on one of the greatest individual performances in postseason history, scoring 63 points in his first game back, a playoff loss to the Boston Celtics in 1986. The following season he scored 3,041 points—the most ever by a guard—and won the first of his six successive scoring titles, averaging 37.1 points per game. In 1987–1988 he became the first player ever to win the Most Valuable Player and Defensive Player of the Year awards in the same season.

Jordan's brilliance on the basketball court was nearly equaled by his success as a commercial spokesperson. Before his rookie season he signed with the Nike sneaker company to promote a signature shoe—the Air Jordan. The shoe was an instant success, establishing Jordan as a viable spokesperson. The commercials in which he starred with filmmaker Spike Lee helped make him a pop icon as well.

Early in his career, critics suggested that Jordan was not a "team" player. But he and the Bulls shook the one-man-team tag in 1990–1991 by defeating Earvin "Magic" Johnson and the Los Angeles Lakers in five games to win the franchise's first NBA championship. The following season, they defeated the Portland Trailblazers in six games to clinch another title, and in 1993 they again won the championship when they defeated the Phoenix Suns in six games.

Jordan was named the NBA's Most Valuable Player three times between 1988 and 1992. During that period he became the most successfully marketed player in the history of team sports, earning roughly sixteen million dollars in commercial endorsements in 1992 alone from such corporations as Nike, McDonald's, Quaker Oats (Gatorade), and General Mills (Wheaties). Even when controversy surrounded Jordan, as it did during the 1992 Olympic Games when he refused to wear a competing sponsor's uniform, or when he incurred sizable debts gambling on golf and poker, he regularly registered as one of the nation's most admired men and one of young people's most revered role models. Jordan's basketball career came to a sudden halt in October 1993 when he announced his retirement in a

Basketball great Michael Jordan, with Ted Leonsis (l) and Abe Pollin at a press conference in Washington, D.C., January 19, 2000. Jordan was named President of Basketball Operations for the Washington Wizards by owner Pollin, and joined Leonsis as an investor in the team. © REUTERS/CORBIS

nationally televised news conference. He said a diminishing love for the game, the pressures of celebrity, and the murder of his father three months earlier contributed to his decision. In February 1994 he signed with the Chicago White Sox of the American League, hoping to work his way up through the White Sox farm system to play Major League Baseball. Unhappy with the progress he was making, Jordan elected to resume his basketball career by returning to the Bulls in 1995.

Jordan quickly proved that he had lost none of his skill. The Bulls finished the season in 1996 with a new NBA won-loss record of 72–10, and went on to win the NBA championship. Jordan won the NBA Most Valuable Payer Award. The same year, Jordan starred in a popular semi-animated movie *Space Jam,* playing opposite Bugs Bunny. Jordan led the Bulls to NBA championships in each of the following two years, and in 1998 won his fifth MVP award. By this time, he was a worldwide celebrity, whose name was known even in countries where basketball is not played. By the end of 1998 Jordan had scored 29,277 points, third on the all-time NBA list, and was first in scoring average with 31.5 points per game. He spoke several times of retiring, but he had not made a definite statement before a player's strike postponed the resumption of NBA play.

On January 13, 1999, Michael Jordan announced his second retirement from basketball. He said on that occasion that he no longer had the desire to play. "Mentally, I'm exhausted," Jordan said. "I know from a career stand-

point I've accomplished everything I could as an individual. Right now, I just don't have the mental challenges that I've had in the past to proceed as a basketball player."

His retirement came after leading the Bulls to their sixth championship in eight seasons in June 1998. Jordan left with the highest career scoring average in the NBA's history. But he was unable to stay away from basketball. A year later he became part owner and president of basketball operations for the NBA's Washington Wizards, and in 2001 he returned to the court as a player-owner. He ended his playing days a third and final time at the end of the 2003 season.

See also Basketball; Olympians; Sports

■ ■ *Bibliography*

Leahy, Michael. *When Nothing Else Matters: Michael Jordan's Last Comeback.* New York: Simon and Schuster, 2004.

Naughton, Jim. *Talking to the Air: The Rise of Michael Jordan.* New York: Random House, 1992.

JIM NAUGHTON (1996)
Updated by publisher 2005

JORDAN, VERNON E., JR.

AUGUST 8, 1935

Born and raised in Atlanta, lawyer and civil rights leader Vernon Eulion Jordan Jr. lived until the age of thirteen in the University Homes Project, the first federally funded housing project in the country. He majored in political science at DePauw University in Indiana. After graduating in 1957 as the only African American in his class, he attended Howard University for his law degree (1960). In 1960 his home state of Georgia admitted him to the bar and he began work as a law clerk in the office of the eminent black civil rights attorney, Donald L. Hollowell. Jordan worked with Hollowell on the landmark 1961 desegregation suit that forced the University of Georgia to admit its first black students. The Georgia branch of the National Association for the Advancement of Colored People hired Jordan as its field secretary from 1961 to 1963. Beginning in 1965, Jordan headed the Voter Education Project (VEP) of the Southern Regional Council, which succeeded in registering approximately two million black voters.

In 1969 Jordan was appointed a fellow of the Institute of Politics at Harvard University's Kennedy School of

Government, and the next year he was named executive director of the United Negro College Fund, where he continued to hone his fund-raising skills. In 1972 he became executive director of the National Urban League. With monies raised from the corporate sector, as well as federal grants, Jordan doubled the size of the league's operating budget and undertook programs in housing, health, education, and job training. He also inaugurated league programs in the areas of energy and the environment. In 1975 Jordan began a policy review journal, *The Urban League Review,* and the next year instituted an annual report, *The State of Black America.*

On May 29, 1980, while returning to his hotel in Fort Wayne, Indiana, following a speech, Jordan was shot in the back by a sniper. He spent more than ninety days in the hospital, but despite his near-fatal wounds, he recovered fully. In August 1982 Joseph Paul Franklin was brought to trial in federal court on charges of violating Jordan's civil rights (Indiana authorities did not file attempted murder charges). Franklin, an avowed racist, had been convicted earlier in 1982 of the murder of two black joggers, a crime for which he was serving four consecutive life sentences. He was nevertheless acquitted of violating Jordan's civil rights.

On December 31, 1981, Jordan resigned his position at the Urban League. While Jordan claimed that he had planned to serve for only ten years, his resignation was widely seen as having been influenced by his attempted assassination. Soon thereafter, he accepted a position as partner in the powerful Washington, D.C., law firm of Akin, Gump, Strauss, Hauer & Feld. He also served on a number of corporate and foundation boards throughout the 1980s and early 1990s. His lucrative corporate and lobbying activities have been controversial among civil rights activists, who have accused him of forsaking the black struggle for personal advantage. Jordan's defenders have responded by pointing to his private lobbying of business and government, notably for the 1991 Civil Rights Act. A close adviser of President Bill Clinton, Jordan headed the president-elect's transition team in 1993, though he refused the office of U.S. attorney general.

Over the following years, Jordan was a visible "first friend," golfing and vacationing with the president and functioning as a behind-the-scenes adviser. In March 1998 Jordan testified to a grand jury investigating Clinton's sexual relationship with Monica Lewinsky that he had helped find Lewinsky a job and a lawyer.

In 2001 Jordan published his autobiography, *Vernon Can Read!: A Memoir.* In addition, Jordan led the negotiating team for Senator John Kerry in setting up a series of debates with President George W. Bush in the 2004 presidential election campaign.

See also National Association for the Advancement of Colored People (NAACP); National Urban League; United Negro College Fund

■ ■ *Bibliography*

"Jordan, Vernon." *Current Biography,* August 1993, pp. 25–29.

Jordan, Vernon E., Jr., with Annette Gordon-Read. *Vernon Can Read!: A Memoir.* New York: Public Affairs, 2001.

Pertman, Adam. "Vernon Jordan: No. 1 FOB on Martha's Vineyard." *Boston Globe,* August 25, 1993, p. 53.

Williams, Marjorie. "Clinton's Mr. Inside." *Vanity Fair* 56 (March 1993): 172–175.

PETER SCHILLING (1996)
Updated by publisher 2005

JORDON, EDWARD

DECEMBER 6, 1800
FEBRUARY 8, 1869

■ ■ ■

Edward Jordon, a free colored (of mixed African and European ancestry), was born in Jamaica's slave society. His father, also named Edward and colored, came from Barbados, where his progressive views had alienated him from the white planter class. Jordon's mother, Grace, was likely a local free colored.

Edward Jordon belonged to the urban middle group of free colored artisans and professionals, who, although more privileged than the mass of enslaved peoples, were barred from enjoying basic civil rights because of their nonwhite status. Accordingly, they could not vote, give evidence in their own defense, nor hold public offices, and in a society where landed property guaranteed status and privilege, the extent of property they could inherit was restricted.

Jordon grew to manhood during a period of great upheaval in the history of the Americas, as the established order of slavery and colonial domination was being challenged by the Haitian Revolution and the independence struggles in Spanish America. From 1793 to 1830 these developments, as well as the growing abolitionist tide in Britain, had emboldened the Jamaican free coloreds, who determinedly campaigned for the acquisition of the civil liberties enjoyed by whites in the slave society.

After a short period as an apprentice tailor, Jordon worked as a clerk in a Kingston mercantile establishment and joined the free colored campaign for civil rights when he was twenty, but he was dismissed from his job because of his political sentiments. After a short stint as a liquor retailer, he switched to printing and journalism, and with his close friend and lifetime political ally, Robert Osoborn, Jordon opened a bookstore in Kingston. Further, in 1828 they established the *Watchman and Jamaica Free Press,* a newspaper that vigorously supported the campaign of the free coloreds who were victorious in 1830, and also championed the abolition of slavery that came in 1834.

In the postslavery period, Jordon abandoned his radical profile and transformed the *Watchman* into the more moderate *Morning Journal,* which consistently supported policies for incremental change. In the assembly, where he represented Kingston from 1834 to 1864, Jordon was the leader of the colored professionals who regarded themselves as Creole "nationalists" who opposed the planters' reactionary programs. In 1861 he was the first nonwhite to be elected speaker of the assembly, and in 1854 he was the first colored man to be elected mayor of Kingston. He also held senior administrative positions that previously had been the exclusive preserve of whites. Accordingly, he was appointed to the Legislative Council in 1852, and in 1864 he was appointed receiver general, then island secretary in 1865.

Jordon's career underscored the coloreds' expanding social and political influence. This alarmed the white planter and mercantile classes, and in their hysteria after the Morant Bay rebellion in 1865, they surrendered Jamaica's near two-hundred-year-old representative constitution and embraced the introduction of crown colony government in 1866, thereby snuffing out all elements of elected politics and reintroducing the practice that barred coloreds from holding senior administrative posts.

Edward Jordon died in 1869, disappointed and embittered by this reactionary development in Jamaica's governance structure. In 1875 his statue, commissioned by his admirers to mark his struggles against racial discrimination, was unveiled in Kingston.

See also Free Blacks, 1619-1860; Haitian Revolution; Morant Bay Rebellion

■ ■ *Bibliography*

Heuman, Gad. *Between Black and White: Race, Politics, and the Free Coloreds in Jamaica, 1792–1865.* Westport, Conn.: Greenwood Press, 1981.

Campbell, Mavis. *The Dynamics of Change in a Slave Society: A Sociopolitical History of the Free Coloreds of Jamaica, 1800–1865.* Rutherford, N.J.: Farleigh Dickinson University Press, 1975.

SWITHIN WILMOT (2005)

JOSHUA, EBENEZER

MAY 23, 1908
MARCH 14, 1991

■ ■ ■ ─────────────

The prominent Caribbean political leader Ebenezer Theodore Joshua was born in Kingstown, the capital city of Saint Vincent and the Grenadines. He received an elementary school education, participated in overseas matriculation exercises, and worked as a primary school teacher, then as a lawyer's clerk, before migrating to other parts of the Caribbean. He ended up in Trinidad, where he became enamored of the politics of Tubal Uriah Butler, a charismatic Caribbean leader for whose party Joshua performed creditably in the national elections of 1950.

Returning to Saint Vincent in 1951, Joshua was invited to join the United Workers and Rate Payers Union, which was about to launch a political assault on colonial Saint Vincent using the leverage that adult suffrage offered. He became part of the union's Eighth Army of Liberation, a political party that captured all eight seats in the first elections held under universal adult suffrage in 1951. Joshua won a seat for the North Windward constituency.

Joshua broke away from the Eighth Army in 1952 and formed the People's Political Party (PPP), which included a trade-union wing, the Federated Industrial and Agricultural Workers Union (FIAWU). Using the vehicle of the PPP-FIAWU, Joshua emerged as a powerful figure who bestrode the political stage during a critical time in the development of the country. His contributions to the shaping and molding of modern Saint Vincent and the Grenadines are incalculable. "Papa Josh," as he was known, was active in political service from 1951 to 1979, a period that began with the establishment of adult suffrage and ended with independence.

Joshua's political career can be neatly divided into three periods: 1951 to 1960, 1961 to 1970, and 1971 to 1979. His greatest achievement occurred during the first period, when he lifted the level of political awareness of the person-in-the-street, raising social consciousness to new heights. But when confronted by stark choices, the second phase saw Joshua reneging on his early promise, seeking out the lines of weakest resistance, and setting himself on a course leading to decline, which accelerated in the third period of his career, as the integrity and fortunes of the PPP took a turn for the worst and the leadership finally lost all credibility.

During the 1950s Joshua was in his element. He acted as the tribune of the people, championing their every cause. Living the simplest of lives, he rode his bicycle and,

ENCYCLOPEDIA *of* AFRICAN~AMERICAN CULTURE *and* HISTORY
second edition

with his wife Ivy, walked from village to village preaching the gospel of anticolonial politics and spreading the word of militant trade unionism. Joshua held regular Wednesday night meetings in Kingstown, hammering home his message by constant repetition. For their part, the people of Saint Vincent and the Grenadines enjoyed Joshua's style, as on their behalf he stood up to the colonial authorities and defiantly twisted the tail of the establishment. Joshua remained in constant touch with the grassroots, taking the pulse of the people and keeping his ear to the ground. One afternoon he would be at Mount Bentick pleading the cause of sugar workers; the next morning he would be at Richmond, "opening" an arrowroot field.

From 1957 to 1961, Joshua concentrated on infrastructural development. A road and school building program, together with the Arnos Vale Airport, bear eloquent testimony to his efforts. After 1960, Joshua denounced socialism and became more business-oriented, self-centered, and even corrupt, as evidenced by the public works scandal, the waiving of ministers' income tax, and the issues surrounding the deep water pier.

The PPP-FIAWU became riddled with internal strife, and Joshua became more conservative and repressive. Among other things, Joshua made a mockery of the affairs of the Kingstown Town Board and resorted to unfair control of the streets in order to hold demonstrations to camouflage from the public his reversal of fortunes. He helped to create an unsavory political climate during the country's approach to independence.

After statehood was achieved in 1979, the PPP's fortunes dipped more sharply as Joshua struggled for political survival. He began to fear the influence of communists, and he cast aspersions on the burgeoning black consciousness movement of the early 1970s. Finally, in desperation, he began to cast about indiscriminately for allies to his cause.

First, in 1972, he joined with James F. Mitchell, who would later organize the New Democratic Party and serve four terms as prime minister, purely as a tactic to buy time and keep the Labour Party at bay. Then, in 1974 Joshua caused consternation among his political associates and panic in his rank-and-file supporters when, without consulting them, he abandoned Mitchell and jettisoned some of his most loyal and devoted followers to enter the PPP into an alliance with the Labour Party, which for the previous twenty-five years he had represented as a malevolent adversary. Three years later, Joshua, who had stood foremost in the vanguard of the movement for self-determination, broke with Labour on the pretext that the country was not yet ready for independence.

In the 1979 elections, held three months after independence was granted, the PPP failed to win a seat, with Joshua himself suffering ignominious defeat in the former PPP bastion of South Central Windward. Six months later, drained and battle-weary, he threw in his political towel.

The story of Joshua represents a classic case of a populist leader whose hold over his people loosened as his charisma waned and his gift of grace wore thin. Joshua left behind few concrete structures, and he did not even leave a functioning political party, for the PPP was but an extension of his own personality and could not survive him.

But for all his weaknesses and shortcomings, Joshua, during the final stage of colonialism, bestirred the ordinary person out of his lethargy, making him alive to his dignity as a worker and assertive of his rights as a person. Joshua, in effect, awoke a slumbering giant who would not go back to sleep. For that, he is assured a place in the pantheon of Vincentian heroes.

See also Butler, Uriah; Politics and Politicians in the Caribbean

KENNETH JOHN (2005)

JOURNALISM

Faced with the challenge of seeking just treatment in a society that systematically restricted the lives of freepeople as well as slaves, African Americans began publishing their own periodicals long before the Civil War, using their words as weapons in a protracted struggle for equality. The crusading editors of early black newspapers comprised an intellectual vanguard with a five-pronged mission: (1) to define the identity of a people who had been stripped of their own culture in a hostile environment; (2) to create a sense of unity by establishing a network of communication among literate blacks and their white supporters throughout the country; (3) to examine issues from a black perspective; (4) to chronicle black achievements that were ignored by the American mainstream; and (5) to further the cause of black liberation.

These objectives, set forth by the founders of one of the oldest black institutions in the United States, underscored the activities of African-American journalists for nearly 150 years. When blacks began to move into the mainstream during the latter part of the twentieth century, assuming positions on general-circulation newspapers and in the broadcast media, many retained a sense of being linked to a larger racial cause. Often they were torn by conflicting loyalties. Were they blacks first or journalists first? Should they strive for respect in the mainstream by

Front page of the New York Age, **Thursday, May 11, 1911.** *Founded by T. Thomas Fortune as the* New York Freeman *in 1884, the* Age *was one of the leading black newspapers in New York City during the first half of the twentieth century.* MANUSCRIPTS, ARCHIVES AND RARE BOOKS DIVISION, SCHOMBURG CENTER FOR RESEARCH IN BLACK CULTURE, THE NEW YORK PUBLIC LIBRARY, ASTOR, LENOX AND TILDEN FOUNDATIONS.

avoiding stories dealing with black topics, or fill in the gaps of coverage that might be left by white reporters? Should they follow the journalistic rule that calls for objectivity and report even events that might be damaging to blacks, or be mindful of the effects their stories might have on attitudes toward African Americans? It was a measure of social change that no such questions would have entered the minds of their predecessors.

ORIGINS

The first African-American newspaper, *Freedom's Journal,* was founded in New York City on March 16, 1827, in response to the persistent attacks on blacks by a proslavery white paper, the *New York Enquirer.* The purpose of this pioneering publication was to encourage enlightenment and to enable blacks in the various states to exchange ideas. Thus it provided a forum for debate on issues that swirled around the institution of slavery. Among these was the question of whether blacks should strive for full citi-

zenship and assimilation in America—a view favored by most blacks at that time—or whether they should follow a course of separation and opt for resettlement in Africa, a position then held mostly by whites who saw this as a way to rid the country of troublesome free blacks.

The two founding editors of *Freedom's Journal* were educated and accomplished freemen who stood on opposite sides of the colonization question. Samuel E. Cornish, an ordained minister who had organized the first African Presbyterian church in the United States, thought blacks should fight for integration in America, while the Jamaican-born John B. Russwurm, who was the nation's second black college graduate (from Bowdoin College) supported repatriation in a part of West Africa that became Liberia. But they were united in their opposition to slavery and appetite for discussion. They clearly set forth their mission in the first issue of *Freedom's Journal,* stating: "We wish to plead our own cause. Too long have others spoken for us. . . . From the press and the pulpit we have suffered much by being incorrectly represented."

Six months later, when their differences over the colonization issue proved insurmountable, Cornish left. Russwurm continued publishing the paper until March 28, 1829. He then settled in Liberia where he remained until his death in 1851, at one time editing a newspaper called *The Liberia Herald*

Two months after Russwurm's departure, Cornish resurrected *Freedom's Journal* on May 29, 1829, changing its name to *The Rights of All* and infusing it with a more militant tone; publication was suspended on October 9 of the same year. Though Cornish was active in the antislavery and black convention movements, he was driven toward journalism. In 1837 he became editor of Philip A. Bell's newspaper, the *Weekly Advocate.* Two months after its debut, the paper was renamed the *Colored American* and was published until 1842. Although the paper was based in New York, there is evidence that a Philadelphia edition also was produced, making it possibly the first African-American publication to serve more than one city with different editions. Scholars of the early black press have noted the quality and originality of the *Colored American,* which was uncompromising in its call for black unity and full citizenship rights for all.

After these first steps had been taken, others began using journalism to establish communication links in a largely illiterate nation and to generate support in the struggle against slavery. While most of these papers were based in New York, the *Alienated American* was launched in Cleveland on April 9, 1853. Martin R. Delany, the first black graduate of Harvard, published his own newspaper, the *Mystery,* in Pittsburgh before he became assistant editor of Frederick Douglass's *North Star*. Other outstanding early publications were Stephen Myer's *Elevator* (Albany, New York, 1842), Thomas Hamilton's *Anglo-American* (New York, 1843), and William Wells Brown's *Rising Sun* (New York, 1847).

The first black newspaper to be published in the South before the Civil War was the *Daily Creole,* which surfaced in New Orleans in 1856 but bowed to white pressure in assuming an anti-abolitionist stance. It was followed near the end of the Civil War by the *New Orleans Tribune,* which appeared in July 1864 and is considered the first daily black newspaper. Published three times a week in both English and French, it was an official organ of Louisiana's Republican Party, then the nation's progressive political wing. The *Tribune* called for bold measures to redress the grievances of bondage, including universal suffrage and payment of weekly wages to ex-slaves.

Most of these newspapers depended on the personal resources of their publishers along with contributions from white sympathizers to supplement the meager income from subscriptions, but prosperous blacks also lent their support. A notable "angel" of the period was James Forten, a Philadelphia veteran of the American Revolution who had amassed a fortune as a sail manufacturer. Forten was a major backer of William Lloyd Garrison, a white journalist who became one of the leading voices in the abolitionist movement through his newspaper the *Liberator,* first published on January 1, 1831.

Of the forty or so black newspapers published before the Civil War, the most influential was the *North Star,* founded and edited by Frederick Douglass in Rochester, New York, on November 1, 1847. The name was that of the most brilliant star in the night sky, Polaris, a reference point for escaping slaves as they picked their way northward to freedom. Douglass is an important historical figure, often not regarded primarily as a journalist, but he, like the black leaders who would follow him, knew how to use the press as a weapon. In the prospectus announcing his new publication, he wrote: "The object of the *North Star* will be to attack slavery in all its forms and aspects; advocate Universal Emancipation; exact the standard of public morality; promote the moral and intellectual improvement of the colored people; and to hasten the day of freedom to our three million enslaved fellow countrymen." Thus he defined the thrust of the early black press.

A PERIOD OF TRANSITION

The number of black newspapers increased dramatically after the end of the Civil War in 1965, as the newly emancipated struggled to survive with no resources and few guaranteed rights. Publications sprang up in states where none had previously existed. Armistead S. Pride, the leading scholar on the black press, determined in the mid-twentieth century that African Americans had published 575 newspapers or periodicals by 1890, the end of the Reconstruction period. Although most were short-lived and many were religious or political publications rather than regular newspapers, some survived—notably the *Philadelphia Tribune,* which was founded in 1884 and continues to be published. It is considered the oldest continuously published black newspaper in the United States. This period also marks the beginning of the *Afro-American,* which originated as a four-page Baptist Church publication in Baltimore on August 13, 1892. After several metamorphoses, it became the highly respected anchor of a nationally distributed newspaper chain.

This heightened journalistic activity was the result of many factors, among them an increase in literacy and greater mobility on the part of blacks, though their position in society as a whole was hardly satisfactory. When federal troops were withdrawn from the South in 1877 as a matter of political expediency, African Americans were left to the mercy of bitter whites who had fought to deny them freedom. Slavery was replaced by the economic bondage of sharecropping. White dominance was sustained through a system of rigidly enforced segregation and terrorism, including lynching, the random torture and hanging of blacks. When southern blacks fled to northern cities in the first wave of the Great Migration, they found themselves trapped in squalid ghettos with few opportunities for work except in the most menial jobs. For these reasons, the black press was still fueled by the spirit of protest, though that spark often had to be veiled.

The pattern for race relations in America had been set in 1895 when Booker T. Washington, a former slave who had founded Tuskegee Institute, a school providing vocational education for blacks, went before the Cotton States' Exposition in Atlanta and proclaimed that it was folly for blacks to seek equal rights: They should pull themselves up by their own bootstraps and make the best of things as they were, getting along with whites by being patient, hardworking, subservient, and unresentful. In one of the most famous metaphors of American history, Washington raised his hand and declared: "In all things that are purely social, we can be as separate as the fingers, yet one as the hand in all things essential to mutual progress." Such rhetoric, calling for a separate but not necessarily equal society, condoned the conservative mood of the era. Ordained by whites to speak for blacks, because of his "Atlanta compromise" Washington came to wield extraordinary power. It extended to the press, as black publishers struggled to keep their papers alive. Most had a small subscription base and

December, 1921   15 cts. a copy.

The MESSENGER

EDITED BY
A. PHILIP RANDOLPH
AND
CHANDLER OWEN

Harding at Birmingham

Cover of **The Messenger,** *December 1921. Black labor leader A. Philip Randolph (1889–1979) founded this socialist journal with his friend Chandler Owen in 1917.* MANUSCRIPTS, ARCHIVES AND RARE BOOKS DIVISION, SCHOMBURG CENTER FOR RESEARCH IN BLACK CULTURE, THE NEW YORK PUBLIC LIBRARY, ASTOR, LENOX AND TILDEN FOUNDATIONS.

advertising was hard to come by. Therefore, they were inordinately dependent on contributions. Washington's critics said that he exercised undue influence over the black press by controlling loans, advertisements, and political subsidies, making certain that his doctrine prevailed.

The journalist most commonly associated with Washington is T. Thomas Fortune, who was editor of he *New York Age* during a period when Washington controlled it financially and used the paper as a conduit for presentation of his views, though Fortune did not share them. Respected as an accomplished writer with a sharp satiric style, Fortune was one of the first of his race to hold an editorial position on a white daily, writing for the *New York Sun* and the *Evening Sun,* leading turn-of-the-century newspapers. Before assuming control of the *Age,* Fortune had published two newspapers of his own, the *Globe* and the *Freeman,* which were considered the best of their type. The *Age* had grown out of a tabloid called the *Rumor,* established in 1890.

Fortune was an activist who thoroughly opposed Washington's willing acquiescence to racism and used the

Age to promulgate his own ideas. He extolled black pride before the arrival of the twentieth century, urging that the term Afro-American be used instead of "negro," then usually spelled with a lowercase *n*. Disdaining political patronage and declaring himself as independent, he had to get along without the political advertising that was the main source of income for black newspapers. As a result, Fortune had to rely increasingly on contributions from Booker T. Washington, who eventually purchased the *Age.* Obliged to write editorials espousing Washington's views, Fortune responded by presenting his own opinions in opposing editorials in the same edition. Researchers credit Fortune with having written or edited all of Washington's books and many of his speeches, but Washington never acknowledged him. Torn by the compromises he was forced to make, Fortune succumbed to mental illness and poverty during the latter part of his career, but he has been called the dean of black journalism.

A few intrepid journalists refused to accept a state of such uneasy compromise. Ida B. Wells-Barnett transcended gender by risking her life to expose racially motivated crimes. She was a teacher in the rural schools of Mississippi and later Tennessee, when she began writing exposés about injustices in the education system. Turning to journalism on a full-time basis, she became part owner and editor of the *Memphis Free Speech.* In May 1892, when three black Memphis businessmen were lynched after a white mob attacked their grocery store, Wells-Barnett charged in her paper that the murders had been instigated by the white business community and called for a boycott of those white businesses. She also wrote that she had purchased a pistol and would use it to protect herself. While Wells-Barnett was out of town to attend a convention, her newspaper office and the building that housed it were burned down. She relocated to New York, where she continued her crusade in Fortune's *New York Age,* of which she became a part owner. She later published extensive documentation of lynchings in *Redbook* magazine, a leading mainstream publication.

Washington's accommodationist views still prevailed at the arrival of the twentieth century, but a more militant tone was set when William Monroe Trotter founded the *Boston Guardian* in 1901 with George Forbes. Both had graduated from college in 1895, Trotter from Harvard and Forbes from Amherst. Trotter quickly became the main force on the paper. The product of an interracial marriage, he had grown up comfortably in a Boston suburb. At Harvard, he had become the first African American inducted into the honor society Phi Beta Kappa and went on to earn his M.A. degree there in 1896. Unwilling to accept any sort of compromise, he demanded absolute equality for blacks and used his paper to consolidate the first organized opposition to Washington and his ideas. Trotter joined with another son of Massachusetts, W. E. B. Du Bois—who is considered by many to be the greatest intellectual produced by black America—in laying groundwork for the Niagara Movement, the forerunner of the National Association for the Advancement of Colored People (NAACP). Trotter then disdained the NAACP for being too little, too late, and too white. He carried the fight for black rights to the international arena, going be fore the League of Nations and the World Peace Conference in Paris, to no avail. Disillusioned and ill, Trotter either jumped or fell to his death from the roof of his Boston home in 1934, when he was sixty-two years old. But he had sounded a defiant note that set the tone for further development of the black press throughout the twentieth century.

Early black newspapers bore little resemblance to their modern counterparts. From the beginning, they had not been intended as instruments of mass communication. They were aimed at a small, educated elite and emphasized commentary over news coverage. Editors exchanged copies of their publications by mail and engaged in debates over issues, with the responses appearing in their next editions. It was assumed that subscribers also read white publications and thus were informed on national events. Yet these papers filled a void by interpreting the news from a black perspective and noting developments of particular interest to African Americans, providing information that was not available elsewhere. This included local coverage of religious and social events, still a mainstay of black newspapers.

GROWTH AND POWER

The modern black press did not come into being until 1905, when Robert S. Abbott founded the *Chicago Defender,* the first African-American newspaper designed to appeal to the masses and, consequently, the first commercially successful black journalistic enterprise. Although Abbott's sole objective was to improve the plight of blacks in America, he realized that he would have to communicate with the common people if he were to help them. In this respect Abbott followed the imperatives that have shaped daily newspapers since the beginning of the twentieth century. It has been assumed, for the most part, that a publication first must capture the attention of the largest number of potential readers by playing up stories that generate immediate interest. Abbott took particular note of the practices of William Randolph Hearst, who had built the largest journalistic empire of the early twentieth century by engaging in sensationalism to boost sales. But in spite of the screaming red headlines and excited tone that

came to mark the *Defender's* style, the paper, at its core, held to the same precepts that have informed black journalism since its inception.

A small, very black man who suffered the indignities imposed on those of his color during a period when dark skin was considered a major social liability even among African Americans, Abbott was a Georgian who settled in Chicago where he decided to publish his own newspaper, although three other black newspapers already were being distributed there. According to Roi Ottley, Abbott's biographer, the publisher started out in a rented room with nothing but a card table, a borrowed chair, and twenty-five cents in capital, intent on producing his newspaper. Abbott, who had a law degree, called it the *Defender* because he intended to fight for the rights of black people. At that time the black population of Chicago was concentrated in so few blocks on the South Side that Abbott could gather the news, sell advertising, and distribute his newspaper on foot by himself. That was a situation he was to change with his paper.

At first Abbott avoided politics and other contentious topics, featuring neighborhood news and personals, but he hit his stride when he began to concentrate on muckraking, publishing exposés of prostitution and other criminal activities in the black community. Adopting the scarlet headlines favored by his white counterparts, Abbott developed a publication so popular that copies were posted in churches and barbershops where blacks congregated, so that the latest stories could be read aloud.

One of the factors that contributed to Abbott's early success was increasing literacy among blacks. By 1910 seven out of ten blacks over the age of ten could read and Chicago's black population had grown to 44,103, though still concentrated in a small area. In 1910, when the *Defender* was in its fifth year, Abbott hired his first paid employee, J. Hockley Smiley, an editor who moved the paper more decidedly toward sensationalism and encouraged the publisher to press for national circulation. White distributors refused to carry black newspapers, but Chicago was a major railroad center, so Smiley suggested that railroad porters and waiters be used to carry bundles of papers to their destinations, smuggling them into the South, where they could be turned over to local black agents. In turn, the railroad workers brought back news, enabling the *Defender* to become the first black publication with a truly national scope. To shore up this thrust, Abbott employed Roscoe Conkling Simmons, a leading narrator, to tour the country, promoting the paper. Since the stance of the *Defender* was militant, with detailed accounts of injustices committed against blacks, participants in this underground distribution system courted danger. Two agents were killed and others were driven from their homes because of their involvement with the *Defender*. Yet Abbott did not back down, engaging the redoubtable Ida B. Wells-Barnett to report on riots, lynchings, and other racial wrongs.

Abbott found his place in history in 1917, during World War I, when he began to publish front-page stories with blazing headlines urging southern blacks to migrate to the North, where they could escape from the indignities of Dixie and acquire higher-paying jobs in industry. The paper offered group railroad rates to migrants and encouraged them to seek personal advice on how to adjust to the big city by following the *Defender's* regular features. Scholars credit the *Defender* with being a major force in stimulating the tide of northern migration after the war, when blacks realized that the rights U.S. soldiers had fought for abroad were not being extended to them at home. More than 300,000 African Americans migrated to the great industrial cities of the North between 1916 and 1918, with 110,000 moving to Chicago alone, tripling the city's black population.

By 1920, the *Defender* claimed its peak circulation of 283,571, with an additional high pass-along rate. Unlike those struggling earlier black publishers, Abbott became a millionaire, moving into his own fully paid-for half-million-dollar plant on Chicago's South Side. With a broad-based national circulation, the *Defender* offered hope and inspiration to poor southern blacks like the young Johnny Johnson, who read the paper as a youth in his native Arkansas during the early 1930s and son moved north with his family to Chicago, where he would build his own publishing empire. Though the paper eventually declined in popularity, due to its failure to keep up with the growing sophistication of blacks, it is still being published. When Abbott died in 1940, one of his nephews, John H. Sengstacke, assumed leadership. In 1956 he converted the *Defender* into a daily; it appeared four times a week with an additional weekend edition.

While Abbott carved out his empire from Chicago, some resourceful publishers in other parts of the country also built journalistic enterprises that cumulatively developed into one of the most powerful institutions in black America.

At least a dozen black newspapers had come and gone in Pittsburgh by 1910, when the lawyer Robert L. Vann drew up incorporation papers for the *Pittsburgh Courier*, a fledgling publication he edited and eventually came to own. Born impoverished in 1879 in Ahoskie, North Carolina, Vann struggled for years to get an education, finally earning both baccalaureate and law degrees from the Western University of Pennsylvania, later renamed the University of Pittsburgh. A relatively small man, like Abbott, he was encouraged by friends to pass for an East Indian because he had straight hair and keen features, but Vann remained staunchly black. Though the *Courier* managed to survive, it did not gain much momentum until 1914, when Ira F. Lewis joined the staff as a sportswriter. He turned out to be a gifted salesman who built advertising and circulation, going on to become business manager of the paper and transforming it into a national institution.

In its editorial tone, the *Pittsburgh Courier* tended to be somewhat less sensational than the *Defender*, commanding attention with its distinctive peach-colored cover page. In front-page editorials, Vann led his crusades, demanding that the huge industrial firms hire African Americans and criticizing unions for denying blacks membership, while the European immigrants who were surging into the labor market were accepted in both cases. He called for better education and housing for blacks and urged them to boycott movie houses and stores that overcharged them or treated them disrespectfully.

A local publication during its early years, the *Courier* began to make national inroads during the 1920s, when Vann improved its quality by retaining some of the most talented black journalists of the period. George S. Schuyler, a figure of the Harlem Renaissance who was called the black H. L. Mencken because of his bitingly satiric prose, began contributing a weekly column and became the chief editorial writer, a position he held for several decades. Schuyler also toured the nation to produce extensive series on the socioeconomic status of black America.

Vann sent Joel A. Rogers, a self-taught historian, to Europe and Africa, where he documented black contributions to Western civilization. Rogers later produced a column called "Your History" and collaborated with an artist on a weekly illustrated feature that stimulated pride among blacks, who had been denied evidence of prior achievements by their race. When Italy invaded Ethiopia in 1935, Rogers became one of the first black war correspondents by covering the conflict from the front. His colorful dispatches captured the attention of African Americans throughout the United States and thus boosted circulation.

Sparkling entertainment and social news were staples, but the *Courier's* forte was its sports coverage. Excellent reportage was provided by W. Rollo Wilson, William G. Nunn Sr., Wendell Smith, and Chester "Ches" Washington, a championship speed typist who went on in the 1970s to become the successful publisher of a chain of newspapers in California. The *Courier* secured its national stature during the 1930s by recognizing the potential of a young pugilist named Joe Louis and maintaining a virtual monopoly on coverage of his activities until long after Louis had become the most popular heavyweight champion in history. As a result, circulation reached 250,000 by 1937, according to figures of the Audit Bureau of Circulation, making the *Courier* competitive with the *Defender* as the nation's leading black weekly.

It was a role of the nation's top black newspapers to bridge the gap separating artists and intellectuals from the masses. The *Defender* published the early poems of the young Chicagoan Gwendolyn Brooks, who would become the first African American to win a Pulitzer Prize, and employed Willard Motley as a youth editor long before he became a best-selling novelist. The poet and humorist Langston Hughes introduced his character Jesse B. Semple (Simple) in its pages. Similarly, the *Courier* featured commentary and reviews by James Weldon Johnson, while W. E. B. Du Bois wrote a column for the paper after he stepped down as editor of the *Crisis,* the official magazine of the NAACP.

Unlike Abbott, who relished his ties to the man in the street and especially fellow migrants from the South, Vann was an aloof, politically driven man who used his paper to promote his own career as a lawyer and to seek control of black patronage. He is perhaps best known for his defection from the Republican Party, which had claimed the loyalties of black voters since the time of Abraham Lincoln. Democrats were strongly identified with their party's southern segregationist faction. By 1932 the country was in the throes of an economic depression and the yet untried Franklin D. Roosevelt was the Democratic presidential candidate. Vann, who thought that the Republicans had taken the black vote for granted without responding to the needs of that constituency, delivered a speech that projected him to national prominence. Calling for the black vote to remain "liquid" rather than allied to a single party, he said, "I see millions of Negroes turning the picture of Lincoln to the wall." The line became a catchphrase in the successful Democratic campaign to get black votes and win the election.

Vann died in 1940, seven months after Robert S. Abbott. Yet he established so firm a foundation for the *Courier* that it retained its popularity for several more years under the management of Ira Lewis, with the publisher's widow, Jesse L. Vann, at the helm. Under editors P. L. Prattis and William G. Nunn, Sr., the crusades continued, with calls for integration of the armed forces during World War II and a "double V" campaign for victory abroad and against discrimination at home. In 1946 the *Courier* published fourteen editions, including local and national editions with branch offices in twelve cities, and was the most

popular black publication even in several cities with their own black newspapers. It attained a circulation of 357,212 in May 1947, a record for audited black newspapers.

Some of the paper's crusades had tangible results. *Courier* sportswriter Wendell Smith, who had been using his column to press for integration of major league baseball since the 1920s, served as the liaison between Jackie Robinson and Branch Rickey, general manager of the Brooklyn Dodgers, resulting in Robinson's joining that team in 1947.

After the death of Ira Lewis in 1948, the *Courier* lapsed into a general decline because of mismanagement and numerous other factors that affected the black press in the 1950s and 1960s. On the brink of financial collapse in 1965, it was purchased by John Sengstacke, owner of the *Defender* chain. Thus the similar but separate missions of Robert S. Abbott and Robert L. Vann converged in a final irony. Continuing publication as the *New Pittsburgh Courier,* it earned some awards for excellence under its new editor-in-chief, Hazel Garland, whose tenure there dated back to the Golden Age of the 1940s, but the *Courier* had become but a shadow of its old self. Sengstacke Publications, which included the *Courier* and other acquisitions, became the largest African-American newspaper chain in the country.

The third member of what could be called a triumvirate of great black national newspapers was the *Afro-American,* which evolved from its beginnings as a Baltimore church publication to become one of the most widely circulated black newspaper in the South and East, with branch offices in Washington, Philadelphia, Richmond, and Newark, New Jersey. Its founder was John H. Murphy, Sr., a former slave and a whitewasher by trade, who created it by merging his own Sunday school sheet with two similar church publications and going on to expand its coverage to include issues and events of interest to the general black public.

When Murphy died in 1922, his five sons took over the operation, with one of them, Carl Murphy, assuming control. Under his leadership, the *Afro-American* grew into a national publication with multiple editions that emphasized solid reportage and took moderate editorial positions. It became the dominant black publication in the Washington-Baltimore-Richmond triangle, focusing on political matters in a part of the country with a heavy concentration of African Americans. Though firmly patriotic in most of its views, the *Afro,* as it was known, demonstrated courage by standing up for the singer/actor Paul Robeson and the scholar/editor W. E. B. Du Bois when both were accused of being Communists during the McCarthy era. The publisher also ignored official pressure and sent the journalist William Worthy to Communist China on assignment after the U.S. State Department had denied him a visa. From 1961 through the 1980s the founder's grandson, John Murphy III, played a major role in the paper's fortunes, especially after the death of Carl Murphy in 1967. Over the years, successive generations of Murphys have stepped forward to assume leadership.

While these were the titans in the era of the popular black press, other newspapers distinguished themselves by serving the needs of their own urban communities. The *Amsterdam News* was established in 1909 in New York City when James H. Anderson began publishing a local sheet with $10 and a dream, giving it the name of the street on which he lived. The paper gained prominence and commercial success after 1936, when it was purchased by two Harlem physicians. One of them, C. B. Powell, assumed control and developed the paper to the point where it had a circulation of more than 100,000 after World War II. The *Norfolk Journal and Guide* achieved a high level of respectability after 1910, when P. B. Young, a twenty-six-year-old North Carolinian, purchased its original entity, a fraternal organ, and transformed it into a general circulation black newspaper. Avoiding sensationalism and maintaining a relatively conservative stance, the *Journal and Guide* was singled out for praise by mainstream scholars, who considered it the most objective of black newspapers. Yet it responded readily to the needs of its readers, launching campaigns that resulted in better housing for black residents and pay scales for black teachers that equaled those of whites. W. O. Walker built the *Cleveland Call and Post* into a "bread-and-butter" paper that focused firmly on local news, while the Scott family, beginning in 1932, built the *Atlanta Daily World* into the nation's oldest black daily, one of only three that survived beyond the 1990s. Across the nation, from the early to mid-twentieth century, it was difficult to find a major city that was not served by a black newspaper.

The reasons for their existence were obvious. Until the late 1950s African Americans were almost totally ignored by mainstream publications, and when they did appear, it was as suspected perpetrators of crime. If news of interest to the black population was included at all, it was in tiny, segregated columns dubbed "Negro" or "Afro-American," or some similar name, placed inconspicuously in back pages. Even reportage on African-American sports or entertainment figures was designed to reinforce prevailing stereotypes. Thus the black press served the palpable needs of a neglected and maligned people. Editors of black newspaper said that they hoped to change society to such an extent that they would put themselves out of business. But when this change began to take place, they were not prepared to cope with the consequences.

THE TIDES OF CHANGE

When the struggle for racial equality blossomed into the civil rights movement, beginning with the Montgomery, Alabama, bus boycott in 1955, mainstream publications took steps toward covering events in which African Americans were the major players. As the movement spread from Montgomery to Birmingham to Little Rock and beyond, white newspaper editors began to realize that they were witnessing one of the biggest stories of the century. Furthermore, they were being challenged for the first time by television, a new medium that could provide more immediate coverage, enhanced by dramatic visual images that captured the action as it happened. This was most forcefully demonstrated on August 28, 1963, when television provided extended live coverage of the historic March on Washington and the Rev. Dr. Martin Luther King's "I Have a Dream" speech. Since each day brought new developments, most black newspapers, limited to weekly publication, were unable to compete. Furthermore, few of them possessed or were willing to commit the resources that would have enabled them to deploy correspondents to the various hot spots throughout the country. Reporters who worked for the black press during that time recalled their frustration at having to cover the movement by telephone or by rewriting accounts that appeared in the leading white-owned papers.

Although the coverage provided by mainstream print and broadcast media was from a white perspective, inroads were made into a territory that had been the exclusive property of the black press. Yet black journalists rarely were employed by the white media. Even in New York City, the nation's media capital, no African Americans held full-time jobs on white newspapers until Lester A. Walton was hired by the *World* in the 1920s. No further advances were made until 1936 when Ted Poston became a staff reporter for the *New York Post*. He risked his life to cover stories in the South, including the trial in Florida of three young black men who were beaten, with a fourth being killed, for the alleged rape of a white woman, a crime that was never proven. Poston won a George Polk award for his stories on this subject and became a legend in the field, but black journalists were still shunned by daily newspapers. In 1955, a year after the Supreme Court school-desegregation decision, *Ebony* magazine found only thirty-one blacks working on white newspapers throughout the country. Black journalists were so rare in the developing medium of television that they were not even counted before 1962, when Mal Goode, a radio newscaster and former advertising salesman for the *Pittsburgh Courier*, was hired by ABC to become the first network correspondent of his race.

No major changes were to occur until the late 1960s, when the nation's black communities went up in flames, from Watts in Los Angeles to Harlem in New York. The 1968 Report of the National Advisory Commission on Civil Disorders, better known as the Kerner Commission Report, analyzed the causes of these upheavals. In a section implicating the media, the report said:

They have not communicated to the majority of their audience—which is white—a sense of the degradation, misery and hopelessness of living in the ghetto. They have not communicated to whites a feeling for the difficulties and frustrations of being a Negro in the United States. They have not shown understanding or appreciation of—and thus have not communicated—a sense of Negro culture, thought or history.

Equally important, most newspaper articles and most television programming ignored the fact that an appreciable part of their audience was black. The world that television and newspapers offered to their black audience was almost totally white, in both appearance and attitude. As we have said, our evidence shows that the so-called "white press" is at best mistrusted and at worst held in contempt by many black Americans. Far too often, the press acts and talks about Negroes as if Negroes do not read the newspapers or watch television, give birth, marry, die and go to PTA meetings.

The riots, as they were transpiring, had driven home a message to white news managers, who realized that their reporters were ill-equipped to enter the alien world of black neighborhoods and to gain confidence of residents to the point where they might discover what was really going on. As the flames of rage spread from the ghettos to central commercial areas, some realized that the destiny of white America was irrevocably linked to that of black America. As a result, some black reporters were hired literally in the heat of the moment. With the strong indictment of the Kerner Commission finding its mark, black reporters were recruited by the mainstream for the first time, most commonly from the black press. By the mid-1970s nearly a hundred African-American journalists were employed by mainstream publications.

Another response to the report was the development of training programs to increase the limited supply of black journalists. The largest of these was a concentrated summer program established at Columbia University in 1968 through a $250,000 grant from the Ford Foundation. Directed by Fred Friendly, former head of CBS News and

a professor at Columbia's Graduate School of Journalism, the program trained members of various minority groups, then placed from twenty to forty of them each year in both print and broadcast jobs. When one of its black graduates, Michele Clark, died in an airplane crash after working her way up to become co-anchor of the *CBS Morning News,* the minority-training program was renamed in her honor. In 1974, after substantial increases in the number of African Americans earning degrees from journalism schools, including Columbia's, this program was discontinued. The following year it was revived through the efforts of Earl Caldwell, a leading African-American journalist. Relocated to the University of California at Berkeley and operated by the Institute for Journalism Education (IJE), the program to train and place members of minorities on mainstream newspapers continued into the early 1990s. Under the guidance of nationally known African-American journalists, among them Nancy Hicks, Robert Maynard and Dorothy Gilliam, the IJE broadened its scope to focus on programs in editing and management training, facilitating movement of black journalists into the upper echelons of the print media.

All of these changes had a devastating effect on black newspapers. Their circulations plummeted as television and mainstream newspapers encroached on their readership by providing more immediate, though often superficial and insensitive, coverage of major events affecting the African-American community. By 1977 the audited circulation of the *Chicago Defender* had shrunk to 34,000 daily and 38,000 for the weekend edition. The *New Pittsburgh Courier* dipped to 30,000 weekly; the *Baltimore Afro-American* averaged 34,000 for two weekday editions and 18,500 for a weekend national edition. A few publications fared somewhat better, but others teetered on the brink of bankruptcy or had disappeared altogether. While more than 300 black newspapers were being published in the early 1960s, only 170 remained by the late 1980s. Their overall quality also declined as most of the top talent defected to the mainstream, where the rewards included salaries that were several times larger, far better benefits, and greater prestige. Television offered not only large salaries but also high visibility and glamour, a heady kind of stardom. After 1970, few aspiring journalists entered the field with the intention of working for the black press.

Exceptions to this grim pattern were two radical newspapers that surfaced during the 1960s in the furor of the Black Revolution. *Muhammad Speaks,* the official organ of the Nation of Islam, otherwise known as the Black Muslins, stemmed from a column called "Mr. Muhammad Speaks" that the sect's leader, Elijah Muhammad, had written for the *Pittsburgh Courier* during the

1950s. When Christian ministers, valuable links in the black press circulation chain, objected to Muhammad's anti-Christian rhetoric, the column was discontinued. Since Muslim followers had employed aggressive tactics to sell the paper on the streets, they took with them a huge chunk of the *Courier's* circulation. The column resurfaced in the *Amsterdam News* during the 1960s, when Malcolm X was galvanizing the black masses not only in Harlem but also throughout the nation. By the early 1970s the Black Muslims were publishing a popular weekly newspaper of their own called *Muhammad Speaks*. It was produced in Chicago, where Elijah Muhammad lived, by a staff of experienced journalists (who were not necessarily Muslims) working out of a well-equipped plant. Featuring African-American news with a militant slant, along with dogma, and distributed through the same pressurized street-selling techniques, *Muhammad Speaks* achieved an unaudited weekly circulation of 400,000 to 600,000, an all-time record for a black newspaper. (Unaudited means that the Audit Bureau of Circulations has not verified these figures.) Circulation dropped sharply after the assassination of Malcolm X in 1965, the death of Elijah Muhammad, which brought on power struggles within the Muslim sect, and a general shift away from overt militancy in the African-American population. However, the paper continued publication under other names, including the *Bilalian News* and later the *Final Call,* into the early twenty-first century. These later publications never approached the success of earlier efforts.

A short-lived but significant polemical newspaper was the *Black Panther,* which achieved an unaudited circulation of 100,000 during the early 1970s, when it was edited by Eldridge Cleaver, author of the autobiographical militant manifesto *Soul on Ice.* Radical in tone, this newspaper attracted an audience in the turbulent antiwar climate of that time by condemning police brutality at home and America's foreign policy abroad, but it ceased publication after the credibility of Panther leaders was broadly questioned.

The sheer volume of news being generated by the movement toward integration and mainstream efforts to recruit African Americans who could cover these events all but obliterated the power previously held by black newspapers. But one genre of black publications flourished. These were the black magazines that had been conceived as commercial enterprises rather than instruments of protest. Thus they were better able to adjust to the demands of an increasingly competitive marketplace.

BLACK MAGAZINES

Early black newspapers so resembled magazines in tone and content that differentiation between the two often was based on frequency of publication. The first black magazines seem to have been subsidized organs that originated in the black church during the early 1840s. The first general-circulation magazine owned independently by African Americans and directed to them was the *Mirror of Liberty,* published by David Ruggles, a New Yorker who was a key figure in the Underground Railroad. Forwarding the cause of abolition, it was published from 1847 to 1849. Other magazines followed. Frederick Douglass, after publishing a series of newspapers, lent his name to an abolitionist magazine, *Douglass' Monthly.* Aimed primarily at British readers, it was issued from 1860 to 1862. A forerunner of popular modern periodicals was *Alexander's Magazine,* a national publication produced in Boston from 1905 to 1909. It emphasized the positive aspects of African-American life, featuring stories about outstanding individuals with commentary on cultural, educational, and political events.

The first African-American magazine to have a lasting impact was the *Crisis,* which was the brainchild of W. E. B. Du Bois. It first appeared in 1910, a year that resonates with significance because of the number of African-American organizations, institutions, and publications spawned at that time. Du Bois, who was one of the original incorporators of the NAACP, assumed the position of director of publications and research for that organization after several previous excursions into journalism. He used the *Crisis*—which remains the official organ of the NAACP—to criticize national policies that impeded the progress of blacks and to educate African Americans in the techniques of protest. After Du Bois resigned his post in 1934 following squabbles with the NAACP leadership, he launched other magazines, the most notable being *Phylon,* a scholarly journal published by Atlanta University, where he spent portions of his career as a professor and head of the sociology department.

Following Du Bois's inspired lead, the National Urban League published *Opportunity,* a journal that documented the literary and artistic accomplishments of the Harlem Renaissance and lasted until 1949. Another important periodical of the post–World War I period was *The Messenger,* a militantly socialist journal edited by Chandler Owen and A. Philip Randolph, the latter of whom was to become the voice of black labor as head of the Brotherhood of Sleeping Car Porters. All of these publications depended on subsidies.

Commercial black magazines—meaning those that were fully self-sustaining through advertising as well as subscriptions—did not surface until the 1940s, a period when general-circulation magazines were one of the main forms of home entertainment. The engaging combination of pictures and words had made *Life* a popular chronicler of the American Dream, while *Time* provided snappily written coverage of weekly events and *The Saturday Evening Post* reinforced mainstream values in fiction and non-fiction. The *Reader's Digest* offered extracts from the era's leading publications, such as the Ladies' Home Journal, which catered to the traditional interests of women. Yet African Americans remained invisible in the pages of these magazines, as they had been in mainstream newspapers.

A veritable revolution in black magazines began in 1942 when John H. Johnson began publishing *Negro Digest,* a monthly periodical roughly the size of the *Reader's Digest,* featuring stories about black accomplishments, news items of interest to African Americans, and provocative original articles by prominent whites addressing black issues. He used it as a cornerstone for the development of the most successful black publishing firm in history. Although other quality mass-circulation black magazines originated in the post–World War II period, Johnson outmaneuvered his competition and thus eliminated it by developing brilliant marketing strategies.

Johnson's climb from poverty to riches was a real Horatio Alger story. He was born poor in 1918 in a tiny Arkansas town on the banks of the Mississippi River. His father was killed in a sawmill accident when he was eight and his mother remarried a year later. Since the town offered no opportunities for a black child to be educated beyond the eighth grade, his mother, Gertrude Johnson Williams, moved her family north in 1933 and worked s a domestic to educate her son. When he graduated from Chicago's DuSable High School as the most outstanding student in the class of 1936, he was offered a scholarship to the University of Chicago but opted to attend part-time while working at Supreme Liberty Life Insurance Company, one of the nation's leading black businesses. One of his tasks was to produce the company's monthly newspaper. Another was to provide digests of news about blacks for the company's president, Harry Pace, who was Johnson's mentor.

When friends relished the nuggets of black-oriented news Johnson shared with them, he conceived the idea of publishing a monthly magazine based on this kind of material. Having no money, he used his mother's new furniture, with her permission, as collateral to borrow $500. With this sum, he paid for the mailing of an introductory subscription letter sent to Supreme's twenty thousand customers in 1942. The resultant magazine, *Negro Digest,* was so popular that Johnson was able to launch another magazine, *Ebony,* in 1945. Stressing the positive aspects of African-American life and using ample pictures to help tell stories, *Ebony* immediately attracted a large, enthusiastic audience.

Along the way, Johnson outstripped his most promising competitor, *Our World,* which was published by John P. Davis, a Harvard Law School graduate. It was launched in 1946, just after *Ebony,* and also was a quality picture magazine printed on slick paper. *Our World* amassed an impressive circulation of 251,599 by 1952, but went bankrupt in 1955 because it could not attract major advertising accounts, the lifeblood of commercial publications. Meanwhile, Johnson used every ounce of ingenuity he could muster to break down the barriers that led white manufacturers to dismiss black magazines as advertising venues. It was essential to his survival and eventually he devised a winning strategy. By Johnson's own admission, he triumphed not so much because he had a better magazine but because he was a more inventive businessman.

Johnson also was adept at changing his tactics as the times demanded. He discontinued *Negro Digest* in 1951 when *Ebony* had usurped its audience, replacing his first publication with *Jet,* a pocket-size weekly newsmagazine that has remained popular over the years. In 1965, when militancy was in vogue, he revived *Negro Digest,* changing its name to *Black World.* Under the editor Hoyt Fuller, it became a prestigious outlet for African-American literature and thought, documenting the developments of what some have called the second black Renaissance. By 1970, when the movement subsided and subscriptions began to fall off, Johnson again discontinued the magazine.

Responding to what he considered to be public taste, Johnson conceived and published an assortment of magazines over the years, among them *Tan Confessions* during the 1950s, which was transformed into *Black Stars* in the 1960s, but more significantly *Ebony Jr.,* an educational magazine for children produced during the late 1960s, *Ebony Africa,* which reflected the African independence movement but was discontinued after a few issues in 1965 when it foundered on differing national, linguistic, and political realities. But over six decades, Johnson has prevailed as the nation's—and world's—leading black publisher, his empire anchored by two stalwarts: *Ebony,* with an audited monthly circulation of 1,707,489 at the end of 2004, and *Jet,* with a weekly circulation of 967,909.

Some criticized Johnson's publications for relying too heavily on entertainment and light features while paying too little attention to major issues. But *Ebony* also had a serious side and provided a nurturing environment for talented black writers. Foremost among these was Lerone Bennett, who joined the staff in 1953. A scholar as well as a journalist, Bennett produced several series of articles that interpreted and dramatized black history in a literary style accessible to the general reader. Most of these articles evolved into popular books, published by Johnson, becoming a mainstay of black studies programs instituted by American colleges and universities during the 1970s.

The legislative gains of the 1960s led to improvements in the overall educational and economic status of African Americans, providing fertile ground for the cultivation of magazines aimed at newly affluent black consumers. A dozen new magazines surfaced in 1970 alone. Two of them became major publications: *Essence* and *Black Enterprise*.

COURTING BLACK WOMEN

Essence: The Magazine for Today's Black Woman was conceived in New York City in the fall of 1968. Russell Goings, an assistant vice president for Shearson, Hamill & Company and one of the few black executives with a Wall Street investment banking and brokerage firm at that time, put together a list of up-and-coming young African-Americans in the corporate world. He then invited them to a series of meetings where they could put forth ideas for new businesses they might want to start. It was Jonathan Blount, age twenty-two, a salesman for New Jersey Bell Yellow Pages, who came up with the idea for a black women's magazine. The idea had come from his godmother. Goings introduced Blount to other young men who liked the idea and formed a team. (Few women attended those meetings.) As a result, Blount, joined by Ed Lewis, age twenty-eight, a star in the executive training program at First City Bank; Clarence Smith, thirty-five, a top salesman at Prudential Insurance; and Cecil Hollingsworth, twenty-eight, who had started a small printing brokerage firm, developed a proposal for a black women's magazine. They became known as the Hollingsworth group, with Ed Lewis serving as chief executive.

They assumed it would take $1.5 million to start the magazine, but being black and having no experience in publishing made it all but impossible for them to get backing. All four had to quit their jobs to concentrate full-time on the project, but presentations on Wall Street and elsewhere, attracted no backers. Somehow they got by on moderate loans that had to be paid back, leaving them little to work with. Finally, in May 1970, or nearly two years later, *Essence* made its debut on newsstands in 145 cities with a press run of 175,000 copies. The new magazine was chock-full of thoughtful articles on important issues by respected authorities along with a cornucopia of fiction, nonfiction, and essays by leading black writers. It was highlighted throughout by beautiful illustrations under the supervision of photographer Gordon Parks. This ap-

proach resonated immediately with the targeted *Essence* audience. However, theirs were not the only opinions that would determine whether the new magazine could survive. White media critics found *Essence* too militant, somehow intimidating. A white writer for *Time* magazine went so far as to state that "After a while, the young, urban, inquisitive and acquisitive Black woman for whom the magazine is intended is going to get tired of being reminded of the longstanding, dehumanizing rape of the Black woman in America." An advertising newsletter menacingly predicted: "Black women's magazines have a shaky future." These comments could drive away advertisers.

Sensing potential problems, the founders dismissed their editor in chief, Ruth N. Ross, a former assistant editor at *Newsweek* who had left her job—a rare one for women of any color in those days—to join their tiny staff. Ross also had come up with the name of *Essence* for the magazine. Originally, the founders had intended to call it *Sapphire,* long a pejorative term for a loud-mouthed black woman. Focus groups of women had voiced their displeasure, but the four young men had found it difficult to come up with a better name. Ross had done so, but her approach was deemed "too black for prime time" after the first issue. Furthermore, her old job at *Newsweek* had closed up after her. But *Essence* thrived. By 1992 *Essence* had an audited circulation of 900,000, and by the end of 2004, it had climbed to 1,063,645, surpassed only by *Ebony*.

BLACK ENTERPRISE

For more than thirty years, *Black Enterprise* magazine, which was founded in 1970 by Earl G. Graves, a former administrative assistant to Robert F. Kennedy, has informed the public—and particularly African Americans—of improved financial opportunities available to them, thus encouraging greater black participation in the economic mainstream. It celebrates the achievements of black entrepreneurs by presenting documented lists of those who have been most successful. Its annual listing of the one hundred biggest black businesses provides a ready reference for determining the progress of African-American entrepreneurs. This magazine has a clear-cut mission and was nearly two years in the planning, with input from a board of advisors that included Whitney Young, Jr., executive director of the Urban League. It is to get African Americans to learn more about money, how to get more of it and how to use it to their own advantage.

Unlike many magazines specializing in financial affairs, *Black Enterprise* takes an upbeat but down-to-earth approach, examining a full range of money matters, from the issues of corporate America to how families handle their finances. *Black Enterprise's* annual listing of the nation's largest black businesses is a ready reference to the financial health and wealth of black capitalists. Much emphasis is placed on self-improvement and ample coverage is provided of regular people who have developed their own start-ups, even on a small scale. Complex matters are explained in understandable terms highlighted by photos of smiling African Americans who have managed to make money work for them. The formula has worked, for the magazine had attained an audited circulation of 508,489 by 2005.

With the expansion of the black middle class, a variety of new magazines were developed to address specific tastes. By 1990 at least twenty-five black-oriented magazines were being published in the United States. Most of the newcomers did not survive. Some deserved a better chance, most notably *Emerge,* a black newsmagazine launched in 1991 by Wilmer Ames, an African-American editor on the *Newsweek* staff. Uncertain in its thrust early on, *Emerge* acquired firmer footing when most of its stock was purchased by Black Entertainment Television (BET), which Bob Johnson had launched in 1980 in Washington, D.C., as the first black-owned national cable network. This was a mismatch of sorts, for BET featured dance videos and catered to tastes of those favoring urban hip-hop culture, while *Emerge* was a newsmagazine. *Emerge* reached its peak in the mid-to late 1990s when George Curry served as editor, offering fearlessly satiric assessments of politics and public affairs with articles by top black writers working in the mainstream. By 1999 it had a monthly circulation of 160,000, but BET wanted a bigger return for its investment and discontinued publication.

MAINSTREAMING

The last decades of the twentieth century brought a dramatic shift toward the mainstreaming of African-American journalists. Beginning in the 1970s, general-circulation daily newspapers and television stations recruited black journalists as they never had before. By 1990 nearly four thousand blacks were employed by daily newspapers, with a few establishing national reputations. Foremost among them was Carl T. Rowan, a senior statesman of journalism who had always worked in the mainstream, starting out in 1948 at the *Minneapolis Tribune.* He held high government posts in the Kennedy and Johnson administrations, then became a syndicated columnist and television panelist. Rowan conducted a historic televised interview with Justice Thurgood Marshall on his retirement from the U.S. Supreme Court in 1991. William Raspberry of the *Washington Post* also gained broad recog-

nition through his syndicated column. Other columnists who became widely known were Earl Caldwell of the *New York Daily News;* Bob Herbert, who became the first African-American columnist for the *New York Times;* Les Payne of *Newsday;* Dorothy Gilliam of the *Washington Post;* Chuck Stone of the *Philadelphia Daily News;* and Clarence Page of the *Chicago Tribune.*

The Gannett Corporation, which was the nation's largest newspaper chain, publishing eighty-seven dailies throughout the country as well as the national *USA Today,* outstripped others by instituting a strong affirmative action program. Under chairman Allen Neuharth, Gannett enforced strict rules ensuring that minorities were included in coverage and that they were consulted as sources for stories that did not necessarily pertain to race. Through the Gannett chain, Robert Maynard, who had spent ten years at the *Washington Post* as a national correspondent, ombudsman, and editorial writer, became the first publisher of a general-market daily, the *Oakland Tribune,* in 1979. Maynard went on to purchase the paper in 1983, another first. Also under the Gannett system, Pam Johnson, who held a Ph.D. in communications, was named publisher of the *Ithaca Journal* in upstate New York in 1981, becoming the first African-American woman to control the affairs of a mainstream daily newspaper.

TELEVISION

Similar changes took place in television, though they did not extend to the higher levels of management. The first black journalist on television was Louis Lomax, a newspaperman and college teacher who entered the relatively new medium in 1958 at WNTA-TV in New York. The author of five books, Lomax produced television documentaries before his death in an automobile accident in 1970. Because of the visual nature of television, it often appeared that blacks were making more progress there than in print journalism. Some shifted easily from one medium to the other. In 1963, a year after Mal Goode became the first African-American commentator on network television news, Bill Matney moved from the *Detroit News,* a daily newspaper, to NBC, where he covered the White House for the network from 1970 to 1972. Yet no African American held a major position in television until 1978, when Max Robinson was the first of his race to become a regular co-anchor for a prime-time network television newscast, heading the national desk in Chicago for the *ABC Nightly News.* Robinson left the network five years later after being demoted and died of AIDS in 1988, but he served as a role model for young blacks aspiring to careers in television news. One of the most durable of network TV newscasters was Ed Bradley, who joined CBS as a stringer in the Paris bureau in 1971, then became a White House correspondent in1976. He later anchored the *CBS Sunday Night News* and later went on to attract a loyal following in his long-term position as one of the chief correspondents for the top-rated *60 Minutes,* a position he still held in 2005. In terms of all-around popularity, the leader was Bryant Gumbel, who shuttled between news and entertainment as host of NBC's *Today* show. Although he had been with the show for fifteen years by 1992, it took him five more years to convince NBC brass to let him take the show to Africa, the only continent other then Antarctica that they had not visited. He was able to do so by compiling a mountain of meticulous research and planning on how it could be done. The weeklong series cost more than $2 million to produce but won an award for Gumbel. His struggle to pull it off highlighted Americans' lack of interest in Africa and its people. An informal survey of network coverage found that Africa got less coverage than California whales trapped in Arctic ice or a virus among North Sea seals.

Progress in television was more uneven for women. Charlayne Hunter-Gault, a former *New Yorker* staffer and *New York Times* reporter, became one of the most visible women journalists on TV in 1978 when she became New York correspondent for the *McNeil-Lehrer Report,* on the Public Broadcast System's nightly news program. During her tenure there, she also became the first African-American woman to anchor a national news program. When Hunter-Gault left PBS to take up residence in South Africa, the public network acquired another heavy hitter. Gwen Ifill, a lawyer and journalist, had been White House correspondent for the *New York Times* before she left in 1994 to join NBC News. After five years at NBC, she was hired by PBS as moderator and managing editor of Washington Week in Review and correspondent for Jim Lehrer's *Nightly NewsHour,* making her the most prominent woman in public television.

Change moved at a slower pace in commercial TV, but by the late 1980s it had become common for local stations to feature black women as anchors, for they were "two-fers," qualifying as diversity hires because of both race and gender. As the twenty-first century settled in, the formula was modified to include Asian and Latino women, sometimes paired with an African-American woman or man as a featured reporter or weather commentator, especially in urban areas. But it was difficult for these women to break into the networks as correspondents. The most successful black woman journalist on television was Carole Simpson, who took a major step in 1989 at ABC, when she became the first African-American woman to anchor an evening newscast on commercial television, appearing on Sunday nights. But these gains were limited. As in print journalism, the real power in broadcasting is held by executive producers and other top managers, who work behind a white curtain where they determine who or what will make it onto the air. In a 1982 survey of the nation's three networks, Michael Massing found that no blacks held high-level management positions. The highest job held by an African American at ABC was an assignment editor on a nightly news show, while at CBS and NBC the top posts were held by bureau chiefs. At all the networks, about 5 percent of the producers and associated producers were black, many in lower-level jobs. The efforts of black reporters were often overshadowed by general policies that resulted in a predominance of negative portrayals of African Americans in the media. While only 15 percent of the poor people in the United States in 1990 were black, newspaper and television coverage, in particular, perpetuated the impression that most criminals, prostitutes, drug addicts, welfare mother, illiterates, and homeless persons were black. On the other hand, hardworking African Americans and those who constituted a large and growing middle class were glossed over. In newspapers, as on television, the problem could be traced to monochromatic leadership. A survey conducted by the American Society of Newspapers in 1985 revealed that almost 95 percent of the journalists on daily newspapers were white and the 92 percent of the nation's newspapers did not have a single minority person in a news executive position. Fifty-four percent of the newspapers had no minority employees at all.

Yet progress was made. A study released in 1999 showed that the percentage of minority television reporters had doubled within that decade. In 1998 they represented 20 percent of those broadcasting as compared to 10 percent in 1991. But there was a disturbing consequence. The increase in black, brown, and tan faces on television has caused many white Americans to believe that all inequities had been corrected. Some even contended that talented whites—and particularly white men—were being denied opportunities they deserved to meet demands for diversity. This led to strained relations in many of the nation's newsrooms.

LEAVING THE FOLD

During the many years when African-American journalists worked almost entirely within the black press, their salaries had not been particularly handsome and the white world had not paid much attention to them, but they commonly had gone about their tasks with a communal spirit, a shared sense of knowing that they were doing something that might make life better for their people. Besides, they could have fun while doing it, for their co-workers as well as the people they usually covered shared a common culture. Of course, there were rivalries at work and some of the same irritations that might be found on any job, but if they got undesirable assignments, were paid less, or passed over for promotions, they could be certain that it was not because of their race. That one factor was a major concern for many African-American journalists who moved into the mainstream. By the early twenty-first century, most black journalists were to be found there.

ON A DIFFICULT COURSE

Life could be uncomfortable at times in the mainstream. Cut off from the fold, fragmented, and dogged by a sense of isolation, these journalists were concerned about their overall ability to effect better and more balanced coverage of African Americans in newsrooms where this might not be a priority. Many were troubled by what they perceived to be an overall assumption of black inferiority and an expectation that their work should emphasize black patholo-gy. Some black journalists were challenged to prove their objectivity, or ability to assume a "white" perspective in their work by digging up dirt about black politicians and leaders, although white reporters were not asked to prove their objectivity. It was assumed. Often black reporters found themselves in a bind, trapped in an uncomfortable place where they would be more likely to achieve success on the job if they wrote negative stories about their own people. This led black people to turn against these journal-ists, at times venting their rage in public meetings. But one ambitious young journalist rode the matter of black pa-thology to fame—or infamy.

Janet Cooke, a talented, twenty-five-year-old writer at *The Washington Post* won a Pulitzer Prize in 1980 for her feature story about an eight-year-old boy named Jimmy whose mother's boyfriend regularly injected him with her-oin, thus feeding the child's addiction, which the live-in lover had instigated. Cooke said she had witnessed the scene. The story appeared on the front page of the *Post* and was picked up by hundreds of other papers, making Cooke an instant journalistic star. When it was discovered that Cooke had fabricated both Jimmy and the story, she was condemned by the public and had to return the Pulitzer, which was the first won by an individual African-American woman journalist. Cooke's caper led many in the journalistic establishment to question the credibility of African-American journalists as a whole, although white journalists were not regarded similarly when those of their color were revealed to be fabricators.

When a similar incident occurred several years later, some feared that black journalists, as a whole, again would have to bear the burden for the misdeeds of an individual. Jayson Blair, a promising twenty-seven-year-old *New York Times* reporter, had been on the fast track, working as a roving national correspondent, after courting the favor of some of the paper's top figures. But in May 2003, it was revealed that Blair had fabricated much of the material in high-profile stories he had written, some related to mov-ing events taking place on the homefront, in other parts of the nation, during the Iraqi war. He had produced them without leaving his apartment, borrowing material from other publications and creating his own details. His feat, which was examined and analyzed extensively, especially by the *Times,* was a major embarrassment to that institu-tion. Blair would be remembered as a miscreant who not only destroyed his own career, but who also took down the *Times'* editor, Howell Raines, who resigned, and the first African-American managing editor at the *Times,* Ger-ald Boyd, who also resigned. Though some conservatives dubbed Blair the "poster child for affirmative action," most pundits of the press linked his misdeeds to a culture in some high-pressure journalistic institutions that places such a premium on fame that people will do almost any-thing to get it.

NABJ

As African-American journalists moved into the main-stream, they took major steps to address their problems. They realized that there could be power in numbers, so they organized. Forty-four African-American newsmen and newswomen founded the National Association of Black Journalists (NABJ) on December 12, 1975, at the Sheraton Park Hotel in Washington, D.C. They came from both black and mainstream firms, from print media (newspapers and magazine) and broadcast (radio and tele-vision). Unlike some journalism organizations, NABJ lim-ited membership to professionals involved in gathering and disseminating the news, excluding professors and those in public relations. Chuck Stone, a flamboyant jour-nalistic figure who had been an editor of several black newspapers, was the guiding force behind creation of the NABJ and served as its first president. At the time, he was a columnist for the *Philadelphia Daily News.* After two years the organization had a membership of more than a thousand. Its leaders went on to develop a scholarship program for journalism students, to present annual awards to outstanding journalists of the year, and to hold lavish annual conventions in various cities where there were member chapters. These affairs included job fairs, panel discussions, speeches by luminaries, screen debuts, and live performances by musical stars. One of the major accomplishments of NABJ has been to have members of its board meet with leaders of the three other major organizations of ethnic journalists: the National Association of Hispanic Journalists, the Asian American Journalists Association, and the Native American Journalists Association. The objective is to work in consort and thus to prevent negative forces in the mainstream from pitting them against each other. These sessions resulted in joint conventions called UNITY, held in 1994 at the Georgia World Congress Center in Atlanta. Six years in the making and budgeted at $1,000,000, the event brought together 6,000 members of all four organizations to share their cultures and concerns. UNITY continued to meet at five-year intervals, with conferences in 1999 and 2004.

Clouds on the Horizon

Wayne Dawkins, who documents NABJ's history, noticed something unexpected when he checked their financial records at the end of 1999. Membership in the organization had reached an all-time high of 3,321 in August 1997 but had dropped to 2,456, down 26 percent in only a year and a half. Perhaps it was just a glitch resulting from the high cost of members having to travel to conventions in western cities for two consecutive years, far from the East and Midwest, where most members live. But this drop-off more likely was a manifestation of a trend others have noticed. Numbers of African Americans and other minorities have been leaving journalism almost as fast as other members of their groups have been entering the field. A 1978 survey by the Dow Jones Newspaper Fund concluded that only one in five minorities who earned journalism degrees got jobs. Some get them, but their unemployment rate is three times that of their white peers. A 1985 study by the IJE, a leader in educating and placing minorities in journalism jobs, tracked a group of graduates over ten years and found that 40 percent of them were planning on leaving the field because of a perceived glass ceiling that did not allow them opportunities to grow, to move up. These comments might be considered in the context of a rancorous and heavily-covered trial in 1987 which grew out of a federal discrimination suit filed by four African-American journalists—three men and one woman—against their employer, the New York *Daily News,* at that time, the nation's most widely circulated newspaper. Some in the industry considered it a suit against the whole industry. The issue was not mere employment or even salary, though it was revealed during the investigation related to the suit that blacks and Hispanics were generally paid less than whites in comparable positions, regardless of performance. But the complaint by the *Daily News* employees had more to do with promotion, recognition, and opportunities to distinguish themselves. They prevailed and

were given a total of $3.1 million in damages and a promise that the *Daily News* would implement an affirmative action program to increase the number of black reporters. Though some considered this a victory, the plaintiffs were permanently scarred by the experience. Joan Shepard, a forty-five-year-old cultural editor who was the lone woman in the case, was found alone in her home in 1998, dead for an unknown length of time, after struggling to establish her own restaurant newsletter.

A Final Note

Progress toward more integrated media seemed to slow after the end of the twentieth century. A study conducted by the Knight Foundation in 2005 found that 73 percent of the larger American newspapers employed fewer non-whites in that year than they had in some earlier year dating back to 1990. They included some of the most highly respected, among them *The New York Times, Washington Post, Wall Street Journal, Baltimore Sun* and *USA Today.* This finding also coincides with the defection of younger journalists from the field, due to frustration at lack of advancement. But Herbert Lowe, a courts reporter for *Newsday* and president of NABJ confirms this finding, saying that much of it has to do with lack of advancement. But other experienced journalists stress a need for those who are dissatisfied to understand that it's not enough just to do a job and to do it well. They have to learn how to play the game, to politick on their own behalf.

Those who are dissatisfied also might try the Black Press. More than two hundred black community newspapers and two dailies are being published, with some, like the *Sacramento Observer* being robust and respected. Someone concerned about preservation might help to restore a historic institution, *The Chicago Defender,* which celebrated its centennial on May 5, 2005. It has been struggling to survive, with circulation down to 15,000 for four weekday editions and 19,000 for a weekend edition. But Tom Picou, long the key executive of the *Defender* and chair of the corporate concern that now owns the newspaper has announced plans to move into electronic media by presenting podcasts of news and interviews.

However, Black media itself might be forced to undergo some changes. In June 2005 the New York Times Company announced that it intended to publish a newspaper for African Americans in Gainesville, Florida, called the *Gainesville Guardian.* The new paper would result from the conversion of a newspaper the Times Company already owns in that area, *The Gainsville Sun.* A black editor already had been chosen and was participating in the planning. The question raised by African-American publishers was whether a newspaper could be considered "black" if it was not owned by blacks. Their response was a resounding "no." One publisher called such publications "white papers in blackface," conveying memories of the insults of minstrelsy. Nonetheless a precedent already had been set. On January 4, 2005, Time Inc. had announced that it had agreed to buy the 51 percent of Essence Communications Partners, the publisher of the magazines *Essence* and *Suede,* that it did not already own. A story in the *New York Times* business section noted that in 2000 Time Inc., which is owned by Time Warner, had purchased 49 percent of Essence Communications. Ed Lewis, founder and chief executive of Essence Communications, was quoted as saying that in the four years of partnership with Time Inc. he had come to trust the company and that he believed that its strategic might would help *Essence* and *Suede* reach more readers. *Black Enterprise* immediately shot back with an article potting: "Are Black Women Losing Their Voice?" The debate is likely to ensue.

See also Abbott, Robert Sengstacke; *Anglo-African, The*; *Baltimore Afro-American*; Black Press in Brazil; *Black World/Negro Digest*; *Chicago Defender*; *Christian Recorder*; Cornish, Samuel E.; *Crisis, The*; Delany, Martin R.; *Ebony*; Forten, James; Fortune, T. Thomas; Douglass, Frederick; *Freedom's Journal*; *Guardian, The*; *Jet*; *Liberator, The*; *Messenger, The*; *Negro World*; *North Star*; *Opportunity: Journal of Negro Life*; *Phylon*; *Pittsburgh Courier*; Schuyler, George S.; Trotter, William Monroe; Washington, Booker T.; Wells-Barnett, Ida B.; *Woman's Era*

■ ■ *Bibliography*

Bennett, Lerone, Jr. *Before the Mayflower: A History of Black America,* 5th ed. Chicago: Johnson Publishing, 1982.

Berger, Warren. "One Year and Counting: Wilmer Ames and 'Emerge'." *Folio* (December 1, 1990): 35.

Britt, Donna. "The Relentlessly Upbeat Woman Behind Spirit of Essence." *Los Angeles Times,* June 3, 1990, p. E14.

Buni, Andrew. *Robert L. Vann of the* Pittsburgh Courier: *Politics and Black Journalism.* Pittsburgh: University of Pittsburgh Press, 1974.

Carmody, Deidre. "Black Magazines See Sales in Unity." *New York Times,* May 4, 1992, p. D9.

Carr, David. "Time Warner Unit to Buy Publisher of Two Magazines." *New York Times,* January 5, 2005, p. C4.

Cohen, Roger. "Black Media Giant's Fire Still Burns." *New York Times,* November 19, 1990, p. D8.

Dann, Martin E. ed. *The Black Press 1827–1890.* New York: Putnam, 1971.

Dates, Janette, L., and William Barlow, eds. *Split Image: African Americans in the Mass Media.* Washington, D.C.: Howard University Press, 1990.

Dawkins, Wayne. *Black Journalists: The NABJ Story.* Merrillville, Ind.: August Press, 1997.

Dawkins, Wayne. *Rugged Waters: Black Journalists Swim the Mainstream.* Newport News, Va.: August Press, 2003.

Gilliam, Dorothy. "What Do Black Journalists Want?" *Columbia Journalism Review* (May/June 1972): 47.

Hicks, Jonathan P. "More New Magazines, and These Beckon to Black Readers." *New York Times,* August 5, 1990, p.20.

Hines, Patricia Mignon, ed. *Essence: 25 Years Celebrating Black Women.* New York: H. N. Abrams, 1995.

Hogan, Lawrence D. *A Black National News Service: The Associated Negro Press and Claude Barnett, 1919–1945.* Rutherford, N.J.: Farleigh Dickinson University Press, 1984.

Johnson, John H., with Lerone Bennett, Jr. *Succeeding Against the Odds.* New York: Warner Books, 1989.

Jones, Alex S. "Oakland Publisher in Uphill Struggle." *New York Times,* June 5, 1985, p. A16.

Jones, Alex S. "Sense of Muscle for Black Journalists," *New York Times,* August 21, 1989, p. D1.

LaBrie, Henry III, ed. *Perspectives of the Black Press: 1974.* Kennebunkport, Me.: Mercer House Press, 1974.

Michaelson, Judith. "Black Journalists Remember Robinson as Role Model." *Los Angeles Times,* December 23, 1988, sect. 6, p. 36.

"Negroes on White Newspapers." *Ebony,* November 1955.

Newkirk, Pamela. *Within the Veil: Black Journalists, White Media.* New York: New York University Press, 2000.

Noble, Gil. *Black Is the Color of My TV Tube.* Secaucus, N.J.: Lyle Stuart, 1981.

Ottley, Roi. *The Lonely Warrior: The Life and Times of Robert S. Abbott.* Chicago: H. Regnery, 1955.

Polski, Harry A., and James Williams, eds. *The Negro Almanac: A Reference Work on the Afro-American,* 5th ed. Detroit: Gale, 1989.

Quintanilla, Michael. "Blacks Seek Changes in Newsrooms." *Los Angeles Times,* August 3, 1990, p. E1.

Scardino, Albert. "Black Papers Retain a Local Role." *New York Times,* July 24, 1989, p. D1.

Shaw, David. "Negative News and Little Else." *Los Angeles Times,* December 11, 1990, p. A1.

Shaw, David. "Newspapers Struggling to Raise Minority Coverage." *Los Angeles Times,* December 12, 1990, p. A1.

Shaw, David. "Critics Cite Need to Lead in Hiring Minorities." *Los Angeles Times,* December 13, 1990, p. A1.

Smith, Roger W. "Black Journalists Deplore Pace of New Media Hires." *Newsday,* March 19, 1988, p. 11.

Smythe, Mabel, ed. *The Black American Reference Book.* Englewood Cliffs, N.J.: Prentice-Hall, 1976.

Strader, Jim. "Black on Black." *Washington Journalism Review* (March 1992): 33–36.

Wells, Ida B. *Crusade for Justice: The Autobiography of Ida B. Wells.* Edited by Alfreda M. Duster. Chicago: University of Chicago Press, 1970.

Williams, Juan. "Being Black, Being Fair: Journalists Have to 'Do the Right Thing' Too.'" *Washington Post,* July 16, 1989, p. B1.

Wolseley, Roland E. *The Black Press U.S.A.* Ames: Iowa State University Press, 1971.

PHYL GARLAND (1996)
Updated by author 2005

JOURNAL OF AFRICAN AMERICAN HISTORY, THE

As soon as he founded the Association for the Study of Negro Life and History (now the Association for the Study of African American Life and History), the African-American historian Carter G. Woodson (1875–1950) hoped to begin publishing a "Quarterly Journal of Negro History." Prior to Woodson's establishment of this publication, white historians controlled the production and distribution of scholarship in black history through the editorial policies they formulated for scholarly journals. In January 1916, just four months after the association was founded, the first issue of the *Journal of Negro History* was published. Several members of Woodson's executive council believed that publishing the journal was too risky, and maintained that he should have obtained greater financial support before launching the new publication. Woodson, however, would not delay publication, for he believed that fund-raising would be easier if potential subscribers and contributors could see the product of his labors. Yet throughout his long career as editor, Woodson had to devote an inordinate amount of his time to fund-raising for the journal, as it was a continual drain on his financial resources. He managed to keep it going and never missed an issue during his thirty-five-year career as editor.

The journal was the centerpiece of Woodson's research program and provided black scholars with an outlet for the publication of their research. Without it, far fewer black scholars would have been able to publish their work. It also served as an outlet for the publication of articles written by white scholars whose interpretations differed from the mainstream of the historical profession.

Through the journal, Woodson promoted black history, combated racist historiography written by white scholars, and provided a vehicle for the publication of articles on the black experience in Africa and the Americas. Woodson formulated an editorial policy that was very inclusive. Topically, the journal provided coverage on all aspects of the black experience: slavery, the slave trade, black culture, the family, religion, the treatment of slaves, resistance to slavery, antislavery and abolitionism, and biographical articles on prominent African Americans. Chronologically, articles covered the sixteenth through the twentieth centuries. Interested amateurs, as well as scholars, published important historical articles in the journal, and Woodson took care to keep this balance between contributors. Most of the early contributors were his black colleagues and associates from the Washington, D.C., public schools, Howard University, and the organizations with which he was affiliated. When he lacked enough articles, Woodson may have written articles and signed his friends' names. He also wrote the majority of book reviews in early issues, sometimes leaving them unsigned or using pseudonyms.

The authors who published in the journal were pioneers of interpretation and method in black history. They used many of the techniques that were later adopted by social historians, beginning in the 1960s. Authors pointed to the positive achievements and contributions of African Americans during slavery, emphasized black struggles against slavery, uncovered the rich cultural traditions that blacks maintained in bondage, and challenged the widely held belief in black inferiority. Many scholars published significant articles that interpreted slavery from the slaves' point of view, rather than from the masters' perspective. This interpretation facilitated a shift in historiography in the mainstream of the historical profession, which would begin to adopt this perspective only in the late 1950s. Among the pathbreaking articles published in the journal were those of Herbert Aptheker, Melville Herskovits, Arthur Link, Kenneth Stampp, and, most notably, Richard Hofstader, whose critique of historian U. B. Phillips appeared in 1944. Also notable was black historians' emphasis on black culture created during slavery. While recognizing the harshness of slavery, these scholars argued that blacks had enough autonomy to create distinctive institutions. They also took note of the African background and the influence of African culture on African-American culture.

Among the many black scholars who published in the *Journal of Negro History* in its early years were John Hope Franklin, Lorenzo Johnson Greene, Rayford Logan, Benjamin Quarles, Charles Wesley, and Eric Williams. Woodson also published more articles by and about women than any of the other major historical journals. He highlighted the publication of documentary source materials that he and his associates had uncovered while doing research; by 1925, at least one-quarter of the journal's space was devoted to the publication of transcripts of primary source materials, thereby encouraging their use by scholars who otherwise would not have known about them.

Without Woodson's efforts, contemporary scholars would have fewer resources for studying African-American history. Woodson retired as editor of the journal in 1950. He was succeeded by Rayford W. Logan (1950–1951), William M. Brewer (1951–1970), W. Augustus Low (1970–1974), Lorraine A. Williams (1975–1976), Alton Hornsby Jr. (1976–2003), and V. P. Franklin, who assumed the editorship in 2003. In 2001 the name of the journal was changed to the *Journal of African American History*.

See also Association for the Study of African American Life and History; *Opportunity: Journal of Negro Life*; Woodson, Carter G.

■ ■ *Bibliography*

Conyers, James L., Jr. *Carter G. Woodson: A Historical Reader.* New York: Garland Publishing, 1999.

Goggin, Jacqueline. *Carter G. Woodson: A Life in Black History.* Baton Rouge, La.: Louisiana State University Press, 1993.

Goggin, Jacqueline. "Countering White Racist Scholarship: Carter G. Woodson and the Journal of Negro History." *Journal of Negro History* 68 (1983): 355–375.

JACQUELINE GOGGIN (1996)
Updated bibliography

JUDAISM

Estimates of the number of black people in the United States who consider themselves Jews or Hebrews range from 40,000 to 500,000. These people can be divided into three groups: individuals who convert to Judaism and join predominantly white congregations, often as a result of intermarriage, such as Julius Lester and the late Sammy Davis Jr.; African Americans who trace their Jewish heritage back to slavery and who worship in either black or white synagogues; and blacks whose attraction to Judaism is based on a racial identification with the biblical Hebrews.

The third group is by far the largest, but it is made up of many independent denominations that have a wide variety of beliefs and practices. The best known are the Black Jews of Harlem, the Temple Beth-El congregations, the Nation of Yahweh, the Original Hebrew Israelite Nation, the Israeli School of Universal Practical Knowledge, the Church of God, and the Nubian Islamic Hebrews. Reconstructionist Black Jews and Rastafarians are two groups whose relationship to Judaism or Hebrewism is so limited that they are best thought of as movements basically rooted in Christianity that have an affinity to the Old Testament and Jewish symbols.

Each of the major groups is unique and will be discussed separately, although they generally have the following characteristics in common: They believe that the ancient Hebrews were black people, that they are their descendants, and that their immediate ancestors were forcibly converted from Judaism to Christianity during slavery. In addition, they believe that they are not converts to Judaism but have discovered or returned to their true religion. On the other hand, they believe that white Jews are either converts to their way of life, descendants of one of the biblical people who they believe started the white race (Edomites, Canaanites, Japhites, or lepers), or that they are imposters altogether. This is the principal reason that some groups consider the term "Jew" anathema and insist on the biblical terms Hebrew or Israelite, or more commonly, Hebrew Israelite. They believe that the enslavement of and discrimination against African Americans were predicted in the Bible and are therefore a combination of divine punishment upon the children of Israel for their sins and the result of the blatant aggression of white people. Hebrew Israelites are messianic and believe that when the messiah comes, retribution will be handed down upon all sinners—but particularly upon white people for their oppression of people of color. Beyond these similarities—which a few Hebrew Israelites strongly oppose—the groups can differ widely according to the degree to which they follow rabbinic traditions, use Hebrew, conduct services, follow dress codes, and incorporate Christian or Islamic beliefs into their theology.

There have been three main phases in the use of elements of the Jewish religion in African-American worship. From exposure to evangelical Protestantism in the early nineteenth century, many African Americans identified with the enslavement, emancipation, and nation building of the Hebrews as depicted in the Bible. Old Testament imagery was a staple of sermons and spirituals. The best known of the latter is undoubtedly "Go Down, Moses," in which the release of the Hebrews from Egyptian captivity is seen as a sign of the redemption of blacks from slavery. This connection to the Jewish people, often strengthened by connections to Pan-African movements such as the one led by Marcus Garvey, provided the impetus for more formal identification as Jews, often outside of a Christian context, in the late nineteenth and early twentieth centuries. Since the 1960s, another period of active black nationalism, there has been renewed identification with elements of the Jewish religion by a number of African-American religious groups. Many of these groups are quite eclectic in their theology and religious borrowings, and are often hostile to mainstream Judaism.

The Black Jews of Harlem is one of the oldest, largest, and best known Hebrew Israelite groups in the United States. The denomination was founded in New York City by Rabbi Arnold J. Ford (1877–1935) and Rabbi Wentworth Arthur Matthew (1892–1973). Ford was the musical director of Garvey's Universal Negro Improvement Association (UNIA). The Black Jews based their nationalism of Ethiopianism on the belief that biblical prophecies about Ethiopia, notably Psalm 68:31 "Ethiopia shall soon stretch out her hands," referred to Ethiopia in connection with the regathering of the Children of Israel as applied specifically to black people. To achieve this Ford tried to create a black Jewish denomination based on beliefs and customs he learned from European Jews. During the early period the group used the term Ethiopian Hebrew rather than Hebrew Israelite. Also, whereas Ford and Matthew emphatically believed that the ancient Hebrews were black, they were less certain about the origins of white Jews and would sometimes refer to them as "our fairer brothers."

In 1923 Ford opened a congregation called Beth B'nai Abraham (House of the Children of Abraham) for black people in Harlem. Rabbi Matthew, who had founded The Commandment Keepers Congregation in Harlem four years earlier, became Ford's student. In 1933 Ford ordained Matthew before leaving for Ethiopia, where he lived the remainder of his life. Matthew quickly instituted the Jewish knowledge he gained from Ford into his services. In the late 1940s he created the Ethiopian Hebrew Rabbinical College in New York City, where he trained and ordained twenty-two other rabbis who carried their blend of black nationalist and orthodox European Judaism to black communities throughout the United States and the Caribbean. By the 1990s, this community was being led by two students of Matthew: Rabbi Levi Ben Levy, who is the chief rabbi of the Israelite Board of Rabbis, and Rabbi Yhoshua Ben Yahonatan, who is the president of the Israelite Council. The rabbis and congregation affiliated with these bodies have limited but cordial relations with mainstream white Jewish congregations in New York. The Black Jews generally conduct their services in both Hebrew and English, observe Jewish holidays such as Hanukkah and Purim, the high holy days, and ceremonies such as Bar and Bat Mitzvah. By the early 1990s, the size of the group was probably less than five thousand, though higher estimates are sometimes given.

The Temple Beth-El congregations, also known as the Church of God and Saints of Christ (CGSC), were founded by William Saunders Crowdy (1847–1908).

Crowdy was born a slave and fought in the Civil War. In 1893 he had a prophetic vision on his farm in Guthrie, Oklahoma, that told him to start a new church that had no affiliation with any religious denomination. The specific doctrines of the church evolved over time and were based on Crowdy's revelations, which he called the "Seven Keys." Crowdy taught that black people were part of the "lost tribes of Israel" and that the Hebraic Laws of the Old Testament, such as Passover, were to be obeyed. Unlike the Black Jews of Harlem, Crowdy did not abandon the use of the New Testament or a belief in Jesus Christ, and he continued practices such as baptism and ritual foot washing. In 1896 he founded his first church in Lawrence, Kansas. Two years later the first CGSC general assembly was held. By 1900 the church had five thousand members. After his death in 1908 the church suffered a split. As a whole, the church was at its height in 1936, when there were over 213 tabernacles in the United States. By the 1990s the number of tabernacles had declined to fifty-three with seven branches in South Africa. Over the years the Christian component of the Beth-El tabernacle has diminished and the Jewish elements have been augmented. The Temple's national headquarters is in Philadelphia, Pennsylvania, and its international headquarters is on a five-hundred-acre farm in Suffolk, Virginia. It has an estimated membership of 38,000.

The Church of God was founded by Prophet F. S. Cherry. The anthropologist Arthur Huff Fauset describes this group in *Black Gods of the Metropolis* (1944). Fauset reports that this group was located at 2132 Nicholas Street in Philadelphia, Pennsylvania. The church had fewer than three hundred members at its founding in the early twentieth century, and there was no mention of affiliate congregations. All that is known about Prophet Cherry is that he was born in the South and worked as a seaman and on the railroads, which allowed him to travel throughout the United States and to many parts of the world. He was self-educated and taught his followers that they were the original Hebrews. They believed that Jesus was the messiah and used the Old and New Testaments in their services. Hebrew and Yiddish were taught in the church's schools, but white Jews were generally thought to be imposters. Saturday was considered to be the Sabbath Day, but services were also held on Sundays. The group celebrated Passover and did not recognize either Christmas or Easter. The eating of pork was prohibited among members of the group, as was the taking of pictures. Prophet Cherry predicted that the new millennium would take place in the year 2000. Whether the denomination still exists is unknown.

The Nation of Yahweh, also known as the Temple of Love, was founded by Hulon Mitchell (1935–), who calls himself Yahweh Ben Yahweh ("God the Son of God"). Yahweh Ben Yahweh was raised in a Pentecostal church; in the 1960s he joined the Nation of Islam before leaving it to start his congregation of Hebrew Israelites in the 1970s. Members of this group believe that the black people of America are the "lost sheep of the House of Israel." They teach that white people are "real devils" and will be destroyed when God restores black people to power. Members of this group are encouraged to wear long white robes and they use the Star of David—though they also believe in Jesus. They believe that black people should not participate in political processes and that there is a government-sponsored plan to commit genocide against African people. By the 1990s the Nation of Yahweh had congregations in thirty-five cities in the United States. Its headquarters is in the Miami area, where members own many businesses, housing units, a printing press, a fleet of buses, and a school. The Nation of Yahweh has been indicted on a number of state and federal charges ranging from extortion to child abuse. In 1992 its leader, Yahweh Ben Yahweh, was convicted of murder and racketeering and sentenced to prison. His followers saw the conviction as a case of political oppression, and most have remained loyal to the group.

The Original Hebrew Israelite Nation was founded by Ben Ammi Carter in Chicago during the 1960s. They attempt to follow what they conceive of as an ancient form of Judaism that includes polygamy. They have developed a unique garb that resembles African and Middle Eastern attire, which includes colorful robes and knitted skullcaps, or turbans. Members of this group are strict vegetarians and believe that they are witnessing the "end of the Gentile age," which is taken to mean the end of a period of white rule. This is the only group of Hebrew Israelites that is Zionist and has attempted to immigrate to Israel. In 1969 the first of 1,500 Hebrew Israelites left Liberia, where they had established a temporary settlement, to found a permanent settlement in Dimona, Israel. Since their identity as Jews was questioned by Israeli authorities, they have not been granted Israeli citizenship under the Law of Return, which guarantees citizenship to persons who are regarded as Jews under rabbinic law. However, some members of this group are allowed to work and own businesses in various cities around the country and perform in a popular musical group at Israeli festivals. As a whole, members of this group have very little contact with either Israelis, Arabs, or Ethiopians—though they still have followers in the United States.

The Nubian Islamic Hebrew Mission, also known as the Ansaaru Allah Community, traces its origin to Mohammed Ahmed Ibn Adulla (1845–1885), the leader of a revolt against British occupation of the Sudan in the 1880s. Mohammed Ahmed was hailed by his followers as the Mahdi, the predicted Khaliyfah (successor) to the Prophet Mohammed. In 1993 the group was lead by As Sayyid Al Imaan Isa Al Haadi Al Hadhi, the alleged great-grandson of the founder. The group organized in the United States in the late 1960s. They believe that they are both Hebrew and Muslim because both nationalities trace their lineage to Abraham, who they believe was a black man. They profess to observe all the laws and holidays of the Torah and the Koran—though Arabic and Islamic beliefs seem to be more prominent. The group's emblem is the Star of David and the inverted crescent. Their headquarters is in Brooklyn, New York, and they have followers in many cities throughout the United States. Members of this group do not recognize Orthodox Muslims as true followers of Islam, nor do they recognize white Jews as Hebrews. They repudiate the Nation of Islam, Malcolm X, and Wallace D. Mohammed as spreading a false Islam to black people. They teach that Abraham is the father of their nation, Jesus was the Messiah, and Mohammed was the last prophet. Members of this group wear white robes, and many are vendors on the streets of New York, where they sell incense, idols, and books, and recruit new members.

The Israeli School of Universal Practical Knowledge was founded in Harlem during the 1960s and claims to have branches throughout the United States. Two of their leaders are Ta-Har, who describes himself as a high priest, and Peter Sherrod, who runs the school. Like most of the other Black Jewish groups, they believe that black people are the only true Hebrew Israelites. White people are generally thought to be evil according to the teachings of this group. They are a paramilitary organization, and their mostly male followers dress in flamboyant garb that is either African in design or altered military fatigues. Their dress is often adorned with big belt buckles and emblems of different kinds, and they often wear turbans and combat boots. They also carry large staffs or wear swords or daggers. They propagate their message from street corners in New York and by means of a public-access cable TV program called "It's Time to Wake Up," which began in the early 1990s. They teach that the Twelve Tribes of Israel correspond to "Negroes (African Americans), West Indians, Haitians, Dominicans, Panamanians, Puerto Ricans, Cubans, North American Indians, Seminole Indians, Brazilians, Argentineans, and Mexicans." They believe that the scriptures predict a violent confrontation between black and white people in which black people will be victorious, and the ancient nation of Israel will be restored.

Rastafarians are sometimes considered a sect of Hebrew Israelites because they believe that Haile Selassie was the messiah and a descendant of King Solomon and the Queen of Sheba. They place particular emphasis on the Old Testament laws concerning the Nazzerites, who were not allowed to cut their hair. This practice has developed into the wearing of dreadlocks that have been popularized by reggae musicians since the 1970s. There are also references to the Lion of Judah and the Star of David in their music.

There are a number of other small religious groups not discussed here that have more in common with Pentecostal "holiness" churches or purely political organizations, which make use of some Jewish elements in their worship. However, with many of these other groups, Judaism or Hebraisms are a minor part of their doctrine and ritual.

See also Pan-Africanism; Rastafarianism; Religion

■ ■ *Bibliography*

Berger, Graenum. *Black Jews in America: A Documentary with Commentary.* New York: Commission on Synagogue Relations, 1978.

Brotz, Howard M. *The Black Jews of Harlem: Negro Nationalism and the Dilemmas of Negro Leadership.* New York: Free Press of Glencoe, 1964.

Fauset, Arthur Huff. *Black Gods of the Metropolis: Negro Religious Cults of the Urban North.* Philadelphia: University of Pennsylvania Press, 1971.

Landing, James E. *Black Judaism: Story of an American Movement.* Durham, N.C.: Carolina Academic Press, 2002.

Onolemhemhen, Durrenda Nash. *The Black Jews of Ethiopia.* Lanham, Md.: Scarecrow Press, 2002.

SHOLOMO BEN LEVY (1996)
Updated Bibliography

JUST, ERNEST

AUGUST 14, 1883
OCTOBER 27, 1941

⊢⊩⊣

Zoologist and educator Ernest Everett Just was born in Charleston, South Carolina, the son of Charles Fraser Just, a carpenter and wharf builder, and his wife, Mary Mathews Cooper Just, a teacher and civic leader. His early education was received at a school run by his mother, the Frederick Deming, Jr. Industrial School. In 1896 he entered the teacher-training program of the Colored Normal, Industrial, Agricultural and Mechanical College (South Carolina State College) in Orangeburg, South Car-

olina. After graduating in 1899 he attended Kimball Union Academy in Meriden, New Hampshire (1900–1903), before proceeding to Dartmouth College. At Dartmouth he majored in biology and minored in Greek and history. He received an A.B., graduating magna cum laude, in 1907.

Essentially, two career options were available to an African American with Just's academic background: teaching in a black institution or preaching in a black church. Just chose the former, beginning his career in the fall of 1907 as an instructor in English and rhetoric at Howard University. In 1909 he taught English and biology, and a year later he assumed a permanent full-time commitment in zoology as part of a general revitalization of the science curriculum at Howard. He also taught physiology in the medical school. A devoted teacher, he served as faculty adviser to a group that was trying to establish a nationwide fraternity of black students. The Alpha chapter of Omega Psi Phi was organized at Howard in 1911, and Just became its first honorary member. In 1912 he married a fellow Howard faculty member, Ethel Highwarden. They had three children—Margaret, Highwarden, and Maribel.

Meanwhile, Just laid plans to pursue scientific research. In 1909 he started studying at the Marine Biological Laboratory (MBL) in Woods Hole, Massachusetts, under the eminent scientist Frank Rattray Lillie, MBL director and head of the zoology department at the University of Chicago. He also served as Lillie's research assistant. Their relationship quickly blossomed into a full and equal scientific collaboration. By the time Just earned a Ph.D. in zoology at the University of Chicago in 1916, he had already coauthored a paper with Lillie and written several on his own.

The two worked on fertilization in marine animals. Just's first paper, "The Relation of the First Cleavage Plane to the Entrance Point of the Sperm," appeared in *Biological Bulletin* in 1912 and was cited frequently as a classic and authoritative study. He went on to champion a theory—the fertilizin theory—first proposed by Lillie, who postulated the existence of a substance called "fertilizin" as the essential biochemical catalyst in the fertilization of the egg by the sperm. In 1915 Just was awarded the NAACP's first Spingarn Medal in recognition of his scientific contributions and "foremost service to his race."

Science was for Just a deeply felt avocation, an activity he looked forward to doing each summer at the MBL as a welcome respite from his heavy teaching and administrative responsibilities at Howard. Under the circumstances his productivity was extraordinary. Within ten years (1919–1928), he published thirty-five articles, mostly relating to his studies on fertilization. Though proud of his output, he yearned for a position or environment in which he could pursue his research full-time.

In 1928 Just received a substantial grant from the Julius Rosenwald Fund that allowed him a change of environment and longer stretches of time for his research. His first excursion, in 1929, took him to Italy, where he worked for seven months at the Stazione Zoologica in Naples. He traveled to Europe ten times over the course of the next decade, staying for periods ranging from three weeks to two years. He worked primarily at the Stazione Zoologica; the Kaiser-Wilhelm Institut für Biologie in Berlin; and the Station Biologique in Roscoff, France.

In Europe Just wrote a book synthesizing many of the scientific theories, philosophical ideas, and experimental results of his career. The book was published under the title *Biology of the Cell Surface* in 1939. Its thesis, that the ectoplasm or cell surface has a fundamental role in development, did not receive much attention at the time but later became a major focus of scientific investigation. Also in 1939 he published a compendium of experimental advice under the title *Basic Methods for Experiments on Eggs of Marine Animals*. In 1940 Just was interned briefly in France following the German invasion and then released to return to America, where he died a year later. Just was featured on a U.S. postage stamp in 1996.

See also Howard University; Science

■ ■ *Bibliography*

Gould, Stephen Jay. "Just in the Middle: A Solution to the Mechanist-Vitalist Controversy." *Natural History* (January 1984): 24–33.

Manning, Kenneth R. *Black Apollo of Science: The Life of Ernest Everett Just.* New York: Oxford University Press, 1983.

KENNETH R. MANNING (1996)

Karenga, Maulana

1941

The activist and educator Ronald McKinley Everett, later known as Maulana Karenga, was born in Parsonburg, Maryland, the youngest of fourteen children of a Baptist minister. He moved to Los Angeles in 1959 and received his B.A. (1963) and M.A. (1964) in political science from the University of California, Los Angeles (UCLA). He became active in local civil rights battles and in 1965 he helped rebuild the Watts community following the riots earlier that year. At that time he embraced cultural nationalism and adopted the African name Maulana (master teacher) Karenga (keeper of the tradition). In 1966 Karenga founded US (indicating *us* as opposed to *them*), a small vanguard nationalist organization that maintained that a black cultural renaissance was the first step in the revolutionary struggle for black power.

Karenga was deeply influenced by Pan-Africanists such as Ghana's Kwame Nkrumah, the American W. E. B. Du Bois, the Negritude movement epitomized by Senegal's Leopold Senghor, and the African socialism pioneered by Tanzania's Julius Nyerere. Domestically, Karenga was influenced by the black nationalist tradition epitomized by Marcus Garvey, the Nation of Islam, and especially Malcolm X. To achieve true liberation, Karenga increasingly argued, African Americans needed to embrace a culture that reflected their African heritage. Karenga called this ideology Kawaida. In effect, Kawaida stressed that black liberation could not be achieved unless black people rejected the cultural values of the dominant white society. Under his leadership, US's guiding principle became "back to black." Members wore traditional African garb, promoted the teaching of Swahili, sponsored Afrocentric events, and often attempted to work in coalitions with other black organizations. Although consisting of fewer than one hundred members, US played an important role in promoting and building independent schools, black studies departments, and black student unions.

Karenga believed that African Americans should base their lives on seven African values: *umoja* (unity), *kujichagulia* (self-determination), *ujima* (collective work and responsibility), *ujamaa* (cooperative economics), *nia* (purpose), *kuumba* (creativity), and *imani* (faith). In 1966 he founded the holiday of Kwanza, a seven-day celebration based on these principles. Karenga coplanned and helped to convene Black Power conferences in Washington, D.C. (1966), Newark, New Jersey (1967), and Philadelphia (1968).

His popularity declined, however, in the late 1960s and early 1970s due to internal turmoil within US as well as intense struggles with the Black Panther Party over the control and direction of the West Coast black nationalist movement. The Black Panther Party viewed socioeconomic struggle, not cultural reaffirmation, as the key to black liberation. Confrontations too often escalated into violence because of both groups' reliance on arms. In 1968, following a bitter debate and violent confrontation over the appointment of a director of the Afro-American Studies Center at UCLA, three US members were ultimately convicted of the shooting deaths of two Black Panthers. In 1976, the FBI admitted to abetting the warfare between US and the Black Panther Party in an attempt to undermine both organizations.

In 1971 Karenga was charged with and later convicted of aggravated assault on two female US members. He received an indeterminate sentence of one to ten years. Upon his release from prison in 1975, he embraced socialism and called for black people to struggle against class, as well as racial, oppression. One year later he received a doctorate in leadership and human behavior from U.S. International University in San Diego.

Throughout the 1990s and during the early twenty-first century, Karenga has remained a vocal proponent of Afrocentrism. He served as director of the African-American Cultural Center in Los Angeles as well as chairman of the black studies department at California State University at Long Beach. In 1993 Karenga earned another doctorate, this one in social ethics, from the University of Southern California. He is the author of numerous articles and texts, including *The Quotable Karenga* (1967), *Introduction to Black Studies* (1982), *Kemet, the African World View: Research and Restoration* (1986), and *Kwanzaa: A Celebration of Family, Community and Culture* (1998).

See also Afrocentrism; Black Power Movement; Black Studies; Du Bois, W. E. B.; Kawaida; Nationalism in the United States in the Nineteenth Century; Pan-Africanism

■ ■ *Bibliography*

Alexander, Victor S. "Interview: Dr. Maulana Ron Karenga." *African Commentary* 1, no. 1 (October 1989): 61–64.

Brown, Scot. *Fighting for US: Maulana Karenga, the US Organization, and Black Cultural Nationalism*. New York: New York University Press. 2003.

Van Deburg, William L. *New Day in Babylon: The Black Power Movement and American Culture, 1965–1975*. Chicago: University of Chicago Press, 1992.

WALDO E. MARTIN JR. (1996)
Updated by author 2005

KAWAIDA

The philosophy of the cultural nationalist theory and movement called kawaida (a Swahili word meaning "tradition" or "reason," pronounced *ka-wa-EE-da*) is a synthesis of nationalist, pan-Africanist, and socialist ideologies. It was created and defined by Maulana Karenga during the height of black pride and self-awareness that characterized the Black Power movement in 1966. Karenga believed that black people needed a change of consciousness before they could mount a political struggle to empower themselves. He argued that the reclamation of an African value system based on the *nguzo saba* (seven principles) of *umoja* (unity), *kujichagulia* (self-determination), *ujima* (collective work and responsibility), *ujamaa* (cooperative economics), *nia* (purpose), *kuumba* (creativity), and *imani* (faith) would serve as a catalyst to motivate, intensify, and sustain the black struggle against racism. This value system, which served as the basis of kawaida, would provide the foundation for a new African-American culture defined in terms of mythology (religion); history; social, economic, and political organization; creative production; and ethos.

Kawaida, the guiding philosophy behind Karenga's California-based cultural nationalist organization, called US, was introduced to a wider audience of African Americans at the National Conference on Black Power in Newark, New Jersey, in 1967. Although some African Americans criticized the ideology for not mounting a revolutionary challenge to the economic status quo, the search for connections to an African past and the ideal of unifying the black nation had widespread appeal.

Amiri Baraka, a writer and militant activist, became the chief spokesperson for the ideology in the late 1960s and was key to its popularization. Baraka believed that kawaida could be used to politicize the black masses, and he supported the creation of community theaters and schools that focused on African cultural values. In the late 1960s he became head of the Temple of Kawaida in Newark, New Jersey, which taught African religions, and he played a key role in the creation of Kawaida Towers, a low- and middle-income housing project in Newark, during the early 1970s. Baraka sought to bridge the gaps between culture, politics, and economics, and by 1974 he had reinterpreted kawaida to include a socialist critique of capitalism.

Kawaida's influence in black America continued to grow, and the ideology provided a basis for the development of theories of Afrocentricity in the late 1970s and 1980s. In the late 1980s, the National Association of Kawaida Organizations (NAKO) was founded under Karenga's direction. NAKO sponsors workshops, forums, and symposia to promote awareness of and appreciation for Africa in the black community. The most influential expression of kawaida is Kwanza, an African-American holiday based on the *nguzo saba,* which Karenga created in 1966.

See also Baraka, Amiri (Jones, LeRoi); Black Power Movement; Karenga, Maulana; Kwanza; Nationalism in the United States in the Nineteenth Century; Pan-Africanism

▪▪ *Bibliography*

Baraka, Imamu Amiri. *Kawaida Studies: The New Nationalism.* Chicago, Ill.: Third World Press, 1972.

Baraka, Imamu Amiri. *Kawaida, National Liberation, and Socialism.* Newark, N.J.: Jihad, 1974.

Huber, Palmer. "Three Black Nationalist Organizations and Their Impact upon Their Times." Ph.D. diss., Claremont Graduate School, 1973.

Karenga, Maulana. *Kawaida Theory: An Introductory Outline.* Inglewood, Calif.: Kawaida Publications, 1980.

Van Deburg, William L. *New Day in Babylon: The Black Power Movement and American Culture, 1965–1975.* Chicago: University of Chicago Press, 1992.

MANSUR M. NURUDDIN (1996)
ROBYN SPENCER (1996)

KECKLEY, ELIZABETH

1818
MAY 26, 1907

Dressmaker Elizabeth Keckley was born Elizabeth Hobbs, to a slave family in Dinwiddie Court House, Virginia. While in her teens she was sold to a North Carolina slaveowner, and in North Carolina she was raped, probably by her owner, and gave birth to a son. At the age of eighteen she was repurchased, along with her son, by the daughter of her original owner and taken to Saint Louis. There she began her career as a dressmaker, supporting her owners and their five children as well as her own son. In Saint Louis she married James Keckley—a slave who convinced her to marry him by claiming to be free—but soon separated from him.

In 1855 Keckley's dressmaking customers lent her $1,200 to purchase her freedom. She established a successful dressmaking business, and in 1860 she moved first to Baltimore and then to Washington, D.C., where she established herself as one of the capital's elite dressmakers. One of her customers was the wife of Jefferson Davis.

Mary Todd Lincoln, the wife of President Abraham Lincoln, became one of Keckley's most loyal customers. Keckley soon made all of the First Lady's clothes, and the two struck up a close friendship. From 1861 to 1865 Keckley worked in the White House as Mary Todd Lincoln's dressmaker and personal maid.

During the Civil War Keckley became active in the abolitionist movement, helping found an organization of black women to assist former slaves seeking refuge in Washington, D.C. The Contraband Relief Association received a $200 donation from Mary Todd Lincoln, and Keckley successfully solicited several prominent abolitionists for financial support, including Wendell Phillips and Frederick Douglass.

After the assassination of President Lincoln, Mary Todd Lincoln and Keckley remained close friends until 1868, when Keckley's diaries were published as a book, *Behind the Scenes; or, Thirty Years a Slave, and Four Years in the White House.* Mary Todd Lincoln considered the book a betrayal and broke off her relationship with Keckley. Even several noted African Americans criticized Keckley for what they believed to be a dishonorable attack on "the Great Emancipator." Nonetheless, the book has long been considered an invaluable resource for scholars of the Lincoln presidency. It reveals much about the personalities of Abraham and Mary Todd Lincoln, their family life, and their opinions about government officials. The memoir also offers an intimate depiction of Keckley's life in slavery, particularly of the sexual violence she endured as a teenager. Although its accuracy has not been questioned, the book's true authorship has been the subject of considerable debate, since its polished prose seems to be at odds with Keckley's lack of formal education.

Keckley's dressmaking business declined as a result of the controversy surrounding the book. In the 1890s she was briefly a teacher of domestic science, but for most of her later years lived in obscurity, supported by a pension paid to her because her son had been killed fighting for the Union army. Keckley died in 1907 in a Washington rest home she had helped found.

See also Abolition; Douglass, Frederick; Slave Narratives

▪▪ *Bibliography*

Fleischner, Jennifer. *Mrs. Lincoln and Mrs. Keckley: The Remarkable Story of the Friendship between the First Lady and a Former Slave.* New York: Broadway, 2003.

Hine, Darlene Clark. *Black Women in America: An Historical Encyclopedia.* Brooklyn, N.Y.: Carlson, 1993.

Keckley, Elizabeth. *Behind the Scenes; or, Thirty Years a Slave, and Four Years in the White House* (1868). New York: Oxford University Press, 1988.

Washington, John E. *They Knew Lincoln.* New York: Dutton, 1942.

THADDEUS RUSSELL (1996)
Updated bibliography

KEITH, DAMON JEROME

JULY 4, 1922

The federal judge Damon Jerome Keith was born and raised in Detroit, Michigan. He earned an A.B. in 1943 from West Virginia State College, then served as a staff sergeant in the U.S. Army from 1943 to 1946. In 1949 he received an LL.B. from Howard University. He returned to Detroit and from 1951 to 1955 worked as an attorney at the Office of the Friend of the Court. In 1956 he received an LL.M. from Wayne State University. Keith was a founding member of the Detroit law firm of Keith, Conyers, Anderson, Brown, and Whals, where he was a full partner from 1964 to 1967. During his years in private practice, he was active in civil rights work as president of the Detroit Housing Commission (1958–1967), chairman of the Michigan Civil Rights Commission (1964–1967), and in other organizations, as well as being an active member in both the Detroit Area Council of the Boy Scouts of America and the Tabernacle Baptist Church.

In 1967 President Lyndon B. Johnson appointed him to the U.S. Federal District Court for Michigan. Among his most important decisions, often referred to by legal scholars as the Keith Decision, was the case of *United States v. U.S. District Court* (1971), in which he ruled that warrantless wiretaps, even those ordered by the president, are unconstitutional.

In 1974 Keith was awarded the National Association for the Advancement of Colored People (NAACP)'s Spingarn Medal. Three years later President Jimmy Carter appointed Keith to the Sixth Circuit, comprising Tennessee, Kentucky, Ohio, and Michigan. In 1979, in a widely noticed opinion, Keith, who has a reputation as a liberal Democrat, ruled in favor of the Detroit Police Department's affirmative action hiring program.

Keith has served as the first vice president of the Detroit chapter of the NAACP. In 1987 Chief Justice William Rehnquist appointed Keith national chair of the Judicial Conference Committee on the Bicentennial of the Constitution. In 1993 Wayne State University established, in Keith's honor, the Damon J. Keith Law Collection, the first archival collection devoted entirely to African-American lawyers and judges.

Keith was awarded the Thurgood Marshall Award in 1997 and the Edward J. Devitt Award for Distinguished Service to Justice in 1998. In 2001 an official portrait of Keith was unveiled in the U.S. Courthouse in Detroit. In 2004, at the age of eighty-two, Keith was still serving on the U.S. Court of Appeals.

See also National Association for the Advancement of Colored People (NAACP); Spingarn Medal

■ ■ *Bibliography*

"Damon Jerome Keith." *Contemporary Black Biography,* Vol. 16. Detroit, Mich.: Gale, 1997.

"Federal Judge Damon Keith Honored by Michigan Governor for Twenty Years on Bench." *Jet,* December 21, 1987, p. 14.

LOUISE P. MAXWELL (1996)
Updated by publisher 2005

KENNEDY, ADRIENNE

SEPTEMBER 13, 1931

The playwright Adrienne Kennedy was born Adrienne Lita Hawkins in Pittsburgh, Pennsylvania, and grew up in Cleveland, Ohio, where she went to public school. She received her Bachelor of Arts in education from Ohio State University in 1952 and shortly thereafter moved to New York City with her husband and child. Over the following ten years, she studied creative writing at various schools, including Columbia University (1954–1956), the New School for Social Research (1957), and the American Theater Wing (1958). The first of Kennedy's plays to be produced, *Funnyhouse of a Negro* (1963), was written while she was attending Edward Albee's workshop at the Circle in the Square. *Funnyhouse,* a one-act play about a young mulatto woman's efforts to come to terms with her mixed-race heritage, opened off-Broadway in 1964. Kennedy wrote two other one-act plays, *A Rat's Mass* and *The Owl Answers,* in 1963, and she received the Stanley Drama Award for *Funnyhouse* and *The Owl Answers* that same year. She won an Obie Award for *Funnyhouse* in 1964.

Kennedy, an avant-garde dramatist, has considered the one-act play to be the most congenial form for exploring conflicts of race, gender, and identity. Her plays tend to be surrealistic and symbolic, rather than naturalistic, and she frequently uses masks or divides a single character's story among several characters or actors in order to convey a sense of racial and psychic disorientation. Kennedy's fourth one-act play, *A Lesson in Dead Language,* was written in 1964. The following year, *A Beast's Story* appeared; it was performed in Westport, Connecticut, but did not open off-Broadway until 1969, when it was billed with *The Owl Answers* under the title *Cities in Bezique.*

Between the years 1967 and 1969, Kennedy was awarded a Guggenheim Memorial Fellowship as well as several writing grants from the Rockefeller Foundation. Her first full-length play, *In His Own Write,* an adaptation of John Lennon's stories and poems, was written in 1967 and produced in London by the National Theatre Company. In 1971 Kennedy joined with five other women playwrights in founding the Women's Theater Council, a cooperative designed to promote the works of women playwrights and provide opportunities for women in other aspects of theater. *An Evening with Dead Essex,* her one-act memorial to Mark Essex, a black New Orleans youth who was murdered by the police, was written two years later.

During the 1970s and early 1980s, Kennedy taught creative writing at Yale, Princeton, and Brown universities and received grants from the National Endowment for the Arts and the Creative Artists Public Service. Her second full-length play, *A Movie Star Has to Star in Black and White,* opened off-off-Broadway in 1976. In 1980, Kennedy was commissioned by the Empire State Youth Theatre Institute in Albany, New York, to write a children's musical, *A Lancashire Lad,* about the boyhood of Charlie Chaplin. That year, she wrote another children's play, *Black Children's Day,* based on the black experience in Rhode Island. In 1981, she was commissioned by the Juilliard School to write a full-length adaptation of the Greek tragedies *Orestes* and *Electra.* The year 1987 marked the appearance of another full-length play, *Diary of Lights,* and the publication of her memoirs, *People Who Led to My Plays.* In 1994, Kennedy was the recipient of the Lila Wallace-Reader's Digest Fund's Writer's Award, which she used to establish an arts and culture program for minority children in Cleveland's inner-city schools.

Kennedy was the Playwright-in-Residence for the 1995-1996 season of the Signature Theatre Company in New York City. The season included the world premieres of the plays *June and Jean in Concert* and *Sleep Deprivation Chamber,* the latter written in conjunction with her son Adam. Both plays won the Obie Award for Best New Play. In 2003 Kennedy received the Lifetime Achievement Award from the Anisfield-Wolf Book Awards. She is also the recipient of an Academy Award in Literature from the American Academy of Arts and Letters.

See also Drama

■ ■ *Bibliography*

Betsko, Kathleen, and Rachel Koenig, eds. *Interviews with Contemporary Women Playwrights.* New York: Beech Tree Books, 1987.

Bryant-Jackson, Paul K., and Lois More Overbeck, eds. *Intersecting Boundaries, The Theater of Adrienne Kennedy.* Minneapolis, University of Minnesota Press, 1992.

Kennedy, Adrienne. *People Who Led To My Plays.* New York: Knopf, 1986.

Kennedy, Adrienne. *The Adrienne Kennedy Reader,* introduction by Werner Sollors. Minneapolis: University of Minnesota Press, 2001.

PAMELA WILKINSON (1996)
Updated bibliography

KENNEDY, IMOGENE QUEENIE

FEBRUARY 8, 1928
MARCH 10, 1998

■ ■ ■

Imogene Elizabeth Dixon (known familiarly as B and Beatrice) was born into a peasant family at Dalvey in Saint Thomas Parish, southeastern Jamaica. Her involvement in African culture was influenced by her maternal grandparents, with whom she grew until prepubescence and who were West Central Africans brought to work on sugar estates in the second half of the nineteenth century. Her experience of Kumina derived largely from ceremonies held by a neighbor, "Man" Parker. Her uncle, Clifford Flemming, was an adherent of Flenkey (or Bongo or Convince), a cult of ancestor communication. Kennedy, however, credited her vocation to mystical inspiration that began with her childhood inclination toward solitude and her eventual self-seclusion in the wall-like roots of a silk-cotton tree, believed to house spirits of the dead. Secreted here for twenty-one days, she saw visions of people and heard voices speaking in "the African language," teaching her words and songs. This language was the Kumina ritual code, consisting of Koongo, Mbundu, and Jamaican English words embedded in Jamaican English grammar and denuded Koongo syntax.

Imogene migrated to Two-Mile, off the Spanish Town Road in west Kingston, in the late 1940s. She initially practiced Kumina with Cyrus Wallace, a Kumina leader, but Kennedy's mother was a Revivalist and also associated with several Revival leaders, including Mallica "Kapo" Reynolds, a painter and sculptor of religious themes. Kennedy indicated that Kumina ceremonies occur within Revival when an "African messenger" (spirit) wishes to "complete its journey," just as Revival adherents rock their bodies in spiritual possession during Kumina. She acknowledged manifesting as a "dove" (peacemaker, conciliator) in the Revival mode of worship, and this accounted for her wearing of blue or blue and white and entering a pool of water during some ceremonies.

During the 1950s, Kennedy attracted the attention of Edward Seaga during his anthropological research into Jamaican religions. By 1963, when the first Jamaica Independence Festival was held, Seaga was the minister of development and welfare and he invited Kennedy to perform Kumina drumming, dances, and songs for secular Jamaican audiences. Her brother was the accomplished lead drummer in her "bands" (religious group), which appeared on television and at cultural events in Jamaica, England, the United States, and Germany.

By the 1960s, Imogene was called Queenie, a title indicating her status as leader of a Kumina group, a healer and counselor to a substantial clientele. Queenie was a graceful dancer, inching forward with mincing steps, her arms outspread, sometimes balancing a water-filled glass on her head. She exuded self-possession and authority in her voice and manner, despite her diminutive figure, and led the singing in a strident, rich contralto. Queenie married Clinton Kennedy on January 31, 1963, had one daughter, raised several other children, and moved from Trench Town, her second Kingston home, to Waterloo, in Saint Catherine parish, in 1975. She died in 1998.

Her accessibility to researchers and the use of her spiritual aura for healing rather than monetary reward have sealed her place in twentieth-century Jamaican cultural history. Among the institutions she assisted artistically are the Jamaican Folk Singers, the Jamaica Memory Bank, the National Dance Theatre Company, and the Jamaica Cultural and Development Commission. The government of Jamaica awarded her the Order of Distinction (Officer Class) in 1983 for "services in the development of African heritage."

See also Creole Languages of the Americas; Kumina; Revivalism

■ ■ *Bibliography*

Brathwaite, Edward Kamau. "Kumina: The Spirit of African Survival." *Jamaica Journal* 42 (1978): 44–63.

Carter, Hazel. "Annotated Kumina Lexicon." *African-Caribbean Institute of Jamaica Research Review* 3 (1996): 84–129.

Lewin, Olive. *"Rock It Come Over": The Folk Music of Jamaica.* Kingston, Jamaica: University of the West Indies Press, 2000.

Seaga, Edward. "Revival Cults in Jamaica: Notes towards a Sociology of Religion." *Jamaica Journal* 3 (1969): 2–13.

Warner-Lewis, Maureen. *The Nkuyu: Spirit Messengers of the Kumina.* Mona, Jamaica: Savacou, 1977.

MAUREEN WARNER-LEWIS (2005)

KERNER REPORT

The Kerner Report was the result of a seven-month study by the National Commission on Civil Disorders, set up to pinpoint the cause of racial violence in American cities during the late 1960s. The eleven-member panel was better known as the Kerner Commission, after its chairman, Governor Otto Kerner of Illinois.

President Lyndon Johnson appointed the commission on July 28, 1967, in the wake of large-scale urban rioting in the United States between 1965 and 1967, which resulted in several deaths and injuries as well as widespread property damage. The commission was charged with tracing the specific events that led up to the violence, finding general reasons for the worsening racial atmosphere in the country, and suggesting solutions to prevent future disorders.

The Kerner Report was submitted to Johnson in February 1968. It concluded, in part, that the violence had its roots in the frustration and anger of poor urban blacks concerning such problems as high unemployment, discrimination, poor schools and health care, and police bias.

Stating that discrimination and segregation were deeply embedded in American society, the report warned that America was "moving toward two societies, one black, one white—separate and unequal." The report recommended a massive national commitment to sweeping reforms to improve education, housing, employment opportunities, and city services in poor black urban areas.

The Reverend Dr. Martin Luther King Jr. called the report "a physician's warning of approaching death, with a prescription for life." The prescription was, however, largely ignored. Many whites thought the report placed too much blame for the riots on societal problems and white racism, and not enough on the lawlessness of black rioters. Johnson accepted the report but did not support its conclusions, and few of the report's recommendations were ever implemented.

See also Red Summer; Riots and Popular Protests

■ ■ *Bibliography*

Carson, Clayborne, ed. *Eyes on the Prize: America's Civil Rights Years.* New York: Penguin, 1987.

Harris, Fred R., and Roger W. Wilkins, eds. *Quiet Riots: Race and Poverty in the United States—The Kerner Report Twenty Years Later.* New York: Pantheon Books, 1988.

Karl, Jonathan, and Kevin Smith. "Thirty Years after Kerner Report, Some Say Racial Divide Wider." CNN Interactive. Available from http://www.cnn.com/US/9803/01/kerner .commission/.

O'Reilly, Kenneth. *Racial Matters: The FBI's Secret File on Black Americans, 1960–1972.* New York: Free Press, 1989.

RENE SKELTON (1996)

KILLENS, JOHN OLIVER

JANUARY 14, 1916
OCTOBER 27, 1987

▌▌▌

The novelist John Oliver Killens was born in Macon, Georgia, to Charles Myles Sr. and Willie Lee (Coleman) Killens. He credits his relatives with fostering in him cultural pride and literary values—his father had him read a weekly column by Langston Hughes; his mother, president of the Dunbar Literary Club, introduced him to poetry; and his great-grandmother filled his boyhood with the hardships and tales of slavery. Such early exposure to criticism, art, and folklore is evident in his fiction, which is noted for its accurate depictions of social classes, its engaging narratives, and its successful layering of African-American history, legends, songs, and jokes.

Killens originally planned to be a lawyer. After attending Edward Waters College in Jacksonville, Florida (1934-1935) and Morris Brown College in Atlanta, Georgia (c. 1935-1936), he moved to Washington, D.C., became a staff member of the National Labor Relations Board, and completed his B.A. through evening classes at Howard University. He studied at the Robert Terrel Law School from 1939 until 1942, when he abandoned his pursuit of a degree and joined the army. His second novel, *And Then We Heard the Thunder* (1963), which deals with racism in the military, is based on his service in the South Pacific. It was nominated for the Pulitzer Prize.

In 1946 Killens returned briefly to his office job at the National Labor Relations Board. In 1947-1948 he organized black and white workers for the Congress of Industrial Organizations (CIO) and was an active member of the Progressive Party. But he soon became convinced that leading intellectuals, the white working class, and the U.S. government were not truly committed to creating a more inclusive society.

In 1948 Killens moved to New York, where he attended writing classes at Columbia University and New York University and met such influential figures as Langston Hughes, Paul Robeson, and W. E. B. Du Bois. While working on his fiction, he wrote regularly for the leftist newspaper *Freedom* (1951–1955). His views at the time, closely aligned with those of the Communist Party, were evident in his 1952 review of Ralph Ellison's novel *Invisible Man*. He attacked the novel as a "decadent mixture . . . a vicious distortion of Negro life." Killens believed that literature should be judged on its potential for improving society: "Art is functional. A Black work of art helps the liberation or hinders it."

Fortunately, Killens had already found some young writers, many with close ties to left-wing or black nationalist organizations, committed to the idea of writing as a vehicle of social protest. With Rosa Guy, John Henrik Clarke, and Walter Christmas, he founded a workshop that became known as the Harlem Writers Guild in the early 1950s.

Killens's *Youngblood* (1954), the first novel published by a guild member, chronicles the struggles of a southern black family in early twentieth-century Georgia. Following the critical praise of this book, Killens toured the country to speak on subjects important to African Americans. In 1955 he went to Alabama to research a screenplay on the Montgomery Bus Boycott and to visit with the Reverend Dr. Martin Luther King Jr. Killens also became close friends with Malcolm X, with whom he founded the Organization for Afro-American Unity in 1964. *Black Man's Burden,* a 1965 collection of political essays, documents his shift from a socialist philosophy to one promoting black nationalism.

Killens's major subject is the violence and racism of American society, and how it hinders black manhood and family. *'Sippi* (1967) is a protest novel about struggle over voting rights in the 1960s. *The Cotillion; or, One Good Bull Is Half the Herd,* published in 1971 and nominated for the Pulitzer Prize, satirizes middle-class African-American values and was the basis for *Cotillion,* a play produced in New York City in 1975. Killens's other plays include *Ballad of the Winter Soldiers* (1964, with Loften Mitchell) and *Lower Than the Angels* (1965). He wrote two screenplays, *Odds Against Tomorrow* (1959, with Nelson Gidding) and *Slaves* (1969, with Herbert J. Biberman and Alida Sherman). He also edited *The Trial Record of Denmark Vesey* (1970) and authored two juvenile novels, *Great Gittin' Up Morning: A Biography of Denmark Vesey* (1972) and *A Man Ain't Nothin' but a Man: The Adventures of John Henry* (1975).

Beginning in the mid-1960s, Killens served as a writer-in-residence at a number of institutions, including Fisk

University (1965-1968), Columbia University (1970-1973), Howard University (1971-1972), Bronx Community College (1979-1981), and Medgar Evers College in the City University of New York (1981-1987). He received numerous awards, included a fellowship from the National Endowment for the Arts (1980) and a Lifetime Achievement Award from the Before Columbus Foundation (1986). Until his death, Killens continued to contribute articles to leading magazines such as *Ebony, Black World, The Black Aesthetic,* and *African Forum. The Great Black Russian: a Novel on the Life and Times of Alexander Pushkin* was published posthumously in 1988.

See also Clarke, John Henrik; Ellison, Ralph; Harlem Writers Guild; Hughes, Langston; King, Martin Luther, Jr.; Literature of the United States; Malcolm X

■ ■ *Bibliography*

Cruse, Harold. *The Crisis of the Negro Intellectual.* New York: Morrrow, 1967. Reprint, New York: New York Review of Books, 2005.

Gayle, Addison, Jr. *The Way of the New World: The Black Novel in America.* Garden City, N.Y.: Anchor Press, 1975.

Obituary. *American Visions* 3 (February 1988): 10.

Obituary. *New York Times,* October 30, 1987.

Wiggins, William H., Jr. "John Oliver Killens." *Dictionary of Literary Biography,* Vol. 33, *Afro-American Fiction Writers After 1955.* Detroit: Gale Research, 1984.

DEKKER DARE (1996)
Updated bibliography

KINCAID, JAMAICA

MAY 25, 1949

┫┣┣

Born Elaine Potter Richardson in St. Johns, Antigua, author Jamaica Kincaid moved to New York at the age of sixteen, ostensibly to become a nurse. Working first as an au pair and then at other odd jobs, she spent brief periods studying photography at New York's School for Social Research and at Franconia College in New Hampshire. She began her career as a writer by conducting a series of interviews for *Ingénue.* From 1974 to 1976 she contributed vignettes about African-American and Caribbean life to *The New Yorker.* In 1976 she became a staff writer for *The New Yorker,* which two years later published "Girl," her first piece of fiction. Most of Kincaid's fiction has first appeared in the magazine, for which she also began to write a gardening column in 1992.

Jamaica Kincaid. AP/WIDE WORLD PHOTOS. REPRODUCED BY PERMISSION.

Kincaid's first volume of stories, *At the Bottom of the River* (1983), has a dreamlike, poetic character. Her early interest in photography, evident in this volume, also undergirds the rest of her work with its emphasis on condensed images. The choice of the short-story form allows her to isolate moments of heightened emotion. Published separately, the stories that make up the novel *Annie John* (1985) string such brief glimpses together to explore a defiant Annie's growing up in Antigua and especially her relationship to her mother. Themes of mother-daughter conflict are central to Kincaid's work and can be extended into metaphorical relations, such as that between the Caribbean island and those who leave it. For those who visit it, *A Small Place* (1988) is an extended essay on contemporary Antigua, an essay directed toward the tourist. Its tone is alternately cynical and wise, its information painful to accept, but its characteristically careful wording entices the reader as much as any poster of island beauty. *Lucy* (1990) combines the vigor of this Antiguan commentary and the embryonic artistic sensibility of *Annie John* into an extended allegory of the colonial relation set in the contemporary period. Lucy Josephine Potter, a young woman from the Caribbean entrusted with caring for four blond children, brazenly charges through her new world until the blank page confronts her with the fragility of her own identity.

Kincaid's colorful personality and life history, perhaps best exemplified in the selection of her assumed name, propel critical interest in her biography. Like many black writers, especially women, she is burdened both with the expectation that she will represent not merely herself but her community and with the assumption that her stories will be true and factual. The insistent presence of the first person in Kincaid's work is a challenge to that combined requirement. Filtering every perception through an individual, even selfish, lens, her stories are not autobiography; only the depth of feeling is. Kincaid has maintained that she is uninterested in literary realism. Borne by her plain-speaking prose, her audacious girl/woman protagonists gain an audience they might never have gotten in life.

Kincaid lives in Bennington, Vermont, with her husband and children. She has taught creative writing at Bennington College and continues to write, publishing *My Garden Book* in 1999, *Talk Stories* in 2001, *Mr. Potter* in 2002, and *Among Flowers: A Walk in the Himalaya* in 2005.

See also Caribbean/North American Writers, Contemporary; Literature

■ ■ *Bibliography*

Bloom, Harold, ed. *Jamaica Kincaid.* New York: Chelsea House, 1998.

Cudjoe, Selwyn R. "Jamaica Kincaid and the Modernist Project: An Interview." In *Caribbean Women Writers: Essays from the First International Conference.* Wellesley, Mass.: Calaloux Publications, 1990, pp. 215–232.

Murdoch, H. Adlai. "Severing the (M)other Connection: The Representation of Cultural Identity in Jamaica Kincaid's *Annie John.*" *Callaloo* 13, no. 2 (spring 1990): 325–340.

Paravisini-Gebert, Lizabeth. *Jamaica Kincaid: A Critical Companion.* Westport, Conn.: Greenwood Press, 1999.

Simmons, Diane. *Jamaica Kincaid.* New York: Macmillan, 1994.

GINA DENT (1996)
Updated by publisher 2005

KING, "B. B."

SEPTEMBER 16, 1925

▪▪▪————————

Born Riley B. King in Itta Bena, Mississippi, blues singer and guitarist B. B. King grew up on a plantation, working as a farmhand. He sang in choirs at school and church be-

fore teaching himself to play the guitar. He moved to Memphis in 1947 and began singing blues in bars. Following a radio appearance with Sonny Boy Williamson (Alex Miller), King began working on Memphis radio station WDIA as "the Pepticon Boy," advertising Pepticon tonic. He later became a disc jockey for WDIA, being billed as "the Blues Boy from Beale Street," gradually becoming "B. B." He began recording in 1949 and had a few local hits. His recording of "Three O'Clock Blues" (1952) was a national hit and allowed him to begin touring the country as a blues singer. By the mid-1960s he had become known as one of the country's greatest blues performers and a leading figure in the urban blues scene, thanks to the praise of many "British invasion" rock musicians, including Eric Clapton and Mick Jagger, who cited his influence. He has continued to record and perform, earning many industry awards, including a Grammy for his 1981 album *There Must Be a Better World Somewhere* and induction into the Rock and Roll Hall of Fame in 1987. In 2004 King Carl XVI Gustaf of Sweden awarded King with the Polar Music Prize for his contributions to the blues, including a cash prize of over $130,000. King's albums continue to be re-released in the 2000s.

The focus of King's music remains his powerful, commanding voice and guitar playing, through which he maintains an emotional urgency while supporting his performance with a full band. Traditional blues arrangements form the backbone of his songs, featuring prominent call-and-response sequences between the guitar and vocals. His guitar playing is characterized by warm, clear tone and lyrical phrases punctuated by a quick, stinging vibrato.

See also Blues, The

■ ■ *Bibliography*

Danchin, Sebastian. *Blues Boy: The Life and Music of B. B. King.* Jackson: University of Mississippi Press, 1998.

George, Nelson. *The Death of Rhythm and Blues.* New York: Pantheon Books, 1988, pp. 49–50.

Sawyer, Charles. *The Arrival of B. B. King: The Authorized Biography.* Garden City, N.Y.: Doubleday, 1980.

DANIEL THOM (1996)
Updated by publisher 2005

KING, CORETTA SCOTT

APRIL 27, 1927

▪▪▪————————

Born in Marion, Alabama, a rural farming community, civil rights activist Coretta Scott attended Lincoln High

Coretta Scott King (seated) is pictured with Rosa Parks, as the two attend the opening of an exhibit of memorabilia of the late Dr. Martin Luther King Jr. at the Schomburg Center, 1986. © BETTMANN/CORBIS

School, a local private school for black students run by the American Missionary Association. After graduating in 1945, she received a scholarship to study music and education at Antioch College in Yellow Springs, Ohio. Trained in voice and piano, she made her concert debut in 1948 in Springfield, Ohio, as a soloist at the Second Baptist Church. Scott officially withdrew from Antioch in 1952 after entering the New England Conservatory of Music in 1951 to continue her music studies.

During her first year at the conservatory, she met the Rev. Dr. Martin Luther King Jr., who was a doctoral candidate at Boston University's school of theology. The two were married on June 18, 1953, despite Martin Luther King Sr.'s opposition to the match because of his disapproval of the Scott family's rural background and his hope that his son would marry into one of Atlanta's elite black families. The couple returned to Boston to continue their studies. The following year, Coretta Scott King received a bachelor's degree in music from the New England Conservatory of Music, and in September the two moved to Montgomery, Alabama, despite Coretta King's misgivings about returning to the racial hostility of Alabama.

Although Coretta King aspired to become a professional singer, she devoted most of her time to raising her children and working closely with her husband after he had assumed the presidency of the Montgomery Improvement Association in 1955. She participated in many major events of the civil rights movement along with her husband, both in the United States and overseas, as well as having to endure the hardships resulting from her husband's position, including his frequent arrests and the bombing of their Montgomery home in 1956.

Early in 1960 the King family moved to Atlanta when King became co-pastor of Ebenezer Baptist Church with his father. Later that year Coretta King aided in her husband's release from a Georgia prison by appealing to presidential candidate John F. Kennedy to intervene on his behalf. In 1962 she became a voice instructor at Morris Brown College in Atlanta, but she remained primarily involved in sharing the helm of the civil rights struggle with her husband. She led marches, directed fund-raising for the Southern Christian Leadership Conference, and gave a series of "freedom concerts" that combined singing, lecturing, and poetry reading. A strong proponent of disarmament, King served as a delegate to the Disarmament Conference in Geneva, Switzerland, in 1962, and in 1966 and 1967 was a cosponsor of the Mobilization to End the War in Vietnam. In 1967, after an extended leave of absence, she received her bachelor of arts degree in music and elementary education from Antioch College.

On April 8, 1968, only four days after her husband was assassinated in Memphis, Coretta King substituted for him in a march on behalf of sanitation workers that he had been scheduled to lead. Focusing her energies on preserving her husband's memory and continuing his struggle, Coretta King also took part in the Poor People's Washington Campaign in the nation's capital during June 1968, serving as the keynote speaker at the main rally at the Lincoln Memorial. In 1969 she helped found and served as president of the Atlanta-based Martin Luther King, Jr. Center for Nonviolent Social Change, a center devoted to teaching young people the importance of nonviolence and to preserving the memory of her husband. In 1969 she also published her autobiography, *My Life with Martin Luther King, Jr.*, and in 1971 she received an honorary doctorate in music from the New England Conservatory.

In 1983 Coretta King led the twentieth-anniversary March on Washington and the following year was elected chairperson of the commission to declare King's birthday a national holiday, which was observed for the first time in 1986. She was active in the struggle to end apartheid, touring South Africa and meeting with Winnie Mandela in 1986 and returning there in 1990 to meet the recently released African National Congress leader, Nelson Mandela.

Coretta King has received numerous awards for her participation in the struggle for civil rights, including the outstanding citizenship award from the Montgomery Improvement Association in 1959 and the Distinguished Achievement Award from the National Organization of Colored Women's Clubs in 1962. Formerly chief executive officer of the Martin Luther King, Jr. Center for Nonviolent Change, Coretta Scott King continues to press for the worldwide recognition of civil rights and human rights.

In October 2004, legislation was passed in Congress to present Coretta Scott King and Martin Luther King, Jr. (posthumously) with the Congressional Gold Medal.

See also Civil Rights Movement, U.S.; King, Martin Luther, Jr.; Montgomery Improvement Association; Poor People's Campaign; Southern Christian Leadership Conference (SCLC)

■ ■ *Bibliography*

Branch, Taylor. *Parting the Waters: America in the King Years, 1954–63.* New York: Simon and Schuster, 1988.

King, Coretta Scott. *My Life with Martin Luther King, Jr.* New York: Holt, Rinehart and Winston, 1969.

LOUISE P. MAXWELL (1996)
Updated by publisher 2005

KING, DON

AUGUST 20, 1931

Boxing promoter Don King was born and raised in Cleveland, Ohio. As a young adult King was involved in organized crime in Cleveland, running an illegal lottery. King also owned a nightclub, and in 1966 he was convicted of manslaughter for killing a former employee during a street fight. After spending four and a half years in an Ohio penitentiary, he was paroled in 1971 and pardoned by the governor of Ohio in 1983.

Soon after his release King began a career as a boxing promoter. By 1972 he was promoting and unofficially managing local fighters, including Earnie Shavers, who went on to become a challenger for the heavyweight championship. In 1973, immediately after George Foreman knocked out Joe Frazier to become heavyweight champion, King talked himself into Foreman's camp and was hired as the new champion's promoter. With his newly established Don King Productions company, King set up Foreman's first defense of the championship, a successful two-round knockout of Ken Norton in Caracas, Venezuela. In 1974 King arranged a match between Foreman and former champion Muhammad Ali in Kinshasa, Zaire. The "Rumble in the Jungle" ended when Foreman was knocked out in the eighth round, but the fight provided Foreman with five million dollars and established King as the sport's most successful promoter.

Based in New York, King went on to promote fights for a number of the greatest boxers of the 1970s, 1980s, and 1990s, including Muhammad Ali, Larry Holmes, Roberto Duran, Mike Tyson, and Julio Cesar Chavez. King copromoted the famous 1975 "Thrilla in Manila" heavyweight championship match between Ali and Frazier. His rise to fame was aided by his flamboyant, often volatile personality and trademark vertical shock of salt-and-pepper hair. In 1984 King branched out from boxing by promoting the multimillion-dollar world tour of the Jacksons, the singing group consisting of Michael Jackson and his brothers.

King's business practices have been the focus of significant controversy. In 1984 King and his longtime secretary Constance Harper were indicted by a federal grand jury, but ultimately acquitted, on twenty-three counts of income tax evasion and conspiracy. In the late 1980s he was investigated, but never indicted, by the Federal Bureau of Investigation and the U.S. Attorney General's office for alleged racketeering in the boxing industry.

From the late 1970s through the early 1990s, King held a virtual monopoly on promotions for major boxing matches, and boxing reformers often pointed to his powerful hold over the industry as an example of the sport's corrupt centralization. He was often criticized for acting as de facto manager for many of the boxers whose fights he promoted. (International boxing bylaws prohibit one person serving as a boxer's promoter and manager because of potential conflicts of interest.) In the most famous instance, he came under intense scrutiny for "advising" both Mike Tyson and Buster Douglas, whose 1990 heavyweight championship fight King promoted. King also was accused by many of his former clients of misappropriating funds from boxing matches. In 1993 he proposed his own seven-point plan to reform boxing, including round-by-round displayed scoring, the elimination of draws, and a prohibition on promoters paying the expenses of judges and referees. King's reform plan, while often mocked as hypocritical, was lauded by many in boxing as a constructive proposal.

King was awarded an honorary doctorate from Shaw University in 1998.

See also Ali, Muhammad; Boxing; Foreman, George; Frazier, Joe; Tyson, Mike

■ ■ *Bibliography*

Lupica, Mike. "Donfire of the Vanities." *Esquire* (March 1991): 52.

Newfield, Jack. *Only in America: The Life and Crimes of Don King.* New York: William Morrow, 1995.

Ziegel, Vic. "The King of Boxing." *Rolling Stone* (January 19, 1984): 13–14.

THADDEUS RUSSELL (1996)
Updated by publisher 2005

KING, IRIS

❚❚❚

1911

2000

King was the eldest child of Thomas and Rebecca Ewart and the sister of the dean of West Indian cricket umpires, Tom Ewart. She grew up in Eastern Kingston. She completed her early education at Kingston Technical School in 1933 and shortly thereafter married S. Herman King. While her first career was that of wife and mother to four children, King drifted immediately into Jamaican party politics. She entered the world of local politics in 1938, the year the People's National Party (PNP) was born, and she became an active political campaigner for this party.

Iris King's life and career were centered around her contributions to public life. In 1947 she was elected a councillor of the Kingston and Saint Andrew Corporation (KSAC). When her term as councillor ended in 1950, she enrolled at Roosevelt University in Chicago for a course in public administration. After three years she earned a degree in municipal administration and political science. *The Sunday Gleaner* of December 28, 1958, observed that because of her degree King could be described as the only trained politician in Jamaica.

King returned to Jamaica from Chicago in 1955 in time to become a candidate in the general elections. She ran against the National Labour Party (NLP) candidate Kenneth George Hill and the Jamaica Labour Party (JLP) candidate Hugh Shearer for the West Kingston seat. King finished a close second to Shearer with 5,246 votes to his 6,383; Hill polled 3,262 votes. Losing the seat to Shearer, King returned to municipal politics, winning back with overwhelming support her seat in the KSAC.

On April 9, 1958, Iris King had the distinction of becoming the first female mayor of the city of Kingston. She was the forty-first person to occupy this chair. Photographs of King from this period show a smiling and well-dressed woman with an expansively warm personality. Newspaper reports consistently remarked on her sincerity and kindness coupled with the toughness required for political life. Just after her election as mayor of Kingston, the April 10, 1958, issue of *The Daily Gleaner* reported: "It was obvious to political observers even from the early days that Iris King would be a force to be reckoned with and that her 'leonine' platform qualities, her kindliness, her toughness and charity, would take her far up the political ladder."

A major reason for the recognition she was given was her work with the underprivileged people of Western

Kingston, where she focused particularly on improving conditions for children. Partly due to this work, she was appointed chair of the Maxfield Park Children's Home, a facility that, as mayor, she both expanded and developed.

After her election as mayor she was invited by the U.S. government to spend two months on a study tour of the United States. The November 2, 1958, issue of Jamaica's *Sunday Gleaner* reported that on October 1, 1958, she was presented with a key to the city of Washington, D.C., by District Commissioner David Karrick during an official ceremony held in her honor.

In 1959 King again entered the election platform as the PNP candidate for the constituency of Kingston West Central against Arthur Smith of the JLP. She won this seat with 7,320 votes against her opponent's 4,894, helping her party to win twenty-nine of the forty-five seats contested that year. She was also named a member of Prime Minister Norman Manley's cabinet. The PNP was defeated in 1962, and King left politics in 1967 and immigrated to the United States, where she obtained employment as a hospital administrator.

Iris King ranks with such pioneer women politicians as Mary Morris Knibb, Rose Leon (the first woman to become a government minister), Edith Dalton James, and Iris Collins-Williams (the first woman elected to the House of Representatives). Although present in political history, the records reveal very little of the contributions of women like King. After her achievements as mayor, parliamentarian, and cabinet member, she faded from the public records and from the memories of many Jamaicans.

See also Dalton-James, Edith; Leon, Rose; Manley, Norman; Morris Knibb, Mary; People's National Party; Politics

■ ■ *Bibliography*

"Her Worship." *The Daily Gleaner* (April 10, 1958).

"Iris King: The Long Ladder of Service." *The Daily Gleaner* (May 3, 1958).

"Iris King—Political Personality 1956." *The Sunday Gleaner* (December 28, 1958).

PATRICIA MOHAMMED (2005)

KING, MARTIN LUTHER, JR.

JANUARY 15, 1929
APRIL 4, 1968

■┼■

This entry consists of two distinct articles. The first, by Clayborne Carson, deals with King's life and work; the second, by David J. Garrow, evaluates King's legacy and influence on a later generation.

LIFE
  Clayborne Carson

LEGACY
  David J. Garrow

LIFE

Martin Luther King Jr. was born in Atlanta as Michael King Jr., the first son of a Baptist minister and the grandson of a Baptist minister. His forebears exemplified the African-American social gospel tradition that would shape his career as a reformer. King's maternal grandfather, the Reverend A. D. Williams, had transformed Ebenezer Baptist Church, a block down the street from his grandson's childhood home, into one of Atlanta's most prominent black churches. In 1906, Williams had joined such figures as Atlanta University scholar W. E. B. Du Bois and African Methodist Episcopal (AME) bishop Henry McNeal Turner to form the Georgia Equal Rights League, an organization that condemned lynching, segregation in public transportation, and the exclusion of black men from juries and state militia. In 1917 Williams helped found the Atlanta branch of the National Association for the Advancement of Colored People (NAACP), later serving as the chapter's president. Williams's subsequent campaign to register and mobilize black voters prodded white leaders to agree to construct new public schools for black children.

After Williams's death in 1931, his son-in-law, Michael King Sr., also combined religious and political leadership. He became president of Atlanta's NAACP, led voter-registration marches during the 1930s, and spearheaded a movement to equalize the salaries of black public school teachers with those of their white counterparts. In 1934, King Sr.—perhaps inspired by a visit to the birthplace of Protestantism in Germany—changed his name (and that of his son) to Martin Luther King.

Despite the younger King's admiration for his father's politically active ministry, he was initially reluctant to accept his inherited calling. Experiencing religious doubts during his early teenage years, he decided to become a minister only after he came into contact with religious leaders who combined theological sophistication with social gospel advocacy. At Morehouse College, which King attended from 1944 to 1948, the college's president, Benjamin E. Mays, encouraged him to believe that Christianity should become a force for progressive social change. A course on the Bible taught by Morehouse professor George Kelsey exposed King to theological scholarship. After deciding to become a minister, King increased his understanding of liberal Christian thought while attending Crozer Theological Seminary in Pennsylvania. Compiling an outstanding academic record at Crozer, he deepened his understanding of modern religious scholarship and eventually identified himself with theological personalism. King later wrote that this philosophical position strengthened his belief in a personal God and provided him with a "metaphysical basis for the dignity and worth of all human personality."

At Boston University, where King began doctoral studies in systematic theology in 1951, his exploration of theological scholarship was combined with extensive interactions with the Boston African-American community. He met regularly with other black students in an informal group called the Dialectical Society. Often invited to give sermons in Boston-area churches, he acquired a reputation as a powerful preacher, drawing ideas from African-American Baptist traditions as well as theological and philosophical writings. While the academic papers he wrote at Boston displayed little originality, King's scholarly training provided him with an exceptional ability to draw upon a wide range of theological and philosophical texts to express his views with force and precision, a talent that would prove useful in his future leadership activities. During his stay in Boston, King also met and began dating Coretta Scott, then a student at the New England Conservatory of Music. On June 18, 1953, the two students were married in Marion, Alabama, where Scott's family lived. During the following academic year, King began work on his dissertation, which was completed during the spring of 1955.

Soon after King accepted his first pastorate at Dexter Avenue Baptist Church in Montgomery, Ala., he had an unexpected opportunity to utilize the insights he had gained from his childhood experiences and academic training. After the NAACP official Rosa Parks was jailed for refusing to give up her bus seat to a white passenger, King accepted the post of president of the Montgomery Improvement Association, which was formed to coordinate a boycott of Montgomery's buses. In his role as the primary spokesman of the boycott, King gradually forged a distinctive protest strategy that involved the mobilization of black churches, the utilization of Gandhian methods of nonviolent protest, and skillful appeals for white support.

After the U.S. Supreme Court outlawed Alabama bus segregation laws in late 1956, King quickly rose to national prominence as a result of his leadership role in the boycott. In 1957 he became the founding president of the Southern Christian Leadership Conference (SCLC), formed to coordinate civil rights activities throughout the South. The publication of King's *Stride Toward Freedom: The Montgomery Story* (1958) further contributed to his rapid emergence as a nationally known civil rights leader. Seeking to forestall the fears of NAACP leaders that his organization might draw away followers and financial support, King acted cautiously during the late 1950s. Instead of immediately seeking to stimulate mass desegregation protests in the South, he stressed the goal of achieving black voting rights when he addressed an audience at the 1957 Prayer Pilgrimage for Freedom in Washington, D.C. During 1959 he increased his understanding of Gandhian ideas during a month-long visit to India as a guest of Prime Minister Jawaharlal Nehru. Early in 1960, King moved his family—which now included two children, Yolanda Denise (born 1955) and Martin Luther III (born 1957)—to Atlanta in order to be nearer SCLC's headquarters in that city and to become copastor—with his father—of Ebenezer Baptist Church. The Kings' third child, Dexter Scott, was born in 1961; their fourth, Bernice Albertine, was born in 1963.

Soon after King's arrival in Atlanta, the lunch counter sit-in movement, led by students, spread throughout the South and brought into existence a new organization, the Student Nonviolent Coordinating Committee (SNCC). SNCC activists admired King but also pushed him toward greater militancy. In October 1960, his arrest during a student-initiated protest in Atlanta became an issue in the national presidential campaign when the Democratic candidate, John F. Kennedy, intervened to secure his release from jail. Kennedy's action contributed to his narrow victory in the November election. During 1961 and 1962, King's differences with SNCC activists widened during a sustained protest movement in Albany, Georgia. King was arrested twice during demonstrations organized by the Albany movement, but when he left jail, and ultimately left Albany, without achieving a victory, his standing among activists declined.

King reasserted his preeminence within the African-American freedom struggle through his leadership of the Birmingham, Alabama, campaign of 1963. Initiated by the

Dr. Martin Luther King Jr. speaks to a large gathering of attentive listeners at a rally in Cleveland, Ohio, 1965. © BETTMANN/CORBIS

SCLC in January, the Birmingham demonstrations were the most massive civil rights protests that had occurred up to that time. With the assistance of Fred Shuttlesworth and other local black leaders, and without much competition from SNCC or other civil rights groups, SCLC officials were able to orchestrate the Birmingham protests to achieve maximum national impact. During May, televised pictures of police using dogs and fire hoses against demonstrators aroused a national outcry. This vivid evidence of the obstinacy of Birmingham officials, combined with Alabama overnor George C. Wallace's attempt to block the entry of black students at the University of Alabama, prompted President John F. Kennedy to introduce major new civil rights legislation. King's unique ability to appropriate ideas from the Bible, the Constitution, and other canonical texts manifested itself when he defended the black protests in a widely quoted letter, written while he was jailed in Birmingham.

King's speech at the August 28, 1963, March on Washington, attended by over 200,000 people, provides another powerful demonstration of his singular ability to

Martin Luther King, Jr.

"I guess it is easy for those who have never felt the stinging darts of injustice to say wait ... There comes a time when the cup of endurance runs over, and men are no longer willing to be plunged into an abyss of injustice where they experience the bleakness of corroding despair."

ORIGINALLY IN A LETTER FROM THE BIRMINGHAM CITY JAIL, DATED APRIL 16, 1963. REPRINTED IN CLAYBORNE CARSON, ED. *EYES OF THE PRIZE: CIVIL RIGHTS READER.* NEW YORK: PENGUIN, 1987, P. 155.

draw on widely accepted American ideals in order to promote black objectives. At the end of his prepared remarks, which announced that African Americans wished to cash the "promissory note" signified in the words of the Constitution and the Declaration of Independence, King began his most quoted oration: "So I say to you, my friends, that even though we must face the difficulties of today and tomorrow, I still have a dream. It is a dream deeply rooted in the American dream . . . that one day this nation will rise up and live out the true meaning of its creed—we hold these truths to be self-evident, that all men are created equal." He appropriated the familiar words of the song "My Country 'Tis of Thee" before concluding: "And when we allow freedom to ring, when we let it ring from every village and every hamlet, from every state and every city, we will be able to speed up that day when all of God's children—black men and white men, Jews and Gentiles, Protestants and Catholics—will be able to join hands and to sing in the words of the old Negro spiritual, 'Free at last, free at last, thank God Almighty, we are free at last.' "

After the March on Washington, King's fame and popularity were at their height. Named *Time* magazine's Man of the Year at the end of 1963, he was awarded the Nobel Peace Prize in December 1964. The acclaim he received prompted FBI director J. Edgar Hoover to step up his effort to damage King's reputation by leaking information gained through surreptitious means about King's ties with former communists and his extramarital affairs.

King's last successful civil rights campaign was a series of demonstrations in Alabama that were intended to dramatize the denial of black voting rights in the deep South. Demonstrations began in Selma, Alabama, early in 1965 and reached a turning point on March 7, when a group of demonstrators began a march from Selma to the state capitol in Montgomery. King was in Atlanta when state policemen, carrying out Governor Wallace's order to stop the march, attacked with tear gas and clubs soon after the procession crossed the Edmund Pettus Bridge on the outskirts of Selma. The police assault on the marchers quickly increased national support for the voting rights campaign. King arrived in Selma to join several thousand movement sympathizers, black and white. President Lyndon B. Johnson reacted to the Alabama protests by introducing new voting rights legislation, which would become the Voting Rights Act of 1965. Demonstrators were finally able to obtain a court order allowing the march to take place, and on March 25 King addressed the arriving protestors from the steps of the capitol in Montgomery.

After the successful voting rights campaign, King was unable to garner similar support for his effort to confront the problems of northern urban blacks. Early in 1966 he launched a major campaign in Chicago, moving into an apartment in the black ghetto. As he shifted the focus of

Dr. Martin Luther King Jr., speaking to reporters in 1968. *King, seen here discussing his disenchantment with President Johnson's Vietnam policies, engendered controversy and criticism for speaking out on political issues that were beyond the realm of civil rights for African Americans.* AP/WIDE WORLD PHOTOS

his activities north, however, he discovered that the tactics used in the South were not as effective elsewhere. He encountered formidable opposition from Mayor Richard Daley, and he was unable to mobilize Chicago's economically and ideologically diverse black populace. He was stoned by angry whites in the suburb of Cicero when he led a march against racial discrimination in housing. Despite numerous well-publicized protests, the Chicago campaign resulted in no significant gains and undermined King's reputation as an effective leader.

His status was further damaged when his strategy of nonviolence came under renewed attack from blacks following a major outbreak of urban racial violence in Los Angeles during August 1965. When civil rights activists reacted to the shooting of James Meredith by organizing "March against Fear" through Mississippi, King was forced on the defensive as Stokely Carmichael and other militants put forward the Black Power slogan. Although King refused to condemn the militants who opposed him, he criticized the new slogan as vague and divisive. As his influence among blacks lessened, he also alienated many white moderate supporters by publicly opposing U.S. intervention in the Vietnam War. After he delivered a major antiwar speech at New York's Riverside Church on April 4, 1967, many of the northern newspapers that had once supported his civil rights efforts condemned his attempt to link civil rights to the war issue.

In November 1967, King announced the formation of a Poor People's Campaign designed to prod the nation's leaders to deal with the problem of poverty. Early in 1968, he and other SCLC workers began to recruit poor people and antipoverty activists to come to Washington, D.C., to lobby on behalf of improved antipoverty programs. This effort was in its early stages when King became involved in a sanitation workers' strike in Memphis. On March 28, as he led thousands of sanitation workers and sympathizers on a march through downtown Memphis, violence broke out and black youngsters looted stores. The violent outbreak led to more criticisms of King's entire antipoverty strategy. He returned to Memphis for the last time early in April. Addressing an audience at Bishop Charles H. Mason Temple on April 3, he sought to revive his flagging movement by acknowledging: "We've got some difficult days ahead. But it doesn't matter with me now. Because I've been to the mountaintop. . . . And I've seen the promised land. I may not get there with you. But I want you to know tonight that we, as a people, will get to the promised land."

The following evening, King was assassinated as he stood on a balcony of the Lorraine Motel in Memphis. A white segregationist, James Earl Ray, was later convicted of the crime. The Poor People's Campaign continued for a few months but did not achieve its objectives. King became an increasingly revered figure after his death, however, and many of his critics ultimately acknowledged his considerable accomplishments. In 1969 his widow, Coretta Scott King, established the Martin Luther King, Jr. Center for Nonviolent Social Change, in Atlanta, to carry on his work. In 1986, a national holiday was established to honor King's birth.

■■ *Bibliography*

Baldwin, Lewis V. *There is a Balm in Gilead: The Cultural Roots of Martin Luther King, Jr.* Minneapolis, Minn.: Fortress Press, 1991.

Branch, Taylor. *Parting the Waters: America in the King Years, 1954-63.* New York: Simon and Schuster, 1988.

Branch, Taylor. *Pillar of Fire: America in the King Years, 1963-65.* New York: Simon & Schuster, 1998.

Fairclough, Adam. *Martin Luther King, Jr.* Athens: University of Georgia Press, 1995.

Garrow, David J. *Bearing the Cross: Martin Luther King and the Southern Christian Leadership Conference.* New York: William Morrow, 1986.

King, Coretta Scott. *My Life with Martin Luther King, Jr.* New York: Holt, Rinehart and Winston, 1969.

King, Martin Luther, Jr. *A Testament of Hope: The Essential Writings and Speeches of Martin Luther King, Jr.*, edited by James Melvin Washington. San Francisco: Harper & Row, 1986.

King, Martin Luther, Jr. *The Autobiography of Martin Luther King, Jr.*, edited by Carson, Claybourne. New York: Warner Books, 1998.

King, Martin Luther, Sr., and Clayton Riley. *Daddy King: An Autobiography.* New York: William Morrow, 1980.

Lewis, David Levering. *King: A Biography.* Urbana: University of Illinois Press, 1978.

Oates, Steven B. *Let the Trumpet Sound: The Life of Martin Luther King, Jr.* New York: Harper & Row, 1982.

Reddick, L. D. *Crusader Without Violence: A Biography of Martin Luther King, Jr.* New York: Harper, 1959.

CLAYBORNE CARSON (1996)
Updated bibliography

LEGACY

The militant political legacy of the Reverend Dr. Martin Luther King Jr. is in eclipse, and his historical reputation is frequently distorted by the popular misconception that he was primarily a philosophical "dreamer," rather than a realistic and often courageous dissident. King's true legacy is not the 1963 March on Washington and his grandly optimistic "I Have a Dream" speech; it is instead his 1968 plan for a massively disruptive but resolutely nonviolent "Poor People's Campaign" aimed at the nation's capital, a protest campaign that came to pass only in a muted and disjointed form after his death.

Some of the distortion of King's popular image is a direct result of how disproportionately he is often presented as a gifted and sanguine speechmaker whose life ought to be viewed through the prism of his "dream." King had used the "I Have a Dream" phrase several times before his justly famous oration, but on numerous occasions in later years King invoked the famous phrase only to emphasize how the "dream" he had had in Washington in 1963 had "turned into a nightmare."

Both the dilution of King's legacy and the misrepresentation of his image are also in part due to the stature accorded his birthday, now a national holiday. Making King an object of official celebration has inescapably led to at least some smoothing of edges and tempering of substance that otherwise would irritate and challenge those Americans who are just as eager to endorse "I Have a Dream" as they are to reject any "Poor People's Campaign."

But another facet of King's erroneous present-day image as a milquetoast moderate, particularly among young people, is directly tied to the greatly increased prominence of Malcolm X. Even before the media booklet that accompanied Spike Lee's 1992 movie *Malcolm X,* popular appreciation of Malcolm X had expanded well beyond anything that had existed in the first two decades following his 1965 death. Even if young people's substantive understanding of Malcolm X's message is oftentimes faulty or nonexistent, among youthful Americans of all races the rise of Malcolm X has vastly magnified the mistaken stereotype that "Malcolm and Martin" were polar opposites.

Far too many people assume that if Malcolm personified unyielding tenacity and determination, King, as his supposed opposite, was no doubt some sort of vainglorious compromiser who spent more time socializing with the Kennedys than fighting for social change. Hardly anything could be further from the truth, for while Malcolm's courageous self-transformation is deserving of far more serious attention and study than it has yet received, King was as selflessly dedicated and utterly principled a public figure as any other in the United States during the twentieth century.

Perhaps King's most remarkable characteristic was how he became a nationally and then internationally famous figure without ever having any egotistical desire to promote himself onto the public stage (unlike virtually every luminary in contemporary America). Drafted by his colleagues in Montgomery, Alabama, in 1955 to serve as the principal spokesperson for the black community's boycott of municipal buses, King was far from eager to be any sort of "leader," and only a deeply spiritual sense of obligation convinced him that he could not refuse this call.

King's resolutely selfless orientation gave his leadership both a public integrity and a private humility that are rare, if not wholly unique, in recent U.S. history. Perhaps the greatest irony generated by the hundreds upon hundreds of King's ostensibly private telephone conversations that were preserved for history by the FBI's indecently intrusive electronic surveillance—and released thanks to the Freedom of Information Act—is that one comes away from a review of King's most unguarded moments with a distinctly heightened, rather than diminished, regard for the man. Time and again, those transcripts show King as exceptionally demanding of himself and as an overly harsh judge of his own actions. How many other public figures, lacking only an FBI director like J. Edgar Hoover to preserve their off-the-cuff comments for posterity, could hope to pass such an ultimate test of civic character?

King's remarkable political courage and integrity were just as dramatically visible on the public stage, however, as in his self-critical private conversations. Unlike almost every other public figure in the country, both then and now, King had no interest in assessing which position on which issue would be the most popular or the most remunerative for organizational fund-raising before he decided how and when to speak his mind.

Nowhere was this more starkly apparent than in King's early decision to speak out against U.S. involvement in Vietnam at a time when President Lyndon B. Johnson's war still had the support of most progressive Democrats. Many liberal newspapers—and even several "mainstream" civil rights organizations—harshly attacked King for devoting his attention to an issue that did not fall within the "black" bailiwick, and while in private King was deeply hurt by such criticism, he had decided to confront the Vietnam issue knowing full well that just such a reaction would ensue.

"Leadership" to King did not mean tailoring one's comments to fit the most recent public opinion poll or shifting one's positions to win greater acclaim or support. King realized, too, that real leadership did not simply comprise issuing press releases and staging news conferences, and he was acutely aware that most real "leaders" of the southern civil rights struggle—unheralded people who performed the crucial task of encouraging others to stand up and take an active part in advancing their own lives and communities—got none of the public attention and awards that flowed to King and a very few others.

King understood that in the modern culture of publicity, the recognition of an individual symbolic figure was inevitable and essential to the movement's popular success, but he always sought to emphasize, as in his Nobel Peace Prize lecture, that he accepted such applause and honors only as a "trustee" on behalf of the thousands of unsung people whose contributions and aspirations he sought to represent. King realized, better than many people at the time, and far better than some subsequent disciples, that the real essence of the movement was indeed the local activists in scores of generally unpublicized locales. In private, King could be extremely self-conscious about how he personally deserved only a very modest portion of all the praise and trophies that came his way.

King would very much welcome the newfound appreciation of Malcolm X, but he would likewise be intensely discomfited by a national holiday that in some hands seems to encourage celebration of King's own persona rather than the movement he came to symbolize. King also would rue how the culture of celebrity has become more and more a culture of violence, and how economic inequality in America is even more pronounced in the 1990s than it was at the time of his death in 1968.

King would also rue his legacy being too often shorn of his post-1965 nonviolent radicalism, as well as the celebration of his image by people who proffered no support to him and the movement when he was alive. But King would not worry about any decline in his own reputation or fame, for he would greatly welcome increased credit and appreciation for those whom the media and history habitually overlook. If Martin Luther King Jr.'s individual image continues gradually to recede, King himself would be happy rather than sad, for personal fame and credit were not something that he sought or welcomed either in 1955 or in 1968.

See also Black Power Movement; Civil Rights Movement, U.S.; King, Coretta Scott; Malcolm X; Mays, Benjamin E.; Meredith, James H.; Montgomery Improvement Association; Montgomery, Ala., Bus Boycott; National Association for the Advancement of Colored People (NAACP); Parks, Rosa; Poor People's Campaign; Shuttlesworth, Fred L.; Southern Christian Leadership Conference (SCLC); Student Nonviolent Coordinating Committee (SNCC); Voting Rights Act of 1965

■ ■ *Bibliography*

Albert, Peter J., and Ronald Hoffman. *We Shall Overcome: Martin Luther King, Jr., and the Black Freedom Struggle.* New York: Pantheon, 1990.

Cone, James H. *Martin and Malcolm and America: A Dream or a Nightmare.* Maryknoll, N.Y.: Orbis, 1991.

Harding, Vincent. *Martin Luther King, the Inconvenient Hero.* Maryknoll, NY: Orbis Books, 1996.

Ivory, Luther D. *Toward a Theology of Radical Involvement: The Theological Legacy of Martin Luther King, Jr.* Nashville, Tenn.: Abingdon Press, 1997.

Miller, Keith D. *Voice of Deliverance: The Language of Martin Luther King, Jr., and Its Sources.* New York: Free Press, 1992.

DAVID J. GARROW (1996)
Updated bibliography

KING, SYDNEY (KWAYANA, EUSI)

1925

Sydney King, who changed his name to Eusi Kwayana, was born in Lusignan, in British Guiana, on a sugar estate. From the age of seven he lived in Buxton on the east coast of British Guiana. Buxton was a village that had come into existence after impecunious planters were forced to sell their estates to the ex-slaves, who were known as Creoles

and who had deliberately deprived the plantations of their labor power. As a young man Kwayana entered the teaching profession. He later became involved in politics when, in 1949, he and a friend organized the Buxton Ratepayers' Association, which forced village councilors to abandon a plan to grant the planters a ninety-nine-year lease for land to construct a canal that would have competed with the existing railway and thus undermined the village economy. During the late 1940s and 1950s, when teachers were subject to arbitrary dismissal for reasons having nothing to do with competence at the hands of school managers who were mostly religious dignitaries, Kwayana used his reputation as a teacher to spread a clandestine message of political independence, particularly among African Guianese villagers in Buxton.

With these experiences Kwayana's transition to more formal politics, which occurred when he became a member of the Political Affairs Committee (PAC), the immediate precursor of the People's Progressive Party (PPP), the colony's first mass-based political party, was not a problematic one. On becoming a member of the party, which made clear its intention to seek political independence from the British for the colony, Kwayana took an active part in the PPP's efforts, designed to educate and mobilize the masses in furtherance of that aim. However, such was the sociopolitical climate that, being a teacher, much of Kwayana's writing on political issues was done anonymously. Thus, most of the passages from a PAC bulletin that were quoted in the inquiry into the 1948 shooting of five sugar estate workers who were protesting against unpalatable working conditions, and that were attributed to the secretary of the PPP at the time, were in fact written by Kwayana (personal correspondence, October 6, 1989). In addition, in his role as a political independence movement intellectual, and along with Martin Carter, perhaps Guyana's most distinguished poet, who at the time was a civil servant and therefore restricted from participating in political activity, Kwayana addressed political meetings in many parts of the colony far from the gaze of colonial officials and was also responsible for composing the PPP's "battle song."

Kwayana subsequently became assistant secretary of the PPP and was described both by one of his party colleagues as "blindly pro-Moscow" and by the then governor as one of the two "most influential and fanatical members of the PPP" for his purported role in a sugar workers' strike offensive in 1953. He was appointed minister of Communications and Works in the short-lived PPP government of 1953. After the dismissal of the PPP government and the suspension of the constitution in October 1953 by the British, Kwayana was at first restricted to Buxton, and then detained from October 1953 to March 1954 at the U.S. World War II air base at Atkinson Field. Following his release from Atkinson Field, he was restricted to the Buxton-Friendship area and ordered to report to the police station there on a daily basis.

After a split in the leadership of the PPP in 1954 involving East Indian Cheddi Jagan and African Forbes Burnham, Kwayana remained with the Jagan faction. He left the party, though, along with two other influential African Guyanese members, after Jagan reneged on a promise to seek the inclusion of the colony in the West Indian Federation on the grounds that it was not in the interest of the East Indian population. After unsuccessfully contesting a seat during the 1957 general elections as an independent candidate, Kwayana subsequently joined the People's National Congress (PNC), which was headed by Burnham. He also served for a while as the editor of the party's newspaper before incurring the displeasure of top party officials for advocating partition as a way of solving the colony's racial problems.

Apparently convinced that the PPP was abandoning its Marxist/class posture in favor of one based on race, especially as a way of winning elections, Kwayana was instrumental in founding both the African Society for Racial Equality (ASRE) and the African Society for Closer Relations with Independent Africa (ASCRIA), because "Black people needed organizing." After a brief rapprochement with Burnham and the PNC, during which time he worked with the Guyana Marketing Corporation, he severed permanently his ties with the party and later became an important figure in the Working People's Alliance (WPA) and served in the House of Assembly as a representative of that political party. Following the decline of the WPA after the death of one of its leaders, Dr. Walter Rodney, on June 13, 1980, Kwayana, as a public intellectual who articulates the concerns of a specific social grouping, continued to speak out against violence in Buxton, the village in which he grew up, as well as other pressing social ills.

See also Burnham, Forbes; People's National Congress; Politics and Politicians in Latin America; Rodney, Walter

■ ■ *Bibliography*

Kwayana, Eusi. "Guyana's Race Problems and My Part in Them." *Rodneyite* 2, no. 3 (August 1992).

Kwayana, Eusi. *Notes on the Guyanese Political Situation,* unpublished, n.d.

MAURICE ST. PIERRE (2005)

KITT, EARTHA MAE

JANUARY 26, 1928

Born on a farm in the town of North, South Carolina, singer and actress Eartha Kitt and her sister Pearl were abandoned as small children by their mother. They were raised in a foster family until 1936, when Eartha moved to New York City to live with her aunt.

In New York Kitt attended the Metropolitan High School (which later became the High School of Performing Arts), and at sixteen she met Katherine Dunham, who granted her a scholarship with Dunham's dance troupe. Kitt toured Europe and Mexico with the troupe, developing a sexually provocative stage presence and a throaty, sensual singing style. When the troupe arrived in Paris, Kitt was offered a job singing at a top nightclub. Orson Welles saw her perform and cast her as "Girl Number Three" in his 1951 stage production of Marlowe's *Doctor Faustus.* After touring Germany with the production and a brief singing engagement in Turkey, Kitt returned to New York. She performed at La Vie en Rose and at the Village Vanguard, where Leonard Sillman saw her and decided to cast her in his Broadway show *New Faces of 1952.* Kitt also appeared in the 1954 film version of *New Faces.* In both versions she sang "C'est Si Bon," "Monotonous," and "Uska Dara," which were recorded for her 1955 album *The Bad Eartha.*

Kitt performed from the mid-1950s through the 1960s in theaters, nightclubs, and cabarets in the United States and abroad, honing her reputation as a "sex kitten." Her stage appearances included *Mrs. Patterson* (1954), a musical produced by Sillman, for which she received a Tony Award nomination, and *Shinbone Alley* (1957). Kitt also appeared in the films *St. Louis Blues* (1958), *The Accused* (1957), and *Anna Lucasta* (1959), which earned her an Oscar nomination. During this period she recorded two notable albums, *Bad but Beautiful* in 1961 and *At the Plaza* in 1965. Kitt also made numerous television appearances, including a stint on the 1960s *Batman* series, in which she played Catwoman.

In 1968 Kitt's career took a dramatic turn when she criticized the war in Vietnam at a White House luncheon hosted by the First Lady, Lady Bird Johnson. As a result she lost bookings and was vilified by conservatives and much of the mainstream press and was investigated by the Central Intelligence Agency and the Federal Bureau of Investigation. Although Kitt's subsequent appearances in Europe were commonly believed to be the result of her being blacklisted in the United States, in fact she maintained a significant presence in American clubs, film, and

Eartha Mae Kitt. *An accomplished and popular stage, film, and television entertainer, Kitt sparked controversy by speaking out against U.S. involvement in Vietnam at a "Woman Doer's Luncheon" hosted at the White House in 1968.* AP/WIDE WORLD PHOTOS. REPRODUCED BY PERMISSION.

television. In 1972 her political reputation took a sharp turn when she performed in South Africa and publicly complimented her white hosts for their hospitality.

In the late 1970s and 1980s Kitt continued her career as a cabaret singer and occasional actor. Her return to Broadway in the 1978 show *Timbuktu* earned her a second Tony nomination. She recorded the album *I Love Men* in 1984 and published two autobiographies during this period, *I'm Still Here* in 1989 and *Confessions of a Sex Kitten* in 1991. Kitt also appeared in a variety of marginal Hollywood films, including *Erik the Viking* in 1989, *Ernest Scared Stupid* in 1991, *Boomerang* in 1992, and *Fatal Instinct* in 1993. A five-compact disc retrospective of her work, entitled *Eartha Quake*, was released in 1993.

Kitt remained active in the decade following the release of her autobiographies and retrospective. In 1996 she portrayed jazz legend Billie Holiday in a one-woman show, *Lady Day at Emerson's Bar and Grill.* In 1998 she portrayed the Wicked Witch in a musical version of *The Wizard of Oz*, and in 2000 she was cast as the Fairy Godmother in a musical version of *Cinderella.* Kitt pursues her hobbies of gardening and needlepoint at her Westchester

County, New York, home. Despite her "sex kitten" image, she has never had plastic surgery.

See also Dunham, Katherine; Music in the United States

■ ■ *Bibliography*

Hine, Darlene Clark, ed. *Black Women in America.* New York: Carlson, 1993.

Kitt, Eartha. *Thursday's Child.* New York: Duell, Sloan and Pearce, 1956.

Kitt, Eartha. *Alone with Me.* Chicago: Henry Regnery, 1976.

Kohn, Martin F. "Mischief and Magic." *Detroit Free Press,* March 3, 2002.

SUSAN MCINTOSH (1996)
THADDEUS RUSSELL (1996)
Updated by publisher 2005

KNIGHT, GLADYS
MAY 28, 1944

Gladys Knight, who was born and raised in Atlanta, Georgia, made her public singing debut at the age of four at Mount Mariah Baptist Church, where her parents were members of the choir. By the time she was five, Knight had performed in numerous Atlanta churches and toured through Florida and Alabama with the Morris Brown Choir. At the age of seven she won the Grand Prize on Ted Mack's nationally televised *Original Amateur Hour.*

In 1952 Knight formed a quartet with her brother Merald "Bubba" Williams and cousins William Guest and Edward Patten. The group, named "The Pips" after James "Pip" Woods, another cousin and the group's first manager, quickly established itself in Atlanta nightclubs. By the late 1950s, the group was a popular fixture on the national rhythm-and-blues circuit. The first recording came in 1961, when Vee Jay Records released the single "Every Beat of My Heart," which became a Top-Ten pop and number one rhythm-and-blues (R&B) hit. The following year Fury Records signed the group, changed its name to Gladys Knight and the Pips, and released their Top-Ten R&B single "Letter Full of Tears."

Though well known in R&B circles, Gladys Knight and the Pips did not become a major crossover act until 1965, when they signed with Motown Records and were featured on the label's touring reviews. Their 1967 Motown single, "I Heard It Through the Grapevine," reached number two on the *Billboard* pop chart. The late 1960s brought the group mass acclaim for its polished, call-and-response singing style and slick, synchronized dance routines. The next big hit came in 1970 with the top-selling single, "You Need Love Like I Do." Six of the group's albums made the R&B charts: *Nitty Gritty* (1970); *Greatest Hits* (1970); *If I Were Your Woman* (1971); *Standing Ovation* (1972); *Neither One of Us* (1972); and *All I Need Is Time* (1972).

In 1972 Gladys Knight and the Pips had another big hit with "Neither One of Us (Wants to Be the First to Say Goodbye)." In 1973 the group switched to the Buddah label for its top forty album, *Imagination,* which included two of the group's most enduring successes, "Midnight Train to Georgia," a number one pop single in 1973, and "I've Got to Use My Imagination." The group won two 1974 Grammy Awards for "Neither One of Us" and "Midnight Train to Georgia."

In the late 1970s the group's popularity began to wane. Legal conflicts with Motown forced Knight to record separately for a brief period in the late 1970s. The group reunited in 1980 and continued touring but was not able to record another chart-topping record until 1988, when "Love Overboard" reached the top twenty on the *Billboard* pop chart. The following year Knight once again left the group, this time voluntarily, to establish a solo career. The following year she released *Good Woman,* a solo LP that was moderately successful on black radio.

In 1993, Knight began appearing in the company of Les Brown, a highly acclaimed speaker best known for his motivational lectures and best-selling book *Living Your Dreams.* The two eventually wed on August 29, 1995, but divorced in 1997. That same year, Knight published her autobiography, *Between Each Line of Pain and Glory: My Life Story.*

After her divorce from Brown, Knight converted to the Mormon religion, engaging actively and visibly in church functions. She also continued to perform on stage and to record. Her collection *At Last* was released in 2001. She produced the album with the assistance of her then sixteen-year-old grandson, Rishawn Newman. The album won a Grammy for Best Traditional R&B Vocal Album in 2001. On April 12 of that year, Knight married William McDowell, a spa manager whom she had met in 1990.

In February 2005, Knight enjoyed a special honor, sharing the Grammy Award for best gospel performance for "Heaven Help Us All" with the late Ray Charles.

See also Music; Rhythm and Blues

■ ■ *Bibliography*

Bloom, Steve. "Gladys Knight in No Man's Land." *Rolling Stone* (June 30, 1988): 23.

Knight, Gladys. *Between Each Line of Pain and Glory: My Life Story.* New York: Hyperion, 1997.

Whitaker, Charles. "Hotter Than Ever: Gladys Knight and the Pips Mark 36 Years of Making Music." *Ebony* (September 1988): 72.

THADDEUS RUSSELL (1996)
Updated by publisher 2005

KOREAN WAR

See Military Experience, African-American

KUMINA

Kumina is a religion centered in Jamaica's southeastern parish, St. Thomas. Its presence was first noted only in the 1950s, but it was likely formulated by West Central African indentured laborers introduced by the British colonial government and British plantation owners between 1845 and 1865. However, its beliefs and rituals are not unrelated to those of Maroons (runaway slaves) in the neighboring parish, Portland, from where migrants settled in northern St. Thomas in the late nineteenth century. During the mid-twentieth century, Kumina spread when its adherents joined population movements into Kingston, the island's capital, and in the second half of the century it moved further westward into St. Catherine Parish.

Kumina is a belief system dedicated to ancestor commemoration. While the human has a spirit that returns at death to its creator, it also has a spirit, *kuyu*, that bridges the grave and the temporal world. This is the spirit with which the believer interacts as a medium and protégé. Within Kumina, no deities are called upon or worshiped, although a divine creator is recognized, named Zaambi, Zaambi Ampungo, Kinzaambi, or anglicized as King Zaambi. This is the creator among many Kongo subgroups of West Central Africa. His element is thunder.

Kumina ceremonies take the form of dancing in a counterclockwise circle around drummers seated on two drums: the *bandu* or *kibandu*, and the *playin' kyas* (cask). The single-headed drums are beaten with the palms, and tonal variation is achieved by imposing and releasing pressure on the drumhead with one heel. The bandu keeps a

2/2 heartthrob, while counterrhythms and rolls are slapped on the cask. Short repetitive songs by the dancers use either the Kongo language or Jamaican Creole English. As the dancing and drumming proceed, participants become possessed by spirits of the departed, persons who had in the near or distant past been community members. Possession behavior involves slumping to the ground, rigidity of features, body tremors or stiffness, and climbing up rafters or trees. Possession, called *mayal*, is interpreted as the return of ancestral spirits to enjoy the life experiences they once knew.

The Kumina ceremony is called a "duty," which translates the Koongo word *kamama*, "to feel obliged to keep a promise or perform a duty." This obligation can result from a dreamed request by an ancestor, or it acknowledges significant rites of passage for an individual either living or dead, such as anniversaries of birth or death, and the "tombing" of graves (their cementing over) a year or two after burial. "Duties" also mark communal anniversaries such as the turn of the year or Emancipation from slavery on August 1, 1838. Ceremonies can also petition help with physical and mental healing, legal matters, and the like. Upright posts in the shed ("bood," or booth) may be wound with ribbons in colors that signify the spiritual mood of the occasion. The head ties and clothes of the principal participants may also bear emblematic colors.

Kumina ceremonies typically start in the early night and last until near dawn. A major recess occurs around midnight when the "table" is "broken." This is a table bearing candles, bread, cakes, and fruits in a borrowing from the Afro-Christian religion Revival; it replicates a communion altar. A reading from the Bible may introduce the bread-breaking segment. The communal meal also includes meat of a goat that had been fed while being led around the circle before being beheaded publicly during the ceremony. Cooked salt-free meat and rice on banana leaves are sacralized by placement in front of the drums and then sited on the ground at the four corners of the premises as offerings to the ancestors. Early in the ceremony the ritual space of the "bood" is demarcated by the "king" or "queen" of the proceedings, who sprays rum libations from the mouth toward its four cardinal points. Kumina's ritual language is an intercalation of Jamaican Creole English and Kongo words and fossilized phrases.

See also Africanisms; Creole Languages of the Americas; Kennedy, Imogene Queenie; Religion; Revivalism

■ ■ *Bibliography*

Bilby, Kenneth, and Fu-Kiau kia Bunseki. *Kumina: A Kongo-Based Tradition in the New World*. Brussels: Centre d'étude et de documentation africaines, 1983.

Carter, Hazel. "Annotated Kumina Lexicon." *African-Caribbean Institute of Jamaica Research Review* 3 (1996): 84–129.

Lewin, Olive. *A Rock It Come Over: The Folk Music of Jamaica*. Kingston, Jamaica: University of the West Indies Press, 2000.

Ryman, Cheryl. "Kumina: Stability and Change." *African-Caribbean Institute of Jamaica Research Review* 1 (1984): 81–128.

Warner-Lewis, Maureen. *The Nkuyu: Spirit Messengers of the Kumina*. Mona, Jamaica: Savacou, 1977.

MAUREEN WARNER-LEWIS (2005)

KWANZA

■ ■ ■

In 1966, at the height of the black self-awareness and pride that characterized the Black Power movement, cultural nationalist Maulana Karenga created the holiday of Kwanza, which means "first fruits" in Swahili. The holiday is derived from the harvest festival of East African agriculturalists. Karenga believed that black people in the diaspora should set aside time to celebrate their African cultural heritage and affirm their commitment to black liberation. His philosophy, called kawaida, formed the ideological basis of Kwanza. The holiday was intended to provide a nonmaterialistic alternative to Christmas and is celebrated from December 26 through January 1. Each day is devoted to one of the seven principles on which kawaida is based: *umoja* (unity), *kujichagulia* (self-determination), *ujima* (collective work and responsibility), *ujamaa* (cooperative economics), *nia* (purpose), *kuumba* (creativity), and *imani* (faith).

The attempt to honor communal heritage through ceremony is central to Kwanza. On each evening of the celebration, family and friends gather to share food and drink. The hosts adorn the table with the various symbols of Kwanza and explain their significance to their guests. First an *mkeka* (straw mat) representing the African-American heritage in traditional African culture is laid down. Upon the mat, a *kinara* (candleholder) is lit with seven candles in memory of African ancestors. Each of the seven candles represents one of the seven values being celebrated. A *kikomba* (cup) is placed on the mat to symbolize the unity of all African peoples, and finally tropical fruits and nuts are laid out to represent the yield of the first harvest.

Although Kwanza was at first limited in practice to cultural nationalists, as more African Americans came to heightened awareness and appreciation of their African heritage the holiday gained wider and more mainstream acceptance. In the 1990s Kwanza came to be celebrated internationally, but it gained its widest acceptance and popularity among African Americans.

See also African Diaspora; Africanisms; Karenga, Maulana; Kawaida

■ ■ *Bibliography*

Karenga, Maulana. *Kwanzaa: Origin, Concepts, Practice.* San Diego: Kawaida Publications, 1977.

Karenga, Maulana. *Kawaida Theory: An Introductory Outline.* Inglewood, Calif.: Kawaida Publications, 1980.

Karenda, Maulana. *Kwanzaa: A Celebration of Family, Community and Culture.* Los Angeles: University of Sankore Press, 1997.

Magubane, Bernard. *The Ties That Bind: African American Consciousness of Africa.* Trenton, N.J.: Africa World Press, 1987.

Weusi-Puryear, Omoniki. "How I Came to Celebrate Kwanza." *Essence,* December 1979, 112, 115, 117.

NANCY YOUSEF (1996)
ROBYN SPENCER (1996)
Updated bibliography

KWAYANA, EUSI

See King, Sydney (Kwayana, Eusi)

LaBelle, Patti (Holt, Patricia Louise)

October 4, 1944

Born and raised in Philadelphia, Pennsylvania, singer Patti LaBelle grew up singing in the choir of the Beaulah Baptist Church. She was sixteen years old when she joined a vocal group called the Ordettes; a year later, LaBelle, Cindy Birdsong (who joined the Supremes as Florence Ballard's replacement in 1967), Nona Hendrix, and Sarah Dash signed on with Newton Records, and named their group the BlueBelles after Newton's subsidiary label, Bluebelle records. After their song "I Sold My Heart to the Junkman" reached the top twenty in 1962, the group was rechristened Patti LaBelle and the BlueBelles.

LaBelle, who is known for her fiery stage presence and outrageous attire—a mixture of leather, feathers, glitter, and enormous fanlike coiffures—received her first big break in 1968, when she and the BlueBelles opened for the Who during their U.S. tour. The following year, she married Armstead Edwards, an educator who enrolled in business courses in order to become her personal manager. In 1971 LaBelle and the BlueBelles became known as simply "LaBelle." Their album *Nightbirds,* with its number one

single "Lady Marmalade," made the top ten in 1973. In 1974 LaBelle became the first black band to perform in New York's Metropolitan Opera House; as the lead singer, Patti LaBelle caused a sensation when she began the show by descending from the ceiling, where she hung suspended, to the stage.

LaBelle went solo in 1977 after personal and artistic differences between the singers caused the band's dissolution the previous year. By the end of the 1970s she had recorded two LPs for Epic Records, and she continued to appear live and record albums throughout the 1980s and early 1990s. In 1985 LaBelle appeared in Pennsylvania to perform in the Live Aid Benefit Rock Concert; her album *Burnin'* earned her a Grammy Award for best rhythm-and-blues performance by a female vocalist in 1991. In 1997 she released the album *Flame,* and her album *Live! One Night Only* (1998) garnered her another Grammy. In 2003 she won a Songwriters Hall of Fame Lifetime Achievement Award.

LaBelle is well known for her support of numerous charitable and social organizations, including Big Sisters and the United Negro College Fund, as well as various urban renewal and homelessness projects in Philadelphia, where she lives. In addition to giving concert performances, she costarred with singer Al Green in a revival of

Your Arms Too Short to Box with God on Broadway in 1982, and appeared in the films *A Soldier's Story* and *Beverly Hills Cop,* in her own television special, and in the television series *A Different World* and *Out All Night.*

The co-author of a book of recipes (*LaBelle Cuisine: Recipes to Sing About,* 1999), LaBelle expanded her career once again to launch a clothing line on the Home Shopping Network (HSN) in November 2003. LaBelle, involved in the creative process for that line of women's clothing, took inspiration from her own wardrobe and stage clothes.

LaBelle has not let her other artistic endeavors impede her musical career. She signed with Def Jam Classics to produce another album, *Timeless Journey,* which was released in 2004.

See also Music in the United States; Rhythm and Blues; United Negro College Fund

■ ■ *Bibliography*

Ebert, Alan. "Girlfriend: A Down Home Diva!" *Essence* 21 (March 1991): 68–70.

Hine, Darlene Clark, ed. *Black Women in America: An Historical Encyclopedia,* Vol. 1. Brooklyn, N.Y.: Carlson, 1993.

LaBelle, Patti. *Don't Block the Blessings.* New York: Riverhead Books, 1996.

PAMELA WILKINSON (1996)
Updated by publisher 2005

LABOR AND LABOR UNIONS

African-American workers' relationship to the organized labor movement has undergone tremendous, if uneven, shifts since the Civil War. Concentrated in southern agriculture or in unskilled occupations before World War I, most black workers simply did not compete directly with whites in the economic sphere. Trade unions were dominated by white workers, whose skills and racial solidarity often enabled them to bar blacks from membership in their associations and employment in certain sectors of the economy. By World War I, however, the efforts of an ever-growing number of urban industrial black workers to advance economically undermined the success of white labor's exclusionary strategy. With the triumph of industrial unionism represented by the rise of the Congress of Industrial Organizations during the Great Depression of the 1930s, an important branch of the labor movement

committed itself to interracial organizing. The modern American labor movement has both reflected and contributed to the nation's changing race relations. While never free of racial tensions or inequality, and while possessing a wide range of unions with different racial policies, practices, and degrees of commitment to racial equality, the labor movement has served as one more arena of black workers' larger struggle for racial equality in the economy.

AGRICULTURE

In the aftermath of the Civil War, the overwhelming number of black workers made their living in southern agriculture as landless sharecroppers and tenant farmers, concentrated at the bottom of the South's economic hierarchy where they exercised little political or economic power. Black agricultural workers launched periodic collective challenges to white planters' authority in the political realm during Reconstruction and the Populist Era in the late 1880s and early 1890s, and in the economic arena in the form of strikes by rural Knights of Labor in the mid-1880s and by various sharecroppers' movements in the 1930s. But their movements and uprisings were quickly crushed. The 1887 strike by some 10,000 Knights of Labor (most of whom were black) working in the Louisiana sugar fields met with fierce state repression, as did the efforts of the black Alabama Share Croppers' Union in the 1930s. Trade unions and other movements found the rural South infertile soil in which to take root and flourish, for many reasons, including the South's racial ideology, black workers' economic weakness arising from their landlessness, the power of the planter class, the commitment of the state to repressing rural labor, and the organized labor movement's lack of interest in agricultural and black workers. The most successful black response to economic and political oppression was short-range mobility within the South and ultimately migration out of the South. Engaged overwhelmingly in rural southern agriculture at the end of the Civil War, African Americans had, by the late twentieth century, become a largely urban people, engaged in manufacturing, transportation, and service trades in the North, South, and West.

NINETEENTH- AND EARLY TWENTIETH-CENTURY TRADE UNIONS

Before and after the Civil War, trade unions of white workers in the North and South viewed skilled and unskilled urban black workers as a threat to their own economic security. Skill, independence, manliness, and a sense of racial superiority defined the contours of these skilled whites' beliefs. In white workers' thinking, black workers (slave or free) might demean a craft by working more cheaply and without regard to union work rules or customs. Accordingly, whites excluded blacks from membership in their organizations, denied blacks access to apprenticeship programs, and occasionally resorted to force to drive blacks out of employment. Immediately after the Civil War, a new, loosely organized, and short-lived national federation of white trade unions, the National Labor Union (1866–1872), eventually admitted black delegates representing black workers to its conventions but went no further. At the same time, most of its constituent members barred blacks from their unions, urging them to organize separately into their own unions. While white workers excluded blacks from white associations, their acceptance, sometimes reluctant, sometimes not, of all-black associations was as far as most white union members were willing to go. The alternative, which was more widely practiced, was white exclusion, nonrecognition, and outright hostility toward blacks. Until the 1930s, exclusion and biracial unionism represented the white labor movement's two dominant tendencies toward African Americans.

In response to their exclusion from white organizations, black workers built upon their communities' larger institutional networks to create all-black unions that championed their members' class and racial interests. Black labor leader Isaac Myers, a Baltimore ship caulker, was a founder of another short-lived association in 1869, the black National Labor Union, which brought together representatives of newly formed black unions, community leaders, and black political (Republican) officials. More enduring, if less recognized, were the dozens of smaller associations that emerged during and after Reconstruction in such southern urban centers as Richmond, Galveston, New Orleans, Mobile, and Savannah.

During the 1880s, the Knights of Labor emerged from obscurity to become the nation's most powerful labor federation. The Knights' ideology was cooperative, inclusive, and egalitarian. The organization embraced all wage earners across lines of skill, gender, religion, ethnicity, and race (with the exception of Asian immigrants). Although there are no precise figures, one contemporary estimated that blacks constituted about 10 percent (roughly 60,000) of the Knights' membership in 1886. Yet the formation of Knights' locals largely followed strict racial lines. The Order, particularly in the South, absorbed already existing black and white locals, and new locals formed along racially distinct lines. This biracial character did not prevent black and white delegates from meeting together or formulating joint strategies, but it did perpetuate existing differences and made expressions of solidarity more difficult. By 1886, the Knights' racial policies came under fierce at-

tack from conservative southern editors, politicians, and employers as well as some white Knights. Playing upon white workers' racial fears, employers "race-baited" the Order, which, for many reasons, went into decline in the late 1880s.

The American Federation of Labor (founded in 1881) succeeded the Knights as the nation's dominant labor organization by the early 1890s. In contrast to the inclusiveness of the Knights, the social bases of the AFL rested on white craft workers who sought to protect their skills and jobs from all newcomers. Craft unions were exclusive, barring workers from membership on the basis of their lack of skills, their sex, race, and in some cases ethnicity. The AFL was formally opposed to racial discrimination in its ranks; in 1892, its New Orleans members participated in an (unsuccessful) interracial general strike on behalf of unskilled black and white workers. But by the turn of the century, AFL leaders tolerated widespread discrimination by its constituent members, explaining that the all-important principle of craft autonomy—which granted considerable power to individual unions—made it impossible for them to intervene in member unions' internal affairs. AFL officials adhered to that principle only selectively, however, for on other issues they did sometimes intervene.

The majority of union internationals in the AFL, as well as the independent, powerful railroad brotherhoods, remained all white, and a minority of union internationals admitted blacks into segregated, second-class unions. Several large internationals defied these trends. The International Longshoremen's Association and the United Mine Workers of America, while embracing biracial unions (all-black and all-white locals), espoused somewhat more egalitarian views and policies. The existence of large numbers of black workers, many of whom were organized, compelled white trade unionists in these fields to reach accommodations with African-American workers. That is, these unions' success and very existence required a coming-to-grips with racial divisions; they could little afford to exclude or ignore black workers.

During the Progressive Era, only the Industrial Workers of the World (IWW) adopted a principled stand against racial discrimination. Far to the left of the AFL, the IWW advocated the formation of industrial unions (all workers in a factory, regardless of craft, would be members of the same union) and the overthrow of capitalism, championing a working-class solidarity that transcended all lines of division. While it gained adherents among black and white southern timber workers and Philadelphia longshoremen before World War I, the IWW confronted massive government and employer repression and declined rapidly during the war.

In the late nineteenth and early twentieth century, maintaining all-white workplaces sometimes brought white workers into sharp conflict with employers and blacks. Employers used white workers' racial beliefs and practices to their own advantage by turning to black workers to break strikes or otherwise undermine union wages and work rules. Black workers, who were barred from certain sectors of employment and union membership, found strikebreaking to be one method of cracking the economic color line and securing new jobs. In this period, there were dozens of instances of small- and large-scale riots and other violence as whites in all-white unions battled black workers imported by employers to undercut union authority and power.

White workers often coexisted easily or uneasily with black workers in their trades, but upon other occasions they sought to drive blacks completely out of those jobs. For instance, the 1894 and 1895 strikes by white New Orleans dock workers and the 1909 strike by white Georgia railroad firemen each sought as its goal the elimination of black workers. During the World War I era, massive labor shortages in the North contributed to an unprecedented migration of African Americans out of the South. Securing a wide foothold in mass-production industries for the first time, black workers confronted often-hostile whites, especially during the postwar economic downturn. Competition for jobs was only one of the many causes of the race riots that exploded in 1919, and black workers suffered discrimination not only at the hands of unions but by employers as well.

Despite the AFL's racial practices and black leaders' condemnation of those practices, numerous black workers formed all-black unions and joined the federation. Generally representing unskilled workers (in such trades as longshoring and mining), these unions were often smaller and weaker than their white counterparts. Nonetheless, they participated in the labor upheavals of the World War I era. The years 1918 and 1919, for instance, witnessed strikes by black female domestic workers and laundry workers in Mobile and Newport News, black male longshoremen in New Orleans, Galveston, Savannah, and Key West, and black (and white) coal miners in West Virginia, Tennessee, Kentucky, Arkansas, and Alabama. These strikes failed less because of white workers' opposition (in some cases, whites and blacks struck together) than because of violent opposition by employers and government. Yet the rare union effort to bridge the racial gap in northern industry, such as the wartime drive by Chicago's multiracial and multiethnic packinghouse workers, failed not only because of the employers' hostility; in the Chicago packinghouses, racial and skill divisions proved too deep for organizers to overcome, dooming the unions' efforts.

Immediately after the war, black unionists demanded that the AFL abolish its color line and actively organize black workers. While the AFL passed lofty resolutions, the behavior of its white affiliates changed little, if at all. Although the AFL eventually did offer organizational backing to the largest all-black union in the United States, the Brotherhood of Sleeping Car Porters, founded in 1925 and led by A. Philip Randolph, it did little to challenge the racism of its other railroad unions, which remained virtually lily-white until the 1960s.

African Americans, like their white native-born and immigrant counterparts, were of many minds on the subject of organized labor. Until the mid-twentieth century, most blacks worked in sectors of the economy (agriculture, domestic service, and common labor) that were not conducive to sustaining trade unions, regardless of the race of the labor force. If no one could deny the institutional racism of organized white labor, African Americans disagreed on such issues as the possibilities of positive institutional change, the relationship between black workers and white industrialists, the union movement's tactics, and the like. Conservative leader Booker T. Washington, along with many business-oriented black newspaper editors and clergymen, were extremely harsh in their evaluation of the AFL, counseling black workers to ally with the industrial leaders in the New South and in the North. Some black workers, excluded from white unions and hence certain job categories, reluctantly or enthusiastically became strikebreakers as the only way to gain access to better jobs. Other black leaders were ideologically flexible, praising organized labor when it opened its doors to blacks, condemning it when it kept those doors closed. Black proponents of black union organizing, like miner Richard L. Davis and longshoreman James Porter, worked within their respective union internationals, attempting to enlist black workers in the labor movement's ranks at the same time they sought to modify white labor's racism. Given white workers' often abusive treatment, a relative lack of skills, and economic subordination, a majority of black workers remained outside of the labor movement (as did a majority of white workers). Black workers who joined trade unions did so for many of the same reasons white workers did: to improve wages and working conditions, to eliminate or reduce abuses, to win a degree of job security and control over the conditions of their labor, and to secure a measure of dignity in their work lives. Black trade unions waged a continual struggle to carve out a place for themselves in an often reluctant labor movement dominated by whites. Until the rise of the Congress of Industrial Organizations in the 1930s, their successes were relatively few and far between.

Industrial Unionism and Unions in Modern America

The formation of the Congress of Industrial Organizations (CIO) in 1935 heralded a gradual transformation in the relationship between organized labor and African-American workers. Breaking away from the AFL, CIO unions advocated industrial unionism and campaigned vigorously to organize basic industry (auto, steel, meat packing, electric, rubber). Committed to organizing all workers, regardless of skill, sex, or race, the CIO both ideologically and practically had to secure the support of black workers, whose presence in basic industry in the North had increased dramatically since the great migration of the World War I era brought hundreds of southern blacks into the northern economy. There was no single CIO perspective or practice on racial issues, for CIO unions' record on racial issues and behavior toward black workers varied by industry and region. During World War II, thousands of white workers (many of whom were themselves newcomers to industry and the labor movement) conducted unofficial, unsanctioned hate strikes against the presence or advancement of black workers in their factories, strikes that were opposed by the federal government and top union leaders. Before and after World War II, left-wing CIO unions maintained the strongest record on civil rights issues and the treatment of black members. Influenced by communist leaders and an active black rank and file, the United Packinghouse Workers, the Farm Equipment Workers, the Food, Tobacco, Agricultural, and Allied Workers, the Mine, Mill, and Smelter Workers, and, by the 1950s and 1960s, the Hospital Workers Union stood at the forefront of those in the labor movement advancing a civil rights agenda. The more centrist United Automobile Workers Union, especially in Detroit, worked in close alliance with black political leaders in the 1940s.

Since 1950, the labor movement's record on issues of black equality has remained checkered. Participating in the anticommunism of the post–World War II era, the CIO purged its left wing, firing communist organizers and expelling unions most active in the struggle for racial equality. The CIO's failed Operation Dixie in 1946 and 1947 left organized labor far weaker and economic segregation far stronger in the South. The merger of the AFL and the CIO in 1955 sealed the labor movement's primary organizational fault line, but on terms that left substantively untouched much of the racial conservatism of the AFL craft unions. Over the next several decades, black trade unionists founded a number of all-black organizations as well as caucuses within various international unions (affecting unions in steel, the garment trade, the

postal service, and education), all of which aimed at advancing African Americans' civil rights by pressuring AFL-CIO officials and employers alike. Since the 1960s, many white AFL unions have continued to discriminate against blacks and have opposed affirmative action strongly, and, in the 1980s, many white unionists participated in the "white backlash" and defected from the Democratic party, becoming "Reagan Democrats" who voted Republican in presidential elections. Yet the united AFL-CIO did create a civil rights department, and some union internationals and locals contributed money and organizers to the civil rights movement of the late 1950s and 1960s. The percentage of blacks in the AFL-CIO continued to rise, reaching roughly 10 percent of the federation's declining membership by 1970. African Americans in unionized jobs earned about 25 percent more than blacks in nonunionized jobs by 1979. By the 1990s, unions containing a large African-American membership include the United Auto Workers, the Service Employees International Union, the American Federation of State, County, and Municipal Employees, and the Hospital Workers Local 1199. During the 1980s, unions with large numbers of black members were active in supporting South Africa's anti-apartheid movement and in lobbying for progressive legislation in health care; a number of unions endorsed Jesse Jackson's 1988 bid for the presidency.

The late 1990s brought union scandals and controversy. In December 1998 Stanley Hill was pressured by the American Federation of State, County and Municipal Employees to take a leave of absence from his longtime position as the executive director of District Council 17. The Manhattan District Attorney was investigating allegations of embezzlement, kickbacks, and vote fraud in District Council 17. Hill announced his retirement eleven weeks later on February 17, 1999. Two of Hill's top aides resigned in December 1998 after admitting that they had taken part in the vote fraud. Although he repeatedly denied any knowledge of the vote rigging, he felt some responsibility for it since some of his key people were involved.

Since the 1960s, deindustrialization and capital flight, the expansion of dead-end and poorly paid jobs in the new "service" economy, an increasingly hostile political environment, and the revival of strong anti-union sentiment in the business community have contributed to the steady and dramatic decline of organized labor. Fighting an uphill battle for its own survival, the labor movement has devoted relatively little attention to making inroads in the economy's fast-growing, low-wage, unskilled sector, which is increasingly dominated by black and other nonwhite workers. Because of its weakness, its narrow vision,

Union appeal for integration, Detroit, 1944. *A truck paneled with signboards arranged to mimic the appearance of a Klansman carries a message sponsored by the San Francisco branch of the NAACP.* PHOTOGRAPHS AND PRINTS DIVISION, SCHOMBURG CENTER FOR RESEARCH IN BLACK CULTURE, THE NEW YORK PUBLIC LIBRARY, ASTOR, LENOX AND TILDEN FOUNDATIONS.

and its adherence to traditional strategies centered primarily on member needs, the labor movement has contributed little to addressing the larger issues of economic decline and postindustrial poverty, which have had tremendously negative effects on the African-American urban working class.

The decline in U.S. manufacturing and the continued outsourcing and offshoring of U.S. jobs to foreign countries has hurt all workers, although at 10.5 percent (as of January 2004), black unemployment is more than twice that of whites. According to U.S. Department of Labor statistics, 20.1 percent of wage and salary workers were union workers in 1983; by 2004 that figure was 12.5 percent, though 15.1 percent of overall membership was African American. In 2005 the Detroit-based International Brotherhood of Teamsters and the Washington, D.C.–based Service Employees International Union (SEIU) broke away from the AFL-CIO, which comprises some sixty unions. This marked the biggest split among the labor organization's 13 million members since its founding in

1955, although the union of Carpenters and Joiners International and its 300,000 members broke away in 2000. The two dissident unions, representing 3.2 million workers, cited declining U.S. union membership and the future direction of organized labor for their decision. Calling themselves the Change to Win Coalition—which also include the Laborers International of North America; the textile, garment, and hotel employees union UNITE HERE; the United Food and Commercial Workers; and the United Farm Workers—the dissident unions prefer a greater focus on organizing workers and merging smaller unions into larger ones, believing that the AFL-CIO devotes too much of its resources to centralization and political lobbying. The coalition represents mostly lower-wage workers in service industries, which now comprise 76 percent of the job market.

See also Black Power Movement; Brotherhood of Sleeping Car Porters; Civil Rights Movement, U.S.; Communist Party of the United States; Economic Condition, U.S.;

League of Revolutionary Black Workers; National Negro Labor Council; Negro American Labor Council; Politics in the United States; Randolph, Asa Philip; Riots and Popular Protests; Urban Poverty in the Caribbean

■■ Bibliography

Anderson, Claud. *Black Labor, White Wealth: The Search for Power and Economic Justice.* Edgewood, Md.: Duncan & Duncan, 1994.

Anderson, Jervis. *A. Philip Randolph: A Biographical Portrait.* Berkeley: University of California Press, 1986.

Arnesen, Eric. *Waterfront Workers of New Orleans: Race, Class, and Politics, 1863-1923.* Urbana: University of Illinois Press, 1994.

Cayton, Horace R., and George S. Mitchell. *Black Workers and the New Unions.* 1939. Reprint, Westport, Conn.: Negro Universities Press, 1970.

Foner, Philip Sheldon. *Organized Labor and the Black Worker, 1619–1981,* 2d ed. New York: International Publishers, 1982.

Gould, William B. *Black Workers in White Unions: Job Discrimination in the United States.* Ithaca, N.Y.: Cornell University Press, 1977.

Harris, William H. *The Harder We Run: Black Workers since the Civil War.* New York: Oxford University Press, 1982.

Hill, Herbert. *Black Labor and the American Legal System: Race, Work and the Law.* Madison: University of Wisconsin Press, 1985.

Honey, Michael Keith. *Black Workers Remember: An Oral History of Segregation, Unionism, and the Freedom Struggle.* Berkeley: University of California Press, 1999.

Jacobson, Julius, ed. *The Negro and the American Labor Movement.* Garden City, N.Y.: Anchor Books, 1968.

Korstad, Robert, and Nelson Lichtenstein. "Opportunities Found and Lost: Labor, Radicals, and the Early Civil Rights Movement." *Journal of American History* 75 (1988): 786–811.

Lewis, Ronald L. *Black Coal Miners in America: Race, Class, and Community Conflict, 1780-1980.* Lexington: University Press of Kentucky, 1987.

Mason, Patrick L., ed. *African Americans, Labor and Society: Organizing for a New Agenda.* Detroit: Wayne State University Press, 2001.

Meier, August, and Elliott Rudwick. *Black Detroit and the Rise of the UAW.* New York: Oxford University Press, 1979.

Miller, Calvin Craig. *A. Philip Randolph: And the African-American Labor Movement.* Greensboro, N.C.: Morgan Reynolds, 2005.

Moreno, Paul D. *Black Americans and Organized Labor: A New History.* Baton Rouge: Louisiana State University Press, 2005.

Obadele-Starks, Ernest. *Black Unionism in the Industrial South.* College Station: Texas A&M University Press, 2000.

Peterson, Kyle. "Labor Schism Could Ignite Union Renewal." (July 28, 2005). Available from <http://www.reuters.com>.

Rachleff, Peter J. *Black Labor in Richmond, 1865–1890.* Urbana: University of Illinois Press, 1984. Reprint, 1988.

Roediger, David R. *The Wages of Whiteness: Race and the Making of the American Working Class.* New York: Verso, 1991.

Spero, Sterling D., and Abram L. Harris. *The Black Worker: The Negro and the Labor Movement.* New York: Columbia University Press, 1931. Reprint, New York: Atheneum, 1968.

Tye, Larry. *Rising from the Rails: Pullman Porters and the Making of the Black Middle Class.* New York: Henry Holt, 2004.

Zieger, Robert H., ed. *Organized Labor in the Twentieth-Century South.* Knoxville: University of Tennessee Press, 1991.

Zieger, Robert H., and Gilbert J. Gall. *American Workers, American Unions: The Twentieth Century.* Baltimore, Md.: Johns Hopkins University Press, 2002.

ERIC ARNESEN (1996)
CHRISTINE TOMASSINI (2005)

LABOV, WILLIAM

DECEMBER 4, 1927

Sociolinguist William Labov was born in Rutherford, New Jersey. Perhaps more than any other person, Labov has shaped the foundation of contemporary sociolinguistics. He made seminal contributions to the study of African-American Vernacular English (AAVE), albeit within the greater context of his global effort to create an inclusive and comprehensive linguistic science.

Labov's academic training began at Harvard University in 1944, where he majored in English and philosophy. After several unsuccessful attempts at other professions, he settled upon work as an industrial chemist in 1949. The experience of his philosophical, English, and scientific training—combined with the no-nonsense production schedules demanded of successful entrepreneurs—proved to be ideally suited to Labov's emerging fascination with linguistic science.

Labov's 1966 dissertation, "The Social Stratification of English in New York City," written at Columbia University, remains one of the most important and influential linguistic studies ever produced. It gave rise to his abiding concern about how best to advance literacy and educational achievement among black students with sophisticated analyses of their linguistic behavior.

Labov, working in collaboration with Paul Cohen, Clarence Robins, and John Lewis, produced *The Nonstandard English of Black and Puerto Rican Speakers in New York City* in 1968. This important study provided the empirical bases for two companion studies that codify Labov's twin tower contributions to racial justice and linguistic science.

Students of AAVE have benefited from "The Logic of Nonstandard English" (1969) and "Contraction, Deletion, and Inherent Variability of the English Copula" (1969). In the former, Labov dispelled some prevalent myths regarding the logical coherence of AAVE. In the latter, he produced a major quantitative study of copula variation (i.e., variants of "is" and "are") among African Americans, and he did so in ways that were compatible with Noam Chomsky and Morris Halle's 1968 formulations for the sound pattern of English. Labov did more than merely describe AAVE; he did so while advancing a comprehensive linguistic science—that is, an empirical linguistic science that is fully inclusive.

These classical sociolinguistic studies remain the gold standard for excellence in AAVE research. Labov used his AAVE expertise in 1979 during the landmark Black English Trial in Ann Arbor, Michigan. Based on that experience he wrote "Objectivity and Commitment in Linguistic Science" (1982) in which he extols the social and educational virtue of the strategic collaboration between linguists, educators, and attorneys in support of young African-American plaintiffs. In this instance the black plaintiffs won their case by confirming that the defendant school district failed to account for potential linguistic barriers to their academic success and their language education in particular. Shortly thereafter he observed linguistic divergence among blacks and whites (Labov and Harris, 1986), which was a precursor to some of the important contemporary research on hip-hop and its linguistic defiance in the face of mainstream American English.

Labov remains extremely active. "How I Got into Linguistics, and What I Got Out of It" and "Coexistent Systems in African American English" provide greater insight into his professional life and recent contributions to studies of African-American English. Other major works include the two-volume *Principles of Linguistic Change,* the first volume (1994) dealing with internal factors and the second with social factors (2001). Intellectual tributes from his students can be found in the two-volume set *Towards a Social Science of Language: Papers in Honor of William Labov.*

See also Educational Psychology and Psychologists; English, African-American; Psychology and Psychologists: Race Issues; Social Psychology, Psychologists, and Race

■ ■ *Bibliography*

Guy, Gregory Guy, John Baugh, Deborah Schiffrin, and Crawford Feagin. *Towards a Social Science of Language: Papers in Honor of William Labov.* Philadelphia: John Benjamins, 1996–1997.

Labov, William. *The Social Stratification of English in New York City.* Washington, D.C.: Center for Applied Linguistics, 1966.

Labov, William. "The Logic of Nonstandard English." In *Georgetown Monograph Series on Language and Linguistics,* vol. 22, edited by J. Alatis. Washington, D.C.: Georgetown University Press, 1969.

Labov, William. "Contraction, Deletion, and Inherent Variability of the English Copula." *Language* 45 (1969): 715–762.

Labov, William. *Language in the Inner-City: Studies in the Black English Vernacular.* Philadelphia: University of Pennsylvania Press, 1972.

Labov, William. *Sociolinguistic Patterns.* Philadelphia: University of Pennsylvania Press, 1972.

Labov, William. "Objectivity and Commitment in Linguistic Science: The Case of the Black English Trial in Ann Arbor." *Language in Society* 11 (1982): 165–202.

Labov, William. *Principles of Linguistic Change.* Volume 1: *Internal Factors.* Oxford, UK: Blackwell, 1994. Volume 2: *Social Factors.* Oxford, UK: Blackwell, 2001.

Labov, William. "How I Got into Linguistics, and What I Got Out of It" (1997). Available from <http://www.ling.upenn.edu/~wlabov/HowIgot.html>.

Labov, William, and Clarence Robins. "A Note on the Relation of Reading Failure to Peer-Group Status in Urban Ghettos." *Teachers College Record* 70 (1969): 395–405.

Labov, William, and Wendel Harris. "DeFacto Segregation of Black and White Vernaculars." In *Diversity and Diachrony,* edited by D. Sankoff, pp. 1–24. Philadelphia: John Benjamins, 1986.

JOHN BAUGH (2005)

LAFAYETTE PLAYERS

The Lafayette Players was the first enduring African-American stock theater company, and it offered the first opportunity for black actors to appear in nonmusical presentations. The group was formed in 1915 as the Anita Bush Players and presented its first play, *The Girl at the Fort,* on November 19, 1915, at the Lincoln Theatre in Harlem. The group was successful, but a dispute with the Lincoln Theatre management led it to transfer to the Lafayette Theater, where it began to present plays on December 27, 1915. By March of the following year, Bush transferred ownership of the players to the Lafayette Theater management and the group became known as the Lafayette Players.

At the height of the Lafayette Players' success, from 1919 to 1921, four traveling companies used the name and were booked on the circuit controlled by the corporate owner. The Lafayette Players was continuously active until 1923, when film undercut live entertainment. The name *Lafayette Players* was used intermittently by various successor groups until 1928; a group was also active under the name in Los Angeles from 1928 to 1932.

The Lafayette Players presented over 250 productions, mostly of abbreviated Broadway plays or classics; only a handful were what were called race plays. The early production schedule called for a new play every week. The presentations almost always shared the bill with vaudeville acts and movies. The most famous among the early players were Charles Gilpin (1878–1930), who played the lead in Eugene O'Neill's *The Emperor Jones* on Broadway in 1920, and Clarence Muse (1889–1979), who had a long career in Hollywood.

See also Drama; Lincoln Theatre; Micheaux, Oscar

▨ ▪ *Bibliography*

Johns, Robert L. "Anita Bush." In *Notable Black American Women,* edited by Jessie Carney Smith. Detroit: Gale,1992.

Peterson, Bernard L., Jr. *The African American Theatre Directory, 1816–1960: A Comprehensive Guide to Early Black Theatre Organizations, Companies, Theatres, and Performing Groups.* Westport, Conn.: Greenwood, 1997.

ROBERT L. JOHNS (1996)
Updated bibliography

LAM, WIFREDO

DECEMBER 8, 1902
SEPTEMBER 11, 1982

▪▪▪

Cuban painter Wifredo Lam was the first artist of color to make an impact on the international art scene. He was born in Sagua le Grande, Cuba. His father was Chinese, his mother of African and Spanish ancestry. After studying art at the Academia San Alejandro in Havana, he left Cuba in 1923 to study art in Spain, where he lived for fifteen years. During this period he set the foundation for his signature style by experimenting with a variety of academic art and modernist tendencies, inspired in particular by the work of Henri Matisse and Pablo Picasso. Lam became involved with the Republican cause in the Spanish Civil War (1936–1939). In 1937 he became ill and was sent to Barcelona to recover, escaping to Paris in 1938 just as the city fell to the Nationalist forces.

In Paris Lam made contact with Picasso, who introduced him to André Breton and the surrealist group. In the context of that movement Lam was able to promote his art internationally. When the German forces advanced on Paris in 1940, Lam began his journey back to Cuba, going first to Marseilles, where in the company of the surrealists he developed a language of hybrid forms that would characterize his unique mature style. He secured passage from Marseilles to Martinique, eventually arriving in Cuba. There, from 1942 to 1945, he created his first masterpieces, most famously *The Jungle* (1942–1943, located in the Museum of Modern Art in New York), which featured a synthesis of Afro-Cuban religious motifs (with references to deities known as *orishas*), European modernism, and ancient alchemical ideas implanted on human, plant, and animal hybrids. Through Breton, who had gone on to New York, Lam was able to exhibit this work in New York during the 1940s. After World War II Lam reconnected with the European art scene, establishing a studio in Italy where he worked for the final twenty-two years of his career.

This was the period of the extensive internationalization of Lam's reputation in Europe, Latin America, the Caribbean, the United States, and even Asia. His style continued to evolve, becoming more schematic and more imaginative as he continually invented variations on his repertoire of thematic motifs: bamboo stalks and tobacco leaves, banana and papaya fruit, inverted cup-heads of Elegua (*orisha* of the crossroads), and the ever-present horse-headed woman (*femme cheval*). Lam became a mentor as well as associate of the new generation of artists in movements such as the CoBrA group (referring to Copenhagen, Brussels, and Amsterdam), the Group Phases, and the International Situationists, who represented the evolution of surrealism after World War II. Lam was unwavering in his conviction that his work was an instrument of political, cultural, and personal liberation. His ultimate legacy was that he demonstrated the potential of issues of identity and nationality within modernism, setting the stage for postmodernism. Lam died in Paris in 1982 after suffering a debilitating stroke in 1978 and is buried in Havana, Cuba.

See also Orisha; Painting and Sculpture

▨ ▪ *Bibliography*

Sims, Lowery Stokes. *Wifredo Lam and the International Avant-Garde.* Austin: University of Texas Press, 2002.

Tonneau-Ryckelynck, Dominique, and Pascaline Dron. *Wifredo Lam, oeuvre gravé et lithographié: Catalogue raisonné.* Gravelines, France: Editions du Musée de Gravelines, 1994.

LOWERY STOKES SIMS (2005)

LAMMING, GEORGE

JUNE 8, 1927

A prominent figure in Caribbean literary history, George Lamming was born in Carrington Village, Barbados. Although overwhelmingly populated by descendants of African slaves brought to the island for plantation labor, Barbados was at the time so self-identified as an anglicized British colony that it was called "Little England." Lamming migrated to London in the great wave of Caribbean migration in the 1950s, but his experiences there as a black man challenged his initial belief that there was limited potential in the Anglophone Caribbean and that a West Indian writer had no choice but to leave for the mother country, England. He returned to Barbados several decades later, where he continues to write, lecture, and travel to various countries. He has published no major fiction after his allegorical novel *Natives of My Person* (1972) but has worked on a dramatic piece on reimagining history in the Americas. Although he began as a short story writer and a poet, Lamming's most important works remain his novels, including *In the Castle of My Skin* (1953), *The Emigrants* (1954), *Of Age and Innocence* (1958), *Season of Adventure* (1960), and *Water with Berries* (1971).

Lamming's entire corpus focuses on various phases of Caribbean colonial history and its aftermath, including what he perceived as the failure of independence movements on the islands. The author himself notes internal connections in theme and substance in his novels, characterizing each of his fictional works as part of a corpus that could be read as one book, although not in chronological order. *In the Castle of My Skin,* published shortly after he migrated to London, is the first in a series that explores the psychological, historical, and political impact of European colonization in the Americas. It became an instant classic and is still the most frequently cited of his novels. It examines the material effects of landlessness and poverty on black villagers in Barbados and the ideological consequences of English colonial education. His second novel, *The Emigrants,* can be read as a sequel to his first, which ends with the betrayal of the labor riots of the 1930s and the departure of the protagonist. *The Emigrants* deals with the mass migration to England and the shocking alienation of the various Caribbean islanders who thought of themselves as British subjects, only to experience racism and hostility from those who saw them as threatening outsiders. *Of Age and Innocence, Season of Adventure,* and *Water with Berries* depict a return to the Caribbean and stress a postcolonial engagement with universal suffrage, independence struggles, and interethnic tensions. The last novel, *Natives of My Person,* moves back in historical time to early European slaving and settlement enterprises on the islands while at the same time suggesting a continued link from that period in history to the later phases of postindependence.

Apart from his fictional work, Lamming is also known for his collection of essays, *The Pleasures of Exile* (1960), which discusses many of the ideas also raised in his novels, including the reinterpretation of Caliban, Shakespeare's monstrous character in *The Tempest,* as a revolutionary slave and tragic hero. One of the earliest challenges to the English canon, Lamming's provocative reading of Caliban went on to become a representative symbol of anticolonial resistance in African, Caribbean, and Latin American literatures, indeed for postcolonial theory in general. While much of his work engages in the task of retrieving and reimagining distorted or obscured history in the Americas in order to seek resolutions and chart a new future, its bleak and weighty conclusions do not lend themselves to naively celebratory readings of the end of slavery in the Caribbean.

See also Caribbean/North American Writers (Contemporary)

■■ *Bibliography*

MAJOR WORKS BY LAMMING

In the Castle of My Skin. 1953. Reprint, Ann Arbor: University of Michigan Press, 1991.

The Emigrants. 1954. Reprint, Ann Arbor: University of Michigan Press, 1994.

Of Age and Innocence. 1958. Reprint, London: Allison and Busby 1981.

Season of Adventure. 1960. Reprint, Ann Arbor: University of Michigan Press, 1999.

The Pleasures of Exile. 1960. Reprint, Ann Arbor: University of Michigan Press, 1992.

Water with Berries. 1971. Reprint, London: Longman Caribbean, 1973.

Natives of My Person. 1972. Reprint, Ann Arbor: University of Michigan Press, 1992.

Conversations: George Lamming Essays, Addresses and Interviews, 1953–1990, edited by Richard Drayton and Andaiye. London: Karia Press, 1992.

Coming, Coming, Home: Conversations II. Philipsburg, St. Martin: House of Nehesi, 1995.

The Sovereignty of the Imagination. Kingston, Jamaica: Arawak Publications, 2004.

OTHER SOURCES

Nair, Supriya. *Caliban's Curse: George Lamming and the Revisioning of History.* Ann Arbor: University of Michigan Press, 1996.

Paquet, Sandra Pouchet. *The Novels of George Lamming.* London: Heinemann, 1982.

Scott, David. "The Sovereignty of the Imagination: An Interview with George Lamming." *Small Axe* 12 (2002): 72–200.

Silva, A. J. Simoes Da. *The Luxury of Nationalist Despair: George Lamming's Fiction as Decolonizing Project.* Amsterdam: Rodopi, 2000.

SUPRIYA NAIR (2005)

LAMPKIN, DAISY

MARCH 1884?
MARCH 10, 1965

▐▐▐

The date and place of birth of Daisy Elizabeth Adams Lampkin, a civil rights leader, are not certain. Some records list her as being born in March 1884 in the District of Columbia (the stepdaughter of John and Rosa Temple), while others list her as born on August 9, 1888, in Reading, Pennsylvania, to George and Rosa Anne (Proctor) Adams. Records become more reliable for her late adolescent years: She finished high school in Reading, moved to Pittsburgh in 1909, and married William Lampkin in 1912.

Daisy Lampkin met *Pittsburgh Courier* publisher Robert L. Vann in 1913, after she had won a cash prize for selling the most copies of the newspaper; with the prize, she purchased stock in the *Courier* corporation. She continued to invest in the *Courier* corporation until 1929, when she began a lifelong tenure as the corporation's vice president.

In 1915 Lampkin became president of the Negro Women's Franchise League; that year, too, she became involved in the National Suffrage League and the women's division of the Republican Party. In July 1924, as president of the National Negro Republican Convention in Atlantic City, she helped pass a strong resolution against lynching. She also took part that year in a black delegation to the White House, led by James Weldon Johnson, to vindicate black soldiers involved in the Houston riot of 1917. She also became a delegate-at-large to the 1924 Republican National Convention in Cleveland, Ohio.

In 1929 Walter White, acting executive secretary of the National Association for the Advancement of Colored People (NAACP), had Lampkin appointed regional field secretary for the organization. She used her positions in the NAACP and the powerful *Courier* corporation to attract new funds and members to both organizations. In 1930 her grassroots political influence helped defeat Roscoe McCullough's reelection bid as senator from Ohio. McCullough had supported the nomination of Judge John J. Parker (who had once opposed black suffrage) to the U.S. Supreme Court.

In 1935 Lampkin was named national field secretary of the NAACP, a post she held until 1947. In this capacity she displayed great skill at raising funds while keeping operating expenses to a minimum. She and White campaigned strongly, although unsuccessfully, for the passage of the 1935 Costigan-Wagner federal antilynching bill. During Franklin Roosevelt's administration, she encouraged blacks to change their voting preferences from the Republican Party to the Democratic Party. However, she supported the Democrats selectively. Under Roosevelt, she supported the party despite the NAACP directives against partisan activity; under Truman, she cited those same directives as a reason to withhold her official support.

Although physical fatigue forced her to resign as national field secretary in 1947, Lampkin continued her fund-raising activities as a member of the NAACP board of directors. She continued to challenge any symbolic or substantive threats to African-American progress, but at the increasing cost of her physical stamina. She supported the Republicans in 1952 when the Democrats ran a segregationist vice presidential candidate, Alabama's John J. Sparkman. She also led a major fund-raising effort for the Delta Sigma Theta sorority's purchase of a $50,000 building that year.

Lampkin remained active in NAACP activities through the early 1960s, receiving the National Council of Negro Women's first Eleanor Roosevelt–Mary McLeod Bethune Award in December 1964. Lampkin died at her home in Pittsburgh in 1965. In 1983 she became the first black woman honored by the state of Pennsylvania with a historical marker, located at the site of her Webster Avenue home. In 1997 she was the recipient of the "Spirit of King" award, which honors civil rights advocates from Pittsburgh who embody the ideals of Dr. Martin Luther King Jr.

See also Johnson, James Weldon; National Association for the Advancement of Colored People (NAACP); National Council of Negro Women; *Pittsburgh Courier*

■■ *Bibliography*

Giddings, Paula. *When and Where I Enter: The Impact of Black Women on Race and Sex in America.* New York: Morrow, 1985.

Giddings, Paula. *In Search of Sisterhood: Delta Sigma Theta and the Challenge of the Black Sorority Movement.* New York: Morrow, 1988.

McKenzie, Edna B. "Daisy Lampkin: A Life of Love and Service." *Pennsylvania Heritage* (Summer 1983): 9–12.

DURAHN TAYLOR (1996)
Updated by publisher 2005

LANGSTON, JOHN MERCER

DECEMBER 14, 1829
NOVEMBER 15, 1897

The politician John Mercer Langston was born in Louisa County, Virginia, the youngest of four children born to Ralph Quarles, a white planter, and Quarles's manumitted slave, Lucy Langston. After the death of their parents in 1834, the Langston children were settled in Ohio. John Mercer began his studies in theology in 1844 at Oberlin College, where he received both a bachelor's and a master's degree. He later read law under Philemon Bliss, a judge from Elyria, Ohio, and passed the state bar examination in 1854.

Langston established a successful law practice in Brownhelm, Ohio, and he participated in local politics. His election as town clerk in 1855 made him the first African American elected by popular vote to a public office. Together with his brothers, Gideon Langston and Charles H. Langston, he made the family name synonymous with black abolitionism in Ohio. He participated in a variety of community activities, from organizing antislavery and reform societies to presiding at local and state black conventions. He was involved in the protests against state black laws, and worked with the Ohio branch of the Underground Railroad to assist escaping slaves. Langston's commitment to social reform included women's rights, temperance, and racial progress through self-reliance. He worked to improve black education in Ohio and supported the black press. His correspondence on current issues appeared frequently in *Frederick Douglass's Paper*, and he also contributed some articles to the *Anglo-African Magazine*.

Langston became disheartened by the deterioration in American race relations in the early 1850s. He began advocating black separatism and emigration, but at the 1854 national emigration convention in Cleveland he surprised delegates with a vigorous defense of integration and an optimistic assessment of the prospects for racial progress and equality in the United States. In the late 1850s he grew increasingly militant and predicted that the issue of slavery would lead to a national conflict. He was among several blacks who conspired with John Brown in the plan to incite a slave insurrection, though he declined to participate directly in the Harpers Ferry raid.

During the Civil War, Langston directed his efforts to the Union cause. His work as the chief recruiting agent in the western states helped fill the ranks of the Union

John Mercer Langston (1829–1897). THE LIBRARY OF CONGRESS

Army's black regiments. He also encouraged the charity of the soldiers' aid societies. The black national convention held in Syracuse, New York, selected him as president of the newly founded National Equal Rights League in 1864.

Contemporaries described Langston as an intelligent, persuasive orator with an "aristocratic style and a democratic temperament." Given these qualities and an impressive career of public service, he established a national reputation. Beginning in 1867, he toured the South as an inspector for the Freedmen's Bureau. His message to southern blacks emphasized educational opportunity, political equality, and economic justice. He organized the law department at Howard University in 1868 and later became the university's acting president. In 1877 he received an appointment as the American consul general to Haiti. After returning to the United States in 1885, he became president of Virginia Normal and Collegiate Institute. As the Democratic Party regained control of Virginia, Langston faced a growing challenge to his civic and political leadership, but he remained in the state that he always had considered his home. In 1888 he ran as an independent in a bitterly contested campaign for a seat in the U.S.

House of Representatives. The House adjudicated in Langston's favor in September 1890, and he held his seat until March 1891. Langston surveyed his distinguished public career in an autobiography, *From the Virginia Plantation to the Nation's Capitol* (1894). In 1996, the state of Virginia recognized John Mercer Langston as one of its distinguished native sons with a historic marker in his birthplace of Louisa County.

See also Black Codes; *Frederick Douglass' Paper*; Free Blacks, 1619–1860; Howard University; Politics in the United States; Underground Railroad

■ ■ *Bibliography*

Cheek, William, and Aimee Lee Cheek. *John Mercer Langston and the Fight for Black Freedom, 1829-1865.* Urbana: University of Illinois Press, 1989.

Ripley, C. Peter, et al., eds. *The Black Abolitonist Papers, Volume 4: The United States, 1847-1858.* Chapel Hill: University of North Carolina Press, 1991.

MICHAEL F. HEMBREE (1996)

LARSEN, NELLA

APRIL 13, 1891
C. MARCH 30, 1964

┠╂┨━━━━━━━━━━━

Born in Chicago, novelist Nella Larsen was the mixed-race child of immigrant parents. Reared in a visibly "white" family, she was a lonely child whose racial identity separated her from both parents and sibling. She compensated for her difference by becoming an avid reader of novels and travelogues and a keen observer of life around her. Although she later claimed her Danish or her West Indian heritages, she became part of an African-American world when she entered the Fisk University Normal High School. She left after a year without receiving either a diploma or a teaching degree. She moved to New York, where in 1915 she completed nurse's training at the Lincoln Hospital School of Nursing. Her career choice enabled her to become self-supporting, working initially for her alma mater, then briefly for Tuskegee Institute's John Andrew Memorial Hospital and later for New York City's Board of Health.

In 1919 Larsen married a research physicist, Dr. Elmer S. Imes, and became part of the upwardly mobile African-American middle class. Disillusioned with the opportunities for African-American females in nursing, she capitalized on her love of books by working for the New York Public Library, a job that enabled her to enter the New York Public Library School in 1922 and introduced her to the emerging coterie of writers in Harlem. Her first publication, a 1923 book review in the *Messenger,* was the result of her work for the library school.

Throughout the 1920s Larsen was active in the Harlem Renaissance. Two of her early stories, "The Wrong Man" and "Freedom," appeared under a pseudonym in 1926. Shortly thereafter, she published two novels, *Quicksand* (1928) and *Passing* (1929), which earned her a considerable reputation as a writer of powerful explorations of female psychology and modern consciousness. *Quicksand* follows the exploits of an educated mulatto, Helga Crane, as she searches for self-definition, social recognition, and sexual expression. *Passing* presents two light-skinned women as antagonists and psychological doubles in a drama of racial passing, class and social mobility, and female desire. Larsen received the Harmon Foundation's Bronze Medal for achievement in literature in 1929 and a Guggenheim Fellowship in creative writing in 1930. She spent her fellowship year in Spain and France researching a novel on racial freedom and writing a novel about her husband's infidelity.

Larsen's literary promise, however, did not achieve full maturity. She ceased publishing during the 1930s after several public humiliations undermined her confidence in her ability. She was accused in *Forum* magazine of plagiarizing *Sanctuary* (1930), and she was sensationalized in the African-American press during her divorce proceedings (1933). By the 1940s, after several efforts at collaborative novels had failed, she gave up all efforts to write and returned to the nursing profession. She continued to work as a nurse in New York hospitals until March 1964, when she was found dead in her apartment. Although nearly forgotten as a writer at the time of her death, Larsen has subsequently achieved renewed visibility as a major modern African-American novelist whose complex representations of gender and race intrigue postmodern readers and resist reductive readings.

See also Harlem Renaissance; Literature

■ ■ *Bibliography*

Davis, Thadious M. *Nella Larsen: Novelist of the Harlem Renaissance.* Baton Rouge: Louisiana State University Press, 1944.

Larsen, Charles R. *Invisible Darkness: Jean Toomer & Nella Larsen.* Iowa City: University of Iowa Press, 1993.

McDowell, Deborah. "Introduction." In *Nella Larsen,* Quicksand *and* Passing. New Brunswick, N.J.: Rutgers University Press, 1986.

Washington, Mary Helen. "Nella Larsen." In *Invented Lives: Narratives of Black Women, 1860–1960*. Garden City, N.Y.: Anchor Press, 1987.

THADIOUS M. DAVIS (1996)
Updated bibliography

LAST POETS

The radical writers' and musicians' group called the Last Poets grew out of the black arts movement of the late 1960s, performing and recording politically and rhythmically charged messages that prefigured the rap music of the 1980s and 1990s. The Last Poets were formed at a May 1968 gathering in Harlem's Mount Morris Park to commemorate Malcolm X. The members of that group— Gylan Kain, Abiodun Oyewole, and David Nelson—went on to sell more than 300,000 copies of their first album, *The Last Poets*, which contained such songs as "New York, New York," "Niggers Are Scared of Revolution," and "When the Revolution Comes." These were heated denunciations of racial oppression in the United States set to stripped-down African, Afro-Cuban, and African-American drumming. Nelson soon left the group and was replaced by Felipe Luciano.

The Last Poets appeared in the film *Right On!* (1969) before an ideological disagreement between Oyewole and Kain caused the members to split into two groups. Kain, Luciano, and Nelson continued to work under the name "Last Poets," as did Oyewole and such new members as Umar Bin Hassan, Suliaman El-Hadi, and Alafia Pudim (later known as Jalaludin Mansur Nuriddin). Albums by the two groups attacked both whites and blacks who compromised on militant positions of black power and social justice, and their comments were often intensified through the use of profanity and offensive language. Despite their initial success, the Last Poets never received a major recording contract and failed to gain a large following. Aside from occasional performances in the United States and Europe, the members of the Last Poets remained cult figures who constantly fought and bickered over the rights to the name.

The rediscovery of the Last Poets by rap musicians in the 1980s helped the members of both ensembles become more active. In 1985, Nuriddin and El-Hadi released *Oh My People*, followed the next year by a book of poems, *Vibes of the Scribes*, and the album *Freedom Express*. In 1990, believing that the success of rap music had paved the way for a comeback, Kain, Nelson, and Oyewole reunited and made a tour of the United States. However, the group failed to recapture its initial popularity. Several albums from Last Poets members, including *Holy Terror* and *Be Bop or Be Dead*, were released in the 1990s. Since then the groups calling themselves the Last Poets (Don Babatunde Eton began playing with Oyewole and Bin Hassan) have continued to perform at concerts, often along with 1970s groups such as the Ohio Players and George Clinton's P-Funk All Stars. The Last Poets' spoken word and drums format continued on the 1994 release *Scatterap/Home*.

See also Black Arts Movement; Dub Poetry Hip-Hop; Poetry, U.S.; Rap

■ ■ *Bibliography*

James, Curtia. "Political Snoozers Beware: The Last Poets Are Back." *Essence* 17 (June 1986): 32.

Mills, David. "The Last Poets: Their Radical Past, Their Hopeful Future, Their Broken Voice." *Washington Post* (December 12, 1993): G1, G4.

Rule, Sheila. "Generation Rap: Interview with A. Oyewole and Ice Cube." *New York Times Magazine* (April 3, 1994): 40–45.

JONATHAN GILL (1996)

LATIMER, LEWIS HOWARD
SEPTEMBER 4, 1848
DECEMBER 11, 1928

Inventor Lewis Howard Latimer was born in Chelsea, Massachusetts, the son of runaway slaves from Virginia. In his youth Latimer worked at a variety of odd jobs, including selling copies of William Lloyd Garrison's *Liberator*, sweeping up in his father's barbershop, hanging paper, and waiting tables. In 1863 he joined the Union navy and worked as a cabin boy aboard the *U.S.S. Massasoit*. He served on the James River in Virginia until the end of the war in 1865.

After the war Latimer returned to Boston, where in 1871 he was hired by patent lawyers Crosby and Gould. Although hired as an office boy, he became an expert mechanical drafter. He also tried his hand at inventing, and on February 10, 1874, he patented a pivot bottom for a water closet for railroad cars. The inventor of the telephone, Alexander Graham Bell, retained Crosby and Gould to handle his patent application, and Latimer helped sketch the drawings for Bell's 1876 patent.

In 1880 Latimer was hired by inventor Hiram Maxim's United States Electric Lighting Company in

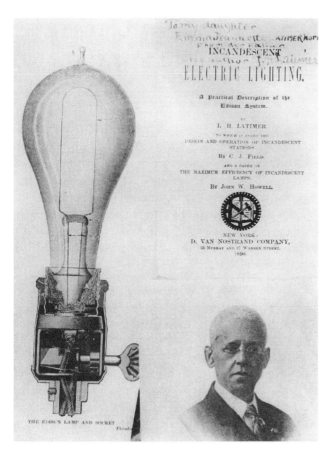

Dr. Lewis Howard Latimer (1848–1928). *Title page of Latimer's book on incandescent electric lighting, including an image of the Edison lamp and socket. A draftsman and engineer, Latimer invented carbon filaments for the Maxim electric incandescent lamp.* PHOTOGRAPHS AND PRINTS DIVISION, SCHOMBURG CENTER FOR RESEARCH IN BLACK CULTURE, THE NEW YORK PUBLIC LIBRARY, ASTOR, LENOX AND TILDEN FOUNDATIONS.

Bridgeport, Connecticut. Maxim was a competitor of Thomas A. Edison, who had patented the incandescent light bulb in 1879. In 1881 Latimer and his colleague Joseph V. Nichols shared a patent for an electric lamp. Latimer's most important invention, patented in 1882, was a carbon filament that increased the brightness and longevity of the lightbulb. Because of its decreased costs, the resulting product made electric lighting more accessible. Latimer also invented a locking rack for hats, coats, and umbrellas in 1896.

From 1880 to 1882 Latimer oversaw the establishment of factories for U.S. Electric's production of the filaments and the installation of electric-light systems in New York City and Philadelphia and later in London. After his return from Britain, he worked for firms in the New York area until he joined the Edison Electric Light Company in 1884. (Edison Electric soon bought out other companies to form General Electric.) There he served as an engineer,

chief draftsman, and an expert witness for Edison in patent infringement lawsuits. Latimer was author of *Incandescent Electric Lighting* (1896), one of the first textbooks on electric lighting. When General Electric and Westinghouse decided that year to pool patents, they created the Board of Patent Control to monitor patent disputes and appointed Latimer to the board. He used his drafting techniques and knowledge of patent law in this capacity until 1911, when the board was disbanded. He then did patent law consulting with the New York firm of Hammer & Schwarz.

Latimer moved to Flushing, New York, in the late nineteenth century and was active in New York City politics and civil rights issues. In 1902 he circulated a petition to New York City Mayor Seth Low, expressing concern about the lack of African-American representation on the school board. He also taught English and mechanical drawing to immigrants at the Henry Street Settlement in 1906. In 1918 Latimer became a charter member of the Edison Pioneers, an honorary group of scientists who had worked for Thomas Edison's laboratories. Latimer's booklet, *Poems of Love and Life,* was privately published by his friends on his seventy-fifth birthday in 1925. Latimer died in Flushing in 1928. On May 10, 1968, a public school in Brooklyn was named in his honor.

See also Inventors and Inventions; Patents and Inventions

■ ■ *Bibliography*

Brodie, James Michael. *Created Equal: The Lives and Ideas of Black American Inventors.* New York: William Morrow, 1993.

Fouche, Rayvon. *Black Inventors in the Age of Segregation.* Baltimore, Md.: Johns Hopkins University Press, 2003.

Haber, Louis. *Black Pioneers of Science and Invention.* New York: Harcourt, Brace & World, 1970.

Hayden, Robert C. *Eight Black American Inventors.* Reading, Mass.: Addison-Wesley, 1972.

Turner, Glennette Tilley. *Lewis Howard Latimer.* Englewood Cliffs, N.J.: Silver Burdett Press, 1991.

ALLISON X. MILLER (1996)
KEVIN PARKER (1996)
Updated bibliography

LAVEAU, MARIE

Two women named Marie Laveau, mother and daughter, were key figures in the practice of voodoo in New Orleans from approximately 1830 until the 1880s. The first Marie

Laveau (b. 1783) built a reputation as a powerful leader in the particular form of West African Dahomean religion that developed in New Orleans. There, voodoo practice centered on several Dahomean deities (vodun) and on healing, herbalism, and divination. In the Louisiana context, elements of Roman Catholicism were blended with the Dahomean tradition as well.

The first Marie Laveau oversaw large ritual gatherings in Congo Square and on the banks of Lake Ponchartrain. In her home she also saw clients who came with health problems, domestic difficulties, and other troubles. Clearly, Laveau was successful in her practice, and black and white residents of the city knew of her skills and solicited them. She was also widely known for visiting and caring for death row prisoners.

Around 1875 Marie Laveau's health began to fail, and her daughter (b. 1827) assumed the public role of Marie Laveau. By the time the first Marie died in 1881, the reputation of her daughter had been solidified. The second Marie continued the craft developed by her mother and other practitioners of voodoo, particularly healing, divining, and providing protective charms for white and black clients. By the last decade of the century, Marie Laveau's practice had declined significantly, as other figures assumed prominence in the city.

The legend of Marie Laveau was kept alive by twentieth-century conjurers who claimed to use Laveau techniques, and it is kept alive through the continuing practice of commercialized voodoo in New Orleans. Each year hundreds of curious tourists and followers visit Marie Laveau's grave in New Orleans, where they present offerings to "the Voodoo Queen."

See also Voodoo

▪ *Bibliography*

Raboteau, Albert J. *Slave Religion: The "Invisible Institution" in the Antebellum South.* New York: Oxford University Press, 1978.

Tallant, Robert. *Voodoo in New Orleans.* New York: Macmillan, 1946.

Ward, Martha. *Voodoo Queen: The Spirited Lives of Marie Laveau.* Jackson: University Press of Mississippi, 2004.

JUDITH WEISENFELD (1996)
Updated by publisher 2005

LAW AND LIBERTY IN ENGLAND AND AMERICA

■ ■ ■

While the concept of freedom has become universal, and basic civil and human rights are considered the minimum standard of existence in society, it was not always so. Law and liberty intersected increasingly in the seventeenth and eighteenth centuries during Britain's domination of the African slave trade, leading to numerous polarities of opinion and raising a host of important questions. For Africans in the Anglo-Atlantic slave societies, liberty was often arbitrated in courts.

The existence, spread, and growing entrenchment of African slavery in the New World in the period of flourishing revolutionary ideologies of liberty constituted a deeply intransigent problem—one that refused to be solved either easily or quickly (because of its deeply profitable nature). Antislavery movements on both sides of the Atlantic stood squarely against proslavery proponents, and the enslaved themselves resisted the institution in countless creative ways. Even after Britain's loss of the American colonies, American law traced its roots to English law; English cases were invoked as legitimate legal precedents. By availing themselves of legal structures on both sides of the Atlantic, the enslaved and their advocates sought and, surprisingly, won relief in the courts.

BEGINNINGS

Political philosophers and legal theorists (such as Grotius, Locke, and Hobbes) initiated discussions about natural law and natural rights—laws and rights inherent in the human condition. The greatest articulation of English law in the eighteenth century was William Blackstone's *Commentaries on the Laws of England* in 1765, contributing an accessibly written, comprehensive view of English common law. In it he commented on natural rights, the rights of persons, and the tendency of the law to favor liberty, additionally insisting that the law of England asserted and preserved the personal liberty of individuals. Furthermore, according to ancient practices, English soil was by definition free soil: A slave or a stranger who set foot on it became, in theory, free. In a sense, the doctrine of English soil at once advanced the cause of liberty and contributed to years of contradictory rulings. It was at the heart of English legal tendencies toward defending personal liberty, yet according to the claims of those in the business of slavery, it threatened personal property.

ENGLAND

The first recorded English case concerning the status of Africans was *Butts v. Penny* (1677). Although the case had not been brought by the Africans involved, it had at its core a problem that would bedevil the courts well into the nineteenth century: Could the enslaved be considered property or were they legal personalities? While it would have been simpler to have declared the enslaved to be property in *all* cases, ridding the courts of ambiguities, no such uniform declaration ensued. There were English laws in abundance concerning villeins—peasants who comprised a bound labor staple doomed to grime and perpetual poverty. The laws concerning villeins were harsh and restrictive, but villeinage and slavery were not the same. As for English slaves, they were not numerous. English law appeared ill prepared to address the question of enslaved Africans. Judicial rulings from the late seventeenth century to the late eighteenth century concerning African slavery were inconsistent as a result both of the inability to equate African bondage with existing forms of English bondage and of the spread of natural rights ideology. Decisions might easily be in favor of liberty or against it.

Early court cases emphasized the non-Christian status of Africans and simultaneously benefited from circular reasoning. Africans were defined as infidels and customarily purchased or sold as merchandise in America; had Africans been Christians, they could not be bought and sold. Africans, therefore, were property because they were saleable, and were saleable because they were property. For a period of years, then, antislavery proponents routinely encouraged Christian baptism as a way to ensure the freeing of slaves in England. (In some circles baptism was considered effective manumission.) However, the mention of buying and selling in the Americas introduced a key ideological and legal qualifier—one that potentially favored dealers in slaves. Legal counsel for masters, merchants, and planters would typically link slave practices with specific geographic locations where those practices were both customary and sanctioned. In this way they could argue for the lawful continued but limited recognition of slavery even in places where there was no slave law per se. Thus, masters would not necessarily jeopardize their supposed right to a slave when they went to certain places in the English Atlantic.

The signal English case, both in terms of trial length and widespread effect of the ruling, was the 1772 *Somerset* case. Its arguments and decision became central to numerous American cases prior to the Civil War. James Somerset had been brought to England in the late 1760s by his owner, Charles Stuart. Eventually, Somerset ran away, but he was found and placed on board a ship bound for the Caribbean plantation colonies to be resold. His allies challenged his forcible detainment with a writ of habeas corpus, beginning a legal process that continued for many months. Arguments about the nature of slavery, Somerset's contested status relative to the law, the question of detainment under duress, the problem of slavery on English soil and the rights of masters abounded. Reluctant to address directly the fundamental question of slavery, Chief Justice Mansfield rendered a decision that focused on Somerset's wrongful detainment and forcible removal from England despite having committed no crime. In short, Mansfield's decision freed James Somerset, but it did not end slavery in England. What was key, however, was Mansfield's language, broadly condemning slavery by insisting that as an institution slavery was so odious that only positive law (a specific legislative act) could support it. The *Somerset* decision posed a significant threat to slavery by questioning the ways in which custom and practice sanctioned slavery despite the lack of laws specifically enacting slavery's existence. The *Somerset* decision, well known to American legal personnel, would have an ongoing effect in America for years to come.

AMERICA

By the end of the eighteenth century, northern states had moved to abolish slavery within their individual borders. Slavery expanded in the South, where a variety of complex laws concerning manumission developed—including, in Virginia, the prohibition of manumission of slaves under or over arbitrarily determined ages. Certain slaves in the 1780s were emancipated as a result of serving in the American War for Independence, although even free African Americans continued to live under social and legal surveillance.

During the early nineteenth century, proslavery ideology consolidated, aided in part by early expressions of North/South polarization as the United States expanded westward with territories applying for statehood. The essential question regarding the admission of territories was this: Would they be slave states or free? This question kept the problem of slavery before the public at a national level, with the tensions playing out in political and legal realms. The existence of geographic areas of freedom so proximate to locales where perpetual bondage held sway contributed to the entrenchment of slavery in the United States, resulting in the increased regulation of fugitive slaves. In addition, slave owners themselves faced a new dilemma: What would happen if they went from their home slavery-sanctioning state to a free state with a slave in tow? Travelers (as slave owners temporarily in free states with their slaves were known) were problematic, for they echoed the

Somerset situation. When a slave owner passed through a free state, was his customary relationship to his slave de facto suspended? Did the relationship persist? Would the relationship be suspended *only* if the enslaved person sought the protection of the local laws? Were states that did not sanction slavery obliged to temporarily admit the presence of that species of bondage into their midst? (This was a question of comity—the courtesy recognition of laws and judicial decisions of one jurisdiction in another jurisdiction.) If so, what constituted "temporary"? One month or three? Six months or a year?

The first major case to address the question concerning the presence of slavery on free soil was *Commonwealth v. Aves* (1836). The *Somerset* decision played a considerable role in the case. An enslaved little girl named Med was brought by her Louisiana mistress, Mrs. Slater, to Boston, Massachusetts. When the child's presence was discovered in the home of Mrs. Slater's father—Thomas Aves, a Boston resident—a writ of habeas corpus was served upon him; Med was being "restrained of her liberty" unlawfully by Aves.

Central to the case were several questions: What was the effect of Louisiana law in Massachusetts? Brought to a free state temporarily, what was the status of a slave in those circumstances? Aves's counsel stressed the preeminence of Louisiana law over local Massachusetts law, for it was under Louisiana law that the child was enslaved; he argued in favor of comity. Arguing against comity, Med's counsel emphasized Massachusetts's long-term commitment to liberty and, following *Somerset*, focused on the undesirability of admitting slavery within specific locales; he insisted that Massachusetts, like England, was a place that favored liberty. The chief justice avoided ruling on the rights of the master but determined that by coming within the limits of Massachusetts, a person was subject to its municipal laws and entitled to the privileges those laws conferred; the little girl won her freedom.

Despite some successes, court rulings throughout the nineteenth century continued on a case-by-case basis. In Connecticut a slave may have successfully obtained freedom (*Jackson v. Bullock,* 1837), while in Mississippi a freed slave's ability to inherit property in a state where she was once a slave would be challenged (*Mitchell v. Wells,* 1859). Enslaved persons who resided for a time in a free locale but returned to the South sometimes sued for their freedom afterwards; prior to the 1840s their liberty was often upheld. However, by the 1850s most southern courts were ill disposed to hold that time spent within geographically free borders transformed a slave into a free person. The legal retrenchment of liberties during the nineteenth century must be viewed in relation to the growing intersec-

tional tensions. Both the infamous 1850 Fugitive Slave Law (upheld by the federal government) and the 1854 Kansas-Nebraska Act (allowing slavery into places where it had been previously prohibited) demonstrated the degree to which the ubiquitous problem of slavery in the United States lay at the heart of sectional strife. The landmark 1857 Dred Scott decision, in which the Missouri Supreme Court reversed an earlier ruling that Scott had become free while living in a free locale (and maintained his liberty even after reentering a slaveholding state), brought the agitation for liberty through the courts to a nadir. Chief Justice Taney's caustic opinion about the inability of people of African descent to be legal personalities and citizens with basic rights reversed an important jurisprudential tenet as well as decades of legal practice *in favorem libertatis* (in favor of liberty). It would take the courts decades to begin to undo and redress the damage.

See also Abolition; *Dred Scott v. Sandford*; Free Blacks, 1619–1860; Slavery and the Constitution

■■ *Bibliography*

Davis, David Brion. *The Problem of Slavery in the Age of Revolution.* Ithaca, N.Y.: Cornell University Press, 1975.

Finkelman, Paul. *The Law of Freedom and Bondage: A Casebook.* New York: Oceana, 1986.

Hall, Kermit L., et. al. *American Legal History: Cases and Materials.* New York: Oxford University Press, 1991.

Higginbotham, A. Leon, Jr. *In the Matter of Color: Race and the American Legal Process.* New York: Oxford University Press, 1978.

Posner, Richard A. *The Problems of Jurisprudence.* Cambridge, Mass.: Harvard University Press, 1990.

Walvin, James. *England, Slaves, and Freedom: 1776–1838.* Jackson: University Press of Mississippi, 1986.

T. K. HUNTER (2005)

LAWRENCE, JACOB

SEPTEMBER 7, 1917
JUNE 9, 2000

■ ■ ■

Born in Atlantic City, New Jersey, painter and draftsman Jacob Armstead Lawrence grew up in Harlem during the Great Depression, and his career owes much to that heritage. Soon after the births of his sister, Geraldine, and brother, William, in Pennsylvania, his parents separated. Seeking domestic work, Lawrence's mother brought her three children to Harlem around 1930. She enrolled them in a day-care program at Utopia House, a settlement house offering children hot lunches and after-school arts-and-crafts activities at nominal cost. The arts program was run by painter Charles Alston, who recognized young Jacob Lawrence's talent and encouraged him.

Lawrence's mother was often on welfare, so Jake, as he was called, took on several jobs as a young teenager to help support the family: He had a paper route, and he worked in a printer's shop and in a laundry. But in the evenings he continued to attend art classes, and he committed himself to painting.

From 1932 to 1937 Lawrence received training in the Harlem Art Workshops, which were supported first by the College Art Association and then by the government under the Federal Art Project of the Works Project Administration. He attended the American Artists School in New York City on scholarship from 1937 to 1939. He was still a student when he had his first one-person exhibition at the Harlem YMCA in February 1938. At twenty-one and twenty-two years of age, he served as an easel painter on "the Project" in Harlem. Swept up in the vigorous social and cultural milieu of the era following the Harlem Renaissance, Lawrence drew upon Harlem scenes and black history for his subjects, portraying the lives and aspirations of African Americans.

By 1936 Lawrence had established work space in the studio of Charles Alston at 306 West 141st Street—the renowned "306" studio that was a gathering place for people in the arts. There Lawrence worked for several years, meeting and learning from such African-American intellectuals as philosopher Alain Locke, writers Langston Hughes and Claude McKay, and painter Aaron Douglas.

Lawrence's first paintings assumed the character of social realism, a popular style of the 1930s. His earliest works date from around 1936 and are typically interior scenes or outdoor views of Harlem activity (e.g., *Street Orator*, 1936; *Interior*, 1937). He was primarily influenced by the other community artists, such as Alston, sculptor Augusta Savage, and sculptor Henry Bannarn, who believed in him and inspired him by their interest in themes of ethnic origin and social injustice.

Lawrence's general awareness of art came from his teachers as well as from books, local exhibitions, and frequent trips to the Metropolitan Museum. When he was a youth, he met painter Gwendolyn Knight, originally from Barbados, and their friendship led to marriage in 1941. Their long relationship was a vital factor in Lawrence's career.

Lawrence's art remained remarkably consistent throughout the decades. His content is presented through either genre (scenes of everyday life) or historical narra-

The Migration Gained in Momentum *(Jacob Lawrence, 1940–1941). Lawrence, one of the most acclaimed African American artists of the twentieth century, painted many scenes of black Americans and their sociopolitical struggles. During the period known as the Great Migration, the subject of Lawrence's painting reproduced here, large numbers of blacks moved from the rural South to the urban North.* THE MUSEUM OF MODERN ART, NEW YORK. GIFT OF MRS. DAVID M. LEVY. PHOTOGRAPH © 2000 THE MUSEUM OF MODERN ART. REPRODUCED BY PERMISSION.

tive, and always by means of simplified, representational forms. He used water-based media applied in vivid color. Lawrence was an expressionist: He tried to convey the feeling he got from his subject through the use of expressionistic distortion and color choice, and often through cubist treatment of form and space.

A distinctive feature of Lawrence's work is his frequent use of the series format to render narrative content. Stimulated by the Harlem community's interest in the stories of legendary black leaders, he created several historical series about these heroic figures, including *Toussaint L'Ouverture* (1937–1938), *Frederick Douglass* (1938–1939), and *Harriet Tubman* (1939–1940). Some of his fifteen series are based on nonhistorical themes, such as *Theater* (1951–1952).

Jacob Lawrence received almost overnight acclaim when his *Migration of the Negro* series was shown at New York's prestigious Downtown Gallery in November 1941. With this exhibition, he became the first African-American artist to be represented by a major New York gallery. By the time he was thirty, he had become widely known as the foremost African-American artist in the country. In 1960 the Brooklyn Museum mounted his first retrospective exhibition, and it traveled throughout the country. In 1974 the Whitney Museum of American Art in New York held a major retrospective of Lawrence's work, which toured nationally. In December 1983 he was elected to the American Academy of Arts and Letters. His third retrospective exhibition, originated by the Seattle Art Museum in 1986, drew record-breaking crowds when it toured the country. For more than forty years, Lawrence also distinguished himself as a teacher of drawing, painting, and design, first at Black Mountain College, North Carolina, in the summer of 1946, then at schools such as Pratt Institute in Saratoga Springs, New York (1955–1970), Brandeis University (spring 1965), and the New School for Social Research, New York (1966–1969).

During World War II Lawrence served in the U.S. Coast Guard (then part of the Navy), first as a steward's mate and then as a combat artist. On coming out of the service, he received a Guggenheim Fellowship to paint a series about his war experiences (*War*, 1946–1947).

Lawrence and his wife spent eight months in Nigeria in 1964, an experience that resulted in his *Nigerian* series (1964). Also in the 1960s he produced powerfully strident works in response to the civil rights conflicts in America (e.g., *Wounded Man*, 1968). When he was appointed professor of art at the University of Washington in 1971, he and his wife moved to Seattle. He retired from teaching in 1987. After about 1968 Lawrence concentrated on works with a Builders theme that place a symbolic emphasis on humanity's aspirations and constructive potential. In 1979 he created the first of his several murals, *Games*, for the Kingdome Stadium in Seattle. In 1990 he was awarded the National Medal of Arts by President George H. W. Bush. In 1999 he and his wife began plans for an art center in Harlem, but he never saw the plan realized, for he died after a long illness in 2000.

Lawrence's work is full of humor, compassion, and pictorial intensity. His central theme is human struggle. Always a social observer with a critical sensibility, he approached his subjects with a quiet didacticism. Although his work is always emotionally autobiographical, his imagery has universal appeal. Lawrence's greatest contribution to the history of art may be his reassertion of painting's narrative function. In his art's ability to speak to us through time of the often neglected episodes of African-American history and the black experience, Lawrence offers a significant link in the traditions of American history painting, American scene painting, and American figural art.

See also Douglas, Aaron; Harlem Renaissance; Hughes, Langston; Locke, Alain Leroy; McKay, Claude; Painting and Sculpture; Savage, Augusta

■ ■ *Bibliography*

Bearden, Romare, and Harry Henderson. *Six Black Masters of American Art.* Garden City, N.Y.: Zenith, 1972.

Brown, Milton W. *Jacob Lawrence.* New York: Dodd, Mead, 1974.

Nesbett, Peter, and Michelle DuBois. *The Complete Jacob Lawrence: Paintings, Drawings and Murals (1935–1999).* Seattle: University of Washington Press, 2000.

Wheat, Ellen Harkins. *Jacob Lawrence, American Painter.* Seattle: University of Washington Press, 1986.

Wheat, Ellen Harkins. "Jacob Lawrence and the Legacy of Harlem." *Archives of American Art Journal* 26, no. 1 (1986): 18–25.

Wheat, Ellen Harkins. *Jacob Lawrence: The Frederick Douglass and Harriet Tubman Series of 1938–40.* Hampton, Va., and Seattle, Wash.: Hampton University Museam: 1991.

ELLEN HARKINS WHEAT (1996)
Updated by publisher 2005

LAWRENCE, MARGARET

AUGUST 19, 1914

Physician Margaret Cornelia Morgan was born in New York City because her mother, Mary Elizabeth Morgan, a teacher, had traveled there in search of the better medical care available to black people in the North. Margaret's father, Sandy Alonzo Morgan, was an Episcopal minister, and the family followed him as he answered calls to minister in Portsmouth, Virginia; New Bern, North Carolina; Widewater, Virginia; and Mound Bayou, Mississippi, before settling in Vicksburg, Mississippi, when Margaret was seven. Certain at a young age that she wanted to be a doctor, Morgan persuaded her parents to allow her to live with relatives in New York City to take advantage of the better educational opportunities there. She attended Wadleigh High School for Girls in New York City and entered Cornell University with a full scholarship in 1932. She was the only African-American undergraduate studying there at the time. Barred from the Cornell dormitories because of her race, she boarded as a live-in maid to a white family. Although her grades and entrance examinations were more than satisfactory, Cornell Medical School refused her admission because she was black. She enrolled in Columbia University, where she earned her M.D. in 1940, and served her medical internship and residency at Harlem Hospital. In 1943 she received an M.S. in Public Health from Columbia. That year she moved with her husband, sociologist Charles Radford Lawrence II, and their baby son to Nashville, where she became a professor at Meharry Medical College.

While in Nashville, Lawrence gave birth to two daughters eighteen months apart, created a Well-Baby Clinic in East Nashville, and maintained a private pediatric practice at home. In 1947, the Lawrence family returned to New York, and Lawrence attended Columbia University's Psychiatric Institute. She was the first African-American trainee at the Columbia Psychoanalytic Clinic for Training and Research, from which she received a Certificate in Psychoanalysis in 1951. That year she moved with her family to Rockland County, New York, where she organized the Community Mental Health Center and had a private psychiatric practice. From 1963 until her retirement in 1984, Lawrence served as a child psychiatrist at Harlem Hospital, directing its Developmental Psychiatry Clinic, and an associate clinical professor of psychiatry at Columbia's College of Physicians and Surgeons.

Lawrence, one of the first black women psychiatrists in the nation, published two books on child psychiatry, *The Mental Health Team in Schools* (1971) and *Young Inner City Families* (1975). She was a Julius Rosenwald Fellow (1942–1943) and a National Institute of Mental Health Fellow (1948–1950). In 1991 her pioneering work developing the "ego-strength" of disadvantaged children was recognized as she received the Camille Cosby World of Children Award. In 1988 Lawrence's achievements were celebrated in an award-winning biography, *Balm in Gilead: Journey of a Healer,* written by her daughter, Sara Lawrence Lightfoot, a professor of education at Harvard University. In 2003 Lawrence received an honorary doctorate from Swarthmore College in Pennsylvania.

See also Psychology and Psychologists: Race Issues; Social Psychology, Psychologists, and Race

■■ *Bibliography*

Christy, Marian. "Dr. Margaret Lawrence: Overcoming All Odds." *Boston Globe,* October 23, 1991, p. 71.

Lightfoot, Sara Lawrence. *Balm in Gilead: Journey of a Healer.* Reading, Mass.: Addison-Wesley, 1988.

"Margaret Cornelia Morgan Lawrence." In *Notable Black American Scientists.* Detroit: Gale, 1998.

SABRINA FUCHS (1996)
LYDIA MCNEILL (1996)
Updated by publisher 2005

LEADBELLY (LEDBETTER, HUDSON WILLIAM)

JANUARY 15, 1888
DECEMBER 6, 1949

The blues singer and guitarist Hudson "Leadbelly" Ledbetter was born and raised near Mooringsport, Louisiana. His birth date is subject to dispute, however (January 21, 1885, and January 29, 1889, are also often given). Leadbelly, as he was known later in life, was still a child when he began to work in the cotton fields of his sharecropper parents. They later bought land across the border in Leigh, Texas, and "Huddie," as he was called, learned to read and write at a local school. During this time he also began to play the windjammer, a Cajun accordion. He also danced and performed music for pay at parties. Ledbetter learned to play the twelve-string guitar, as well as shoot a revolver, in his early teens, and he began to frequent the red-light district of Fannin Street in Shreveport, Louisiana, where he performed for both black and white audiences.

By the time he left home for good in 1906, Ledbetter had a reputation for hard work, womanizing, violence, and musical talent. In 1908 Ledbetter, who had already fathered two children with Margaret Coleman, married Aletta Henderson and settled down in Harrison County, Texas, where he worked on farms and became a song leader in the local Baptist church. Ledbetter also claimed to have attended Bishop College, in Marshall, Texas, during this time. In 1910 Ledbetter and his family moved to Dallas, and Ledbetter began to frequent the Deep Ellum neighborhood, where he began playing professionally with Blind Lemon Jefferson (1897–1929). The two were inseparable for five years.

In 1915 Ledbetter was jailed and sentenced to a chain gang for possessing a weapon. He escaped, and for several years he lived under the pseudonym Walter Boyd. In 1917 he shot and killed a man in a fight, and the next year he was sentenced to up to thirty years for murder and assault with intent to kill. He served time at the Shaw State Farm Prison, in Huntsville, Texas, from 1918 to 1925. That year, when Governor Pat Neff visited the prison, Leadbelly made up a song on the spot asking to be released and convinced Neff to set him free. By this time Ledbetter was known as "Leadbelly," a corruption of his last name that also referred to his physical toughness. In the late 1920s Leadbelly supported himself by working as a driver and maintenance worker in Houston and around Shreveport. He also continued to perform professionally. In 1930 he was again jailed, this time for attempted homicide in Mooringsport. He had served three years when the ethnomusicologist John Lomax (1915–2002) came to the notorious Louisiana State Penitentiary at Angola to record music by the prisoners. Lomax, impressed by Leadbelly's musicianship, lobbied for his release, which came in 1934. Lomax hired him as a driver and set him on a career as a musician. In 1935 Leadbelly married Martha Promise.

Leadbelly made his first commercial recordings in 1935, performing "C.C. Rider," "Bull Cow," "Roberta Parts I and II," and "New Black Snake Moan." Thereafter, aside from another prison term during 1939 and 1940 for assault, Leadbelly enjoyed enormous success as a professional musician, performing and recording to consistent acclaim. In the late 1930s and throughout the 1940s, he appeared at universities and political rallies on both the East and West coasts, as well as on radio and film, and he was a key element and influence in the growth of American folk and blues music. He became a fixture of the folk music scene in Greenwich Village, near his home on New York's Lower East Side, and was often associated with left-wing politics.

Leadbelly was best known for his songs about prison and rural life in the South. However, his repertory was vast and included blues, children's tunes, cowboy and work songs, ballads, religious songs, and popular songs. Although his audiences were generally white (Leadbelly made only a few recordings for the "race" market of African-American record buyers), he addressed matters of race in songs such as "Scottsboro Boys" (1938) and "Bourgeois Blues" (1938). His powerful voice was capable of considerable sensitivity and nuance, and his twelve-string guitar playing was simple, yet vigorous and percussive. Among his most popular and enduring songs, some of which were recorded by Lomax for the Library of Congress, are "Goodnight Irene" (1934), "The Midnight Special" (1934), "Rock Island Line" (1937), "Good Morning Blues" (1940), and "Take This Hammer" (1940). He recorded in 1940 with the Golden Gate Quartet, a gospel vocal group. From 1941 to 1943 Leadbelly performed regularly on the U.S. Office of War Information's radio programs, and in 1945 he appeared in Pete Seeger's short documentary film *Leadbelly*. He made a trip to Paris shortly before his death in New York City at the age of sixty-one from amyotrophic lateral sclerosis (Lou Gehrig's disease). The 1976 film *Leadbelly* was based on his life story. In 1988 Leadbelly was inducted into the Rock and Roll Hall of Fame.

See also Jefferson, Blind Lemon

▪ ▪ *Bibliography*

Addeo, Edward, and Richard Garvin. *The Midnight Special: The Legend of Leadbelly*. New York: B. Geis, 1971.

Obrecht, Jas. "Lead Belly: King of the 12-String Blues." *Guitar Player* 30, no. 8 (August 1996): 55-64.

Snyder, Jared. "Leadbelly and His Windjammer: Examining the African American Button Accordion Tradition." *American Music* 12, no. 2 (summer 1994): 148-156.

Ward, Geoffrey C. "Leadbelly." *American Heritage* 44, no. 6 (October 1993): 10-11.

Wolfe, Charles, and Kip Lornell. *The Life and Legend of Leadbelly*. New York: HarperCollins, 1992.

JONATHAN GILL (1996)

LEAGUE OF REVOLUTIONARY BLACK WORKERS

▪ ▪ ▪

Growing out of the merger of the Dodge Revolutionary Union Movement (DRUM) and other Revolutionary Union Movement (RUM) organizations, the League of Revolutionary Black Workers was formed in the aftermath of a wildcat strike by about four thousand workers at the main Dodge automobile plant in Hamtramck, Michigan, on May 2, 1968. Automobile production had increased during the previous five years, and many young African Americans had been hired. However, almost all black workers were placed under older white men, many of whom expressed racist views. There were struggles about safety rules and promotion of blacks into positions of authority in the workplace and in the United Auto Workers (UAW) union. DRUM, organized barely a year after the massive Detroit riot of 1967, was formed to respond to these problems.

DRUM started a newsletter, *Drum,* organized several rallies and strikes, and led the organization of RUMs at different Detroit factories. In early 1969 DRUM merged with several auto RUMs in Detroit and Mahwah, New Jersey, including FRUM (Ford), CADRUM (Cadillac), and ELRUM (Chrysler Eldon Avenue Plant), as well as such nonautomotive groups as Birmingham steelworkers, to form the League of Revolutionary Black Workers. The league remained a small operation, with never more than a few hundred members. Its leaders combined socialist theory and civil rights organization. In mid-1969, the league associated itself with James Forman, who used funds raised by the Black Economic Development Conference to fund a league staff. Leaders came from the Detroit activist community, notably African-American lawyers Mike Hamlin and Ken Cockrel and revolutionaries General Gordon Baker and John Watson, who had turned the Wayne State University daily *South End* into a radical organ and printed their journal *Inner City Voice* on its presses. They also joined with Forman's publishing house, Black Star Press, to print league pamphlets. Members formed a film collective, which put out a feature-length documentary, *Finally Got the News* (1970).

By 1970, however, the entire movement was disintegrating. The car industry slumped after 1969, and many of the young workers who were core league supporters were laid off. The league became more a discussion group than a union and never devised a consistent program. Its members alienated many black workers with their Marxist rhetoric. In 1970 there was a schism. One faction, mostly plant organizers, tried to solidify unionization efforts and ran union slates in 1970 and 1971 in an unsuccessful attempt to unseat the white UAW leadership. This earned the movement the enmity of union leaders. Meanwhile, the "outside" radicals formed a Black Workers Congress in hopes that the league would be a central unit and sponsor the organization of RUMs on a Maoist model. The league did not affiliate, and the Black Workers Congress was "taken over" by the Stalinist Communist Labor Party. By May 1973 the league and the RUMs were gone; members returned to the UAW or joined more radical organizations. The league did leave a legacy of African-American political awareness, and it increased the number of black foremen and UAW leaders in Detroit.

See also Labor and Labor Unions

■ ■ *Bibliography*

Buhle, Jari Jo, Paul Buhle, and Daniel Georgahas. *Encyclopedia of the American Left.* New York: Garland, 1990.

Fine, Sidney. *Violence in the Model City: The Cavanagh Administration, Race Relations, and the Detroit Riot of 1967.* Ann Arbor: University of Michigan Press, 1989.

Geschwender, James. *Class, Race, and Worker Insurgency: The League of Revolutionary Black Workers.* New York: Cambridge University Press, 1977.

ALANA J. ERICKSON (1996)

LEE, DON L.

See Madhubuti, Haki R. (Lee, Don L.)

LEE, SPIKE

MARCH 20, 1957

Filmmaker Shelton Jackson "Spike" Lee was born in Atlanta, Georgia, to William Lee, a jazz musician and composer, and Jacqueline Shelton Lee, a teacher of art and literature. The oldest of five children, Lee grew up in Brooklyn, New York, with brothers David, Chris, and Cinque, and sister Joie. Lee's family environment was imbued with a strong sense of black history. Like his father and grandfather, Lee attended Morehouse College, and graduated with a B.A. in 1979. Upon graduating, Lee enrolled in New York University's Tisch School of the Arts, where he received an M.F.A. in film production in 1983. While at New York University Lee produced several student films: *The Answer* (1980), *Sarah* (1981), and *Joe's Bed-Stuy Barbershop: We Cut Heads* (1982). *Joe's Bed-Stuy Barbershop,* his M.F.A. thesis film, was awarded a Student Academy Award by the Academy of Motion Picture Arts and Sciences in 1982, was broadcast by some public television stations, and received critical notice in *Variety* and the *New York Times.*

Lee has produced over two dozen films. In virtually all of the films he has been director, writer, actor, and producer. Lee's first feature-length film was the highly acclaimed comedy *She's Gotta Have It* (1986), which he shot in twelve days on location in Brooklyn at a cost of $175,000, financed partly by his grandmother. The film eventually grossed $8 million. The action of the film centers on a sexually liberated young black woman who is having affairs simultaneously with three men. Interspersed with these scenes, she and the film's characters debate her conduct from ideological perspectives then current in the black community; such topics as hip-hop, color differences, sexual codes, and interracial relationships are raised. This debate spilled over into the national media. Controversy was to become a hallmark of Lee's work. *She's Gotta Have It* is characterized by disjointed narrative syn-

Film director Spike Lee. PHOTOGRAPH BY CHRYSTYNA CZAJKOWSKY. AP/WIDE WORLD PHOTOS. REPRODUCED BY PERMISSION

tax, mock-cinema verité technique, active camera movement, and disregard for autonomy of text. Lee has often employed the same actors and film technicians in many films, giving them a repertory effect.

Lee's second film, *School Daze* (1988), was financed by Columbia Pictures for $6.5 million and grossed more than $15 million. It also dealt with a controversial topic, the conflict at a southern black college between light-skinned students who seek assimilation into mainstream America and dark-skinned students who identify with Africa.

In 1989 Lee produced *Do the Right Thing*, which was set in Brooklyn. The film was produced for $6 million and grossed $30 million. *Do the Right Thing* focused on the relationship between an Italian-American family that operates a pizzeria in the Bedford-Stuyvesant neighborhood and the depressed black community that patronizes it. The film chronicles the racial tensions and events over a period of one day, climaxes in a riot in which one black youth is killed, and ends with the complete destruction of the pizzeria.

This highly successful film was followed by *Mo' Better Blues* (1990), the story of the love affairs, personal growth,

and development of a jazz musician in New York City. *Jungle Fever* (1991), also set in New York, was Lee's treatment of interracial relationships, centering on an affair between a married black architect and his Italian-American secretary.

Lee's most ambitious film to date has been *Malcolm X,* which was released in November 1992. In this film Lee departed from his earlier technique and employed the traditional style and approach of the Hollywood epic biography. Produced by Warner Brothers, *Malcolm X* was three hours long and cost $34 million, though it had originally been budgeted for $28 million. By the end of 1994 it had grossed $48.1 million. In a highly publicized initiative, Lee raised part of the additional funds needed from black celebrities Bill Cosby, Oprah Winfrey, Earvin "Magic" Johnson, Michael Jordan, Janet Jackson, and Prince, among others. Denzel Washington, who portrayed Malcolm X, was nominated for an Academy Award as best actor. Lee based his film on an original screenplay, written by James Baldwin and Arnold Perl in 1968, that was based on *The Autobiography of Malcolm X* as told to Alex Haley.

In 1994 Lee collaborated with his siblings Joie and Cinque Lee in the production of *Crooklyn,* the story of a large, working-class black family growing up in Brooklyn.

In the following years, he continued to produce idiosyncratic and well-crafted films about the black experience. *Get on the Bus* (1996) celebrated the diversity and ideals of the Million Man March. *Four Girls and a Church* (1997) was a touching documentary about four girls murdered in a church bombing in Birmingham in 1963. *He Got Game* (1998) explored the relationship between a teenage basketball star and his estranged father. Major releases after the turn of the century include *Bamboozled* (2000), *25th Hour* (2002), and *She Hate Me* (2004).

Spike Lee's film career has generated a film company, Forty Acres and a Mule; a chain of retail outlets that sell paraphernalia from his films; and a series of television commercials, ten of them with basketball star Michael Jordan. He also serves as artistic director of the graduate division of the Kanbar Institute of Film and Television at New York University's Tisch School of the Arts.

See also Film; Malcolm X

■■ *Bibliography*

Arnold, Darren. *The Pocket Essential Spike Lee.* New York: Pocket Books, 2003.

Lee, Spike. *Spike Lee's* Gotta Have It: *Inside Guerilla Filmmaking.* New York: Simon and Schuster, 1987.

Lee, Spike. *Uplift the Race: The Construction of* School Daze. New York: Simon and Schuster, 1988.

Lee, Spike. *By Any Means Necessary: The Trials and Tribulations of the Making of* Malcolm X. New York: Hyperion, 1992.

Lee, Spike, with Lisa Jones. Do the Right Thing: *The New Spike Lee Joint.* New York: Fireside Press, 1989.

ROBERT CHRISMAN (1996)
Updated by publisher 2005

LEON, ROSE

1912
1999

Rose Agatha Leon was Jamaica's first notable female politician, emerging in the formative period of Jamaica's modern political system. She had the distinction of serving in the governments of the two main political parties and of being a founding member of Jamaica's party, legislative, and ministerial systems at both the local and central levels.

Leon was a member of the Jamaica Labour Party (JLP, formed in 1943), serving as party chair from 1948 to 1960. In that role, she was among those credited with creating a revised constitution for the party in 1951 and with attempts to reform the party along more democratic lines throughout the 1950s, a role that eventually brought her into serious conflict with the leader, Alexander Bustamante, and cost her membership in the party.

As chairperson of the JLP, Madame Leon, as she was called, was determined to make the party into more than a caucus of candidates approved by the powerful Bustamante, as it was believed to have been, and into one with a broadened organizational structure and a popular base with a branch system. She succeeded in establishing a number of new branches, bringing in thousands of new members and increasing the presence of the middle class in the JLP. The party's central committee was strengthened, a proper party office was acquired, and its executive became more professional. By 1957 the party's newspaper hailed the organizational work as a "revolution."

During this period, Leon also sought elective office. Although she had been unsuccessful as a candidate in Jamaica's first local government elections under adult suffrage (in which Jamaicans aged twenty-one and over exercised the right to vote), which had been held in 1947, she was successful in 1951 and 1956.

Leon was also a founding member of Jamaica's legislature and a successful candidate in Jamaica's second general elections, in 1949. When Jamaica achieved ministerial government in 1953, she was one of the first ministers to serve as minister of health and housing, from 1953 to 1955. Although the JLP lost the 1955 elections, Leon won her seat but she was subsequently unseated for violating an election law.

By the end of the 1950s, Leon had fallen out with Alexander Bustamante, the JLP's dominant personality, over the authoritarian way in which he led the party. After the general election of 1959—which the party lost—Leon continued her earlier efforts to reform the party and substitute collective leadership for Bustamante's personality cult. She sought the post of second deputy leader, but Bustamante accused her and other reformers of trying to usurp his power. Things came to a head at the party's 1960 and 1961conferences. Leon resigned in bitterness in 1961 and her attempt to build collective leadership was defeated.

Leon ran as an independent candidate in Jamaica's 1962 elections but lost. By 1967 she had joined the rival People's National Party (PNP) but failed to win a seat in the general elections that year. She made her way up the party's ranks by winning a seat in local government elections in 1969 and became deputy mayor of Kingston and Saint Andrew (the administrative capital), serving from 1969 to 1971. She won a parliamentary seat for the PNP in 1972 and served as minister of local government from 1972 to 1976. Although she narrowly lost her seat in 1976, she served as special adviser to the minister of social security from 1977 to 1980.

When the government changed, Leon retired from political life. Trained in cosmetic chemistry, she operated a cosmetics business and a travel agency. As a manufacturer of beauty products and partner in the Leon School of Beauty Culture since 1940, she was a member of the Jamaica Manufacturers Association. She was also a member of the Association of Local Government, the Jamaica Federation of Women, the Commonwealth Parliamentary Association, and the National Council for the Aged.

Leon was killed in an attempted robbery at her home in 1999. She was eighty-seven.

See also Bustamante, Alexander; Jamaica Labour Party; People's National Party; Politics and Politicians in the Caribbean

■ ■ *Bibliography*

Eaton, George. *Alexander Bustamante and Modern Jamaica.* Kingston, Jamaica: LMH, 1995.

ROBERT MAXWELL BUDDAN (2005)

LEONARD, SUGAR RAY

MAY 17, 1956

Named after the musician Ray Charles, boxer Ray Charles "Sugar Ray" Leonard was born in Wilmington, North Carolina, and spent his childhood in Palmer Park, Maryland, just outside Washington, D.C. Leonard took his nickname from "Sugar Ray" Robinson, the former middleweight champion. By the time he was twenty years old, Leonard had completed one of the most successful amateur boxing careers in modern history. During a tour of Moscow in 1974 with the U.S. National Boxing Team, judges awarded the decision to Leonard's Soviet opponent, who then spontaneously turned around, marched across the canvas, and handed the award to Leonard. Leonard's 145–5 amateur record culminated with his winning the light-welterweight gold medal at the Montreal Olympics in 1976. His lightning-quick punches and charismatic style made Leonard an instant television and crowd favorite.

The following year Leonard turned professional. With Janks Morton as coach and Mike Trainor as promoter, Leonard rose rapidly in the professional ranks by defeating such top-ranked fighters as Rafael Rodriguez, Floyd Mayweather, Armando Muniz, and Adolfo Viruet. In 1979 Leonard won both the North American Boxing Federation and World Boxing Council's (WBC) welterweight championships by knocking out Pete Ranzany and Wilfred Benitez.

Leonard's two most famous fights as a welterweight were in 1980. In June he lost his WBC crown by decision to Roberto Duran in Montreal. In November he won it back in New Orleans, in what came to be called the "*no mas*" (no more) fight, a reference to Duran's cryptic announcement to Leonard when he abruptly quit in the middle of the eighth round for no apparent reason. A year later Leonard took on Tommy Hearns, the undefeated welterweight champion of the World Boxing Association, and knocked him out in fourteen rounds, thereby becoming the undisputed welterweight champion. Leonard was named "Sportsman of the Year" by *Sports Illustrated* in 1981.

After a three-year retirement because of an eye injury sustained in 1984, Leonard returned to the ring in 1987 as a middleweight, dethroning Marvin Hagler as WBC champion in a controversial twelve-round split decision in Las Vegas. The victory over Hagler increased his career earnings to $53 million. In 1988 Leonard knocked out Canadian Don Lalonde, the WBC light heavyweight champion, which earned him both the WBC light-heavyweight

and super middleweight titles, making him the first boxer ever to win at least a share of titles in five different weight classes. His thirty-seven professional bouts over fourteen years included thirty-five wins, twenty-five by knockout.

After retiring again in 1991, Leonard worked as a commentator on boxing broadcasts and appeared in several television commercials. He returned to the ring at the age of forty-one in March 1997, but he was pounded by Hector Camacho and retired again following the loss. Leonard was inducted into the International Boxing Hall of Fame that same year.

In 2001, at the age of 47, Leonard launched Sugar Ray Leonard Boxing, LLC. As chairman of the board, he provided overall leadership and worked with fighters, promoters, television executives, venues, and boxing commissioners to plan boxing events. Leonard dissolved the company in 2004.

See also Ali, Muhammad; Boxing; Foreman, George; Frazier, Joe; Tyson, Mike

■ ■ *Bibliography*

Porter, David L., ed. *Biographical Dictionary of American Sports: Basketball and Other Indoor Sports.* Westport, Conn.: Greenwood Press, 1989.

Raz, Tahl. "Sugar Ray Leonard's Toughest Fight." *Inc.* (June 2003). Available from <http://www.inc.com/magazine/20030601/25524.html>.

"Sportsman of the Year." *Sports Illustrated* (December 28, 1981): 34–41.

NANCY YOUSEF (1996)
THADDEUS RUSSELL (1996)
Updated by publisher 2005

LESBIAN, GAY, BISEXUAL AND TRANSGENDER RIGHTS MOVEMENT

See Gay Men; Lesbians

LESBIANS

The presence of lesbians as a diverse and vibrant segment of the black community is often overlooked or even denied in most literature concerning African Americans. This neglect is rooted historically in the long-standing negative perceptions and hostile treatment of lesbians and gay men within American society as a whole, by blacks as well as whites. The black church has often been hostile to homosexuality, viewing it as a sin or a form of mental illness. Perhaps because of the prominence of the black church, much of the discussion of sexual preference by prominent black leaders has been caustically homophobic. Some elements in the black nationalist movement, in an effort to assert patriarchal social relations and to equate the advancement of black people with the achievement of "black manhood," have issued harsh denunciations of homosexuality. Some black scholars and activists have argued that homosexuality is a manifestation of internalized racism, or have claimed that the identity is exclusively European, reflecting white cultural values. Still others have attacked the lesbian and gay rights movement, fearing that its claims would undercut demands for racial equality and diminish the legitimacy of civil rights activism.

At the same time, some observers have suggested that the black community, historically diverse because of the confines of segregation, may have displayed greater tolerance for homosexuality than society at large. Black lesbian writers and critics, including Ann Shockley, Barbara Smith, and Jewelle Gomez, have pointed to an unspoken acknowledgement of lesbianism in black life, in spite of public disavowal and disdain. Prominent black lesbian activists have connected their efforts to a long tradition of struggle for liberation among African Americans, and some black ministers and civil rights leaders, such as the Reverend Jesse Jackson, have lent wholehearted support to the lesbian and gay movement's quest for equality and justice.

Until recently, lesbians have been marginalized in black discourse and have rarely been viewed outside of stereotypes. However, black lesbians are making themselves more visible and embracing their sexuality as a positive aspect of their identities. At the same time, they are openly challenging widespread prejudices that distort their lives, asserting their contributions to the history of African Americans and continuing to play an integral role in their communities.

The history of lesbians in the United States can best be characterized as an emergence of visibility. Lesbianism has been difficult to document historically, largely because of the silence and hostility surrounding lesbian existence (and women's sexuality more generally). Women who loved women did not always wish to claim an explicitly lesbian identity, nor were they necessarily able to do so. Moreover, disagreement persists over the very definition of lesbian identity. Some argue that only women's sexual and romantic involvement with other women can be properly considered as lesbianism. Others insist that platonic intimacy between close women friends—particularly in historical periods, such as the Victorian era, in which women lacked a language to openly describe these relationships—may have constituted lesbianism as well.

Black women's own lifestyle choices, frequently shaped by their lack of economic options, have also obscured the existence of lesbianism. Many black lesbians—including prominent figures whose histories of involvement with women are well-known, such as blues singer Ma Rainey—were married, perhaps as a means to achieve economic well-being or as a "cover" to thwart suspicions of their same-sex relationships. Others were "passing" women who lived and worked as men for many years precisely in order to attain economic independence, courting and even marrying other women. Some of these women were eventually "discovered." Annie Lee Grant, for example, was exposed as a woman in Mississippi in 1954 after having lived as a man for fifteen years; at the time, she was engaged to another woman. Certainly many others lived out their lives without detection. Nella Larsen's seminal novel *Passing* (1969) treats another dilemma of racial and sexual identity in its implication of a romantic relationship between two black women passing for white.

In many cases, one can only speculate about women whose personal histories are noticeably silent on the subject of their sexuality. Women who were "unconventional" may or may not have been explicitly "lesbian" in the contemporary understanding of the term. For example, Mary Fields, born a slave in Tennessee in the 1830s, dressed as a man and worked as a stagecoach driver and in other traditionally male-dominated employment. Whether or not she was a lesbian is not clear.

With the formation of an organized and self-identified black lesbian community, it is possible to determine more explicitly the nature and meaning of black lesbian existence. For black lesbians, such a form of community has only been traced as far back as the 1920s. That traces emerge in this period is indicative of the transformations black communities underwent as a result of the Great Migration, for the movement of single black women to northern urban centers—particularly Chicago, Detroit, and New York City—forced them to create and sustain support systems for their survival. At the same time, it enabled them to escape the intense scrutiny and regulation to which they were subjected in small southern towns and cities.

These circumstances were particularly conducive and crucial to the development of a black lesbian community, for the ability to make connections demanded some level of autonomy economically and socially. Thus, in communities such as Harlem, a number of social settings—bars, clubs, "buffet flat" gatherings, and rent parties—were lesbian-oriented. At the same time, some social spaces frequented by straight people also tolerated, if not welcomed, the presence of lesbians and gay men. Black women in Harlem socialized with each other, worked with each other, and even married each other in large public ceremonies, either with one woman "passing" and using a male name, or with a gay male friend acting as a surrogate.

The flourishing of literary and cultural expression in 1920s Harlem also added to the visibility and viability of lesbian life. Many of the literati of the so-called Harlem Renaissance were lesbians, among them poet and playwright Angelina Weld Grimké and writer Alice Moore Dunbar-Nelson. Many women blues singers and other entertainers who rose to fame during the same period also participated, often quite openly, in sexual relationships with other women; Bessie Smith, Ma Rainey, Ethel Waters, Alberta Hunter, and Josephine Baker, among others, all had lesbian relationships at some point in their lives.

These Harlem sophisticates frequented the lavish gatherings hosted by A'Lelia Walker (heiress daughter of washerwoman-turned-millionaire Madame C. J. Walker), who surrounded herself with prominent lesbian and gay artists and performers. And they flocked to the Clam House, a Harlem social club, to see the performances of entertainer Gladys Bentley, a male impersonator who publicly married another woman. (In later years, Bentley underwent hormone treatments, married a man, and renounced her past life.) Some whites also traveled to Harlem to participate in the lesbian and gay scene, participating in what they perceived as a looser and more tolerant atmosphere.

If the personal lives of Harlem's luminaries gave visibility and legitimacy to lesbian existence within their own circles, their influence was extended to the wider community through their work. Black lesbians were portrayed in some Renaissance-era fiction, including Wallace Thurman's *The Blacker the Berry* (1929) and white author Blair Niles's *Strange Brother* (1931). Blues songs also contained lyrics that explicitly recognized and asserted lesbian sexuality, particularly Bessie Jackson's "BD Women's Blues" and Ma Rainey's "Prove It On Me Blues." While lesbian and gay male identity was not always presented in a positive light—often the depiction drew on prevalent stereotypes or reflected ambivalent attitudes within the community—the themes introduced by blueswomen clearly legitimized women's quest for economic and sexual independence from men.

The emergence of visibility was further influenced by the changes wrought by the entry of the United States into World War II in 1941, when women flooded the job market to replace men who went off to war. Despite continuing discrimination against black women, those black women who were able to participate in either civilian or military workplaces attained a greater measure of economic and sexual independence and were able to meet and socialize with each other. Although little scholarly research has been done to illuminate the experience of black lesbians specifically during World War II, given the preponderance of lesbians in the military at that time, it is certain that among the four thousand black women who served in the Women's Army Corps—separated from men and from white women—a good number were probably lesbians.

By the end of the war, lesbians and gay men in general had expanded their social networks. In urban communities such as New York's Greenwich Village and Harlem, black lesbians participated in an active, though clandestine, social milieu (often interracial) that centered around house parties. Bars catered to a lesbian crowd as well, but were often notorious for their discriminatory treatment of black women patrons. Lesbians who were part of the "gay girls" scene have pointed to the significance of these early efforts by lesbians to come together, as friends as well as lovers, across racial lines.

At the same time, some lesbians and gay men began to identify and critique their oppression in a political way. The 1950s was marked by both political and sexual repression, in which a virulent anticommunism was explicitly linked to fears about racial equality and "deviant" sexual behavior. Still, by mid-decade two organizations—the Mattachine Society and the Daughters of Bilitis—had formed to address the civil rights of gay men and lesbian women, respectively. Although these two groups were an important precursor to the lesbian and gay liberation movement that was forged in the late 1960s, their memberships were small and they zealously protected the confidentiality of those they reached. Their activities touched few blacks, but several anonymous letters to Daughters of Bilitis's publication *The Ladder,* expressing support for the group's efforts, have been traced to playwright Lorraine Hansberry, acclaimed author of *A Raisin in the Sun* (1959).

It was through the civil rights, Black Power, and women's and gay liberation movements of the 1960s that many black lesbians first gained the experience of collective identity and action that was pivotal for the emergence of a politicized and organized black lesbian community. For the most part, the civil rights and Black Power movements posed no fundamental challenge to patriarchal gender relations. While black women played a significant role in the black liberation struggle, both in leadership and at the grassroots level, they often faced sexist discrimination and exclusion from decision-making. Thus, while many black women were empowered by their experience of activism, at the same time they were limited and constrained. Those who hoped to redefine the meaning of liberation in ways that would challenge traditional gender norms were often isolated and attacked as a divisive force detracting from the struggle against racism. Although critical of the black liberation movement, many black women continued to identify with it; thus, activists such as Pauli Murray and Barbara Jordan remained publicly silent about their relationships with women.

By the late 1960s, activist white women were also developing a critique of the oppression and exploitation of women based on their work in civil rights and the New Left, and they were beginning to organize on their own. But white women began to define their struggle as a distinctive women's liberation movement, largely autonomous from other movements in which they had participated. At the same time, they sought unity among women through universalizing women's experiences. However, many black women felt alienated by the affirmation of inclusiveness that did not necessarily speak to their experiences or interests. To the extent that the women's movement began to respond to the racism within its own ranks, it was due to the courageous initiative of black women.

By the early 1970s black women were developing a broader conception of feminism that spoke to their specific concerns and took into account the intersections of race, sex, and class. As black feminist discourse began to take shape, and as a visible gay liberation movement began to emerge, the way was opened for the development of an identifiable and organized black lesbian community.

Black lesbians have become a more visible force in American culture than ever, creating the basis for black lesbian organizing and establishing links with other lesbians of color in the search for common ground. In 1974 black women in Boston formed the Combahee River Collective and issued a classic statement of commitment to struggle against "racial, sexual, heterosexual, and class oppression." Other groups, including Salsa Soul Sisters of New York City and the Sapphire Sapphos of Washington, D.C., have also carried out political and educational work. The National Coalition of Black Gays (now the National Coalition of Black Lesbians and Gays) sponsored the first National Third World Lesbian and Gay Conference in 1979; a year later, the first Black Lesbian Conference was held. Black lesbians have also been at the forefront in initi-

ating a number of political and literary publications, including *Azalea, Moja: Black and Gay,* and the *Third World Women's Gay-zette.* The magazines *Venus* and *Women in the Life* appeal to a popular readership for lesbians of African descent.

Also since the 1970s, black lesbians—including Cheryl Clarke, Anita Cornwell, Jewelle Gomez, Gloria Hull, Audre Lorde, Pat Parker, Ann Shockley, Barbara Smith, and many others—have pioneered work in black feminist theory, literary criticism, poetry, and fiction. They have increased the visibility of black lesbians not only through their own public presence but also through their writing, some of which was showcased in several important collections of black women's writing: *Conditions Five: The Black Women's Issue* (1979), *Home Girls: A Black Feminist Anthology* (1983), and *Afrekete: An Anthology of Black Lesbian Writing* (1995), the latter named for a motif in Lorde's work. Love relationships between women have been depicted in such widely acclaimed works as Gloria Naylor's *Women of Brewster Place* (1982) and Alice Walker's *The Color Purple* (1982). In addition to being depicted in the film adaptations of Naylor's and Walker's novels, black lesbians have independent and mainstream filmmakers like Cheryl Dunye (*The Watermelon Woman,* 1996) and Angela Robinson to represent them behind the camera.

That much of this cultural outpouring both celebrates black lesbian existence and portrays the tragic dimensions of persistent oppression reflects the reality of black lesbians' lives. Visibility can heighten society's level of tolerance, but it often carries an increased threat of violence as well, and "coming out" is not always an option among black lesbians whose survival and livelihood are at stake. Black lesbians are all too aware of forms of repression to which they are disproportionately vulnerable, as demonstrated by the outrage at the state of Oklahoma's execution of Wanda Jean Allen, a disabled black lesbian, in 2001, and the murder of Sakia Gunn, a black lesbian youth, in New Jersey in 2003. Many black lesbians continue to struggle both inside their relationships and within their communities for the right to live and love as they choose.

Increased visibility for black lesbians has illuminated the issues facing women, African Americans, and gay, lesbian, bisexual, and transgendered (GLBT) people in America. In major cities across the nation, annual Black GLBT Pride events are an alternative and a complement to gay pride festivals. Women attending these events cite HIV/AIDS, hate-crime violence, and marriage and domestic partnership among their primary political concerns. The devastating effects of AIDS on gays and blacks—and the consequent homophobic response throughout the country—have intensified black lesbians' organizing efforts. Cathy Cohen, author of *The Boundaries of Blackness* (1999), was one of the most prominent voices to address the importance of HIV/AIDS to black Americans of all genders, sexualities, and social classes. With rates of HIV infection among African-American women on the rise, women's advocates have seen the need to organize their own responses to the epidemic while they continue their crucial roles as strong allies and insightful critics for other segments in the communities affected by the epidemic. Along with these serious concerns, women participating in black GLBT events and organizations address their experiences facing job discrimination, finding spirituality, and raising children, challenges that persist for all African Americans. From proud parents and their children to activist elders like Ruth Ellis, who lived to be the oldest lesbian in America, black lesbians have attained visibility and shown themselves to be valuable members of society as a whole. They are not only affirming their lives but also ensuring the recognition they deserve.

See also Gay Men

■ ■ *Bibliography*

Battle, Juan, Cathy J. Cohen, Gerard Fergerson, and Suzette Audam. "Say It Loud: I'm Black and I'm Proud: Black Pride Survey 2000." New York: Policy Institute of the National Gay and Lesbian Task Force, 2002.

Bentley, Gladys. "I Am a Woman Again." *Ebony* (August 1952): 92–98.

Cohen, Cathy J. *The Boundaries of Blackness: AIDS and the Breakdown of Black Politics.* Chicago: University of Chicago Press, 1999.

Cooper, Gary. "Stagecoach Mary." *Ebony* (October 1977).

Cornwell, Anita. *Black Lesbian in White America.* Tallahassee, Fla.: Naiad, 1983.

D'Emilio, John, and Estelle B. Freedman. *Intimate Matters: A History of Sexuality in America.* New York: Harper, 1988; 2d ed, Chicago: University of Chicago Press, 1997.

Faderman, Lillian. *Odd Girls and Twilight Lovers: A History of Lesbian Life in Twentieth-Century America.* New York: Columbia University Press, 1991.

Garber, Eric. "A Spectacle in Color: The Lesbian and Gay Subculture of Jazz Age Harlem." In *Hidden from History: Reclaiming the Gay and Lesbian Past,* edited by Martin B. Duberman, Martha Vicinus, and George Chauncey Jr. New York: New American Library, 1989.

Gomez, Jewelle, and Barbara Smith. "Talking About It: Homophobia in the Black Community: A Dialogue." *Feminist Review* 34 (Spring 1990): 47–55.

Lorde, Audre. *Zami: A New Spelling of My Name.* Trumansburg, N.Y.: Crossing Press, 1982.

Lorde, Audre. *I Am Your Sister: Black Women Organizing Across Sexualities.* Freedom Organizing Series #3. New York: Kitchen Table–Women of Color Press, 1985.

Mays, Vickie M., Susan D. Cochran, and Sylvia Rhue. "The Impact of Perceived Discrimination on the Intimate Relationships of Black Lesbians." *Journal of Homosexuality* 25, no. 4 (1993): 1–14.

McKinley, Catherine E., and L. Joyce DeLaney. *Afrekete: An Anthology of Black Lesbian Writing.* New York: Anchor, 1995.

Omosupe, Ekua. "Black/Lesbian/Bulldogger." *Differences: A Journal of Feminist Cultural Studies* 3, no. 2 (Summer 1991): 101–111.

Pokorski, Doug. "Activist Ruth Ellis Dead at Age 101." *State Journal-Register,* Springfield, Ill. (October 13, 2000): 13.

Smith, Barbara, ed. *Home Girls: A Black Feminist Anthology.* New York: Kitchen Table–Women of Color Press, 1983. Reprint, New Brunswick, N.J.: Rutgers University Press, 2000.

"The Woman Who Lived as a Man for 15 Years." *Ebony* (November 1954): 93–98.

ALYCEE JEANNETTE LANE (1996)
ANDRÉ CARRINGTON (2005)

LESTER, JULIUS

JANUARY 27, 1939

The son of a Methodist minister, Julius Lester, a writer and professor, was born in St. Louis, Missouri. In 1960 he received his bachelor's degree from Fisk University, and from 1966 to 1968 he was director of the Newport Folk Festival in Newport, Rhode Island. For seven years, from 1968 to 1975, he was the host and producer of a live talk show on WBAI-FM in New York. From 1968 to 1970 Lester was a lecturer at the New School for Social Research in New York City. From 1971 to 1973 he was also host of a live television show, *Free Time,* on WNET-TV in New York. Lester has been a professor at the University of Massachusetts at Amherst in the department of Afro-American Studies (1971–1988) and then in the departments of Comparative Literature and Near Eastern and Judaic Studies. From 1982 to 1984 Lester also served at the University of Massachusetts as the acting director and associate director of the Institute for Advanced Studies in the Humanities. In 1985 he was writer-in-residence at Vanderbilt University.

Lester's serious scholarly side is well evidenced in the long introduction he wrote as editor of the two-volume anthology *The Seventh Son: The Thoughts and Writings of W. E. B. Du Bois* (1971). *To Be a Slave* (1969) was nominated for the Newbery Award, and *The Long Journey Home: Stories from Black History* (1972) was a National Book Award finalist. Other works written and edited by Lester, which make clear the diversity of his interests, include (with Pete Seeger) *The 12-String Guitar as Played by*

Leadbelly (1965), *Look Out Whitey! Black Power's Gon' Get Your Mama!* (1968), *Black Folktales* (1969), *Search for the New Land: History as a Subjective Experience* (1969), *Revolutionary Notes* (1969), *The Knee-High Man and Other Tales* (1972), *Two Love Stories* (1972), *Who I Am* (1974), *All Is Well: An Autobiography* (1976), *This Strange New Feeling* (1982), *The Lord Remember Me* (1984), and *Uncle Remus: Tales from the Briar Patch,* 4 vols. (1999).

Lester's early work basically falls into two categories, one encompassing African-American history and the other recreating tales and legends from African-American folklore. In both cases, Lester deals with white oppression and the historical basis for the relationship between the African-American community and the mainstream white community. While his earliest work was sometimes criticized as "antiwhite," Lester was later credited with stressing the broader implications of the civil rights era for all Americans.

Lester has had a long record of being embroiled in controversies and of dramatic turns in his search for moral verities. This is perhaps best exemplified by the events following the publication in 1988 of *Lovesong: Becoming a Jew. Lovesong* is, among other things, Lester's account of how a hesitant early fascination with Judaism in the late 1970s led finally to an official conversion in 1983. In *Lovesong,* however, Lester accuses the late James Baldwin of making anti-Semitic remarks in a 1984 University of Massachusetts class discussion. The accusation led to furious conflicts on the campus and eventually to his estrangement from the University of Massachusetts' department of Afro-American Studies.

Lester has continued to write prolifically, adding especially to his growing list of highly regarded books for children and young adults. Characters featured in these works typically fall into two categories: those drawn from Afro-American folklore and those drawn from black or Judaic history. Recent titles include *John Henry* (1994), *The Man Who Knew Too Much: A Moral Tale from the Baila of Zambia* (1994), *Sam and the Tigers: A New Retelling of Little Black Sambo* (1996), *From Slave Ship to Freedom Road* (1998), *Black Cowboy, Wild Horses: A True Story* (1998), *The Blues Singers: Ten Who Rocked the World* (2001), *The Autobiography of God* (2003), and *Let's Talk about Race* (2003).

See also Baldwin, James; Folk Heroes and Characters, U.S.; Judaism; Literature of the United States

■ ■ *Bibliography*

"Julius Lester." *Authors and Artists for Young Adults*, vol. 51. Detroit, Mich.: Gale, 2003.

Lehman, David. "A Conversion." *Partisan Review* (spring 1990): 321–325.

Lester, Julius. "Black and White—Together." *Salgamundi* (winter 1989): 174–181.

AMRITJIT SINGH (1996)
Updated by publisher 2005

LEWIS, ARTHUR

JANUARY 23, 1915
JUNE 15, 1991

Sir Arthur Lewis had a notable career as a public intellectual in the field of development economics, and in the process broke through many of the racial barriers that existed in higher education against persons of African descent. For his contributions to the field of development economics, he was awarded the Nobel Prize in 1979. In addition to his many academic achievements, he made a mark in public affairs, serving as a frequent consultant to the British Colonial Office during and immediately after World War II. He then became Ghana's first chief economic adviser and, after that, the first vice-chancellor of the University of the West Indies. In recognition of his work as the vice-chancellor, Queen Elizabeth knighted him in 1963. In the academic world, he held chaired professorships in political economy at the University of Manchester and Princeton University.

Born on the island of St. Lucia in the British West Indies, William Arthur Lewis displayed a brilliance in the classroom that enabled him to win a highly competitive and prestigious West Indian government scholarship to pursue undergraduate studies in Britain. He entered the London School of Economics (LSE) in 1933 to work for a B.A. degree in commerce. After achieving first-class honors in the undergraduate program in 1937, he became a Ph.D. candidate at LSE and completed his thesis in 1940. With war preparations drawing many of the regular LSE faculty away from their teaching and advising responsibilities, the school's administration asked Lewis to become an assistant lecturer in 1938, thus making him LSE's first black faculty member.

Lewis taught at the London School of Economics from 1938 to 1948, introducing the school's first course in what was then called colonial economics, a field that soon was referred to as development economics. After being turned down for a chaired professorship at Liverpool University in 1947 on racial grounds and through the intervention of the vice-chancellor of that institution,

Lewis was appointed the Stanley Jevons Professor of Political Economy at the University of Manchester in 1948. Lewis's professorial appointment at Manchester marked the first time that a black person had held a chair in a British university.

Lewis made his most important scholarly contributions to the emerging field of development economics during his Manchester years (1948–1957). His writings were so influential that many of his peers soon began to describe him as the founding figure of the field. They credited his publications with stimulating broad interest in development economics and providing new perspectives for examining the economies of the less developed parts of the world. Unquestionably, his major work, for which he received the Nobel Prize in 1979, was an article published in 1954 in the journal *Manchester Studies* under the title, "Economic Development with Unlimited Supplies of Labour." In this article Lewis outlined the way that the developed world had first begun to achieve rapid economic growth and suggested that this same process could be repeated in the rest of the world. Central to his argument was a belief that in poor countries a sharp division existed between the traditional and modern economic sectors. In poor economies, a traditional sector housed a large workforce, many of whose members made little or no contribution to the output of that sector. In contrast, in the modern sector labor was highly productive. The key to economic success, then, was to stimulate the modern sector, the economic progress of which was likely to be rapid and successful because workers could easily be drawn out of the traditional sector even at relatively low wages and without any loss of output in the traditional sector. The Lewis model, also known as the dual model, became an instant success. Using its guidelines, economic planners all over the world sought to promote industrial development by attracting workers away from the agricultural sector into the modern, industrializing part of the economy.

Lewis followed the publication of this article with an equally well-received overview of development economics, *The Theory of Economic Growth,* also published in 1954 and destined to become the handbook of development economics in this period. In colleges and universities around the world and in ministries of finance and governmental and international planning organizations, these two publications provided the guidelines for promoting economic growth.

Even while Lewis was publishing these and other works, he made his talents available to government agencies. During and after World War II he advised the British Colonial Office about the ways Britain could alter its economic relations with colonial territories in preparation for the day when the British empire would devolve power to nationalist leaders. From 1950 to 1952 he served as a director of the Colonial Development Corporation, a British agency that identified potentially profitable projects in colonial areas in which to invest. He also advised colonial governments moving toward independence. At the request of the Ministry of Finance of the Gold Coast, he conducted an inquiry into the prospects of industrialization in that country and published an influential report on the topic in 1953, *Industrialization and the Gold Coast Economy.* When the Gold Coast became independent in 1957, he became that country's chief economic adviser, serving in that capacity for a little less than two years, during which time he helped to shape Ghana's first Five-Year Development Plan (1959–1963). After leaving Ghana, he became principal of the University College of the West Indies in 1959, and when the University College became a full-fledged independent university in 1961 (the University of the West Indies), he became its first vice-chancellor.

Although Lewis believed in the obligations of an intellectual to be a public servant, he experienced many disappointments in his dealing with government officials. He resigned as the secretary of the British Colonial Office's Colonial Economic Advisory Committee in 1943, protesting that the Colonial Office's vision of economic development was too conventional. The Colonial Office terminated his appointment as a director of the Colonial Development Corporation in 1952, in large part because of Lewis's criticism of Britain's failure to decolonize the white settler territories in British Africa. In Ghana he and the Ghanaian nationalist leader and prime minister, Kwame Nkrumah, did not see eye to eye on development priorities, and he resigned his position in late 1958 before his two-year contract had expired. Finally, he left the vice-chancellorship of the University of the West Indies to take up a professorship of political economy at Princeton University in 1963 because his efforts to promote the political federation of the British West Indies had failed and left him exhausted.

At Princeton University, where he remained until he retired in 1983, Lewis continued his distinguished career as an economist. His most notable publications were *The Evolution of the International Economic Order* (1977) and *Growth and Fluctuations, 1870–1913* (1978). He also took time away from teaching and academic responsibilities to be head of the Caribbean Development Bank from 1970 to 1973. Lewis continued to be an active scholar until his death at the age of seventy-six.

See also Education in the Caribbean; University of the West Indies

▪▪ *Bibliography*

Frimpong-Ansah, J. H. "Professor Sir W. Arthur Lewis: A Patriarch of Development Economics." Paper presented at the annual conference of the Development Studies Association. Manchester, UK: University of Manchester, 1987.

Lewis, W. Arthur. *The Theory of Economic Growth.* Homewood, Ill.: Richard D. Irwin, 1955.

Lewis, Sir Arthur. "Autobiographical Note," *Social and Economic Studies* (Mona, Jamaica) 29. no. 4 (1980, pp. 1-4).

Meier, Gerald M., and Dudley Seers, eds. "Sir Arthur Lewis." In *Pioneers in Development: A World Bank Publication.* New York: Oxford University Press, 1984, pp. 119–137.

ROBERT L. TIGNOR (2005)

LEWIS, EDMONIA

c. 1844
c. 1909

▮▮▮

Information on the sculptor Edmonia Lewis's life is sparse and difficult to verify. She was often inconsistent in her own accounts of her early days. Born in upstate New York around 1844, the daughter of a Chippewa mother and a black father, Lewis, who was given the Indian name Wildfire, and her older brother, Sunrise, were orphaned when she was five. Raised by maternal aunts, she described her youth as something of an idyll, in which she lived in the wild, fished for food, and made moccasins to sell. She was able, as well, to study at a school near Albany.

With financial help from her brother, Lewis attended Oberlin College, where her studies included drawing and painting. In a dramatic incident, she was accused of the attempted murder, by poisoning, of two classmates who were stricken shortly after enjoying a hot drink she had prepared. While the young women lay ill, Lewis was abducted by a mob and severely beaten. After her recovery and subsequent vindication in the courts, she ended her studies and moved to Boston in order to pursue a career in the arts.

There she found encouragement and support from the abolitionist William Lloyd Garrison, the writer Lydia Maria Child, the sculptor Edward Brackett, with whom she studied, and a community of friends and patrons of the arts, many of whom were active in the abolitionist movement. Her bust of Robert Gould Shaw (1864), the Boston Brahmin and Civil War hero who died leading black troops into battle, was a great success. Sales of copies of that work enabled her to finance a trip to Europe, where, after traveling in England, France, and Italy, she settled in a studio once occupied by the sculptor Antonio Canova on the Via Della Frezza in Rome.

Studio portrait of sculptor Edmonia Lewis, c. 1870s. Lewis's neoclassical works, termed ideal because her imagery was often based on narratives from literature, mythology, and the Bible, often centered on abolitionist themes and the precarious social position of newly freed blacks. PHOTOGRAPHS AND PRINTS DIVISION, SCHOMBURG CENTER FOR RESEARCH IN BLACK CULTURE, THE NEW YORK PUBLIC LIBRARY, ASTOR, LENOX AND TILDEN FOUNDATIONS.

A friend of the sculptors Anne Whitney and Harriet Hosmer and the actress Charlotte Cushman, Lewis was a member of the group of British and American expatriate women artists whom Henry James called the "white, marmorean flock." About Lewis, he wrote: "One of the sisterhood . . . was a Negress, whose color, picturesquely contrasting with that of her plastic material, was the pleading agent of her fame."

James's opinion notwithstanding, Lewis's work was much in demand during the heyday of what were called the literary sculptors. Her studio, listed in the best guidebooks, was a fashionable stop for Americans and others on the grand tour, many of whom ordered busts of family members or of literary and historical figures to adorn their mantels and front parlors.

The first African American to gain an international reputation as a sculptor, Lewis was a prolific artist. The catalog of her work runs to over sixty items, not all of which have been located. Her early work in Boston included portrait medallions and busts of major abolitionists such as John Brown, Maria Weston Chapman, and Garrison. There was also a small statue, now lost, showing the black hero Sgt. William H. Carney holding aloft the flag at the battle of Fort Wagner.

In Rome, she executed such major works as "Forever Free" (1867), a depiction of a slave couple hearing the news of emancipation, and "Hagar" (1868–1875), about which she said, "I have a strong feeling for all women who have struggled and suffered." Henry Wadsworth Longfellow's poem "Song of Hiawatha" had made him a literary folk hero and inspired numerous artists, and Lewis drew on that familiar resource with groups such as "The Marriage of Hiawatha" (1867) and "The Old Arrow-Maker and His Daughter" (1867). These works seemed to patrons all the more authentic coming from the hand of a young woman who was part Indian and was reputed to have grown up in the wild.

Lewis's considerable celebrity reached its height with the unveiling of her "Death of Cleopatra" (1876) at the Philadelphia Centennial Exhibition. That monumental work, a life-sized depiction of Cleopatra on her throne, was praised for the horrifying verisimilitude of the moment when the snake's poison takes hold, and for Lewis's attempt to depict the authentic Egyptian queen from a study of historic coins, medals, and other records.

In the 1880s, as the vogue for late neoclassical sculpture declined, references to Lewis dwindled as well. Although it is known that she was living in Rome as late as 1909, it is not certain where and when she died.

See also Painting and Sculpture

■ ■ *Bibliography*

Blodget, Geoffrey. "John Mercer Langston and the Case of Edmonia Lewis: Oberlin 1862." *Journal of Negro History* 53, no. 3 (July 1968): 201–218.

Buick, Kirsten P. "The Ideal Works of Edmonia Lewis." *American Art*, summer, 1995: 5–19.

Richardson, Marilyn. "Vita: Edmonia Lewis." *Harvard Magazine* 88, no. 4 (March-April 1986): 40–41.

Wolfe, Rinna Evelyn. *Edmonia Lewis: Wildfire in Marble.* Parsippany, N.J.: Dillon, 1998.

MARILYN RICHARDSON (1996)
Updated bibliography

LEWIS, JOHN

FEBRUARY 21, 1940

■ ■ ■

Civil rights activist and politician John Lewis was born near the town of Troy, in Pike County, Alabama. Lewis grew up on a small farm and was one of ten children in a poor sharecropping family. He had been drawn to the ministry since he was a child, and in fulfillment of his lifelong dream he entered the American Baptist Theological Seminary in Nashville, Tennessee, in 1957. He received his B.A. four years later. As a seminary student, Lewis participated in nonviolence workshops and programs taught by James Lawson—a member of the Fellowship of Reconciliation (FOR), a pacifist civil rights organization. Lewis became a field secretary for FOR and attended the Highlander Folk School, an interracial adult education center in Tennessee that was committed to social change, where he was deeply influenced by Septima Clark, the director of education.

Lewis became an active participant in the growing civil rights movement and a member of the Nashville Student Movement. Along with Diane Nash Bevel, James Bevel, and other African-American students, he participated in the Nashville desegregation campaigns of 1960. Lewis was one of the founding members of the Student Nonviolent Coordinating Committee (SNCC) in 1960 and played a leading role in organizing SNCC participation in the Congress of Racial Equality's (CORE) freedom rides. He led freedom rides in South Carolina and Alabama, where he and the other protesters were violently attacked by southern whites.

Lewis rose to a leadership position within SNCC, serving as national chairman from 1963 to 1966. During the 1963 March on Washington, Lewis—representing SNCC—delivered a highly controversial speech that criticized the federal government's consistent failure to protect civil rights workers, condemned the civil rights bill as "too little, too late," and called on African Americans to participate actively in civil rights protests until "the unfinished revolution of 1776 is complete." Although he had acceded to the march organizers' and other participants' request and allowed his speech to be severely edited to tone down its militant rhetoric, it was still considered by most people in attendance to be the most radical speech of the day.

In March 1965 Lewis marched with Rev. Dr. Martin Luther King Jr. in Selma, Alabama, to agitate for a voting rights act that would safeguard African Americans' access to the franchise. He was one of the many participants severely beaten by state troopers on what became known as Bloody Sunday. By 1966 Lewis's continued advocacy of nonviolence had made him an anachronism in the increasingly militant SNCC. He resigned from the organization in June of that year, to be succeeded as chairperson by Stokely Carmichael. Lewis continued his civil rights activities as part of the Field Foundation from 1966 to 1967 and worked as director of community organization projects for the Southern Regional Council. In 1970 he was appointed director of the Voter Education Project, which promoted black empowerment through greater participation in electoral politics.

Lewis became more directly involved in the political arena six years later, when President Carter appointed him to serve on the staff of ACTION—a government agency that coordinated volunteer activities. From 1981 to 1986 he served on the Atlanta City Council. In 1986, in a bitter race, he challenged and defeated Julian Bond—another civil rights veteran—for an Atlanta congressional seat. In Congress Lewis became an influential member of the House Ways and Means Committee. He was an advocate of civil rights and was highly praised for his political acumen. In 1998 he was reelected from Georgia's Fifth Congressional District for a seventh term.

In 2004 Lewis was a recipient of the Freedom Award, given by the National Civil Rights Museum.

See also Bevel, James; Carmichael, Stokely; Civil Rights Movement, U.S.; Clark, Septima; Congress of Racial Equality (CORE); Nash, Diane; Politics in the United States; Student Nonviolent Coordinating Committee (SNCC)

■ ■ *Bibliography*

Carson, Clayborne. *In Struggle: SNCC and the Black Awakening of the 1960s.* Cambridge, Mass.: Harvard University Press, 1981.

Garrow, David. *Bearing the Cross: Martin Luther King, Jr. and the Southern Christian Leadership Conference.* New York: Morrow, 1986.

Lewis, John, with Michael D'Orso. *Walking with the Wind: A Memoir of the Movement.* New York: Simon & Schuster, 1998.

MARSHALL HYATT (1996)
Updated by publisher 2005

LIBERATION THEOLOGY

The term *liberation theology* was first used by Latin-American priests and theologians (mainly Catholic) and U.S. African-American clergy and theologians (mainly Protestant) during the latter part of the 1960s. It refers to an interpretation of the Bible and the Christian faith from the standpoint of the poor and their struggles for justice in society. Without knowledge of the political activities and theological reflections of each other, Latin-American priests working among the masses and U.S. African-American ministers working with exploited blacks began to claim that God was involved in the history of oppressed people, empowering them to fight against poverty and racism.

Latin Americans focused their concern primarily on economic exploitation, particularly the great gap between large poor majorities and rich landowners. African Americans focused their concern primarily on racial oppression, the extreme dehumanization of black people arising from 244 years of slavery and more than a hundred years of segregation. Both Latin Americans and U.S. African Americans, however, emphasized that the world should not be the way it is and that it is therefore the task of Christians to change it.

LIBERATION THEOLOGY IN LATIN AMERICA

A key moment in the development of Latin-American liberation theology was a meeting of priests in Chimbote, Peru, in July 1968. A Peruvian priest and theologian, Gustavo Gutierrez, made the first statement on liberation theology, delivering a paper entitled "Toward a Theology of Liberation." He outlined the methodology for which liberation theology has become famous. "Theology is a reflection—that is, . . . a second act . . . that comes after action. Theology is not first; the commitment is first." Theology, therefore, does not tell people what to do; rather, it arises out of what they do. For Christians, therefore, the truth of the gospel of Jesus is discovered only in practice.

One month after the Chimbote meeting, the well-known Second General Conference of Latin American Bishops was held at Medellín, Colombia, from August 26 to September 6, 1968. The Medellín conference marked a turning point in the history of the Church in Latin America analogous to the impact of the Second Vatican Council on the Roman Catholic Church worldwide. At Medellín, the Latin American Bishops, with much encouragement from Gutierrez and other theological advisers, "discovered" the world of the poor, the exploited masses who "hunger and thirst after justice." This inspired a continent-wide preferential option for the poor.

While the Medellín conference is often cited as the beginning of liberation theology, Gustavo Gutierrez's *A Theology of Liberation* is regarded as its most influential text.

Published in Spanish in 1971 and translated into English in 1973, the continuing and worldwide influence of this book is the major reason Gutierrez has been called the "father of liberation theology." The book is an extended interpretation of his Chimboté paper on liberation theology. In it, Gutierrez emphasizes that liberation theology is not a reflection on the abstract and timeless truths about God; rather, it is chiefly a new way of doing theology, a "critical reflection on historical praxis." Liberation theology "does not stop with reflecting on the world, but tries to be part of the process through which the world is transformed" (Gutierrez, 1973, p.15).

LIBERATION THEOLOGY IN THE UNITED STATES

The key moment in the development of black liberation theology was the publication of the Black Power statement in the *New York Times* on July 31, 1966, by an ad hoc committee of radical black clergy who later organized themselves as the National Conference of Black Christians (NCBC). In this statement, they opposed the white church's rejection of Black Power as unchristian and instead expressed their solidarity with the urban black poor in their communities, affirming the need for black self-determination and empowerment. Two years later, responding to the widespread Black Power movement in the black communities throughout the United States, James Cone published an essay titled "Christianity and Black Power." He defined the liberating message of Black Power as the message of Christ. Cone deepened the theological meaning of Black Power in the book *Black Theology and Black Power* (1969). During the same year, using Cone's book as the main source of their deliberations, the Theological Commission of the NCBC issued an official statement on "Black Theology," defining it as a "theology of black liberation." One year later, Cone's *A Black Theology of Liberation* (1970) was published, making liberation the organizing principle of his theological perspective.

Like Latin-American liberation theology, black theology also emphasized praxis. It was defined as a specific kind of obedience that organizes itself around a social theory of reality in order to implement in society the freedom inherent in faith. If faith is the belief that God created all for freedom, then praxis is the social theory used to analyze what must be done for the historical realization of freedom. To sing about freedom and to pray for its coming is not enough. Freedom must be actualized in history by oppressed peoples who accept the intellectual challenge to analyze the world for the purpose of changing it.

LIBERATION THEOLOGY IN AFRICA AND ASIA

Soon after the appearance of liberation theology in Latin America and in African-American communities in the United States, other expressions of it appeared in Africa, in Asia, and among women in all groups. Black and contextual theologies of liberation were created by Christian communities struggling against apartheid in South Africa, with Desmond Tutu and Alan Boesak as prominent leaders. African theology appeared in other parts of Africa with an emphasis on indigenization and Africanization. John Mbiti of Kenya and Engelbert Mveng of Cameroon were prominent interpreters. An Asian liberation theology emerged out of Christian communities encountering the overwhelming poverty and the multifaceted religiousness of the continent. Aloysius Pieris of Sri Lanka and Samuel Rayan of India were important representatives.

LIBERATION THEOLOGY AMONG WOMEN

Responding to their struggles against sexism, women on all continents began to develop theologies of liberation out of their experience. In the United States, Mary Daly and Rosemary Ruether were among the leading voices in initiating the development of feminist theology; Delores Williams and Jacquelyn Grant helped to create a womanist theology out of black women's experience; and Ada Marie Isasi-Diaz made a similar contribution to the development of a feminist theology among Hispanics. Mercy Amba Oduyoye of Ghana, Chung Hyun-Kyung of South Korea, and Elsa Tamez of Mexico reflected on the liberating presence of God in the struggles of third-world women against patriarchal mechanisms of domination in the global context of the church and the society.

THE UNITY OF THIRD WORLD THEOLOGIANS

Recognizing the commonality of their concerns, theologians of liberation in Latin America, Africa, Asia, and among U.S. minorities met in Dar es Salaam, Tanzania, in August 1976 and created the Ecumenical Association of Third World Theologians (EATWOT). Their concern was to break with theological models inherited from the West and to develop a new way of doing theology that would interpret the gospel in a more meaningful way to peoples of the third world and promote their struggles of liberation. In more than twenty-five years of dialogue, visiting each others' places of struggle, liberation theologians have debated one another about the most important starting point for doing Christian theology. Latin Americans have emphasized their struggle to overcome economic structures of domination, pointing to the wide gap between the rich and poor among nations and within nations and stressing the need for theology to make use of the social sciences in analyzing the world of the poor. Africans have talked about their struggle against "anthropological poverty" and the "despoiling of human beings not only of what they have but of everything that constitutes their essence—their identity, history, language, and dignity" (Mveng, 1983, p. 220). They have also stressed the need to liberate theology from the cultural captivity of the West. Asians have emphasized the need to develop a theological method that combines the analyses of religion, culture, politics, and economics. U.S. minorities, the smallest group in the association, have reminded all of the importance of race analysis in the doing of theology.

In their dialogues, which have often been intense, liberation theologians in EATWOT have learned much from each other. They have published eight volumes, including Sergio Torres and Virginia Fabella (eds.), *The Emergent Gospel: Theology From the Underside of History* (1978); Virginia Fabella and Sergio Torres (eds.), *Irruption of the Third World: Challenge to Theology* (1983); Virginia Fabella and Sergio Torres (eds.), *Doing Theology in a Divided World* (1985); Virginia Fabella and Mercy Amba Oduyoye (eds.), *With Passion and Compassion: Third World Women Doing Theology* (1988); K. C. Abraham (ed.), *Third World Theologies: Commonalities and Divergences* (1990); and K. C. Abraham and Bernadette Mbuy-Beya (eds.), *Spirituality of the Third World* (1994).

All liberation theologians agree that the Christian gospel can best be understood and interpreted in the context of one's participation in the struggles of the poor for justice. Faith is not primarily intellectual assent to truths about God; rather, it is a commitment to God and to human beings, especially the poor. Theology, therefore, is a reflection on the commitment that Christians make in their effort to put into practice the demands of faith.

The contrast between liberation theologies and the dominant theologies of Europe and North America is quite revealing. The identity of the dominant theologies has been strongly influenced by the European Enlightenment and secularism, creating the problem of the unbeliever. The central task of theology, therefore, is to make the Christian faith intelligible in a world that can be explained without God.

The identity of liberation theologies has been defined by oppression—poverty, racism, colonialism, and sexism—creating the problem of the nonperson. In this context, theology asks, what is the relationship between salvation and the struggle for justice in society? Faith demands not only that it be understood, but that salvation be realized in the social, economic, and political lives of people.

Theologies of liberation have also emerged among gays, lesbians, and transsexual people and among other oppressed groups. Liberation theology is not limited to one group or continent but found wherever oppressed people of faith are empowered intellectually to reflect on their fight for freedom.

See also Black Power Movement; Catholicism in the Americas; Protestantism in the Americas

■■ *Bibliography*

Boff, Leonardo, and Clodovis Boff. *Introducing Liberation Theology.* Maryknoll, N.Y.: Orbis, 1987.

Cone, James H. *For My People: Black Theology and the Black Church.* Maryknoll, N.Y.: Orbis, 1984.

Gutierrez, Gustavo. *A Theology of Liberation: History, Politics, and Salvation.* Translated and edited by Caridad Inda and John Eagleson, Maryknoll, N.Y.: Orbis, 1973.

Hennelly, Alfred T., ed. *Liberation Theology: A Documentary History.* Maryknoll, N.Y.: Orbis, 1990.

Mveng, Englebert. "Third World Theology—What Theology? What Third World?: Evaluation by an African Delegate." In *Irruption of the Third World: Challenge to Theology,* edited by Virginia Fabella and Sergio Torres. Maryknoll, N.Y.: Orbis, 1983.

Wilmore, Gayraud S., and James H. Cone. *Black Theology: A Documentary History, 1966–1979.* Maryknoll, N.Y.: Orbis, 1979.

JAMES H. CONE (1996)
Updated by author 2005

LIBERATOR, THE

The Liberator, an abolitionist newspaper, was begun in 1831 by William Lloyd Garrison (1805–1879) and Isaac Knapp (1804–1843) in Boston. Garrison used *The Liberator* for over thirty years to voice his scathing indictments of the slave system and of the country that allowed it to flourish. It complemented his work in the New England Anti-Slavery Society and the American Anti-Slavery Society, which he founded in 1832 and 1833, respectively. From the start, *The Liberator,* which was published weekly, received substantial African-American support. Of its 450 initial subscribers, roughly 400 were black. One was Philadelphian James Forten, who urged Garrison to "plead our cause" and expose "the odious system of slavery." A deeply religious Baptist and pacifist, Garrison aimed at bringing people to the cause of abolition through "moral suasion." He therefore avoided politics and called for immediate, rather than gradual, abolition. "I am in earnest—I will not equivocate—I will not excuse—I will not retreat a single inch—AND I WILL BE HEARD," pledged Garrison in the first issue. In the early years of the paper, this was a radical stance, even among antislavery advocates.

The publication of *The Liberator* brought furious reaction from southern politicians, who passed legislation banning its circulation. Columbia, South Carolina, offered a reward of $5,000 for the arrest and conviction of Garrison or Knapp. In October 1831 the corporation of Georgetown, D.C., forbade any free black to take *The Liberator* out of the post office. Offenders would be punished by fine and imprisonment, and if they did not pay, were to be sold into slavery for four months. Despite its inflammatory appeal, *The Liberator*'s circulation remained relatively small, particularly among the white population. In its fourth year, nearly three-quarters of the two thousand subscribers were African Americans. Knapp, whose contributions to the paper were more in terms of publishing and trying, unsuccessfully, to keep the paper financially afloat, left in 1839. Wanting to try his hand at writing editorials, he published his own abolitionist paper, *Knapp's Liberator,* in January 1842, but this proved unsuccessful.

The Liberator contained some of the most important writings on the abolitionist cause. Aside from Garrison's fiery editorials, it published the writings of John Rankin, Oliver Johnson, Wendell Phillips, and English abolitionist George Thompson. With these writers, *The Liberator* continued its fight: opposing colonization (which Garrison perceived as a plot to strengthen slavery by removing free blacks from the country) and rallying boycotts against the products of slavery. In 1842 Garrison called for a "Repeal of the Union." The U.S. Constitution, he wrote, was "a Convenant with Death and an Agreement with Hell." This quickly became *The Liberator*'s motto. When secession became a reality in 1861, however, it was the slaveholders who wanted to leave the Union. At first, Garrison celebrated their departure. But as the Civil War progressed, he shifted his position and used *The Liberator* to pressure President Abraham Lincoln for abolition. Significantly, the new motto of the paper became, "Proclaim liberty throughout the land, to all the inhabitants thereof." Garrison cheered the issuance of the Emancipation Proclamation, writing "Glory Hallelujah!," but he kept working, hoping to secure the freedom of slaves in border states. With the passing of the Thirteenth Amendment, Garrison believed the mission of the paper accomplished. "Great and marvelous are thy works, Lord God Almighty!" he wrote in one of the last issues. On December 29, 1865, *The Liberator,* the most influential and important abolitionist newspaper, ceased publication.

See also Abolition; Civil War, U.S.; Slavery and the Constitution

■ ■ *Bibliography*

Grimké, Archibald Henry. *William Lloyd Garrison the Abolitionist.* 1891. Reprint. New York: Negro University Press, 1969.

Merrill, Walter McIntosh. *Against Wind and Tide, a Biography of William Lloyd Garrison.* Cambridge, Mass.: Harvard University Press, 1963.

Mott, Frank Luther. *A History of American Magazines.* 5 vols. Cambridge, Mass.: Harvard University Press, 1967.

WALTER FRIEDMAN (1996)

LIELE, GEORGE

c. 1750
1820

┅━┅━┅━

Born into slavery in Virginia, George Liele, a Baptist minister, was taken by his owner, Henry Sharp, to Burke County, Georgia, in 1773. Sharp, a Baptist deacon, supported Liele's conversion the following year, and Buckhead Creek Baptist Church certified him to minister to slaves on surrounding plantations. Thus, Liele became one of the first licensed black preachers in North America. He was emancipated on the eve of the American Revolution. When Sharp, a Tory, was killed in the war, his heirs attempted to reenslave Liele, but British officers whom Liele had served protected him. In 1777 Liele gathered at one of the first black Baptist churches in America at Yama Craw, near Savannah. Among those who heard him preach were the influential black Baptists David George and Andrew Bryan.

When the British evacuated Savannah in 1782, Liele indentured himself in exchange for passage to Jamaica. Upon working out his indenture, he was given his free papers in 1784 and began to preach, first in a private home, and then publicly, after obtaining a grant of toleration from the Jamaican Assembly. In Jamaica, Liele faced strong opposition from Anglican authorities. He was tried and acquitted on a charge of sedition, and was also imprisoned for debts he acquired while building a church in Kingston. Nevertheless, his congregation grew. By 1791 Liele estimated that he had baptized four hundred people in Jamaica, including a few whites. In addition to his ministry, Liele established and promoted a free school, and earned his living as a farmer and transporter of goods. A founding father of the African Baptist faith in two countries, he died in Jamaica in 1820.

See also Baptists; Free Blacks, 1619–1860

■■ *Bibliography*

"George Liele." *Notable Black American Men*. Detroit: Gale, 1998.

Kaplan, Sidney, and Emma Nogrady Kaplan. *The Black Presence in the Era of the American Revolution*. Amherst: University of Massachusetts Press, 1989.

Logan, Rayford W., and Michael R. Winston, eds. *Dictionary of American Negro Biography*. New York: Norton, 1982.

Sobel, Mechal. *Trabelin' On: The Slave Journey to an Afro-Baptist Faith*. Westport, Conn.: Greenwood Press, 1979.

BENJAMIN K. SCOTT (1996)
Updated by publisher 2005

LIGHBOURNE, ROBERT

NOVEMBER 29, 1909
DECEMBER 28, 1995

▮▮▮——————

Industrialist, politician, and administrator Robert Lighbourne was born in Morant Bay, St. Thomas. His father, a politician and a wealthy landowner, sent him to England to further his studies after his high school education at Jamaica College. Robert later became a manufacturer in Birmingham, producing ploughshares for Ferguson tractors, as well as other essential equipment needed for World War II. After hurricane Charlie devastated Jamaica in 1951, Lighbourne's managerial skills in organizing relief for the island attracted the attention of the Jamaican authorities, and he was invited home to assist in the rebuilding of the country. He first assisted at Jamaica Welfare Ltd, a national development project founded in 1943. Lighbourne's first significant impact as an industrialist came in 1951 when he became the first managing director of the newly established Industrial Development Corporation, a position he held until 1955.

The Jamaica Labour Party (JLP), the political party in power, capitalized on Lighbourne's reputation by having him run for elective office in his home parish of Western St. Thomas, in the West Indian federal elections of 1958. Lighbourne won his seat but resigned after one year because of his disenchantment with the federation and to prepare for Jamaica's 1959 general elections.

Lighbourne became the first minister of trade and industry in independent Jamaica, serving from 1962 to 1972, where he displayed exceptional managerial skills. His stellar achievement remains the successful negotiation of the Commonwealth Sugar Agreement of 1968, which paved the way for preferential treatment of Commonwealth products to Britain. He also initiated scientific research into the extraction of iron ore out of Jamaican red mud and served as chairman of the World Sugar Conference in 1968. In Jamaica he initiated the First Industrial Incentives Act; the Export Industry Encouragement Act and the New Companies Act; the Jamaica Industrial Development Center; the Jamaican Bureau of Standards; and the Industrial Apprentice Scheme, and he positioned Jamaica in joining CARIFTA (Caribbean Free Trade Association). Jamaica also became an independent member of the General Agreement on Tariffs and Trade (GATT). Lighbourne also introduced the Jamaica Industrial Apprentice Scholars Scheme, which from 1963 to 1974 sent over 120 young high school graduates to the United Kingdom to become engineers. In the 1960s he even proposed to OPEC that it should establish a two-tiered price structure, which gave developing countries the benefit of a lower price than that charged to developed countries, since increasing oil prices would damage their fragile economies.

Despite not being chosen as the new leader of the JLP when a vacancy occurred, he nevertheless contested the 1972 general elections and won his constituency of Western St. Thomas for the JLP. He resigned from the JLP not long after but remained an independent member of Jamaica's parliament until 1976. Lighbourne even formed his own political party, the United Party, in 1974, but it dissolved after a year. In July 1990 the Jamaican government appointed Lighbourne as a special envoy with the rank of ambassador in the area of foreign affairs and trade. He died on December 28, 1995, at eighty-six.

See also Jamaica Labour Party; Politics and Politicians in the Caribbean

■■ *Bibliography*

Eaton, George E. *Alexander Bustamante and Modern Jamaica*. Kingston, Jamaica: Kingston Publishers Limited, 1975.

Lighbourne, Robert. Papers. National Library of Jamaica, Kingston.

DAVE GOSSE (2005)

LIGON, GLENN

APRIL 20, 1960

▮▮▮——————

Glenn Ligon is an African-American visual artist who uses language to question issues pertaining to race, sexuality,

Portrait of American installation artist Glenn Ligon, 1998. JOHN
JONAS GRUEN/GETTY IMAGES

and identity. Born in the Bronx, New York, in 1960, he studied at Wesleyan College, where he received his B.A, and at the Rhode Island School of Design. During the 1980s and 1990s, Ligon was among a cadre of black and Latino artists who began using structuralist and post-structuralist theory to deconstruct commonly held assumptions about race, sexuality, and gender. In many of his works, Ligon focuses specifically on language as an ironically self-sufficient system for negotiating issues concerning identity formation.

Ligon's works frequently appropriate sections from historically significant literature, as well as euphemisms from African-American popular culture and folklore tradition. In this way, Ligon is able to examine the relationship between language and meaning, and to explore the implications of subjectivity and intent. Ligon thus combines speech with conceptualist and minimalist strategies in multimedia prints, paintings, and installations that incorporate language as an important component of his visual art. In 1998 Ligon began his *Stranger in the Village* series of drawings and paintings. In this series which continued until 2004, Ligon often stenciled excerpts of

James Baldwin's classic text onto a canvas and then covered the text with multiple layers of coal dust, rendering the author's statement partly illegible. Where Baldwin elaborates on the experience of being an outsider—as the only black man to have visited an isolated Swiss village—Ligon's encrusted paintings intimate a mounting tension synonymous with the author's testimonial. As the artist has commented on the importance of text in his work: "Text demands to be read, and perhaps the withdrawal of the text, the frustration of the ability to decipher it, reflects a certain pessimism on my part about the ability and the desire to communicate. Also, literature has been a treacherous site for black Americans because literary production has been so tied with the project of proving our humanity through the act of writing" (Firstenberg, p. 43).

From 1994 to 1998, Ligon worked on a project titled *Feast of Scraps*, through which he critiqued the notion of identity and sentiment associated with the family photo album by creating such an album filled with vintage gay pornography. The photographs are captioned with statements such as "Mother Knew" and "Brother." By incorporating images with subversive texts, Ligon puts before the viewer a union of identities commonly associated with notions of both morality and immorality—identities that are secretly acknowledged yet excluded from both the verbal discourses and visual artifacts that make up familial identity. Through this process, Ligon also called attention to the irony inherent in the highly selective and exclusionary practices with which people construct and legitimate familial and larger historical narratives. Ligon revisited the family photo album for his web-based project, *Annotations* (2000), a digital twenty-page album that is itself linked to multiple layers of visual information, including photos, hand-written narratives, and audio clips. It was Ligon's intention for this progression to mimic the ways in which memory works, through reminiscence, correlation, and suggestion. Moreover, in *Annotations*, references to race and African-American history are continual subtexts for the work as a whole. Periodically, images containing texts (such as "Harlem is Burning") are juxtaposed with subversive imagery referencing the photographer Edward Steichen's 1955 exhibition and publication, *The Family of Man*.

See also Art in the United States, Contemporary; Painting and Sculpture

■ ■ *Bibliography*

Firstenberg, Lauri. "Neo-Archival and Textual Modes of Production: An Interview with Glenn Ligon." *Art Journal* 60, no. 1 (spring 2001): 43.

Golden, Thelma. *Black Male: Representations of Masculinity in Contemporary American Art.* New York: Whitney Museum of American Art, 1994.

Ligon, Glenn. *Un/becoming.* Philadelphia: Institute of Contemporary Art, University of Pennsylvania, 1998.

Ligon, Glenn. *Coloring: New Work by Glenn Ligon.* Minneapolis: Walker Art Center, 2001.

LERONN BROOKS (2005)

LINCOLN, ABBEY

AUGUST 6, 1930

The actress and jazz singer Abbey Lincoln was born Anne Marie Woolridge in Chicago, Illinois. In high school she toured Michigan with a dance band; in 1951 she moved to California and sang in nightclubs as Gaby Lee. After a club residency in Hawaii (1952–1954), she returned to California and began singing in Hollywood nightclubs. In 1956 she made her recording debut with Benny Carter's orchestra and changed her name to Abbey Lincoln. During the 1950s and 1960s, she sang with the jazz group led by Max Roach (to whom she was married until 1971) and helped popularize his "Freedom Now Suite" (1960), one of the musical hallmarks of the civil rights movement.

During the 1970s Lincoln toured Europe, Asia, and Africa as a soloist. As an actress she appeared in *Nothing but a Man* (1964), which won the top film award at the First World Festival of Negro Arts in Dakar, Senegal. She also made appearances in Jean Genet's play *The Blacks* and was a member of the road company of the musical *Jamaica.* Lincoln was also active in television and radio. In 1975 she adopted the name Aminata Moseka and in her lyrics expressed political positions devoted to the advancement of the culture and arts of African Americans. In 1991, in a comeback as a jazz diva, she recorded the album *You Gotta Pay the Band,* for which she penned five of the songs. Critics considered it one of the best examples of her work.

Lincoln enjoyed a prolific output through the 1990s, creating a large, distinctive catalog of new material on Verve Records. Beginning with *The World Is Falling Down* and ending with *Over the Years,* an album that serves as a summation of her long and varied career, Lincoln released seven albums for the Verve label between 1990 and 2000. She presented a stunning three-night retrospective of her career at New York's Jazz at the Lincoln Center in March of 2002.

See also Jazz; Roach, Max

■ ■ *Bibliography*

Jones, Lisa. "'Late Bloomer' in Her Prime." *New York Times* (August 4, 1991).

JAMES E. MUMFORD (1996)
Updated by publisher 2005

LINCOLN THEATRE

Located on 135th Street just off Lenox Avenue in New York City, the Lincoln Theatre was Harlem's premier center of popular entertainment from the turn of the century until the Great Depression. Its predecessor was the Nickelette, a storefront nickelodeon presenting fifteen-minute segments of live entertainment on a makeshift stage. One early performer, around 1903, was Baby Florence, the child singer and dancer who grew up to be Florence Mills, the Broadway and London star. The Nickelette was purchased in 1909 by Maria C. Downs, who doubled the seating to three hundred and named the theater after Abraham Lincoln. Harlem was becoming increasingly black, but most theaters segregated or refused admission to African Americans. Downs turned the Lincoln into a headquarters for black shows and audiences, a policy so successful that she constructed the building with a seating capacity of 850 in 1915.

Although the theater placed some emphasis on serious drama—with the Anita Bush Stock Company, for example, before it moved to the rival Lafayette—the Lincoln during the 1910s and 1920s became the focal point for down-home, even raucous, vernacular entertainment that particularly appealed to recent working-class immigrants from the South. As the New York showcase of the Theatre Owners Booking Association (TOBA), it drew all the big names of black vaudeville: Bessie Smith, Bert Williams, Alberta Hunter, Ethel Waters, and Butterbeans and Susie. The Lincoln was the only place in New York where Ma Rainey ever sang. Mamie Smith was appearing there in Perry Bradford's *Maid of Harlem* when she made the first commercial recording of vocal blues by a black singer.

Because it housed a live orchestra, the Lincoln also became a venue for jazz musicians. Don Redman performed there in 1923 with Billy Paige's Broadway Syncopators. Lucille Hegamin and her Sunny Land Cotton Pickers featured a young Russell Procope on clarinet in 1926, the same year Fletcher Henderson with his Roseland Orchestra played there. Perhaps the name most closely identified with the Lincoln was the composer and stride pianist Thomas "Fats" Waller, who imitated the theater's piano and organ player while still a child and was hired for twenty-three dollars a week in 1919 to replace her; he was then fifteen years old. When he failed to find financial backing to produce his opera *Treemonisha*, Scott Joplin paid for a single performance at the Lincoln. Unable to afford an orchestra, he provided the only accompaniment himself on the piano.

A steady stream of white show-business writers and composers, including George Gershwin and Irving Berlin, joined the black audiences at the Lincoln, not only to be entertained but to find new ideas and new tunes. More than one melody, dance step, or comedy routine that originated with a black vaudeville act wound up in a white Broadway musical. The Lincoln did not survive the economic disaster of the Great Depression and the changing tastes of the Harlem community, where more sophisticated people began to refer to it as "the Temple of Ignorance." Downs sold the theater in 1929 to Frank Shiffman, who turned it into a movie house. Later, a renovated Lincoln Theatre housed the Metropolitan AME Church.

See also Blues, The; Harlem, New York; Jazz

■ ■ *Bibliography*

Newman, Richard. "The Lincoln Theatre." *American Visions* 6, no. 4 (August 1991): 29–32.

RICHARD NEWMAN (1996)

LINCOLN UNIVERSITY
▬■▬

Lincoln University is located in southern Chester County, four miles north of Oxford, Pennsylvania. Founded in 1854, the university is the oldest extant black institution of higher learning in the United States. The university was founded by John Miller Dickey, a white senior pastor of the Oxford Presbyterian Church. Before founding Lincoln University, Dickey had shown concern for the welfare of African Americans. In 1850 he contributed decisively to the liberation of two sisters, Rachel and Elizabeth Parker, who had been kidnapped in Oxford for sale into slavery. Dickey also supported the American Colonization Society and felt that emancipated Africans should return to the African continent as missionaries. In 1852 Dickey made unsuccessful attempts to place James Ralston Amos, an African American and the treasurer of the fund for "Negro Church" building established by Richard Allen in 1794, into Princeton University Seminary and also at a religious academy managed by the Presbyterian Synod of Philadelphia. Frustrated by a failed effort to secure admission for

a "colored" student in a "white" institution, Dickey sought a solution in establishing an institution for "colored" men.

The institution Dickey established was originally chartered by the state of Pennsylvania as Ashmun Institute, named in honor of Jehudi Ashmun, the first governor of Liberia. After the Civil War and in recognition of the role that President Abraham Lincoln played in the emancipation of the enslaved, Ashmun Institute was renamed Lincoln University. The educational curriculum was originally conceived to include not only all aspects of liberal arts but also law, medicine, and theology. Financial problems and declining enrollment, however, necessitated the closing of the seminary as well as the schools of law and medicine. The university's charters of 1854 and 1866 restricted admission to male students. However, in 1953 the university amended its charter to permit coeducation. In 1972 Lincoln University became a state-related institution within Pennsylvania's Commonwealth System of Higher Education and was placed on the same basis for state aid as Temple University and the University of Pittsburgh as well as Pennsylvania State University.

Lincoln University has played a vital role in the training of leaders, not only among African Americans but also among Africans. In the first hundred years of its existence, Lincoln University graduated twenty percent of the African-American doctors and more than ten percent of the African-American attorneys in the United States. In the words of Dr. Niara Sudarkasa, the eleventh president of Lincoln University, "Lincoln University's alumni roster reads like a section of Who's Who of the Twentieth Century." Its distinguished alumni include Thurgood Marshall, who not only argued successfully the historic school desegregation case before the Supreme Court in 1954 but also became the first African-American appointed to the Supreme Court, and the poet Langston Hughes, who was in Lincoln University's class of 1929. Two former heads of state in Africa were educated at Lincoln University: Kwame Nkrumah, Ghana's first prime minister, graduated in 1939, and Nnamdi Azikiwe, Nigeria's first president, was in Lincoln University's class of 1930. Lincoln's alumni have been presidents of thirty-six colleges and universities.

Lincoln's positive impact has particularly been felt in the Commonwealth of Pennsylvania, where many of its graduates have distinguished themselves as educators, physicians, judges, lawyers, and scientists. Lincoln's graduates include Harry W. Bass, Pennsylvania's first African-American legislator; Robert N. C. Nix, the state's first African-American congressman; Herbert Millen, the state's first African-American judge; and Roy C. Nichols, the first African-American bishop of the United Methodist Church.

Lincoln University has continued the tradition of educating students from Africa who return to their continent to assume leadership positions. Namibia's first independence government cabinet had at least six Lincoln University graduates. This impressive record of Lincoln's national and international alumni in various fields of human endeavor testifies to the value of a preparation solidly rooted in an education for freedom.

Since the 1960s Lincoln University has intensified its tradition of international involvement. In 1961 the U.S. State Department sponsored the African Languages and Area Studies Program at the university. From 1963 to 1971 the United States Peace Corps Training Program prepared volunteers on Lincoln University's campus and sent them to Africa and the Caribbean. Sudarkasa, an internationally recognized anthropologist and the first African-American female to be appointed as Lincoln's president, highlighted the international focus of Lincoln University. Under her leadership Lincoln established the Center for Public Policy and Diplomacy, the Center for the Study of Critical Languages, and the Center for the Comparative Study of the Humanities. These centers have become focal points for international studies at the university. Also, in addition to the European languages that are traditionally taught in colleges, Lincoln also teaches Chinese, Japanese, Russian, and Arabic languages.

Dr. Horace Mann Bond, a graduate of Lincoln University, was the institution's first African-American president. He served from 1945 to 1957. Dr. Bond was succeeded by Dr. Marvin Wachman, who was white. After Dr. Wachman, the succeeding presidents—Dr. Herman Branson (1970–1985), Dr. Sudarkasa (1987–1998), and Dr. Ivory V. Nelson (1999–)—have been black.

Lincoln University's student population traditionally numbered about fourteen hundred, but by 2005 the number had risen to about two thousand. Students are recruited from various social, economic, and national backgrounds. The university has continued to expand the physical facilities on its 350 acres of land.

See also Bethune-Cookman College; Dillard University; Fisk University; Howard University; Morehouse College; Spelman College; Tuskegee University; Wilberforce University

■■ *Bibliography*

Bond, Horace Mann. *Education for Freedom: A History of Lincoln University, Pennsylvania.* Lincoln, Penn.: Lincoln University, 1976.

Carr, George B. *John Miller Dickey.* Philadelphia: Westminster Press, 1929.

Lewis, Thomas E. "Lincoln University—The World's First Negro School of Higher Learning." *Philadelphia Bulletin* (August 26, 1951): 3.

Sudarkasa, Niara. "Lincoln University's International Dimension." In *Education for International Competence in Pennsylvania,* edited by Andrew Dinniman and Burkart Holzner. Harrisburg: Pennsylvania Department of Education, 1988.

LEVI A. NWACHUKU (1996)
Updated by publisher 2005

LISBOA, ANTÔNIO FRANCISCO

c. 1738
NOVEMBER 18, 1814

Born in Vila Rica (now Ouro Prêto), Minas Gerias, Brazil, Antônio Francisco Lisboa, the illegitimate son of Manuel Francisco Lisboa, a Portuguese architect and master carpenter, and his African slave Isabel, was an architect, sculptor, and wood carver. Lisboa is considered the most notable artist of the colonial period in Brazil. His biography has often been mythologized in twentieth-century Brazilian history and used to solidify an artistic national heritage. Between 1796 and 1804, working primarily in wood and soapstone, the mulatto artist created an extraordinary number of baroque sculptures. Lisboa apprenticed in the workshops of his father, his uncle Antonio Francisco Pombal, and the draftsman João Gomes Batista of the Lisbon Mint. All of these European artists resided in the prosperous Captaincy of Minas Gerais in the early eighteenth century, at the height of the Brazilian gold boom. Master Lisboa never left Brazil and, according to documentary sources, only made one trip to Rio de Janeiro to resolve a paternity suit. His relative isolation makes it all the more extraordinary that he adapted refined German and French rococo forms and styles in his sculptural and decorative works. His knowledge of European styles probably came from theoretical architectural treatises and ornamental engravings. Southern Germanic religious prints, particularly those by the Augsburg-based Klauber brothers, influenced Lisboa's artistic oeuvre.

At a young age, Lisboa became one of the most respected artists of the Captaincy, producing his first works in wood and stone at fourteen, and working until his death. His fame only increased with the onset of an unidentifiable disease (possibly leprosy, syphilis, or viral influenza) around the age of forty. In response to his condition, which led to the progressive deformation of his

Basilica do Bom Jesus de Matozinhos, Congonhas do Campo, Brazil. *Antônio Francisco Lisboa, dubbed O Aleijadinho ("the little cripple"), created the sculptures decorating the basilica with tools strapped to his wrists, as he suffered from the effects of a progressively debilitating disease that affected the use of his limbs and hands.* © JACK FIELDS/CORBIS

limbs, he was nicknamed O Aleijadinho ("the little cripple"). The disease caused him intense suffering, although he was able to keep the use of his thumbs and index fingers, essential for the more precise movements of sculpting. Nonetheless, Lisboa had an extremely prolific career and produced the majority of his documented work after the onset of the disease.

The vast majority of Lisboa's architectural and sculptural works are located in the Minas Gerais cities of Ouro Prêto, São João del Rei, Sabará and Cogonhas do Campo. Many of his statues are now in Brazilian museums (São Paulo, Museu de Arte Sacra; Ouro Prêto, Museu de Inconfidência) and religious centers, as well as in private collections.

Lisboa received most of his commissions in the 1770s, immediately before the onset of his disease. His first large-scale work in soapstone was for the portal of the Church of Carmo of Sabará in 1770. In the 1780s he completed the internal ornamentation for the church. The Church of St. Francis of Assisi in Ouro Prêto, another important commission, most thoroughly embodies Lisboa's architec-

tural and ornamentational concepts. His highly original architectural design combines a Portuguese mannerist rectangular church with a curvilinear plan after Francesco Borromini. The prestige and success of this project led to many more architectural commissions.

Lisboa's most important sculptural legacy lies in the pilgrimage church of Bom Jesus de Matozinhos, Congonhas do Campo. Aleijadinho and his assistants sculpted a total of sixty-six life-size figures of Christ's Passion (1796–1799). These sculptures stand in six chapels forming the *Via Sacra,* or Way of the Cross, ending on a sacred hill. At the top of the hill lie twelve life-size soapstone sculptures of the Old Testament prophets (1800–1805). The ensemble of statues is emotionally evocative in the tradition of medieval religious drama, allowing worshipers to participate in the staging of sacred theater as they climb the stairway and view the sculptures from varying angles.

Called "the new Praxiteles" by his fellow artists, Lisboa died in Vila Rica at the age of seventy-six, having never accumulated great wealth or social prestige.

See also Painting and Sculpture

■ ■ *Bibliography*

Bazin, Germain. *L'Architecture religieuse baroque au Brésil*, 2 vols. São Paulo, Brazil: Museu de Arte, 1956–1958. (catalogue raisonné)

Ribeiro de Oliveira, Myriam Andrade. *O Aleijandinho e sua oficina*. São Paulo, Brazil: Editora Capivara, 2002. (in Portuguese and English)

AMY J. BUONO (2005)

LITERACY EDUCATION

Literacy is a process by which one expands one's knowledge of reading and writing in order to develop one's thinking and learning for the purpose of understanding oneself and the world. This process is fundamental to achieving competence in every educational subject. Since literacy is a necessary foundation for educational achievement and it has not always been legal for black people to be literate in the Americas, an understanding of historical approaches to literacy education for black children can elucidate larger relationships between individuals, communities, and the world. In an effort to ensure children's success and ability to be self-determined in a largely literate society, approaches to literacy education have included multilingual, multicultural, and multimedia resources.

The institution of slavery and subsequent racialization that situated Africans in America in isolated speech communities contributed to the development of what is now termed African American English (AAE). Many scholars have noted the effects of slavery on literacy education; they have also noted the effects that isolation had on language acquisition and development (Baugh, 1999; Morgan, 2002; Rickford and Rickford, 2000; Smitherman, 2000). Just as efforts were made to categorize enslaved Africans as inferior to European settlers, similar campaigns were also made to stigmatize the language of African Americans. The outcome of these subjugation strategies contributes to negative language attitudes concerning AAE today. Negative language attitudes can be a barrier to literacy education because literacy draws upon the linguistic and cultural knowledge of language learners as they create and interpret texts. In response, various researchers have empirically countered trends to designate AAE (and the related inferences regarding the cognitive abilities of African Americans) as different and somehow deficient compared to a European-centered norm. Moreover, educators have combated such educational practices by incorporating culturally and linguistically relevant curricula.

Enslaved Africans developed strategies to acquire and maintain literacy. Despite legislation forbidding literacy, some enslaved Africans were nevertheless literate in various languages, such as Arabic, English, French, Spanish, and Portuguese. After Emancipation and the passing of amendments that secured citizenship rights, examples of literacy education in schools began to emerge. Efforts such as the use of spirituals and other cultural materials to facilitate multiple literacies of black youth are evident throughout the era of segregation (Yasin, 1999). As integration policies began to be enforced, the number of black schoolteachers declined, as did linguistically and culturally relevant literacy education. During the 1970s, with civil rights legislation and the advent of the Black Power movement, there were increased efforts to include alienated African-American learners from language study. Civil rights legislation, Title VI in particular, protected students against discrimination and also served as the basis for cases (e.g., *Lau v. Nichols*) that protected the rights of other language minorities in the United States. Ensuring equitable education for African-American children did not end with legal and policy changes. The Black Power movement revolutionized societal values and perspectives regarding African culture, language, and history. Such attitude shifts were reflected in curricula that were intended to support African-American youth. Theories of how to best make curricula culturally and linguistically relevant flourished.

SESD APPROACHES TO LITERACY

One of the most noted programmatic changes in literacy education resulted in readers for Standard English as a Second Dialect (SESD). These programs approached the literacy of African-American children much like English as a Second Language (ESL) programs approach nonnative English speakers: They introduced standard English (SE) grammatical structures while attempting to respect students' home dialects/languages. SESD programs were launched in urban areas around the United States, such as Los Angeles, Chicago, Washington, D.C., and Detroit, as well as in rural areas where large numbers of African-American children were schooled (e.g., north and central Florida). Similar programs were initiated in urban areas throughout the Caribbean as well. According to Marcyliena Morgan, in Chicago and Florida, for example, the curriculum of SESD programs included (a) culturally relevant material such as "dialect stories and folk tales . . . , (b) grammatical exercises that reviewed AAE exclusively, (c) grammatical exercises that tested General English (GE) exclusively, and (d) contrastive exercises that included both forms" (Morgan, 2002, p. 141). Morgan criticizes SESD programs for not adequately informing students' parents about the functions of dialect readers and how they are used to teach standard literacy. Such priming was necessary given the nation's history of stigmatizing African-American language varieties. This lack of collaboration with community constituents eventually led to the decline of the SESD, although numerous studies attested to their success. Morgan observes that "these readers were an innovation that actually contradicted everything that the community—and most Americans—expected to happen in a classroom. No one had been socialized around dialect readers and with the notion that a quality education included them—especially when integrated educational institutions had worked so hard to exclude black children culturally" (2002, p. 141).

Despite initial community rejection, programs that are philosophically similar to the SESD programs emerged. The unified school districts of Ann Arbor, Los Angeles, and Oakland are noted for implementing such literacy programs (e.g., the Language Development Program for African American Students in Los Angeles). Though these programs received negative and ill-informed media coverage, they were praised by many professionals for being linguistically sound, and these programs are considered a legal right by various organizations ranging from the National Council of Teachers of English (NCTE) and the Linguistic Society of America (LSA) to the United Nations Educational, Scientific, and Cultural Organization (UNESCO). The social uproar that followed the Oakland Resolution, which is popularly referred to as the "Ebonics debate," is instructive for understanding pervasive stereotypes and prejudice regarding the languages and cultures of African Americans. It is also indicative of how negative language attitudes can continue to affect literacy strategies via the "miseducation" of the masses through the media. Experts have responded by educating both the public and policymakers about the utility of AAE for literacy education.

Marcyliena Morgan (2002) and John Rickford (2000) outline these histories in detail by explaining—case by case—how knowledge of AAE can positively and empirically increase the literacies of black children. However, because literacy involves knowledge of culture and language, multilingual, AAE-informed educational programs are not the only ones designed to facilitate literacy among black children. Recently, literacy efforts that include multicultural education, critical pedagogy, and even popular cultural approaches that use hip-hop have emerged.

Multicultural Education

Multicultural education is a process of school reform that ensures equitable education for all students by embracing diversity and affirming pluralism in pedagogical practice.

Some scholars posit that critical pedagogy is an underlying philosophy of multicultural education, but various scholars define the concept differently (Bank and Banks, p. 48). Most agree that the goal of multicultural education is social change. James Banks and Cherry McGee Banks (2004, p. 20) describe the five dimensions of multicultural education as content integration, knowledge construction, prejudice reduction, equity pedagogy, and empowering school culture and social structure.

Critical Pedagogy

Critical pedagogy was introduced by Paulo Freire and Donaldo Macedo (1987) in their seminal work regarding literacy as empowerment for oppressed peoples. Henry Giroux developed the concept of critical pedagogy into a field of literacy research that has important implications concerning the education of black children. Giroux writes that "pedagogy in the critical sense illuminates the relationship among knowledge, authority and power. . . . [It is] about the knowledge and practices that teachers, cultural workers, and students might engage in together" (p. 30). This perspective corresponds to the goals of literacy education explained above. Teaching children to use reading and writing in an effort to expand how they make sense of their worlds entails criticism (assessing the strengths and weaknesses) of current knowledge production, authority, and power relations.

If Giroux is correct, then perhaps the future of literacy education lies in strategies that encompass aspects of youth culture, such as popular culture and hip-hop in particular, in order to further make literacy education appealing and relevant to youths' lived experiences. Indeed, teachers can design curricula utilizing hip-hop to facilitate youth-centered discussions about literacy (Morgan, 2001; Smitherman, 2000; Yasin, 1999). Educational scholars have noted this utility as they have researched teachers who guide students through identification of specific literary terms and grammatical concepts by studying hip-hop lyrics as texts or as bases for lessons on intertextuality (e.g., Ladson-Billings, pp. 82–84; Mahiri, pp. 111–117; Yasin, pp. 213–217). The educators featured in these studies often use hip-hop as an exercise in "translation" and as a supplement to using AAE-informed literacy approaches in the classroom. Therefore, these contemporary strategies combine and build upon the approaches to literacy education highlighted above in the SESD programs, multicultural education and critical pedagogy.

Given the myriad approaches to literacy education for black children, one might hope that their implementation will eventually erase negative language attitudes that impede educational achievement and community success.

Just as the enslaved Africans innovated in their efforts to ensure literacy—even when it was illegal—educators and other experts concerned with the literacy of black children will probably continue to innovate as they strive to improve community conditions and bridge educational achievement disparities.

See also Education in the United States; English, African-American

▪ ▪ *Bibliography*

Banks, James, and Cherry A. McGee Banks, eds. *Multicultural Education: Issues and Perspectives.* Hoboken, N.J.: John Wiley, 2004.

Baugh, John. *Out of the Mouths of Slaves: African American Language and Educational Malpractice.* Austin: University of Texas Press, 1999.

Freire, Paulo, and Donaldo Macedo. *Literacy: Reading the Word and the World.* London: Bergin and Garvey, 1987.

Giroux, Henry. *Disturbing Pleasures: Learning Popular Culture.* New York: Routledge, 1994.

Ladson-Billings, Gloria. *The Dreamkeepers: Successful Teachers of African American Children.* San Francisco: Jossey-Bass, 1994.

Mahiri, Jabari. *Shooting for Excellence: African American and Youth Culture in New Century Schools.* New York: Teachers College Press, 1998.

Morgan, Marcyliena. "'Nuttin' but a G thang': Grammar and Language Ideology in Hip Hop Identity." In *Sociocultural and Historical Contexts of African American English,* edited by Sonja L. Lanehart. Philadelphia: John Benjamins North America, 2001.

Morgan, Marcyliena. *Language, Discourse, and Power in African American Culture.* Cambridge: Cambridge University Press, 2002.

Rickford, John R., and Russell J. Rickford. *Spoken Soul: The Story of Black English.* New York: Wiley, 2000.

Smitherman, Geneva. *Talkin' That Talk: Language, Culture, and Education in African America.* London: Routledge, 2000.

Yasin, Jon A. "Rap in the African-American Music Tradition: Cultural Assertion and Continuity." In *Race and Ideology: Language, Symbolism, and Popular Culture,* edited by Arthur K. Spears. Detroit: Wayne State University Press, 1999.

DAWN-ELISSA T. I. FISCHER (2005)

Cover of the Messenger, *November, 1923. During its early years the editorial policy of the* Messenger *was one of militant socialism, but by 1923 the journal was taking a more favorable view of the accomplishments of the black middle class.* MANUSCRIPTS, ARCHIVES AND RARE BOOKS DIVISION, SCHOMBURG CENTER FOR RESEARCH IN BLACK CULTURE, THE NEW YORK PUBLIC LIBRARY, ASTOR, LENOX AND TILDEN FOUNDATIONS.

an African-American context from its beginning to the mid-1990s. The second article by Shelly Eversley offers an update on changes in the field in the late-twentieth and early-twenty-first centuries.

LITERARY CRITICISM
   David Lionel Smith

SCHOLARSHIP IN THE TWENTY-FIRST CENTURY
   Shelly Eversley

LITERARY CRITICISM, U.S.

▪┨▪

This entry consists of two distinct articles. The first by David Lionel Smith provides an overview of Literary Criticism in

OVERVIEW

In his *Notes on the State of Virginia,* Thomas Jefferson, to illustrate his assertions of Negro inferiority, remarked, "Religion indeed has produced a Phyllis Whately [sic; reference is to Phillis Wheatley], but it could not produce a poet. The compositions published under her name are below the dignity of criticism" (p. 189). Jefferson's attitude of dismissal extended equally to the writers Jupiter Hammon and Ignatius Sancho and to every other black person. Though his discussion of Wheatley's work falls short, by his own admission, of literary criticism, it initiates a tradition of disparagement in which European-American critics use ideology as a grounds for judging African-American writing inferior. Not surprisingly, the work of African-American critics has often been conceived, at least implicitly, in response to such critical chauvinism.

African-American literary criticism should be understood to comprise several interlocking categories of writing: criticism of works by African Americans, criticism by African Americans, and criticism of African-American works by African-American critics. Furthermore, criticism includes literary biography, literary history, literary theory, and cultural theory as well as analyses of specific literary works. Thus African-American literary criticism is a broadly defined genre, and because the racial category "black" or "African American" has always been heavily laden with social values, literary criticism has been one of the realms in which questions of racial values and racial identity have always been articulated and contested.

The explicitly Euro-chauvinist tradition that uses literary criticism as a pretext for assertions of white supremacy and black inferiority, initiated by Jefferson and perpetuated through the late twentieth century, has its vigorously antagonistic counterpart in the tradition that commits itself to demonstrating through criticism the distinctiveness and integrity of African-American artists and culture. Despite their sharp disagreements, these two traditions hold in common the premise that the race of the author should be a major consideration for the critic. This presumption, needless to say, has not generally been inflicted upon European-American authors, and such differential treatment has provoked anger or anxiety in many black writers. Ironically, this passion or its absence has manifested itself in writers' works and has in turn shaped the critical responses to their works. Such are the literary burdens of race.

In one sense, Jefferson's overtly dismissive comments are anomalous to the critical tradition. If work is "below the dignity of criticism," why would a critic lower himself to it? More typically, racial chauvinism has been expressed in the form of condescending praise. For example, in 1926, just as the Harlem Renaissance was beginning, John Nelson published *The Negro Character in American Literature*, the first full-length study of this subject. Nelson took particular delight in the comic and sentimental portraits of black people in works by turn-of-the-century writers such as Thomas Nelson Page, Irwin Russell, and Joel Chandler Harris:

[the Negro's] irresistible gaiety, his gift for dance and song, his spontaneity and childish delight in gay colors and all forms of display, his love of high-sounding words, his fondness for chicken and watermelon, his gullibility, his excuse-making powers, his whimsicality, his illogicalness and superstition, his droll philosophy, his genial shiftlessness and laziness, his "superb capacity for laughter" — these traits were appreciated as never before, were revalued and pronounced delightful.

In other words, Nelson loved minstrelsy. Nelson' comments are noteworthy because they both reflect the attitudes of many critics and indicate implicitly the kind of portrayals of black people that critics found acceptable, even in works by black writers: colorful and comical.

The impatience of such critics with black writers who rendered more serious or realistic depictions of African-American life is articulated by David Littlejohn in *Black on White: A Critical Survey of Writing by American Negroes* (1966):

A white reader is saddened, then burdened, then numbed by the deadly sameness, the bleak wooden round of ugly emotions and situations; the same frustrated dreams, the same issues and charges and formulas and events repeated over and over, in book after book . . .the responding spirit is dulled, finally, bored by the iteration of hopelessness, the sordid limitation of the soul in the tight closet of the black imagination.

By contrast, Littlejohn praises Gwendolyn Brooks because she is "far more a poet than a Negro." The implication, clearly, is that "Negro" and "poet" are somehow antithetical. Such remarks illustrate the continuity of racially dismissive and condescending attitudes in American literary criticism over a span of two centuries. African-American writers and critics have produced their work fully cognizant that many highly educated white Americans continue to espouse such views.

Not surprisingly, then, the most conspicuous African-American critical tradition has been polemical. This polemical tradition has been primarily concerned to use literary criticism as a means of addressing social issues, not as a form of aesthetic engagement. In the nineteenth century, African-American criticism belonged almost exclusively to this genre; but there was relatively little of it, since the quantity of African-American literature was small and was primarily limited to the black periodical press. Not until after the turn of the century did the social and economic conditions exist to support a class of black professional critics. Thus the criticism published during the nineteenth century was generally the work of activists who published work in various genres. Frederick Douglass, for example, sometimes commented on books, but he was not a literary critic. Similarly, characters in the fiction of Frances E. W. Harper and Pauline Hopkins sometimes discuss books, but this is not what we mean by literary criticism, either.

Kelly Miller, a professor and administrator at Howard University, published fine, erudite, vigorously argued, and elegantly balanced essays on a broad range of topics. His collection *Race Adjustments* (1908) includes essays on Thomas Dixon's *The Leopard's Spots* and *Walt Whitman*. The essay on The Leopard's Spots, a novel that sold over a million copies, challenges the racist views and historical accuracy of Dixon's narrative about Reconstruction. Furthermore, Miller contests Dixon's bigoted and inaccurate depiction of African Americans and racial politics at the turn of the century. In this essay, the critic appears in the guise of racial spokesman and defender. By contrast, "What Walt Whitman Means to the Negro" allows Miller to display his literary erudition and sensibility as well as to make a social point. He celebrates Whitman's work because of its democratic inclusiveness, such that "all are welcome; none are denied, shunned, avoided, ridiculed, or made to feel ashamed" (p. 204). Furthermore, he asserts:

> Whitman has a special meaning to the Negro, not only because of his literary portrayal; he has lessons also. He inculcates the lesson of ennobling self-esteem. He teaches the Negro that "there is no sweeter fat than sticks to his own bones." He urges him to accept nothing that "insults his own soul" (p. 208).

These comments reflected Miller's own grounding in a late nineteenth-century culture in which moral issues were a paramount concern for literary critics.

That same predisposition is conspicuous in the literary criticism of the most influential African-American literary critic of Miller's generation: W. E. B. Du Bois. Du Bois is not generally regarded as a literary critic, but in judging intellectuals trained in the late nineteenth century, disciplinary categories of the late twentieth century can be misleading. Like Kelly Miller and Charles Waddell Chesnutt, Du Bois was a "man of letters." He published distinguished writing in virtually every genre. As editor of *The Crisis* for twenty-five years, he was easily the most widely read African-American writer of the early twentieth century. In his articles, columns, and commentaries, Du Bois addressed virtually every issue, event, and publication of relevance to African Americans.

It was not merely the quantity of his output nor the size of his audience, however, that made Du Bois so influential. Rather, Du Bois's accomplishments as a scholar and activist, his incomparable erudition, his elegant writing style and refined literary sensibility, and his intense passion for truth, justice, and beauty all combined to make him authoritative and compelling. Thus his judgments about particular artists or works carried extraordinary weight. Du Bois used his enormous prestige to endorse and publicize the works of black writers, including Harlem Renaissance figures such as Countee Cullen, Langston Hughes, and Jessie Fauset.

The essay that best represents Du Bois as a visionary and inspirational critic is his "Criteria of Negro Art" (1926). In it he reiterates his belief, earlier expressed in *The Souls of Black Folk* (1903), that black people have a special calling to revive in a debased, materialist nation an appreciation for beauty and higher values:

> Who shall let this world be beautiful? Who shall restore to men the glory of sunsets and the peace of quiet sleep? We black folk may help for we have within us as a race new stirrings; stirrings of the beginning of a new appreciation of joy, a new desire to create, of a new will to be; as though in this morning of group life we had awakened from some sleep that at once dimly mourns the past and dreams a splendid future. . . .

After declaring the unity of beauty with truth and justice, Du Bois concludes with a prophecy: "The ultimate art coming from black folk is going to be just as beautiful, and beautiful largely in the same ways, as the art that comes from white folk, or yellow, or red; but the point today is that until the art of the black folk compels recognition they will not be rated as human." For Du Bois, then, the creation of black art and the struggle for social justice were inseparable, and by implication, artists should be understood as warriors in this struggle, not deserters from it. This formulation encourages young artists to pursue their own aesthetic visions and offers them protection against charges of irrelevance or frivolity, such as political pragmatists have often advanced against art. While Du Bois did not hesitate to criticize particular works bluntly and even harshly, his broader critical impact was as a champion of literary art. As a critic, he exerted a major influence on artists of the Harlem Renaissance; and as a model of intellectual activism, he influenced the radical critics of the 1930s and 1960s.

Though Du Bois was the preeminent African-American critic and intellectual life of the Harlem Renaissance decade (the 1920s), several other notable critics of African-American writing emerged during that period. James Weldon Johnson deserves to be remembered alongside Du Bois as a truly exemplary figure who exerted influence in several fields. He was a poet, novelist, essayist, songwriter, civil rights leader, and diplomat, and though he is not usually described as a literary critic, his preface to the first edition of *The Book of American Negro Poetry* (1921) is one of the seminal essays on African-American poetry.

Johnson's preface serves a number of purposes at once. It identifies the major styles and tendencies of African-American artistic expression and assesses the relationship of black culture to the broader American and international cultures. It considers the relationship between vernacular culture and fine art traditions and does so with a refreshingly uncondescending appreciation of black popular arts such as the blues and the cakewalk. And not least, it provides a concise historical overview of African-American poetry from Jupiter Hammon and Phillis Wheatley to Langston Hughes and other poets born about the turn of the century. In effect, the essay sets a broad context with its detailed discussions of eighteenth- and nineteenth-century poets and other aesthetic forms, though the anthology actually begins with Paul Laurence Dunbar. In its time *The Book of American Negro Poetry* was important for introducing many poets who were unfamiliar to the reading public. Its preface endures, however, as one of the best and most insightful discussions of the African-American poetic tradition.

Another distinguished and influential critic of the 1920s was Alain Leroy Locke, a philosopher, essayist, editor, art collector, critic, and the first African-American Rhodes scholar. Like Du Bois, Locke was a man of broad interests and influence. He is most commonly remembered as the editor of the *New Negro* (1925), a volume that announced and sought to define the cultural explosion known subsequently as the Harlem Renaissance. At the time it was more often called "the New Negro Movement," and Alain Locke was regarded as its midwife and intellectual leader.

Locke's literary essays of the 1920s reflect a fundamental conflict between two antagonistic intellectual tendencies. On the one hand, Locke was deeply committed to empirical social science and to an understanding of race in social and cultural terms. This tendency is expressed in his introductory essay, "The New Negro," when he argues that the Negro Renaissance should be understood in relation to recent migration from the rural South, the black response to urban social conditions, and a political consciousness developed from struggles over race, labor, eco-

nomics, and related issues. In this sense, he argues, developments in Harlem should be understood in the context of national and international developments, and Harlem would become a "race capital" because "Harlem has the same role to play for the New Negro as Dublin has had for the New Ireland or Prague for the New Czechoslovakia" (p. 7).

On the other hand, Locke's thinking also reveals a strain of romantic primitivism, a tendency that some scholars attribute to his close association with the white philanthropist and Negrophile Charlotte Osgood Mason. "Godmother," as she insisted she be called, believed that white civilization was decadent and doomed unless it could be infused with the vitality inherent in "primitive" cultures, such as black and Native American. Thus she undertook to subsidize African-American artists, and with Locke as her talent scout, she became a patroness to Langston Hughes, Zora Neale Hurston, Aaron Douglas, and others. Locke, himself, received considerable largesse from Godmother, enabling him to travel to Europe annually and helping him to acquire what developed into a major collection of African art. "Negro Youth Speaks," Locke's introduction to the literature section of the volume, argues:

> Art cannot disdain the gift of a natural irony, of a transfiguring imagination, of rhapsodic Biblical speech, of dynamic musical swing, of cosmic emotion such as only the gifted pagans knew, of a return to nature, not by way of the forced and worn formula of Romanticism, but through the closeness of an imagination that has never broken kinship with nature (p. 52).

Since Locke published this primitivist manifesto in 1925 and did not meet Mrs. Mason until 1926, perhaps their relationship would be more aptly described as a confluence of like minds. Mrs. Mason doubtless encouraged this aspect of Locke's thinking, but she did not initiate it.

By the late 1930s Locke repudiated primitivism, returning to an emphasis on social experience as the basis of black cultural expression. Locke might be more aptly described as a cultural critic than as a literary critic, strictly speaking. Nevertheless, his literary influence was substantial because of his essays, anthologies, correspondence, social activity, and his role as a procurer of patronage. In addition to *The New Negro*, he also published *Plays of Negro Life* (1927), coedited with T. Montgomery Gregory.

Another influential anthologist of this period was William Stanley Braithwaite. Unlike Locke, Braithwaite was himself a creative writer—a poet—and his purview was not exclusively or even primarily African American.

Raised by very fair-skinned parents who encouraged young William not to associate with black people, Braithwaite eventually developed into a poet whose work betrayed virtually no evidence of his African-American background. He developed a substantial reputation as an essayist and reviewer for leading literary magazines such as *Atlantic Monthly, North American Review,* and *Scribner's.* His greatest fame and influence, however, accrued from his several poetry anthologies, such as *The Book of Elizabethan Verse,* and the series of annual compilations that he edited from 1913 to 1929, called *Anthology of Magazine Verse.* In this editorial capacity, he helped to bring national attention to such younger writers as Carl Sandburg, Edgar Lee Masters, and Vachel Lindsay. Though he was celebrated by African-Americans—for example, he won the Spingarn Medal in 1918—many of his readers were unaware that he was black. Braithwaite was unique in enjoying a successful literary career in which his race was neither a stigma nor a premise of his professional identity.

During the 1920s the first serious histories of black literature began to appear. Foremost among them was Benjamin Brawley's *The Negro Genius* (1937), originally published in 1918 as *The Negro in Literature and Art.* Benjamin Griffith Brawley was a professor of literature with degrees from Chicago and Harvard, who spent the bulk of his teaching career at Shaw University and Howard. He published textbooks on English literature and a biography of Paul Laurence Dunbar, but *The Negro Genius* was his most enduring work. As its original title suggests, *The Negro Genius* was actually a history of African Americans in all of the arts: literature, drama, visual arts, and music. Brawley's objective was to trace the various manifestations of African-American creative talent, and his book is virtually an encyclopedia of black artists, offering brief introductory essays on each, in chronological order.

The Negro Genius has embedded within it a kind of racial theory, distinguishing between the inherent gifts of "people of mixed blood" and "blacks":

> People of mixed blood have given us the college presidents, the administrators, the Government employees; but the blacks are the singers and seers. Black slaves gave us the spirituals; modern composers of a lighter hue transcribe them. . . . In other words, the mixed element in the race may represent the Negro's talent, but it is upon the black element that he must rely for his genius (pp. 8-9).

"Negro genius" is, according to Brawley, "lyrical, imaginative, subjective." Though Brawley makes such claims in a spirit of race pride, vindicating dark-skinned people, racial theory cuts in both directions. If the aesthetic is black, the scientific must be white. If genius is racial, the lack of genius must also be racial. Brawley's larger intention is to celebrate African-American achievement; but framing the argument in racial terms simply perpetuates the basis for invidious hierarchies, which has always been the primary function of racial ideology. As a critical premise this notion is also flawed, because it encourages the critic to appreciate the lyricism of black artists but not their formal designs. It stereotypes black artists even as it celebrates them. Nevertheless, *The Negro Genius* did a valuable service by providing a broad, concise, and readily accessible account of African-American artistic achievement.

Another notable work of this period was *The Negro Author and His Development* (1930) by Vernon Loggins, which unlike Brawley's work focused exclusively on black literature. The most sophisticated history of African-American literature published during this era, however, was *To Make a Poet Black* (1939) by J. Saunders Redding. Indeed, no book is more deserving to be regarded as the classic African-American literary history. Redding's book is distinguished by its literary style, its conceptual design, its high aesthetic standards, and its vigorous critical argument. Unlike Brawley, who was constrained by the essentially apologetic conception of *The Negro Genius* to praise the authors he discussed in order to persuade a doubting audience that black people are capable of creating serious art, Redding defined for himself a critical agenda, committed to analyzing and evaluating the work of black writers.

Redding begins with an acknowledgment of the conflicting social imperatives that have bedeviled black writers, the sharply opposed expectations of black and white audiences. As a consequence of this conflict, Redding argues, "Negro writers have been obliged to have two faces." These two impulses Redding defines as, first, the aesthetic quest for honest, well-crafted self-expression, and second, the political quest to contribute to the advancement of one's oppressed race. In Redding's own concise description, "these two necessities can be traced with varying degrees of clarity—now one and now the other predominant—like threads through the whole cloth" (p. 3). This describes aptly a trait that has characterized African-American writing throughout its history, and accordingly it provides a set of terms that Redding can use cogently and consistently to analyze texts from Jupiter Hammon to Sterling Brown.

While he addresses the writers' work with a sympathetic understanding of their circumstances and an appreciation of their particular talents and achievements, Redding never relinquishes his commitment to the primacy of aesthetic concerns. For him this means that literature should be not just skillfully wrought but also honest, passionate, and purposeful. Thus, while he acknowledges Phillis Wheatly as a talented and important poet, he deplores her glib religiosity, her acceptance of slavery, and her failure to identify with the plights of other slaves as attitudes that undermine her art:

> It is this negative, bloodless, unracial quality in Phillis Wheatley that makes her seem superficial, especially to members of her own race. Hers is a spirit-denying-the-flesh attitude that somehow cannot seem altogether real as the essential quality and core of one whose life should have made her sensitive to the very things she denies. In this sense none of her poetry is real (p. 11).

For similar reasons, he criticizes the work of William Stanley Braithwaite, dismissing it as "the most outstanding example of perverted energy that the period from 1903 to 1917 produced" (p. 89). Braithwaite's work, he argues, "is pretty and skillful poetry, but it is not poetry afire with the compelling necessity for expression. No passion (even slightly remembered in tranquility) of pain or joy, no spring of pure personal knowledge or conviction justifies it" (p. 91). For Redding, neither deficient literary technique nor deficient moral fervor is acceptable, and both of these poets lack the latter.

In the early fiction of Charles Chesnutt, Redding finds work that meets his high standards. He declares: "His early career was a great artistic success, for he did the one thing needful to the American Negro writer: He worked dangerous, habit-ridden material with passive calm and fearlessness. . . . He exposed the Negro to critical analysis" (p. 76). The terms that he uses to convey praise reflect Redding's insistence on originality, honesty, and cogency. The poems and prefaces of James Weldon Johnson, especially in *God's Trombones*, also embody for Redding the mature achievement of African-American writing:

> Aside from the beauty of the poems, the essay which prefaces them is of the first importance for it definitely hails back from the urban and sophisticated to the earthy exuberance of the Negro's kinship with the earth, the fields, the suns and rains of the South. Discarding the "mutilations of dialect," Mr. Johnson yet retains the speech forms, the idea patterns, and the rich racial flavor (p. 121).

Revealingly, Redding places Johnson out of chronological sequence at the end of the book, just before Sterling Brown and Zora Neale Hurston. These writers represent for him the most promising achievements of African-

American writing. *To Make a Poet Black* is a monumental work of African-American literary criticism because it is the first book-length history of African-American literature that breaks entirely with the tradition of racial apologetics, devoting itself instead to a sustained examination of how social pressures, cultural traditions, and personal sensibility interact in the making of African-American literary art.

Sterling A. Brown was a major poet of his generation and a major critic as well. *The Negro in American Fiction* (1937) and *Negro Poetry and Drama* (1937) are exhaustive works on their respective topics. Brown's critical approach is primarily that of descriptive bibliography. His books are immensely useful, but they provide concise summaries or assessments rather than detailed discussions of individual works. A major concern of both books is "to show how attitudes to Negro life have developed in American thinking" (*Negro Poetry*, p. 2). Thus Brown surveys both black and white writers, assessing how African Americans have been depicted in literary works. Unlike Redding, he does not emphasize aesthetic evaluation. Nevertheless, these are works of formidable scholarship, and they have remained important to students of race in American literature, though they are not so pertinent to theoretical or evaluative concerns as *To Make a Poet Black*.

In 1939 the College Language Association (CLA) was formed to provide a professional outlet for African-American literary scholars, who were in effect excluded from the Modern Language Association (MLA). Like the MLA, the CLA held annual meetings and published a journal, which for many years was the primary outlet for scholarship by black critics. The formation of the CLA was an important event, since it marked the emergence of African-American literary scholars as a professional class. Two of the most prominent of the black academic critics during this period were Nick Aaron Ford (1904–1982), author of *The Contemporary Negro Novel* (1936), and Hugh Gloster (1911–), who wrote *Negro Voices in American Fiction* (1948). Blyden Jackson (1910–) is also a member of this generation, but he did not publish his most important book, the first volume of a general history of African-American writing, until 1989, after his retirement. *A History of Afro-American Literature: The Long Beginning, 1746-1895* is a monumental achievement. A model of thorough and detailed scholarship, it supersedes all other histories of African-American literature and establishes Jackson as a preeminent scholar in the field at a time when others of his generation are regarded as forebears, not contemporaries. Jackson's lengthy bibliographical essay alone, which encompasses the entire fields of historical and literary scholarship on African Americans from the beginnings to the 1980s, makes his book an indispensable reference work.

These scholars of the 1930s and 1940s taught in black colleges, and the heavy course loads in those institutions limited their opportunities for research and writing. Thus, with a few exceptions, the literary scholars of this generation exerted their influence primarily through their articles, professional associations, and teaching, not through books. Ironically, however, most black colleges did not offer courses on black literature. (Sterling Brown at Howard was a pioneering exception.) English professors were expected to do research and writing on "canonical" (i.e., white) authors; and this remained the case even through the 1960s. The work of a few outstanding critics notwithstanding, then, the volume of criticism on African-American writers remained limited. Only in the 1980s, with the full integration of American universities, the gradual development of African-American literature courses as regular components in English department curricula, and the erosion of racist and elitist attitudes within the academy did it become possible for a generation of scholars to turn their full attention to the study of African-American literature.

Meanwhile, during the next two decades, the most important works of African-American criticism were written by literary artists, such as Richard Wright, James Baldwin, and Ralph Ellison; and their most famous literary essays were polemical pieces that echoed the larger debate between Marxists and liberals over the value and function of art. For instance, Richard Wright's essay "Blueprint for Negro Writing" (1937), rejecting black nationalist attitudes and most previous black literature, declares a Marxist agenda for African-American fiction. By the time he wrote "How Bigger Was Born" (1940), his meditation on Native Son, Wright's thinking had begun to manifest existentialist ideas that would dominate his work of the late forties and fifties. Wright's most sustained treatment of black writers, and one of his finest critical essays, is "The Literature of the Negro in the United States," which was published in a French periodical and later included in his book White Man, Listen! (1957). In any case, the unprecedented success of Native Son made Wright the preeminent African-American literary figure of the 1940s. His forthright identification with the Left seemed to convey an imperative for all black writers.

Not surprisingly, some writers took exception. James Baldwin's essays "Everybody's Protest Novel" (1949) and "Many Thousands Gone" (1951) reject the entire tradition of protest fiction, from Uncle Tom's Cabin to Native Son. In Baldwin's view, protest fiction dehumanizes characters by subsuming individual psychology and experience to so-ciological generalizations. Baldwin argues instead for fiction that foregrounds the individual perspective. One may debate how accurately Baldwin describes Wright and other protest writers, but clearly these two essays anticipate the character of Baldwin's own fiction and essays.

Ralph Ellison also distanced himself from Wright, but he did so by asserting his own alternative, humanist vision rather than by attacking Wright. Ellison's most famous skirmish was an exchange with the leftist critic Irving Howe, whose "Black Boys and Native Sons" (1963) chided with Baldwin, Ellison, and others for deviating from the activist model of Wright's fiction. Ellison's two-installment rejoinder, combined in his collection Shadow and Act into a single essay called "The World and the Jug," is a devastating deflation of Howe's argument. Ellison's importance as a critic, however, transcends such debates. With a few exceptions, Ellison's essays are not concerned with African-American literature but rather with issues of literary art more broadly framed. He does, however, give detailed attention to African-American music and comic traditions. As a theorist of the relationship between vernacular culture and high art, Ellison has been among our most sophisticated thinkers. Essays such as "Change the Joke and Slip the Yoke" and "The Little Man at Chehaw Station" are classic inquiries into African-American sensibility and the nature of American culture. The work collected in Shadow and Act and Going to the Territory demonstrates that Ellison was unsurpassed as a literary essayist.

The prominence of Baldwin and Ellison notwithstanding, the 1950s and early 1960s was a relatively moribund period in the history of African-American literary criticism. Though many talented black critics were active during this period, surprisingly little was published on African-American literature. One exceptional critic whose work, ironically, corresponds to this quiescent period is Nathan A. Scott Jr. (1925–). A brilliant and prolific critic with degrees in both divinity and literature, Scott used his books to explore the manifestations of moral, psychological, and existential conflicts in modern literature. His works include Rehearsals of Discomposure: Alienation and Reconciliation in Modern Literature (1952); The Tragic Vision and the Christian Faith (1957); and Negative Capability: Studies in the New Literature and the Religious Situation (1969). Scott taught at Howard from 1948 to 1955, at the University of Chicago for twenty years, and subsequently at the University of Virginia. Though he published a splendid essay on Richard Wright, "The Dark and Haunted Tower of Richard Wright" (1964), Scott, arguably the most acclaimed and distinguished African-American literary critic of his generation, seldom turned his attention to black writers.

Several other critics of this generation were instrumental in moving the study of black literature from black colleges, where heavy teaching and administrative demands made the completion of book projects very difficult, to the major and predominantly white research universities. That group includes Richard Barksdale (University of Illinois), George Kent (University of Chicago), Charles T. Davis (Yale), and Darwin T. Turner (University of Iowa). Though all of these critics published important essays, they were most influential as teachers, mentors, and professional colleagues—daunting scholarly models who set very high standards and proposed collective agendas for the future study of African-American literature. All of them published books after they moved to the universities, but Kent, Davis, and Turner all died prematurely, leaving major scholarly manuscripts unfinished. Nevertheless, the scholars who established black literary studies in the universities in the 1970s laid the basis for the blossoming of that field in the late 1980s and 1990s.

Mainstream academic critics, however, were not the only important critics of African-American literature during that period, and they were certainly not the most conspicuous. During the late 1960s a school of black nationalist criticism developed, and it was for a time predominant in setting the canon and shaping critical attitudes. The most influential critics of this group included Hoyt Fuller, the editor of *Negro Digest*: creative writers such as Amiri Baraka, Carolyn Rodgers, Haki Madhubuti, and Larry Neal; and academics such as Addison Gayle and Stephen Henderson. These black aesthetic critics shared a belief that literature and criticism should be socially relevant, providing a critique of racist white society and advancing the struggle for black consciousness, black solidarity, and black liberation. They favored writing that addressed political and racial issues and preferred polemics to introspection, collectivity to subjectivity, and didacticism to humor.

The critics of this movement exercised their influence through conventional publications, but because of the vogue for public meetings during this era of heightened political passions, lectures and conferences were frequent and heavily attended. Thus the oral presentation of literary arguments acquired a special importance during the black arts movement. The social and political conditions created a large and avid audience for books on black topics, and this resulted in a proliferation of anthologies, new works, and reissues. Anthologies such as *Black Fire* by Amiri Baraka and Larry Neal, *Black Expression and The Black Aesthetic* by Addison Gayle, and *Understanding the New Black Poetry* by Stephen Henderson were very influential in shaping critical opinion. Furthermore, literary criticism and literary polemics were prominent features of important intellectual journals such as *Negro Digest/Black World* and *The Black Scholar* as well as literary magazines such as *Cricket* and *The Journal of Black Poetry*. Suddenly African-American literary critics had more outlets and a broader audience than had ever existed before.

Even serious scholarly books began to be directed toward a general audience. George Kent's *Blackness and the Adventure of Western Culture* (1972), a collection of essays on twentieth-century black writers, was published by Third World Press in Chicago as the first book of literary scholarship to be issued by a black publisher. Full-scale literary histories such as Addison Gayle's *The Way of the New World* (1975) and Eugene B. Redmond's *Drumvoices: The Mission of Afro-American Poetry* (1976) were published by major publishing houses and issued in mass market paperback editions. The black arts movement made literary criticism a popular genre.

At the same time, the black arts movement provoked opposition among academic critics that was soon to repudiate black aesthetic criteria as the basis of critical discourse. Black arts critics succeeded in articulating critical principles that were appropriate to the concerns of a black nationalist politics, but unfortunately these principles, seeking to incorporate only those works that seemed properly "black," defined a very narrow literary canon that excluded most extant African-American writing. Black arts critics were especially concerned with the relationship between vernacular culture and literary expression. Ironically, this had been the predominant preoccupation of the African-American critical tradition, most of which the black arts critics rejected. Despite their dismissive attitude toward their critical forebears, the black arts critics were not able to develop a black aesthetic theory that could respond adequately to the complexities of sophisticated literary texts. Consequently, critics who wished to take seriously the black literary tradition were obliged to move beyond the narrow limits imposed by black arts theory.

This process of critical rebellion was marked by several publications of the late 1970s, most notably, the anthology of *Chant of Saints* (1979), edited by Michael S. Harper and Robert B. Stepto, and *Afro-American Literature: The Reconstruction of Instruction* (1979), edited by Dexter Fisher and Robert B. Stepto. The latter was especially important. It developed from a two-week seminar on African-American literature sponsored by the Modern Language Association in 1977, and like the seminar, it was intended to reappropriate and reformulate the teaching and scholarship in the field. The volume features essays by Stepto, Melvin Dixon, Henry Louis Gates Jr., Sherley Anne Williams, Robert Hemenway, and Robert G. O'Meally, all of whom would gain recognition in the 1980s as major critics of African-American literature. This book, which includes designs for courses and recommends areas for future inquiry, represents the successful coup that displaced black nationalist hegemony over African-American literary studies. By focusing attention on questions of narrative structure, generic convention, literary form, and rhetorical design, Reconstruction redirected black literary critics into the academic mainstream.

The book was also notable because it represented the emergence of Henry Louis Gates Jr., whose three essays in this collection brought him national prominence within the profession. Gates was the most conspicuous and arguably the most influential African-American literary critic of the 1980s and early 1990s. His most important work of criticism was The Signifying Monkey: A Theory of African-American Literary Criticism (1988), a synthetic work that used ethnolinguistic scholarship, folklore studies, and literary theory to explore "the relation of the black vernacular tradition to the Afro-American literary tradition. The book attempts to identify a theory of criticism that is inscribed within the black vernacular tradition and that in turn informs the shape of the Afro-American literary tradition" (p. xix). Gates argues that the signifying monkey derives from the messenger and trickster figure Esu-Elegbara (Legba) of the Yoruba tradition and manifests itself in literature as "Signifyin(g)," which represents "moments of self-reflexiveness" (p. xxi). Gates identifies this self-reflexiveness in the "intertexuality" through which black texts speak to and signify upon each other. Ironically, though Gates explicitly rejects the black arts critics, his endeavor to derive from African-American culture a theory of black literature represents the most thorough, scholarly, and intellectually compelling realization of what the black arts critics attempted and failed to achieve.

Despite the singularity and importance of The Signifying Monkey, Gates has exerted his greatest influence through his extensive editorial work and his vast energies as a publicist and entrepreneur for African-American literary studies. His compilations of literary criticism, such as Black Literature and Literary Theory (1984), and "The Schomburg Library of Nineteenth-Century Black Women Writers," of which he is general editor, have shaped the work of a generation of graduate students.

While Gates was clearly the most influential African-American literary critic in the final two decades of the twentieth century, the books published by Houston A. Baker Jr. constitute the most sustained, wide-ranging, and detailed inquiry into African-American literature by any critic. In a series of books beginning with Long Black Song (1972), Baker has addressed nearly all of the major Afri-can-American texts, authors, and literary movements, as well as the most compelling issues associated with the study of African-American writing and culture. Furthermore, Baker has been an assiduous student of literary theory, and each of his books has reflected his careful engagement with current and emerging forms of theory or interpretive method, seeking always to examine the pertinence of such academic trends to the study of black expressive culture. Baker's distinctive combination of vernacular culture and high theory in the reading of black texts is most compellingly demonstrated in The Journey Back (1980) and Blues, Ideology, and Afro-American Literature (1984).

Beginning his career during the era of the black arts critics, Baker shared many of their basic concerns and priorities; yet his work always displayed a scholarly thoroughness and theoretical sophistication that distinguished it from that group. Baker's work represents both the continuity of African-American critical traditions and the integration of black critics into the professional discourse of European-American criticism. Baker's unique position within the academy was aptly acknowledged when in 1992 he became the first African-American president of the Modern Language Association.

Though literary theory was the preeminent concern of academic critics from the late 1970s to the early 1990s, distinguished work continued to be done in literary history and literary biography. Two of the most significant scholarly events of this period were the publications of two exemplary biographies: Robert Hemenway's Zora Neale Hurston: A Literary Biography (1977) and Arnold Rampersad's two volume biography A Life of Langston Hughes (1986 and 1988). Also during these years the number of black Ph.D.s increased dramatically, and correspondingly. African-American literary scholars found employment at virtually all of the major colleges and universities. Given the emphasis on scholarly publication as a necessity of professional survival, it was inevitable that the quality and quantity of publications by black critics would also increase dramatically. Thus the critics who have published excellent work in this field since 1980 are far too numerous to enumerate. Two journals were the primary venues for black literary scholarship during these years: African-American Review (originally called Negro American Literature Forum and subsequently Black American Literature Forum) and Callaloo. Furthermore, the study of black writers became surprisingly fashionable during the early 1990s, and for the first time, journals on American literature began to publish work on black literature with some frequency.

The most significant and pervasive new direction of African-American literary studies from the mid-1980s to the mid-1990s was the entry of large numbers of black women into the profession and the proliferation of work on black women writers. During the 1970s a small group of black women began to acquire national reputations as literary scholars, notably Barbara Christian, Thadious Davis, Trudier Harris, Nellie McKay, Hortense Spillers, Eleanor Taylor, and Kenny Williams. By the mid-1990s the black women entering the profession outnumbered the black men substantially. Black women writers such as Harriet Jacobs, Frances E. W. Harper. Zora Neale Hurston, Alice Walker, and Toni Morrison, too long undervalued, began to acquire a secure place in American literature syllabi and in the pages of scholarly journals.

The creative capacity of African-Americans is no longer open to dispute, nor is it necessary to justify the study of African-American texts. Thus African-American literary criticism has at last escaped the onus of racial apologetics. In general, black critics remain deeply interested in the relationship between social experience—whether this means racial and gender identity or cultural knowledge and conditioning—and literary expression. This will likely remain the case as long as black critics experience social pressures that distinguish them from their white counterparts. Nevertheless, as awareness increases of various possibilities of African-American racial experience, critical judgments regarding the relationship between race and writing will doubtless become more and more vexed.

See also Baldwin, James; Baraka, Amiri (Jones, LeRoi); Black Arts Movement; *Black World/Negro Digest*; Braithwaite, William Stanley; Brawley, Benjamin Griffith; Brown, Sterling Allen; *The Crisis*; Du Bois, W. E. B.; Ellison, Ralph; Gates, Henry Louis, Jr.; Harlem Renaissance; Johnson, James Weldon; Literature of the United States; Locke, Alain Leroy; Neal, Larry; *New Negro*; Redding, Jay Saunders; Wright, Richard

■ ■ *Bibliography*

Baker, Houston A., Jr. *The Journey Back: Issues in Black Literature and Criticism.* Chicago: University of Chicago Press, 1980.

Baker, Houston A., Jr. *Blues, Ideology, and Afro-American Literature: A Vernacular Theory.* Chicago: University of Chicago Press, 1984.

Baker, Houston A., Jr., and Patricia Redmond, eds. *Afro-American Literary Study in the 1990s.* Chicago: University of Chicago Press, 1989.

Bell, Bernard W. *The Afro-American Novel and Its Tradition.* Amherst, Mass.: University of Massachusetts Press, 1987.

Brawley, Benjamin. *The Negro Genius.* New York: Dodd Mead & Company, 1937.

Brown, Sterling A. *The Negro in American Fiction.* Washington, D.C.: The Associates in Negro Folk Education, 1937.

Brown, Sterling A. *Negro Poetry and Drama.* Washington, D.C.: The Associates in Negro Folk Education, 1937.

Carby, Hazel V. *Reconstructing Womanhood: The Emergence of the Afro-American Woman Novelist.* New York: Oxford University Press, 1987.

Christian, Barbara. *Black Feminist Criticism: Perspectives on Black Women Writers.* New York: Pergamon Press, 1985. Reprint, New York: Teachers College Press, 1997.

Davis, Arthur P. *From the Dark Tower: Afro-American Writers, 1900-1960.* Washington, D.C.: Howard University Press, 1974.

Earvin, Hazel Arnet, ed. *African American Literary Criticism, 1773-2000.* New York: Twayne Publishers, 1999.

Fisher, Dexter, and Robert B. Stepto, eds. *Afro-American Literature: The Reconstruction of Instruction.* New York: Modern Language Association of America, 1979.

Gates, Henry Louis, Jr. *Black Literature and Literary Theory.* New York: Methuen, 1984.

Gates, Henry Louis, Jr. *Figures in Black: Words, Signs, and the "Racial" Self.* New York: Oxford University Press, 1987.

Gates, Henry Louis, Jr. *Reading Black, Reading Feminist: A Critical Anthology.* New York: Meridian Book, 1990.

Gayle, Addison, Jr., ed. *The Black Aesthetic.* Garden City, N.Y.: Doubleday, 1971.

Henderson, Stephen. *Understanding the New Black Poetry: Black Speech and Black Music as Poetic References.* New York: Morrow, 1973.

Jackson, Blyden. *A History of Afro-American Literature. Vol. 1, The Long Beginning, 1746-1895.* Baton Rouge, La.: Louisiana State University Press, 1989.

Napier, Winston. *African American Literary Theory: A Reader.* New York: New York University Press, 2000.

Pryse, Marjorie, and Hortense J. Spillers, eds., *Conjuring: Black Women, Fiction, and Literary Tradition.* Bloomington: Indiana University Press, 1985.

Redding, J. Saunders. *To Make a Poet Black.* Ithaca, N. Y.: Cornell University Press, 1988.

Redmond, Eugene B. *Drumvoices: The Mission of Afro-American Poetry.* Garden City, N.Y.: Anchor Press, 1976.

Stepto, Robert B. *From Behind the Veil: A Study of Afro-American Narrative.* Urbana: University of Illinois Press, 1979.

Turner, Darwin T. "Afro-American Literary Critics." *Black World* 19, no. 9 (1970): 54-67.

Weixlmann, Joe, and Houston A. Baker, eds. *Studies in Black American Literature 3: Black Feminist Criticism and Critical Theory.* Greenwood, Fla.: Penkevill Pub. Co., 1988.

DAVID LIONEL SMITH (1996)
Updated bibliography

SCHOLARSHIP IN THE TWENTY-FIRST CENTURY

Literary criticism in the early twenty-first century accepts and interrogates historical and political influences on African-American literature. This willingness to read literature within specific cultural contexts has led to the emergence of literary cultural studies. Thus African-American literary criticism has developed even more sophisticated, interdisciplinary approaches to literature by welcoming new ways to explore and critique gender, sexuality, class, nation, and culture within the entire history of African-American literature.

Cultural and historical approaches to literary criticism have reevaluated claims that, for instance, do not recognize the impact of Frederick Douglass on American and African-American letters. While past critics generally understood Douglass primarily as a political activist, newer critics are rereading Douglass as a crucial figure in the American Renaissance of the nineteenth century and as a major influence in African-American letters. Saidiya V. Hartman's *Scenes of Subjection: Terror, Slavery, and Self-Making in Nineteenth-Century America* (1997) and Fred Moten's *In the Break: The Aesthetics of the Black Radical Tradition* (2003) consciously accept intersections of politics and aesthetics as they also position Douglass at the very beginning of their inquiries. Like many of their peers, Hartman and Moten use interdisciplinarity to produce an African-American literary criticism within and beyond the color-line. Even as they position black American literature at the center of their investigations, they also use critical tools such as Marxist theory, psychoanalysis, visual theory, and the law to interrogate and extend the limits of African-American literary criticism.

In her book *Queering the Color Line: Race and the Invention of Homosexuality in American Culture* (2000), Siobhan B. Somerville argues that race and sexuality are related categories, both crucially dependent on the color-line. Her readings of novels by Pauline Hopkins, James Weldon Johnson, and Jean Toomer mark an important development in African-American literary criticism in which race, sexuality, and gender together are necessary concerns. Besides Somerville's views, Robert F. Reid-Pharr's *Conjugal Union: The Body, the House, and the Black American* (1999) explores antebellum African-American literature through lenses of race, sexuality, gender, and class. Feminist literary critics have helped to open these new ways of thinking through gender, sexuality, and class. Carla Peterson, Valerie Smith, Hortense J. Spillers, Claudia Tate, and Cheryl A. Wall are some of the most influential scholars of the 1980s and 1990s. Their work continues to shape the most recent developments in African-American literary criticism.

The question of subjectivity as a political and aesthetic concern has influenced recent developments. Since the publication of Paul Gilroy's *The Black Atlantic: Modernity and Double Consciousness* (1993), literary criticism has even more carefully explored the internationalisms of African-American authors. Brent Hayes Edwards's *The Practice of Diaspora: Literature, Translation, and the Rise of Black Internationalism* (2003) and Michelle M. Wright's *Becoming Black: Creating Identity in the African Diaspora* (2004), for example, have theorized Black American subjectivity and Black American literature within the transnational context of an African diaspora. These internationalist perspectives within African-American literary criticism have helped reshape discussions of the Harlem Renaissance, W. E. B. Du Bois, and Richard Wright even as they recover black women intellectuals and authors who have always been a forceful presence in the making of African-American literature.

▪ ▪ *Bibliography*

Dubey, Madhu. *Signs and Cities: Black Literary Postmodernism.* Chicago: University of Chicago Press, 2003.

Edwards, Brent Hayes. *The Practice of Diaspora: Literature, Translation, and the Rise of Black Internationalism.* Cambridge, Mass.: Harvard University Press, 2003.

Moten, Fred. *In the Break: The Aesthetics of the Black Radical Tradition.* Minneapolis: University of Minnesota Press, 2003.

Reid-Pharr, Robert F. *Conjugal Union: The Body, the House, and the Black American.* New York: Oxford University Press, 1999.

Rushdy, Ashraf A. *Remembering Generations: Race and Family in Contemporary African American Fiction.* Chapel Hill: University of North Carolina Press, 2001.

Somerville, Siobhan B. *Queering the Color Line: Race and the Invention of Homosexuality in American Culture.* Durham, N.C.: Duke University Press, 2000.

Spillers, Hortense J. *Black, White, and in Color: Essays on American Literature and Culture.* Chicago: University of Chicago Press, 2003.

Tate, Claudia. *Psychoanalysis and Black Novels: Desire and the Protocols of Race.* New York: Oxford University Press, 1998.

SHELLY EVERSLEY (2005)

LITERARY MAGAZINES
▪▪▪

Literary magazines and journals have occupied a position of great importance in the development of African-American literature. Since their appearance in the nineteenth century, such magazines have served as outlets for writers who would otherwise have had few opportunities to publish their work. They have been important forums for discussion of the literary aesthetics of black literature and catalysts of change in black culture and politics. The influence of black literary journals is especially notable given their small numbers and the difficult conditions in which they were generally produced. With scarce financial support and limited readership, most black literary journals rarely survived long enough to publish more than a few issues. Magazines and journals that concentrated on literary work while maintaining a more general focus on society and politics occasionally offered more stable platforms for literary publication, but literature was often the first thing to be eliminated from such publications during times of financial distress.

Another important factor in the difficulty of sustaining African-American literary magazines has been the often factional and highly politicized nature of black intellectual and literary debate. Politics has always been integral to African-American literature. Many of the most important literary magazines were considered by their creators to be primarily political publications; their contents often contained much that would not conventionally be considered literature, in the sense of poetry, drama, and narrative fiction. The abolitionist journalism of the early nineteenth century, the political editorials of W. E. B. Du Bois, and the ongoing debates over the proper role of the arts in black culture have all made significant contributions to black literature and provide important examples of the varied and often apparently extraliterary writing that has appeared in black literary magazines. One theme that frequently recurs in the history of black literary magazines is the ongoing debate over the relationship between literary aesthetics and cultural politics, a debate that often led to attempts to avoid or transcend the apparent dichotomy between "art as propaganda" and "art for art's sake." More important, it can be seen as a sustained effort to develop a literature that can bridge the gap between the two.

The earliest African-American journals were published in the northern centers of the free black population in the 1820s. Avowedly abolitionist and opposed to racial discrimination, they established the foundation on which later black protest journalism was built. The first black periodical was *Freedom's Journal* (1827), followed by the *National Reformer* (1833), the *Mirror of Liberty* (1837), an early incarnation of the *Colored American Magazine* (1837–1841), and *Douglass' Monthly* (1858–1861). These early journals had a strong political focus and usually served as mouthpieces for their publishers. A notable exception to this practice was the *Anglo-African* magazine (1859–1862). The *Anglo-African* and the associated *Weekly Anglo-African* newspaper (1859–1865) were more diversified in approach, and their inclusion of contending political perspectives and literary efforts made them the most influential African-American journals of their day. The *Anglo-African* magazine was also the first African-American journal to include substantial works of literary prose, initiating the early development of a black literary aesthetic. Because of the difficulty African Americans encountered in finding publishing opportunities, these magazines afforded one of the only venues for black authors. Martin Delany's novel *Blake; or, The Huts of America,* for example, was serialized in the *Anglo-African* magazine in 1859–1860 but was not published in book form until 1970. Other notable contributors to *Anglo-African* magazine included Frederick Douglass, John Langston, Daniel Payne, Frances Ellen Watkins Harper, and William Wells Brown.

After the Civil War and the failure of radical Reconstruction, the optimism of the abolitionists was eroded. Although African-American newspapers flourished during the last quarter of the nineteenth century, literary magazines virtually vanished during this period. As the century approached its close, Booker T. Washington emerged as the pre-eminent leader of African Americans. He made substantial efforts to gain control of the African-American journals and thus to eliminate opposition within the African-American community to his accommodationist position. By the first decade of the twentieth century, Washington's views were endorsed by most of the notable journals of the time, including *Southern Workmen* (1872–1910), *Colored Citizen* (1900), *Age* (1900), and most notably, *Colored American* magazine (1900–1909). *Colored American,* edited in its opening years by Pauline Hopkins, was the first significant African-American literary journal of the twentieth century, publishing the works of such notable writers as William Stanley Braithwaite, Benjamin Brawley, James Corrothers, Angelina Weld Grimké, and Paul Laurence Dunbar. Until 1904, when Washington succeeded in having Hopkins dismissed from her post, its varied contents—politics, business, religion, history, and fiction—reflected strong opposition to his views.

Despite Washington's takeover of *Colored American,* the opposition was at this time gaining strength under the leadership of W. E. B. Du Bois. A number of new journals reflecting Du Bois's ideas were established, the most important of which were *Voice of the Negro* (1904–1907), *Moon Illustrated Weekly* (1905–1906), and *Horizon* (1907–1910). *Voice of the Negro,* edited by J. Max Barber, was the first African-American magazine edited in the South, and *Moon* and *Horizon* were Du Bois's first journalistic platforms. While none of these journals was able to survive for long (because opposition to Washington virtually eliminated any possibility of substantial financial support), they served an important role in developing a radical aesthetic of explicit and energetic political protest.

All the journals, whether influenced by Washington or Du Bois, included literary pieces in addition to social

OPPORTUNITY
Journal of Negro Life

JUNE
1925

15 CENTS
the copy

Cover of Opportunity *magazine, June 1925. Published by the National Urban League,* Opportunity *provided African Americans a stable venue for literary work and critical discussion.* PHOTOGRAPHS AND PRINTS DIVISION, SCHOMBURG CENTER FOR RESEARCH IN BLACK CULTURE, THE NEW YORK PUBLIC LIBRARY, ASTOR, LENOX AND TILDEN FOUNDATIONS.

and political commentary, and debate over the appropriate aesthetic for African-American literature intensified in this decade. Hopkins and Du Bois, recalling the energetic protest journalism of the abolitionists, attempted to develop a direct and audacious style of writing that would reinforce the radically confrontational political themes of their literary work. After 1904, however, the pro-Washington magazines, such as *Alexander's* and *Colored American,* generally avoided such provocative positions, placing less emphasis on explicitly political themes and favoring instead light poetry and popular fiction written with conventional restraint and intended to provide entertainment or to describe some exemplary achievement.

By the time of Washington's death in 1915 the sort of conventional literature favored by those magazines under his influence was rapidly losing ground to the energetically and provocatively modern style fostered by Du Bois and such journals as *The Crisis* (1910–) and *Opportunity* (1923–1949), published by the National Association

for the Advancement of Colored People and the National Urban League, respectively. These journals, financially supported by social and political organizations involved in race relations, provided for the first time not only a stable forum for black literary work and critical discussion, but also a substantial, national black readership. As a result of this support and wide exposure, a remarkable number of young writers, including Arna Bontemps, Countee Cullen, Langston Hughes, Zora Neale Hurston, and Claude McKay, gained national recognition. This new generation of writers moved beyond traditional concerns with countering white prejudices and opposing related political views to address themselves to issues of African-American self-definition.

Over the next two decades, black literature experienced an unprecedented degree of aesthetic experimentation and development as African-American writers turned their attention to articulating the identity of the "New Negro," the term chosen by Alain Locke as the title of his landmark 1925 anthology of the period's poetry and prose. As Locke observed in 1928, "Yesterday it was the rhetorical flush of partisanship, challenged and on the defensive. . . . Nothing is more of a spiritual gain in the life of the Negro than the quieter assumption of his group identity and heritage; and contemporary Negro poetry registers this incalculable artistic and social gain" (Locke, 1928, p. 11). The organizational journals and a host of little literary magazines were the primary vehicles for this development and the ensuing controversy.

The first, and in many ways the most influential, of the organizational journals was *The Crisis.* Du Bois's sponsorship of young writers and his own development of an energetic, modern style of writing made him the most important figure in the early growth of the modern black literary aesthetic that would reach maturity in the Harlem Renaissance. Along with Jessie Fauset, the literary editor of *The Crisis* from 1919 to 1926, Du Bois provided critical early support and exposure for the unprecedented numbers of young, educated black writers. The quick national success of *The Crisis* was encouraging, and its example was followed by the launching of *Stylus* (1916–1941) and *New Era* (1916), both smaller literary magazines. *Stylus* was established at Howard University by Locke and Montgomery Gregory, and *New Era* was a short-lived attempt by Pauline Hopkins to revive the early form of *Colored American* magazine.

Despite Du Bois's central role in the early development of the Harlem Renaissance, his increasingly emphatic insistence that literature concern itself with political and moral issues had distanced him from many of the younger generation by the mid-1920s. As Du Bois lost influence, dominance of the expanding literary scene shifted to Charles Spurgeon Johnson, the editor of *Opportunity* from 1923 to 1928. Unlike Du Bois and, to some extent, Fauset, Charles Johnson did not insist that literary aesthetics be tied to the political and moral values of the prosperous, educated, black middle class—those Du Bois called the "Talented Tenth." Instead, he asserted that self-expression and artistic freedom were the paramount concerns for the new literature, and *Opportunity*'s support of more radical young writers of the time marked the maturation of the Harlem Renaissance.

The more general cultural vitality of the Harlem Renaissance brought further attention to black literary development through a number of special issues of essentially white periodicals, including *Palms* (1926), *Carolina* magazine (1927–1929), and *Survey Graphic* (1925), much of which was reprinted in Locke's anthology *The New Negro* (1925).

With the success of the organizational magazines and the attention garnered by the special numbers of white periodicals, the African-American literary community had become optimistic enough to launch a number of independent little literary magazines. *New Era* and *Stylus* were followed in the mid-1920s by numerous other independent journals, including *Harlem* (1926) and the more conservative *Black Opals* (1927–1928) and *Saturday Evening Quill* (1926–1930). However, in many ways the most notable of the little magazines of this era was *Fire!!* (1926), the first exclusively literary, independent black magazine. Edited by Wallace Thurman, the first and only issue of *Fire!!* caused substantial controversy upon publication because of its energetically antipuritanical position. Rather than presenting conventional portraits of exemplary, middle-class African Americans, the magazine attempted to put forward a new radical aesthetic that concerned itself with many of the aspects of African-American life considered to be disreputable, such as prostitution and homosexuality.

The radical themes of *Fire!!* were more than a simply aesthetic rejection of the practices of the Talented Tenth. The focus on lower-class black life also reflected the growing influence of socialist political theory among the black writers of the 1920s. In 1926 Thurman had served a brief term as editor of the era's third influential organizational journal, the *Messenger* (1917–1928), which had begun as a radical socialist magazine and eventually became allied with the mainstream labor movement (In 1925 it became the official organ of the Brotherhood of Sleeping Car Porters.) Despite its early rejection of the importance of black literary efforts, the *Messenger* became a significant supporter of many of the more radical Harlem Renaissance writers after it came under the editorial control of George Schuyler and Theophilus Lewis in 1923. With the exception of Thurman's brief stint as editor, Schuyler and Lewis maintained control of the magazine until its demise five years later, and under their leadership the *Messenger* provided support for literature that reflected the growing interest in the life of the black lower class.

The literary renaissance of the 1920s turned out to be unexpectedly short-lived. With the onset of the next decade, economic hardship made financial survival difficult for journals, and their numbers decreased sharply. While *The Crisis* and *Opportunity* were able to survive, both experienced such financial difficulties that they sharply curtailed their support of literature. The depressed economic situation also had its impact on literary aesthetics; both the primarily middle-class aesthetic of the organizational journals and the radical aesthetic style of some of the little magazines seemed increasingly out of touch with the problems of the Great Depression. The radical writers' focus on the life of the lower classes, however, now came to the fore as the foundation for much of the black literature of the 1930s. In *Challenge* (1934–1937), edited by Dorothy West, and *New Challenge* (1937), edited by West, Marion Minus, and Richard Wright, a new generation of black writers (including Wright and Ralph Ellison) developed a literary aesthetic that linked radical socialism to folklore and to the experience of the working class. While such work foregrounded politics to a degree that had not been seen since the early writing of Du Bois and Pauline Hopkins, the socialist orientation of the new literature focused on class tensions as much as it did on race.

With the onset of World War II, the political position of most African-American journals shifted to liberal anticommunism, and the journals focused their attentions on the legal struggle to achieve integration, an emphasis that would remain dominant throughout the 1940s and most of the 1950s. At the same time, many black authors found it increasingly easy to publish in mainstream literary journals. For instance, James Baldwin's famous attack on Richard Wright and the black protest tradition, "Many Thousands Gone" (1949), appeared not in an African-American literary magazine but in *Partisan Review*. The diversity and unity of human experience became the primary thematic concerns, and notions of an independent or oppositional black literary aesthetic were minimized. Many mainstream publications were opened to black writers for the first time, although such interest was limited to formulaic entertainment pieces. Only two small journals, *Negro Quarterly* (1942–1944) and *Negro Story* (1944–1946), existed during the war, and *The Crisis* and *Opportunity* continued to serve as important outlets for serious literary work.

However, both experienced further financial strain and erosion of circulation during wartime, and neither journal was able to maintain a significant role in literary development after the war. *Opportunity* had reached particularly desperate straits, and it ceased publication in 1949. *Phylon* (1940–), a journal published by Atlanta University and started by W. E. B. Du Bois, took over the position left open by *Crisis* and *Opportunity* in the late 1940s and maintained its influence through the next decade.

The era's aesthetic trend toward the white mainstream was not conducive to independent little black magazines, and their scarcity during this period eventually became a cause for concern among black writers. By the end of the 1940s, the predominant aesthetic emphasis on the universality of human experience began to be perceived by some as a potentially negative influence on African-American culture, drawing it into the mainstream while diluting its identity. *Harlem Quarterly* (1949–1950) and *Voices* (1950) were short-lived efforts to counteract this trend; they attempted to answer the need for a journal of black fiction about African-American life in particular. *Free Lance* (1953–1976) and *Yugen* (1958–1963), the earliest platforms for LeRoi Jones (later known as Imamu Amiri Baraka), addressed the same problem in the next decade, though neither of these journals was exclusively concerned with African-American interests and literature.

By the middle of the 1960s, the black arts movement and black political militance created a climate in which the rejection of Western cultural norms and values in favor of an independent African-American cultural identity became the basis for a new black literature. The return to a literary aesthetic of opposition and protest was carried out through a new renaissance of independent small journals, including the *Liberator* (1961–1971), *Soulbook* (1964–1976), *Black Dialogue* (1964–1970), the *Journal of Black Poetry* (1966–1973), and the more moderate *Umbra* (1963–1975). *Negro Digest* (1942–1970) also lent support to this perspective after a shift in its editorial position in the middle of the decade. The aesthetic position that developed in the small journals of this decade was part of the larger attempt by the black arts movement to disengage African-American artistic culture from the Western tradition and to form a new black cultural consciousness. Fundamentally political, the black aesthetic combined language and form indigenous to the African-American experience with revolutionary, nationalistic political critique.

The black arts movement peaked at the end of the 1960s, just as *Negro Digest* adopted its new title, *Black World* (1970–1976). The decline of the movement, and of the Black Power movement in general, was gradual and not immediately noticeable. In the early years of the 1970s, a number of new magazines and journals were established as part of the movement, including *Nommo* (1969–1970), *Black Creation* (1970–1975), *Black Review* (1971–1972), *Kitaba Cha Jua* (1974–1976), and *First World* (1977–1980). However, as the general political climate cooled and the movement splintered and slowed, financial support for such journals became scarce. Few survived.

By the middle of the 1970s, the pendulum had swung away from radical oppositional politics, and the new emphasis became the necessity of establishing a strong and consistent critical and theoretical base for a separate black literary aesthetic. A number of university publications, such as *Hambone* (1974–), *Callaloo* (1976–), and *Black American Literature Forum* (1967, 1976–), played a central role in the development of this new aesthetic, providing academic critics (such as Henry Louis Gates and Houston Baker) with an unprecedented degree of influence in the African-American literary community. Other literary magazines and journals that contributed to this development include *Obsidian/Obsidian II/Obsidian III* (1975–), *Y'Bird* (1977–1978), *Quilt* (1980–1984), *Sage: A Scholarly Journal on Black Women* (1984–), *Catalyst* (1986–), *Shooting Star Review* (1986–), and *Konch* (1990).

At the same time that more recent literary journals have reflected an increasingly academic orientation, they have also displayed a significant shift toward greater diversity of focus and opinion. Unlike the literary debates of earlier periods, that of the 1980s and early 1990s did not reveal any particular dominant concern, but rather began to confront the internal heterogeneity of the African-American literary community. This heterogeneity accounts in part for the relatively large number of literary journalssince the 1960s.

While established literary journals such as *Callaloo* continued to hold a dominant position in the late 1990s and into the new century, the expansion of the Internet has provided new outlets for African-American poets and fiction writers, allowing publishers to disseminate the work of both new and established writers at a far lower cost. The Cave Canem organization, which is "committed to the discussion and cultivation of new voices in African American poetry," was formed in 1996, and many members of its "faculty" edit Web publications such as *Ambulant*. FYAH!!, dedicated to a "new generation of Black wordsmiths," is an online magazine that publishes the work of such poets as India Savage Anderson, who has also published in the quarterly e-magazine *Mosaic,* founded in 1998. *Mosaic* has become a leading publisher of new and established African-American and other writers, including Staceyann Chin, Colson Whitehead, Major Jackson, Willie

Perdomo, Colin Channer, Roger Bonair-Agard, Sonia Sanchez, bell hooks, and Haki Madhubuti. Another online project that has provided a forum for new writers is *Voices from the Gap: Women Artists and Writers of Color,* published at the University of Minnesota. Online publications such as *VelvetIllusion* reflect a more internationalist perspective, featuring the work not only of African Americans but also of people of color throughout the world.

Another development, one that reflects the growing reach of a distinctly African-American literature, is the prominence of publications that not only review the work of African-American writers but that themselves publish some of that work. One of the most widely read is the *African American Review,* published since 1967 at St. Louis University (the journal was originally titled *Negro American Literature Forum;* In 1976 it became the *Black American Literature Forum;* and it took on the current title in 1992). The *African American Review* is the official publication of the Division on Black American Literature and Culture of the Modern Language Association. It has published work by such writers as Houston A. Baker, Jr., Henry Louis Gates, Jr., Trudier Harris, Arnold Rampersad, Hortense Spillers, Amiri Baraka, Gwendolyn Brooks, Rita Dove, Charles Johnson, Toni Morrison, and Ishmael Reed. A more recent review is *Black Issues Book Review,* published since 1999. The success of these mainstream publications help firmly entrench African-American voices in the contemporary literary landscape.

See also Baraka, Amiri (Jones, LeRoi); Black Arts Movement; *Black World/Negro Digest; Crisis, The;* Du Bois, W. E. B.; Fauset, Jessie Redmon; Harlem Renaissance; Hopkins, Pauline Elizabeth; Johnson, Charles Spurgeon; *Liberator, The; Messenger, The;* New Negro; *Opportunity: Journal of Negro Life; Phylon;* Schuyler, George S.; Thurman, Wallace; Washington, Booker T.

■ ■ *Bibliography*

Bontemps, Arna, ed. *The Harlem Renaissance Remembered.* New York: Dodd, Mead, 1972.

Bullock, Penelope. *The Afro-American Free Press, 1838–1909.* Baton Rouge: Louisiana State University Press, 1981.

Hutton, Frankie. *The Early Black Press in America, 1827–1860.* Westport, Conn.: Greewood Press, 1993.

Johnson, Abby Arthur, and Ronald M. Johnson. *Propaganda and Aesthetics: The Literary Politics of African-American Magazines in the Twentieth Century.* Amherst: University of Massachusetts Press, 1979.

Kornweibel, Theodore, Jr. *No Crystal Stair: Black Life and* The Messenger, *1917–1928.* Westport, Conn.: Greenwood Press, 1975.

Lewis, David Levering. *When Harlem Was in Vogue.* New York: Oxford University Press, 1979.

Locke, Alain. "The Message of the Negro Poets." *Carolina* 28 (May 1928).

Wolseley, Roland E. *The Black Press, U.S.A.,* 2d ed. Ames: Iowa State University Press, 1990.

MATTHEW BUCKLEY (1996)
MICHAEL O'NEAL (2005)

LITERATURE

This entry consists of seven articles examining literature from several distinct geographic perspectives.

LITERATURE OF FRENCH GUIANA
Karen Smyley Wallace

LITERATURE OF HAITI
J. Michael Dash

LITERATURE OF MARTINIQUE AND GUADELOUPE
H. Adlai Murdoch

LITERATURE OF SURINAME
Ineke Phaf-Rheinberger

LITERATURE OF THE ENGLISH-SPEAKING CARIBBEAN
Faith Smith

LITERATURE OF THE NETHERLANDS ANTILLES
Ineke Phaf-Rheinberger

LITERATURE OF THE UNITED STATES
Arnold Rampersad
Stefanie Dunning

LITERATURE OF FRENCH GUIANA

French Guiana is France's oldest overseas possession (dating from the seventeenth century). Along with Martinique, Guadeloupe, and Reunion, it has been a department of France since 1946. Yet, unlike these other French overseas departments, it is the only French territory on the American mainland. French Guiana (approximately 35,000 square miles), is located in the equatorial forest zone of South America. The country is bounded on the north by the Atlantic Ocean, to the east and the south by Brazil, and to the west by Suriname. Because of its complex and treacherous geography, it was particularly well suited to function as a penal colony, which it was from 1852 until 1938. This part of French Guiana's history was dramatically depicted in Henri Charrière's l969 novel, *Papillon,* and in the 1973 movie of the same name.

Although the country is small, the literary landscape of French Guiana is broad and mirrors faithfully the complexities of its diverse population, which comprises persons of mixed white, Amerindian, and African descent (Creoles), as well as descendants of Arawak and Carib Indians. From this perspective, there is not one literature, but several literary components that make up this vast body of works. Under this umbrella are pieces written in French by writers who reside in France, works in French by writers who reside in Guiana, works written in Creole, and, to some extent, works emerging from the *Bushinenge* and *Amerindian* communities found along the border of Suriname. It is not surprising then, that conflicts about identity—including color, class, language, and ethnicity—appear frequently as themes within the literature. Their objective is to carve out a more accurate definition of the Guianese self—what is referred to as their *guyanité*. While debate continues around this critical issue, most contemporary scholars from that region tend to agree that a writer's ability to express the Guianese experience is more important than the geographical community from which he or she emerges.

Among French Guiana's many writers, Alfred Parépou (author of the first novel in Creole, *Atipa* [1885]) is less well known outside of the country, though his contribution to this body of literature is considerable. By writing exclusively in Creole, he was able to accurately portray daily life in the Guianese community and vividly capture the spirit of its inhabitants. René Maran (winner of the 1921 Prix Goncourt for his novel *Batouala)* is more familiar to readers outside of French Guiana. Although he was born in Martinique (in 1887) to Guianese parents and lived most of his life in France (he died in Paris in 1960), Maran is still acclaimed as one of French Guiana's most notable writers. His pioneering novel, *Batouala,* which unapologetically portrayed the realities of the colonial system in French West Africa, remains a classic. The reader's attention is artfully turned away from the European colonizer, and the story is told instead through the eyes of the indigenous people of Oubangui-Chari. By bringing them to center stage, he brought meaning to their customs, traditions, and values. It is because of his innovative approach that René Maran is considered to be one of the important precursors of the *Négritude* movement.

Perhaps the most memorable of writers from French Guiana is Léon-Gontran Damas (1912–1978), who, along with Aimé Césaire (Martinique) and Léopold Sédar Senghor (Senegal), was one of the principal founders of the *Négritude* movement. Damas was a native of the capital city, Cayenne. After the death of his mother, in 1913, he was raised by his aunt, the formidable *Man Gabi,* whose penchant for strict adherence to the codes of bourgeois behavior were vividly brought to life in the poem "Hoquet." Damas continued his secondary studies in Martinique, at the renowned Lycée Schoelcher, where he first met Aimé Césaire. He then went on to continue his studies in Paris, where he became inspired by the liberated thinking current among young African and Caribbean students. Together with Césaire and Senghor, he helped to establish the journal *L'Etudiant noir* (1934), an important vehicle for the articulation of these new thoughts. In 1937 Damas published a collection of poems titled *Pigments,* which both symbolized and launched the *Négritude* movement. His literary portfolio includes essays, such as *Retour de Guyane* (1938); poetic collections, such as *Veillées noires* (1942), *Graffiti* (1953), and *Black Label* (1956); and an anthology of works by poets from the French colonies (1957).

Damas was both inspired and intrigued by the racial problems in America. In his poetry, he showed a particular ability to comprehend the pain and suffering caused by racial prejudice, Jim Crow, and lynching, as well as to communicate the essence of the blues and jazz. His memorable syncopated style captures the frustrations of the blacks of the period as they sought to exist within white societies. Many of his poems are dedicated to black American artists, writers, and musicians such as Langston Hughes, Claude McKay, Countee Cullen, Alain Locke, Richard Wright, Louis Armstrong, and others. Eventually, Damas settled in the United States, where he lectured and taught at many universities. He was eventually named Distinguished Professor of African Literature at Howard University, in Washington. D.C., a position he held until his death in 1978.

Another of French Guiana's giants was Bertène Juminer (1927–2003), who was acclaimed for his novel *Les bâtards* (1961), which describes the psychological struggle of an Antillean who leaves home to study in metropolitan France, and who later returns to Guiana and attempts to readjust to that society. Juminer is also noted for his contributions as an academic and a physician, and as a man of conviction who fought tirelessly for the betterment of Guiana and the French West Indies.

French Guiana's contemporary literary landscape continues to expand and includes the poet and dramatist Elie Stephenson (*Où se trouvent les orangers*, 2000), and the poet and novelist Serge Patient (*Le Nègre du Gouverneur*, 2001).

See also Caribbean/North American Writers (Contemporary); Creole Languages of the Americas; Literature of Martinique and Guadeloupe; Literature of Suriname; Négritude

■ ■ *Bibliography*

Burton, Richard, and Fred Reno, eds. *French and West Indian: Martinique, Guadeloupe, and French Guiana Today.* Charlottesville: University Press of Virginia, 1995.

Ormerod, Beverly. *An Introduction to the French Caribbean Novel.* London: Heinemann, 1985.

KAREN SMILEY WALLACE (2005)

LITERATURE OF HAITI

Created out of a revolutionary war that drove the French out of colonial St. Domingue in 1804, Haitian literature has been inspired as much by the need to affirm the uniqueness of the Haitian nation as by its redemptive mission in a world dominated by colonialism and slavery. The nationalist impulse in early Haitian verse is enhanced by the Romantic movement's insistence on the poet's national genius as well as the influence of the natural environment over individual sensibility. This need to express a particularly Haitian worldview in literature is elaborated during the twenty-three years of Jean-Pierre Boyer's presidency and given its most articulate expression in the verse of Oswald Durand, whose *Rires et Pleurs* (Laughter and tears; 1896) is a celebration of Haitian flora and fauna. He is the first writer to successfully experiment with the use of Creole, especially in the poem "Choucoune," which was eventually put to music. This trend also paves the way for the emergence of Haitian prose writing at the turn of the century. Haiti's early novels are either political satires or sympathetic depictions of peasant life. The conventions of realism are apparent in the novels by Frédéric Marcelin, Justin Lhérisson, and Antoine Innocent published at the turn of the century. The end of the nineteenth century also saw a backlash against what was considered an overly parochial approach to literary creativity. The group of poets associated with the journal *La ronde* (1898–1902) fiercely criticized narrow nationalism and regionalism in Haitian writing and advocated a more cosmopolitan and eclectic approach to literature.

Early Haitian literature was also postcolonial in the sense that it called into question the racial and cultural values and beliefs on which the colonial system was based. Haitian writers were, therefore, also acutely aware of the dangers of celebrating Haitian exceptionalism, given the degree of international ostracism suffered by the new state. Henry Christophe's secretary, Le Baron de Vastey, published one of the first critiques of European colonization in his essay *Le système colonial dévoile* (The colonial system unmasked; 1814). A keen awareness of the fetishizing of race and nation in the colonial system led later essayists to abandon the rhetoric of racial and cultural difference for arguments that favor a nonessentializing universalism. The essayist Anténor Firmin's *De l'égalité des races humaines* (The equality of the human races; 1885) is a two-volume response to the ideas of racial difference and racial perfectibility put forward by Joseph-Arthur de Gobineau in Paris. His *Lettres de St. Thomas* (1910), published in exile, argued against xenophobia in Haitian politics and the need to create an "Antillean Confederation" in order to ensure national survival.

Chronic instability at the beginning of the twentieth century and the spread of U.S. imperialism in the northern Caribbean led to Haiti being occupied by U.S. Marines from 1915 to 1934. The neocolonial nature of the occupation had the effect of uniting Haitians, who had been divided by class and color, around the ideals of race and nation. A young radical group of writers began to dominate intellectual life from the 1920s. They were much involved in street protests, militant journalism, and the cultural nationalism expressed in the journals *La nouvelle ronde* (1925), *La trouee* (1927), and *La revue indigene* (1927–1928). The poetry published in these journals ranged from the fashionably bohemian poems of Émile Roumer and Carl Brouard to more socially conscious writing from Jacques Roumain. Roumain introduced and translated the writers of the Harlem Renaissance and contemporary Latin America and founded the Haitian Communist Party in 1934. The ideas of the anthropologist Jean Price-Mars, who spoke of the need to recognize peasant culture and to reform the Haitian elite, was a shaping force at the time.

Roumain's conception of peasant resistance in the context of international proletarian revolt would leave an indelible mark on succeeding generations of writers. His two best-known posthumously published works, *Bois d'ébène* (Ebony wood; 1945) and *Gouverneurs de la rosée* (Masters of the dew; 1944) exemplify this insertion of the Haitian peasantry in the context of a global modernity. Roumain, who founded the Bureau d'Ethnologie in 1941, is well known for the successful use of a Creole-inflected French in the latter novel to approximate the authentic voice of the peasantry, but he also introduces into their culture Spanish words that introduce concepts of worker solidarity and labor revolt.

At the end of World War II Haiti experienced a period of intellectual effervescence with the visits of Aimé Césaire, Nicolás Guillén, Alejo Carpentier, and André Breton. The outburst of literary and political radicalism at this rivaled that of the American occupation. The pro-American mulatto president at the time was overthrown in protests led by student activists of the journal *La ruche*. Jacques Stephen Alexis and René Depestre, two of the leading student activists, were influenced by Roumain's Marxism as well as surrealist ideas. Alexis came to prominence in the 1956 Congress of Black and African Writers in Paris when he challenged the monolithic racial theories of Négritude with his essay on "marvellous realism," which promoted a more hemispheric definition of Haitian culture. Depestre challenged Aimé Césaire by advocating the ideas of Louis Aragon in defining a national poetics in Haiti. Both writers would run foul of the regime of *noiriste* intellectual François Duvalier, who came to power in 1957.

Alexis's novels, produced between 1955 and his death in 1961 at the hands of Duvalier's Macoutes, used a combination of socialist realism and fantasy to depict the lives of the Haitian working class. His sweeping, largely historically based fiction tried to cover all of Haiti's changing society. The question of regional identity is raised in Alexis's last novel, *L'espace d'un cillement* (The flicker of an eyelid; 1959), in which the protagonists are Cuban and the action takes place in a brothel on the outskirts of Port au Prince that is frequented by American marines. Alexis's oeuvre marks fiction created during the Duvalier years. The novelist, dramatist, and painter Franck Étienne's best-known work is the Creole novel *Dezafi* (1975), which describes the horrors of a zombified Haiti under Duvalier. His novels borrow Alexis's use of fantasy and advocate experimentation with form, which Étienne called a *spiraliste* poetics. Pierre Clitandre's *Cathédrale du mois d'août* (Cathedral of the August heat; 1982) is also a successful depiction of the urban poor's world of magic, misery, and desperate optimism.

Duvalierism also created an exodus of Haitian intellectuals, and beginning in the 1970s there has been an increasing Haitian diaspora in cities such as Montreal, Miami, and New York. Explicit anti-Duvalierist protest writing flourished in exile in a way it could not among writers who remained in Haiti. One of the major anti-Duvalier texts was actually written in Haiti, but it led to the exile of its author. Marie Chauvet's *Amour colère folie* (Love anger madness; 1968) brilliantly evoked not only the nightmare of state brutality but the complacency of the elite as well as the impotence of writers and intellectuals under Duvalier. Strident protest fiction was produced by Depestre, Étienne, and Anthony Phelps. The Duvalier dynasty proved to be very resistant to change, and Haitian writing in the diaspora became less centered on political protest and more focused on the experience of cultural displacement and the redefinition of Haitian identity. Even though there were attempts in the novels of Jean Métellus, Depestre, and the Creole poetry of Félix Morisseau-Leroy to return nostalgically to the native land, a younger generation of writers explored the freedoms and influences of being Haitian writers in the United States and Canada.

Two 1985 novels by Jean-Claude Charles and Dany Laferrière were the first to evoke Haiti's new transnational preoccupations. *Manhattan Blues* and *Comment faire l'amour avec un nègre sans se fatiguer* (How to make love to a Negro without getting tired) ushered in a new kind literature that is as much autobiographical fiction as travel writing. In Canada the novels *Passages* (1991) and *Les urnes scelles* (The sealed urns; 1995) by the late Émile Ollivier treat the difficulty of return and the hybridized space of the Haitian diaspora. This diaspora has also produced a number of major writers in English, many of whom are women. The most outstanding of these is Edwidge Danticat, whose successful first novel, *Breath Eyes Memory* (1994), deals with a young Haitian woman's personal experience of the clash of modernity and tradition. Her later works took on larger political themes. *The Farming of Bones* (1998) deals with the massacre of Haitian cane cutters in the Dominican Republic in 1937, *The Dew Breaker* (2004) with the difficulty of facing the ghosts of the Duvalierist past for those Haitians who have grown up outside of Haiti.

See also Canadian Writers in French; Caribbean/North American Writers (Contemporary); Creole Languages of the Americas; Danticat, Edwidge; Négritude; Women Writers of the Caribbean

■ ■ *Bibliography*

Dash, Michael. *Literature and Ideology in Haiti: 1915–1961.* New York: Macmillan, 1981.

Dash, Michael. *Culture and Customs of Haiti.* Westport, Conn.: Greenwood, 2001.

Garret, Naomi. *The Renaissance of Haitian Poetry.* Paris: Presence Africaine, 1963.

Hoffmann, Leon. *Histoire de la littérature d'Haïti.* Paris: EDICEF, 1995.

"Haiti: The Literature and Culture." *Callaloo* 15, nos. 2 and 3 (1992).

J. MICHAEL DASH (2005)

LITERATURE OF MARTINIQUE AND GUADELOUPE

The award of the *Prix Goncourt*, France's foremost literary prize, to Patrick Chamoiseau of Martinique in 1992 for his novel *Texaco* highlighted the increase in literary output and artistic visibility that had characterized work from the region since the 1970s. Paradoxically, it also tended to highlight the geopolitical ambivalence of the status as French Overseas Department imposed on these territories in 1946, which arguably has provided the region some of its recent impetus toward asserting a nonmetropolitan identity. Given this legal limbo, these islands are neither independent nations nor territories fully integrated into the French mainland. However, after their colonization by France in 1635, documented literary output in these islands dates back at least to the mid-eighteenth century, and until the early twentieth century much of this production was the work of metropolitan settlers. This shift in discursive emphasis will prove the central point in this analysis.

COLONIALISM AND EMANCIPATION

The period that followed the European arrival was characterized by a preoccupation with colonization and settlement in order to enhance profit margins from agriculture. As virtual corollaries to this process, the indigenous Carib and Arawak Indian populations succumbed to overwork and Western disease and disappeared within a century of colonization and were replaced by African slave labor on a massive scale. In time they would be followed by other arrivals, including East Asian, Chinese, and Syro-Lebanese. Literature during this period consisted largely of European travel writing and a relative absence of a colonized voice. Even though the first generation of Creoles had already appeared, most literary endeavors of the period were the work of Europeans, written for metropolitan consumption. Indeed, whites virtually monopolized writing from these territories for centuries, especially since most slave laws forbade teaching slaves to read or write. Catholic priest Père Labat's 1742 work, *Nouveau voyage aux isles d'Amérique* (New voyage to the American islands), falls into this category. An exception that proves the rule is the "Speech made by a Black at Guardaloupe" (1709), a critique that provides an opening onto the world of the slave more than a century before emancipation in 1848. The harrowing picture it provided of the contemporary treatment of slaves became grist for the mill of anti-slavery discourse.

An exception to this pattern would be *Les Bambous: Fables de La Fontaine travesties en patois martiniquais* (Bamboo: La Fontaine's fables rendered in Martinican Creole), published in 1846 by François Achille Marbot. *Les Bambous* was the work of an indigenous author and a groundbreaking text in terms of its valorization and transcription of the Creole language that had been formed on the plantation through the exchanges both between the varied African ethnic groups and between these groups and their owners. Its scope, however, was limited because it was a translation of a classic metropolitan text, breaking down relatively few barriers as a result. In general, the midcentury era became marked by strong tendencies toward literary mimetism, encouraging island poets (in large part members of the planter class) to imitate the styles and themes of their more established metropolitan counterparts. This so-called "*doudouiste*" period produced such notables as Daniel Thaly (1879–1950) and Victor Duquesnay (1870–1920), whose works took the soaring flights of metropolitan romantic fancy as their models, praising the incomparable delights of the island's flora and fauna, its light and shadow. The result was an ongoing dichotomy between a vibrant lived Creole culture and its exclusion from modes of expression in local arts and letters, the result of a virtual monopoly of contemporary poesis by colonial barriers of race and class.

NÉGRITUDE, ANTILLANITÉ, CRÉOLITÉ

The twentieth century saw the emergence of the white Guadeloupean Saint-John Perse as a major poet, and his collection *Anabase* (1924) would eventually help to secure him the Nobel Prize for literature. Indeed, French Caribbean writing, such as it was, had become associated almost exclusively with whites. However, the postwar period of the 1920s and 1930s saw a marked shift in emphasis with regard to both writer and theme. A literary and cultural upheaval was produced by the launching in Paris of the *Négritude* movement, led by Martinique's Aimé Césaire and Senegal's Léopold Sédar Senghor, itself partly inspired by the publication in 1928 of the folklore collection *Ainsi parla l'oncle* (Thus spoke the uncle) by Haiti's Dr. Jean Price-Mars. The appearance in 1939 of Césaire's *Cahier d'un retour au pays natal* (Notebook of a return to the homeland) cleared the way for indigenous black Caribbean writers to finally express their Francophone identity. But given the *Négritude* movement's unfortunate construction in terms of a common or shared black essence, the better to contest long-standing claims of French universalism, it would ultimately be charged with ignoring the West Indian specificities of the French Overseas Departments.

The context provided by the Algerian war of independence during the 1950s, and its attendant corollaries of decolonization, brought the revolutionary writings of Martinique's Frantz Fanon to worldwide prominence. But the ambiguities of distance and domination brought about by French Caribbean departmentalization in 1946 would, over time, highlight the islands' lived dichotomies of Caribbean particularism and French universalism that even Césaire's rewriting of regional revolutionary history in the Haitian-themed *La tragédie du Roi Christophe* (The tragedy of King Christophe) could not completely eradicate. The burgeoning *antillanité,* or Caribbeanness, movement was, in a sense, born of these very contradictions and omissions. Meanwhile, the appearance of such works as Simone Schwarz-Bart's landmark novel *Pluie et vent sur Télumée Miracle* (The bridge of beyond) and her outstanding play *Ton beau capitaine* (Your handsome captain), Myriam Warner-Vieyra's *Juletane,* and Daniel Maximin's *L'isolé soleil* (Lone sun), all of Guadeloupe, and *L'autre qui danse* (The other who dances) by Martinique's Suzanne Dracius-Pinalie in the 1970s and 1980s, continued to demonstrate the dynamism and inventiveness of French Caribbean literary production.

Edouard Glissant's theory of *antillanité,* first propounded in his *Discours antillais* (Caribbean discourse) in 1981, draws on the common Caribbean experience of uprooting, transformation, and cultural exchange to posit a principle of creativity grounded in the composite, where fragmentation and pluralism enable a new geopolitical vision for French Caribbean identity. Meanwhile, the writings of Guadeloupe's Maryse Condé, the prolific author of over a dozen novels, including *En attendant le bonheur* (Heremakhonon), *Moi, Tituba, sorcière noire de Salem* (I, Tituba, black witch of Salem), and *Traversée de la mangrove* (Crossing the mangrove), insisted on the centrality of women to the literary and cultural Caribbean canon. In addition, Xavier Orville's novels of the same period inscribed themes of poverty and social injustice within a framework of folk history to invoke issues of identity and collective memory within a Martinican framework.

The extent to which Glissant's articulation of *antillanité* provided a basis for Jean Bernabé, Patrick Chamoiseau, and Raphaël Confiant to construct their *Eloge de la créolité* (In praise of Creoleness) in 1989 is well known. In theoretical terms, however, the rather programmatic folkloric framework embraced by *créolité* makes it much more contested than its precursor. More artistically than geopolitically focused, it takes the compound ethnic, linguistic, and cultural structures undergirding the Creole language as the enabling metaphor for a broad-based aesthetic framework, valorizing the creative expression of diversity in the Caribbean Creole mosaic over the exclusionary oneness implicit in Western universalism. From a linguistic perspective, Jean Bernabé's pioneering work on the grammatical structures of French Creole has led both to its rehabilitation as a *langue véhiculaire* and to its increased acceptance in both the literary and the pedagogical domains.

Finally, it should be noted that whereas male writers certainly have dominated the literary output of these islands over time, this pattern has been overturned with the relative ascendancy of female writers since the early 1980s. Geopolitical perspectives can also be somewhat divergent, as very generally Guadeloupeans are seen as hewing to a more autonomous mind-set than their Martinican counterparts. Taken together, these authors trace the trajectory of tensions and hierarchies that frame the task of defining an indigenous yet hybrid French Caribbean identity; despite daunting geopolitical odds, their evolving vision of regional realities has helped create a permanent place in the pantheon of letters for the islands of Guadeloupe and Martinique.

See also Caribbean/North American Writers (Contemporary); Caribbean Theater, Anglophone; Césaire, Aimé; Chamoiseau, Patrick; Condé, Maryse; Creole Languages of the Americas; Glissant, Edouard; Literature of Haiti; Négritude; Women Writers of the Caribbean

▪ ▪ *Bibliography*

Arnold, A. James. *Modernism and Negritude: The Poetry and Poetics of Aimé Césaire.* Cambridge: Harvard University Press, 1981.

Balutansky, Kathleen M., and Marie-Agnès Sourieau, eds. *Caribbean Creolizations: Reflections on the Cultural Dynamics of Language, Literature, and Identity.* Gainesville: University Press of Florida, 1998.

Bernabé, Jean, Patrick Chamoiseau, and Rafaël Confiant. *Eloge de la Créolité/In Praise of Creoleness.* Bilingual edition, translated by M. B. Taleb-Khyar. Paris: Gallimard, 1993.

Britton, Celia. *Edouard Glissant and Postcolonial Theory.* Charlottesville: University Press of Virginia, 1999.

Burton, Richard D. E. *Le roman marron: études sur la littérature martiniquaise contemporaine.* Paris: L'Harmattan, 1997.

Burton, Richard D. E., and Fred Reno, eds. *French and West Indian: Martinique, Guadeloupe and French Guiana Today.* London: Macmillan Caribbean, 1995.

Chamoiseau, Patrick, and Raphaël Confiant. *Lettres Créoles: Tracées antillaises et continentales de la littérature, 1635–1975.* Paris: Hatier, 1991.

Condé, Maryse. *La Parole des femmes: Essai sur des romancières des antilles de langue française.* Paris: L'Harmattan, 1979.

Dash, J. Michael. *Edouard Glissant.* New York: Cambridge University Press, 1995.

Glissant, Edouard. *Le Discours antillais.* Paris: Seuil, 1981.

Glissant, Edouard. *Caribbean Discourse: Selected Essays.* Translated by J. Michael Dash. Charlottesville: University of Virginia Press, 1989.

Glissant, Edouard. *Poétique de la relation.* Paris: Gallimard, 1990. *Poetics of Relation.* Translated by Betsy Wing. Ann Arbor: University of Michigan Press, 1997.

Haigh, Sam, ed. *An Introduction to Caribbean Francophone Writing: Guadeloupe and Martinique*. Oxford, U.K.: Berg, 1999.

Murdoch, H. Adlai. *Creole Identity in the French Caribbean Novel*. Gainesville: University Press of Florida, 2001.

Rosello, Mireille. *Littérature et identité créole aux Antilles*. Paris: Editions Karthala, 1992.

H. ADLAI MURDOCH (2005)

LITERATURE OF SURINAME

Suriname, located on the north Atlantic coast of South America, is the country in which Maroon experiences have been most visible throughout history. The Maroons are descendants of former slaves who escaped from their plantations and reconstructed their African cultural heritage in the rain forest. They have also at times engaged in armed resistance against the military forces of the various governments of the nation.

This heroic history is rarely addressed in literary works by contemporary writers of Maroon descent, such as Doris Vrede, André Pakosie, and Julian With. These writers publish their work in Dutch and deal with contemporary issues of injustice, discrimination, and the dramatic changes occurring in their village communities.

The first Maroon author, Johannes King (1830–1899), wrote in Sranan, the main Creole language of Suriname. He was an autodidact and a member of the Moravian Church. The Moravian Mission always promoted the use of Sranan and was instrumental in its development as a literary language. The schoolmaster "Papa" Koenders, who published the magazine *Foetoeboi* in the 1940s, belonged to the Moravian Church, as did Sophie Redmond (1907–1955), a medical doctor and an author of theater texts. The country's most important poet, Trefossa (1916–1975), was also a Moravian. Jan Voorhoeve (1923–1983), a well-known linguist, was sent by the Moravians to study Sranan culture in postwar Paramaribo. Voorhoeve found a tabooed but flourishing tradition in which storytelling was considered to be a serious specialization, and the songs, dances, and musical performances were extremely rich with reminiscences of the times of slavery. Sranan was identified with strategies of resistance and survival, and it became the political language for the nationalist politicians before independence in 1975. Eddy Bruma, a lawyer and politician, has composed theater pieces and poems about the Maroon heroes.

Sranan serves as a connection to the African-American past in Suriname, and important poets such as Johanna Schouten-Elsenhout (1910–1992) and Michaël Slory (b. 1935) have helped maintain that connection. Nonetheless, the first critical approach to Surinamese history told from the slave's point of view was written in Dutch: In 1934, Anton de Kom (1898–1945) published *We Slaves from Surinam*, which was censored by the Dutch authorities.

In his early novels, Albert Helman (1903–1996) addressed the cruelties and injustice of slavery in plantation society in the seventeenth century. The writer Dobru (1935–1983), meanwhile, created humorous but critical narrative sketches about the everyday life of the poor in Paramaribo. Dobru also was a poet, and his poem "Wan bon" (One tree) is considered a second national anthem in Suriname.

In the 1950s and 1960s, Sranan and Surinamese Dutch were explicitly forbidden in the educational system of Suriname. Edgar Cairo (1948–2000) felt this to be such a painful experience that he struggled against its humiliating effects in his critical essays, poems, and narratives. Although Cairo wrote in Dutch (he lived most of his life in Holland), his native Sranan tongue strongly influences his syntax and grammar. In fact, many Surinamese writers have published their work in the Netherlands since the 1970s. Poetry, theater, novels, radio plays, and short stories are all represented. Clark Accord was particularly successful with his 1999 novel *De koningin van Paramaribo: kroniek van Maxi Linder* (The queen of Paramaribo: Chronicle of Maxi Linder), a tale about a famous prostitute. His work was immediately adapted to theater. Ellen Ombre (b. 1948) describes her experience of blackness from a female perspective, intertwined with the contemporary history of Africa. Her first novel, *Een negerjood in moederland* (A Negro Jew in the mother country), was published in 2004. Cynthia McLeod (b. 1936) has authored several historical novels. She discovered that the richest woman of Paramaribo in the eighteenth century was black, and she published her extensive archival research on this woman, Elisabeth Samson (1715–1771), whose parents were both slaves. McLeod also wrote a novel based on her own life, *De vrije negerin Elisabeth. Gevangene van kleur* (The free Negro woman Elisabeth. Prisoner of color; 2000). Astrid Roemer's characters, in contrast, are pure fiction, though clearly recognizable as Surinamese. Roemer (b. 1947) has written an impressive trilogy about life in Paramaribo in the second half of the past century. The trilogy comprises *Gewaagd leven* (Life at risk; 1996), *Lijken op liefde* (Looking like love; 1997), and *Was getekend* (Signed; 1998). Authors such as Ombre and Roemer do not identify themselves as Dutch or European, and they do not seem to find meaning in, or draw inspiration from, European literature. However, one of the most innovative poets writing in Dutch, Hans Faverey (1933–1990), a black Surinamese, seemed to consider his work a part of Dutch literature.

Finally, Surinamese literature shares features with literature from the rest of the black diaspora. Critics have drawn connections, for example, between African-American women writers in the United States and women writers in Suriname. Furthermore, Surinamese literature has shared with Brazilian and Angolan literature an interest in analyzing the attitudes of that economically well-off sector of the population in each of these societies known as Creoles—particularly their attitudes towards slavery and the slave trade. Unlike Angolan and Brazilian writers, however, Surinamese literature also focuses on the Maroons and on their dynamic interplay with other ethnic groups in Surinam's extraordinarily rich social landscape.

See also Literature of Guyane; Literature of the Netherlands Antilles; Maroon Arts

■■ *Bibliography*

Arnold, A. James, ed. *History of Literature in the Caribbean,* Volume 2: *English- and Dutch-Speaking Regions,* edited by Vera M. Kutzinski and Ineke Phaf-Rheinberger. Amsterdam and Philadelphia: J. Benjamins, 2001.

Drie, Aleks de. *Wan tori fu mi eygi srefi,* edited by Trudi Guda. Paramaribo, Suriname: Ministerie voor Onderwijs, Wetenschappen en Cultuur, 1984.

Neck-Yoder, Hilda van, ed. "Caribbean Literature of Suriname, the Netherlands Antilles, Aruba, and the Netherlands." *Callaloo* 21, no. 3 (1998).

Voorhoeve, Jan, and Ursy M. Lichtveld, eds. *Creole Drum: An Anthology of Creole Literature in Surinam,* translated by Vernie A. February. New Haven, Conn.: Yale University Press, 1975.

INEKE PHAF-RHEINBERGER (2005)

LITERATURE OF THE ENGLISH-SPEAKING CARIBBEAN

"Two sterling works are the most a young country like this can be expected to produce in a limited number of years, and—to tell the whole truth—they are all the public, in its present state, can put up with." This sentiment, from a June 1871 *Trinidad Chronicle* editorial, notes that only infrequently did the "tender stem of Creole Literature, languishing in an as yet wild and barren soil," produce "something ripe and substantial" rather than "watery, sour, or husky fruit"—not an atypical sentiment for the nineteenth- and twentieth-century Anglophone Caribbean. The lament of the absence of anything but a small, insufficiently literate or "cultured" reading public, and the lack of writers able to or interested in rendering a "Creole" reality, usefully flags issues of inadequacy, authenticity, and taste that have continued to resonate in discussions of the region's writers.

A relatively small percentage of competent and interested readers must be put, first, in the context of a relatively small population across the region, and then also in the context of an interest in books for the purpose of commerce or of gaining accreditation—the surest way to stifle pleasurable reading—as well as a deep suspicion of "political" or "ideological" sentiments. But the notion that "literariness" and pleasurable, leisured reading ought somehow to be cleanly separated from the taint of politics, examinations, or the market has haunted literary aesthetes in the region and across the globe, and it is precisely around definitions of "culture" that commentators within and outside the region have deemed the Caribbean a "wild and barren soil."

The extraordinarily rich cultural production of the mass of Caribbean people has been disparaged as "noise" in letters to the editor from the nineteenth century until today. It has also been disparaged in punitive legal codes, not least of all because the language of this "noise" has mainly been in the Creole languages of the region. A restrictive definition of *literacy* cannot accommodate the Caribbean's keen interpretation of signs, dreams, graffiti, West African masquerade, the King James Bible, the Rastafarian *Promise Key,* political and religious utopias, imperial edicts and wars, seditious broadsides, L. W. de Laurence's books of magic, Marcus Garvey's newspaper *Negro World,* Haile Selassie's speeches, missionary hymns, the Ramayana, Congolese Nsibidi script, "high canonical" and "trash" literary publications, current news from across the globe, and the absorption of all of this and more into the rhythms of daily life in societies that have never had the luxury of pretending that they are closed. To the consternation of those who condemn this "noise," the achievement of producing two Nobel laureates of literature—Derek Walcott from Saint Lucia in 1992 and V. S. Naipaul from Trinidad in 2004—has to be qualified by the fact that the region's popular musicians are much better known and more often cited around the world.

Yet, if it is true that narrow definitions of culture, literature, and society have ensured that the creativity of the lower echelons of Caribbean society has been scorned (Cooper, 1993), it has also meant that a lettered elite, anxious about its distance from this stratum of society and recognizing in its "noise" the key to challenging metropolitan definitions of the region's people as debased and inhuman, has focused on it intensely in its fiction and poetry—some have even called the focus voyeuristic (Hodge, 1972). Thus, for some critics, poetic personae and fictional characters and narrators who use Creole speech, for instance, are genuinely "Creole," Caribbean, or politically engaged, and those who do not are inauthentic. Is Jamaican-born poet Claude McKay's *Constab Ballads* (1912) more authentic for being written in Jamaican Creole than his sonnets, or, for that matter, than the poetry of his compatriots: Philip Sherlock celebrating blackness and nationalism in the 1950s in iambic pentameter ("Across the sand I saw a black man stride / To fetch his fishing gear and broken things"), or the coolly ironic poetry of Edward Baugh, Mervyn Morris, Velma Pollard, and Dennis Scott in the 1970s and 1980s?

Jamaican author Louise "Miss Lou" Bennett was honored in 2003 in national ceremonies in Jamaica that were attended by a middle class that had criticized her for using Creole in the public domain decades earlier. This only means that the boundaries of acceptability have shifted to include her and not others. But it is also surely just as wrong to assume that anything uttered in Creole is inherently oppositional or progressive. Countries and territories such as Saint Lucia and Curaçao (Netherlands Antilles) have long led the way in using Creole languages for a range of purposes. Perhaps it is less useful to make unequivocal judgments about authenticity than to recognize the enormous diversity of voices and perspectives in the literature of the region, and to note the particular stakes for each critic in the assessment of this diversity.

What counted as "substantial Creole Literature" for the 1871 editor quoted above—"two sterling works" published shortly before by Antoine Léotaud on the birds of Trinidad and John Jacob Thomas on Trinidad's Creole language—suggests some characteristics of the region's literary history. Both Léotaud, who was white, and Thomas, who was black, were delineating a "Creole" Trinidadian landscape. This is a reminder that white, functionally-white, Indo-Caribbean, and other writers not usually classified as black have contributed powerful interpretations of Caribbean life and the impact of the Afro-Caribbean presence in particular: such writers include H. G. De Lisser, Samuel Selvon, Jean Rhys, V. S. Naipaul, Robert Antoni, Sharlow, Lawrence Scott, Ian Macdonald, and Anthony Winkler, to name a few.

Léotaud's and Thomas's texts posed a Francophone challenge to the Anglophone hegemony of British rule, but Thomas also sought to insert dark-skinned, working-class Trinidadians who spoke little else beside Creole into Trini-

dad's cultural matrix as legitimate culture-bearers rather than uncivilized tabulae rasae fit only for labor. This vindication of people of African descent in Trinidad led Thomas to publish *Froudacity: West Indian Fables by James Anthony Froude* (1889), which refuted the racism of Victorian historian James Anthony Froude's *English in the West Indies, or, The Bow of Ulysses* (1888). Thomas's book was similar to Haitian writer Joseph-Anténor Firmin's *De l'égalité des races humaines* (Equality of the human races; 1885), which challenged Count Arthur Gobineau's theories of racial inequality. It also resembled the two-volume *Glimpses of the Ages or the "Superior" and "Inferior" Races, So-Called, Discussed in the Light of Science and History* (1905/1908) by Jamaican-born Theophilus Scholes. Their desire to challenge metropolitan perspectives—"writing back to empire"—has been a key trope in much of the region's fiction and poetry.

Firmin, who wanted the French language to have the same nationalistic and cultural significance as the Spanish language did for Latin Americans, would not have agreed with Thomas's championing of Creole. On the other hand, dictionaries and grammars are written by scholarly elites for consumption by other elites, and Thomas was as committed to speaking on behalf of working-class Trinidadians as any of his counterparts. As "one of Her Majesty's Ethiopic subjects," he affirmed the validity of the Caribbean in the context of British colonialism. If those who traveled to England in the 1930s, 1940s, and 1950s were more ambivalent, London was still viewed as the inevitable place to be consecrated as a serious writer. As critics have pointed out, authenticating the novel or poem as truly "West Indian" as opposed to "British," and ensuring that Caribbean male writers would be equal to or better than the English writers against whom they were often measured, frequently involved the use of male characters and poetic personae who would keep metropolitan and local women in line, and also respect but ultimately contain the energies of the unlettered working class, and so usher the nascent nation into being (Edmondson, 1999).

A critical factor in the experience and delineation of a regional "West Indian" sensibility was the *Caribbean Voices* radio program broadcast by the British Broadcasting Corporation from 1945 to 1958. Founded by Jamaican poet Una Marson, prospective writers were inspired to produce their own work after hearing on the radio the poetry of Eric Roach from Trinidad and Tobago; or the Saint Vincentians Danny Williams, Owen Campbell, and Shake Keane; or the performance of Walcott's play *Henri Christophe* (1950) on Sunday afternoons. The output of literature by Caribbean writers during this period and into the 1960s is phenomenal, and includes the work of, among many others, C. L. R. James, George Lamming, Edgar Mittelholzer, Garth St. Omer, Vic Reid, Neville Dawes, Namba Roy, Sylvia Wynter, and Orlando Patterson. They published their work abroad, or in journals across the region (such as *Kyk-Over-al* in Guyana, *Bim* in Barbados, *Beacon* in Trinidad, *Focus* in Jamaica), or in newspapers such as Trinidad's *Guardian*. They also joined members of various literary and debating societies, poetry leagues, and artists' collectives, were galvanized by the labor strikes of the 1930s and calls for federation and independence, and became inspired to explore the region's history of enslavement and revolution.

At the same time, writers such as Rosa Guy, who helped found the Harlem Writers Guild, Claude McKay, Eric Walrond, Jamaica Kincaid, and Michelle Cliff migrated to the United States rather than to Europe. In one sense, the presence of so many Caribbean writers today in that location has diminished the impact of London, but in another sense it signals the shift in the center of gravity from one English-speaking empire to another. In addition, immigrants to England or their children—including Linton Kwesi Johnson, Caryl Phillips, Andrea Levy, Fred D'Aguiar, and Zadie Smith—are winning accolades for rewriting an England that is fully theirs, just as Olive Senior, Austin Clarke, M. Nourbese Philip, and Ramabai Espinet are rewriting both the Canada to which they have relocated and the Caribbean.

Because writers across the French-, English-, and Spanish-speaking Caribbean have had such an enormous impact on theorizations of anticolonial and postcolonial politics and poetics, and have been affirmed as "the best writers in English today," it is often the case that their specific Caribbean contexts are minimized or ignored. For some, this underlines the importance of analyzing writers in terms of their respective nations. And certainly it is hard to imagine the explorations of the interior by Jan Carew and Wilson Harris, or the critiques of political authoritarianism by Martin Carter in the 1960s and 1970s and Oonya Kempadoo more recently, as other than Guyanese, or the explorations of calypso and Carnival in the fiction of C. L. R. James, Earl Lovelace, and Marion Patrick Jones as other than Trinidadian. Studies like those by Selwyn Cudjoe (2003) and Barbara Lalla (1996) take up this national perspective, but even Lalla explores the significance of the outcast and homelessness in Jamaican literature as "a national fiction within the Caribbean aesthetic."

Any purely national focus is always in tension with other perspectives. *New World Quarterly, Savacou, Trinidad and Tobago Review* (formerly *Tapia*), the *Journal of West Indian Literature, Small Axe,* and *Anthurium* and other journals have had a regional focus, as did the London-based Caribbean Artists Movement of the 1960s. In addition, the University of the West Indies in Jamaica and other institutions have fostered this regional consciousness. Not just Europe and the United States, but the migration of people in the English-speaking Caribbean to Panama and Cuba has affected the outlook of the region's writers, as has the continuing impact of the Cuban and Grenadian revolutions. If the annual Commonwealth Writers' Prize is one way for Caribbean writers to receive recognition, so is Cuba's Casa de las Américas award.

Africa and the African diaspora constitute another focus, and the novels of writers such as Paule Marshall and Erna Brodber use this prism to explore the impact of culture and nation on the Caribbean psyche. Vic Reid's 1958 novel *The Leopard* is set in Kenya, and both Neville Dawes and Kamau Brathwaite lived in West Africa. More than physical location, however, there is a continuing discussion about Africa's impact on Caribbean aesthetics, and as more and more empirical research emerges, the parameters of these debates will shift accordingly (Warner-Lewis, 2002).

Regardless of their linguistic origin and place of residence within or outside of the region, women writers across the Caribbean are being read and analyzed as a constituency. From that perspective, Kempadoo, for instance, critiques the nation in the specific register of the sexual violence done to women's and children's bodies (Francis, 2004). Other writers, such as Patricia Powell, question the ways in which the postcolonial nation polices the sexual identities of its citizens.

Today, debates about what constitutes "good" and "bad" literature continue with the publication of Caribbean urban and historical romance novels and thrillers, as well as the recovery and re-publication of forgotten nineteenth-century novels. As metropolitan literati applaud the region's writers, younger writers chafe at the old-fashioned preoccupations of their predecessors. It is possible to see older writers and younger writers, such as novelist Garfield Ellis and spoken-word artists Staceyann Chin and Roger Bonair-Agard, performing together at such events as the annual Calabash Literary Festival in Jamaica, organized by novelist Colin Channer and playwright, poet, and critic Kwame Dawes.

If some commentators still worry about "watery, sour, or husky fruit," they do so in a context in which the meanings of *Caribbean, English-speaking,* and *literature* are heatedly and eagerly debated.

See also Bennett, Louise; Brathwaite, Edward Kamau; Brodber, Erna; Canadian Writers in English; Carew, Jan; Caribbean/North American Writers (Contemporary);

Caribbean Theater, Anglophone; Clarke, Austin; Creole Languages of the Americas; Dub Poetry; Harris, Wilson; Hearne, John (Caulwell, Edgar); James, C. L. R.; Kincaid, Jamaica; Lamming, George; Lovelace, Earl; Mais, Roger; Marson, Una; Prince, Mary; Seacole, Mary; Sherlock, Philip; Slave Narratives of the Caribbean and Latin America; Walcott, Derek Alton; Williams, Francis; Wynter, Sylvia

■ ■ *Bibliography*

Breiner, Laurence A. *An Introduction to West Indian Poetry.* New York and Cambridge, U.K.: Cambridge University Press, 1998.

Cooper, Carolyn. *Noises in the Blood: Orality, Gender, and the "Vulgar" Body of Jamaican Popular Culture.* London: Macmillan, 1993.

Cudjoe, Selwyn R. *Beyond Boundaries: The Intellectual Tradition of Trinidad and Tobago in the Nineteenth Century.* Wellesley, Mass.: Callaloux, 2003.

Dawes, Kwame. *Natural Mysticism: Towards a New Reggae Aesthetic in Caribbean Writing.* Leeds, U.K.: Peepal Tree, 1999.

Edmondson, Belinda. *Making Men: Gender, Literary Authority, and Women's Writing in Caribbean Narrative.* Durham, N.C.: Duke University Press, 1999.

Firmin, Joseph-Anténor. *The Equality of the Human Races* (1885). Translated by Asselin Charles; edited by Carolyn Fluehr-Lobban. New York: Garland, 2000.

Firmin, Joseph-Anténor. *Lettres de Saint Thomas: Études sociologiques, historiques, et littéraires* (1910). Port-au-Prince, Haiti: Éditions Fardin, 1986.

Francis, Donette A. "Uncovered Stories: Politicizing Sexual Histories in Third Wave Caribbean Women's Writings." *Black Renaissance Noire* 6, no. 1 (2004): 61–81.

Hodge, Merle. "Peeping Tom in the Nigger Yard." Review of C. L. R. James's *Minty Alley. Tapia* (April 2, 1972): 11–12.

Lalla, Barbara. *Defining Jamaican Fiction: Marronage and the Discourse of Survival.* Tuscaloosa: University of Alabama Press, 1996.

Philip, Michel Maxwell. *Emmanuel Appadocca, or, Blighted Life: A Tale of the Boucaneers* (1854). Amherst: University of Massachusetts Press, 1997.

Thomas, John Jacob. *The Theory and Practice of Creole Grammar* (1869). London: New Beacon, 1969.

Thomas, John Jacob. *Froudacity: West Indian Fables by James Anthony Froude* (1889). London: New Beacon, 1969.

Warner-Lewis, Maureen. *Central Africa in the Caribbean: Transcending Time, Transforming Cultures.* Kingston, Jamaica: University of the West Indies Press, 2002.

FAITH LOIS SMITH (2005)

LITERATURE OF THE NETHERLANDS ANTILLES

Papiamentu is the native language of the populations of Curaçao, Bonaire, and Aruba, while Dutch is the overall language for justice, administration, and education. This language division plays an important role. Papiamentu is an exploratory laboratory for linguistic research on Creole languages. Its oral literature is full of regional traditions, such as the Anancy stories, also found in other Caribbean countries and performed with music and dance. The artist and writer Ellis Juliana is especially relevant in this respect. He even writes haikus in Papiamentu, giving expression to the unlimited possibilities of its poetical potential. He also worked as a collector of the oral history heritage.

Literature in Curaçao began to be written in Spanish around 1900. Neither black experience nor Papiamentu culture were central to this literature. By the time that Cola Debrot published his short novel *Mijn zuster de negerin* (My Sister the Negro) in 1935 in Dutch, this prejudice had come under attack. Debrot claimed that the African-American population belonged to the same Dutch-speaking family. But only when literature in Papiamentu became a real issue did the relationship with the cultural background of slavery and Africa start to be addressed explicitly. Frank Martinus Arion wrote a classical novel on this theme, *Doubleplay: The History of an Amazing World Record* (1998). The book contains an important reference to 1795, when Tula and Carpata led an armed revolt against slavery. They had contacts with the French islands and the Papiamentu speakers in Coro, the coastal city of Venezuela, where a similar revolt was undertaken in that same year.

Latin America, however, is no role model for the black experience in the Netherlands Antilles. Pierre Lauffer makes it clear in *Patria* (1944), one of the first published poetry volumes in Papiamentu, that Curaçao was his homeland. In 1957 Frank Martinus Arion introduced *Négritude* into Dutch-Antillean literature. His epic poem *Stemmen uit Afrika* (1957) echoes black voices in the forest, through which white tourists are passing. Although Arion writes in Dutch, he has other work published in Papiamentu. He also cofounded the first primary school in Papiamentu, the Kolegio Erasmo, in 1987, with a strong program on African-American heritage. In addition, Arion is an outspoken defender of Papiamentu's Portuguese origins, thus documenting intimate connections with Lusophone Africa.

The coexistence of Papiamentu with Dutch literature became reality after May 30, 1969, the historical date of the radical workers' protests. They accused the authorities of having discriminated against the cultural heritage of the islanders. Writers immediately took up this point. When writing in Dutch, like Arion, they emphasize the exquisite African-American details of the Papiamentu culture. And when writing in Papiamentu, authors display its rich variety for the creation of different images and word combinations. This is the subject in the novel *De langste maand* (1994) by Diana Lebacs. She views the island's culture through the eyes of a white Dutch camera team and elaborates the subsequent chain of misunderstandings.

Whereas Bonaire joins Curaçao in emphasizing the African-American heritage, Aruban authors are not particularly eager to consider this tradition. The relationship is more explicitly dealt with in St. Maarten, where the House of Nehesi regularly publishes works about black issues. The people of St. Maarten speak English, and this explains why the Nehesi editing house seeks to forge more connections with the English-speaking countries in the Caribbean than with their counterparts in the Leeward Islands. The Barbados-born Kamau Brathwaite and George Lamming are some of the authors in their publication program. The most outstanding writer and personality is the poet, journalist, and editor Lasana M. Sekou. He constantly deals with politics and migration and defines his own literary work as the search for liberation. Some of his publications are *Born Here* (1986), *Love Songs Make You Cry* (1989), and *Quimbé—Poetics of Sound* (1991).

See also Brathwaite, Edward Kamau; Caribbean/North American Writers (Contemporary); Creole Languages of the Americas; Lamming, George; Literature of Suriname

■ ■ *Bibliography*

Arion, Frank Martinus. *Double Play: The History of an Amazing World Record.* 1973. Translated from Dutch by Paul Vincent. London: Faber and Faber, 1998.

Arnold, A. James, ed. *History of Literature in the Caribbean.* Vol. 2: *English- and Dutch-Speaking Regions.* Edited by Vera M. Kutzinski and Ineke Phaf-Rheinberger. Philadelphia, Pa.: Benjamins, 2001.

Debrot, Cola. *Literature of the Netherlands Antilles.* Willemstad, Netherlands Antilles: Departement van Cultuur en Opvoeding van de Nederlandse Antillen, 1964.

Neck-Yoder, Hilda van, ed. Special Issue on Caribbean Literature from Suriname, the Netherlands Antilles, Aruba, and the Netherlands. *Callaloo* 21, no. 3 (1998).

Smith, Wycliffe. *Windward Island Verse: A Survey of Poetry in the Dutch Windward Islands.* St. Maarten: Offsetdrukkerij Montero, 1981.

INEKE PHAF-RHEINBERGER (2005)

LITERATURE OF THE UNITED STATES

African-American literature, like African-American culture in general, was born out of the harsh realities of black life in North America. Although the African presence in the Americas preceded both slavery and its predecessor, indentured service (which began for blacks in North America with the landing of nineteen Africans from a Dutch ship at Jamestown, Virginia, in 1619), blacks lived virtually from the start under severe pressures that tended to erode their African identity, although many important features of African culture and personality unquestionably persisted. These pressures also prevented the easy acquisition by blacks of the more complex aspects of European civilization. Except in rare circumstances, literacy among blacks was discouraged or forbidden on pain of punishment by the law courts, by slave owners, or by vigilante force. On the other hand, because the determination of blacks to become free and to acquire power (essentially one and the same idea) is as old as their presence in North America, the ability to read and write became quickly established as essential to the political and economic future of the group.

The earliest black writing reveals a combination of factors and influences that set African-American literature on its way. The desire for freedom and power was shaped at the start by religious rather than secular rhetoric, so that the Bible was the most important text in founding the new literature. Gradually, religious arguments and images gave way in the nineteenth century to political and social protest that eschewed appeals to scriptural authority. As blacks, increasingly estranged from their African cultural identities, sought to understand and represent themselves in the New World, they drew more and more on the wide range of European literatures to find the models and characters they would adapt to tell their own stories. Rich forms of culture developed in folktales and other works of the imagination, as well as in music, dance, and the other arts. A major aspect of African-American literature, broadly defined, is the persisting influence of oral traditions rooted in the African cultural heritage; these traditions have probably affected virtually all significant artistic meditations by African Americans on their social and political realities and aspirations.

The first significant black American writing emerged toward the end of the eighteenth century with the poet Phillis Wheatley. Born in Africa but reared as a slave in Boston, Wheatley was anomalous in that she was encouraged by her white owners not only to read and write but also to compose literature. Like the other black poet of note writing about the same time, Jupiter Hammon, Wheatley was strongly influenced by Methodism. Unlike Hammon, however, she responded to secular themes as, for example, in celebrating George Washington and the American struggle for independence. Her volume *Poems on Various Subjects, Religious and Moral* (London, 1773) was the first book published by a black American and only the second volume of poetry published by any American woman.

One consequence of the religious emphasis in early black American writing was a tendency to deny, in the face of God's omnipotence, the authenticity of the individual self and the importance of earthly freedom and economic power. In autobiography, the first literary assertion of the emerging African-American identity came in the eighteenth century from a writer ultimately committed to religion—Olaudah Equiano, born in Africa and sold into slavery in the West Indies, North America, and Great Britain. His volume *The Interesting Narrative of the Life of Olaudah Equiano, or Gustavus Vassa, the African* (London, 1789) became the model for what would emerge as the most important single kind of African-American writing: the slave narrative.

Also in the eighteenth century appeared the first of another significant strain—the essay devoted primarily to the exposition of the wrongs visited on blacks in the New World and to the demand for an end to slavery and racial discrimination. In 1791, the gifted astronomer and almanac maker Benjamin Banneker addressed an elegant letter of protest to Thomas Jefferson, then secretary of state and later president of the United States. Banneker appealed to Jefferson, as a man of genius who had opposed slavery (even as he continued to own slaves) and as a signer of the Declaration of Independence, to acknowledge the claims of blacks to equal status with white Americans.

Although the United States formally abolished the importation of slaves in 1807, the first half of the nineteenth century paradoxically saw the deepening of the hold of slavery on American life, primarily because the invention of the cotton gin revived slavery as an economic force in the South. In response, African-American writers increasingly made the quest for social justice their principal theme. In 1829, George Moses Horton of North Carolina, who enjoyed unusual freedom for a slave, became the first black American to protest against slavery in verse when he published his volume *The Hope of Liberty*. Far more significant, however, was David Walker's Appeal, in *Four Articles* (1829), in which he aggressively expounded arguments against slavery and racism and attacked white claims to civilization even as that civilization upheld slavery. Walker's writing may have encouraged the most fa-

mous of all slave insurrections, led by Nat Turner in Virginia the following year, when some sixty whites were killed.

The founding by the white radical William Lloyd Garrison of the antislavery newspaper the *Liberator* in 1831 helped to galvanize abolitionism as a force among both whites and blacks. In particular, abolitionism stimulated the growth in popularity of slave narratives. A major early example was *A Narrative of the Adventures and Escape of Moses Roper* (1837), but the most powerful and effective was undoubtedly *Narrative of the Life of Frederick Douglass, an American Slave* (1845), which enjoyed international success and made Frederick Douglass a leader in the antislavery crusade. One New England observer, Ephraim Peabody, hailed the narratives as representing a "new department" in literature; another, Theodore Parker, declared that they were the only native American form of writing and that "all the original romance of Americans is in them, not in the white man's novel." Slave narratives were certainly a major source of material and inspiration for the white writer Harriet Beecher Stowe when she published, in the wake of the Fugitive Slave Act of 1850, her epochal novel *Uncle Tom's Cabin* (1852). This novel, which offered the most expansive treatment of black character and culture seen to that point in American literature, would itself have a profound effect on black writing.

One autobiography largely ignored in its time, but later hailed as a major work, was Harriet Jacobs's *Incidents in the Life of a Slave Girl* (1861), published under the pseudonym Linda Brent. In its concern for the fate of black women during and after slavery, and its emphasis on personal relationships rather than on the acquisition of power, *Incidents in the Life* anticipated many of the concerns that would distinguish the subsequent writing of African-American women. The publication of a previously undiscovered manuscript by Henry Louis Gates in 2002, *The Bondwoman's Narrative, by Hannah Crafts, a Fugitive Slave*, changed the terrain of early African-American literature. Characterized by Gates as a novel rather than a slave narrative, this work is now understood to be the first novel written by an African-American woman. Like Jacobs's narrative, *The Bondswoman's Narrative* relies upon the conventions of sentimentality and the themes of religion so prevalent in nineteenth-century writing.

Other important writers of the antebellum period who sounded notes of protest against social injustice were escaped slaves such as William Wells Brown and Henry Highland Garnet, as well as the freeborn John Brown Russwurm (from Jamaica, West Indies) and Martin R. Delany. Of these writers, the most versatile was certainly Brown, who published as a poet, fugitive slave narrator, essayist, travel writer, dramatist, historian, and novelist. Responding to the implicit challenge of *Uncle Tom's Cabin,* Brown published the first novel by an African American, *Clotel; or, The President's Daughter* (London, 1853), in which he drew on the rumor of a long-standing affair between Thomas Jefferson and a slave. *Uncle Tom's Cabin* and *Clotel* helped to establish the main features of the black novel in the nineteenth century. These include an emphasis on the question of social justice for African Americans, on light-skinned heroes and heroines, and on plots marked by melodrama and sentimentality rather than realism.

Almost as versatile as Brown, and in some respects the representative African-American writer of the second half of the nineteenth century, was the social reformer Frances Ellen Watkins Harper. As with the vast majority of black writers before and after the Civil War and the heyday of the abolitionist movement, Harper maintained her career by printing and distributing her own texts, almost entirely without the opportunities and rewards that came from white publishers. Her major source of her fame was her poetry, although she depended technically on the lead of traditional American poets of the age, such as Longfellow and Whittier. Antislavery sentiment formed the core of her first book, *Poems on Miscellaneous Subjects* (1854), which went through almost two dozen editions in twenty years. Harper also published the first short story by an African American, "The Two Offers," in 1859; the biblical narrative *Moses, a Story of the Nile* (1869); and a novel about an octoroon heroine, *Iola Leroy, or Shadows Uplifted* (1892). Although Harper's limitations as a novelist are clear, *Iola Leroy* raises significant questions about the place of women in African-American culture.

While opposition to slavery was an enormous stimulus to African-American writing of the time, the Civil War itself went largely unreflected in black poetry, fiction, or drama. William Wells Brown published *The Negro in the American Rebellion: His Heroism and His Fidelity* (1867), and a generation later the historian George Washington Williams offered his *History of the Negro Troops in the War of Rebellion* (1888). In some respects, however, the most powerful document to emerge from that watershed event in African-American history is the *Journal of Charlotte Forten* (1854–1892) (published in abridged form in 1953) by Charlotte Forten Grimké. The journal records events in Forten's life from her school days in Salem, Massachusetts (she was born in Philadelphia, the granddaughter of a wealthy black sail-maker active in the abolitionist cause), through her two years as a volunteer teacher in the Sea Islands off South Carolina during the war. Also illuminating is the autobiography of Elizabeth Keckley, *Behind the Scenes; or Thirty Years a Slave, and Four Years in the White House* (1868), which culminates in an account of her service as a seamstress to Mary Todd Lincoln, when Keckley strove to use her insider's position to assist other blacks and the war effort in general.

Although it is possible to see black literature of the 1850s as constituting a flowering or even a renaissance of writing, the two decades after the Civil War saw no rich development of the field. Reconstruction was a period of promise but also of disillusionment for blacks. It was followed by a dramatic worsening in their social, economic, and political status, culminating in the U.S. Supreme Court decisions *Williams v. Mississippi* (1895) and *Plessy v. Ferguson* (1896). These and other decisions effectively nullified the Fifteenth Amendment to the U.S. Constitution, which gave black freedmen the right to vote. Soon, black Americans had also essentially lost the right to associate freely with whites in virtually the entire public sphere.

The rise of segregation and of vigilante repression after Reconstruction diminished, but did not destroy, black American literature. With the rise of black newspapers and journals (as exemplified at the turn of the century by *The Voice of the Negro* and *The Colored American*), formed in response to the barriers to integration, there was another upsurge in literary creativity. In 1884, the poet Albery A. Whitman published probably his finest work, *Rape of Florida,* a long narrative poem in Spenserian stanzas that showed off his considerable lyrical gift. In 1899, Sutton Griggs published *Imperium in Imperio,* the first of five privately printed novels that gave expression to Griggs's startlingly nationalistic ideas about the future of black America. Another important figure was Pauline Hopkins, who served as editor of *The Colored American.* However, the major new talents of the age were the fiction writer Charles W. Chesnutt and the poet and novelist Paul Laurence Dunbar.

Between 1887 and 1900, Chesnutt kept his racial identity a secret from his readers while he built his reputation as a gifted writer of poems, articles, and short stories in magazines (including the prestigious *Atlantic Monthly*) and newspapers that served mainly whites. Several of his short stories, including "The Goophered Grapevine," drew on the black folklore of the antebellum South, which Chesnutt treated with imagination and sympathy but also with a shrewd awareness of the harsh realities of slavery. In 1900 came the first of his three novels, *The House Behind the Cedars,* followed by *The Marrow of Tradition* (1901) and *The Colonel's Dream* (1905). Folklore dominated his collection of stories *The Conjure Woman* (1899), but Chesnutt also boldly explored in realist fashion the racial tensions of his day, as in his use of the infamous Wilmington, North Carolina, riot of 1898 in *The Marrow of Tradition.*

Dunbar, on the other hand, published from the start as an African-American writer. Starting out with the collection *Majors and Minors* (1895), he achieved national fame as a poet—the first black American to do so—with his volume *Lyrics of Lowly Life* (1896). This volume sported a glowing introduction by William Dean Howells, the distinguished white novelist, critic, and editor. In 1899 came another collection, *Lyrics from the Hearthside.* Drawing on the stereotypes of black life formed by the black minstrel tradition, as well as on the so-called plantation tradition, which sought to glorify the antebellum culture of the South, Dunbar was an acknowledged master of dialect verse. Such poems found a ready audience among whites and, perhaps more uneasily, among blacks. Unwittingly, Howells had pointed to the essential lack of authenticity of black dialect verse. He praised Dunbar for writing poetry that explored the range of African-American character, which Howells saw as being "between appetite and emotion, with certain lifts far beyond and above it." Eventually Dunbar regretted Howells's endorsement. In his brief poem "The Poet," he seemed to deplore the fact that for all his valiant attempts to compose dignified poems in standard English, the world had "turned to praise / A jingle in a broken tongue."

Nevertheless, dialect poems became a staple of black literature, especially in the hands of writers such as John Wesley Holloway and James D. Corrothers; Dunbar's verse, in both dialect and standard English, became enshrined within African-American culture as beloved recitation pieces. He also published four volumes of short stories and four novels, few of which are memorable. Genial collections of stories such as *Folks from Dixie* (1898) and *In Old Plantation Days* mainly gave comfort to those Americans who would remember the "good old days" of slavery. His novels, too, were rather weakly constructed—except for the last, *The Sport of the Gods* (1902). Here Dunbar, emphasizing black characters in his novels for the first time, helped to break new ground in black fiction by dwelling on the subject of urban blight in the North.

Dunbar was admired and imitated by many black poets of the age, but his misgivings about dialect verse came to be widely shared. One of his most gifted admirers, James Weldon Johnson, himself later an influential poet, anthologist, novelist, and autobiographer, credited a reading of Whitman's *Leaves of Grass* around 1900 with alerting him to the limitations of dialect verse. However, by far the most influential publication for the future of African-American literature to appear in Dunbar's day was W. E.

B. Du Bois's epochal *The Souls of Black Folk* (1903). With essays on black history and culture, as well as a short story and a prose elegy on the death of his young son, Du Bois virtually revolutionized Afro-American self-portrayal in literature.

Du Bois directly challenged the most popular recent book by a black American, Booker T. Washington's autobiography, *Up from Slavery* (1901). Washington's story tells of his rise from slavery to his acknowledged position as a powerful black American (he was the major consultant on black public opinion for most of the leading whites of his day). The autobiography comforted whites, especially white southerners, by urging blacks to concede the right to vote and to associate freely with whites. Criticizing Washington, *The Souls of Black Folk* offered a far more complex definition of black American history, culture, and character. In elegant prose, it fused a denunciation of slavery and racism with equally detailed descriptions of the heroism of blacks in facing the vicissitudes of American life. The most striking passage of Du Bois's book was probably his identification of an essential "double consciousness" in the African American—"an American, a Negro; two souls, two thoughts, two unreconciled strivings; two warring ideals in one dark body, whose dogged strength alone keeps it from being torn asunder."

Along with his other books of history, sociology, biography, and fiction between 1897 and 1920, Du Bois's work as editor of *The Crisis* (founded in 1910), the official magazine of the newly formed NAACP, unquestionably helped to pave the way for the flowering of African-American writing in the 1920s. Influenced by *The Souls of Black Folk,* James Weldon Johnson explored the question of "double consciousness" in his novel *The Autobiography of an Ex-Coloured Man* (1912), which has been described as the first significantly psychological novel in African-American fiction. He also published an influential volume of verse, *Fifty Years and Other Poems* (1917, celebrating the anniversary of the Emancipation Proclamation in 1913), and an even more significant anthology, *Book of American Negro Poetry* (1922), which included dialect verse but consciously set new standards for younger writers. Another important anticipatory figure was the poet Fenton Johnson of Chicago, with his modernist compositions that deplored the pieties and hypocrisy of western civilization. The Jamaican-born Claude McKay, in a body of poetry highlighted by his *Spring in New Hampshire* (1920) and *Harlem Shadows* (1922), combined conventional lyricism with racial assertiveness. His best-known poem, the 1919 sonnet "If We Must Die," was widely read by blacks as a brave call to strike back at white brutality, especially at the bloody antiblack riots that year in Chicago and elsewhere.

Jean Toomer's *Cane* (1923), an avant-garde pastiche of fiction, poetry, and drama, captivated the younger writers and intellectuals with its intensely lyrical dramatization of the psychology of blacks at a major turning point in their American history.

The Crisis, the *Messenger* (founded in 1917 by the socialists A. Philip Randolph and Chandler Owen), and *Opportunity* (founded in 1923 by Charles S. Johnson for the National Urban League) consciously sought to stimulate literature as an adjunct to a more aggressive political and cultural sense among blacks. Marcus Garvey's *Negro World,* with its "back-to-Africa" slogan, also added to the sense of excitement among black Americans at the coming of a new day, especially with the mass migration to the North from the segregated South. In some respects, the culmination of these efforts was Alain Locke's *The New Negro* (1925). A revised version of a special Harlem number of the national magazine *Survey Graphic* (March 1925), this collection of essays, verse, and fiction by a variety of writers announced the arrival of a new generation and a new spirit within black America.

Among writers born in the twentieth century, the poets Countee Cullen, starting with *Color* (1925), and Langston Hughes, with *The Weary Blues* (1926) and *Fine Clothes to the Jew* (1927), set new standards in verse. Cullen offered highly polished poems that combined his reverence for traditional forms (he was influenced by the English poets John Keats and A. E. Housman, in particular) with his deep resentment of racism. Less reverential about literary tradition, and guided by the American examples of Whitman and Carl Sandburg, Hughes experimented with fusions of traditional verse and blues and jazz forms native to black culture. Also during what is often called the Harlem Renaissance (although the literary movement was certainly felt elsewhere) came the work of poets such as Georgia Douglas Johnson, Anne Spencer, Gwendolyn Bennett, and Arna Bontemps, as well as Sterling A. Brown, who also rooted his poetry in the lives of the southern black folk and in the blues idiom. Several of these writers were reticent about race as a subject in verse, let alone forms influenced by blues and jazz. For the others, however, the new spirit was perhaps captured best by Hughes in his essay "The Negro Artist and the Racial Mountain" (*Nation,* 1926). Dismissing the reservations of both blacks and whites, Hughes declared that "we younger Negro artists who create now intend to express our individual dark-skinned selves without fear or shame. . . .We know we are beautiful. And ugly too."

Later in the 1920s and in the early 1930s, fiction supplanted poetry as the most powerful genre among black writers. In 1924, Jessie Fauset, the literary editor of *The Crisis* and ultimately the most prolific black novelist of the period, published her first book, *There Is Confusion,* set in the refined, educated black middle class from which she had come. The same year also saw Walter White's *The Fire in Flint,* on the subject of lynching. In 1928, Claude McKay published *Home to Harlem,* which antagonized some older blacks by emphasizing what they saw as hedonism. Nella Larsen's *Quicksand* (1928) and *Passing* (1929) sensitively treated the consciousness of African-American women teased and taxed by conflicts about color, class, and gender. Du Bois's *Dark Princess* (1928) sought to examine some of the global political implications of contemporary black culture. Wallace Thurman's *The Blacker the Berry* (1929) probed color consciousness within the black world, and in *Infants of the Spring* (1932) he satirized aspects of the new movement. Langston Hughes's *Not without Laughter* (1930) told of a young black boy growing up with his grandmother and her daughters in the Midwest. Other noteworthy novels include Bontemps's *God Sends Sunday* (1931), George Schuyler's *Black No More* (1931), and Cullen's *One Way to Heaven* (1932).

A major feature of the New York flowering had been the close dependence of the younger black writers on personal relationships with whites—not only editors but wealthy patrons. If the role of white patronage in the movement would remain a much-debated matter, the financial collapse of Wall Street in 1929 and the onset of the Great Depression certainly helped to end the renaissance. Many black writers, like their white counterparts, began to find radical socialism and the Communist Party appealing. Setting aside the blues, Langston Hughes, who lived in the Soviet Union for a year (1932–1933), wrote a series of propaganda poems for the radical cause; and even Countee Cullen found the Communist Party attractive.

On the other hand, probably the greatest single work of this decade—Zora Neale Hurston's second novel, *Their Eyes Were Watching God* (1937)—went against the grain of radical socialism or the overt assertion of racial pride. A lover of black folk culture as well as a trained ethnographer, Hurston set in the rural South her highly poetic story of a black woman's search for an independent sense of identity and self-fulfillment; the narrative abounds in examples of folk sayings, humor, and wisdom. Ignored in its day, her novel would eventually be hailed as a masterpiece.

In poetry, both Margaret Walker's *For My People* (1942) and Melvin B. Tolson's *Rendezvous with America* (1944) reflected the radical populism and socialist influence of the 1930s, when both began to write seriously. Again, however, the outstanding work came in fiction. In Chicago, Richard Wright, not long from Mississippi and

Tennessee, had started out as a propaganda poet for the Communist Party, then turned to fiction. In 1938, his first collection of short stories, *Uncle Tom's Children,* set in the South, showed great promise that was realized two years later, when *Native Son* appeared. A Book-of-the-Month Club main selection, the novel became a national bestseller (the first by an African-American writer). *Native Son* was unprecedented in American literature. Its bleak picture of black life in an urban setting—Chicago—and the brutishness and violence of its central character, Bigger Thomas, who kills two young women, drew on extreme realism and naturalism to express Wright's sense of a crisis in American—and African-American—culture. His brilliant autobiography, *Black Boy* (1945), also a bestseller, set his individual determination to be an artist against the backdrop of almost unrelieved hostility from both whites and blacks in the South; it confirmed Wright's status as the most renowned black American writer.

In 1947, Wright emigrated with his family to Paris, where he lived until his death in 1960. *Native Son,* however, with its emphasis on black fear, rage, and violence in an urban, northern setting, left its mark on the next generation of African-American novelists. William Attaway's *Blood on the Forge* (1941), Chester Himes's *If He Hollers Let Him Go* (1945), Anne Petry's *The Street* (1946), and Willard Motley's *Knock on Any Door* (1947) all showed Wright's influence. On the other hand, the most successful (at least in terms of book sales) of African-American writers, the novelist Frank Yerby, also started his career in the 1940s, but on a completely different footing. Eschewing black culture and the idea of racial protest as sources of inspiration, Yerby established his reputation mainly with romances of the South, starting with his enormously popular *The Foxes of Harrow* (1946).

In a sense, Wright and his admirers, on the one hand, and Yerby, on the other, were enacting the latest stage of the essential political and aesthetic debate among African-American intellectuals, which pitted the merits of racial awareness and protest against the allure of integration within white America as the major goal. Yerby represented one extreme response to this question; the career of the gifted poet Gwendolyn Brooks illustrated a more moderate position. She won the Pulitzer Prize in 1950 for her volume *Annie Allen* (1949), which appeared to confirm not only the unprecedented degree of acceptability of black literature by whites but also Brooks's wisdom and insight in mixing, as she did, "high" or learned modernist technique with a commitment to African-American subject matter. Her first volume, *A Street in Bronzeville* (1945), in which she drew on the same Chicago setting on which *Native Son* is based, exemplifies this strategy.

In fiction, an even more acclaimed fusion of modernism and black material came with Ralph Ellison's novel *Invisible Man* (1952), which won the prestigious National Book Award for fiction. Ellison had attended Tuskegee Institute for two years. There he had been drawn to modernist literature, especially as epitomized by T. S. Eliot's epochal poem *The Waste Land* and James Joyce's *Ulysses.* In New York, he had become friends with Richard Wright. In the following years, Ellison schooled himself in virtually all aspects of modernist literary criticism and technique, including advanced uses of folk material, and deepened his understanding of his relationship to the mainstream American literary tradition going back to Emerson, Melville, and Whitman. In *Invisible Man,* his unnamed hero struggles with fundamental questions of identity as a naive young black man making his way in the American world. At times baffled and confused, hurt and alienated, Ellison's hero nevertheless is sustained by a recognizably American vivaciousness and optimism. This last quality perhaps accounted in part for the success of the book among many white critics, as well as with many blacks, when it appeared.

Another pivotal figure in the late 1940s and the early 1950s was James Baldwin, who more clearly than Brooks or Ellison defined himself in opposition to earlier writers, and in particular to the master figure of Wright. Deploring what he saw as the commitment of black writing to forms of protest, Baldwin attacked *Native Son* in the celebrated essay "Everybody's Protest Novel" (*Partisan Review,* 1949), which is ostensibly concerned mainly with Harriet Beecher Stowe's *Uncle Tom's Cabin.* According to Baldwin, both novels dehumanize their black characters; art must rise, he argued, above questions of race and politics if it is to be successful. In his own first novel, *Go Tell It on the Mountain* (1953), set almost entirely within a black American community, a troubled adolescent struggles against a repressive background of storefront Pentecostal religion to assert himself in the face of his brutal, insensitive father and passive, victimized mother. Baldwin's second novel, *Giovanni's Room* (1956), on the individual's search for identity in the face of homophobia, included no black characters at all.

In 1954, the U.S. Supreme Court decision *Brown v. Board of Education* appeared to signal the end of segregation across the United States. Instead, it set in motion sharpening conflicts over the standing questions concerning race, identity, and art as the civil rights movement carried the struggle to the strongholds of segregation in the South. These conflicts in the 1950s and the early 1960s (in the era before the distinctive rise of Black Power as a philosophy, with its attendant black arts movement) certainly stimulated the growth of African-American literature. Some older black writers, such as Hughes, Wright, Tolson, and Brooks, published effectively in this period. Hughes brought out five collections of stories based on his popular character "Simple," drawn from his columns in the weekly *Chicago Defender,* as well as several other books, including his second volume of autobiography, *I Wonder as I Wander* (1956). Ellison's collection of essays, *Shadow and Act* (1964), on the interplay between race and culture, consolidated his reputation as a leading intellectual. Baldwin became celebrated as an essayist with dazzling collections such as *Notes of a Native Son* (1956) and *Nobody Knows My Name* (1961). His novel *Another Country* (1962), with its exploration of the themes of miscegenation and bisexuality among blacks and whites, was a bestseller. In focusing primarily on whites, however, *Another Country* perhaps epitomized the integrationist impulse that was soon to pass from African-American writing.

In the theater, Lorraine Hansberry's *A Raisin in the Sun* (1959) dramatized in timely fashion the conflicts of integration within a black family rising in the world. This play became the longest-running drama by an African American in the history of Broadway, as well as an acclaimed motion picture. When Hansberry won the New York Drama Critics Circle Award, she became the first black American and the youngest woman to do so. Other playwrights of the 1950s included the indefatigable Langston Hughes, who broke ground with gospel plays such as *Black Nativity* and *Jericho-Jim Crow,* as well as younger writers such as Alice Childress (*Mojo, a Black Love Story,* 1971), William Branch (*In Splendid Error,* 1953), Loften Mitchell (*A Land beyond the River,* 1957), and the actor-dramatist Ossie Davis, whose *Purlie Victorious* (1961) was a solid commercial success.

Although the civil rights struggle was being waged mainly in the South, a major disquieting voice boldly challenging racism in the United States was that of Malcolm X. *The Autobiography of Malcolm X,* cowritten with Alex Haley and published in the year of Malcolm's assassination (1965), was hailed almost at once as a classic work that combined spiritual autobiography with racial and political polemic. The work tells of Malcolm's rise from a life of crime and sin to deliverance through his conversion to the Nation of Islam, then his repudiation of that sect in favor of a more inclusive vision of world and racial unity. Malcolm's work appeared to stimulate a series of highly significant autobiographies that demonstrated once again the centrality of this genre to black culture. Claude Brown's *Manchild in the Promised Land* (1965) is an often harrowing account of its author's determination to climb from a life of juvenile delinquency in Harlem. Anne

Moody's autobiography, *Coming of Age in Mississippi* (1969), chronicles her troubled evolution from a small-town southern girlhood into a life as a militant worker in the tumultuous civil rights movement; it illuminates both her individual growth and some of the weaknesses of the movement as it affected many idealistic young blacks. Maya Angelou's *I Know Why the Caged Bird Sings* (1970) is a lyrical but also realistic autobiography of a woman whose indomitable human spirit triumphs over adversity, including her rape as a child.

Although Malcolm X's *Autobiography* appeared finally to repudiate racial separation, it had a major impact on the separatist ideal that informed the next major stage in the evolution of African-American culture. In 1965, in a break with the integrationist ideal of all the major civil rights organizations, younger black leaders began to rally around the cry of Black Power. In this move, they were supported brilliantly by certain writers and artists. In 1964, LeRoi Jones, soon to be known as Amiri Baraka, had staged *Dutchman* and *The Slave,* two plays that anticipated this turnabout. A graduate of Howard University, Jones had begun his career as a bohemian poet in Greenwich Village, where he had edited the magazine *Yugen* and helped to edit *The Floating Bear* and *Kulchur.* All of these journals featured the work of avant-garde poets, almost all of them white. Exploring the sensibility of a bohemian poet, his first volume of verse, *Preface to a Twenty-Volume Suicide Note* (1961), touched only lightly on the theme of race. *Dutchman* and *The Slave,* however, laid bare Jones's deepening hatred of white culture and of African-American artists and intellectuals who resisted the evidence of white villainy. He soon left Greenwich Village for Harlem, where he founded the Black Arts Repertory Theatre School, which barred whites. Jones transformed himself into an ultraradical black artist, an extreme cultural nationalist whose art would be determined almost entirely by the conflicts of race and by the connection between blacks and Africa.

Vividly expounded by Baraka and by other theorists (several of them poets) such as Ron Karenga and Larry Neal, radical cultural nationalism became the dominant aesthetic among younger blacks. Baraka's collection of new poems, *Black Magic* (1969), defined the artistic temper of the movement. These and other poems of the age voiced their radical opinions in blunt, often profane and even obscene language inspired by an easy familiarity with black street idioms and jazz rhythms, conveyed through typographic and other stylistic innovations. A spurning of all persons and things white and a romantic questing for kinship with Africa—the proclaimed fountainhead of all genuine spirituality—characterized the writing of these cultural nationalists. Addison Gayle Jr.'s *The Black Aesthetic* (1971), an edited collection of essays on literature and the other arts by black writers, gave another name and another degree of focus to the movement, even though several of the essays did not readily endorse the new radical nationalist position. Undoubtedly the most respected journal sympathetic to the new movement, imaginatively edited by Hoyt Fuller, was the monthly *Black World* (formerly called *Negro Digest,* and published by the parent company of *Ebony* magazine).

Baraka's attempt to form a theater committed to the politically purposeful expression of African-American values encouraged black playwrights to be bolder than ever. However, the existence Off-Broadway of the Negro Ensemble Company, led by Douglas Turner Ward, with a vision often in conflict with Baraka's, ensured variety among the writers. The result was probably the most prolific period in the history of African-American theater. Baldwin's *Blues for Mister Charlie* (1964) and *The Amen Corner* (staged on Broadway in 1965) reflected the new militancy and cynicism of black artists as they viewed the American landscape. Hansberry's *The Sign in Sidney Brustein's Window* (first staged in 1964) explored the minds and reactions of white liberals in contemporary New York. Adrienne Kennedy's *Funnyhouse of a Negro* (1964-1969) revealed her interest in expressionism and violence as she pursued questions of identity and personality. Charles Gordone's realist *No Place to Be Somebody* (1969) won a Pulitzer Prize for drama, the first by a black American. Other playwrights included Ted Shine, Douglas Turner Ward, Ed Bullins, Philip Hayes Dean, Ron Milner, and Richard Wesley. Lonne Elder III wrote the acclaimed *Ceremonies in Dark Old Men* (1969), and Charles Fuller later enjoyed a commercial hit with *A Soldier's Play* (1981) about blacks in the military. In 1975, Ntozake Shange's brilliant staging of her "choreopoem" *For Colored Girls Who Have Considered Suicide / When the Rainbow Is Enuf* captivated audiences as it anticipated a theme of rising importance, the feminist revaluation by women of their role in American and African-American culture.

In spite of successes on stage and in fiction, poetry became the most popular genre of the new black writers of the late 1960s. One encouraging development was the rise of small black-owned publishing houses, especially Dudley Randall's Broadside Press and Naomi Long Madgett's Lotus Press, which brought out the work of several poets in cheap editions that reached a wide audience among blacks. In this way, Sonia Sanchez, Nikki Giovanni, Don L. Lee (later known as Haki Madhubuti), Mari Evans, Lucille Clifton, Jayne Cortez, Etheridge Knight, Conrad Kent Rivers, Samuel Allen, June Jordan, Carolyn Rodgers, Ted

Joans, Audre Lorde, and other writers acquired relatively large followings. Indeed, the relationship of poets to the black population in general had virtually no counterpart in the white world, where poetry had long passed almost entirely into the hands of academics. Among black poets less committed to populist and nationalist expression, the most outstanding were probably Jay Wright and Robert Hayden. Hayden's first volume had appeared in 1940; his *Selected Poems* (1966) showed his commitment to an allusive poetry of reflection and painstaking art, even as he probed subjects as disparate as the African slave trade, the Holocaust, and the landscapes of Mexico. Somewhere between the populist poets and the gravely meditative Hayden was Michael S. Harper, in whose several books of verse, such as *Dear John, Dear Coltrane* (1970) and *Nightmare Becomes Responsibility* (1975), one finds a lively interest in contemporary black culture, including jazz, as well as a deeply humane cosmopolitanism in the face of personal tragedy and the brutalities of racism.

With the exception of the work of a few poets, however, fiction by black writers exhibited a more sophisticated impulse than did poetry. Novelists such as Ishmael Reed and William Melvin Kelley broke relatively new ground in black fiction with work that often satirized whites and their culture, aspirations, and pretensions. Reed's *Yellow Back Radio Broke-Down* (1969) and *Mumbo Jumbo* (1972) are rich in diverse forms of parody, as are Kelley's *dem* (1967) and *Dunfords Travels Everywheres* (1970). Novelists such as William Demby, Jane Phillips, Charlene H. Polite, and Clarence Major also represented the commitment to narrative experimentalism that coexisted, sometimes uneasily, with the realist tradition in black American literature. More traditional in technique but equally rooted in an affection for black American culture is the fiction of Ernest Gaines, notably *The Autobiography of Miss Jane Pittman* (1971).

John A. Williams, with ten novels (as well as other books) published so far, was the most prolific black novelist of the era. Emphasizing the travails of blacks in white America but often with reference to international conspiracy, espionage, and genocide, his books include *The Man Who Cried I Am* (1967*)*, *Sons of Darkness, Sons of Light* (1969), and *!Click Song* (1982). Another major figure, but one with different concerns, was Paule Marshall, whose publishing career spanned more than three decades. Born in Brooklyn but keenly aware of her Caribbean ancestry, she has explored her experience between these worlds in *Brown Girl, Brownstones* (1959), *The Chosen Place, the Timeless People* (1969), and *Praisesong for the Widow* (1983). The poet Margaret Walker's historical novel *Jubilee* (1966) was probably the single most popular work of fiction published by a black woman in the 1960s. Other fiction writers of the age include John Oliver Killens, Al Young, and Cecil Brown. Gayl Jones's novel *Corregidora* (1975) was praised for its lyrical examination of sexual fear and rage, and Toni Cade Bambara's collection of stories *Gorilla, My Love* (1972) richly reflected the wide range of personalities and styles within black America. Writers who established themselves as urban realists included Nathan Heard, Robert D. Pharr, Louise Meriwether, and George Cain.

By the late 1970s, the high point of the Black Power, black arts, and black aesthetic movements had clearly passed. However, all had left an indelible mark on the consciousness of the African-American writer. Virtually no significant black writer in any major form now defined him- or herself without explicit, extensive reference in some form to race and the history of race relations in the United States. On the other hand, gender began to rival race as a rallying point for an increasing number of women writers, most of whom addressed their concern for the black woman as a figure doubly imperiled on the American scene. Zora Neale Hurston's *Their Eyes Were Watching God* and, to a lesser extent, Harriet Jacobs's *Incidents in the Life of a Slave Girl* became recognized as fountainhead texts for black women, who were finally seen as having their own distinct line within the greater tradition of American writing.

The most influential black feminist fiction writer of this period was Alice Walker, who gained critical attention with her poetry and with her novels *The Third Life of Grange Copeland* (1970) and *Meridian* (1976). However, *The Color Purple* (1981), with its exploration of the role of incest, male brutality against women, black "womanist" feeling (Walker's chosen term, in contrast to "feminist"), and lesbianism as a liberating force, against a backdrop covering both the United States and Africa, became an international success. The novel, which won Walker the Pulitzer Prize for fiction, appealed to black and white women alike, as well as to many men, although its critical portraiture of black men led some to see it as divisive. Gloria Naylor's *The Women of Brewster Place* (1982), the interrelated stories of seven black women living in a decaying urban housing project, was also hailed as a striking work of fiction; her *Linden Hills* (1985) and *Mama Day* (1988) brought her further recognition. Audre Lorde also contributed to black feminist literature, and expanded her considerable reputation as a poet with her autobiography, or "biomythography," *Zami: A New Spelling of My Name* (1982), which dealt frankly with her commitment to lesbianism as well as to black culture. With poetry, literary criticism, and her widely admired historical novel *Dessa Rose*

(1986), Sherley Anne Williams established herself as a versatile literary artist. Earlier fiction writers, such as Toni Cade Bambara and Paule Marshall, also published with distinction in a new climate of interest in women's writing. Bambara's *The Salt Eaters* (1980) and *Marshall's Daughters* (1991) found receptive audiences.

The most critically acclaimed black American writer of the 1980s, however, was Toni Morrison. Without being drawn personally into the increasingly acrimonious debate over feminism, she nevertheless produced perhaps the most accomplished body of fiction yet produced by an African-American woman. Starting with *The Bluest Eye* (1970), then with *Sula* (1973), *Song of Solomon* (1977), *Tar Baby* (1981), and—garnering enormous praise—*Beloved* (1987), Morrison's works consistently find their emotional and artistic center in the consciousness of black women. *Beloved,* based on an incident in the nineteenth century in which a black mother killed her child rather than allow her to grow up as a slave, won Morrison the Pulitzer Prize for fiction in 1988. Her sixth novel, *Jazz,* appeared in 1992. In 1993 Morrison became the first black woman to be awarded the Nobel Prize for literature.

In some respects, the existence of a chasm between black female and male novelists was more illusion than reality. Certainly they were all participants in a maturing of the African-American tradition in fiction, marked by versatility and range, in the 1980s. In science fiction, for example, Samuel R. Delany, Octavia Butler, and Steven Barnes produced notable work, as did Virginia Hamilton in the area of children's literature. David Bradley in the vivid historical novel *The Chaneysville Incident* (1981), and John Edgar Wideman in a succession of novels and stories set in the black Homewood section of Pittsburgh where he grew up, rivaled the women novelists in critical acclaim. Charles Johnson's novels *Oxherding Tale* (1982) and *Middle Passage* (1990; winner of the National Book Award) exuberantly challenged the more restrictive forms of cultural nationalism. Without didacticism, and with comic brilliance, Johnson's work reflects his abiding interests in Hindu and Buddhist religious and philosophical forms as well as in the full American literary tradition, including the slave narrative and the works of mid-nineteenth-century American writers.

The shift away from fundamental black cultural nationalism to more complex forms of expression was strongly reflected in the waning popularity of poetry. Most of the black-owned presses either went out of business or were forced by a worsening economic climate to cut back severely on their lists. The work of the most acclaimed new poet of the 1980s, Rita Dove, showed virtually no debt to the cultural-nationalist poets of the previous generation.

While Dove's verse indicated her interest in and even commitment to the exploration of aspects of black culture, it also indicated a conscious desire to explore more cosmopolitan themes; from the start, her art acknowledged formalist standards and her sense of kinship with the broad tradition of American and European poetry. In 1987, she won the Pulitzer Prize for poetry (the first African American to do so since Gwendolyn Brooks in 1950) with *Thomas and Beulah,* a volume that drew much of its inspiration from her family history in Ohio. She was named U.S. poet laureate in 1993. This shift from black cultural nationalism was also evident in some of the most important works such as Colson Whitehead's novel *The Intuitionist* (1999). It is often compared in style and theme to Ralph Ellison's *Invisible Man.* Undoubtedly indebted to the gains made by the prominence of black feminist writers like Morrison and Walker, Whitehead's novel features a female protagonist whose experiences as an elevator inspector force her to confront the realities of racism, sexism, and classism. Edward P. Jones's novel *The Known World,* which won the Pulitzer Prize in 2004, also defies the cultural binarism of nationalism by demonstrating the inextricable connections between black and white people during slavery.

Sealing the wide prestige enjoyed by African-American writers late in the twentieth century, a major playwright appeared in the 1980s to match the recognition gained by writers such as Morrison and Walker. August Wilson, with *Fences* (1986), *Ma Rainey's Black Bottom* (1988), *The Piano Lesson* (Pulitzer Prize, 1990), and *Two Trains Running* (1992), was hailed for the power and richness of his dramas of black life. George C. Wolfe, especially with *The Colored Museum and Jelly's Last Jam* (1992), also enjoyed significant critical success as a dramatist. Suzan-Lori Parks emerged in the 1990s as a major voice in theater with the staging of her plays *The America Play* and *Venus.* Her 2002 play *Topdog/Underdog,* about the difficulties of being African American and about family life, won her the 2002 Pulitzer Prize in drama.

By the last decade of the twentieth century, the study of African-American literature had become established across the United States as an important part of the curriculum in English departments and programs of African-American studies. This place had been created in part by the merit of the literature, but more clearly in response to demands by black students starting in the 1960s. Still later, the prestige of black literature was reinforced in the academic community through widespread acceptance of the idea that race, class, and gender played a far greater role in the production of culture than had been acknowledged. The academic study and criticism of African-American

writing also flourished. In addition to the work of anthologists, who had helped to popularize black writers since the 1920s, certain essays and books had helped to chart the way for later critics. Notable among these had been the work of the poet-scholar Sterling Brown in the 1920s and 1930s, especially his groundbreaking analysis of the stereotypes of black character in American literature. More comprehensively, a white scholar, Vernon Loggins, had brought out a study of remarkable astuteness and sympathy, *The Negro Author: His Development in America to 1900* (1931).

In 1939, J. Saunders Redding, himself a novelist and autobiographer of note, published a landmark critical study, *To Make a Poet Black;* with Arthur P. Davis, he also edited *Cavalcade,* one of the more important of African-American anthologies. Later, Robert Bone's *The Negro Novel in America* (1958; revised edition, 1965) laid the foundation for the future study of African-American fiction. In the 1960s and 1970s academics such as Darwin Turner, Addison Gayle Jr., Houston A. Baker Jr., Mary Helen Washington, George Kent, Stephen Henderson, and Richard Barksdale led the reevaluation of black American literature in the context of the more radical nationalist movement. In biography, the French scholar Michel Fabre and Robert Hemenway contributed outstanding studies of Richard Wright and Zora Neale Hurston, respectively. Another French scholar, Jean Wagner, published the most ambitious study of black verse, *Black Poets of the United States* (1973). Still later, other academics such as Barbara Christian, Hortense Spillers, Frances Smith Foster, Donald Gibson, Thadious Davis, Trudier Harris, Robert B. Stepto, Robert G. O'Meally, Richard Yarborough, Deborah McDowell, Hazel V. Carby, William L. Andrews, Nellie Y. McKay, Gloria Hull, and Henry Louis Gates Jr. provided an often rich and imaginative counterpart in criticism and scholarship to the achievement of African-American creative writers of the past and present. Gates's *The Signifying Monkey* (1988), which explores the relationship between the African and African-American vernacular traditions and literature, became perhaps the most frequently cited text in African-American literary criticism. The turn toward poststructuralism in the work of many of the aforementioned scholars enabled the rise of cultural studies to predominate in important literary criticism of the 1990s and early 2000s. The work of Robert Reid-Pharr, Philip Brian Harper, Marlon B. Ross, Jennifer DeVere Brody, Wahneema Lubiano, and Sharon Holland represent examinations into black culture that rely upon complex theoretical paradigms to interpret African-American literature and culture. The analysis of black culture in the work of these critics increasingly considers not only questions of race, gender, and class but also of sexuality. In 1991,

Houston A. Baker Jr. became the first African American to serve as president of the Modern Language Association, the most important organization of scholars and critics of literature and language in the United States.

See also Angelou, Maya; Baldwin, James; Bambara, Toni Cade; Baraka, Amiri (Jones, LeRoi); Bontemps, Arna; Brooks, Gwendolyn; Chesnutt, Charles W.; Cullen, Countee; Dialect Poetry; Drama; Du Bois, W. E. B.; Dunbar, Paul Laurence; Ellison, Ralph; Harlem Renaissance; Hughes, Langston; Hurston, Zora Neale; Johnson, James Weldon; Locke, Alain Leroy; Morrison, Toni; Slave Narratives; Toomer, Jean; Walker, Alice; Wheatley, Phillis; Wright, Richard

■■ *Bibliography*

Anderson, Jervis. *This Was Harlem: 1900–1950.* New York: Farrar, Straus, Giroux, 1981.

Bone, Robert. *The Negro Novel in America.* New Haven, Conn.: Yale University Press, 1965.

Bontemps, Arna, ed. *The Harlem Renaissance Remembered.* New York: Dodd, Mead, 1972.

Craft, Hannah. *The Bondwoman's Narrative.* Edited by Henry Louis Gates. New York: Warner Books, 2002.

Cullen, Countee, ed. *Caroling Dusk: An Anthology of Verse by Negro Poets.* New York: Harper, 1929.

Davis, Arthur P. *From the Dark Tower: Afro-American Writers 1900–1960.* Washington, D.C.: Howard University Press, 1981.

Honey, Maureen, ed. *Shadowed Dreams: Women's Poetry of the Harlem Renaissance.* New Brunswick, N.J.: Rutgers University Press, 1989.

Huggins, Nathan I. *Harlem Renaissance.* New York: Dodd, Mead, 1971.

Huggins, Nathan I., ed. *Voices from the Harlem Renaissance.* New York: Oxford University Press, 1976.

Hughes, Langston. *The Big Sea.* New York: Hill and Wang, 1940.

Hughes, Langston, and Arna Bontemps, eds. *Poetry of the Negro, 1746–1970.* Garden City, N.Y.: Anchor, 1970.

Ikonne, Chidi. *From Du Bois to Van Vechten: The Early Negro Literature, 1903–1926.* Westport, Conn.: Greenwood Press, 1981.

Jones, Edward P. *The Known World.* New York: Amistad, 2003.

Johnson, James Weldon. *Along This Way.* New York: Penguin, 1990.

Kellner, Bruce, ed. *The Harlem Renaissance: A Historical Dictionary for the Era.* New York: Methuen, 1987.

Knopf, Marcy. *The Sleeper Wakes: Harlem Renaissance Stories by Women.* New Brunswick, N.J.: Rutgers University Press, 1993.

Lewis, David Levering. *When Harlem Was in Vogue.* New York: Oxford University Press, 1989.

Locke, Alain, ed. *The New Negro.* New York: Arno Press, 1968.

McKay, Claude. *A Long Way from Home.* New York: Harcourt, Brace, and World, 1970.

Osofsky, Gilbert. *Harlem: The Making of a Ghetto.* New York: Harper and Row, 1963.

Parks, Suzan-Lori. *The America Play and Other Works.* New York: Theatre Communications Group, 1995.

Parks, Suzan-Lori. *Venus: A Play.* New York: Theatre Communications Group, 1997.

Parks, Suzan-Lori. *Topdog/Underdog.* New York: Theatre Communications Group, 2001.

Perry, Margaret. *Silence to the Drums: A Survey of the Literature of the Harlem Renaissance.* Bloomington: Indiana University Press, 1985.

Rampersad, Arnold. *The Life of Langston Hughes: Vol. 1, 1902–1941: I Too Sing America.* New York: Oxford University Press, 1986.

Studio Museum in Harlem. *Harlem Renaissance Art of Black America.* New York: Author, 1987.

Wagner, Jean. *Black Poets of the United States.* Translated by Kenneth Douglas. Urbana: University of Illinois Press, 1973.

Whitehead, Colson. *The Intuitionist.* New York: Anchor Books, 1999.

Wintz, Cary D. *Black Culture and the Harlem Renaissance.* Houston, Tex.: Rice University Press, 1988.

ARNOLD RAMPERSAD (1996)
STEFANIE DUNNING (2005)

LITTLE RICHARD (PENNIMAN, RICHARD)

DECEMBER 25, 1935

Born to a devout Seventh-Day Adventist family, Richard Penniman, best known as Little Richard, began singing and playing piano in the church. He left home at thirteen to start a musical career. In 1951 he made some recordings with various jump-blues bands but with little success. Shortly thereafter, however, he began recording for Specialty Records, where he was to have six hits, beginning with "Tutti Frutti" (1954), that outlined the style that became rock and roll. In 1957 he left his music career behind and enrolled at Oakwood College in Huntsville, Alabama, following an "apocalyptic vision." He received a B.A. and became a minister in the Seventh-Day Adventist church. Inspired by the "British invasion," he returned to rock and roll in 1964, but he was unable to recapture his early success. During the 1970s he brought his flamboyant act to the Las Vegas showroom circuit, billing himself as the "bronze Liberace." Little Richard returned to the church in the early 1980s, but his influence on rock and roll was not forgotten. In 1986 he was among the first artists inducted into the newly established Rock and Roll Hall of Fame, an honor that helped restore his celebrity status in the late 1980s. He has a star on the Hollywood Walk of Fame, and his hometown of Macon, Georgia, has named a boulevard in his honor. In 2003, Little Richard was inducted into the Songwriters Hall of Fame. The following year, his album *Get Down with It: The Okeh Sessions* was released.

Little Richard's style—defined by his Specialty recordings—featured frenetic, shrieking vocals, suggestive lyrics, and boogie-woogie-style piano performed at a remarkably fast tempo. His flamboyant stage persona and extravagant costumes also became a significant part of his act.

See also Music in the United States

■■ *Bibliography*

"Little Richard." In *St. James Encyclopedia of Popular Culture.* Detroit: St. James Press, 2000.

Morthland, John. "Little Richard." In *New Grove Dictionary of American Music,* vol. 3. New York: Macmillan, 1986.

"Rock's Top Ten: Little Richard." *Rolling Stone* 467 (February 13, 1986): 37.

White, Charles. *The Life and Times of Little Richard.* New York: Harmony, 1984.

DANIEL THOM (1996)
Updated by publisher 2005

L. L. COOL J (SMITH, JAMES TODD)

JANUARY 14, 1968

■ ■ ■

Musician, actor, and writer L(adies) L(ove) Cool J(ames) is the largest selling rap musician to date, with more than twenty million albums sold worldwide. Born in St. Albans, Queens, New York, and raised by his grandparents, he began rapping at age nine. On his thirteenth birthday, he received DJ equipment as a gift from his grandfather. Cool J arrived on the music scene in 1985 with his first hit record, "I Can't Live Without My Radio." "Rock the Bells" soon followed, and in 1986, he achieved his first million-selling album, *Radio.*

In 1987 his second album, *Bigger and Deffer,* contained the first rap ballad, "I Need Love." *Walking with a*

Panther (1989) met with negative critical response but still sold more than five hundred thousand copies. The follow-up, *Mama Said Knock You Out* (1990), won a Grammy Award for best rap solo performance, remaining on the *Billboard* charts for over a year and selling more than one million units. *14 Shots to the Dome* (1993) became another platinum album for the artist, and he won his second Grammy for best rap solo performance for his single, "Hey Lover."

L. L. Cool J released three more successful albums in the mid-1990s: *Mr. Smith,* 1995; *All World,* 1996; and *Phenomenon,* 1997. *Phenomenon* was followed by a three-year break from the recording studio while the rapper focused on his film acting career. During this time he appeared in the films *Halloween: H20* (1998), *Deep Blue Sea* (1999), *Any Given Sunday* (1999), *In Too Deep* (1999), and *Charlie's Angels* (2000). Returning to the studio while continuing to act, Cool J released the album *G.O.A.T. Featuring James T. Smith: The Greatest Hits of All Time* in 2000. *G.O.A.T.* quickly climbed to the top of the music charts. Cool J returned to the screen with the films *Kingdom Come* (2001), *Roller Ball* (2002), *Deliver Us from Eva* (2003), *S.W.A.T.* (2003), and *Mindhunters* (2004), among others.

Continuing to juggle his careers in music and in film, Cool J released the collection *10* in 2002. A single from this album, "Luv U Better," became one of his biggest hits. Cool J re-signed his contract with Def Jam in 2003, continuing his relationship of more than two decades with the groundbreaking label.

Cool J's accomplishments include fifteen New York Music Awards, ten Soul Train Awards, and a *Billboard* Music Award. In 1998, he published an autobiography, *I Make My Own Rules.*

See also Hip Hop; Music in the United States; Rap

■■ *Bibliography*

George, Nelson. *Hip-Hop America.* New York: Viking, 1998.

L.L. Cool J, with Karen Hunter. *I Make My Own Rules.* New York: St. Martin's, 1997.

Rose, Tricia. *Black Noise: Rap Music and Black Culture in Contemporary America.* Hanover, N.H.: University Press of New England, 1994.

RACHEL ZELLARS (1996)
Updated by publisher 2005

Alain Locke (1885–1954). Locke was considered a brilliant scholar whose activities provided depth and coherence to the study of black culture. His highly regarded anthology The New Negro, *a collection of poems, stories, essays, and pictures of African and African-American art, gave Locke the role of primary interpreter of the New Negro movement.* THE LIBRARY OF CONGRESS

LOCKE, ALAIN LEROY

SEPTEMBER 13, 1885
JUNE 9, 1954

Best known for his literary promotion of the Harlem Renaissance of the 1920s, philosopher Alain Locke was a leading spokesman for African-American humanist values during the second quarter of the twentieth century. Born into what he called the "smug gentility" and "frantic respectability" of Philadelphia's black middle class, Locke found himself propelled toward a "mandatory" professional career that led to his becoming the first African-American Rhodes scholar, a Howard University professor for over forty years, a self-confessed "philosophical midwife" to a generation of black artists and writers between the world wars, and the author of a multifaceted array of books, essays, and reviews.

Locke was descended from formally educated free black ancestors on both maternal and paternal sides. Mary and Pliny Locke provided their only child with an extraor-

dinarily cultivated environment, partly to provide "compensatory satisfactions" for the permanently limiting effects imposed by a childhood bout with rheumatic fever. His mother's attraction to the ideas of Felix Adler brought about Locke's entry into one of the early Ethical Culture schools; his early study of the piano and violin complemented the brilliant scholarship that won him entry to Harvard College in 1904 and a magna cum laude citation and election to Phi Beta Kappa upon graduation three years later.

Locke's undergraduate years, during Harvard's "golden age of philosophy," culminated with his being selected a Rhodes scholar from Pennsylvania (the only African American so honored during his lifetime) and studying philosophy, Greek, and humane letters at Oxford and Berlin from 1907 to 1911. There Locke developed his lasting "modernist" interests in the creative and performing arts, and close relationships with African and West Indian students that gave him an international perspective on racial issues. Locke's singular distinction as a black Rhodes scholar kept a national focus on his progress when he returned to the United States in 1912 to begin his long professional career at Howard University. His novitiate there as a teacher of English and philosophy was coupled with an early dedication to fostering Howard's development as an "incubator of Negro intellectuals" and as a center for research on worldwide racial and cultural contacts and colonialism. He managed simultaneously to complete a philosophy dissertation in the field of axiology on "The Problem of Classification in Theory of Value," which brought him a Ph.D. from Harvard in 1918. In 1924 he spent a sabbatical year in Egypt collaborating with the French Oriental Archeological Society for the opening at Luxor of the tomb of Tutankhamen.

On his return in 1925, Locke encountered the cycle of student protests then convulsing African-American colleges and universities, including Hampton, Fisk, and Lincoln, as well as Howard. Subsequently dismissed from Howard because of his allegiances with the protestors, he took advantage of the three-year hiatus in his Howard career to assume a leadership role in the emerging Harlem Renaissance by first editing the March 1925 special "Harlem number" of *Survey Graphic* magazine. Its immediate success led him to expand it into book form later that year in the stunning anthology *The New Negro*, which—with its cornucopia of literature, the arts, and social commentary—gave coherent shape to the New Negro movement and gave Locke the role of a primary interpreter.

More than just an interpreter, mediator, or "liaison officer" of the New Negro movement, however, Locke became its leading theoretician and strategist. Over the following fifteen years, and from a staggering diversity of sources in traditional and contemporary philosophy, literature, art, religion, and social thought, he synthesized an optimistic, idealistic cultural credo, a "New Negro formulation" of racial values and imperatives that he insisted was neither a formula nor a program but that confronted the paradoxes of African-American culture, charting what he thought was a unifying strategy for achieving freedom in art and in American life.

Locke's formulation was rooted, like the complex and sometimes competing ideological stances of W. E. B. Du Bois, in the drive to apply the methods of philosophy to the problems of race. It fused Locke's increasingly sophisticated "cultural racialism" with the new cultural pluralism advocated by Jewish-American philosopher Horace Kallen (a colleague during Locke's Harvard and Oxford years) and by Anglo-American literary radicals such as Randolph Bourne and V. F. Calverton. Locke adapted Van Wyck Brooks's and H. L. Mencken's genteel critical revolt against Puritanism and Philistinism to analogous problems facing the emergent but precarious African-American elite; and he incorporated into his outlook the Whitmanesque folk ideology of the 1930s and 1940s "new regionalism." Finally, Locke's credo attempted to turn the primitivist fascination with the art and culture of Africa to aesthetic and political advantage by discovering in it a "useable past" or "ancestral legacy" that was both classical and modern, and by urging an African-American cultural mission "apropos of Africa" that would combine the strengths of both Garveyism and Du Bois's Pan-African congresses.

In the course of doing so, Alain Locke became a leading American collector and critic of African art, clarifying both its dramatic influence on modernist aesthetics in the West and its import as "perhaps the ultimate key for the interpretation of the African mind." In conjunction with the Harmon Foundation, he organized a series of African-American art exhibitions; in conjunction with Montgomery Gregory and Marie Moore-Forrest, he played a pioneering role in the developing national black theater movement by promoting the Howard University Players and by coediting with Gregory the 1927 watershed volume *Plays of Negro Life: A Source-Book of Native American Drama.* From the late 1920s to mid-century, Locke published annual *Opportunity* magazine reviews of scholarship and creative expression that constitute in microcosm an intellectual history of the New Negro era.

With the onset of the worldwide depression in 1929 and the end of the 1920s "vogue for things Negro," Locke viewed the New Negro movement to be shifting, in lockstep, from a "Renaissance" phase to a "Reformation." His commitment to adult-education programs led him to publish, for the Associates in Negro Folk Education, *The Negro and His Music* and *Negro Art: Past and Present* in 1936 and a lavish art-history volume, *The Negro in Art: A Pictorial Record of the Negro Artists and the Negro Theme in Art,* in 1940. A return to formal work in philosophy found him producing a series of essays in the 1930s and 1940s on cultural pluralism. Moreover, he revived his early interest in the scientific study of global race relations by coediting with Bernhard Stern *When Peoples Meet: A Study in Race and Culture Contacts* (1942). During a year as an exchange professor in Haiti, Locke had begun a potential magnum opus on the cultural contributions of African Americans, which occupied the last decade of his life, when his preeminence as a scholar and the lessening of segregation in American higher education kept him in demand as a visiting professor and lecturer within the United States and abroad. The effects of his lifelong heart ailments led to Locke's death in 1954. His uncompleted opus, *The Negro in American Culture,* was completed and published posthumously by Margaret Just Butcher, daughter of a Howard colleague.

See also Du Bois, W. E. B.; Garvey, Marcus; Harlem Renaissance; Howard University; New Negro

▪ ■ *Bibliography*

Baker, Houston. *Modernism and the Harlem Renaissance.* Chicago: University of Chicago Press, 1987.

Harris, Leonard, ed. *The Philosophy of Alain Locke: Harlem Renaissance and Beyond.* Philadelphia: Temple University Press, 1989.

Harris, Leonard, ed. *The Critical Pragmatism of Alain Locke: A Reader on Value Theory, Aesthetics, Community, Culture, Race, and Education.* Lanham, Md.: Rowman & Littlefield, 1999.

Kofi Cain, Rudolph Alexander. *Alain Leroy Locke: Race, Culture, and the Education of African American Adults.* Amsterdam, Netherlands: Rodopi, 2003.

Lewis, David Levering. *When Harlem Was in Vogue.* New York: Penguin, 1997.

Linnemann, Russell J. *Alain Locke: Reflections on a Modern Renaissance Man.* Baton Rouge: Louisiana State University Press, 1982.

Posnock, Ross. *Color and Culture: Black Writers and the Making of the Modern Intellectual.* Cambridge, Mass.: Harvard University Press, 1998.

Stewart, Jeffrey, ed. *The Critical Temper of Alain Locke: A Selection of His Essays on Art and Culture.* New York: Garland, 1983.

Tidwell, J. Edgar, and John S. Wright. "Alain Locke: A Comprehensive Bibliography of His Published Writings." *Callaloo* 4 (1981): 175–192.

Washington, Johnny. *Alain Locke and His Philosophy: A Quest for Cultural Pluralism.* Westport, Conn.: Greenwood, 1986.

Washington, Johnny. *A Journey into the Philosophy of Alain Locke.* Westport, Conn.: Greenwood, 1994.

JOHN S. WRIGHT (1996)
Updated bibliography

LOGAN, RAYFORD W.

JANUARY 7, 1897
NOVEMBER 4, 1982

The historian Rayford Whittingham Logan, the son of Arthur C. and Martha Logan, was born and raised in Washington, D.C. Although his family was poor, it had social status and connections owing to Arthur's position as butler to the Republican senator from Connecticut. Logan was educated at the prestigious but segregated M Street (later Dunbar) High School, whose faculty included Carter G. Woodson and Jessie Fauset, and whose alumni included Charles Houston, William Hastie, and Charles Drew; his secondary education was conscious preparation not only for college but also for race leadership. He attended Williams College (graduating Phi Beta Kappa in 1917) and then joined the army, rose to lieutenant, and was injured in combat.

World War I was a turning point for Logan. Like most African Americans, he had expected that participation in the conflict would lead to full citizenship rights. But the extreme racism of army life angered him. After the armistice he demobilized in France, remaining there for five years. Because he avoided white American tourists, he experienced the freedom of a society that appeared to harbor little animus toward people of color. While an expatriate, he began a lifelong association with W. E. B. Du Bois and became a leading advocate of Pan-Africanism, helping to articulate a program for racial equality in the United States and the protection and development of Africans.

In 1924 Logan returned to the United States with a desire to pursue an academic career and merge it with civil rights activism. While working toward an M.A. at Williams (1927) and a Ph.D. from Harvard (1936), Logan taught at Virginia Union University (1925–1930), where he was the first to introduce courses on imperialism and black history, and at Atlanta University (1933–1938). Both were elite, historically black colleges. He also spent two years as Woodson's assistant at the Association for the Study of Negro Life and History (now the Association for the Study of African American Life and History). Along

with Du Bois, Woodson was a seminal influence on Logan's scholarship. In the 1930s he worked closely with Du Bois on the *Encyclopedia of the Negro* project. In 1938 he moved to Howard University, where he remained until he retired in 1974. Logan developed a strong scholarly and political interest in Haiti and the European powers' administration of their African colonies. His dissertation on Haiti and the United States broke new scholarly ground on the issue of race and diplomacy. He witnessed firsthand the 1934 end of the American occupation of the island republic, and in 1941 the Haitian government awarded him the Order of Honor and Merit with the rank of commander for his scholarship and advocacy. In the same year his study *The Diplomatic Relations of the United States with Haiti, 1776–1891* was published. His articles on colonial abuses in Africa and the African Diaspora appeared in the *Journal of Negro History,* the *Journal of Negro Education,* and the *Pittsburgh Courier.*

The thrust of Logan's scholarship and activism was to promote the dignity and equality of black people around the world and to expose the racial hypocrisy of American democracy. He organized voter registration drives in Richmond and Atlanta in the 1920s and 1930s, campaigned against the segregated military in the 1940s, and was a leader in A. Philip Randolph's March on Washington Movement (participating in the final negotiations that led to Executive Order 8802, which prohibited discrimination in the Defense Department and established the Fair Employment Practices Committee (FEPC), a condition set by leaders of the movement to call off the march). In 1944 he edited *What the Negro Wants,* a collection of essays by fourteen prominent African Americans that helped to put squarely before a national, interracial audience the demand for a total end to segregation. He championed, in close association with Du Bois, the cause of African and Third World decolonization in the post–World War II era; between 1948 and 1950 he was the principal adviser on international affairs for the National Association for the Advancement of Colored People (NAACP). His most renowned work, *The Negro in American Life and Thought: The Nadir, 1877–1901* (1954), established an analytical framework that historians continue to find useful. Logan spent his last decade compiling and editing, with Michael R. Winston, the *Dictionary of American Negro Biography* (1982), an important reference work that was inspired by Du Bois's unfinished *Encyclopedia of the Negro.*

An intellectual of considerable talent, Logan also hoped to be a major civil rights figure. But in part because of his abrasive personality and aversion to accepting the organizational discipline of others, and in part because his views were at times more strident than those of the mainstream advancement organizations, he could more often be found on the margins, in the role of the prophet who received little recognition. This conundrum allowed Logan the luxury of being an incisive critic but prevented him from consistently implementing his often farsighted plans and from accumulating the recognition he felt he deserved from both African Americans and white Americans. Nevertheless, he was awarded the Spingarn Medal by the NAACP in 1980. He died in Washington, D.C., in 1982.

See also Association for the Study of African American Life and History; Du Bois, W. E. B.; Haitian Revolution; Howard University; National Association for the Advancement of Colored People; Pan-Africanism; Randolph, Asa Philip; Spingarn Medal; Woodson, Carter G.

■ ■ *Bibliography*

Janken, Kenneth Robert. *Rayford W. Logan and the Dilemma of the African-American Intellectual.* Amherst: University of Massachusetts Press, 1993.

Meier, August, and Elliott Rudwick. *Black History and the Historical Profession, 1915–1980.* Urbana: University of Illinois Press, 1986.

KENNETH ROBERT JANKEN (1996)

LONGBRIDGE-BUSTAMANTE, GLADYS

MARCH 8, 1912

■■■

Through her work for the betterment of the working class and of children, and through her association and partnership with one of Jamaica's leading politicians, Sir Alexander Bustamante, Lady Gladys Bustamante contributed a great deal to the building of independent Jamaica. She has been acclaimed as a woman of quiet strength and courage, of dedication and loyalty, qualities she has demonstrated in her faithful service to her employer and husband throughout his struggle for workers' rights and self-government, and in her persistence in the face of adversity.

Lady Bustamante was born Gladys Maud Longbridge in Ashton, Westmoreland, the child of James Longbridge and Rebecca Blackwood-Longbridge. Her grandparents raised her from an early age, as her mother had migrated to Cuba and her father worked as an overseer in the parish of St. Mary. She attended primary school in Ashton until she was fifteen, and later she attended the now defunct Tu-

torial Secondary and Commercial College in Kingston. She studied accounting, shorthand, typewriting, music, and Spanish. She was raised as a Moravian, but she later became a Roman Catholic.

Lady Bustamante began her working life in 1928 as a pupil teacher in her old school in Ashton, before going to Kingston to further her education there. She worked for a brief time in Montego Bay in 1934 before returning to Kingston, where she was temporarily employed at the Arlington House Hotel and Restaurant as a typist, clerk, and cashier. In 1936, at the age of twenty-four, she accepted a job in Bustamante's Loan and Securities Company. She served as Alexander Bustamante's secretary for twenty-seven years both in his business and in his later work in trade unionism and politics. She served in that capacity until he became the first prime minister of independent Jamaica in 1962, the same year that she became his wife (he was seventy-eight years old at the time).

It was in Montego Bay that Lady Bustamante became aware of the sharp class and race divide in Jamaica, and her work at the hotel had allowed her to overhear discussions of many of the leading players in the evolving movement toward self-government. This exposure informed her interest in changing the circumstances of the working class, but it was her engagement as Bustamante's secretary that catapulted her into nation building. Just a few years after she entered his employ, in 1938, the workers' riots in Jamaica pushed her employer into trade unionism and politics and placed her in the path of greatness. She was unsuccessful, however, in her one attempt to be elected to political office. While she did not serve in the nation's parliament, she was very much in the forefront of the birth of the nation, for she was actively involved in the initiating of the activities that would lead to independence. Following independence, she continued to use her position as the wife of the prime minister to great influence. For example, she was instrumental in the changing of the regulation that prevented women from working after marriage.

Lady Bustamante adopted her husband's interest in trade unionism and politics, making his life's work hers. She is reported to have challenged the police in defense of Bustamante during the 1938 uprising, and she was actually placed on the list for those to be sent to a detention camp. She was beside him throughout his fight with the Colonial Office for equity in the workplace, adult suffrage, and the achievement of nationhood. Her position not only allowed her to gain invaluable knowledge, but she was also able to help him in processing the information he received and in deciding on the best course of action. She refused to be an office-based secretary and accompanied him on his visits with workers and to meetings. She mingled with crowds and received first-hand knowledge of the people's plight and of their responses to Bustamante's speeches. This must have stood him in good stead in his political life, and he often credited her with his success.

Her exposure to the world of the working class made her into a trade union advocate. This, and her frequent travels into rural Jamaica with Sir Alexander as he laid the foundations for the Bustamante Industrial Trade Union (BITU) and the Jamaica Labour Party (JLP), made her eminently suitable to serve as a trustee, and as treasurer, of the BITU. She also led the BITU while Bustamante, then her employer, was in detention. She also served in the upper echelons of the JLP (founded in 1943). She was a member of the executive committee and a trustee of the party's Old Age Pension Committee, before becoming a life member in 1977.

Lady Bustamante's awareness of the needs of the poor and destitute led her into social work. She has served as patron of the Bustamante Hospital for Children for several years. She has not only worked for the betterment of the families of port workers, she has sought to uplift the communities in the sugar belt and worked to improve the care of children of destitute parents. While she has no children of her own, she has acted as godmother for some fifty-three children. Her treats (parties) for children and the indigent during the holiday season are well known.

Lady Bustamante has received renown both as wife of a former prime minister and national hero of Jamaica and in her own right as humanitarian and social worker. Her work has been recognized both inside and outside of Jamaica. In 1979 she received the nation of Jamaica's fourth highest honor, the Order of Jamaica (OJ), only the second woman to do so. Her other honors include the Harmony in the Homes Movement Model Family Trophy for widows (1985), awarded to her because of her exemplary family life. She also received the Golden Orchid Award from the government of Venezuela. Appreciation has been shown by the Lion Club of Kingston (1968), Committee for Christian Education of New York and Jamaica, the New York Freedom League (1984), and Young Jamaica. In addition, a hybrid bougainvillea was named for her—the Lady Bustamante is strawberry red in color. In more recent years she has served as patron of the Women Trade Fair and Exhibition. She lives in her home, Belencita, in Irish Town in the St. Andrew Hills.

See also Bustamante, Alexander

■ ■ *Bibliography*

Bustamante, Lady Gladys Maud. *The Memoirs of Lady Bustamante*. Kingston, Jamaica: Kingston Publishers Ltd., 1997.

Guy, Henry A., and Lavern Bailey. *Women of Distinction in Jamaica*. Kingston, Jamaica: Caribbean Herald, 1977.

Guy, Henry A., et al. *Women in the Caribbean*. Kingston, Jamaica: Henry A. Guy, 1966.

Jamaica Directory of Personalities, 1992-1993. 4th ed. Kingston, Jamaica: Selecto Publications Ltd., 1993.

Lambie, Shelly. "Lady B: Great Faith in My Jamaicans." *Sunday Gleaner* (July 31, 1983).

Marbella, Margua. "Lady B Honoured in New York and Sir Alex Remembered." *Gleaner* (March 24, 1984).

Neita, Hartley. "Saluting an Outstanding Matriarch of Jamaica." *Gleaner* (March 11, 1996).

ALERIC J. JOSEPHS (2005)

LORDE, AUDRE

FEBRUARY 18, 1934
NOVEMBER 17, 1992

The poet, novelist, and teacher Audre Geraldine Lorde was born in Harlem to West Indian parents. She described herself as "a black lesbian feminist mother lover poet." The exploration of pain, rage, and love in personal and political realms pervades her writing. Perhaps because Lorde did not speak until she was nearly five years old and also suffered from impaired vision, her passions were equally divided between a love of words and imagery and a devotion to speaking the truth, no matter how painful. Her objective, she stated, was to empower and encourage toward speech and action those in society who are often silenced and disfranchised.

Lorde published her first poem while in high school, in *Seventeen* magazine. She studied for a year (1954) at the National University of Mexico, before returning to the United States to earn a bachelor of arts degree in literature and philosophy from Hunter College in 1959. She went on to receive a master's degree from the Columbia School of Library Science in 1960. During this time she married attorney Edward Ashley Rollins and had two children, Elizabeth and Jonathan. Lorde and Rollins divorced in 1970. Juggling her roles as black woman, lesbian, mother, and poet, she was actively involved in causes for social justice. Throughout this period she was a member of the Harlem Writers Guild.

An important juncture in Lorde's life occurred in 1968, when she published her first collection of poetry, *The First Cities,* and also received a National Endowment for the Arts Residency Grant, which took her to Tougaloo College in Mississippi. This appointment represented the beginning of Lorde's career as a full-time writer and teacher. Returning to New York, she continued to teach and publish. In 1973, her third book, *From a Land Where Other People Live,* was nominated for the National Book Award for Poetry. It was praised for its attention to racial oppression and injustice around the world. She spent ten years on the faculty of John Jay College of Criminal Justice and then became professor of English at her alma mater, Hunter College, in 1980. She wrote three more books of poetry before the appearance of *The Black Unicorn* (1978), for which she received the widest acclaim and recognition. It fuses themes of motherhood and feminism while placing African spiritual awakening and black pride at its center.

Lorde's devotion to honesty and outspokenness is evident in the works she produced in the 1980s. She published her first nonpoetry work, *The Cancer Journals* (1980), so she could share the experience of her cancer diagnosis, partial mastectomy, and apparent triumph over the disease with as wide an audience as possible. *Zami: A New Spelling of My Name* (1982) was enthusiastically received as her first prose fiction work. Self-described as a "biomythography," it is considered a lyrical and evocative autobiographical novel. She was a founding member of both Women of Color Press and Sisters in Support of Sisters in South Africa.

Sister Outsider (1984), a collection of speeches and essays spanning the years 1976 to 1984, details Lorde's evolution as a black feminist thinker and writer. In 1986, she returned to poetry with *Our Dead behind Us.* Another work, *Burst of Light* (1988), which won an American Book Award, chronicles the spread of Lorde's cancer to her liver, and presents a less hopeful vision of the future than *The Cancer Journals.* Lorde's poetry appeared regularly in magazines and journals and has been widely anthologized. In 1991 she became the poet laureate of New York State. She died in St. Croix, U.S. Virgin Islands.

See also Caribbean/North American Writers (Contemporary); Literature of the United States; Poetry, U.S.

■ ■ *Bibliography*

"Audre Lorde." In *Gay and Lesbian Biography.* Detroit: St. James Press, 1997.

"Audre Lorde." In *Black Literature Criticism.* Detroit: Gale, 1992.

Christian, Barbara. "Dynamics of Difference." *Women's Review of Books* 1, no. 11 (August 1984): 6–7.

Obituary. *New York Times,* November 20, 1992.

Stepto, R. B. "Audre Lorde: The Severed Daughter." In *American Women Poets,* edited by Harold Bloom. New York: Chelsea House, 1986.

NICOLE R. KING (1996)
Updated bibliography

LOUIS, JOE

MAY 13, 1914
APRIL 12, 1981

■ ■ ■

Boxer Joe Louis Barrow was born to a sharecropping couple in Chambers County, Alabama, the seventh of eight children. Louis's father, Munroe Barrow, was placed in a mental institution when Louis was two, apparently unable to cope with the strain of the dirt-farming life. (It has been suggested by a few observers that Louis's mental and emotional problems in later life may have resulted from congenital causes rather than blows in the prize ring.) Louis's father died in Searcy State Hospital for the Colored Insane nearly twenty years later, never having learned that his son had become a famous athlete.

Lillie Barrow, Louis's mother, remarried a widower with a large family of his own named Pat Brooks, who, in 1920, moved the family to Mt. Sinai, Alabama. In 1926 Brooks migrated north to Detroit to work for the Ford Motor Company. The family, like many other African-American families of this period of the Great Migration, followed suit soon after, settling in Detroit's burgeoning black ghetto.

At the time of the move to Detroit, Louis was twelve years old. He was big for his age, but because of his inadequate education in the South and his lack of interest in and affinity for school, he was placed in a lower grade than his age would have dictated. Consequently, he continued to be an indifferent student and eventually went to work when his stepfather was laid off by Ford at the beginning of the depression.

Like many poor, unskilled, undereducated, ethnic urban boys of the period, Louis drifted into boxing largely as an opportunity to make money and to release his aggression in an organized, socially acceptable way. Although his stepfather was opposed to his entry into athletics, his mother supported and encouraged him.

Competing as a light heavyweight, Louis started his amateur career in 1932 but lost badly in his first fight and did not return to the ring until the following year. Following this brief hiatus, however, Louis quickly rose to prominence in boxing and African-American or "race" circles.

By 1933 he compiled an amateur record of fifty wins, forty-three by knockout, and only four losses. In 1934, shortly after winning the light heavyweight championship of the Amateur Athletic Union, Louis turned professional and moved up to the heavyweight division. His managers were two black numbers runners, John Roxborough and Julian Black. Louis's trainer was a white man, the former lightweight fighter Jack Blackburn.

Thanks to generous coverage by the black press, Louis was already a familiar figure in the black neighborhoods of northern cities by 1934. At a time when color bars prohibited blacks from competing with whites in every major professional sport other than boxing, Louis became a symbol of black aspirations in white America. Through the prime of his career, Louis's fights were major social events for African Americans, and spontaneous celebrations would erupt in urban ghettos after his victories.

At the start of his professional career, Louis faced a number of obstacles in trying to win the heavyweight title. First, under a "gentlemen's agreement," no black fighter had been permitted to fight for that title since Jack Johnson, the first black heavyweight champion. Johnson lost the title in Havana, Cuba, to Jess Willard in 1915. Second, Louis had an entirely black support and management team, making it difficult for him to break into boxing's big market in New York City and to get a crack at the name fighters against whom he had to compete if he were to make a name for himself.

Louis's managers overcame the first problem by making sure that Louis did not in any way act like or remind his white audience or white sportswriters of Johnson, who scandalized white public opinion with his marriages to white women and other breaches of prevailing racial mores. Louis was not permitted to be seen in the company of white women, never gloated over his opponents, was quiet and respectful, and generally was made to project an image of cleanliness and high moral character. The second problem was solved when Mike Jacobs, a fight promoter in New York City, decided to take on Madison Square Garden's monopoly on boxing with his 20th Century Sporting Club and formed a partnership with Louis's managers to promote him with the intention of guiding him to the championship.

Louis, 6'1", with a fighting weight around two hundred pounds, soon amassed a glittering record. Starting in his first professional bout, a first-round knockout of Jack Kracken on July 4, 1934, to his winning the heavyweight title in an eighth-round knockout of Jim Braddock on June 22, 1937, Louis recorded thirty wins, twenty-five by knockout, and one loss. The most memorable of his fights during this period included the easy knockouts of former heavyweight champions Max Baer and Primo Carnera in 1935. Louis's one loss during this period was critically important in his career and in American cultural history. On June 19, 1936, the German Max Schmeling knocked out Louis, then a world-class challenger for the heavyweight crown, in twelve rounds, giving the highly touted black fighter his first severe beating as a professional. This loss greatly reduced Louis's standing with white sportswriters, who had previously built him up almost to the point of invincibility. (The writers had given him a string of alliterative nicknames, including the "Tan Tornado" and the "Dark Destroyer," but it was the "Brown Bomber" that stuck.) However, Louis's loss was also a watershed as it marked a slow change on the part of white sportswriters, who began to stop patronizing him and slowly grew to treat him more fully as a human being.

The loss also set up a rematch with Schmeling on June 22, 1938, after Louis had become champion by defeating Braddock the previous year. The second bout with Schmeling was to become one of the most important fights in American history. It was not Louis's first fight with political overtones. He had fought the Italian heavyweight Primo Carnera (beating him easily) as Italy was beginning its invasion of Ethiopia, and both fighters became emblems of their respective ethnicities; Louis, oddly enough, became both a nationalistic hero for blacks while being a kind of crossover hero for non-Italian, antifascist whites. By 1938 Hitler was rapidly taking over Europe and Nazism had clearly become a threat to both the United States and the world generally. Schmeling was seen as the symbol of Nazism, an identification against which he did not fight very hard. Indeed, Schmeling seemed eager to exploit the racial overtones of the fight as a way of getting a psychological edge on Louis. Louis became an emblem not simply of black America, but also, like Jesse Owens in Berlin a few years earlier, of antitotalitarian America itself, of its ideology of opportunity and freedom. Perhaps in some sense no one could better bear the burden of America's utopian vision of itself as an egalitarian paradise than a champion black prizefighter, combining both the myths of class mobility with racial uplift. Under the scrutiny of both their countries and most of the rest of the world, Louis knocked out Schmeling in two minutes of the first round.

Following the second Schmeling bout, Louis embarked on a remarkable string of title defenses, winning seventeen fights over four years, fifteen by knockout. Because of the general lack of talent in the heavyweight division at the time and the ease of Louis's victories, his opponents were popularly referred to as "The Bum of the Month Club." The only serious challenge came from Billy Conn in 1941, who outboxed the champion for twelve

Pvt. Joe Louis says_

"We're going to do our part ... and we'll win because we're on God's side"

A war poster depicting boxer Joe Louis, who was drafted for the U.S. military in 1942. Attending a fundraising dinner for the Navy Relief Society early that same year, Louis uttered the phrase captured in this poster, the last few words of which became a rallying cry across America during World War II. © CORBIS. REPRODUCED BY PERMISSION.

rounds before succumbing to Louis's knockout punch in the thirteenth.

During World War II, Louis in some ways matured deeply as a man and came into his own as an American icon and hero. When the war began, he was twenty-seven and at his prime as a fighter. When it ended, he was thirty-one, beginning to slip as a champion athlete, and, probably, he was not as interested in boxing as he had been. However, he had become something of an elder statesman among blacks who were also prominent in popular culture. Younger black athletes such as Jackie Robinson and Sugar Ray Robinson looked up to and respected him. Both men had served in the segregated armed forces with him, and he helped them bear with dignity the hostilities and humiliations that were often visited upon them as black soldiers. Louis became self-consciously political at that time; he campaigned for Republican presidential candidate Wendell Wilkie in 1940.

Louis was drafted January 12, 1942, but remained active as a boxer, continuing to fight professionally during the war. He contributed his earnings to both the Army and the Navy Relief Funds. While this was a wise move politically, it was disastrous for Louis financially. (In fact, even before he joined the service, he contributed the purse from his Buddy Baer fight on January 9, 1942, to the Navy Relief Fund.)

"We're going to do our part, and we will win," Louis intoned at a Navy Relief Society dinner on March 10, 1942, "because we are on God's side." This moment, perhaps more than any other in Louis's career, signaled the complete transformation of the image of the man in the mind of the white public. Louis had risen from the sullen, uneasy "colored boy" from black Detroit who was considered in 1935 the wunderkind of boxing, to become in seven years the mature, patriotic American who could speak both to and for his country. Louis could now not simply address his audience but command it. He could, as one pundit put it, "name the war." Louis's phrase, "We're on God's side," became one of the most famous phrases in American oratory during the Second World War. Ironically, however, Louis had misremembered his lines. He was supposed to say the more commonplace, "God's on our side," yet it is this cunning combination of the inadvertent and the opportunistic, the serendipitous and the intentional, that marks Louis's career in its later phase.

After the war, Louis's abilities as a fighter diminished as his earnings evaporated in a mist of high living and alleged tax evasion. After winning a rematch against Jersey Joe Walcott on June 25, 1948—only the second black fighter against whom Louis defended his title, indicating how much of a presence white fighters were in the sport well into the twentieth century—on the heels of winning an earlier controversial match on December 5, 1947, that most observers felt he had lost, Louis retired from the ring in 1949. At that time he made a deal with the unsavory Jim Norris and the International Boxing Club, which resulted in the removal of an old, sick Mike Jacobs from the professional boxing scene. Louis's deal with Norris created an entity called Joe Louis Enterprises that would sign up all the leading contenders for the heavyweight championship and have them exclusively promoted by Norris's International Boxing Club. Louis received $150,000 and became a stockholder in the IBC. He was paid $15,000 annually to promote boxing generally and the IBC bout specifically. In effect, Louis sold his title to a gangster-controlled outfit that wanted and eventually obtained for a period in the 1950s virtual control over both the management and promotion of all notable professional fighters in the United States. By 1950, however, an aged Louis, reflexes shot and legs gimpy, was forced back into the ring because of money problems. He lost to Ezzard Charles in a fifteen-round decision on September 27. On October 26, 1951, his career ended for good when he was knocked out in eight rounds by the up-and-coming Rocky Marciano.

In sixty-six professional bouts, Louis lost only three times (twice in the last two years of his career) and knocked out forty-nine of his opponents. He was elected to the Boxing Hall of Fame in 1954.

After his career, Louis, like many famous athletes who followed him, lived off of his reputation. He certainly never considered the idea of returning to the ordinary work world he left in the early 1930s when he became a fighter. He was hounded by the Internal Revenue Service for back taxes, began taking drugs, particularly cocaine, suffered a number of nervous breakdowns, and seemed often at loose ends, despite a third marriage to a woman of considerable maturity and substance, Martha Jefferson. Eventually, in part as a result of his second marriage (his second wife, Marva Trotter, was a lawyer for Teamster boss Jimmy Hoffa), Louis wound up working in Las Vegas as a casino greeter, playing golf with high-rolling customers and serving as a companion for men who remembered him in his glory years.

On April 12, 1981, the day after he attended a heavyweight championship match between Larry Holmes and Trevor Berbick, Louis collapsed at his home in Las Vegas and died of a massive heart attack. He was, without question, one of the most popular sports figures of the twentieth century. In 1993 Louis appeared on a U.S. postage stamp.

See also Boxing; Charles, Ezzard; Owens, Jesse; Robinson, Jackie; Robinson, Sugar Ray; Walcott, Jersey Joe

■ ■ *Bibliography*

Anderson, Jervis. "Black Heavies." *American Scholar* 47 (1978): 387–395.

Barrow, Joe Louis, Jr., and Barbara Munder. *Joe Louis: 50 Years an American Hero*. New York: McGraw-Hill, 1988.

Edmonds, Anthony. *O. Joe Louis*. Grand Rapids, Mich: Erdmanns, 1973.

Grombach, John V. *The Saga of Sock*. New York: Barnes, 1949.

Louis, Joe, with Edna and Art Rust. *Joe Louis: My Life*. New York: Harcourt Brace Jovanovich, 1978. Reprint, Hopewell, N.J.: Ecco Press, 1997.

Mead, Chris. *Champion: Joe Louis, Black Hero in White America*. New York: Penguin Books, 1985.

Mead, Chris. *Champion Joe Louis*. New York: Robson Books, Parkwest Publications, 1995.

Nagler, Barney. *Brown Bomber: The Pilgrimage of Joe Louis*. New York: World Pub., 1972.

Wright, Richard. "High Tide in Harlem: Joe Louis as a Symbol of Freedom." *New Masses* (July 5, 1938): 18–20.

GERALD EARLY (1996)
Updated bibliography

LOVELACE, EARL

JULY 13, 1935

❙❙❙

The writer Earl Lovelace was born in Toco, Trinidad, in 1935 and grew up in Tobago. He was educated in Tobago, Trinidad, and the United States, and in 1964 he won the British Petroleum Independence Literary Award with the manuscript of *While Gods Are Falling* (1965). That impressive debut was followed by the publication of *The Schoolmaster* (1968), *The Dragon Can't Dance* (1979), *The Wine of Astonishment* (1982), *Jestina's Calypso and Other Plays* (1984), *A Brief Conversion and Other Stories* (1988), and *Crawfie the Crapaud* (a children's story, 1997). *Salt*, a novel that dazzles with its humanistic and multicultural ethos, was published in 1996 and went on to win the prestigious Commonwealth Writers Prize in 1997. *Growing in the Dark: Selected Essays* (edited and introduced by Funso Aiyejina) was published in 2003. These essays, which span 1967 to 2002, confirm Lovelace as one of the most consistent and perceptive organic and original thinkers, writers, and aesthetes from the Caribbean region.

Lovelace has the distinction of being one of the few West Indian writers of his generation to live and write out of the region at a time when metropolitan exile was the more lucrative option. In his journey from being a new writer in 1964 to becoming a nationally and internationally celebrated writer, Lovelace has worked as a forest ranger, agricultural assistant, proofreader, journalist, resident playwright and director of grassroots theatre groups, and university lecturer. He has always been an avid reader of books and an astute student of people, and these interests have served his commitment to writing about Trinidad and Tobago and the Caribbean.

Lovelace's work celebrates people's desire to belong, their need to claim and understand their landscape and history, and the impulse to recognize the human dignity inherent in both, in spite of whatever human failings may exist. He has championed the language and culture of the folk, whom he envisions as the most instinctive and versatile culture bearers and culture creators in the region. His persistence in his commitment to his craft is matched by a compassion in the presentation of his characters and their struggle for self-apprehension and self-realization.

Lovelace's compassion is born out of his self-identification with the people among whom he lived and worked, men and women who demonstrated their love of life and an awareness that each person must be responsible for the world he or she lives in, a philosophy that has directed his abiding desire to create fictions in which the multiplicity of voices and perspectives of a multicultural society are properly ventilated.

In recognition of his contribution to literature and culture, Lovelace has won several awards over the years, including the Pegasus Literary Award for his outstanding contribution to the Arts in Trinidad and Tobago (1966), a Guggenheim Fellowship (1980), Trinidad and Tobago's Chaconia (Gold) Medal (1988), and the University of the West Indies' Honorary Doctor of Letters (2002).

See also Caribbean/North American Writers (Contemporary); Literature of the English-Speaking Caribbean

■ ■ *Bibliography*

Aiyejina, Funso. "Lovelace's Prospect: Masquerade or Masquerader?" *Trinidad and Tobago Review* 16, nos. 7–9 (1994): 7–10.

Aiyejina, Funso. "Novelypso: Indigenous Narrative Strategies in Earl Lovelace's Fiction." *Trinidad and Tobago Review* 22, nos. 7–8 (2000): 15–17.

Cary, Norman Reed. "Salvation, Self, and Solidarity in the Work of Earl Lovelace." *World Literature Written in English* 28, no. 1 (1988): 103–114.

Down, Lorna. "In a Native Voice: The Folk as Subject in Lovelace's Fiction." *Caribbean Studies* 27, nos. 3/4 (1994): 377–389.

Hodge, Merle. "Dialogue and Narrative Voice in Earl Lovelace's 'The Schoolmaster'." *Journal of West Indian Literature* 8, no. 1 (1998): 56–72.

Meek, Sandra. "The 'Penitential Island': The Question of Liberation in Earl Lovelace's 'Salt'." *Journal of Caribbean Studies* 15, no. 3 (2000/2001): pp. 273–297.

Nair, Supriya. "Diasporic Roots: Imagining a Nation in Earl Lovelace's 'Salt'." *South Atlantic Quarterly* 100, no. 1 (2001): 259–285.

O'Callaghan, Evelyn. "The Modernization of the Trinidadian Landscape in the Novels of Earl Lovelace." *Ariel: A Review of International English Literature* 20, no. 1 (1989): 41–54.

Sunitha, K. T. "The Discovery of Selfhood in Earl Lovelace's Fiction." *Commonwealth Novel in English* 5, no. 1 (Spring 1992): 27–37.

FUNSO AIYEJINA (2005)

LOWERY, JOSEPH E.

OCTOBER 6, 1924

▮▮▮ ────────────────

Born and raised in Huntsville, Alabama, Joseph Echols Lowery, who served as president of the Southern Christian Leadership Conference (SCLC), attended Knoxville College in Tennessee from 1939 to 1941. In the 1940s he studied theology at Paine Theological Seminary in Augusta, Georgia, and was ordained a minister by the United Methodist Church. From 1952 to 1961 he served as pastor of the Warren Street Methodist Church in Mobile, Alabama, where he developed a politically active ministry and helped sponsor lower- and middle-class housing developments for African Americans. In January 1957 Lowery was invited by the Rev. Dr. Martin Luther King Jr., and the Rev. Fred Shuttlesworth to become a founding member of the SCLC.

Lowery remained one of the SCLC's central leaders through the heyday of the civil rights movement. He first gained national attention, however, in 1962 when the city commissioners of Montgomery, Alabama, successfully sued Lowery, three other SCLC leaders, and the *New York Times* for libel over the organization's advertisement in the newspaper attacking the racist policies of the Montgomery city government. The case, *New York Times Co. v. Sullivan* (1964), became a landmark in libel jurisprudence when the U.S. Supreme Court reversed the Alabama court's decision in favor of the plaintiffs. Lowery served as a chief organizer of the pivotal desegregation campaigns in Birmingham in 1963 and Selma in 1965. In 1965 he moved to Birmingham to become pastor of St. Paul's Methodist Church and assumed a leadership position in the Alabama Christian Movement for Human Rights, a civil rights organization allied with the SCLC.

In 1968 Lowery moved to Atlanta, where he became pastor of Central United Methodist Church and emerged as the leader of the moderate faction within the SCLC. In 1977 he wrested control from the militant wing, led by Hosea Williams, and was elected president of the organization in 1977. As president he was accused by the Williams faction of transforming the SCLC into a "middle-class clique of blacks," yet under Lowery's leadership the organization underwent a period of revitalized activism.

In 1978 and 1979 Lowery led a protest of a Mississippi energy company for buying coal from South Africa and directed a support march for the "Wilmington Ten," a group of civil rights activists who had been jailed for alleged conspiracy to murder white segregationists. During this time the SCLC also led a support march for Tommie Lee Hines, a mentally retarded black youth who the organization believed was wrongly convicted of raping a white woman in Decatur, Alabama. During the march for Hines, members of the Ku Klux Klan opened fire on the marchers, injuring four and barely missing Lowery and his wife. In 1979 Lowery was severely criticized by American Jewish organizations after he led a delegation of African-American clergy to Lebanon, where they met with Palestine Liberation Organization (PLO) leader Yasir Arafat and called for the establishment of a Palestinian homeland, reduction of U.S. aid to Israel, and PLO recognition of Israel as a nation.

In the 1980s Lowery continued to broaden the SCLC's activities beyond traditional civil rights issues. He oversaw the organization's involvement with Haitian refugees seeking political asylum in the United States, protested U.S. policy in Central America, supported the anti-apartheid movement, and reinitiated the Operation Breadbasket economic program, which raised money for black-owned enterprises. Through the decade the group also conducted Crusade for the Ballot, a program that significantly increased the black vote in the South through increased voter registrations. In 1986 Lowery transferred to the Cascade United Methodist Church, where he finished his career as a minister.

In the early 1990s the SCLC under Lowery's leadership continued to serve as a national coordinating agency for local civil rights organizations and conducted a national "Stop the Killing" campaign to protest gang violence. Lowery retired from the ministry in 1992 but nevertheless continued to serve as president of the SCLC until his retirement in July 1997. He remained active in community affairs, notably as a member of the board of MARTA, Atlanta's transit system.

Lowery has been the recipient of numerous honors. He was named one of the nation's greatest black preachers by *Ebony* magazine, and the Joseph E. Lowery Institute for Justice and Human Rights was established at Clark Atlanta University.

See also Civil Rights Movement, U.S.; King, Martin Luther, Jr.; Shuttlesworth, Fred L.; Southern Christian Leadership Conference (SCLC); Williams, Hosea Lorenzo

■ ■ *Bibliography*

Branch, Taylor. *Parting the Waters: America in the King Years, 1954–1963.* New York: Simon and Schuster, 1988.

Current Biography Yearbook. New York: H. W. Wilson, 1982.

Fairclough, Adam. *To Redeem the Soul of America: The Southern Christian Leadership Conference and Martin Luther King, Jr.* Athens: University of Georgia Press, 1987.

THADDEUS RUSSELL (1996)
Updated by publisher 2005

LOWNDES COUNTY FREEDOM ORGANIZATION

■ ■ ■

In the early spring of 1965, in Lowndes County, Alabama, the black activist Stokely Carmichael (1941–1998) and other members of the civil rights organization called the Student Nonviolent Coordinating Committee (SNCC) created the Lowndes County Freedom Organization (LCFO). Lowndes County, a rural farming area just south of Montgomery, at that time had a population of fifteen thousand, of which over 70 percent were black. However, white supremacy was the cornerstone of law and society, historically enforced by violence and open intimidation. The black population was poor and politically voiceless. As a result of the violent intimidation, none of the blacks in the county was registered to vote in elections, thus maintaining the white dominance.

SNCC had devoted considerable energy to registering blacks to vote in the Deep South from 1961 to 1965. In 1964, SNCC created the Mississippi Freedom Democratic Party (MFDP) to represent black voters in the Democratic Party. However, the MFDP failed to gain acceptance at the 1964 Democratic National Convention held in Atlantic City, New Jersey. In reaction to the racism dominant in the Alabama Democratic Party, Carmichael decided the time was right to counter the political domination and create an independent black political party. He believed the drive for racial integration was just another form of white supremacy. Carmichael argued that blacks should speak for themselves, using their own words and ideas, and gain independence in their own communities.

An unusual Alabama state law provided that any group of citizens who nominated candidates for county offices and won at least 20 percent of the vote could be formally recognized as a county political party. Carmichael and SNCC began organizing in several counties, including the mostly black Lowndes County. On May 3, 1965, five new county freedom organizations met to nominate candidates for the offices of sheriff and tax assessor, and for school boards.

The LCFO adopted the image of a black panther, in contrast to the Alabama Democratic Party's white rooster symbol. The panther symbolized power, dignity, and determination. The determination was soon evident: at a May 8 local election, nine hundred of almost two thousand registered black voters in Lowndes County voted, despite risking their personal safety. In recognition of the risk involved, the LCFO's saying at the time was "Vote the panther, then go home." The LCFO was successful in electing some black officials.

The LCFO was a landmark organization not only for transforming the goals of civil rights advocates from integration to liberation, but also for introducing the black panther image, which was later adopted by the militant Black Panther organization in Oakland, California. The LCFO represented the growing differences within the civil rights movement over desired goals and how to achieve them. The peaceful civil-disobedience tactics of Martin Luther King Jr. and the Southern Christian Leadership Conference (SCLC) were increasingly challenged by the more confrontational strategies of SNCC. The SCLC urged blacks in Lowndes County to remain in the Democratic Party and fight for change within the organization. Instead, independent black political activity developed.

See also Black Panther Party for Self-Defense; Carmichael, Stokely; King, Martin Luther, Jr.; Mississippi Freedom Democratic Party; Southern Christian Leadership Conference (SCLC); Student Nonviolent Coordinating Committee (SNCC)

■ ■ *Bibliography*

Carmichael, Stokely. "Power and Racism: What We Want." *Black Scholar* 27 (1997): 52–57. (Reprint of 1966 essay).

Carmichael, Stokely, and Charles V. Hamilton. *Black Power: The Politics of Liberation in America.* New York: Random House, 1967.

Cone, James H. *Risks of Faith: The Emergence of a Black Theology of Liberation, 1968–1998.* Boston, Mass.: Beacon Press, 1999.

Hall, Raymond L. *Black Separatism in the United States.* Hanover, N.H.: University Press of New England, 1978.

Stanton, Mary. *From Selma to Sorrow: The Life and Death of Viola Liuzzo.* Athens: University of Georgia Press, 1998.

RICHARD C. HANES (1996)

LUCY FOSTER, AUTHERINE
OCTOBER 15, 1929

■■■

Student civil rights activist Autherine Lucy was born in Shiloh, Alabama. She attended public schools there and in Linden, Alabama, before attending Selma University and Miles College in Birmingham, from which she graduated in 1952. In September of that year, she and a friend, Pollie Myers, a civil rights activist with the NAACP, applied to the University of Alabama. Lucy later said that she wanted a second undergraduate degree, not for political reasons but to get the best possible education in the state. Although the women were accepted, their admittance was rescinded when the authorities discovered they were not white.

Backed by the NAACP, Lucy and Myers charged the University of Alabama with racial discrimination in a court case that took almost three years to resolve. While waiting, Lucy worked as an English teacher in Carthage, Mississippi, and as a secretary at an insurance company. In July 1955, in the wake of the 1954 U.S. Supreme Court decision in *Brown v. Board of Education,* the University of Alabama was ordered by a federal district court to admit Myers and Lucy.

On January 30, 1956, the university admitted Lucy but rejected Myers on the grounds that a child she had conceived before marriage made her an unsuitable student. Lucy registered on February 3, becoming the first African American to be accepted as a student at the 136-year-old University of Alabama.

The university's decision was met with resistance by many students, Tuscaloosa citizens, and the Ku Klux Klan. Crosses were burned nightly on the campus grounds, and mobs rioted at the university in what was, to date, the most violent post-*Brown* anti-integration demonstration. On the third day of classes, after white student mobs pelted Lucy with rotten produce and threatened to kill her, she was suspended from school on the grounds that her own safety and that of other students required it. The NAACP filed suit protesting this, and the federal courts ordered that Lucy be reinstated after the university had taken adequate measures to protect her. However, on that same day, February 29, Lucy was expelled from the University of Alabama on the grounds that she had maligned its officials by taking them to court. The NAACP, feeling that further legal action was pointless, did not contest this decision. Lucy, tired and scared, acquiesced.

In April 1956, in Dallas, Lucy married Hugh Foster, a divinity student (and later a minister) whom she had met at Miles College. For some months afterward she was a civil rights advocate, making speeches at NAACP meetings around the country. But by the end of the year, her active involvement in the civil rights movement had ceased.

For the next seventeen years, Lucy and her family lived in various cities in Louisiana, Mississippi, and Texas. Her notoriety made it difficult at first for her to find employment as a teacher. The Fosters moved back to Alabama in 1974, and Lucy obtained a position in the Birmingham school system.

In April 1988 Autherine Lucy's expulsion was annulled by the University of Alabama. She enrolled in the graduate program in education the following year and received an M.A. degree in May 1992. In the course of the commencement ceremonies, the University of Alabama named an endowed fellowship in her honor.

See also *Brown v. Board of Education of Topeka, Kansas*; Civil Rights Movement, U.S.

■ ■ *Bibliography*

Clark, E. Culpepper. *The Schoolhouse Door: Segregation's Last Stand at the University of Alabama*. New York: Oxford University Press, 1993.

Kluger, Richard. *Simple Justice: The History of* Brown v. Board of Education *and Black America's Struggle for Equality*. New York: Knopf, 1976. 2d ed., New York: Knopf, 2004.

QADRI ISMAIL (1996)
Updated bibliography

LUPERÓN, GREGORIO

SEPTEMBER 8, 1839
MAY 21, 1897

Gregorio Luperón was an Afro-Dominican soldier and politician who was acclaimed as a national hero during the War of Restoration (1861–1865) against Spain.

Born in 1839 in Puerto Plata, the young Luperón sold goods from the store run by his mother, Nicolasa, an English-speaking immigrant. His industry impressed a local timber merchant, who made him overseer when he was only fourteen. Largely self-taught, Luperón availed himself of his employer's library.

In March 1861, almost two decades after its foundation, the Dominican Republic was annexed by Spain, its former colonial ruler. While some members of the elite supported this move, it launched a series of rebellions.

Luperón, then aged twenty-two, was jailed following a fight with an annexationist. He escaped and fled to Haiti and the United States. He returned to the island to take part in an unsuccessful uprising in 1863. Later, during the siege of Santiago, Luperón's bravery, charisma, and oratory caught the attention of his superiors, and he was made a general.

When a provisional government was set up, Luperón became supreme chief of operations. During the War of Restoration, in which many Dominicans of African descent participated, Luperón's strategic and leadership abilities came to the fore. With fewer men, arms, and supplies than the Spaniards, he resorted to guerrilla tactics. These unorthodox methods led his superiors to relieve him of his command.

The war ended in 1865 when the Spaniards withdrew, and Luperón accepted the vice presidency of a provisional government. When General Buenaventura Báez was restored to power in October, Luperón declared his opposition and was expelled from the country.

After a successful uprising against Báez, the country was ruled by a triumvirate of military leaders, of whom Luperón was the most prominent. A government was elected but it was overthrown in 1868, and Báez was reinstated. He soon began to advocate the country's annexation by the United States.

Luperón went abroad to organize against Báez. He helped Ulises Espaillat win the 1876 election and accepted the post of war and navy minister. A series of rebellions in the south forced Espaillat's resignation, and Báez returned to power. Luperón went into exile again.

Luperón returned after Báez went into exile in 1878 and headed a provisional government. Its fourteen months of progressive rule were followed by a period of political unrest. Luperón supported Ulises Heureaux, his former lieutenant and an Afro-Dominican war hero, in the 1886 elections. However, it soon became clear that Heureaux was a brutal dictator. Dominican liberals rallied round Luperón, who stood against Heureaux in the 1888 elections. Realizing that the elections would be rigged, Luperón withdrew his candidacy and fled to Puerto Rico. He unsuccessfully attempted to launch a campaign against Heureaux. While in exile in Saint Thomas he became seriously ill. A contrite Heureaux visited his former mentor and commanding officer and persuaded him to return home. He died in Puerto Plata on May 21, 1897.

Luperón wrote a number of pamphlets and articles. His *Notas autobiográficas y apuntes históricos sobre la República Dominicana desde la Restauración a nuestros días* (1895–1896) is a three-volume work about his life and the period of the restoration.

See also Maroon Societies in the Caribbean; Politics and Politicians in the Caribbean

■ ■ *Bibliography*

Moya Pons, Frank. *The Dominican Republic: A National History.* New Rochelle, N.Y.: Hispaniola Books, 1995.

CHRISTINE AYORINDE (2005)

LYNCH, JOHN ROY

1847
NOVEMBER 2, 1939

Politician and lawyer John Roy Lynch was born a slave on a Louisiana plantation, later moved to Mississippi with his mother, and became free when Union forces occupied Natchez in 1863. At the end of the Civil War he was the proprietor of a thriving photographic business while attending evening classes. In 1867 he became active in politics, joining a Republican club in Natchez and supporting the new state constitution. In 1869 he was elected to the lower house of the Mississippi legislature, where he made a quite favorable impression; three years later his colleagues elevated him to the position of speaker. In 1873 he ran for Congress and won.

As one of the vigorous supporters of the Civil Rights Bill of 1875, Lynch became widely known. Reelected in 1874, he was defeated in 1876. After successfully contesting the election in 1880, he returned to Congress but was defeated once more in 1882. In 1884 he delivered the keynote address at the Republican National Convention, the first African American to be so honored. Subsequently he managed his Mississippi plantation, served as fourth auditor of the Treasury, was paymaster of volunteers in the Spanish-American War, and practiced law in Mississippi, Washington, D.C., and Chicago. In 1913 he published *The Facts of Reconstruction* to refute the claims of so-called scientific historians of Reconstruction. Lynch died in his Chicago home and was buried with full military honors at Arlington National Cemetery.

See also Politics in the United States

■ ■ *Bibliography*

Lynch, John Roy. *Reminiscences of an Active Life: The Autobiography of John Roy Lynch.* Edited by John Hope Franklin. Chicago: University of Chicago Press, 1970.

JOHN HOPE FRANKLIN (1996)

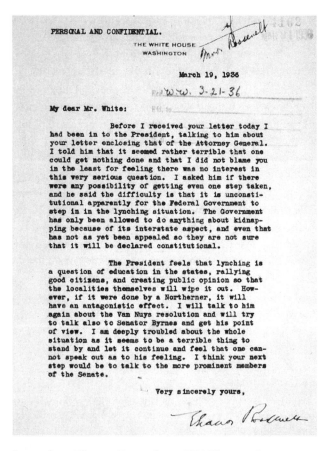

Letter from Eleanor Roosevelt to NAACP executive secretary Walter White, March 19, 1936. *The First Lady's letter outlines her efforts in lobbying for federal action against lynchings.* THE LIBRARY OF CONGRESS

LYNCHING

Although rooted in an older and broader tradition of vigilantism, the term *lynching* is primarily associated with the killing of African Americans by white mobs in the period from the Civil War to the middle of the twentieth century. By most accounts, the practice originated on the Revolutionary War frontier when Colonel Charles Lynch and other prominent citizens of Bedford County, Virginia, organized informally to apprehend and punish Tories and other lawless elements throughout the community.

LYNCHING IN ANTEBELLUM AMERICA

"Lynch law" subsequently spread to other parts of the country, but it became especially prevalent in less-settled frontier areas with poorly developed legal institutions. Initially, lynch mobs punished alleged lawbreakers and enforced community mores through whippings, tarring and feathering, and, on occasion, extralegal executions by hanging or shooting. Victims were mostly white and

The Crisis, August, 1919. Lynching announcements from the New Orleans States and the Jackson Daily News are reprinted in the NAACP journal. GENERAL RESEARCH AND REFERENCE DIVISION, SCHOMBURG CENTER FOR RESEARCH IN BLACK CULTURE, THE NEW YORK PUBLIC LIBRARY, ASTOR, LENOX AND TILDEN FOUNDATIONS.

ranged from outlaws and horse thieves in frontier areas to Catholics, immigrants, and abolitionists in northern cities.

Blacks were by no means immune to mob action and sometimes received harsher treatment than white victims, but lynching had not yet attained its special association with race. Even under slavery, the lynching of blacks was relatively infrequent. The economic self-interest and paternalistic attitudes of masters, combined with a rigid system of slave control, normally militated against widespread mob violence against slaves, although in the aftermath of slave rebellions, mobs sought out and ruthlessly punished suspected conspirators.

Lynching after the Civil War

After the Civil War, lynching spread rapidly and became a systematic feature of the southern system of white su-

premacy. Mob-inflicted deaths increased during Reconstruction as southern whites resorted to violence to restore white control over ex-slaves. The practice reached epidemic proportions in the late 1880s and 1890s, averaging more than 150 incidents per year in the latter decade, and began to decline after the turn of the century.

Overall, between 1882, when the *Chicago Tribune* began recording lynchings, and 1968, an estimated 4,742 persons died at the hands of lynch mobs. Although whites continued to be victimized on occasion, African-American men and women accounted for the overwhelming majority (some 72 percent) of known lynchings after 1882. By the 1920s, 90 percent of all victims were black, and 95 percent of all lynchings occurred in southern states.

Southern whites justified lynching as a necessary response to black crime and an inefficient legal system, but virtually any perceived transgression of the racial boundaries or threat to the system of white supremacy could provoke mob action. The alleged offenses of lynching victims ranged from such actual crimes as murder, assault, theft, arson, and rape to such trivial breaches of the informal etiquette of race as "disrespect" toward whites and failing to give way to whites on the sidewalks.

The most frequent justification, however, was the charge of rape or sexual assault of white women by black men. Although fewer than 26 percent of all lynchings involved even the allegation of sexual assault, the mythology of rape and images of the "black beast" despoiling white womanhood dominated the southern rationale for lynching by the 1890s and inflamed mobs to ever-increasing brutality.

The Nature of Lynchings

Lynchings took various forms, ranging from hangings and shootings administered by small groups of men in secret, to posses meting out summary justice at the conclusion of a manhunt, to large public spectacles with broad community participation. The classic public lynchings for which the South became so notorious always involved torture and mutilation and ended in death for the victim, either by hanging, or, increasingly, by being burned alive. The lynching ritual characteristically included prior notice of the event, the selection of a symbolically significant location, and the gathering of a large crowd of onlookers, including women and children.

Mobs typically sought to elicit confessions from their victims and frequently allowed them to pray before the final act of the drama. Lynchers often left the bullet-ridden bodies of hanging victims on public display as a warning to other potential transgressors. In both hangings and

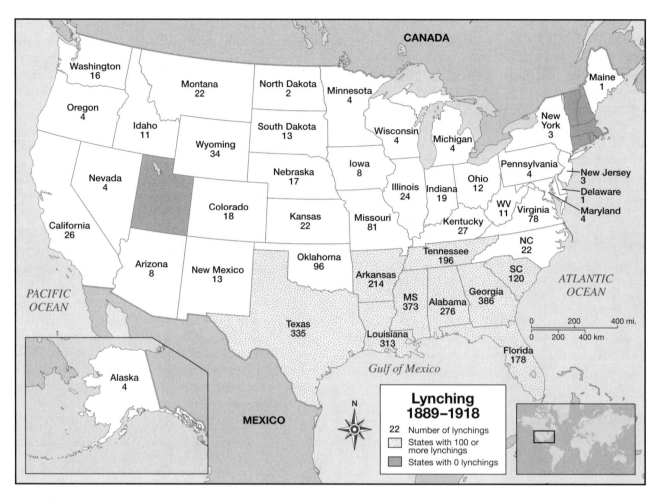

Map of the United States, showing the number of lynchings by state over a thirty-year period beginning in 1918. *About 75 percent of the 3200 blacks who were lynched during these years were killed in the nine southern states that are partially shaded.* MAP BY XNR PRODUCTIONS. THE GALE GROUP.

burnings, mobs tortured, mutilated, castrated (in the case of males), and even dismembered their victims. The victim of the alleged crime or a victim's close relative often played a prominent role in the ritual. A particularly gruesome feature of lynchings was the taking of souvenirs in the form of body pieces, bone fragments salvaged from the ashes, or photographs.

The social composition of southern mobs remains obscure. Some have argued that lynch mobs were composed primarily of lower-class whites, but most scholars agree that the upper class and community leaders at the very least condoned the mob's actions and not uncommonly were themselves participants. Police were rarely effective in preventing lynchings, even when they tried, and mob members were almost never identified and prosecuted. Authorities typically attributed lynchings to "persons unknown."

THE SOCIAL FORCES BEHIND LYNCHING

Lynching was ultimately a product of racism and the caste system it sustained, but social, economic, and political conditions shaped the rhythms and geographical distribution of the practice. Early twentieth-century investigators linked lynchings to such factors as rural isolation, poorly developed legal institutions, broad economic fluctuations, the price of cotton, the ratio of blacks to whites in the population, the structure of county government, revivalism, and the seasonality of southern crops. In his classic study *The Tragedy of Lynching* (1933), Arthur Raper concluded that lynchings were most likely to occur in the poorest, most sparsely populated southern counties, and especially in recently settled ones where blacks constituted less than 25 percent of the population.

Extending these earlier findings, modern social scientists have viewed lynching variously as a form of "scape-

A banner announcing a lynching flies from a window of the NAACP headquarters in New York City, 1936. Since the organization's founding in 1909, the NAACP drew attention to every one of the thousands of lynchings occurring in the United States between that year and the late 1930s. THE LIBRARY OF CONGRESS.

goating" in which white aggression and frustration was displaced onto blacks during periods of economic decline, either as a consequence of direct economic competition between whites and blacks or as a manifestation of repressive justice in response to a "boundary crisis" precipitated by Populist Party efforts to unite lower-class whites and blacks in the 1890s.

While acknowledging some connection between lynching and populism, historians generally attribute the sudden emergence of lynching as a prominent feature of

race relations in the 1880s and 1890s to broader and more complex forces. Jacquelyn Dowd Hall has argued that in addition to being a form of "repressive justice" designed to preserve the caste system, lynching served to dramatize "hierarchical power relationships based on gender and race" (Hall, 1979, p. 156). It reinforced racial boundaries for black men and helped maintain caste solidarity for whites generally, but it also reinforced notions of female vulnerability and subordination in a patriarchal society. Joel Williamson (1984) also stressed the association between lynching and sex roles, but he attributed the growth

A 1934 crime conference sponsored by the Daughters of the American Revolution failed to address lynching in its program, sparking a silent protest outside DAR Memorial Hall in Washington, D.C. © BETTMANN/CORBIS. REPRODUCED BY PERMISSION.

of lynching in the late nineteenth century to the convergence of a radical strain of racism, deep-seated economic trouble, and white male anxiety over the perceived erosion of their ability to provide materially for their women and families. The pathological obsession with the black rapist, and the firestorm of lynchings it produced in the 1890s, thus constituted a kind of "psychic compensation" for male feelings of inadequacy (Williamson, 1984, p. 115). Edward L. Ayers traces the epidemic of lynchings to a "widespread and multifaceted crisis" rooted in the economic depression of the 1890s. That depression contributed to the growth of crime and vagrancy, particularly among blacks, thereby feeding the submerged fears and anxieties of southern whites (Ayers, 1984, pp. 250–253).

LYNCHING IN THE TWENTIETH CENTURY

The number of lynchings declined gradually in the first three decades of the twentieth century, dropped dramatically after the early 1930s, but continued sporadically well into the 1950s. The emergence of vocal opposition to lynching, both inside and outside the South, contributed to its demise, as did fundamental changes in southern society and in race relations. Some blacks, and a few white liberals, spoke out against the horrors of lynching in the

late nineteenth century, most notably Ida B. Wells (1862–1931), a black woman activist from Memphis who sought to mobilize public opinion against mob violence through newspaper editorials and lectures. After 1909, the National Association for the Advancement of Colored People (NAACP), under the leadership of W. E. B. Du Bois, James Weldon Johnson, Walter White, and others, investigated and publicized lynchings, pressured political leaders to speak out, and lobbied for antilynching legislation. Some states passed laws against lynching, but they were largely ineffective. Despite decades of effort, and near success in 1922, 1937, and 1940, no federal antilynching legislation was ever enacted. Within the South, opposition to lynching centered on two interracial organizations: the Commission on Interracial Cooperation, founded in 1919, and the Association of Southern Women for the Prevention of Lynching, founded by Jessie Daniel Ames in 1930.

The modernization of southern society and the institutionalization of other forms of repression also hastened the decline of lynching. New roads, electricity, telephones, automobiles, and other social changes transformed the most isolated and lynching-prone areas of the South. Business leaders worked to change the violent image of the region in an effort to encourage investment and economic development. And law enforcement officials became more effective in preventing lynchings. Beginning in the late nineteenth century, furthermore, the emergence of alternative forms of racial control—segregation, disfranchisement, and tenant farming—made lynching less essential to the preservation of white supremacy.

There is also evidence that the decline of lynching was accompanied by an increase in "legal" executions of blacks in the South, often with the mere formality of a trial, and that other forms of violence against blacks increased as the incidence of lynching waned in the twentieth century. African Americans would continue to be killed in the name of white supremacy, particularly at the height of the civil rights movement, but lynching, in the classic sense of the earlier era, appears to have ended with the murder of Emmett Till in 1955 and of Mack Charles Parker in 1959.

In 2005 Senators Mary Landrieu of Louisiana and George Allen from Virginia raised a proposal to apologize for the Senate's failure to pass antilynching legislation. The nonbinding proposal, formally apologizing to victims of lynching and their families, was passed in the U.S. Senate without objection in June 2005.

See also National Association for the Advancement of Colored People (NAACP); Till, Emmett

■ ■ *Bibliography*

Ayers, Edward L. *Vengeance and Justice: Crime and Punishment in the Nineteenth-Century South.* New York: Oxford University Press, 1984.

Hall, Jacquelyn Dowd. *Revolt against Chivalry: Jessie Daniel Ames and the Women's Campaign against Lynching.* New York: Columbia University Press, 1979.

McGovern, James R. *Anatomy of a Lynching: The Killing of Claude Neal.* Baton Rouge: Louisiana State University Press, 1982.

Raper, Arthur F. *The Tragedy of Lynching.* 1933. Reprint, New York, 1969.

Tolnay, Stewart Emory, and E. M. Beck. *A Festival of Violence: An Analysis of Southern Lynchings, 1882–1930.* Urbana: University of Illinois Press, 1995.

Wells-Barnett, Ida B. *On Lynchings.* 1892. Reprint, Amherst N.Y.: Humanity Books, 2002.

Whitfield, Stephen J. *A Death in the Delta: The Story of Emmett Till.* New York: Free Press, 1988.

Williamson, Joel. *The Crucible of Race: Black-White Relations in the American South Since Emancipation.* New York: Oxford University Press, 1984.

Zangrando, Robert L. *The NAACP Crusade against Lynching, 1909-1950.* Philadelphia: Temple University Press, 1980.

L. RAY GUNN (1996)
Updated bibliography

6/08